EXPANDED VERSION

BUSINESS

NINTH EDITION

WILLIAM M. PRIDE
Texas A&M University

ROBERT J. HUGHES
Richland College, Dallas County Community College

JACK R. KAPOOR
College of DuPage

With Additional Content

INTRODUCTION TO THE EFFECT OF DISASTERS ON BUSINESS

by Carmen Powers

From Becoming a Master Employee by Dave Ellis:

CAREER PLANNING

MASTERING WORK

HOUGHTON MIFFLIN COMPANY
Boston   New York

BUSINESS, NINTH EDITION
by William M. Pride, Robert J. Hughes and Jack R. Kapoor
Copyright © 2008 by Houghton Mifflin Company. All rights reserved.

Vice President, Executive Publisher: George Hoffman
Sponsoring Editor: Katie Rose
Senior Marketing Manager: Mike Schenk
Marketing Coordinator: Erin Lane
Senior Development Editor: Joanne Dauksewicz
Editorial Assitant: John Powers
Senior Project Editor: Tamela Ambush
Editorial Assistant: Joanna Carter
Senior Art and Design Coordinator: Jill Haber Atkins
Cover Design Manager: Anne S. Katzeff
Senior Photo Editor: Jennifer Meyer Dare
Composition Buyer: Chuck Dutton

INTRODUCTION TO THE EFFECT OF DISASTERS ON BUSINESS
by Carmen Powers
Copyright © 2006 by Houghton Mifflin Company. All rights reserved.

BECOMING A MASTER EMPLOYEE
by Dave Ellis
Copyright © 2006 by Houghton Mifflin Company. All rights reserved.

Publisher: Patricia A. Coryell
Senior Sponsoring Editor: Mary Finch
Development Editor: Shani B. Fisher
Editorial Associate: Andrew Sylvester
Senior Project Editor: Cathy Labresh Brooks
Editorial Assistant: Neil Reynolds
Composition Buyer: Sarah Ambrose
Art and Design Manager: Jill Haber
Manufacturing Manager: Karen Banks
Marketing Manager: Elinor Gregory
Marketing Assistant: Evelyn Yang

Custom Publishing Editor: Dan Luciano
Custom Publishing Production Manager: Christina Battista
Project Coordinator: Jen Feltri

Cover Image: Martin Luckner/stock.xchng

ISBN-13: 978-0-618-89493-2
ISBN-10: 0-618-89493-4
N-07682

5 6 7 8 9 – CCI – 08 07

Houghton Mifflin
Custom Publishing

222 Berkeley Street • Boston, MA 02116

Address all correspondence and order information to the above address.

Brief Contents

Contents

3   Exploring Global Business   75

Part 2   Trends in Business Today   113

4   Navigating the World of e-Business   114

5   Choosing a Form of Business Ownership   147

6   Small Business, Entrepreneurship, and Franchises   181

Part 3 Management and Organization **217**

7 Understanding the Management Process **218**

8 Creating a Flexible Organization **245**

9   Producing Quality Goods and Services   **275**

Part 4   Human Resources   **311**

10   Attracting and Retaining the Best Employees   **312**

11 Motivating and Satisfying Employees and Teams   347

Part 5   Marketing   411

Part 6   Information for Business Strategy and Decision Making   549

18 Using Accounting Information

Part 7   Finance and Investment

19 Understanding Money, Banking, and Credit

20 Mastering Financial Management   663

21 Understanding Personal Finances and Investments   695

A GUIDE TO

BUSINESS

NINTH EDITION

A Word from the Authors

Dear Business Professors and Business Students

Meeting Needs! Just two words, but they say a lot about business and this *Business* textbook. As authors, we believe this important concept is true in business and education. For nine editions, we have been keenly aware that our customers are instructors *and* students. With each revision, we have asked instructors for suggestions that would help professors teach better and help students learn more efficiently. And with each edition, we have incorporated these suggestions and ideas to create what has become a best selling Introduction to Business text. We are also proud to say that we have included extensive student feedback in our text and program features. In the ninth edition, for example, student focus groups have helped us to shorten our boxes, make better use of our learning objectives throughout the text and program, and add more opportunities for test preparation. We can only say *thank you* for your suggestions, ideas, and support. Without you—both instructors and students—we would have no reason to write an Introduction to Business text.

We invite you to examine the visual guide that follows to see how Pride/Hughes/Kapoor can help invite students into business and succeed in life.

Sincerely,

WMP, RJH, JRK

BUSINESS

PRIDE | HUGHES | KAPOOR

9th edition

PRIDE | HUGHES | KAPOOR
Business

The BEST program for beginning a business education

Chapter 1

Exploring the World of Business and Economics

LEARNING OBJECTIVES

WHAT you will be able to do once you complete this chapter:

1 **Discuss** your future in the world of business.

2 **Define** *business* and identify potential risks and rewards.

3 **Define** *economics* and describe the two types of economic systems: capitalism and command economy.

4 **Identify** the ways to measure economic performance.

5 **Outline** the four types of competition.

6 **Summarize** the factors that affect the business environment and the challenges that American businesses will encounter in the future.

WHY this chapter matters

Studying business will help you to choose a c...[become a successful employee, perhaps start...own business, and become a better-informed...consumer and investor.

FOR HELP with studying this chapter, visit the Online Student Center:

www.college.hmco.com/PIC/pridebusiness9e

Online Study Center

From the first page to the last, *Business*, Ninth Edition, provides students with a solid foundation in the functional areas of business—management, marketing, accounting, finance, and information technology. At the beginning of every chapter, students will find a simple guide to success in the course—a succinct preview of what they will learn in the chapter, why it is important, and where they can go (**Online Student Center**) for help with understanding and further study of key concepts.

Sparking student interest, **Inside Business** opening cases make the world of business come alive. And, because every story has a beginning and an end, the students are brought back to the case later in the chapter. This way, readers can revisit their first impressions and better understand the significance of these events after reading the chapter materials.

Inside Business
Frito-Lay Competes in a Healthy Way

For market-leader Frito-Lay, the snack business is healthier than ever—both the profits and the products. Every year, consumers around the world spend $90 billion on crackers, chips, and cookies; Americans alone spend $3 billion on just chips. Frito-Lay's $10 billion in annual sales represents a hefty bite of the lucrative and highly competitive global snack market.

In some parts of the country, regional rivals that have a strong local following challenge the four main Frito-Lay brands of Dorito's, Lay's, Tostitos, and Cheetos. Herr's potato chips sell well on the East Coast, for example, and Ballreich's potato chips are a favorite in the Midwest. Frito-Lay is also feeling more competitive heat from Kraft and other global food giants that have introduced bite-sized versions of their well-known cookie and cracker brands. In addition, sales of organic and natural snacks are sky-rocketing as consumers pay closer attention to nutritional value and what goes into the foods

DID YOU KNOW?

While Frito-Lay has more than 15 major brands that each generate more than $100 million in sales each year, the company continues to examine the way it does business and the way it treats both its customers and its employees.

commitment to health and wellness by reformulating its entire snack line. Studies show that eating less *trans* fat can help to reduce bad cholesterol and the risk of heart disease, which is why the U.S. Food and Drug Administration (FDA) recently required food manufacturers to list *trans*-fat content on the Nutrition Facts label. Frito-Lay didn't wait for the labeling directive. Its experts cooked up *trans*-fat-free snacks nearly three years before the FDA requirement went into effect.

Being the first snack maker to get rid of *trans* fat gave Frito-Lay a competitive edge as it kicked off its health and wellness initiative.

Today, the company uses a green "Smart Spot" symbol to call attention to approximately 100 Frito-Lay snacks that have particular nutritional benefits or are lower in fat, salt, or sugar. It is expanding into nuts and seeds offerings to provide healthy snack alternatives and to meet the competition from natural foods. Just as the world of business is always changing, Frito-Lay is always changing to stay one snack ahead of its rivals.[1]

For more information about this company, go to **www.fritolay.com**.

RETURN TO   Inside Business

Frito-Lay knows that tastes change every day, that competitors change every day, and therefore, that it must earn its success one day at a time. Although the company commands a 65 percent share of the salty-snack market, its food experts are always in the kitchen developing new snacks. From Dorito's Guacamole-flavored Tortilla Chips and Light Lay's Potato Chips to Oberto Beef Jerky Crisps and Dorito's Black Pepper Jack, Frito-Lay offers a wide variety of choices to tempt more palates away from rival snacks.

To attract hungry consumers who otherwise might munch on cookies or crackers, management

recently beefed up the Frito-Lay advertising budget by 50 percent—to a whopping $150 million. Teens who like intensely flavored and vividly colored snacks are a main target, as are adults who want snacks with nutrition benefits. Clearly, Frito-Lay is doing everything it can to ensure healthier products and profits in its future.

Questions

1. What customer needs do you think Frito-Lay aims to satisfy with its assortment of snacks?
2. How does Frito-Lay use product differentiation to compete with other food manufacturers?

EFFECTIVE learning aids "map" content . . .

Part 3

Management and Organization

This part of the book deals with the organization—the "thing" that is a business. We begin with a discussion of the management functions involved in developing and operating a business. Next, we analyze the organization's elements and structure. Then we consider a firm's operations that are related to the production of goods and services.

7 Understanding the Management Process
8 Creating a Flexible Organization
9 Producing Quality Goods and Services

Learning is easier when students know where they are going. **Part Introductions** provide concise descriptions of the material to follow, while **Learning Objectives** at the beginning of each chapter map out the material they will master. These objectives are then reinforced in the margins of the chapter and serve as the chapter summary's organizational framework.

LEARNING OBJECTIVES

WHAT you will be able to do once you complete this chapter:

1 **Define** what management is.

2 **Describe** the four basic management functions: planning, organizing, leading and motivating, and controlling.

3 **Distinguish** among the various kinds of managers in terms of both level and area of management.

4 **Identify** the key management skills and the managerial roles.

5 **Explain** the different types of leadership.

6 **Discuss** the steps in the managerial decision-making process.

7 **Describe** how organizations benefit from total quality management.

8 **Summarize** what it takes to become a successful manager today.

What Is Management?

1 LEARNING OBJECTIVE
Define what management is.

management the process of coordinating people and other resources to achieve the goals of an organization

Management is the process of coordinating people and other resources to achieve the goals of an organization. As we saw in Chapter 1, most organizations make use of four kinds of resources: material, human, financial, and informational (see Figure 7.1).

Material resources are the tangible, physical resources an organization uses. For example, General Motors uses steel, glass, and fiberglass to produce cars and trucks on complex machine-driven assembly lines. A college or university uses books, classroom buildings, desks, and computers to educate students. And the Mayo Clinic uses beds, operating room equipment, and diagnostic machines to provide health care.

Perhaps the most important resources of any organization are its *human resources*—people. In fact, some firms live by the philosophy that their employees are their most important assets. One such firm is Southwest Airlines. Southwest treats its employees with the same respect and attention it gives its passengers. Southwest selectively seeks employees with upbeat attitudes and promotes from within 80 percent of the time. In decision making, everyone who will be affected is encouraged to get involved in the process. In an industry in which deregulation, extreme price competition, and fluctuating fuel costs have eliminated several major competitors, Southwest keeps growing and making a profit because of its employees. Many experts would agree with Southwest's emphasis on employees. Evidence suggests that the way employees are developed and managed may have more impact on an organization than other vital components such as marketing, sound financial decisions about large expenditures,

►► CHAPTER REVIEW

Summary

1

Define what management is.

Management is the process of coordinating people and other resources to achieve the goals of an organization. Managers are concerned with four types of resources—material, human, financial, and informational.

2

Describe the four basic management functions: planning, organizing, leading and motivating, and controlling.

Managers perform four basic functions. Management functions do not occur according to some rigid, preset timetable, though. At any time, managers may engage in a number of functions simultaneously. However, each function tends to lead naturally to others. First, managers engage in planning—determining where the firm should be going and how best to get there. Three types of plans, from the broadest to the most specific, are strategic plans, tactical plans,

the best interests of the organization. In addition, managers control ongoing activities to keep the organization on course. There are three steps in the control function: setting standards, measuring actual performance, and taking corrective action.

3

Distinguish among the various kinds of managers in terms of both level and area of management.

Managers—or management positions—may be classified from two different perspectives. From the perspective of level within the organization, there are top managers, who control the fortunes of the organization; middle managers, who implement strategies and major policies; and first-line managers, who supervise the activities of operating employees. From the viewpoint of area of management, managers most often deal with the areas of finance, operations, marketing, human resources, and administration.

4

Identify the key management skills and the managerial roles.

Text features SPARK interest . . .

Learning happens when the content is engaging and meaningful. The writing style, design, and illustration program build enthusiasm and facilitate greater understanding of key concepts.

>> **FIGURE 3.4**

THE EVOLVING EUROPEAN UNION

Initial core (1957)
Middle years (joined 1973-95)
Newest members (joined 2004)

Disney's Magical Express! Like magic, guests and their baggage are whisked from the Orlando International Airport to the Walt Disney World Resort. Complementary round-trip shuttle service to one of 22 hotels in the Orlando, Florida area is just one of the many services Disney provides to make a guest's stay more enjoyable.

service economy an economy in which more effort is devoted to the production of services than to the production of goods

some of its own products, buys other merchandise from suppliers, and operates a credit division, an insurance company, an entertainment division, and a medical equipment division. Smaller firms, by contrast, may use one production process. For example, Texas-based Advanced Cast Stone, Inc., manufactures one basic product: building materials made from concrete.

The Increasing Importance of Services

The application of the basic principles of operations management to the production of services has coincided with a dramatic growth in the number and diversity of service businesses. In 1900, only 28 percent of American workers were employed in service firms. By 1950, this figure had grown to 40 percent, and by September 2005, it had risen to 83 percent.[2] In fact, the American economy is now characterized as a **service economy** (see Figure 9.2). A service economy is one in which more effort is devoted to the production of services than to the production of goods.

Today, the managers of restaurants, laundries, real estate agencies, banks, movie theaters, airlines, travel bureaus, and other service firms have realized that they can benefit from the experience of manufacturers. And yet the production of services is very different from the production of manufactured goods in the following four ways:

1. Services are consumed immediately and, unlike manufactured goods, cannot be stored. For example, a hair stylist cannot store completed haircuts.
2. Services are provided when and where the customer desires the service. In many cases customers will not travel as far to obtain a service.
3. Services are usually labor-intensive because the human resource is often the most important resource used in the production of services.
4. Services are intangible, and it is therefore more difficult to evaluate customer satisfaction.[3]

>> **FIGURE 9.2**

SERVICE INDUSTRIES

The growth of service firms has increased so dramatically that we live in what is now referred to as a service economy.

Percent of American workers employed by service industries

Year	Percent
1975	72%
1985	76%
1995	80%
2005	83%

Source: U.S. Bureau of Labor Statistics website: **www.bls.gov**; accessed October 30, 2005.

Copyright © Houghton Mifflin Company.

The Basis for International Business

International business encompasses all business activities that involve exchanges across national boundaries. Thus a firm is engaged in international business when it buys some portion of its input from or sells some portion of its output to an organization located in a foreign country. (A small retail store may sell goods produced in some other country. However, because it purchases these goods from American distributors, it is not engaged in international trade.)

1 LEARNING OBJECTIVE
Explain the economic basis for international business.

international business all business activities that involve exchanges across national boundaries

Absolute and Comparative Advantage

Some countries are better equipped than others to produce particular goods or services. The reason may be a country's natural resources, its labor supply, or even customs or a historical accident. Such a country would be best off if it could *specialize* in the production of such products because it can produce them most efficiently. The country could use what it needed of these products and then trade the surplus for products it could not produce efficiently on its own.

Saudi Arabia thus has specialized in the production of crude oil and petroleum products; South Africa, in diamonds; and Australia, in wool. Each of these countries is said to have an absolute advantage with regard to a particular product. An **absolute advantage** is the ability to produce a specific product more efficiently than any other nation.

One country may have an absolute advantage with regard to several products, whereas another country may have no absolute advantage at all. Yet it is still worthwhile for these two countries to specialize

absolute advantage the ability to produce a specific product more efficiently than any other nation

Exploiting absolute advantage. Saudi Arabia has long specialized in the production of crude oil and petroleum products. Because of their natural oil resources, Saudi Arabia and other countries in the Middle East enjoy an absolute advantage—their ability to produce petroleum products more efficiently than in any other area of the world. Here, President Bush meets with Saudi Crown Prince Abdullah to persuade him to help curb skyrocketing oil prices that are hurting American families and businesses.

The MOST current and relevant information . . .

YOUR CAREER

Making the Most of a Mentor Relationship

If you've been thinking about meeting with a *mentor*—an experienced person who becomes an informal advisor to another employee—ask yourself:

1. What do you want to learn, and why?
2. Are you open to advice and ready to be challenged?
3. Are you willing to share your hopes and concerns?
4. How do you plan to act on what you learn?

Whether you want to be a more effective employee or build your own business, a mentor can provide

spot. This relationship is one way I'm going to continue to grow personally and professionally."

ENTREPRENEURIAL CHALLENGE

When Should Entrepreneurs Use Outsourcing?

Small businesses are not necessarily sending jobs overseas when they choose outsourcing. For entrepreneurs and established companies alike, outsourcing can mean hiring local or national vendors to handle specialized functions such as payroll, manufacturing, information technology, and food services. Before outsourcing, an entrepreneur should ask:

- Is the fu... tive tha... only?

- Does my company have the people, expertise, and equipment to do the job more efficiently than an outsource vendor?
- Can my company weather the possible disruption if an outsource vendor experiences supply, labor, technical, or weather problems?
- How will the vendor handle any liability issues that might arise in managing the outsourced function?
- How long has the vendor been in business, and what do its customers say about its performance?
- Is the outsourcing contract too expensive, too re... ...y?
- ...eed to do to manage the ...y?

EXAMINING ETHICS

Can Businesses Keep Your Personal Information Safe?

Is your personal data safe from theft and fraud? Both ethical and legal questions are mounting after security breaches such as these:

- CitiFinancial, a loan company, shipped a computer tape containing data on 3.9 million customers, but it never arrived.
- Bank of America shipped a tape containing records of 1.2 million federal employees, but it never arrived.
- Ameritrade, a brokerage firm, shipped tapes containing account information on 200,000 clients, but they never arrived.
- CardSystems, which processes credit-card transactions, found that hackers accessed computer data on 240,000 accounts.
- DSW Shoe Warehouse, a shoe retailer, found that hackers stole 1.4 million customers' credit-card numbers from its system.

Experts advise businesses to encrypt data for secure storage, change passwords frequently, hold data no longer than necessary, and disclose security breaches promptly. As lawmakers address this growing problem, you can protect yourself by checking bank and credit records and reporting any unauthorized

Throughout the text, special features help students relate to the concepts being presented and bring them up-to-date with what is happening in their world.

Box features in this edition are brief, to-the-point, and fun to read, reflecting themes that most instructors believe to be important:

Your Career
Entrepreneurial Challenge
Examining Ethics
Business Around the World
BizTech

Business Around the World

Flying the Frightening Skies

Terrorism in the sky has changed the way people travel and the way businesses operate, sending ripples throughout the global economy. After police thwarted a plot to bomb several jets flying between Great Britain and the United States, British Airways canceled 1,100 flights, stranding thousands of passengers and leaving 20,000 pieces of luggage in limbo. Airline stock prices nosedived and airports were in turmoil as stricter security forced travelers to check all bags. Trying to recoup some of its lost revenue, one airline even sued the U.K. government.

BizTech

Different Paths to e-Profits

Three of the world's largest high-tech firms have pursued different paths to profits.

Amazon. Founded as an online bookstore, Amazon.com was unprofitable in the early years but today rings up $7 billion annually selling everything from diamonds to DVDs. Offering free shipping on purchases of $25 or more cuts into profits but encourages repeat business. Amazon also

eBay. eBay pioneered online auctions in 1995 and was profitable from the start. Why? Because it doesn't actually own what it sells but does receive a commission on every transaction. Now more than 150 million people worldwide use eBay to buy and sell all kinds of goods and services. The firm recently bought Skype, a

Google. This well-known search site opened for business in 1998 and was profitable by the end of 2001. Google makes most of its money selling advertising links alongside search results. With services such as Froogle shopping search and Google Earth maps—plus new technologies—Google wants to attract more users and keep them

Spotlights highlight current facts of interest. The **Using the Internet** feature reminds students about the wealth of information available at their fingertips.

@ USING THE INTERNET

The Business for Social Responsibility Organization website at **www.bsr.org/** provides a good overview of business ethics and proper social behavior. Be sure to explore the Global Business Responsibility Resource Center, the organization's gateway to useful reports, research, and links to related sites.

SPOTLIGHT

Personal calls on the job

Time that workers spend on personal telephone calls per day.

- Don't make personal calls **4.8%**
- 31 to 60 minutes **1%**
- 11 to 30 minutes **17.3%**
- 1 to 10 minutes **76.9%**

Tools for SUCCESS . . .

Students can be sure they've studied effectively and fully comprehend key concepts with the complete end-of-chapter materials. The Summary, organized around chapter learning objectives, provides a review of important concepts. Marginal Key Terms are revisited with page references. Review Questions reinforce definitions and concepts, and Discussion Questions promote critical thinking.

Two end-of-chapter cases including one video case focus on recognizable organizations and allow students to consider the real-world implications of concepts covered in the chapter.

▶▶ CHAPTER REVIEW

Summary

1

Discuss your future in the world of business.

For many years, people in business—both employees and managers—assumed that prosperity would continue. When the bubble burst, a large number of these same people then began to ask the question: Wh... this is a fair question, it is diffic... a college student taking busin... employee just starting a career... difficult to answer. And yet ther... there for people who are willin... learn, and possess the ability to...

2

Define *business* and identify po... rewards.

Business is the organized effort of ind... sell, for a profit, the goods and servi... needs. Four kinds of resources—ma... rpes... d ma... ll bus... the p... busin... of los...

Key Terms

You should now be able to define and give an example relevant to each of the following terms.

free enterprise (4)
cultural (or workplace) diversity (6)
business (9)
profit (11)
stakeholders (11)
economics (11)
microeconomics (12)
macroeconomics (12)
economy (12)
factors of production (12)
entrepreneur (13)
capitalism (13)
invisible hand (13)
market economy (14)
mixed economy (14)
consumer products (15)
command economy (15)

Review Questions

1. List all the activities involved in operations management.
2. What is the difference between an analytical and a synthetic manufacturing process? Give an example of each type of process.
3. In terms of focus, magnitude, and number, characterize the production processes used by a local pizza parlor, a dry-cleaning establishment, and an auto repair shop.
4. Describe how research and development lead to new products.
5. Explain why product extension and refinement are important.
6. What are the major elements of design planning?
7. What factors should be considered when selecting a site for a new manufacturing facility?
8. What is the objective of operational planning? What four steps are used to accomplish this objective?

Discussion Questions

1. Why would Rubbermaid—a successful U.S. company—need to expand and sell its products to customers in foreign countri...
2. Do certain kinds of firms... of operations managemen...
3. Is it really necessary for... search and development... and operations control?
4. How are the four areas... related?
5. In what ways can employe... of a firm's products?
6. Is operations managem... organizations such as co... why not?

▶▶ CASE 2.2

Wal-Mart Goes Green

A turnaround is underway at Wal-Mart. The largest and most powerful retailer in U.S. history is highly profitable—but it is also the target of intense criticism. Critics say that it offers low employee pay, works hard to avoid unionization, sells merchandise made in overseas sweatshops, and doesn't do enough to protect the environment. In recent years, however, Wal-Mart has been listening harder and making changes to show how good a corporate citizen it can be.

As an example, the company is determined to do business in a "greener" way. Meetings with the Natural Resources Defense Council and Conservation International have helped Wal-Mart identify ways to make its operations more ecofriendly. Such changes go well beyond image building because they directly affect how the chain's global suppliers operate. CEO H. Lee Scott, Jr., explains: "As we do the right thing, we have an impact across so many industries, so many countries. And we are finding tremendous cost savings while doing

By reducing the amount of packaging on some of its imported toys, Wal-Mart and its suppliers saved lots of trees and lots of fuel. Moreover, because the toys were less bulky, they could be shipped in fewer containers, shaving more than $1 million from Wal-Mart's annual transportation budget. In addition, two new "green" stores are serving as laboratories for energy conservation techniques such as generating heat from leftover fat used to fry chickens. Such changes not only help the environment, but they also boost the retailer's bottom line while polishing its public image.

Being big allows Wal-Mart to make a difference in a big way. Consider the company's response to the devastation caused by hurricane Katrina, one of America's worst natural disasters. With hundreds of thousands of people forced to flee flooded areas of Louisiana and Mississippi, Wal-Mart opened its wallet wide and contributed $17 million in cash to jump-start relief efforts. It also donated all kinds of products to help evacuees, aid workers, and law enforcement officials.

One hundred Wal-Mart trucks rolled into the Gulf

▶▶ VIDEO CASE 9.1

Cutting-Edge Production at Remington

Remington—long known for its shavers—has been associated with a number of manufacturing "firsts." It produced the first commercial typewriter in 1873. the first

2003, Remington was acqu... which also owns Rayovac... products, and many other na...

Today, Remington offe... shavers, hair trimmers, hair dryers, curling irons, and other small appliances for personal grooming. Its prod-

BUILDING SKILLS FOR CAREER SUCCESS

1. Exploring the Internet

Socially responsible business behavior can be as simple as donating unneeded older computers to schools, mentoring interested learners in good business practices, or supplying public speakers to talk about career opportunities. Students, as part of the public at large, perceive a great deal of information about a company, its employees, and its owners by the positive social actions taken and perhaps even more by actions not taken. Microsoft donates millions of dollars of computers and software to educational institutions every year. Some people consider this level of corporate giving to be insufficient given the scale of the wealth of the corporation. Others believe that firms have no obligation to give back any more than they wish and that recipients should be grateful. Visit the text website for updates to this exercise.

Assignment

1. Select any firm involved in high technology and the Internet such as Microsoft or IBM.

Unfortunately, many employees currently are struggling with such issues. The moral dilemmas that arise when employees find their own ethical values incompatible with the work they do every day are causing a lot of stress in the workplace, and furthermore, these dilemmas are not being discussed. There exists an ethics gap. You already may have faced a similar situation in your workplace.

Assignment

1. In small groups with your classmates, discuss your answers to the following questions:
   a. If you were faced with any of the preceding situations, what would you do?
   b. Would you complete work you found morally unacceptable, or would you leave it undone and say nothing?
   c. If you spoke up, what would happen to you or your career? What would be the risk?
   d. What are your options?

Journal Exercises and Building Skills for Career Success drive home an awareness of the skills students will need to be successfully employed. These exercises focus on students' writing, Internet, critical thinking, team-building, communication, and career exploration. In addition, Career Snapshots (video clips found in the Online Student Center) provide interesting and personal anecdotes of how several successful business professionals got their start.

APPLICATION and RELEVANCE...

→ PREP TEST

Matching Questions

____ 1. It is a process for converting a product idea into an actual product.

____ 2. Raw materials are broken into different components.

____ 3. Its focus is minimizing holding costs and potential stock-out costs.

____ 4. It is created by converting materials, people, finances, and information into finished goods.

____ 5. A set of statistical techniques that is used to monitor all aspects of the production process.

____ 6. Work is accomplished mostly by equipment.

____ 7. Input from workers is used to improve the workplace.

____ 8. Output per unit of time is measured per worker.

____ 9. Computers are the main tool used in the development of products.

a. analytical process
b. capital-intensive technology
c. computer-aided design
d. design planning
e. form utility
f. inventory control
g. just-in-time inventory system
h. productivity
i. quality circle
j. statistical quality control (SQC)

Students like to know if they've really "gotten it." Will they know enough to do well on the next test? Will they make an "A"? Never before have they had so many opportunities to find out.

A **Prep Test** at the end of every chapter allows students to immediately check how much they have retained after reading the chapter.

Also, **Running a Business**, an end-of-part **continuing video case**, and **Building a Business Plan** give students an opportunity to virtually experience planning and running a small business.

►► RUNNING A BUSINESS PART I

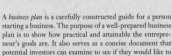

The Rise of Finagle A Bagel

Would bagels sell in Hong Kong? Laura Beth Trust and Alan Litchman planned to find out. Trust was in Hong Kong working in the garment manufacturing industry, and Litchman was in real estate, but they were eager to start their own business. They were particularly interested in running a business where they would have direct customer contact and be able to get first-hand feedback about their products and services. And no matter what kind of business they started, it would be a family undertaking: The two entrepreneurs recently had decided to get married.

Looking around Hong Kong, Litchman and Trust noticed numerous Western-style food chains such as McDonald's, Pizza Hut, KFC, and Starbucks but no bagel places. Yet they believed that Hong Kong's sophisticated, multicultural population would welcome authentic New York–style bagels. Although both the entrepreneurs had

three owners agr
sibilities and coll
pansion. Within
pleted a deal to b
sole owners and

The business
to bagels. Today
downtown Bosto
Finagle A Bagel
the owners recen
ters and producti
is where tens of t
along with enou
much larger netw

Branding the Ba

Over time, the

BUILDING A BUSINESS PLAN PART I

A *business plan* is a carefully constructed guide for a person starting a business. The purpose of a well-prepared business plan is to show how practical and attainable the entrepreneur's goals are. It also serves as a concise document that potential investors can examine to see if they would like to invest or assist in financing a new venture. A business plan should include the following twelve components:

- Introduction
- Executive summary
- Benefits to the community
- Company and industry
- Management team
- Manufacturing and operations plan
- Labor force
- Marketing plan
- Financial plan
- Exit strategy
- Critical risks and assumptions

Warning: Don't rush this step. This step often requires much thought, but it is well worth the time and effort. As an added bonus, you are more likely to develop a quality business plan if you really want to open this type of business.

Now that you have decided on a specific type of business, it is time to begin the planning process. The goal for this part is to complete the introduction and benefits-to-the-community components of your business plan.

Before you begin, it is important to note that the business plan is not a document that is written and then set aside. It is a living document that an entrepreneur should refer to continuously in order to ensure that plans are being carried through appropriately. As the entrepreneur begins to execute the plan, he or she should monitor the business environment continuously and make changes to the plan to address any challenges or opportunities that were not foreseen originally.

Throughout this course you will, of course, be building your knowledge about business. Therefore, it will be appropriate for you to continually revisit parts of the plan that you have already written in order to refine them based on your

---

Business | Exploring the World of Business and Economics - Microsoft Internet Explorer

File Edit View Favorites Tools Help

HOUGHTON MIFFLIN
college division

Online Study C

Business, Ninth Edition Pride | Hughes | Kapoor

[Navigate By Chapter ▼]   Discipline Home | Bookstore | Contact Us

Chapter 1
● Prepare For Class
● Improve Your Grade
● ACE the Test

● General Resources
● Site Map

Product Information Center > Student Home > Chapter 1 > Improve Your Grade

📖 **Improve Your Grade**

Work with these documents and activities to master chapter learning objectives. Some content requires software plugins. Visit our Plugin Help Center for help with downloading plugins.

Exploring the World of Business and Economics

To access protected content denoted by the **Your Guide to an "A"** icon, please use the code in the passkey that came with new copies of your text. If you purchased a used textbook, the **Your Guide to an "A"** passkey is available for purchase through your bookstore or through the Houghton Mifflin's eCommerce bookstore. Please note that all content in chapter 1 is available without a passkey.

∷Learning Objective Su
Here you can find a cop
help you study.

🔊 Audio Chapter Revie
Review the chapter w
chapter, and the othe

🔊 Flashcards
Review important term

🔊 Crossword Puzzle
Fill out this fun crossw

Your Guide to an A ROADMAP

- ACE+ — Practice to ACE the test!
- Flashcards — Review key terms!
- Audio Chapter Reviews — Quick MP3s on the go!
- Games — Test prep with Asteroids, Hangman, and Crosswords!

If students want additional practice, there's much more in the **Online Student Center**. In addition to chapter summaries, glossary, Internet activities, and career information, the Your Guide to an "A" online study guide provides premium study tools, including **downloadable mp3 audio summaries** and **audio tests**, **interactive flashcards**, **ACE practice quizzes** (four per chapter), and fun games, like **Hangman**, **Asteroids**, and **Crosswords**, to test their knowledge.

The BEST resources to meet your UNIQUE teaching needs . . .

Instructors who teach large classes, have multiple sections per semester, and just want some new and innovative ideas for teaching Introduction to Business, have plenty of materials to choose from.

It's Strictly Business Telecourse Guide

For those students enrolled in the It's Strictly Business Telecourse, this guide provides the necessary correlation between the video lessons and the textbook, including assignments, learning objectives, key terms, text focus points, video focus points, and practice tests.

Instructor's Resource Manual

Completely expanded, updated, and redesigned to be a one-stop resource for instructors, this 2-volume manual includes (1) a special section that contains helpful advice for teaching the Introduction to Business course; (2) a transition guide for each chapter located within each chapter, where it is easy to find and use; (3) a quick reference guide that details all packaged features for the chapter and where they can be found (in text or online); (4) a large-type comprehensive lecture outline that instructors can place on a desk or podium and glance down to read; (5) key figures from the text reproduced in a comprehensive lecture outline for easy identification; (6) additional examples, teaching tips, discussion starters, debate issues, suggested questions corresponding to boxed inserts, and interesting quotes the instructor can use to make lectures and classroom time more effective; (7) reproduction of all overhead transparencies and PowerPoint slides so teachers can easily see what is available; and (8) a unique section of classroom exercises—written by Carmen Powers (Monroe Community College; Kaplan University)—that includes homework and in-class activities that provide innovative opportunities for collaborative experiential learning. Step-by-step instructions, time estimates, handouts, and other teaching aids are also available for quick and easy course preparation.

Chapter 1 Exploring the World of Business and Economics

I. **BUSINESS: A DEFINITION**

   A. *Business* is the organized effort of individuals to produce and sell, for a profit, the goods and services that satisfy society's needs. To be successful, a business must be organized, it must satisfy needs, and it must earn a profit.

PowerPoint Slide 1-3 (Figure 1.1)

The Organized Effort of Individuals

Combining Resources

Copyright © Houghton Mifflin Company. All rights reserved.

   B.   **The Organized Effort of Individuals.** For a business to be organized, it must combine four kinds of resources: material, human, financial, and informational. (See Figure 1.1.)

     1. Material resources include the raw materials used in manufacturing processes, as well as buildings and machinery.

     2. Human resources are the people who furnish their labor to the business in return for wages.

     3. The financial resource is the money required to pay employees, purchase materials, and generally keep the business operating.

Test Bank

Written and class-tested by the text's authors, the *Test Bank* contains over 5,000 items. Each chapter includes essay, true/false, multiple-choice and scenario (mini-case) questions. An item-information column in the *Test Bank* specifies details about each question, such as learning objective tie-in, learning level, answer, level of difficulty, and text page reference.

HMClassPrep® with HMTesting CD-ROM

 This CD provides a variety of teaching resources in an electronic format that allows for easy customization to meet specific instructional needs. Files on the CD include PowerPoint slides, Word files from the *Instructor's Resource Manual* (including exercise handouts), Business Plan Teacher Guidelines and Classroom Response System content. The electronic version of the printed *Test Bank* allows instructors to easily create and edit tests. The program includes an online testing feature instructors can use to administer tests via their local area network or over the Web. It also has a gradebook feature that lets users set up classes, record and track grades from tests or assignments, analyze grades, and produce class and individual statistics.

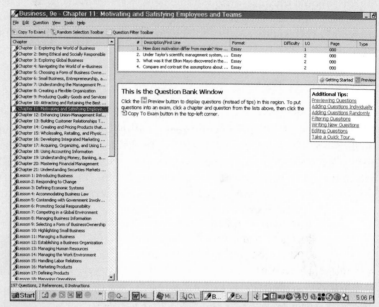

Online Teaching Center

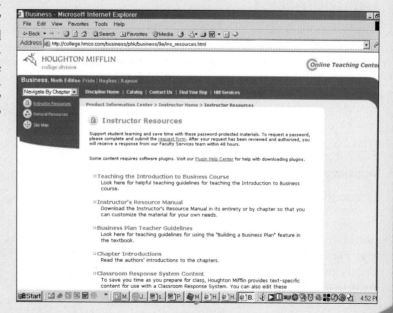 This password-protected site includes valuable tools to help instructors design and prepare for the course. The contents include modules for teaching Introduction to Business, sample syllabi, a SCANS correlation chart to show how the text's contents meet SCANS competency requirements, PowerPoint slides, an online Video Guide, "Master the Class" interactive PowerPoint game, and Word files from the *Instructor's Resource Manual*. In addition, 3 Appendixes and 4 Learning Modules appear online for those instructors who wish to customize their courses with supplementary materials. The three appendixes are entitled "Careers in Business," "Risk Management and Insurance," and "Business Law, Regulation, and Taxation." The four learning modules include "Crisis Management: The Effects of Disasters on Business," "Sports Marketing," "Customer Relationship Management," and "Marketing Ethics."

Online/Distance Learning Support

Instructors can create and customize online course materials to use in distance learning, distributed learning, or as a supplement to traditional classes. The *Blackboard®* and *WebCT®* course materials that accompany the text include a variety of study aids for students, written and gradable homework, as well as course management tools for instructors.

Classroom Response System (CRS)

Using state-of-the-art wireless technology and text-specific content, a Classroom Response System provides a convenient and inexpensive way to gauge student comprehension, deliver quizzes or exams, and provide "on-the-spot" assessment. Various answering modes, question types, and display options mean that a CRS is as functional as you want it to be. Content available in the Online Teaching Center includes multiple choice questions customized for reviewing key content in the text. Instructors may edit existing questions and/or create their own.

PowerPoint Slides

These presentations, available on the instructor's website and *HM ClassPrep®* CD, provide a complete lecture for each chapter, including key figures and tables from the text. An enhanced version of the slides includes supplemental figures and in-class activities for instructors who wish to lecture beyond the textbook content and add interactivity to class time. Instructors can use these presentations as is, or can edit, delete, and add to them to suit their specific class needs.

Business: A Definition

- The organized effort of individuals to produce and sell, for a profit, the goods and services that satisfy society's needs

1 - 9

Transparencies

This package includes over 300 color transparencies—some drawn from the text and more than 150 from outside sources. Supplemental transparencies for each chapter include a chapter outline, a class exercise, a debate issue, and a multiple-choice quiz. Additional transparencies for each chapter include definitions and figures not found in the text.

Videos and DVDs

  Video modules that correlate to the chapters in the textbook help instructors bring their lectures to life by providing thought-provoking insights into real-world companies, products, and issues. Each chapter module includes four segments: a chapter overview, two key concept segments, and a segment supporting the end-of-chapter video case. There are also seven videos to support the end-of-part "Running a Business" continuing case.

Acknowledgments

We thank Brahm Canzer at John Abbot College for helping us develop technology-related materials for the text and supplements. We thank Carmen Powers of Monroe Community College and Kaplan University for her many valuable contributions to the *Instructor's Resource Manual*. We thank Kathryn Hegar of Mountain View College for developing many of the online study guide elements behind the *Your Guide to an "A"* passkey. We thank Peggy Borchardt of Richland College for providing the SCANS correlation. We thank John Drea at Western Illinois University for creating the "Master the Class" review game. We thank Mary C. Greene, MATESOL, UC Extension and San Jose State University, for her review of the text for accessibility to non-native speakers. We thank the R. Jan LeCroy Center for Educational Telecommunications of the Dallas County Community College District for the Telecourse partnership and providing the related student and instructor materials. Finally, we thank the following people for technical assistance: Susan Kahn, Tammy Lemke, Dana Egg, Brooke Arnold, Clarissa Means, Samia Qaiyum, Kari Kelley, Laura Henderson, Megan O'Leary, Marian Wood, Theresa Kapoor, Kathryn Thumme, Karen Tucker, and Dave Kapoor.

A special Faculty Advisory Board assisted us in making decisions both large and small throughout the entire development process of the text and the instructional package. For being "on-call" and available to answer questions and make valuable suggestions, we are grateful to those who participated:

Maria Aria
Camden County College

Harold Babson
Columbus State Community College

Frank Barber
Cuyahoga Community College

Paul Callahan
Cincinnati State University

Peter Dawson
Collin County Community College

Richard Ghidella
Citrus College

Debbie Gilliard
Metropolitan State College

John Humphreys
Eastern New Mexico University

David Kroeker
Tabor College

Bruce Kusch
Brigham Young University

J. B. Locke
University of Mobile

Monty Lynn
Abilene Christian University

Douglas McCabe
Georgetown University

Barry McCarthy
Irvine Valley College

Tony Mifsud
Rowan Cabarrus Community College

Nancy Ray-Mitchaell
McLennan Community College

Gary Mrozinski
Broome Community College

Jeffrey D. Penley
Catawba Valley Community College

Anthony Slone
Elizabeth Community & Technical College

Raymond Sparks
Pima College

Paula Thompson
Florida Institute of Technology

Martin Welc
Saddleback College

Kenneth Wendeln
Indiana University

For the generous gift of their time and for their thoughtful and useful comments and suggestions, we are indebted to the following reviewers of this and previous editions. Their suggestions have helped us improve and refine the text as well as the whole instructional package.

David V. Aiken
Hocking College

Phyllis C. Alderdice
Jefferson Community College

Marilyn Amaker
Orangeburg-Calhoun Technical College

Harold Amsbaugh
North Central Technical College

Carole Anderson
Clarion University

Lydia E. Anderson
Fresno City College

Maria Aria
Camden County College

James O. Armstrong, II
John Tyler Community College

Ed Atzenhoefer
Clark State Community College

Harold C. Babson
Columbus State Community College

Xenia P. Balabkins
Middlesex County College

Gloria Bemben
Finger Lakes Community College

Charles Bennett
Tyler Junior College

Patricia Bernson
County College of Morris

Robert W. Bitter
Southwest Missouri State University

Angela Blackwood
Belmont Abbey College

Wayne Blue
Allegany College of Maryland

Mary Jo Boehms
Jackson State Community College

Stewart Bonem
Cincinnati Technical College

James Boyle
Glendale Community College

Steve Bradley
Austin Community College

Lyle V. Brenna
Pikes Peak Community College

Tom Brinkman
Cincinnati Technical College

Robert Brinkmeyer
University of Cincinnati

Harvey S. Bronstein
Oakland Community College

Edward Brown
Franklin University

Joseph Brum
Fayetteville Technical Institute

Janice Bryan
Jacksonville College

Howard R. Budner
Manhattan Community College

Clara Buitenbos
Pan American University

C. Alan Burns
Lee College

Frank Busch
Louisiana Technical University

Joseph E. Cantrell
DeAnza College

Brahm Canzer
John Abbot College

Don Cappa
Chabot College

Robert Carrel
Vincennes University

Richard M. Chamberlain
Lorain County Community College

Bruce H. Charnov
Hofstra University

Lawrence Chase
Tompkins Cortland Community College

Felipe Chia
Harrisburg Area Community College

Michael Cicero
Highline Community College

William Clarey
Bradley University

Robert Coiro
LaGuardia Community College

Don Coppa
Chabot College

Robert J. Cox
Salt Lake Community College

Susan Cremins
Westchester Community College

Bruce Cudney
Middlesex Community College

Andrew Curran
Antonelli Institute of Art and Photography

Gary Cutler
Dyersburg State Community College

Rex R. Cutshall
Vincennes University

John Daily
St. Edward's University

Brian Davis
Weber State University

Gregory Davis
Georgia Southwestern State University

Helen M. Davis
Jefferson Community College

Harris D. Dean
Lansing Community College

Wayne H. Decker
Memphis State University

Sharon Dexter
Southeast Community College

William M. Dickson
Green River Community College

M. Dougherty
Madison Area Technical College

Michael Drafke
College of DuPage

Richard Dugger
Kilgore College

Sam Dunbar
Delgado Community College

Robert Elk
Seminole Community College

Pat Ellebracht
Northeastern Missouri State University

Pat Ellsberg
Lower Columbia College

John H. Espey
Cecil Community College

Carleton S. Everett
Des Moines Area Community College

Frank M. Falcetta
Middlesex County College

Thomas Falcone
Indiana University of Pennsylvania

Janice Feldbauer
Austin Community College

Coe Fields
Tarrant County Junior College

Carol Fischer
University of Wisconsin—Waukesha

Larry A. Flick
Three Rivers Community College

Gregory F. Fox
Erie Community College

Michael Fritz
Portland Community College at Rock Creek

Fred Fry
Bradley University

Eduardo F. Garcia
Laredo Junior College

Arlen Gastineau
Valencia Community College

Carmine Paul Gibaldi
St. John's University

Edwin Giermak
College of DuPage

R. Gillingham
Vincennes University

Robert Googins
Shasta College

Karen Gore
Ivy Technical State College

W. Michael Gough
DeAnza College

Cheryl Davisson Gracie
Washtenaw Community College

Joseph Gray
Nassau Community College

Michael Griffin
University of Massachusetts—Dartmouth

Ricky W. Griffin
Texas A & M University

Stephen W. Griffin
Tarrant County Junior College

Roy Grundy
College of DuPage

John Gubbay
Moraine Valley Community College

Rick Guidicessi
Des Moines Area Community College

Ronald Hadley
St. Petersburg Junior College

Carnella Hardin
Glendale Community College

Aristotle Haretos
Flagler College

Keith Harman
National-Louis University

Richard Hartley
Solano Community College

Richard Haskey
University of Wisconsin

Carolyn Hatton
Cincinnati State University

Linda Hefferin
Elgin Community College

Sanford Helman
Middlesex County College

Victor B. Heltzer
Middlesex County College

Ronald L. Hensell
Mendocino College

Leonard Herzstein
Skyline College

Donald Hiebert
Northern Oklahoma College

Nathan Himelstein
Essex County College

L. Duke Hobbs
Texas A & M University

Charles Hobson
Indiana University Northwest

Marie R. Hodge
Bowling Green State University

Gerald Hollier
University of Texas—Brownsville

Jay S. Hollowell
Commonwealth College

Townsend Hopper
Joseph Hrebenak
Community College of Allegheny County—Allegheny

James L. Hyek
Los Angeles Valley College

James V. Isherwood
Community College of Rhode Island

Charleen S. Jaeb
Cuyahoga Community College

Sally Jefferson
Western Illinois University

Jenna Johannpeter
Belleville Area College

Gene E. A. Johnson
Clark College

Carol A. Jones
Cuyahoga Community College

Pat Jones
Eastern New Mexico University

Robert Kegel
Cypress College

Isaac W. J. Keim, III
Delta College

George Kelley
Erie Community College

Marshall Keyser
Moorpark College

Betty Ann Kirk
Tallahassee Community College

Edward Kirk
Vincennes University

Judith Kizzie
Clinton Community College

Karl Kleiner
Ocean County College

Clyde Kobberdahl
Cincinnati Technical College

Connie Koehler
McHenry County College

Robert Kreitner
Arizona State University

Patrick Kroll
University of Minnesota, General College

Kenneth Lacho
University of New Orleans

John Lathrop
New Mexico Junior College

R. Michael Lebda
DeVry Institute of Technology

Martin Lecker
SUNY Rockland Community College

George Leonard
St. Petersburg Junior College

Marvin Levine
Orange County Community College

Chad Lewis
Everett Community College

Jianwen Liao
Robert Morris College

Ronnie Liggett
University of Texas at Arlington

William M. Lindsay
Northern Kentucky University

Carl H. Lippold
Embry-Riddle Aeronautical University

Thomas Lloyd
Westmoreland County Community College

Paul James Londrigan
Mott Community College

Kathleen Lorencz
Oakland Community College

Fritz Lotz
Southwestern College

Robert C. Lowery
Brookdale Community College

Anthony Lucas
Community College of Allegheny County—Allegheny

Sheldon A. Mador
Los Angeles Trade and Technical College

Joan Mansfield
Central Missouri State University

Gayle J. Marco
Robert Morris College

John Martin
Mt. San Antonio Community College

Irving Mason
Herkimer County Community College

John F. McDonough
Menlo College

Catherine McElroy
Bucks County Community College

L. J. McGlamory
North Harris County College

Charles Meiser
Lake Superior State University

Ina Midkiff-Kennedy
Austin Community College—Northridge

Edwin Miner
Phoenix College

Jim Moes
Johnson County Community College

Dominic Montileone
Delaware Valley College

Linda Morable
Dallas County Community Colleges

Charles Morrow
Cuyahoga Community College

T. Mouzopoulos
American College of Greece

W. Gale Mueller
Spokane Community College

C. Mullery
Humboldt State University

Robert J. Mullin
Orange County Community College

Patricia Murray
Virginia Union University

Robert Nay
Stark Technical College

James Nead
Vincennes University

Jerry Novak
Alaska Pacific University

Grantley Nurse
Raritan Valley Community College

Gerald O'Bryan
Danville Area Community College

Larry Olanrewaju
Virginia Union University

David G. Oliver
Edison Community College

John R. Pappalardo
Keene State College

Dennis Pappas
Columbus Technical Institute

Roberta F. Passenant
Berkshire Community College

Clarissa M. H. Patterson
Bryant College

Kenneth Peissig
College of Menominee Nation

Constantine Petrides
Manhattan Community College

Donald Pettit
Suffolk County Community College

Norman Petty
Central Piedmont Community College

Joseph Platts
Miami-Dade Community College

Gloria D. Poplawsky
University of Toledo

Greg Powell
Southern Utah University

Fred D. Pragasam
SUNY at Cobleskill

Peter Quinn
Commonwealth College

Kimberly Ray
North Carolina A & T State University

Robert Reinke
University of South Dakota

William Ritchie
Florida Gulf Coast University

Kenneth Robinson
Wesley College

John Roisch
Clark County Community College

Rick Rowray
Ball State University

Jill Russell
Camden County College

Karl C. Rutkowski
Pierce Junior College

Martin S. St. John
Westmoreland County Community College

Ben Sackmary
Buffalo State College

Eddie Sanders, Jr.
Chicago State University

P. L. Sandlin
East Los Angeles College

Nicholas Sarantakes
Austin Community College

Wallace Satchell
St. Philip's College

Warren Schlesinger
Ithaca College

Marilyn Schwartz
College of Marin

Jon E. Seely
Tulsa Junior College

John E. Seitz
Oakton Community College

J. Gregory Service
Broward Community College—North Campus

Lynne M. Severance
Eastern Washington University

Dennis Shannon
Southwestern Illinois College

Richard Shapiro
Cuyahoga Community College

Raymond Shea
Monroe Community College

Lynette Shishido
Santa Monica College

Cindy Simerly
Lakeland Community College

Anne Smevog
Cleveland Technical College

James Smith
Rocky Mountain College

David Sollars
Auburn University Montgomery

Carl Sonntag
Pikes Peak Community College

Russell W. Southhall
Laney College

John Spence
University of Southwestern Louisiana

Rieann Spence-Gale
Northern Virginia Community College

Nancy Z. Spillman
President, Economic Education Enterprises

Richard J. Stanish
Tulsa Junior College

Jeffrey Stauffer
Ventura College

Jim Steele
Chattanooga State Technical Community College

William A. Steiden
Jefferson Community College

E. George Stook
Anne Arundel Community College

W. Sidney Sugg
Lakeland Community College

Lynn Suksdorf
Salt Lake Community College

Richard L. Sutton
University of Nevada—Las Vegas

Robert E. Swindle
Glendale Community College

William A. Syvertsen
Fresno City College

Lynette Teal
Ivy Technical State College

Raymond D. Tewell
American River College

George Thomas
Johnston Technical College

Karen Thomas
St. Cloud University

Judy Thompson
Briar Cliff College

William C. Thompson
Foothill Community College

James B. Thurman
George Washington University

Patric S. Tillman
Grayson County College

Frank Titlow
St. Petersburg College

Charles E. Tychsen
Northern Virginia Community College—Annandale

Ted Valvoda
Lakeland Community College

Robert H. Vaughn
Lakeland Community College

Frederick A. Viohl
Troy State University

C. Thomas Vogt
Allan Hancock College

Loren K. Waldman
Franklin University

Stephen R. Walsh
Providence College

Elizabeth Wark
Springfield College

John Warner
The University of New Mexico—Albuquerque

Randy Waterman
Dallas County Community Colleges

W. J. Waters, Jr.
Central Piedmont Community College

Philip A. Weatherford
Embry-Riddle Aeronautical University

Jerry E. Wheat
Indiana University, Southeast Campus

Elizabeth White
Orange County Community College

Benjamin Wieder
Queensborough Community College

Ralph Wilcox
Kirkwood Community College

Charlotte Williams
Jones County Junior College

Larry Williams
Palomar College

Paul Williams
Mott Community College

Steven Winter
Orange County Community College

Wallace Wirth
South Suburban College

Amy Wojciechowski
West Shore Community College

Nathaniel Woods
Columbus State Community College

Gregory J. Worosz
Schoolcraft College

Marilyn Young
Tulsa Junior College

Many talented professionals at Houghton Mifflin have contributed to the development of *Business*, Ninth Edition. We are especially grateful to George Hoffman, Katie Rose, Mike Schenk, Erin Lane, Joanne Dauksewicz, Amy Galvin, John Powers, Tamela Ambush, Joanna Carter, and Jill Haber. Their inspiration, patience, support, and friendship are invaluable.

Part 1

The Environment of Business

In Part 1 of *Business,* first, we begin with an examination of the world of business and economics. Next, we discuss ethical and social responsibility issues that affect business firms and our society. Then we explore the increasing importance of international business.

1 Exploring the World of Business and Economics

2 Being Ethical and Socially Responsible

3 Exploring Global Business

Exploring the World of Business and Economics

LEARNING OBJECTIVES

WHAT you will be able to do once you complete this chapter:

1 Discuss your future in the world of business.

2 Define *business* and identify potential risks and rewards.

3 Define *economics* and describe the two types of economic systems: capitalism and command economy.

4 Identify the ways to measure economic performance.

5 Outline the four types of competition.

6 Summarize the factors that affect the business environment and the challenges that American businesses will encounter in the future.

WHY this chapter matters

Studying business will help you to choose a career, become a successful employee, perhaps start your own business, and become a better-informed consumer and investor.

FOR HELP with studying this chapter, visit the Online Student Center:

www.college.hmco.com/PIC/pridebusiness9e

Online Study Center

For market-leader Frito-Lay, the snack business is healthier than ever—both the profits and the products. Every year, consumers around the world spend $90 billion on crackers, chips, and cookies; Americans alone spend $3 billion on just chips. Frito-Lay's $10 billion in annual sales represents a hefty bite of the lucrative and highly competitive global snack market.

In some parts of the country, regional rivals that have a strong local following challenge the four main Frito-Lay brands of Dorito's, Lay's, Tostitos, and Cheetos. Herr's potato chips sell well on the East Coast, for example, and Ballreich's potato chips are a favorite in the Midwest. Frito-Lay is also feeling more competitive heat from Kraft and other global food giants that have introduced bite-sized versions of their well-known cookie and cracker brands. In addition, sales of organic and natural snacks are skyrocketing as consumers pay closer attention to nutritional value and what goes into the foods they eat. Still, more Americans are more overweight than ever.

As a result, Frito-Lay has decided to show its

DID YOU KNOW?

While Frito-Lay has more than 15 major brands that each generate more than $100 million in sales each year, the company continues to examine the way it does business and the way it treats both its customers and its employees.

commitment to health and wellness by reformulating its entire snack line. Studies show that eating less *trans* fat can help to reduce bad cholesterol and the risk of heart disease, which is why the U.S. Food and Drug Administration (FDA) recently required food manufacturers to list *trans*-fat content on the Nutrition Facts label. Frito-Lay didn't wait for the labeling directive. Its experts cooked up *trans*-fat-free snacks nearly three years before the FDA requirement went into effect. Being the first snack maker to get rid of *trans* fat gave Frito-Lay a competitive edge as it kicked off its health and wellness initiative.

Today, the company uses a green "Smart Spot" symbol to call attention to approximately 100 Frito-Lay snacks that have particular nutritional benefits or are lower in fat, salt, or sugar. It is expanding into nuts and seeds offerings to provide healthy snack alternatives and to meet the competition from natural foods. Just as the world of business is always changing, Frito-Lay is always changing to stay one snack ahead of its rivals.[1]

For more information about this company, go to **www. fritolay.com**.

Wow! What a challenging world we live in. Just for a moment, think about the changes that both individuals and businesses have experienced since the beginning of the twenty-first century. The economy took a nosedive and now shows signs of recovery. We have experienced the tragic events of September 11 and have begun a war on terrorism. The stock market lost approximately a third of its value and then began to rebound. There have been hurricanes that affected not only the people who live in the coastal areas of the country but also businesses and consumers around the globe. The cost of energy has risen. There were a large number of business failures—especially in high-technology industries. And yet, make no mistake about it, our economic system will survive. In fact, our economy continues to adapt and change to meet the challenges of an ever-changing world.

Since the last edition of *Business* was published three years ago, we have seen businesses examine how they do business. Think for a moment about Frito-Lay, the corporation profiled in the Inside Business opening case for this chapter. The firm's snack foods don't magically appear on store shelves. There is a whole lot more to producing Fritos corn chips and other snack foods than most consumers can imagine. And once the firm's products are produced, they must be distributed and marketed to consumers in order to generate sales in a very competitive business world. While Frito-Lay, now a division of PepsiCo, has more than 15 major brands that each generate more than $100 million in sales each year, the company continues to examine the way it does business and the way it treats both its customers and its employees.[2] As a result of constantly working to improve the way it does business, Frito-Lay is an excellent example of what American business should be doing.

Our economic system provides an amazing amount of freedom that allows businesses that range in size from the small corner grocer to Frito-Lay to adapt to changing business environments. Within certain limits, imposed mainly to ensure public safety, the owners of a business can produce any legal good or service they choose and attempt to sell it at the price they set. This system of business, in which individuals decide what to produce, how to produce it, and at what price to sell it, is called **free enterprise.** Our free-enterprise system ensures, for example, that Dell Computer can buy parts from Intel and software from Microsoft and manufacture its own computers. Our system gives Dell's owners and stockholders the right to make a profit from the company's success. It gives Dell's management the right to compete with Hewlett-Packard and IBM. And it gives computer buyers the right to choose.

In this chapter we look briefly at what business is and how it got that way. First, we discuss your future in business and explore some important reasons for studying business. Then we define *business*, noting how business organizations satisfy needs and earn profits. Next, we examine how capitalism and command economies answer four basic economic questions. Then our focus shifts to how the nations of the world measure economic performance and the four types of competitive situations. Next, we look at the events that helped shape today's business system, the current business environment, and the challenges that businesses face.

free enterprise the system of business in which individuals are free to decide what to produce, how to produce it, and at what price to sell it

Your Future in the Changing World of Business

1 LEARNING OBJECTIVE
Discuss your future in the world of business.

The key word in this heading is *changing*. When faced with both economic problems and increasing competition not only from firms in the United States but also from international firms located in other parts of the world, employees and managers now began to ask the question: What do we do now? Although this is a fair question, it is difficult to answer. Certainly, for a college student taking business courses or a beginning employee just starting a career, the question is even more difficult to answer. And yet there are still opportunities out there for people who are willing to work hard, continue to learn, and possess the ability to adapt to change. Let's begin our discussion in this section with three basic concepts.

- What do you want?
- Why do you want it?
- Write it down!

During a segment on the Oprah Winfrey television show, Joe Dudley, one of the world's most successful black business owners, gave the preceding advice to anyone who wants to succeed in business. And his advice is an excellent way to begin our discussion of what free enterprise is all about. What is so amazing about Dudley's success is that he started a manufacturing business in his own kitchen, with his wife and children serving as the new firm's only employees. He went on to develop his own line of hair-care products and to open a chain of beauty schools and beauty supply stores. Today Mr. Dudley has built a multimillion-dollar empire and is president of Dudley Products, Inc—one of the most successful minority-owned companies in the nation. Not only a successful business owner, he is also a winner of the Horatio Alger Award—an award given to outstanding individuals who have succeeded in the face of adversity.[3] While many people would say that Joe Dudley was just lucky or happened to be in the right place at the right time, the truth is that he became a success because he had a dream and worked hard to turn his dream into a reality. He would be the first to tell you that you have the same opportunities that he had. According to Mr. Dudley, "Success is a journey, not just a destination."[4]

Whether you want to obtain part-time employment to pay college and living expenses, begin your career as a full-time employee, or start a business, you must *bring something to the table* that makes you different from the next person. Employers and our capitalistic economic system are more demanding than ever before. Ask yourself: What can I do that will make employers want to pay me a salary? What skills do I have that employers need? With these two questions in mind, we begin the next section with another basic question: Why study business?

Why Study Business?

The potential benefits of higher education are enormous. To begin with, there are economic benefits. Over their lifetimes, college graduates on average earn much more than high school graduates. And while lifetime earnings are substantially higher for college graduates, so are annual income amounts—see the nearby Spotlight feature.

The nice feature of education and knowledge is that once you have it, no one can take it away. It is yours to use for a lifetime. In this section we explore what you may expect to get out of this business course and text. You will find at least four quite compelling reasons for studying business.

@ USING THE INTERNET

To find out the details about a specific career, expected growth in an industry, training and other qualifications, and earnings, visit the *Occupational Outlook Handbook* published by Bureau of Labor Statistics at **www.bls.gov.**

For Help in Choosing a Career   What do you want to do with the rest of your life? Someplace, sometime, someone probably has asked you this same question. And like many people, you may find it a difficult question to answer. This business course will introduce you to a wide array of employment opportunities. In private enterprise, these range from small, local businesses owned by one individual to large companies such as American Express and Marriott International that are owned by thousands of stockholders. There are also employment opportunities with federal, state, county, and local governments and with not-for-profit organizations such as the Red Cross and Save the Children. For help in deciding what career might be right for you, read Appendix A: Careers in Business, which appears on the text website. There is also information about researching a career and the steps necessary to perform a job search. To view this information:

1. Make an Internet connection and go to **http://college.hmco.com/ business/phk/business/9e/student_home.html.**
2. Click on the General Resources link and choose Appendix A.

SPOTLIGHT

Who makes the most money!

The amount of education you have can make a difference. Dollar amounts represent median yearly income for each group.

$88,216

$50,600

$35,023

$27,526

High school graduate | Some college, no degree | Bachelor's degree | Professional degree

Source: *2004–2005 Statistical Abstract of the United States.*

In addition to career information in Appendix A on the text website, a number of additional websites provide information about career development. For more information, visit the following sites:

- Career Builder at **www.careerbuilder.com**
- Career One Stop at **www.careeronestop.org**
- Monster at **monster.com**
- Yahoo! Hot Jobs at **http://hotjobs.yahoo.com**

One thing to remember as you think about what your ideal career might be is that a person's choice of a career ultimately is just a reflection of what he or she values and holds most important. What will give one individual personal satisfaction may not satisfy another. For example, one person may dream of a career as a corporate executive and becoming a millionaire before the age of thirty. Another may choose a career that has more modest monetary rewards but that provides the opportunity to help others. One person may be willing to work long hours and seek additional responsibility in order to get promotions and pay raises. Someone else may prefer a less demanding job with little stress and more free time. What you choose to do with your life will be based on what you feel is most important. And the *you* is a very important part of that decision.

To Be a Successful Employee Deciding on the type of career you want is only a first step. To get a job in your chosen field and to be successful at it, you will have to develop a plan, or road map, that ensures that you have the skills and knowledge the job requires. You will be expected to have both the technical skills needed to accomplish a specific task and the ability to work well with many types of people in a culturally diverse work force. **Cultural** (or **workplace**) **diversity** refers to the differences among people in a work force owing to race, ethnicity, and gender. These skills, together with a working knowledge of the American business system and an appreciation for a culturally diverse workplace, can give you an inside edge when you are interviewing with a prospective employer.

cultural (or workplace) diversity differences among people in a work force owing to race, ethnicity, and gender

This course, your instructor, and all the resources available at your college or university can help you to acquire the skills and knowledge you will need for a successful career. But don't underestimate your part in making your dream a reality. It will take hard work, dedication, perseverance, and time management to achieve your goals. Communication skills are also important. Today, most employers are looking for employees who can compose a business letter and get it in mailable form. They also want employees who can talk with customers and use e-mail to communicate with people within and outside the organization. Employers also will be interested in any work experience you may have had in

A business owner with a big smile. Alison McDaniel, pictured in the center with two employees, is one of thousands of female business owners in Alaska. Starting Alison's Relocations, Inc. was an uphill battle, but she now believes her success is the result of determination, hard work, and the skills she obtained while working for larger companies in the transport industry.

YOUR CAREER

Making the Most of a Mentor Relationship

If you've been thinking about meeting with a *mentor*—an experienced person who becomes an informal advisor to another employee—ask yourself:

1. What do you want to learn, and why?
2. Are you open to advice and ready to be challenged?
3. Are you willing to share your hopes and concerns?
4. How do you plan to act on what you learn?

Whether you want to be a more effective employee or build your own business, a mentor can provide guidance, help to solve on-the-job problems, and widen your network of contacts. Jeannie Alexander, a senior auditor at KPMG, sought out a mentor because, she says, "I was comfortable in my own little

spot. This relationship is one way I'm going to continue to grow personally and professionally." Having a mentor is no substitute for training. However, with the right mentor, says Camellia Poplarski, a regional sales director for Eli Lilly, "you learn things that are not in any book."

cooperative work/school programs, during summer vacations, or in part-time jobs during the school year. These things can make a difference when it is time to apply for the job you really want.

To Start Your Own Business Some people prefer to work for themselves, and they open their own businesses. To be successful, business owners must possess many of the same skills that successful employees have. And they must be willing to work hard and put in long hours.

It also helps if your small business can provide a product or service that customers want. For example, Mark Cuban started a small Internet company called Broadcast.com that provided hundreds of live and on-demand audio and video programs ranging from rap music to sporting events to business events over the Internet. When Cuban sold Broadcast.com to Yahoo! Inc., he became a billionaire. Today he is an expert on how the Internet will affect society in the future and believes that there is a real need for all companies, not just technology companies, to provide something that their customers want. If they do not do that, their company could very well fail.[5]

Unfortunately, many small-business firms fail; 70 percent of them fail within the first five years. Typical reasons for business failures include undercapitalization (not enough money), poor business location, poor customer service, unqualified or untrained employees, fraud, lack of a proper business plan, and failure to seek outside professional help. The material in Chapter 6 and selected topics and examples throughout this text will help you to decide whether you want to open your own business. This material also will help you to overcome many of these problems.

To Become a Better Informed Consumer and Investor The world of business surrounds us. You cannot buy a home, a new Grand Prix from the local Pontiac dealer, a Black & Decker sander at an ACE Hardware store, a pair of jeans at the Gap, or a hot dog from a street vendor without entering a business transaction. Because you no doubt will engage in business transactions almost every day of your life, one very good reason for studying business is to become a more fully informed consumer. Many people also rely on a basic understanding of business to help them to invest for the future. According to Julie Stav, Hispanic stockbroker-turned-author/radio personality, "Take $25, add to it drive plus determination and then watch it multiply into an empire."[6] The author of *Get Your Share*, a *New York Times* best-seller, believes that it is important to learn the basics about the economy and business, stocks, mutual funds, and other alternatives before investing your money. And while this is an obvious conclusion, just dreaming of being rich doesn't make it happen. In fact, like many facets of life, it takes planning and determination to establish the type of investment program that will help you to accomplish your financial goals.

Special Note to Students

It is important to begin reading this text with one thing in mind: *This business course does not have to be difficult.* In fact, *learning about business and how you can be involved as an employee, business owner, consumer, or investor can be fun!*

We have done everything possible to eliminate the problems that students encounter in a typical class. All the features in each chapter have been evaluated and recommended by instructors with years of teaching experience. In addition, business students were asked to critique each chapter component. Based on this feedback, the text includes the following features:

- *Your Guide to Success in Business* is placed at the beginning of each chapter and provides helpful suggestions for mastering chapter content.
- *Learning objectives* appear at the beginning of each chapter.
- *Inside Business* is a chapter-opening case that highlights how successful companies do business on a day-to-day basis.
- *Margin notes* are used throughout the text to reinforce both learning objectives and key terms.
- *Boxed features* highlight career information, starting a business, ethical behavior, global issues, and the impact of technology on business today.
- *Spotlight* features highlight interesting facts about business and society and often provide a real-world example of an important concept within a chapter.
- *Using the Internet* features provide useful web addresses that relate to chapter material.
- *End-of-chapter materials* provide questions about the opening case, a chapter summary, a list of key terms, review and discussion questions, a journal exercise, and two cases. The last section of every chapter is entitled Building Skills for Career Success and includes exercises devoted to exploring the Internet, developing critical-thinking skills, building team skills, researching different careers, and improving communication skills.
- *End-of-part materials* provide a continuing video case about the Finagle A Bagel Company that operates a chain of retail outlets in the northeastern section of the United States. Also at the end of each major part is an exercise designed to help you to develop the components that are included in a typical business plan.

In addition to the text, a number of student supplements will help you to explore the world of business. We are especially proud of the website that accompanies this edition. There, you will find online study aids, including interactive study tools, practice tests, audio reviews for each chapter, flashcards, and other resources. If you want to take a look at the Internet support materials available for this edition of *Business*,

1. Make an Internet connection and go to **http://college.hmco.com/business/ phk/business/9e/student_home.html.**
2. Click on the Navigate by Chapter link and choose Prepare for Class, Improve Your Grade, or ACE the test.

As authors, we want you to be successful. We know that your time is valuable and that your schedule is crowded with many different activities. We also appreciate the fact that textbooks are expensive. Therefore, we want you to use this text and get the most out of your investment. In order to help you get off to a good start, a number of

> > **TABLE 1.1**

SEVEN WAYS TO USE THIS TEXT AND ITS RESOURCES

1. Prepare before you go to class.	Early preparation is the key to success in many of life's activities. Certainly, early preparation can help you to participate in class, ask questions, and improve your performance on exams.
2. Read the chapter.	Although it may seem like an obvious suggestion, many students never take the time to really read the material. Find a quiet space where there are no distractions, and invest enough time to become a "content expert."
3. Underline or highlight important concepts.	Make this text yours. Don't be afraid to write on the pages of your text. It is much easier to review material if you have identified important concepts.
4. Take notes.	While reading, take the time to jot down important points and summarize concepts in your own words. Also, take notes in class.
5. Apply the concepts.	Learning is always easier if you can apply the content to your real-life situation. Think about how you could use the material either now or in the future.
6. Practice critical thinking.	Test the material in the text. Do the concepts make sense? To build critical-thinking skills, answer the questions that accompany the cases at the end of each chapter. Also, many of the exercises in the Building Skills for Career Success require critical thinking.
7. Prepare for exams.	Allow enough time to review the material before exams. Check out the summary and review questions at the end of the chapter. Then use the resources on the text website.

suggestions for developing effective study skills and using this text are provided in Table 1.1. Why not take a look at these suggestions and use them to help you succeed in this course and earn a higher grade. Remember what Joe Dudley said, "Success is a journey, not a destination."

Since a text always should be evaluated by the students and instructors who use it, we would welcome and sincerely appreciate your comments and suggestions. Please feel free to contact us by using one of the following e-mail addresses:

Bill Pride: **w-pride@tamu.edu**
Bob Hughes: **bhughes@dcccd.edu**
Jack Kapoor: **kapoorj@cdnet.cod.edu**

Business: A Definition

Business is the organized effort of individuals to produce and sell, for a profit, the goods and services that satisfy society's needs. The general term *business* refers to all such efforts within a society (as in "American business") or within an industry (as in "the steel business"). However, *a business* is a particular organization, such as Kraft Foods, Inc., or Cracker Barrel Old Country Stores. To be successful, a business must perform three activities. It must be organized. It must satisfy needs. And it must earn a profit.

2 LEARNING OBJECTIVE
Define *business* and identify potential risks and rewards.

business the organized effort of individuals to produce and sell, for a profit, the products and services that satisfy society's needs

The Organized Effort of Individuals

For a business to be organized, it must combine four kinds of resources: material, human, financial, and informational. *Material* resources include the raw materials used in manufacturing processes, as well as buildings and machinery. For example, Sara Lee Corporation needs flour, sugar, butter, eggs, and other raw materials to produce the food products it sells worldwide. In addition, this Chicago-based company needs human, financial, and informational resources. *Human* resources are the people who furnish their labor to the business in return for wages. The *financial* resource is the

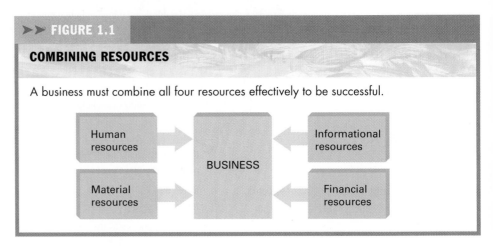

>> **FIGURE 1.1**

COMBINING RESOURCES

A business must combine all four resources effectively to be successful.

money required to pay employees, purchase materials, and generally keep the business operating. And *information* is the resource that tells the managers of the business how effectively the other resources are being combined and used (see Figure 1.1).

Today, businesses usually are organized as one of three specific types. *Manufacturing businesses* process various materials into tangible goods, such as delivery trucks or towels. Intel, for example, produces computer chips that, in turn, are sold to companies that manufacture computers. *Service businesses* produce services, such as haircuts, legal advice, or tax preparation. And some firms called *marketing intermediaries* buy products from manufacturers and then resell them. Sony Corporation is a manufacturer that produces stereo equipment, among other things. These products may be sold to a marketing intermediary such as Best Buy or Circuit City, which then resells the manufactured goods to consumers in their retail stores.

Satisfying Needs

The ultimate objective of every firm must be to satisfy the needs of its customers. People generally do not buy goods and services simply to own them; they buy products and services to satisfy particular needs. Some of us may feel that the need for transportation is best satisfied by an air-conditioned BMW with stereo compact-disc player, automatic transmission, power seats and windows, and remote-control side mirrors. Others may believe that a Ford Focus with a stick shift will do just fine. Both products are available to those who want them, along with a wide variety of other products that satisfy the need for transportation.

When firms lose sight of their customers' needs, they are likely to find the going rough. However, when businesses understand their customers' needs and work to satisfy those needs, they are usually successful. Back in 1962, Sam Walton opened his first discount store in Rogers, Arkansas. Although the original store was quite different from the Wal-Mart Superstores you see today, the basic ideas of providing customer service and offering goods that satisfied needs at low prices are part of the reason why this firm has grown to become the largest retailer in the world. Today, Wal-Mart provides its products and services to more than 135 million customers each week. Although it currently has more than 3,600 retail stores in the United States and almost 1,600 retail stores in nine different countries, this highly successful discount-store organization continues to open new stores to meet the needs of its customers around the globe.[7]

Low carbs and diet drinks can equal fat profits. Many restaurant owners have found that one way to improve sales and profits is to meet the needs of diet-conscious consumers.

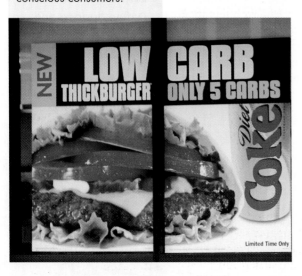

Business Profit

A business receives money (sales revenue) from its customers in exchange for goods or services. It also must pay out money to cover the expenses involved in doing business. If the firm's sales revenues are greater than its expenses, it has earned a

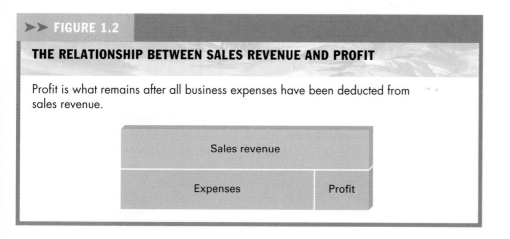

>> FIGURE 1.2

THE RELATIONSHIP BETWEEN SALES REVENUE AND PROFIT

Profit is what remains after all business expenses have been deducted from sales revenue.

Sales revenue	
Expenses	Profit

profit. More specifically, as shown in Figure 1.2, **profit** is what remains after all business expenses have been deducted from sales revenue. A negative profit, which results when a firm's expenses are greater than its sales revenue, is called a *loss*. A business cannot continue to operate at a loss for an indefinite period of time. Management and employees must find some way to increase sales revenues and/or reduce expenses in order to return to profitability. If some specific actions aren't taken to eliminate losses, a firm may be forced to file for bankruptcy protection. In some cases, the pursuit of profits is so important that some corporate executives, including those from such corporations as Enron, WorldCom, and Adelphia Communications have fudged their profit figures to avoid disappointing shareholders, directors, Wall Street analysts, lenders, and other stakeholders. The term **stakeholders** is used to describe all the different people or groups of people who are affected by the policies, decisions, and activities made by an organization.

The profit earned by a business becomes the property of its owners. Thus, in one sense, profit is the reward business owners receive for producing goods and services that consumers want. Profit is also the payment that business owners receive for assuming the considerable risks of ownership. One of these is the risk of not being paid. Everyone else—employees, suppliers, and lenders—must be paid before the owners.

A second risk that owners undertake is the risk of losing whatever they have invested into the business. A business that cannot earn a profit is very likely to fail, in which case the owners lose whatever money, effort, and time they have invested. Although there have been business failures in all industries in recent years, firms in the high-tech industry have experienced a large number of failures. Simply put, here is what happened: In the 1990s, there were a large number of investors who wanted to cash in on the technology boom and often would provide initial financing for new high-tech start-up firms. These start-up firms used the money to expand their business operations, hoping that they could generate enough sales revenues to pay their expenses and eventually earn profits before they burned through their initial financing. During the first part of the twenty-first century, however, for many of these firms, including Kozmo.com, Pets.com, Quokka Sports, and NBCi, bankruptcy, a merger, or absorption by a large corporation was the result of continually operating at a loss.[8]

To satisfy society's needs and make a profit, a business must operate within the parameters of a nation's economic system. In the next section we define economics and describe two different types of economic systems.

profit what remains after all business expenses have been deducted from sales revenue

stakeholders all the different people or groups of people who are affected by the policies and decisions made by an organization

Types of Economic Systems

Economics is the study of how wealth is created and distributed. By *wealth*, we mean "anything of value," including the products produced and sold by business. *How wealth is distributed* simply means "who gets what." Experts often use economics to explain the choices we make and how those choices change as we cope with the demands of every-day life. In simple terms, individuals, businesses, governments, and society must make

3 LEARNING OBJECTIVE
Define economics and describe the two types of economic systems: capitalism and command economy.

economics the study of how wealth is created and distributed

BizTech

Different Paths to e-Profits

Three of the world's largest high-tech firms have pursued different paths to profits.

Amazon. Founded as an online bookstore, Amazon.com was unprofitable in the early years but today rings up $7 billion annually selling everything from diamonds to DVDs. Offering free shipping on purchases of $25 or more cuts into profits but encourages repeat business. Amazon also charges a commission when other merchants make a sale through its site—much like eBay.

eBay. eBay pioneered online auctions in 1995 and was profitable from the start. Why? Because it doesn't actually own what it sells but does receive a commission on every transaction. Now more than 150 million people worldwide use eBay to buy and sell all kinds of goods and services. The firm recently bought Skype, a company that specializes in online telephone communications.

Google. This well-known search site opened for business in 1998 and was profitable by the end of 2001. Google makes most of its money selling advertising links alongside search results. With services such as Froogle shopping search and Google Earth maps—plus new technologies—Google wants to attract more users and keep them on Google sites for as long as possible.

---

decisions that reflect what is important to each group at a particular time. For example, you want to take a weekend trip to some exotic vacation spot, and you also want to begin an investment program. Because of your financial resources, though, you cannot do both. You must decide what is most important. Business firms, governments, and to some extent society face the same types of decisions. And each group must deal with scarcity when making important decisions. In this case, *scarcity* means "lack of resources"—money, time, natural resources, etc.—that are needed to satisfy a want or need.

Today, experts often study economic problems from two different perspectives: microeconomics and macroeconomics. **Microeconomics** is the study of the decisions made by individuals and businesses. Microeconomics, for example, examines how the prices of homes affect the number of homes built and sold. On the other hand, **macroeconomics** is the study of the national economy and the global economy. Macroeconomics examines the economic effect of taxes, government spending, interest rates, and similar factors on a nation and society.

The decisions that individuals, business firms, government, and society make and the way in which people deal with the creation and distribution of wealth determine the kind of economic system, or **economy,** that a nation has.

Over the years, the economic systems of the world have differed in essentially two ways: (1) the ownership of the factors of production and (2) how they answer four basic economic questions that direct a nation's economic activity. **Factors of production** are the resources used to produce goods and services. There are four such factors:

- *Land and natural resources*—elements in their natural state that can be used in the production process to make appliances, automobiles, and other products. Typical examples include crude oil, forests, minerals, land, water, and even air.
- *Labor*—the time and effort that we use to produce goods and services. It includes human resources such as managers and employees.
- *Capital*—the facilities, equipment, and machines used in the operation of organizations. While most people think of capital as just money, it also can be the manufacturing equipment on a Ford automobile assembly line or a computer used in the corporate offices of Ace Hardware.
- *Entrepreneurship*—the resources that organize land, labor, and capital. It is the

microeconomics the study of the decisions made by individuals and businesses

macroeconomics the study of the national economy and the global economy

economy the way in which people deal with the creation and distribution of wealth

factors of production resources used to produce goods and services

willingness to take risks and the knowledge and ability to use the other factors of production efficiently. An **entrepreneur** is a person who risks his or her time, effort, and money to start and operate a business.

A nation's economic system significantly affects all the economic activities of its citizens and organizations. This far-reaching impact becomes more apparent when we consider that a country's economic system determines how the factors of production are used to meet the needs of society. Today, two different economic systems exist: capitalism and command economies. The way each system answers the four basic economic questions below determines a nation's economy.

1. What goods and services—and how much of each—will be produced?
2. How will these goods and services be produced?
3. For whom will these goods and services be produced?
4. Who owns and who controls the major factors of production?

Capitalism

Capitalism is an economic system in which individuals own and operate the majority of businesses that provide goods and services. Capitalism stems from the theories of the eighteenth-century Scottish economist Adam Smith. In his book *Wealth of Nations*, published in 1776, Smith argued that a society's interests are best served when the individuals within that society are allowed to pursue their own self-interest. In other words, people will work hard and invest long hours to produce goods and services only if they can reap the rewards of their labor—more pay or profits in the case of a business owner. According to Smith, when an individual is acting to improve his or her own fortunes, he or she indirectly promotes the good of his or her community and the people in that community. Smith went on to call this concept the "invisible hand." The **invisible hand** is a term created by Adam Smith to describe how an individual's own personal gain benefits others and a nation's economy. For example, the only way a small-business owner who produces shoes can increase personal wealth is to sell shoes to customers. To become even more prosperous, the small-business owner must hire workers to produce even more shoes. According to the invisible hand, people in the small-business owner's community not only would have shoes, but some workers also would have jobs working for the shoemaker. Thus the success of people in the community and, to some extent, the nation's economy is tied indirectly to the success of the small-business owner.

Adam Smith's capitalism is based on four fundamental issues illustrated in Figure 1.3. First, Smith argued that the creation of wealth is properly the concern of private individuals, not government. Second, private individuals must own the resources used to create wealth. Smith argued that the owners of resources should be free to determine how these resources are used. They also should be free to enjoy the income, profits, and other benefits they might derive from the ownership of these resources. Third,

entrepreneur a person who risks time, effort, and money to start and operate a business

capitalism an economic system in which individuals own and operate the majority of businesses that provide goods and services

invisible hand a term created by Adam Smith to describe how an individual's own personal gain benefits others and a nation's economy

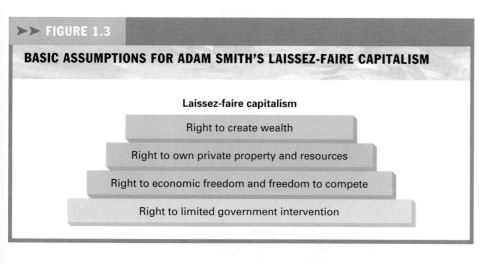

>> **FIGURE 1.3**

BASIC ASSUMPTIONS FOR ADAM SMITH'S LAISSEZ-FAIRE CAPITALISM

Laissez-faire capitalism

Right to create wealth

Right to own private property and resources

Right to economic freedom and freedom to compete

Right to limited government intervention

Smith contended that economic freedom ensures the existence of competitive markets that allow both sellers and buyers to enter and exit as they choose. This freedom to enter or leave a market at will has given rise to the term *market economy*. A **market economy** (sometimes referred to as a *free-market economy*) is an economic system in which businesses and individuals decide what to produce and buy, and the market determines quantities sold and prices. Finally, in Smith's view, the role of government should be limited to providing defense against foreign enemies, ensuring internal order, and furnishing public works and education. With regard to the economy, government should act only as rule maker and umpire. The French term *laissez-faire* describes Smith's capitalistic system and implies that there should be no government interference in the economy. Loosely translated, this term means "let them do" (as they see fit).

Capitalism in the United States

Our economic system is rooted in the laissez-faire capitalism of Adam Smith. However, our real-world economy is not as laissez-faire as Smith would have liked because government participates as more than umpire and rule maker. Our economy is, in fact, a **mixed economy**, one that exhibits elements of both capitalism and socialism.

In a mixed economy, the four basic economic questions discussed at the beginning of this section (what, how, for whom, and who) are answered through the interaction of households, businesses, and governments. The interactions among these three groups are shown in Figure 1.4.

Households   Households, made up of individuals, are the consumers of goods and services, as well as owners of some of the factors of production. As *resource owners*, the members of households provide businesses with labor, capital, and other resources.

>> **FIGURE 1.4**

THE CIRCULAR FLOW IN OUR MIXED ECONOMY

Our economic system is guided by the interaction of buyers and sellers, with the role of government being taken into account.

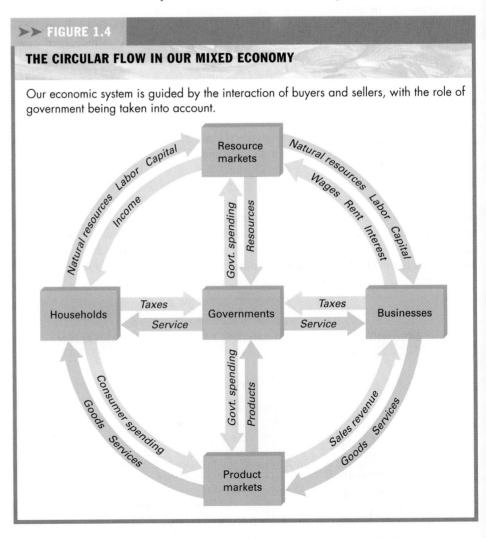

In return, businesses pay wages, rent, and dividends and interest, which households receive as income.

As *consumers*, household members use their income to purchase the goods and services produced by business. Today, approximately 70 percent of our nation's total production consists of **consumer products** — goods and services purchased by individuals for personal consumption. (The remaining third is purchased by businesses and governments.[9]) This means that consumers, as a group, are the biggest customers of American business.

Businesses   Like households, businesses are engaged in two different exchanges. They exchange money for natural resources, labor, and capital and use those resources to produce goods and services. Then they exchange their goods and services for sales revenue. This sales revenue, in turn, is exchanged for additional resources, which are used to produce and sell more goods and services. Thus the circular flow of Figure 1.4 is continuous.

Along the way, of course, business owners would like to remove something from the circular flow in the form of profits. And households try to retain some income as savings. But are profits and savings really removed from the flow? Usually not! When the economy is running smoothly, households are willing to invest their savings in businesses. They can do so directly by buying stocks in businesses, by purchasing shares in mutual funds that purchase stocks in businesses, or by lending money to businesses. They also can invest indirectly by placing their savings in bank accounts. Banks and other financial institutions then invest these savings as part of their normal business operations.

When business profits are distributed to business owners, these profits become household income. (Business owners are, after all, members of households.) And, as we saw, household income is retained in the circular flow as either consumer spending or invested savings. Thus business profits, too, are retained in the business system, and the circular flow is complete. How, then, does government fit in?

Governments   The framers of our Constitution desired as little government interference with business as possible. At the same time, the Preamble to the Constitution sets forth the responsibility of government to protect and promote the public welfare. Local, state, and federal governments discharge this responsibility through regulation and the provision of services. The numerous government services are important but either (1) would not be produced by private business firms or (2) would be produced only for those who could afford them. Typical services include national defense, police and fire protection, education, and construction of roads and highways. To pay for all these services, governments collect a variety of taxes from households (such as personal income taxes and sales taxes) and from businesses (corporate income taxes).

Figure 1.4 shows this exchange of taxes for government services. It also shows government spending of tax dollars for resources and products required to provide those services.

Actually, with government included, our circular flow looks more like a combination of several flows. In reality, it is. The important point is that together the various flows make up a single unit—a complete economic system that effectively provides answers to the basic economic questions. Simply put, the system works.

Command Economies

Before we discuss how to measure a nation's economic performance, we look quickly at another economic system called a *command economy*. A **command economy** is an economic system in which the government decides what goods and services will be produced, how they will be produced, for whom available goods and services will be produced, and who owns and controls the major factors of production. The answers to all four basic economic questions are determined, at least to some degree, through

Let's make a deal (or a market economy). In order to increase sales and reduce inventory, General Motors uses employee discount pricing for everyone. This practical example of a market economy illustrates how businesses (who decide what to produce) and individuals (who decide what to buy) interact in the real world.

consumer products goods and services purchased by individuals for personal consumption

command economy an economic system in which the government decides what goods and services will be produced, how they will be produced, for whom available goods and services will be produced, and who owns and controls the major factors of production

centralized government planning. Today, two types of economic systems—*socialism* and *communism*—serve as examples of command economies.

Socialism   In a *socialist* economy, the key industries are owned and controlled by the government. Such industries usually include transportation, utilities, communications, banking, and industries producing important materials such as steel. Land, buildings, and raw materials also may be the property of the state in a socialist economy. Depending on the country, private ownership of smaller businesses is permitted to varying degrees. People usually may choose their own occupations, but many work in state-owned industries.

What to produce and how to produce it are determined in accordance with national goals, which are based on projected needs and the availability of resources. The distribution of goods and services—who gets what—is also controlled by the state to the extent that it controls rents and wages. Among the professed aims of socialist countries are the equitable distribution of income, the elimination of poverty, the distribution of social services (such as medical care) to all who need them, and the elimination of the economic waste that supposedly accompanies capitalistic competition. The disadvantages of socialism include increased taxation and loss of incentive and motivation for both individuals and business owners.

Today, many of the nations that traditionally have been labeled as socialist nations, including France, the Netherlands, Sweden, and India, are transitioning to a free-market economy. And currently, many countries that once were thought of as communist countries are now often referred to as socialist countries. Examples of former communist countries often referred to as socialists (or even capitalist) include most of the nations that were formerly part of the Union of Soviet Socialist Republics (USSR), China, and Vietnam. Other, more authoritarian countries actually may have socialist economies; however, we tend to think of them as communist because of their almost total lack of freedom.

Communism   If Adam Smith was the father of capitalism, Karl Marx was the father of communism. In his writings during the mid-nineteenth century, Marx advocated a classless society whose citizens together owned all economic resources. All workers then would contribute to this *communist* society according to their ability and would receive benefits according to their need.

Since the breakup of the Soviet Union and economic reforms in China and most of the Eastern European countries, the best remaining examples of communism are North Korea and Cuba. Today these so-called communist economies seem to practice a strictly controlled kind of socialism. The government owns almost all economic resources. The basic economic questions are answered through centralized state planning, which sets prices and wages as well. Emphasis is placed on the production of goods the government needs rather than on the products that consumers might want, so there are frequent shortages of consumer goods. Workers have little choice of jobs, but special skills or talents seem to be rewarded with special privileges. Various groups of professionals (bureaucrats, university professors, and athletes, for example) fare much better than, say, factory workers.

Measuring Economic Performance

4 LEARNING OBJECTIVE
Identify the ways to measure economic performance.

Today, it is hard to turn on the radio, watch the news on television, or read the newspaper without hearing or seeing something about the economy. Consider for just a moment the following questions:

- Are U.S. workers as productive as workers in other countries?
- Is the gross domestic product for the United States increasing or decreasing?
- What is the current balance of trade for our country?
- Why is the unemployment rate important?

The information needed to answer these questions, along with the answers to other similar questions, is easily obtainable from many sources. More important, the answers to these and other questions can be used to gauge the economic health of a nation.

The Importance of Productivity in the Global Marketplace

One way to measure a nation's economic performance is to assess its productivity. **Productivity** is the average level of output per worker per hour. An increase in productivity results in economic growth because a larger number of goods and services are produced by a given labor force. Productivity growth in the United States has increased dramatically over the last several years. For example, overall productivity growth averaged 3.8 percent for the period from 2001 through 2004.[10] (*Note:* At the time of publication, 2004 was the last year that complete statistics were available.) This is an extraordinary statistic when compared against historical standards. And yet, before you think that all the nation's economic problems are over, consider the following questions:

productivity the average level of output per worker per hour

Question: *How does productivity growth affect the economy?*

Answer: Because of productivity growth, it now takes just 90 workers to produce what 100 workers produced in 2001.[11] As a result, employers have reduced costs, earned more profits, and/or sold their products for less. Finally, productivity growth helps American business to compete more effectively with other nations in a competitive world.

Question: *How does a nation improve productivity?*

Answer: Reducing costs and enabling employees to work more efficiently are at the core of all attempts to improve productivity. For example, productivity in the United States is expected to improve dramatically as more economic activity is transferred onto the Internet, reducing costs for servicing customers and handling routine ordering functions between businesses. Other methods that can be used to increase productivity are discussed in detail in Chapter 9.

Question: *Is productivity growth always good.*

Answer: While economists always point to increased efficiency and the ability to produce goods and services for lower costs as a positive factor, a number of factors must be considered before reaching conclusions. First, fewer workers producing more goods and services can lead to higher unemployment rates. In this case, increased productivity is good for employers but not good for unemployed workers seeking jobs in a very competitive work environment. Second, at least part of the upturn in productivity during the 2001–2004 period was the result of employers facing the economic uncertainties after September 11, prospects of a lengthy recession, the war on terrorism in Afghanistan and Iraq, and unrest in the Middle East. Because of these uncertainties, employers refused to hire more workers and pushed existing employees to produce more. As these same employers begin to hire more workers, productivity growth could decline.[12]

Employers in Japan, China, Korea, and other countries throughout the world are also concerned

SPOTLIGHT

The changing U.S. labor force

The importance of valuing diversity is apparent as the U.S. labor force is projected to become increasingly diverse.

12:15 P.M.

	2005	2020
White, non-Hispanic	73%	68%
Hispanic	11%	14%
African American	11%	11%
Asian American	5%	6%

Source: Diversity Central, **www.diversitycentral.com**, and *Workforce 2020*, Hudson Institute.

about productivity. For example, consider the economic growth of China. About 200 years ago, Napoleon returned from China and said, "That is a sleeping dragon. Let him sleep! If he wakes up he will shake the world."[13] Today, China is awake and is shaking the world. Increased productivity has enabled the Chinese to manufacture products that range from trinkets to sophisticated electronic and computer products. And China is just one country. There are many other countries that understand the economic benefits of increased productivity.

@ USING THE INTERNET

For more information about the current GDP and other economic information, you may want to access the U.S. Bureau of Economic Analysis at **www.bea.gov** or the U.S. Bureau of Labor Statistics at **www.bls.gov.**

gross domestic product (GDP) the total dollar value of all goods and services produced by all people within the boundaries of a country during a one-year period

inflation a general rise in the level of prices

deflation a general decrease in the level of prices

Important Economic Indicators that Measure a Nation's Economy

In addition to productivity, a measure called *gross domestic product* can be used to measure the economic well-being of a nation. **Gross domestic product (GDP)** is the total dollar value of all goods and services produced by all people within the boundaries of a country during a one-year period. For example, the value of automobiles produced by employees in both an American-owned General Motors plant and a Japanese-owned Toyota plant *in the United States* are both included in the GDP for the United States. The U.S. GDP was $11,734 billion in 2004.[14]

The GDP figure facilitates comparisons between the United States and other countries because it is the standard used in international guidelines for economic accounting. It is also possible to compare the GDP for one nation over several different time periods. This comparison allows observers to determine the extent to which a nation is experiencing economic growth. For example, government experts project that GDP will grow to $12,638 billion by the year 2012.[15]

To make accurate comparisons of the GDP for different years, we must adjust the dollar amounts for inflation. **Inflation** is a general rise in the level of prices. (The opposite of inflation is deflation.) **Deflation** is a general decrease in the level of prices. By using inflation-adjusted figures, we are able to measure the *real* GDP for a nation. In effect, it is now possible to compare the products and services produced by a nation in constant dollars—dollars that will purchase the same amount of goods and services. Figure 1.5 depicts the GDP of the United States in current dollars and the *real* GDP

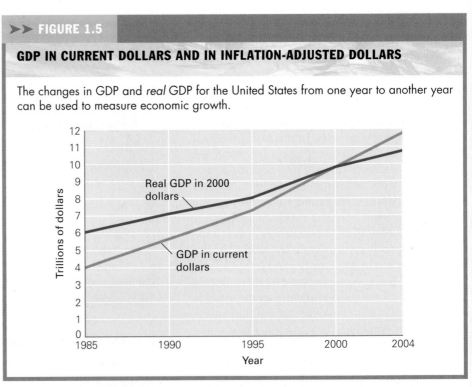

➤➤ FIGURE 1.5

GDP IN CURRENT DOLLARS AND IN INFLATION-ADJUSTED DOLLARS

The changes in GDP and *real* GDP for the United States from one year to another year can be used to measure economic growth.

Source: U.S. Bureau of Economic Analysis website at **www.bea.gov,** accessed September 29, 2005.

in inflation-adjusted dollars. Note that between 1985 and 2004, America's *real* GDP grew from $6,053 billion to $10,756 billion.[16]

In addition to GDP and *real* GDP, other economic measures exist that can be used to evaluate a nation's economy. The **consumer price index (CPI)** is a monthly index that measures the changes in prices of a fixed basket of goods purchased by a typical consumer in an urban area. Goods listed in the CPI include food and beverages, transportation, housing, utilities, clothing, medical care, recreation, education and communication, and other goods and services. Economists often use the CPI to determine the effect of inflation on not only the nation's economy but also consumers. Another monthly index is the producer's price index. The **producer price index (PPI)** measures prices at the wholesale level. Since changes in the PPI reflect price increases or decreases at the wholesale level, the PPI is an accurate predictor of both changes in the CPI and prices that consumers will pay for many everyday necessities. Some additional terms are described in Table 1.2. Like the measures for GDP, these measures can be used to compare one economic statistic over different periods of time.

The Business Cycle

All industrialized nations of the world seek economic growth, full employment, and price stability. However, a nation's economy fluctuates rather than grows at a steady pace every year. In fact, if you were to graph the economic growth rate for a country such as the United States, it would resemble a roller coaster ride with peaks (high points) and troughs (low points). These fluctuations generally are referred to as the **business cycle,** that is, the recurrence of periods of growth and recession in a nation's economic activity. The changes that result from either growth or recession affect the amount of products and services that consumers are willing to purchase and, as a result, the amount of products and services produced. Generally, the business cycle consists of four states: the peak (sometimes called prosperity), recession, the trough, and recovery (sometimes called *expansion*).

During the *peak period*, unemployment is low, and total income is relatively high. As long as the economic outlook remains prosperous, consumers are willing to buy products and services. In fact, businesses often expand and offer new products and

The frustrating search for employment. Often unemployment rates are just one more economic statistic—unless *you're* the one unemployed. In this photo, eager job seekers line up to attend a job expo in New York.

consumer price index (CPI) a monthly index that measures the changes in prices of a fixed basket of goods purchased by a typical consumer in an urban area

producer price index (PPI) an index that measures prices at the wholesale level

business cycle the recurrence of periods of growth and recession in a nation's economic activity

> > TABLE 1.2

COMMON MEASURES USED TO EVALUATE A NATION'S ECONOMIC HEALTH

Economic Measure	Description
1. Balance of trade	The total value of a nation's exports minus the total value of its imports over a specific period of time.
2. Bank credit	A statistic that measures the lending activity of commercial financial institutions.
3. Corporate profits	The total amount of profits made by corporations over selected time periods.
4. Inflation rate	An economic statistic that tracks the increase in prices of goods and services over a period of time. This measure usually is calculated on a monthly or annual basis.
5. National income	The total income earned by various segments of the population, including employees, self-employed individuals, corporations, and other types of income.
6. New housing starts	The total number of new homes started during a specific time period.
7. Prime interest rate	The lowest interest rate that banks charge their most creditworthy customers.
8. Productivity rate	An economic measure that tracks the increase and decrease in the average level of output per worker.
9. Unemployment rate	The percentage of a nation's labor force that is unemployed at any time.

services during the peak period in order to take advantage of consumers' increased buying power.

Economists define a **recession** as two or more consecutive three-month periods of decline in a country's GDP. Because unemployment rises during a recession, total buying power declines. The pessimism that accompanies a recession often stifles both consumer and business spending. As buying power decreases, consumers tend to become more value conscious and reluctant to purchase frivolous items. In response to a recession, many businesses focus on the products and services that provide the most value to their customers. Economists define a **depression** as a severe recession that lasts longer than a recession. A depression is characterized by extremely high unemployment rates, low wages, reduced purchasing power, lack of confidence in the economy, and a general decrease in business activity.

Economists refer to the third phase of the business cycle as the *trough*. The trough of a recession or depression is the turning point when a nation's output and employment bottom out and reach their lowest levels. To offset the effects of recession and depression, the federal government uses both monetary and fiscal policies. **Monetary policies** are the Federal Reserve's decisions that determine the size of the supply of money in the nation and the level of interest rates. Through **fiscal policy,** the government can influence the amount of savings and expenditures by altering the tax structure and changing the levels of government spending.

Although the federal government collects almost $2 trillion in annual revenues, the government often spends more than it receives, resulting in a **federal deficit.** For example, the government had a federal deficit for each year between 2002 and 2004. The total of all federal deficits is called the **national debt.** Today, the U.S. national debt is about $7.5 trillion, or approximately $26,000 for every man, woman, and child in the United States.[17]

Some experts believe that effective use of monetary and fiscal policies can speed up recovery and reduce the amount of time the economy is in recession. *Recovery* (or *expansion*) is movement of the economy from depression or recession to prosperity. High unemployment rates decline, income increases, and both the ability and the willingness to buy rise.

Types of Competition

Our capitalist system ensures that individuals and businesses make the decisions about what to produce, how to produce it, and what price to charge for the product. Mattel, Inc., for example, can introduce new versions of its famous Barbie doll, license the Barbie name, change the doll's price and method of distribution, and attempt to produce and market Barbie in other countries or over the Internet at **www.mattel.com.** Our system also allows customers the right to choose between Mattel's products and those produced by competitors.

Competition like that between Mattel and other toy manufacturers is a necessary and extremely important by-product of capitalism. Business **competition** is essentially a rivalry among businesses for sales to potential customers. In a capitalistic economy, competition also ensures that a firm will survive only if it serves its customers well by providing products and services that meet needs. Economists recognize four different degrees of competition ranging from ideal, complete competition to no competition at all. These are perfect competition, monopolistic competition, oligopoly, and monopoly. For a quick overview of the different types of competition, including numbers of firms and examples for each type, look at Table 1.3.

Perfect Competition

Perfect (or pure) competition is the market situation in which there are many buyers and sellers of a product, and no single buyer or seller is powerful enough to affect the price of that product. Note that this definition includes several important ideas. First, we are discussing the market for a single product, say, bushels of wheat. Second,

---

recession two or more consecutive three-month periods of decline in a country's GDP

depression a severe recession that lasts longer than a recession

monetary policies Federal Reserve decisions that determine the size of the supply of money in the nation and the level of interest rates

fiscal policy government influence on the amount of savings and expenditures; accomplished by altering the tax structure and by changing the levels of government spending

federal deficit a shortfall created when the federal government spends more in a fiscal year than it receives

national debt the total of all federal deficits

5 LEARNING OBJECTIVE
Outline the four types of competition.

competition rivalry among businesses for sales to potential customers

perfect (or pure) competition the market situation in which there are many buyers and sellers of a product, and no single buyer or seller is powerful enough to affect the price of that product

>> **TABLE 1.3**

FOUR DIFFERENT TYPES OF COMPETITION

The number of firms determines the degree of competition within an industry.

Type of Competition	Number of Business Firms or Suppliers	Real-World Examples
1. Perfect	Many	Corn, wheat, peanuts
2. Monopolistic	Many	Clothing, shoes
3. Oligopoly	Few	Automobiles, cereals
4. Monopoly	One	Software protected by copyright, local public utilities

all sellers offer essentially the same product for sale. Third, all buyers and sellers know everything there is to know about the market (including, in our example, the prices that all sellers are asking for their wheat). And fourth, the overall market is not affected by the actions of any one buyer or seller.

When perfect competition exists, every seller should ask the same price that every other seller is asking. Why? Because if one seller wanted 50 cents more per bushel of wheat than all the others, that seller would not be able to sell a single bushel. Buyers could—and would—do better by purchasing wheat from the competition. On the other hand, a firm willing to sell below the going price would sell all its wheat quickly. But that seller would lose sales revenue (and profit) because buyers actually are willing to pay more.

In perfect competition, then, sellers—and buyers as well—must accept the going price. The price of each product is determined by the actions of *all buyers and all sellers together* through the forces of supply and demand.

The Basics of Supply and Demand

The **supply** of a particular product is the quantity of the product that producers are willing to sell at each of various prices. Producers are rational people, so we would expect them to offer more of a product for sale at higher prices and to offer less of the product at lower prices, as illustrated by the supply curve in Figure 1.6.

The **demand** for a particular product is the quantity that buyers are willing to purchase at each of various prices. Buyers, too, are usually rational, so we would expect them—as a group—to buy more of a product when its price is low and to buy less of the product when its price is high, as depicted by the demand curve in Figure 1.6.

supply the quantity of a product that producers are willing to sell at each of various prices

demand the quantity of a product that buyers are willing to purchase at each of various prices

The Equilibrium, or Market, Price

There is always one certain price at which the demanded quantity of a product is exactly equal to the quantity of that product produced. Suppose that producers are willing to *supply* 2 million bushels of wheat at a price of $4 per bushel and that buyers are willing to *purchase* 2 million bushels at a price of $4 per bushel. In other words, supply and demand are in balance, or in equilibrium, at the price of $4. Economists call this price the *market price*. The **market price** of any product is the price at which the quantity demanded is exactly equal to the quantity supplied. If suppliers produce 2 million bushels, then no one who is willing to pay $4 per bushel will have to go without wheat, and no producer who is willing to sell at $4 per bushel will be stuck with unsold wheat.

market price the price at which the quantity demanded is exactly equal to the quantity supplied

In theory and in the real world, market prices are affected by anything that affects supply and demand. The *demand* for wheat, for example, might change if researchers suddenly discovered that it offered a previously unknown health benefit. Then buyers would demand more wheat at every price. Or the *supply* of wheat might change if new technology permitted the production of greater quantities of wheat from the same amount of acreage. Other changes that can affect competitive prices are shifts in buyer tastes, the development of new products, fluctuations in income owing to inflation or recession, or even changes in the weather that affect the production of wheat.

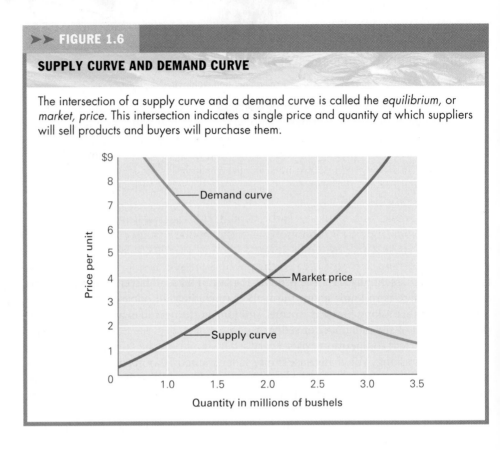

➤➤ FIGURE 1.6

SUPPLY CURVE AND DEMAND CURVE

The intersection of a supply curve and a demand curve is called the *equilibrium,* or *market, price.* This intersection indicates a single price and quantity at which suppliers will sell products and buyers will purchase them.

Perfect competition is quite rare in today's world. Many real markets, however, are examples of monopolistic competition.

Monopolistic Competition

monopolistic competition a market situation in which there are many buyers along with a relatively large number of sellers who differentiate their products from the products of competitors

product differentiation the process of developing and promoting differences between one's products and all similar products

Monopolistic competition is a market situation in which there are many buyers along with a relatively large number of sellers. The various products available in a monopolistically competitive market are very similar in nature, and they are all intended to satisfy the same need. However, each seller attempts to make its product different from the others by providing unique product features, an attention-getting brand name, unique packaging, or services such as free delivery or a "lifetime" warranty.

Product differentiation is the process of developing and promoting differences between one's products and all similar products. It is a fact of life for the producers of many consumer goods, from soaps to clothing to furniture to shoes. A furniture manufacturer such as Thomasville sees what looks like a mob of competitors, all trying to chip away at its market. By differentiating each of its products from all similar products produced by competitors, Thomasville obtains some limited control over the market price of its product.

Oligopoly

oligopoly a market (or industry) in which there are few sellers

An **oligopoly** is a market (or industry) situation in which there are few sellers. Generally, these sellers are quite large, and sizable investments are required to enter into their market. Examples of oligopolies are the automobile, car rental, cereal, and farm implement industries.

Because there are few sellers in an oligopoly, the market actions of each seller can have a strong effect on competitors' sales and prices. If General Motors, for example, reduces its automobile prices, Ford, DaimlerChrysler, Toyota, and Nissan usually do the same to retain their market shares. In the absence of much price competition, product differentiation becomes the major competitive weapon; this is very evident in the advertising of the major auto manufacturers. For instance, when General Motors began offering employee-discount pricing, Ford and Chrysler also launched competitive financing deals.

Monopoly

A **monopoly** is a market (or industry) with only one seller. In a monopoly, there is no close substitute for the product or service. Because only one firm is the supplier of a product, it would seem that it has complete control over price. However, no firm can set its price at some astronomical figure just because there is no competition; the firm soon would find that it had no customers or sales revenue either. Instead, the firm in a monopoly position must consider the demand for its product and set the price at the most profitable level.

    Classic examples of monopolies in the United States are public utilities. Each utility firm operates in a **natural monopoly,** an industry that requires a huge investment in capital and within which any duplication of facilities would be wasteful. Natural monopolies are permitted to exist because the public interest is best served by their existence, but they operate under the scrutiny and control of various state and federal agencies. While many public utilities are still classified as natural monopolies, there is increased competition in many industries. For example, there have been increased demands for consumer choice when selecting a company that provides electrical service to both homes and businesses.

    A legal monopoly—sometimes referred to as a *limited monopoly*—is created when the federal government issues a copyright, patent, or trademark. Each of these exists for a specific period of time and can be used to protect the owners of written materials, ideas, or product brands from unauthorized use by competitors that have not shared in the time, effort, and expense required for their development. Because Microsoft owns the copyright on its popular Windows software, it enjoys a limited-monopoly position. Except for natural monopolies and monopolies created by copyrights, patents, and trademarks, federal antitrust laws prohibit both monopolies and attempts to form monopolies.

monopoly a market (or industry) with only one seller

natural monopoly an industry requiring huge investments in capital and within which any duplication of facilities would be wasteful and thus not in the public interest

American Business Today

While our economic system is far from perfect, it provides Americans with a high standard of living compared with people in other countries throughout the world. **Standard of living** is a loose, subjective measure of how well off an individual or a society is mainly in terms of want satisfaction through goods and services. Also, our economic system offers solutions to many of the problems that plague society and provides opportunity for people who are willing to work and to continue learning.

    To understand the current business environment and the challenges ahead, it helps to understand how business developed.

Early Business Development

Our American business system has its roots in the knowledge, skills, and values that the earliest settlers brought to this country. Refer to Figure 1.7 for an overall view of our nation's history, the development of our business system, and some major inventions that influenced the nation and our business system.

    The first settlers in the New World were concerned mainly with providing themselves with basic necessities—food, clothing, and shelter. Almost all families lived on farms, and the entire family worked at the business of surviving. They used their surplus for trading, mainly by barter, among themselves and with the English trading ships that called at the colonies. **Barter** is a system of exchange in which goods or services are traded directly for other goods and/or services without using money. As this trade increased, small-scale business enterprises began to appear. Some settlers were able to use their skills and their excess time to work under the domestic system of production. The **domestic system** was a method of manufacturing in which an entrepreneur

6 LEARNING OBJECTIVE
Summarize the factors that affect the business environment and the challenges American businesses will encounter in the future.

standard of living a loose, subjective measure of how well off an individual or a society is mainly in terms of want satisfaction through goods and services

barter a system of exchange in which goods or services are traded directly for other goods and/or services without using money

domestic system a method of manufacturing in which an entrepreneur distributes raw materials to various homes, where families process them into finished goods to be offered for sale by the merchant entrepreneur

distributed raw materials to various homes, where families would process them into finished goods. The merchant entrepreneur then offered the goods for sale.

Then, in 1789, a young English apprentice mechanic named Samuel Slater decided to sail to America. At this time, British law forbade the export of machinery, technology, and skilled workers. To get around the law, Slater painstakingly memorized the plans for Richard Arkwright's water-powered spinning machine, which had

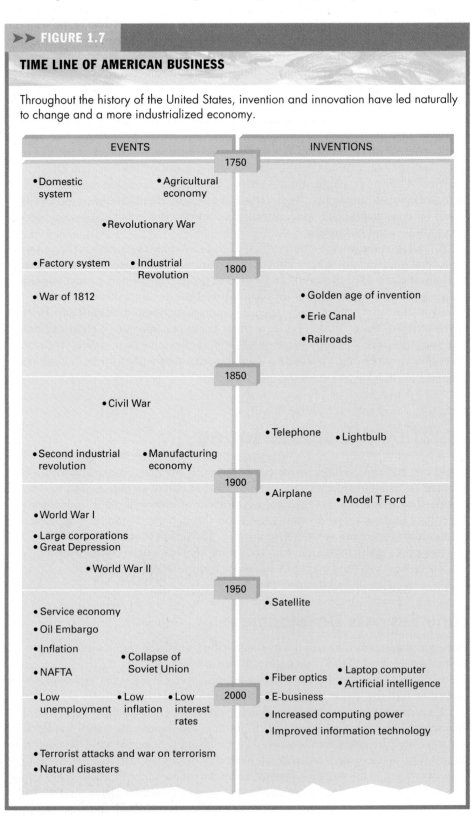

➤➤ FIGURE 1.7

TIME LINE OF AMERICAN BUSINESS

Throughout the history of the United States, invention and innovation have led naturally to change and a more industrialized economy.

EVENTS	INVENTIONS
1750	
• Domestic system • Agricultural economy	
• Revolutionary War	
• Factory system • Industrial Revolution **1800**	
• War of 1812	• Golden age of invention
	• Erie Canal
	• Railroads
1850	
• Civil War	
	• Telephone • Lightbulb
• Second industrial revolution • Manufacturing economy	
1900	• Airplane • Model T Ford
• World War I	
• Large corporations	
• Great Depression	
• World War II	
1950	• Satellite
• Service economy	
• Oil Embargo	
• Inflation	
• Collapse of Soviet Union	
• NAFTA	• Laptop computer
	• Fiber optics • Artificial intelligence
• Low unemployment • Low inflation • Low interest rates **2000**	• E-business
	• Increased computing power
	• Improved information technology
• Terrorist attacks and war on terrorism	
• Natural disasters	

revolutionized the British textile industry, and left England disguised as a farmer. A year later he set up a textile factory in Pawtucket, Rhode Island, to spin raw cotton into thread. Slater's ingenuity resulted in America's first use of the **factory system** of manufacturing, in which all the materials, machinery, and workers required to manufacture a product are assembled in one place. The Industrial Revolution in America was born. A manufacturing technique called *specialization* was used to improve productivity. **Specialization** is the separation of a manufacturing process into distinct tasks and the assignment of the different tasks to different individuals.

The years from 1820 to 1900 were the golden age of invention and innovation in machinery. Elias Howe's sewing machine became available to convert materials into clothing. The agricultural machinery of John Deere and Cyrus McCormick revolutionized farm production. At the same time, new means of transportation greatly expanded the domestic markets for American products. Many business historians view the period from 1870 to 1900 as the second Industrial Revolution. Certainly, many characteristics of our modern business system took form during this time period.

The Twentieth Century

Industrial growth and prosperity continued well into the twentieth century. Henry Ford's moving automotive assembly line, which brought the work to the worker, refined the concept of specialization and helped spur on the mass production of consumer goods. Fundamental changes occurred in business ownership and management as well. No longer were the largest businesses owned by one individual; instead, ownership was in the hands of thousands of corporate shareholders who were willing to invest in—but not to operate—a business.

The Roaring Twenties ended with the sudden crash of the stock market in 1929 and the near collapse of the economy. The Great Depression that followed in the 1930s was a time of misery and human suffering. People lost their faith in business and its ability to satisfy the needs of society without government involvement. After Franklin D. Roosevelt became president in 1933, the federal government devised a number of programs to get the economy moving again. In implementing these programs, the government got deeply involved in business for the first time.

The economy was on the road to recovery when World War II broke out in Europe in 1939. The need for vast quantities of war materials spurred business activity and technological development. This rapid economic pace continued after the war, and the 1950s and 1960s witnessed both increasing production and a rising standard of living.

In the mid-1970s, however, a shortage of crude oil led to a new set of problems for business. As the cost of petroleum products increased, a corresponding price increase took place in the cost of energy and the cost of goods and services. The result was inflation at a rate well over 10 percent per year during the early 1980s. Interest rates also increased dramatically, so both businesses and consumers reduced their borrowing. Business profits fell as the purchasing power of consumers was eroded by inflation and high interest rates.

By the early 1990s, unemployment numbers, inflation, and interest—all factors that affect business—were now at record lows. In turn, business took advantage of this economic prosperity to invest in information technology, cut costs, and increase flexibility and efficiency. The

factory system a system of manufacturing in which all the materials, machinery, and workers required to manufacture a product are assembled in one place

specialization the separation of a manufacturing process into distinct tasks and the assignment of the different tasks to different individuals

Economic prosperity after World War II. For nearly 30 years after World War II, the United States became the most productive nation in the world. Fueled by economic prosperity, Americans bought homes, automobiles, and other consumer goods that made the American standard of living the envy of the world.

Internet became a major force in the economy, with computer hardware, software, and Internet service providers taking advantage of the increased need for information. e-Business—a topic we will continue to explore throughout this text—became an accepted method of conducting business. **e-Business** is the organized effort of individuals to produce and sell through the Internet, for a profit, the products and services that satisfy society's needs. As further evidence of the financial health of the new economy, the stock market enjoyed the longest period of sustained economic growth in our history. Unfortunately, by the last part of the twentieth century, a larger number of business failures and declining stock values were initial signs that larger economic problems were on the way.

e-Business the organized effort of individuals to produce and sell through the Internet, for a profit, the products and services that satisfy society's needs

A New Century: 2000 and Beyond

According to many economic experts, the first few years of the twenty-first century might be characterized as the best of times and the worst of times rolled into one package. On the plus side, technology became available at an affordable price. Both individuals and businesses now could access information with the click of a button. They also could buy and sell merchandise online.

In addition to information technology, the growth of service businesses and increasing opportunities for global trade also changed the way American firms do business in the twenty-first century. Because they employ over eighty percent of the American work force, service businesses are a very important component of our economy.[18] As a result, service businesses must find ways to improve productivity and cut costs while at the same time providing jobs for an even larger portion of the work force.

On the negative side, it is hard to watch television, surf the web, listen to the radio, or read the newspaper without hearing some news about the economy. Even though many of the economic indicators described in Table 1.2 on page 19 remain strong or show signs of improvement, there is still a certain amount of pessimism surrounding the economy.

The Current Business Environment

Before reading on, answer the following question:

In today's competitive business world, which of the following environments affects business?

    a. The competitive environment
    b. The global environment
    c. The technological environment
    d. The economic environment
    e. All the above

The correct answer is "e." All the environments listed affect business today. For example, businesses operate in a *competitive environment*. As noted earlier in this chapter, competition is a basic component of capitalism. Every day business owners must figure out what makes their businesses successful and how their businesses are different from the competition. Often the answer is contained in the basic definition of business on page 9. Just for a moment, review the definition:

> *Business* is the organized effort of individuals to produce and sell, for a profit, the goods and services that satisfy society's needs.

Note the phrase *satisfy society's needs*. Those three words say a lot about how well a successful firm competes with competitors. If you meet customer needs, then you have a better chance at success.

Related to the competitive environment is the *global environment*. Not only do American businesses have to compete with other American businesses, but they also must compete with businesses from all over the globe. According to global experts, China is the fastest-growing economy in the world. And China is not alone. Other countries around the world also compete with U.S. firms. There once was a time when the label "Made in the United States" gave U.S. businesses an inside edge both at home and in the global marketplace. Now, other countries manufacture and sell goods. According to Richard Haass, president of the Council on Foreign Relations, "There will be winners and losers from globalization. We win every time we go shopping because prices are lower. Choice is greater because of globalization. But there are losers. There are people who will lose their jobs either to foreign competition or [to] technological innovation."[19]

While both foreign competition and technological innovation have changed the way we do business, the *technology environment* for U.S. businesses has never been more challenging. While many of us take technological change for granted, it does change the way we do business. Changes in manufacturing equipment, communication with customers, and distribution of products are all examples of how technology has changed everyday business practices. And the technology will continue to change. New technology will require businesses to spend additional money to keep abreast of an ever-changing technology environment.

In addition to the competitive, global, and technology environments, the *economic environment* always must be considered when making business decisions. While many people believe that business has unlimited resources, the truth is that managers and business owners realize that there is never enough money to fund all the activities a business might want to fund. This fact is especially important when the nation's economy takes a nosedive or an individual firm's sales revenue and profits are declining.

When you look back at the original question we asked at the beginning of this section, clearly, each different type of environment affects the way a business does *business*. As a result, there are always opportunities for improvement and challenges that must be considered.

Business Around the World

Flying the Frightening Skies

Terrorism in the sky has changed the way people travel and the way businesses operate, sending ripples throughout the global economy. After police thwarted a plot to bomb several jets flying between Great Britain and the United States, British Airways canceled 1,100 flights, stranding thousands of passengers and leaving 20,000 pieces of luggage in limbo. Airline stock prices nosedived and airports were in turmoil as stricter security forced travelers to check all bags. Trying to recoup some of its lost revenue, one airline even sued the U.K. government.

The new rules slowed business travelers and hurt airport retailers that cater to international travelers who buy duty-free products before flying home. In time, more delays and more frustration could push passengers toward other modes of travel. For now, analysts predict a surge in charter flights and in business travel through private carriers.

The Challenges Ahead

There it is—the American business system in brief. When it works well, it provides jobs for those who are willing to work, a standard of living that few countries can match, and many opportunities for personal advancement. However, like every other system devised by humans, it is not perfect. Our business system may give us prosperity, but it also gave us the Great Depression of the 1930s and the economic problems of the 1970s, the late 1980s, and the first part of the twenty-first century.

Obviously, the system can be improved. Certainly there are plenty of people who are willing to tell us exactly what *they* think the American economy needs. But these people provide us only with conflicting opinions. Who is right and who is wrong? Even the experts cannot agree.

The experts do agree, however, that several key issues will challenge our economic system (and our nation) over the next decade. Some of the questions to be resolved include

- How can we encourage Iraq and Afghanistan to establish a democratic and free society and resolve possible conflict with North Korea and other countries throughout the world?
- How can we create a more stable economy and create new jobs?
- As a nation, how can we develop a disaster crisis management program that will help people in times of peril?
- How can we meet the challenges of managing culturally diverse work forces to address the needs of a culturally diverse marketplace?
- How can we make American manufacturers more productive and more competitive with foreign producers who have lower labor costs?
- How can we preserve the benefits of competition and small businesses in our American economic system?
- How can we encourage economic growth and at the same time continue to conserve natural resources, protect our environment, and meet the needs of society?
- How can we best market American-made products in foreign nations?
- How can we meet the needs of two-income families, single parents, older Americans, and the less fortunate?

The answers to these questions are anything but simple. In the past, Americans always have been able to solve their economic problems through ingenuity and creativity. Now, as we continue the journey through the twenty-first century, we need that same ingenuity and creativity not only to solve our current problems but also to compete in the global marketplace.

According to economic experts, if we as a nation can become more competitive, we may solve many of our current domestic problems. As an added bonus, increased competitiveness also will enable us to meet the economic challenges posed by other industrialized nations of the world. The way we solve these problems will affect our own future, our children's future, and that of our nation. Within the American economic and political system, the answers are ours to provide.

The American business system is not perfect by any means, but it does work reasonably well. We discuss some of its problems in Chapter 2 as we examine the topics of social responsibility and business ethics.

RETURN TO Inside Business

Frito-Lay knows that tastes change every day, that competitors change every day, and therefore, that it must earn its success one day at a time. Although the company commands a 65 percent share of the salty-snack market, its food experts are always in the kitchen developing new snacks. From Dorito's Guacamole-flavored Tortilla Chips and Light Lay's Potato Chips to Oberto Beef Jerky Crisps and Dorito's Black Pepper Jack, Frito-Lay offers a wide variety of choices to tempt more palates away from rival snacks.

To attract hungry consumers who otherwise might munch on cookies or crackers, management recently beefed up the Frito-Lay advertising budget by 50 percent—to a whopping $150 million. Teens who like intensely flavored and vividly colored snacks are a main target, as are adults who want snacks with nutrition benefits. Clearly, Frito-Lay is doing everything it can to ensure healthier products and profits in its future.

Questions

1. What customer needs do you think Frito-Lay aims to satisfy with its assortment of snacks?
2. How does Frito-Lay use product differentiation to compete with other food manufacturers?

➤➤ CHAPTER REVIEW

Summary

1

Discuss your future in the world of business.

For many years, people in business—both employees and managers—assumed that prosperity would continue. When the bubble burst, a large number of these same people then began to ask the question: What do we do now? Although this is a fair question, it is difficult to answer. Certainly, for a college student taking business courses or a beginning employee just starting a career, the question is even more difficult to answer. And yet there are still opportunities out there for people who are willing to work hard, continue to learn, and possess the ability to adapt to change. To be sure, employers and our capitalistic economic system are more demanding than ever before. As you begin this course, ask yourself: What can I do that will make employers want to pay me a salary? What skills do I have that employers need? The kind of career you choose ultimately will depend on your own values and what you feel is most important in life. But deciding on the kind of career you want is only a first step. To get a job in your chosen field and to be successful at it, you will have to develop a plan, or road map, that ensures that you have the necessary skills and the knowledge the job requires to become a better employee. By studying business, you also may decide to start your own business and become a better consumer and investor.

2

Define *business* and identify potential risks and rewards.

Business is the organized effort of individuals to produce and sell, for a profit, the goods and services that satisfy society's needs. Four kinds of resources—material, human, financial, and informational—must be combined to start and operate a business. The three general types of businesses are manufacturers, service businesses, and marketing intermediaries. Profit is what remains after all business expenses are deducted from sales revenue. It is the payment that owners receive for assuming the risks of business—primarily the risks of not receiving payment and of losing whatever has been invested in the firm.

3

Define *economics* and describe the two types of economic systems: capitalism and command economy.

Economics is the study of how wealth is created and distributed. An economic system must answer four questions: What goods and services will be produced? How will they be produced? For whom will they be produced? Who owns and who controls the major factors of production? Capitalism (on which our economic system is based) is an economic system in which individuals own and operate the majority of businesses that provide goods and services. Capitalism stems from the theories of Adam Smith. Smith's pure laissez-faire capitalism is an economic system in which the factors of production are owned by private entities, and all individuals are free to use their resources as they see fit; prices are determined by the workings of supply and demand in competitive markets; and the economic role of government is limited to rule maker and umpire.

Our economic system today is a mixed economy. In the circular flow that characterizes our business system (see Figure 1.4), households and businesses exchange resources for goods and services, using money as the medium of exchange. In a similar manner, government collects taxes from businesses and households and purchases products and resources with which to provide services.

In a command economy, government, rather than individuals, owns the factors of production and provides the answers to the three other economic questions. Socialist and communist economies are—at least in theory—command economies. In the real world, however, communists seem to practice a strictly controlled kind of socialism.

Identify the ways to measure economic performance.

One way to evaluate the performance of an economic system is to assess changes in productivity, which is the average level of output per worker per hour. Gross domestic product (GDP) also can be used to measure a nation's economic well-being and is the total dollar value of all goods and services produced by all people within the boundaries of a country during a one-year period. This figure facilitates comparisons between the United States and other countries because it is the standard used in international guidelines for economic accounting. It is also possible to adjust GDP for inflation and thus to measure *real* GDP. In addition to GDP, other economic indicators include a nation's balance of trade, bank credit, corporate profits, consumer price index (CPI), inflation rate, national income, new housing starts, prime interest rate, producer price index (PPI), productivity rate, and unemployment rate.

A nation's economy fluctuates rather than grows at a steady pace every year. These fluctuations generally are referred to as the business cycle. Generally, the business cycle consists of four states: the peak (sometimes referred to as prosperity), recession, the trough, and recovery. Some experts believe that effective use of monetary policy (the Federal Reserve's decisions that determine the size of the supply of money and the level of interest rates) and fiscal policies (the government's influence on the amount of savings and expenditures) can speed up recovery and even eliminate depressions for the business cycle.

Outline the four types of competition.

Competition is essentially a rivalry among businesses for sales to potential customers. In a capitalist economy, competition works to ensure the efficient and effective operation of business. Competition also ensures that a firm will survive only if it serves its customers well. Economists recognize four degrees of competition. Ranging from most to least competitive, the four degrees are perfect competition, monopolistic competition, oligopoly, and monopoly. The factors of supply and demand generally influence the price that consumers pay producers for goods and services.

Summarize the factors that affect the business environment and the challenges American businesses will encounter in the future.

Since its beginnings, American business has been based on private ownership of property and freedom of enterprise. From this beginning, through the Industrial Revolution of the early nineteenth century, and to the phenomenal expansion of American industry in the nineteenth and early twentieth centuries, our government maintained an essentially laissez-faire attitude toward business. However, during the Great Depression of the 1930s, the federal government began to provide a number of social services to its citizens. Government's role in business has expanded considerably since that time.

During the 1970s, a shortage of crude oil led to higher prices and inflation. In the 1980s, business profits fell as the consumers' purchasing power was eroded by inflation and high interest rates. By the early 1990s, the U.S. economy began to show signs of improvement and economic growth. Unemployment numbers, inflation, and interest—all factors that affect business—were now at record lows. Fueled by investment in information technology, the stock market enjoyed the longest period of sustained economic growth in our history. Increased use of the Internet and e-business now is changing the way that firms do business. Other factors that affect the way firms do business include the increasing importance of services and global trade. Unfortunately, by the last part of the 1990s, a larger number of business failures and declining stock values were initial signs that more economic problems were on the way as we entered the twenty-first century.

Now more than ever before, the way a business operates is affected by the competitive environment, global environment, technological environment, and economic environment. As a result, business has a number of opportunities for improvement and challenges for the future. According to the experts, if we as a nation can become more competitive, we may solve many of our current domestic problems. As an added bonus, increased competitiveness also will enable us to meet the economic challenges posed by other industrialized nations of the world.

Key Terms

You should now be able to define and give an example relevant to each of the following terms.

free enterprise (4)
cultural (or workplace) diversity (6)
business (9)
profit (11)
stakeholders (11)
economics (11)
microeconomics (12)
macroeconomics (12)
economy (12)
factors of production (12)
entrepreneur (13)
capitalism (13)
invisible hand (13)
market economy (14)
mixed economy (14)
consumer products (15)
command economy (15)
productivity (17)
gross domestic product (GDP) (18)
inflation (18)
deflation (18)
consumer price index (CPI) (19)
producer price index (PPI) (19)
business cycle (19)
recession (20)
depression (20)
monetary policies (20)
fiscal policy (20)
federal deficit (20)
national debt (20)
competition (20)
perfect (or pure) competition (20)
supply (21)
demand (21)
market price (21)
monopolistic competition (22)
product differentiation (22)
oligopoly (22)
monopoly (23)
natural monopoly (23)
standard of living (23)
barter (23)
domestic system (23)
factory system (25)
specialization (25)
e-business (26)

Review Questions

1. What reasons would you give if you were advising someone to study business?
2. What factors affect a person's choice of careers?
3. Describe the four resources that must be combined to organize and operate a business. How do they differ from the economist's factors of production?
4. What distinguishes consumers from other buyers of goods and services?
5. Describe the relationship among profit, business risk, and the satisfaction of customers' needs.
6. What are the four basic economic questions? How are they answered in a capitalist economy?
7. Explain the invisible hand of capitalism.
8. Describe the four basic assumptions required for a laissez-faire capitalist economy.
9. Why is the American economy called a mixed economy?
10. Based on Figure 1.4, outline the economic interactions between business and households in our business system.
11. How does capitalism differ from socialism and communism?
12. Define gross domestic product. Why is this economic measure significant?
13. How is the producer price index related to the consumer price index?
14. What are the four steps in a typical business cycle? How are monetary and fiscal policy related to the business cycle?
15. Choose three of the economic measures described in Table 1.2 and describe why these indicators are important when measuring a nation's economy.
16. Identify and compare the four forms of competition.
17. Explain how the equilibrium, or market, price of a product is determined.
18. Four different environments that affect business were described in Chapter 1. Choose one of the environments and explain how it affects a small electronics manufacturer located in Oregon.
19. What do you consider the most important challenges that will face people in the United States in the years ahead?

Discussion Questions

1. In what ways have the economic problems that the nation has experienced in the past three years affected business firms? In what ways have these problems affected employees?
2. What factors caused American business to develop into a mixed economic system rather than some other type of economic system?
3. Does an individual consumer really have a voice in answering the basic economic questions?
4. Is gross domestic product a reliable indicator of a nation's economic health? What might be a better indicator?
5. Discuss this statement: "Business competition encourages efficiency of production and leads to improved product quality."
6. In our business system, how is government involved in answering the four basic economic questions? Does government participate in the system or interfere with it?
7. Choose one of the challenges listed on page 28 and describe possible ways that business and society could help to solve or eliminate the problem in the future.

►► VIDEO CASE 1.1

Stonyfield Farm's "Yogurt on a Mission"

Stonyfield Farm's "Yogurt on a Mission" is changing the culture of at least one multinational corporation. Stonyfield Farm, founded in New Hampshire in 1983, began with a few Jersey cows. Today it owns the third largest-selling yogurt brand in America. The company's extensive line of organic foods includes refrigerated yogurts, ice cream, frozen yogurt, soft-serve yogurt, cultured soy snacks, and drinkable yogurts. All its products meet rigorous guidelines for organic certification because the ingredients are produced without synthetic fertilizers or pesticides, antibiotics, and hormones. Although organic foods were not as popular when Stonyfield was established, they currently account for a whopping $9 billion in yearly sales.

Stonyfield is pursuing a five-part mission to (1) support family farmers, (2) be profitable, (3) offer quality products, (4) protect the environment, and (5) be a great place for employees to work. All Stonyfield's decisions and actions reflect this ambitious mission. Managers are dedicated to using only the highest-quality ingredients to make all-natural food products that are both healthy and tasty. They use product packaging to educate customers about environmental causes such as global warming and recycling. They also are firmly committed to the family farms that supply organic milk for Stonyfield's products, paying a higher price so that the farmers can survive even when competing yogurt makers cut the amount they pay for milk. And they ensure that workplace conditions allow employees the opportunity to develop their skills and advance into new positions.

Following company policy to "reduce, reuse, recycle," Stonyfield's personnel always look for the most environmentally friendly ways to operate. For example, the company currently recycles 60 percent of its yogurt plant's waste. However, CEO Gary Hirshberg wants to increase that recycling level to 80 percent or higher. Even milk that does not meet the company's strict quality standards is not wasted—it goes to local farmers, who feed it to their pigs. The company also collects used yogurt cups and turns them over to a company that recycles the plastic into handles for razors and toothbrushes.

Stonyfield's continuing success proves that caring for the environment can be profitable. Using less energy or water actually lowers operating costs. Similarly, reducing or recycling waste lowers waste-removal costs. Just as important, communicating with customers about environmental issues creates a closer connection and builds sales by reinforcing brand loyalty. In fact, Stonyfield's sales have been growing rapidly, and it donates 10 percent of its profits to environmental causes every year.

Hirshberg is also using his entrepreneurial talents to move into the lucrative fast-food market with O'Natural's restaurants. The chain serves healthy fast food in a comfortable, family-friendly setting—with environmental education as a side dish. "We call it 'fast food with a mission,'" the CEO states.

Now Stonyfield is entering a new phase of its business life. In 2001, France's Groupe Danone—maker of Dannon, the world's best-selling yogurt—acquired a 40 percent holding in Stonyfield. In 2004, Groupe Danone increased that stake to 80 percent. If Stonyfield's president leaves the company, Groupe Danone will keep donating 10 percent of Stonyfield's profits to environmental causes for at least a decade afterward.

Groupe Danone's chairman sees Stonyfield as a model for doing business in the future. "We are driven by social values similar to Gary's," he notes. "We have to think not only in terms of economics, but also in terms of social responsibility." This fits with Hirshberg's long-term view of socially responsible businesses and healthier customers: "If you make the right choices, then future generations will have a healthier planet and healthier, more enjoyable lives."[20]

For more information about this company, go to **www.stonyfield.com.**

Questions

1. As a business, what needs does Stonyfield satisfy for its customers?
2. Does the yogurt market reflect monopolistic competition or an oligopoly? Support your answer by discussing how Stonyfield's diverse product line helps it to compete.
3. Why would a firm like Stonyfield embrace environmental causes and the concept of increasing sales and profits?
4. From the perspective of business profit, should Groupe Danone keep contributing to environmental causes for many years after Hirshberg leaves? Why?

►► CASE 1.2

Wipro Vies to Bring Business to Bangalore

As global demand rises for technology and engineering services, Wipro, Ltd., wants to bring much of the business to Bangalore. The Indian company—which has offices across Europe, Asia, and the United States—writes software, handles back-office operations, and designs high-tech products for some of the world's largest corporations. When Fiat wanted a satellite navigation system for its Alfa Romeo sports cars, it hired Wipro. Nokia, Morgan Stanley, Cisco, Honeywell, and General Motors are among the 420 other companies that have drawn on Wipro's expertise.

Wipro is prospering from the trend toward outsourcing, in which companies reduce their costs by sending projects or jobs to countries where labor costs are lower. Skilled technology professionals in India are paid far less than their counterparts in Western Europe and the United States. Although Wipro raises salaries regularly and offers employees stock and other benefits, "the cost advantage is still in India's favor," observes the chief marketing officer. This is why some companies hire Wipro or its main Indian competitors, Tata Consultancy Services and Infosys Technologies, to perform functions such as providing technical support to customers.

In only six years, Wipro's annual sales have soared from $150 million to nearly $2 billion. To keep up with this explosive growth, the company hires three new employees every hour of every business day. In 2002, 14,000 people were on the payroll; today, nearly 42,000 are on the payroll, including several thousand who work on assignment for months at a time at customers' offices in the United States, Japan, or Europe.

By hiring Wipro to deal with operational nuts and bolts such as processing paperwork, business customers can focus on the tasks that make a difference to *their* customers. Florida's E-OPS, for example, is a start-up company that markets mortgage-processing services to banks. Instead of having their own employees fill out forms, make multiple copies, and send documents to different departments and organizations, banks seeking to cut costs and save time can hire E-OPS. Wipro does the actual processing, whereas E-OPS concentrates on signing new customers and meeting their needs. "It's amazing that you can run a national company with just a handful of employees, and Wipro does the rest," says the CEO of E-OPS.

As Wipro expands its menu of services, it faces tough competition not only from Indian firms but also from IBM, Accenture, and other corporations with decades of experience in working with a global customer base. Profits are healthy, and customers are satisfied, yet Wipro is constantly on the lookout for ways to improve. Not long ago, Wipro managers toured a nearby Toyota factory and came away with ideas for reconfiguring workspaces, boosting employee involvement, and more—ideas that took quality to a new level and hiked efficiency by more than 40 percent.

Wipro is also investing in new facilities for specialized services, both in India and in other countries. One of the newest is a software-development center in Beijing's high-tech district. A senior Wipro manager points out that China is best known as the world's factory, but in the future, "there will be a shift toward the knowledge or services sector." By opening a development center now, the company will have the time to study the foreign companies that plan to do business in China and figure out how to profit from tomorrow's opportunities. Around the world and around the clock, Wipro is pushing hard to bring more business to Bangalore.[21]

For more information about this company, go to **www.wipro.com.**

Questions

1. How is Wipro using the factors of production to fuel global growth?
2. What are the advantages and disadvantages of using a manufacturer like Toyota as a role model for a service business like Wipro?
3. What effect might the trend toward outsourcing have on the economy of India? What effect might this trend have on the economy of the United States?

→ CHAPTER 1: JOURNAL EXERCISE

Discovery statement: Much of the information in Chapter 1 was designed to get you to think about what it takes to be a successful employee in the competitive business world.

Assume that you are now age 25 and are interviewing for a position as a management trainee in a large corporation. Also assume that this position pays $40,000 a year. Describe what steps you would take to prepare for this interview.

_____

_____

_____

_____

Assuming that you get the management trainee position, describe the personal traits or skills that you have that will help you to become successful.

_____

_____

_____

_____

Now describe the one personal skill or trait that you feel needs improvement. How would you go about improving your weakness?

_____

_____

_____

_____

BUILDING SKILLS FOR CAREER SUCCESS

1. Exploring the Internet

The Internet is a global network of computers that can be accessed by anyone in the world. For example, your school or firm most likely is connected to the web. You probably have private access through a commercial service provider such as America Online, AT&T Yahoo!, or a host of other smaller Internet service providers.

To familiarize you with the wealth of information available through the Internet and its usefulness to business students, this exercise focuses on information services available from a few popular "search engines" used to explore the web. Each of the remaining chapters in this text also contains an Internet exercise that is in some way associated with the topics covered in the chapter. After completing these exercises, not only will you be familiar with a variety of sources of business information, but you also will be better prepared to locate information you might need in the future.

To use one of these search engines, enter its _Internet address_ in your web browser. The addresses of some popular search engines are

www.ask.com
www.google.com
www.msn.com
www.yahoo.com

Visit the text website for updates to this exercise.

Assignment

1. Examine the ways in which two search engines present categories of information on their opening screens. Which search engine was better to use in your opinion? Why?

2. Think of a business topic that you would like to know more about, for example,

careers, gross domestic product, or another concept introduced in this chapter. Using your preferred search engine, explore a few articles and reports provided on your topic. Briefly summarize your findings.

2. Developing Critical-Thinking Skills

Under capitalism, competition is a driving force that allows the market economy to work, affecting the supply of goods and services in the marketplace and the prices consumers pay for those goods and services. Let's see how competition works by pretending that you want to buy a new car.

Assignment

1. Brainstorm the following questions:
   a. Where would you go to get information about new cars?
   b. How will you decide on the make and model of car you want to buy, where to buy the car, and how to finance it?
   c. How is competition at work in this scenario?
   d. What are the pros and cons of competition as it affects the buyer?
2. Record your ideas.
3. Write a summary of the key points you learned about how competition works in the marketplace.

3. Building Team Skills

Over the past few years, employees have been expected to function as productive team members instead of working alone. People often believe that they can work effectively in teams, but many people find working with a group of people to be a challenge. Being an effective team member requires skills that encourage other members to participate in the team endeavor.

College classes that function as teams are more interesting and more fun to attend, and students generally learn more about the topics in the course. If your class is to function as a team, it is important to begin building the team early in the semester. One way to begin creating a team is to learn something about each student in the class. This helps team members to feel comfortable with each other and fosters a sense of trust.

Assignment

1. Find a partner, preferably someone you do not know.
2. Each partner has two to three minutes to answer the following questions:
   a. What is your name, and where do you work?
   b. What interesting or unusual thing have you done in your life? (Do not talk about work or college; rather, focus on such things as hobbies, travel, family, and sports.)
   c. Why are you taking this course, and what do you expect to learn? (Satisfying a degree requirement is not an acceptable answer.)
3. Introduce your partner to the class. Use one to two minutes, depending on the size of the class.

4. Researching Different Careers

In this chapter, *entrepreneurship* is defined as the willingness to take risks and the knowledge and ability to use the other factors of production efficiently. An *entrepreneur* is a person who risks his or her time, effort, and money to start and operate a business. Often people believe that these terms apply only to small business operations, but recently, employees with entrepreneurial attitudes have advanced more rapidly in large companies.

Assignment

1. Go to the local library or use the Internet to research how large firms, especially corporations, are rewarding employees who have entrepreneurial skills.
2. Find answers to the following questions:
   a. Why is an entrepreneurial attitude important in corporations today?
   b. What makes an entrepreneurial employee different from other employees?
   c. How are these employees being rewarded, and are the rewards worth the effort?
3. Write a two-page report that summarizes your findings.

5. Improving Communication Skills

Most jobs today require good writing skills. Written communications in the workplace range from the simple task of jotting down telephone messages to the more complex tasks of writing memos, newspaper articles, policy manuals, and technical journals. Regardless of the type of communication, the writer must convey the correct information to the reader in a clear, concise, and courteous manner. This involves using effective writing skills, which can be improved through practice. You can begin improving your skills by writing in a journal on a regular basis.

Assignment

1. Each week during the semester, write your thoughts and ideas in a journal. Include business terms you learned during the week, and give an example of how each term is used in the business world. Also, do one of the following:

   a. Ask someone, preferably a person working in business, a question based on a topic in the class assignment for the week. Record the answers, and comment on your perceptions about the topic in your journal.

   b. Read a newspaper article relating to a topic covered in the class assignment for the week. Summarize your thoughts on the topic in your journal, specifically discussing what you learned.

2. Ask your instructor for guidelines and due dates for the completed journal and the summary you will prepare at the end of the semester.

→ PREP TEST

Matching Questions

____ 1. Materials, machinery, and workers are assembled in one place.

____ 2. The government spends more than it receives.

____ 3. System of exchange.

____ 4. The process of distinguishing Colgate from Crest toothpaste.

____ 5. The average level of output per worker per hour.

____ 6. A study of how wealth is created and distributed.

____ 7. An organized effort to produce and sell goods and services for a profit.

____ 8. A system where individuals own and operate the majority of businesses.

____ 9. A person who take the risks and invests in a business.

____ 10. Value of all goods and services produced within a country during a one-year period.

a. capitalism
b. economics
c. federal deficit
d. productivity
e. product differentiation
f. business
g. factory system
h. entrepreneur
i. gross domestic product
j. barter

True/False Questions

T F

11. ○ ○ The majority of small business firms are successful within the first five years.

12. ○ ○ For a business to be organized, it must combine four categories of resources: workers, natural resources, capital, and ownership.

13. ○ ○ The equilibrium price means that the supply and demand for a product are in balance.

14. ○ ○ Under communism, individual consumers determine what will be produced.

15. ○ ○ Ford Motor Company and General Motors use product differentiation in the marketplace.

T F

16. ○ ○ If a firm's sales revenues exceed its expenses, the firm has earned a profit.

17. ○ ○ Fiscal policy determines the level of interest rates.

18. ○ ○ The main objective of business firms should be to satisfy the needs of their customers.

19. ○ ○ Adam Smith is the father of communism and advocated a classless society.

20. ○ ○ A business cycle consists of four states: peak, recession, trough, and recovery.

Multiple-Choice Questions

21. Demand is a
    a. relationship between prices and the quantities purchased by buyers.
    b. relationship between prices and the quantities offered by producers.
    c. quantity of goods available for purchase.
    d. price the consumer is willing to pay.
    e. by-product of communism.

22. The process of separating work into distinct tasks is called
    a. bartering.
    b. networking.
    c. specialization.
    d. a factory system.
    e. a domestic system.

23. What term implies that there shall be no government interference in the economy?
    a. market economy
    b. free-market economy

    c. command economy
    d. laissez-faire
    e. socialism

24. When the level of prices in an economy rise, it's called
    a. prosperity.
    b. recession
    c. depression.
    d. recovery.
    e. inflation.

25. The total of all federal deficits is called
    a. depression.
    b. fiscal policy.
    c. gross domestic product
    d. national debt.
    e. business cycle.

Fill-in-the-Blank Questions

26. A system in which raw materials are distrib-uted to various homes to be processed into goods is called a(n) _____ system.

27. _____ is a necessary and extremely important by-product of free enterprise.

28. The differences among people in a work force owing to race, ethnicity, and gender is referred to as _____.

29. _____ is the study of decisions made by individuals and businesses.

30. A term created by Adam Smith to describe how an individual's own personal gain benefits others and a nation's economy is the concept of the _____ _____.

Online Study Center

FOR MORE **test practice, use the interactive ACE quizzes available at the Online Student Center: www.college.hmco.com/PIC/pridebusiness9e.**

Answers on p. PT1.

Being Ethical and Socially Responsible

LEARNING OBJECTIVES

WHAT you will be able to do once you complete this chapter:

1 Understand what is meant by *business ethics*.

2 Identify the types of ethical concerns that arise in the business world.

3 Discuss the factors that affect the level of ethical behavior in organizations.

4 Explain how ethical decision making can be encouraged.

5 Describe how our current views on the social responsibility of business have evolved.

6 Explain the two views on the social responsibility of business and understand the arguments for and against increased social responsibility.

7 Discuss the factors that led to the consumer movement and list some of its results.

8 Analyze how present employment practices are being used to counteract past abuses.

9 Describe the major types of pollution, their causes, and their cures.

10 Identify the steps a business must take to implement a program of social responsibility.

WHY this chapter matters

Business ethics and social responsibility issues have become extremely relevant in today's business world. Business schools are teaching business ethics to help prepare future managers to be more responsible and more responsive to stakeholders. Increasingly, more corporations are developing ethics and social responsibility programs than ever before.

FOR HELP with studying this chapter, visit the Online Student Center:

www.college.hmco.com/PIC/pridebusiness9e

Online Study Center

Home Depot, the world's largest retailer of home-improvement products, is on a mission to build higher sales along with stronger communities. The chain was founded in Atlanta in 1979 and currently operates 2,000 warehouse-size stores and showrooms across North America, each filled from floor to ceiling with thousands of items for home construction and repair. Home Depot's industry dominance and financial strength—it rings up more than $73 billion in annual sales—put real muscle behind the company's social responsibility agenda.

High on the list of worthwhile causes is affordable housing. Working with Habitat for Humanity, Rebuilding Together, and other groups, Home Depot sponsors building projects, provides money and materials, and encourages volunteers to get involved. Since 1991, it has helped construct hundreds of new homes and renovate more than 20,000 housing units for disabled and elderly residents.

Another major program is Team Depot, which encourages employees in every company store and facility to donate time to community projects. Home Depot employees have volunteered to fix up parks, re-

DID YOU KNOW?

The Home Depot, the world's largest home-improvement retailer, committed more than $9 million to the victims of hurricanes Katrina, Rita, and Wilma, and its employees donate two million hours of volunteer time to community causes each year?

furbish schools, build playgrounds, create walking trails, and help on many other local projects. After hurricanes caused flooding and severe damage throughout the Gulf Coast, Home Depot volunteers quickly joined the cleanup effort. The year before, Home Depot volunteers spruced up youth centers and helped rebuild other facilities after hurricanes tore through Florida.

In any given year, Home Depot volunteers devote two million hours to helping in their communities. The company is also one of a number of corporations active in an ambitious campaign to promote volunteerism among their employees and managers. The campaign has set a goal of getting 6.4 million new volunteers within twenty-four months.

Whenever Team Depot volunteers get to work on a local project, they look for ways to get newcomers involved—and the community benefits.

"Giving back to communities where we work and live is a fundamental part of Home Depot culture," says CEO Bob Nardelli.[1]

For more information about this company, go to **www.homedepot.com.**

Obviously, organizations like Home Depot want to be recognized as responsible corporate citizens. Such companies recognize the need to harmonize their operations with environmental demands and other vital social concerns. Not all firms, however, have taken steps to encourage a consideration of social responsibility and ethics in their decisions and day-to-day activities. Some managers still regard such business practices as a poor investment, in which the cost is not worth the return. Other managers— indeed, most managers—view the cost of these practices as a necessary business expense, similar to wages or rent.

Most managers today, like those at Home Depot, are finding ways to balance a growing agenda of socially responsible activities with the drive to generate profits. This also happens to be a good way for a company to demonstrate its values and to attract like-minded employees, customers, and stockholders. In a highly competitive business environment, an increasing number of companies are, like Home Depot, seeking to set themselves apart by developing a reputation for ethical and socially responsible behavior.

We begin this chapter by defining *business ethics* and examining ethical issues. Next, we look at the standards of behavior in organizations and how ethical behavior can be encouraged. We then turn to the topic of social responsibility. We compare and contrast two present-day models of social responsibility and present arguments for and against increasing the social responsibility of business. After that, we examine the major elements of the consumer movement. We discuss how social responsibility in business has affected employment practices and environmental concerns. Finally, we consider the commitment, planning, and funding that go into a firm's program of social responsibility.

Business Ethics Defined

Ethics is the study of right and wrong and of the morality of the choices individuals make. An ethical decision or action is one that is "right" according to some standard of behavior. **Business ethics** is the application of moral standards to business situations. Recent court cases involving unethical behavior have helped to make business ethics a matter of public concern. In one such case, Copley Pharmaceutical, Inc., pled guilty to federal criminal charges (and paid a $10.65 million fine) for falsifying drug manufacturers' reports to the Food and Drug Administration. In another much-publicized case, lawsuits against tobacco companies have led to $246 billion in settlements, although there has been only one class-action lawsuit filed on behalf of all smokers. That case, *Engle* v. *R. J. Reynolds* could cost tobacco companies an estimated $500 billion. In yet another case, Adelphia Communications Corp., the nation's fifth-largest cable television company agreed to pay $715 million to settle federal investigations stemming from rampant earnings manipulation by its founder John J. Rigas and his son, Timothy J. Rigas. Prosecutors and government regulators charged that the Rigases had misappropriated Adelphia funds for their own use and had failed to pay the corporation for securities they controlled.[2]

1 LEARNING OBJECTIVE
Understand what is meant by *business ethics.*

ethics the study of right and wrong and of the morality of the choices individuals make

business ethics the application of moral standards to business situations

Ethical Issues

Ethical issues often arise out of a business's relationship with investors, customers, employees, creditors, or competitors. Each of these groups has specific concerns and usually exerts pressure on the organization's managers. For example, investors want management to make sensible financial decisions that will boost sales, profits, and returns on their investments. Customers expect a firm's products to be safe, reliable, and reasonably priced. Employees demand to be treated fairly in hiring, promotion, and compensation decisions. Creditors require accounts to be paid on time and the accounting information furnished by the firm to be accurate. Competitors expect the firm's competitive practices to be fair and honest. Consider TAP Pharmaceutical

2 LEARNING OBJECTIVE
Identify the types of ethical concerns that arise in the business world.

EXAMINING ETHICS

Can Businesses Keep Your Personal Information Safe?

Is your personal data safe from theft and fraud? Both ethical and legal questions are mounting after security breaches such as these:

- CitiFinancial, a loan company, shipped a computer tape containing data on 3.9 million customers, but it never arrived.
- Bank of America shipped a tape containing records of 1.2 million federal employees, but it never arrived.
- Ameritrade, a brokerage firm, shipped tapes containing account information on 200,000 clients, but they never arrived.
- CardSystems, which processes credit-card transactions, found that hackers accessed computer data on 240,000 accounts.
- DSW Shoe Warehouse, a shoe retailer, found that hackers stole 1.4 million customers' credit-card numbers from its system.

Experts advise businesses to encrypt data for secure storage, change passwords frequently, hold data no longer than necessary, and disclose security breaches promptly. As lawmakers address this growing problem, you can protect yourself by checking bank and credit records and reporting any unauthorized activity.

Products, Inc., whose sales representatives offered every urologist in the United States a big-screen TV, computers, fax machines, and golf vacations if the doctors prescribed TAP's new prostate cancer drug Lupron. Moreover, the sales representatives sold Lupron at cut-rate prices or gratis while defrauding Medicare. Recently, the federal government won an $875 million judgment against TAP.[3]

Business people face ethical issues every day, and some of these issues can be difficult to assess. Although some types of issues arise infrequently, others occur regularly. Let's take a closer look at several ethical issues.

Fairness and Honesty

Fairness and honesty in business are two important ethical concerns. Besides obeying all laws and regulations, business people are expected to refrain from knowingly deceiving, misrepresenting, or intimidating others. The consequences of failing to do so can be expensive. Recently, for example, Keith E. Anderson and Wayne Anderson, the leaders of an international tax shelter scheme known as Anderson's Ark and Associates, were sentenced to as many as twenty years in prison. The Andersons, among their associates, were ordered to pay over $200 million in fines and restitution.[4] In yet another 2005 case, the accounting firm PriceWaterhouseCoopers LLP agreed to pay the U.S. government $42 million to resolve allegations that it made false claims in connection with travel reimbursements it collected for several federal agencies.[5]

In another case, a Florida Chevrolet dealer promised a "free four-day, three-night vacation to Acapulco" to anyone who bought a car or van. A customer purchased a van, but when the vacation voucher arrived, it was really a time-share sales promotion filled with numerous conditions and restrictions. The customer sued, and the jury awarded $1,768 in compensatory and $667,000 in punitive damages.[6]

Personal data security breaches have become a major threat to personal privacy in the new millennium. Can businesses keep your personal data secure?

Organizational Relationships

A business person may be tempted to place his or her personal welfare above the welfare of others or the welfare of the organization. For example, in late 2002, former CEO of Tyco International, Ltd., Leo Dennis Kozlowski was indicted for misappropriating $43 million in corporate funds to make philanthropic contributions in his own name, including $5 million to Seton Hall University, which named its new business-school building Kozlowski Hall. Furthermore, according to Tyco, the former CEO took $61.7 million in interest-free relocation loans without the board's permission. He allegedly used the money to finance many personal luxuries, including a $15 million yacht and a $3.9 million Renoir painting, and to throw a $2 million party for his wife's birthday.[7] Relationships with customers and coworkers often create ethical problems. Unethical behavior in these areas includes taking credit for others' ideas or work, not meeting one's commitments in a mutual agreement, and pressuring others to behave unethically.

Conflict of Interest

Conflict of interest results when a business person takes advantage of a situation for his or her own personal interest rather than for the employer's interest. Such conflict may occur when payments and gifts make their way into business deals. A wise rule to remember is that anything given to a person that might unfairly influence that person's business decision is a bribe, and all bribes are unethical.

For example, Nortel Networks Corporation does not permit its employees, officers, and directors to accept any gifts or to serve as directors or officers of any organization that might supply goods or services to Nortel Networks. However, Nortel employees may work part time with firms that are not competitors, suppliers, or customers. At AT&T, employees are instructed to discuss with their supervisors any investments that may seem improper. Verizon Communications forbids its employee and executives from holding a "significant" financial stake in vendors, suppliers, or customers.

At Procter & Gamble Company (P&G), all employees are obligated to act at all times solely in the best interests of the company. A conflict of interest arises when an employee has a personal relationship or financial or other interest that could interfere with this obligation or when an employee uses his or her position with the company for personal gain. P&G requires employees to disclose all potential conflicts of interest and to take prompt actions to eliminate a conflict when the company asks them to do so. Receiving gifts, entertainment, or other gratuities from people with whom P&G does business generally is not acceptable because doing so could imply an obligation on the part of the company and potentially pose a conflict of interest.

Communications

Business communications, especially advertising, can present ethical questions. False and misleading advertising is illegal and unethical, and it can infuriate customers. Sponsors of advertisements aimed at children must be especially careful to avoid misleading messages. Advertisers of health-related products also must take precautions to guard against deception when using such descriptive terms as *low fat*, *fat free*, and *light*. In fact, the Federal Trade Commission has issued guidelines on the use of these labels.

Factors Affecting Ethical Behavior

Is it possible for an individual with strong moral values to make ethically questionable decisions in a business setting? What factors affect a person's inclination to make either ethical or unethical decisions in a business organization? Although the answers to these questions are not entirely clear, three general sets of factors do appear to influence the standards of behavior in an organization. As shown in Figure 2.1, the sets consist of individual factors, social factors, and opportunity.

Several individual factors influence the level of ethical behavior in an organization. How much an individual knows about an issue is one factor: A decision maker with a greater amount of knowledge regarding a situation may take steps to avoid ethical problems, whereas a less-informed person may take action unknowingly that leads to an ethical quagmire. An individual's moral values and central, value-related attitudes also clearly influence his or her business behavior. Most people join organizations to accomplish personal goals. The types of personal goals an individual aspires to and the manner in which these goals are pursued have a significant impact on that individual's behavior in an organization. The actions of specific individuals in scandal-plagued companies such as Adelphia, Arthur Andersen, Enron, Halliburton, Qwest, and WorldCom often raise questions about individuals' personal character and integrity.

A person's behavior in the workplace, to some degree, is determined by cultural norms, and these social factors vary from one culture to another. For example, in some countries it is acceptable and ethical for customs agents to receive gratuities for performing ordinary, legal tasks that are a part of their jobs, whereas in other countries

3 LEARNING OBJECTIVE
Discuss the factors that affect the level of ethical behavior in organizations.

>> **FIGURE 2.1**

FACTORS THAT AFFECT THE LEVEL OF ETHICAL BEHAVIOR IN AN ORGANIZATION

LEVEL OF ETHICAL BEHAVIOR

| Individual factors | Social factors | Opportunity |

Source: Based on O. C. Ferrell and Larry Gresham, "A Contingency Framework for Understanding Ethical Decision Making in Marketing," *Journal of Marketing*, Summer 1985, p. 89.

these practices would be viewed as unethical and perhaps illegal. The actions and decisions of coworkers constitute another social factor believed to shape a person's sense of business ethics. For example, if your coworkers make long-distance telephone calls on company time and at company expense, you might view that behavior as acceptable and ethical because everyone does it. The moral values and attitudes of "significant others"—spouses, friends, and relatives, for instance—also can affect an employee's perception of what is ethical and unethical behavior in the workplace. Even the Internet presents new challenges for firms whose employees enjoy easy access to sites through convenient high-speed connections at work. An employee's behavior online can be viewed as offensive to coworkers and possibly lead to lawsuits against the firm if employees engage in unethical behavior on controversial websites not related to their job. As a result, research by Websense and the Center for Internet Studies reveals that nearly two out of three companies nationwide have disciplined employees and that nearly one out of three have fired employees for Internet misuse in the workplace.[8] Interestingly, one recent survey of employees found that most workers assume that their use of technology at work will be monitored. A large majority of employees approved of most monitoring methods such as monitoring faxes and e-mail, tracking web use, and even recording telephone calls.

Opportunity refers to the amount of freedom an organization gives an employee to behave unethically if he or she makes that choice. In some organizations, certain company policies and procedures reduce the opportunity to be unethical. For example, at some fast-food restaurants, one employee takes your order and receives your payment, and another fills the order. This procedure reduces the opportunity to be unethical because the person handling the money is not dispensing the product, and the person giving out the product is not handling the money. The existence of an ethical code and the importance management places on this code are other determinants of opportunity (codes of ethics are discussed in more detail in the next section). The degree of enforcement of company policies, procedures, and ethical codes is a major force affecting opportunity. When violations are dealt with consistently and firmly, the opportunity to be unethical is reduced.

Do you make personal telephone calls on company time? Many individuals do. Although most employers limit personal calls to a few min-

SPOTLIGHT

Personal calls on the job

Time that workers spend on personal telephone calls per day.

Don't make personal calls
4.8%

31 to 60 minutes
1%

11 to 30 minutes
17.3%

1 to 10 minutes
76.9%

Source: At-A-Glance survey of 1,385 office workers. Margin of error +2.7 percentage points. O.C. Ferrell, John Fraedrich and Linda Ferrell, *Business Ethics*, 6th ed. Copyright © 2005 by Houghton Mifflin Company. Reprinted with permission.

utes, some make personal calls in excess of thirty minutes. Whether or not you use company time and equipment to make personal calls is an example of a personal ethical decision.

Now that we have considered some of the factors believed to influence the level of ethical behavior in the workplace, let's explore what can be done to encourage ethical behavior and to discourage unethical behavior.

Encouraging Ethical Behavior

Most authorities agree that there is room for improvement in business ethics. A more problematic question is: Can business be made more ethical in the real world? The majority opinion on this issue suggests that government, trade associations, and individual firms indeed can establish acceptable levels of ethical behavior.

The government can encourage ethical behavior by legislating more stringent regulations. For example, the landmark **Sarbanes-Oxley Act of 2002** provides sweeping new legal protection for those who report corporate misconduct. At the signing ceremony, President George W. Bush stated, "The act adopts tough new provisions to deter and punish corporate and accounting fraud and corruption, ensure justice for wrongdoers, and protect the interests of workers and shareholders." Among other things, the law deals with corporate responsibility, conflicts of interest, and corporate accountability. However, rules require enforcement, and the unethical business person frequently seems to "slip something by" without getting caught. Increased regulation may help, but it surely cannot solve the entire ethics problem.

Trade associations can and often do provide ethical guidelines for their members. These organizations, which operate within particular industries, are in an excellent position to exert pressure on members who stoop to questionable business practices. For example, recently, a pharmaceutical trade group adopted a new set of guidelines to halt the extravagant dinners and other gifts sales representatives often give to physicians. However, enforcement and authority vary from association to association. And because trade associations exist for the benefit of their members, harsh measures may be self-defeating.

Codes of ethics that companies provide to their employees are perhaps the most effective way to encourage ethical behavior. A **code of ethics** is a written guide to acceptable and ethical behavior as defined by an organization; it outlines uniform policies, standards, and punishments for violations. Because employees know what is expected of them and what will happen if they violate the rules, a code of ethics goes a long way toward encouraging ethical behavior. However, codes cannot possibly cover every situation. Companies also must create an environment in which employees recognize the importance of complying with the written code. Managers must provide direction by fostering communication, actively modeling and encouraging ethical decision making, and training employees to make ethical decisions.

During the 1980s, an increasing number of organizations created and implemented ethics codes. In a recent survey of *Fortune* 1000 firms, 93 percent of the companies that responded reported having a formal code of ethics. Some companies are now even taking steps to strengthen their codes. For example, to strengthen its accountability, the Healthcare Financial Management Association recently revised its code to designate contact persons who handle reports of ethics violations, to clarify how its board of directors should deal with violations of business ethics, and to guarantee a fair hearing process. S. C. Johnson & Son, makers of

4 LEARNING OBJECTIVE
Explain how ethical decision making can be encouraged.

Sarbanes-Oxley Act of 2002 provides sweeping new legal protection for employees who report corporate misconduct

code of ethics a guide to acceptable and ethical behavior as defined by the organization

Meet senators Sarbanes and Oxley. Senators Paul Sarbanes and Michael Oxley look on as President Bush signs the landmark Sarbanes-Oxley Act of 2002. The new law adopts tough new provisions to deter and punish corporate and accounting fraud and corruption. It imposes tough penalties for violators and protects the whistle-blowers who report corporate misconduct.

CORPORATE RESPONSIBILITY

whistle-blowing informing the press or government officials about unethical practices within one's organization

Pledge, Drano, Windex, and many other household products, is another firm that recognizes that it must behave in ways the public perceives as ethical; its code includes expectations for employees and its commitment to consumers, the community, and society in general. As shown in Figure 2.2, included in the ethics code of electronics giant Texas Instruments (TI) are issues relating to policies and procedures; laws and regulations; relationships with customers, suppliers, and competitors; conflicts of interest; handling of proprietary information; and code enforcement.

Assigning an ethics officer who coordinates ethical conduct gives employees someone to consult if they are not sure of the right thing to do. An ethics officer meets with employees and top management to provide ethical advice, establishes and maintains an anonymous confidential service to answer questions about ethical issues, and takes action on ethics-code violations.

Sometimes even employees who want to act ethically may find it difficult to do so. Unethical practices can become ingrained in an organization. Employees with high personal ethics then may take a controversial step called *whistle-blowing*. **Whistle-blowing** is informing the press or government officials about unethical practices within one's organization.

The year 2002 was labeled as the "Year of the Whistle-blower." Consider Joe Speaker, a 40-year-old acting chief financial officer (CFO) at Rite Aid Corp. in 1999. He discovered that inventories at Rite Aid had been overvalued and that millions in expenses had not been reported properly. Further digging into Rite Aid's books revealed that $541 million in earnings over the previous two years were really $1.6 billion in losses. Mr. Speaker was a main government witness when former Rite Aid Corp. Chairman and CEO Martin L. Grass went on trial. Mr. Speaker is among dozens of corporate managers who have blown the whistle. Enron's Sherron S. Watkins and WorldCom's Cynthia Cooper are now well-known whistle-blowers and *Time* magazine's persons of the year 2002. According to Linda Chatman Thomsen, deputy director for enforcement at the Securities and Exchange Commission, "Whistle-blowers give us an insider's perspective and have advanced our investigation immeasurably." Stephen Meagher, a former federal prosecutor who represents whistle-blowers, calls Watkins and Cooper national champions and says, "The business of whistle-blowing is booming."[9]

Whistle-blowing could have averted disaster and prevented needless deaths in the *Challenger* space shuttle disaster, for example. How could employees have known about life-threatening problems and let them pass? Whistle-blowing, on the other hand, can have serious repercussions for employees: Those who "blow whistles" sometimes lose their jobs. However, the Sarbanes-Oxley Act of 2002 protects whistle-blowers who report corporate misconduct. Any executive who retaliates against a whistle-blower can be held criminally liable and imprisoned for up to ten years.

Retaliations do occur, however. For example, in 2005, the U.S. Court of Appeals for the 8th Circuit unanimously upheld the right of Jane Turner, a twenty-five-year veteran FBI agent, to obtain monetary damages and a jury trial against the FBI. The court held that Ms. Turner presented sufficient facts to justify a trial by jury based on the FBI's retaliatory transfer of Ms. Turner from her investigatory position in Minot, North Dakota, to a demeaning desk job in Minneapolis. Kris Kolesnik, executive director of the National Whistle Blower Center, said, "Jane Turner is an American hero. She refused to be silent when her co-agents committed misconduct in a child rape case. She refused to be silent when her co-agents stole property from Ground Zero. She paid the price and lost her job. The 8th Circuit Court did the right thing and insured that justice will take place in her case."[10]

When firms set up anonymous hotlines to handle ethically questionable situations, employees actually may be more likely to engage in whistle-blowing. When firms instead create an environment that educates employees and nurtures ethical behavior, fewer ethical problems arise, and ultimately, the need for whistle-blowing is greatly reduced.

>> **FIGURE 2.2**

DEFINING ACCEPTABLE BEHAVIOR: TEXAS INSTRUMENTS' CODE OF ETHICS

Texas Instruments encourages ethical behavior through an extensive training program and a written code of ethics and shared values.

TEXAS INSTRUMENTS CODE OF ETHICS

"Integrity is the foundation on which TI is built. There is no other characteristic more essential to a TIer's makeup. It has to be present at all levels. Integrity is expected of managers and individuals when they make commitments. They are expected to stand by their commitments to the best of their ability.

One of TI's greatest strengths is its values and ethics. We had some early leaders who set those values as the standard for how they lived their lives. And it is important that TI grew that way. It's something that we don't want to lose. At the same time, we must move more rapidly. But we don't want to confuse that with the fact that we're ethical and we're moral. We're very responsible, and we live up to what we say."

Tom Engibous, President and CEO
Texas Instruments, 1997

We Respect and Value People By:

Treating others as we want to be treated.

- Exercising the basic virtues of respect, dignity, kindness, courtesy and manners in all work relationships.
- Recognizing and avoiding behaviors that others may find offensive, including the manner in which we speak and relate to one another and the materials we bring into the workplace, both printed and electronically.
- Respecting the right and obligation of every TIer to resolve concerns relating to ethics questions in the course of our duties without retribution and retaliation.
- Giving all TIers the same opportunity to have their questions, issues and situations fairly considered while understanding that being treated fairly does not always mean that we will all be treated the same.
- Trusting one another to use sound judgment in our use of TI business and information systems.
- Understanding that even though TI has the obligation to monitor its business information systems activity, we will respect privacy by prohibiting random searches of individual TIers' communications.
- Recognizing that conduct socially and professionally acceptable in one culture and country may be viewed differently in another.

We Are Honest By:

Representing ourselves and our intentions truthfully.

- Offering full disclosure and withdrawing ourselves from discussions and decisions when our business judgment appears to be in conflict with a personal interest.
- Respecting the rights and property of others, including their intellectual property. Accepting confidential or trade secret information only after we clearly understand our obligations as defined in a nondisclosure agreement.
- Competing fairly without collusion or collaboration with competitors to divide markets, set prices, restrict production, allocate customers or otherwise restrain competition.
- Assuring that no payments or favors are offered to influence others to do something wrong.
- Keeping records that are accurate and include all payments and receipts.
- Exercising good judgment in the exchange of business courtesies, meals and entertainment by avoiding activities that could create even the appearance that our decisions could be compromised.
- Refusing to speculate in TI stock through frequent buying and selling or through other forms of speculative trading.

Source: Courtesy of Texas Instruments, **www.ti.com/corp/docs/company/citizen/ethics/brochure/ intergrity.shtml**; accessed September 21, 2005.

It is difficult for an organization to develop ethics codes, policies, and procedures to deal with all relationships and every situation. When no company policy or procedures exist or apply, a quick test to determine if a behavior is ethical is to see if others—

coworkers, customers, and suppliers—approve of it. Ethical decisions always will withstand scrutiny. Openness and communication about choices often will build trust and strengthen business relationships. Table 2.1 provides some general guidelines for making ethical decisions.

Social Responsibility

social responsibility the recognition that business activities have an impact on society and the consideration of that impact in business decision making

Social responsibility is the recognition that business activities have an impact on society and the consideration of that impact in business decision making. In the first few days after hurricane Katrina hit New Orleans, Wal-Mart delivered $20 million in cash (including $4 million to employees displaced by the storm), 100 truckloads of free merchandise, and food for 100,000 meals. The company also promised a job elsewhere for every one of its workers affected by the catastrophe. Obviously, social responsibility costs money. It is perhaps not so obvious—except in isolated cases—that social responsibility is also good business. Customers eventually find out which firms are acting responsibly and which are not. And just as easily as they cast their dollar votes for a product made by a company that is socially responsible, they can vote against the firm that is not.

Consider the following examples of organizations that are attempting to be socially responsible:

- Social responsibility can take many forms—including flying lessons. Through Young Eagles, underwritten by S. C. Johnson, Phillips Petroleum, Lockheed Martin, Jaguar, and other corporations, 22,000 volunteer pilots have taken a half million youngsters on free flights designed to teach flying basics and inspire excitement about flying careers. Young Eagles is just one of the growing number of education projects undertaken by businesses building solid records as good corporate citizens.
- The General Mills Foundation is one of the nation's largest company-sponsored foundations. According to Chris Shea, president of General Mills Foundation and Community Action, "Now, more than ever, we need to focus on our responsibility to reach out and enrich the communities we serve—to discover the areas of greatest need and address them with breakthrough ideas, championship people, and financial resources." For example, recently, General Mills donated over $20 million of its products to America's Second Harvest, the nation's largest domestic hunger-relief organization. Through a network of over 200 food banks and food-rescue programs, America's Second Harvest provides emergency food assistance to more than twenty-three million hungry Americans each year, eight million of whom are children.
- Dell employees contributed more than $2 million to the Asian tsunami relief effort. Globally, Dell employees are dedicating thousands of hours and donating millions of dollars every year to organizations such as the International Red Cross, Habitat for Humanity, United Way, Second Harvest, and Earth Share. Through the company's One Dell: One Community program, employees combine team building and volunteerism to benefit local communities. Last year the program culminated with Global Community Involvement Month, when nearly 18,000 employees

ConAgra Foods Kids Cafe fights child hunger.
Corporate social responsibility may cost money, but it is also good business. ConAgra Foods, one of North America's largest packaged food companies, is the national sponsor of Kids Cafes, which provide free meal service programs for children at-risk of hunger. Children who participate in Kids Cafe programs report earning better grades in school, having more energy, less fatigue, and improved concentration.

≫≫ TABLE 2.1

GUIDELINES FOR MAKING ETHICAL DECISIONS

1. Listen and learn.	Recognize the problem or decision-making opportunity that confronts your company, team, or unit. Don't argue, criticize, or defend yourself—keep listening and reviewing until you are sure that you understand others.
2. Identify the ethical issues.	Examine how coworkers and consumers are affected by the situation or decision at hand. Examine how you feel about the situation, and attempt to understand the viewpoint of those involved in the decision or in the consequences of the decision.
3. Create and analyze options.	Try to put aside strong feelings such as anger or a desire for power and prestige and come up with as many alternatives as possible before developing an analysis. Ask everyone involved for ideas about which options offer the best long-term results for you and the company. Then decide which option will increase your self-respect even if, in the long run, things don't work out the way you hope?
4. Identify the best option from your point of view.	Consider it and test it against some established criteria, such as respect, understanding, caring, fairness, honesty, and openness.
5. Explain your decision and resolve any differences that arise.	This may require neutral arbitration from a trusted manager or taking "time out" to reconsider, consult, or exchange written proposals before a decision is reached.

Source: Tom Rusk with D. Patrick Miller, "Doing the Right Thing," *Sky* (Delta Airlines), August 1993, pp. 18–22.

from twenty-eight countries volunteered time in their communities. During the year-end holidays, U.S. Dell employees donated 545,000 pounds of food, which provided more than 716,000 meals for hungry families. Employee food-bank support helped to earn the company the Group Volunteer of the Year Award from America's Second Harvest, the nation's largest hunger-relief organization. The Dell Foundation, the company's corporate giving division, offers several grant opportunities that provide funds for health and human services, education, literacy, and technology-access programs for youth around the world.[11]

In 2004, IBM contributed $144 million in equipment, technical services, and cash to not-for-profit organizations and educational institutions worldwide. In addition, IBM employees and retirees personally contributed $56 million to nearly 18,000 nonprofit agencies and schools. IBM's On Demand Community portal supports education and community organizations in more than eighty countries by sharing IBM technology and know-how in volunteer engagements. More than 40,000 IBM employees and retirees have registered, and they volunteered a million hours in 2004.

IBM launched the World Community Grid in November 2004. It combines excess processing power from thousands of computers into a virtual supercomputer. This grid enables researchers to gather and analyze unprecedented quantities of data aimed at advancing research on genomics, diseases, and natural disasters. The first project, the Human Proteome Folding Project, assists in identifying cures for diseases such as malaria and tuberculosis and has registered 85,000 devices around the world to date.

In the wake of natural disasters, IBM's Crisis Response Team works

Children's Miracle Network. More than 20 years ago, Marriott International, Inc. became the first corporate sponsor of the Nationwide Children's Miracle Network, and since then Marriott has contributed more than $25 million to help children who need hospitalization. Most funds are raised through Marriott Pride, a program in which employees play a role in their communities.

with local governments to deploy appropriate technologies, services, and solutions to help affected communities. In the last ten years, this team has contributed to relief operations in the wake of more than seventy major disasters, including the earthquake in Gujarat, India, in 2001, the attacks of September 11, 2001, in the United States, and most recently, the tsunami that struck Southeast Asia. Within hours of that tragedy, IBM was working in India, Indonesia, Sri Lanka, and Thailand to establish secure wireless systems, operate relief sites, and deploy applications to track displaced and missing persons. IBM's commitment of $3 million in services and equipment for relief efforts was supplemented by $1.2 million in donations by IBM employees.[12]

- General Electric Company (GE) has a long history of supporting the communities where its employees work and live through GE's unique combination of resources, equipment, and employees' and retirees' hearts and souls. Today GE's responsibility extends to communities around the world. The GE family reacted quickly to respond to the needs of thousands of survivors after the tsunami in Southeast Asia. For example, GE employees around the world donated a total of $3.8 million to the Red Cross/Red Crescent and UNICEF for tsunami relief efforts, which was matched by the GE Foundation and augmented by an additional $1.1 million in grants. GE donated more than $10 million in equipment and services, including two water-purification systems to Indonesia that have the capacity to provide potable water for tens of thousands of people daily. Two telethons hosted by GE-owned NBC Universal on its television stations and its broadcast and cable platforms raised approximately $32 million. In total, the GE family donated more than $19 million and helped raise millions more.

    The GE family continued its strategic philanthropic efforts as well. It completed the first year of a five-year $20 million project to improve the infrastructure of hospitals and clinics in Africa with donations of health-care and power-generation equipment, water-filtration systems, appliances, and lighting. The GE Foundation invested in improving the quality of and access to education with a total of $52 million in grants worldwide. Many of those efforts were bolstered by the work of GE volunteers.

    In 2004, contributions from the GE Foundation, GE businesses, and GE employees and retirees totaled over $150 million and more than one million volunteer hours for key community initiatives. GE was honored to receive broad recognition for its citizenship initiatives. GE received the Catalyst Award for excellence in developing and promoting women and the Executive Leadership Council Award for excellence in its work with African-American employees. In addition, GE was added to the Dow Jones Sustainability Index, joining a highly selective group of companies representing the top 10 percent in sixty industry groups across thirty-four countries chosen for their environmental, social, and economic programs.[13]

- At Merck & Co., Inc., the Patient Assistance Program makes the company's medicines available to low-income Americans and their families at no cost. When patients don't have health insurance or a prescription drug plan and are unable to afford the Merck medicines their doctors prescribe, they can work with their physicians to contact the Merck Patient Assistance Program. For nearly 50 years, Merck has provided its medicines completely free of charge to people in need through this program. Patients can get information through **www.merck.com** or by calling a toll-free number, 1-800-727-5400, or from their physician's office. For eligible patients, the medicines are shipped directly to their home or the prescribing physician's office. Each applicant may receive up to one year of medicines, and patients may reapply to the program if their need continues. In 2004, this program delivered 6.7 million prescriptions to nearly 700,000 people.

    Merck reacted quickly in response to the tsunami tragedy that struck Asia and the eastern coast of Africa. The company contributed a total of more than $10 million, including $3 million to the American Red Cross, the U.S. Fund for UNICEF and several local agencies. Its donation also includes more than $7.4 million in medicines.[14]

- 3M is a company of dedicated employees who also strive to be good citizens. 3M Community Giving is about the collective effort of 3M, the 3M Foundation, and 3M employees and retirees in giving cash, products, and time to meet ongoing and emergency community needs. Most recently, 3M employees and retirees around the world stepped forward in an unprecedented way to help with relief efforts in the Southeast Asian and African countries devastated by the undersea earthquake and ensuing tsunami. 3M's global gift totaled nearly $4.7 million. This includes $757,000 from 3M employees and retirees globally, $200,000 donated by 3M's international companies, $500,000 in matching funds from the 3M Foundation to selected relief agencies, and $3.2 million in products from 3M locations around the world.

  In 2004, 3M's Office Supplies Division contributed to breast cancer awareness and research by constructing the World's Largest Pink Ribbon, a seventy-foot-high ribbon constructed entirely of 75,000 pink Post-it Super Sticky Notes, in New York City's Times Square. This eye-catching ribbon attracted attention worldwide. With this effort, 3M contributed $300,000 to the City of Hope—a world-renowned cancer research facility—in 2004, and the company continued to support this cause further in 2005.[15]

- AT&T has built a tradition of supporting education, health and human services, the environment, public policy, and the arts in the communities it serves since Alexander Graham Bell founded the company over a century ago. Since 1984, AT&T has invested more than $600 million in support of education. Currently, more than half the company's contribution dollars, employee volunteer time, and community-service activities is directed toward education. In 1995, AT&T created the AT&T Learning Network, a $150 million corporate commitment to support the education of children in schools across the nation by providing the latest technology and cash grants to schools and communities. Since 1911, AT&T has been a sponsor of the Telephone Pioneers of America, the world's largest industry-based volunteer organization consisting of nearly 750,000 employees and retirees from the telecommunications industry. Each year the pioneers volunteer millions of hours and raise millions of dollars for health and human services and the environment.[16]

- Education programs often link social responsibility with corporate self-interest. For example, Bayer and Merck, two major pharmaceuticals firms, promote science education as a way to enlarge the pool of future employees. Students who visit the Bayer Science Forum in Elkhart, Indiana, work alongside scientists conducting a variety of experiments. And workshops created by the Merck Institute for Science Education show teachers how to put scientific principles into action through hands-on experiments.

These are just a few illustrations from the long list of companies big and small that attempt to behave in socially responsible ways. In general, people are more likely to want to work for and buy from such organizations.

The Evolution of Social Responsibility in Business

Business is far from perfect in many respects, but its record of social responsibility today is much better than in past decades. In fact, present demands for social responsibility have their roots in outraged reactions to the abusive business practices of the early 1900s.

During the first quarter of the twentieth century, businesses were free to operate pretty much as they chose. Government protection of workers and consumers was minimal. As a result, people either accepted what business had to offer or they did without. Working conditions often were deplorable by today's standards. The average work week in most industries exceeded sixty hours, no minimum-wage law existed, and

5 LEARNING OBJECTIVE
Describe how our current views on the social responsibility of business have evolved.

SPOTLIGHT

Best corporate citizens

1. CUMMINS, INC.
2. GREEN MOUNTAIN COFFEE ROASTERS, INC.
3. ST PAUL TRAVELERS COS., INC.
4. NUVEEN INVESTMENTS, INC.
5. INTEL CORP.
6. WELLS FARGO & CO.
7. HEWLETT-PACKARD CO.
8. PROCTER & GAMBLE CO.
9. NOVELL, INC.
10. XEROX CORP.

Cummins, Inc., the Columbus, Indiana engine maker, is in the number one spot because it is "the best in the world" when it comes to air-emissions reduction research.

Source: Reprinted with permission from *Business Ethics*, P.O. Box 8439, Minneapolis, MN 55408 USA, **www.business-ethics.com**, Spring 2005, p. 22.

caveat emptor a Latin phrase meaning "let the buyer beware"

employee benefits were almost nonexistent. Work areas were crowded and unsafe, and industrial accidents were the rule rather than the exception. To improve working conditions, employees organized and joined labor unions. During the early 1900s, however, businesses—with the help of government—were able to use court orders, brute force, and even the few existing antitrust laws to defeat union attempts to improve working conditions.

During this period, consumers generally were subject to the doctrine of **caveat emptor,** a Latin phrase meaning "let the buyer beware." In other words, "what you see is what you get," and if it is not what you expected, too bad. Although victims of unscrupulous business practices could take legal action, going to court was very expensive, and consumers rarely won their cases. Moreover, no consumer groups or government agencies existed to publicize their consumers' grievances or to hold sellers accountable for their actions.

Prior to the 1930s, most people believed that competition and the action of the marketplace would, in time, correct abuses. Government therefore became involved in day-to-day business activities only in cases of obvious abuse of the free-market system. Six of the more important business-related federal laws passed between 1887 and 1914 are described in Table 2.2. As you can see, these laws were aimed more at encouraging competition than at correcting abuses, although two of them did deal with the purity of food and drug products.

The collapse of the stock market on October 29, 1929, triggered the Great Depression and years of dire economic problems for the United States. Factory production fell by almost one-half, and up to 25 percent of the nation's work force was unemployed. Before long, public pressure mounted for government to "do something" about the economy and about worsening social conditions.

Soon after Franklin D. Roosevelt was inaugurated as president in 1933, he instituted programs to restore the economy and improve social conditions. Laws were

> **TABLE 2.2**

EARLY GOVERNMENT REGULATIONS THAT AFFECTED AMERICAN BUSINESS

Government Regulation	Major Provisions
Interstate Commerce Act (1887)	First federal act to regulate business practices; provided regulation of railroads and shipping rates
Sherman Antitrust Act (1890)	Prevented monopolies or mergers where competition was endangered
Pure Food and Drug Act (1906)	Established limited supervision of interstate sale of food and drugs
Meat Inspection Act (1906)	Provided for limited supervision of interstate sale of meat and meat products
Federal Trade Commission Act (1914)	Created the Federal Trade Commission to investigate illegal trade practices
Clayton Antitrust Act (1914)	Eliminated many forms of price discrimination that gave large businesses a competitive advantage over smaller firms

passed to correct what many viewed as the monopolistic abuses of big business, and various social services were provided for individuals. These massive federal programs became the foundation for increased government involvement in the dealings between business and society.

As government involvement has increased, so has everyone's awareness of the social responsibility of business. Today's business owners are concerned about the return on their investment, but at the same time most of them demand ethical behavior from employees. In addition, employees demand better working conditions, and consumers want safe, reliable products. Various advocacy groups echo these concerns and also call for careful consideration of our earth's delicate ecological balance. Managers therefore must operate in a complex business environment—one in which they are just as responsible for their managerial actions as for their actions as individual citizens. Interestingly, today's high-tech and Internet-based firms fare relatively well when it comes to environmental issues, worker conditions, the representation of minorities and women in upper management, animal testing, and charitable donations.

Two Views of Social Responsibility

Government regulation and public awareness are *external* forces that have increased the social responsibility of business. But business decisions are made *within* the firm—and there, social responsibility begins with the attitude of management. Two contrasting philosophies, or models, define the range of management attitudes toward social responsibility.

The Economic Model

According to the traditional concept of business, a firm exists to produce quality goods and services, earn a reasonable profit, and provide jobs. In line with this concept, the **economic model of social responsibility** holds that society will benefit most when business is left alone to produce and market profitable products that society needs. The economic model has its origins in the eighteenth century, when businesses were owned primarily by entrepreneurs or owner-managers. Competition was vigorous among small firms, and short-run profits and survival were the primary concerns.

To the manager who adopts this traditional attitude, social responsibility is someone else's job. After all, stockholders invest in a corporation to earn a return on their investment, not because the firm is socially responsible, and the firm is legally obligated to act in the economic interest of its stockholders. Moreover, profitable firms pay federal, state, and local taxes that are used to meet the needs of society. Thus managers who concentrate on profit believe that they fulfill their social responsibility indirectly through the taxes paid by their firms. As a result, social responsibility becomes the problem of government, various environmental groups, charitable foundations, and similar organizations.

The Socioeconomic Model

In contrast, some managers believe that they have a responsibility not only to stockholders but also to customers, employees, suppliers, and the general public. This broader view is referred to as the **socioeconomic model of social responsibility,** which places emphasis not only on profits but also on the impact of business decisions on society.

Recently, increasing numbers of managers and firms have adopted the socioeconomic model, and they have done so for at least three reasons. First, business is dominated by the corporate form of ownership, and the corporation is a creation of society. If a corporation does not perform as a good citizen, society can and will demand changes. Second, many firms have begun to take pride in their social responsibility records, among them Starbucks Coffee, Hewlett-Packard, Colgate-Palmolive, and Coca-Cola. Each of these companies is a winner of a Corporate Conscience Award

6 LEARNING OBJECTIVE
Explain the two views on the social responsibility of business and understand the arguments for and against increased social responsibility.

economic model of social responsibility the view that society will benefit most when business is left alone to produce and market profitable products that society needs

socioeconomic model of social responsibility the concept that business should emphasize not only profits but also the impact of its decisions on society in the areas of environmental concern, responsiveness to employees, equal opportunity, and community involvement. And of course, many other corporations are much more socially responsible today than they were ten years ago. Third, many business people believe that it is in their best interest to take the initiative in this area. The alternative may be legal action brought against the firm by some special-interest group; in such a situation, the firm may lose control of its activities.

The Pros and Cons of Social Responsibility

Business owners, managers, customers, and government officials have debated the pros and cons of the economic and socioeconomic models for years. Each side seems to have four major arguments to reinforce its viewpoint.

Arguments for Increased Social Responsibility Proponents of the socioeconomic model maintain that a business must do more than simply seek profits. To support their position, they offer the following arguments:

1. Because business is a part of our society, it cannot ignore social issues.
2. Business has the technical, financial, and managerial resources needed to tackle today's complex social issues.
3. By helping resolve social issues, business can create a more stable environment for long-term profitability.
4. Socially responsible decision making by firms can prevent increased government intervention, which would force businesses to do what they fail to do voluntarily.

These arguments are based on the assumption that a business has a responsibility not only to its stockholders but also to its customers, employees, suppliers, and the general public.

Arguments Against Increased Social Responsibility Opponents of the socioeconomic model argue that business should do what it does best: earn a profit by manufacturing and marketing products that people want. Those who support this position argue as follows:

1. Business managers are responsible primarily to stockholders, so management must be concerned with providing a return on owners' investments.
2. Corporate time, money, and talent should be used to maximize profits, not to solve society's problems.
3. Social problems affect society in general, so individual businesses should not be expected to solve these problems.
4. Social issues are the responsibility of government officials who are elected for that purpose and who are accountable to the voters for their decisions.

These arguments obviously are based on the assumption that the primary objective of business is to earn profits and that government and social institutions should deal with social problems.

Table 2.3 compares the economic and socioeconomic viewpoints in terms of business emphasis. Today, few firms are either purely economic or purely socioeconomic in outlook; most have chosen some middle ground between the two extremes. However, our society generally seems to want—and even to expect—some degree of social responsibility from business. Thus, within this middle ground, businesses are leaning toward the socioeconomic view. In the next several sections we look at some results of this movement in four specific areas: consumerism, employment practices, concern for the environment, and implementation of social responsibility programs.

> > > **TABLE 2.3**

A COMPARISON OF THE ECONOMIC AND SOCIOECONOMIC MODELS OF SOCIAL RESPONSIBILITY AS IMPLEMENTED IN BUSINESS

Economic Model Primary Emphasis		Socioeconomic Model Primary Emphasis
1. Production		1. Quality of life
2. Exploitation of natural resources		2. Conservation of natural resources
3. Internal, market-based decisions	Middle ground	3. Market-based decisions, with some community controls
4. Economic return (profit)		4. Balance of economic return and social return
5. Firm's or manager's interest		5. Firm's and community's interests
6. Minor role for government		6. Active government

Source: Adapted from Keith Davis, William C. Frederick, and Robert L. Blomstron, *Business and Society: Concepts and Policy Issues* (New York: McGraw-Hill, 1980), p. 9. Used by permission of McGraw-Hill Book Company.

Consumerism

Consumerism consists of all activities undertaken to protect the rights of consumers. The fundamental issues pursued by the consumer movement fall into three categories: environmental protection, product performance and safety, and information disclosure. Although consumerism has been with us to some extent since the early nineteenth century, the consumer movement became stronger in the 1960s. It was then that President John F. Kennedy declared that the consumer was entitled to a new "bill of rights."

The Six Basic Rights of Consumers

President Kennedy's consumer bill of rights asserted that consumers have a right to safety, to be informed, to choose, and to be heard. Two additional rights added since 1975 are the right to consumer education and the right to courteous service. These six rights are the basis of much of the consumer-oriented legislation passed during the last forty years. These rights also provide an effective outline of the objectives and accomplishments of the consumer movement.

The Right to Safety The consumers' right to safety means that the products they purchase must be safe for their intended use, must include thorough and explicit directions for proper use, and must be tested by the manufacturer to ensure product quality and reliability. There are several reasons why American business firms must be concerned about product safety. Federal agencies such as the Food and Drug Administration and the Consumer Product Safety Commission have the power to force businesses that make or sell defective products to take corrective actions. Such actions include offering refunds, recalling defective products, issuing public warnings, and reimbursing consumers—all of which can be expensive. Business firms also should be aware that consumers and the government have been winning an increasing number of product-liability lawsuits against sellers of defective products. Moreover, the amount of the awards in these suits has been increasing steadily. Fearing the outcome of numerous lawsuits filed around the nation, tobacco giants Philip Morris and R. J. Reynolds, which for decades had denied that cigarettes cause illness, began negotiating in 1997 with state attorneys general, plaintiffs' lawyers, and antismoking activists. The tobacco giants proposed sweeping curbs on their sales and advertising practices and the payment of hundreds of billions of dollars in compensation. Yet another major reason for improving product safety is consumers' demand for safe products. People simply will stop buying a product they believe is unsafe or unreliable.

7 LEARNING OBJECTIVE

Discuss the factors that led to the consumer movement and list some of its results.

consumerism all activities undertaken to protect the rights of consumers

The FDA's main concern: safety first! A growing number of Americans obtain their medicines from abroad, often seeking out suppliers in Canada. But the U.S. Food and Drug Administration cannot ensure the safety of drugs purchased from these sources. Here, Peter Pitts of the FDA distributes public information pamphlets warning of the dangers of obtaining drugs from foreign countries. According to the FDA, of the drugs being promoted as "Canadian," 85 percent actually came from 27 other countries around the globe. Many of these drugs were found to be counterfeit.

The Right to Be Informed The right to be informed means that consumers must have access to complete information about a product before they buy it. Detailed information about ingredients and nutrition must be provided on food containers, information about fabrics and laundering methods must be attached to clothing, and lenders must disclose the true cost of borrowing the money they make available to customers who purchase merchandise on credit.

In addition, manufacturers must inform consumers about the potential dangers of using their products. Manufacturers that fail to provide such information can be held responsible for personal injuries suffered because of their products. For example, Maytag provides customers with a lengthy booklet that describes how they should use an automatic clothes washer. Sometimes such warnings seem excessive, but they are necessary if user injuries (and resulting lawsuits) are to be avoided.

The Right to Choose The right to choose means that consumers must have a choice of products, offered by different manufacturers and sellers, to satisfy a particular need. The government has done its part by encouraging competition through antitrust legislation. The greater the competition, the greater is the choice available to consumers.

Competition and the resulting freedom of choice provide additional benefits for customers by reducing prices. For example, when personal computers were introduced, they cost over $5,000. Thanks to intense competition and technological advancements, personal computers today can be purchased for less than $500.

The Right to Be Heard This fourth right means that someone will listen and take appropriate action when customers complain. Actually, management began to listen to consumers after World War II, when competition between businesses that manufactured and sold consumer goods increased. One way that firms got a competitive edge was to listen to consumers and provide the products they said they wanted and needed. Today, businesses are listening even more attentively, and many larger firms have consumer relations departments that can be contacted easily via toll-free phone numbers. Other groups listen, too. Most large cities and some states have consumer affairs offices to act on citizens' complaints.

Additional Consumer Rights In 1975, President Gerald Ford added to the consumer bill of rights the right to consumer education, which entitles people to be fully informed about their rights as consumers. In 1994, President Bill Clinton added a sixth right, the right to service, which entitles consumers to convenience, courtesy, and responsiveness from manufacturers and sellers of consumer products.

Major Consumerism Forces

The major forces in consumerism are individual consumer advocates and organizations, consumer education programs, and consumer laws. Consumer advocates, such as Ralph Nader, take it on themselves to protect the rights of consumers. They band together into consumer organizations, either independently or under government sponsorship. Some organizations, such as the National Consumers' League and the Consumer Federation of America, operate nationally, whereas others are active at state and local levels. They inform and organize other consumers, raise issues, help businesses to develop consumer-oriented programs, and pressure lawmakers to enact consumer protection laws. Some consumer advocates and organizations encourage consumers to boycott products and businesses to which they have objections. Today, the consumer movement has adopted corporate-style marketing and addresses a broad range of issues. Current campaigns include efforts (1) to curtail the use of animals for testing purposes, (2) to reduce liquor and cigarette billboard advertising in low-income, inner-city neighborhoods, and (3) to encourage recycling.

Educating consumers to make wiser purchasing decisions is perhaps one of the most far-reaching aspects of consumerism. Increasingly, consumer education is becoming a part of high school and college curricula and adult-education programs. These programs cover many topics—for instance, what major factors should be considered when buying specific products, such as insurance, real estate, automobiles, appliances and furniture, clothes, and food; the provisions of certain consumer-protection laws; and the sources of information that can help individuals become knowledgeable consumers.

Major advances in consumerism have come through federal legislation. Some laws enacted in the last forty-four years to protect your rights as a consumer are listed and described in Table 2.4. Most business people now realize that they ignore consumer issues only at their own peril. Managers know that improper handling of consumer complaints can result in lost sales, bad publicity, and lawsuits.

Employment Practices

Managers who subscribe to the socioeconomic view of business's social responsibility, together with significant government legislation enacted to protect the buying public, have broadened the rights of consumers. The last four decades have seen similar progress in affirming the rights of employees to equal treatment in the workplace.

Everyone should have the opportunity to land a job for which he or she is qualified and to be rewarded on the basis of ability and performance. This is an important issue for society, and it also makes good business sense. Yet, over the years, this opportunity has been denied to members of various minority groups. A **minority** is a racial, religious, political, national, or other group regarded as different from the larger group of which it is a part and that is often singled out for unfavorable treatment.

The federal government responded to the outcry of minority groups during the 1960s and 1970s by passing a number of laws forbidding discrimination in the workplace. (These laws are discussed in Chapter 10 in the context of human resources management.) Now, forty-three years after passage of the first of these (the Civil

8 LEARNING OBJECTIVE
Analyze how present employment practices are being used to counteract past abuses.

minority a racial, religious, political, national, or other group regarded as different from the larger group of which it is a part and that is often singled out for unfavorable treatment

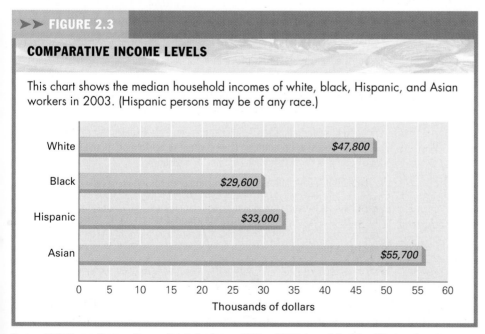

▶▶ FIGURE 2.3

COMPARATIVE INCOME LEVELS

This chart shows the median household incomes of white, black, Hispanic, and Asian workers in 2003. (Hispanic persons may be of any race.)

White — $47,800
Black — $29,600
Hispanic — $33,000
Asian — $55,700

Thousands of dollars

Source: U.S. Census Bureau, *Current Population Survey,* 2003 and 2004 Annual Social and Economic Supplements; **http://www.census.gov/hhes/www/img/incpov03/fig07.jpg**; accessed October 7, 2005.

>> **TABLE 2.4**

MAJOR FEDERAL LEGISLATION PROTECTING CONSUMERS SINCE 1960

Legislation	Major Provisions
Federal Hazardous Substances Labeling Act (1960)	Required warning labels on household chemicals if they are highly toxic
Kefauver-Harris Drug Amendments (1962)	Established testing practices for drugs and required manufacturers to label drugs with generic names in addition to trade names
Cigarette Labeling Act (1965)	Required manufacturers to place standard warning labels on all cigarette packages and advertising
Fair Packaging and Labeling Act (1966)	Called for all products sold across state lines to be labeled with net weight, ingredients, and manufacturer's name and address
Motor Vehicle Safety Act (1966)	Established standards for safer cars
Wholesome Meat Act (1967)	Required states to inspect meat (but not poultry) sold within the state
Flammable Fabrics Act (1967)	Extended flammability standards for clothing to include children's sleepwear in sizes 0 to 6X
Truth in Lending Act (1968)	Required lenders and credit merchants to disclose the full cost of finance charges in both dollars and annual percentage rates
Child Protection and Toy Act (1969)	Banned toys with mechanical or electrical defects from interstate commerce
Credit Card Liability Act (1970)	Limited credit-card holder's liability to $50 per card and stopped credit-card companies from issuing unsolicited cards
Fair Credit Reporting Act (1971) Act (1972)	Required credit bureaus to provide credit reports to consumers regarding their own credit files; also provided for correction of incorrect information
Consumer Product Safety Commission Act (1972)	Established the Consumer Product Safety Commission
Trade Regulation Rule (1972)	Established a "cooling off" period of 72 hours for door-to-door sales
Fair Credit Billing Act (1974)	Amended the Truth in Lending Act to enable consumers to challenge billing errors
Equal Credit Opportunity Act (1974)	Provided equal credit opportunities for males and females and for married and single individuals
Magnuson-Moss Warranty-Federal Trade Commission Act (1975)	Provided for minimum disclosure standards for written consumer-product warranties for products that cost more than $15
Amendments to the Equal Credit Opportunity Act (1976, 1994)	Prevented discrimination based on race, creed, color, religion, age, and income when granting credit
Fair Debt Collection Practices Act (1977)	Outlawed abusive collection practices by third parties
Drug Price Competition and Patent Restoration Act (1984)	Established an abbreviated procedure for registering certain generic drugs
Orphan Drug Act (1985)	Amended the original 1983 Orphan Drug Act and extended tax incentives to encourage the development of drugs for rare diseases
Nutrition Labeling and Education Act (1990)	Required the Food and Drug Administration to review current food labeling and packaging focusing on nutrition label content, label format, ingredient labeling, food descriptors and standards, and health messages
Telephone Consumer Protection Act (1991)	Prohibited the use of automated dialing and prerecorded-voice calling equipment to make calls or deliver messages
Consumer Credit Reporting Reform Act (1997)	Placed more responsibility for accurate credit data on credit issuers; required creditors to verify that disputed data are accurate and to notify a consumer before reinstating the data
Children's Online Privacy Protection Act (2000)	Placed parents in control over what information is collected online from their children under age 13; required commercial website operators to maintain the confidentiality, security, and integrity of the personal information collected from children

Rights Act of 1964), abuses still exist. An example is the disparity in income levels for whites, blacks, Hispanics, and Asians, as illustrated in Figure 2.3. Lower incomes and higher unemployment rates also characterize Native Americans, handicapped persons, and women. Responsible managers have instituted a number of programs to counteract the results of discrimination

Affirmative Action Programs

An **affirmative action program** is a plan designed to increase the number of minority employees at all levels within an organization. Employers with federal contracts of more than $50,000 per year must have written affirmative action plans. The objective of such programs is to ensure that minorities are represented within the organization in approximately the same proportion as in the surrounding community. If 25 percent of the electricians in a geographic area in which a company is located are black, then approximately 25 percent of the electricians it employs also should be black. Affirmative action plans encompass all areas of human resources management: recruiting, hiring, training, promotion, and pay.

Unfortunately, affirmative action programs have been plagued by two problems. The first involves quotas. In the beginning, many firms pledged to recruit and hire a certain number of minority members by a specific date. To achieve this goal, they were forced to consider only minority applicants for job openings; if they hired non-minority workers, they would be defeating their own purpose. However, the courts have ruled that such quotas are unconstitutional even though their purpose is commendable. They are, in fact, a form of discrimination called *reverse discrimination.*

The second problem is that although most such programs have been reasonably successful, not all business people are in favor of affirmative action programs. Managers not committed to these programs can "play the game" and still discriminate against workers. To help solve this problem, Congress created (and later strengthened) the **Equal Employment Opportunity Commission (EEOC),** a government agency with the power to investigate complaints of employment discrimination and sue firms that practice it.

The threat of legal action has persuaded some corporations to amend their hiring and promotional policies, but the discrepancy between men's and women's salaries still exists, as illustrated in Figure 2.4. For more than forty years, women have consistently earned only about 70 cents for each dollar earned by men.

Training Programs for the Hard-Core Unemployed

For some firms, social responsibility extends far beyond placing a help-wanted ad in the local newspaper. These firms have assumed the task of helping the **hard-core unemployed,** workers with little education or vocational training and a long history of unemployment. For example, a few years ago, General Mills helped establish Siyeza, a frozen soul-food processing plant in North Minneapolis. Through the years, Siyeza has provided stable, high-quality full-time jobs for a permanent core of eighty unemployed or underemployed minority inner-city residents. In addition, groups of up to a hundred temporary employees are called in when needed. Recently, Siyeza had a regular payroll of almost $1.9 million and is an example of the persistent commitment necessary to make positive changes in the community.[17] In the past, such workers often were turned down routinely by personnel managers, even for the most menial jobs.

Obviously, such workers require training; just as obviously, this training can be

affirmative action program a plan designed to increase the number of minority employees at all levels within an organization

Equal Employment Opportunity Commission (EEOC) a government agency with power to investigate complaints of employment discrimination and power to sue firms that practice it

hard-core unemployed workers with little education or vocational training and a long history of unemployment

The women of Wal-Mart. Are female Wal-Mart employees paid less than comparable male employees? Do female employees receive fewer promotions than their male counterparts? Betty Dukes (right), a former employee believes so. She has filed a nationwide sex discrimination class action lawsuit, Dukes v. Wal-Mart Stores, Inc. U.S. District Court Judge Martin Jenkins described the case as "historic, dwarfing other employment cases that came before it." The suit charges that Wal-Mart discriminates against its female retail employees in pay and promotions. The class action includes more than 1.6 million current and former female employees.

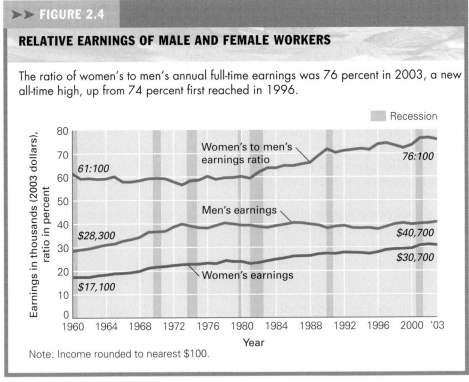

>> **FIGURE 2.4**

RELATIVE EARNINGS OF MALE AND FEMALE WORKERS

The ratio of women's to men's annual full-time earnings was 76 percent in 2003, a new all-time high, up from 74 percent first reached in 1996.

Note: Income rounded to nearest $100.

Source: U.S. Census Bureau, *Current Population Survey*, 1961 to 2004 Annual Social and Economic Supplements; **http://www.census.gov/hhes/www/img/incpov03/fig12.jpg**; accessed October 7, 2005.

expensive and time-consuming. To share the costs, business and community leaders have joined together in a number of cooperative programs. One particularly successful partnership is the **National Alliance of Business (NAB),** a joint business-government program to train the hard-core unemployed. The alliance's 5,000 members include companies of all sizes and industries, their CEOs and senior executives, as well as educators and community leaders. NAB, founded in 1968 by President Lyndon Johnson and Henry Ford II, is a major national business organization focusing on education and work force issues.

National Alliance of Business (NAB) a joint business-government program to train the hard-core unemployed

Concern for the Environment

9 LEARNING OBJECTIVE
Describe the major types of pollution, their causes, and their cures.

pollution the contamination of water, air, or land through the actions of people in an industrialized society

The social consciousness of responsible business managers, the encouragement of a concerned government, and an increasing concern on the part of the public have led to a major effort to reduce environmental pollution, conserve natural resources, and reverse some of the worst effects of past negligence in this area. **Pollution** is the contamination of water, air, or land through the actions of people in an industrialized society. For several decades, environmentalists have been warning us about the dangers of industrial pollution. Unfortunately, business and government leaders either ignored the problem or were not concerned about it until pollution became a threat to life and health in America. Today, Americans expect business and government leaders to take swift action to clean up our environment—and to keep it clean.

Effects of Environmental Legislation

As in other areas of concern to our society, legislation and regulations play a crucial role in pollution control. The laws outlined in Table 2.5 reflect the scope of current environmental legislation: laws to promote clean air, clean water, and even quiet work and living environments. Of major importance was the creation of the Environmental Protection Agency (EPA), the federal agency charged with enforcing laws designed to protect the environment.

When they are aware of a pollution problem, many firms respond to it rather than wait to be cited by the EPA. Other owners and managers, however, take the position that environmental standards are too strict. (Loosely translated, this means that compliance with present standards is too expensive.) Consequently, it often has been necessary for the EPA to take legal action to force firms to install antipollution equipment and to clean up waste storage areas.

Experience has shown that the combination of environmental legislation, voluntary compliance, and EPA action can succeed in cleaning up the environment and keeping it clean. However, much still remains to be done.

The race to save the planet and its inhabitants. Phelps Dodge Tyrone, Inc., which operates the 9,400-acre Tyrone copper mine in southwest New Mexico, pleaded guilty to a misdemeanor charge of violating the Migratory Bird Treaty Act on August 30, 2005. Many dead birds were found near water contaminated by the mining process.

Water Pollution The Clean Water Act has been credited with greatly improving the condition of the waters in the United States. This success comes largely from the control of pollutant discharges from industrial and wastewater treatment plants. Although the quality of our nation's rivers, lakes, and streams has improved significantly in recent years, many of these surface waters remain severely polluted. Currently, one of the most serious water-quality problems results from the high level of toxic pollutants found in these waters.

Among the serious threats to people posed by water pollutants are respiratory irritation, cancer, kidney and liver damage, anemia, and heart failure. Toxic pollutants also damage fish and other forms of wildlife. In fish, they cause tumors or reproductive problems; shellfish and wildlife living in or drinking from toxin-ladened waters

>>> **TABLE 2.5**

SUMMARY OF MAJOR ENVIRONMENTAL LAWS

Legislation	Major Provisions
National Environmental Policy Act (1970)	Established the Environmental Protection Agency (EPA) to enforce federal laws that involve the environment
Clean Air Amendment (1970)	Provided stringent automotive, aircraft, and factory emission standards
Water Quality Improvement Act (1970)	Strengthened existing water pollution regulations and provided for large monetary fines against violators
Resource Recovery Act (1970)	Enlarged the solid-waste disposal program and provided for enforcement by the EPA
Water Pollution Control Act Amendment (1972)	Established standards for cleaning navigable streams and lakes and eliminating all harmful waste disposal by 1985
Noise Control Act (1972)	Established standards for major sources of noise and required the EPA to advise the Federal Aviation Administration on standards for airplanes
Clean Air Act Amendment (1977)	Established new deadlines for cleaning up polluted areas; also required review of existing air-quality standards
Resource Conservation and Recovery Act (1984)	Amended the original 1976 act and required federal regulation of potentially dangerous solid-waste disposal
Clean Air Act Amendment (1987)	Established a national air-quality standard for ozone
Oil Pollution Act (1990)	Expanded the nation's oil-spill prevention and response activities; also established the Oil Spill Liability Trust Fund
Clean Air Act Amendments (1990)	Required that motor vehicles be equipped with onboard systems to control about 90 percent of refueling vapors

ENTREPRENEURIAL CHALLENGE

It's 6am, Do You Know Where Your Coffee Came From?

Fair trade earns small growers in Africa, South and Central America, and other regions more money for crops certified as grown in an ecofriendly manner. The idea is to encourage sustainable agriculture and ensure that farmers get a fair price for coffee beans, cocoa beans, and other foods. Some facts about fair trade:

- From 1998 to 2005, U.S. imports of fair-trade coffee topped seventy-four million pounds, earning growers $60 million in additional revenue.
- Fair-trade coffee is sold in 20,000 U.S. stores.
- Starbucks buys more than two million pounds of fair-trade-certified coffee every year.
- All espresso beverages sold by Dunkin' Donuts are made from fair-trade coffee.
- The United Kingdom is the world's largest market for fair-trade produce, with annual sales exceeding $250 million.

In the United States, TransFair USA (**www.transfairusa.org**) oversees fair-trade certification of imported produce; in the United Kingdom, the Fairtrade Foundation (**www.fairtrade.org.uk**) oversees certification.

also have suffered genetic defects. Recently, the Pollution Control Board of Kerala in India ordered Coca Cola to close its major bottling plant. For years, villagers in the nearby areas had accused Coke of depleting local groundwater and producing other local pollution. The village council president said, "We are happy that the government is finally giving justice to the people who are affected by the plant."

The task of water cleanup has proved to be extremely complicated and costly because of pollution runoff and toxic contamination. And yet improved water quality is not only necessary; it is also achievable. Consider Cleveland's Cuyahoga River. A few years ago the river was so contaminated by industrial wastes that it burst into flames one hot summer day! Now, after a sustained community cleanup effort, the river is pure enough for fish to thrive in.

Another serious issue is acid rain, which is contributing significantly to the deterioration of coastal waters, lakes, and marine life in the eastern United States. Acid rain forms when sulfur emitted by smokestacks in industrialized areas combines with moisture in the atmosphere to form acids that are spread by winds. The acids eventually fall to the earth in rain, which finds its way into streams, rivers, and lakes. The acid-rain problem has spread rapidly in recent years, and experts fear that the situation will worsen if the nation begins to burn more coal to generate electricity. To solve the problem, investigators first must determine where the sulfur is being emitted. The costs of this vital investigation and cleanup are going to be high. The human costs of having ignored the problem so long may be higher still.

Air Pollution   Aviation emissions are a potentially significant and growing percentage of greenhouse gases that contribute to global warming. Aircraft emissions are significant for several reasons. First, jet aircraft are the main source of human emissions deposited directly into the upper atmosphere, where they may have a greater warming effect than if they were released at the earth's surface. Second, carbon dioxide—the primary aircraft emission—is the main focus of international concern. For example, it survives in the atmosphere for nearly 100 years and contributes to global warming, according to the Intergovernmental Panel on Climate Change. The carbon dioxide emissions from worldwide aviation roughly equal those of some industrialized countries. Third, carbon dioxide emissions, combined with other gases and particles emitted by jet aircraft, could have two to four times as great an effect on the atmosphere as carbon dioxide alone. Fourth, the Intergovernmental Panel recently concluded that the rise in aviation emissions owing to the growing demand for air travel would not be fully offset by reductions in emissions achieved solely through technological improvements.

Usually, two or three factors combine to form air pollution in any given location. The first factor is large amounts of carbon monoxide and hydrocarbons emitted by motor vehicles concentrated in a relatively small area. The second is the smoke and other pollutants emitted by manufacturing facilities. These two factors can be eliminated in part through pollution-control devices on cars, trucks, and smokestacks.

A third factor that contributes to air pollution—one that cannot be changed—is the combination of weather and geography. The Los Angeles Basin, for example, combines just the right weather and geographic conditions for creating dense smog. Los Angeles has strict regulations regarding air pollution. Even so, Los Angeles still struggles with air pollution problems because of uncontrollable conditions.

How effective is air pollution control? The EPA estimates that the Clean Air Act and its amendments eventually will result in the removal of fifty-six billion pounds of pollution from the air each year, thus measurably reducing lung disease, cancer, and other serious health problems caused by air pollution. Other authorities note that we have already seen improvement in air quality. A number of cities have cleaner air today than they did thirty years ago. Even in southern California, bad air quality days have dropped to less than forty days a year, about 60 percent lower than just a decade ago. Numerous chemical companies have recognized that they must take responsibility for operating their plants in an environmentally safe manner; some now devote considerable capital to purchasing antipollution devices. For example, 3M's pioneering Pollution Prevention Pays (3P) program, designed to find ways to avoid the generation of pollutants, marked its thirtieth anniversary in 2005. Since 1975, more than 5,600 employee-driven 3P projects have prevented the generation of more than 2.2 billion pounds of pollutants and produced first-year savings of nearly $1 billion. In recognition of 3M's commitment to environment, 2004 was the fifth year that 3M was selected for inclusion in the Dow Jones Sustainability Index and the fourth year that 3M was named the leader in its industry group. This index rates companies on their proactive corporate policies and practices in managing the economic, environmental, and social aspects of doing business around the world.[18]

Land Pollution   Air and water quality may be improving, but land pollution is still a serious problem in many areas. The fundamental issues are (1) how to restore damaged or contaminated land at a reasonable cost and (2) how to protect unpolluted land from future damage.

The land pollution problem has been worsening over the past few years because modern technology has continued to produce increasing amounts of chemical and radioactive waste. U.S. manufacturers produce an estimated forty to sixty million tons of contaminated oil, solvents, acids, and sludges each year. Service businesses, utility companies, hospitals, and other industries also dump vast amounts of wastes into the environment.

Individuals in the United States contribute to the waste-disposal problem, too. A shortage of landfills, owing to stricter regulations, makes garbage disposal a serious problem in some areas. Incinerators help to solve the landfill-shortage problem, but they bring with them their own problems. They reduce the amount of garbage but also leave tons of ash to be buried—ash that often has a higher concentration of toxicity than the original garbage. Other causes of land pollution include strip-mining of coal, nonselective cutting of forests, and the development of agricultural land for housing and industry.

To help pay the enormous costs of cleaning up land polluted with chemicals and toxic wastes, Congress created a $1.6 billion Superfund in 1980. Originally, money was to flow into the Superfund from a tax paid by 800 oil and chemical companies that produce toxic waste. The EPA was to use the money in the Superfund to finance the cleanup of hazardous waste sites across the nation. To replenish the Superfund, the EPA had two options: It could sue companies guilty of dumping chemicals at specific waste sites, or it could negotiate with guilty companies and thus completely avoid the legal system. During the 1980s, officials at the EPA came under fire because they preferred negotiated settlements. Critics referred to these settlements as "sweetheart deals" with industry. They felt that the EPA should be much more aggressive in reducing land pollution. Of course, most corporate executives believe that cleanup efficiency and quality might be improved if companies were more involved in the process. Many firms, including Delphi Automotive Systems Corporation and 3M, have modified or halted the production and sale of products that have a negative impact on the environment. For example, after tests showed that ScotchGuard does not decompose in the environment, 3M announced a voluntary end to production of the forty-year-old product, which had generated $300 million in sales.

BizTech

Reduce, Reuse, Recycle Your e-Waste

Electronic waste—*e-waste*—is a growing problem as technology advances and personal computers become obsolete at a rapid rate.

Tons of Trash

Since the personal computer (PC) was invented in 1985, more than sixty million have been sent to landfills as Americans trade up to newer, faster models. The National Safety Council estimates that by 2009, 136,000 PCs will be thrown away every day. Because some of the metals in PCs can leach into soil and water, pollution is a real concern.

Recycling Options

The major computer manufacturers all offer recycling programs. For a modest fee, Hewlett-Packard, Dell, and other companies will send you a shipping label and arrange to pick up your old PC. Or nonprofits such as the National Cristina Foundation and Per Scholas may take your PC if it's not too outdated.

Find Out More

For more information on e-waste and PC recycling, check Earth 911 (**www.earth911.org**), the Rethink Initiative (**rethink.ebay.com**), or the Computer Takeback Campaign (**www.computertakeback.com**).

Noise Pollution   Excessive noise caused by traffic, aircraft, and machinery can do physical harm to human beings. Research has shown that people who are exposed to loud noises for long periods of time can suffer permanent hearing loss. The Noise Control Act of 1972 established noise emission standards for aircraft and airports, railroads, and interstate motor carriers. The act also provided funding for noise research at state and local levels.

Noise levels can be reduced by two methods. The source of noise pollution can be isolated as much as possible. (Thus many metropolitan airports are located outside the cities.) And engineers can modify machinery and equipment to reduce noise levels. If it is impossible to reduce industrial noise to acceptable levels, workers should be required to wear earplugs to guard against permanent hearing damage.

Who Should Pay for a Clean Environment?

Governments and businesses are spending billions of dollars annually to reduce pollution—over $35 billion to control air pollution, $25 billion to control water pollution, and $12 billion to treat hazardous wastes. To make matters worse, much of the money required to purify the environment is supposed to come from already depressed industries, such as the chemical industry. And a few firms have discovered that it is cheaper to pay a fine than to install expensive equipment for pollution control.

Who, then, will pay for the environmental cleanup? Many business leaders offer one answer—tax money should be used to clean up the environment and to keep it clean. They reason that business is not the only source of pollution, so business should not be forced to absorb the entire cost of the cleanup. Environmentalists disagree. They believe that the cost of proper treatment and disposal of industrial wastes is an expense of doing business. In either case, consumers probably will pay a large part of the cost—either as taxes or in the form of higher prices for goods and services.

Implementing a Program of Social Responsibility

10 LEARNING OBJECTIVE
Identify the steps a business must take to implement a program of social responsibility.

A firm's decision to be socially responsible is a step in the right direction—but only the first step. The firm then must develop and implement a program to reach this goal. The program will be affected by the firm's size, financial resources, past record in the area of social responsibility, and competition. Above all, however, the program must have the firm's total commitment or it will fail.

Developing a Program of Social Responsibility

An effective program for social responsibility takes time, money, and organization. In most cases, developing and implementing such a program will require four steps: securing the commitment of top executives, planning, appointing a director, and preparing a social audit.

Commitment of Top Executives Without the support of top executives, any program will soon falter and become ineffective. For example, the Boeing Company's Ethics and Business Conduct Committee is responsible for the ethics program. The committee is appointed by the Boeing board of directors, and its members include the company chairman and CEO, the president and chief operating officer, the presidents of the operating groups, and senior vice presidents. As evidence of their commitment to social responsibility, top managers should develop a policy statement that outlines key areas of concern. This statement sets a tone of positive support and later will serve as a guide for other employees as they become involved in the program.

Planning Next, a committee of managers should be appointed to plan the program. Whatever form their plan takes, it should deal with each of the issues described in the top managers' policy statement. If necessary, outside consultants can be hired to help develop the plan.

Appointment of a Director After the social responsibility plan is established, a top-level executive should be appointed to implement the organization's plan. This individual should be charged with recommending specific policies and helping individual departments to understand and live up to the social responsibilities the firm has assumed. Depending on the size of the firm, the director may require a staff to handle the program on a day-to-day basis. For example, at the Boeing Company, the director of ethics and business conduct administers the ethics and business conduct program.

The Social Audit At specified intervals, the program director should prepare a social audit for the firm. A **social audit** is a comprehensive report of what an organization has done and is doing with regard to social issues that affect it. This document provides the information the firm needs to evaluate and revise its social responsibility program. Typical subject areas include human resources, community involvement, the quality and safety of products, business practices, and efforts to reduce pollution and improve the environment. The information included in a social audit should be as accurate and as quantitative as possible, and the audit should reveal both positive and negative aspects of the program.

social audit a comprehensive report of what an organization has done and is doing with regard to social issues that affect it

Today, many companies listen to concerned individuals within and outside the company. For example, the Boeing Ethics Line listens to and acts on concerns expressed by employees and others about possible violations of company policies, laws, or regulations, such as improper or unethical business practices, as well as health, safety, and environmental issues. Employees are encouraged to communicate their concerns, as well as ask questions about ethical issues. The Ethics Line is available to all Boeing employees, including Boeing subsidiaries. It is also available to concerned individuals outside the company.

Funding the Program

We have noted that social responsibility costs money. Thus, just like any other corporate undertaking, a program to improve social responsibility must be funded. Funding can come from three sources:

1. Management can pass the cost on to consumers in the form of higher prices.

2. The corporation may be forced to absorb the cost of the program if, for example, the competitive situation does not permit a price increase. In this case, the cost is treated as a business expense, and profit is reduced.
3. The federal government may pay for all or part of the cost through tax reductions or other incentives.

RETURN TO   Inside Business

Even as Home Depot volunteers donate their time, the company donates cash and supplies through its philanthropic arm, The Home Depot Foundation. The foundation has an annual budget of about $25 million to support a variety of good causes, including disaster relief, job training, youth services, and United Way activities. After devastating hurricanes hit Florida and the Gulf Coast, the retailer donated

$4.6 million in cash and supplies to the cleanup effort.

Environmental protection is another area where Home Depot has become active. The company pledged to stop selling products made from lumber logged in endangered rainforests following a series of activist protests in the late 1990s. It also began giving preference to "certified wood"—wood products that come from nonendangered forests. With Home Depot leading the way, competitors quickly followed suit. Home Depot now requires certification from its suppliers and stocks ecofriendly substitutes so that customers have more choices.

Questions

1. Why would customers, employees, and shareholders prefer to be involved with a company such as Home Depot that wants to build stronger communities?
2. Does Home Depot's social responsibility agenda also address one or more of the basic rights of consumers? Explain your answer.

►► CHAPTER REVIEW

Summary

1

Understand what is meant by *business ethics*.

Ethics is the study of right and wrong and of the morality of choices. Business ethics is the application of moral standards to business situations.

2

Identify the types of ethical concerns that arise in the business world.

Ethical issues arise often in business situations out of relationships with investors, customers, employees, creditors, or competitors. Business people should make every effort to be fair, to consider the welfare of customers and others within the firm, to avoid conflicts of interest, and to communicate honestly.

3

Discuss the factors that affect the level of ethical behavior in organizations.

Individual, social, and opportunity factors all affect the level of ethical behavior in an organization. Individual factors include knowledge level, moral values and attitudes, and personal goals. Social factors include cultural norms and the actions and values of coworkers and significant others. Opportunity factors refer to the amount of leeway that exists in an organization for employees to behave unethically if they so choose.

4

Explain how ethical decision making can be encouraged.

Governments, trade associations, and individual firms all can establish guidelines for defining ethical behavior. Governments can pass stricter regulations. Trade associations provide ethical guidelines for their members. Companies provide codes of ethics—written guides to acceptable and ethical behavior as defined by an organization—and create an atmosphere in which ethical behavior is encouraged. An ethical employee working in an unethical environment may resort to whistle-blowing to bring a questionable practice to light.

5

Describe how our current views on the social responsibility of business have evolved.

In a socially responsible business, management realizes that its activities have an impact on society and considers that impact in the decision-making process. Before the 1930s, workers, consumers, and government had very little influence on business activities; as a result, business leaders gave little thought to social responsibility. All this changed with the Great Depression. Government regulations, employee demands, and consumer awareness combined to create a demand that businesses act in socially responsible ways.

6

Explain the two views on the social responsibility of business and understand the arguments for and against increased social responsibility.

The basic premise of the economic model of social responsibility is that society benefits most when business is left alone to produce profitable goods and services. According to the socioeconomic model, business has as much responsibility to society as it has to its owners. Most managers adopt a viewpoint somewhere between these two extremes.

7

Discuss the factors that led to the consumer movement and list some of its results.

Consumerism consists of all activities undertaken to protect the rights of consumers. The consumer movement generally has demanded—and received—attention from business in the areas of product safety, product information, product choices through competition, and the resolution of complaints about products and business practices. Although concerns over consumer rights have been around to some extent since the early nineteenth century, the movement became more powerful in the 1960s when President John F. Kennedy initiated the consumer "bill of rights." The six basic rights of consumers include the right to safety, the right

to be informed, the right to choose, the right to be heard, and the rights to consumer education and courteous service.

8

Analyze how present employment practices are being used to counteract past abuses.

Legislation and public demand have prompted some businesses to correct past abuses in employment practices—mainly with regard to minority groups. Affirmative action and training of the hard-core unemployed are two types of programs that have been used successfully.

9

Describe the major types of pollution, their causes, and their cures.

Industry has contributed to the noise pollution and the pollution of our land and water through the dumping of wastes and to air pollution through vehicle and smokestack emissions. This contamination can be cleaned up and controlled, but the big question is: Who will pay? Present cleanup efforts are funded partly by government tax revenues, partly by business, and in the long run by consumers.

10

Identify the steps a business must take to implement a program of social responsibility.

A program to implement social responsibility in a business begins with total commitment by top management. The program should be planned carefully, and a capable director should be appointed to implement it. Social audits should be prepared periodically as a means of evaluating and revising the program. Programs may be funded through price increases, reduction of profit, or federal incentives.

Key Terms

You should now be able to define and give an example relevant to each of the following terms:

ethics (41)
business ethics (41)
Sarbanes-Oxley Act of 2002 (45)
code of ethics (45)
whistle-blowing (46)
social responsibility (48)
caveat emptor (52)
economic model of social responsibility (53)
socioeconomic model of social responsibility (53)
consumerism (55)
minority (57)
affirmative action program (59)
Equal Employment Opportunity Commission (EEOC) (59)
hard-core unemployed (59)
National Alliance of Business (NAB) (60)

pollution (60)

social audit (65)

Review Questions

1. Why might an individual with high ethical standards act less ethically in business than in his or her personal life?
2. How would an organizational code of ethics help to ensure ethical business behavior?
3. How and why did the American business environment change after the Great Depression?
4. What are the major differences between the economic model of social responsibility and the socioeconomic model?
5. What are the arguments for and against increasing the social responsibility of business?
6. Describe and give an example of each of the six basic rights of consumers.
7. There are more women than men in the United States. Why, then, are women considered a minority with regard to employment?
8. What is the goal of affirmative action programs? How is this goal achieved?
9. What is the primary function of the Equal Employment Opportunity Commission?
10. How do businesses contribute to each of the four forms of pollution? How can they avoid polluting the environment?
11. Our environment *can* be cleaned up and kept clean. Why haven't we simply done so?
12. Describe the steps involved in developing a social responsibility program within a large corporation.

Discussion Questions

1. When a company acts in an ethically questionable manner, what types of problems are caused for the organization and its customers?
2. How can an employee take an ethical stand regarding a business decision when his or her superior already has taken a different position?
3. Overall, would it be more profitable for a business to follow the economic model or the socioeconomic model of social responsibility?
4. Why should business take on the task of training the hard-core unemployed?
5. To what extent should the blame for vehicular air pollution be shared by manufacturers, consumers, and government?
6. Why is there so much government regulation involving social responsibility issues? Should there be less?

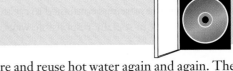

►► VIDEO CASE 2.1

At New Belgium Brewing, Greater Efficiency is Blowing in the Wind

New Belgium Brewing (NBB), America's first wind-powered brewery, aims to make both a better beer and a better society. Founded by husband-and-wife entrepreneurs Jeff Lebesch and Kim Jordan, the company offers European-style beers under intriguing brands such as Fat Tire and Sunshine Wheat. Lebesch hatched the idea for brewing his own beers after sipping local beers while touring Belgium on bicycle. Returning home with a special yeast strain, Lebesch experimented in his basement and came up with a beer he dubbed Fat Tire Amber Ale in honor of his bicycle trip.

By 1991, he and his wife were bottling and delivering five Belgian-style beers to liquor stores and other retailers in and around their hometown of Fort Collins, Colorado. Within a few years, sales had grown so rapidly that NBB needed much more space. Lebesch and Jordan moved the operation into a former railroad depot and then moved again into a new state-of-the-art brewery.

Not only is the 80,000-square-foot facility highly automated for efficiency, but it is also designed with the environment in mind. For example, sun tubes bring daylight to areas that lack windows, which reduces the brewery's energy requirements. As another energy-saving example, the brewery's kettles have steam condensers to

capture and reuse hot water again and again. The biggest energy-conservation measure is a special cooling device that reduces the need for air conditioning in warm weather. In the office section, NBB employees reuse and recycle paper and as many other supplies as possible.

Soon after opening the new brewery, the entire staff voted to convert it to wind power, which is kinder to the environment because it does not pollute or require scarce fossil fuels. In addition to saving energy and natural resources, NBB is actually transforming the methane from its waste stream into energy through the process of cogeneration. It also has found ways to cut carbon dioxide emissions and reuse brewing by-products as cattle feed. Going further, NBB donates $1 to charitable causes for every barrel of beer it sells—which translates into more than $200,000 per year. Moreover, it donates the proceeds of its annual Tour de Fat biking event to non-profit bicycling organizations.

Employee involvement is a key element of NBB's success. Lebesch and Jordan have unleashed the entrepreneurial spirit of the work force through employee ownership. Employees share in decisions, serve as taste testers, and receive detailed information about NBB's financial performance, including costs and profits. Being empowered as part owners not only motivates employees, but it also gives them a great sense of pride in their work. And reminiscent of the bicycle trip that prompted

Lebesch to brew his own beers, all employees receive a cruising bicycle on the first anniversary of joining the company.

Still, customers are most concerned with the taste of NBB's beers, which have won numerous awards and have attracted a large, loyal customer base in twelve states. In the last five years, Fat Tire's annual sales have grown from 0.9 million cases to 2.6 million cases. Many people become customers after hearing about the beer from long-time fans, and as its popularity grows, the word spreads even further. NBB does some advertising, but its budget is tiny compared with deep-pocketed rivals such as Anheuser-Busch and Miller Brewing. Instead of glitzy commercials on national television, NBB uses a low-key approach to show customers that the company is comprised of "real people making real beer."

Today, the company employs 140 people and is the sixth largest selling draft beer in America. Clearly, sales and profits are vital ingredients in NBB's long-term recipe, but they are not the only important elements. Jordan stresses that the company is not just about making beer—it is about creating what she calls "magic." Reflecting on her continued involvement in NBB, she says: "How do you support a community of people? How do you show up in the larger community? How do you strive to be a business role model? That's the part that keeps me really engaged here."

In fact, NBB has integrated social responsibility into its operations so successfully that it recently received an award from *Business Ethics* magazine. The award cited the company's "dedication to environmental excellence in every part of its innovative brewing process." Jordan, Lebesch, and all the NBB employee-owners can take pride in their efforts to build a better society as well as a better beer.[19]

For more information about this company, go to **www.newbelgium.com**.

Questions

1. What do you think Kim Jordan means when she talks about how New Belgium Brewing strives to be a "business role model," not just a beer maker?
2. Given New Belgium Brewing's emphasis on social responsibility, what would you suggest the company look at when preparing a social audit?
3. Should businesses charge more for products that are produced using more costly but environmentally friendly methods such as wind power? Should consumers pay more for products that are *not* produced using environmentally friendly methods because of the potential for costly environmental damage? Explain your answers.

▸▸ CASE 2.2

Wal-Mart Goes Green

A turnaround is underway at Wal-Mart. The largest and most powerful retailer in U.S. history is highly profitable—but it is also the target of intense criticism. Critics say that it offers low employee pay, works hard to avoid unionization, sells merchandise made in overseas sweatshops, and doesn't do enough to protect the environment. In recent years, however, Wal-Mart has been listening harder and making changes to show how good a corporate citizen it can be.

As an example, the company is determined to do business in a "greener" way. Meetings with the Natural Resources Defense Council and Conservation International have helped Wal-Mart identify ways to make its operations more ecofriendly. Such changes go well beyond image building because they directly affect how the chain's global suppliers operate. CEO H. Lee Scott, Jr., explains: "As we do the right thing, we have an impact across so many industries, so many countries. And we are finding tremendous cost savings while doing better things for the environment. Packaging is one of the simple things, and shame on us for not having done it earlier."

By reducing the amount of packaging on some of its imported toys, Wal-Mart and its suppliers saved lots of trees and lots of fuel. Moreover, because the toys were less bulky, they could be shipped in fewer containers, shaving more than $1 million from Wal-Mart's annual transportation budget. In addition, two new "green" stores are serving as laboratories for energy conservation techniques such as generating heat from leftover fat used to fry chickens. Such changes not only help the environment, but they also boost the retailer's bottom line while polishing its public image.

Being big allows Wal-Mart to make a difference in a big way. Consider the company's response to the devastation caused by hurricane Katrina, one of America's worst natural disasters. With hundreds of thousands of people forced to flee flooded areas of Louisiana and Mississippi, Wal-Mart opened its wallet wide and contributed $17 million in cash to jump-start relief efforts. It also donated all kinds of products to help evacuees, aid workers, and law enforcement officials.

One hundred Wal-Mart trucks rolled into the Gulf Coast right after the hurricane, loaded with bottled water, flashlights, batteries, ready-to-eat foods, and other basics. Store pharmacies filled prescriptions without charge for people with emergency medical needs. To help family members find each other via the Internet, Wal-Mart donated 150 computers to temporary shelters housing evacuees. To help employees displaced by the storm, the retailer paid out $4 million in cash assistance and fielded questions on a toll-free emergency hotline number.

This quick and generous response brought media attention and attracted praise from many observers. In one glowing newspaper report, a marketing expert was quoted as saying: "Wal-Mart has raised the ante for every company in the country. This is going to change the face of corporate giving." Indeed, the media coverage has gone a long way toward showing that Wal-Mart has a heart. "We have never claimed to be flawless," the CEO said afterward, adding that "we have always demanded that we as a company do care. If anything, this week has shown we do care."

Low prices and high volume will continue to be at the center of Wal-Mart's strategy. At the same time, more changes are ahead as Wal-Mart expands its inspection of the overseas factories where its merchandise is made and starts addressing other controversies that affect its reputation. The CEO knows that his company cannot afford to stand still: "We have to continue to evolve in how we operate and how we interface with society."[2]

For more information about this company, go to **www.walmart.com.**

Questions

1. When Wal-Mart's CEO tells a reporter, "We have never claimed to be flawless," does he seem to be demonstrating a strong commitment to social responsibility?
2. What areas would you recommend that Wal-Mart management examine when preparing a social audit, and why?
3. Considering the reaction to Wal-Mart's disaster-relief donations, should the company raise its prices so that it can fund more corporate giving? Explain your answer.

→ CHAPTER 2: JOURNAL EXERCISE

Discovery statement: This chapter was devoted mostly to business ethics, ethical concerns that arise in the business world, personal ethics, and social responsibility of business.

Assume that you are an accountant at ABC Corporation, where you question the company's accounting practices. What legal and managerial changes would you suggest to prevent the use of accounting tricks to manipulate corporate earnings?

_____

_____

_____

_____

Assume that your manager refuses to incorporate any of your suggestions. Would you blow the whistle? Why or why not?

_____

_____

_____

_____

_____

Suppose that you blow the whistle and get fired. Which law might protect your rights, and how would you proceed to protect yourself?

_____

_____

_____

_____

_____

BUILDING SKILLS FOR CAREER SUCCESS

1. Exploring the Internet

Socially responsible business behavior can be as simple as donating unneeded older computers to schools, mentoring interested learners in good business practices, or supplying public speakers to talk about career opportunities. Students, as part of the public at large, perceive a great deal of information about a company, its employees, and its owners by the positive social actions taken and perhaps even more by actions not taken. Microsoft donates millions of dollars of computers and software to educational institutions every year. Some people consider this level of corporate giving to be insufficient given the scale of the wealth of the corporation. Others believe that firms have no obligation to give back any more than they wish and that recipients should be grateful. Visit the text website for updates to this exercise.

Assignment

1. Select any firm involved in high technology and the Internet such as Microsoft or IBM. Examine their website and report their corporate position on social responsibility and giving as they have stated it. What activities are they involved in? What programs do they support, and how do they support them?

2. Search the Internet for commentary on business social responsibility, form your own opinions, and then evaluate the social effort demonstrated by the firm you have selected. What more could the firm have done?

2. Developing Critical-Thinking Skills

Recently, an article entitled "Employees Coming to Terms with Moral Issues on the Job" appeared in a big-city newspaper. It posed the following situations:

You are asked to work on a project you find morally wrong.

Important tasks are left undone because a coworker spends more time planning a social event than working on a proposal.

Your company is knowingly selling defective merchandise to customers.

Unfortunately, many employees currently are struggling with such issues. The moral dilemmas that arise when employees find their own ethical values incompatible with the work they do every day are causing a lot of stress in the workplace, and furthermore, these dilemmas are not being discussed. There exists an ethics gap. You already may have faced a similar situation in your workplace.

Assignment

1. In small groups with your classmates, discuss your answers to the following questions:

   a. If you were faced with any of the preceding situations, what would you do?

   b. Would you complete work you found morally unacceptable, or would you leave it undone and say nothing?

   c. If you spoke up, what would happen to you or your career? What would be the risk?

   d. What are your options?

   e. If you were a manager rather than a lower-level employee, would you feel differently and take a different approach to the issue? Why?

2. In a written report, summarize what you learned from this discussion.

3. Building Team Skills

A firm's code of ethics outlines the kinds of behaviors expected within the organization and serves as a guideline for encouraging ethical behavior in the workplace. It reflects the rights of the firm's workers, shareholders, and consumers.

Assignment

1. Working in a team of four, find a code of ethics for a business firm. Start the search by asking firms in your community for a copy of their codes, by visiting the library, or by searching and downloading information from the Internet.

2. Analyze the code of ethics you have chosen, and answer the following questions:

   a. What does the company's code of ethics say about the rights of its workers, shareholders, consumers, and suppliers? How does the code reflect the company's attitude toward competitors?

   b. How does this code of ethics resemble the information discussed in this chapter? How does it differ?

   c. As an employee of this company, how would you personally interpret the code of ethics? How might the code influence your behavior within the workplace? Give several examples.

4. Researching Different Careers

Business ethics has been at the heart of many discussions over the years and continues to trouble employees and shareholders. Stories about dishonesty and wrongful behavior in the workplace appear on a regular basis in newspapers and on the national news.

Assignment

Prepare a written report on the following:

1. Why can it be so difficult for people to do what is right?

2. What is your personal code of ethics? Prepare a code outlining what you believe is morally right. The document should include guidelines for your personal behavior.

3. How will your code of ethics affect your decisions about

   a. The types of questions you should ask in a job interview?

   b. Selecting a company in which to work?

5. Improving Communication Skills

Businesses with programs of social responsibility provide a wealth of services to groups in their communities, such as schools, libraries, city governments, and service and civic organizations. If you are not aware of the businesses in your community that are doing this, you might be surprised at what is happening.

Assignment

1. Identify several businesses in your community that are providing services to local institutions and organizations.

2. Prepare a table using the following columns to indicate what services they provide, what the impact of these services has been on your community, and in what ways they make a difference to the organization or institution receiving the services:

   Column 1: Name of company providing services

   Column 2: Types of services provided

   Column 3: Organizations or institutions receiving services

   Column 4: Impact in the community

   Column 5: Difference within the organization

3. Summarize your philosophy of business's social responsibility. As an employee, how would you feel about helping your company fulfill its social responsibility within the community? Why? Is this a fair job requirement? Explain.

→ **PREP TEST**

Matching Questions

___ 1. Its focus is to protect the rights of consumers.

___ 2. A group singled out for unfavorable treatment.

___ 3. According to this view, social responsibility is the government's job.

___ 4. It reflects how businesses deal with societal issues.

___ 5. "Businesses have a responsibility to society" is its premise.

___ 6. "What you see is what you get" is its essence.

___ 7. Moral standards are applied to business.

___ 8. Employees' expected behavior on the job is described.

___ 9. It is a study of right and wrong.

___ 10. Employees tell government officials about unethical practices in their workplace.

a. business ethics
b. caveat emptor
c. code of ethics
d. consumerism
e. economic model
f. ethics
g. minority
h. social responsibility
i. socioeconomic model
j. whistle-blowing

True/False Questions

T F

11. ○ ○ Demands for social responsibility are a direct result of the U.S. involvement in the Vietnam war.

12. ○ ○ An internal business force that affects decisions concerning social responsibility is government regulation.

13. ○ ○ By helping resolve social issues, businesses can prevent increased government intervention.

14. ○ ○ Employees generally find it easy to assess ethical issues.

15. ○ ○ In consumerism, the right to safety means that products have been tested by the manufacturer to ensure quality and reliability.

16. ○ ○ Employees with federal contracts of more than $50,000 per year must have written affirmative action plans.

T F

17. ○ ○ The economic model of social responsibility is used exclusively by IBM and Johnson & Johnson.

18. ○ ○ An argument against increased social responsibility is that corporate time, money, and talent should be used to maximize profits, not to solve society's problems.

19. ○ ○ National Alliance of Business is a locally sponsored program that offers scholarships to academically successful students.

20. ○ ○ A corporate code of ethics provides guidelines for acceptable and ethical behavior in business operations.

Multiple-Choice Questions

21. John Ameron has no marketable skills, a chronic record of unemployment, and did not complete high school. Which organization could best help him?
    a. National Alliance of Business
    b. American Federation of Labor
    c. Chamber of Commerce
    d. Equal Employment Opportunity Commission
    e. Consumer Product Safety Commission

22. This act prevents mergers where competition is endangered.
    a. Interstate Commerce Act
    b. Sherman Antitrust Act
    c. Federal Trade Commission Act
    d. Clayton Act
    e. Truth in Lending Act

23. Which of the following programs ensures that minorities are represented within the organization in approximately the same proportion as in the surrounding community?
    a. National Alliance of Business
    b. Affirmative Action Program
    c. Equal Employment Opportunity Program
    d. Hard-Core Unemployment Program
    e. All the above.

24. Proponents of the socioeconomic model of social responsibility argue that
    a. corporate time, money, and talent should be used to maximize profits, not to solve society's problems.
    b. by helping to resolve social issues, businesses can create a more stable environment for long-term profitability.
    c. social issues are the responsibility of government officials elected by the people.
    d. individual businesses are not equipped to solve social problems that affect society in general.
    e. business managers are primarily responsible to stockholders.

25. Carol Randal has the educational requirements, experience, and skills to be promoted to the next management level in an insurance company. Overhearing a conversation between two other employees, she learns that the person who was promoted to the position had been with the firm less than a year, was currently working on completing his degree next semester, and lacked skills in several areas. She should file a complaint with the
    a. Equal Employment Opportunity Commission.
    b. National Alliance of Business.
    c. union.
    d. National Organization for Women.
    e. Federal Trade Commission.

Fill-in-the-Blank Questions

26. The act that eliminated many forms of price discrimination that gave large businesses a competitive advantage over smaller firms was the _____ Act.

27. A firm's comprehensive report of its social issues is a _____.

28. A partnership of business and community leaders, with a focus on education and workforce issues, is the _____.

29. Workers with little education or vocational training and a long history of unemployment are _____ unemployed workers.

30. The contamination of water, air, or land through the actions of people in an industrialized society is called _____.

Online Study Center

FOR MORE **test practice, use the interactive ACE quizzes available at the Online Student Center: www.college.hmco.com/PIC/pridebusiness9e.**

Answers on p. PT1.

Exploring Global Business

WHAT you will be able to do once you complete this chapter:

1 Explain the economic basis for international business.

2 Discuss the restrictions nations place on international trade, the objectives of these restrictions, and their results.

3 Outline the extent of international trade and identify the organizations working to foster it.

4 Define the methods by which a firm can organize for and enter into international markets.

5 Describe the various sources of export assistance.

6 Identify the institutions that help firms and nations finance international business.

WHY this chapter matters

Free trade—are you for it or against it? Why? Even though most economists support free-trade policies, public support for these policies can be lukewarm at best, and certain groups are adamantly opposed to free trade. These groups allege that "trade harms large segments of U.S. workers," "trade degrades the environment," and "trade exploits poor countries."

FOR HELP with studying this chapter, visit the Online Student Center:

www.college.hmco.com/PIC/pridebusiness9e

Online Study Center

H.J. Heinz has been a major force in global business for more than 120 years. Henry John Heinz started the Pittsburgh-based company in 1869, before the public was accustomed to the commercial marketing of preserved foods in cans and jars. Heinz reasoned that selling horseradish in jars would allow buyers to see the product's high quality. In fact, sales were so strong that the company began selling pickles, sauerkraut, vinegar, tomato ketchup, and other condiments in Heinz-branded jars.

Heinz sailed to England in 1886 to place his products in London shops. Ten years later, he opened the company's first international office near the Tower of London. To ensure freshness and quality, Heinz built local factories to make what became known as the "57 Varieties" of products for European markets and, later, for markets on other continents.

By the mid-1950s, however, Heinz was ready to change its recipe for international success. Instead of constructing factories to serve new markets, the company expanded by buying local firms—a

DID YOU KNOW?

H.J. Heinz Company markets its brands in 200 countries, and it produces more than 1.4 billion bottles of ketchup every year?

strategy it still follows today. Not long ago, Heinz bought a ketchup company in Russia and acquired HP Foods from France's Group Danone. That deal brought it saucemakers Lea & Perrins and Amoy, which sell condiments in 75 countries. Even as Heinz refocuses on its best-selling global brands, it is seeking corporate buyers for less-profitable businesses from earlier international acquisitions, such as talcum powder (India) and prepared produce (Europe).

Today, Heinz's worldwide revenue exceeds $9 billion annually, driven by sales of such popular brands as Ore-Ida, Weight Watchers, Smart Ones, and Wyler's. The Heinz brand remains the biggest seller, accounting for $3 billion in annual revenue. Along with increasing consumption in areas where its products are already strong sellers, the company is working to build its business in high-population-growth countries such as China and India. What will Heinz stock in its global pantry tomorrow?[1]

For more information about this company, go to **www.heinz.com**.

Heinz is just one of a growing number of U.S. companies, large and small, that are doing business with firms in other countries. Some companies, such as Coca-Cola, sell to firms in other countries; others, such as Pier 1 Imports, buy goods around the world to import into the United States. Whether they buy or sell products across national borders, these companies are all contributing to the volume of international trade that is fueling the global economy.

Theoretically, international trade is every bit as logical and worthwhile as interstate trade between, say, California and Washington. Yet nations tend to restrict the import of certain goods for a variety of reasons. For example, in the early 2000s, the United States restricted the import of Mexican fresh tomatoes because they were undercutting price levels of domestic fresh tomatoes.

Despite such restrictions, international trade has increased almost steadily since World War II. Many of the industrialized nations have signed trade agreements intended to eliminate problems in international business and to help less-developed nations participate in world trade. Individual firms around the world have seized the opportunity to compete in foreign markets by exporting products and increasing foreign production, as well as by other means.

Signing the Trade Act of 2002, President George W. Bush remarked, "Trade is an important source of good jobs for our workers and a source of higher growth for our economy. Free trade is also a proven strategy for building global prosperity and adding to the momentum of political freedom. Trade is an engine of economic growth. In our lifetime, trade has helped lift millions of people and whole nations out of poverty and put them on the path of prosperity.[2]

We describe international trade in this chapter in terms of modern specialization, whereby each country trades the surplus goods and services it produces most efficiently for products in short supply. We also explain the restrictions nations place on products and services from other countries and present some of the possible advantages and disadvantages of these restrictions. We then describe the extent of international trade and identify the organizations working to foster it. We describe several methods of entering international markets and the various sources of export assistance available from the federal government. Finally, we identify some of the institutions that provide the complex financing necessary for modern international trade.

The Basis for International Business

International business encompasses all business activities that involve exchanges across national boundaries. Thus a firm is engaged in international business when it buys some portion of its input from or sells some portion of its output to an organization located in a foreign country. (A small retail store may sell goods produced in some other country. However, because it purchases these goods from American distributors, it is not engaged in international trade.)

Absolute and Comparative Advantage

Some countries are better equipped than others to produce particular goods or services. The reason may be a country's natural resources, its labor supply, or even customs or a historical accident. Such a country would be best off if it could *specialize* in the production of such products because it can produce them most efficiently. The country could use what it needed of these products and then trade the surplus for products it could not produce efficiently on its own.

Saudi Arabia thus has specialized in the production of crude oil and petroleum products; South Africa, in diamonds; and Australia, in wool. Each of these countries is said to have an absolute advantage with regard to a particular product. An **absolute advantage** is the ability to produce a specific product more efficiently than any other nation.

One country may have an absolute advantage with regard to several products, whereas another country may have no absolute advantage at all. Yet it is still worthwhile for these two countries to specialize

Exploiting absolute advantage. Saudi Arabia has long specialized in the production of crude oil and petroleum products. Because of their natural oil resources, Saudi Arabia and other countries in the Middle East enjoy an absolute advantage—their ability to produce petroleum products more efficiently than in any other area of the world. Here, President Bush meets with Saudi Crown Prince Abdullah to persuade him to help curb skyrocketing oil prices that are hurting American families and businesses.

and trade with each other. To see why this is so, imagine that you are the president of a successful manufacturing firm and that you can accurately type ninety words per minute. Your assistant can type eighty words per minute but would run the business poorly. Thus you have an absolute advantage over your assistant in both typing and managing. However, you cannot afford to type your own letters because your time is better spent in managing the business. That is, you have a **comparative advantage** in managing. A comparative advantage is the ability to produce a specific product more efficiently than any other product.

Your assistant, on the other hand, has a comparative advantage in typing because he or she can do that better than managing the business. Thus you spend your time managing, and you leave the typing to your assistant. Overall, the business is run as efficiently as possible because you are each working in accordance with your own comparative advantage.

The same is true for nations. Goods and services are produced more efficiently when each country specializes in the products for which it has a comparative advantage. Moreover, by definition, every country has a comparative advantage in *some* product. The United States has many comparative advantages—in research and development, high-technology industries, and identifying new markets, for instance.

comparative advantage the ability to produce a specific product more efficiently than any other product

Exporting and Importing

Suppose that the United States specializes in producing corn. It then will produce a surplus of corn, but perhaps it will have a shortage of wine. France, on the other hand, specializes in producing wine but experiences a shortage of corn. To satisfy both needs—for corn and for wine—the two countries should trade with each other. The United States should export corn and import wine. France should export wine and import corn.

Exporting is selling and shipping raw materials or products to other nations. The Boeing Company, for example, exports its airplanes to a number of countries for use by their airlines. Figure 3.1 shows the top ten merchandise-exporting states in this country.

exporting selling and shipping raw materials or products to other nations

>> FIGURE 3.1

THE TOP TEN MERCHANDISE-EXPORTING STATES

Texas and California accounted for over one-fourth of all 2004 U.S. merchandise exports.

Billions of dollars, 2004 merchandise exports

State	Exports
Texas	$117.2
California	$109.9
New York	$44.4
Michigan	$35.6
Washington	$33.8
Ohio	$31.2
Illinois	$30.2
Florida	$28.9
Massachusetts	$21.8
Louisiana	$19.9

Total 2004 U.S. exports: $817.9 billion

Source: **www.ita.doc.gov/td/industry/otea/usfth/aggregate/H04T11.html**; accessed September 21, 2005.

Importing is purchasing raw materials or products in other nations and bringing them into one's own country. Thus buyers for Macy's department stores may purchase rugs in India or raincoats in England and have them shipped back to the United States for resale.

Importing and exporting are the principal activities in international trade. They give rise to an important concept called the *balance of trade*. A nation's **balance of trade** is the total value of its exports *minus* the total value of its imports over some period of time. If a country imports more than it exports, its balance of trade is negative and is said to be *unfavorable*. (A negative balance of trade is unfavorable because the country must export money to pay for its excess imports.) In 2004, the United States imported $1,470 billion worth of merchandise and exported $819 billion worth. It thus had a trade deficit of $651 billion. A **trade deficit** is a negative balance of trade (see Figure 3.2). However, the United States has consistently enjoyed a large and rapidly growing surplus in services. For example, in 2004, the United States imported $296 billion worth and exported $344 billion worth of services, thus creating a favorable balance of $48 billion.[3]

importing purchasing raw materials or products in other nations and bringing them into one's own country

balance of trade the total value of a nation's exports minus the total value of its imports over some period of time

trade deficit a negative balance of trade

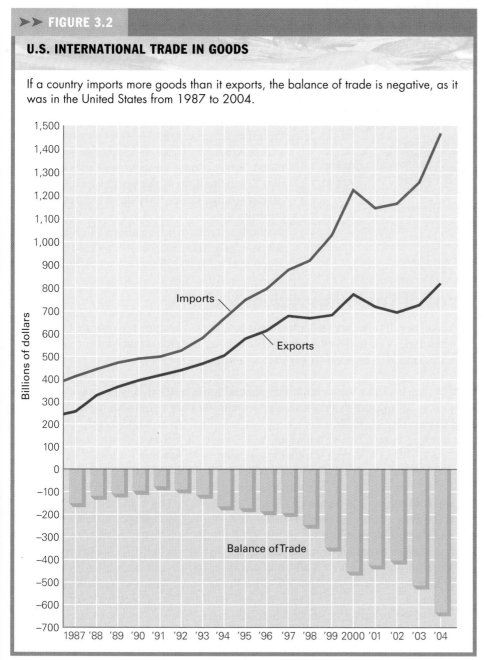

>> **FIGURE 3.2**

U.S. INTERNATIONAL TRADE IN GOODS

If a country imports more goods than it exports, the balance of trade is negative, as it was in the United States from 1987 to 2004.

Source: U.S. Department of Commerce, International Trade Administration, **www.ita.doc.gov/td/industry/otea/usfth/aggregate/H04T03.html;** accessed September 21, 2005.

balance of payments the total flow of money into a country minus the total flow of money out of that country over some period of time

On the other hand, when a country exports more than it imports, it is said to have a *favorable* balance of trade. This has consistently been the case for Japan over the last two decades or so.

A nation's **balance of payments** is the total flow of money into a country *minus* the total flow of money out of that country over some period of time. Balance of payments therefore is a much broader concept than balance of trade. It includes imports and exports, of course. But it also includes investments, money spent by foreign tourists, payments by foreign governments, aid to foreign governments, and all other receipts and payments.

A continual deficit in a nation's balance of payments (a negative balance) can cause other nations to lose confidence in that nation's economy. A continual surplus may indicate that the country encourages exports but limits imports by imposing trade restrictions.

SPOTLIGHT

The growing deficit

After a small surplus in 1991, the U.S. balance of payments has consistently run large deficits since 1992.

Year	Deficit in billions of dollars
1996	−125
1998	−214
2000	−416
2002	−475
2004	−668
2005	−805

Source: U.S. Department of Commerce, Bureau of Economic Analysis, *News Release,* **www.bea.doc.gov/bea/Articles/2005/ 07July/0705_ita%;** accessed March 14, 2006.

Restrictions to International Business

Specialization and international trade can result in the efficient production of want-satisfying goods and services on a worldwide basis. As we have noted, international business generally is increasing. Yet the nations of the world continue to erect barriers to free trade. They do so for reasons ranging from internal political and economic pressures to simple mistrust of other nations. We examine first the types of restrictions that are applied and then the arguments for and against trade restrictions.

Types of Trade Restrictions

2 LEARNING OBJECTIVE
Discuss the restrictions nations place on international trade, the objectives of these restrictions, and their results.

Nations generally are eager to export their products. They want to provide markets for their industries and to develop a favorable balance of trade. Hence most trade restrictions are applied to imports from other nations.

import duty (tariff) a tax levied on a particular foreign product entering a country

Tariffs Perhaps the most commonly applied trade restriction is the customs (or import) duty. An **import duty** (also called a **tariff**) is a tax levied on a particular foreign product entering a country. For example, the United States imposes a 2.2 percent import duty on fresh Chilean tomatoes, an 8.7 percent if tomatoes are dried and packaged, and nearly 12 percent if tomatoes are made into ketchup or salsa. The two types of tariffs are revenue tariffs and protective tariffs; both have the effect of raising the price of the product in the importing nations, but for different reasons. *Revenue tariffs* are imposed solely to generate income for the government. For example, the United States imposes a duty on Scotch whiskey solely for revenue purposes. *Protective tariffs,* on the other hand, are imposed to protect a domestic industry from competition by keeping the price of competing imports level with or higher than the price of similar domestic products. Because fewer units of the product will be sold at the increased price, fewer units will be imported. The French and Japanese agricultural sectors would both shrink drastically if their nations abolished the protective tariffs that keep the price of imported farm products high. Today, U.S. tariffs are the lowest in history, with average tariff rates on all imports of under 3 percent.

dumping exportation of large quantities of a product at a price lower than that of the same product in the home market

Some countries rationalize their protectionist policies as a way of offsetting an international trade practice called *dumping.* **Dumping** is the exportation of large quantities of a product at a price lower than that of the same product in the home market.

Cuba embargo fading away. The United States' trade embargo against Cuba has been criticized by many noted economists, politicians, academicians, farm leaders, and business people. However, the United States is the largest source of humanitarian assistance to Cuba. Since 2001, the U.S. government has licensed the export of $5 billion in agricultural commodities to Cuba. Has the time come to end the trade embargo and lift the ban on travel to Cuba by American citizens? "Ending the embargo is the right thing to do," says Iowa Agriculture Secretary Patty Judge.

Thus dumping drives down the price of the domestic item. Recently, for example, the Pencil Makers Association, which represents eight U.S. pencil manufacturers, charged that low-priced pencils from Thailand and the People's Republic of China were being sold in the United States at less than fair-value prices. Unable to compete with these inexpensive imports, several domestic manufacturers had to shut down. To protect themselves, domestic manufacturers can obtain an antidumping duty through the government to offset the advantage of the foreign product. In 2005, for example, the U.S. Department of Commerce imposed preliminary antidumping duties of up to 30 percent on a variety of steel products imported from Europe, Japan, and Russia, 29 percent on Canadian soft lumber, and up to 60 percent on orange juice from Brazil.

Nontariff Barriers

A **nontariff barrier** is a nontax measure imposed by a government to favor domestic over foreign suppliers. Nontariff barriers create obstacles to the marketing of foreign goods in a country and increase costs for exporters. The following are a few examples of government-imposed nontariff barriers:

- An **import quota** is a limit on the amount of a particular good that may be imported into a country during a given period of time. The limit may be set in terms of either quantity (so many pounds of beef) or value (so many dollars' worth of shoes). Quotas also may be set on individual products imported from specific countries. Once an import quota has been reached, imports are halted until the specified time has elapsed.
- An **embargo** is a complete halt to trading with a particular nation or in a particular product. The embargo is used most often as a political weapon. At present, the United States has import embargoes against Iran and North Korea—both as a result of extremely poor political relations.
- A **foreign-exchange control** is a restriction on the amount of a particular foreign currency that can be purchased or sold. By limiting the amount of foreign currency importers can obtain, a government limits the amount of goods importers can purchase with that currency. This has the effect of limiting imports from the country whose foreign exchange is being controlled.
- A nation can increase or decrease the value of its money relative to the currency of other nations. **Currency devaluation** is the reduction of the value of a nation's currency relative to the currencies of other countries.

    Devaluation increases the cost of foreign goods while it decreases the cost of domestic goods to foreign firms. For example, suppose that the British pound is worth $2. Then an American-made $2,000 computer can be purchased for £1,000. However, if the United Kingdom devalues the pound so that it is worth only $1, that same computer will cost £2,000. The increased cost, in pounds, will reduce the import of American computers—and all foreign goods—into England.

nontariff barrier a nontax measure imposed by a government to favor domestic over foreign suppliers

import quota a limit on the amount of a particular good that may be imported into a country during a given period of time

embargo a complete halt to trading with a particular nation or in a particular product

foreign-exchange control a restriction on the amount of a particular foreign currency that can be purchased or sold

currency devaluation the reduction of the value of a nation's currency relative to the currencies of other countries

On the other hand, before devaluation, a £500 set of English bone china will cost an American $1,000. After the devaluation, the set of china will cost only $500. The decreased cost will make the china—and all English goods—much more attractive to U.S. purchasers. Bureaucratic red tape is more subtle than the other forms of nontariff barriers. Yet it can be the most frustrating trade barrier of all. A few examples are unnecessarily restrictive application of standards and complex requirements related to product testing, labeling, and certification.

Another type of nontariff barrier is related to cultural attitudes. Cultural barriers can impede acceptance of products in foreign countries. For example, illustrations of feet are regarded as despicable in Thailand. When customers are unfamiliar with particular products from another country, their general perceptions of the country itself affect their attitude toward the product and help to determine whether they will buy it. Because Mexican cars have not been viewed by the world as being quality products, Volkswagen, for example, may not want to advertise that some of its models sold in the United States are made in Mexico. Many retailers on the Internet have yet to come to grips with the task of designing an online shopping site that is attractive and functional for all global customers. According to a study by Forrester Research, 46 percent of all orders to U.S.-based sites placed by people living outside the United States went unfilled owing to process failures. Given that the Forrester study suggests that the average website gets 30 percent of its traffic and 10 percent of its orders from non-U.S. customers, the results suggest that an enormous loss of potential export sales will continue until websites better reflect local-buyer culture and behavior. [4]

Reasons for Trade Restrictions

Various reasons are advanced for trade restrictions either on the import of specific products or on trade with particular countries. We have noted that political considerations usually are involved in trade embargoes. Other frequently cited reasons for restricting trade include the following:

- *To equalize a nation's balance of payments.* This may be considered necessary to restore confidence in the country's monetary system and in its ability to repay its debts.
- *To protect new or weak industries.* A new, or *infant*, industry may not be strong enough to withstand foreign competition. Temporary trade restrictions may be used to give it a chance to grow and become self-sufficient. The problem is that once an industry is protected from foreign competition, it may refuse to grow, and "temporary" trade restrictions will become permanent. For example, a recent report by the General Accounting Office (GAO), the congressional investigative agency, has accused the federal government of routinely imposing quotas on foreign textiles without "demonstrating the threat of serious damage" to U.S. industry. The GAO said that the Committee for the Implementation of Textile Agreements sometimes applies quotas even though it cannot prove the textile industry's claims that American companies have been hurt or jobs eliminated.
- *To protect national security.* Restrictions in this category generally apply to technological products that must be kept out of the hands of potential enemies. For example, strategic and defense-related goods cannot be exported to unfriendly nations.
- *To protect the health of citizens.* Products may be embargoed because they are dangerous or unhealthy (e.g., farm products contaminated with insecticides).
- *To retaliate for another nation's trade restrictions.* A country whose exports are taxed by another country may respond by imposing tariffs on imports from that country.
- *To protect domestic jobs.* By restricting imports, a nation can protect jobs in domestic industries. However, protecting these jobs can be expensive. For example, to protect 9,000 jobs in the U.S. carbon-steel industry costs $6.8 billion, or $750,000 per job. In addition, Gary Hufbauer and Ben Goodrich, economists at

the Institute for International Economics, estimate that the tariffs could temporarily save 3,500 jobs in the steel industry, but at an annual cost to steel users of $2 billion, or $584,000 per job saved. Yet recently the United States imposed tariffs of up to 30 percent on steel imported from Brazil, China, Japan, Russia, and the European Union.[5] Similarly, it is estimated that we spent more than $100,000 for every job saved in the apparel manufacturing industry—jobs that seldom paid more than $15,000 a year.

Reasons Against Trade Restrictions

Trade restrictions have immediate and long-term economic consequences—both within the restricting nation and in world trade patterns. These include

- *Higher prices for consumers.* Higher prices may result from the imposition of tariffs or the elimination of foreign competition, as described earlier. For example, imposing quota restrictions and import protections adds $25 billion annually to U.S. consumers' apparel costs by directly increasing costs for imported apparel.
- *Restriction of consumers' choices.* Again, this is a direct result of the elimination of some foreign products from the marketplace and of the artificially high prices that importers must charge for products that still *are* imported.
- *Misallocation of international resources.* The protection of weak industries results in the inefficient use of limited resources. The economies of both the restricting nation and other nations eventually suffer because of this waste.
- *Loss of jobs.* The restriction of imports by one nation must lead to cutbacks—and the loss of jobs—in the export-oriented industries of other nations. Furthermore, trade protection has a significant effect on the composition of employment. U.S. trade restrictions—whether on textiles, apparel, steel, or automobiles—benefit only a few industries while harming many others. The gains in employment accrue to the protected industries and their primary suppliers, and the losses are spread across all other industries. A few states gain employment, but many other states lose employment.

YOUR CAREER

Are You Ready for a Global Job?

Would you be successful in an international job assignment? Ask yourself:

1. How do I react to new and unfamiliar situations?
2. What strengths, skills, and knowledge do I have to offer?
3. Am I accepting of different cultures and viewpoints?
4. How will an overseas assignment help me personally and professionally?

Although some multinationals use English as their global business language, employees who want to work abroad may have to know the local language (or at least be able to understand basic phrases). Robyn Glennon, whose first overseas job was in Prague, sums up her experience this way: "Every day was a challenge—the language, the people, the homesickness. But I was learning something new every day."

The Extent of International Business

Restrictions or not, international business is growing. Although the worldwide recessions of 1991 and 2001–2002 slowed the rate of growth, globalization is a reality of our time. Since the early 1980s, total trade in goods accounted for 36 percent of world gross domestic product (GDP); 23 years later, that ratio increased to 50 percent.[6] In the United States, international trade now accounts for over one-fourth of GDP. As trade barriers decrease, new competitors enter the global marketplace, creating more choices for consumers and new opportunities for job seekers. International business will grow along with the expansion of commercial use of the Internet.

3 LEARNING OBJECTIVE
Outline the extent of international trade and identify the organizations working to foster it.

The World Economic Outlook for Trade

While the U.S. economy had been growing steadily until 2000 and recorded the longest peacetime expansion in the nation's history, the worldwide recession has slowed the rate of growth. The International Monetary Fund (IMF), an international bank with 184 member nations, estimated that the U.S. economy grew by slightly less than 4.2 percent in 2004 and, despite hurricanes Katrina and Rita, by 3.5 percent in 2005 and 3.3 percent in 2006. However, global growth in 2004 was the highest in three decades when world output increased by over 5 percent.[7] International experts expected global economic growth of 4.3 percent in 2005 and 2006, despite the high oil prices and two hurricanes in the United States. At this rate of growth, world production of goods and services will double by the year 2020.

Canada and Western Europe Our leading export-import partner, Canada, is projected to show the fastest growth. The inflation rate in Canada is about half the U.S. rate, and our exports to Canada are booming. Economic growth of 2.9 percent in 2005 and 3.2 percent in 2006 was predicted for Canada. However, economies in Western Europe have been growing slowly. Only the United Kingdom enjoyed 1.9 percent economic growth in 2005 with the lowest level of unemployment in 20 years; the economies of Germany, France, and Italy all grew by less than 1.0 percent in 2005 and 1.2 percent in 2006. Recent growth in Austria, Belgium, the Netherlands, and Portugal has been slow, whereas growth in Greece, Ireland, and Spain has been stronger.

Mexico and South America Our second-largest export-import partner, Mexico, suffered its sharpest recession ever in 1995, but its growth rate in 2005 was about 4.0 percent. In general, however, the Latin American economies grew 4.1 percent in 2005 versus 5.6 percent in 2004. The economies of Argentina, Uruguay, Paraguay, Brazil, Venezuela, Ecuador, Peru, and a few other countries in that region have been sluggish owing to political, economic, and financial market problems. Future growth of about 4.0 percent is projected for the region.

This lumber is made for exporting. Southland Log Homes of Irmo, South Carolina, manufactures quality log homes and has sales offices throughout the United States. Southland homes have been built in more than 43 states and 13 foreign countries. Exporting homes now accounts for about 18 percent of the company's sales, the majority of which are sold to Japan.

Japan Japan's economy is regaining momentum. Stronger consumer demand and business investment make Japan less reliant on exports for growth. The first half of 2005 saw very strong growth, and the IMF estimated the growth at 2 percent for 2005 and 2006.

Asia The economic recovery in Asia increased significantly in 2005. For example, in China and India, the GDP increased 9.0 and 7.0 percent, respectively. Even in the hardest-hit economies in the region, Singapore and Taiwan Province of China, the recovery continued in 2005. Growth in Asia is expected to moderate somewhat to about 7.8 percent in 2005 and 7.2 percent in 2006.

China's emergence as a global economic power has been among the most dramatic economic developments of recent decades. From 1980 to 2004, China's economy averaged a real GDP growth rate of 9.5 percent and became the world's sixth-largest economy. China's total share in world trade expanded from 1 percent in 1980 to almost 6 percent in 2003. By 2004, China had become the third-largest trading nation in dollar terms, behind the United States and Germany and just ahead of Japan.[8] China's growth is estimated to be 8.2 percent in 2006.

Central and Eastern Europe and Russia After World War II, trade between the United States and the communist nations of central and Eastern Europe was minimal. The United States maintained high tariff barriers on imports from most of these countries and also restricted its exports. However, since the disintegration of the Soviet Union and the collapse of communism, trade between the United States and central and Eastern Europe has expanded substantially.

The countries that made the transition from communist to market economies quickly have recorded positive growth for several years—those that did not continue to struggle. Among the nations that have enjoyed several years of positive economic growth are the member countries of the Central European Free Trade Association (CEFTA): Hungary, the Czech Republic, Poland, Slovenia, and the Republic of Slovakia. An average growth of 4.3 percent is projected for this region.

U.S. exports to central and Eastern Europe and Russia will increase, as will U.S. investment in these countries, as demand for capital goods and technology opens new markets for U.S. products. There already has been a substantial expansion in trade between the United States and the Czech Republic, the Republic of Slovakia, Hungary, and Poland. Table 3.1 shows the growth rates from 2003 to 2006 for most regions of the world.

Exports and the U.S. Economy   Globalization represents a huge opportunity for all countries—rich or poor. The fifteen-fold increase in trade volume over the past forty-eight years has been one of the most important factors in the rise of living standards around the world. During this time, exports have become increasingly important to the U.S. economy. Exports as a percentage of U.S. GDP have increased steadily since 1985, except in the 2001 recession. And our exports to developing and newly industrialized countries are on the rise. Table 3.2 shows the value of U.S. merchandise exports to and imports from each of the nation's ten major trading partners. Note that Canada and Mexico are our best partners for our exports; Canada and China, for imports.

>> TABLE 3.1

GLOBAL GROWTH REMAINS STRONG

Growth has been led by developing countries and emerging markets.

	2003	2004	Projected 2005	Projected 2006
		(annual percent change)		
World	4.0	5.1	4.3	4.3
United States	2.7	4.2	3.5	3.3
Euro area	0.7	2.0	1.2	1.8
United Kingdom	2.5	3.2	1.9	2.2
Japan	1.4	2.7	2.0	2.0
Canada	2.0	2.9	2.9	3.2
Other advanced economies	2.5	4.4	3.2	3.9
Newly industrialized Asian economies	3.1	5.6	4.0	4.7
Developing countries and emerginig markets	6.5	7.3	6.4	6.1
Africa	4.6	5.3	4.5	5.9
Asia	8.1	8.2	7.8	7.2
CIS	7.9	8.4	6.0	5.7
Middle East	6.5	5.5	5.4	5.0
Western Hemisphere	2.2	5.6	4.1	3.8

Source: Republished with permission of International Monetary Fund, from *World Economic Outlook*, October, 3, 2005, p. 293; permission conveyed through Copyright Clearance Center, Inc.

> > **TABLE 3.2**

VALUE OF U.S. MERCHANDISE EXPORTS AND IMPORTS, 2004

Rank/Trading Partner	Exports ($ billions)	Rank/Trading Partner	Imports ($ billions)
1 Canada	190.2	1 Canada	256.0
2 Mexico	110.8	2 China	196.7
3 Japan	54.4	3 Mexico	155.8
4 United Kingdom	35.9	4 Japan	129.6
5 China	34.7	5 Germany	77.2
6 Germany	31.4	6 United Kingdom	46.4
7 South Korea	26.3	7 South Korea	46.2
8 Netherlands	24.3	8 Taiwan	34.6
9 Taiwan	21.7	9 France	31.8
10 France	21.2	10 Malaysia	28.2

Source: U.S. Department of Commerce, International Trade Administration, **http://www.ita.doc.gov/td/ industry/otea/usfth/aggregate/H04T11.html,** September 21, 2005.

Figure 3.3 shows the U.S. goods export and import shares in 2004. Major U.S. exports and imports are manufactured goods, agricultural products, and mineral fuels.

The General Agreement on Tariffs and Trade and the World Trade Organization

General Agreement on Tariffs and Trade (GATT) an international organization of 132 nations dedicated to reducing or eliminating tariffs and other barriers to world trade

At the end of World War II, the United States and twenty-two other nations organized the body that came to be known as *GATT*. The **General Agreement on Tariffs and Trade (GATT)** was an international organization of 132 nations dedicated to reducing or eliminating tariffs and other barriers to world trade. These 132 nations accounted for 90 percent of the world's merchandise trade. GATT, headquartered in Geneva, Switzerland, provided a forum for tariff negotiations and a means for settling international trade disputes and problems. *Most-favored-nation status* (MFN) was the famous principle of GATT. It meant that each GATT member nation was to be treated equally by all contracting nations. MFN therefore ensured that any tariff reductions or other trade concessions were extended automatically to all GATT members. From 1947 to 1994, the body sponsored eight rounds of negotiations to reduce trade restrictions. Three of the most fruitful were the Kennedy Round, the Tokyo Round, and the Uruguay Round.

The Kennedy Round (1964–1967)   In 1962, the U.S. Congress passed the Trade Expansion Act. This law gave President John F. Kennedy the authority to negotiate reciprocal trade agreements that could reduce U.S. tariffs by as much as 50 percent. Armed with this authority, which was granted for a period of five years, President Kennedy called for a round of negotiations through GATT.

These negotiations, which began in 1964, have since become known as the *Kennedy Round.* They were aimed at reducing tariffs and other barriers to trade in both industrial and agricultural products. The participants succeeded in reducing tariffs on these products by an average of more than 35 percent. They were less successful in removing other types of trade barriers.

The Tokyo Round (1973–1979)   In 1973, representatives of approximately one hundred nations gathered in Tokyo for another round of GATT negotiations. The *Tokyo Round* was completed in 1979. The participants negotiated tariff cuts of 30 to 35 percent, which were to be implemented over an eight-year period. In addition, they

>> **FIGURE 3.3**

U.S. GOODS EXPORT AND IMPORT SHARES IN 2004

About 44 percent of our exports and 42 percent of our imports in 2004 were from Canada, Mexico, and Japan and Canada, China, and Mexico, respectively.

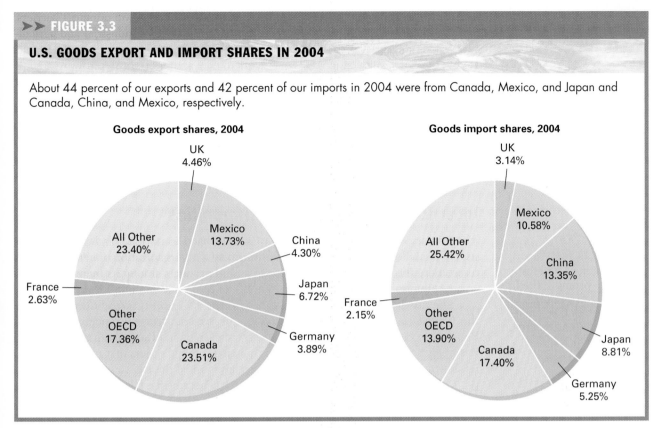

Source: Federal Reserve Bank of St. Louis, *National Economic Trends*, September 2005, p. 18.

were able to remove or ease such nontariff barriers as import quotas, unrealistic quality standards for imports, and unnecessary red tape in customs procedures.

World Trade Organization (WTO) powerful successor to GATT that incorporates trade in goods, services, and ideas

The Uruguay Round (1986–1993)   In 1986, the *Uruguay Round* was launched to extend trade liberalization and widen the GATT treaty to include textiles, agricultural products, business services, and intellectual-property rights. This most ambitious and comprehensive global commercial agreement in history concluded overall negotiations on December 15, 1993, with delegations on hand from 109 nations. The agreement included provisions to lower tariffs by greater than one-third, to reform trade in agricultural goods, to write new rules of trade for intellectual property and services, and to strengthen the dispute-settlement process. These reforms were expected to expand the world economy by an estimated $200 billion annually.

The Uruguay Round also created the **World Trade Organization (WTO)** on January 1, 1995. The WTO was established by GATT to oversee the provisions of the Uruguay Round and resolve any resulting trade disputes. Membership in the WTO obliges 148 member nations to observe GATT rules. The WTO has judicial powers to mediate among members disputing the new rules. It incorporates trade in goods, services, and ideas and exerts more binding authority than GATT.

The Doha Round (2001)   On November 14, 2001, in Doha, Qatar, the WTO members agreed to further reduce trade barriers through multilateral trade negotiations over the next three years.

SPOTLIGHT

Now and forever

Countries that are key trading partners with other countries tend to remain so.

Country	Number of key trading partners
United States	90
Germany	83
United Kingdom	79
Netherlands	73
France	68
Italy	65
Japan	57

Source: Republished with permission of International Monetary Fund, from *Direction of Trade Statistics*, September 2005, p. 50; permission conveyed through Copyright Clearance Center, Inc.

This new round of negotiations will focus on industrial tariffs and nontariff barriers, agriculture, services, and easing trade rules. U.S. exporters of industrial and agricultural goods and services should have improved access to overseas markets. The Doha Round has set the stage for WTO members to take an important step toward significant new multilateral trade liberalization. It is a difficult task, but the rewards—lower tariffs, more choices for consumers, and further integration of developing countries into the world trading system—are sure to be worth the effort. If all global trade barriers were eliminated, approximately 500 million people could be lifted out of poverty in 15 years. Developing countries would gain about $200 billion annually in income.[9] There are encouraging signs that major developing countries are assuming an important leadership role in helping the Doha Round succeed.

International Economic Communities

economic community an organization of nations formed to promote the free movement of resources and products among its members and to create common economic policies

The primary objective of the WTO is to remove barriers to trade on a worldwide basis. On a smaller scale, an **economic community** is an organization of nations formed to promote the free movement of resources and products among its members and to create common economic policies. A number of economic communities now exist.

The *European Union* (EU), also known as the *European Economic Community* and the *Common Market*, was formed in 1957 by six countries—France, the Federal Republic of Germany, Italy, Belgium, the Netherlands, and Luxembourg. Its objective was freely conducted commerce among these nations and others that might later join. As shown in Figure 3.4, many more nations have joined the EU since then.

On May 1, 2004, the fifteen nations of the EU became the EU25 as Cyprus, Malta, and eight Eastern European countries became new members. More countries, such as Romania and Bulgaria, may join in 2007, and Turkey and the Balkan countries may follow later. The EU is now an economic force, with a collective economy larger than that of the United States or Japan.

Since January 2002, twelve member nations of the EU are participating in the new common currency, the euro. The euro is the single currency of the European Monetary Union nations. But three EU members, Denmark, the United Kingdom, and Sweden, still keep their own currencies.

A second community in Europe, the *European Economic Area* (EEA), became effective in January 1994. This pact consists of Iceland, Norway, and the fifteen member nations of the EU. The EEA, encompassing an area inhabited by more than 395 million people, allows for the free movement of goods throughout all seventeen countries.

The *North American Free Trade Agreement* (NAFTA) joined the United States with its first- and second-largest trading partners, Canada and Mexico. Implementation of NAFTA on January 1, 1994, created a market of over 436 million people. This market consists of Canada (population 33 million), the United States (297 million), and Mexico (106 million). Since 1994, trade among the three countries has increased more than 200 percent. Mexico's exports have increased threefold, with nearly 90 percent coming to the United States. From 1993 to 2003, U.S.–Mexico total trade increased 189 percent, from $81.4 billion to $235.5 billion.[10]

NAFTA is built on the Canadian Free Trade Agreement (FTA), signed by the United States and Canada in 1989, and on the substantial trade and investment reforms undertaken by Mexico since the mid-1980s. Initiated by the Mexican government, formal negotiations on NAFTA began in June 1991 among the three governments. The support of NAFTA by President Bill Clinton, past U.S. Presidents Ronald Reagan and Jimmy Carter, and Nobel Prize–winning economists provided the impetus for U.S. congressional ratification of NAFTA in November 1993. NAFTA will gradually eliminate all tariffs on goods produced and traded among Canada, Mexico, and the United States to provide for a totally free-trade area by 2009. Chile is expected to become the fourth member of NAFTA, but political forces may delay its entry into the agreement for several years.

The *Central American Free Trade Agreement* (CAFTA) was created in 2003 by the United States and four Central American countries—El Salvador, Guatemala, Honduras, and Nicaragua. CAFTA immediately eliminates tariffs on nearly 80 percent

>> FIGURE 3.4

THE EVOLVING EUROPEAN UNION

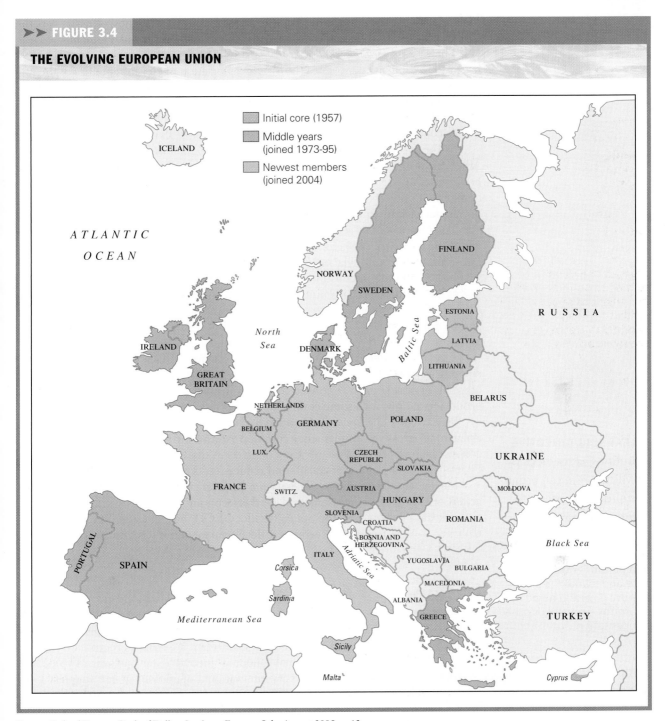

Initial core (1957)

Middle years
(joined 1973-95)

Newest members
(joined 2004)

Source: Federal Reserve Bank of Dallas, *Southwest Economy*, July–August 2005, p. 12.

of U.S. exports and is expected to generate billions of dollars in increased sales of U.S. goods and farm exports.[11] The *Association of Southeast Asian Nations* (ASEAN), with headquarters in Jakarta, Indonesia, was established in 1967 to promote political, economic, and social cooperation among its seven member countries: Indonesia, Malaysia, Philippines, Singapore, Thailand, Brunei, and Vietnam. In January 1992, ASEAN agreed to create a free-trade area known as the *ASEAN Free Trade Area* (AFTA). AFTA countries have a population of more than 550 million people, and their trade totals $750 billion.

The *Pacific Rim*, referring to countries and economies bordering the Pacific Ocean, is an informal, flexible term generally regarded as a reference to East Asia, Canada, and the United States. At a minimum, the Pacific Rim includes Canada, Japan, China, Taiwan, and the United States. It also may include Australia, Brunei, Cambodia, Hong Kong/Macau, Indonesia, Laos, North Korea, South Korea,

Malaysia, New Zealand, the Pacific Islands, the Philippines, Russia (or the Commonwealth of Independent States), Singapore, Thailand, and Vietnam.

The *Commonwealth of Independent States* (CIS) was established in December 1991 by the newly independent states (NIS) as an association of eleven republics of the former Soviet Union: Russia, Ukraine, Belarus (formerly Byelorussia), Moldova (formerly Moldavia), Armenia, Azerbaijan, Uzbekistan, Turkmenistan, Tajikistan, Kazakhstan, and Kyrgystan (formerly Kirghiziya). The Baltic states did not join. Georgia maintained observer status before joining the CIS in November 1993.

In the western hemisphere, the *Caribbean Basin Initiative* (CBI) is an inter-American program led by the United States to give economic assistance and trade preferences to Caribbean and Central American countries. CBI provides duty-free access to the U.S. market for most products from the region and promotes private-sector development in member nations.

The *Common Market of the Southern Cone* (MERCOSUR) was established in 1991 under the Treaty of Asuncion to unite Argentina, Brazil, Paraguay, and Uruguay as a free-trade alliance; Bolivia and Chile joined as associates in 1996. The alliance represents over 230 million consumers—63 percent of South America's population, making it the third-largest trading bloc behind NAFTA and the EU. Like NAFTA, MERCOSUR promotes "the free circulation of goods, services and production factors among the countries" and established a common external tariff and commercial policy.[12]

The *Organization of Petroleum Exporting Countries* (OPEC) was founded in 1960 in response to reductions in the prices that oil companies were willing to pay for crude oil. The organization was conceived as a collective-bargaining unit to provide oil-producing nations with some control over oil prices.

In May 2005, the *Economic Community of West African States* (ECOWAS) approved a plan to progressively implement a common external tariff (CET). The agreement increases the number of West African countries in the CET from eight to fifteen (see Figure 3.5). The plan lowers tariffs and reduces costs for importers.[13]

Finally, the *Organization for Economic Cooperation and Development* (OECD) is a group of twenty-four industrialized market-economy countries of North America, Europe, the Far East, and the South Pacific. OECD, headquartered in Paris, was established in 1961 to promote economic development and international trade.

4 LEARNING OBJECTIVE

Define the methods by which a firm can organize for and enter into international markets.

licensing a contractual agreement in which one firm permits another to produce and market its product and use its brand name in return for a royalty or other compensation

Methods of Entering International Business

A firm that has decided to enter international markets can do so in several ways. We will discuss several different methods. These different approaches require varying degrees of involvement in international business. Typically, a firm begins its international operations at the simplest level. Then, depending on its goals, it may progress to higher levels of involvement.

Licensing

Licensing is a contractual agreement in which one firm permits another to produce and market its product and use its brand name in return for a royalty or other compensation. For example, Yoplait yogurt is a French yogurt licensed for production in the United States. The Yoplait brand maintains an appealing French image, and in return, the U.S. producer pays the French firm a percentage of its income from sales of the product.

Licensing is especially advantageous for small manufacturers wanting to launch a well-known domestic brand internationally. For example, all Spalding sporting products are licensed worldwide. The licensor, the Questor Corporation,

> **FIGURE 3.5**

WEST AFRICAN CET MEMBERS

The common external tariff (CET) simplifies the structure of tariffs, with a top bracket of 20 percent on finished goods, 10 percent on intermediate goods, 5 percent on basic necessities and raw materials, and no tariff on social goods such as medicines and publications.

New CET countries
Existing CET countries

Canary Islands
WESTERN SAHARA
ALGERIA
ATLANTIC OCEAN
MAURITANIA
MALI
NIGER
Cape Verde
SENEGAL
GAMBIA
GUINEA-BISSAU
GUINEA
BOURKINA FASO
BENIN
NIGERIA
SIERRA LEONE
IVORY COAST
LIBERIA
TOGO
GHANA
CAMEROON

Source: The U.S. Agency for International Development, "7 More West African Countries Cut Tariffs, Boost Trade Pact," *Frontlines*, September 2005, p. 13.

owns the Spalding name but produces no goods itself. The German firm of Lowenbrau has used licensing agreements, including one with Miller in the United States, to increase its beer sales worldwide without committing capital to building breweries.[14] Licensing thus provides a simple method for expanding into a foreign market with virtually no investment. On the other hand, if the licensee does not maintain the licensor's product standards, the product's image may be damaged. Another possible disadvantage is that a licensing arrangement may not provide the original producer with any foreign marketing experience.

Exporting

A firm also may manufacture its products in its home country and export them for sale in foreign markets. As with licensing, exporting can be a relatively low-risk method of entering foreign markets. Unlike licensing, however, it is not a simple method; it opens up several levels of involvement to the exporting firm.

At the most basic level, the exporting firm may sell its products outright to an *export-import merchant*, which is essentially a merchant wholesaler. The merchant assumes

Samsung's mobile world. Samsung Electronics Co., Ltd., the world's third largest cell phone maker, made history with a record-breaking 55,000-square-foot wrap of the Stardust Resort and Casino on the Las Vegas strip. The wrap promoted two of Samsung's ultra-thin multi-media cell phones destined for the U.S. market.

all the risks of product ownership, distribution, and sale. It may even purchase the goods in the producer's home country and assume responsibility for exporting the goods. An important and practical issue for domestic firms dealing with foreign customers is securing payment. This is a two-sided issue that reflects the mutual concern rightly felt by both parties to the trade deal: The exporter would like to be paid before shipping the merchandise, whereas the importer obviously would prefer to know that it has received the shipment before releasing any funds. Neither side wants to take the risk of fulfilling its part of the deal only later to discover that the other side has not. The result would lead to legal costs and complex, lengthy dealings wasteful of everyone's resources. This mutual level of mistrust is in fact good business sense and has been around since the beginning of trade centuries ago. The solution then was as it still is today—for both parties to use a mutually trusted go-between who can ensure that the payment is held until the merchandise is in fact delivered according to the terms of the trade contract. The go-between representatives employed by the importer and exporter are still, as they were in the past, the local domestic banks involved in international business.

Here is a simplified version of how it works. After signing contracts detailing the merchandise sold and terms for its delivery, an importer will ask its local bank to issue a **letter of credit** for the amount of money needed to pay for the merchandise. The letter of credit is issued "in favor of the exporter," meaning that the funds are tied specifically to the trade contract involved. The importer's bank forwards the letter of credit to the exporter's bank, which also normally deals in international transactions. The exporter's bank then notifies the exporter that a letter of credit has been received in its name, and the exporter can go ahead with the shipment. The carrier transporting the merchandise provides the exporter with evidence of the shipment in a document called a **bill of lading.** The exporter signs over title to the merchandise (now in transit) to its bank by delivering signed copies of the bill of lading and the letter of credit.

In exchange, the exporter issues a **draft** from the bank, which orders the importer's bank to pay for the merchandise. The draft, bill of lading, and letter of credit are sent from the exporter's bank to the importer's bank. Acceptance by the importer's bank leads to return of the draft and its sale by the exporter to its bank, meaning that the exporter receives cash and the bank assumes the risk of collecting the funds from the foreign bank. The importer is obliged to pay its bank on delivery of the merchandise, and the deal is complete.

In most cases, the letter of credit is part of a lending arrangement between the importer and its bank, and of course, both banks earn fees for issuing of letters of credit and drafts and for handling the import-export services for their clients. Furthermore, the process incorporates the fact that both importer and exporter will have different local currencies and might even negotiate their trade in a third currency. The banks look after all the necessary exchanges. For example, the vast majority of international business is negotiated in U.S. dollars, even though the trade may be between countries other than the United States. Thus, although the importer may end up paying for the merchandise in its local currency and the exporter may receive payment in another local currency, the banks involved will exchange all necessary foreign funds in order to allow the deal to take place.

The exporting firm instead may ship its products to an *export-import agent*, which for a commission or fee arranges the sale of the products to foreign intermediaries. The agent is an independent firm—like other agents—that sells and may perform other marketing functions for the exporter. The exporter, however, retains title to the products during shipment and until they are sold.

An exporting firm also may establish its own *sales offices*, or *branches*, in foreign countries. These installations are international extensions of the firm's distribution system. They represent a deeper involvement in international business than the other exporting techniques we have discussed—and thus they carry a greater risk. The exporting firm maintains control over sales, and it gains both experience in and knowledge of foreign markets. Eventually, the firm also may develop its own sales force to operate in conjunction with foreign sales offices.

letter of credit issued by a bank on request of an importer stating that the bank will pay an amount of money to a stated beneficiary

bill of lading document issued by a transport carrier to an exporter to prove that merchandise has been shipped

draft issued by the exporter's bank, ordering the importer's bank to pay for the merchandise, thus guaranteeing payment once accepted by the importer's bank

Joint Ventures

A *joint venture* is a partnership formed to achieve a specific goal or to operate for a specific period of time. A joint venture with an established firm in a foreign country provides immediate market knowledge and access, reduced risk, and control over product attributes. However, joint-venture agreements established across national borders can become extremely complex. As a result, joint-venture agreements generally require a very high level of commitment from all the parties involved.

A joint venture may be used to produce and market an existing product in a foreign nation or to develop an entirely new product. Recently, for example, Archer Daniels Midland Company (ADM), one of the world's leading food processors, entered into a joint venture with Gruma SA, Mexico's largest corn flour and tortilla company. Besides a 22 percent stake in Gruma, ADM also received stakes in other joint ventures operated by Gruma. One of them will combine both companies' U.S. corn flour operations, which account for about 25 percent of the U.S. market. ADM also has a 40 percent stake in a Mexican wheat flour mill. ADM's joint venture increased its participation in the growing Mexican economy, where ADM already produces corn syrup, fructose, starch, and wheat flour.

Venturing into a joint venture. Archer Daniels Midland Company (ADM) and Volkswagen AG formed a joint research alliance to develop and use biodiesel fuels for the automotive industry. ADM is a world leader in renewable fuels. Volkswagen and ADM are now testing a blend of 20 percent biodiesel in order to provide ever-cleaner alternative and sustainable fuel choices.

Totally Owned Facilities

At a still deeper level of involvement in international business, a firm may develop *totally owned facilities*, that is, its own production and marketing facilities in one or more foreign nations. This *direct investment* provides complete control over operations, but it carries a greater risk than the joint venture. The firm is really establishing a subsidiary in a foreign country. Most firms do so only after they have acquired some knowledge of the host country's markets.

Direct investment may take either of two forms. In the first, the firm builds or purchases manufacturing and other facilities in the foreign country. It uses these facilities to produce its own established products and to market them in that country and perhaps in neighboring countries. Firms such as General Motors, Union Carbide, and Colgate-Palmolive are multinational companies with worldwide manufacturing facilities. Colgate-Palmolive factories are becoming *Eurofactories*, supplying neighboring countries as well as their own local markets.

A second form of direct investment in international business is the purchase of an existing firm in a foreign country under an arrangement that allows it to operate independently of the parent company. When Sony Corporation (a Japanese firm) decided to enter the motion-picture business in the United States, it chose to purchase Columbia Pictures Entertainment, Inc., rather than start a new motion-picture studio from scratch.

Strategic Alliances

A **strategic alliance,** the newest form of international business structure, is a partnership formed to create competitive advantage on a worldwide basis. Strategic alliances are very similar to joint ventures. The number of strategic alliances is growing at an estimated rate of about 20 percent per year. In fact, in the automobile and computer industries, strategic alliances are becoming the predominant means of competing.

strategic alliance a partnership formed to create competitive advantage on a worldwide basis

International competition is so fierce and the costs of competing on a global basis are so high that few firms have all the resources needed to do it alone. Thus individual firms that lack the internal resources essential for international success may seek to collaborate with other companies.

An example of such an alliance is the New United Motor Manufacturing, Inc. (NUMMI), formed by Toyota and General Motors to make automobiles of both firms. This enterprise united the quality engineering of Japanese cars with the marketing expertise and market access of General Motors.[15]

Trading Companies

trading company provides a link between buyers and sellers in different countries

A **trading company** provides a link between buyers and sellers in different countries. A trading company, as its name implies, is not involved in manufacturing or owning assets related to manufacturing. It buys products in one country at the lowest price consistent with quality and sells to buyers in another country. An important function of trading companies is taking title to products and performing all the activities necessary to move the products from the domestic country to a foreign country. For example, large grain-trading companies operating out of home offices both in the United States and overseas control a major portion of the world's trade in basic food commodities. These trading companies sell homogeneous agricultural commodities that can be stored and moved rapidly in response to market conditions. The best-known U.S. trading company is Sears World Trade, which specializes in consumer goods, light industrial items, and processed foods.[16]

Countertrade

countertrade an international barter transaction

In the early 1990s, many developing nations had major restrictions on converting domestic currency into foreign currency. Exporters therefore had to resort to barter agreements with importers. **Countertrade** is essentially an international barter transaction in which goods and services are exchanged for different goods and services. Examples include Saudi Arabia's purchase of ten 747 jets from Boeing with payment in crude oil, Philip Morris's sale of cigarettes to Russia in return for chemicals used to make fertilizers, and Iraq's barter of crude oil for warships from Italy.

Multinational Firms

multinational enterprise a firm that operates on a worldwide scale without ties to any specific nation or region

A **multinational enterprise** is a firm that operates on a worldwide scale without ties to any specific nation or region. The multinational firm represents the highest level of involvement in international business. It is equally "at home" in most countries of the world. In fact, as far as the operations of the multinational enterprise are concerned, national boundaries exist only on maps. It is, however, organized under the laws of its home country.

Table 3.3 shows the ten largest foreign and U.S. public multinational companies; the ranking is based on a composite score reflecting each company's best three out of four rankings for sales, profits, assets, and market value. Table 3.4 describes steps in entering international markets.

According to the chairman of the board of Dow Chemical Company, a multinational firm of U.S. origin, "The emergence of a world economy and of the multinational corporation has been accomplished hand in hand." He sees multinational enterprises moving toward what he calls the "anational company," a firm that has no nationality but belongs to all countries. In recognition of this movement, there already have been international conferences devoted to the question of how such enterprises would be controlled.

Sources of Export Assistance

5 LEARNING OBJECTIVE
Describe the various sources of export assistance.

In September 1993, President Bill Clinton announced the *National Export Strategy* (NES) to revitalize U.S. exports. Under the NES, the *Trade Promotion Coordinating Committee* (TPCC) assists U.S. firms in developing export-promotion programs. The

>> **TABLE 3.3**

THE TEN LARGEST FOREIGN AND U.S. MULTINATIONAL CORPORATIONS

2004 Rank	Company	Business	Country	Revenue ($ millions)
1	Wal-Mart Stores	General merchandiser	United States	287,989
2	BP	Energy	United Kingdom	285,059
3	ExxonMobil	Energy	United States	270,772
4	Royal Dutch/Shell Group	Energy	Netherlands/United Kingdom	268,690
5	General Motors	Automobiles	United States	193,517
6	DaimlerChrysler	Automobiles	Germany	176,687
7	Toyota Motor	Automobiles	Japan	172,616
8	Ford Motor	Automobiles	United States	172,233
9	General Electric	Electricity and electronics	United States	152,866
10	Total	Energy	France	152,609

Source: *Fortune* Global 500, July 25, 2005, p.119. Copyright © 2005 Time, Inc., **www.fortune.com**. All rights reserved.

export services and programs of the nineteen TPCC agencies can help American firms to compete in foreign markets and create new jobs in the United States. An overview of selected export-assistance programs follows:

- *U.S. Export Assistance Centers (USEACs).* USEACs are federal export-assistance offices. They provide assistance in export marketing and trade finance by integrating in a single location the counselors and services of the U.S. and Foreign Commercial Services of the Department of Commerce, the Export-Import Bank, the Small Business Administration, and the U.S. Agency for International Development: **www.sba.gov/oit/export/useac.html.**
- *International Trade Administration (ITA), U.S. Department of Commerce.* ITA offers assistance and information to exporters through its units, which include (1) domestic and overseas commercial officers, (2) country experts, and (3) industry experts. Each unit promotes products and offers services and programs for the U.S. exporting community: **www.ita.doc.gov/.**
- *U.S. and Foreign Commercial Services (US&FCS).* To help U.S. firms compete more effectively in the global marketplace, the US&FCS has a network of trade specialists in over eighty countries worldwide. US&FCS offices provide information on foreign markets, agent/distributor location services, and trade leads, as well as counseling on business opportunities, trade barriers, and prospects abroad: **www.export.gov/.**

Business Around the World

Discount Airlines Are Flying High

Discount airlines are taking off all over the world, expanding the reach of air travel as they compete aggressively with established carriers and each other. A sample:

- Ireland: Ryanair, among the fastest-growing and most-profitable airlines on the planet, concentrates on Western European destinations.
- India: By connecting smaller cities, Air Deccan, the country's first discount airline, is fueling a tourism boom in southern areas.
- Thailand: One-Two-Go, a subsidiary of Orient Thai Airlines, flies from Bangkok to other Thai cities and to southern China.
- Malaysia: One way that AirAsia keeps fares low is by selling food, beverages, merchandise, and other extras.

In an industry where profitability is notoriously inconsistent, how many of these airlines will still be flying in five years?

>> TABLE 3.4

STEPS IN ENTERING INTERNATIONAL MARKETS

Step	Activity	Marketing Tasks
1	Identify exportable products	Identify key selling features
		Identify needs that they satisfy
		Identify the selling constraints that are imposed
2	Identify key foreign markets for the products	Determine who the customers are
		Pinpoint what and when they will buy
		Do market research
		Establish priority, or "target," countries
3	Analyze how to sell in each priority market (methods will be affected by product characteristics and unique features of country/market)	Locate available government and private-sector resources
		Determine service and backup sales requirements
4	Set export prices and payment terms, methods, and techniques	Establish methods of export pricing
		Establish sales terms, quotations, invoices, and conditions of sale
		Determine methods of international payments, secured and unsecured
5	Estimate resource requirements and returns	Estimate financial requirements
		Estimate human resources requirements (full- or part-time export department or operation?)
		Estimate plant production capacity
		Determine necessary product adaptations
6	Establish overseas distribution Network	Determine distribution agreement and other key marketing decisions (price, repair policies, returns, territory, performance, and termination)
		Know your customer (use U.S. Department of Commerce international marketing services)
7	Determine shipping, traffic, and documentation procedures and requirements	Determine methods of shipment (air or ocean freight, truck, rail)
		Finalize containerization
		Obtain validated export license
		Follow export-administration documentation procedures
8	Promote, sell, and be paid	Use international media, communications, advertising, trade shows, and exhibitions
		Determine the need for overseas travel (when, where, and how often?)
		Initiate customer follow-up procedures
9	Continuously analyze current marketing, economic, and political situations	Recognize changing factors influencing marketing strategies
		Constantly reevaluate

Source: U.S. Department of Commerce, International Trade Administration, Washington, D.C.

- *Export Legal Assistance Network (ELAN)*. ELAN is a nationwide group of attorneys with experience in international trade who provide free initial consultations to small businesses on export-related matters: **www.fita.org/elan/** or **www.export-legal-assistance.org/**.

- *Advocacy Center*. The Advocacy Center, established in November 1993, facilitates high-level U.S. official advocacy to assist U.S. firms competing for major projects and procurements worldwide. The center is directed by the Trade Promotion Coordinating Committee: **www.ita.doc.gov/advocacy**.

Awarding the Export Achievement Certificate. Congressman Richard W. Pombo presents Simpson Manufacturing Company of California with the U.S. Department of Commerce's Export Achievement Certificate. Working with the Oakland U.S. Export Assistance Center of the U.S. Commercial Service, Simpson recently added Japan and China to its list of export markets. Simpson designs, engineers, and manufactures structural connectors, anchors, and other products for the construction industry.

- *Trade Information Center (TIC)*. This information center was established as a comprehensive source for U.S. companies seeking information on federal programs and activities that support U.S. exports, including information on overseas markets and industry trends. This center maintains a computerized calendar of U.S. government–sponsored domestic and overseas trade events: **www.ita.doc.gov/td/tic/** or call 1-800-USA-TRADE.

- *STATUSA/Internet*. A comprehensive collection of business, economic, and trade information available on the web. Through this site, a firm can access the National Trade Data Bank (NTDB), daily trade leads and economic news, *Commerce Business Daily*, and the latest economic press releases and statistical series from the federal government. For more information on this low-cost service, call 1-800-STAT-USA (1-800-782-8872) or visit **www.stat-usa.gov/**.

- *TRADESTATS*. This is a comprehensive source for U.S. export and import data, both current and historical. Maintained by the Commerce Department's Office of Trade and Economic Analysis, this website contains total U.S. trade statistics by country and commodity, state and metropolitan area export data, and trade and industry statistics. Much of these data are downloadable: **www.ita.doc.gov/td/industry/otea/**.

- *Selected SBA market research–related general resources*. The Small Business Administration (SBA) publishes many helpful guides to assist small and medium-sized companies, including *Marketing for Small Business: An Overview*, *Researching Your Market*, and *Breaking into the Trade Game* or the videos *Marketing: Winning Customers with a Workable Plan* and *The Basics of Exporting*. Contact the Small Business Answer Desk at 1–800-UASK-SBA (1–800–827–5722) or visit **www.sba.gov/oit/**.

- *National Trade Data Bank (NTDB)*. The NTDB contains international economic and export-promotion information supplied by over twenty U.S. agencies. Data are updated daily on the Internet (**www.stat-usa.gov/tradtest.nsf**) and monthly on CD-ROM. The CD-ROM version is available for use at over 1,000 libraries throughout the country. The NTDB contains data from the Departments of Agriculture (Foreign Agriculture Service), Commerce (Bureau of Census, Bureau of Economic Analysis, International Trade Administration, and National Institute for Standards and Technology), Energy, and Labor (Bureau of Labor Statistics); the Central Intelligence Agency; the Export-Import Bank; the Federal Reserve System; the U.S. International Trade Commission; the Overseas Private Investment Corporation; the Small Business Administration; and the U.S. Trade Representative.

These and other sources of export information enhance the business opportunities of U.S. firms seeking to enter expanding foreign markets. Another vital entry factor is financing.

ENTREPRENEURIAL CHALLENGE

Connecting Global Partners

Entrepreneurs seeking to expand internationally now can connect online with potential buyers, distributors, and partners in other countries. Here are a few of the many sites that specialize in global matchmaking:

U.S. government sites. Small businesses can use the databases on the U.S. Commercial Service site (**www.buyusa.gov**) and the U.S. Government Export Portal (**www.export.gov**) to locate qualified buyers by country.

Small Business Exporters Association. The association's website (**www.sbea.org**) links to lists of possible trading partners and reports on the business situation in specific countries.

JETRO. The Japan External Trade Organization site (**www.jetro.org**) offers business matchmaking services, in-person or videoconference meetings with Japanese firms, and more.

Alibaba.com. Companies looking for suppliers and buyers in China can check **www.alibaba.com**, run by a Chinese Internet firm, for background information and contact details.

Although not every matchmaking effort leads to a sale, some have been quite successful. QualityCare, a Virginia company that sells medical supplies, located an Egyptian distributor through the U.S. Export Assistance Center. Now the company's products are available in thousands of pharmacies in Egypt and several other Middle Eastern countries.

Financing International Business

International trade compounds the concerns of financial managers. Currency exchange rates, tariffs and foreign-exchange controls, and the tax structures of host nations all affect international operations and the flow of cash. In addition, financial managers must be concerned both with the financing of their international operations and with the means available to their customers to finance purchases.

Fortunately, along with business in general, a number of large banks have become international in scope. Many have established branches in major cities around the world. Thus, like firms in other industries, they are able to provide their services where and when they are needed. In addition, financial assistance is available from U.S. government and international sources.

Several of today's international financial organizations were founded many years ago to facilitate free trade and the exchange of currencies among nations. Some, such as the Inter-American Development Bank, are internationally supported and focus on developing countries. Others, such as the Export-Import Bank, are operated by one country but provide international financing.

The Export-Import Bank of the United States

The **Export-Import Bank of the United States,** created in 1934, is an independent agency of the U.S. government whose function it is to assist in financing the exports of American firms. *Eximbank*, as it is commonly called, extends and guarantees credit to overseas buyers of American goods and services and guarantees short-term financing for exports. It also cooperates with commercial banks in helping American exporters to offer credit to their overseas customers. In 2004, the Eximbank, supported 3,107 U.S. export sales. It authorized $13.3 billion in loan guarantees and export credit insurance supporting $17.8 billion of U.S. exports to markets around the world.[17]

Multilateral Development Banks

A **multilateral development bank (MDB)** is an internationally supported bank that provides loans to developing countries to help them grow. The most familiar is the World Bank, which operates worldwide. Four other MDBs operate primarily in Central and South America, Asia, Africa, and Eastern and Central Europe. All five are supported by the industrialized nations, including the United States.

The *Inter-American Development Bank* (IDB), the oldest and largest regional bank, was created in 1959 by ten Latin American countries and the United States. Forty-seven member countries—twenty-six borrowing countries in Latin America and the Caribbean and twenty-one nonborrowing countries, including the United States, Japan, Canada, sixteen European countries, and Israel—now own the bank, which is headquartered in Washington, D.C. The IDB makes loans and provides technical advice and assistance to countries.[18]

6 LEARNING OBJECTIVE
Identify the institutions that help firms and nations finance international business.

Export-Import Bank of the United States an independent agency of the U.S. government whose function it is to assist in financing the exports of American firms

multilateral development bank (MDB) an internationally supported bank that provides loans to developing countries to help them grow

With sixty-four member nations, the *Asian Development Bank* (ADB), created in 1966 and headquartered in the Philippines, promotes economic and social progress in Asian and Pacific regions. The U.S. government is the second-largest contributor to the ADB's capital, after Japan. Recently, the ADB approved $5.4 billion for seventy-two loans in twenty-two countries; India received the largest loan of $1.5 billion, followed by China and Pakistan.[19]

The *African Development Bank* (AFDB), also known as *Banque Africaines de Developpment*, was established in 1964 with headquarters in Abidjan, Ivory Coast. Its members include fifty-three African and twenty-four non-African countries from the Americas, Europe, and Asia. The AFDB's goal is to foster the economic and social development of its African members. The bank pursues this goal through loans, research, technical assistance, and the development of trade programs.

Established in 1991 to encourage reconstruction and development in the Eastern and Central European countries, the London-based *European Bank for Reconstruction and Development* (EBRD) is owned by sixty countries and two intergovernmental institutions. Its loans are geared toward developing market-oriented economies and promoting private enterprise.[20]

The International Monetary Fund

The **International Monetary Fund (IMF)** is an international bank with 184 member nations that makes short-term loans to developing countries experiencing balance-of-payment deficits. This financing is contributed by member nations, and it must be repaid with interest. Loans are provided primarily to fund international trade.

International Monetary Fund (IMF) an international bank with 184 member nations that makes short-term loans to developing countries experiencing balance-of-payment deficits

RETURN TO Inside Business

The way Heinz handles its international business has evolved over the years. It preferred totally owned facilities when first entering foreign markets and later began acquiring foreign businesses. These days, Heinz's fifty-nation global strategy also includes strategic alliances and licensing. For example, it licenses the Weight Watchers brand for diet foods and the Jack Daniels brand for barbecue sauces. In an alliance with Walkers Snack Foods, Heinz sauces add a saucy flavor to chips sold in the United Kingdom.

Perhaps the biggest challenge for Heinz is boosting ketchup sales in markets where it already dominates. "What we have to do," explains CEO William R. Johnson, "is convince people there are different ways to use ketchup." Thanks to Heinz, many Swedish consumers now pour ketchup on their pasta. Getting more Americans to eat eggs with ketchup and more Russians to eat fish with ketchup will only add to the company's global profits.

Questions

1. Was Heinz a multinational firm when it first built a factory in England? Is it a multinational firm today?
2. To fuel growth without the expense of direct investment, should Heinz license its brand in countries where it has no presence? Support your answer.

►► CHAPTER REVIEW

Summary

1

Explain the economic basis for international business.

International business encompasses all business activities that involve exchanges across national boundaries. International trade is based on specialization, whereby each country produces the goods and services that it can produce more efficiently than any other goods and services. A nation is said to have a comparative advantage relative to these goods. International trade develops when each nation trades its surplus products for those in short supply.

A nation's balance of trade is the difference between the value of its exports and the value of its imports. Its balance of payments is the difference between the flow of money into and out of the nation. Generally, a negative balance of trade is considered unfavorable.

2

Discuss the restrictions nations place on international trade, the objectives of these restrictions, and their results.

Despite the benefits of world trade, nations tend to use tariffs and nontariff barriers (import quotas, embargoes, and other restrictions) to limit trade. These restrictions typically are justified as being needed to protect a nation's economy, industries, citizens, or security. They can result in the loss of jobs, higher prices, fewer choices in the marketplace, and the misallocation of resources.

3

Outline the extent of international trade and identify the organizations working to foster it.

World trade is generally increasing. Trade between the United States and other nations is increasing in dollar value but decreasing in terms of our share of the world market. The General Agreement on Tariffs and Trade (GATT) was formed to dismantle trade barriers and provide an environment in which international business can grow. Today, the World Trade Organization (WTO) and various economic communities carry on that mission.

4

Define the methods by which a firm can organize for and enter into international markets.

A firm can enter international markets in several ways. It may license a foreign firm to produce and market its products. It may export its products and sell them through foreign intermediaries or its own sales organization abroad. Or it may sell its exports outright to an export-import merchant. It may enter into a joint venture with a foreign firm. It may establish its own foreign subsidiaries. Or it may develop into a multinational enterprise. Generally, each of these methods represents an increasingly deeper level of involvement in international business, with licensing being the simplest and the development of a multinational corporation the most involved.

5

Describe the various sources of export assistance.

Many government and international agencies provide export assistance to U.S. and foreign firms. The export services and programs of the nineteen agencies of the U.S. Trade Promotion Coordinating Committee (TPCC) can help U.S. firms to compete in foreign markets and create new jobs in the United States. Sources of export assistance include U.S. Export Assistance Centers, the International Trade Administration, U.S. and Foreign Commercial Services, Export Legal Assistance Network, Advocacy Center, National Trade Data Bank, and other government and international agencies.

6

Identify the institutions that help firms and nations finance international business.

The financing of international trade is more complex than that of domestic trade. Institutions such as the Eximbank and the International Monetary Fund have been established to provide financing and ultimately to increase world trade for American and international firms.

Key Terms

You should now be able to define and give an example relevant to each of the following terms:

international business (77)
absolute advantage (77)
comparative advantage (78)
exporting (78)
importing (79)
balance of trade (79)
trade deficit (79)
balance of payments (80)
import duty (tariff) (80)
dumping (80)
nontariff barrier (81)
import quota (81)
embargo (81)

foreign-exchange control (81)
currency devaluation (81)
General Agreement on Tariffs and Trade (GATT) (86)
World Trade Organization (WTO) (87)
economic community (88)
licensing (90)
letter of credit (92)
bill of lading (92)
draft (92)
strategic alliance (93)
trading company (94)
countertrade (94)
multinational enterprise (94)
Export-Import Bank of the United States (98)
multilateral development bank (MDB) (98)
International Monetary Fund (IMF) (99)

Review Questions

1. Why do firms engage in international trade?
2. What is the difference between an absolute and a comparative advantage in international trade? How are both types of advantages related to the concept of specialization?
3. What is a favorable balance of trade? In what way is it "favorable"?
4. List and briefly describe the principal restrictions that may be applied to a nation's imports.
5. What reasons generally are given for imposing trade restrictions?
6. What are the general effects of import restrictions on trade?
7. Define and describe the major objectives of the World Trade Organization (WTO) and the international economic communities.

8. Which nations are the principal trading partners of the United States? What are the major U.S. imports and exports?
9. The methods of engaging in international business may be categorized as either direct or indirect. How would you classify each of the methods described in this chapter? Why?
10. In what ways is a multinational enterprise different from a large corporation that does business in several countries?
11. List some key sources of export assistance. How can these sources be useful to small business firms?
12. In what ways do Eximbank, multilateral development banks, and the IMF enhance international trade?

Discussion Questions

1. The United States restricts imports but, at the same time, supports the WTO and international banks whose objective is to enhance world trade. As a member of Congress, how would you justify this contradiction to your constituents?
2. What effects might the devaluation of a nation's currency have on its business firms? On its consumers? On the debts it owes to other nations?
3. Should imports to the United States be curtailed by, say, 20 percent to eliminate our trade deficit? What might happen if this were done?
4. When should a firm consider expanding from strictly domestic trade to international trade? When should it consider becoming further involved in international trade? What factors might affect the firm's decisions in each case?
5. How can a firm obtain the expertise needed to produce and market its products in, for example, the EU?

►► VIDEO CASE 3.1

IDG Profits Globally from Local Differences

For more than four decades, International Data Group (IDG) has prospered by allowing each of its publishing, online, research, and conference businesses to find their own keys to success, nation by nation. A business idea that works spectacularly well in one country may fail miserably in another. This is why IDG's careful focus on meeting local needs—in the local language—makes all the difference in fulfilling the company's mission of spreading the computer revolution around the world.

All of IDG's businesses deal with information about technology. Its newspapers and magazines, such as *PCWorld* and *ComputerWorld*, keep business people up-to-date on technology developments. The company maintains 400 technology news websites and manages hundreds of technology conferences and exhibitions every year, such as the popular MacWorld Expo. In addition, its International Data Corporation unit specializes in researching and analyzing worldwide technology trends for business clients.

IDG's combined annual revenue from operations in eighty-five countries soon will reach $3 billion. The company is looking ahead to even higher revenue as different units expand to meet growing demand for timely technology information in Southeast Asia, China, and other areas. In each country, local interests and language preferences shape the goods and services offered by IDG's local businesses. Moreover, the company sometimes teams up with local government agencies to develop and launch new offerings. For example, it has partnered with the Ministry of Science and Technology to produce information technology conferences in Vietnam.

Unlike multinational corporations that embrace the "one size fits all" strategy, the IDG businesses in each country are expected to be entrepreneurs, investigating what their customers want and need. Top executives have given local managers the authority to make decisions based on local trends and changes. As one example, the unit in South Korea decided to introduce online services before offering magazine subscriptions because it found that most local business people rely on high-speed Internet and web-enabled cell phones to access information. IDG is not only looking at the outcome in South Korea, but it is also considering how this approach might work in other areas. Thus, in the future, IDG might decide to deliver technology news solely through wireless media in some countries rather than relying on more traditional print media.

In China, IDG is already one of the top international publishers because of its joint ventures with local companies, which publish *ComputerWorld China* and other magazines in Chinese. IDG's success here has led other U.S. publishers to seek its help in launching Chinese editions of popular U.S. consumer magazines such as *Cosmopolitan*. Having gained in-depth market knowledge and forged close ties with local businesses, IDG began investing in Chinese high-tech companies in the early 1990s. Over the years, some of these firms went bankrupt, whereas others began selling stock or became acquisition targets—vastly increasing the value of IDG's investment stake.

CEO Patrick Kenealy says that his job is to let the best ideas of IDG's businesses rise to the surface and then "help everyone share best practices." However, he and his management team recognize the potential for misinterpretation when employees from different cultures try to communicate. Because IDG's local employees speak so many languages, presentations for multinational internal audiences are made in English. Even when employees are using the same language—English—employees from the United States, United Kingdom, and Australia may not glean the same meaning from a presentation or report. This is why Gigi Wang, senior vice president of strategy, stresses that "it's not what you say that's important; it's what the listener hears."[21]

For more information about this company, go to **www.idg.com**.

Questions

1. What are some of the advantages and disadvantages of IDG's intense focus on meeting local needs and using the local language in every country?
2. Why do you think that IDG partners with government agencies rather than with private firms in some countries?
3. Considering that IDG's main product is information, which trade restrictions might affect its profitability?

►► CASE 3.2

Coca-Cola Pours into New Countries

Coca-Cola's red and white logo is a familiar sight all over the world, from Argentina to Zimbabwe. Battling rival PepsiCo as well as regional soft-drink manufacturers, the Atlanta-based beverage company has long viewed global markets as critical to its push for profits. It established operations in Canada and Central America before 1910, and today its products are available in more than 200 nations.

The company earns nearly three-quarters of its revenue outside the United States. However, growth in worldwide sales volume has slowed in recent years. As a result, Coca-Cola's senior managers are looking at ways to build sales in markets that previously seemed less promising because of low income levels, high inflation, currency fluctuations, volatile political conditions, supply and energy shortages, or other complications.

Few people in rural northern India, for example, can afford costly products such as kitchen appliances on the area's average monthly income of about $42. Even large-size soft drinks are out of reach for many. After losing millions of dollars as it gained first-hand knowledge of the market, however, Coca-Cola hit on the dual strategy of adjusting the bottle size—to make its sodas more affordable for buyers—and putting its products in as many outlets as possible.

Now Indians can buy a tiny 200-milliliter bottle of Coca-Cola for the equivalent of 12 cents at thousands of bus-stop stands, neighborhood grocery stores, and food stalls. The deputy president of Coca-Cola India explains the company's outlet-by-outlet drive for distribution: "Our hands are firmly in the dust here. It's the only way we can capture this market." And the drive has been successful: Coca-Cola has captured more than 50 percent of the market for carbonated soft drinks in India.

China is another fast-growing market where Coca-Cola is boosting sales by getting its beverages into as many stores and stands as possible. At one time, the company had to use pedicabs and other creative transportation methods to move beverages from bottling plants to outlets around Shanghai and other big cities. As the company built more bottling plants, it contracted with hundreds of thousands of distributors to get its beverages into local outlets. Thanks to this extensive distribution system, Coca-Cola sells nearly $2 billion worth of soft drinks in China every year. China soon will overtake Brazil as the company's third-largest market (behind the United States and Mexico).

Coca-Cola's business in Brazil has been up and down as the country's economic situation has changed. After years of high inflation, the economy improved, and Brazilians began buying more soft drinks. Coca-Cola responded to stiff competition from low-priced local brands by cutting prices. However, the move hurt profitability and failed to spark a significant sales rally, so Coca-Cola changed tactics. As it did in India, the company started offering soft drinks in smaller bottles, each size carrying a correspondingly small price tag. Thinking small made all the difference: Coca-Cola's sales and profits are bubbling in Brazil.

Africa has proven to be a much bigger challenge. Runaway inflation, frequent power outages, and ongoing supply shortages have sapped Coca-Cola's profits in Zimbabwe and several other African nations. Despite the obstacles, the company is determined to continue doing business in those markets. It is moving ahead with plans to expand the number of stores that sell Coca-Cola beverages as a long-term foundation for future prof-

itability. When and where consumers get thirsty, Coca-Cola will have its bottles and cans in a convenient outlet. "We want to be everywhere, and will be there forever," says Alex Cummings, president of Coca-Cola's Africa operations.[22]

For more information about this company, go to **www.cocacola.com**.

Questions

1. Why might a country in Latin America or Africa resist Coca-Cola's efforts to expand local sales?
2. Does the United States have a comparative advantage in soft drinks? Explain.
3. Knowing that smaller sizes have helped Coca-Cola increase sales and profits in India and China, do you think it should use the same approach in the United States? Why?

→ CHAPTER 3: JOURNAL EXERCISE

Discovery statement: This chapter was designed to excite you about international business and how trade among nations affects our daily lives.

Assume that your friend, who recently lost his job in the automobile industry, is critical of imported Toyotas, Hondas, and Volkswagens. How would you respond to his resentment of imported goods?

_____

_____

_____

What specific reasons will you offer to your friend that international trade is beneficial to society as a whole?

_____

_____

_____

_____

_____

Ask your friend what might be some consequences if the trade among nations was banned.

_____

_____

_____

_____

BUILDING SKILLS FOR CAREER SUCCESS

1. Exploring the Internet

A popular question debated among firms actively involved on the Internet is whether or not there exists a truly global Internet-based customer, irrespective of any individual culture, linguistic, or nationality issues. Does this Internet-based universal customer see the Internet and products sold there in pretty much the same way? If so, then one model might fit all customers. For example, although Yahoo.com translates its web pages so that they are understood around the world, the pages look pretty much the same regardless of which international site you use. Is this good strategy, or should the sites reflect local customers differently? Visit the text website for updates to this exercise.

Assignment

1. Examine a website such as Yahoo's (**www.yahoo.com**) and its various international versions that operate in other languages around the world. Compare their similarities and differences as best you can, even if you do not understand the individual languages.
2. After making your comparison, do you now agree that there are indeed universal Internet products and customers? Explain your decision.

2. Developing Critical-Thinking Skills

Suppose that you own and operate an electronics firm that manufactures transistors and integrated circuits. As foreign competitors enter the market and undercut your prices, you realize that your high labor costs are hindering your ability to compete. You are concerned about what to do and are open for suggestions. Recently, you have been trying to decide whether to move your plant to Mexico, where labor is cheaper.

Assignment

1. Questions you should consider in making this decision include the following:
   a. Would you be better off to build a new plant in Mexico or to buy an existing building?
   b. If you could find a Mexican electronics firm similar to yours, would it be wiser to try to buy it than to start your own operation?
   c. What are the risks involved in directly investing in your own facility in a foreign country?
   d. If you did decide to move your plant to Mexico, how would you go about it? Are there any government agencies that might offer you advice?
2. Prepare a two-page summary of your answers to these questions.

3. Building Team Skills

The North American Trade Agreement among the United States, Mexico, and Canada went into effect on January 1, 1994. It has made a difference in trade among the countries and has affected the lives of many people.

Assignment

1. Working in teams and using the resources of your library, investigate NAFTA. Answer the following questions:
   a. What are NAFTA's objectives?
   b. What are its benefits?
   c. What impact has NAFTA had on trade, jobs, and travel?
   d. Some Americans were opposed to the implementation of NAFTA. What were their objections? Have any of these objections been justified?
   e. Has NAFTA influenced your life? How?
2. Summarize your answers in a written report. Your team also should be prepared to give a class presentation.

4. Researching Different Careers

Today, firms around the world need employees with special skills. In some countries such employees are not always available, and firms then must search abroad for qualified applicants. One way they can do this is through global work force databases. As business and trade operations continue to grow globally, you may one day find yourself working in a foreign country, perhaps for an American company doing business there or for a foreign company. In what foreign country would you like to work? What problems might you face?

Assignment

1. Choose a country in which you might like to work.

2. Research the country. The National Trade Data Bank (NTDA) is a good place to start. Find answers to the following questions:

   a. What language is spoken in this country? Are you proficient in it? What would you need to do if you are not proficient?

   b. What are the economic, social, and legal systems like in this nation?

   c. What is its history?

   d. What are its culture and social traditions like? How might they affect your work or your living arrangements?

3. Describe what you have found out about this country in a written report. Include an assessment of whether you would want to work there and the problems you might face if you did.

5. Improving Communication Skills

Working in a foreign country, even for a short time, can affect your career significantly. While there are benefits, there also may be many obstacles to overcome. How would you deal with the obstacles, and would it be worth the trouble? If you could work in another country for at least three years, how would it affect your career?

Assignment

1. Read newspaper articles and periodicals to find answers to the following questions:

   a. What would be the benefits of working in a foreign country for a three-year period? How might it advance your career?

   b. What obstacles might this experience present? How would you deal with them? Compare the benefits with the obstacles and record the findings in your journal.

→ PREP TEST

Matching Questions

____ 1. A country produces a specific product more efficiently than any other product.

____ 2. It measures the total flow of money into a country minus the total flow of money out of a country.

____ 3. It is the process of buying goods from foreign countries.

____ 4. An unfavorable balance of trade is created.

____ 5. A limit imposed on a particular imported good.

____ 6. The process of reducing the value of a nation's currency.

____ 7. Countries with a balance of payments deficit can be assisted by this entity.

____ 8. Where trade disputes are resolved.

____ 9. An international barter transaction where goods are traded for different goods.

____ 10. Importers request banks to issue this document.

a. balance of payments
b. comparative advantage
c. countertrade
d. currency devaluation
e. import quota
f. International Monetary Fund
g. importing
h. letter of credit
i. trade deficit
j. World Trade Organization

True/False Questions

T F

11. ○ ○ The euro is the single currency of the European Monetary Union nations.

12. ○ ○ Licensing is a way to distribute goods internationally.

13. ○ ○ Under the direct-investment approach, domestic firms are not allowed to purchase foreign firms.

14. ○ ○ A tariff has the effect of raising the price of the product in the exporting nation.

15. ○ ○ If a country imports more than it exports, its balance of trade is said to be favorable.

T F

16. ○ ○ The European Free Trade Association is known as the Common Market.

17. ○ ○ Import quotas may be stated in terms of either the quantity or the value of the product.

18. ○ ○ Balance of payments is a much broader concept than balance of trade.

19. ○ ○ The Eximbank makes short-term loans to countries experiencing balance-of-payments deficits.

20. ○ ○ Cultural attitudes can form nontariff barriers that impede acceptance of products in foreign countries.

Multiple-Choice Questions

21. The agreement joining Mexico, the United States, and Canada on January 1, 1994, is called the
    a. Canadian Free Trade Agreement (FTA).
    b. Pacific Rim.
    c. North American Free Trade Agreement (NAFTA).
    d. Organization for Economic Cooperation and Development (OECD).
    e. Commonwealth of Independent States (CIS).

22. An internationally supported bank that provides loans to developing countries for growth is the
    a. Eximbank.
    b. World Bank.
    c. African Development Bank.
    d. European Bank for Reconstruction and Development.
    e. Inter-American Development Bank.

23. When Saudi Arabia specializes in the production of crude oil and petroleum products, it is practicing the concept of
    a. international business.
    b. comparative advantage.
    c. restricting trade.
    d. absolute advantage.
    e. licensing.

24. A goal of OPEC is to
    a. increase the supply of oil.
    b. control the prices of crude oil.
    c. reduce the oversupply of oil.
    d. deregulate the oil industry.

25. When Michelle from Texas flies to Mexico on a Mexican airline and buys silver jewelry to bring home, she is
    a. decreasing the trade deficit.
    b. being disloyal and unpatriotic.
    c. contributing to the negative balance of payments.
    d. buying American-made goods.
    e. buying American-produced services.

Fill-in-the-Blank Questions

26. When a country has the ability to produce a specific product more efficiently than any other nation, it has a/an _____ advantage.

27. A business that conducts transactions in a foreign country is engaging in _____ business.

28. _____ is a contractual agreement that allows expanding one's business operations into a foreign country.

29. An exporter issues a _____ from the bank, which orders the importer's bank to pay for the merchandise.

30. An _____ is a complete halt to trading with a particular nation.

Online Study Center

FOR MORE **test practice, use the interactive ACE quizzes available at the Online Student Center: www.college.hmco.com/PIC/pridebusiness9e.**

Answers on p. PT1.

The Rise of Finagle A Bagel

Would bagels sell in Hong Kong? Laura Beth Trust and Alan Litchman planned to find out. Trust was in Hong Kong working in the garment manufacturing industry, and Litchman was in real estate, but they were eager to start their own business. They were particularly interested in running a business where they would have direct customer contact and be able to get first-hand feedback about their products and services. And no matter what kind of business they started, it would be a family undertaking: The two entrepreneurs recently had decided to get married.

Looking around Hong Kong, Litchman and Trust noticed numerous Western-style food chains such as McDonald's, Pizza Hut, KFC, and Starbucks but no bagel places. Yet they believed that Hong Kong's sophisticated, multicultural population would welcome authentic New York–style bagels. Although both the entrepreneurs had MBA degrees from the Sloan School of Management, neither had any restaurant experience or knew how to make a bagel. Still, because they sensed a profitable opportunity and possessed solid business skills, Trust and Litchman decided to move ahead. The two incorporated a company, found a partner, and then returned to the United States to investigate the bagel business. As part of their research, they approached two knowledgeable experts for advice.

One of the bagel experts was Larry Smith, who in 1982 had cofounded a tiny cheesecake store in Boston's historic Quincy Market. When business was slow, the store began selling bagels topped with leftover cream cheese. By the late 1980s, this sideline was doing so well that Smith and his partners changed their focus from cheesecakes to bagels and changed the store's name from Julian's Cheesecakes to Finagle A Bagel. They relocated the store from a cramped 63-square-foot storefront into a more spacious 922-square-foot space in the same busy market complex. Soon so many customers were lining up for bagels that the owners began opening additional Finagle A Bagel stores around downtown Boston.

New Ownership, New Growth

By the time Trust and Litchman met Smith, he was operating six successful bagel stores, was ringing up $10 million in annual sales, and was looking for a source of capital to open more stores. Therefore, instead of helping the entrepreneurs launch a business in Hong Kong, Smith suggested that they stay and become involved in Finagle A Bagel. Because Litchman and Trust had roots in the Boston area, the opportunity to join a local bagel business was appealing both personally and professionally. Late in 1998, they bought a majority stake in Finagle A Bagel from Smith. The

three owners agreed on how to divide management responsibilities and collaborated on plans for more aggressive expansion. Within a few years, Trust and Litchman completed a deal to buy the rest of the business and became the sole owners and copresidents.

The business has grown every year since the conversion to bagels. Today, Finagle A Bagel operates twenty stores in downtown Boston and the surrounding suburbs. Because Finagle A Bagel outgrew its original production facilities, the owners recently purchased a new corporate headquarters and production center in Newton, Massachusetts. This is where tens of thousands of bagels are prepared every day, along with enough cream cheese and cookies to supply a much larger network of stores.

Branding the Bagel

Over time, the owners have introduced a wide range of bagels, sandwiches, salads, and soups linked to the core bagel product. Bagels are baked fresh every day, and the stores receive daily deliveries of fresh salad fixings and other ingredients. Employees make each menu item to order while the customer watches. Some of the most popular offerings include a breakfast bagel pizza, salads with bagel-chip croutons, and BLT (bacon-lettuce-tomato) bagel sandwiches.

Finagle A Bagel is also boosting revenues by wholesaling its bagels to thousands of universities, hospitals, and corporate cafeterias. In addition, it sells several varieties of bagels under the Finagle A Bagel brand to the Shaw's Market grocery chain. Shaw's has been expanding in New England through mergers and acquisitions, opening new opportunities for its bagel supplier. "As they grow, we grow with them," comments Litchman. "More importantly, it gets our name into markets where we're not. And we can track the sales and see how we're doing." If a particular Shaw's supermarket registers unusually strong bagel sales, the copresidents will consider opening a store in or near that community.

The Bagel Economy

Although Finagle A Bagel competes with other bagel chains in and around Boston, its competition goes well beyond restaurants in that category. "You compete with a person selling a cup of coffee; you compete with a grocery store selling a salad," Litchman notes. "People only have so many 'dining dollars' and you need to convince them to spend those dining dollars in your store." Finagle A Bagel's competitive advantages are high-quality, fresh products, courteous and competent employees, and clean, attractive, and inviting restaurants.

During a recent economic recession, Boston's tourist traffic slumped temporarily, and corporate customers cut back on catering orders from Finagle A Bagel. After the company's sales revenues remained flat for about a year, they began inching up as the economy moved toward recovery. Now the business sells more than $20 million worth of bagels, soups, sandwiches, and salads every year.

Social Responsibility Through Bagels

Social responsibility is an integral part of Finagle A Bagel's operations. Rather than simply throw away unsold bagels at the end of the day, the owners donate the bagels to schools, shelters, and other nonprofit organizations. When local nonprofit groups hold fund-raising events, the copresidents contribute bagels to feed the volunteers. Over the years, Finagle A Bagel has provided bagels to bicyclists raising money for St. Jude Children's Research Hospital, to swimmers raising money for breast cancer research, and to people building community playgrounds. Also, the copresidents are strongly committed to being fair to their customers by offering good value and a good experience. "Something that we need to remember and instill in our people all the time," Trust emphasizes, "is that customers are coming in, and your responsibility is to give them the best that you can give them."

Even with 320-plus employees, the copresidents find that owning a business is a nonstop proposition. "Our typical day never ends," says Trust. They are constantly visiting stores, dealing with suppliers, reviewing financial results, and planning for the future. Despite all these responsibilities, this husband-and-wife entrepreneurial team enjoys applying their educational background and business experience to build a company that satisfies thousands of customers every day.

Questions

1. How has the business cycle affected Finagle A Bagel?
2. What is Finagle A Bagel doing to differentiate itself from competitors that want a share of customers' dining dollars?
3. Why would Finagle A Bagel donate bagels to local charities rather than give them away to customers or employees?
4. If you wanted to open a bagel restaurant in Hong Kong, would you license the Finagle A Bagel brand? Why or why not?

A *business plan* is a carefully constructed guide for a person starting a business. The purpose of a well-prepared business plan is to show how practical and attainable the entrepreneur's goals are. It also serves as a concise document that potential investors can examine to see if they would like to invest or assist in financing a new venture. A business plan should include the following twelve components:

- Introduction
- Executive summary
- Benefits to the community
- Company and industry
- Management team
- Manufacturing and operations plan
- Labor force
- Marketing plan
- Financial plan
- Exit strategy
- Critical risks and assumptions
- Appendix

A brief description of each of these sections is provided in Chapter 6 (see also Table 6.4 on page 195).

This is the first of seven exercises that appear at the ends of each of the seven major parts in this textbook. The goal of these exercises is to help you work through the preceding components to create your own business plan. For example, in the exercise for this part, you will make decisions and complete the research that will help you to develop the introduction for your business plan and the benefits to the community that your business will provide. In the exercises for Parts 2 through 7, you will add more components to your plan and eventually build a plan that actually could be used to start a business. The flowchart shown in Figure 3.6 gives an overview of the steps you will be taking to prepare your business plan.

The First Step: Choosing Your Business

One of the first steps for starting your own business is to decide what type of business you want to start. Take some time to think about this decision. Before proceeding, answer the following questions:

- Why did you choose this type of business?

- Why do you think this business will be successful?

- Would you enjoy owning and operating this type of business?

Warning: Don't rush this step. This step often requires much thought, but it is well worth the time and effort. As an added bonus, you are more likely to develop a quality business plan if you really want to open this type of business.

Now that you have decided on a specific type of business, it is time to begin the planning process. The goal for this part is to complete the introduction and benefits-to-the-community components of your business plan.

Before you begin, it is important to note that the business plan is not a document that is written and then set aside. It is a living document that an entrepreneur should refer to continuously in order to ensure that plans are being carried through appropriately. As the entrepreneur begins to execute the plan, he or she should monitor the business environment continuously and make changes to the plan to address any challenges or opportunities that were not foreseen originally.

Throughout this course you will, of course, be building your knowledge about business. Therefore, it will be appropriate for you to continually revisit parts of the plan that you have already written in order to refine them based on your more comprehensive knowledge. You will find that writing your plan is not a simple matter of starting at the beginning and moving chronologically through to the end. Instead, you probably will find yourself jumping around the various components, making refinements as you go. In fact, the second component—the executive summary—should be written last, but because of its comprehensive nature and its importance to potential investors, it appears after the introduction in the final business plan. By the end of this course, you should be able to put the finishing touches on your plan, making sure that all the parts create a comprehensive and sound whole so that you can present it for evaluation.

The Introduction Component

1.1. Start with the cover page. Provide the business name, street address, telephone number, web address (if any), name(s) of owner(s) of the business, and the date the plan is issued.

1.2. Next, provide background information on the company and include the general nature of the business: retailing, manufacturing, or service; what your product or service is; what is unique about it; and why you believe that your business will be successful.

1.3. Then include a summary statement of the business's financial needs, if any. You probably will need to revise your financial needs summary after you complete a detailed financial plan later in Part 6.

>> FIGURE 3.6

BUSINESS PLAN

The progressive steps in writing a business plan.

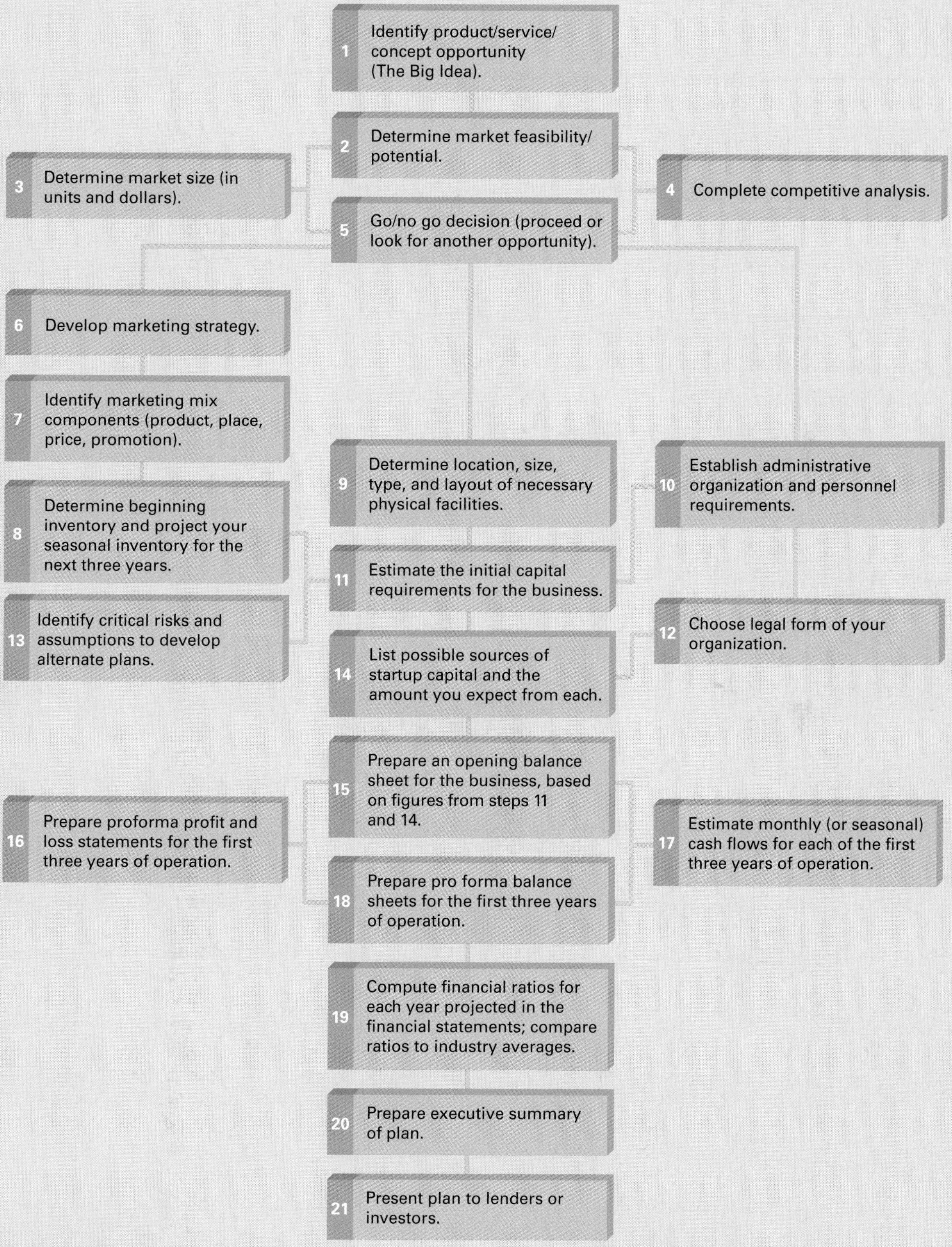

1 Identify product/service/concept opportunity (The Big Idea).

2 Determine market feasibility/potential.

3 Determine market size (in units and dollars).

4 Complete competitive analysis.

5 Go/no go decision (proceed or look for another opportunity).

6 Develop marketing strategy.

7 Identify marketing mix components (product, place, price, promotion).

8 Determine beginning inventory and project your seasonal inventory for the next three years.

9 Determine location, size, type, and layout of necessary physical facilities.

10 Establish administrative organization and personnel requirements.

11 Estimate the initial capital requirements for the business.

12 Choose legal form of your organization.

13 Identify critical risks and assumptions to develop alternate plans.

14 List possible sources of startup capital and the amount you expect from each.

15 Prepare an opening balance sheet for the business, based on figures from steps 11 and 14.

16 Prepare proforma profit and loss statements for the first three years of operation.

17 Estimate monthly (or seasonal) cash flows for each of the first three years of operation.

18 Prepare pro forma balance sheets for the first three years of operation.

19 Compute financial ratios for each year projected in the financial statements; compare ratios to industry averages.

20 Prepare executive summary of plan.

21 Present plan to lenders or investors.

Source: Hatten, Timothy, *Small Business Management*, Third Edition. Copyright © 2006 by Houghton Mifflin Company. Reprinted with permission.

1.4. Finally, include a statement of confidentiality to keep important information away from potential competitors.

The Benefits to the Community Component

In this section, describe the potential benefits to the community that your business could provide. Chapter 2 in your textbook, "Being Ethical and Socially Responsible," can help you in answering some of these questions. At the very least, address the following issues:

1.5. Describe the number of skilled and nonskilled jobs the business will create, and indicate how purchases of supplies and other materials can help local businesses.

1.6. Next, describe how providing needed goods or services will improve the community and its standard of living.

1.7. Finally, state how your business can develop new technical, management, or leadership skills; offer attractive wages; and provide other types of individual growth.

Review of Business Plan Activities

Read over the information that you have gathered. Because the Building a Business Plan exercises at the end of Parts 2 through 7 are built on the work you do in Part 1, make sure that any weaknesses or problem areas are resolved before continuing. Finally, write a brief statement that summarizes all the information for this part of the business plan.

Part 2

Trends in Business Today

In Part 2 of *Business* we look at several trends that influence how and where business is conducted. First, we investigate the exploding world of e-business. Then we move to a very practical aspect of business: how businesses are owned. Issues related to ownership are particularly interesting in today's world, where large global businesses coexist with small businesses. Finally, because the majority of businesses are small, we look at specific issues related to small business.

Navigating the World of e-Business

WHAT you will be able to do once you complete this chapter:

1 Explain the meaning of e-business.

2 Explore the basic framework of e-business.

3 Describe the fundamental models of e-business.

4 Understand the factors that influence an e-business plan.

5 Discuss the social and legal concerns of e-business.

6 Explore the growth trends, future opportunities, and challenges of e-business.

WHY this chapter matters

Today, the Internet and e-business are changing the way you live and the way business does business. As a result, there are many career opportunities available in e-business. In fact, many people dream of a career in the quick-paced e-business industry.

FOR HELP with studying this chapter, visit the Online Student Center:

www.college.hmco.com/PIC/pridebusiness9e

Online Study Center

Few e-businesses can triumph in direct competition with the world's largest retailer. Yet this is exactly what happened when Wal-Mart got out of the online DVD-rental business after three years and sent customers to Netflix. Blockbuster, the biggest name in the movie rental industry, is actively building its online DVD-rental operation—yet Netflix remains the market leader. How did Netflix become such an e-business power?

CEO Reed Hastings started thinking about online DVD rentals after he had to pay a local Blockbuster store $40 in late fees for an overdue movie rental. A successful software entrepreneur, Hastings thought about using technology to run a DVD-rental business that would not require movies to be returned by specific due dates. He also wanted to make the rental experience more efficient and convenient for customers. His solution: Post the inventory of DVDs available for rent on the Internet, and let customers build a list of movies they want to see. After customers build their list of movies, Netflix does the rest. This e-business rushes the DVDs to customers, who can keep them as long as they like. When ready, the customer sends the DVDs back, and Netflix sends additional titles on the customer's "queue." By the way, Netflix pays the shipping and postage.

When Netflix debuted in 1997, videocassettes dominated movie rentals, and a mere 2 percent of U.S. households owned a DVD player. At first, Netflix offered about 900 DVD titles, but it continued to expand its selection as the DVD format caught on. Four years later, 39 percent of U.S. households owned a DVD player, and the DVD-rental industry had grown to $3 billion in annual revenue. Today, most movies are issued on DVD, and the industry rings up more than $8 billion in annual rental revenue.

Netflix now offers more than 60,000 titles; with multiple copies of popular movies, its total inventory exceeds 40 million DVDs. Customers pay a monthly subscription fee to have one DVD at home at a time, three at home, or more. The basic plan for one movie at a time is $9.99 per month. The most popular plan is $17.99 per month that enables customers to obtain three movies at a time. Today, because of the goal of making it easier for customers to rent DVDs and

sophisticated software, extensive inventory, and nationwide network of distribution centers, Netflix continues to grow its customer base. In fact, Neflix is so good at what it does that even Wal-Mart, known for its efficiency, could not compete—despite its lower subscription fee.[1]

For more information about this company, go to **www.netflix.com**.

Think for a moment what your life would be like if it weren't for the Internet? Everyday tasks such as using the web to obtain the weather forecast or movie reviews or tracking the value of your investments would be much more difficult. And today, more and more people are buying *and* selling merchandise through the Internet. In fact, the Internet is so popular that it is changing the way both large and small businesses do business. Netflix, the company showcased in the Inside Business opening case, is a good example of a company that is meeting the needs of customers by using the Internet. This firm exists because of commercial activity on the web. Like other well-known firms, such as Yahoo!, eBay, Amazon, and Google, Netflix owes its very existence to the Internet. Quite simply, without the Internet, there would be no Netflix, Yahoo!, Amazon, or Google. Most firms, on the other hand, have developed or will develop an Internet presence by transferring some of their business practices to the Internet. This was the route taken by Disney, which found new opportunities by placing some of its products, entertainment, and information content online.

There is a fundamental difference between businesses that invented themselves on the Internet, such as MSN, and previously established firms that have transferred only some of their activities to the Internet, such as the Gap. Firms with no history but the one defined on the Internet make their business decisions with a clear focus on the online world. There is no concern for interfering with other established business activity. By contrast, firms such as the Gap are very concerned about how development on the Internet will affect their current retail store sales, costs, customer relations, and so forth.

This chapter examines the development of both types of businesses and provides a foundation for understanding how and why Internet activities will change the way businesses function in the future. We also take a closer look at how firms conduct business on the Internet and what growth opportunities may be available to both new and existing firms. Before exploring this new and exciting arena for business competition, however, let's begin by defining e-business.

Defining e-Business

1 LEARNING OBJECTIVE
Explain the meaning of e-business.

e-business (electronic business) the organized effort of individuals to produce and sell, for a profit, the goods and services that satisfy society's needs through the facilities available on the Internet

In Chapter 1 we defined *business* as the organized effort of individuals to produce and sell, for a profit, the goods and services that satisfy society's needs. In a simple sense, then, **e-business,** or **electronic business,** can be defined as the organized effort of individuals to produce and sell, for a profit, the goods and services that satisfy society's needs *through the facilities available on the Internet.* And just as we distinguished between any *individual business* and the general term *business,* which refers to all such efforts within a society, we recognize both the individual *e-business,* such as eBay or Google, and the general concept of *e-business.* As you will see in the remainder of this chapter and throughout this book, e-business is transforming key business activities, such as buying and selling products and services, building better supplier and customer relationships, and improving general business operations—often at a lower cost than more traditional methods.

Sometimes people use the term *e-commerce* instead of *e-business.* In a strict sense, *e-business* is used when one is speaking about all business activities and practices conducted on the Internet by an individual firm or industry. On the other hand, **e-commerce** is a part of e-business; the term refers only to buying and selling activities conducted online. These activities may include identifying suppliers, selecting products or services, making purchase commitments, completing financial transactions, and obtaining service.[2] We generally use the term *e-business* because of its broader definition and scope.

e-commerce buying and selling activities conducted online

Organizing e-Business Resources

As noted in Chapter 1, to be organized, a business must combine *human, material, informational,* and *financial resources.* This is true of e-business, too (see Figure 4.1), but in this case, the resources may be more specialized than in a typical business. For example, people who can design, create, and maintain websites are only a fraction of the specialized human resources required by e-businesses. Material resources must include specialized computers, sophisticated equipment and software, and high-speed Internet connection lines. Computer programs that track the number of customers to view a firm's website are generally among the specialized informational resources required. Financial resources, the money required to start and maintain the firm and allow it to grow, usually reflect greater participation by individual entrepreneurs and investors willing to invest in a high-tech firm instead of conventional financial sources such as banks. In an effort to reduce the cost of specialized resources that are used in e-business, many firms have turned to outsourcing. **Outsourcing** is the process of finding outside vendors and suppliers that provide professional help, parts, or materials at a lower cost. For example, a firm that needs specialized software to complete a project may turn to an outside firm located in another part of the United States, India, or some Eastern European country.

Satisfying Needs Online

Think for a moment, why do people use the Internet? For most people, the Internet can be used to purchase products or services and as a source of information and interaction with other people. Today, more people use the Internet to satisfy these needs than ever before, and the number of people who use the Internet will continue to grow in the years to come. Because of this explosive growth of the Internet, let's start with two basic assumptions. First, the Internet has created some new customer needs that did not exist before creation of the Internet. Second, e-businesses can satisfy those needs, as well as

Call centers go global. When you call for technical support, the person on the other end of the phone may be in another country. The two technical support employees in this photo are located in Dakar, Senegal. Today, many American firms have outsourced technical support, software development, and many other business activities to workers in other nations in order to reduce costs.

outsourcing the process of finding outside vendors and suppliers that provide professional help, parts, or materials at a lower cost

>> **FIGURE 4.1**

COMBINING E-BUSINESS RESOURCES

While all businesses use four resources (human, material, informational, and financial), these resources typically are more specialized when used in an e-business.

HUMAN RESOURCES
- Web site designers
- Programmers
- Web masters

INFORMATIONAL RESOURCES
- Customer tracking systems
- Order fulfillment and tracking systems
- Online content-monitoring systems

BUSINESS

MATERIAL RESOURCES
- Computers
- Software
- High-speed Internet connection lines

FINANCIAL RESOURCES
- Investors interested in supporting e-business firms
- Electronic payment from customers

more traditional ones. For example, Amazon.com gives customers anywhere in the world access to the same virtual store of books, DVDs, and CDs. And at eBay's global auction site, customers can, for a small fee, buy and sell almost anything. In each of these examples, customers can use the Internet to purchase a product or service.

Internet users also can access print media, such as newspapers and magazines, and radio and television programming at a time and place convenient to them. In addition to offering such a wide selection of content, the Internet provides the opportunity for *interaction*. In other words, communication is now an active two-way street between the online program and the viewer. CNN.com and other news-content sites encourage dialogue among viewers in chat rooms and exchanges with the writers of articles posted to the site. In contrast to the passive situation they encounter with traditional media such as television or radio, customers can respond to Internet programming by requesting more information about a product or posing specific questions, which may lead to purchasing a product or service.

Finally, the Internet allows customers to choose the content they are offered. For example, individuals can custom design daily online newspapers and magazines with articles that are of interest to them. Knowing what is of interest to a customer allows an Internet firm to direct appropriate, *smart advertising* to a specific customer. For example, someone wanting to read articles about the New York Yankees might be a potential customer for products and services related to baseball. For the advertiser, knowing that its advertisements are being directed to the most likely customers represents a better way to spend advertising dollars.

revenue stream a source of revenue flowing into a firm

Creating e-Business Profit

While firms can't increase profits magically, they can increase their profits either by increasing sales revenue or by reducing expenses through a variety of e-business activities.

Increasing Sales Revenue Each source of sales revenue flowing into a firm is referred to as a **revenue stream.** One way to increase revenues is to sell merchandise on the Internet. Online merchants can reach a global customer base twenty-four hours a day, seven days a week because the opportunity to shop on the Internet is virtually unrestricted. The removal of barriers that might keep customers from conventional stores is a major factor in increasing sales-revenue potential for e-businesses, as such firms as Barnesandnoble.com and Landsend.com have demonstrated. And yet the simple redirection of in-store sales to an online revenue stream is not desirable. For example, shifting revenues earned from customers inside a real store to revenues earned from those same customers online does not create any real new revenue for a firm. The goal is to find new customers and generate new sales so that total revenues are increased.

Intelligent informational systems also can help to generate sales revenue for Internet firms such as Amazon.com. Such systems store information about each customer's purchases, along with a variety of other information about the buyer's preferences. Using this information, the system can assist the customer the next time he or she visits the website. For example, if the customer has bought a Clay Aiken or

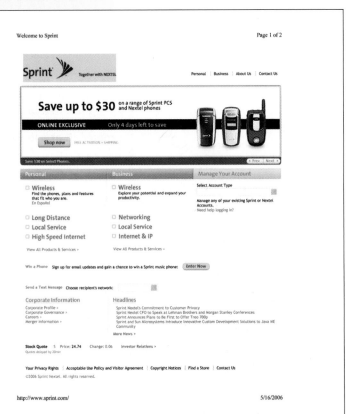

Kelly Clarkson CD in the past, the system might suggest CDs by similar artists who have appeared on the popular televised talent search program *American Idol*.

While some customers in certain situations may not make a purchase online, the existence of the firm's website and the services and information it provides may lead to increased sales in the firm's physical stores. For example, Toyota.com can provide basic comparative information for shoppers so that they are better prepared for their visit to an automobile showroom.

In addition to selling products or services online, e-business revenue streams are created by advertising placed on web pages and by subscription fees charged for access to online services and content. For example, Hoover's Online (**www.hoovers.com**), a comprehensive source for company and industry information, makes some of its online content free for anyone who visits the site, but more detailed data are available only by paid subscription. In addition, it receives revenue from companies that are called *sponsors*, who advertise their products and services on Hoover's website.

Many Internet firms that distribute news, magazine and newspaper articles, and similar content generate revenue primarily from advertising sponsors and commissions earned from sellers of products linked to the site. Online shopping malls, for example, now provide groups of related vendors of electronic equipment and computer hardware and software with a new method of selling their products and services. In many cases the vendors share online sales revenues with the site owners.

Reducing Expenses Reducing expenses is the second major way in which e-business can help to increase profitability. Providing online access to information customers want can reduce the cost of dealing with customers. For example, besides displaying seat availability and taking customer reservations on their websites, most airlines provide updated scheduling and pricing information, as well as promotional material. This reduces the costs of dealing with customers through a call center operated by employees and of mailing brochures, which may be outdated within weeks or easily misplaced by customers. Sprint Nextel (**www.sprint.com**) is just one company that maintains an extensive website where potential customers can learn more about cell phone products and services and current customers can access personal account information, send e-mail questions to customer service, and purchase additional products or services. With such extensive online services, SprintPCS does not have to maintain as many physical store locations as it would without these online services. For more information on the advantages and disadvantages of e-business, look at Table 4.1

We examine more examples of how e-business contributes to profitability throughout this chapter, especially as we focus on some of the business models for activity on the Internet.

> > **TABLE 4.1**

ADVANTAGES AND DISADVANTAGES OF E-BUSINESS

Advantages	Disadvantages
Increases productivity for both customers and employees by saving time and money	Requires specialized knowledge to use
Allows for communications at a more convenient place and time through e-mail and other software	User must have Internet access
Provides access to information anytime anywhere	May be perceived as an undesirable means of communications compared with direct contact between people
Allows firms to profitably serve small markets	May result in lost customers or sales if online sales experience is unsatisfactory
Facilitates online shopping for customers located around the globe	Online promotional efforts such as e-mail and pop-up advertising may be annoying
Inexpensive methods to promote the firm and its products to current and potential customers	

A Framework for Understanding e-Business

2 LEARNING OBJECTIVE
Explore the basic framework of e-business.

World Wide Web (the web) the Internet's multimedia environment of audio, visual, and text data

digitized data that have been converted to a type of signal that computers and telecommunications equipment that make up the Internet can understand

The Internet was conceived originally as an elaborate military communications network that would allow vital messages to be transmitted in the event of war. Should one element of the network be destroyed, the system was designed to ensure that an alternative route could be found in the remaining network so that messages could be sent to people who would use the information to make vital decisions. Before 1994, the U.S. National Science Foundation, the agency that funded and regulated use of the Internet, restricted its use to noncommercial activities, such as e-mail communication and the sharing of data among university researchers. However, as the potential commercial benefits of the Internet became increasingly obvious, a growing list of commercially interested groups demanded that the doors be opened to business activity. At about the same time, new technology emerged that simplified use of the Internet and allowed the addition of multimedia content. This multimedia environment of audio, visual, and text data came to be known as the **World Wide Web** (or more simply, **the web**). Figure 4.2 presents some of the major events that have occurred during the relative brief history of the Internet.

Today, the Internet can be envisioned as a large network of computers that pass small, standardized packets of electronic data from one station to another until they are delivered to their final destination. In a sense, the Internet is the equivalent of the telephone network. However, instead of transmitting just voice communications, the Internet can transfer a variety of multimedia data at high speed around the world. To be transferred over the Internet, data need to be **digitized,** which means converted to a type of signal that computers and telecommunications equipment that make up the Internet can understand.

>> FIGURE 4.2

A BRIEF HISTORY OF THE INTERNET AND E-BUSINESS

As a result of creation of the World Wide Web, the use of technology for both e-business and traditional business has increased dramatically in the last fifteen years.

YEAR	INVENTIONS
1960s	• Paul Baran and his team at the Rand Corporation develop communication system for the U.S. military.
1990s	• The World Wide Web is created
1994	• Yahoo!
1995	• Amazon.com, eBay, CompuServ, AOL, and Prodigy
1998	• Google
1999	• Napster and online file sharing, First online banking
2000s	
2000	• The Intenet meltdown and many dot com failures
2001	• AOL acquires Time Warner, Apple introduces iPod
2003	• Apple opens iTunes
2005	• eBay acquires Skype.com

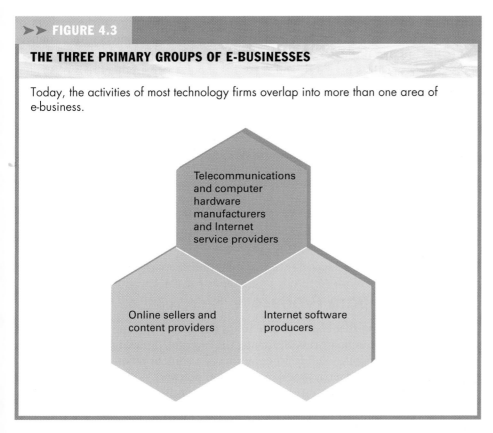

➤➤ FIGURE 4.3

THE THREE PRIMARY GROUPS OF E-BUSINESSES

Today, the activities of most technology firms overlap into more than one area of e-business.

Telecommunications and computer hardware manufacturers and Internet service providers

Online sellers and content providers

Internet software producers

Internet service providers (ISPs) provide customers with a connection to the Internet through various phone plugs and cables

There's more to a laptop than meets the eye! While some would say these laptop computers are pretty, the truth is that regardless of what the computers look like, they must process data into information. Here, Ken Musgrave and Steve Gluskoter, both directors of industrial design for Dell, display the latest laptop models, which have features that enable Dell to compete in the very competitive computer industry.

Most firms involved in e-business today fall more or less into one of three primary groups as defined by their e-business activities (see Figure 4.3):

- Telecommunications and computer hardware manufacturers and Internet service providers
- Internet software producers
- Online sellers and content providers

In this section we examine these three groups and also look at how e-business facilitates both global and small-business operations.

Telecommunications and Computer Hardware Manufacturers and Internet Service Providers

The telecommunications and computer hardware manufacturers that helped to build the Internet, together with Internet service providers, supply the physical infrastructure of the industry today. Lucent Technologies, Cisco Systems, and Nortel Networks produce most of the telecommunications hardware that allows the Internet to work. Companies such as Sony, Apple, and Dell produce many of the computers used by consumers, and companies such as Sun, IBM, and Hewlett Packard manufacture servers that control corporate computer networks. **Internet service**

providers (ISPs), which buy their technological capability from the makers of telecommunications and hardware manufacturers, provide customers with a connection to the Internet through various phone plugs and cables. While many people recognize the larger ISPs like AOL and AT&T Yahoo!, there are hundreds of smaller ISPs in both urban and rural areas that also provide access to the Internet. Furthermore, recent developments in technologies using wireless networks within office buildings and small clusters of buildings such as college campuses are helping to create a more readily accessible Internet using a variety of communications devices. These devices, along with new technology such as Voice over Internet Protocol (VoIP), allow such firms as Vonage (**www.vonage.com**) to provide cheaper telephone services over the Internet. Now anyone with a high-speed Internet connect and a VoIP device can speak to anyone else who is similarly equipped without paying any long-distance or other connect charges. According to some analysts, VoIP is the "next big thing" on the Internet, and the $300 billion dollar a year American telephone industry is facing collapse owing to the superior features and cheaper prices now available from VoIP providers.[3]

Internet Software Producers

Producers of software that enable people to do things on the Internet are the second primary group of e-business firms. Searching the Internet, browsing websites, sending e-mail messages, shopping, and viewing multimedia content online are activities that require specialized computer programs. Browser software is the single most basic product for user interaction on the Internet. Currently, the dominant browser is Microsoft's Internet Explorer, followed well back by Netscape and Mozilla's Firefox.

In addition to browser software, many people use search-engine software to find information on the Internet. Popular search engines include google.com, yahoo.com, msn.com, aol.com, lycos.com, netscape.com, and hundreds of lesser-known sites that enable users to search the Internet for needed information. By entering key words and phrases, users are guided to available online information. These search engines earn a great deal of their revenues by selling advertisements associated with key words to firms that wish to have their links displayed on the screen after a search.

Today, e-mail is considered a standard communication software tool for all business people. Whether for internal or external communication, the benefits from using e-mail often make it the easiest Internet-based software solution to rationalize from a cost standpoint. More advanced and complex communications solutions might include customer relationship and supply-chain management software. Several large firms now sell complete **customer relationship management (CRM) software** solutions that incorporate a variety of methods that can be used to manage communication with customers and share important information with all of a firm's employees. And just as CRM software solutions help firms to create more efficient relationships with their customers, **supply-chain management (SCM) software** solutions focus on ways to improve communication between the suppliers and users of materials and components. By providing their production requirements and planning information directly to their suppliers, manufacturers can reduce inventories, improve delivery schedules, and reduce costs, which can quickly show up as improved profitability. For example, Dell Computer's SCM software (**https://valuechain.dell.com**) virtually eliminates the need for the firm to maintain any inven-

customer relationship management (CRM) software software solutions that incorporate a variety of methods that can be used to manage communication with customers and share important information with all of a firm's employees

supply-chain management (SCM) software software solutions that focus on ways to improve communication between the suppliers and users of materials and components

SPOTLIGHT

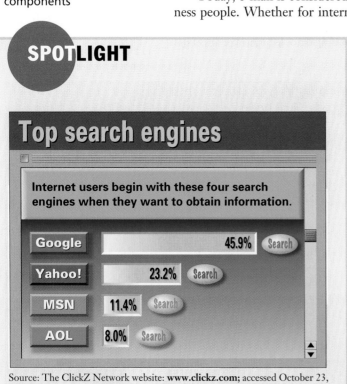

Top search engines

Internet users begin with these four search engines when they want to obtain information.

Google	45.9%	Search
Yahoo!	23.2%	Search
MSN	11.4%	Search
AOL	8.0%	Search

Source: The ClickZ Network website: **www.clickz.com**; accessed October 23, 2005.

tory because suppliers are tied directly into Dell's new manufacturing facility in Round Rock, Texas. Manufacturing schedules and parts orders are revised every two hours. Suppliers must keep an agreed-on level of inventory for Dell on hand at nearby local warehouses. As a result, 95 percent of Dell's PCs are built and shipped to customers within twelve hours of their orders being entered into the system. The new software has improved productivity by 160 percent and reduced errors in orders by 50 percent.[4]

Online Sellers and Content Providers

The third primary group of e-businesses—online sellers and content providers—consists of all the firms that customers actually interact with on websites. In this area of e-business, we have just begun to see the development of strategies for reaching out to existing and new customers. As noted earlier, some e-businesses, such as eBay and Google, owe their existence to the Internet. They offer products and services that can be found only online. In contrast, other firms—among them the Gap, Nike, Restoration Hardware, and Wal-Mart—have moved only some of their business practices to the Internet. These firms use the Internet to sell merchandise, provide information to customers, and supplement their regular retail sales efforts and other traditional business activities.

Although the Internet is changing constantly, it is clear that both ISPs and businesses are scrambling to take advantage of the Internet's ability to provide customers with information. Time Warner's decision to merge with AOL is a case in point. By arranging for online distribution of interesting content that formerly was distributed through traditional magazines, radio, and television, Time Warner has found new opportunities for revenue growth.

In fact, the greatest opportunities for entrepreneurs on the Internet are often in the production of a service or content. Anyone with a good idea that might appeal to a global audience stands a chance of successfully launching an e-business. As the short history of the Internet indicates, we are only at the beginning of new and exciting applications that can be delivered online.

Global e-Business

All three primary groups of e-business firms are in a race to capture global business revenues. Telecommunications firms are competing to build infrastructure in countries all over the world. For example, in poor countries where telephone poles have never existed, ground-based wireless systems are now providing instant state-of-the-art communication. In many places, large, global ISPs and software producers such as AOL are competing against better-known local firms. And online sellers and content producers are selling their merchandise and services to customers all over the globe.

The ability to customize content for individual customer needs makes the Internet an adaptable tool for global enterprise. Consider Berlitz's website (**www.berlitz.com**), which allows anyone in the world to jump quickly to a website designed in the viewer's preferred language. By clicking on the appropriate icon, viewers can move forward to a website created to meet their needs in their own language. Once there, the viewer can examine Berlitz's wide range of products and services, including multimedia language-learning material, online translation services, and referrals to local Berlitz classroom-based instruction services. This global strategy, which reaches out to the world and yet allows for viewer customization, is at the heart of e-business. And the marketplace is growing. According to research conducted by *Computer Industry Almanac*, about one billion people, or one sixth of the world's population, now use the Internet, and this number will grow to 1.3 billion by 2007. The United States still ranks highest among individual countries with almost 200 million users, but China, at 100 million users, now ranks second.[5]

Business Around the World

e-Businesses Go Globetrotting

How easy is it to take an e-business global? Here's how PearlParadise.com in California and Handango in Texas addressed the challenges first hand.

PearlParadise.com

Owner Jeremy Shepherd imports pearl jewelry from Asia and then sells it to customers all over the world. One challenge was earning customer trust. To do this, Shepherd joined the Safe Shopping Network and had his site's security verified by Geo-Trust and other firms. Receiving payment was another challenge. To avoid being stung by credit-card fraud, Shepherd verifies billing addresses and card numbers before shipping to customers in Asia and Eastern Europe.

Handango

The first challenge for this cell phone software retailer was figuring out how to "avoid the carpet-bagger image of outsiders trying to own a market they don't understand." Handango solved the problem by registering local website addresses (ending in *.co.uk* for Great Britain, for example). Handango also had to adapt to non-U.S. buying preferences. For instance, Japanese buyers like paying for online purchases in local stores. Therefore, Handango formed an alliance with a Japanese e-business that had existing store relationships. When it set up sites in Germany, China, and Korea, the company adapted payment methods to local preferences as well.

Small e-Business

Based on early experience, the Internet will continue to be a powerful tool for small business. According to a report by Access Markets International (AMI) Partners and *Inc.* magazine, small-business online activity got off to a very quick start. Research showed that an estimated 400,000 U.S. small businesses sold their products and services on e-business sites in 1998, and this number jumped 50 percent to 600,000 in 1999. During the same period, the dollar amount of online transactions grew more than 1,000 percent, increasing from $2 billion to $25 billion. Interestingly, a significant number of small firms—six out of ten—were reluctant to sell their products online at the time because of security concerns, technology challenges, or the belief that their products were unsuited for online selling.[6]

However, despite these early concerns, online activity continues to grow. According to a recent American Express survey, 66 percent of small businesses already had integrated the Internet into their processes as a tool to help them run their businesses, using it for making travel plans; purchasing office supplies, equipment, or other business services; conducting industry or market research; marketing or advertising; networking with other entrepreneurs; purchasing goods from wholesalers; and managing accounts and making payments.[7]

Although large firms dominate e-business, the remarkable thing about the Internet is how accessible it is to small businesses. The relatively low cost of going online means that the Internet is open to thousands of small businesses seeking opportunities to sell their services or products internationally. And many small online magazines, or **e-zines,** as they are often called, have found their special audiences through the virtual world of online publishing. In fact, many small publications that began online have gone on to create print versions of their e-zines.

Writers such as Stephen King and recording artists such as Sarah McLachlan have discovered that they can earn higher profits by dealing directly with customers online

e-zines small online magazines

rather than through conventional middlemen such as wholesalers and retail distributors. The Internet also has given unknown artists a new venue for finding an audience; after reading or listening to a sample of their work, newfound fans can order books or CDs directly or download and create their own copies. And software producers such as Kazaa and the original Napster were quick to provide users with the technology they could use to download copyrighted materials. Although both firms challenged traditional methods of entertainment distribution, they also have been at the center of legal concerns over ownership of distribution rights to content on the Internet. In 2001, through lawsuits filed in American courts by music distribution firms, Napster was forced to cease illegal file-sharing activities conducted by users of its software. Still, its brand recognition was so pervasive that the firm was relaunched as a legitimate music store. More information about what firms in the publishing and music industries are doing about Internet-based distribution methods and protecting their property is provided later in this chapter.

Fundamental Models of e-Business

One way to get a better sense of how businesses are adapting to the opportunities available on the Internet is to identify e-business models. A **business model** represents a group of common characteristics and methods of doing business to generate sales revenues and reduce expenses. Each of the models discussed below represents a primary e-business model. All the models focus on the identity of a firm's customers.

Business-to-Business (B2B) Model

Many e-businesses can be distinguished from others simply by their customer focus. For instance, some firms use the Internet mainly to conduct business with other businesses. These firms generally are referred to as having a **business-to-business, or B2B, model.** Currently, the vast majority of e-business is B2B in nature.

When examining B2B business firms, two clear types emerge. In the first type, the focus is simply on facilitating sales transactions between businesses. For example, Dell manufactures computers to specifications that customers enter on the Dell website. The vast majority of Dell's online orders are from corporate clients who are well informed about the products they need and are looking for fairly priced, high-quality computer products that will be delivered quickly. Basically, by building only what is ordered, Dell reduces storage and carrying costs and rarely is stuck with unsold inventory. By dealing directly with Dell, customers eliminate costs associated with wholesalers and retailers, thereby helping to reduce the price they pay for equipment.

A second, more complex type of B2B model involves a company and its suppliers. Today, suppliers use the Internet to bid on products and services they wish to sell to a customer, learn about the customer's rules and procedures that must be followed, and so forth. Likewise, firms seeking specific items now can ask for bids on their websites and choose from available suppliers through the online system. For example, both General Motors and Ford have developed B2B models to link thousands of suppliers that sell the automobile makers parts worth billions of dollars each year. While the B2B sites are expensive to start and maintain, there are significant savings for General Motors and Ford—much like the savings that other firms involved in B2B models experience. Specifically, savings for both automobile manufacturers come primarily from the elimination of manual labor and the errors created by the repetitive entry of data by employees. For instance, under the old system, Ford might fax an order for parts to a supplier. The supplier would fill out another order form and send a copy to Ford for confirmation. The data would have to be entered in each company's computer system each step of the way. However, under the new system, the supplier has access to Ford's inventory of parts and

3 LEARNING OBJECTIVE

Describe the fundamental models of e-business.

business model represents a group of common characteristics and methods of doing business to generate sales revenues and reduce expenses

business-to-business (B2B) model firms that conduct business with other businesses

@ **USING THE INTERNET**

To find information about e-business careers, including educational requirements and salaries, go to
www.bls.gov
www.careerbuilder.com
http://hotjobs.yahoo.com
www.job.com
www.monster.com

can place bids for parts online. Ford eliminates the labor costs of data entry and much of the order-processing costs by connecting suppliers to the system.

Given the potential savings, it is no wonder that many other manufacturers and their suppliers are beginning to use the same kind of B2B systems that are used by the automakers. In fact, suppliers know that to be a "preferred" supplier for a large firm that may purchase large quantities of parts, supplies, or raw materials, they must be tied into the purchaser's B2B system. For example, in 2005, Ford announced that it would reduce the number of suppliers that provide the firm with the $70 billion of car parts and $20 billion of other supplies and increase the volume of purchases with those that remained connected to its system.[8]

Business-to-Consumer (B2C) Model

business-to-consumer (B2C) model firms that focus on conducting business with individual buyers

In contrast to the B2B model, firms such as Amazon and eBay clearly are focused on individual buyers and so are referred to as having a **business-to-consumer, or B2C, model.** In a B2C situation, understanding how consumers behave online is critical to a firm's success. Typically, a business firm that uses a B2C model must answer the following questions:

- Will consumers use websites merely to simplify and speed up comparison shopping?
- Will customers purchase services and products online or end up buying at a traditional retail store?
- What sorts of products and services are best suited for online consumer shopping?
- Which products and services are simply not good choices at this stage of online development?

No doubt as more consumers make use of online environments, an increasing amount of research will help to explain how best to meet their needs. For example, on-line grocery shopping has failed to impress both customers and most retailers who have attempted to create an online presence. However, research also suggests that specialty grocery Internet retailing of more-difficult-to-find products is another matter. The Piggly Wiggly and Dick's Supermarkets chains in Wisconsin, northern Illinois, and Iowa, are partnering with a division of Kehe Foods, which supplies specialty items such as ethnic foods, gourmet items, and natural foods. As a result, customers will be able to choose from more than 30,000 items, many of which aren't available in area stores.[9]

In addition to providing round-the-clock global access to all kinds of products and services, B2C firms often make a special effort to build long-term relationships with their customers. Often firms will make a special effort to make sure that the customer is satisfied and that problems, if any, are quickly solved. While a "little special attention" may increase the cost of doing business for a B2C firm, the customer's repeated purchases will repay the investment many times over. Specialized software also can help to build good customer relationships. Tracking the decisions and buying preferences as customers navigate a website, for instance, helps management to make well-informed decisions about how best to serve such customers. In essence, this is Amazon.com's selling approach. By tracking and analyzing customer data, Amazon can provide individualized service to its customers.

Today, B2B and B2C models are the most popular business models for e-business. And yet, there are other business models that perform specialized e-business activities to generate revenues. Most of the business models described in Table 4.2 are modified versions of the B2B and B2C models.

Creating an e-Business Plan

4 LEARNING OBJECTIVE
Understand the factors that influence an e-business plan.

The approach taken to creating an e-business plan will depend on whether you are establishing a new Internet business or adding an online component to an existing business. In this section we consider some important factors that affect both situations.

> > **TABLE 4.2**

OTHER BUSINESS MODELS THAT PERFORM SPECIALIZED E-BUSINESS ACTIVITIES

Although modified versions of B2B or B2C, the following business models perform specialized e-business activities to generate revenues:

Advertising e-business model	Advertisements that are displayed on a firm's website in return for a fee. Examples include pop-up and banner advertisements on search engines and other popular Internet sites.
Brokerage e-business model	Online marketplaces where buyers and sellers are brought together to facilitate exchange of goods and services. Examples include eBay (**www.ebay.com**), which provides a site for buying and selling virtually anything.
Consumer-to-consumer model	Peer-to-peer software that allows individuals to share information over the Internet. Examples include Morpheus (**www.morpheus.com**), which allows users to exchange audio, documents, photos, or video files.
Subscription and pay-per-view e-business models	Content that is available only to users who pay a fee to gain access to a website. Examples include investment information provided by Standard & Poor's (**www.standardandpoors.com**) and business research provided by Forrester Research, Inc. (**www.forrester.com**).

Starting Up a New Internet Business from Scratch

For a new Internet business, a good e-business plan should provide detailed answers to basic questions. To begin, the planners need to determine if an Internet business will meet the needs of customers. Furthermore, the planning process should provide information that can help to identify and select groups of potential buyers, direct development of the online product or service, as well as the promotion, pricing, and distribution effort. The start-up planning also should indicate whether the potential market will generate enough sales and profits to make the new venture worthwhile. The answers to these questions will determine what type of business model (B2B, B2C, or one of the specialized models described in Table 4.2) is appropriate for the new Internet business. Sometimes more than one business model is appropriate. For example, British children's author J. K. Rowling used the Internet to launch her international marketing effort for *Harry Potter and the Goblet of Fire*. The book launch became an event, with advance sales of 5.3 million copies.[10] Although mainly intended as a promotional effort to both bookstores and consumers, the website used both a B2B model and a B2C model. Eventually, many of these sales took place through Amazon.com and Barnesandnoble.com as customers ordered online and had the books shipped as gifts to children for their summertime reading enjoyment. The website has grown since its inception and now serves as a site for ongoing marketing and advertising of new titles.

Is Harry Potter magic? Although author J.K. Rowling has enjoyed tremendous success with the Harry Potter books, there is still need to get the word out about each new addition to the series. When Harry Potter books are published, both a B2B and a B2C business model are used to generate publicity. The result: Millions of books are presold before hitting the shelves in bookstores around the globe.

Building an Online Presence for an Existing Business

A business that already has a physical location and a customer base often looks at e-business as a way to expand sales to current customers and to add new customers who are beyond the reach of the firm's geographic location. For example, retail firms such as Radio Shack, Sears, and many others have turned to the Internet to sell more products or to lead customers to physical stores in order to purchase products or services. Both customers who are seeking the convenience of shopping online and those who are simply using the website to view a retailer's merchandise and promotions before buying in a retail store can use the firm's website to satisfy their personal shopping needs. Although developing an online presence may seem like a logical extension of what a firm already does, there are important factors that must be considered before using the Internet to sell products or services or to provide information to customers. To see how starting a new Internet business differs from building an online presence for an existing business, look at Figure 4.4. In the remainder of this section we examine how these factors can change the way an existing business firm develops an online presence.

Are Online Customers Really Different?   For an existing business, one of the first concerns is how an online customer differs from a customer who walks into its physical stores. For example, customers who visit the J.C. Penney website may be different from customers who visit a department store located in a shopping mall in a large metropolitan area. The online customers may live in a rural area, earn more or less money, and have different needs when compared with shoppers in a metropolitan area. If the customers are different with different needs, the task of develop-

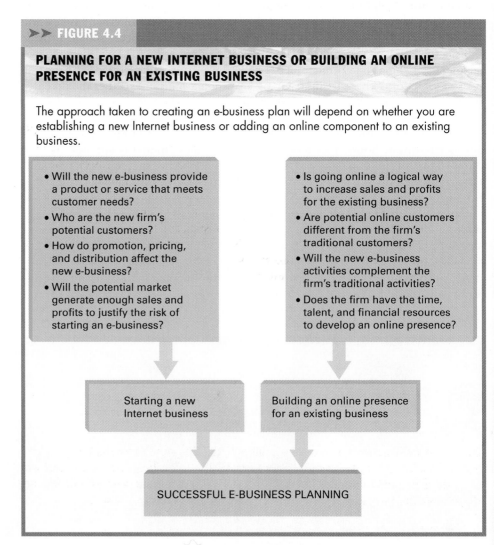

>> **FIGURE 4.4**

PLANNING FOR A NEW INTERNET BUSINESS OR BUILDING AN ONLINE PRESENCE FOR AN EXISTING BUSINESS

The approach taken to creating an e-business plan will depend on whether you are establishing a new Internet business or adding an online component to an existing business.

- Will the new e-business provide a product or service that meets customer needs?
- Who are the new firm's potential customers?
- How do promotion, pricing, and distribution affect the new e-business?
- Will the potential market generate enough sales and profits to justify the risk of starting an e-business?

- Is going online a logical way to increase sales and profits for the existing business?
- Are potential online customers different from the firm's traditional customers?
- Will the new e-business activities complement the firm's traditional activities?
- Does the firm have the time, talent, and financial resources to develop an online presence?

Starting a new Internet business

Building an online presence for an existing business

SUCCESSFUL E-BUSINESS PLANNING

ing appropriate strategies to meet their needs is more complex. On the other hand, if both types of customers are similar with similar needs, many of the same methods used in the firm's physical stores can be transferred to the web. Advertising, pricing, and shipping methods, for instance, that are already in place can be used on the firm's website.

Generally, existing firms that want to sell products or services throughout the world face additional problems when going online. For instance, besides the obvious differences in language, a website selling a product such as clothing or footwear must provide standardized sizes that are used in different nations around the world. In fact, designing a website that can communicate successfully to individual customers in other nations can be a challenge for online vendors that is far greater than eliminating language barriers or simply ensuring the display of proper size references to customers.

How e-Business Can Help Traditional Business Activities   The development of a firm's e-business activities should be guided by one key objective: to complement the existing non-Internet-based business plan. The e-business plan must be in line with the firm's overall goals and objectives. If customer satisfaction, for example, is considered a weakness, providing information online and allowing customers to contact customer service employees by e-mail may reduce or eliminate the problem. But be warned: Developing e-business activities that can be used to solve or reduce a firm's problems can be a complex process that takes time.

YOUR CAREER

The New Role of Chief Privacy Officer

Earthlink, the U.S. Census Bureau, and many other organizations with an online presence have appointed a chief privacy officer (CPO) to oversee privacy issues. What does a CPO do?

1. Develop and enforce rules governing how sensitive data are collected, protected, and shared.
2. Ensure that privacy policies are legally and ethically appropriate.
3. Investigate and respond to stakeholder inquiries regarding data privacy.
4. Train the work force in privacy safeguards.
5. Monitor compliance with privacy policies.

The U.S. Census Bureau's CPO meets with government officials, privacy groups, and other stakeholders to understand privacy concerns and strengthen the agency's policies accordingly. At Highmark, a health insurance firm, CPO Kimberly Gray sums up her role this way: "All of us who are involved with privacy are concerned from a customer-trust perspective—first and foremost, making sure we're doing the right thing for our customers."

Complexity and Time Concerns   Every business must be prepared to allow sufficient time for customers, suppliers, and staff to adapt to the new e-business methods. Online solutions such as introducing e-mail or a simple company website to help the staff to communicate better with one another, customers, and suppliers can be developed and installed quickly without undue delay, cost, or disruption of current work responsibilities. However, as the complexity of the plan increases, so too does the amount of time (and money) required to design, install, and test the new technology— and then to train the staff to use it. All this is further complicated by the need to educate customers and suppliers, who will be expected to change to a new method of placing orders, making requests for information, and other typical business activities. Internet banking, for instance, has grown in popularity, but it takes time for customers to get used to the procedures required to bank online. A strong customer-support system is critical to help customers who may be confused about the online screen options, computer and connection problems, security, and anything else with which they may need assistance.

Social and Legal Concerns

The social and legal concerns of an e-business extend beyond those shared by all businesses. In addition to the issues presented in Chapter 2, e-businesses must deal with the special circumstances of operating in a new frontier—one without borders and without much in the way of control by government or any organization.

5 LEARNING OBJECTIVE
Discuss the social and legal concerns of e-business.

Ethics and Social Responsibility

Socially responsible and ethical behavior by individuals and businesses on the Internet are major concerns. For example, an ethically questionable practice in cyberspace is the unauthorized access and use of information discovered through computerized tracking of users once they are connected to the Internet. Essentially, a user may visit a web page and unknowingly receive a small piece of software code called a **cookie.** This cookie can track where the user goes on the Internet and measure how long the user stays at any particular website. Although this type of software may produce valuable customer information, it also can be viewed as an invasion of privacy, especially since users may not even be aware that their movements are being monitored.

cookie a small piece of software sent by a website that tracks an individual's Internet use

The special circumstances of social interaction in an online environment are also a matter of increasing concern. For example, in some cases, people engaging in online chat rooms will reveal personal information that they would never reveal in face-to-face settings. People may buy things, say things, and do things that they otherwise would not because of the effect of the online environment. But none of this should be surprising. People behave differently when they are on vacation, at a party, or watching a baseball game in a stadium. The environment has an effect on us, whether it is a physical environment or one created in cyberspace.

A number of issues about privacy and the distribution of questionable online content, such as pornographic and hate literature, will remain issues of concern in the foreseeable future. Most ISPs and browsers allow users to block out websites identified as adult in nature, and many chat rooms are supervised so that unacceptable language or behavior can be terminated. Nonetheless, given the openness of the Internet and the relative absence of regulation, online users will have to develop their own strategies for handling difficult ethical and social situations.

Privacy and Confidentiality Issues

Besides the unauthorized use of cookies on users' computers to track their online behavior, there are several other threats to users' privacy and confidentiality. According to research by the University of Denver's Privacy Foundation Workplace Surveillance Project, more than one-third of the forty million U.S. employees who work online—about fourteen million—are under continuous surveillance by their employers.[11]

log-file records files that store a record of the websites visited

Monitoring an employee's **log-file records,** which record the websites visited, may be intended to help employers police unauthorized Internet use on company time; however, the same records also can give a firm the opportunity to observe what otherwise might be considered private and confidential information. Today, legal experts suggest that at the very least, employers need to disclose and publicize the level of surveillance to their employees and consider the corporate motivation for monitoring employees' behavior.

data mining the practice of searching through data records looking for useful information

Some firms also practice data mining. **Data mining** refers to the practice of searching through data records looking for useful information. Customer registration forms typically require a variety of information before a user is given access to a site. When this is combined with customer-transaction records, data-mining analysis can provide what might be considered private and confidential information about individuals or groups. For example, suppose that a website offering free access to health information requires users to fill out a registration form before they are granted access to the site. As a result of this voluntary disclosure, website operators can easily uncover correlations between users' age and gender and specific health topics and issues. The website operators then conceivably could sell this information to pharmaceutical firms. The information sold might suggest that there is a large group of potential customers over the age of 50 who have a high level of interest in a particular type of medication that the firm manufactures. Once this information is obtained, the pharmaceutical firm could begin a marketing campaign "to educate" potential customers about the benefits of its products.

Advocates for better control of how information is collected and distributed to interested third parties such as businesses point to the potential misuse of information—intentionally or otherwise. If an individual, for instance, frequents a website that provides information about a life-threatening disease, an insurance company might refuse to insure this individual, thinking that there is a higher risk associated with someone who wants more information about this disease.

The ability to collect and analyze personal data is critical for the industry if it is going to compete for advertisers' spending, so it must learn to do this ethically. To help deal with this issue and to support industry self-regulation, the U.S. Federal Trade Commission (FTC) approved the formation of the Network Advertising Initiative (NAI). The NAI, which is made up of Internet advertisers, was established to set rules and guidelines for the collection and use of personal data. By requiring the consent of users and making the process somewhat more open to scrutiny, the NAI has helped to make online data collection more ethical than it used to be and lends support to the argument that the Internet can regulate itself without undue government interference.

Security Concerns and Cybercrime

Because the Internet today often is regarded as an unregulated frontier, both individual and business users must be particularly aware of online risks and dangers. One particular problem, **computer viruses,** which can originate anywhere in the world, are software codes designed to disrupt normal computer operations. Their potentially devastating effects have given rise to a software security industry. Norton's antivirus program, distributed by Symantec (**www.symantec.com**), is only one of several well-known products that help to screen out incoming files containing unwanted viruses. Although not a security violation in the same sense as releasing a computer virus, **spamming,** the sending of massive amounts of unsolicited e-mail, also may be considered if not a security issue, then certainly an ethical issue. Sorting through what many recipients view as *junk e-mail* is, if nothing else, a waste of resources that cost individuals time and their employers money. As long as undesirable data can be transmitted easily, viruses and other forms of online harassment will remain a security issue and a business opportunity for firms such as Symantec, which must continuously revise its software to deal with newly issued viruses.

In addition to these risks, individual users and businesses must watch for criminal activities. According to data published by the Privacy Rights Clearinghouse, nearly 51 million Americans had some of their personal information compromised in a six-month period beginning in February 2005. One of the largest security breaches occurred when Bank of America lost a backup tape that contained personal information about 1.2 million individuals.[12] As a result of these and similar security breaches, consumers are buying less online because of concerns about identity theft, according to a survey conducted by the Conference Board in New York. The survey found that 70 percent of consumers have installed additional software on their PCs, and 41 percent said that they're purchasing less online.[13] Most consumers are also concerned about fraud. Because the Internet allows easy creation of websites, access from anywhere in the world, and anonymity for users, it is almost impossible to know with certainty that the website, organization, or individuals that you believe you are interacting with are what they seem. As always, *caveat emptor* ("let the buyer beware") is good advice to follow whether on the Internet or not.

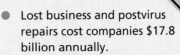
computer viruses software codes that are designed to disrupt normal computer operations

spamming the sending of massive amounts of unsolicited e-mail

secure electronic transaction (SET) an encryption process developed by MasterCard, Visa, IBM, Microsoft, and Netscape that prevents merchants from ever actually seeing any transaction data, including the customer's credit-card number

copyright legal right to control content ownership

To alleviate consumer concerns about online purchasing, the major credit-card organizations such as MasterCard and Visa use various programs to protect cardholders against fraudulent use of their cards on the Internet. For example, the **secure electronic transaction (SET)** encryption process, which was developed by MasterCard, Visa, IBM, Microsoft, and Netscape, prevents merchants from ever actually seeing any transaction data, including the customer's credit-card number.

Digital Property and Copyright Concerns

A major concern for businesses that use the Internet to distribute content is the legal right to control content ownership, commonly referred to as **copyright** laws. Most affected by this issue are the music and publishing industries. Both have had difficulties dealing with new technologies that have allowed individuals to make copies of their content. Early predictions about how the Internet would increase distribution for the entertainment industry have proven to be widely optimistic thus far. According to research conducted by Jupiter Media Metrix in 2001, the $40 billion global music industry was expected to include over $6 billion of annual online sales by 2006.[14] However, the Recording Industry of America (RIAA) reported that legal online downloading of singles and albums totaled less that $200 million of sales for the first half of 2005, suggesting that illegal downloading remained a problem for industry members.[15] With software easily available from such firms as MP3 (**www.mp3.com**) and Kazaa (**www.kazaa.com**), and Limewire (**www.limewire.com**), any Internet user can create a file of a song online and then send it to someone else, without ever paying the copyright owner. As far as the music industry is concerned, every copy of a song passed along freely on the Internet represents lost sales revenue from a customer who otherwise would make a purchase. As a means of dealing with this problem, some music companies have begun to sign distribution contracts with firms such as MP3 in order to gain more control over the distribution of their content. Others have sought a solution by establishing a software mechanism of their own that allows the distribution of music online but prevents its free distribution by those who are unauthorized. For example, MusicNet (**www.musicnet.com**), a service backed by music and technology companies, was established to control legal distribution of the firms' content.

However, the industry appears to be gradually coming around to experimenting with different pricing strategies in an effort to confront the price issue head-on, as illustrated by Rhapsody.com, which offers customers unlimited downloads for a flat fee of $9.99 per month instead of the benchmark 99-cent price per single and $9.99 per album. At the same time, the industry has taken a strong and somewhat controversial approach to illegal downloading by taking individuals and organizations to court for copyright violations. For example, in 2005, the RIAA announced another round of targeted lawsuits against individuals at the following schools: Boston University, Columbia University, Georgia Institute of Technology, Harvard University, Massachusetts Institute of Technology, Princeton University, Rochester Institute of Technology, University of California–Berkeley, University of California–Los Angeles, and other major universities across the nation.[16]

In addition to problems in the music and publishing industries, available technology makes it quite easy to copy and use a company name or recognized trademark, such as McDonald's golden arches, without permission. Most firms post information about how their names and

Sweet music! That's how many music lovers describe Rhapsody.com. For a low monthly fee, users have unrestricted access to Rhapsody's 1.5 million-song catalog. At a time when the music industry is taking legal action to protect its copyrighted material, it is refreshing to see new pricing strategies that are not only consumer friendly, but also legal.

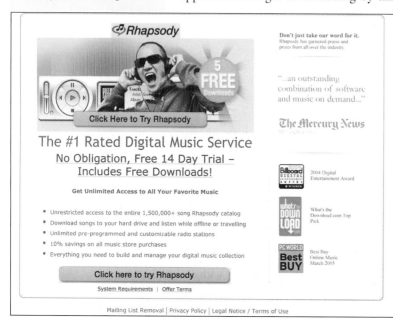

trademarks may be used legally and under what circumstances links to their sites can be made. However, there are many people who see the Internet as an open and unregulated environment and believe that no government or company should be able to control the distribution of information once it reaches the Internet. To combat this problem, most firms will take legal steps, if necessary, to protect their property, including brand names and trademarks, from unauthorized use.

Government Regulation and Taxation

For the most part, government regulators have come to view the Internet as just an extension of regular business activity of firms operating in their jurisdictions. To the extent that online business activities resemble traditional business activities, the same rules and regulations apply whether businesses exist entirely or only partially online. Therefore, when it comes to the collection of sales taxes on products and services sold online, you would think that online firms would be responsible for collecting sales taxes and then remitting them to local and state governments. This is not the case, and although state and local governments are working toward a uniform sales-tax policy for online sales, online vendors are legally treated like mail-order companies, which collect sales taxes only if they have a physical presence in the customer's state. American buyers are expected to pay local *use* taxes on products bought in other states, but the responsibility for paying the use tax is the customer's, not the firm selling a product or service. To help sort out the complex details about where the buyer, store, and warehouses are located and other factors related to the operations of the seller, several states have come together in a cooperative effort referred to as the *Streamlined Sales Tax Project*. To find updates on sales taxation for online sales, visit **www.streamlinedsalestax.org.**

Another area of concern is the sale and distribution of restricted products such as prescription drugs. The Internet allows anyone to obtain medications online and, in some cases, with only a claim to a prescription and a credit card. It is, however, the legal responsibility of the online pharmacist to verify the validity of the order and to look for abusive patterns, such as doctors prescribing unusually large quantities of certain drugs for one patient. Nonetheless, the fact that prescription drugs can be bought online with relatively little difficulty opens the way for drugs being sold in the illicit drug market.

Although it should be emphasized that most firms attempt to ensure that their online activity is fair and legal, the Internet presents a great opportunity for illegal activity in which profit is a major motivator. In the absence of stricter government control, legal and ethical issues in the online environment will become even more pronounced as more firms move their traditional businesses to the Internet.

The Future of e-Business: Growth, Opportunities, and Challenges

Since the beginning of commercial activity on the Internet, developments in e-business have been rapid and formidable with spectacular successes such as eBay, Google, and Yahoo!. However, the slowdown in e-business activity that began in 2000 caused a shakeout of excessive optimism in this new-business environment. By 2003, most firms involved in e-business used a more intelligent approach to development. Today, we can safely say that the long-term view held by the vast majority of analysts is that the Internet will continue to expand along with related technologies. For example, according to Forrester Research, Inc., the popularity and growth of consumer broadband access to the Internet have pushed marketers to allocate more money to advertising online in order to reach customers who are moving to the web and away from traditional media such as television and radio. As a result, Forrester predicts that by 2010, more than $26 billion, or about 8 percent of all advertising spending, will be online.[17]

LEARNING OBJECTIVE
Explore the growth trends, future opportunities, and challenges of e-business.

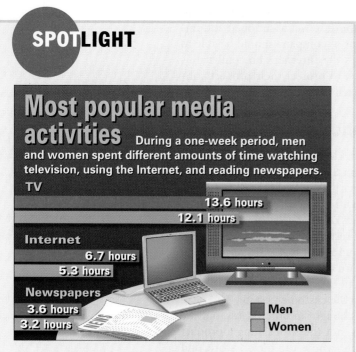
Internet Growth Potential

To date, only a small percentage of the global population uses the Internet. Current estimates suggest that about one billion of the six billion people in the world use the web, and only about 60 percent of them are active users. Clearly, there is much more growth opportunity. Americans comprise 20 percent of all users—the largest group online.[18] Of the almost 300 million people making up the American population, 185 million use the Internet—140 million actively. And more than 40 percent of Americans enjoy fast broadband access at home, suggesting future development of more online activity requiring high-speed service such as downloading entertainment content and games.[19] American men spend about 6.7 hours online, and women, 5.3 hours, each week. Checking e-mail is the reason for going online 90 percent of the time for both men and women, although men also are motivated to check news and look for job and career information, whereas women tend to be more interested in getting movie information, sharing photographs, and playing games. After checking e-mail, searching the web is the second most popular activity because people seem to have developed an interest in exploring a wide variety of topics available through the Internet. Consequently, it should be no surprise that time passed watching television has declined in popularity as Internet use has increased.[20]

The popularity of websites varies depending on the country and the research firm's methodology. Because users' preferences change over time, these ratings, like those of television and radio shows, are meaningful only if they are current. Up-to-date usage statistics, ratings, and rankings are available from firms that perform market research. For example, Nielsen//NetRatings, Inc., reported that Yahoo! was the most popular website brand in February 2005, with about ninety-three million "unique visitors." (A *unique visitor* is a single person who visited at least once during the month; repeat visits by the same person are not counted.) Microsoft followed Yahoo!, with ninety million unique visitors, and MSN ranked third, with eighty-nine million. Other well-known brands followed, including AOL, Google, and eBay.[21]

Even with any future economic downturn, the Internet will continue to offer great opportunities for growth. Firms that adapt existing business models to an online environment will continue to dominate development. Books, CDs, clothing, hotel accommodations, car rentals, and travel reservations are products and services well suited to online buying and selling. These products or services will continue to be sold in the traditional way, as well as in a more cost-effective and efficient fashion over the Internet.

While there are many examples of how the Internet can be used to distribute new and unique products, consider how the Internet is changing the entertainment industry. Use of the Internet to webcast any content that was designed for television and radio is commonplace today, allowing news services such as CNN to reach a global audience 24/7 over the Internet. With the introduction of Apple's iPod technology, a new type of communications called *podcasting* emerged that allows individuals to obtain any form of content from music to lectures for downloading from a website. Then they can listen on MP3 players, such as Apple's iPod. New websites that cater to special-interest areas of podcasting are

@ USING THE INTERNET

What do e-business players read to keep up-to-date on other people, ideas, and trends in the fast-paced world of e-business? Although there has been an information explosion owing to the Internet, the answer is likely to include the following:

Wired: **www.wired.com**

Fast Company: **www.fastcompany.com**

The Industry Standard: **www.thestandard.com**

CNET News: **www.news.com**

ZDNet: **www.zdnet.com**

popping up daily. To get a general understanding of the phenomenon, check out Apple's podcast area located at **www.apple.com/itunes/podcasts/.**

Environmental Forces Affecting e-Business

Although the environmental forces at work are complex, it is useful to think of them as either internal or external forces that affect an e-business. Internal environmental forces are those that are closely associated with the actions and decisions taking place within a firm. As shown in Figure 4.5, typical internal forces include a firm's planning activities, organizational structure, human resources, management decisions, information database, and available financing. For example, a shortage of skilled employees needed for a specialized project can undermine a firm's ability to sell its services to clients. Unlike the external environmental forces affecting the firm, internal forces such as this one are more likely to be under the direct control of management. In this case, management can either hire the needed staff or choose to pass over a prospective project.

In contrast, external environmental forces are factors affecting e-business planning that originate from outside the organization. These forces are unlikely to be controllable by an e-business firm. Instead, managers and employees of an e-business firm generally will react to these forces, attempting to shield the organization from any undue negative effects and finding ways to take advantage of opportunities in the ever-changing e-business environment. The primary external environmental forces affecting e-business planning include globalization, society, demographic, economic, competitive, technological, and political and legal forces.

> ▶▶ **FIGURE 4.5**

INTERNAL AND EXTERNAL FORCES THAT AFFECT AN E-BUSINESS

Today, managers and employees of an e-business must respond to internal forces within the organization and external forces outside the organization.

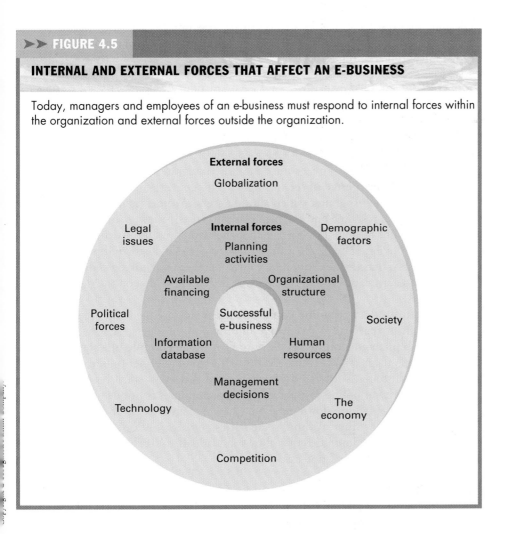

It's a small world after all.
Padmasree Warrior and Anson Chen, two Motorola executives, show off a new cell phone that has all the latest technological features at a press conference in Bangalore, India. Motorola, a leader in telecommunications, realizes that it must manufacture products for a global market: If it doesn't, a competitor will.

No discussion about the future of e-business would be complete without mentioning four specific external forces—globalization, convergence of technologies, online communities, and partnering online—that are already changing e-business firms around the globe.

Globalization
Globalization is currently the focus of a great deal of discussion and debate—and with good reason. For many people, globalization is a positive force that is drawing the people of the world together to live under universally shared standards of culture, communication, technologies, and economics. To others, globalization represents a threat to their national cultures, identities, languages, and even their way of life. Regardless of whether you think globalization is good or bad, the Internet exemplifies globalization because a person with a computer and Internet access in North America, Europe, Africa, or Asia can access information and conduct business online with anyone with similar access anyplace in the world.

Because of globalization, it is not uncommon to find software engineers in India doing programming for American-based firms that are selling products to German customers. Along with this collaboration by workers on the production of globally distributed products and services comes the transfer of business methods used in different parts of the world. In addition, jobs that previously would not have been available to engineers in India or any other nation in the world because of geography, trade barriers, and other restrictive factors are now made accessible because the Internet creates a virtual workplace that allows individuals anywhere to be part of a global network of production and marketing efforts.

convergence of technologies the overlapping of capabilities and the merging of products and services into one fully integrated interactive system

Convergence of Technologies
As webcasting and podcasting illustrate, the borders of telecommunications technologies for electronic distribution of sound, images, and text have become less clear. Today we can send and receive e-mail from pagers, interact with the Internet from a small screen on a cell phone, and even have visually active telephone conversations. This phenomenon of overlapping capabilities and the merging of products and services into one fully integrated interactive system is referred to as the **convergence of technologies.** This convergence is leading the way to interactive television programs, which allow viewers to select their preferences in the way a program is presented and the products advertised. Viewers of a cooking show, for example, might be able to select whether they would prefer instructions for regular or nonfat cooking. The profile of the viewer's personal tastes and preferences can be maintained so that the next time the viewer watches the cooking show, the profile can be entered automatically and the appropriate data provided on the screen.

online communities groups of individuals or firms that want to exchange information, products, or services over the Internet

Online Communities
Online communities, which are made up of groups of individuals or firms that want to exchange information, products, or services over the Internet, are a phenomenon that is likely to grow. One example of a thriving online community is iVillage.com, a commercial site for women. Other online communities include buyers' groups, such as OnVia.com, a site that helps small businesses secure government contracts online. Online learning communities continue to evolve as sites in a wide variety of fields, allowing people who share an interest or concern to communicate with each other. Yahoo!'s Geocities.com is only one portal to a huge selection of online communities that allows individuals to freely create communities for friends, family members, and associates.

Partnering Online
While opportunities for independent e-business effort will continue, online partnerships, which can benefit both large and small firms, are likely to be increasingly common. By playing a role within a larger entity, small firms can

enjoy competitive advantage and increase their market penetration. A review of the major e-business sites, including those of IBM, Microsoft, and Oracle, indicates that the e-business approach taken by these firms involves local smaller-business firms.

Many Internet firms have been able to realize rapid growth through partnerships with smaller firms. For example, Amazon.com pays its website partners a commission on items bought by users whom the partners send to Amazon. Suppose that an online learning community made up of Spanish students and small vendors of related products and services had a link on its web page that takes viewers to Amazon.com. By connecting with Amazon.com, the site can earn revenue and at the same time satisfy users who might not find what they are looking for within the learning community's limited selection. The learning community's range of products thus is extended automatically to the wide selection carried by Amazon, and both Amazon and the learning community benefit.

This chapter has presented an overview of the fast-paced, emerging world of e-business. Throughout this book you will find more e-business references and examples as they apply to the different aspects of business, such as management, marketing, and finance. Chapter 17 covers the more technological side of e-business, focusing on such topics as web pages, software, and the communications system that makes up the Internet. In Chapters 5 and 6 we examine issues related to forms of business ownership and special considerations surrounding small business.

RETURN TO   Inside Business

Netflix serves more than four million subscribers and brings in nearly $50 million in annual rental fees. The firm's website is always adding features to help customers choose movies, rate DVDs they've rented, and see what friends are renting. Once a customer rates a number of movies, Netflix's software analyzes this information and suggests other movies that the customer might enjoy. "If the Starbucks' secret is a smile when you get your latte, ours is that the website adapts to the individual's taste," says the CEO. Personalization works: Fewer than 5 percent of subscribers drop out during a typical three-month period.

Although online DVD rentals are increasingly popular, rental stores are not disappearing. Blockbuster remains a key competitor, and McDonald's is putting Redbox DVD kiosks in hundreds of its restaurants and in other stores to rent movies for $1 per night. So what will Netflix do next? Stay tuned.

Questions

1. Of the questions in Figure 4.4, which do you think might explain Netflix's actions in the online DVD rental business?
2. Of the questions in Figure 4.4, which do you think might explain Wal-Mart's decision to close its online DVD rental business?

➤➤ CHAPTER REVIEW

Summary

1

Explain the meaning of e-business.

e-Business, or electronic business, can be defined as the organized effort of individuals to produce and sell, for a profit, the goods and services that satisfy society's needs *through the facilities available on the Internet.* The term *e-business* refers to all business activities and practices conducted on the Internet by an individual firm or the general concept of e-business. On the other hand, *e-commerce* is a part of e-business; the term refers only to online buying and selling activities. The human, material, information, and financial resources that any business requires are highly specialized for e-business. In an effort to reduce the cost of e-business resources, many firms have turned to outsourcing.

Using e-business activities, it is possible to satisfy new customer needs created by the Internet as well as traditional ones in unique ways. Meeting customer needs is especially important when an e-business is trying to earn profits by increasing sales and reducing expenses. Each source of revenue flowing into the firm is referred to as a *revenue stream.*

2

Explore the basic framework of e-business.

The Internet was conceived originally as an elaborate military communications network that would allow vital messages to be transmitted in the event of war. However, the commercial benefits of the Internet became increasingly obvious. As technology emerged that simplified use of the Internet and allowed the addition of audio, visual, and text data, the new multimedia environment became known as the World Wide Web (or more simply the web).

Most firms involved in e-business fall more or less into one of three primary groups as defined by their e-business activities: (1) telecommunications and computer hardware manufacturers and Internet service providers, which together supply the physical infrastructure of the Internet, (2) producers of Internet software, which provide users with the ability to do things on the Internet, and (3) online sellers and content providers. The Internet still would be limited to communication between individuals and among groups of special-interest researchers were it not for the activity of online sellers and content producers. In this area of e-business we have just begun to see the development of online strategies for reaching out to existing and new customers. The special characteristics of e-business provide increased opportunity for firms to reach global markets and for small businesses to start up and grow.

3

Describe the fundamental models of e-business.

e-Business models focus attention on the identity of a firm's customers. Firms that use the Internet mainly to conduct business with other businesses generally are referred to as having a business-to-business, or B2B, model. Currently, the vast majority of e-business is B2B in nature. When examining B2B business firms, two clear types emerge. In the first type of B2B, the focus is simply on facilitating sales transactions between businesses. A second, more complex type of the B2B model involves a company and its suppliers. In contrast to the focus of the B2B model, firms such as Amazon and eBay clearly are focused on individual buyers and so are referred to as having a business-to-consumer, or B2C, model. In a B2C situation, understanding how consumers behave online is critical to the firm's success. And successful B2C firms often make a special effort to build long-term relationships with their customers. While B2B and B2C models are the most popular e-business models, there are other models that perform specialized e-business activities to generate revenues (see Table 4.2).

4

Understand the factors that influence an e-business plan.

The approach taken to creating an e-business plan will depend on whether you are establishing a new Internet business or adding an online component to an existing business. For a new Internet business, a good e-business plan should provide detailed answers to basic questions about potential customers and their needs. Once the answers and initial research have been completed, it is time to choose a business model. Options include the B2B model, the B2C model, or one of the specialized models.

It is also quite common for an existing business to add e-business activities. A business that already has a physical location and a customer base generally looks at e-business as a way to expand sales to current customers and to add new customers who are beyond the reach of the firm's geographic location. Although developing an online presence may seem like a logical extension of what the firm already does, there are important factors that must be considered before using the Internet to sell products or services or to provide information to customers. These factors include determining if online customers are really different from traditional customers, how e-business can help traditional business activities, and complexity and time concerns when implementing new e-business activities.

5

Discuss the social and legal concerns of e-business.

The social and legal concerns of an e-business extend beyond those shared by all businesses. e-Businesses must deal with the special circumstances of operating in a new frontier—one without borders and with limited control by government or any other organization. As a result, consumers, businesses, and the government are all learning how to deal with issues related to ethics, social responsibility, privacy, confidentiality, security, cybercrime, digital property and copyright concerns, and government regulation and taxation.

6

Explore the growth trends, future opportunities, and challenges of e-business.

Since the advent of commercial activity on the Internet, developments in e-business have been rapid and formidable. Clearly, the slowdown in e-business activity that began in 2000 caused a shakeout of excessive optimism in this new-business environment. By 2003, most firms involved in e-business used a more intelligent approach to development. Still, the long-term view held by the vast majority of analysts is that the Internet will continue to expand along with related technologies. Although the environmental forces at work are complex, it is useful to think of them as either internal or external forces that affect an e-business. Internal environmental forces are those that are closely associated with the actions and decisions taking place within a firm. In contrast, external environmental forces are those factors affecting an e-business originating outside an organization. No discussion about the future of e-business would be complete without mentioning four specific external forces—globalization, convergence of technologies, online communities, and partnering online—that are already changing e-business firms around the globe.

Key Terms

You should now be able to define and give an example relevant to each of the following terms:

e-business (electronic business) (116)
e-commerce (116)
outsourcing (117)
revenue stream (118)
World Wide Web (the web) (120)
digitized (120)
Internet service providers (ISPs) (121)
customer relationship management (CRM) software (122)
supply-chain management (SCM) software (122)
e-zines (124)
business model (125)
business-to-business (B2B) model (125)

business-to-consumer (B2C) model (126)
cookie (130)
log-file records (130)
data mining (130)
computer viruses (131)
spamming (131)
secure electronic transaction (SET) (132)
copyright (132)
convergence of technologies (136)
online communities (136)

Review Questions

1. What are four major factors contained in the definition of e-business?
2. How does e-business differ from e-commerce?
3. How do e-businesses generate revenue streams?
4. What roles do telecommunications firms and Internet service providers play in e-business?
5. How do software producers contribute to e-business?
6. What does the term *content providers* mean?
7. Why does e-business represent a global opportunity to reach customers?
8. How can small businesses use the Internet to increase sales?
9. What are the two fundamental e-business models?
10. What concerns should be considered when creating an e-business plan?
11. Give an example of an unethical use of the Internet by a business or an individual.
12. What has been the general level of involvement of governments in e-business to date?
13. What is the difference between internal and external forces that affect an e-business? How do they change the way an e-business operates?
14. What does *convergence of technologies* mean?
15. What are online communities?
16. How can partnering with other e-businesses help firms to compete on the Internet?

Discussion Questions

1. Can advertising provide enough revenue for an e-business to succeed in the long run?
2. Is outsourcing good for an e-business firm? the firm's employees? Explain your answer.
3. What distinguishes the B2B and B2C e-business models?
4. How would planning differ for starting a new Internet business when compared with adding an e-business component to an existing business?
5. Pick two or three specific social, ethical, and legal issues facing e-business and discuss how they affect Internet users. From the standpoint of an e-business, how should these same issues be resolved?
6. Discuss the role of government and regulatory agencies in e-business.
7. Do you think that the Internet will continue to grow as fast as it has in the past? Why?

►► VIDEO CASE 4.1

Travelocity Takes e-Business a Long Way

One of the original online travel agency sites, Travelocity, has been bookmarked by millions of people seeking low prices on airline tickets, hotel rooms, cruises, and rental cars. The site books $5 billion worth of travel annually to destinations near and far. Customers can search for flights on six major carriers, read descriptions before reserving at one of 20,000 participating hotels, compare car-rental prices, and click to browse and buy specially priced travel packages.

Travelocity began its e-business life as a site for finding the lowest airfares. However, Jeff Glueck, its chief marketing officer, notes that the company actually makes its money on hotel rooms and travel packages, not on airline tickets. This is why the site goes beyond emphasizing price to feature vacation packages and hotel choices more prominently—a change that has increased sales of these lucrative offerings dramatically.

Intense competition from Expedia and other online rivals has prompted Travelocity to find new ways of differentiating itself and keeping customers loyal. CEO Michelle Peluso says that the company is particularly interested in crating "an emotional connection with customers, one that builds more trust and bookings." Instead of focusing solely on low prices, Travelocity has invested $80 million in its "Roaming Gnome" multimedia ad campaign. The colorful garden gnome attracts attention in a crowded marketplace. It also brings personality and humor to the message that Travelocity stands for the whole travel experience, not just low prices.

In addition, the site has posted a Customer Bill of Rights guaranteeing customers that "everything about your booking will be right, or we'll work with our partners to make it right and right away." Although many e-businesses offer customer service by live chat, e-mail, and FAQ (frequently asked questions) pages, Travelocity encourages customers to call if something goes wrong with their travel arrangements so that company representatives can fix the problem. Peluso observes that customers whose problems are resolved satisfactorily have a 90 percent return rate, compared with an 80 percent rate for customers who have a good experience.

Not long ago, Travelocity had the opportunity to put the spotlight on its guarantee when it posted a superlow airfare for flights to Fiji. The rock-bottom price was supposed to apply to companion tickets only, but because the fare was posted in error, travelers were unsure initially whether Travelocity really would issue the tickets. The company decided to honor the fare, despite the mistake, to prove its commitment to taking care of customers. This brought a lot of positive media coverage, further enhancing Travelocity's reputation.

The company recently redesigned its website so that customers can find exactly what they want and have more tools for planning all aspects of a trip. For example, customers can buy tickets to city tours, price travel insurance, buy gift certificates, check flight status, read about different destinations, and read what travelers have to say about the hotels.

Before making major changes to the site, Travelocity conducts usability testing to see how customers react to new features and to uncover problems customers might encounter when trying to buy. For example, the company learned that many people forgot their passwords and clicked away at the last minute because they needed the password to complete a purchase. To solve this problem, Travelocity removed the requirement and allowed customers to buy without inputting a password. Sales soared by 10 percent almost overnight, increasing revenue by millions of dollars.

Travelocity operates a number of other travel sites, including holidayautos.com, lastminute.com, showtickets.com, and site59.com. The company has been branching out into corporate travel services and specialized travel sites for international markets. It also provides travel services for the members of AARP and other organizations. Where in the world will Travelocity's Roaming Gnome turn up next?[22]

For more information about this company, go to **www.travelocity.com**.

Questions

1. Each year Travelocity helps millions of customers find low prices on airline tickets, hotel rooms, cruises, and rental cars by providing a website that is easy to use. What type of business model is Travelocity using? Support your answer.
2. Today, competition between Internet travel firms such as Travelocity, Expedia, and other online travel agencies has never been greater. What steps has Travelocity taken to retain its market share and increase revenues and profits?
3. Why would Travelocity publicize the availability of telephone customer service when higher call volume raises the company's costs?
4. AARP, an association for consumers over 50 years old, has partnered with Travelocity to offer travel services to members through a site called "AARP Passport powered by Travelocity." From Travelocity's perspective, what are the pros and cons of having both the AARP and the Travelocity name on this travel site?

➤➤ CASE 4.2

Countrywide Plans for "Clicks and Bricks"

As online lending transforms the home-mortgage business, Countrywide Financial Corp. is leading the way by combining electronic efficiency with personal service. Banks such as Wells Fargo and Washington Mutual traditionally have used their branch networks as a springboard to lending money for home ownership. As Internet usage spread to more households, specialized sites drew the attention of consumers seeking the convenience of shopping for a mortgage from home or office. Now Countrywide, founded as a mortgage company in 1969, has leapfrogged the banks and mortgage sites to become the country's biggest home-mortgage lender, thanks in part to its e-business productivity.

Countrywide was barely a year old when cofounders Angelo Mozilo and David Loeb moved their headquarters from New York to take advantage of the home-construction boom in suburban Los Angeles. At the time, Countrywide offered only two types of mortgages; today, it offers nearly 200 types to accommodate the needs of home buyers in small and large communities alike. To remain competitive with the major banks, the company has always put a premium on efficiency. In the 1980s, it pioneered the use of PCs to service its fast-growing mortgage volume. In the 1990s, it replaced the mountain of paperwork needed to apply for a mortgage with a completely electronic process, slashing the application time to just a few minutes.

The Internet has increased the pressure on Countrywide—and helped it become even more productive without sacrificing personal service. Since early in the Internet age, specialized brokerage e-business sites such as LendingTree.com have put the spotlight on lenders competing for the consumer's business. That's when Countrywide decided "that the Internet was a channel for doing business, not the be-all and end-all," says Richard Jones, chief technology officer. "We thought that 'clicks and bricks' was the answer."

In line with this approach, Countrywide developed its e-business to supplement its national network of loan offices and call centers. Over time, it expanded its online presence to include credit-education materials, mortgage descriptions, interest-rate data, application processing updates, account information, and links to mortgage-related sites and services. By 2000, Countrywide was receiving 18 percent of its applications online.

Now the company operates more than 100 sites for consumers and 150 for employees. Prospective home owners can take their time browsing for mortgage and insurance products; current customers can quickly and easily set up electronic mortgage payments, check loan balances, and find out about other Countrywide services. When people need a mortgage, they have the option of applying online (which takes about 10 minutes), calling toll-free, sending an e-mail, or visiting a Countrywide office. Those who apply online receive a follow-up call from a Countrywide mortgage expert, who stays in touch to keep customers informed at every step of the process.

This "clicks and bricks" model allows the company to combine paperless efficiency with personal service. Because mortgage loans are complex and involve a significant amount of money, the majority of Countrywide's mortgage applications still come in by phone or through an office, not via the web. However, because of the information and services available online, Countrywide's websites receive nearly 1.5 million hits per month.

As the number-one U.S. mortgage company, Countrywide has assets totaling $104 billion. And because of its competitive rates and home mortgage options, one out of every eight U.S. home owners with a mortgage does business with Countrywide. Not content to maintain the status quo, the company aims to double its market share by 2010. Its "clicks and bricks" strategy is clearly paying off in productivity and profitability.[23]

For more information about this company, go to **www.countrywide.com**.

Questions

1. Improving efficiency improves Countrywide's bottom line. What are the advantages and disadvantages of offering customers inducements to apply online?
2. Why would Countrywide not want to participate in a brokerage e-business site that brings multiple lenders together with prospective borrowers?
3. How do you think the complexity of mortgage loans affected Countrywide's decision to pursue a "clicks and bricks" strategy?
4. What would you do to help Countrywide compete even more effectively with specialized mortgage websites such as LendingTree.com?

→ CHAPTER 4: JOURNAL EXERCISE

Discovery statement: Today, more and more people use the Internet to purchase products or services. And yet, many people are reluctant to make online purchases because of identity and privacy issues. Still others are "afraid" of the technology.

Have you ever used the Internet to purchase a product or service? _____ Yes _____ No

If you answered yes, why did you purchase on-line as compared with purchasing the same product or service in a traditional retail store?

_____

_____

_____

_____

_____

In your own words, describe whether the on-line shopping experience was a pleasant one. What factors contributed to your level of satisfaction or dissatisfaction?

_____

_____

_____

_____

_____

If you answered no, describe why you prefer to shop in a traditional retail store as compared with shopping on the web.

_____

_____

_____

_____

_____

BUILDING SKILLS FOR CAREER SUCCESS

1. Exploring the Internet

To thrive, all websites need visitors. Without the revenue that comes from firms that buy banner advertising on websites or the subscription fees paid by viewers, the necessary cash to create, maintain, and grow simply would not exist. What attracts viewers varies according to their lifestyle, age, gender, and information requirements. Many online communities focus on the interests of a selected target audience. MarthaStewart.com and iVillage.com are two well-known sites catering mostly to college-educated women interested in leisure, parenting, business, nutrition, and the like. However, these are only two sites in a sea of choices. Visit the text website for updates to this exercise.

Assignment

1. Identify and describe two or more websites with content that attracts you and keeps you returning on a regular basis.
2. How would you describe the target audience for these sites?
3. What advertisements are typically displayed?

2. Developing Critical-Thinking Skills

Although the variety of products available to online shoppers is growing quickly, many people are reluctant to make purchases over the Internet. For a variety of reasons, some individuals are uncomfortable with using the Internet for this purpose, whereas others do so easily and often. The considerations involved in making a B2B purchase decision differ from those involved in making a personal purchase. However, the experience of buying office supplies from Staples.com for a business might influence an individual to visit other online sites to shop for personal items.

Assignment

1. Which sorts of products or services do you think would be easy to sell online? What kinds of things do you think would be difficult to purchase online? Explain your thinking.
2. Have you ever purchased anything over the Internet? Explain why you have or have not.
3. Explain how the considerations involved in buying office supplies from Staples.com for a business might differ from those involved in making a personal purchase.

3. Building Team Skills

An interesting approach taken by Yahoo.com and several other websites is to provide viewers with the tools needed to create a personal web page or community. Yahoo's GeoCities site (**http://geocities.yahoo.com**) provides simple instructions for creating a site and posting your own content, such as articles and photographs.

Assignment

1. Working in a group, examine some of the GeoCities communities and personal web pages. Discuss which sites you think work well and which do not. Explain your reasoning.
2. Develop an idea for your own website. Draw a sketch of how you would like the site to appear on the Internet. You may use ideas that look good on other personal pages.
3. Who is your target audience, and why do you think they will want to visit the site?

4. Researching Different Careers

The Internet offers a wide assortment of career opportunities in business, as well as in Internet-related technologies. As firms seek opportunities online, new e-businesses are springing up every day. In many cases these firms want people with a fresh outlook on how e-business can succeed, and they prefer individuals without preconceived notions about how to proceed. Website managers, designers, creative artists, and content specialists are just a few of the positions available. Many large online job sites, such as Monster.com, can help you to find out about employment opportunities in e-business and the special skills required for various jobs.

Assignment

1. Identify a website that provides information about careers in e-business.
2. Summarize the positions that appear to be in high demand in e-business.
3. What are some of the special skills required to fill these jobs?
4. What salaries and benefits typically are associated with these positions?
5. Which job seems most appealing to you personally? Why?

5. Improving Communication Skills

Describing websites in summary form can be difficult because of the mix of information involved. A useful exercise is to create a table that can serve not only as an organizational tool for the information but also as a means of quick comparison.

Assignment

1. Create a table that will compare seven websites you have visited. Place the title of one type of information at the head of each column. For example, you might start with the firm's name in the first column, the type of product or service it sells online in the second column, and so forth.
2. Enter short descriptive data in each column.
3. Write a descriptive summary of the table you have prepared identifying a few of the outstanding characteristics listed in the data.

→ PREP TEST

Matching Questions

___ 1. All business activities that are conducted on the Internet.

___ 2. Small online magazines that bring customers a wide selection of information.

___ 3. It provides the legal right to control content ownership.

___ 4. The activities of Internet users can be tracked by a piece of software.

___ 5. Its focus is to facilitate sales transactions between businesses.

___ 6. Amazon.com makes a special effort to build long-term relationships with its customers.

___ 7. It is an encryption process that prevents merchants from seeing transactions.

___ 8. A practice of searching data records for useful information.

___ 9. It is predicted to lead to interactive television programs.

___ 10. Connections to the Internet are provided.

a. business-to-business model

b. business-to-consumer model

c. convergence of technologies

d. cookie

e. copyright

f. data mining

g. e-business

h. e-zines

i. Internet service providers (ISPs)

j. secure electronic transaction (SET)

True/False Questions

T F

11. ○ ○ Intelligent information systems generate sales revenue for Internet firms.

12. ○ ○ Companies such as SprintPCS reduce their expenses by offering product information online.

13. ○ ○ Netscape Communicator is the dominant browser.

14. ○ ○ The ability to customize content for individual customer's needs makes the Internet an adaptable tool for global enterprise.

15. ○ ○ Regardless if you are creating a completely new e-business or adding an online component to an existing business, planning is the same.

16. ○ ○ Computerized tracking of users connected to the Internet is an accepted socially responsibile activity of an Internet retailer.

T F

17. ○ ○ Special government rules and regulations apply to business activities conducted online versus traditional business activities.

18. ○ ○ The most exciting prospect for businesses and customers is not the creation of new and unique products and services but the conversion of existing processes to e-business processes.

19. ○ ○ The Internet creates a virtual workplace.

20. ○ ○ Many Internet firms have found it unprofitable to partner with smaller firms.

Multiple-Choice Questions

21. The Exciting Lighting Company is a successful company that has a good physical location and an excellent customer base of consumers and builders. It has just gone online with its products. What does this company expect to gain from its e-commerce activities?
    a. Expand sales to current customers
    b. Add new customers beyond the local geographic area
    c. Provide information on its products
    d. Render faster customer service
    e. All the above

22. A customer tracking system is an example of e-business _____ resources.
    a. human
    b. informational
    c. material
    d. financial
    e. specialized

23. Google provides a service to Internet users. If it is to survive, it must create an e-business revenue stream. How can Google do this?
    a. Sell products online
    b. Place advertising on web pages
    c. Charge subscription fees for access to some online services
    d. Sell services over the Internet
    e. All the above

24. Supply-chain management (SCM) software allows manufacturers to
    a. increase inventories.
    b. extend delivery schedules.
    c. reduce cost.
    d. maintain productivity.
    e. standardize errors.

25. Groups of individuals or firms that want to exchange information, products, or services over the Internet are
    a. partnerships.
    b. online communities.
    c. cookies.
    d. e-zines.
    e. business models.

Fill-in-the-Blank Questions

26. The Internet's multimedia environment of audio, visual, and text data is known as the _____.

27. Data converted to a signal that computers and telecommunications equipment can understand have been _____.

28. Software codes designed to disrupt normal computer operations are computer _____.

29. Records that store the websites visited by employees are called _____ records.

30. The _____ management software focuses on improving communications between suppliers and users of materials and components.

Online Study Center

FOR MORE **test practice, use the interactive ACE quizzes available at the Online Student Center:**
www.college.hmco.com/PIC/pridebusiness9e.

Answers on p. PT1.

Choosing a Form of Business Ownership

LEARNING OBJECTIVES

WHAT you will be able to do once you complete this chapter:

1 Describe the advantages and disadvantages of sole proprietorships.

2 Explain the different types of partners and the importance of partnership agreements.

3 Describe the advantages and disadvantages of partnerships.

4 Summarize how a corporation is formed.

5 Describe the advantages and disadvantages of a corporation.

6 Examine special types of corporations, including S-corporations, limited-liability companies, government-owned corporations, and not-for-profit corporations.

7 Discuss the purpose of a cooperative, joint venture, and syndicate.

8 Explain how growth from within and growth through mergers can enable a business to expand.

WHY this chapter matters

There's a good chance that during your lifetime you will work for a business or even start your own business. With this fact in mind, the material in this chapter can help you to understand how and why businesses are organized and how you can become a successful employee or entrepreneur.

FOR HELP with studying this chapter, visit the Online Student Center:

www.college.hmco.com/PIC/pridebusiness9e

Online Study Center

From light bulbs and locomotives to pumps and plastics, General Electric (GE) has achieved spectacular growth in its more than 100 years as a corporation. Born from the 1892 merger of Edison General Electric and the Thomson-Houston Electric Company, GE originally emphasized the manufacture and sale of Thomas A. Edison's many inventions. Today, the Connecticut-based firm generates more than $152 billion in annual revenue, nearly half from foreign operations.

GE is already one of the largest corporations in the United States, yet it must keep growing to meet the investment expectations of the 5 million stockholders who fund its activities through their ownership of the company's 10.6 billion outstanding shares. In the march toward profitable growth, GE businesses have produced engines for jet planes, developed monitoring systems to track the health of astronauts in space, and made movies and programs to entertain millions of people around the world. The company provides business and consumer credit programs of all

DID YOU KNOW?

Today it's common to hear of profitable companies. It is less common to hear of profitable companies that are held in high regard by their competitors. And yet, General Electric has managed to do both—earn both profits and respect.

types and also works with scientists to identify promising medical breakthroughs.

Growth is, in fact, one of CEO Jeffrey Immelt's top four priorities. Another priority is execution, which means successfully translating growth plans into action. A third priority is hiring and training the right people for the right jobs. Because the work force of 300,000 employees includes talented experts skilled in managing each of the businesses that make up the GE family, the corporation is better positioned for execution and growth.

The fourth priority is good corporate citizenship. Immelt recognizes that the best employees want to work for "a company that's doing great things in the world." Given GE's enormous size and global reach, the company can make a real difference in areas such as environmental protection—and that's why it is always feeling pressure to do even more. How will GE face these challenges in its second century?[1]

For more information about this company, go to **www.ge.com**.

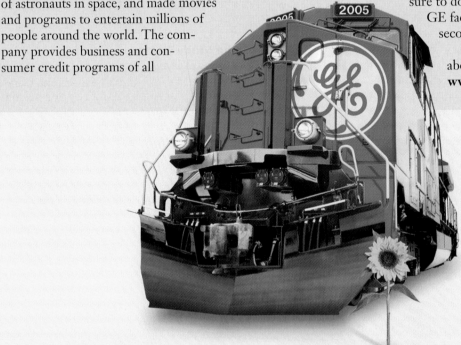

While most of us think of General Electric (or simply GE) as the corporation that manufactures light bulbs, it is so much more. Consider three facts about this global giant. First, it is a corporation. GE chose the corporate form of ownership because it offers a number of advantages when compared with other forms of ownership. We'll discuss each of the major forms of ownership in this chapter. Second, GE is profitable. While some would-be business owners think that if they incorporate, their business will automatically be profitable, the fact is that there's more to earning a profit than the type of ownership you choose. In today's competitive business world, any corporation, sole proprietorship, *or* partnership must produce products and services that customers want. Finally, GE is a good corporate citizen. The company is committed to giving back resources to the communities in which it operates. In today's competitive environment, it's common to hear of profitable companies. It is less common to hear of profitable companies that are held in high regard by their competitors. And yet, GE has managed to do both—earn both profits and respect.

Many people dream of opening a business, and one of the first decisions they must make is what form of ownership to choose. We begin this chapter by describing the three common forms of business ownership: sole proprietorships, partnerships, and corporations. We discuss how these types of businesses are formed and note the advantages and disadvantages of each. Next, we consider several types of business ownership usually chosen for special purposes, including S-corporations, limited-liability companies, government-owned corporations, not-for-profit corporations, cooperatives, joint ventures, and syndicates. We conclude the chapter with a discussion of how businesses can grow through internal expansion or through mergers with other companies.

Sole Proprietorships

A **sole proprietorship** is a business that is owned (and usually operated) by one person. Although a few sole proprietorships are large and have many employees, most are small. Sole proprietorship is the simplest form of business ownership and the easiest to start. In most instances, the owner (the *sole* proprietor) simply decides that he or she is in business and begins operations. Some of today's largest corporations, including Ford Motor Company, H.J. Heinz Company, and J.C. Penney Company, started out as tiny—and in many cases, struggling—sole proprietorships.

As you can see in Figure 5.1, there are more than 18.3 million sole proprietorships in the United States. They account for 71.6 percent of the country's business firms. Although the most popular form of ownership when compared with partnerships and corporations, they rank last in total sales revenues. As shown in Figure 5.2, sole proprietorships account for just over $1 trillion, or about 4.4 percent, of total sales.

Sole proprietorships are most common in retailing, service, and agriculture. Thus the clothing boutique, corner grocery, television-repair shop down the street, and small, independent farmer are likely to be sole proprietorships. In addition to more traditional sole proprietorships, many entrepreneurs have started their own consulting services firms. Not only can they pick and choose which job assignments to accept, but they also have found that they can earn more money by not working exclusively for one firm as a salaried employee.

Advantages of Sole Proprietorships

Most of the advantages of sole proprietorships arise from the two main characteristics of this form of ownership: simplicity and individual control.

Ease of Start-up and Closure Sole proprietorship is the simplest and cheapest way to start a business. Often, start-up requires no contracts, agreements, or other legal documents. Thus a sole proprietorship can be, and most often is, established

1 LEARNING OBJECTIVE
Describe the advantages and disadvantages of sole proprietorships.

sole proprietorship a business that is owned (and usually operated) by one person

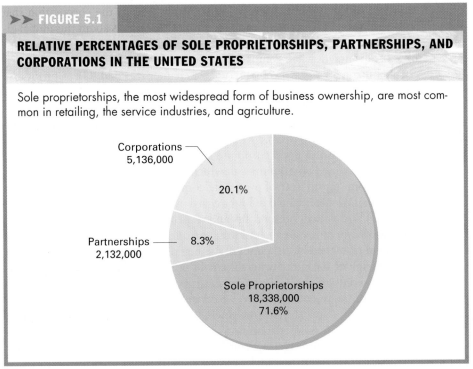

>> FIGURE 5.1

RELATIVE PERCENTAGES OF SOLE PROPRIETORSHIPS, PARTNERSHIPS, AND CORPORATIONS IN THE UNITED STATES

Sole proprietorships, the most widespread form of business ownership, are most common in retailing, the service industries, and agriculture.

Corporations
5,136,000

20.1%

Partnerships
2,132,000

8.3%

Sole Proprietorships
18,338,000
71.6%

Source: U.S. Bureau of the Census, *Statistical Abstract of the United States*, 124th ed., Washington, D.C., 2004, p. 484 (**www.census.gov**).

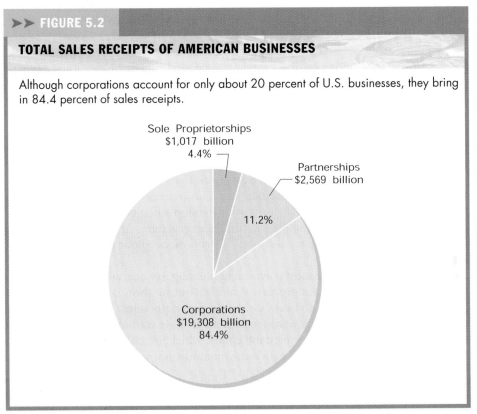

>> FIGURE 5.2

TOTAL SALES RECEIPTS OF AMERICAN BUSINESSES

Although corporations account for only about 20 percent of U.S. businesses, they bring in 84.4 percent of sales receipts.

Sole Proprietorships
$1,017 billion
4.4%

Partnerships
$2,569 billion

11.2%

Corporations
$19,308 billion
84.4%

Source: U.S. Bureau of the Census, *Statistical Abstract of the United States*, 124th ed., Washington, D.C. 2004, p. 484 (**www.census.gov**).

without the services of an attorney. The legal requirements often are limited to registering the name of the business and obtaining any necessary licenses or permits.

If the enterprise does not succeed, the firm can be closed as easily as it was opened. Creditors must be paid, of course, but generally, the owner does not have to go through any legal procedure before hanging up an "Out of Business" sign.

Pride of Ownership

A successful sole proprietor is often very proud of her or his accomplishments—and rightfully so. In almost every case the owner deserves a great deal of credit for assuming the risks and solving the day-to-day problems associated with operating sole proprietorships. Unfortunately, the reverse is also true. When the business fails, it is often the sole proprietor who is to blame.

Retention of All Profits

Because all profits become the personal earnings of the owner, the owner has a strong incentive to succeed. This direct financial reward attracts many entrepreneurs to the sole proprietorship form of business and, if the business succeeds, is a source of great satisfaction.

Flexibility of Being Your Own Boss

A sole proprietor is completely free to make decisions about the firm's operations. Without asking or waiting for anyone's approval, a sole proprietor can switch from retailing to wholesaling, move a shop's location, open a new store, or close an old one. Suppose that the sole proprietor of an appliance store finds that many customers now prefer to shop on Sunday afternoons. He or she can make an immediate change in business hours to take advantage of this information (provided that state laws allow such stores to open on Sunday). The manager of a store in a large corporate chain such as Best Buy Company or Circuit City may have to seek the approval of numerous managers and company officials before making such a change.

No Special Taxes

Profits earned by a sole proprietorship are taxed as the personal income of the owner. As a result, sole proprietors must report certain financial information on their personal tax returns and make estimated quarterly tax payments to the federal government. Thus a sole proprietorship does not pay the special state and federal income taxes that corporations pay.

Profits for proprietors

As a reward for taking the risks of opening a business, proprietors receive profits. The amounts below are for all proprietors.

In billions of dollars

$797.7

$938.7

2002   Today

Source: The U.S. Department of Commerce and the Bureau of Economic Analysis. Website: **www.bea.gov**; accessed May 2, 2006.

Disadvantages of Sole Proprietorships

The disadvantages of a sole proprietorship stem from the fact that these businesses are owned by one person. Some capable sole proprietors experience no problems. Individuals who start out with few management skills and little money are most at risk for failure.

Unlimited Liability

Unlimited liability is a legal concept that holds a business owner personally responsible for all the debts of the business. There is legally no difference between the debts of the business and the debts of the proprietor. If the business fails, or if the business is involved in a lawsuit and loses, the owner's personal property—including savings and other assets—can be seized (and sold if necessary) to pay creditors.

Unlimited liability is perhaps the major factor that tends to discourage would-be entrepreneurs with substantial personal wealth from using this form of business organization.

unlimited liability a legal concept that holds a business owner personally responsible for all the debts of the business

Lack of Continuity

Legally, the sole proprietor *is* the business. If the owner retires, dies, or is declared legally incompetent, the business essentially ceases to exist. In many cases, however—especially when the business is a profitable enterprise—the owner's

Once a sole proprietor, now a corporation. Ayisha Bennett began her career as a fashion designer as a sole proprietorship. Now, after phenomenal success designing clothing that is not only trend setting, but also soft and comfortable, her company, Envi, is incorporated.

heirs take it over and either sell it or continue to operate it. The business also can suffer if the sole proprietor becomes ill and cannot work for an extended period of time. If the owner, for example, has a heart attack, there is often no one who can step in and manage the business. An illness can be devastating if the sole proprietor's personal skills are what determine if the business is a success or a failure.

Lack of Money Banks, suppliers, and other lenders usually are unwilling to lend large sums of money to sole proprietorships. Only one person—the sole proprietor—can be held responsible for repaying such loans, and the assets of most sole proprietors usually are limited. Moreover, these assets may have been used already as the basis for personal borrowing (a home mortgage or car loan) or for short-term credit from suppliers. Lenders also worry about the lack of continuity of sole proprietorships: Who will repay a loan if the sole proprietor dies? Finally, many lenders are concerned about the large number of sole proprietorships that fail—a topic discussed in Chapter 6.

The limited ability to borrow money can prevent a sole proprietorship from growing. It is the main reason that many business owners, when in need of relatively large amounts of capital, change from a sole proprietorship to a partnership or corporate form of ownership.

Limited Management Skills The sole proprietor is often the sole manager—in addition to being the only salesperson, buyer, accountant, and on occasion, janitor. Even the most experienced business owner is unlikely to have expertise in all these areas. Consequently, unless he or she obtains the necessary expertise by hiring employees, assistants, or consultants, the business can suffer in the areas in which the owner is less knowledgeable. For the many sole proprietors who cannot hire the help they need, there just are not enough hours in the day to do everything that needs to be done.

Difficulty in Hiring Employees The sole proprietor may find it hard to attract and keep competent help. Potential employees may feel that there is no room for advancement in a firm whose owner assumes all managerial responsibilities. And when those who *are* hired are ready to take on added responsibility, they may find that the only way to do so is to quit the sole proprietorship and go to work for a larger firm or start up their own businesses. The lure of higher salaries and increased benefits (especially hospitalization) also may cause existing employees to change jobs.

Beyond the Sole Proprietorship

Like many others, you may decide that the major disadvantage of a sole proprietorship is the limited amount that one person can do in a workday. One way to reduce the effect of this disadvantage (and retain many of the advantages) is to have more than one owner.

2 LEARNING OBJECTIVE
Explain the different types of partners and the importance of partnership agreements.

partnership a voluntary association of two or more persons to act as co-owners of a business for profit

Partnerships

A person who would not think of starting and running a business alone may enthusiastically seize the opportunity to enter into a business partnership. The U.S. Uniform Partnership Act defines a **partnership** as a voluntary association of two or more persons to act as co-owners of a business for profit. For example, in 1990, two young African-American entrepreneurs named Janet Smith and Gary Smith started Ivy Planning Group—a company that provides strategic planning and performance measurement for clients. Today, more than 15 years later, the company has evolved into a multimillion-dollar company that has hired a diverse staff of employees and provides cultural diversity training for *Fortune* 500 firms and federal government agencies. In recognition of its efforts, Ivy Planning Group has been honored by DiversityBusiness.com as one of the top 50 minority-owned companies and by *Black Enterprise* and *Working Woman* magazines. And Ms Smith was named "1 of 50 Most Influential Minorities in Business" by Minority Business and Professionals Network.[2]

As shown in Figures 5.1 and 5.2, there are approximately 2.1 million partnerships in the United States, and this type of ownership accounts for about $2.6 trillion in sales receipts each year. Note, however, that this form of ownership is much less common than the sole proprietorship or the corporation. In fact, as Figure 5.1 shows, partnerships represent only about 8 percent of all American businesses. Although there is no legal maximum on the number of partners a partnership may have, most have only two. Large accounting, law, and advertising partnerships, however, are likely to have multiple partners. Regardless of the number of people involved, a partnership often represents a pooling of special managerial skills and talents; at other times, it is the result of a sole proprietor's taking on a partner for the purpose of obtaining more capital.

Types of Partners

All partners are not necessarily equal. Some may be active in running the business, whereas others may have a limited role.

General Partners

A **general partner** is a person who assumes full or shared responsibility for operating a business. General partners are active in day-to-day business operations, and each partner can enter into contracts on behalf of the other partners. He or she also assumes unlimited liability for all debts, including debts incurred by any other general partner without his or her knowledge or consent. A **general partnership** is a business co-owned by two or more general partners who are liable for everything the business does. To avoid future liability, a general partner who withdraws from the partnership must give notice to creditors, customers, and suppliers.

general partner a person who assumes full or shared responsibility for operating a business

general partnership a business co-owned by two or more general partners who are liable for everything the business does

Limited Partners

A **limited partner** is a person who contributes capital to a business but who has no management responsibility or liability for losses beyond his or her investment in the partnership. A **limited partnership** is a business co-owned by one or more general partners who manage the business and limited partners who invest money in it. Limited partnerships may be formed to finance real estate, oil and gas, motion-picture, and other business ventures. Typically, the general partner or partners collect management fees and receive a percentage of profits. Limited partners receive a portion of profits and tax benefits.

limited partner a person who contributes capital to a business but has no management responsibility or liability for losses beyond the amount he or she invested in the partnership

Because of potential liability problems, special rules apply to limited partnerships. These rules are intended to protect customers and creditors who deal with limited partnerships. For example, prospective partners in a limited partnership must file a formal declaration, usually with the secretary of state or at their county courthouse, that describes the essential details of the partnership and the liability status of each partner involved in the business. At least one general partner must be responsible for the debts of the limited partnership. Also, some states prohibit the use of the limited partner's name in the partnership's name.

limited partnership a business co-owned by one or more general partners who manage the business and limited partners who invest money in it

A special type of limited partnership is referred to as a *master limited partnership*. A **master limited partnership (MLP)** (sometimes referred to as a *publicly traded partnership*, or PTP) is a business partnership that is owned and managed like a corporation but often taxed like a partnership. This special ownership arrangement has a major advantage: Units of ownership in MLPs can be sold to investors to raise capital and often are traded on organized security exchanges. Because MLP units can be traded on an exchange, investors can sell their units of ownership at any time, hopefully for a profit. For more information on MLPs, visit the Coalition of Publicly

master limited partnership (MLP) a business partnership that is owned and managed like a corporation but often taxed like a partnership

Two people with one goal. When Angela Craig and Al Brent created B.A. Kid, they had one goal in mind: Create an online retail store that sells educational and fun toys for kids of all ages. Because of their commitment and their ability to agree on major business issues, the website **www.bakid.com** is now successful, reaching customers around the globe.

Traded Partnerships website at **www .ptpcoalition.org.**

Originally, there were tax advantages to forming an MLP because profits from this special type of partnership were reported as personal income. MLPs thus avoided the double taxation paid on corporate income. Today, the Internal Revenue Service has limited many of the tax advantages of MLPs. While there are exceptions, most MLPs typically involve exploration for natural resources, oil or natural gas wells, or distribution companies for oil, natural gas, propane, or home heating oil.

The Partnership Agreement

Articles of partnership are an agreement listing and explaining the terms of the partnership. Although both oral and written partnership agreements are legal and can be enforced in the courts, a written agreement has an obvious advantage: It is not subject to lapses of memory.

Figure 5.3 shows a typical partnership agreement. The partnership agreement should state who will make the final decisions, what each partner's duties will be, and the investment each partner will make. The partnership agreement also should state how much profit or loss each partner receives or is responsible for. Finally, the partnership agreement should state what happens if a partner wants to dissolve the partnership or dies. Although the people involved in a partnership can draft their own agreement, most experts recommend consulting an attorney.

When entering into a partnership agreement, partners would be wise to let a neutral third party—a consultant, an accountant, a lawyer, or a mutual friend—assist with any disputes that might arise.

Advantages of Partnerships

3 LEARNING OBJECTIVE
Describe the advantages and disadvantages of partnerships.

Partnerships have many advantages. The most important are described below.

Ease of Start-up   Partnerships are relatively easy to form. As with a sole proprietorship, the legal requirements often are limited to registering the name of the business and obtaining any necessary licenses or permits. It may not even be necessary to prepare written articles of partnership, although doing so is generally a good idea.

Availability of Capital and Credit   Because partners can pool their funds, a partnership usually has more capital available than a sole proprietorship does. This additional capital, coupled with the general partners' unlimited liability, can form the basis for a better credit rating. Banks and suppliers may be more willing to extend credit or grant larger loans to such a partnership than to a sole proprietor. This does not mean that partnerships can borrow all the money they need. Many partnerships have found it hard to get long-term financing simply because lenders worry about the possibility of management disagreements and lack of continuity.

Personal Interest   General partners are very concerned with the operation of the firm—perhaps even more so than sole proprietors. After all, they are responsible for the actions of all other general partners, as well as for their own. The pride of ownership from solving the day-to-day problems of operating a business—with the help of another person(s)—is a strong motivating force and often makes all the people involved in the partnership work harder to become more successful.

➤➤ **FIGURE 5.3**

ARTICLES OF PARTNERSHIP

Articles of partnership is a written or oral agreement that lists and explains the terms of a partnership.

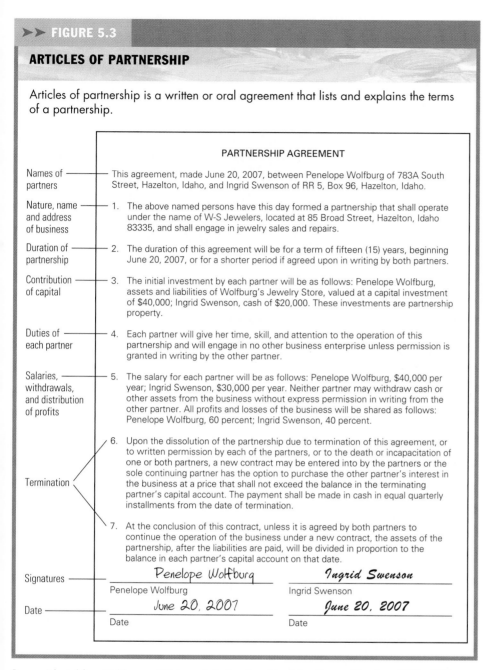

PARTNERSHIP AGREEMENT

Names of partners — This agreement, made June 20, 2007, between Penelope Wolfburg of 783A South Street, Hazelton, Idaho, and Ingrid Swenson of RR 5, Box 96, Hazelton, Idaho.

Nature, name and address of business — 1. The above named persons have this day formed a partnership that shall operate under the name of W-S Jewelers, located at 85 Broad Street, Hazelton, Idaho 83335, and shall engage in jewelry sales and repairs.

Duration of partnership — 2. The duration of this agreement will be for a term of fifteen (15) years, beginning June 20, 2007, or for a shorter period if agreed upon in writing by both partners.

Contribution of capital — 3. The initial investment by each partner will be as follows: Penelope Wolfburg, assets and liabilities of Wolfburg's Jewelry Store, valued at a capital investment of $40,000; Ingrid Swenson, cash of $20,000. These investments are partnership property.

Duties of each partner — 4. Each partner will give her time, skill, and attention to the operation of this partnership and will engage in no other business enterprise unless permission is granted in writing by the other partner.

Salaries, withdrawals, and distribution of profits — 5. The salary for each partner will be as follows: Penelope Wolfburg, $40,000 per year; Ingrid Swenson, $30,000 per year. Neither partner may withdraw cash or other assets from the business without express permission in writing from the other partner. All profits and losses of the business will be shared as follows: Penelope Wolfburg, 60 percent; Ingrid Swenson, 40 percent.

6. Upon the dissolution of the partnership due to termination of this agreement, or to written permission by each of the partners, or to the death or incapacitation of one or both partners, a new contract may be entered into by the partners or the sole continuing partner has the option to purchase the other partner's interest in the business at a price that shall not exceed the balance in the terminating partner's capital account. The payment shall be made in cash in equal quarterly installments from the date of termination.

Termination

7. At the conclusion of this contract, unless it is agreed by both partners to continue the operation of the business under a new contract, the assets of the partnership, after the liabilities are paid, will be divided in proportion to the balance in each partner's capital account on that date.

Signatures — *Penelope Wolfburg*   *Ingrid Swenson*
Penelope Wolfburg   Ingrid Swenson

Date — *June 20, 2007*   *June 20, 2007*
Date   Date

Source: Adapted from Goldman and Sigismond, *Business Law*, 6th edition. Boston: Houghton Mifflin, 2004. Copyright © 2004 by Houghton Mifflin Company. Reprinted with permission.

Combined Business Skills and Knowledge Partners often have complementary skills. The weakness of one partner—in manufacturing, for example—may be offset by another partner's strength in that area. Moreover, the ability to discuss important decisions with another concerned individual often relieves some pressure and leads to more effective decision making.

Retention of Profits As in a sole proprietorship, all profits belong to the owners of the partnership. The partners share directly in the financial rewards and therefore are highly motivated to do their best to make the firm succeed. As noted, the partnership agreement should state how much profit or loss each partner receives or is responsible for.

No Special Taxes Although a partnership pays no income tax, the Internal Revenue Service requires partnerships to file an annual information return that states

ENTREPRENEURIAL CHALLENGE

Incubators Give Entrepreneurs a Head Start

Business incubators want to give entrepreneurs a head start on success. Why would a small-business owner seek space in an incubator?

- To rent reasonably priced, well-equipped office or manufacturing space
- To obtain free help from technical experts and other specialists
- To gain access to low-cost loans and grants
- To learn from other entrepreneurs using the incubator
- To gain access to the local talent and facilities

Since 1980, the number of North American incubators has increased from 12 to 1,000. Many are located on university campuses or in urban neighborhoods where economic development is a priority.

Among the pioneers was Rensselaer Polytechnic Institute in Troy, New York, which has had an 80 percent success rate in launching new businesses. Participating in an incubator is no guarantee of success, but it can provide a solid foundation on which to grow.

the names and addresses of all partners involved in the business. The return also must provide information about income and expenses and distributions made to each partner. Then each partner is required to report his or her share of profit (or loss) from the partnership business on his or her individual tax return and is taxed on his or her share of the profit—in the same way a sole proprietor is taxed.

Disadvantages of Partnerships

Although partnerships have many advantages when compared with sole proprietorships and corporations, they also have some disadvantages, which anyone thinking of forming a partnership should consider.

Unlimited Liability   As we have noted, each *general* partner has unlimited liability for all debts of the business. Each partner is legally and personally responsible for the debts and actions of any other partner, even if that partner did not incur those debts or do anything wrong. General partners thus run the risk of having to use their personal assets to pay creditors. *Limited* partners, however, risk only their original investment.

Today, many states allow partners to form a *limited-liability partnership* (LLP), in which a partner may have limited-liability protection from legal action resulting from the malpractice of the other partners. Most states that allow LLPs restrict this type of ownership to certain types of professionals such as accountants, architects, attorneys, and similar professionals. (Note the difference between a limited partnership and a limited-liability partnership. A limited partnership must have at least one general partner that has unlimited liability. On the other hand, all partners in a limited-liability partnership may have limited liability for the malpractice of the other partners.)

Management Disagreements   What happens to a partnership if one of the partners brings a spouse or a relative into the business? What happens if a partner wants to withdraw more money from the business? Notice that each of the preceding situations—and for that matter, most of the other problems that can develop in a partnership—involves one partner doing something that disturbs the other partner(s). This human factor is especially important because business partners—with egos, ambitions, and money on the line—are especially susceptible to friction. When partners begin to disagree about decisions, policies, or ethics, distrust may build and get worse as time passes—often to the point where it is impossible to operate the business successfully.

Lack of Continuity   Partnerships are terminated if any one of the general partners dies, withdraws, or is declared legally incompetent. However, the remaining partners can purchase that partner's ownership share. For example, the partnership agreement may permit surviving partners to continue the business after buying a deceased partner's interest from his or her estate. However, if the partnership loses an owner whose specific management or technical skills cannot be replaced, it is not likely to survive.

Frozen Investment   It is easy to invest money in a partnership, but it is sometimes quite difficult to get it out. This is the case, for example, when remaining partners are unwilling to buy the share of the business that belongs to a partner who retires or wants to relocate to another city. To avoid such difficulties, the partnership agreement should include some procedure for buying out a partner.

In some cases, a partner must find someone outside the firm to buy his or her share. How easy or difficult it is to find an outsider depends on how successful the business is and how willing existing partners are to accept a new partner.

Beyond the Partnership

The main advantages of a partnership over a sole proprietorship are the added capital and management expertise of the partners. However, some of the basic disadvantages of the sole proprietorship also plague the general partnership. One disadvantage in particular—unlimited liability—can cause problems. A third form of business ownership, the corporation, overcomes this disadvantage.

@ USING THE INTERNET

Where can you find out more about starting and managing a business? The Small Business Administration (SBA) website explores a number of business topics that are beneficial to new businesses as well as those currently in operation. The site answers typical questions such as which legal form is best and how to get financing and has an SBA answer desk where you can submit written questions about any specific concerns. Your gateway to the SBA is at **www.sbaonline.sba.gov.**

Corporations

4 LEARNING OBJECTIVE
Summarize how a corporation is formed.

Back in 1837, William Procter and James Gamble—two sole proprietors—formed a partnership called Procter & Gamble and set out to compete with fourteen other soap and candle makers in Cincinnati, Ohio. Then, in 1890, Procter & Gamble incorporated to raise additional capital for expansion that eventually allowed the company to become a global giant. While not all sole proprietorships and partnerships become corporations, there are reasons why business owners choose the corporate form of ownership. Let's begin with a definition of a corporation. Perhaps the best definition of a corporation was given by Chief Justice John Marshall in a famous Supreme Court decision in 1819. A corporation, he said, "is an artificial being, invisible, intangible, and existing only in contemplation of the law." In other words, a **corporation** (sometimes referred to as a *regular* or *C-corporation*) is an artificial person created by law, with most of the legal rights of a real person. These include the rights to start and operate a business, to buy or sell property, to borrow money, to sue or be sued, and to enter into binding contracts. Unlike a real person, however, a corporation exists only on paper.

There are 5.1 million corporations in the United States. They comprise only about 20 percent of all businesses, but they account for 84.4 percent of sales revenues (see Figures 5.1 and 5.2). Table 5.1 lists the seven largest U.S. industrial corporations, ranked according to sales.

corporation an artificial person created by law with most of the legal rights of a real person, including the rights to start and operate a business, to buy or sell property, to borrow money, to sue or be sued, and to enter into binding contracts

>> **TABLE 5.1**

THE SEVEN LARGEST U.S. INDUSTRIAL CORPORATIONS, RANKED BY SALES

Rank 2004	Rank 2003	Company	Revenues ($ millions)	Profits ($ millions)	Assets ($ millions)
1	1	Wal-Mart Stores, Bentonville, AR	288,189.0	10,267.0	120,624.0
2	2	EXXON Mobil, Irving, TX	270,772.0	25,330.0	195,256.0
3	3	General Motors Detroit, MI	193,517.0	2,805.0	479,603.0
4	4	Ford Motor, Dearborn, MI	172,233.0	3,487.0	292,654.0
5	5	General Electric, Fairfield, CT	152,363.0	16,593.0	750,330.0
6	6	ChevronTexaco, San Ramon, CA	147,967.0	13,328.0	93,208.0
7	7	ConocoPhillips, Houston, TX	121,663.0	8,129.0	92,861.0

Source: *Fortune* April 18, 2005, p. F-1. Copyright © 2005 Time, Inc. All rights reserved.

Corporate Ownership

stock the shares of ownership of a corporation

stockholder a person who owns a corporation's stock

The shares of ownership of a corporation are called **stock.** The people who own a corporation's stock—and thus own part of the corporation—are called **stockholders** or sometimes *shareholders.* Once a corporation has been formed, it may sell its stock to individuals or other companies that want to invest in the corporation. It also may issue stock as a reward to key employees in return for certain services or as a return to investors (in place of cash payments).

closed corporation a corporation whose stock is owned by relatively few people and is not sold to the general public

A **closed corporation** is a corporation whose stock is owned by relatively few people and is not sold to the general public. As an example, Mr. and Mrs. DeWitt Wallace owned virtually all the stock of Reader's Digest Association, making it one of the largest corporations of this kind. A person who wishes to sell the stock of a closed corporation generally arranges to sell it *privately* to another stockholder or a close acquaintance.

open corporation a corporation whose stock can be bought and sold by any individual

Although founded in 1922 as a closed corporation, the Reader's Digest Association became an open corporation when it sold stock to investors for the first time in 1990. An **open corporation** is one whose stock can be bought and sold by any individual. Examples of open corporations include General Motors, Microsoft, and Wal-Mart.

Forming a Corporation

Although you may think that incorporating a business guarantees success, it does not. There is no special magic about placing the word *Incorporated* or the abbreviation *Inc.* after the name of a business. Unfortunately, like sole proprietorships or partnerships, incorporated businesses can go broke. The decision to incorporate a business therefore should be made only after carefully considering whether the corporate form of ownership suits your needs better than the sole proprietorship or partnership forms.

If you decide that the corporate form is the best form of organization for you, most experts recommend that you begin the incorporation process by consulting a lawyer to be sure that all legal requirements are met. While it may be possible to incorporate a business without legal help, it is well to keep in mind the old saying, "A man who acts as his own attorney has a fool for a client." Table 5.2 lists some aspects of starting and running a business that may require legal help.

Where to Incorporate A business is allowed to incorporate in any state that it chooses. The decision on where to incorporate usually is based on two factors: (1) the cost of incorporating in one state compared with the cost in another state and (2) the advantages and disadvantages of each state's corporate laws and tax structure. Most small and medium-sized businesses are incorporated in the state where they do the

> > **TABLE 5.2**

TEN ASPECTS OF BUSINESS THAT MAY REQUIRE LEGAL HELP

1. Choosing either the sole proprietorship, partnership, or corporate form of ownership
2. Constructing a partnership agreement
3. Obtaining a corporate charter
4. Registering a corporation's stock
5. Obtaining a trademark, patent, or copyright
6. Filing for licenses or permits at the local, state, and federal levels
7. Purchasing an existing business or real estate
8. Creating valid contracts
9. Hiring employees and independent contractors
10. Extending credit and collecting debts

most business. The founders of larger corporations or of those that will do business nationwide often compare the benefits that various states provide to corporations. Some states are more hospitable than others, and some offer fewer restrictions, lower taxes, and other benefits to attract new firms. Delaware is often chosen by corporations that do business in more than one state because of its low organizational costs.[3]

An incorporated business is called a **domestic corporation** in the state in which it is incorporated. In all other states where it does business, it is called a **foreign corporation.** Sears Holdings Corporation, the parent company of Sears and Kmart, is incorporated in Deleware, where it is a domestic corporation. In the remaining forty-nine states, Sears is a foreign corporation. Sears must register in all states where it does business and also pay taxes and annual fees to each state. A corporation chartered by a foreign government and conducting business in the United States is an **alien corporation.** Volkswagen AG, Sony Corporation, and the Royal Dutch/Shell Group are examples of alien corporations.

domestic corporation a corporation in the state in which it is incorporated

foreign corporation a corporation in any state in which it does business except the one in which it is incorporated

alien corporation a corporation chartered by a foreign government and conducting business in the United States

The Corporate Charter   Once a home state has been chosen, the incorporator(s) submits *articles of incorporation* to the secretary of state. When the articles of incorporation are approved, they become the firm's corporate charter. A **corporate charter** is a contract between a corporation and the state in which the state recognizes the formation of the artificial person that is the corporation. Usually the charter (and thus the articles of incorporation) includes the following information:

corporate charter a contract between a corporation and the state in which the state recognizes the formation of the artificial person that is the corporation

- The firm's name and address
- The incorporators' names and addresses
- The purpose of the corporation
- The maximum amount of stock and types of stock to be issued
- The rights and privileges of stockholders
- The length of time the corporation is to exist

To help you to decide if the corporate form of organization is the right choice, you may want to review the material available on the Yahoo! Small Business website (**http://smallbusiness.yahoo.com**). In addition, before making a decision to organize your business as a corporation, you may want to consider two additional areas: stockholders' rights and the importance of the organizational meeting.

common stock stock owned by individuals or firms who may vote on corporate matters but whose claims on profit and assets are subordinate to the claims of others

Stockholders' Rights   There are two basic types of stock. Owners of **common stock** may vote on corporate matters. Generally, an owner of common stock has one vote for each share owned. However, any claims of common-stock owners on profit and assets of the corporation are subordinate to the claims of others. The owners of **preferred stock** usually have no voting rights, but their claims on dividends are paid before those of common-stock owners. While large corporations may issue both common and preferred stock, generally small corporations issue only common stock.

preferred stock stock owned by individuals or firms who usually do not have voting rights but whose claims on dividends are paid before those of common-stock owners

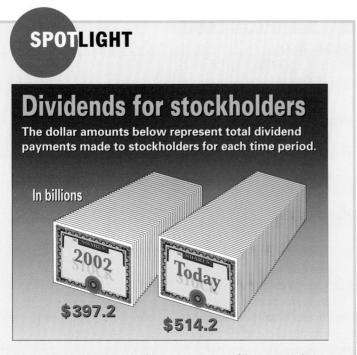

SPOTLIGHT

Dividends for stockholders

The dollar amounts below represent total dividend payments made to stockholders for each time period.

In billions

2002   **$397.2**

Today   **$514.2**

Source: The U.S. Department of Commerce, Bureau of Economic Analysis website: **www.bea.gov;** accessed May 2, 2006.

Perhaps the most important right of owners of both common and preferred stock is to share in the profit earned by the corporation through the payment of dividends. A **dividend** is a distribution of earnings to the stockholders of a corporation. Other rights include receiving information about the corporation, voting on changes to the corporate charter, and attending the corporation's annual stockholders' meeting, where they may exercise their right to vote.

Because common stockholders usually live all over the nation, very few actually may attend a corporation's annual meeting. Instead, they vote by proxy. A **proxy** is a legal form listing issues to be decided at a stockholders' meeting and enabling stockholders to transfer their voting rights to some other individual or individuals. The stockholder can register a vote and transfer voting rights simply by signing and returning the form. Today, most corporations also allow stockholders to exercise their right to vote by proxy by accessing the Internet or using a toll-free phone number.

Organizational Meeting   As the last step in forming a corporation, the incorporators and original stockholders meet to adopt corporate by-laws and elect their first board of directors. (Later, directors will be elected or reelected at the corporation's annual meetings.) The board members are directly responsible to the stockholders for the way they operate the firm.

dividend a distribution of earnings to the stockholders of a corporation

proxy a legal form listing issues to be decided at a stockholders' meeting and enabling stockholders to transfer their voting rights to some other individual or individuals

board of directors the top governing body of a corporation, the members of which are elected by the stockholders

Corporate Structure

The organizational structure of most corporations is more complicated than that of a sole proprietorship or partnership. This is especially true as the corporation begins to grow and expand. In a corporation, both the board of directors and the corporate officers are involved in management.

Board of Directors   As an artificial person, a corporation can act only through its directors, who represent the corporation's stockholders. The **board of directors** is the top governing body of a corporation, and are elected by the stockholders. Board members can be chosen from within the corporation or from outside it. *Note:* For a small corporation, only one director is required in most states although you can choose to have more.

Directors who are elected from within the corporation are usually its top managers—the president and executive vice presidents, for example. Those elected from outside the corporation

What's Bill Gates doing in Beijing? While most people around the world recognize Bill Gates as the co-founder and chairman of Microsoft—a corporation with an American corporate charter—Mr. Gates has been elevated to "rock star" status in many countries around the globe because of the corporation's software products.

generally are experienced managers or entrepreneurs with proven leadership ability and/or specific talents the organization seems to need. In smaller corporations, majority stockholders usually serve as board members.

The major responsibilities of the board of directors are to set company goals and develop general plans (or strategies) for meeting those goals. The board also is responsible for the firm's overall operation.

Corporate Officers **Corporate officers** are appointed by the board of directors. The chairman of the board, president, executive vice presidents, corporate secretary, and treasurer are all corporate officers. They help the board to make plans, carry out strategies established by the board, hire employees, and manage day-to-day business activities. Periodically (usually each month), they report to the board of directors. And at the annual meeting, the directors report to the stockholders. In theory, then, the stockholders are able to control the activities of the entire corporation through its directors because they are the group that elects the board of directors (see Figure 5.4).

corporate officers the chairman of the board, president, executive vice presidents, corporate secretary, treasurer, and any other top executive appointed by the board of directors

Advantages of Corporations

Back in October 2000, Manny Ruiz decided that it was time to start his own company. With the help of a team of media specialists, he founded Hispanic PR Wire. In a business where hype is the name of the game, Hispanic PR Wire is the real thing and has established itself as the nation's leading news distribution service reaching U.S. Hispanic media and opinion leaders. Today, the business continues to build on its early success.[4] Mr. Ruiz chose to incorporate this business because it provided a number of advantages that other forms of business ownership did not offer. Typical advantages include limited liability, ease of raising capital, ease of transfer of ownership, perpetual life, and specialized management.

5 LEARNING OBJECTIVE
Describe the advantages and disadvantages of a corporation.

Limited Liability One of the most attractive features of corporate ownership is **limited liability.** With few exceptions, each owner's financial liability is limited to the amount of money he or she has paid for the corporation's stock. This feature arises from the fact that the corporation is itself a legal being, separate from its owners. If a corporation fails, creditors have a claim only on the corporation's assets, not on the owners' personal assets. Because it overcomes the problem of unlimited liability connected with sole proprietorships and general partnerships, limited liability is one of the chief reasons why entrepreneurs often choose the corporate form of organization.

limited liability a feature of corporate ownership that limits each owner's financial liability to the amount of money that he or she has paid for the corporation's stock

Ease of Raising Capital The corporation is by far the most effective form of business ownership for raising capital. Like sole proprietorships and partnerships, corporations can borrow from lending institutions. However, they also can raise additional sums of money by selling stock. Individuals are more willing to invest in corporations than in other forms of business because of limited liability, and they can sell their stock easily—hopefully for a profit.

Ease of Transfer of Ownership Accessing a brokerage firm website or a telephone call to a stockbroker is all that is required to put stock up for sale. Willing buyers are available for most stocks at the market price. Ownership is transferred when the

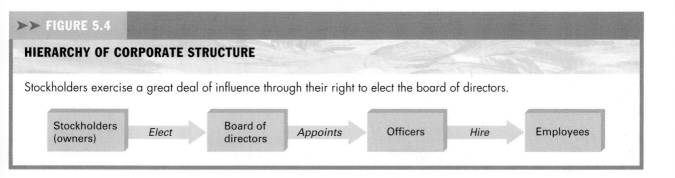

>> FIGURE 5.4

HIERARCHY OF CORPORATE STRUCTURE

Stockholders exercise a great deal of influence through their right to elect the board of directors.

Stockholders (owners) → *Elect* → Board of directors → *Appoints* → Officers → *Hire* → Employees

YOUR CAREER

Corporations Depend on Investor Relations

Check the website of any public company and you'll find a link to investor relations. Whenever an open corporation announces its financial results or schedules an annual shareholders' meeting, the investor relations department is in the lead. A career in investor relations typically involves

- Answering reporters' and analysts' questions about the stock price
- Discussing the corporation's future plans with investors
- Reviewing financial statements with top executives
- Understanding government rules concerning financial disclosures
- Writing parts of the annual report to shareholders

This fast-paced career requires excellent communication skills, familiarity with financial data, a "big picture" mentality, and the ability to think on your feet. Every corporation's situation is different, and the stock market's gyrations add even more spice. Barbara Gasper, who heads investor relations for Ford Motor Company, says that her biggest challenge is "dealing with Wall Street in a period of uncertainty, not just for Ford but for the entire industry."

sale is made, and practically no restrictions apply to the sale and purchase of stock issued by an open corporation.

Perpetual Life   Since it is essentially a legal "person," a corporation exists independently of its owners and survives them. The withdrawal, death, or incompetence of a key executive or owner does not cause the corporation to be terminated. Sears, Roebuck, which started as a partnership in 1887 and incorporated in 1893, is one of the nation's largest retailing corporations, even though its original owners, Richard Sears and Alvah Roebuck, have been dead for decades.

Specialized Management   Typically, corporations are able to recruit more skilled, knowledgeable, and talented managers than proprietorships and partnerships. This is so because they pay bigger salaries, offer excellent fringe benefits, and are large enough to offer considerable opportunity for advancement. Within the corporate structure, administration, human resources, finance, marketing, and operations are placed in the charge of experts in these fields.

Disadvantages of Corporations

Like its advantages, many of a corporation's disadvantages stem from its legal definition as an artificial person or legal entity. The most serious disadvantages are described below. (See Table 5.3 for a comparison of some of the advantages and disadvantages of a sole proprietorship, general partnership, and corporation.)

Difficulty and Expense of Formation   Forming a corporation can be a relatively complex and costly process. The use of an attorney usually is necessary to complete the legal forms and apply to the state for a charter. Charter fees, attorney's fees, registration costs

---

>> **TABLE 5.3**

SOME ADVANTAGES AND DISADVANTAGES OF A SOLE PROPRIETORSHIP, PARTNERSHIP, AND CORPORATION

	Sole Proprietorship	General Partnership	Regular (C) Corporation
Protecting against liability for debts	Difficult	Difficult	Easy
Raising money	Difficult	Difficult	Easy
Ownership transfer	Difficult	Difficult	Easy
Preserving continuity	Difficult	Difficult	Easy
Government regulations	Few	Few	Many
Formation	Easy	Easy	Difficult
Income taxation	Once	Once	Twice

associated with selling stock, and other organizational costs can amount to thousands of dollars for even a medium-sized corporation. The costs of incorporating, in terms of both time and money, discourage many owners of smaller businesses from forming corporations.

Government Regulation and Increased Paperwork

A corporation must meet various government standards before it can sell its stock to the public. Then it must file many reports on its business operations and finances with local, state, and federal governments. In addition, the corporation must make periodic reports to its stockholders about various aspects of the business. To prepare all the necessary reports, even small corporations often need the help of an attorney, certified public accountant, and other professionals on a regular basis. In addition, a corporation's activities are restricted by law to those spelled out in its charter.

Conflict Within the Corporation   Because a large corporation may employ thousands of employees, some conflict is inevitable. For example, the pressure to increase sales revenue, reduce expenses, and increase profits, often leads to increased stress and tension for both managers and employees. This is especially true when a corporation operates in a competitive industry, attempts to develop and market new products, or must downsize the workforce to reduce employee salary expense.

Double Taxation   Corporations must pay a tax on their profits. In addition, stockholders must pay a personal income tax on profits received as dividends. Corporate profits thus are taxed twice—once as corporate income and a second time as the personal income of stockholders. *Note:* Both the S-corporation and the limited-liability company discussed in the next section are taxed like a partnership but still provide limited liability.

Lack of Secrecy   Because open corporations are required to submit detailed reports to government agencies and to stockholders, they cannot keep their operations confidential. Competitors can study these corporate reports and then use the information to compete more effectively. In effect, every public corporation has to share some of its secrets with its competitors.

@ USING THE INTERNET

o find information about management and employee salaries paid by corporations, go to the following websites:
Bureau of Labor Statistics at **www.bls.gov**
CareerBuilder at **www.careerbuilder.com**
Monster at **www.monster.com**

Special Types of Business Ownership

In addition to the sole proprietorship, partnership, and the regular corporate form of organization, some entrepreneurs choose other forms of organization that meet their special needs. Additional organizational options include S-corporations, limited-liability companies, government-owned corporations, and not-for-profit corporations.

S-corporations

If a corporation meets certain requirements, its directors may apply to the Internal Revenue Service for status as an S-corporation. An **S-corporation** is a corporation that is taxed as though it were a partnership. In other words, the corporation's income is taxed only as the personal income of stockholders. Corporate profits of losses "pass through" the business and are reported on the owners' personal income tax returns.

Becoming an S-corporation can be an effective way to avoid double taxation while retaining the corporation's legal benefit of limited liability. To qualify for the special status of an S-corporation, a firm must meet the following criteria[5]:

1. No more than 100 stockholders are allowed.
2. Stockholders must be individuals, estates, or exempt organizations.

6 LEARNING OBJECTIVE
Examine special types of corporations, including S-corporations, limited-liability companies, government-owned corporations, and not-for-profit corporations.

S-corporation a corporation that is taxed as though it were a partnership

3. There can be only one class of outstanding stock.
4. The firm must be a domestic corporation eligible to file for S-corporation status.
5. There can be no nonresident-alien stockholders.
6. All stockholders must agree to the decision to form an S-corporation.

Limited-Liability Companies

In addition to the traditional forms of business ownership already covered, a new form of ownership called a *limited-liability company* has been approved in all fifty states—although each state's laws may differ. A **limited-liability company (LLC)** is a form of business ownership that combines the benefits of a corporation and a partnership while avoiding some of the restrictions and disadvantages of those forms of ownership. Chief advantages of an LLC are as follows:

1. LLCs with at least two members are taxed like a partnership and thus avoid the double taxation imposed on most corporations. LLCs with just one member are taxed like a sole proprietorship.
2. Like a corporation, it provides limited-liability protection. An LLC thus extends the concept of personal-asset protection to small-business owners.
3. The LLC type of organization provides more management flexibility when compared with corporations. A corporation, for example, is required to have directors and corporate officers that follow guidelines established by the corporate charter. By comparison, an LLC is generally run by the owners or managers, who make all management decisions.

Although many experts believe that the LLC is nothing more than a variation of the S-corporation, there is a difference. An LLC is not restricted to 100 stockholders—a common drawback of the S-corporation. LLCs are also less restricted and have more flexibility than S-corporations in terms of who can become an owner. Although the owners of an LLC must file articles of organization with their state's secretary of state, they are not hampered by lots of Internal Revenue Service rules and government regulations that apply to corporations. As a result, experts are predicting that LLCs may become one of the most popular forms of business ownership available. In fact, new LLC companies now outnumber corporate formations in several states.[6] For help in understanding the differences between a regular corporation, S-corporation, and limited-liability company, see Table 5.4.

Government-Owned Corporations

A **government-owned corporation** is owned and operated by a local, state, or federal government. The Tennessee Valley Authority (TVA), the National Aeronautics and Space Administration (NASA), and the Federal Deposit Insurance Corporation (FDIC) are all government-owned corporations. They are operated by the U.S. government. In addition, most municipal bus lines and subways are run by city-owned corporations.

A government corporation usually provides a service the business sector is reluctant or unable to offer. Profit is secondary in such corporations. In fact, they may continually operate at a loss, particularly if they are involved in public transportation. Their main objective is to ensure that a particular service is available.

Not-for-Profit Corporations

A **not-for-profit corporation** (sometimes referred to as *nonprofit*) is a corporation organized to provide a social, educational, religious, or other service rather than to earn a profit. Various charities, museums, private schools, and colleges are organized in this

An LLC doesn't have to be small. Cingular Wireless, the largest wireless company in the United States, is a joint venture of AT&T and BellSouth and is organized as a limited liability company (LLC). In this photo, sales associate Cedric Washington uses the company's latest PDA to talk with one of the LLC's 54 million customers.

limited-liability company (LLC) a form of business ownership that combines the benefits of a corporation and a partnership while avoiding some of the restrictions and disadvantages of those forms of ownership

government-owned corporation a corporation owned and operated by a local, state, or federal government

not-for-profit corporation a corporation organized to provide a social, educational, religious, or other service rather than to earn a profit

>> **TABLE 5.4**

SOME ADVANTAGES AND DISADVANTAGES OF A REGULAR CORPORATION, S-CORPORATION, AND LIMITED-LIABILITY COMPANY

	Regular (C) Corporation	S-Corporation	Limited Liability Company
Double taxation	Yes	No	No
Limited liability and personal-asset protection	Yes	Yes	Yes
Management and ownership flexibility	No	No	Yes
Restrictions on the number of owners/stockholders	No	Yes	No
Internal Revenue Service tax regulations	Many	Many	Fewer

way, primarily to ensure limited liability. Habitat for Humanity is a not-for-profit corporation and was formed to provide homes for qualified low-income people who could not afford housing. Even though this corporation may receive more money than it spends, any surplus funds are "reinvested" in building activities to provide low-cost housing. It is a not-for-profit corporation because its primary purpose is to provide a social service. Other examples include the Public Broadcasting System (PBS), the Girl Scouts, and the Red Cross.

Cooperatives, Joint Ventures, and Syndicates

Today, three additional types of business organizations—cooperatives, joint ventures, and syndicates—are used for special purposes. Each of these forms of organization is unique when compared with more traditional forms of business ownership.

Cooperatives

A **cooperative** is an association of individuals or firms whose purpose is to perform some business function for its members. The cooperative can perform its function more effectively than any member could by acting alone. For example, cooperatives purchase goods in bulk and distribute them to members; thus the unit cost is lower than it would be if each member bought the goods in a much smaller quantity.

Although cooperatives are found in all segments of our economy, they are most prevalent in agriculture.

7 LEARNING OBJECTIVE
Discuss the purpose of a cooperative, joint venture, and syndicate.

cooperative an association of individuals or firms whose purpose is to perform some business function for its members

Entrepreneurial zeal at the New York Museum of Modern Art. When the New York Museum of Modern Art (often referred to as MoMa) sold the air rights over its Manhattan location for millions, the income from the sale helped finance a new wing, which doubled the size of the museum. The air space was then used for the construction of a private forty-four-story residential tower.

Farmers use cooperatives to purchase supplies, to buy services such as trucking and storage, and to process and market their products. Ocean Spray Cranberries, Inc., for example, is a cooperative of some 650 cranberry growers and more than 100 citrus growers spread throughout the country.

Joint Ventures

joint venture an agreement between two or more groups to form a business entity in order to achieve a specific goal or to operate for a specific period of time

A **joint venture** is an agreement between two or more groups to form a business entity in order to achieve a specific goal or to operate for a specific period of time. Both the scope of the joint venture and the liabilities of the people or businesses involved usually are limited to one project. Once the goal is reached, the period of time elapses, or the project is completed, the joint venture is dissolved.

Corporations, as well as individuals, may enter into joint ventures. Major oil producers often have formed a number of joint ventures to share the extremely high cost of exploring for offshore petroleum deposits. In the entertainment industry, Walt Disney formed a joint venture with Pixar Animation Studios to create movies. Finally, Japanese consumer electronics manufacturer Sony and Swedish telecom giant Ericsson have formed a joint venture to manufacture and market mobile communications equipment. Now, after more than four years, the joint venture is profitable and projects even larger sales revenues and profits in the immediate future.[7]

Syndicates

syndicate a temporary association of individuals or firms organized to perform a specific task that requires a large amount of capital

A **syndicate** is a temporary association of individuals or firms organized to perform a specific task that requires a large amount of capital. The syndicate is formed because no one person or firm is willing to put up the entire amount required for the undertaking. Like a joint venture, a syndicate is dissolved as soon as its purpose has been accomplished.

Syndicates are used most commonly to underwrite large insurance policies, loans, and investments. To share the risk of default, banks have formed syndicates to provide loans to developing countries. Stock brokerage firms usually join together in the same way to market a new issue of stock. For example, Morgan Stanley, Credit Suisse First Boston, and other Wall Street firms formed a syndicate to sell shares of stock in Google. The initial public offering (IPO) was one of the largest in U.S. history—too large for Morgan Stanley and Credit Suisse First Boston to handle without help from other Wall Street firms. (An *initial public offering* is the term used to describe the first time a corporation sells stock to the general public.)

Corporate Growth

8 LEARNING OBJECTIVE
Explain how growth from within and growth through mergers can enable a business to expand.

Growth seems to be a basic characteristic of business. One reason for seeking growth has to do with profit: A larger firm generally has greater sales revenue and thus greater profit. Another reason is that in a growing economy, a business that does not grow is actually shrinking relative to the economy. A third reason is that business growth is a means by which some executives boost their power, prestige, and reputation.

Growth poses new problems and requires additional resources that first must be available and then must be used effectively. The main ingredient in growth is capital—and as we have noted, capital is most readily available to corporations. Thus, to a great extent, business growth means corporate growth.

Growth from Within

Most corporations grow by expanding their present operations. Some introduce and sell new but related products. Others expand the sale of present products to new geographic markets or to new groups of consumers in geographic markets already served. Currently, Wal-Mart has over 3,600 stores in the United States and over 1,600 stores in nine different countries and has long-range plans for expanding into additional international markets.[8]

Growth from within, especially when carefully planned and controlled, can have relatively little adverse effect on a firm. For the most part, the firm continues to do what it has been doing, but on a larger scale. For instance, Larry Ellison, cofounder and CEO of Oracle Corporation of Redwood City, California, built the firm's annual revenues up from a mere $282 million in 1988 to approximately $12 billion today.[9] Much of this growth has taken place since 1994 as Oracle capitalized on its global leadership in information management software.

Growth Through Mergers and Acquisitions

Another way a firm can grow is by purchasing another company. The purchase of one corporation by another is called a **merger.** An *acquisition* is essentially the same thing as a merger, but the term usually is used in reference to a large corporation's purchases of other corporations. Although most mergers and acquisitions are friendly, hostile takeovers also occur. A **hostile takeover** is a situation in which the management and board of directors of a firm targeted for acquisition disapprove of the merger.

When a merger or acquisition becomes hostile, a corporate raider—another company or a wealthy investor—may make a tender offer or start a proxy fight to gain control of the target company. A **tender offer** is an offer to purchase the stock of a firm targeted for acquisition at a price just high enough to tempt stockholders to sell their shares. Corporate raiders also may initiate a proxy fight. A **proxy fight** is a technique used to gather enough stockholder votes to control a targeted company.

merger the purchase of one corporation by another

hostile takeover a situation in which the management and board of directors of a firm targeted for acquisition disapprove of the merger

tender offer an offer to purchase the stock of a firm targeted for acquisition at a price just high enough to tempt stockholders to sell their shares

proxy fight a technique used to gather enough stockholder votes to control a targeted company

Standoff or merger? Although many mergers become hostile, the merger between CSX Transportation and Conrail was a friendly horizontal merger. In this photo, two train engines, one from each company, meet nose-to-nose, and an executive from each company christens the merger with champagne while employees look down from a bridge in Jacksonville, Florida.

If the corporate raider is successful and takes over the targeted company, existing management usually is replaced. Faced with this probability, existing management may take specific actions sometimes referred to as "poison pills," "shark repellents," or "porcupine provisions" to maintain control of the firm and avoid the hostile takeover. Whether mergers are friendly or hostile, they are generally classified as *horizontal*, *vertical*, or *conglomerate* (see Figure 5.5).

Horizontal Mergers   A *horizontal merger* is a merger between firms that make and sell similar products or services in similar markets. The merger between Oracle and PeopleSoft is an example of a horizontal merger because both firms are in the software industry. This type of merger tends to reduce the number of firms in an industry—and thus may reduce competition. For this reason, each merger may be reviewed carefully by federal agencies before it is permitted.

Vertical Mergers   A *vertical merger* is a merger between firms that operate at different but related levels in the production and marketing of a product. Generally, one of the merging firms is either a supplier or a customer of the other. A vertical merger occurred when IBM acquired Candle Corporation—an IBM business partner since 1976. At the time of the merger, Candle Corporation, a privately held software and consulting company, was a leading provider of software solutions to help customers develop, deploy, and manage their enterprise infrastructure. At the same time, IBM needed this type of software to add to its own line of software products and remain competitive in the ever-changing software industry. Rather than develop its own software or purchase needed software from Candle Corporation, it simply purchased the company.[10]

Conglomerate Mergers   A *conglomerate merger* takes place between firms in completely different industries. One of the largest conglomerate mergers in recent history occurred when Procter & Gamble merged with Gillette. While both companies were known for their consumer products, Procter & Gamble is the manufacturer and dis-

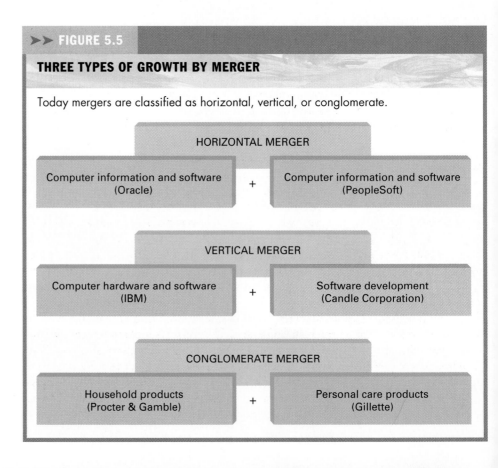

➤➤ **FIGURE 5.5**

THREE TYPES OF GROWTH BY MERGER

Today mergers are classified as horizontal, vertical, or conglomerate.

HORIZONTAL MERGER

Computer information and software (Oracle)   +   Computer information and software (PeopleSoft)

VERTICAL MERGER

Computer hardware and software (IBM)   +   Software development (Candle Corporation)

CONGLOMERATE MERGER

Household products (Procter & Gamble)   +   Personal care products (Gillette)

Business Around the World

International Mergers and Acquisitions Face Protectionism

Cross-border mergers and acquisitions are nothing new. One of the highest-profile acquisitions in the auto industry was the deal in which Germany's Daimler-Benz bought U.S.-based Chrysler to form DaimlerChrysler. However, corporations increasingly face protectionism as they seek growth across international borders. Two examples:

France
Just the rumor that the U.S. snack firm PepsiCo. might try to acquire Groupe Danone spurred government officials to say that they want Danone to remain under French ownership. In fact, France will protect ten industries (including casinos and defense firms) from cross-border takeovers. The minister for industry notes, however, that "our policy is not to oppose by principle every acquisition of a French company."

United States
China National Offshore Oil Company (CNOOC), owned by China, tried to buy California's Unocal. Congress opposed the move, citing the need to protect the country's energy producers, and CNOOC withdrew its bid (leaving Chevron to buy Unocal). "It's a tremendous precedent setter for a government to interfere and declare that national security is at stake," comments an oil industry expert. What is this going to mean for American oil companies [that want to invest in natural resources in different nations] from Algeria to Zanzibar?

---

tributor for many household products, and Gillette is well known for personal-care products. According to Procter & Gamble, the addition of Gillette's products "will broaden the ways in which we can continue to provide the kinds of helpful solutions to assist our customers in taking care of their families, their homes—and themselves!"[11]

Current Merger Trends

Economists, financial analysts, corporate managers, and stockholders still hotly debate whether takeovers are good for the economy—or for individual companies—in the long run. One thing is clear, however: There are two sides to the takeover question. Takeover advocates argue that for companies that have been taken over, the purchasers have been able to make the company more profitable and productive by installing a new top-management team and by forcing the company to concentrate on one main business.

Takeover opponents argue that takeovers do nothing to enhance corporate profitability or productivity. These critics argue that threats of takeovers have forced managers to devote valuable time to defending their companies from takeover, thus robbing time from new-product development and other vital business activities. This, they believe, is why U.S. companies may be less competitive with companies in such countries as Japan, Germany, and South Korea, where takeovers occur only rarely. Finally, the opposition argues that the only people who benefit from takeovers are investment bankers, brokerage firms, and takeover "artists," who receive financial rewards by manipulating U.S. corporations rather than by producing tangible products or services.

Most experts now predict that mergers and acquisitions during the first part of the twenty-first century will be the result of cash-rich companies looking to acquire businesses that will enhance their position in the marketplace. Analysts also anticipate more mergers that involve companies or investors from other countries. Regardless of the companies involved or where the companies are from, future mergers and acquisitions will be driven by solid business logic, the desire to compete in the international marketplace, and the explosion of information technology.

leveraged buyout (LBO) a purchase arrangement that allows a firm's managers and employees or a group of investors to purchase the company

Finally, experts predict more leveraged buyouts in the future. A **leveraged buyout (LBO)** is a purchase arrangement that allows a firm's managers and employees or a group of investors to purchase the company. (LBO activity is sometimes referred to as *taking a firm private*.) To gain control of a company, LBOs usually rely on borrowed money to purchase stock from existing stockholders. The borrowed money is later repaid through the company's earnings, sale of assets, or money obtained from selling more stock.

Whether they are sole proprietorships, partnerships, corporations, or some other form of business ownership, most U.S. businesses are small. In the next chapter we focus on these small businesses. We examine, among other things, the meaning of the word *small* as it applies to business and the place of small business in the American economy.

RETURN TO   Inside Business

General Electric (GE) consistently ranks first or second among the most admired corporations in the United States and the world. It also has been named one of the best U.S. companies for working women. A good reputation lays a solid foundation for profitable growth, but it also raises expectations about what one of America's largest corporations can and should be doing on issues such as environmental protection and poverty.

CEO Jeffrey Immelt is committed to doing more. Under Immelt, GE has acquired alternative-energy companies and

spent millions to improve health care in poor nations. Decades after one of its plants discharged chemicals into an upstate New York river—a legal practice at the time—GE has begun a massive, multiyear environmental cleanup. As Immelt observes: "It's up to us to use our platform to be a good citizen. Because not only is it a nice thing to do, it's a business imperative."

Questions

1. What are the advantages and disadvantages of GE investing millions of dollars of its shareholders' money in corporate citizenship projects with no immediate profit payback?
2. Would you like to work for a corporation like GE? Why or why not?

►► CHAPTER REVIEW

Summary

1

Describe the advantages and disadvantages of sole proprietorships.

In a sole proprietorship, all business profits become the property of the owner, but the owner is also personally responsible for all business debts. A successful sole proprietorship can be a great source of pride for the owner. When comparing different types of business ownership, the sole proprietorship is the simplest form of business to enter, control, and leave. It also pays no special taxes. Perhaps for these reasons, 71.6 percent of all American business firms are sole proprietorships.

Sole proprietorships nevertheless have disadvantages, such as unlimited liability and limits on one person's ability to borrow or to be an expert in all fields. As a result, this form of ownership accounts for only 4.4 percent of total revenues when compared with partnerships and corporations.

2

Explain the different types of partners and the importance of partnership agreements.

Like sole proprietors, general partners are responsible for running the business and for all business debts. Limited partners receive a share of the profit in return for investing in the business. However, they are not responsible for business debts beyond the amount they have invested. It is also possible to form a master limited partnership (MLP) and sell units of ownership to raise capital. Regardless of the type of partnership, it is always a good idea to have a written agreement (or articles of partnership) setting forth the terms of a partnership.

3

Describe the advantages and disadvantages of partnerships.

Although partnership eliminates some of the disadvantages of sole proprietorship, it is the least popular of the major forms of business ownership. The major advantages of a partnership include ease of start-up, availability of capital and credit, personal interest, combined skills and knowledge, retention of profits, and possible tax advantages. The effects of management disagreements are one of the major disadvantages of a partnership. Other disadvantages include unlimited liability (in a general partnership), lack of continuity, and frozen investment. By forming a limited partnership, the disadvantage of unlimited liability may be eliminated for the limited partner(s). This same disadvantage may be eliminated for partners that form a limited-liability partnership. Of course, special requirements must be met if partners form either the limited partnership or the limited-liability partnership.

4

Summarize how a corporation is formed.

A corporation is an artificial person created by law, with most of the legal rights of a real person, including the right to start and operate a business, to own property, to borrow money, to be sued or sue, and to enter into contracts. With the corporate form of ownership, stock can be sold to individuals to raise capital. The people who own a corporation's stock—and thus own part of the corporation—are called stockholders or sometimes shareholders. Generally, corporations are classified as closed corporations (few stockholders) or open corporations (many stockholders).

The process of forming a corporation is called incorporation. Most experts believe that the services of a lawyer are necessary when making decisions about where to incorporate and about obtaining a corporate charter, issuing stock, holding an organizational meeting, and all other legal details involved in incorporation. In theory, stockholders are able to control the activities of the corporation because they elect the board of directors who appoint the corporate officers.

5

Describe the advantages and disadvantages of a corporation.

Perhaps the major advantage of the corporate form is limited liability—stockholders are not liable for the corporation's debts beyond the amount they paid for its stock.

Other important advantages include ease of raising capital, ease of transfer of ownership, perpetual life, and specialized management. A major disadvantage of a large corporation is double taxation: All profits are taxed once as corporate income and again as personal income because stockholders must pay a personal income tax on the profits they receive as dividends. Other disadvantages include difficulty and expense of formation, government regulation, conflict within the corporation, and lack of secrecy.

6

Examine special types of corporations, including S-corporations, limited-liability companies, government-owned corporations, and not-for profit corporations.

S-corporations are corporations that are taxed as though they were partnerships but that enjoy the benefit of limited liability. To qualify as an S-corporation, a number of criteria must be met. A limited-liability company (LLC) is a form of business ownership that provides limited liability and has fewer government restrictions. LLCs with at least two members are taxed like a partnership and thus avoid the double taxation imposed on most corporations. LLCs with just one member are taxed like a sole proprietorship. When compared with a regular corporation or an S-corporation, an LLC is more flexible. Government-owned corporations provide particular services, such as public transportation, to citizens. Not-for-profit corporations are formed to provide social services rather than to earn profits.

7

Discuss the purpose of a cooperative, joint venture, and syndicate.

Three additional forms of business ownership—the cooperative, joint venture, and syndicate—are used by their owners to meet special needs, and each may be owned by either individuals or firms. A cooperative is an association of individuals or firms whose purpose is to perform some business function for its members. A joint venture is formed when two or more groups form a business entity in order to achieve a specific goal or to operate for a specific period of time. Once the goal is reached, the joint venture is dissolved. A syndicate is a temporary association of individuals or firms organized to perform a specific task that requires large amounts of capital. Like a joint venture, a syndicate is dissolved as soon as its purpose has been accomplished.

8

Explain how growth from within and growth through mergers can enable a business to expand.

A corporation may grow by expanding its present operations or through a merger or acquisition. Although most mergers are friendly, hostile takeovers also occur. A hostile takeover is a situation in which the management and board of directors of a firm targeted for acquisition disapprove of the merger. Mergers generally are classified as horizontal, vertical, or conglomerate mergers.

While economists, financial analysts, corporate managers, and stockholders debate the merits of mergers, some trends should be noted. First, experts predict that future mergers will be the result of cash-rich companies looking to acquire businesses that will enhance their position in the marketplace. Second, more mergers are likely to involve foreign companies or investors. Third, mergers will be driven by business logic, the desire to compete in the international marketplace, and the explosion of information technology. Finally, more leveraged buyouts are expected.

Key Terms

You should now be able to define and give an example relevant to each of the following terms:

sole proprietorship (149)
unlimited liability (151)
partnership (152)
general partner (153)
general partnership (153)
limited partner (153)
limited partnership (153)
master limited partnership (MLP) (153)
corporation (157)
stock (158)
stockholder (158)
closed corporation (158)
open corporation (158)
domestic corporation (159)
foreign corporation (159)
alien corporation (159)
corporate charter (159)
common stock (159)
preferred stock (159)
dividend (160)
proxy (160)
board of directors (160)
corporate officers (161)
limited liability (161)
S-corporation (163)
limited-liability company (LLC) (164)
government-owned corporation (164)
not-for-profit corporation (164)
cooperative (165)
joint venture (166)
syndicate (166)
merger (167)

hostile takeover (167)
tender offer (167)
proxy fight (167)
leveraged buyout (LBO) (170)

Review Questions

1. What is a sole proprietorship? What are the major advantages and disadvantages of this form of business ownership?
2. How does a partnership differ from a sole proprietorship? Which disadvantages of sole proprietorship does the partnership tend to eliminate or reduce?
3. What is the difference between a general partner and a limited partner?
4. What issues should be included in a partnership agreement? Why?
5. Explain the difference between
   a. an open corporation and a closed corporation.
   b. a domestic corporation, a foreign corporation, and an alien corporation.
6. Outline the incorporation process, and describe the basic corporate structure.
7. What rights do stockholders have?
8. What are the primary duties of a corporation's board of directors? How are directors selected?
9. What are the major advantages and disadvantages associated with the corporate form of business ownership?
10. How do an S-corporation and a limited-liability company differ?
11. Explain the difference between a government-owned corporation and a not-for-profit corporation.
12. Why are cooperatives formed? Explain how they operate.
13. In what ways are joint ventures and syndicates alike? In what ways do they differ?
14. What is a hostile takeover? How is it related to a tender offer and a proxy fight?
15. Describe the three types of mergers.

Discussion Questions

1. If you were to start a business, which ownership form would you choose? What factors might affect your choice?
2. Why might an investor choose to become a partner in a limited-liability partnership business instead of purchasing the stock of an open corporation?
3. Discuss the following statement: "Corporations are not really run by their owners."
4. What kinds of services do government-owned corporations provide? How might such services be provided without government involvement?
5. Is growth a good thing for all firms? How does management know when a firm is ready to grow?

►► VIDEO CASE 5.1

Bay Partners Sticks to Venture-Capital Basics

All businesses—sole proprietorships, partnerships, and corporations—need money. And money is the business of Bay Partners, a venture-capital firm with headquarters in Cupertino, California. For more than twenty-five years, Bay Partners has been investing in up-and-coming high-tech companies connected with innovative goods and services. Its investments are typically in the range of $1 million to $10 million. In addition, the partners of Bay Partners have been active participants in one or more technology start-ups over the years. Therefore, they have the knowledge and the background to help each company in which they invest by serving as consultants, mentors, and financial advisors.

Not every company is a candidate for the funding and specialized assistance that the partners offer. As smart investors, they are extremely particular about which enterprises they choose to support. First, they look at the size of the market opportunity and how fast the market is growing. Ideally, Bay Partners would prefer to invest in entrepreneurial companies offering products for larger, faster-growing markets.

Next, Bay Partners looks at the managers who are running the company. Do these people have the expertise, experience, drive, and dedication to make the company successful? As the business grows, can they attract a team of talented employees who are customer-oriented and flexible enough to adjust to rapid, often unexpected changes?

The product is another important part of the evaluation process. The partners consider whether the good or service will meet customers' needs and whether customers will have to alter their behavior drastically to use the product. Can the company communicate with customers about its innovation? What kind of competitive situation is the company likely to confront in the marketplace? The development process is also analyzed to be sure that the entrepreneurs have realistic plans and schedules for creating, testing, manufacturing, and introducing new products and technologies. Generally, Bay Partners invests in companies that are about to bring tested technologies to market rather than those with unproven ideas.

Finally, Bay Partners takes a good look at each company's business plan. Because the partners have been entrepreneurs, they understand the many challenges a company faces as it implements its business plan. Thus the partners do not focus exclusively on projected sales volume and revenue goals. In addition, they think about the plan as a whole. If it does not seem realistic, it is unlikely to be workable once the company is funded. This is critical because the partners do not make money unless the companies in which they invest make money.

The partners in Bay Partners like the excitement of working with new discoveries, of watching a business grow, and of helping entrepreneurs achieve their dreams. They do not invest in every company they analyze, but they do give entrepreneurs feedback on their ideas. In some cases the partners will work with budding entrepreneurs to shape a promising concept into a business plan with potential. Currently, the venture-capital firm's portfolio of investments includes Intraspect (produces collaboration software), Guidewire (produces transaction-processing software), NanoGram Devices (produces medical components), and PatchLink (offers application security).

Despite their extensive analysis, the partners are well aware of the risks—and the stress—they will encounter through their investments. Ultimately, when the partners decide they are going to invest, they make a long-term commitment of expertise as well as money to help the business succeed. For example, three media executives formed Sportvision as a corporation in 1998. Their plan was to enhance the viewers' experience of sports events aired on television and the web. Professional baseball, football, basketball, hockey, golf, racing, and other sports have used Sportvision's technology over the years. Even though the company received venture-capital funding from Bay Partners a number of years ago and is well beyond the start-up phase, at least one of the three founders talks with a Bay Partners' contact every week to discuss strategy, hiring, and other operational matters.[12]

For more information about this company, go to **www.baypartners.com.**

Questions

1. Imagine that you are a venture capitalist considering whether to invest as a part owner in a start-up corporation with a promising but unproven technology. You know that the owners have limited financial liability if the corporation fails. How would this affect your investment decision?
2. The partners of Bay Partners are very particular about which businesses they choose to support. What factors do they consider before making a decision to provide venture-capital and management assistance to a start-up company?
3. Why would the partners at Bay Partners want to stay involved in a start-up company once a decision is made to provide venture capital? From the entrepreneur's standpoint, is this continued involvement good or bad? Explain your answer.
4. If you were an entrepreneur seeking venture capital backing, what questions would you ask before accepting an investment from Bay Partners?

►► CASE 5.2

Stockholders Make Their Voices Heard at Disney

How much influence do stockholders wield over decisions made by and about the board of directors? Many stockholders of Walt Disney have been pushing for more say in key corporate governance issues such as how the board of directors is chosen and how corporate officers are supervised. Little by little, their voices have been heard. Disney has made a number of changes to the way directors are elected, reduced the size of its board, increased the number of independent members, and separated the role of chairman of the board from the role of chief executive officer.

Stockholders were looking forward to new leadership and new ideas when Michael Eisner was named CEO of Disney in the mid-1980s. The company's earnings were down, and its movies weren't drawing the huge audiences that management had hoped for. Eisner and his management team supercharged the theme park business, brought the company into the television industry by buying Cap Cities ABC, and put the magic back into Disney movies.

More than a decade into Eisner's revival of the Magic Kingdom's fortunes, however, some stockholders were grumbling. Disney had to write off millions that it had invested in its go.com Internet initiative as it changed its online strategy. Profits at the ABC Network were not up to par, and theme-park attendance was down following the terrorist attacks of 2001. Roy Disney, the last member of the Disney family to serve as a director, complained publicly about Eisner's management and the company's lagging share price. Eventually, he and another director resigned from the board and continued to push for management changes.

Eisner came under even more pressure when the cable company Comcast launched an unsolicited acquisition bid for Disney. As the company struggled against this unwanted takeover attempt—which it ultimately rebuffed—stockholders showed their displeasure with the CEO's performance. Eisner was running unopposed for reelection to the board, usually a routine event for a CEO who is also serving as chairman of the board. At this annual meeting, however, the CEO received a "withhold" vote from 45 percent of the shares.

Shareholders' voices were heard: The Disney board took the chairman's title away from Eisner that night, although he remained a director. No longer would the CEO be able to chair Disney's board of directors.

Within months, Eisner announced he would soon retire. In preparation, the board scheduled a meeting with officials of major pension funds, which own sizable blocks of Disney stock, to hear their concerns about corporate governance and to discuss choosing Eisner's successor.

In the next few months, the board cut the total number of directors and added a new director considered to be independent of the company's management. It committed to rotating members among the board's committees to bring new viewpoints to such key areas of corporate governance as executive compensation. And most important, it changed the voting rules to require any director who receives a majority of "withhold" votes to submit a letter of resignation. George J. Mitchell, who replaced Eisner as chairman of the board, said in announcing the new voting rules: "Today's action is the latest in a series of steps we have taken to further strengthen Disney's corporate governance practices."

Meanwhile, capping months of debate over choosing a new CEO, the board finally named Robert A. Iger, who served as president under Eisner. More than two decades after taking the helm, Eisner stepped down as CEO and simultaneously resigned from the board. Iger quickly made peace with Roy Disney, who was named director emeritus and announced that he would support the new CEO. What will stockholders say as the new Disney era unfolds?[13]

For more information about this company, go to **www.disney.com.**

Questions

1. Generally, stockholders of a large corporation such as Disney are fairly complacent with existing management. And yet, these same stockholders eventually changed the way that Disney was managed. In this case, what actions provoked stockholders to become so vocal?
2. After Michael Eisner received such a high percentage of "withhold" votes, do you think the Disney board should have taken additional steps beyond taking away his chairmanship title?
3. Do you agree with the Disney board's decision to meet with the managers of large pension funds that own sizable blocks of Disney stock? Why or why not?
4. Why is it important for a board to have a certain number of directors who are not corporate officers and have no personal connection with corporate officers? What can board members who are outside the corporation contribute to the overall management of a large corporation?

→ CHAPTER 5: JOURNAL EXERCISE

Discovery statement: Today, many people work for a sole proprietorship, partnership, or corporation. Still others decide to become entrepreneurs and start their own business.

Assume that you are now age 25 and have graduated from college. Would you prefer to work in someone else's business or one that you would start? Explain your answer.

_____

_____

_____

_____

_____

Assuming that you have decided to start your own small business, what special skills and experience will you need to be successful? (*Note:* You may want to talk with someone who owns a business before answering this question.)

_____

_____

_____

_____

Now describe where and how you could obtain the skills and experience you need to be successful.

_____

_____

_____

_____

_____

BUILDING SKILLS FOR CAREER SUCCESS

1. Exploring the Internet

Arguments about mergers and acquisitions often come down to an evaluation of who benefits and by how much. Sometimes the benefits include access to new products, talented management, new customers, or new sources of capital. Often the debate is complicated by the involvement of firms based in different countries.

The Internet is a fertile environment for information and discussion about mergers. The firms involved will provide their view about who will benefit and why it is either a good thing or not. Journalists will report facts and offer commentary as to how they see the future result of any merger, and of course, chat rooms located on the websites of many jour-

nals promote discussion about the issues. Visit the text website for updates to this exercise.

Assignment

1. Using an Internet search engine such as Google or Yahoo!, locate two or three sites providing information about a recent merger (use a keyword such as *merger*).

2. After examining these sites and reading journal articles, report information about the merger, such as the dollar value, the reasons behind the merger, and so forth.

3. Based on your assessment of the information you have read, do you think the merger is a good idea or not for the firms involved, the employees, the investors, the

industry, and society as a whole? Explain your reasoning.

2. Developing Critical-Thinking Skills

Suppose that you are a person who has always dreamed of owning a business but never had the money to open one. Since you were old enough to read a recipe, your mother allowed you to help in the kitchen. Most of all, you enjoyed baking and decorating cakes. You liked using your imagination to create cakes for special occasions. By the time you were in high school, you were baking and decorating wedding cakes for a fee. Also assume that after high school you started working full time as an adjuster for an insurance company. Your schedule now allows little time for baking and decorating cakes. Finally, assume that you inherited $250,000 and that changes at your job have created undue stress in your life. What should you do?

Assignment

1. Discuss the following points:
   a. What career options are available to you?
   b. If you decide to open your own business, what form of ownership would be best for your business?
   c. What advantages and disadvantages apply to your preferred form of business ownership?
2. Prepare a two-page report summarizing your findings.

3. Building Team Skills

Using the scenario in Exercise 2, suppose that you have decided to quit your job as an insurance adjuster and open a bakery. Your business is now growing, and you have decided to add a full line of catering services. This means more work and responsibility. You will need someone to help you, but you are undecided about what to do. Should you hire an employee or find a partner? If you add a partner, what type of decisions should be made to create a partnership agreement?

Assignment

1. In a group, discuss the following questions:
   a. What are the advantages and disadvantages of adding a partner versus hiring an employee?
   b. Assume that you have decided to form a partnership. What articles should be included in a partnership agreement?
   c. How would you go about finding a partner?
2. Summarize your group's answers to these questions, and present them to your class.
3. As a group, prepare an articles-of-partnership agreement. Be prepared to discuss the pros and cons of your group's agreement with other groups from your class, as well as to examine their agreements.

4. Researching Different Careers

Many people spend their entire lives working in jobs that they do not enjoy. Why is this so? Often it is because they have taken the first job they were offered without giving it much thought. How can you avoid having this happen to you? First, you should determine your "personal profile" by identifying and analyzing your own strengths, weaknesses, things you enjoy, and things you dislike. Second, you should identify the types of jobs that fit your profile. Third, you should identify and research the companies that offer those jobs.

Assignment

1. Take two sheets of paper and draw a line down the middle of each sheet, forming two columns on each page. Label column 1 "Things I Enjoy or Like to Do," column 2 "Things I Do Not Like Doing," column 3 "My Strengths," and column 4 "My Weaknesses."
2. Record data in each column over a period of at least one week. You may find it helpful to have a relative or friend give you input.
3. Summarize the data, and write a profile of yourself.
4. Take your profile to a career counselor at your college or to the public library and ask for help in identifying jobs that fit your profile. Your college may offer testing to assess your skills and personality. The Strong-Campbell Interest Inventory and the Myers-Briggs Personality Inventory can help you to assess the kind of work you may enjoy. The Internet is another resource.
5. Research the companies that offer the types of jobs that fit your profile.
6. Write a report on your findings.

5. Improving Communication Skills

If businesses are to succeed, they must change continually. Change takes many forms. Every week newspapers report on companies taking steps to organize into larger units or to downsize into smaller units. This chapter has discussed several strategies that effect change in organizations. They include mergers and acquisitions, hostile takeovers, and leveraged buyouts.

Assignment

1. Read articles illustrating how one or more of these strategies has caused an organization to change.

2. Write a two-page report covering the following:

   a. Explain in your own words what led up to this change.

   b. How will this change affect the company itself, its consumers, its employees, its investors, and its industry?

   c. What opportunities does this change create, and what problems do you forecast?

→ PREP TEST

Matching Questions

___ 1. It is an association of two or more business owners.

___ 2. AT&T is an example of this type of corporation.

___ 3. This type of ownership is the easiest type of business to start.

___ 4. A person who invests only capital in a partnership.

___ 5. The concept of being personally responsible for all debts of a business.

___ 6. An entity or artificial being with most legal rights of a person.

___ 7. It describes the purpose of the corporation.

___ 8. A process that is used in purchasing another firm.

___ 9. Type of business used to fulfill a specific purpose in conducting business transactions.

___ 10. A company chartered in a foreign country doing business in the United States.

a. alien corporation
b. corporate charter
c. corporation
d. joint venture
e. limited partner
f. merger
g. open corporation
h. partnership
i. sole proprietorship
j. unlimited liability

True/False Questions

T F

11. ○ ○ Unlimited liability is an advantage of a sole proprietorship.

12. ○ ○ The Federal Deposit Insurance Corporation (FDIC) is an example of a open corporation.

13. ○ ○ Cooperatives are owned by their members.

14. ○ ○ Syndicates are formed to underwrite large loans for business expansions.

15. ○ ○ The articles of partnership is a written contract describing the terms of a partnership.

T F

16. ○ ○ Preferred stockholders have voting rights.

17. ○ ○ The S-corporation form of organization allows a corporation to avoid double taxation.

18. ○ ○ Cooperatives are more prevalent in the banking industry.

19. ○ ○ At least one general partner must be responsible for the debts of the limited partnership.

20. ○ ○ The board of directors is directly responsible to the shareholders.

Multiple-Choice Questions

21. During college, Elyssa Wood earned extra money by using her culinary skills to cater special parties. After graduation, she decided to turn her part-time job into a full-time business that she plans to expand in the future. In the meantime, she wants to maintain complete control of the business. She will *most likely* organize the business as a

    a. limited partnership.

    b. corporation.

    c. general partnership.

    d. sole proprietorship.

    e. cooperative.

22. Which of the following is *not* an advantage of a corporate form of ownership?

    a. It is easier to raise capital.

    b. Ownership can be transferred easily and quickly.

    c. The death of an owner does not terminate the corporation.

    d. Profits are taxed twice.

    e. The liability of the owners is limited.

23. A corporation incorporated in Texas doing business in New York is known in

    a. New York as a domestic corporation.

    b. Texas as a foreign corporation.

    c. Texas as a domestic corporation.

    d. New York as an alien corporation.

    e. All the above.

24. PepsiCo acquired Pizza Hut. What type of merger was this?

    a. Limited

    b. Syndicate

    c. Joint venture

    d. Horizontal

    e. Vertical

25. J. R. Imax, a financial investor, wants to control the Simex Company. So far he has been unsuccessful in purchasing enough stock to give him control. To reach his goal, which technique should he use to gather enough stockholder votes to control the company?

    a. Stock offer

    b. Liability takeover

    c. Merger

    d. Acquisition

    e. Proxy fight

Fill-in-the-Blank Questions

26. A corporation whose stock is owned by relatively few people is called a(an) _____ corporation.

27. When groups need large sums of money for a job, they are likely to establish a _____.

28. A technique used to gather enough stockholder votes to control a company is called a _____.

29. The ability to combine skills and knowledge is an advantage of a _____ type of ownership.

30. A _____ merger takes place between firms in completely different industries.

Online Study Center

FOR MORE **test practice, use the interactive ACE quizzes available at the Online Student Center:**
www.college.hmco.com/PIC/pridebusiness9e.

Small Business, Entrepreneurship, and Franchises

WHAT you will be able to do once you complete this chapter:

1 Define what a small business is and recognize the fields in which small businesses are concentrated.

2 Identify the people who start small businesses and the reasons why some succeed and many fail.

3 Assess the contributions of small businesses to our economy.

4 Judge the advantages and disadvantages of operating a small business.

5 Explain how the Small Business Administration helps small businesses.

6 Appraise the concept and types of franchising.

7 Analyze the growth of franchising and franchising's advantages and disadvantages.

WHY this chapter matters

America's small businesses drive the U.S. economy. Small businesses represent 99.7 percent of all employer firms, and there is a good probability that you will work for a small business or perhaps even start your own business. This chapter can help you to become a good employee or a successful entrepreneur.

FOR HELP with studying this chapter, visit the Online Student Center:

www.college.hmco.com/PIC/pridebusiness9e

Online Study Center

Inside Business
Carol's Daughter Grows Up With Beauty

Carol's Daughter has quite a story to tell about building a small business into an international enterprise. Founder Lisa Price, whose mother was named Carol, began her business by mixing fragrances and skin lotions in her New York City kitchen. In 1999, after years of selling her beauty products at events such as the DanceAfrica bazaar and the International African Arts Festival, Price opened her first Carol's Daughter store in Brooklyn, New York.

The Brooklyn store is still open and doing well, managed by Price's son, Aerol Hutson. Carol's Daughter also publishes a catalog and sells online. One reason the business has thrived is because Price is very responsive to customers' suggestions about new products. At one point she was offering 1,000 different items in her store and her seasonal catalogs.

These days, however, Carol's Daughter has grown into much more than a family business. Six years after the grand store opening in

DID YOU KNOW?

Carol's Daughter received a $10 million investment from celebrities such as Will Smith, Jada Pinkett Smith, Steve Stoute, and Thalia?

Brooklyn, Carol's Daughter celebrated a star-studded store opening in the heart of Harlem. Now, with celebrity backing, the company is building its name from coast to coast and beyond.

These ambitious expansion plans took shape after an investment group, headed by record executive and marketing expert Steve Stoute, put $10 million into Carol's Daughter. The investors include actor Will Smith, his wife Jada Pinkett Smith, singer Thalia, rapper Jay-Z, and other celebrities. Stoute explains, "Our job [as investors] is to nurture this business's growth—to take it from a crawl to a walk." To do this, the investors are going beyond financial backing. "I was thrilled several years ago when I learned that Jada used our products," Price says. "Now she's appearing in our advertising. We used to shoot the catalog in my kitchen; now we can use the best photographers. It's a dream come true."[1]

For more information about this company go to **www .carolsdaughter.com**.

Just as Lisa Price's empire grew from mixing fragrances and skin lotions in her New York City kitchen, most businesses start small. Unlike Price's empire, most small businesses that survive usually stay small. They provide a solid foundation for our economy—as employers, as suppliers and purchasers of goods and services, and as taxpayers.

In this chapter we do not take small businesses for granted. Instead, we look closely at this important business sector—beginning with a definition of small business, a description of industries that often attract small businesses, and a profile of some of the people who start small businesses. Next, we consider the importance of small businesses in our economy. We also present the advantages and disadvantages of smallness in business. We then describe services provided by the Small Business Administration, a government agency formed to assist owners and managers of small businesses. We conclude the chapter with a discussion of the pros and cons of franchising, an approach to small-business ownership that has become very popular in the last thirty years.

Small Business: A Profile

The Small Business Administration (SBA) defines a **small business** as "one which is independently owned and operated for profit and is not dominant in its field." How small must a firm be not to dominate its field? That depends on the particular industry it is in. The SBA has developed the following specific "smallness" guidelines for the various industries, as shown in Table 6.1.[2] The SBA periodically revises and simplifies its small-business size regulations.

Annual sales in the millions of dollars may not seem very small. However, for many firms, profit is only a small percentage of total sales. Thus a firm may earn only $40,000 or $50,000 on yearly sales of $1 million—and that *is* small in comparison with the profits earned by most medium-sized and large firms. Moreover, most small firms have annual sales well below the maximum limits in the SBA guidelines.

The Small-Business Sector

In the United States, it typically takes four days and $210 to establish a business as a legal entity. The steps include registering the name of the business, applying for tax IDs, and setting up unemployment and workers' compensation insurance. In Japan, however, a typical entrepreneur spends more than $3,500 and thirty-one days to follow eleven different procedures (see Table 6.2).

A surprising number of Americans take advantage of their freedom to start a business. There are, in fact, about twenty-three million businesses in this country. Only just over 17,000 of these employ more than 500 workers—enough to be considered large.

Interest in owning or starting a small business has never been greater than it is today. During the last decade, the number of small businesses in the United States has increased 49 percent, and for the last few years, new-business formation in the United States has broken successive records, except during the 2001–2002 recession. Recently, nearly 581,000 new businesses were incorporated. Furthermore, part-time entrepreneurs have increased fivefold in recent years; they now account for one-third of all small businesses.[3]

**1 LEARNING OBJECTIVE
Define** what a small business is and recognize the fields in which small businesses are concentrated.

small business one that is independently owned and operated for profit and is not dominant in its field

> > **TABLE 6.1**

INDUSTRY GROUP-SIZE STANDARDS

Small business size standards are usually stated in number of employees or average annual sales. In the United States, 99.7 percent of all businesses are considered small.

Industry Group	Size Standard
Manufacturing	500 employees
Wholesale trade	100 employees
Agriculture	$750,000
Retail trade	$6.5 million
General & heavy construction (except dredging)	$31 million
Dredging	$18.5 million
Special trade contractors	$13 million
Travel agencies	$3.5 million (commissions & other income)
Business and personal services except	$6.5 million
• Architectural, engineering, surveying, and mapping services	$4.5 million
• Dry cleaning and carpet cleaning services	$4.5 million

Source: **www.sba.gov/size/indexwhatsnew.html#%inf/IFR**, accessed December 13, 2005.

>> TABLE 6.2

ESTABLISHING A BUSINESS AROUND THE WORLD

The entrepreneurial spirit provides the spark that enriches the U.S. economy. The growth will continue if lawmakers resist the urge to overregulate entrepreneurs and provide policies that foster free enterprise.

	Number of Procedures	Time (days)	Cost (US$)	Minimum Capital (% per Capita Income)
Australia	2	2	402	0
Belgium	7	56	2,633	75.1
Canada	2	3	127	0
Denmark	4	4	0	52.3
France	10	53	663	32.1
Germany	9	45	1,341	103.8
Greece	16	45	8,115	145.3
Ireland	3	12	2,473	0
Italy	9	23	4,565	49.6
Japan	11	31	3,518	71.3
Netherlands	7	11	3,276	70.7
New Zealand	3	3	28	0
Norway	4	24	1,460	33.1
Portugal	11	95	1,360	43.4
Spain	11	115	2,366	19.6
Sweden	3	16	190	41.4
Switzerland	6	20	3,228	33.8
United Kingdom	6	18	264	0
United States	5	4	210	0

Sources: World Bank (2004); as found in *Inside the Vault,* Federal Reserve Bank of St. Louis, Fall 2004, p. 1.

Statistically, over 70 percent of new businesses can be expected to fail within their first five years.[4] The primary reason for these failures is mismanagement resulting from a lack of business know-how. The makeup of the small-business sector thus is constantly changing. Despite the high failure rate, many small businesses succeed modestly. Some, like Apple Computer, Inc., are extremely successful—to the point where they can no longer be considered small. Taken together, small businesses are also responsible for providing a high percentage of the jobs in the United States. According to some estimates, the figure is well over 50 percent.

Industries that Attract Small Businesses

Some industries, such as auto manufacturing, require huge investments in machinery and equipment. Businesses in such industries are big from the day they are started—if an entrepreneur or group of entrepreneurs can gather the capital required to start one.

By contrast, a number of other industries require only a low initial investment and some special skills or knowledge. It is these industries that tend to attract new businesses. Growing industries, such as outpatient-care facilities, are attractive because of their profit potential. However, knowledgeable entrepreneurs choose areas with which they are familiar, and these are most often the more established industries.

Small enterprise spans the gamut from corner newspaper vending to the development of optical fibers. The owners of small businesses sell gasoline, flowers, and coffee to go. They publish magazines, haul freight, teach languages, and program computers. They make wines, movies, and high-fashion clothes. They build new homes and restore old ones. They fix appliances, recycle metals, and sell used cars. They drive cabs and fly planes. They make us well when we are ill, and they sell us the products of corporate giants. In fact, 74 percent of real estate, rental, and leasing industries; 76 percent of the businesses in the arts, entertainment, and recreational services; and 90 percent of the construction industries are dominated by small businesses.[5] The various kinds of businesses generally fall into three broad categories of industry: distribution, service, and production.

Distribution Industries   This category includes retailing, wholesaling, transportation, and communications—industries concerned with the movement of goods from producers to consumers. Distribution industries account for approximately 33 percent of all small businesses. Of these, almost three-quarters are involved in retailing, that is, the sale of goods directly to consumers. Clothing and jewelry stores, pet shops, bookstores, and grocery stores, for example, are all retailing firms. Slightly less than one-quarter of the small distribution firms are wholesalers. Wholesalers purchase products in quantity from manufacturers and then resell them to retailers.

Service Industries   This category accounts for over 48 percent of all small businesses. Of these, about three-quarters provide such nonfinancial services as medical and dental care; watch, shoe, and TV repairs; haircutting and styling; restaurant meals; and dry cleaning. About 8 percent of the small service firms offer financial services, such as accounting, insurance, real estate, and investment counseling. An increasing number of self-employed Americans are running service businesses from home.

Production Industries   This last category includes the construction, mining, and manufacturing industries. Only about 19 percent of all small businesses are in this group, mainly because these industries require relatively large initial investments. Small firms that do venture into production generally make parts and subassemblies for larger manufacturing firms or supply special skills to larger construction firms.

The People in Small Businesses: The Entrepreneurs

The entrepreneurial spirit is alive and well in the United States. A recent study revealed that the U.S. population is quite entrepreneurial when compared with those of other countries. More than 70 percent of Americans would prefer being an entrepreneur to working for someone else. This compares with 46 percent of adults in Western Europe and 58 percent of adults in Canada. Another study on entrepreneurial activity for 2002 found that of thirty-six countries studied, the United States was in the top third in entrepreneurial activity and was the leader when compared with Japan, Canada, and Western Europe.[6]

Small businesses typically are managed by the people who started and own them. Most of these people have held jobs with other firms and still could be so employed if they wanted. Yet owners of small businesses would rather take the risk of starting and operating their own firms, even if the money they make is less than the salaries they otherwise might earn.

Researchers have suggested a variety of personal factors as reasons why people go into business for themselves. One that is cited often is the "entrepreneurial spirit"—the desire to create a new business. For example, Nikki Olyai always knew that she wanted to create and develop her own business. Her father, a successful businessman in Iran, was her role model. She came to the United States at the age of seventeen and lived with a host family in Salem, Oregon, attending high school there. Undergraduate and graduate degrees in computer science led her to start Innovision Technologies while she held two other jobs to keep the business going and took care of her four-year-old son. Recently, Nikki Olyai was honored by the Women's Business Enterprise National Council's "Salute to Women's Business Enterprises" as one of eleven top

2 LEARNING OBJECTIVE
Identify the people who start small businesses and the reasons why some succeed and many fail.

Teens tagging with a high-powered CO2 laser. Meet Kyle Grossman and his sisters, Kacie and Colby. These young siblings from Boca Raton, Florida, specialize in engraving digital photographs onto aluminum dog tags with a high-powered CO2 laser. Their business, Unlimited Dog Tags, is now off the ground and running.

successful firms. Innovision Technologies specializes in information technology, systems analysis and assessment, project management, and quality assurance. For three consecutive years her firm was selected as a "Future 50 of Greater Detroit Company."[7] Other factors, such as independence, the desire to determine one's own destiny, and the willingness to find and accept a challenge certainly play a part. Background may exert an influence as well. In particular, researchers think that people whose families have been in business (successfully or not) are most apt to start and run their own businesses. Those who start their own businesses also tend to cluster around certain ages—more than 70 percent are between 24 and 44 years of age[8] (see Figure 6.1).

High-tech teen entrepreneurship is definitely exploding. "There's not a period in history where we've seen such a plethora of young entrepreneurs," comments Nancy F. Koehn, associate professor of business administration at Harvard Business School. Still, teen entrepreneurs face unique pressures in juggling their schoolwork, their social life, and their high-tech workload. Some ultimately quit school, whereas others quit or cut back on their business activities. Melissa Sconyers, a web designer, chose to shrink her workload: "I had lost touch with my friends. I had to remember I am a teenager."[9] Or Consider Brian Hendricks at Winston Churchill High School in Potomac, Maryland. He is the founder of StartUpPc and VB Solutions, Inc. StartUpPc, founded in 2001, sells custom-built computers and computer services for home users, home offices, small businesses, and students. Brian's services include design, installation of systems, training, networking, and on-site technical support. In October 2002, Brian founded VB Solutions, Inc., which develops and customizes websites and message boards. The firm sets up advertising contracts and counsels website owners on site improvements. The company has designed corporate ID kits, logos, and websites for clients from all over the world. Brian learned at a very young age that working for yourself is one of the best jobs avail-

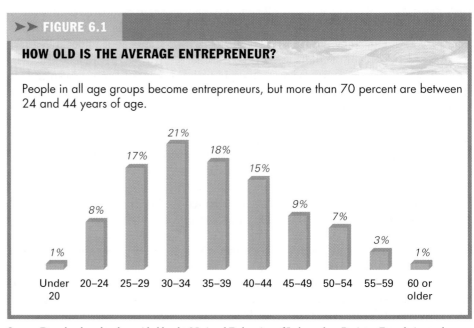

>> FIGURE 6.1

HOW OLD IS THE AVERAGE ENTREPRENEUR?

People in all age groups become entrepreneurs, but more than 70 percent are between 24 and 44 years of age.

Under 20	20–24	25–29	30–34	35–39	40–44	45–49	50–54	55–59	60 or older
1%	8%	17%	21%	18%	15%	9%	7%	3%	1%

Source: Data developed and provided by the National Federation of Independent Business Foundation and sponsored by the American Express Travel Related Services Company, Inc.

BizTech

Goodbye Cell Phone, Hello Wi-Fi Phone?

Wi-Fi phones—which route calls via wireless Internet access—are a cutting-edge way for small businesses to cut communication costs. Here are the pros and cons:

Advantages

Wi-Fi phones work in any area that has wireless Internet access, such as a company's private network or a public Wi-Fi hot spot in a hotel, school, or coffee

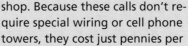

shop. Because these calls don't require special wiring or cell phone towers, they cost just pennies per minute or, in many cases, are free. Not only are Wi-Fi calls cheaper than cell phone calls, they are often clearer. And in the near future, Wi-Fi videoconferencing will bring voices and images together in a single call.

Disadvantages

Callers need specially equipped phones and must log into a wireless network to make or receive calls. Moreover, experts warn that public Wi-Fi hot spots may not be secure. Just as important, the standards and technology are relatively new and are still evolving. Therefore, small businesses must consider one final disadvantage: A souped-up Wi-Fi phone that is state-of-the-art today could, in a matter of months, become a useless paperweight.

able. According to Brian, a young entrepreneur must possess "the five P's of entrepreneurship"—planning, persistence, patience, people, and profit. Brian knows what it takes to be a successful entrepreneur. His accolades include Junior Achievement's "National Youth Entrepreneur of the Year" and SBA's 2005 "Young Entrepreneur of the Year" awards.[10]

Finally, there must be some motivation to start a business. A person may decide that he or she simply has "had enough" of working and earning a profit for someone else. Another may lose his or her job for some reason and decide to start the business he or she has always wanted rather than seek another job. Still another person may have an idea for a new product or a new way to sell an existing product. Or the opportunity to go into business may arise suddenly, perhaps as a result of a hobby, as was the case with Cheryl Strand. Strand started baking and decorating cakes from her home while working full time as a word processor at Clemson University. Her cakes became so popular that she soon found herself working through her lunch breaks and late into the night to meet customer demand.

After deciding to start her own business, Strand contacted the Clemson University Small Business Development Center. The center helped her prepare for the business start-up and develop a loan package—complete with a detailed business plan and financial statements for presentation at local banks. Strand obtained the $10,000 she needed. Since then, Cakes by Cheryl has doubled in size and has increased sales by approximately 56 percent per year. It now offers fresh breads, deli sandwiches, a tempting line of baked goods, and catering and carry-out services.

Cheryl Strand is one of a growing number of women who are small-business owners. Women are 51 percent of the U.S. population, and according to the SBA, they owned at least 50 percent of all small businesses in 2005. Women already own 66 percent of the home-based businesses in this country, and the number of men in home-based businesses is growing rapidly.

According to the SBA, 6.5 million women-owned businesses in the United States provide over 7.2 million jobs and generate $950.6 billion in sales annually.[11] Furthermore, women-owned businesses in the United States have proven that they are more successful; over 40 percent have been in business for twelve years or more. According to Dun and Bradstreet, women-owned businesses are financially sound and creditworthy, and their risk of failure is lower than average.

Just over one-half of small businesses are home-based and 91 percent have no employees. About 60 percent of home-based businesses are in service industries,

16 percent in construction, 14 percent in retail trade, and the rest in manufacturing, finance, transportation, communications, wholesaling, and other industries.[12]

In some people, the motivation to start a business develops slowly as they gain the knowledge and ability required for success as a business owner. Knowledge and ability—especially management ability—are probably the most important factors involved. A new firm is very much built around the entrepreneur. The owner must be able to manage the firm's finances, its personnel (if there are any employees), and its day-to-day operations. He or she must handle sales, advertising, purchasing, pricing, and a variety of other business functions. The knowledge and ability to do so are acquired most often through experience working for other firms in the same area of business.

Why Small Businesses Fail

Small businesses are prone to failure. Capital, management, and planning are the key ingredients in the survival of a small business, as well as the most common reasons for failure. Businesses can experience a number of money-related problems. It may take several years before a business begins to show a profit. Entrepreneurs need to have not only the capital to open a business but also the money to operate it in its possibly lengthy start-up phase. One cash-flow obstacle often leads to others. And a series of cash-flow predicaments usually ends in a business failure. This scenario is played out all too often by small and not-so-small start-up Internet firms that fail to meet their financial backers' expectations and so are denied a second wave of investment dollars to continue their drive to establish a profitable online firm. For example, in one month alone, Digital Entertainment Network shut its video-streaming site, clothing distributor boo.com closed after spending more than $100 million in only six months of business, and healthshop.com shut its doors completely after failing to meet its investors' expectations.[13]

Many entrepreneurs lack the management skills required to run a business. Money, time, personnel, and inventory all need to be managed effectively if a small business is to succeed. Starting a small business requires much more than optimism and a good idea.

Success and expansion sometimes lead to problems. Frequently, entrepreneurs with successful small businesses make the mistake of overexpansion. Fast growth often results in dramatic changes in a business. Thus the entrepreneur must plan carefully and adjust competently to new and potentially disruptive situations.

Every day, and in every part of the country, people open new businesses. For example, recently, 581,000 new businesses opened their doors, but at the same time, 576,200 businesses closed their business and 34,317 businesses declared bankruptcy.[14] Although many fail, others represent well-conceived ideas developed by entrepreneurs who have the expertise, resources, and determination to make their businesses succeed. As these well-prepared entrepreneurs pursue their individual goals, our society benefits in many ways from their work and creativity. Such billion-dollar companies as Apple Computer, McDonald's Corporation, and Procter & Gamble are all examples of small businesses that expanded into industry giants.

The Importance of Small Businesses in Our Economy

3 LEARNING OBJECTIVE
Assess the contributions of small businesses to our economy.

This country's economic history abounds with stories of ambitious men and women who turned their ideas into business dynasties. The Ford Motor Company started as a one-man operation with an innovative method for industrial production. L. L. Bean, Inc., can trace its beginnings to a basement shop in Freeport, Maine. Both Xerox and Polaroid began as small firms with a better way to do a job.

Sikorsky still flying high. Igor Sikorsky, the Russian-born scientist, engineer, pilot, and entrepreneur, made aviation history with his mix of genius and determination. After a lifetime of challenges, achievements, and honors, he died in 1972 at the age of 83. Today, Sikorsky Aircraft continues his dream of vertical flight, and his tradition of technical innovation.

Providing Technical Innovation

Invention and innovation are part of the foundations of our economy. The increases in productivity that have characterized the past 200 years of our history are all rooted in one principal source: new ways to do a job with less effort for less money. Studies show that the incidence of innovation among small-business workers is significantly higher than among workers in large businesses. Small firms produce two and a half times as many innovations as large firms relative to the number of persons employed. In fact, small firms employ 41 percent of all high-tech workers such as scientists, engineers, and computer specialists. No wonder small firms produce thirteen to fourteen times more patents per employee than large patenting firms.[15]

According to the U.S. Office of Management and Budget, more than half the major technological advances of the twentieth century originated with individual inventors and small companies. Even just a sampling of those innovations is remarkable:

- Air conditioning
- Airplane
- Automatic transmission
- FM radio
- Heart valve
- Helicopter
- Instant camera
- Insulin
- Jet engine
- Penicillin
- Personal computer
- Power steering

Perhaps even more remarkable—and important—is that many of these inventions sparked major new U.S. industries or contributed to an established industry by adding some valuable service.

Providing Employment

Small firms traditionally have added more than their proportional share of new jobs to the economy. Recently, the U.S. economy created over three million new jobs. Seven out of the ten industries that added the most new jobs were small-business-dominated industries. Small businesses creating the most new jobs in 2004 included business services, leisure and hospitality services, and special trade contractors. Small firms hire a larger proportion of employees who are younger workers, older workers, women, or workers who prefer to work part time. Furthermore, small businesses provide 67 percent of workers with their first jobs and initial on-the-job training in basic skills. According to the SBA, small businesses represent about 99 percent of all employers, employ about 50 percent of the private work force, and provide about two-thirds of the net new jobs added to our economy.[16]

Small businesses thus contribute significantly to solving unemployment problems. Table 6.3 shows the industries that are generating the most new jobs and the small-business shares in those industries.

Providing Competition

Small businesses challenge larger, established firms in many ways, causing them to become more efficient and more responsive to consumer needs. A small business cannot, of course, compete with a large firm in all respects. But a number of small firms, each competing in its own particular area and its own particular way, together have the desired competitive effect. Thus several small janitorial companies together add up to reasonable competition for the no-longer-small ServiceMaster.

Filling Needs of Society and Other Businesses

By their nature, large firms must operate on a large scale. Many may be unwilling or unable to meet the special needs of smaller groups of consumers. Such groups create almost perfect markets for small companies, which can tailor their products to these groups and fill their needs profitably. A prime example is a firm that modifies automobile controls to accommodate handicapped drivers.

Small firms also provide a variety of goods and services to each other and to much larger firms. Sears, Roebuck purchases merchandise from approximately 12,000 sup-

---

>> **TABLE 6.3**

INDUSTRIES GENERATING THE MOST JOBS

This ranking is based on the change (increase) in number of jobs from 2003 to 2004. The small-business share of new jobs is greatest in construction and leisure and hospitality services.

Industry	Annual Employment 2003	Increase from 2004	Percent Small Business
Construction	6,920,000	200,000	85.1
Financial services	8,050,000	80,000	40.2
Professional and business services	16,450,000	460,000	44.2
Leisure and hospitality services	12,320,000	196,000	61.2
Trade, transportation, and utilities	25,480,000	200,000	47.1

Source: The U.S. Small Business Administration, Office of Advocacy, using data from the U.S. Department of Commerce, Bureau of the Census, U.S. Department of Labor, Bureau of Labor Statistics, February 10, 2005.

ENTREPRENEURIAL CHALLENGE

When Should Entrepreneurs Use Outsourcing?

Small businesses are not necessarily sending jobs overseas when they choose outsourcing. For entrepreneurs and established companies alike, outsourcing can mean hiring local or national vendors to handle specialized functions such as payroll, manufacturing, information technology, and food services. Before outsourcing, an entrepreneur should ask:

- Is the function so strategically important or sensitive that it must be handled by my own staff only?

- Does my company have the people, expertise, and equipment to do the job more efficiently than an outsource vendor?
- Can my company weather the possible disruption if an outsource vendor experiences supply, labor, technical, or weather problems?
- How will the vendor handle any liability issues that might arise in managing the outsourced function?
- How long has the vendor been in business, and what do its customers say about its performance?
- Is the outsourcing contract too expensive, too restrictive, or too lengthy?
- What will my company need to do to manage the outsource vendor properly?

pliers—and most of them are small businesses. General Motors relies on more than 32,000 companies for parts and supplies and depends on more than 11,000 independent dealers to sell its automobiles and trucks. Large firms generally buy parts and assemblies from smaller firms for one very good reason: It is less expensive than manufacturing the parts in their own factories. This lower cost eventually is reflected in the price that consumers pay for their products.

It is clear that small businesses are a vital part of our economy and that, as consumers and as members of the labor force, we all benefit enormously from their existence. Now let us look at the situation from the viewpoint of the owners of small businesses.

The Pros and Cons of Smallness

Do most owners of small businesses dream that their firms will grow into giant corporations—managed by professionals—while they serve only on the board of directors? Or would they rather stay small, in a firm where they have the opportunity (and the responsibility) to do everything that needs to be done? The answers depend on the personal characteristics and motivations of the individual owners. For many, the advantages of remaining small far outweigh the disadvantages.

4 LEARNING OBJECTIVE
Judge the advantages and disadvantages of operating a small business..

Advantages of Small Business

Small-business owners with limited resources often must struggle to enter competitive new markets. They also have to deal with increasing international competition. However, they enjoy several unique advantages.

Personal Relationships with Customers and Employees   For those who like dealing with people, small business is the place to be. The owners of retail shops get to know many of their customers by name and deal with them on a personal basis.

Farm fresh, home-grown decorations with a personal touch. What do corn stalks, straw bales, pumpkins, and gourds have in common? They're all part of the autumnal decorations crafted by Sarah Hodge of Farm Girls Decorations in Janesville, Wisconsin. Hodge and her partner, Tammy Waller, create customized harvest displays for homes and businesses. The supplies for their decorations are grown locally at Hodge's mother's farm, The Good Acres, and Waller's Silverstone farm.

Through such relationships, small-business owners often become involved in the social, cultural, and political life of the community.

Relationships between owner-managers and employees also tend to be closer in smaller businesses. In many cases the owner is a friend and counselor as well as the boss.

These personal relationships provide an important business advantage. The personal service small businesses offer to customers is a major competitive weapon—one that larger firms try to match but often cannot. In addition, close relationships with employees often help the small-business owner to keep effective workers who might earn more with a larger firm.

Ability to Adapt to Change Being his or her own boss, the owner-manager of a small business does not need anyone's permission to adapt to change. An owner may add or discontinue merchandise or services, change store hours, and experiment with various price strategies in response to changes in market conditions. And through personal relationships with customers, the owners of small businesses quickly become aware of changes in people's needs and interests, as well as in the activities of competing firms.

Simplified Record Keeping Many small firms need only a simple set of records. Record keeping might consist of a checkbook, a cash-receipts journal in which to record all sales, and a cash-disbursements journal in which to record all amounts paid out. Obviously, enough records must be kept to allow for producing and filing accurate tax returns.

Independence Small-business owners do not have to punch in and out, bid for vacation times, take orders from superiors, or worry about being fired or laid off. They are the masters of their own destinies—at least with regard to employment. For many people, this is the prime advantage of owning a small business.

Other Advantages According to the SBA, the most profitable companies in the United States are small firms that have been in business for more than ten years and employ fewer than twenty people. Small-business owners also enjoy all the advantages of sole proprietorships, which were discussed in Chapter 5. These include being able to keep all profits, the ease and low cost of going into business and (if necessary) going out of business, and being able to keep business information secret.

Disadvantages of Small Business

Personal contacts with customers, closer relationships with employees, being one's own boss, less cumbersome record-keeping chores, and independence are the bright side of small business. In contrast, the dark side reflects problems unique to these firms.

Risk of Failure As we have noted, small businesses (especially new ones) run a heavy risk of going out of business—about two out of three close their doors within the first six years. Older, well-established small firms can be hit hard by a business recession mainly because they do not have the financial resources to weather an extended difficult period.

Limited Potential   Small businesses that survive do so with varying degrees of success. Many are simply the means of making a living for the owner and his or her family. The owner may have some technical skill—as a hair stylist or electrician, for example—and may have started a business to put this skill to work. Such a business is unlikely to grow into big business. Also, employees' potential for advancement is limited.

Limited Ability to Raise Capital   Small businesses typically have a limited ability to obtain capital. Figure 6.2 shows that most small-business financing comes out of the owner's pocket. Personal loans from lending institutions provide only about one-fourth of the capital required by small businesses. About 70 percent of all new firms begin with less than $25,000 in total capital, according to Census Bureau and Federal Reserve surveys. In fact, almost half of new firms begin with less than $10,000, usually provided by the owner or family members and friends.[17]

Although every person who considers starting a small business should be aware of the hazards and pitfalls we have noted, a well-conceived business plan may help to avoid the risk of failure. The U.S. government is also dedicated to helping small businesses make it. It expresses this aim most actively through the SBA.

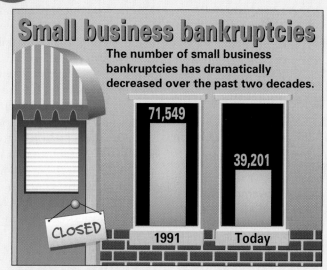

SPOTLIGHT

Small business bankruptcies

The number of small business bankruptcies has dramatically decreased over the past two decades.

71,549 — 1991
39,201 — Today

Source: U.S. Census Bureau, U.S. Department of Labor, Employment, and Training Administration, Administrative Office of the U.S. Courts, 2004; **www.sba.gov/advo/**, October 2005.

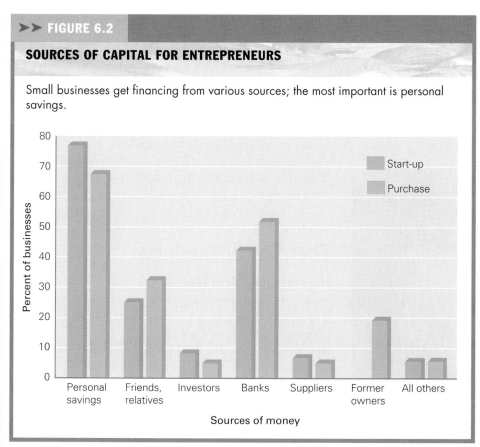

▶▶ FIGURE 6.2

SOURCES OF CAPITAL FOR ENTREPRENEURS

Small businesses get financing from various sources; the most important is personal savings.

Legend: Start-up, Purchase

Y-axis: Percent of businesses
X-axis: Sources of money — Personal savings, Friends, relatives, Investors, Banks, Suppliers, Former owners, All others

Source: Data developed and provided by the National Federation of Independent Business Foundation and sponsored by the American Express Travel Related Services Company, Inc.

Developing a Business Plan

Lack of planning can be as deadly as lack of money to a new small business. Planning is important to any business, large or small, and never should be overlooked or taken lightly. A **business plan** is a carefully constructed guide for the person starting a business. Consider it as a tool with three basic purposes: communication, management, and planning. As a communication tool, a business plan serves as a concise document that potential investors can examine to see if they would like to invest or assist in financing a new venture. It shows whether a business has the potential to make a profit. As a management tool, the business plan helps to track, monitor, and evaluate the progress. The business plan is a living document; it is modified as the entrepreneur gains knowledge and experience. It also serves to establish timelines and milestones and allows comparison of growth projections against actual accomplishments. Finally, as a planning tool, the business plan guides a business person through the various phases of business. For example, the plan helps to identify obstacles to avoid and to establish alternatives. According to Robert Krummer, Jr., chairman of First Business Bank in Los Angeles, "The business plan is a necessity. If the person who wants to start a small business can't put a business plan together, he or she is in trouble."

business plan a carefully constructed guide for the person starting a business

5 LEARNING OBJECTIVE
Explain how the Small Business Administration helps small businesses.

Small Business Administration (SBA) a governmental agency that assists, counsels, and protects the interests of small businesses in the United States

Components of a Business Plan

Table 6.4 shows the twelve sections that a business plan should include. Each section is further explained at the end of each of the seven major parts in the text. The goal of each end-of-the part exercise is to help a business person create his or her own business plan. When constructing a business plan, the business person should strive to keep it easy to read, uncluttered, and complete. Like other busy executives, officials of financial institutions do not have the time to wade through pages of extraneous data. The business plan should answer the four questions banking officials and investors are most interested in: (1) What exactly is the nature and mission of the new venture? (2) Why is this new enterprise a good idea? (3) What are the business person's goals? (4) How much will the new venture cost?

The great amount of time and consideration that should go into creating a business plan probably will end up saving time later. For example, Sharon Burch, who was running a computer software business while earning a degree in business administration, had to write a business plan as part of one of her courses. Burch has said, "I wish I'd taken the class before I started my business. I see a lot of things I could have done differently. But it has helped me since because I've been using the business plan as a guide for my business." Table 6.5 provides a business plan checklist. Accuracy and realistic expectations are crucial to an effective business plan. It is unethical to deceive loan officers, and it is unwise to deceive yourself.

Nailing down a successful business. Hanh Nguyen is one of a growing number of minority women who are small business owners. Hanh is an entrepreneur from Saigon, Vietnam, who wants her manicure business in Memphis, Tennessee, to succeed. She is determined to adjust to a new lifestyle in America and to learn a new language and the "American Way" of doing business. She even named her business "Kathy's Nails," after her newly adopted first name.

The Small Business Administration

The **Small Business Administration (SBA),** created by Congress in 1953, is a governmental agency that assists, counsels, and protects the interests of small businesses in the United States. It helps people get into business and stay in business. The agency provides assistance to owners and managers of prospective, new, and established small businesses. Through more than 1,000 offices and resource centers throughout the nation, the SBA provides both financial assistance and management counseling. Recently, the SBA provided training, technical assistance, and education to

> > **TABLE 6.4**

COMPONENTS OF A BUSINESS PLAN

1. *Introduction.* Basic information such as the name, address, and phone number of the business; the date the plan was issued; and a statement of confidentiality to keep important information away from potential competitors.

2. *Executive Summary.* A one- to two-page overview of the entire business plan, including a justification why the business will succeed.

3. *Benefits to the Community.* Information on how the business will have an impact on economic development, community development, and human development.

4. *Company and Industry.* The background of the company, choice of the legal business form, information on the products or services to be offered; and examination of the potential customers, current competitors, and the business's future.

5. *Management Team.* Discussion of skills, talents, and job descriptions of management team, managerial compensation, management training needs, and professional assistance requirements.

6. *Manufacturing and Operations Plan.* Discussion of facilities needed, space requirements, capital equipment, labor force, inventory control, and purchasing requirement.

7. *Labor Force.* Discussion of the quality of skilled workers available and the training, compensation, and motivation of workers.

8. *Marketing Plan.* Discussion of markets, market trends, competition, market share, pricing, promotion, distribution, and service policy.

9. *Financial Plan.* Summary of the investment needed, sales and cash-flow forecasts, breakeven analysis, and sources of funding.

10. *Exit Strategy.* Discussion of a succession plan or going public. Who will take over the business?

11. *Critical Risks and Assumptions.* Evaluation of the weaknesses of the business and how the company plans to deal with these and other business problems.

12. *Appendix.* Supplementary information crucial to the plan, such as résumés of owners and principal managers, advertising samples, organization chart, and any related information.

Source: Adapted from Timothy S. Hatten, *Small Business Management: Entrepreneurship and Beyond,* 3d ed. Copyright © 2006 by Houghton Mifflin Company, pp. 108–120. Reprinted with permission.

over two million small businesses. It helps small firms to bid for and obtain government contracts, and it helps them to prepare to enter foreign markets.

SBA Management Assistance

Statistics show that most failures in small business are related to poor management. For this reason, the SBA places special emphasis on improving the management ability of the owners and managers of small businesses. The SBA's Management Assistance Program is extensive and diversified. It includes free individual counseling, courses, conferences, workshops, and a wide range of publications. Recently, the SBA provided management and technical assistance to nearly one million small businesses through its 1,000 Small Business Development Centers and 11,000 volunteers from the Service Corps of Retired Executives.[18]

Management Courses and Workshops The management courses offered by the SBA cover all the functions, duties, and roles of managers. Instructors may be teachers from local colleges and universities or other professionals, such as management consultants, bankers, lawyers, and accountants. Fees for these courses are quite low. The most popular such course is a general survey of eight to ten different areas of business management. In follow-up studies, business people may concentrate in-depth

> > **TABLE 6.5**

BUSINESS PLAN CHECKLIST

1. Does the executive summary grab the reader's attention and highlight the major points of the business plan?

2. Does the business-concept section clearly describe the purpose of the business, the customers, the value proposition, and the distribution channel and convey a compelling story?

3. Do the industry and market analyses support acceptance and demand for the business concept in the marketplace and define a first customer in depth?

4. Does the management-team plan persuade the reader that the team could implement the business concept successfully? Does it assure the reader that an effective infrastructure is in place to facilitate the goals and operations of the company?

5. Does the product/service plan clearly provide details on the status of the product, the timeline for completion, and the intellectual property that will be acquired?

6. Does the operations plan prove that the product or service could be produced and distributed efficiently and effectively?

7. Does the marketing plan successfully demonstrate how the company will create customer awareness in the target market and deliver the benefit to the customer?

8. Does the financial plan convince the reader that the business model is sustainable—that it will provide a superior return on investment for the investor and sufficient cash flow to repay loans to potential lenders?

9. Does the growth plan convince the reader that the company has long-term growth potential and spin-off products and services?

10. Does the contingency and exit-strategy plan convince the reader that the risk associated with this venture can be mediated? Is there an exit strategy in place for investors?

Source: Kathleen R. Allen, *Launching New Ventures: An Entrepreneurial Approach*, 4th ed. Copyright © 2006 by Houghton Mifflin Company, p. 197. Reprinted with permission.

on one or more of these areas depending on their particular strengths and weaknesses. The SBA occasionally offers one-day conferences. These conferences are aimed at keeping owner-managers up-to-date on new management developments, tax laws, and the like.

The Small Business Training Network (SBTN) is an online training network consisting of eighty-three SBA-run courses, workshops, and resources. Recently, the SBA site (**www.sba.gov/training**) hosted more than one million visitors and trained nearly 2.5 million small-business owners.[19]

Service Corps of Retired Executives (SCORE) a group of retired business people who volunteer their services to small businesses through the SBA

 USING THE INTERNET

So How Do You Connect with the SBA?

The Internet is a great source of information for learning what assistance is available from the Small Business Administration. Do you want financial assistance or management counseling, do you want to bid for and obtain government contracts, do you want to enter foreign markets, or do you want to learn how to write a business plan? You can find answers to frequently asked questions at **www.sba.gov/advo/stats/sbfaq.html.**

SCORE The **Service Corps of Retired Executives (SCORE),** created in 1964, is a group of more than 11,000 retired business people including over 2,000 women who volunteer their services to small businesses through the SBA. The collective experience of SCORE volunteers spans the full range of American enterprise. These volunteers have worked for such notable companies as Eastman Kodak, General Electric, IBM, and Procter & Gamble. Experts in areas of accounting, finance, marketing, engineering, and retailing provide counseling and mentoring to entrepreneurs.

A small-business owner who has a particular problem can request free counseling from SCORE. An assigned counselor visits the owner in his or her establishment and, through careful observation, analyzes the business situation and the problem. If the problem is complex, the counselor may call on other volunteer experts to assist. Finally, the counselor offers a plan for solving the problem and helping the owner through the critical period.

Consider the plight of Elizabeth Halvorsen, a mystery writer from Minneapolis. Her husband had built up the family advertising and graphic arts firm for seventeen years when he was called in 1991 to serve in the Persian Gulf War. The only one left behind who could run the business was Mrs. Halvorsen, who admittedly had no business experience. Enter SCORE. With a SCORE management expert at her side, she kept the business on track. In 2004, SCORE volunteers served 468,000 small-business people like Mrs. Halvorsen.[20]

Help for Minority-Owned Small Businesses
Americans who are members of minority groups have had difficulty entering the nation's economic mainstream. Raising money is a nagging problem for minority business owners, who also may lack adequate training. Members of minority groups are, of course, eligible for all SBA programs, but the SBA makes a special effort to assist those who want to start small businesses or expand existing ones. For example, the Minority Business Development Agency awards grants to develop and increase business opportunities for members of racial and ethnic minorities. In 2004, over 4.1 million minority-owned firms in the United States provided over 4.8 million jobs and generated $694.1 billion in sales.[21]

Helping women become entrepreneurs is also a special goal of the SBA. Emily Harrington, one of nine children, was born in Manila, the Philippines. She arrived in the United States in 1972 as a foreign-exchange student. Convinced that there was a market for hard-working, dedicated minorities and women, she launched Qualified Resources, Inc. *Inc.* magazine selected her firm as one of "America's Fastest Growing Private Companies" just six years later. Harrington credits the SBA with giving her the technical support that made her first loan possible. Finding a SCORE counselor who worked directly with her, she refined her business plan until she got a bank loan. Before contacting the SBA, Harrington was turned down for business loans "by all the banks I approached," even though she worked as a manager of loan credit and collection for a bank. Later, Emily Harrington was SBA's winner of the local, regional, and national Small Business Entrepreneurial Success Award for Rhode Island, the New England region, and the nation! For several years in a row, Qualified Resources, Inc., was named one of the fastest-growing private companies in Rhode Island. Now with over 100 Women's Business Centers, entrepreneurs like Harrington can receive training and technical assistance, access to credit and capital, federal contracts, and international markets.[22]

Small-Business Institutes
Small-business institutes (SBIs), created in 1972, are groups of senior and graduate students in business administration who provide management counseling to small businesses. SBIs have been set up on over 520 college campuses as another way to help business owners. The students work in small groups guided by faculty advisers and SBA management-assistance experts. Like SCORE volunteers, they analyze and help solve the problems of small-business owners at their business establishments.

Small-Business Development Centers
Small-business development centers (SBDCs) are university-based groups that provide individual counseling and practical training to owners of small businesses. SBDCs draw from the resources of local, state, and federal governments, private businesses, and universities. These groups can provide managerial and technical help, data from research studies, and other types of specialized assistance of value to small businesses. In 2005,

small-business institutes (SBIs) groups of senior and graduate students in business administration who provide management counseling to small businesses

small-business development centers (SBDCs) university-based groups that provide individual counseling and practical training to owners of small businesses

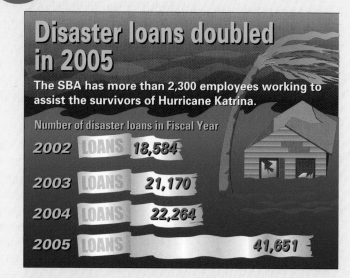

SPOTLIGHT

Disaster loans doubled in 2005

The SBA has more than 2,300 employees working to assist the survivors of Hurricane Katrina.

Number of disaster loans in Fiscal Year

2002 LOANS 18,584
2003 LOANS 21,170
2004 LOANS 22,264
2005 LOANS 41,651

Source: The SBA FY2005 Performance and Accountability Report, **sba.gov/2005PAR.pdf/**, accessed March 28, 2006.

Cool idea is a hot business. Want a party for kids where parents can have fun too? Then go to a party at Little Scoops, and let the fun begin. Little Scoops does all the planning, set-up, and cleaning, while you sit back and enjoy the party. Since 2001, Michelle Violetto and Tanya Ehrlich have hosted hundreds of parties and opened nine additions to their business. Both partners credit SCORE's volunteer counselors for their success. Violetto says, "We have lots of female friends who have started their own businesses. We refer them all to SCORE."

there were over 1,100 SBDC locations, primarily at colleges and universities, assisting people such as Kathleen DuBois. After scribbling a list of her abilities and the names of potential clients on a napkin in a local restaurant, Kathleen DuBois decided to start her own marketing firm. Beth Thornton launched her engineering firm after a discussion with a colleague in the ladies room of the Marriott. When Richard Shell was laid off after twenty years of service with Nisource (Columbia Gas), he searched the Internet tirelessly before finding the right franchise option. Introduced by mutual friends, Jim Bostic and Denver McMillion quickly connected, built a high level of trust, and combined their diverse professional backgrounds to form a manufacturing company. Although these entrepreneurs took different routes in starting their new businesses in West Virginia, all of them turned to the West Virginia Small Business Development Center for the technical assistance to make their dreams become a reality.[23]

SBA Publications   The SBA issues management, marketing, and technical publications dealing with hundreds of topics of interest to present and prospective managers of small firms. Most of these publications are available from the SBA free of charge. Others can be obtained for a small fee from the U.S. Government Printing Office.

SBA Financial Assistance

Small businesses seem to be constantly in need of money. An owner may have enough capital to start and operate the business. But then he or she may require more money to finance increased operations during peak selling seasons, to pay for required pollution-control equipment, to finance an expansion, or to mop up after a natural disaster such as a flood or a terrorist attack. For example, the Supplemental Terrorist Activity Relief (STAR) program has made $3.7 billion in loans to 8,202 small businesses harmed or disrupted by the September 11 terrorist attacks. In October 2005, the SBA guaranteed loans of up to $150,000 to small businesses affected by hurricanes Katrina and Rita.[24] The SBA offers special financial-assistance programs that cover all these situations. However, its primary financial function is to guarantee loans to eligible businesses.

Regular Business Loans   Most of the SBA's business loans are actually made by private lenders such as banks, but repayment is partially guaranteed by the agency. That is, the SBA may guarantee that it will repay the lender up to 90 percent of the loan if the borrowing firm cannot repay it. Guaranteed loans approved on or after October 1, 2002, may be as large as $1.5 million (this loan limit may be increased in the future). The average size of an SBA-guaranteed business loan is about $300,000, and its average duration is about eight years. In 2004, the SBA approved approximately $20 billion in guaranteed loans.[25]

venture capital money that is invested in small (and sometimes struggling) firms that have the potential to become very successful

Small-Business Investment Companies   **Venture capital** is money that is invested in small (and sometimes struggling) firms that have the potential to become very successful. In many cases, only a lack of capital keeps these firms from rapid and solid growth. The people who invest in such firms expect that their investments will grow with the firms and become quite profitable.

The popularity of these investments has increased over the past twenty-five years, but most small firms still have difficulty obtaining venture capital. To help such businesses, the SBA licenses, regulates, and provides financial assistance to **small-business investment companies (SBICs).**

An SBIC is a privately owned firm that provides venture capital to small enterprises that meet its investment standards. Such small firms as America Online, Apple Computer, Federal Express, Compaq Computer, Intel Corporation, Outback Steakhouse, and Staples, Inc., all were financed through SBICs during their initial growth period. SBICs are intended to be profit-making organizations. The aid the SBA offers allows them to invest in small businesses that otherwise would not attract venture capital. In 2004, SBICs financed 4,462 firms, providing them with over $2.8 billion in capital. Since Congress created the program in 1958, SBICs have financed over 150,000 small businesses for a total of about $39.0 billion.[26]

We have discussed the importance of the small-business segment of our economy. We have weighed the advantages and drawbacks of operating a small business as compared with a large one. But is there a way to achieve the best of both worlds? Can one preserve one's independence as a business owner and still enjoy some of the benefits of "bigness"? Let's take a close look at franchising.

small-business investment companies (SBICs) privately owned firms that provide venture capital to small enterprises that meet their investment standards

6 LEARNING OBJECTIVE
Appraise the concept and types of franchising.

franchise a license to operate an individually owned business as though it were part of a chain of outlets or stores

franchising the actual granting of a franchise

franchisor an individual or organization granting a franchise

franchisee a person or organization purchasing a franchise

Franchising

A **franchise** is a license to operate an individually owned business as if it were part of a chain of outlets or stores. Often the business itself is also called a *franchise*. Among the most familiar franchises are McDonald's, H & R Block, AAMCO Transmissions, GNC (General Nutrition Centers), and Dairy Queen. Many other franchises carry familiar names; this method of doing business has become very popular in the last thirty years or so. It is an attractive means of starting and operating a small business.

What Is Franchising?

Franchising is the actual granting of a franchise. A **franchisor** is an individual or organization granting a franchise. A **franchisee** is a person or organization purchasing a franchise. The franchisor supplies a known and advertised business name, management skills, the required training and materials, and a method of doing business. The franchisee supplies labor and capital, operates the franchised business, and agrees to abide by the provisions of the franchise agreement. Table 6.6 lists some items that would be covered in a typical franchise agreement.

Franchising: One way to begin. The Singer Sewing Company was one of the first large firms to distribute its sewing machines through franchising. In 2001, Singer celebrated the 150th anniversary of Isaac Singer's patent on the first practical sewing machine. In 1870, the Red "S" girl trademark made her debut and was destined to become one of the best-known emblems in the world.

> > **TABLE 6.6**

MCDONALD'S CONVENTIONAL FRANCHISE AGREEMENT AS OF NOVEMBER 2005

McDonald's (Franchisor) Provides	Individual (Franchisee) Supplies
1. Nationally recognized trademarks and an established reputation for quality	1. Total investment of approximately $494,750 to $1,030,500, which includes initial franchise fee of $45,000
2. Designs and color schemes for restaurants, signs, and equipment	2. Approximate cash requirement of 40 percent of total investment; a minimum of $200,000 of nonborrowed personal funds
3. Specifications for certain food products	3. A monthly base rent or rent based on a percentage of monthly sales
4. Proven methods of inventory and operations control	4. A minimum of 4 percent of gross sales annually for marketing and advertising
5. Bookkeeping, accounting, and policies manuals specially geared toward a franchised restaurant	5. Payment of a service fee of 4 percent of monthly gross sales to McDonald's
6. A franchise term of up to twenty years	6. Payment of a variable rent percent of monthly gross sales to McDonald's based on McDonald's investment and/or sales
7. Formal training program completed on a part-time basis in approximately eighteen to twenty-four months in a McDonald's restaurant	7. Kitchen equipment, seating, decor, lighting, and signs in conformity with McDonald's standards (included in total investment figure)
8. Five weeks of classroom training, including two weeks at Hamburger University	8. Taxes, insurance, and maintenance costs on the restaurant building and land
9. Ongoing regional support services and field service staff	9. Commitment to ensuring high-quality standards and upholding the McDonald's reputation
10. Research and development of labor-saving equipment and methods	
11. Monthly bulletins, periodicals, or meetings to inform franchisees about management and marketing techniques	
12. Site selection (purchase or lease) and development, including building	

Source: "McDonald's Conventional Franchise Agreement as of November 2005," from *McDonald's Franchising*, McDonald's Corporation, Oak Brook, IL, **www.mcdonalds.com/corp/franchise**, accessed November 7, 2005. Used with permission from McDonald's Corporation.

Types of Franchising

Franchising arrangements fall into three general categories. In the first approach, a manufacturer authorizes a number of retail stores to sell a certain brand-name item. This type of franchising arrangement, one of the oldest, is prevalent in sales of passenger cars and trucks, farm equipment, shoes, paint, earth-moving equipment, and petroleum. About 90 percent of all gasoline is sold through franchised, independent retail service stations, and franchised dealers handle virtually all sales of new cars and trucks. In the second type of franchising arrangement, a producer licenses distributors to sell a given product to retailers. This arrangement is common in the soft-drink industry. Most national manufacturers of soft-drink syrups—the Coca-Cola Company, Dr. Pepper/Seven-Up Companies, PepsiCo, Royal Crown Companies, Inc.—franchise independent bottlers who then serve retailers. In a third form of franchising, a franchisor supplies brand names, techniques, or other services instead of a complete product. Although the franchisor may provide certain production and distribution services, its primary role is the careful development and control of marketing strategies. This approach to franchising, which is the most typical today, is used by Holiday Inns, Howard Johnson Company, AAMCO Transmissions, McDonald's, Dairy Queen, Avis, Hertz Corporation, KFC (Kentucky Fried Chicken), and SUBWAY, to name but a few.

7 LEARNING OBJECTIVE

Analyze the growth of franchising and franchising's advantages and disadvantages.

The Growth of Franchising

Franchising, which began in the United States around the time of the Civil War, was used originally by large firms, such as the Singer Sewing Company, to distribute their products. Franchising has been increasing steadily in popularity since the early 1900s, primarily for filling stations and car dealerships; however, this retailing strategy has experienced enormous growth since the mid-1970s. A new franchise opens every eight minutes somewhere in the United States.[27] The franchise proliferation generally has paralleled the expansion of the fast-food industry. As Table 6.7 shows, five of *Entrepreneur* magazine's top-rated franchises for 2005 were in this category.

Of course, franchising is not limited to fast foods. Hair salons, tanning parlors, and dentists and lawyers are expected to participate in franchising arrangements in growing numbers. Franchised health clubs, pest exterminators, and campgrounds are already widespread, as are franchised tax preparers and travel agencies. The real estate industry also has experienced a rapid increase in franchising.

Also, franchising is attracting more women and minority business owners in the United States than ever before. One reason is that special outreach programs designed to encourage franchisee diversity have developed. Consider Angela Trammel, a young mother of two. She had been laid off from her job at the Marriott after 9/11. Since she was a member of a Curves Fitness Center and liked the concept of empowering women to become physically fit, she began researching the cost of purchasing a Curves franchise and ways to finance the business. "I was online looking for financing, and I linked to Enterprise Development Group in Washington, D.C. I knew that they had diverse

>> TABLE 6.7

ENTREPRENEUR'S TOP TEN FRANCHISES IN 2005

Rank	Franchise	Total Investment	Franchise Fee	Royalty Fee	Net-Worth Requirement	Cash Requirement	Comments
1	SUBWAY	$70,000–$220,000	$12,500	8%	$30,000–$90,000	$30,000–$90,000	20-year renewable term
2	Curves for Women	$36,400–$42,900	$39,900	5%	$75,000	$50,000	5-year renewable term
3	Quizno's Franchise Co.	$208,400–$243,800	$25,000	7%	$125,000	$60,000	15-year renewable term; renewable fee $1,000
4	Jackson Hewitt Tax Service	$51,700–$85,500	$25,000	15%	$100,000–$200,000	$50,000	10-year renewable term
5	UPS Store	$138,700–$245,500	$29,950	5%	—	—	10-year renewable term; renewal fee: 25% of current fee
6	Sonic Drive In Restaurants	$710,000–$2,300,000	$30,000	1%–5%	$1,000,000	$500,000	20-year renewable term; renewal fee 10 years for $6,000
6	Taco Bell Corp.	$3,000,000	$45,000	5.5%	—	—	—
7	Jani-King	$11,300–$34,100	$8,600–$16,300	10%	Varies	Varies	20-year renewable term
8	7-Eleven, Inc.	Varies	Varies	Varies	Varies	Varies	15-year renewable term
9	Dunkin Donuts	$255,700–$1,100,000	$40,000–$80,000	5.9%	$1,300,000	$750,000	—
10	RE/MAX Int'l	$20,000–$200,000	$10,000–$25,000	Varies	—	—	5-year renewable term; renewal fee varies

Source: Reprinted with permission from *Entrepreneur* Magazine, November 2005, **www.entrepreneur.com**.

clients." The cost for the franchise was $19,500, but it took $60,000 to open the doors to her fitness center. "Applying for a loan to start the business was much harder than buying a house," said Trammel. Just three years later, Angela and her husband, Ernest, own three Curves Fitness Centers with twelve employees. Recently, giving birth to her third child, she has found the financial freedom and flexibility needed to care for her busy family. In fact, within a three-year period, the Trammel's grew their annual household income from $80,000 to $250,000.[28] Franchisors such as Wendy's, McDonald's, Burger King, and Church's Chicken all have special corporate programs to attract minority and women franchisees. Just as important, successful women and minority franchisees are willing to get involved by offering advice and guidance to new franchisees.

Herman Petty, the first black McDonald's franchisee, remembers that the company provided a great deal of help while he worked to establish his first units. In turn, Petty traveled to help other black franchisees, and he invited new franchisees to gain hands-on experience in his Chicago restaurants before starting their own establishments. Petty also organized a support group, the National Black McDonald's Operators Association, to help black franchisees in other areas. Today, this support group has thirty-three local chapters and more than 330 members across the country. "We are really concentrating on helping our operators to be successful both operationally and financially," says Craig Welburn, the McDonald's franchisee who leads the group.

Dual-branded franchises, in which two franchisors offer their products together, are a new small-business trend. For example, in 1993, pleased with the success of its first cobranded restaurant with Texaco in Beebe, Arkansas, McDonald's now has over 400 cobranded restaurants in the United States. Also, an agreement between franchisors Doctor's Associates, Inc., and TCBY Enterprises, Inc., now allows franchisees to sell SUBWAY sandwiches and TCBY yogurt in the same establishment.

Are Franchises Successful?

Franchising is designed to provide a tested formula for success, along with ongoing advice and training. The success rate for businesses owned and operated by franchisees is significantly higher than the success rate for other independently owned small businesses. In a recent nationwide Gallup poll of 944 franchise owners, 94 percent of franchisees indicated that they were very or somewhat successful, only 5 percent believed that they were very unsuccessful or somewhat unsuccessful, and 1 percent did not know. Despite these impressive statistics, franchising is not a guarantee of success for either franchisees or franchisors. Too rapid expansion, inadequate capital or management skills, and a host of other problems can cause failure for both franchisee and franchisor. Thus, for example, the Dizzy Dean's Beef and Burger franchise is no longer in business. Timothy Bates, a Wayne State University economist, warns, "Despite the hype that franchising is the safest way to go when starting a new business, the research just doesn't bear that out." Just consider Boston Chicken, which once had more than 1,200 restaurants before declaring bankruptcy in 1998.

Advantages of Franchising

Franchising plays a vital role in our economy and soon may become the dominant form of retailing. Why? Because franchising offers advantages to both the franchisor and the franchisee.

To the Franchisor   The franchisor gains fast and well-controlled distribution of its products without incurring the high cost of constructing and operating its own outlets. The franchisor thus has more capital available to expand production and to use for advertising. At the same time, it can ensure, through the franchise agreement, that outlets are maintained and operated according to its own standards.

The franchisor also benefits from the fact that the franchisee—a sole proprietor in most cases—is likely to be very highly motivated to succeed. The success of the franchise means more sales, which translate into higher royalties for the franchisor.

To the Franchisee The franchisee gets the opportunity to start a business with limited capital and to make use of the business experience of others. Moreover, an outlet with a nationally advertised name, such as Radio Shack, McDonald's, or Century 21 Real Estate, has guaranteed customers as soon as it opens.

If business problems arise, the franchisor gives the franchisee guidance and advice. This counseling is primarily responsible for the very high degree of success enjoyed by franchises. In most cases, the franchisee does not pay for such help.

The franchisee also receives materials to use in local advertising and can take part in national promotional campaigns sponsored by the franchisor. McDonald's and its franchisees, for example, constitute one of the nation's top twenty purchasers of advertising. Finally, the franchisee may be able to minimize the cost of advertising, supplies, and various business necessities by purchasing them in cooperation with other franchisees.

Disadvantages of Franchising

The main disadvantage of franchising affects the franchisee, and it arises because the franchisor retains a great deal of control. The franchisor's contract can dictate every aspect of the business: decor, design of employee uniforms, types of signs, and all the details of business operations. All Burger King French fries taste the same because all Burger King franchisees have to make them the same way.

Contract disputes are the cause of many lawsuits. For example, Rekha Gabhawala, a Dunkin' Donuts franchisee in Milwaukee, alleged that the franchisor was forcing her out of business so that the company could profit by reselling the downtown franchise to someone else; the company, on the other hand, alleged that Gabhawala breached the contract by not running the business according to company standards. In another case, Dunkin' Donuts sued Chris Romanias, its franchisee in Pennsylvania, alleging that Romanias intentionally underreported gross sales to the company. Romanias, on the other hand, alleged that Dunkin' Donuts, Inc., breached the contract because it failed to provide assistance in operating the franchise. Other franchisees claim that contracts are unfairly tilted toward the franchisors. Yet others have charged that they lost their franchise and investment because their franchisor would not approve the sale of the business when they found a buyer.

To arbitrate disputes between franchisors and franchisees, the National Franchise Mediation Program was established in 1993 by thirty member firms, including Burger King Corporation, McDonald's Corporation, and Wendy's International, Inc. Negotiators have since resolved numerous cases through mediation. Recently, Carl's Jr. brought in one of its largest franchisees to help set its system straight, making most franchisees happy for the first time in years. The program also helped PepsiCo settle a long-term contract dispute and renegotiate its franchise agreements.

Because disagreements between franchisors and franchisees have increased in recent years, many franchisees have been demanding government regulation of franchising. In 1997, to avoid government regulation, some of the largest franchisors proposed a new self-policing plan to the Federal Trade Commission.

Franchise holders pay for their security, usually with a one-time franchise fee and continuing royalty and advertising fees, collected as a percentage of sales. As Table 6.6 shows, a McDonald's franchisee pays an initial franchise fee of $45,000, an annual fee of 4 percent of gross sales (for advertising), and a monthly fee of 4 percent of gross sales. In Table 6.7 you can see how much money a franchisee needs to start a new franchise for selected organizations. In some fields, franchise agreements are not uniform. One franchisee may pay more than another for the same services.

Even success can cause problems. Sometimes a franchise is so successful that the franchisor opens its own outlet nearby, in direct competition—although franchisees may fight back. For example, a court recently ruled that Burger King could not enter into direct competition with the franchisee because the contract was not specific on the issue. A spokesperson for one franchisor contends that the company "gives no geographical protection" to its franchise holders and thus is free to move in on them. Franchise operators work hard. They often put in ten- and twelve-hour days, six days a week. The International Franchise Association advises prospective franchise purchasers to investigate before investing and to approach buying a franchise cautiously. Franchises

Business Around the World

Do's and Don't's of International Franchising.

Small businesses that are thinking about transplanting a franchise from one country to another should think about these dos and don'ts:

Do	Don't
● Find out what support the franchisor offers in each country.	● Assume that customers everywhere need or want what the franchise offers.
● Check trade laws before buying a franchise in another country.	● Expect hiring, training, and marketing practices to be identical in all countries.
● Thoroughly research the competitive situation.	● Underestimate the amount of money needed to fund international operations.
● Understand the laws and regulations governing franchising in each country.	● Forget that strong local management is needed to keep an international franchise going.

Doug Howard, CEO of Drama Kids International, the U.S. franchisor of an Australian-based drama program, stresses that franchisees can import a franchise successfully "as long as they are passionate about the basic concept, are prepared for a reasonable and necessary testing period, and realize that numerous changes—and sometimes dramatic challenges—are part of the process."

vary widely in approach as well as in products. Some, such as Dunkin' Donuts and Baskin-Robbins, demand long hours. Others, such as Great Clips hair salons and Albert's Family Restaurants, are more appropriate for those who do not want to spend many hours at their stores.

Global Perspectives in Small Business

For small American businesses, the world is becoming smaller. National and international economies are growing more and more interdependent as political leadership and national economic directions change and trade barriers diminish or disappear. Globalization and instant worldwide communications are rapidly shrinking distances at the same time that they are expanding business opportunities. According to a recent study, the Internet is increasingly important to small-business strategic thinking, with more than 50 percent of those surveyed indicating that the Internet represented their most favored strategy for growth. This was more than double the next-favored choice, strategic alliances reflecting the opportunity to reach both global and domestic customers. The Internet and online payment systems enable even very small businesses to serve international customers. In fact, technology now gives small businesses the leverage and power to reach markets that were once limited solely to large corporations. No wonder the number of businesses exporting their goods and services has tripled since 1990, with two-thirds of that boom coming from companies with fewer than twenty employees.[29]

The SBA offers help to the nation's small-business owners who want to enter the world markets. The SBA's efforts include counseling small firms on how and where to market overseas, matching U.S. small-business executives with potential overseas customers, and helping exporters to secure financing. The agency brings small U.S. firms into direct contact with potential overseas buyers and partners. The U.S. Commercial Service, a Commerce Department division, aids small and medium-sized businesses in selling overseas. The division's global network includes over 107 offices in the United States and 151 others in eighty-three countries around the world.[30]

International trade will become more important to small-business owners as they face unique challenges in the new century. Small businesses, which are expected to remain the dominant form of organization in this country, must be prepared to adapt to significant demographic and economic changes in the world marketplace.

This chapter ends our discussion of American business today. From here on we shall be looking closely at various aspects of business operations. We begin, in the next chapter, with a discussion of management—what management is, what managers do, and how they work to coordinate the basic economic resources within a business organization.

RETURN TO Inside Business

Although the beauty business is crowded and competitive, Carol's Daughter is making a splash with its unique products and its celebrity investors. Within months of investing in the company, Jada Pinkett Smith and Thalia appeared in its advertising. Founder Lisa Price also has used some of the funding for new product packaging. "The line has become what I always wanted it to be," she says. "No compromises."

The company recently revamped its catalog and website and dropped slower-selling products to make room for new items. Even as it plans showcase stores in major cities, Carol's Daughter is selling products through a select net-

work of U.S. and London specialty stores. Steve Stoute, who put the investment group together, is thinking about the company's long-term potential: "We're not stopping at skin care or hair care. We'll go into household goods like fabric and dishwashing liquids." In the future, says Stoute, Carol's Daughter will be "a billion-dollar opportunity."

Questions

1. If you were working on a business plan for Carol's Daughter, what potential risks would you mention, and how would you suggest that the company deal with them?
2. What are the arguments for and against Carol's Daughter granting franchises? Would you recommend that Lisa Price grant franchises? Explain your answer.

▶▶ CHAPTER REVIEW

Summary

Define what a small business is and recognize the fields in which small businesses are concentrated.

A small business is one that is independently owned and operated for profit and is not dominant in its field. There are about twenty-three million businesses in this country, and more than 90 percent of them are small businesses. Small businesses employ more than half the nation's work force, even though about 70 percent of new businesses can be expected to fail within five years. More than half of all small businesses are in retailing and services.

2

Identify the people who start small businesses and the reasons why some succeed and many fail.

Such personal characteristics as independence, desire to create a new enterprise, and willingness to accept a challenge may encourage individuals to start small businesses. Various external circumstances, such as special expertise or even the loss of a job, also can supply the motivation to strike out on one's own. Poor planning and lack of capital and management experience are the major causes of small-business failures.

Assess the contributions of small businesses to our economy.

Small businesses have been responsible for a wide variety of inventions and innovations, some of which have given rise to new industries. Historically, small businesses have created the bulk of the nation's new jobs. Further, they have mounted effective competition to larger firms. They provide things that society needs, act as suppliers to larger firms, and serve as customers of other businesses, both large and small.

4

Judge the advantages and disadvantages of operating a small business.

The advantages of smallness in business include the opportunity to establish personal relationships with customers and employees, the ability to adapt to changes quickly, independence, and simplified record keeping. The major disadvantages are the high risk of failure, the limited potential for growth, and the limited ability to raise capital.

5

Explain how the Small Business Administration helps small businesses.

The Small Business Administration (SBA) was created in 1953 to assist and counsel the nation's millions of small-business owners. The SBA offers management courses and workshops; managerial help, including one-to-one counseling through SCORE; various publications; and financial assistance through guaranteed loans and SBICs. It places special emphasis on aid to minority-owned businesses, including those owned by women.

6

Appraise the concept and types of franchising.

A franchise is a license to operate an individually owned business as though it were part of a chain. The franchisor provides a known business name, management skills, a method of doing business, and the training and required materials. The franchisee contributes labor and capital, operates the franchised business, and agrees to abide by the provisions of the franchise agreement. There are three major categories of franchise agreements.

7

Analyze the growth of franchising and franchising's advantages and disadvantages.

Franchising has grown tremendously since the mid-1970s. The franchisor's major advantage in franchising is fast and well-controlled distribution of products with minimal capital outlay. In return, the franchisee has the opportunity to open a business with limited capital, to make use of the business experience of others, and to sell to an existing clientele. For this, the franchisee usually must pay both an initial franchise fee and a continuing royalty based on sales. He or she also must follow the dictates of the franchise with regard to operation of the business.

Worldwide business opportunities are expanding for small businesses. The SBA assists small-business owners in penetrating foreign markets. The next century will present unique challenges and opportunities for small-business owners.

Key Terms

You should now be able to define and give an example relevant to each of the following terms:

small business (183)
business plan (194)
Small Business Administration (SBA) (194)
Service Corps of Retired Executives (SCORE) (196)
small-business institutes (SBIs) (197)
small-business development centers (SBDCs) (197)
venture capital (198)
small-business investment companies (SBICs) (199)
franchise (199)
franchising (199)
franchisor (199)
franchisee (199)

Review Questions

1. What information would you need to determine whether a particular business is small according to SBA guidelines?
2. Which two areas of business generally attract the most small businesses? Why are these areas attractive to small business?
3. Distinguish among service industries, distribution industries, and production industries.
4. What kinds of factors encourage certain people to start new businesses?
5. What are the major causes of small-business failure? Do these causes also apply to larger businesses?
6. Briefly describe four contributions of small business to the American economy.
7. What are the major advantages and disadvantages of smallness in business?
8. What are the major components of a business plan? Why should an individual develop a business plan?
9. Identify five ways in which the SBA provides management assistance to small businesses.
10. Identify two ways in which the SBA provides financial assistance to small businesses.
11. Why does the SBA concentrate on providing management and financial assistance to small businesses?
12. What is venture capital? How does the SBA help small businesses to obtain it?
13. Explain the relationships among a franchise, the franchisor, and the franchisee.
14. What does the franchisor receive in a franchising agreement? What does the franchisee receive? What does each provide?
15. Cite one major benefit of franchising for the franchisor. Cite one major benefit of franchising for the franchisee.

Discussion Questions

1. Most people who start small businesses are aware of the high failure rate and the reasons for it. Why, then, do some take no steps to protect their firms from failure? What steps should they take?
2. Are the so-called advantages of small business really advantages? Wouldn't every small-business owner like his or her business to grow into a large firm?
3. Do average citizens benefit from the activities of the SBA, or is the SBA just another way to spend our tax money?
4. Would you rather own your own business independently or become a franchisee? Why?

►► VIDEO CASE 6.1

No Funny Business at Newbury Comics

The two college students who started Newbury Comics have become serious business owners. Mike Dreese and John Brusger started Newbury Comics in 1978 with $2,000 and a valuable comic book collection. Their first store was actually a tiny apartment on Boston's popular Newbury Street, which they rented for $260 per month. Three decades later, the company operates twenty-six stores in Massachusetts, Maine, New Hampshire, and Rhode Island. It still does business on Newbury Street—in a spacious storefront that rents for $23,000 per month.

How did Newbury Comics grow into a multimillion-dollar business? First, the owners identified a need that they could fill. They understood what kind of comic books collectors were interested in buying, and they enjoyed dealing with these customers. They also realized that customer needs can change, which is why they have tested hundreds of new items over the years.

Second, Reese and Brusger thought of their business as a business. As much as they liked comics, they recognized the profit potential of carrying other products. Over time, they started stocking music and added movies, novelty items, and clothing accessories. They were among the first U.S. stores to import recordings by European groups such as U2. Today, comic books account for only a fraction of Newbury Comics' revenue, whereas CDs and DVDs account for about 70 percent of the revenue.

Third, the entrepreneurs didn't do everything themselves—they knew when to delegate to others. As Newbury Comics expanded beyond comics and opened new stores, the owners hired professionals to negotiate leases, make buying decisions, and select the exact merchandise assortment for each store. They also hired technology experts to design systems for tracking what was in stock, what had been sold, how much the company was spending, and how much each store was contributing to total sales. Now, if a new CD or DVD is selling particularly well, the buyer will know within three minutes—in plenty of time to reorder and satisfy customer demand.

Fourth, Reese and Brusger have paid close attention to Newbury Comics' financial situation. They're careful to pay suppliers on time, and in exchange, they can get fast-selling products even when supplies are limited. Consider what happened during the Pokemon fad. Newbury Comics originally ordered a small quantity of cards, which quickly sold out. Every time it placed another order, it sent the supplier a check by express delivery. By the height of the fad, when demand was so high that the supplier could not fill every retailer's order, Newbury Comics still got its shipment. By the time the fad faded, the company had sold $4 million worth of Pokemon cards and made more than $2 million in profits.

Newbury Comics remains profitable, although Dreese notes that sales growth has slowed during the past few years. As a result, he says, "We have all had to grow up a little" and improve the way Newbury Comics operates. The company has formalized its store payroll budgets, assigned employees to check the quality of customer service at each store, and begun offering more products for sale online.

Despite the company's success, Dreese does not expect to expand beyond New England. He knows that a key strength is being able to restock quickly—and that means locating stores within a half-day's drive of the distribution center in Brighton, Massachusetts. Because Newbury Comics owns six trucks, it can resupply every store at least three times a week. Many competitors are far bigger, but no competitor knows its customers and its products better than the team at Newbury Comics.[31]

For more information about this company, go to **www.newburycomics.com**.

Questions

1. This chapter cites five advantages of small business. Which of these seem to apply to the owners' experience with Newbury Comics?
2. This chapter cites three disadvantages of small business. Based on what you know of Newbury Comics, which of these is likely to be the biggest problem in the coming years?
3. Newbury Comics was started without a formal business plan. If you were writing its plan today, what critical risks and assumptions would you examine—and why?

▶▶ CASE 6.2

Teen Tycoons

Elise MacMillan and her brother, Evan MacMillan, founded their Chocolate Farm company when she was in elementary school and he was in middle school. Skylar Schipper and his best friend, Coy Funk, started Manure Gourmet when they were in eighth grade. Camille Winbush, who appears on television in *The Bernie Mac* show, opened an ice cream shop when she was 13 years old. And these are not the only teens turning entrepreneurial these days. So many teenagers want to run their own companies that the Small Business Administration has created a special website with tips, tools, and success stories (**www.sba.gov/teens/**).

Elise MacMillan was 10 and Evan MacMillan was 13 when they became small business owners. Evan was serving on the advisory board of the Young Americans Bank in Denver and urged Elise, who loves cooking with chocolate, to sell her treats at the bank's Young Entrepreneurs Marketplace. After her animal-shaped chocolates sold out, the siblings teamed up to form the Chocolate Farm. Evan developed a business plan, which won the new company a $5,000 bank loan. He also created a website while Elise concentrated on developing more chocolate products.

Very quickly the Chocolate Farm outgrew the MacMillan's kitchen as it filled orders from all over the United States. The teens rented space in a Denver small-business incubator and used the center's commercial kitchen to make chocolate products in larger batches. Their fast-growing company was selected for an Ernst & Young Entrepreneur of the Year Award and also has been featured in *People* and other publications. Although the Chocolate Farm now has 40 employees, Elise remains in charge of product development as she completes high school, and Evan handles finance and administration as well as juggling a full-time college schedule. Elise's advice to other teen entrepreneurs is: "While you're young is a really good time to take risks."

Manure Gourmet got started when Coy Funk and his mother packaged sheep manure as fertilizer to auction off at a school fundraiser. The manure raised so much money that, says Coy, "we started thinking about turning this into a business." He and his friend Skylar

Schipper began picking up manure from farms and barns around their hometown of Stillwater, Oklahoma, drying it, and packaging it with names like "Cow Wow." They hired a tech-savvy friend to design their Manure Gourmet website and opened for business.

To date, the company has sold more than 150,000 pounds of manure and is planning for wider distribution and new products. Being teenage entrepreneurs selling an unusual product has only helped the partners build their business. A recent appearance on the *Tonight* show brought 2,000 new visitors to their site. Skylar comments, "Who would have guessed there'd be so much interest in manure?"

Television viewers know Camille Winbush as Vanessa Thomkins; customers of Baked Ice in Pasadena, California, know her as the owner and a hard worker. Camille has been acting since she was 2. At 13, she decided to start a shop featuring ice cream sandwiches made with fresh-baked cookies. She scouted a suitable location in the busy historic district, "next to a restaurant and, even better, right down the street from the train station," she says.

Now that the shop is open, her aunt is the manager, a cousin works there part time, and Camille helps close up and clean up after she leaves the television studio. "It's very hard work, but it's still a lot of fun," she says. In the next few years, Camille plans to keep her acting career going strong as she builds her business by opening Baked Ice shops in other cities.[32]

For more information about these companies, go to **www.thechocolatefarm.com** and **http://manuregourmet.com**.

Questions

1. What entrepreneurial pitfalls should Camille Winbush watch for as she grows Baked Ice into a multicity enterprise?
2. Imagine yourself as a banker reviewing the original Chocolate Farm loan application. Which components of the founders' business plan would you have examined most closely—and why?
3. Would you advise Manure Gourmet's owners to remain small or go for faster growth? Explain your answer.

→ CHAPTER 6: JOURNAL EXERCISE

Discovery statement: One of the objectives in this chapter was to make you aware of the advantages and disadvantages of owning a franchise.

Assume that after evaluating your skills, experience, and financial situation, you have determined to purchase a franchise in your community. Identify and describe sources where you can obtain information on what the franchise package should contain.

_____

_____

_____

_____

_____

List at least five reasons why you should choose franchising rather than starting a new, independent business.

_____

_____

_____

_____

_____

Identify issues you need to be aware of as a franchisee.

_____

_____

_____

_____

_____

Make a list of possible advantages and disadvantages of the franchise you are considering. What are your rights and your obligations as a franchisee?

_____

_____

_____

_____

_____

_____

BUILDING SKILLS FOR CAREER SUCCESS

1. Exploring the Internet

Perhaps the most challenging difficulty for small businesses is operating with scarce resources, especially people and money. To provide information and point small-business operators in the right direction, many Internet sites offer helpful products and services. Although most are sponsored by advertising and may be free of charge, some charge a fee, and others are a combination of both. The SBA within the U.S. Department of Commerce provides a wide array of free information and resources. You can find your way to the SBA through **www.sbaonline.sba.gov** or **www.sba.gov.** Visit the text website for updates to this exercise.

Assignment

1. Describe the various services provided by the SBA site.
2. What sources of funding are there?
3. What service would you like to see improved? How?

2. Developing Critical-Thinking Skills

Small businesses play a vital role in our economy. They not only contribute to technological innovation and to the creation of many new jobs, but they also ensure that customers have an alternative to the products and services offered by large firms. In addition, by making parts for large firms at a lower cost than the large firms could make the parts themselves, they help to keep the lid on consumer prices. Regardless of our need for them, many small businesses fail within their first five years. Why is this so?

Assignment

1. Identify several successful small businesses in your community.
2. Identify one small business that has failed.
3. Gather enough information about those businesses to answer the following questions:
   a. What role do small businesses play in your community?
   b. Why are they important?
   c. Why did the business fail?
   d. What was the most important reason for its failure?
   e. How might the business have survived?
4. Summarize what you have learned about the impact of small businesses on your community. Give the summary to your instructor.

3. Building Team Skills

A business plan is a written statement that documents the nature of a business and how that business intends to achieve its goals. Although entrepreneurs should prepare a business plan *before* starting a business, the plan also serves as an effective guide later on. The plan should concisely describe the business's mission, the amount of capital it requires, its target market, competition, resources, production plan, marketing plan, organizational plan, assessment of risk, and financial plan.

Assignment

1. Working in a team of four students, identify a company in your community that would benefit from using a business plan, or create a scenario in which a hypothetical entrepreneur wants to start a business.
2. Using the resources of the library or the Internet and/or interviews with business owners, write a business plan incorporating the information in Table 6.4.
3. Present your business plan to the class.

4. Researching Different Careers

Many people dream of opening and operating their own businesses. Are you one of them? To be successful, entrepreneurs must have certain characteristics; their profiles generally differ from those of people who work for someone else. Do you know which personal characteristics make some entrepreneurs succeed and others fail? Do you fit the successful entrepreneur's profile? What is your potential for opening and operating a successful small business?

Assignment

1. Use the resources of the library or the Internet to establish what a successful entrepreneur's profile is and to determine whether your personal characteristics fit that profile. Internet addresses that can help you are **www.smartbiz.com/sbs/arts/ieb1.html** and **www.sba.gov** (see "Starting Your Business" and "FAQs"). These sites have quizzes online that can help you to assess your personal characteristics. The SBA also has helpful brochures.
2. Interview several small-business owners. Ask them to describe the characteristics they think are necessary for being a successful entrepreneur.
3. Using your findings, write a report that includes the following:
   a. A profile of a successful small-business owner
   b. A comparison of your personal characteristics with the profile of the successful entrepreneur
   c. A discussion of your potential as a successful small-business owner

5. Improving Communication Skills

Franchising is a method of doing business that has grown steadily in popularity since the early 1900s. It offers entrepreneurs who want to start a business certain opportunities and advantages. If you started a business, would a franchise be an option?

Assignment

1. Choose a franchise business in your community, preferably one of those listed in Table 6.7.
2. Investigate the business by interviewing the franchise owner. Ask the following questions:
   a. Why did you decide to open a franchise business?
   b. What are the advantages or disadvantages of having a franchise agreement over opening a new business or buying an existing business?
   c. When you were deciding whether to become a franchisee, what were some of your major concerns? What type of research did you do?
   d. What key things does the franchisor provide for you? What are your obligations to the franchisor?
   e. What advice would you give a person who was thinking about becoming a franchisee?
3. Write a two-page report summarizing the information you have gathered.

→ PREP TEST

Matching Questions

____ 1. Seniors and graduate students provide counseling services to small businesses.

____ 2. In 1953, Congress created this entity to assist small businesses.

____ 3. They are university-based groups that provide training to small-business owners.

____ 4. A group of retired business people who counsel small businesses.

____ 5. A guide used to seek financing for starting a business.

____ 6. It is the one who opens and operates a franchise business.

____ 7. Subway and McDonald's are examples.

____ 8. An investment used by small firms that have a potential for rapid growth.

____ 9. It is a method of doing business.

____ 10. It grants the operating license.

a. business plan
b. franchise
c. franchising
d. franchisee
e. franchisor
f. Service Corps of Retired Executives (SCORE)
g. Small Business Administration (SBA)
h. Small-Business Development Center (SBDC)
i. Small-Business Institute (SBI)
j. venture capital

True/False Questions

T   F

11. ○ ○ The main reason small businesses fail is poor management skills of the owners.

12. ○ ○ SBA loans are made by private banks for a duration of approximately twenty-five years.

13. ○ ○ SCORE counselors analyze problems for small businesses and offer plans for resolution.

14. ○ ○ A small business must be independently owned, operated for profit, and not dominant in its field.

15. ○ ○ The failure rate of small businesses is very small.

T   F

16. ○ ○ Owners of small businesses usually find it difficult to adjust to change.

17. ○ ○ The primary reason for failures of new businesses is mismanagement that results from a lack of business know-how.

18. ○ ○ The SBA loan-guarantee program guarantees loans for up to 100 percent of the loan.

19. ○ ○ A disadvantage of franchising is that the franchisee retains a great deal of control over the operations of the franchisor.

20. ○ ○ The franchisor pays the franchisee a royalty on gross sales.

Multiple-Choice Questions

21. People go into business for themselves because of
    a. an entrepreneurial spirit.
    b. independence.
    c. a willingness to accept a challenge.
    d. a desire to determine one's own destiny.
    e. all the above.

22. You have decided to open a carpet-cleaning business and have engaged in a contract with Chem-Dry. You and the company have drawn up an agreement that allows you to use the company's name and its proven method of doing business, to receive training, and to use its advertising materials. In this agreement, Chem-Dry is the _____, and you are the _____.
    a. franchisor; franchisee
    b. entrepreneur; corporation
    c. entrepreneur; local chain
    d. employee; employer
    e. corporation; manager

23. While in college, Randy and Fred spent many hours working on special projects using the computer, which they enjoyed. After graduation, they decided to put their computer skills to work and start a business helping companies design web pages. To secure financial backing, the bank will want to review their

    a. franchise contract
    b. business plan
    c. will
    d. scholastic records
    e. finances

24. Which statement reflects the main advantage for opening a small business?
    a. Financing can be obtained easily.
    b. Operating a small business is risky but offers challenge.
    c. Managing a small business offers flexibility and independence.
    d. Help is readily available from many sources.
    e. Record keeping is not complicated.

25. An advantage for the franchisee includes which of the following?
    a. Provides an opportunity to start a business with limited capital
    b. Can take part in national promotional campaigns
    c. Offers the ability to minimize the cost of supplies
    d. Receives guidance and advice concerning problems
    e. All of the above

Fill-in-the-Blank Questions

26. A Small-Business _____ Company is a privately owned firm that pro-vides venture capital.

27. About two out of three new businesses close their doors within the first _____ years.

28. In a franchise operation, the _____ pays royalties to the par-ent company.

29. Disputes between franchisors and franchisees are settled by the National _____ Program.

30. The Marriott Hotel is an example of a _____ industry.

Online Study Center

FOR MORE **test practice, use the interactive ACE quizzes available at the Online Student Center: www.college.hmco.com/PIC/pridebusiness9e.**

Answers on p. PT1.

Finagle A Bagel: A Fast-Growing Small Business

Finagle A Bagel, a fast-growing small business co-owned by Alan Litchman and Laura Trust, is at the forefront of one of the freshest concepts in the food-service business: fresh food. Each of the twenty stores bakes a new batch of bagels every hour, and each receives new deliveries of cheeses, vegetables, fruits, and other ingredients every day. Rather than prepackage menu items, store employees make everything to order so that they can satisfy the specific needs of each *guest* (Finagle A Bagel's term for a customer). As a result, customers get fresh food prepared to their exact preferences—whether it's extra cheese on a bagel pizza or no onions in a salad—along with prompt, friendly service.

"Every sandwich, every salad is built to order, so there's a lot of communication between the customers and the cashiers, the customers and the sandwich makers, the customers and the managers," explains Trust. This allows Finagle A Bagel's store employees ample opportunity to build customer relationships and encourage repeat business. Many, like Mirna Hernandez of the Tremont Street store in downtown Boston, are so familiar with what certain customers order that they spring into action when regulars enter the store. "We know what they want, and we just ring it in and take care of them," she says. Some employees even know their customers by name and make conversation as they create a sandwich or fill a coffee container.

Buying and Building the Business and Brand

The combination of a strong local following and favorable brand image is what attracted the entrepreneurs to Finagle A Bagel. Looking back, Litchman says that he and his wife recognized that building a small business would require more than good business sense. "It has a lot to do with having a great brand and having great food and reinforcing the brand every day," he remembers. "That's one of the key things that we bought."

To further reinforce the brand and reward customer loyalty, Finagle A Bagel created the Frequent Finagler card. Cardholders receive one point for every dollar spent in a Finagle A Bagel store and can redeem accumulated points for coffee, juice, sandwiches, or other rewards. To join, customers visit the company's website (**www.finagleabagel.com**) and complete a registration form asking for name, address, and other demographics. Once the account is set up, says Litchman, "It's a web-based program where customers can log on, check their points, and receive free gifts by mail. The Frequent Finagler is our big push right now to use technology as a means of generating store traffic."

Bagels Online?

Soon Litchman plans to expand the website so that customers can order food and catering services directly online. Although some competitors already invite online orders, Finagle A Bagel has a more extensive menu, and its fresh-food concept is not as easily adapted to e-commerce. "In our stores, all the food is prepared fresh, and it is very customized," Litchman notes. "This entails a fair amount of interaction between employees and customers: 'What kind of croutons do you want? What kind of dressing? What kind of mustard?' When we're ready to go in that direction, it is going to be a fairly sizable technology venture for us to undertake."

Finagle A Bagel occasionally receives web or phone orders from customers hundreds or thousands of miles away. Still, the copresidents have no immediate plans to expand outside the Boston metropolitan area. Pointing to regional food-service firms that have profited by opening more stores in a wider geographic domain, Trust says, "We see that the most successful companies have really dominated their area first. Cheesecake Factory is an example of a company that's wildly successful right now, but they were a concept in California for decades before they moved beyond that area. In-and-Out Burger is an outstanding example of a food-service company in the west that's done what we're trying to do. They had seventeen stores at one time, and now they have hundreds of stores. They're very successful, but they never left their backyard. That's kind of why we're staying where we are."

Financing a Small Business

Some small businesses achieve rapid growth through franchising. The entrepreneurs running Finagle A Bagel resisted franchising for a long time. "When you franchise, you gain a large influx of capital," says Trust, "but you begin to lose control over the people, the place, and the product." Since the beginning, the owners and their senior managers routinely popped into different Finagle A Bagel stores every day to check quality and service. Now the company says that it will begin granting franchises in the near future and institute a stringent quality-control regimen to maintain the highest standards wherever the brand name appears.

As a corporation, Finagle a Bagel could, as some other small businesses do, raise money for growth through an initial public offering (IPO) of corporate stock. The copresidents prefer not to transform their company into an open corporation at this time. "Going public is very tricky in the food-service business," Trust observes. "Some people have done it very successfully; others have not." The copresidents want to maintain total control over the pace and direction of growth rather than feeling pressured to meet the growth expectations of securities analysts and shareholders. Running a fast-growing small business is their major challenge for now.

Questions

1. Why would Finagle A Bagel maintain a business-to-customer (B2C) website even though it is not yet set up to process online orders from individuals?

2. Do you agree with Finagle A Bagel's plan to franchise its fresh-food concept and brand name? Support your answer.
3. Although opening new stores is costly, the copresidents have chosen not to raise money through an IPO. Do you agree with this decision? Discuss the advantages and disadvantages.
4. If you were writing the executive summary of Finagle A Bagel's business plan to show to lenders, what key points would you stress?

BUILDING A BUSINESS PLAN PART II

After reading Part 2, "Trends in Business Today," you should be ready to tackle the company and industry component of your business plan. In this section you will provide information about the background of the company, choice of the legal business form, information on the product or services to be offered, and descriptions of potential customers, current competitors, and the business's future. Chapter 5 in your textbook, "Choosing a Form of Business Ownership," and Chapter 6, "Small Business, Entrepreneurship, and Franchising," can help you to answer some of the questions in this part of the business plan.

The Company and Industry Component

The company and industry analysis should include the answers to at least the following questions:

2.1. What is the legal form of your business? Is your business a sole proprietorship, a partnership, or a corporation?
2.2. What licenses or permits you will need, if any?
2.3. Is your business a new independent business, a takeover, an expansion, or a franchise?
2.4. If you are dealing with an existing business, how did your company get to the point where it is today?

2.5. What does your business do, and how does it satisfy customers' needs?
2.6. How did you choose and develop the products or services to be sold, and how are they different from those currently on the market?
2.7. What industry do you operate in, and what are the industry-wide trends?
2.8. Who are the major competitors in your industry?
2.9. Have any businesses recently entered or exited? Why did they leave?
2.10. Why will your business be profitable, and what are your growth opportunities?
2.11. Does any part of your business involve e-business?

Review of Business Plan Activities

Make sure to check the information you have collected, make any changes, and correct any weaknesses before beginning Part 3. *Reminder:* Review the answers to questions in the preceding part to make sure that all your answers are consistent throughout the business plan. Finally, write a summary statement that incorporates all the information for this part of the business plan.

Part 3

Management and Organization

This part of the book deals with the organization—the "thing" that is a business. We begin with a discussion of the management functions involved in developing and operating a business. Next, we analyze the organization's elements and structure. Then we consider a firm's operations that are related to the production of goods and services.

7 **Understanding the Management Process**

8 **Creating a Flexible Organization**

9 **Producing Quality Goods and Services**

Understanding the Management Process

WHAT you will be able to do once you complete this chapter:

1 Define what management is.

2 Describe the four basic management functions: planning, organizing, leading and motivating, and controlling.

3 Distinguish among the various kinds of managers in terms of both level and area of management.

4 Identify the key management skills and the managerial roles.

5 Explain the different types of leadership.

6 Discuss the steps in the managerial decision-making process.

7 Describe how organizations benefit from total quality management.

8 Summarize what it takes to become a successful manager today.

WHY this chapter matters

Most of the people who read this chapter will not spend much time at the bottom of organizations. They will advance upward and become managers. Thus an overview of the field of management is essential.

FOR HELP with studying this chapter, visit the Online Student Center:

www.college.hmco.com/PIC/pridebusiness9e

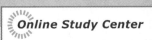
Online Study Center

Inside Business
Do Founders Make Good CEOs?

Should an entrepreneur who starts a company remain CEO for years and years? Founders, such as Pierre Omidyar (eBay), Fred Smith (FedEx), and Jerry Yang and David Filo (Yahoo!), approached this question in different ways. Omidyar served as eBay's CEO for a few years, whereas Smith remained FedEx's CEO for more than thirty years. Yang and Filo gave up day-to-day responsibilities at Yahoo! to concentrate on specific management roles. In deciding how to proceed, each took into consideration how his capabilities, training, and knowledge would affect the company's future.

Pierre Omidyar developed the software and website for eBay in 1995. He quickly recognized the difficulty of juggling both technology and business, so he hired Jeff Skoll as eBay's first president. As the company continued its explosive growth, Omidyar wooed Meg Whitman away from Hasbro to become CEO in 1998. A year later, with Whitman settled into her role, Omidyar withdrew from official management duties, although he continues as an advisor and a board member. Whitman's executive abilities have been credited with building eBay

into the world's busiest and best-known Internet auction site. Bringing in professional management was the right decision for eBay and for Omidyar, who, with his wife, now runs a philanthropic foundation.

Fred Smith has been CEO of FedEx since founding the express delivery company in 1971. Building on an idea he first outlined in a college term paper, the former Marine officer believed that an efficient, reliable overnight shipping service would draw a loyal customer following. He started FedEx knowing that he would have to compete with two well-established rivals: the U.S. Postal Service and UPS.

Under Smith's visionary leadership, FedEx thrived and became profitable within a few years. He has kept up the growth momentum by pushing for changes in government regulations, arranging acquisitions, and adding new services. Being both founder and CEO has taught Smith that "being an entrepreneur doesn't mean 'jump off a ledge and make a parachute on the way down.'"[1]

For more information about these companies, go to **www.ebay.com, www.fedex.com** and **www.yahoo.com.**

DID YOU KNOW?

Founders of some successful companies don't have jobs for life.

The different leadership paths employed by the founders at eBay, FedEx, and Yahoo! illustrate that management can be one of the most exciting and rewarding professions available today. Depending on its size, a firm may employ a number of specialized managers who are responsible for particular areas of management, such as marketing, finance, and operations. That same organization also includes managers at several levels within the firm. In this chapter we define *management* and describe the four basic management functions of planning, organizing, leading and motivating, and controlling. Then we focus on the types of managers with respect to levels of responsibility and areas of expertise. Next, we focus on the skills of effective managers and the different roles managers must play. We examine several styles of leadership and explore the process by which managers make decisions. We also describe how total quality management can improve customer satisfaction. We conclude the chapter with a discussion of what it takes to be a successful manager today.

What Is Management?

Management is the process of coordinating people and other resources to achieve the goals of an organization. As we saw in Chapter 1, most organizations make use of four kinds of resources: material, human, financial, and informational (see Figure 7.1).

Material resources are the tangible, physical resources an organization uses. For example, General Motors uses steel, glass, and fiberglass to produce cars and trucks on complex machine-driven assembly lines. A college or university uses books, classroom buildings, desks, and computers to educate students. And the Mayo Clinic uses beds, operating room equipment, and diagnostic machines to provide health care.

Perhaps the most important resources of any organization are its *human resources*—people. In fact, some firms live by the philosophy that their employees are their most important assets. One such firm is Southwest Airlines. Southwest treats its employees with the same respect and attention it gives its passengers. Southwest selectively seeks employees with upbeat attitudes and promotes from within 80 percent of the time. In decision making, everyone who will be affected is encouraged to get involved in the process. In an industry in which deregulation, extreme price competition, and fluctuating fuel costs have eliminated several major competitors, Southwest keeps growing and making a profit because of its employees. Many experts would agree with Southwest's emphasis on employees. Evidence suggests that the way employees are developed and managed may have more impact on an organization than other vital components such as marketing, sound financial decisions about large expenditures, production, or use of technology.[2]

Financial resources are the funds an organization uses to meet its obligations to investors and creditors. A 7-Eleven convenience store obtains money from customers at the check-out counters and uses a portion of that money to pay its suppliers. Citicorp, a large New York bank, borrows and lends money. Your college obtains money in the form of tuition, income from its endowments, and state and federal grants. It uses the money to pay utility bills, insurance premiums, and professors' salaries.

Finally, many organizations increasingly find that they cannot afford to ignore *information*. External environmental conditions—including the economy, consumer markets, technology, politics, and cultural forces—are all changing so rapidly that a business that does not adapt probably will not survive. And to adapt to change, the business must know what is changing and how it is changing. Most companies gather information about their competitors to increase their knowledge about changes in their industry and to learn from other companies' failures and successes.

It is important to realize that the four types of resources described earlier are only general categories of resources. Within each category are hundreds or thousands of more specific resources. It is this complex mix of specific resources—and not simply "some of each" of the four general categories—that managers must coordinate to produce goods and services.

Another interesting way to look at management is in terms of the different functions managers perform. These functions have been identified as planning, organizing,

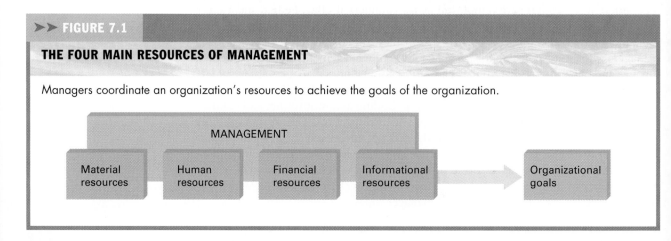

>> **FIGURE 7.1**

THE FOUR MAIN RESOURCES OF MANAGEMENT

Managers coordinate an organization's resources to achieve the goals of the organization.

MANAGEMENT

| Material resources | Human resources | Financial resources | Informational resources | → | Organizational goals |

leading and motivating employees, and controlling. We look at each of these management functions in the next section.

Basic Management Functions

A couple of years ago, AOL was struggling financially because it was losing significant market shares to competitors such as Yahoo! and Google. At the time, AOL was primarily providing Internet service to dial-up customers. To turn the company around, top management had to make significant changes that included redesigning its format to offer a Yahoo!-like portal. In addition, this change forced AOL to provide customers with its rich content for free. These major changes have resulted in a turnaround for AOL. Now AOL is a financially sound organization.[3]

Management functions such as those just described do not occur according to some rigid, preset timetable. Managers do not plan in January, organize in February, lead and motivate in March, and control in April. At any given time, managers may engage in a number of functions simultaneously. However, each function tends to lead naturally to others. Figure 7.2 provides a visual framework for a more detailed discussion of the four basic management functions. How well managers perform these key functions determines whether a business is successful.

Planning

Planning, in its simplest form, is establishing organizational goals and deciding how to accomplish them. It is often referred to as the "first" management function because all other management functions depend on planning. Organizations such as Nissan, Houston Community Colleges, and the U.S. Secret Service begin the planning process by developing a mission statement.

An organization's **mission** is a statement of the basic purpose that makes that organization different from others. Google's mission statement is "to organize the world's information and make it universally accessible and useful."[4] Houston Community College System's mission is to provide an education for local citizens. The mission of the Secret Service is to protect the life of the president. Once an organization's mission has been described in a mission statement, the next step is to develop organizational goals and objectives, usually through strategic planning. **Strategic planning** is the process of establishing an organization's major goals and objectives and allocating the resources to achieve them. Such is the case with MinuteClinic, a quick-fix medical clinic that focuses on efficiency in treating minor ailments. MinuteClinic's strategic plan deals with the quick diagnosis and treatment of medical problems such as the flu, a sore throat, or an eye infection and does not allocate any resources to treating serious medical problems such as chest pains or broken bones.[5]

2 LEARNING OBJECTIVE
Describe the four basic management functions: planning, organizing, leading and motivating, and controlling.

planning establishing organizational goals and deciding how to accomplish them

mission a statement of the basic purpose that makes an organization different from others

strategic planning the process of establishing an organization's major goals and objectives and allocating the resources to achieve them

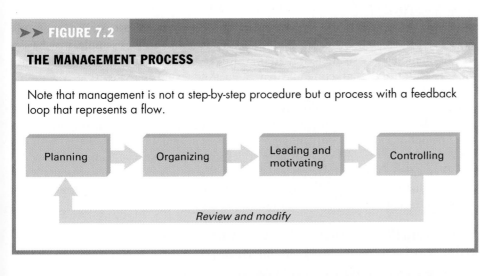

>> FIGURE 7.2

THE MANAGEMENT PROCESS

Note that management is not a step-by-step procedure but a process with a feedback loop that represents a flow.

Planning → Organizing → Leading and motivating → Controlling

Review and modify

The mission of Southwest Airlines. Southwest Airlines is dedicated to the highest quality of customer service, delivered with a sense of warmth, friendliness, individual pride, and company spirit.

goal an end result that an organization is expected to achieve over a one- to ten-year period

objective a specific statement detailing what an organization intends to accomplish over a shorter period of time

Establishing Goals and Objectives   A **goal** is an end result that an organization is expected to achieve over a one- to ten-year period. For example, DaimlerChrysler's goal in Europe is to sell 200,000 units by 2009.[6] An **objective** is a specific statement detailing what the organization intends to accomplish over a shorter period of time.

Goals and objectives can deal with a variety of factors, such as sales, company growth, costs, customer satisfaction, and employee morale. Whereas a small manufacturer may focus primarily on sales objectives for the next six months, a large firm may be more interested in goals for several years ahead. Under the leadership of CEO Will Manzer, Eastern Mountain Sports (EMS) has a goal to return to its roots as a hardcore sports gear provider. Over years of declining profits, EMS has blurred its image by shifting to "soft" merchandise that appeals to a broader market. The company's managers know that goals take time to achieve, and they are willing to invest to reach their goal of becoming the edgy outfitter they once were. They are taking action with objectives such as dropping all their "soft" merchandise, hiring hardcore sporting enthusiasts, and stocking gear for even the most fringe sports out there (e.g., kite skiing, ice climbing, and high-speed sledding).[7] Finally, goals are set at every level of an organization. Every member of an organization—the president of the company, the head of a department, and an operating employee at the lowest level—has a set of goals that he or she hopes to achieve.

The goals developed for these different levels must be consistent. However, it is likely that some conflict will arise. A production department, for example, may have a goal of minimizing costs. One way to do this is to produce only one type of product and offer "no frills." Marketing may have a goal of maximizing sales. One way to implement this goal is to offer customers a wide range of products and options. As part of goal setting, the manager who is responsible for *both* departments must achieve some sort of balance between conflicting goals. This balancing process is called *optimization*.

The optimization of conflicting goals requires insight and ability. Faced with the marketing-versus-production conflict just described, most managers probably would not adopt either viewpoint completely. Instead, they might decide on a reasonably diverse product line offering only the most widely sought-after options. Such a compromise would seem to be best for the whole organization.

Establishing Plans to Accomplish Goals and Objectives   Once goals and objectives have been set for the organization, managers must develop plans for achieving them. A **plan** is an outline of the actions by which an organization intends to accomplish its goals and objectives. Just as it has different goals and objectives, the organization also develops several types of plans, as shown in Figure 7.3.

Resulting from the strategic planning process, an organization's **strategic plan** is its broadest plan, developed as a guide for major policy setting and decision making. Strategic plans are set by the board of directors and top management and generally are designed to achieve the long-term goals of the organization. Thus a firm's strategic plan defines what business the company is in or wants to be in and the kind of company it is or wants to be. When the U.S. Surgeon General issued a report linking smoking and cancer, top management at Philip Morris Companies recognized that the company's survival was being threatened. Executives needed to develop a strategic plan to diversify into nontobacco products.

The Internet has challenged traditional strategic thinking. For example, reluctant to move from a face-to-face sales approach to a less personal website approach, Allstate has created an Internet presence to support its established sales force.

In addition to strategic plans, most organizations also employ several narrower kinds of plans. A **tactical plan** is a smaller-scale plan developed to implement a strategy. Most tactical plans cover a one- to three-year period. If a strategic plan will take five years to complete, the firm may develop five tactical plans, one covering each year. Tactical plans may be updated periodically as dictated by conditions and experience. Their more limited scope permits them to be changed more easily than strategies. In an attempt to fulfill its diversification strategy, Philip Morris developed individual tactical plans to purchase several non-tobacco-related companies such as General Foods, Kraft Foods, and Miller Brewing.

An **operational plan** is a type of plan designed to implement tactical plans. Operational plans usually are established for one year or less and deal with how to accomplish the organization's specific objectives. Assume that after Philip Morris purchased Kraft Foods, managers adopted the objective of increasing sales of Kraft's

plan an outline of the actions by which an organization intends to accomplish its goals and objectives

strategic plan an organization's broadest plan, developed as a guide for major policy setting and decision making

tactical plan a smaller-scale plan developed to implement a strategy

operational plan a type of plan designed to implement tactical plans

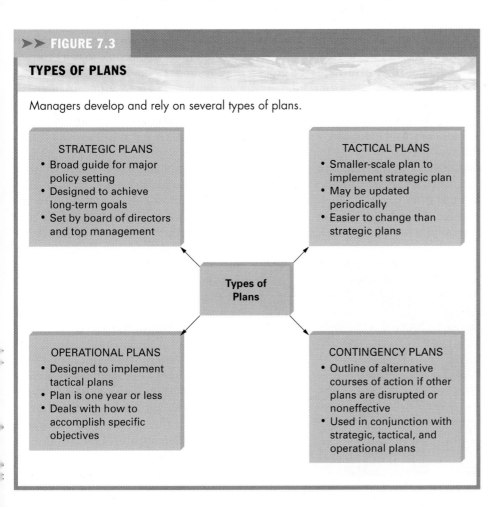

>> **FIGURE 7.3**

TYPES OF PLANS

Managers develop and rely on several types of plans.

STRATEGIC PLANS
- Broad guide for major policy setting
- Designed to achieve long-term goals
- Set by board of directors and top management

TACTICAL PLANS
- Smaller-scale plan to implement strategic plan
- May be updated periodically
- Easier to change than strategic plans

Types of Plans

OPERATIONAL PLANS
- Designed to implement tactical plans
- Plan is one year or less
- Deals with how to accomplish specific objectives

CONTINGENCY PLANS
- Outline of alternative courses of action if other plans are disrupted or noneffective
- Used in conjunction with strategic, tactical, and operational plans

Cheez Whiz by 5 percent the first year. A sales increase this large does not just happen, however. Management must develop an operational plan that describes certain activities the firm can undertake over the next year to increase sales. Specific components of the operational plan might include newspaper and television advertising, reduced prices, and coupon offers—all designed to increase sales.

Regardless of how hard managers try, sometimes business activities do not go as planned. Today, most corporations also develop contingency plans along with strategies, tactical plans, and operational plans. A **contingency plan** is a plan that outlines alternative courses of action that may be taken if an organization's other plans are disrupted or become ineffective. Remember that one reason for Philip Morris's purchase of Kraft was to diversify into nontobacco products. If it became impossible to purchase Kraft, Philip Morris could fall back on contingency plans to purchase other companies.

Organizing the Enterprise

After goal setting and planning, the second major function of the manager is organization. **Organizing** is the grouping of resources and activities to accomplish some end result in an efficient and effective manner. Consider the case of an inventor who creates a new product and goes into business to sell it. At first, the inventor will do everything on his or her own—purchase raw materials, make the product, advertise it, sell it, and keep business records. Eventually, as business grows, the inventor will need help. To begin with, he or she might hire a professional sales representative and a part-time bookkeeper. Later, it also might be necessary to hire sales staff, people to assist with production, and an accountant. As the inventor hires new personnel, he or she must decide what each person will do, to whom each person will report, and how each person can best take part in the organization's activities. We discuss these and other facets of the organizing function in much more detail in Chapter 8.

Leading and Motivating

The leading and motivating function is concerned with the human resources within an organization. Specifically, **leading** is the process of influencing people to work toward a common goal. **Motivating** is the process of providing reasons for people to work in the best interests of an organization. Together, leading and motivating are often referred to as **directing**.

We have already noted the importance of an organization's human resources. Because of this importance, leading and motivating are critical activities. Obviously, different people do things for different reasons—that is, they have different *motivations*. Some are interested primarily in earning as much money as they can. Others may be spurred on by opportunities to get promoted. Part of a manager's job, then, is to determine what factors motivate workers and to try to provide those incentives to encourage effective performance. For example, Nissan's CEO, Carlos Ghosn, has been successful at motivating his employees to give their best efforts. His leadership style involves never punishing or giving orders to his employees. Through his leadership, Ghosn has helped Nissan to exceed its three-year Nissan Revival goals in just two years.[8] Owing to the success of his leadership, Ghosn has taken on an unprecedented challenge in the auto industry. He has assumed the duties of CEO of Renault SA in France, and he remains the head of Nissan in Japan. Ghosn is trying to leverage his leadership and motivation skills to run two automakers simultaneously in different parts of the world.[9]

A lot of research has been done on both motivation and leadership. As you

contingency plan a plan that outlines alternative courses of action that may be taken if an organization's other plans are disrupted or become ineffective

organizing the grouping of resources and activities to accomplish some end result in an efficient and effective manner

leading the process of influencing people to work toward a common goal

motivating the process of providing reasons for people to work in the best interests of an organization

directing the combined processes of leading and motivating

Creating a satisfying work environment can be challenging. Some organizations attempt to create highly satisfying work environments. This CareerBuilder.com advertisement indicates that the career services provider has highly satisfying jobs available.

will see in Chapter 11, research on motivation has yielded very useful information. Research on leadership has been less successful. Despite decades of study, no one has discovered a general set of personal traits or characteristics that makes a good leader. Later in this chapter we discuss leadership in more detail.

Controlling Ongoing Activities

Controlling is the process of evaluating and regulating ongoing activities to ensure that goals are achieved. To see how controlling works, consider a rocket launched by NASA to place a satellite in orbit. Do NASA personnel simply fire the rocket and then check back in a few days to find out whether the satellite is in place? Of course not. The rocket is monitored constantly, and its course is regulated and adjusted as needed to get the satellite to its destination.

The control function includes three steps (see Figure 7.4). The first is *setting standards* with which performance can be compared. The second is *measuring actual performance* and comparing it with the standard. And the third is *taking corrective action* as necessary. Notice that the control function is circular in nature. The steps in the control function must be repeated periodically until the goal is achieved. For example, suppose that Southwest Airlines establishes a goal of increasing profits by 12 percent. To ensure that this goal is reached, Southwest's management might monitor its profit on a monthly basis. After three months, if profit has increased by 3 percent, management might be able to assume that plans are going according to schedule. Probably no action will be taken. However, if profit has increased by only 1 percent after three months, some corrective action would be needed to get the firm on track. The particular action that is required depends on the reason for the small increase in profit.

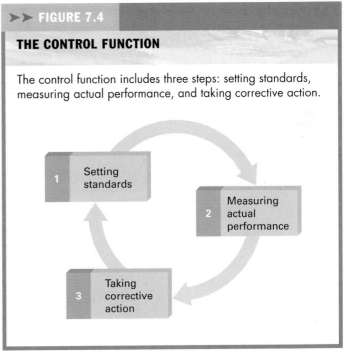

>> **FIGURE 7.4**

THE CONTROL FUNCTION

The control function includes three steps: setting standards, measuring actual performance, and taking corrective action.

1 Setting standards

2 Measuring actual performance

3 Taking corrective action

controlling the process of evaluating and regulating ongoing activities to ensure that goals are achieved

---

What Makes an Ethical Leader?

Business leaders at all levels face ethical issues as they juggle responsibilities to customers, investors, colleagues, employees, competitors, regulators, and other groups. Do you have what it takes to be an ethical leader? Ask yourself:

1. Do I set a good example for others by acting ethically every day?
2. Do I tolerate questionable or unethical behavior around me?
3. Do I act honestly and fairly, with my company's long-term priorities and interests in mind, rather than putting myself first?
4. If my company has an ethical code, do I understand and apply it every day?

5. If there is no ethical code, can I play a role in helping my company to develop and adopt one?

Ethical leaders can influence individual behavior and, over time, shape a company's culture of ethics. Kevin McManus, a plant manager for DaVinci Gourmet, explains: "Each time we allow people to behave in an inappropriate manner, we are essentially telling them that such behavior is OK. By simply speaking up, we might have a significant impact on people and their desire to repeat unethical behavior in the future."

Would you like your manager's job?

Over 70% of workers do not wish to have their manager's job.

Yes 26% 3% No 71%

Don't know

Manager

Source: Office Team Survey, **www.officeteam.com/PressRoom ?LOBName=OT&releaseid=1564.**

top manager an upper-level executive who guides and controls the overall fortunes of an organization

3 LEARNING OBJECTIVE Distinguish among the various kinds of managers in terms of both level and area of management.

Kinds of Managers

Managers can be classified in two ways: according to their level within an organization and according to their area of management. In this section we use both perspectives to explore the various types of managers.

Levels of Management

For the moment, think of an organization as a three-story structure (as illustrated in Figure 7.5). Each story corresponds to one of the three general levels of management: top managers, middle managers, and first-line managers.

Top Managers A **top manager** is an upper-level executive who guides and controls the overall fortunes of an organization. Top managers constitute a small group. In terms of planning, they are generally responsible for developing the organization's mission. They also determine the firm's strategy. Michael Dell, founder of Dell Computers, determined the need for a direct-to-consumer computer company. Many analysts attribute Michael Dell's long-term success to the significant amount of time he spends with customers that helps him to make effective strategy and product decisions. Dell has continued to gain market share at a time when computer industry sales have decreased.[10] It takes years of hard work, long hours, and perseverance, as well as talent and no small share of good luck, to reach the ranks of top management in large companies. Common job titles associated with top managers are president, vice president, chief executive officer (CEO), and chief operating officer (COO).

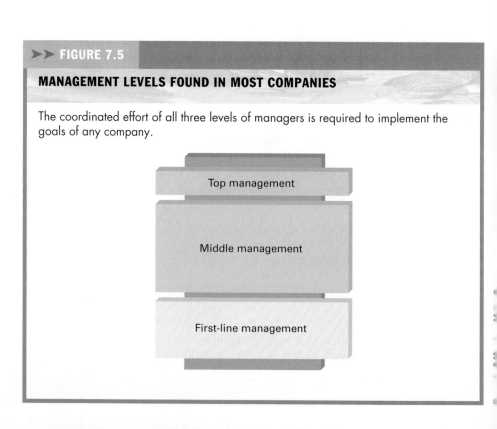

>> FIGURE 7.5

MANAGEMENT LEVELS FOUND IN MOST COMPANIES

The coordinated effort of all three levels of managers is required to implement the goals of any company.

Top management

Middle management

First-line management

Top management. Carlos Ghosn is the CEO of Nissan Motor Company. In this photo, he is surrounded by Nissan employees in Japan.

Middle Managers Middle managers probably make up the largest group of managers in most organizations. A **middle manager** is a manager who implements the strategy and major policies developed by top management. Middle managers develop tactical plans and operational plans, and they coordinate and supervise the activities of first-line managers. Titles at the middle-management level include division manager, department head, plant manager, and operations manager.

First-Line Managers A **first-line manager** is a manager who coordinates and supervises the activities of operating employees. First-line managers spend most of their time working with and motivating their employees, answering questions, and solving day-to-day problems. Most first-line managers are former operating employees who, owing to their hard work and potential, were promoted into management. Many of today's middle and top managers began their careers on this first management level. Common titles for first-line managers include office manager, supervisor, and foreman.

middle manager a manager who implements the strategy and major policies developed by top management

first-line manager a manager who coordinates and supervises the activities of operating employees

Areas of Management Specialization

Organizational structure also can be divided into areas of management specialization (see Figure 7.6). The most common areas are finance, operations, marketing, human resources, and administration. Depending on its mission, goals, and objectives, an organization may include other areas as well—research and development (R&D), for example.

Financial Managers A **financial manager** is primarily responsible for an organization's financial resources. Accounting and investment are specialized areas within financial management. Because financing affects the operation of the entire firm, many of the CEOs and presidents of this country's largest companies are people who got their "basic training" as financial managers.

Operations Managers An **operations manager** manages the systems that convert resources into goods and services. Traditionally, operations management has been

financial manager a manager who is primarily responsible for an organization's

operations manager a manager who manages the systems that convert resources into goods and services

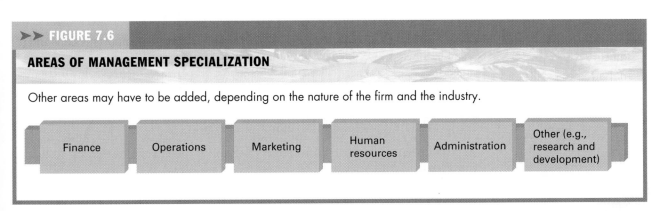

▶▶ FIGURE 7.6

AREAS OF MANAGEMENT SPECIALIZATION

Other areas may have to be added, depending on the nature of the firm and the industry.

| Finance | Operations | Marketing | Human resources | Administration | Other (e.g., research and development) |

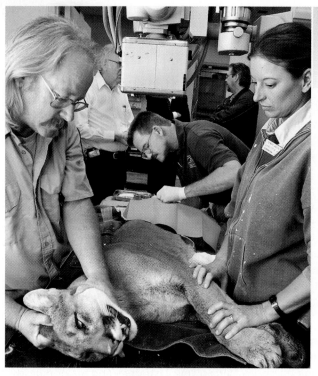

Is holding down a lion a part of your job? First line managers at the Henry Doorly Zoo in Omaha, Nebraska, hold down a sedated mountain lion while the zoo veterinarian performs minor surgery.

equated with manufacturing—the production of goods. However, in recent years, many of the techniques and procedures of operations management have been applied to the production of services and to a variety of nonbusiness activities. As with financial management, operations management has produced a large percentage of today's company CEOs and presidents.

Marketing Managers   A **marketing manager** is responsible for facilitating the exchange of products between an organization and its customers or clients. Specific areas within marketing are marketing research, product management, advertising, promotion, sales, and distribution. A sizable number of today's company presidents have risen from the ranks of marketing management.

marketing manager a manager who is responsible for facilitating the exchange of products between an organization and its customers or clients

human resources manager a person charged with managing an organization's human resources programs

administrative manager a manager who is not associated with any specific functional area but who provides overall administrative guidance and leadership

Human Resources Managers   A **human resources manager** is charged with managing an organization's human resources programs. He or she engages in human resources planning; designs systems for hiring, training, and evaluating the performance of employees; and ensures that the organization follows government regulations concerning employment practices. Some human resources managers are making effective use of technology. For example, over one million job openings are posted on Monster.com, which attracts about eighteen million visitors monthly.[11]

Administrative Managers   An **administrative manager** (also called a *general manager*) is not associated with any specific functional area but provides overall administrative guidance and leadership. A hospital administrator is an example of an administrative manager. He or she does not specialize in operations, finance, marketing, or human resources management but instead coordinates the activities of specialized managers in all these areas. In many respects, most top managers are really administrative managers.

Whatever their level in the organization and whatever area they specialize in, successful managers generally exhibit certain key skills and are able to play certain managerial roles. However, as we shall see, some skills are likely to be more critical at one level of management than at another.

What Makes Effective Managers?

4 LEARNING OBJECTIVE
Identify the key management skills and the managerial roles.

In general, effective managers are those who (1) possess certain important skills and (2) are able to use those skills in a number of managerial roles. Probably no manager is called on to use any particular skill *constantly* or to play a particular role *all the time*. However, these skills and abilities must be available when they are needed.

Key Management Skills

The skills that typify effective managers fall into three general categories: technical, conceptual, and interpersonal.

Assistance for HR managers. A number of human resource specialists are available to assist companies with their human resources decisions and activities.

Technical Skills

A **technical skill** is a specific skill needed to accomplish a specialized activity. For example, the skills engineers and machinists need to do their jobs are technical skills. First-line managers (and, to a lesser extent, middle managers) need the technical skills relevant to the activities they manage. Although these managers may not perform the technical tasks themselves, they must be able to train subordinates, answer questions, and otherwise provide guidance and direction. A first-line manager in the accounting department of the Hyatt Corporation, for example, must be able to perform computerized accounting transactions and help employees complete the same accounting task. In general, top managers do not rely on technical skills as heavily as managers at other levels. Still, understanding the technical side of a business is an aid to effective management at every level.

Conceptual Skills

Conceptual skill is the ability to think in abstract terms. Conceptual skill allows a manager to see the "big picture" and understand how the various parts of an organization or idea can fit together. These skills are useful in a wide range of situations, including the optimization of goals described earlier. They are usually more useful for top managers than for middle or first-line managers.

technical skill a specific skill needed to accomplish a specialized activity

conceptual skill the ability to think in abstract terms

Business Around the World

PepsiCo Faces a Credibility Crisis in India

Although New York-based PepsiCo has decades of experience in global business, it faced a credibility crisis in India just as Indra Nooyi was named the company's first woman CEO in 2006. The trouble began in 2003 when a local group, the Centre for Science and Environment (CSE), said bottled waters sold by Pepsi and rival Coca-Cola were pesticide-laced.

The crisis came to a head three years later when CSE said that Pepsi's and Coke's colas contained

high pesticide residue. This prompted protests throughout the country, and several Indian states banned the beverages even though Pepsi and Coke insisted

that their products met stringent purity standards. However, CSE's target was not just the big multinationals—it also wanted the government to do more to protect public health.

Pepsi may have reacted too slowly. "They got behind the curve, and now they are chasing the crisis," said one consultant.

But management needed to assess the situation's political and cultural nuances before responding. What else can Nooyi do to restore consumer confidence and show India that Pepsi's products are safe?

interpersonal skill the ability to deal effectively with other people

Interpersonal Skills

An **interpersonal skill** is the ability to deal effectively with other people, both inside and outside an organization. Examples of interpersonal skills are the ability to relate to people, understand their needs and motives, and show genuine compassion. One reason why Mary Kay Ash, founder of Mary Kay Cosmetics, has been so successful is her ability to motivate her employees and to inspire their loyalty to her vision for the firm. And although it is obvious that a CEO such as Mary Kay Ash must be able to work with employees throughout the organization, what is not so obvious is that middle and first-line managers also must possess interpersonal skills. For example, a first-line manager on an assembly line at Procter & Gamble must rely on employees to manufacture Tide detergent. The better the manager's interpersonal skills, the more likely the manager will be able to lead and motivate those employees. When all other things are equal, the manager able to exhibit these skills will be more successful than the arrogant and brash manager who does not care about others.

Managerial Roles

Research suggests that managers must, from time to time, act in ten different roles if they are to be successful.[12] (By *role*, we mean a set of expectations that one must fulfill.) These ten roles can be grouped into three broad categories: decisional, interpersonal, and informational.

decisional role a role that involves various aspects of management decision making

Decisional Roles

A **decisional role** involves various aspects of management decision making. The decisional role can be subdivided into four specific managerial roles. In the role of *entrepreneur*, the manager is the voluntary initiator of change. For example, the CEO of DuPont decided to put more financial resources into its Experimental Station, a large R&D center, to increase new products. This entrepreneurial emphasis on R&D led to the creation of Sorona, a synthetic fiber that could be used for clothing, car upholstery, and carpeting. DuPont hopes that these decisions will pay great dividends in the long run.[13] A second role is that of *disturbance handler*. A manager who settles a strike is handling a disturbance. Third, the manager also occasionally plays the role of *resource allocator*. In this role, the manager might have to decide which departmental budgets to cut and which expenditure requests to approve. The fourth role is that of *negotiator*. Being a negotiator might involve settling a dispute between a manager and a worker assigned to the manager's work group.

interpersonal role a role in which the manager deals with people

informational role a role in which the manager either gathers or provides information

Interpersonal Roles

Dealing with people is an integral part of the manager's job. An **interpersonal role** is a role in which the manager deals with people. Like the decisional role, the interpersonal role can be broken down according to three managerial functions. The manager may be called on to serve as a *figurehead*, perhaps by attending a ribbon-cutting ceremony or taking an important client to dinner. The manager also may have to play the role of *liaison* by serving as a go-between for two different groups. As a liaison, a manager might represent his or her firm at meetings of an industry-wide trade organization. Finally, the manager often has to serve as a *leader*. Playing the role of leader includes being an example for others in the organization as well as developing the skills, abilities, and motivation of employees.

Informational Roles

An **informational role** is one in which the manager either gathers or provides information. The informational role can be subdivided as follows: In the role of *monitor*, the manager actively seeks information that may be of

SPOTLIGHT

How quickly supervisors respond to employees

Office workers were asked how long it generally takes their boss to respond to them.

- Before closing that day 29%
- Within an hour or two 36%
- Immediately 27%
- I am lucky if they respond without several prompts 8%

Source: *USA Today*, March 27, 2002, p. A1.

value to the organization. For example, a manager who hears about a good business opportunity is engaging in the role of monitor. The second informational role is that of *disseminator*. In this role, the manager transmits key information to those who can use it. As a disseminator, the manager who heard about a good business opportunity would tell the appropriate marketing manager about it. The third informational role is that of *spokesperson*. In this role, the manager provides information to people outside the organization, such as the press, television reporters, and the public.

Leadership

Leadership has been defined broadly as the ability to influence others. A leader has power and can use it to affect the behavior of others. Leadership is different from management in that a leader strives for voluntary cooperation, whereas a manager may have to depend on coercion to change employee behavior.

Formal and Informal Leadership

Some experts make distinctions between formal leadership and informal leadership. Formal leaders have legitimate power of position. They have *authority* within an organization to influence others to work for the organization's objectives. Informal leaders usually have no such authority and may or may not exert their influence in support of the organization. Both formal and informal leaders make use of several kinds of power, including the ability to grant rewards or impose punishments, the possession of expert knowledge, and personal attraction or charisma. Informal leaders who identify with the organization's goals are a valuable asset to any organization. However, a business can be brought to its knees by informal leaders who turn work groups against management.

Styles of Leadership

For many years, leadership was viewed as a combination of personality traits, such as self-confidence, concern for people, intelligence, and dependability. Achieving a consensus on which traits were most important was difficult, however, and attention turned to styles of leadership behavior. In the last few decades, several styles of leadership have been identified: authoritarian, laissez-faire, and democratic.[14] The **authoritarian leader** holds all authority and responsibility, with communication usually moving from top to bottom. This leader assigns workers to specific tasks and expects orderly, precise results. The leaders at UPS employ authoritarian leadership. At the other extreme is the **laissez-faire leader,** who gives authority to employees. With the laissez-faire style, subordinates are allowed to work as they choose with a minimum of interference. Communication flows horizontally among group members. Leaders at Apple Computer employ a laissez-faire leadership style to give employees as much freedom as possible to develop new products. The **democratic leader** holds final responsibility but also delegates authority to others, who determine work assignments. In this leadership style, communication is active upward and downward. Employee commitment is high because of participation in the decision-making process. Managers for both Wal-Mart and Saturn have used democratic leadership to encourage employees to become more than just rank-and-file workers.

Which Managerial Leadership Style Is Best?

Today, most management experts agree that no "best" managerial leadership style exists. Each of the styles described—authoritarian, laissez-faire, and democratic—has advantages and disadvantages. Democratic leadership can motivate employees to work effectively because they are implementing *their own* decisions. However, the decision-making process in democratic leadership takes time that subordinates could be devoting to the work itself.

5 LEARNING OBJECTIVE
Explain the different types of leadership.

leadership the ability to influence others

authoritarian leader one who holds all authority and responsibility, with communication usually moving from top to bottom

laissez-faire leader one who gives authority to employees and allows subordinates to work as they choose with a minimum of interference; communication flows horizontally among group members

democratic leader one who holds final responsibility but also delegates authority to others, who help to determine work assignments; communication is active upward and downward

Although hundreds of research studies have been conducted to prove which leadership style is best, there are no definite conclusions. The "best" leadership seems to occur when the leader's style matches the situation. Each of the leadership styles can be effective in the right situation. The *most* effective style depends on interaction among employees, characteristics of the work situation, and the manager's personality.

Managerial Decision Making

6 LEARNING OBJECTIVE
Discuss the steps in the managerial decision-making process.

decision making the act of choosing one alternative from a set of alternatives

Decision making is the act of choosing one alternative from a set of alternatives.[15] In ordinary situations, decisions are made casually and informally. We encounter a problem, mull it over, settle on a solution, and go on. Managers, however, require a more systematic method for solving complex problems. As shown in Figure 7.7, managerial decision making involves four steps: (1) identifying the problem or opportunity, (2) generating alternatives, (3) selecting an alternative, and (4) implementing and evaluating the solution.

Identifying the Problem or Opportunity

problem the discrepancy between an actual condition and a desired condition

A **problem** is the discrepancy between an actual condition and a desired condition—the difference between what is occurring and what one wishes would occur. For example, a marketing manager at Campbell Soup Company has a problem if sales revenues for Campbell's Hungry Man frozen dinners are declining (the actual condition). To solve this problem, the marketing manager must take steps to increase sales revenues (desired condition). Most people consider a problem to be "negative"; however, a problem also can be "positive." A positive problem should be viewed as an "opportunity."

Although accurate identification of a problem is essential before it can be solved or turned into an opportunity, this stage of decision making creates many difficulties for managers. Sometimes managers' preconceptions of the problem prevent them from seeing the actual situation. They produce an answer before the proper question has been asked. In other cases, managers overlook truly significant issues by focusing on unimportant matters. Also, managers may mistakenly analyze problems in terms of symptoms rather than underlying causes.

Effective managers learn to look ahead so that they are prepared when decisions must be made. They clarify situations and examine the causes of problems, asking whether the presence or absence of certain variables alters a situation. Finally, they consider how individual behaviors and values affect the way problems or opportunities are defined.

Generating Alternatives

After a problem has been defined, the next task is to generate alternatives. The more important the decision, the more attention is devoted to this stage. Managers should be open to fresh, innovative ideas as well as obvious answers.

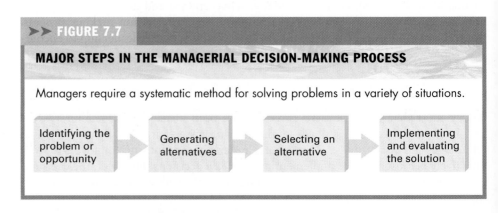

▶▶ FIGURE 7.7

MAJOR STEPS IN THE MANAGERIAL DECISION-MAKING PROCESS

Managers require a systematic method for solving problems in a variety of situations.

Identifying the problem or opportunity → Generating alternatives → Selecting an alternative → Implementing and evaluating the solution

Certain techniques can aid in the generation of creative alternatives. Brainstorming, commonly used in group discussions, encourages participants to produce many new ideas. Other group members are not permitted to criticize or ridicule. Another approach, developed by the U.S. Navy, is called "Blast! Then Refine." Group members tackle a recurring problem by erasing all previous solutions and procedures. The group then re-evaluates its original objectives, modifies them if necessary, and devises new solutions. Other techniques—including trial and error—are also useful in this stage of decision making.

Selecting an Alternative

Final decisions are influenced by a number of considerations, including financial constraints, human and informational resources, time limits, legal obstacles, and political factors. Managers must select the alternative that will be most effective and practical. At times, two or more alternatives or some combination of alternatives will be equally appropriate. After considering several alternatives to become more competitive, IBM management decided to outsource the manufacturing of more products such as disk drives and even low-end servers. Most recently, IBM decided to sell off its PC division to China's top PC maker, Lenovo.[16]

Managers may choose solutions to problems on several levels. The coined word "satisfice" describes solutions that are only adequate and not ideal. When lacking time or information, managers often make decisions that "satisfice." Whenever possible, managers should try to investigate alternatives carefully and select the ideal solution.

YOUR CAREER

The Heat Is On—and You're the Decision Maker

Do you know how to make a decision when the pressure is on? Here are some tips for building your decision-making skills:

- *Stay calm.* Getting panicky can distract you from key information and prompt hasty decisions. Calming your anxiety before attacking a problem will help you to make a better decision.
- *Look for a pattern.* Is the current problem similar to one you solved in the past? If you can identify a similar pattern, you can apply the same decision guidelines you used previously or modify them for the current situation.
- *Simplify, simplify, simplify.* Even if a problem seems complex, you usually can find a simple way to organize the symptoms and analyze possible alternatives and outcomes.
- *Use your intuition.* You won't always have enough data or reliable data to make decisions. Keep an open mind, analyze the data at hand, and ask experts or experienced managers for input. Then let your intuition point you toward the best decision under the circumstances.

Implementing and Evaluating the Solution

Implementation of a decision requires time, planning, preparation of personnel, and evaluation of results. Managers usually deal with unforeseen consequences even when they have carefully considered the alternatives.

The final step in managerial decision making entails evaluating the effectiveness of a decision. If the alternative that was chosen removes the difference between the actual condition and the desired condition, the decision is judged effective. If the problem still exists, managers may select one of the following choices:

- Decide to give the chosen alternative more time to work.
- Adopt a different alternative.
- Start the problem identification process all over again.

Failure to evaluate decisions adequately may have negative consequences. Hewlett Packard's former CEO, Carly Fiorina, suffered negative consequences after the controversial merger with Compaq Computer did not help the company's earnings performance. Because Hewlett Packard's hardware units still were not highly competitive against the market leaders, Fiorina was replaced.[17]

Managing Total Quality

7 LEARNING OBJECTIVE
Describe how organizations benefit from total quality management.

total quality management (TQM) the coordination of efforts directed at improving customer satisfaction, increasing employee participation, strengthening supplier partnerships, and facilitating an organizational atmosphere of continuous quality improvement

The management of quality is a high priority in some organizations today. Major reasons for a greater focus on quality include foreign competition, more demanding customers, and poor financial performance resulting from reduced market shares and higher costs. Over the last few years, several U.S. firms have lost the dominant competitive positions they had held for decades.

Total quality management is a much broader concept than just controlling the quality of the product itself (which is discussed in Chapter 9). **Total quality management (TQM)** is the coordination of efforts directed at improving customer satisfaction, increasing employee participation, strengthening supplier partnerships, and facilitating an organizational atmosphere of continuous quality improvement. For TQM programs to be effective, management must address each of the following components:

- *Customer satisfaction.* Ways to improve include producing higher-quality products, providing better customer service, and showing customers that the company cares.
- *Employee participation.* This can be increased by allowing employees to contribute to decisions, develop self-managed work teams, and assume responsibility for improving the quality of their work.
- *Strengthening supplier partnerships.* Developing good working relationships with suppliers can ensure that the right supplies and materials will be delivered on time at lower costs.
- *Continuous quality improvement.* This should not be viewed as achievable through one single program that has a target objective. A program based on continuous improvement has proven to be the most effective long-term approach.

Although many factors influence the effectiveness of a TQM program, two issues are crucial. First, top management must make a strong commitment to a TQM program by treating quality improvement as a top priority and giving it frequent attention. Firms that establish a TQM program but then focus on other priorities will find that their quality-improvement initiatives will fail. Second, management must coordinate the specific elements of a TQM program so that they work in harmony with each other.

Although not all U.S. companies have TQM programs, these programs provide many benefits. Overall financial benefits include lower operating costs, higher return on sales and on investments, and an improved ability to use premium pricing rather than competitive pricing.

What It Takes to Become a Successful Manager Today

8 LEARNING OBJECTIVE
Summarize what it takes to become a successful manager today.

Everyone hears stories about the corporate elite who make salaries in excess of $1 million a year, travel to and from work in chauffeur-driven limousines, and enjoy lucrative pension plans that provide for a luxurious lifestyle after they retire. Although management obviously can be a rewarding career, what is not so obvious is the amount of time and hard work needed to achieve the impressive salaries and perks.

A Day in the Life of a Manager

Organizations pay managers for performance. As already pointed out, managers coordinate an organization's resources. They also perform the four basic management functions: planning, organizing, leading and motivating, and controlling. And managers make decisions and then implement and evaluate those decisions. This heavy workload requires that managers work long hours, and most do not get paid overtime. Typically, the number of hours increases as a manager advances.

Today's managers have demanding jobs. Managers spend a great deal of time talking with people on an individual basis. The purpose of these conversations is usually to obtain information or to resolve problems. In addition, a manager often spends time in meetings with other managers and employees. In most cases, the purpose of the meetings—some brief and some lengthy—is to resolve problems. And if the work is not completed by the end of the day, the manager usually packs his or her unfinished tasks in a briefcase.

Skills Required for Success

To be successful in today's competitive business environment, you must possess a number of skills. Some of these skills—technical, conceptual, and interpersonal skills—were discussed earlier in this chapter. However, you also need "personal" skills. Oral and written communication skills, computer skills, and critical-thinking skills may give you the edge in getting an entry-level management position.

- *Oral communication skills.* Because a large part of a manager's day is spent conversing with others, the ability to speak *and* listen is critical. Oral communication skills are used when a manager makes sales presentations, conducts interviews, and holds press conferences.
- *Written communication skills.* A manager's ability to prepare letters, e-mails, memos, sales reports, and other written documents may spell the difference between success and failure.
- *Computer skills.* Most employers do not expect you to be an expert computer programmer, but they do expect that you should know how to use a computer to prepare written and statistical reports and to communicate with other managers and employees.
- *Critical-thinking skills.* Employers expect managers to use the steps for effective managerial decision making. They also expect managers to use critical-thinking skills to identify problems correctly, generate reasonable alternatives, and select the "best" alternatives to solve problems.

@ USING THE INTERNET

TBetterManagement.com is an excellent resource for anyone that wants to improve their management skills. BetterManagement offers free access to thousands of articles, webcasts, surveys, and seminars designed to grow management skills and effectiveness. It also offers a free email newsletter to subscribers who want automatic access to management news. To explore these features and become a better manager, visit: **bettermanagement.com.**

The Importance of Education and Experience

Although most experts agree that management skills must be learned on the job, the concepts that you learn in business courses lay the foundation for a successful career. In addition, successful completion of college courses or obtaining a degree can open doors to job interviews and career advancement.

There are methods you can use to "beef up" your résumé and to capitalize on your work experience. First, obtain summer jobs that provide opportunities to learn about the field that interests you. Chosen carefully, part-time jobs can provide work experience that other job applicants may not have. Some colleges and universities sponsor cooperative work/school programs that give students college credit for job experience. Even with solid academics and work experience, many would-be managers find it difficult to land the "right" job. Often they start in an entry-level position to gain more experience.

In the next chapter we examine the organizing function of managers in some detail. We look specifically at various organizational forms that today's successful businesses use. As with many factors in management, how a business is organized depends on its goals, strategies, and personnel.

RETURN TO   Inside Business

Whereas eBay's Pierre Omidyar and FedEx's Fred Smith founded their companies and served as CEOs, Yahoo!'s Jerry Yang and David Filo chose a different management path. After incorporating the Internet search company Yahoo! in 1995, the cofounders hired Tim Koogle, a seasoned technology executive, as CEO. Under his guidance, Yahoo! became a public corporation and a household name. Terry Semel, the next CEO, ex-panded the business glob-ally and added new revenue-producing services.

     Filo and Yang share the title of Chief Yahoo but have carved out specific management roles. Yang is a director and works with top management on strategy issues; Filo leads Yahoo!'s technical side. Although the founders offer input on major decisions, the CEO and board of directors have the final say. This arrangement has helped Yahoo! weather the ups and downs of the dot-com world while making the most of its founders' personal and professional strengths.

Questions

1. Of the key management skills, which were Pierre Omidyar and Fred Smith applying when they founded their companies? Which did Omidyar seek in a CEO?
2. Without the CEO title, what kind of leadership can David Filo and Jerry Yang offer Yahoo!? Explain your answer.

►► CHAPTER REVIEW

Summary

1

Define what management is.

Management is the process of coordinating people and other resources to achieve the goals of an organization. Managers are concerned with four types of resources—material, human, financial, and informational.

2

Describe the four basic management functions: planning, organizing, leading and motivating, and controlling.

Managers perform four basic functions. Management functions do not occur according to some rigid, preset timetable, though. At any time, managers may engage in a number of functions simultaneously. However, each function tends to lead naturally to others. First, managers engage in planning—determining where the firm should be going and how best to get there. Three types of plans, from the broadest to the most specific, are strategic plans, tactical plans, and operational plans. Managers also organize resources and activities to accomplish results in an efficient and effective manner, and they lead and motivate others to work in

the best interests of the organization. In addition, managers control ongoing activities to keep the organization on course. There are three steps in the control function: setting standards, measuring actual performance, and taking corrective action.

3

Distinguish among the various kinds of managers in terms of both level and area of management.

Managers—or management positions—may be classified from two different perspectives. From the perspective of level within the organization, there are top managers, who control the fortunes of the organization; middle managers, who implement strategies and major policies; and first-line managers, who supervise the activities of operating employees. From the viewpoint of area of management, managers most often deal with the areas of finance, operations, marketing, human resources, and administration.

4

Identify the key management skills and the managerial roles.

Effective managers tend to possess a specific set of skills and to fill three basic managerial roles. Technical, conceptual, and interpersonal skills are all important, although the relative importance of each varies with the level of management within the organization. The primary managerial roles can be classified as decisional, interpersonal, or informational.

5

Explain the different types of leadership.

Managers' effectiveness often depends on their styles of leadership—that is, their ability to influence others, either formally or informally. Leadership styles include the authoritarian "do-it-my-way" style, the laissez-faire "do-it-your-way" style, and the democratic "let's-do-it-together" style.

6

Discuss the steps in the managerial decision-making process.

Decision making, an integral part of a manager's work, is the process of developing a set of possible alternative solutions to a problem and choosing one alternative from among the set. Managerial decision making involves four steps: Managers must accurately identify problems, generate several possible solutions, choose the solution that will be most effective under the circumstances, and implement and evaluate the chosen course of action.

7

Describe how organizations benefit from total quality management.

Total quality management (TQM) is the coordination of efforts directed at improving customer satisfaction, increasing employee participation, strengthening supplier partnerships, and facilitating an organizational atmosphere of continuous quality improvement. To have an effective TQM program, top management must make a strong, sustained commitment to the effort and must be able to coordinate all the program's elements so that they work in harmony. Overall financial benefits of TQM include lower operating costs, higher return on sales and on investment, and an improved ability to use premium pricing rather than competitive pricing.

8

Summarize what it takes to become a successful manager today.

Organizations pay managers for their performance. Managers coordinate resources. They also plan, organize, lead, motivate, and control. They make decisions that can spell the difference between an organization's success and failure. To complete their tasks, managers work long hours at a hectic pace. To be successful, they need personal skills

(oral and written communication skills, computer skills, and critical-thinking skills), an academic background that provides a foundation for a management career, and practical work experience.

Key Terms

You should now be able to define and give an example relevant to each of the following terms:

management (220)
planning (221)
mission (221)
strategic planning (221)
goal (222)
objective (222)
plan (223)
strategic plan (223)
tactical plan (223)
operational plan (223)
contingency plan (224)
organizing (224)
leading (224)
motivating (224)
directing (224)
controlling (225)
top manager (226)
middle manager (227)
first-line manager (227)
financial manager (227)
operations manager (227)
marketing manager (228)
human resources manager (228)
administrative manager (228)
technical skill (229)
conceptual skill (229)
interpersonal skill (230)
decisional role (230)
interpersonal role (230)
informational role (230)
leadership (231)
authoritarian leader (231)
laissez-faire leader (231)
democratic leader (231)
decision making (232)
problem (232)
total quality management (TQM) (234)

Review Questions

1. Define the term *manager* without using the word *management* in your definition.
2. What is the mission of a neighborhood restaurant? Of the Salvation Army? What might be reasonable objectives for these organizations?
3. What does the term *optimization* mean?
4. How do a strategic plan, a tactical plan, and an operational plan differ? What do they all have in common?
5. What exactly does a manager organize, and for what reason?

6. Why are leadership and motivation necessary in a business in which people are paid for their work?
7. Explain the steps involved in the control function.
8. How are the two perspectives on kinds of managers—that is, level and area—different from each other?
9. In what ways are management skills related to the roles managers play? Provide a specific example to support your answer.
10. Compare and contrast the major styles of leadership.
11. Discuss what happens during each of the four steps of the managerial decision-making process.
12. What are the major benefits of a total quality management program?
13. What personal skills should a manager possess in order to be successful?

2. Which of the management functions, skills, and roles do not apply to the owner-operator of a sole proprietorship?
3. Which leadership style might be best suited to each of the three general levels of management within an organization?
4. According to this chapter, the leadership style that is *most* effective depends on the interaction among the employees, the characteristics of the work situation, and the manager's personality. Do you agree or disagree? Explain your answer.
5. Do you think that people are really as important to an organization as this chapter seems to indicate?
6. As you learned in this chapter, managers often work long hours at a hectic pace. Would this type of career appeal to you? Explain your answer.

Discussion Questions

1. Does a healthy firm (one that is doing well) have to worry about effective management? Explain.

▶▶ VIDEO CASE 7.1

VIPdesk Is at Your Service

Need restaurant reservations, home repairs, sports tickets, or a perfect gift for someone special? VIPdesk's expert team of concierges is always on call to help customers. Mary Naylor created VIPdesk based on years of experience providing on-site concierge services for the employees of corporations. Recognizing the opportunity to cost-effectively serve more customers through the Internet, Naylor established her first concierge website in 1996.

Today, VIPdesk handles concierge services for more than twenty million users, and it is the leading provider of "live" web-based concierge services. Companies such as Van Kampen offer VIPdesk's services as a reward to outstanding employees. In addition, corporate clients such as MasterCard, Citibank, and General Motors' OnStar offer VIPdesk's concierge services to select customers all over the United States.

When Naylor was planning VIPdesk, she knew that she might not get all the investment funding she needed to expand rapidly in the early years. Therefore, she developed several strategic plans with a range of goals and objectives, tactics, budgets, and performance measures. When she received only one-third of the funding she wanted, she implemented a slower-growth plan.

Naylor launched VIPdesk with six corporate customers and twenty-five managers and employees. As the business grew, she hired more employees to serve as concierges. Some worked in the Oregon call center; others worked from home on a part-time basis during periods of peak demand. These part-timers brought an in-depth knowledge of local resources they could tap to satisfy users in their area. Over time, corporate customers began asking VIPdesk to coordinate additional services, such as employee performance rewards. Through customer surveys, Naylor identified new opportunities for increasing use of VIPdesk's services. Soon she hired a chief strategy officer with the conceptual skills to prepare long-term plans.

Interpersonal skills are extremely important for Naylor because she deals with investors, employees, customers, suppliers, and others everyday. Although she relies on skilled specialists to maintain the company's website and other technical tasks, she has the vision to understand what technology can do for her business. This is why she offers access to her concierge services via the Internet, e-mail, or a toll-free telephone number.

No matter how users reach VIPdesk, they receive fast and professional help. Among the most common requests are help with travel arrangements, auto rentals, theater and sports tickets, personal shopping, and other errands. "In effect, what we provide to the customer is a virtual personal assistant," says the CEO.

Naylor works closely with managers to plan for staffing when VIPdesk gets ready to sign a new corporate customer. First, they look at the number of users who will be covered under the contract. "Then we can look at how much usage we expect or how many requests will be placed from a population of a given size." With this information, she and her managers can determine how many concierges might be needed to accommodate the requests.

Competition is increasing all the time, but VIPdesk offers banks a way to reward people for carrying their credit cards. "It can cost less than a key chain or some token item that a corporation may give as a gift to a customer," Naylor observes. With so many banks trying to woo and win cardholders, VIPdesk should have a bright future ahead.[18]

For more information about this company, go to **www.vipdesk.com.**

Questions

1. Why would operations managers be particularly important in a business such as VIPdesk?
2. At what management level would you expect a chief strategy officer to be positioned in VIPdesk's hierarchy?
3. Based on what you know about VIPdesk, identify one potential threat for which you believe Naylor should have a contingency plan. Explain your answer.

►► CASE 7.2

New Leadership, New Opportunities for Hewlett Packard

Hewlett Packard (HP) was born in somebody's garage. Over six decades later, the company founded by Bill Hewlett and Dave Packard annually sells $82 billion worth of computers, printers, data storage systems, and digital cameras. Yet, in all these years, only six CEOs have led the company—and only two CEOs have been outsiders.

The first was Carly Fiorina, brought from Lucent Technologies to become CEO in 1999. Fiorina's bold strategy included the acquisition of Compaq in 2002 to create an integrated technology superpower. Within three years, however, HP's financial performance was not hitting the expected heights. And although HP was the world's largest printer maker, competitor Dell had surged ahead to become America's top PC company. The board of directors forced Fiorina out as HP continued losing PC market share and replaced her with another outsider: Mark Hurd, the CEO of business technology firm NCR.

Hurd knew that planning would be vitally important to putting HP back on track. He began digging into the company's current strategy, learning about its various businesses, and meeting with employees and managers at all levels. He quickly realized that HP would be better positioned for future opportunities if he and his management team looked closely at organizing, leading and motivating, and controlling.

One of Hurd's early decisions was to step back from Fiorina's integration strategy and refocus the company on individual products. To do this, he organized PCs into one division and printer products into another. Because many large companies prefer to buy complete systems, however, HP continued its integrated sales approach for these customers, sending a team of product experts to assess needs and recommend solutions.

Starting at the top, the CEO tackled the function of leading and motivating. "When you look at the ability to build a great company and great management teams, management is really a team sport," he said after joining HP. "On a personal-style basis, I believe in very engaged management." He added, "I like to move through multiple levels of the company, and I like my management to do that. Great companies have boards, CEOs, and management that all have one script."

Hurd discovered strong motivation throughout the work force: "If there's anything that struck me in coming to HP, it's the desire on the part of employees to see this company succeed." This was important because "when a company has the kind of passion that HP-ers have, it shows up not only inside the company in a positive way but it bleeds into how we support and treat our customers," he said. And this made Hurd enthusiastic about his job: "The CEO actually gets motivated by the employees, sometimes. Everyone thinks the CEO doesn't have emotion around all this stuff, but I get motivated by it, too."

Hurd made controlling a high priority to adjust HP's day-to-day activities for top performance. However, he didn't want employees confused or distracted by having to check too many standards and measure too many activities. Therefore, he established a specific set of standards for assessing performance based on efficiency, revenue, profitability, and other key measures.

In his first year as CEO, Hurd improved HP's financial results and continued to make changes designed to position the company for future growth. Still, high-tech businesses operate within a notoriously uncertain environment, so Hurd will have to apply all his management expertise to continue HP's good performance.[19]

For more information about this company, go to **www.hp.com.**

Questions

1. Do you think that Mark Hurd was emphasizing decisional roles, interpersonal roles, or informational roles when he became HP's CEO—and why?
2. How can Hurd apply the management function of controlling to improve HP's decision-making process?
3. From a management perspective, what are the benefits and limitations of appointing an outsider as CEO?

→ CHAPTER 7: JOURNAL EXERCISE

Discovery statement: This chapter discussed the critical management function of leading and motivating others to work in the best interests of an organization. Think about your current job or a job that you had previously. Who is the most outstanding leader with whom you have worked?

What was his or her position and in what capacity did you work with the person?

_____

_____

_____

_____

_____

What are this person's outstanding leadership qualities?

_____

_____

_____

_____

_____

Select the most outstanding leadership quality above and provide an example that demonstrates this quality.

_____

_____

_____

_____

_____

Do most of your coworkers view this person as being an outstanding leader too? Explain.

_____

_____

_____

_____

_____

BUILDING SKILLS FOR CAREER SUCCESS

1. Exploring the Internet

Most large companies call on a management consulting firm for a variety of services, including employee training, help in the selection of an expensive purchase such as a computer system, recruitment of employees, and direction in reorganization and strategic planning.

Large consulting firms generally operate globally and provide information to companies considering entry into foreign countries or business alliances with foreign firms. They use their websites, along with magazine-style articles, to celebrate achievements and present their credentials to clients. Business students can acquire an enormous amount of up-to-date information in the field of management by perusing these sites.

Assignment

1. Explore each of the following websites:

   Accenture: **www.accenture.com**
   BearingPoint (formerly KPMG Consulting):
   www.bearingpoint.com

Cap Gemini Ernst & Young:
  www.capgemini.com
  Visit the text website for updates to this exercise.

2. Judging from the articles and notices posted, what are the current areas of activities of one of these firms?

3. Explore one of these areas in more detail by comparing postings from each firm's site. For instance, if "global business opportunities" appears to be a popular area of management consulting, how has each firm distinguished itself in this area? Who would you call first for advice?

4. Given that consulting firms are always trying to fill positions for their clients and to meet their own recruitment needs, it is little wonder that employment postings are a popular area on their sites. Examine these in detail. Based on your examination of the site and the registration format, what sort of recruit are they interested in?

2. Developing Critical Thinking Skills

As defined in the chapter, an organization's mission is a statement of the basic purpose that makes the organization different from others. Clearly, a mission statement, by indicating the purpose of a business, directly affects the company's employees, customers, and stockholders.

Assignment

1. Find the mission statements of three large corporations in different industries. The Internet is one source of mission statements. For example, you might search these sites:

   www.kodak.com
   www.benjerry.com
   www.usaa.com

2. Compare the mission statements on the basis of what each reflects about the philosophy of the company and its concern for employees, customers, and stockholders.

3. Which company would you like to work for and why?

4. Prepare a report on your findings.

3. Building Team Skills

Over the past few years, an increasing number of employees, stockholders, and customers have been demanding to know what their companies are about. As a result, more companies have been taking the time to analyze their operations and to prepare mission statements that focus on the purpose of the company. The mission statement is becoming a critical planning tool for successful companies. To make effective decisions, employees must understand the purpose of their company.

Assignment

1. Divide into teams and write a mission statement for one of the following types of businesses:

   Food service, restaurant
   Banking
   Airline
   Auto repair
   Cabinet manufacturing

2. Discuss your mission statement with other teams. How did the other teams interpret the purpose of your company? What is the mission statement saying about the company?

3. Write a one-page report on what you learned about developing mission statements.

4. Researching Different Careers

A successful career requires planning. Without a plan, or roadmap, you will find it very difficult, if not impossible, to reach your desired career destination. The first step in planning is to establish what your career goal is. You then must set objectives and develop plans for accomplishing those objectives. This kind of planning takes time, but it will pay off later.

Assignment

Complete the following statements:
1. My career goal is to

_____

_____ .

  This statement should encapsulate what you want to accomplish over the long run. It may include the type of job you want and the type of business or industry you want to work in. Examples include the following:

- My career goal is to work as a top manager in the food industry.
- My career goal is to supervise aircraft mechanics.
- My career goal is to win the top achievement award in the advertising industry.

2. My career objectives are to

_____

_____ .

Objectives are benchmarks along the route to a career destination. They are more specific than a career goal. A statement about a career objective should specify what you want to accomplish, when you will complete it, and any other details that will serve as criteria against which you can measure your progress. Examples include the following:

- My objective is to be promoted to supervisor by January 1, 20xx.
- My objective is to enroll in a management course at Main College in the spring semester 20xx.
- My objective is to earn an A in the management course at Main College in the spring semester 20xx.
- My objective is to prepare a status report by September 30 covering the last quarter's activities by asking Charlie in Quality Control to teach me the procedures.

3. Exchange your goal and objectives statements with another class member. Can your partner interpret your objectives correctly?

Are the objectives concise and complete? Do they include criteria against which you can measure your progress? If not, discuss the problem and rewrite the objective.

5. Improving Communication Skills

Being a successful employee today requires personal and managerial skills. Without proficiency in these skills, promotions and other rewards are unlikely to be forthcoming. To be competitive, employees must assess their skill levels periodically and, when necessary, work to improve them. How do your personal and managerial skills measure up?

Assignment

1. Rate yourself and have at least two other people rate you on the skills listed in the following table.

2. Prepare a plan for improving your weak areas. The plan should specify exactly how, where, and when you will accomplish your goal. It also should include criteria for measuring your level of improvement.

SKILLS ASSESSMENT

	Below Average	Average	Above average	Specific Examples
Personal skills				
Oral communication skills				
Written communication skills				
Computer skills				
Critical-thinking skills				
Managerial skills				
Conceptual skills				
Technical skills				
Interpersonal skills				
Decision-making skills				

→ PREP TEST

Matching Questions

____ 1. It is the process of accomplishing objectives through people.

____ 2. Its purpose is to implement a strategy.

____ 3. It is a process of establishing an organization's goals and objectives.

____ 4. The ability to influence others is what it is about.

____ 5. A combination of leading and motivating is the essence of this process.

____ 6. It is a process of influencing people to work.

____ 7. This person delegates authority.

____ 8. A distribution handler settles a strike is an example.

____ 9. A vast amount of time is spent motivating employees.

____ 10. It is needed to work a computer.

a. decisional role
b. directing
c. first-line manager
d. laissez-faire leader
e. leadership
f. leading
g. management
h. strategic planning
i. tactical plan
j. technical skill

True/False Questions

T F

11. ○ ○ Developing self-managed work teams is a way to increase employee participation and to improve quality in the workplace.

12. ○ ○ As managers carry out their functions, the first step is to control, the second to organize, and the third to plan.

13. ○ ○ Operational plans aimed at increasing sales would include specific advertising activities.

14. ○ ○ Measuring actual performance is the first step in the control process.

15. ○ ○ Optimization is the process for balancing conflicting goals.

T F

16. ○ ○ An organization's mission is the means by which it fulfills its purpose.

17. ○ ○ A democratic leader makes all the decisions and tells subordinates what to do.

18. ○ ○ Top managers rely on technical skills more than managers at other levels.

19. ○ ○ Brainstorming is a common technique used to generate alternatives in solving problems.

20. ○ ○ Implementation of a decision requires time, planning, preparation of personnel, and evaluation of results.

Multiple-Choice Questions

21. The process of developing a set of goals and committing an organization to them is called
    a. organizing.
    b. planning.
    c. optimizing.
    d. controlling.
    e. directing.

22. Who is responsible for developing a firm's mission?
    a. Top managers
    b. First-level managers
    c. Operations managers
    d. Middle managers
    e. Supervisors

23. Acme Houseware established a goal to increase its sales by 20 percent in the next year. To ensure that the firm reaches its goal, the sales reports are monitored on a weekly basis. When sales show a slight decline, the sales manager takes actions to correct the problem. Which management function is the manager using?

    a. Leading
    b. Controlling
    c. Directing
    d. Organizing
    e. Planning

24. The chief executive officer of Southwest Airlines provides the company with leadership and overall guidance and is responsible for developing its mission and establishing its goals. Which area of management is being used?
    a. Human resources
    b. Operations
    c. Financial
    d. Administrative
    e. Marketing

25. Establishing a structure to carry out plans is called
    a. organizing.
    b. directing.
    c. leading.
    d. planning.
    e. influencing.

Fill-in-the-Blank Questions

26. The first step in the managerial decisional-making process is _____ an opportunity.

27. The most important resources in an organization are its _____ resources.

28. Visualizing an idea and turning it into a profitable business involves _____ skill.

29. The plan designed to implement tactical plans is a/an _____ plan.

30. An organization's _____ is its broadest plan, developed as a guide for major policy setting and decision making.

Online Study Center

FOR MORE test practice, use the interactive ACE quizzes available at the Online Student Center: www.college.hmco.com/PIC/pridebusiness9e.

Answers on p. PT1.

Creating a Flexible Organization

WHY this chapter matters

To operate a business at an acceptable level of profitability, those in charge must create an organization that not only operates efficiently but also is able to attract resources, such as employees, and be able to develop long-term relationships with customers.

FOR HELP with studying this chapter, visit the Online Student Center:

www.college.hmco.com/PIC/pridebusiness9e

Online Study Center

Global Hyatt doesn't do things like other hotels. The Pritzker family, which controls the company, has deliberately kept it smaller than major competitors. Marriott and Hilton each manage over 2,000 hotels worldwide. In contrast, Global Hyatt's annual revenue of $6 billion comes from fewer than 500 hotels.

Another difference is the freedom that Global Hyatt gives each hotel's management team to experiment and innovate. Nick Pritzker, who oversees real estate and development, explains that "at every hotel, there are people coming up with new ideas and implementing [them]." In fact, Global Hyatt wants each individual hotel's personality to shine—even though most hotel companies emphasize consistency of service and design. When the Hyatt West Hollywood was renovated, management installed recording studios in some of its suites to echo the area's "rock star" personality.

Being a little different has advantages. "The Four Seasons and Ritz-Carlton do everything the same, from Miami Beach to Chicago," observes Bernd Chorengel, international division head. "We say every hotel is different. When I wake up in the morning after traveling halfway around the world and the curtains are closed, I'll know where I am."

DID YOU KNOW?

Being a smaller company like Global Hyatt has some major advantages when competing against bigger organizations.

Increasingly, hotel companies are going after larger customer bases by offering a variety of lodgings at different prices. Global Hyatt concentrates on luxury and full-range hotels and resorts under the Park Hyatt, Grand Hyatt, and Hyatt Regency brands. As all-suite hotels became popular, it acquired AmeriSuites, renamed it Hyatt Place, and updated the design.

Global Hyatt management faced another decision regarding organization. Each hotel brand had its own sales force calling on corporate travel buyers. Would this confuse corporate customers? Was it a good use of resources? Management had to decide whether to keep all the sales forces separate or create a single sales organization.[1]

For more information about this company, go to **www.hyatt.com.**

To survive and to grow, companies such as Global Hyatt must constantly look for ways to improve their methods of doing business. Managers at Global Hyatt, like those at many other organizations, deliberately reorganized the company to achieve its goals and to create satisfying products that foster long-term customer relationships.

When firms are organized, or reorganized, the focus is sometimes on achieving low operating costs. Other firms, such as Nike, emphasize providing high-quality products to ensure customer satisfaction. A firm's organization influences its performance. Thus the issue of organization is important.

We begin this chapter by examining the business organization—what it is and how it functions in today's business environment. Next, we focus one by one on five characteristics that shape an organization's structure. We discuss job specialization within a company, the grouping of jobs into manageable units or departments, the delegation of power from management to workers, the span of management, and establishment of a chain of command. Then we step back for an overall view of four approaches to organizational structure: the bureaucratic structure, the matrix structure, the cluster structure, and the network structure. Finally, we look at the network of social interactions—the informal organization—that operates within the formal business structure.

What Is an Organization?

We used the term *organization* throughout Chapter 7 without really defining it mainly because its everyday meaning is close to its business meaning. Here, however, let us agree that an **organization** is a group of two or more people working together to achieve a common set of goals. A neighborhood dry cleaner owned and operated by a husband-and-wife team is an organization. IBM and Home Depot, which employ thousands of workers worldwide, are also organizations in the same sense. Although each corporation's organizational structure is more complex than the dry-cleaning establishment, all must be organized to achieve their goals.

An inventor who goes into business to produce and market a new invention hires people, decides what each will do, determines who will report to whom, and so on. These activities are the essence of organizing, or creating, the organization. One way to create this "picture" is to create an organization chart.

LEARNING OBJECTIVE
Understand what an organization is and identify its characteristics.

organization a group of two or more people working together to achieve a common set of goals

Developing Organization Charts

An **organization chart** is a diagram that represents the positions and relationships within an organization. An example of an organization chart is shown in Figure 8.1. Each rectangle represents a particular position or person in the organization. At the top is the president; at the next level are the vice presidents. The solid vertical lines connecting the vice presidents to the president indicate that the vice presidents are in the chain of command. The **chain of command** is the line of authority that extends from the highest to the lowest levels of the organization. Moreover, each vice president reports directly to the president. Similarly, the plant managers, regional sales managers, and accounting department manager report to the vice presidents. The chain of command can be short or long. For example, at Royer's Roundtop Café, an independent restaurant in Roundtop, Texas, the chain of command is very short. Bud Royer, the owner, is responsible only to himself and can alter his hours or change his menu quickly. On the other hand, the chain of command at McDonald's is long. Before making certain types of changes, a McDonald's franchisee seeks permission from regional management, which, in turn, seeks approval from corporate headquarters.

In the chart, the connections to the directors of legal services, public affairs, and human resources are shown as broken lines; these people are not part of the direct chain of command. Instead, they hold *advisory*, or *staff*, positions. This difference will be examined later in this chapter when we discuss line and staff positions.

Most smaller organizations find organization charts useful. They clarify positions and reporting relationships for everyone in the organization, and they help managers to track growth and change in the organizational structure. For two reasons, however, many large organizations, such as ExxonMobil, Kellogg, and Procter & Gamble, do not maintain complete, detailed charts. First, it is difficult to chart even a few dozen positions accurately, much less the thousands that characterize larger firms. And second, larger organizations are almost always changing parts of their structure. An organization chart would be outdated before it was completed. However, organization must exist even without a chart in order for a business to be successful. Technology is helping large companies implement up-to-date organization charts. Workstream, Inc., is a provider of enterprise workforce management software and has signed big-name clients. Carol Caruso, an organizational design specialist at Mercedes-Benz USA, reported that the software saves time and effort in communicating organizational structure. Aside from providing organization charts, the software also will support human resources processes such as workflow approval and succession planning.[2]

organization chart a diagram that represents the positions and relationships within an organization

chain of command the line of authority that extends from the highest to the lowest levels of an organization

Five Steps for Organizing a Business

When a firm is started, management must decide how to organize the firm. These decisions are all part of five major steps that sum up the organizing process. The five steps are as follows:

>> FIGURE 8.1

A TYPICAL CORPORATE ORGANIZATION CHART

A company's organization chart represents the positions and relationships within the organization and shows the managerial chains of command.

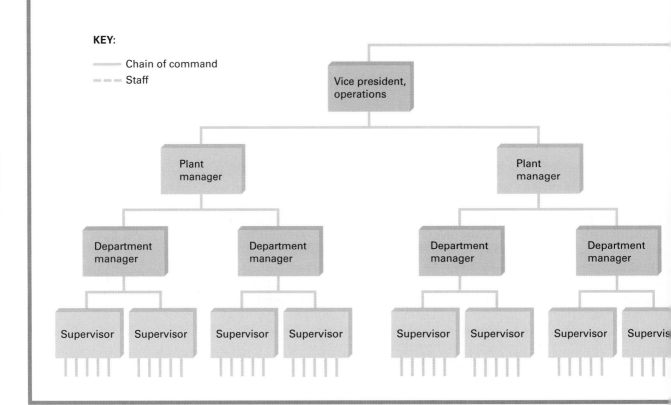

1. *Job design.* Divide the work that is to be done by the entire organization into separate parts, and assign those parts to positions within the organization.
2. *Departmentalization.* Group the various positions into manageable units or departments.
3. *Delegation.* Distribute responsibility and authority within the organization.
4. *Span of management.* Determine the number of subordinates who will report to each manager.
5. *Chain of command.* Establish the organization's chain of command by designating the positions with direct authority and those that are support positions.

In the next several sections we discuss major issues associated with these steps.

Job Design

2 LEARNING OBJECTIVE
Explain why job specialization is important.

In Chapter 1 we defined *specialization* as the separation of a manufacturing process into distinct tasks and the assignment of different tasks to different people. Here we are extending that concept to *all* the activities performed within an organization.

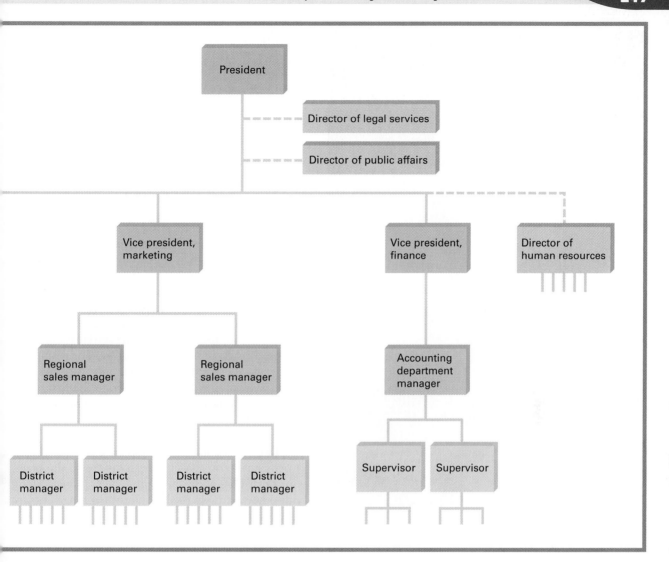

Job Specialization

Job specialization is the separation of all organizational activities into distinct tasks and the assignment of different tasks to different people. Adam Smith, the eighteenth-century economist whose theories gave rise to capitalism, was the first to emphasize the power of specialization in his book, *The Wealth of Nations.* According to Smith, the various tasks in a particular pin factory were arranged so that one worker drew the wire for the pins, another straightened the wire, a third cut it, a fourth ground the point, and a fifth attached the head. Smith claimed that ten men were able to produce 48,000 pins per day. Before specialization, they could produce only 200 pins per day because each worker had to perform all five tasks!

job specialization the separation of all organizational activities into distinct tasks and the assignment of different tasks to different people

The Rationale for Specialization

For a number of reasons, some job specialization is necessary in every organization because the "job" of most organizations is too large for one person to handle. In a firm such as DaimlerChrysler, thousands of people are needed to manufacture automobiles. Others are needed to sell the cars, control the firm's finances, and so on.

    Second, when a worker has to learn one specific, highly specialized task, that individual should be able to learn it very efficiently. Third, a worker repeating the same job does not lose time changing from operations, as the pin workers did when producing complete pins. Fourth, the more specialized the job, the easier it is to design specialized equipment. And finally, the more specialized the job, the easier is the job training.

Job specialization. At the Lindt & Spruengli Chocolate Factory in Switzerland, workers sort chocolates into boxes. These workers' jobs are the result of job specialization, which increases the productivity of this factory.

Alternatives to Job Specialization

Unfortunately, specialization can have negative consequences as well. The most significant drawback is the boredom and dissatisfaction employees may feel when repeating the same job. Bored employees may be absent from work frequently, may not put much effort into their work, and may even sabotage the company's efforts to produce quality products.

To combat these problems, managers often turn to job rotation. **Job rotation** is the systematic shifting of employees from one job to another. For example, a worker may be assigned a different job every week for a four-week period and then return to the first job in the fifth week. Job rotation provides a variety of tasks so that workers are less likely to become bored and dissatisfied.

Two other approaches—job enlargement and job enrichment—also can provide solutions to the problems caused by job specialization. These topics, along with other methods used to motivate employees, are discussed in Chapter 11.

job rotation the systematic shifting of employees from one job to another

3 LEARNING OBJECTIVE
Identify the various bases for departmentalization.

departmentalization the process of grouping jobs into manageable units

departmentalization by function grouping jobs that relate to the same organizational activity

departmentalization by product grouping activities related to a particular product or service

Departmentalization

After jobs are designed, they must be grouped together into "working units," or departments. This process is called *departmentalization*. More specifically, **departmentalization** is the process of grouping jobs into manageable units. Several departmentalization bases are used commonly. In fact, most firms use more than one. Today, the most common bases for organizing a business into effective departments are by function, by product, by location, and by customer.

By Function

Departmentalization by function groups jobs that relate to the same organizational activity. Under this scheme, all marketing personnel are grouped together in the marketing department, all production personnel in the production department, and so on.

Most smaller and newer organizations departmentalize by function. Supervision is simplified because everyone is involved in the same activities, and coordination is easy. The disadvantages of this method of grouping jobs are that it can lead to slow decision making and that it tends to emphasize the department over the whole organization.

By Product

Departmentalization by product groups activities related to a particular good or service. This approach is used often by older and larger firms that produce and sell a variety of products. Each department handles its own marketing, production, financial management, and human resources activities.

Departmentalization by product makes decision making easier and provides for the integration of all activities associated with each product. However, it causes some duplication of specialized activities—such as finance—from department to department. And the emphasis is placed on the product rather than on the whole organization.

By Location

Departmentalization by location groups activities according to the defined geographic area in which they are performed. Departmental areas may range from whole countries (for international firms) to regions within countries (for national firms) to areas of several city blocks (for police departments organized into precincts). Departmentalization by location allows the organization to respond readily to the unique demands or requirements of different locations. Nevertheless, a large administrative staff and an elaborate control system may be needed to coordinate operations in many locations.

departmentalization by location grouping activities according to the defined geographic area in which they are performed

By Customer

Departmentalization by customer groups activities according to the needs of various customer populations. A local Chevrolet dealership, for example, may have one sales staff to deal with individual consumers and a different sales staff to work with corporate fleet buyers. The obvious advantage of this approach is that it allows the firm to deal efficiently with unique customers or customer groups. The biggest drawback is that a larger-than-usual administrative staff is needed.

departmentalization by customer grouping activities according to the needs of various customer populations

Combinations of Bases

Many organizations use more than one of these departmentalization bases.

Take a moment to examine Figure 8.2. Notice that departmentalization by customer is used to organize New-Wave Fashions, Inc., into three major divisions: men's,

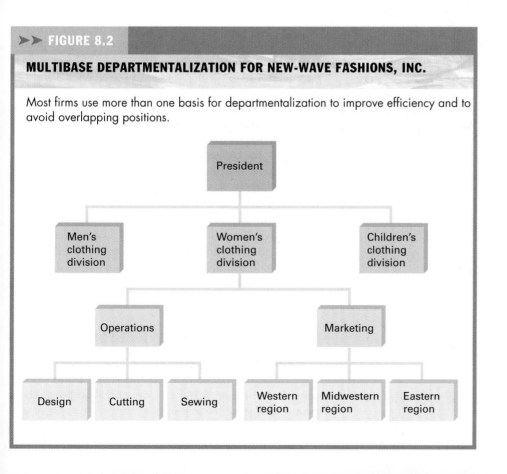

➤➤ **FIGURE 8.2**

MULTIBASE DEPARTMENTALIZATION FOR NEW-WAVE FASHIONS, INC.

Most firms use more than one basis for departmentalization to improve efficiency and to avoid overlapping positions.

women's, and children's clothing. Then functional departmentalization is used to distinguish the firm's production and marketing activities. Finally, location is used to organize the firm's marketing efforts.

Delegation, Decentralization, and Centralization

4 LEARNING OBJECTIVE
Explain how decentralization follows from delegation.

The third major step in the organizing process is to distribute power in the organization. **Delegation** assigns part of a manager's work and power to other workers. The degree of centralization or decentralization of authority is determined by the overall pattern of delegation within the organization.

delegation assigning part of a manager's work and power to other workers

Delegation of Authority

Because no manager can do everything, delegation is vital to completion of a manager's work. Delegation is also important in developing the skills and abilities of subordinates. It allows those who are being groomed for higher-level positions to play increasingly important roles in decision making.

responsibility the duty to do a job or perform a task

authority the power, within an organization, to accomplish an assigned job or task

accountability the obligation of a worker to accomplish an assigned job or task

decentralized organization an organization in which management consciously attempts to spread authority widely in the lower levels of the organization

Steps in Delegation The delegation process generally involves three steps (see Figure 8.3). First, the manager must *assign responsibility*. **Responsibility** is the duty to do a job or perform a task. In most job settings, a manager simply gives the worker a job to do. Typical job assignments might range from having a worker prepare a report on the status of a new quality control program to placing the person in charge of a task force. Second, the manager must *grant authority*. **Authority** is the power, within the organization, to accomplish an assigned job or task. This might include the power to obtain specific information, order supplies, authorize relevant expenditures, or make certain decisions. Finally, the manager must *create accountability*. **Accountability** is the obligation of a worker to accomplish an assigned job or task.

Note that accountability is created, but it cannot be delegated. Suppose that you are an operations manager for Target and are responsible for performing a specific task. You, in turn, delegate this task to someone else. You nonetheless remain accountable to your immediate supervisor for getting the task done properly. If the other person fails to complete the assignment, you—not the person to whom you delegated the task—will be held accountable.

Barriers to Delegation For several reasons, managers may be unwilling to delegate work. Many managers are reluctant to delegate because they want to be sure that the work gets done. Another reason for reluctance stems from the opposite situation. The manager fears that the worker will do the work well and attract the approving notice of higher-level managers. Finally, some managers do not delegate because they are so disorganized that they simply are not able to plan and assign work effectively.

Decentralization of Authority

The pattern of delegation throughout an organization determines the extent to which that organization is decentralized or centralized. In a **decentralized organization,** management consciously attempts to spread authority widely across various organization levels. A

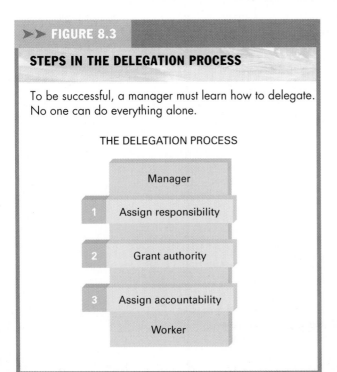

>> FIGURE 8.3

STEPS IN THE DELEGATION PROCESS

To be successful, a manager must learn how to delegate. No one can do everything alone.

THE DELEGATION PROCESS

Manager

1 Assign responsibility

2 Grant authority

3 Assign accountability

Worker

Delegation. A manager at Intel uses the process of delegation. She assigns responsibility and accountability, and grants authority to the worker.

centralized organization an organization that systematically works to concentrate authority at the upper levels of the organization

centralized organization, on the other hand, systematically works to concentrate authority at the upper levels. For example, many publishers of college-level textbooks are centralized organizations, with authority concentrated at the top. Large organizations may have characteristics of both decentralized and centralized organizations. Wal-Mart centralizes its operations in Bentonville, Arkansas, but usually permits tremendous independence in stocking the stores with items local customers want. The top-management team in Bentonville focuses primarily on the top 20 percent and bottom 20 percent of its stores and tends to leave the rest alone.[3]

A number of factors can influence the extent to which a firm is decentralized. One is the external environment in which the firm operates. The more complex and unpredictable this environment, the more likely it is that top management will let lower-level managers make important decisions. After all, lower-level managers are closer to the problems. Another factor is the nature of the decision itself. The riskier or more important the decision, the greater is the tendency to centralize decision making. A third factor is the abilities of lower-level managers. If these managers do not have strong decision-making skills, top managers will be reluctant to decentralize. And, in contrast, strong lower-level decision-making skills encourage decentralization. Finally, a firm that traditionally has practiced centralization or decentralization is likely to maintain that posture in the future.

In principle, neither decentralization nor centralization is right or wrong. What works for one organization may or may not work for another. Kmart Corporation and McDonald's are very successful—and both practice centralization. But decentralization has worked very well for General Electric and Sears. Every organization must assess its own situation and then choose the level of centralization or decentralization that will work best.

The Span of Management

The fourth major step in organizing a business is establishing the **span of management** (or **span of control**), which is the number of workers who report directly to one manager. For hundreds of years,

5 LEARNING OBJECTIVE
Understand how the span of management describes an organization.

span of management (or **span of control**) the number of workers who report directly to one manager

ENTREPRENEURIAL CHALLENGE

Five Ways to Improve Delegation

Accustomed to doing everything alone, entrepreneurs may have difficulty delegating. By learning to delegate, entrepreneurs benefit from the skills and knowledge of others—and create more time to build the business. Experts suggest these five ways to improve delegation:

1. *Identify tasks that can be delegated.* Which tasks are so important that only the owner can deal with them? Which can be delegated to capable employees?
2. *Explain the purpose of each task.* Articulate not only what must be done, but why. Understanding how the business will benefit gives employees context.
3. *Provide the appropriate tools.* Be sure that employees have the information, equipment, contacts, and training to complete their tasks.
4. *Focus on the outcome.* Instead of dictating every action, focus on coaching toward the desired outcome. This allows employees to apply their creativity and hone their skills.
5. *Invest the time.* Although delegating can be time-consuming at first, investing the time upfront will save lots of time later.

Business Around the World

Multinationals Grapple with Global Authority

Gucci Group—the London-based luxury goods company—and Toyota Motor—the Japanese automaker—are both aiming for profitable long-term growth. However, each multinational organization uses a different pattern of delegation to achieve its goals.

Gucci Group. Can CEO Robert Polet double the company's revenue within seven years while returning high-end brands such as

Yves Saint Laurent to profitability within three years? Polet believes that decentralization is the answer. By making the top manager of each brand division its CEO, Polet says that he has "unleashed so much energy, so much creativity, which I think is at the root of our growth."

Toyota Motor. Until recently, Toyota designed cars for each country or region, built local factories in each market, and

worked with local suppliers. Now the world's second-largest automaker is centralizing design and sharing parts to keep expenses down and speed up new-product

introductions. Factory employees still have authority to make improvements in their plants. Under centralization, however, employees from foreign facilities must perfect their skills during visits to a training facility in Japan.

theorists have searched for an ideal span of management. When it became apparent that there is no perfect number of subordinates for a manager to supervise, they turned their attention to the general issue of whether the span should be wide or narrow. This issue is complicated because the span of management may change by department within the same organization. For example, the span of management at FedEx varies within the company. Departments in which workers do the same tasks on a regular basis—customer service agents, handlers and sorters, couriers—usually have a span of management of fifteen to twenty employees per manager. Groups performing multiple and different tasks are more likely to have smaller spans of management consisting of five or six employees.[4] Thus FedEx uses a wide span of control in some departments and a narrower one in others.

Wide and Narrow Spans of Control

A *wide* span of management exists when a manager has a larger number of subordinates. A *narrow* span exists when the manager has only a few subordinates. Several factors determine the span that is better for a particular manager (see Figure 8.4). Generally, the span of control may be wide when (1) the manager and the subordinates are very competent, (2) the organization has a well-established set of standard operating procedures, and (3) few new problems are expected to arise. The span should be narrow when (1) workers are physically located far from one another, (2) the manager has much work to do in addition to supervising workers, (3) a great deal of interaction is required between supervisor and workers, and (4) new problems arise frequently.

Organizational Height

The span of management has an obvious impact on relations between managers and workers. It has a more subtle but equally important impact on the height of the organization. **Organizational height** is the number of layers, or levels, of management in a firm. The span of management plays a direct role in determining the height of the

organizational height the number of layers, or levels, of management in a firm

organization, as shown in Figure 8.4. If spans of management are wider, fewer levels are needed, and the organization is *flat*. If spans of management generally are narrow, more levels are needed, and the resulting organization is *tall*.

In a taller organization, administrative costs are higher because more managers are needed. Communication among levels may become distorted because information has to pass up and down through more people. When companies are cutting costs, one option is to decrease organizational height in order to reduce related administrative expenses. When Raytheon, a high-tech defense supplier, needed to reduce its enormous cost structure, the CEO decided to eliminate an entire layer of management, resulting in a flatter organization.[5] Although flat organizations avoid these problems, their managers may perform more administrative duties simply because there are fewer managers. Wide spans of management also may require managers to spend considerably more time supervising and working with subordinates.

6 LEARNING OBJECTIVE
Understand how the chain of command is established by using line and staff management.

Chain of Command: Line and Staff Management

Establishing the chain of command is another step in organizing a business. It reaches from the highest to the lowest levels of management. A **line management position** is part of the chain of command; it is a position in which a person makes decisions and gives orders to subordinates to achieve the goals of the organization. A **staff management position,** by contrast, is a position created to provide support, advice, and expertise to someone in the chain of command. Staff managers are not part of the chain of command but do have authority over their assistants (see Figure 8.5).

line management position a part of the chain of command; it is a position in which a person makes decisions and gives orders to subordinates to achieve the goals of the organization

staff management position a position created to provide support, advice, and expertise within an organization

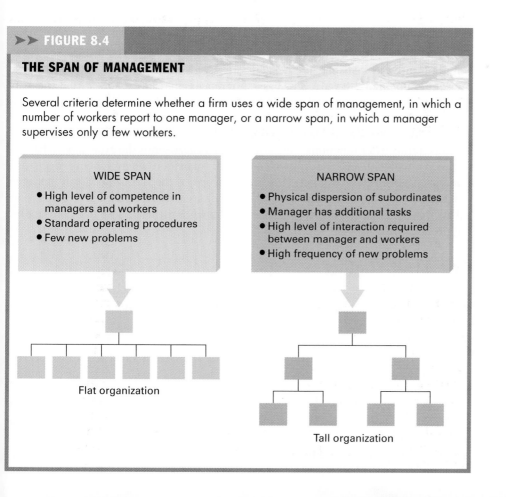

▶▶ FIGURE 8.4

THE SPAN OF MANAGEMENT

Several criteria determine whether a firm uses a wide span of management, in which a number of workers report to one manager, or a narrow span, in which a manager supervises only a few workers.

WIDE SPAN
- High level of competence in managers and workers
- Standard operating procedures
- Few new problems

NARROW SPAN
- Physical dispersion of subordinates
- Manager has additional tasks
- High level of interaction required between manager and workers
- High frequency of new problems

Flat organization

Tall organization

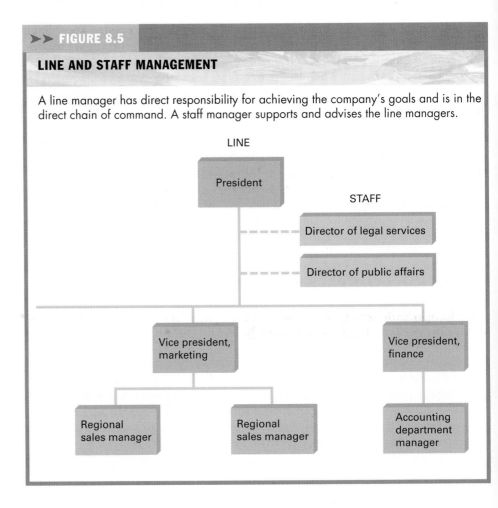

>> FIGURE 8.5

LINE AND STAFF MANAGEMENT

A line manager has direct responsibility for achieving the company's goals and is in the direct chain of command. A staff manager supports and advises the line managers.

Line and Staff Positions Compared

Both line and staff managers are needed for effective management, but the two positions differ in important ways. The basic difference is in terms of authority. Line managers have *line authority*, which means that they can make decisions and issue directives relating to the organization's goals.

Staff managers seldom have this kind of authority. Instead, they usually have either advisory authority or functional authority. *Advisory authority* is the expectation that line managers will consult the appropriate staff manager when making decisions. Functional authority is stronger. *Functional authority* is the authority of staff managers to make decisions and issue directives about their areas of expertise. For example, a legal adviser for Nike can decide whether to retain a particular clause in a contract but not product pricing.

Line-Staff Conflict

For a variety of reasons, conflict between line managers and staff managers is fairly common in businesses. Staff managers often have more formal education and sometimes are younger (and perhaps more ambitious) than line managers. Line managers may perceive staff managers as a threat to their own authority and thus may resent them. For their part, staff managers may become annoyed or angry if their expert recommendations—in public relations or human resources management, for example—are not adopted by line management.

Fortunately, there are several ways to minimize the likelihood of such conflict. One way is to integrate line and staff managers into one team. Another is to ensure that the areas of responsibility of line and staff managers are clearly defined. Finally, line and staff managers both can be held accountable for the results of their activities.

Before studying the next topic—forms of organizational structure—you may want to review the five organization-shaping characteristics that we have just discussed. See Table 8.1 for a summary.

Forms of Organizational Structure

Up to this point we have focused our attention on the major characteristics of organizational structure. In many ways this is like discussing the parts of a jigsaw puzzle one by one. It is time to put the puzzle together. In particular, we discuss four basic forms of organizational structure: bureaucratic, matrix, cluster, and network.

The Bureaucratic Structure

The term *bureaucracy* is used often in an unfavorable context to suggest rigidity and red tape. This image may be negative, but it does capture some of the essence of the bureaucratic structure.

A **bureaucratic structure** is a management system based on a formal framework of authority that is outlined carefully and followed precisely. A bureaucracy is likely to have the following characteristics:

1. A high level of job specialization
2. Departmentalization by function
3. Formal patterns of delegation
4. A high degree of centralization
5. Narrow spans of management, resulting in a tall organization
6. Clearly defined line and staff positions with formal relationships between the two

7 LEARNING OBJECTIVE
Describe the four basic forms of organizational structure: bureaucratic, matrix, cluster, and network.

bureaucratic structure a management system based on a formal framework of authority that is outlined carefully and followed precisely

---

> > **TABLE 8.1**

FIVE CHARACTERISTICS OF ORGANIZATIONAL STRUCTURE

Dimension	Purpose
Job design	To divide the work performed by an organization into parts and assign each part a position within the organization.
Departmentalization	To group various positions in an organization into manageable units. Departmentalization may be based on function, product, location, customer, or a combination of these bases.
Delegation	To distribute part of a manager's work and power to other workers. A deliberate concentration of authority at the upper levels of the organization creates a centralized structure. A wide distribution of authority into the lower levels of the organization creates a decentralized structure.
Span of management	To set the number of workers who report directly to one manager. A narrow span has only a few workers reporting to one manager. A wide span has a large number of workers reporting to one manager.
Line and staff management	To distinguish between those positions that are part of the chain of command and those that provide support, advice, or expertise to those in the chain of command.

The many policies and procedures of a bureaucracy. The United States Postal Service is a bureaucracy. It has many policies and procedures in place that affect both workers and customers.

Perhaps the best examples of contemporary bureaucracies are government agencies, colleges and universities. Consider the very rigid college entrance and registration procedures. The reason for such procedures is to ensure that the organization is able to deal with large numbers of people in an equitable and fair manner. We may not enjoy them, but regulations and standard operating procedures guarantee uniform treatment.

Another example of a bureaucratic structure is the U.S. Postal Service. Like colleges and universities, the Postal Service relies on procedures and rules to accomplish the organization's goals. However, the Postal Service has streamlined some of its procedures and initiated new services in order to compete with FedEx, UPS, and other delivery services. As a result, customer satisfaction has begun to improve.

The biggest drawback to the bureaucratic structure is lack of flexibility. A bureaucracy has trouble adjusting to change and coping with the unexpected. Because today's business environment is dynamic and complex, many firms have found that the bureaucratic structure is not an appropriate organizational structure.

The Matrix Structure

matrix structure an organizational structure that combines vertical and horizontal lines of authority, usually by superimposing product departmentalization on a functionally departmentalized organization

cross-functional team a team of individuals with varying specialties, expertise, and skills that are brought together to achieve a common task

When the matrix structure is used, individuals report to more than one superior at the same time. The **matrix structure** combines vertical and horizontal lines of authority. The matrix structure occurs when product departmentalization is superimposed on a functionally departmentalized organization. In a matrix organization, authority flows both down and across.

To understand the structure of a matrix organization, consider the usual functional arrangement, with people working in departments such as engineering, finance, and marketing. Now suppose that we assign people from these departments to a special group that is working on a new project as a team—a cross-functional team. A **cross-functional team** consists of individuals with varying specialties, expertise, and skills that are brought together to achieve a common task. Frequently, cross-functional teams are charged with the responsibility of developing new products. For example, Ford Motor Company assembled a special project team to design and manufacture its global cars. The manager in charge of a team is usually called a *project manager*. Any individual who is working with the team reports to *both* the project manager and the individual's superior in the functional department (see Figure 8.6).

Cross-functional team projects may be temporary, in which case the team is disbanded once the mission is accomplished, or they may be permanent. These teams often are empowered to make major decisions. Campbell Soup Company recently broadened its innovation group into a permanent cross-functional work team to develop innovative new products and marketing techniques. Campbell's has encountered stiff competition in the soup industry and hopes that this team will create ways to increase the per capita soup consumption in the United States.[6] When a cross-functional team is employed, prospective team members may receive special training because effective teamwork can require different skills. For cross-functional teams to be successful, team members must be given specific information on the job each performs. The team also must develop a sense of cohesiveness and maintain good communications among its members.

Matrix structures offer advantages over other organizational forms. Added flexibility is probably the most obvious advantage. The matrix structure also can increase productivity, raise morale, and nurture creativity and innovation. In addition, employees experience personal development through doing a variety of jobs.

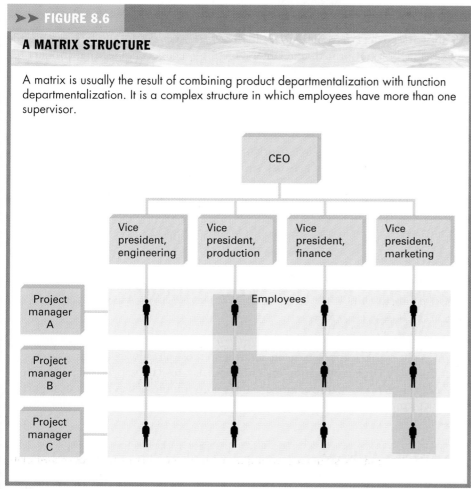

Source: Ricky W. Griffin, *Management*, 8th ed. Copyright © 2005 by Houghton Mifflin Company. Adapted with permission.

The matrix structure also has disadvantages. Having employees report to more than one supervisor can cause confusion about who is in charge. Like committees, teams may take longer to resolve problems and issues than individuals working alone. Other difficulties include personality clashes, poor communication, undefined individual roles, unclear responsibilities, and finding ways to reward individual and team performance simultaneously. Because more managers and support staff may be needed, a matrix structure may be more expensive to maintain.

The Cluster Structure

A **cluster structure** is a type of business that consists primarily of teams with no or very few underlying departments. This type of structure is also called *team* or *collaborative*. In this type of organization, team members work together on a project until it is finished, and then the team may remain intact and be assigned another project, or team members may be reassigned to different teams, depending on their skills and the needs of the organization. In a cluster organization, the operating unit is the team, and it remains relatively small. If a team becomes too large, it can be split into multiple teams, or individuals can be assigned to other existing teams.

The cluster organizational structure has both strengths and weaknesses. Keeping the teams small provides the organization with the flexibility necessary to change directions quickly, to try new techniques, and to explore new ideas. Some employees in these types of organizations express concerns regarding job security and the increased amount of stress that arises owing to the fact that changes occur rapidly.[7]

cluster structure an organization that consists primarily of teams with no or very few underlying departments

The Network Structure

network structure an organization in which administration is the primary function, and most other functions are contracted out to other firms

In a **network structure** (sometimes called a *virtual organization*), administration is the primary function performed, and other functions such as engineering, production, marketing, and finance are contracted out to other organizations. Frequently, a network organization does not manufacture the products it sells. This type of organization has a few permanent employees consisting of top management and hourly clerical workers. Leased facilities and equipment, as well as temporary workers, are increased or decreased as the needs of the organization change. Thus there is rather limited formal structure associated with a network organization.

An obvious strength of a network structure is flexibility that allows the organization to adjust quickly to changes. Some of the challenges faced by managers in network-structured organizations include controlling the quality of work performed by other organizations, low morale and high turnover among hourly workers, and the vulnerability associated with relying on outside contractors.

Additional Factors That Influence an Organization

8 LEARNING OBJECTIVE
Summarize the use of corporate culture, intrapreneurship, committees, coordination techniques, informal groups, and the grapevine.

As you might expect, other factors in addition to those already covered in this chapter affect the way a large corporation operates on a day-to-day basis. To get a "true picture" of the organizational structure of a huge corporation such as Marriott, for example, which employs over 133,000 people,[8] you need to consider the topics discussed in this section.

Corporate Culture

corporate culture the inner rites, rituals, heroes, and values of a firm

Most managers function within a corporate culture. A **corporate culture** is generally defined as the inner rites, rituals, heroes, and values of a firm. An organization's culture has a powerful influence on how employees think and act. It also can determine public perception of the organization.

Corporate culture—let the good times roll (and fly)! Southwest Airlines employees celebrate a new Southwest Airlines route. Southwest Airlines' corporate culture values altruism, humor, hard work, and fun.

Corporate culture generally is thought to have a very strong influence on a firm's performance over time. Hence it is useful to be able to assess a firm's corporate culture. Common indicators include the physical setting (building, office layouts), what the company says about its corporate culture (in advertising and news releases), how the company greets guests (does it have formal or informal reception areas?), and how employees spend their time (working alone in an office or working with others).

Goffee and Jones have identified four distinct types of corporate cultures (see Figure 8.7). One is called the *networked culture*, characterized by a base of trust and friendship among employees, a strong commitment to the organization, and an informal environment. The *mercenary culture* embodies the feelings of passion, energy, sense of purpose, and excitement for one's work. The term *mercenary* does not imply that employees are motivated to work only for the money, but this is part of it. In this culture, employees are very intense, focused, and determined to win. In the *fragmented culture*, employees do not become friends, and they work "at" the organization, not "for" it. Employees have a high degree of autonomy, flexibility, and equality. The *communal culture* combines the positive traits of the networked culture and the mercenary culture—those of friendship, commitment, high focus on performance, and high energy. People's lives revolve around the product in this culture, and success by anyone in the organization is celebrated by all.[9]

Some experts believe that cultural change is needed when a company's environment changes, when the industry becomes more competitive, the company's performance is mediocre, and when the company is growing or is about to become a truly large

SPOTLIGHT

Should coworkers date?

About half say *yes*, and about half say *no*.

Yes 45%

5% Don't know

No 50%

Source: Maritz poll.

>> **FIGURE 8.7**

TYPES OF CORPORATE CULTURES

Which corporate culture would you choose?

High

Sociability

Low

Low   Solidarity   High

Networked Culture
- Extrovert energized by relationships
- Tolerant of ambiguities and have low needs for structure
- Can spot politics and act to stop "negative" politics
- Consider yourself easygoing, affable, and loyal to others

Communal Culture
- You consider yourself passionate
- Strong need to identify with something bigger than yourself
- You enjoy being in teams
- Prepared to make sacrifices for the greater good

Fragmented Culture
- Are a reflective and self-contained introvert
- Have a high autonomy drive and strong desire to work independently
- Have a strong sense of self
- Consider yourself analytical rather than intuitive

Mercenary Culture
- Goal-oriented and have an obsessive desire to complete tasks
- Thrive on competitive energy
- Keep "relationships" out of work—develop them only to achieve your goals
- Keep things clear-cut and see the world in black and white

Source: "Types of Corporate Culture," in Rob Goffee and Gareth Jones, *The Character of a Corporation* (New York: HarperCollins, 1998). Copyright © 1998 by Rob Goffee and Gareth Jones. Reprinted by permission of HarperCollins Publishers, Inc.

BizTech

High-Tech Firms Practice Cubicle Culture

Paul Otellini, Intel's CEO, works at a desk in a cubicle, not in a fancy corner office. Meg Whitman, eBay's CEO, is also a cubicle dweller. Why would the CEO of a large corporation sit in a cubicle?

- *To set the tone for a collegial corporate culture.* Even the

most successful company will have difficulty maintaining peak performance if employees don't work together. Seeing the CEO working in a cube sends a strong message about pulling together for the common good.

- *To improve communications at all levels.* E-mail and instant messaging may be speedy, but a quick chat in the CEO's

cube can get important information out and stop unfounded rumors. Cube-dwelling CEOs also get a better sense of what employees think and feel.

- *To put a human face on management.* Working in a cube demonstrates that CEOs are people. Employees see a family photo or hear clicking of the keyboard and come to realize that the CEO is "one of us."

---

organization. For example, the PC industry has become highly competitive as PC sales stagnated. Fast growth used to be Dell's top concern, but now Michael Dell and other executives are focusing on developing the company's culture. "The Soul of Dell" is the computer giant's guide to corporate culture and ethics, and management hopes that a strong culture will increase employee loyalty and the success of the company.[10] Organizations in the future will look quite different. Experts predict that tomorrow's businesses will be comprised of small, task-oriented work groups, each with control over its own activities. These small groups will be coordinated through an elaborate computer network and held together by a strong corporate culture. Businesses operating in fast-changing industries will require leadership that supports trust and risk taking. Creating a culture of trust in an organization can lead to increases in growth, profit, productivity, and job satisfaction. A culture of trust can retain the best people, inspire customer loyalty, develop new markets, and increase creativity.

intrapreneur an employee who pushes an innovative idea, product, or process through an organization

Another area where corporate culture plays a vital role is the integration of two or more companies. Business leaders often cite the role of corporate cultures in the integration process as one of the primary factors affecting the success of a merger or acquisition. Experts note that corporate culture is a way of conducting business both within the company and externally. If two merging companies do not address differences in corporate culture, they are setting themselves up for missed expectations and possibly failure.[11]

USING THE INTERNET

Winning Workplaces is a non-profit organization that provides consulting services and other resources to businesses. Its goal is to assist organizations in the creation of profitable businesses, happier employees, and a healthy corporate culture. Winning Workplaces offers inexpensive toolkits designed to improve an organization's corporate culture and increase employee job satisfaction. For more information, please visit: **winningworkplaces.org.**

Intrapreneurship

Since innovations and new-product development are important to companies, and since entrepreneurs are innovative people, it seems almost natural that an entrepreneurial character would surface prominently in many of today's larger organizations. An **intrapreneur** is an employee who takes responsibility for pushing an innovative idea, product, or process through an organization.[12] An intrapreneur possesses the confidence and drive of an entrepreneur but is allowed to use organizational resources for idea development. For example, Art Fry, inventor of the colorful Post-it-Notes that Americans can't live without, is a devoted advocate of intrapreneurship. Nurturing his notepad idea at

Minnesota Mining and Manufacturing (3M) for years, Fry speaks highly of the intrapreneurial commitment at 3M. Fry indicates that an *intrapreneur* is an individual who does not have all the skills to get the job done and thus has to work within an organization, making use of its skills and attributes.

Committees

Today, business firms use several types of committees that affect organizational structure. An **ad hoc committee** is created for a specific short-term purpose, such as reviewing the firm's employee benefits plan. Once its work is finished, the ad hoc committee disbands. A **standing committee** is a relatively permanent committee charged with performing a recurring task. A firm might establish a budget review committee, for example, to review departmental budget requests on an ongoing basis. Finally, a **task force** is a committee established to investigate a major problem or pending decision. A firm contemplating a merger with another company might form a task force to assess the pros and cons of the merger. Governments also use task forces to deal with special problems and issues. Enron became the first public company to ever have a government task force created specifically for investigating it. Of course, this was not the type of task force any company wants around because the members included Internal Revenue Service (IRS) and Federal Bureau of Investigation (FBI) agents as well as many attorneys.[13]

Committees offer some advantages over individual action. Their several members are able to bring information and knowledge to the task at hand. Furthermore, committees tend to make more accurate decisions and to transmit their results through the organization more effectively. However, committee deliberations take longer than individual actions. In addition, unnecessary compromise may take place within the committee. Or the opposite may occur, as one person dominates (and thus negates) the committee process.

Coordination Techniques

A large organization is forced to coordinate organizational resources to minimize duplication and to maximize effectiveness. One technique is simply to make use of the **managerial hierarchy,** which is the arrangement that provides increasing authority at higher levels of management. One manager is placed in charge of all the resources being coordinated. That person is able to coordinate them by virtue of the authority accompanying his or her position.

Resources also can be coordinated through rules and procedures. For example, a rule can govern how a firm's travel budget is allocated. This particular resource, then, would be coordinated in terms of that rule.

In complex situations, more sophisticated coordination techniques may be called for. One approach is to establish a liaison. A *liaison* is a go-between—a person who coordinates the activities of two groups. Suppose that General Motors is negotiating a complicated contract with a supplier of steering wheels. The supplier might appoint a liaison whose primary responsibility is to coordinate the contract negotiations. Finally, for *very* complex coordination needs, a committee could be established. Suppose that General Motors is in the process of purchasing the steering-wheel supplier. In this case, a committee might be appointed to integrate the new firm into General Motors' larger organizational structure.

The Informal Organization

So far we have discussed the organization as a formal structure consisting of interrelated positions. This is the organization that is shown on an organization chart. There

Improving coordination. Technologically advanced communication products allow managers to coordinate the activities of workers.

ad hoc committee a committee created for a specific short-term purpose

standing committee a relatively permanent committee charged with performing some recurring task

task force a committee established to investigate a major problem or pending decision

managerial hierarchy the arrangement that provides increasing authority at higher levels of management

Informal groups. Informal groups, such as the Cigna employees' coed softball league in Manhattan, can be a source of information and camaraderie for participants. Although informal groups can sometimes create problems for an organization, they can also provide significant benefits.

is another kind of organization, however, that does not show up on any chart. We define this **informal organization** as the pattern of behavior and interaction that stems from personal rather than official relationships. Firmly embedded within every informal organization are informal groups and the notorious grapevine.

informal organization the pattern of behavior and interaction that stems from personal rather than official relationships

informal group a group created by the members themselves to accomplish goals that may or may not be relevant to an organization

Informal Groups

An **informal group** is created by the group members themselves to accomplish goals that may or may not be relevant to the organization. Workers may create an informal group to go bowling, form a union, get a particular manager fired or transferred, or for lunch. The group may last for several years or a few hours.

Informal groups can be powerful forces in organizations. They can restrict output, or they can help managers through tight spots. They can cause disagreement and conflict, or they can help to boost morale and job satisfaction. They can show new people how to contribute to the organization, or they can help people to get away with substandard performance. Clearly, managers should be aware of these informal groups. Those who make the mistake of fighting the informal organization have a major obstacle to overcome.

grapevine the informal communications network within an organization

The Grapevine

The **grapevine** is the informal communications network within an organization. It is completely separate from—and sometimes much faster than—the organization's formal channels of communication. Formal communications usually follow a path that parallels the organizational chain of command. Information can be transmitted through the grapevine in any direction—up, down, diagonally, or horizontally across the organizational structure. Subordinates may pass information to their bosses, an executive may relay something to a maintenance worker, or there may be an exchange of information between people who work in totally unrelated departments. Grapevine information may be concerned with topics ranging from the latest management decisions to gossip.

How should managers treat the grapevine? Certainly it would be a mistake to try to eliminate it. People working together, day in and day out, are going to communicate. A more rational approach is to recognize its existence. For example, managers should respond promptly and aggressively to inaccurate grapevine information to minimize the damage that such misinformation might do. Moreover, the grapevine can come in handy when managers are on the receiving end of important communications from the informal organization.

In the next chapter we apply these and other management concepts to an extremely important business function: the production of goods and services.

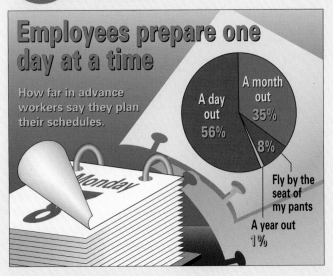

SPOTLIGHT

Employees prepare one day at a time

How far in advance workers say they plan their schedules.

A day out 56%

A month out 35%

8%

Fly by the seat of my pants

A year out 1%

Source: *USA Today*, October 10, 2002, p. B1.

RETURN TO Inside Business

Global Hyatt has been gearing up for faster growth and taking a fresh look at how its organization supports these expansion plans. Within Global Hyatt, Hyatt Corporation is responsible for U.S. and Caribbean hotels and resorts, whereas Hyatt International Corporation is responsible for properties elsewhere. Jobs at each hotel in these two divisions are grouped by function (reservations, housekeeping, banquet services, corporate sales, and so on).

When Global Hyatt expanded into all-suite hotels, it was able to offer corporations a wider choice of accommodations and room rates for their business travelers. However, management discovered a high degree of overlap among the corporate accounts served by the sales forces of all the U.S. hotels. After months of discussion, the company created a single U.S. sales force, organized by customer. Global Hyatt now has "one contact representing all the brands for each corporate customer," says Ty Helms, head of the sales force.

Questions

1. Why would Global Hyatt use departmentalization by customer to organize its U.S. sales force rather than departmentalization by location or product?
2. Considering how Global Hyatt is organized, would you expect it to have a narrow span or wide span of management? Why?

►► CHAPTER REVIEW

Summary

1

Understand what an organization is and identify its characteristics.

An organization is a group of two or more people working together to achieve a common set of goals. The relationships among positions within an organization can be illustrated by means of an organization chart. Five specific characteristics—job design, departmentalization, delegation, span of management, and chain of command—help to determine what an organization chart and the organization itself look like.

2

Explain why job specialization is important.

Job specialization is the separation of all the activities within an organization into smaller components and the assignment of those different components to different people. Several factors combine to make specialization a useful technique for designing jobs, but high levels of specialization may cause employee dissatisfaction and boredom. One technique for overcoming these problems is job rotation.

3

Identify the various bases for departmentalization.

Departmentalization is the grouping of jobs into manageable units. Typical bases for departmentalization are by function, product, location, or customer. Because each of these bases provides particular advantages, most firms—especially larger ones—use a combination of different bases in different organizational situations.

4

Explain how decentralization follows from delegation.

Delegation is the assigning of part of a manager's work to other workers. It involves the following three steps: (a) assigning responsibility, (b) granting authority, and (c) creating accountability. A decentralized firm is one that delegates as much power as possible to people in the lower management levels. In a centralized firm, on the other hand, power is systematically retained at the upper levels.

5

Understand how the span of management describes an organization.

The span of management is the number of workers who report directly to a manager. Spans generally are characterized as wide (many workers per manager) or narrow (few workers per manager). Wide spans generally result in flat organizations (few layers of management); narrow spans generally result in tall organizations (many layers of management).

Understand how the chain of command is established by using line and staff management.

A line position is one that is in the organization's chain of command or line of authority. A manager in a line position makes decisions and gives orders to workers to achieve the goals of the organization. On the other hand, a manager in a staff position provides support, advice, and expertise to someone in the chain of command. Staff positions may carry some authority, but it usually applies only within staff areas of expertise.

7

Describe the four basic forms of organizational structure: bureaucratic, matrix, cluster, and network.

There are four basic forms of organizational structure. The bureaucratic structure is characterized by formality and rigidity. With the bureaucratic structure, rules and procedures are used to ensure uniformity. The matrix structure may be visualized as product departmentalization superimposed on functional departmentalization. With the matrix structure, an employee on a cross-functional team reports to both the project manager and the individual's supervisor in a functional department. A cluster structure is an organization that consists primarily of teams with very few underlying functional departments. In an organization with a network structure, the primary function performed internally is administration, and other functions are contracted out to other firms.

Summarize the use of corporate culture, intrapreneurship, committees, coordination techniques, informal groups, and the grapevine.

Corporate culture—the inner rites, rituals, heroes, and values of a firm—is thought to have a very strong influence on a firm's performance over time. An intrapreneur is an employee in an organizational environment who takes responsibility for pushing an innovative idea, product, or process through the organization. Additional elements that influence an organization include the use of committees and the development of techniques for achieving coordination among various groups within the organization. Finally, both informal groups created by group members and an informal communication network called the grapevine may affect an organization and its performance.

Key Terms

You should now be able to define and give an example relevant to each of the folslowing terms:

organization (247)
organization chart (247)
chain of command (247)
job specialization (249)
job rotation (250)
departmentalization (250)
departmentalization by function (250)
departmentalization by product (250)
departmentalization by location (251)
departmentalization by customer (251)
delegation (252)
responsibility (252)
authority (252)
accountability (252)
decentralized organization (252)
centralized organization (253)
span of management (or span of control) (253)
organizational height (254)
line management position (255)
staff management position (255)
bureaucratic structure (257)
matrix structure (258)
cross-functional team (258)
cluster structure (259)
network structure (260)
corporate culture (260)
intrapreneur (262)
ad hoc committee (263)
standing committee (263)
task force (263)
managerial hierarchy (263)
informal organization (264)
informal group (264)
grapevine (264)

Review Questions

1. In what way do organization charts create a picture of an organization?
2. What is the chain of command in an organization?
3. What determines the degree of specialization within an organization?
4. Describe how job rotation can be used to combat the problems caused by job specialization.
5. What are the major differences among the four departmentalization bases?
6. Why do most firms employ a combination of departmentalization bases?
7. What three steps are involved in delegation? Explain each.
8. How does a firm's top management influence its degree of centralization?

9. How is organizational height related to the span of management?
10. What are the key differences between line and staff positions?
11. Contrast the bureaucratic and matrix forms of organizational structure.
12. What are the differences between the cluster structure and the network structure?
13. What is corporate culture? Describe the major types.
14. Which form of organizational structure probably would lead to the strongest informal organization? Why?
15. How may the managerial hierarchy be used to coordinate the organization's resources?

Discussion Questions

1. Explain how the five steps of the organizing process determine the characteristics of the resulting organization. Which steps are most important?
2. Which kinds of firms probably would operate most effectively as centralized firms? As decentralized firms?
3. How do decisions concerning span of management, the use of committees, and coordination techniques affect organizational structure?
4. How might a manager go about formalizing the informal organization?

▶▶ VIDEO CASE 8.1

Organizing for Success at Green Mountain Coffee Roasters

Even with a work force of 600, Green Mountain Coffee Roasters, based in Waterbury, Vermont, stays as entrepreneurial as when Bob Stiller founded the company in 1981 with one coffee shop and a handful of employees. The original plan was to open a series of coffee shops throughout New England. By the time Green Mountain Coffee had grown to twelve shops, profitability was struggling, so Stiller switched to importing, roasting, and wholesaling high-quality coffee beans to stores, food-service professionals, and restaurants around the country. Today his company brews up profits from $137 million in annual sales to Aramark Food Service, McDonald's New England outlets, Wild Oats Market groceries, Publix supermarkets, and 7,000 other businesses.

Jobs at Green Mountain Coffee are departmentalized into six functions: sales and marketing, operations, human resources, finance, information systems, and social responsibility. The organization chart shows how specialized jobs are linked by a distinct chain of command leading to CEO Bob Stiller at the top. What the chart doesn't show, however, is how collaboration and communication among all levels—rather than strict hierarchy—gives the company a decision-making edge.

This is a flat organization, with only four levels between a corporate salesperson and the CEO. In line with the company's collaborative culture, decisions are made by inviting employees from different functions and different levels to offer their input. Decisions may take a little more time under this system, but they're more informed and usually yield a better solution to the problem than if handled by a single manager or a tiny group.

For a particularly challenging decision, Green Mountain Coffee relies on a "constellation" of communication to collect ideas from around the organization. Managers frequently post decision data on the corporate computer system and ask coworkers for comments. They also exchange a blizzard of e-mail messages and

call cross-functional meetings, when necessary, to share information and opinions. Ultimately, the manager closest to the situation is responsible for evaluating all the data and making the decision, guided by the company's values.

Green Mountain Coffee's values are revealed in its mission statement: "We create the ultimate coffee experience in every life we touch from tree to cup—transforming the way the world understands business." Because the company buys from hundreds of coffee growers and sells to thousands of businesses as well as thousands of consumers who order by mail or online, it touches a lot of lives. Social responsibility ranks high on Green Mountain Coffee's corporate agenda. It is known for donating considerable cash, coffee, and volunteer time to the communities it serves in the United States and in coffee-producing nations.

Every year the company flies dozens of employees to Central America to see how coffee beans are grown, meet the growers, and learn about the farming communities. "The effect is profound," says Stephen Sabol, vice president of development. "The knowledge of the care that goes into the coffee is important, but when [employees] see the social part of it, and how dependent these growers are on us being a quality partner, it hits right home—the obligation we have to do well." After one of these "Coffee Source Trips," employees come back to work with renewed energy and dedication.

Green Mountain Coffee Roasters not only has been cited as one of the fastest-growing companies in the United States, but it also has been named among the most socially responsible. The CEO recognizes that his company must do well in order to do good. "To help the world, we have to be successful," Stiller says. "If we help the world and go out of business, we're not going to help anybody."[14]

For more information about this company, go to **www.greenmountaincoffee.com.**

Questions

1. How is Green Mountain Coffee's "constellation" of communication likely to affect the informal organization?
2. Does Green Mountain Coffee appear to have a network, communal, mercenary, or fragmented culture? Support your answer.
3. Is Green Mountain Coffee a centralized or decentralized organization? How do you know?

►► CASE 8.2

Saturn: Still a Different Kind of Company?

Saturn was only an idea in 1983—General Motors' new idea about how to organize a car company. The idea was to give the company and its employees a lot more autonomy instead of imposing the rigid rules and conventions under which auto factories normally operated. Yet, since 1990, when the Saturn plant opened in Spring Hill, Tennessee, GM has changed the organization little by little. Is today's Saturn still a different kind of car company?

The Saturn project went into high gear after GM and the United Auto Workers came to agreement about having plant employees take a more active role. Instead of operating under an inflexible system of narrow job specialization, the plan was for Saturn's employees to work in teams and handle a variety of tasks as needed. The new company was to be managed as a separate entity and therefore hired its own engineers, developed its own vehicles, and purchased its own supplies and raw materials. GM also built Saturn a new state-of-the-art plant at a cost of $3.5 billion. And to reinforce Saturn's independence from the GM hierarchy, its top manager was designated its CEO.

By the time the first sedans started rolling off the assembly line, Saturn had established itself as a different kind of car company. Customers welcomed the "no haggle, no hassle" pricing policy as a change from the back-and-forth price negotiation they usually had to endure when buying a car. Just as important, Saturn's dealers put extra emphasis on service and satisfaction, making customers feel especially appreciated.

Such a mystique surrounded Saturn that happy customers began dropping by the factory to thank the employees. Saturn soon channeled their enthusiasm into a "homecoming" festival at Spring Hill that drew more than 40,000 customers from all over the United States. The CEO even gave the bride away when the employees of two competing Saturn dealers decided to hold their wedding at Spring Hill. Sales soared, and the plant strained to keep up with demand. For a time, Saturn was more than just a car company—it was a national phenomenon.

By end of the 1990s, however, Saturn had lost its novelty. While GM's officials debated whether to invest in new models, tastes were changing. Competitors' sport-utility vehicles (SUVs) and light pickup trucks had captured the public's imagination and gained market share at Saturn's expense. Eventually, Saturn did introduce the Vue SUV, but it was unable to generate the same kind of magic as the company's original sedan.

Meanwhile, GM was under great pressure to improve its financial performance, and top management was determined to cut costs worldwide. In the past, the president of each region (North America, Europe, Latin America, and Asia-Pacific) was responsible for that region's product development and other key functions. As a result, corporate officials could request but not order changes that would lower costs, such as following one set of engineering standards. By centralizing engineering, purchasing, and product development, the corporate office gained direct control to squeeze out redundancies.

This move toward centralization touched Saturn as well. Although the Spring Hill plant was highly efficient, maintaining a separate engineering staff for Saturn was costly. Thus GM moved Saturn's engineers to Michigan, where they joined the corporate design staff. In addition, GM eliminated the CEO title at Saturn and began managing the brand in the same way as Chevrolet and all other brands in the corporate lineup. In the future, the Spring Hill factory may very well manufacture Chevrolets, whereas Saturns may be produced in Ohio or Mexico. Already the Saturn minivan is being made in Georgia. With all these changes, is Saturn still a new kind of car company?[15]

For more information about this company, go to **www.saturn.com** and **www.gm.com**.

Questions

1. In a factory such as Saturn's, where certain tasks must be completed in exactly the same way to produce each car, why would the company *not* push for job specialization?
2. Does GM appear to be organized by function, product, location, customer, or more than one of these departmentalization bases?
3. How does eliminating the CEO position at Saturn affect the chain of command at GM?

→ CHAPTER 8: JOURNAL EXERCISE

Discovery statement: This chapter described the powerful influence that a corporate culture has on an organization.

Assume that after leaving school, you are hired by your "dream company." What are the major corporate culture dimensions of your dream company?

_____

_____

_____

_____

_____

Before accepting a job at your "dream company," how will you find out about the company's corporate culture?

_____

_____

_____

_____

_____

From Figure 8.7, identify the type of corporate culture that you prefer and explain why?

_____

_____

_____

_____

_____

Thinking back to previous jobs that you have had, describe the worst corporate culture you have ever experienced.

_____

_____

_____

_____

_____

_____

BUILDING SKILLS FOR CAREER SUCCESS

1. Exploring the Internet

After studying the various organizational structures described in this chapter and the reasons for employing them, you may be interested in learning about the organizational structures in place at large firms. As noted in the chapter, departmentalization typically is based on function, product, location, and customer. Many large firms use a combination of these organizational structures successfully. You can gain a good sense of which organizational theme prevails in an industry by looking at several corporate sites.

Assignment

1. Explore the website of any large firm that you believe is representative of its industry, and find its organization chart or a description of its organization. Create a brief organization chart from the information you have found.

2. Describe the bases on which this firm is departmentalized.

2. Developing Critical-Thinking Skills

A firm's culture is a reflection of its most basic beliefs, values, customs, and rituals. Because it can have a powerful influence on how employees think and act, this culture also can have a powerful influence on a firm's performance. The influence may be for the better, of course, as in the case of Southwest Airlines, or it may be for the worse, as in the case of a bureaucratic organization whose employees feel hopelessly mired in red tape. When a company is concerned about mediocre performance and declining sales figures, its managers would do well to examine the cultural environment to see what might be in need of change.

Assignment

1. Analyze the cultural environment in which you work. (If you have no job, consider your school as your workplace and your instructor as your supervisor.) Ask yourself and your coworkers (or classmates) the following questions and record the answers:

   a. Do you feel that your supervisors welcome your ideas and respect them even when they may disagree with them? Do you take pride in your work? Do you feel that your work is appreciated? Do you think that the amount of work assigned to you is reasonable? Are you compensated adequately for your work?

   b. Are you proud to be associated with the company? Do you believe what the company says about itself in its advertisements? Are there any company policies or rules, written or unwritten, that you feel are unfair? Do you think that there is an opportunity for you to advance in this environment?

   c. How much independence do you have in carrying out your assignments? Are you ever allowed to act on your own, or do you feel that you have to consult with your supervisor on every detail?

   d. Do you enjoy the atmosphere in which you work? Is the physical setting pleasant? How often do you laugh in an average workday? How well do you get along with your supervisor and coworkers?

   e. Do you feel that the company cares about you? Will your supervisor give you time off when you have some pressing personal need? If the company had to downsize, how do you think you would be treated?

2. Using the responses to these questions, write a two-page paper describing how the culture of your workplace affects your performance and the overall performance of the firm. Point out the cultural factors that have the most beneficial and negative effects. Include your thoughts on how negative effects could be reversed.

3. Building Team Skills

An organization chart is a diagram showing how employees and tasks are grouped and how the lines of communication and authority flow within an organization. These charts can look very different depending on a number of factors, including the nature and size of the business, the way it is departmentalized, its patterns of delegating authority, and its span of management.

Assignment

1. Working in a team, use the following information to draw an organization chart: The KDS Design Center works closely with two home-construction companies, Amex and Highmass. KDS's role is to help customers select materials for their new homes and to ensure that their selections are communicated accurately to the builders. The company is also a retailer of wallpaper, blinds, and drapery. The retail department, the Amex accounts, and the Highmass accounts make up KDS's three departments. The company has the following positions:

   President
   Executive vice president
   Managers, 2
   Appointment coordinators, 2
   Amex coordinators, 2
   Highmass coordinators, 2
   Consultants/designers for the Amex and Highmass accounts, 15
   Retail positions, 4
   Payroll and billing personnel, 1

2. After your team has drawn the organization chart, discuss the following:

   a. What type of organizational structure does your chart depict? Is it a bureaucratic, matrix, cluster, or network structure? Why?

   b. How does KDS use departmentalization?

   c. To what extent is authority in the company centralized or decentralized?

d. What is the span of management within KDS?

e. Which positions are line positions and which are staff? Why?

3. Prepare a three-page report summarizing what the chart revealed about relationships and tasks at the KDS Design Center and what your team learned about the value of organization charts. Include your chart in your report.

4. Researching Different Careers

In the past, company loyalty and ability to assume increasing job responsibility usually ensured advancement within an organization. While the reasons for seeking advancement (the desire for a better-paying position, more prestige, and job satisfaction) have not changed, the qualifications for career advancement have. In today's business environment, climbing the corporate ladder requires packaging and marketing yourself. To be promoted within your company or to be considered for employment with another company, it is wise to improve your skills continually. By taking workshops and seminars or enrolling in community college courses, you can keep up with the changing technology in your industry. Networking with people in your business or community can help you to find a new job. Most jobs are filled through personal contacts. Who you know can be important.

A list of your accomplishments on the job can reveal your strengths and weaknesses. Setting goals for improvement helps to increase your self-confidence.

Be sure to recognize the signs of job dissatisfaction. It may be time to move to another position or company.

Assignment

Are you prepared to climb the corporate ladder? Do a self-assessment by analyzing the following areas, and summarize the results in a two-page report.

1. Skills
   - What are your most valuable skills?
   - What skills do you lack?
   - Describe your plan for acquiring new skills and improving your skills.
2. Networking
   - How effectively are you at using a mentor?

- Are you a member of a professional organization?
- In which community, civic, or church groups are you participating?
- Whom have you added to your contact list in the last six weeks?

3. Accomplishments
   - What achievements have you reached in your job?
   - What would you like to accomplish? What will it take for you to reach your goal?
4. Promotion or new job
   - What is your likelihood for getting a promotion?
   - Are you ready for a change? What are you doing or willing to do to find another job?

5. Improving Communication Skills

Delegation of authority involves giving another person responsibility for performing a task and the authority or power needed to accomplish the task. The person doing the delegating, however, remains responsible, or accountable, for seeing that the job is done properly. Delegating work is important not only because it is often the only way a manager can accomplish everything that needs to be accomplished but also because it gives lower-level employees the opportunity to improve their skills. For a variety of reasons, managers sometimes fail to delegate authority. They may feel that their subordinates are not competent to perform the work properly, or they may feel that their subordinates are too competent, in which case they would pose a threat to the manager. And some managers are simply too disorganized to delegate their work.

Assignment

1. Arrange an interview with the manager of a business in your community. Prepare a list of questions you will ask in the interview. They should focus on the following topics:
   a. What is the general pattern of delegation in the company?
   b. To what extent is the organization centralized or decentralized?
   c. How much work does this manager delegate? What are the kinds of tasks delegated?

d. What are the benefits of delegating work? What are the drawbacks?

e. Does this manager experience any difficulties in delegating? If so, what are they? Has the manager thought of any ways to resolve them?

2. Write a two-page report on the results of your interview.

→ PREP TEST

Matching Questions

____ 1. Two or more people working toward a common goal.

____ 2. The line of authority from highest to lowest levels.

____ 3. It investigates problems.

____ 4. Line and staff positions are clearly defined.

____ 5. The process of grouping similar things together.

____ 6. The process of giving authority to subordinates.

____ 7. The duty to do a job or perform a task.

____ 8. The power to do an assigned task.

____ 9. One who works within a firm to develop ideas.

____ 10. An informal communications network.

a. authority
b. bureaucratic structure
c. chain of command
d. delegation
e. departmentalization
f. grapevine
g. intrapreneur
h. organization
i. responsibility
j. task force

True/False Questions

T F

11. ○ ○ A benefit of specialization is improved efficiency and increased productivity.

12. ○ ○ Job rotation involves assigning an employee more tasks and greater control.

13. ○ ○ Accountability is created, not delegated.

14. ○ ○ Many firms find that by using matrix organization, the motivation level is lowered, and personal growth of employees is limited.

15. ○ ○ The power to make decisions is granted through authority

T F

16. ○ ○ Line positions support staff positions in decision making.

17. ○ ○ Ad hoc committees can be used effectively to review a firm's employee benefits plan.

18. ○ ○ The span of management should be wide when a great deal of interaction is required between the supervisor and worker.

19. ○ ○ Functional authority is being practiced when staff managers exercise the authority to make decisions and issue directives.

20. ○ ○ A cluster structure is also called team or collaborative.

Multiple-Choice Questions

21. A committee is organized to review applications for scholarships. The group will award two scholarships to recent high school graduates. What type of committee would work best?
    a. Ad hoc committee
    b. Task force
    c. Liaison committee
    d. Standing committee
    e. Self-managed team

22. ABC Distributors is reorganizing to better control costs. The company decided to group hospitals, schools, and churches together into one department. Which departmentalization base is the company using?
    a. Location
    b. Function
    c. Basis
    d. Product
    e. Customer

23. A supervisor assigned to Wendy, the most proficient employee in the accounting department, a project on cost control that was due in three weeks. For Wendy to be accountable for the project, what must Wendy be given?

    a. Responsibility
    b. Power
    c. Authority
    d. Training
    e. Control

24. A narrow span of control works best when
    a. subordinates are located close together.
    b. the manager has few responsibilities outside of supervision.
    c. little interaction is required between the manager and the worker.
    d. new problems arise frequently.
    e. few problems arise on a daily basis.

25. The process of dividing work to be done by an entire organization into separate parts and assigning the parts to positions within the organization is called
    a. departmentalization.
    b. delegation.
    c. job design.
    d. specialization.
    e. organizing.

Fill-in-the-Blank Questions

26. A budget review committee is an example of a/an _____ committee

27. When primary functions are contracted to other organizations, the firm uses a _____ structure.

28. When employees from different departments work on a project, the team is called a/an _____ team.

29. A firm's values and rituals are key components of the corporate _____.

30. A _____ management position is directly responsible for accomplishing objectives of the firm.

Online Study Center

FOR MORE test practice, use the interactive ACE quizzes available at the Online Student Center: **www.college.hmco.com/PIC/pridebusiness9e.**

Answers on p. PT1.

Producing Quality Goods and Services

www.college.hmco.com/PIC/pridebusiness9e

LEARNING OBJECTIVES

WHAT you will be able to do once you complete this chapter:

1 **Explain** the nature of production.

2 **Outline** how the conversion process transforms raw materials, labor, and other resources into finished products or services.

3 **Describe** how research and development lead to new products and services.

4 **Discuss** the components involved in planning the production process.

5 **Explain** how purchasing, inventory control, scheduling, and quality control affect production.

6 **Summarize** how productivity and technology are related.

WHY this chapter matters

Think for a moment about the products and services you bought in the past week. If it weren't for the activities in this chapter, those products and services would not be available. And there wouldn't be any automobiles, clothing, or food on the shelves at the supermarket. In reality, life as we know it today would not exist if it weren't for production.

FOR HELP with studying this chapter, visit the Online Student Center:

www.college.hmco.com/PIC/pridebusiness9e

Online Study Center

The solution to Hyundai Motor's problem of how to sell more cars in the United States comes down to one word: *quality*. "Quality is crucial to our survival. According to Hyundai's top management, we have to get it right, no matter what the cost!" Because they believe they can improve quality, management has set a goal of selling one million cars annually in the United States by the end of this decade. Achieving that goal will be a real challenge for a company that sold fewer than 90,000 cars in the U.S. market in 1998 and whose brand "was worse than nothing," in the words of Hyundai's head of marketing strategy.

Hyundai entered the U.S. market in 1986 with a low-priced sedan for budget-conscious buyers. When this model developed one quality problem after another, however, the company's reputation suffered—and sales plummeted. After Chung Mong Koo, the son of Hyundai's founder, was named chairman in 1998, he concluded that the only way to reverse the sales slide was by making a major investment in quality.

DID YOU KNOW?

Hyundai entered the U.S. market in 1986 with a low-priced sedan for budget-conscious buyers. Now, 20 years later, the South Korean auto maker has set a goal of selling one million cars annually in the United States.

To improve quality, management first reorganized the product-development process so that engineers, designers, and plant managers created new vehicles as a team. By examining and re-examining every blueprint and prototype before a new model went into production, the team was able to prevent many quality problems and boost manufacturing productivity. Hyundai also delayed the launch of new models until every defect was cleared up. Even though the delays meant lost sales revenue in the short run, managers recognized that higher quality would mean higher revenue in the long run.

As evidence of its commitment to quality, Hyundai began offering a ten-year, 100,000-mile warranty. Buyers started coming back, the automaker's sales rebounded, and over time, the poor-quality image faded. Today Hyundai sells more than 400,000 vehicles every year in the United States, and sales are climbing steadily. Can it achieve its million-car goal by the end of the decade?[1]

For more information about this company, go to **www.hyundai-motor.com**.

Can Hyundai sell one million automobiles each year in the competitive U.S. auto market? Good question! Certainly the company's tarnished reputation of the 1990s is now improving because of Hyundai's improved product quality. And yet it must constantly look for ways to improve its methods of doing business to improve not only quality but also manufacturing productivity. The fact is that no industry illustrates this chapter's content—the production of quality goods and services—better than the automobile industry. Auto manufacturers, such as Hyundai, take all kinds of raw materials—steel, aluminum, rubber, plastic, vinyl, and leather—and transform them into fine-tuned cars that are sold to demanding customers around the globe. Today people expect more when purchasing an automobile, and now Hyundai is working to produce a product that people want.

We begin this chapter with an overview of operations management—the activities required to produce goods and services that meet the needs of customers. In this section we also discuss competition in the global marketplace and careers in operations management.

Next, we describe the conversion process that makes production possible and also note the growing role of services in our economy. Then we examine more closely three important aspects of operations management: developing ideas for new products, planning for production, and effectively controlling operations after production has begun. We close the chapter with a look at productivity trends and ways that productivity can be improved through the use of technology.

What Is Production?

1 LEARNING OBJECTIVE
Explain the nature of production.

Have you ever wondered where a new pair of Levi jeans comes from? Or a new Mitsubishi big-screen color television, Izod pullover sweater, or Uniroyal tire for your car? Even factory service on a Hewlett Packard notebook computer or a Maytag clothes dryer would be impossible if it weren't for the activities described in this chapter. In fact, these products and services and millions of others like them would not exist if it weren't for production activities.

Let's begin this chapter by reviewing what an operating manager does. In Chapter 7 we described an *operations manager* as a person who manages the systems that convert resources into goods and services. This area of management is usually referred to as **operations management,** which consists of all the activities managers engage in to produce goods and services.

operations management all activities managers engage in to produce goods and services

To produce a product or service successfully, a business must perform a number of specific activities. For example, suppose that an organization such as Toyota has an idea for a new Toyota Highlander Hybrid sport-utility vehicle (SUV) that will cost in excess of $30,000 and features a new gas/electric engine. Marketing research must determine not only if customers are willing to pay the price for this product but also what special features they want. Then Toyota's operations managers must turn the concept into reality.

Toyota's managers cannot just push the "start button" and immediately begin producing the new automobile. Production must be planned. As you will see, planning takes place both *before* anything is produced and *during* the production process.

Managers also must concern themselves with the control of operations to ensure that the organization's goals are achieved. For a product such as Toyota's Highlander Hybrid SUV, control of operations involves a number of important issues, including product quality, performance standards, the amount of inventory of both raw materials and finished products, and production costs.

We discuss each of the major activities of operations management later in this chapter. First, however, let's take a closer look at American manufacturers and how they compete in the global marketplace.

Competition in the Global Marketplace

After World War II, the United States became the most productive country in the world. For almost thirty years, until the late 1970s, its leadership was never threatened. By then, however, manufacturers in Japan, Germany, Great Britain, Italy, Korea, Sweden, and other industrialized nations were offering U.S. firms increasing competition. And now the Chinese are manufacturing everything from sophisticated electronic equipment and automobiles to less expensive everyday items—often for lower cost than the same goods can be manufactured in other countries. As a result, the goods Americans purchase may have been manufactured in the United States *or* in other countries around the globe and shipped to the United States. Competition has never been fiercer, and in some ways the world has never been smaller.

In an attempt to regain a competitive edge on foreign manufacturers, U.S. firms have taken another look at the importance of improving quality and meeting the needs of their customers. The most successful U.S. firms also have focused on the following:

1. Motivating employees to cooperate with management and improve productivity

Career outlook in manufacturing

Between now and 2012, the need for employees in the manufacturing sector of the economy is expected to decrease as manufacturers find ways to become more productive.

Total number of employees for each year (in millions)

16.8   15.3   15.1

1992   2002   2012

Source: "2002–12 Employment Projections," U.S. Bureau of Labor Statistics website: **www.bls.gov.**

2. Reducing production costs by selecting suppliers that offer higher-quality raw materials and components at reasonable prices
3. Replacing outdated equipment with state-of-the-art manufacturing equipment
4. Using computer-aided and flexible manufacturing systems that allow a higher degree of customization
5. Improving control procedures to help ensure lower manufacturing costs
6. Building new manufacturing facilities in foreign countries where labor costs are lower

Although competing in the global economy is a major challenge, it is a worthwhile pursuit. For most firms, competing in the global marketplace is not only profitable, but it is also an essential activity that requires the cooperation of everyone within the organization.

Careers in Operations Management

Although it is hard to provide information about specific career opportunities in operations management, some generalizations do apply to this management area. First, you must appreciate the manufacturing process and the steps required to produce a product or service. A basic understanding of mass production and the difference between an analytical process and a synthetic process is essential. **Mass production** is a manufacturing process that lowers the cost required to produce a large number of identical or similar products over a long period of time. An **analytical process** breaks raw materials into different component parts. For example, a barrel of crude oil refined by Marathon Oil Corporation—a Texas-based oil and chemical refiner—can be broken down into gasoline, oil and lubricants, and many other petroleum by-products. A **synthetic process** is just the opposite of the analytical one; it combines raw materials or components to create a finished product. Black & Decker uses a synthetic process when it combines plastic, steel, rechargeable batteries, and other components to produce a cordless drill.

Once you understand that operations managers are responsible for producing tangible products or services that customers want, you must determine how you fit into the production process. Today's successful operations managers must

1. be able to motivate and lead people.
2. understand how technology can make a manufacturer more productive and efficient.
3. appreciate the control processes that help lower production costs and improve product quality.
4. understand the relationship between the customer, the marketing of a product, and the production of a product.

If operations management seems like an area you might be interested in, why not do more career exploration? You could take an operations management course if your college or university offers one, or you could obtain a part-time job during the school year or a summer job in a manufacturing company.

mass production a manufacturing process that lowers the cost required to produce a large number of identical or similar products over a long period of time

analytical process a process in operations management in which raw materials are broken into different component parts

synthetic process a process in operations management in which raw materials or components are combined to create a finished product

The Conversion Process

To have something to sell, a business must convert resources into goods and services. The resources are materials, finances, people, and information—the same resources discussed in Chapters 1 and 7. The goods and services are varied, ranging from consumer products to heavy manufacturing equipment to fast food. The purpose of this conversion of resources into goods and services is to provide utility to customers. **Utility** is the ability of a good or service to satisfy a human need. Although there are four types of utility—form, place, time, and possession—operations management focuses primarily on form utility. **Form utility** is created by converting raw materials, people, finances, and information into finished products. The other types of utility—place, time, and possession—are discussed in Chapter 13.

But how does the conversion take place? How does Kellogg convert wheat, corn, sugar, salt, and other ingredients; money from previous sales and stockholders' investments; production workers and managers; and economic and marketing forecasts into cereal products? How does New York Life Insurance convert office buildings, insurance premiums, actuaries, and mortality tables into life insurance policies? They do so through the use of a conversion process like the one illustrated in Figure 9.1. As indicated by our New York Life Insurance example, the conversion process is not limited to manufacturing products. The conversion process also can be used to produce services.

Manufacturing Using a Conversion Process

The conversion of resources into products and services can be described in several ways. We limit our discussion here to three: the focus or major resource used in the conversion process, its magnitude of change, and the number of production processes employed.

Focus   By the *focus* of a conversion process we mean the resource or resources that make up the major or most important *input*. For a bank such as Citibank, financial resources are the major resource. A chemical and energy company such as Chevron concentrates on material resources. A college or university is concerned primarily with information. And a temporary employment service focuses on the use of human resources.

Magnitude of Change   The *magnitude* of a conversion process is the degree to which the resources are physically changed. At one extreme lie such processes as the one by which the Glad Products Company, a subsidiary of the Clorox Corporation, produces Glad Cling Wrap. Various chemicals in liquid or powder form are combined to form long, thin sheets of plastic Glad Cling Wrap. Here, the original resources are totally unrecognizable in the finished product. At the other extreme, Southwest Airlines produces *no* physical change in its original resources. The airline simply provides a service and transports people from one place to another.

Number of Production Processes   A single firm may employ one production process or many. In general, larger firms that make a variety of products use multiple production processes. For example, General Electric manufactures

2 LEARNING OBJECTIVE
Outline how the conversion process transforms raw materials, labor, and other resources into finished products or services.

utility the ability of a good or service to satisfy a human need

form utility utility created by converting raw materials, people, finances, and information into finished products

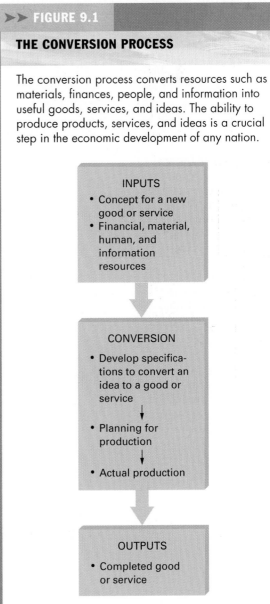

▶▶ FIGURE 9.1

THE CONVERSION PROCESS

The conversion process converts resources such as materials, finances, people, and information into useful goods, services, and ideas. The ability to produce products, services, and ideas is a crucial step in the economic development of any nation.

INPUTS
• Concept for a new good or service
• Financial, material, human, and information resources

CONVERSION
• Develop specifications to convert an idea to a good or service
• Planning for production
• Actual production

OUTPUTS
• Completed good or service

some of its own products, buys other merchandise from suppliers, and operates a credit division, an insurance company, an entertainment division, and a medical equipment division. Smaller firms, by contrast, may use one production process. For example, Texas-based Advanced Cast Stone, Inc., manufactures one basic product: building materials made from concrete.

The Increasing Importance of Services

The application of the basic principles of operations management to the production of services has coincided with a dramatic growth in the number and diversity of service businesses. In 1900, only 28 percent of American workers were employed in service firms. By 1950, this figure had grown to 40 percent, and by September 2005, it had risen to 83 percent.[2] In fact, the American economy is now characterized as a **service economy** (see Figure 9.2). A service economy is one in which more effort is devoted to the production of services than to the production of goods.

Today, the managers of restaurants, laundries, real estate agencies, banks, movie theaters, airlines, travel bureaus, and other service firms have realized that they can benefit from the experience of manufacturers. And yet the production of services is very different from the production of manufactured goods in the following four ways:

1. Services are consumed immediately and, unlike manufactured goods, cannot be stored. For example, a hair stylist cannot store completed haircuts.
2. Services are provided when and where the customer desires the service. In many cases customers will not travel as far to obtain a service.
3. Services are usually labor-intensive because the human resource is often the most important resource used in the production of services.
4. Services are intangible, and it is therefore more difficult to evaluate customer satisfaction.[3]

Disney's Magical Express!
Like magic, guests and their baggage are whisked from the Orlando International Airport to the Walt Disney World Resort. Complementary round-trip shuttle service to one of 22 hotels in the Orlando, Florida area is just one of the many services Disney provides to make a guest's stay more enjoyable.

service economy an economy in which more effort is devoted to the production of services than to the production of goods

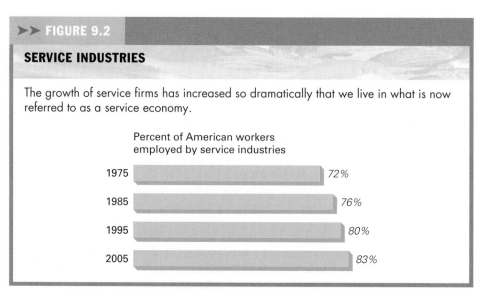

>> FIGURE 9.2

SERVICE INDUSTRIES

The growth of service firms has increased so dramatically that we live in what is now referred to as a service economy.

Percent of American workers employed by service industries

Year	Percent
1975	72%
1985	76%
1995	80%
2005	83%

Source: U.S. Bureau of Labor Statistics website: **www.bls.gov**; accessed October 30, 2005.

Although it is often more difficult to measure customer satisfaction, today's successful service firms work hard at providing the services customers want. Compared with manufacturers, service firms often listen more carefully to customers and respond more quickly to the market's changing needs. Other suggestions for improving the quality of customer service are provided in the nearby Your Career feature.

In an effort to meet increased demands for customer service, businesses ranging from small mom-and-pop firms to large *Fortune* 500 companies are developing new ways to provide services and meet customer needs. For example, Dell is a well-known manufacturer of computer equipment. In order to be successful, it must gather as much information as possible about the customer in order to meet the needs of each individual customer. Want to buy a new Dell Latitude computer? All you have to do is to go to the Dell website and work through a series of steps designed to determine how the computer will be used. Still have questions? By using an 800 phone number, you can contact a customer service representative who will help you to make a decision. Service after the sale is also important because Dell maintains an ongoing dialogue with its customers to understand customer concerns and problems and to identify customers who are ready to buy more of the firm's products.[4]

Now that we understand something about the production process that is used to transform resources into goods and services, we can consider three major activities involved in operations management. These are product development, planning for production, and operations control.

YOUR CAREER

Five Tips for Customer Service Success

Good customer service is an important element when a firm is trying to improve the quality of the customer's experience. Experts offer these five tips for delivering top-notch customer service:

1. *Smile.* You're the face of the company when you face a customer, so maintain a friendly attitude.
2. *Show courtesy.* Customers appreciate polite, respectful treatment. Whether you're answering a question or listening to a complaint, show consideration for the customer's viewpoint.
3. *Communicate.* A common gripe is that businesses fail to communicate. Take a moment to explain to the customer what you're going to do (and why, if appropriate).
4. *Be responsive.* Respond quickly. If you can't answer a question or solve a problem, make it your business to find someone who can—as soon as possible.
5. *Be responsible.* Follow up to be sure the customer's request has been fulfilled or the problem has been solved. Good customer service is *your* responsibility.

Where Do New Products and Services Come From?

No firm can produce a product or service until it has an idea. In other words, someone first must come up with a new way to satisfy a need—a new product or an improvement in an existing product. Starbucks' milkshake-like coffee drink, Apple's iPod, and Yamaha's Jet Ski began as an idea. While no one can predict with 100 percent accuracy what types of products will be available in the next five years, it is safe to say that companies will continue to introduce new products that will change the way we take care of ourselves, interact with others, and find the information and services we need.

3 LEARNING OBJECTIVE
Describe how research and development lead to new products and services.

Research and Development

How did we get personal computers and DVD players? We got them the same way we got light bulbs and automobile tires—from people working with new ideas. Thomas Edison created the first light bulb, and Charles Goodyear discovered the vulcanization process that led to tires. In the same way, scientists and researchers working in businesses and universities have produced many of the newer products we already take for granted.

These activities generally are referred to as *research and development*. For our purposes, **research and development (R&D)** are a set of activities intended to identify new ideas that have the potential to result in new goods and services.

Today, business firms use three general types of R&D activities. *Basic research* consists of activities aimed at uncovering new knowledge. The goal of basic research is scientific advancement, without regard for its potential use in the development of goods and services. *Applied research*, in contrast, consists of activities geared toward discovering new knowledge with some potential use. *Development and implementation* are research activities undertaken specifically to put new or existing knowledge to use in producing goods and services. The 3M Company has always been known for its development and implementation research activities. At the end of the twentieth century, the company had developed more than 55,000 products designed to make people's lives easier. Does a company like 3M quit innovating because it has developed successful products? No, not at all! Just recently the 3M company used development and implementation when it created a new line of Nexcare braces and supports for sport-related injuries, arthritic joints, and pain caused by repetitive-motion injuries. For people with knee, ankle, elbow, wrist, or back injuries, the new products are reducing both immediate pain and the time required for healing. There is even a line of Nexcare youth braces and supports for smaller customers—kids that twist their joints in sports activities or just playing around.[5]

Product Extension and Refinement

When a brand-new product is first marketed, its sales are zero and slowly increase from that point. If the product is successful, annual sales increase more and more rapidly until they reach some peak. Then, as time passes, annual sales begin to decline, and they continue to decline until it is no longer profitable to manufacture the product. (This rise-and-decline pattern, called the *product life cycle*, is discussed in more detail in Chapter 14.)

If a firm sells only one product, when that product reaches the end of its life cycle, the firm will die too. To stay in business, the firm must, at the very least, find ways to refine or extend the want-satisfying capability of its product. Consider television sets. Since they were introduced in the late 1930s, television sets have been constantly *refined* so that they now provide clearer, sharper pictures with less dial adjusting. During the same time, television sets also were *extended*. There are color sets, television-only sets, and others that include VCR and DVD players. There are even television sets that allow their owners to access the Internet. And the latest development—high-definition (HD) television—is already available. Although initial prices were high, prices now have dropped and are more affordable.

Each refinement or extension results in an essentially "new" product whose sales make up for the declining sales of a product that was introduced earlier. When consumers discovered that the original five varieties of Campbell's Soup were of the highest quality, as well as inexpensive, the soups were an instant success. Although one of the most successful companies at the beginning of the 1900s, Campbell's had to continue to innovate, refine, and extend its product line. For example, many consumers in the United States live in what is called an on-the-go society. To meet this need, Campbell's Soup has developed ready-to-serve products that can be popped into a microwave at work or school. In other countries, customer feedback is also used to adapt products to meet the needs of local customers. For example, Liebig Pur, a thick

Research efforts create more fuel-efficient SUVs.
Although many car buyers love SUVs, they hate the cost of filling up at the pump. To help solve this problem, Ford, General Motors, Honda, Toyota, and other automobile makers are using research and development activities to develop automobiles powered by hybrid engines, which combine the best of gasoline and electric motors. In addition, some automobiles, such as the Ford Escape pictured here, operate on Ethanol, a fuel produced from American-grown corn.

research and development (R&D) a set of activities intended to identify new ideas that have the potential to result in new goods and services

ENTREPRENEURIAL CHALLENGE

A Small Business Makes a Big Breakthrough

Can a small business make a big breakthrough? Here's how a small business changed the toothbrush industry by creating the SpinBrush.

- *Identify a need.* Four Ohio entrepreneurs were searching for product ideas when they noticed the high price of electric toothbrushes. If they could offer a battery-operated toothbrush at a fraction of the price, wouldn't many consumers switch from ordinary toothbrushes?

- *Develop the product.* Over the next eighteen months, the entrepreneurs designed and refined the battery-powered SpinBrush. When they got the cost below $5, they began production.

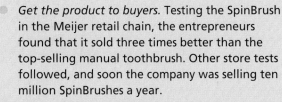

- *Get the product to buyers.* Testing the SpinBrush in the Meijer retail chain, the entrepreneurs found that it sold three times better than the top-selling manual toothbrush. Other store tests followed, and soon the company was selling ten million SpinBrushes a year.

SpinBrush's success caught the eye of Procter & Gamble, which bought out the entrepreneurs and expanded distribution to thirty-five countries. Now owned by Church & Dwight, which also makes Mentadent and Close-up toothpastes, SpinBrush dominates the battery-powered toothbrush industry.

vegetable soup, is sold in cartons with a long shelf life in France.[6] In a similar fashion, Jell-O was introduced to the public in 1897 and was acquired by General Foods Corporation, which later became Kraft Foods. One of Kraft Foods' newer products, Jell-O Pudding Snacks, is still based on Jell-O and produces sales of more than $100 million annually.[7] For most firms, extension and refinement are expected results of their development and implementation effort. Most often they result from the application of new knowledge to existing products. For instance, improved technology affects the content companies can distribute on the Internet. The Disney Corporation currently has a clear advantage over competitors because much of its content is animation. Animation is the easiest content to transfer to the Internet.

Planning for Production

Only a few of the many ideas for new products, refinements, and extensions ever reach the production stage. For those ideas that do, however, the next step is planning for production. Once a new product idea has been identified, planning for production involves three major phases: design planning, facilities planning and site selection, and operational planning (see Figure 9.3).

4 LEARNING OBJECTIVE
Discuss the components involved in planning the production process.

Design Planning

When the R&D staff at Compaq Computers recommended to top management that the firm produce and market an affordable notebook computer, the company could not simply swing into production the next day. Instead, a great deal of time and energy had to be invested in determining what the new computer would look like, where and how it would be produced, and what options would be included. These decisions are a part of design planning. **Design planning** is the development of a plan for converting a product idea into an actual product or service. The major decisions involved in design planning deal with product line, required capacity, and use of technology.

design planning the development of a plan for converting a product idea into an actual product or service

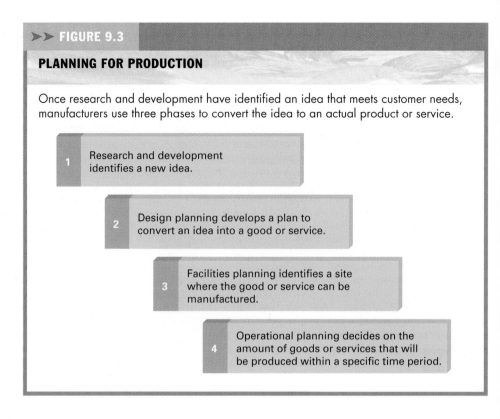

> ➤➤ **FIGURE 9.3**

PLANNING FOR PRODUCTION

Once research and development have identified an idea that meets customer needs, manufacturers use three phases to convert the idea to an actual product or service.

1   Research and development identifies a new idea.

2   Design planning develops a plan to convert an idea into a good or service.

3   Facilities planning identifies a site where the good or service can be manufactured.

4   Operational planning decides on the amount of goods or services that will be produced within a specific time period.

product line a group of similar products that differ only in relatively minor characteristics

Product Line

A **product line** is a group of similar products that differ only in relatively minor characteristics. During the design-planning stage, a computer manufacturer such as Compaq needs to determine how many different models to produce and what major options to offer. A restaurant chain such as Pizza Hut must decide how many menu items to offer.

An important issue in deciding on the product line is to balance customer preferences and production requirements. For this reason, marketing managers play an important role in making product-line decisions. Typically, marketing personnel want a "long" product line that offers customers many options. Because a long product line with more options gives customers choice, it is easier to sell products that meet the needs of individual customers. On the other hand, production personnel generally want a "short" product line because products are easier to produce. With a short product line, the production process is less complex because there are fewer options, and most products are produced using the same basic steps. In many cases the actual choice between a long and short product line involves balancing customer preferences with the cost and problems associated with a more complex production process.

Once the product line has been determined, each distinct product within the product line must be designed. **Product design** is the process of creating a set of specifications from which a product can be produced. When designing a new product, specifications are extremely important. For example, product engineers for Whirlpool Corporation must make sure that a new frost-free refrigerator keeps food frozen in the freezer compartment. At the same time, they must make sure that lettuce and tomatoes do not freeze in the crisper section of the refrigerator. The need for a complete product design is fairly obvious; products that work cannot be manufactured without it. But services should be designed carefully as well—and *for the same reason.*

product design the process of creating a set of specifications from which a product can be produced

capacity the amount of products or services that an organization can produce in a given time

Required Production Capacity

Capacity is the amount of products or services that an organization can produce in a given period of time. (For example, the capacity of a Saab automobile assembly plant might be 300,000 cars per year.) Operations managers—again working with the firm's marketing managers—must determine the required capacity. This, in turn, determines the size of the production facility. If the facility is built with too much capacity, valuable resources (plant, equipment, and money) will lie idle. If the facility offers insufficient capacity, additional capacity may have to be added later when it is much more expensive than in the initial building stage.

Capacity means about the same thing to service businesses. For example, the capacity of a restaurant such as the Hard Rock Cafe in Nashville, Tennessee, is the number of customers it can serve at one time. As with the manufacturing facility described earlier, if the restaurant is built with too much capacity—too many tables and chairs—valuable resources will be wasted. If the restaurant is too small, customers may have to wait for service; if the wait is too long, they may leave and choose another restaurant.

Use of Technology   During the design-planning stage, management must determine the degree to which *automation* will be used to produce a product or service. Here, there is a tradeoff between high initial costs and low operating costs (for automation) and low initial costs and high operating costs (for human labor). Ultimately, management must choose between a labor-intensive technology and a capital-intensive technology. A **labor-intensive technology** is a process in which people must do most of the work. Housecleaning services and the New York Yankees baseball team, for example, are labor-intensive. A **capital-intensive technology** is a process in which machines and equipment do most of the work. A Motorola automated assembly plant is capital-intensive.

One solution to the nation's energy needs. Although windmills have been around for a long time, interest in wind turbines as a means to generate electricity has increased in recent years. This "new-fangled" windmill began as an idea and evolved through a design planning phase. Then, exacting specifications were used to create a product design, which enabled engineers to build a high-tech product that generates electricity.

Facilities Planning and Site Selection

Once initial decisions have been made about a new product line, required capacity, and the use of technology, it is time to determine where the products or services are going to be produced. Generally, a business will choose to produce a new product in an existing factory as long as (1) the existing factory has enough capacity to handle customer demand for both the new product and established products and (2) the cost of refurbishing an existing factory is less than the cost of building a new one.

After exploring the capacity of existing factories, management may decide to build a new production facility. Once again, a number of decisions must be made. Should all the organization's production capacity be placed in one or two large facilities? Or should it be divided among several smaller facilities? In general, firms that market a wide variety of products find it more economical to have a number of smaller facilities. Firms that produce only a small number of products tend to have fewer but larger facilities.

In determining where to locate production facilities, management must consider a number of variables, including the following:

- Locations of major customers and transportation costs to deliver finished products
- Geographic locations of suppliers of parts and raw materials
- Availability and cost of skilled and unskilled labor
- Quality of life for employees and management in the proposed location
- The cost of both land and construction required to build a new production facility
- Local and state taxes, environmental regulations, and zoning laws

labor-intensive technology a process in which people must do most of the work

capital-intensive technology a process in which machines and equipment do most of the work

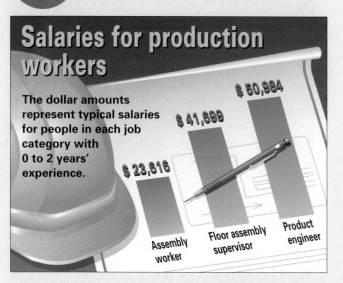

SPOTLIGHT

Salaries for production workers

The dollar amounts represent typical salaries for people in each job category with 0 to 2 years' experience.

$ 23,616 — Assembly worker

$ 41,699 — Floor assembly supervisor

$ 50,984 — Product engineer

Source: The Monster website: **www.monster.com**; accessed October 28, 2005.

- The amount of financial support, if any, offered by local and state governments
- Special requirements, such as great amounts of energy or water used in the production process

It may, of course, be impossible to find the perfect location for a production facility. In fact, the choice of a location often involves balancing the most important variables for each production facility. Before making a final decision about where a proposed plant will be located and how it will be organized, two other factors—human resources and plant layout—should be examined.

Human Resources   Several issues involved in facilities planning and site selection fall within the province of the human resources manager. Thus, at this stage, human resources and operations managers work closely together. For example, suppose that a U.S. firm such as Reebok International wants to lower labor costs by constructing a sophisticated production plant in China. The human resources manager will have to recruit managers and employees with the appropriate skills who are willing to relocate to a foreign country or develop training programs for local Chinese workers or both.

plant layout the arrangement of machinery, equipment, and personnel within a production facility

Plant Layout   **Plant layout** is the arrangement of machinery, equipment, and personnel within a production facility. Three general types of plant layout are used (see Figure 9.4).

The *process layout* is used when different operations are required for creating small batches of different products or working on different parts of a product. The plant is arranged so that each operation is performed in its own particular area. An auto repair facility at a local automobile dealership provides an example of a process layout. The various operations may be engine repair, body work, wheel alignment, and safety inspection. Each operation is performed in a different area. If you take your Lincoln Navigator for a wheel alignment, your car "visits" only the area where alignments are performed.

Can anyone put all the pieces back together? For a product like a Boeing Jetliner, there are literally thousands of parts that must be assembled to build just one plane. Boeing, one of the world's largest aircraft manufacturers, uses a fixed position layout to construct a jetliner because the product is too large and difficult to move during the assembly process.

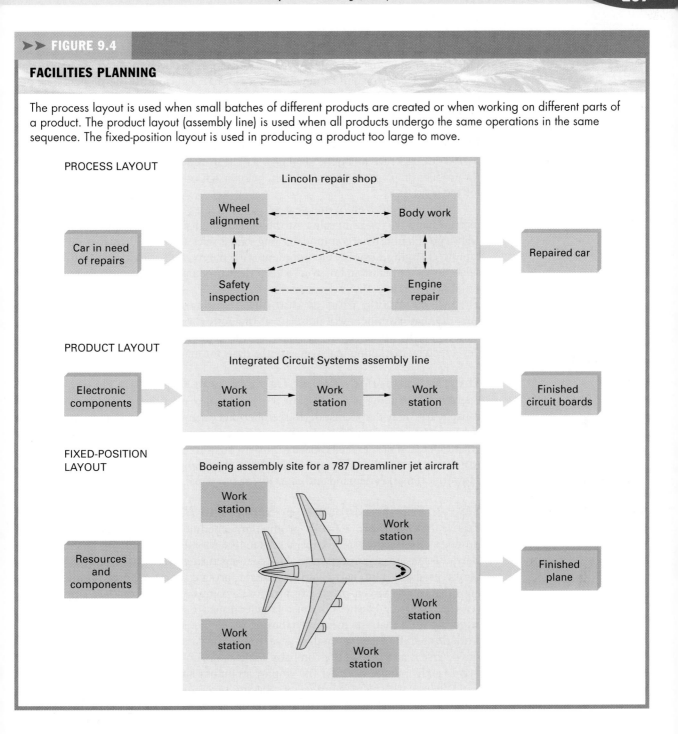

>> **FIGURE 9.4**

FACILITIES PLANNING

The process layout is used when small batches of different products are created or when working on different parts of a product. The product layout (assembly line) is used when all products undergo the same operations in the same sequence. The fixed-position layout is used in producing a product too large to move.

PROCESS LAYOUT

Lincoln repair shop

Car in need of repairs → Wheel alignment ⇄ Body work / Safety inspection ⇄ Engine repair → Repaired car

PRODUCT LAYOUT

Integrated Circuit Systems assembly line

Electronic components → Work station → Work station → Work station → Finished circuit boards

FIXED-POSITION LAYOUT

Boeing assembly site for a 787 Dreamliner jet aircraft

Resources and components → Work station / Work station / Work station / Work station / Work station → Finished plane

A *product layout* (sometimes referred to as an *assembly line*) is used when all products undergo the same operations in the same sequence. Workstations are arranged to match the sequence of operations, and work flows from station to station. An assembly line is the best example of a product layout. For example, Pennsylvania-based Integrated Circuit Systems, Inc., uses a product layout to manufacture components for consumer and business electronic products.

A *fixed-position layout* is used when a very large product is produced. Aircraft manufacturers and shipbuilders apply this method because of the difficulty of moving a large product such as an airliner or ship. The product remains stationary, and people and machines are moved as needed to assemble the product. Boeing, for example, uses the fixed-position layout to build 787 Dreamliner jet aircraft at its Everett, Washington, manufacturing facility.

Operational Planning

Once the product has been designed and a decision has been made to use an existing production facility or build a new one, operational plans must be developed. The objective of operational planning is to decide on the amount of products or services each facility will produce during a specific period of time. Four steps are required.

Step 1: Selecting a Planning Horizon
A **planning horizon** is simply the time period during which an operational plan will be in effect. A common planning horizon for production plans is one year. Then, before each year is up, management must plan for the next.

A planning horizon of one year generally is long enough to average out seasonal increases and decreases in sales. At the same time, it is short enough for planners to adjust production to accommodate long-range sales trends. Firms that operate in a rapidly changing business environment with many competitors may find it best to select a shorter planning horizon to keep their production planning current.

Step 2: Estimating Market Demand
The *market demand* for a product is the quantity that customers will purchase at the going price. This quantity must be estimated for the time period covered by the planning horizon. Sales projections developed by marketing managers are the basis for market-demand estimates.

Step 3: Comparing Market Demand with Capacity
The third step in operational planning is to compare the estimated market demand with the facility's capacity to satisfy that demand. (Remember that capacity is the amount of products or services that an organization can produce in a given time.) One of three outcomes may result: Demand may exceed capacity, capacity may exceed demand, or capacity and demand may be equal. If they are equal, the facility should be operated at full capacity. However, if market demand and capacity are not equal, adjustments may be necessary.

Step 4: Adjusting Products or Services to Meet Demand
The biggest reason for changes to a firm's production schedule is changes in the amount of products or services that a company sells to its customers. For example, Indiana-based Berry Plastics uses an injection-molded manufacturing process to produce all kinds of plastic products. One particularly successful product line for Berry Plastics is drink cups that can be screen-printed to promote a company or the company's products or services.[8] If Berry Plastics obtains a large contract to provide promotional mugs to a large fast-food chain such as Whataburger or McDonald's, the company may need to work three shifts a day, seven days a week until the contract is fulfilled. Unfortunately, the reverse is also true. If the company's sales force does not generate new sales, there may be only enough work for the employees on one shift.

When market demand exceeds capacity, several options are available to a firm. Production of products or services may be increased by operating the facility overtime with existing personnel or by starting a second or third work shift. For manufacturers, another response is to subcontract or outsource a portion of the work to other producers. If the excess demand is likely to be permanent, the firm may expand the current facility or build another facility.

What happens when capacity exceeds market demand? Again, there are several options. To reduce output temporarily, workers may be laid off and part of the facility shut down. Or the facility may be operated on a shorter-than-normal work week for as long as the excess capacity persists. To adjust to a permanently decreased demand, management may shift the excess capacity of a manufacturing facility to the production of other goods or services. The most radical adjustment is to eliminate the excess capacity by selling unused facilities.

Operations Control

We have discussed the development of an idea for a product or service and the planning that translates that idea into the reality. Now we are ready to push the "start button" to begin the production process and examine four important areas of operations control: purchasing, inventory control, scheduling, and quality control (see Figure 9.5).

Purchasing

Purchasing consists of all the activities involved in obtaining required materials, supplies, components (or subassemblies), and parts from other firms. Levi Strauss must purchase denim cloth, thread, and zippers before it can produce a single pair of jeans. Similarly, Nike, Inc., must purchase leather, rubber, cloth for linings, and laces before manufacturing a pair of athletic shoes. For all firms, the purchasing function is far from routine, and its importance should not be underestimated. For some products, purchased materials make up more than 50 percent of their wholesale costs. To improve their purchasing systems, aerospace giants Boeing, BAE Systems, Lockheed Martin, and Raytheon jointly developed an online exchange that links more than 37,000 suppliers, hundreds of airlines, and national governments into a single web-based marketplace for parts. These four firms have used the Internet trading exchange to purchase parts and supplies valued at approximately $70 billion each year since 2000. According to Boeing, "By using a single e-marketplace, all of us—manufacturers, suppliers, airline and government customers, and service providers—can significantly lower transaction costs and deliver more value."[9]

The objective of purchasing is to ensure that required materials are available when they are needed, in the proper amounts, and at minimum cost. Generally, the company with purchasing needs and suppliers must develop a working relationship built on trust. In addition to a working relationship built on trust, many companies believe that purchasing is one area where they can promote diversity. For example, AT&T (the communications giant that was known as SBC Communications until 2005) has developed a Supplier Diversity Program that includes minorities, women, and disabled veteran business enterprises. Goals for the AT&T program include purchasing a total of 21.5 percent of all products and services from these three groups. As a result of its Supplier Diversity Program, the company spends almost $2 billion each year with diverse suppliers and is now recognized as one of the nation's leading companies in supplier diversity.[10]

Purchasing personnel should be on the lookout constantly for new or backup suppliers, even when their needs are being met by their present suppliers, because problems such as strikes and equipment breakdowns can cut off the flow of purchased materials from a primary supplier at any time.

5 LEARNING OBJECTIVE
Explain how purchasing, inventory control, scheduling, and quality control affect production.

purchasing all the activities involved in obtaining required materials, supplies, components, and parts from other firms

---

▶▶ FIGURE 9.5

FOUR ASPECTS OF OPERATIONS CONTROL

Implementing the operations control system in any business requires the effective use of purchasing, inventory control, scheduling, and quality control.

OPERATIONS CONTROL

| Purchasing | Inventory control | Scheduling | Quality control |

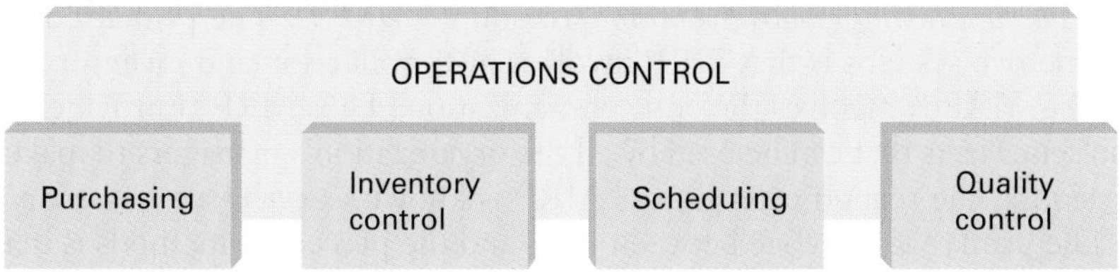

The choice of suppliers should result from careful analysis of a number of factors. The following are especially critical:

- *Price.* Comparing prices offered by different suppliers is always an essential part of selecting a supplier. Even tiny differences in price add up to enormous sums when large quantities are purchased.
- *Quality.* Purchasing specialists always try to buy materials at a level of quality in keeping with the type of product being manufactured. The minimum acceptable quality is usually specified by product designers.
- *Reliability.* An agreement to purchase high-quality materials at a low price is the purchaser's dream. But such an agreement becomes a nightmare if the supplier does not deliver.
- *Credit terms.* Purchasing specialists should determine if the supplier demands immediate payment or will extend credit. Also, does the supplier offer a cash discount or reduction in price for prompt payment?
- *Shipping costs.* One of the most overlooked factors in purchasing is the geographic location of the supplier. Low prices and favorable credit terms offered by a distant supplier can be wiped out when the buyer must pay the shipping costs. Above all, the question of who pays the shipping costs should be answered before any supplier is chosen.

Inventory Control

Can you imagine what would happen if a Coca-Cola manufacturing plant ran out of the company's familiar red and white aluminum cans? It would be impossible to complete the manufacturing process and ship the cases of Coke to retailers. Management would be forced to shut the assembly line down until the next shipment of cans arrived from a supplier. In reality, operations managers for Coca-Cola realize the disasters that a shortage of needed materials can cause and will avoid this type of problem if at all possible. The simple fact is that shutdowns are expensive because costs such as rent, wages, and insurance still must be paid.

Operations managers are concerned with three types of inventories. A *raw-materials inventory* consists of materials that will become part of the product during the production process. The *work-in-process inventory* consists of partially completed products. The *finished-goods inventory* consists of completed goods.

Associated with each type of inventory are a *holding cost*, or storage cost, and a *stock-out cost*, the cost of running out of inventory. **Inventory control** is the process of managing inventories in such a way as to minimize inventory costs, including both holding costs and potential stock-out costs. Today, computer systems are being used to keep track of inventories, provide periodic inventory reports, and alert managers to impending stock-outs.

One of the most sophisticated methods of inventory control used today is materials requirements planning. **Materials requirements planning (MRP)** is a computerized system that integrates production planning and inventory control. One of the great advantages of an MRP system is its ability to juggle delivery schedules and lead times effectively. For a complex product such as an automobile or airplane, it is virtually impossible for individual managers to oversee the hundreds of parts that go into the finished product. However, a manager using an MRP system can arrange both order and delivery schedules so that materials, parts, and supplies arrive when they are needed.

Two extensions of MRP are used by manufacturing firms today. The first is known as *manufacturing resource planning*, or simply *MRP II*. The primary difference between the two systems is that MRP involves just production and inventory personnel, whereas MRP II involves the entire organization. Thus MRP II provides a single common set of facts that can be used by all the organization's managers to make effective decisions. The second extension of MRP is known as *enterprise resource planning* (ERP). The primary difference between ERP and the preceding methods is that ERP software is more sophisticated and can monitor not only inventory and production

inventory control the process of managing inventories in such a way as to minimize inventory costs, including both holding costs and potential stock-out costs

materials requirements planning (MRP) a computerized system that integrates production planning and inventory control

processes but also quality, sales, and even such variables as inventory at a supplier's location.

Because large firms can incur huge inventory costs, much attention has been devoted to inventory control. The just-in-time system being used by some businesses is one result of all this attention. A **just-in-time inventory system** is designed to ensure that materials or supplies arrive at a facility just when they are needed so that storage and holding costs are minimized. The customer must specify what will be needed, when, and in what amounts. The supplier must be sure that the right supplies arrive at the agreed-on time and location. For example, managers using a just-in-time inventory system at a Toyota assembly plant determine the number of automobiles that will be assembled in a specified time period. Then Toyota purchasing personnel order *just* the parts needed to produce those automobiles. In turn, suppliers deliver the parts *in time* or when they are needed on the assembly line.

Without proper inventory control, it is impossible for operations managers to schedule the work required to produce goods that can be sold to customers.

> **just-in-time inventory system** a system designed to ensure that materials or supplies arrive at a facility just when they are needed so that storage and holding costs are minimized

Scheduling

Scheduling is the process of ensuring that materials and other resources are at the right place at the right time. The materials and resources may be moved from a warehouse to the workstations, they may move from station to station along an assembly line, or they may arrive at workstations "just in time" to be made part of the work in process there.

As our definition implies, both place and time are important to scheduling. (This is no different from, say, the scheduling of classes. You cannot attend your classes unless you know *both* where and when they are held.) The *routing* of materials is the sequence of workstations that the materials will follow. Assume that Drexel-Heritage— one of America's largest and oldest furniture manufacturers—is scheduling production of an oval coffee table made from cherry wood. Operations managers would route the needed materials (wood, screws, packaging materials, and so on) through a series of individual workstations along an assembly line. At each workstation, a specific task would be performed, and then the partially finished coffee table would move to the next workstation. When routing materials, operations managers are especially concerned with the sequence of each step of the production process. For the coffee table, the top and legs must be cut to specifications before the wood is finished. (If the wood were finished before being cut, the finish would be ruined, and the coffee table would have to be stained again.)

When scheduling production, managers also are concerned with timing. The *timing* function specifies when the materials will arrive at each station and how long they will remain there. For the cherry coffee table, it may take workers thirty minutes to cut the table top and legs and another thirty minutes to drill the holes and assemble the table. Before packaging the coffee table for shipment, it must be finished with cherry stain and allowed to dry. This last step may take as long as three days depending on weather conditions and humidity.

Whether or not the finished product requires a simple or complex production process, operations managers are responsible for monitoring schedules—called *follow-up*—to ensure that the work flows according to a timetable. For complex products, many operations managers prefer to use Gantt charts or the PERT technique.

> **scheduling** the process of ensuring that materials and other resources are at the right place at the right time

Scheduling Through Gantt Charts   Developed by Henry L. Gantt, a **Gantt chart** is a graphic scheduling device that displays the tasks to be performed on the vertical axis and the time required for each task on the horizontal axis. Gantt charts

- allow you to determine how long a project should take.
- lay out the order in which tasks need to be completed.
- determine the resources needed.
- monitor progress of different activities required to complete the project.

> **Gantt chart** a graphic scheduling device that displays the tasks to be performed on the vertical axis and the time required for each task on the horizontal axis

A Gantt chart that describes the activities required to build three dozen golf carts is illustrated in Figure 9.6. Gantt charts usually are not suitable for scheduling extremely complex situations. Nevertheless, using them forces a manager to plan the steps required to get a job done and to specify time requirements for each part of the job.

Scheduling via PERT   Another technique for scheduling a complex process or project and maintaining control of the schedule is **PERT (Program Evaluation and Review Technique).** To use PERT, we begin by identifying all the major *activities* involved in the project. For example, the activities involved in producing your textbook are illustrated in Figure 9.7.

All events are arranged in a sequence. In doing so, we must be sure that an event that must occur before another event in the actual process also occurs before that event on the PERT chart. For example, the manuscript must be edited before the type is set. Therefore, in our sequence, the event "edit manuscript" must precede the event "set type."

Next, we use arrows to connect events that must occur in sequence. We then estimate the time required for each activity and mark it near the corresponding arrow. The sequence of production activities that take the longest time from start to finish is called the **critical path.** The activities on this path determine the minimum time in which the process can be completed. These activities are the ones that must be scheduled and controlled carefully. A delay in any one of them will cause a delay in completion of the project as a whole.

The critical path runs from event 1 to event 4 to event 5. It then runs through events 6, 8, and 9 to the finished book at event 10. Note that even a six-week delay in preparing the cover will not delay the production process. However, *any* delay in an activity on the critical path will hold up publication. Thus, if necessary, resources could be diverted from cover preparation to, say, making up of pages or preparing pages for printing.

PERT (Program Evaluation and Review Technique) a scheduling technique that identifies the major activities necessary to complete a project and sequences them based on the time required to perform each one

critical path the sequence of production activities that takes the longest time from start to finish

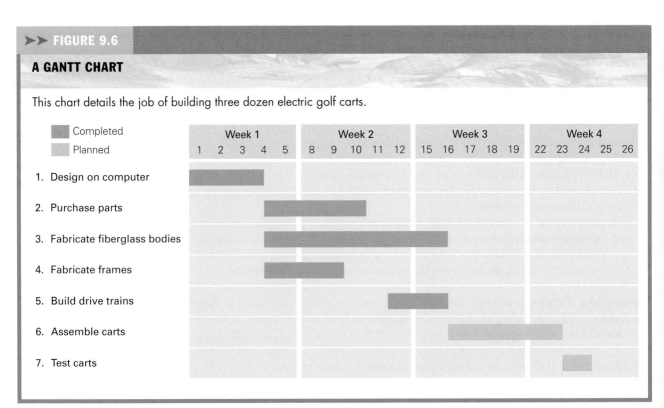

►► FIGURE 9.6

A GANTT CHART

This chart details the job of building three dozen electric golf carts.

Source: Robert Kreitner, *Management,* 9th ed. Copyright © 2004 by Houghton Mifflin Company. Reprinted with permission.

➤➤ **FIGURE 9.7**

SIMPLIFIED PERT DIAGRAM FOR PRODUCING THIS BOOK

A PERT diagram identifies the activities necessary to complete a given project and arranges the activities based on the total time required for each to become an event. The activities on the critical path determine the minimum time required.

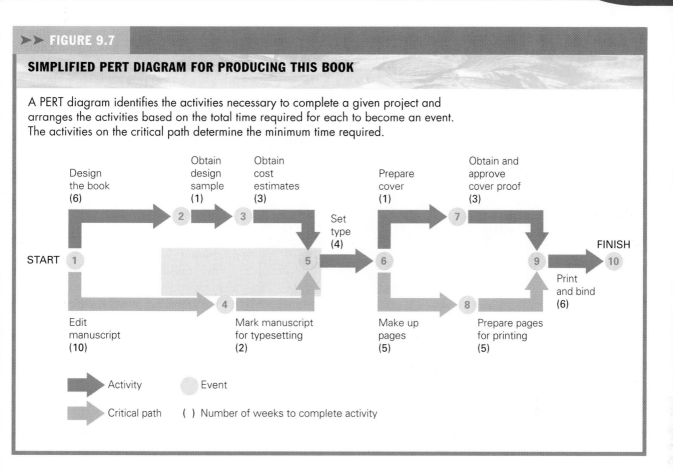

Quality Control

As mentioned earlier in this chapter, American business firms that compete in the very competitive global marketplace have taken another look at the importance of improving quality. Today there is even a national quality award. The **Malcolm Baldrige National Quality Award** is given by the President of the United States to organizations that apply and are judged to be outstanding in specific managerial tasks that lead to improved quality for both products and services. Winners include Texas Nameplate Company, Boeing, Motorola, 3M Dental Products Division, Richland Communtiy College (part of the Dallas Community College District), and many others. For many organizations, using the Baldrige criteria results in

- better employee relations,
- higher productivity,
- greater customer satisfaction,
- increased market share, and
- improved profitability.[11]

Malcolm Baldrige National Quality Award an award given by the President of the United States to organizations that apply and are judged to be outstanding in specific managerial tasks that lead to improved quality for both products and services

While winning the "Baldrige" can mean prestige and lots of free media coverage, the winners all have one factor in common: They use quality control to improve their firm's products or services.

Quality control is the process of ensuring that goods and services are produced in accordance with design specifications. The major objective of quality control is to see that the organization lives up to the standards it has set for itself on quality. Some firms, such as Mercedes-Benz and Neiman Marcus, have built their reputations on quality. Customers pay more for their products in return for assurances of high quality. Other firms adopt a strategy of emphasizing lower prices along with reasonable (but not particularly high) quality.

Many U.S. firms use two systems to gather statistical information about the quality of their products and study the way they operate. **Statistical process control**

quality control the process of ensuring that goods and services are produced in accordance with design specifications

statistical process control (SPC) a system that uses sampling to obtain data that are plotted on control charts and graphs to see if the production process is operating as it should and to pinpoint problem areas

Sometimes quality is a team effort. Customers who purchase Louis Vuitton leather goods expect high-quality products that are both stylish and worth the price. To ensure that its products are all high quality, Louis Vuitton employees are trained to inspect both work in progress and all finished products before they ever leave the firm's manufacturing facility in Ducey, France.

statistical quality control (SQC) a set of specific statistical techniques used to monitor all aspects of the production process to ensure that both work in progress and finished products meet the firm's quality standards

inspection the examination of the quality of work in process

Six Sigma a disciplined approach that relies on statistical data and improved methods to eliminate defects for a firm's products and services

quality circle a team of employees who meet on company time to solve problems of product quality

(SPC) is a system that uses sampling to obtain data that are plotted on control charts and graphs to see if the production process is operating as it should and to pinpoint problem areas. **Statistical quality control (SQC),** a similar technique, is a set of specific statistical techniques used to monitor all aspects of the production process to ensure that both work in progress and finished products meet the firm's quality standards. A firm can use the information provided by both these to correct problems in the production process and to improve the quality of its products.

Increased effort is also being devoted to **inspection,** which is the examination of the quality of work in process. Inspections are performed at various times during production. Purchased materials may be inspected when they arrive at the production facility. Subassemblies and manufactured parts may be inspected before they become part of a finished product. And finished goods may be inspected before they are shipped to customers. Items that are within design specifications continue on their way. Those that are not within design specifications are removed from production.

Improving Quality Through Employee Participation Historically, efforts to ensure quality increased the costs associated with making that good or service. For this reason, quality and productivity were viewed as conflicting: One was increased at the other's expense. Over the years, more and more managers have realized that quality is an essential "ingredient" of the good or service being provided. This view of quality provides several benefits. The number of defects decreases, which causes profits to increase. Making products right the first time reduces many of the rejects and much of the rework. And making employees responsible for quality often eliminates the need for inspection. An employee is indoctrinated to accept full responsibility for the quality of his or her work.

Because of increased global competition, many American manufacturers have adopted a goal that calls for better quality in their products. As noted in Chapter 7, a *total quality management* (TQM) program coordinates the efforts directed at improving customer satisfaction, increasing employee participation, strengthening supplier partnerships, and facilitating an organizational atmosphere of continuous quality improvement. Firms such as American Express, AT&T, Motorola, and Hewlett Packard all have used TQM to improve product quality and, ultimately, customer satisfaction. Another technique that businesses may use to improve not only quality but also overall performance is Six Sigma. **Six Sigma** is a disciplined approach that relies on statistical data and improved methods to eliminate defects for a firm's products and services. While many experts agree that Six Sigma is similar to TQM, Six Sigma often has more top-level support, more training for employees, much more teamwork, and a new corporate attitude or culture.[12] The companies that developed, refined, and have the most experience with Six Sigma are Motorola, General Electric, Allied Signal, and Honeywell. While each of these companies is a corporate giant, the underlying principles of Six Sigma can be used by all firms regardless of size. For more information about Six Sigma go to **www.isixsigma.com.**

The use of a **quality circle,** a team of employees who meet on company time to solve problems of product quality, is another way manufacturers are achieving better quality at the operations level. Quality circles have been used successfully in such companies as IBM, Northrop Grumman Corporation, and Compaq Computers.

World Quality Standards: ISO 9000 and ISO 14000 Different companies have different perceptions of quality. Without a common standard of quality, however, customers may be at the mercy of manufacturers and vendors. As the number of companies competing in the world marketplace has increased, so has the seriousness of this problem. To deal with it, the **International Organization for Standardization** (a nongovernmental organization in Geneva, Switzerland, with a membership of 156 countries) brought together a panel of quality experts to define what methods a company must use to produce a quality product.

In 1987, the panel published ISO 9000 (*iso* is Greek for "equal"), which sets the guidelines for quality management procedures that businesses must use to receive certification. This certification, issued by independent auditors, serves as evidence that a company meets the standards for quality control procedures in design, production processes, product testing, training of employees, record keeping, and correction of defects.

Although certification is not a legal requirement to do business globally, the organization's 156 member countries have approved the ISO standards. In fact, ISO 9000 is so prevalent in the European Community that many customers refuse to do business with noncertified companies. As an added bonus, companies completing the certification process often discover new, cost-efficient ways to improve their existing quality control programs.

As a continuation of this standardization process, the International Organization for Standardization has developed ISO 14000. ISO 14000 is a family of international standards for incorporating environmental concerns into operations and product standards. As with ISO 9000 certification, ISO 14000 requires that a company's procedures be documented by independent auditors. It also requires that a company develop an environmental management system that will help it to achieve environmental goals, objectives, and targets. Both the ISO 9000 and ISO 14000 family of standards are updated periodically. For example, ISO 9001:2000 reflects new standards for quality when compared with the original ISO standards.

International Organization for Standardization a nongovernmental organization in Geneva, Switzerland, with a membership of 156 countries that develops standards for products to facilitate trade across national borders

@ USING THE INTERNET

There are several web-based gateway sources of information and journals devoted to quality management and production issues such as the National Association of Manufacturers (**www.nam.org**), *Quality Digest* (**www.qualitydigest.com**), and *Industry Week* (**www.industryweek.com/**).

Management of Productivity and Technology

No coverage of production and operations management would be complete without a discussion of productivity. Productivity concerns all managers, but it is especially important to operations managers, the people who must oversee the creation of a firm's goods or services. We define **productivity** as the average level of output per worker per hour. Hence, if each worker at plant A produces seventy-five units per day and each worker at plant B produces only seventy units per day, the workers at plant A are more productive. If one bank teller serves twenty-five customers per hour and another serves twenty-eight per hour, the second teller is more productive.

6 LEARNING OBJECTIVE
Summarize how productivity and technology are related.

productivity the average level of output per worker per hour

Productivity Trends

Overall productivity growth for the business sector averaged 3.8 percent for the period 2001–2004.[13] More specifically, manufacturing productivity in 2004 increased 4.7 percent. (*Note:* At the time of publication, 2004 was the last year that complete statistics were available.) Our productivity growth rate was ranked the sixth-largest increase among the fourteen countries for which comparable data are available—the United States, Canada, Japan, Korea, Taiwan, Australia, and eight European countries. Our *rate of productivity growth* is lagging behind the productivity growth rates of such countries as Korea, Taiwan, Sweden, Japan, and the United Kingdom.[14]

Several factors have been cited as possible causes of the reduction in America's productivity growth rate. First, the economic slowdown the United States has experienced since 2000 and the terrorist attacks that occurred on September 11, 2001, have

Business Around the World

Steering Toward Higher Productivity

In the global drive for profits, Toyota, Nissan, and Honda are boosting productivity in their U.S. assembly plants to shave hundreds of dollars from each vehicle's manufacturing costs. General Motors, Ford, and Chrysler are also steering toward higher plant productivity to cut costs:

- *Toyota.* Toyota's average assembly time is just under 28 hours per vehicle, thanks to cutting-edge manufacturing systems and employees experienced in solving production glitches.
- *Nissan.* On average, Nissan can assemble a vehicle in under 30 hours. However, productivity is rising as its plants gain experience building new-model SUVs and pickup trucks.
- *Honda.* Honda plants need an average of 32 hours to build a vehicle—and they can change quickly to producing whatever models are most popular.
- *General Motors.* The U.S. automaker can assemble a vehicle, on average, in just over 34 hours.
- *Chrysler.* The U.S. division of DaimlerChrysler needs an average of nearly 36 hours to build a vehicle.
- *Ford.* Based on recent improvements, Ford can assemble a vehicle in approximately 37 hours.

caused many businesses to reduce the rate of investment in new equipment and technology. As workers have had to use increasingly outdated equipment, their ability to increase productivity has declined.

Another important factor that has hurt the U.S. productivity growth rate is the tremendous growth of the service sector in the United States. While this sector grew in the number of employees and economic importance, its productivity levels did not grow. Today, many economic experts agree that improving service-sector productivity is the next major hurdle facing U.S. business.

Finally, increased government regulation is frequently cited as a factor affecting productivity. Federal agencies such as the Occupational Safety and Health Administration (OSHA) and the Food and Drug Administration (FDA) are increasingly regulating business practices. Often the time employees spend complying with government reporting requirements can reduce productivity growth rates.

Improving Productivity Growth Rates

Several techniques and strategies have been suggested to improve current productivity growth rates. For example, various government policies that may be hindering productivity could be eliminated or at least modified.

In addition, increased cooperation between management and labor could improve productivity. When unions and management work together, quite often the result is improved productivity. In a related area, many managers believe that increased employee motivation and participation can enhance productivity.

Still another potential solution to productivity problems is to change the incentives for work. Many firms simply pay employees for their time, regardless of how much or how little they produce. By changing the reward system so that people are paid for what they contribute rather than for the time they put in, it may be possible to motivate employees to produce at higher levels.

Finally, business must invest more money in facilities, equipment, and employee training. There is hard evidence that investments in technological innovations are linked to job growth, higher employee wages, new products, *and* increased productivity. While building a new factory or purchasing new equipment does not guarantee that a firm's productivity will increase, many companies such as Ford Motor Company, Honeywell International, Deere & Company, and IBM have experienced dramatic increases in productivity when employees can use state-of-the-art equipment. Once a business has made a commitment to invest in facilities and equipment, the next step is to train employees to use the new equipment. In turn, the employees' ability to use new equipment and new technology will increase productivity. To see how different types of technology can improve productivity, read the next section.

The Impact of Computers and Robotics on Production

automation the total or near-total use of machines to do work

Automation, a development that has been revolutionizing the workplace, is the total or near-total use of machines to do work. The rapid increase in automated procedures has been made possible by the microprocessor, a silicon chip that led to the production of desktop computers for businesses, homes, and schools. In factories, microprocessors

Does this product meet design specifications? Today, firms use computers to aid in the design and manufacture of many products, including this jet engine. In this photo, an engineer compares a computer image that aided in the design of the engine with the actual product to determine if it meets or exceeds product design specifications.

are used in robotics and in computer manufacturing systems.

Robotics

Robotics is the use of programmable machines to perform a variety of tasks by manipulating materials and tools. Robots work quickly, accurately, and steadily. For example, Illumina, Inc., a San Diego company, uses robots to screen blood samples and identify DNA quirks that cause diseases. The information then is sold to some of the world's largest pharmaceutical companies, where it is used to alter existing prescription drugs, develop new drug therapies, and customize diagnoses and treatments for all kinds of serious diseases. As an added bonus, Illumina's robots can work 24 hours a day at much lower costs than if human lab workers performed the same tests.[15] Robots are especially effective in tedious, repetitive assembly-line jobs such as this, as well as in handling hazardous materials. They are also useful as artificial "eyes" that can check the quality of products as they are being processed on the assembly lines. To date, the automotive industry has made the most extensive use of robotics, but robots also have been used to mine coal, inspect the inner surfaces of pipes, assemble computer components, provide certain kinds of patient care in hospitals, and clean and guard buildings at night.

robotics the use of programmable machines to perform a variety of tasks by manipulating materials and tools

Computer Manufacturing Systems

People are quick to point out how computers have changed their everyday lives, but most people do not realize the impact computers have had on manufacturing. In simple terms, the factory of the future has already arrived. For most manufacturers, the changeover began with the use of computer-aided design and computer-aided manufacturing. **Computer-aided design (CAD)** is the use of computers to aid in the development of products. Using CAD, Ford speeds up car design, Canon designs new cameras and photocopiers, and American Greetings creates new birthday cards. **Computer-aided manufacturing (CAM)** is the use of computers to plan and control manufacturing processes. A well-designed CAM system allows manufacturers to become much more productive. Not only are a greater number of products produced, but speed and quality also increase. Toyota, Hasbro, Oneida, and Apple Computer all have used CAM to increase productivity.

computer-aided design (CAD) the use of computers to aid in the development of products

computer-aided manufacturing (CAM) the use of computers to plan and control manufacturing processes

If you are thinking that the next logical step is to combine the CAD and CAM computer systems, you are right. Today, the most successful manufacturers use CAD and CAM together to form a computer-integrated manufacturing system. Specifically, **computer-integrated manufacturing (CIM)** is a computer system that not only helps to design products but also controls the machinery needed to produce the finished product. For example, Liz Claiborne, Inc., uses CIM to design clothing, to establish patterns for new fashions, and then to cut the cloth needed to produce the finished product. Other advantages of using CIM include improved flexibility, more efficient scheduling, and higher product quality—all factors that make a production facility more

computer-integrated manufacturing (CIM) a computer system that not only helps to design products but also controls the machinery needed to produce the finished product

competitive in today's global economy. Furthermore, specialized management software from firms such as Maxager.com enables managers to optimize plant operations by providing information about manufacturing costs. Instead of simply guessing which product lines are most profitable, the software uses machinery performance data to analyze profits, including the opportunity costs of the machinery used to produce the products. As a result, client firms such as Motorola believe that paybacks in improved production schedules and the product-selection process are well worth the investment.[16]

Flexible Manufacturing Systems Manufacturers have known for a number of years that the old-style, traditional assembly lines used to manufacture products present a number of problems. For example, although traditional assembly lines turn out extremely large numbers of identical products economically, the system requires expensive, time-consuming retooling of equipment whenever a new product is to be manufactured. This type of manufacturing is often referred to as a continuous process. **Continuous process** is a manufacturing process in which a firm produces the same product(s) over a long period of time. Now it is possible to use flexible manufacturing systems to solve such problems. A **flexible manufacturing system (FMS)** combines robotics and computer-integrated manufacturing in a single production system. Instead of having to spend vast amounts of time and effort to retool the traditional mechanical equipment on an assembly line for each new product, an FMS is rearranged simply by reprogramming electronic machines. Because FMSs require less time and expense to reprogram, manufacturers can produce smaller batches of a variety of products without raising the production cost. Flexible manufacturing is sometimes referred to as an intermittent process. An **intermittent process** is a manufacturing process in which a firm's manufacturing machines and equipment are changed to produce different products. When compared with the continuous process (longer production runs), an intermittent process has a shorter production run.

For most manufacturers, the driving force behind flexible manufacturing systems is the customer. In fact, the term *customer-driven production* is often used by operations managers to describe a manufacturing system that is driven by customer needs and what customers want to buy. For example, advanced software and a flexible manufacturing system have enabled Dell Computer to change to a more customer-driven manufacturing process. The process starts when a customer phones a sales representative on a toll-free line or accesses Dell's website. Then the representative or the customer enters the specifications for the new product directly into a computer. The order then is sent to a nearby plant. Once the order is received, a team of employees with the help of a reprogrammable assembly line can build the product just the way the customer wants it. Products include desktop computers, notebook computers, and other Dell equipment.[17] Although the costs of designing and installing an FMS such as this are high, the electronic equipment is used more frequently and efficiently than the machinery on a traditional assembly line.

Technological Displacement Automation is increasing productivity by cutting manufacturing time, reducing error, and simplifying retooling procedures. Many of the robots being developed for use in manufacturing will not replace human employees. Rather, these robots will work with employees in making their jobs easier and help to prevent accidents. No one knows, however, what the effect will be on the work force. Some experts estimate that automation will bring new changes to more than half of all jobs within the next ten years. Total unemployment may not increase, but many workers will be faced with the choice of retraining for new jobs or seeking jobs in other sectors of the economy. Government, business, and education will have to cooperate to prepare workers for new roles in an automated workplace.

The next chapter discusses many of the issues caused by technological displacement. In addition, a number of major components of human resources management are described, and we see how managers use various reward systems to boost motivation, productivity, and morale.

continuous process a manufacturing process in which a firm produces the same product(s) over a long period of time

flexible manufacturing system (FMS) a single production system that combines robotics and computer-integrated manufacturing

intermittent process a manufacturing process in which a firm's manufacturing machines and equipment are changed to produce different products

RETURN TO   Inside Business

Hyundai Motor has used strict quality control to improve its public image and its sales in the United States. In addition to its long-term goal of selling one million cars annually in the United States, the company has a worldwide goal of overtaking Toyota as the world's top-quality automaker. To achieve these ambitious targets, Hyundai has invested billions of dollars in computer-aided design facilities and highly automated assembly plants. For example, the recently opened Alabama plant uses computer-aided manufacturing to produce Sonata sedans and Santa Fe SUVs.

Hyundai's top executives personally inspect new vehicle designs and prototypes to check the quality of even the smallest detail, such as the gearshift lever. They are keenly aware that maintaining a reputation for quality will allow Hyundai to broaden its appeal and move into higher-profit products such as upscale sedans. According to Hyundai's management team, "We will make ourselves an invincible competitor".

Questions

1. What competitive factors led to Hyundai's decision to improve product quality?
2. Why would assigning engineers, designers, and plant managers to create new vehicles as a team improve manufacturing productivity as well as product quality?

▶▶ CHAPTER REVIEW

Summary

1

Explain the nature of production.

Operations management consists of all the activities that managers engage in to create goods and services. Operations are as relevant to service organizations as to manufacturing firms. Generally, three major activities are involved in producing goods or services: product development, planning for production, and operations control. Today, U.S. manufacturers are forced to compete in an ever-smaller world to meet the needs of more demanding customers. In an attempt to regain a competitive edge, they have taken another look at the importance of improving quality and meeting the needs of their customers. They also have used new techniques to motivate employees, reduced production costs, replaced outdated equipment, used computer-aided and flexible manufacturing systems, improved control procedures, and built new manufacturing facilities in foreign countries where labor costs are lower. Competing in the global economy is not only profitable, but it is also an essential activity that requires the cooperation of everyone within an organization.

2

Outline how the conversion process transforms raw materials, labor, and other resources into finished products or services.

A business transforms resources into goods and services in order to provide utility to customers. Utility is the ability of a good or service to satisfy a human need. Form utility is created by converting raw materials, people, finances, and information into finished products. Conversion processes vary in terms of the major resources used to produce goods and services (focus), the degree to which resources are changed (magnitude), and the number of production processes that a business uses. The application of the basic principles of operations management to the production of services has coincided with the growth and importance of service businesses in the United States.

3

Describe how research and development lead to new products and services.

Operations management often begins with product research and development (R&D). The results of R&D may be entirely new products or extensions and refinements of existing products. R&D activities are classified as basic research (aimed at uncovering new knowledge), applied research (discovering new knowledge with some potential use), and development and implementation (using new or existing knowledge to produce goods and services). If a firm sells only one product, when that product reaches the end of its life cycle, the firm will die, too. To stay in business, the firm must, at the very least, find ways to refine or extend the want-satisfying capability of its product.

Discuss the components involved in planning the production process.

Planning for production involves three major phases: design planning, facilities planning and site selection, and operational planning. First, design planning is undertaken to address questions related to the product line, required production capacity, and the use of technology. Production facilities, site selection, human resources, and plant layout, then must be considered. Operational planning focuses on the use of production facilities and resources. The steps for operational planning include (a) selecting a planning horizon, (b) estimating market demand, (c) comparing market demand with capacity, and (d) adjusting production of products or services to meet demand.

Explain how purchasing, inventory control, scheduling, and quality control affect production.

The major areas of operations control are purchasing, inventory control, scheduling, and quality control. Purchasing involves selecting suppliers. The choice of suppliers should result from careful analysis of a number of factors, including price, quality, reliability, credit terms, and shipping costs. Inventory control is the management of stocks of raw materials, work in process, and finished goods to minimize the total inventory cost. Today, most firms use a computerized system to maintain inventory records. In addition, many firms use a just-in-time inventory system, in which materials or supplies arrive at a facility just when they are needed so that storage and holding costs are minimized. Scheduling ensures that materials and other resources are at the right place at the right time—for use within the facility or for shipment to customers. Both Gantt charts and PERT can be used to improve a firm's ability to schedule the production of products. Quality control guarantees that products meet the design specifications for those products. The major objective of quality control is to see that the organization lives up to the standards it has set for itself on quality. Some firms, such as Mercedes-Benz and Neiman Marcus, have built their reputations on quality. Customers pay more for their products in return for assurances of high quality. Other firms adopt a strategy of emphasizing lower prices along with reasonable (but not particularly high) quality.

Summarize how productivity and technology are related.

The productivity growth rate in the United States has fallen behind the pace of growth in some of the other industrialized nations in recent years. Several factors have been cited as possible causes for this disturbing trend, and managers have begun to explore solutions for overcoming them. Possible solutions include less government regulation, increased cooperation between management and labor, increased employee motivation and participation, new incentives for work, and additional investment by business to fund new or renovated facilities, equipment, employee training, and the use of technology.

Automation, the total or near-total use of machines to do work, has for some years been changing the way work is done in U.S. factories. A growing number of industries are using programmable machines called robots to perform tasks that are tedious or hazardous to human beings. Computer-aided design, computer-aided manufacturing, and computer-integrated manufacturing use computers to help design and manufacture products. The flexible manufacturing system combines robotics and computer-integrated manufacturing to produce smaller batches of products more efficiently than on the traditional assembly line. Instead of having to spend vast amounts of time and effort to retool the traditional mechanical equipment on an assembly line for each new product, an FMS is rearranged simply by reprogramming electronic machines. Because FMSs require less time and expense to reprogram, manufacturers can produce smaller batches of a variety of products without raising the production cost.

Key Terms

You should now be able to define and give an example relevant to each of the following terms:

operations management (277)
mass production (278)
analytical process (278)
synthetic process (278)
utility (279)
form utility (279)
service economy (280)
research and development (R&D) (282)
design planning (283)
product line (284)
product design (284)
capacity (284)
labor-intensive technology (285)
capital-intensive technology (285)
plant layout (286)
planning horizon (288)
purchasing (289)
inventory control (290)
materials requirements planning (MRP) (290)

Review Questions

1. List all the activities involved in operations management.
2. What is the difference between an analytical and a synthetic manufacturing process? Give an example of each type of process.
3. In terms of focus, magnitude, and number, characterize the production processes used by a local pizza parlor, a dry-cleaning establishment, and an auto repair shop.
4. Describe how research and development lead to new products.
5. Explain why product extension and refinement are important.
6. What are the major elements of design planning?
7. What factors should be considered when selecting a site for a new manufacturing facility?
8. What is the objective of operational planning? What four steps are used to accomplish this objective?

9. If you were an operations manager, what would you do if market demand exceeded the production capacity of your manufacturing facility? What action would you take if the production capacity of your manufacturing facility exceeded market demand?
10. Why is selecting a supplier so important?
11. What costs must be balanced and minimized through inventory control?
12. How can materials requirements planning (MRP), manufacturing resource planning (MRP II), and enterprise resource planning (ERP) help to control inventory and a company's production processes?
13. How does the just-in-time-inventory system help to reduce inventory costs?
14. Explain in what sense scheduling is a *control* function of operations managers.
15. How can management and employees use statistical process control, statistical quality control, inspection, and quality circles to improve a firm's products?
16. How might productivity be measured in a restaurant? In a department store? In a public school system?
17. How can CIM and FMS help a manufacturer to produce products?

Discussion Questions

1. Why would Rubbermaid—a successful U.S. company—need to expand and sell its products to customers in foreign countries?
2. Do certain kinds of firms need to stress particular areas of operations management? Explain.
3. Is it really necessary for service firms to engage in research and development? In planning for production and operations control?
4. How are the four areas of operations control interrelated?
5. In what ways can employees help to improve the quality of a firm's products?
6. Is operations management relevant to nonbusiness organizations such as colleges and hospitals? Why or why not?

►► VIDEO CASE 9.1

Cutting-Edge Production at Remington

Remington—long known for its shavers—has been associated with a number of manufacturing "firsts." It produced the first commercial typewriter in 1873, the first electric dry shaver in 1937, and the first cordless shaver in 1960. In fact, one of the best-remembered ads of the 1980s featured then-owner Victor Kiam shaving with a Remington shaver while saying to the camera, "I liked the shaver so much, I bought the company." Despite several changes in ownership, management, and focus, once the company began making shavers, it never stopped. In

2003, Remington was acquired by Spectrum Brands, which also owns Rayovac batteries, Vigoro lawn-care products, and many other name-brand products.

Today, Remington offers a wide variety of electric shavers, hair trimmers, hair dryers, curling irons, and other small appliances for personal grooming. Its products are available in North and South America, Europe, Asia, Australia, and New Zealand, where the company's products are sold through drug, department, and discount stores, as well as through online retailers. The company's website not only provides product and service details, but it also invites customers to click and buy direct from the manufacturer.

Remington uses marketing research to gain an in-depth understanding of its customers' needs so as to develop new technology and product designs to meet those needs. Its products have changed dramatically over the years, but not men's beards. Yet what men and women are looking for in shavers has evolved over time. For example, knowing that some women prefer to shave in the shower or bath and others prefer to shave before or after bathing, Remington has introduced a line of wet/dry shavers. For maximum convenience and flexibility, some of these shavers operate on household batteries, whereas others are recharged using an electric adapter. Other trends affecting Remington's product lineup are changing lifestyles and an aging population.

New products, new technology, and new production methods are all helping Remington meet the needs of customers all over the world. In fact, new technology is just as important as product styling. Not long ago Remington won a favorable ruling from the European Court of Justice in a battle over three-headed rotary razors. Philips trademarked the three-headed design in the 1960s. Decades later, it sued Remington for introducing a three-headed razor of its own, saying that three heads were part of the Philips brand. Remington won by arguing that a trademark cannot cover improved technical performance. In other words, although the hourglass Coca-Cola bottle does not improve the beverage's taste, the three-headed design does improve a razor's shaving ability.

Once Remington has completed a new design, the product is manufactured and assembled overseas. Some products may have up to a hundred components, which adds complexity to the production process. Nonetheless, the company continues to make the cutting parts in the United States so that it has tighter control over quality. Using specialized machinery, production workers punch blades out of steel and make cutters out of miles of aluminum coil. One shaver may require as many as seventy-five blades and three cutters, carefully manufactured, ground for sharpness, and tested before assembly.

To meet global demand for Remington shavers, the plant must turn out one million blades per day. Therefore, plant managers must plan in advance to buy and store supplies and materials, have everything in place when and where needed, and inspect the finished blades to ensure quality. Then the blades go to the foreign factories, where they are incorporated into shavers and trimmers. After production is complete, the finished products are transported to an international network of independent distributors for delivery to retail outlets in dozens of countries.

Under Spectrum Brands, Remington has moved its blade production from Connecticut to Wisconsin. The parent company employs 10,000 people worldwide and rings up nearly $3 billion in annual sales. Remington continues to be a strong competitor to Braun, Philips, Panasonic, and other makers of electric shaving products. However, now that Braun has the financial and marketing power of Procter & Gamble behind it, Remington will face even greater competitive challenges in the coming years. To keep sales and profits growing, the company must keep introducing innovative products to meet customer needs and continue to fine-tune its production methods for ever-higher productivity and quality.[18]

For more information about this company, go to **www.remington-products.com.**

Questions

1. Which plant layout would you suggest that Remington use when making blades in its U.S. factory? Why?
2. Why would Remington choose to produce only blades in the United States rather than assembling entire shavers as well?
3. What is the focus of the conversion process in Remington's U.S. factory?

▸▸ CASE 9.2

Bank of America Banks on Superstringent Quality

Bank of America has a "secret weapon" for quality control: Six Sigma. This superstringent approach to quality can reduce the number of mistakes or defects in the production and delivery of goods and services to a mere 3.4 defects per *million* units. At this level, 99.99966 percent of the output is perfect. Just as important, Six Sigma helps companies to focus on improving the quality of operations that affect customers.

Six Sigma, popularized by manufacturers such as Motorola, General Electric, Allied Signal, and Honeywell, has spread to many other industries in recent years. Yet Bank of America is one of the few banking giants to adopt the process on a large scale. Why? Part of the reason is the difficulty in using statistics to measure quality in the context of customer relationships. As a Bank of America senior vice president explains: "It's often harder to measure some of the attributes of financial services. It's not as tangible as a product."

The bank decided to examine specific business processes that touch its customers in a significant way. One operation that makes a big difference to many small businesses and consumers is how quickly deposits are posted to their accounts. Because banks typically don't post deposits made after 2 p.m. until the following day, customers usually don't have immediate access to their money. Bank of America used Six Sigma techniques to identify and eliminate bottlenecks in back-office processing operations so that it could credit late-afternoon deposits on the same day. Now customers who make deposits at a branch as late as 5 p.m. can count on seeing these transactions posted the same day.

Six Sigma has helped Bank of America improve quality in many areas. For example, its research showed that online banking customers wanted to be able to view account credits and debits just a few minutes after completing a transaction. The bank used Six Sigma to analyze its functions and determine how to add this feature. Once the new capability was in place, the bank conducted another survey and found that 77 percent of its online banking customers reported higher satisfaction. Moreover, because these customers could get more information online, they didn't visit or call local branches as often—which cut Bank of America's costs by nearly $4 million a year.

Since 2001, Bank of America has boosted its bottom line by more than $2 billion and increased both customer satisfaction and loyalty by applying Six Sigma techniques. "What we're finding is that by improving quality of service, customers have fewer problems, and that makes them more loyal to us," notes Bank of America's quality and productivity executive. And satisfied customers tell their friends. Referrals from current customers brought Bank of America 500,000 new accounts during its second year of Six Sigma activity, 1.2 million new accounts during the third year, and 2 million new accounts during the fourth year.

To find out whether the bank is delivering the highest level of service quality day in and day out, it surveys 90,000 branch customers every year and conducts telephone interviews with 10,000 customers every three months. Managers also get immediate feedback from the thousands of calls placed to customer service centers every day. "It's a great learning tool and a building block for us to deliver better processes," says Randall King, a senior vice president.

Still, with 5,900 branches, Bank of America operates the largest branch system in the United States. An organization of that size can always find one more process to fine-tune or one more problem to solve. This is why the bank encourages employees to share their successes at an annual Best of Six Sigma Expo.[19]

For more information about this company, go to **www.bankofamerica.com.**

Questions

1. The Six Sigma approach uses statistical data and improved operating methods to eliminate defects for a firm's products or services. What type of "defects" would a bank want to eliminate? Explain your answer.
2. What effect has Six Sigma had on Bank of America's productivity and customer satisfaction?
3. What criteria should the bank use to select projects for the Best of Six Sigma Expo? Why?

→ CHAPTER 9: JOURNAL EXERCISE

Discovery statement: Today, people purchase all kinds of products ranging from inexpensive items used everyday to expensive, sophisticated products including electronics, automobiles, and even housing. In each case, customers like to think they are "getting their money's worth" when they purchase a product or service.

Describe a recent purchase that you made. Be sure to include the cost and why you made the purchase.

_____

_____

_____

_____

Given the cost of the product or service, were you satisfied? Why?

_____

_____

_____

_____

_____

Do you think that the quality of this product or service was acceptable or unacceptable? Explain your answer.

_____

_____

_____

_____

_____

How could the manufacturer or provider of the service improve the quality of the product or service?

_____

_____

_____

_____

_____

BUILDING SKILLS FOR CAREER SUCCESS

1. Exploring the Internet

Improvements in the quality of products and services is an ever-popular theme in business management. Besides the obvious increase to profitability to be gained by such improvements, a company's demonstration of its continuous search for ways to improve operations can be a powerful statement to customers, suppliers, and investors. Two of the larger schools of thought in this field are Six Sigma and the European-based International Organization for Standardization. Visit the text website for updates to this exercise.

Assignment

1. Use Internet search engines to find more information about each of these topics.

2. From the information on the Internet, can you tell whether there is any real difference between these two approaches?

3. Describe one success story of a firm that realized improvement by adopting either approach.

2. Developing Critical-Thinking Skills

Plant layout—the arrangement of machinery, equipment, and personnel within a production facility—is a critical ingredient in a company's success. If the layout is inefficient, productivity and, ultimately, profits will suffer. The purpose of the business dictates the type of layout that will be most efficient. There are three general types: process layout, product layout, and fixed-position layout.

Assignment

1. For each of the following businesses, identify the best type of layout:

   One-hour dry cleaner
   Health club
   Auto repair shop
   Fast-food restaurant
   Shipyard that builds supertankers
   Automobile assembly plant

2. Prepare a two-page report explaining why you chose these layouts and why proper plant layout is important.

3. Building Team Skills

Suppose that you are planning to build a house in the country. It will be a brick, one-story structure of approximately 2,000 square feet, centrally heated and cooled. It will have three bedrooms, two bathrooms, a family room, a dining room, a kitchen with a breakfast nook, a study, a utility room, an entry foyer, a two-car garage, a covered patio, and a fireplace. Appliances will operate on electricity and propane fuel. You have received approval and can be connected to the cooperative water system at any time. Public sewerage services are not available; therefore, you must rely on a septic system. You want to know how long it will take to build the house.

Assignment

1. Identify the major activities involved in the project, and sequence them in the proper order.

2. Estimate the time required for each activity, and establish the critical path.

3. Working in a group, prepare a PERT diagram to show the steps involved in building your house.

4. Present your PERT diagram to the class, and ask for comments and suggestions.

4. Researching Different Careers

Because service businesses are now such a dominant part of our economy, job seekers sometimes overlook the employment opportunities available in production plants. Two positions often found in these plants are quality control inspector and purchasing agent.

Assignment

1. Using the *Occupational Outlook Handbook* at your local library or on the Internet (**http://stats.bls.gov/oco/home.htm**), find the following information for the jobs of quality control inspector and purchasing agent:

   Job description, including main activities and responsibilities
   Job outlook
   Earnings and working conditions
   Training and qualifications

2. Look for other production jobs that may interest you, and compile the same sort of information about them.

3. Summarize in a two-page report the key things you learned about jobs in production plants.

5. Improving Communication Skills

Total quality management (TQM) is a much broader concept than just controlling the quality of a single product. It is a philosophy that places quality at the center of everything a company does. In particular, TQM is aimed at improving customer satisfaction, increasing employee participation, strengthening supplier partnerships, and facilitating an organizational atmosphere of continuous quality improvement. For TQM to work successfully, it must start with a company's mission statement, be ingrained in the company's goals and objectives, and be implemented through the strategies that ultimately satisfy customer needs. Today, many companies use TQM.

Assignment

1. Read articles or use the Internet to find out how at least two different companies implement TQM.

2. Prepare a three-page report on your findings. The report should include answers to the following questions:

   a. Exactly how does each company focus on quality?

   b. How are the TQM programs of these two companies alike? How do they differ?

   c. How will TQM influence their operations in the twenty-first century?

   d. Using quality as a criterion, which company would you rather work for? Why?

→ PREP TEST

Matching Questions

___ 1. It is a process for converting a product idea into an actual product.

___ 2. Raw materials are broken into different components.

___ 3. Its focus is minimizing holding costs and potential stock-out costs.

___ 4. It is created by converting materials, people, finances, and information into finished goods.

___ 5. A set of statistical techniques that is used to monitor all aspects of the production process.

___ 6. Work is accomplished mostly by equipment.

___ 7. Input from workers is used to improve the workplace.

___ 8. Output per unit of time is measured per worker.

___ 9. Computers are the main tool used in the development of products.

___ 10. Supplies arrive when needed to minimize storage and holding costs.

a. analytical process
b. capital-intensive technology
c. computer-aided design
d. design planning
e. form utility
f. inventory control
g. just-in-time inventory system
h. productivity
i. quality circle
j. statistical quality control (SQC)

True/False Questions

T F

11. ○ ○ Capacity is the degree to which input resources are physically changed by the conversion process.

12. ○ ○ The rise-and-decline pattern of sales for an existing product is called the product life cycle.

13. ○ ○ Operations management is the process of creating a set of specifications from which the product can be produced.

14. ○ ○ A purchasing agent need not worry about a tiny difference in price when a large quantity is being bought.

15. ○ ○ The critical path is the shortest path through the sequence of activities in a PERT diagram.

T F

16. ○ ○ When workstations are arranged to match the sequence of operations, a process layout is being used.

17. ○ ○ Work-in-process inventories are completed goods awaiting shipment to customers.

18. ○ ○ The purpose of research and development is to identify new ideas that have the potential to result in new goods and services.

19. ○ ○ For a food-processing plant such as Kraft Foods, capacity refers to the number of employees working on an assembly line.

20. ○ ○ Labor-intensive technology is accompanied by low initial costs and high operating costs.

Multiple-Choice Questions

21. One worker in Department A produces forty-five units of work per day on a computer, whereas a coworker produces only forty units of work per day on a computer. Since the first worker produces more units, that worker has a
    a. lower capacity to use technology.
    b. higher productivity rate.
    c. desire to help the coworker.
    d. computer-integrated system.
    e. computer-aided system.

22. Services differ from the production of manufactured goods in all ways *except* that services
    a. are consumed immediately and cannot be stored.
    b. aren't as important as manufactured products to the U.S. economy.
    c. are provided when and where the customer desires the service.
    d. are usually labor-intensive.
    e. are intangible, and it's more difficult to evaluate customer service.

23. The goal of basic research is to
    a. uncover new knowledge without regard for its potential use.
    b. discover new knowledge with regard for potential use in development.
    c. discover knowledge for potential use.
    d. put new or existing knowledge to use.
    e. combine ideas.

24. Two important components of scheduling are
    a. lead time and planning.
    b. designing and arranging.
    c. monitoring and controlling.
    d. place and time.
    e. logistics and flow.

25. A common planning horizon for production activities is
    a. one day.
    b. a week.
    c. a month.
    d. six months.
    e. one year.

Fill-In the Blank Questions

26. A scheduling tool displaying tasks on the vertical axis and time requirements on the horizontal axis is called a/an _____ chart.

27. A _____ manufacturing system combines robotics and computer-integrated manufacturing in a single-production system.

28. The process of acquiring materials, supplies, components, and parts from other firms is known as _____.

29. Statistical _____ control plots data on charts to help identify problems.

30. The amount of products that a firm can produce in a given time is called _____.

Online Study Center

FOR MORE **test practice, use the interactive ACE quizzes available at the Online Student Center:**
www.college.hmco.com/PIC/pridebusiness9e.

Answers on p. PT1.

Finagle A Bagel's Management, Organization, and Production Finesse

"We don't have a traditional corporate organizational chart," states Heather Robertson, Finagle A Bagel's director of marketing, human resources, and research and development. When she hires new employees, Robertson draws the usual type of organization chart showing the copresidents on the top and the store employees on the bottom. Then she turns it upside down, explaining: "The most important people in our stores are the crew members, and the store manager's role is to support those crew members. Middle management's role is to support the store managers. And the copresidents' responsibility is to support us," referring to herself and her middle-management colleagues.

In short, the copresidents and all the people in corporate headquarters work as a team to help the general managers (who run the stores) and their crew members. Every store strives to achieve preset sales goals within budget guidelines. Higher-level managers are available to help any general manager whose store's performance falls outside the expected ranges. Moreover, each general manager is empowered to make decisions that will boost sales and make the most of opportunities to build positive relationships with local businesses and community organizations. "We want our general managers to view the store as their business," copresident Laura Trust emphasizes. "If a general manager wants to do something that will alleviate a store problem or increase sales, we give him [or her] the leeway to do it."

Many Bagels, One Factory

Although the copresidents decentralized authority for many store-level decisions, they achieved more efficiency by centralizing the authority and responsibility for food procurement and preparation. For example, headquarters handles payroll, invoices, and many other time-consuming activities on behalf of all the stores. This reduces the paperwork burden on general managers and frees them to concentrate on managing store-level food service to satisfy customers.

Finagle A Bagel also decided to centralize production and supply functions in its recently opened Newton headquarters, where the factory has enough capacity to supply up to 100 stores. "We outgrew our old facility, and we wanted to find some place we could expand our operations," copresident Laura Trust explains. Production employees prepare and shape dough for 100,000 bagels and mix 2,000 pounds of flavored cream cheese spreads every day. In addition, they slice 1,500 pounds of fruit every week. Then they gather whatever each store needs—raw dough, salad fixings, packages of condiments, or plastic bowls—and load it on the truck for daily delivery.

Baking Bagels and More

Once the raw dough reaches a store, crew members follow the traditional New York–style method of boiling and baking bagels in various varieties, ranging from year-round favorites such as sesame to seasonal offerings such as pumpkin raisin. In line with Finagle A Bagel's fresh-food concept, the stores bake bagels every hour and tumble them into a line of bins near the front counter. Each store has a unique piece of equipment, dubbed the "bagel buzz saw," to slice and move bagels to the sandwich counter after customers have placed their orders. This equipment not only helps to prevent employee accidents and speeds food preparation, but it also entertains customers as they wait for their sandwiches.

Finagle A Bagel is constantly introducing new menu items to bring customers back throughout the day. One item the company has perfected is the bagel pizza. Earlier bagel pizzas turned out soggy, but the newest breakfast pizzas are both crunchy and tasty. The central production facility starts by mixing egg bagel dough, forms it into individual flat breads, grills the rounds, and ships them to the stores. There, a crew member tops each round with the customer's choice of ingredients, heats it, and serves it toasty fresh.

Managing a Bagel Restaurant

Finagle A Bagel's general managers stay busy from the early morning, when they open the store and help crew members to get ready for customers, to the time they close the store at night after one last look to see whether everything is in order for the next day. General managers such as Paulo Pereira, who runs the Harvard Square Finagle A Bagel in Cambridge, must have the technical skills required to run a fast-paced food-service operation.

General managers also need good conceptual skills so that they can look beyond each individual employee and task to see how everything should fit together. One way Pereira does this is by putting himself in the customer's shoes. He is constantly evaluating how customers would judge the in-store experience, from courteous, attentive counter service to the availability of fresh foods, clean tables, and well-stocked condiment containers.

Just as important, Pereira—like other Finagle A Bagel general managers—must have excellent interpersonal skills to work effectively with customers, crew members, colleagues, and higher-level managers. Pereira knows that he can't be successful without being able to work well with other people, especially those he supervises. "You need to have a good crew behind you to help you every single hour of the day," he says. "Every employee needs to feel special and appreciated. I try to treat employees as fairly as possible, and I try to accommodate their needs."

Questions

1. What does Finagle A Bagel's upside-down organization chart suggest about the delegation of authority and coordination techniques within the company?
2. Is Finagle A Bagel a tall or flat organization? How do you know?
3. What values seem to permeate Finagle A Bagel's corporate culture?
4. Why would Finagle A Bagel build a dough factory that has more capacity than the company needs to supply its stores and its wholesale customers?

BUILDING A BUSINESS PLAN PART III

Now you should be ready to provide evidence that you have a management team with the necessary skills and experience to execute your business plan successfully. Only a competent management team can transform your vision into a successful business. You also should be able to describe your manufacturing and operations plans. The three chapters in Part 3 of your textbook, "Understanding the Management Process," "Creating a Flexible Organization," and "Producing Quality Goods and Services," should help you in answering some of the questions in this part of the business plan.

The Management Team Component

The management team component should include the answers to at least the following questions:

3.1. How is your team balanced in technical, conceptual, interpersonal, and other special skills needed in your business?
3.2. What will be your style of leadership?
3.3. How will your company be structured? Include a statement of the philosophy of management and company culture.
3.4. What are the key management positions, compensation, and key policies?
3.5. Include a job description for each management position, and specify who will fill that position. *Note:* Prepare an organization chart and provide the résumé of each key manager for the appendix.
3.6. What other professionals, such as a lawyer, an insurance agent, a banker, and a certified public accountant, will you need for assistance?

The Manufacturing and Operations Plans Component

If you are in a manufacturing business, now is a good time to describe your manufacturing and operations plans, space requirements, equipment, labor force, inventory control, and purchasing requirements. Even if you are in a service-oriented business, many of these questions still may apply.

The manufacturing and operations plan component should include the answers to at least the following questions:

3.7. What are the advantages and disadvantages of your planned location in terms of

- Wage rates
- Unionization
- Labor pool
- Proximity to customers and suppliers
- Types of transportation available
- Tax rates
- Utility costs
- Zoning requirements

3.8. What facilities does your business require? Prepare a floor plan for the appendix. Will you rent, lease, or purchase the facilities?
3.9. Will you make or purchase component parts to be assembled into the finished product? Make sure to justify your "make-or-buy decision."
3.10. Who are your potential subcontractors and suppliers?
3.11. How will you control quality, inventory, and production? How will you measure your progress?
3.12. Is there a sufficient quantity of adequately skilled people in the local labor force to meet your needs?

Review of Business Plan Activities

Be sure to go over the information you have gathered. Check for any weaknesses, and resolve them before beginning Part 4. Also review all the answers to the questions in Parts 1, 2, and 3 to be certain that all answers are consistent throughout the entire business plan. Finally, write a brief statement that summarizes all the information for this part of the business plan.

309

Part 4

Human Resources

This part of *Business* is concerned with the most important and least predictable of all resources—people. We begin by examining the human resources efforts that organizations use to hire, develop, and retain their best employees. Then we discuss employee motivation and satisfaction. Finally, we look at organized labor and probe the sometimes controversial relationship between business management and labor unions.

Attracting and Retaining the Best Employees

LEARNING OBJECTIVES

WHAT you will be able to do once you complete this chapter:

1 Describe the major components of human resources management.

2 Identify the steps in human resources planning.

3 Describe cultural diversity and understand some of the challenges and opportunities associated with it.

4 Explain the objectives and uses of job analysis.

5 Describe the processes of recruiting, employee selection, and orientation.

6 Discuss the primary elements of employee compensation and benefits.

7 Explain the purposes and techniques of employee training, development, and performance appraisal.

8 Outline the major legislation affecting human resources management.

WHY this chapter matters

Being able to understand how to attract and keep the right people is crucial. Also, you can better understand about your own interactions with your coworkers.

FOR HELP with studying this chapter, visit the Online Student Center:

www.college.hmco.com/PIC/pridebusiness9e

Online Study Center

The makeup of the McDonald's work force—from burger builders to board members—shows the world's largest restaurant chain as a diversity leader. Mirroring the communities in which it operates, McDonald's hires people of every race and ethnicity, as well as people with disabilities. Women are well represented at all levels—nearly half of McDonald's middle managers are women—and seniors often work alongside teenagers.

DID YOU KNOW?

Companies such as McDonald's go to considerable efforts to have a diverse work force.

"We have a tremendous diversity," confirms Don Thompson, executive vice president and chief operations officer for McDonald's. As a result, the company has "an even stronger ability to tap into and respond to the diversity that our customers represent." In fact, the company's policy of inclusion extends beyond the work force. No other fast-food company has as many minority and women franchisees. What's more, the company buys $3 billion worth of goods and services every year from suppliers owned by women and minorities.

McDonald's launched its diversity strategy thirty years ago, with a series of seminars to educate employees about ongoing changes in the work force. This diversity training has been offered, with updates and revisions, ever since. Next, the company began offering career-development workshops especially for women, African-American, Hispanic, and Asian employees, later adding a White Male Forum. McDonald's also instituted a GenderSpeak program to address differences in male-female communication.

On their own, employees have been forming groups such as the Home Office Asian Network and McDonald's Black Employee Network. When the company formalized its diversity plans, these networks joined together to become the National McDonald's Diversity Advisory Council. Today the group, which includes franchisees and suppliers, meets regularly to discuss new diversity initiatives. Pat Harris, McDonald's chief diversity officer, notes that diversity is "the right thing to do"—but "it's also a business imperative."[1]

For more information about this company, go to **www.mcdonalds.com.**

i'm lovin' it™

McDonald's encourages the hiring and training of employees with diverse ethnic backgrounds. Hiring a diverse mix of employees helps the company to serve a diverse customer base. For many companies, these are important factors to consider when attracting, motivating, and retaining the appropriate mix of human resources.

We begin our study of human resources management (HRM) with an overview of how businesses acquire, maintain, and develop their human resources. After listing the steps by which firms match their human resources needs with the supply available, we explore several dimensions of cultural diversity. Then we examine the concept of job analysis. Next, we focus on a firm's recruiting, selection, and orientation procedures as the means of acquiring employees. We also describe forms of employee compensation that motivate employees to remain with a firm and to work effectively. Then we discuss methods of employee training, management development, and performance appraisal. Finally, we consider legislation that affects HRM practices.

Human Resources Management: An Overview

human resources management (HRM) all the activities involved in acquiring, maintaining, and developing an organization's human resources

The human resource is not only unique and valuable, but it is also an organization's most important resource. It seems logical that an organization would expend a great deal of effort to acquire and make full use of such a resource. This effort is known as *human resources management* (HRM). It also has been called *staffing* and *personnel management*.

Human resources management (HRM) consists of all the activities involved in acquiring, maintaining, and developing an organization's human resources. As the definition implies, HRM begins with acquisition—getting people to work for the organization. The acquisition process can be quite competitive for certain types of qualified employees. For example, brokerage houses such as JPMorgan, Citigroup, and Merrill Lynch are building their specialized algorithmic-trading teams by recruiting experienced employees from other brokerage firms.[2] Next, steps must be taken to keep these valuable resources. (After all, they are the only business resources that can leave an organization.) Finally, the human resources should be developed to their full capacity.

HRM Activities

Each of the three phases of HRM—acquiring, maintaining, and developing human resources—consists of a number of related activities. Acquisition, for example, includes planning, as well as the various activities that lead to hiring new personnel. Altogether this phase of HRM includes five separate activities. They are as follows:

- *Human resources planning*—determining the firm's future human resources needs
- *Job analysis*—determining the exact nature of the positions
- *Recruiting*—attracting people to apply for positions
- *Selection*—choosing and hiring the most qualified applicants
- *Orientation*—acquainting new employees with the firm

Maintaining human resources consists primarily of encouraging employees to remain with the firm and to work effectively by using a variety of HRM programs, including the following:

- *Employee relations*—increasing employee job satisfaction through satisfaction surveys, employee communication programs, exit interviews, and fair treatment
- *Compensation*—rewarding employee effort through monetary payments
- *Benefits*—providing rewards to ensure employee well-being

The development phase of HRM is concerned with improving employees' skills and expanding their capabilities. The two important activities within this phase are

- *Training and development*—teaching employees new skills, new jobs, and more effective ways of doing their present jobs
- *Performance appraisal*—assessing employees' current and potential performance levels

These activities are discussed in more detail shortly, when we have completed this overview of HRM.

Responsibility for HRM

In general, HRM is a shared responsibility of line managers and staff HRM specialists. In very small organizations, the owner handles all or most HRM activities. As a firm grows in size, a human resources manager is hired to take over staff responsibilities.

In firms as large as Disney, HRM activities tend to be very highly specialized. There are separate groups to deal with compensation, benefits, training and development, and other staff activities.

Specific HRM activities are assigned to those who are in the best position to perform them. Human resources planning and job analysis usually are done by staff specialists, with input from line managers. Similarly, recruiting and selection are handled by staff experts, although line managers are involved in hiring decisions. Orientation programs are devised by staff specialists and carried out by both staff specialists and line managers. Compensation systems (including benefits) most often are developed and administered by the HRM staff. However, line managers recommend pay increases and promotions. Training and development activities are the joint responsibility of staff and line managers. Performance appraisal is the job of the line manager, although HRM personnel design the firm's appraisal system in many organizations.

Rewarding employees. Appropriate employee rewards help to attract and retain employees. This Continental Airlines flight attendant was awarded with a new Ford Explorer under the airline's perfect attendance program. Over the last decade, Continental Airlines has awarded almost 100 new vehicles to employees as a part of this program.

Human Resources Planning

Human resources planning is the development of strategies to meet a firm's future human resources needs. The starting point is the organization's overall strategic plan. From this, human resources planners can forecast future demand for human resources. Next, the planners must determine whether the needed human resources will be available. Finally, they have to take steps to match supply with demand.

Forecasting Human Resources Demand

Planners should base forecasts of the demand for human resources on as much relevant information as available. The firm's overall strategic plan will provide information about future business ventures, new products, and projected expansions or contractions of specific product lines. Information on past staffing levels, evolving technologies, industry staffing practices, and projected economic trends also can be helpful.

HRM staff use this information to determine both the number of employees required and their qualifications. Planners use a wide range of methods to forecast specific personnel needs. For example, with one simple method, personnel requirements are projected to increase or decrease in the same proportion as sales revenue. Thus, if a 30 percent increase in sales volume is projected over the next two years, then up to a 30 percent increase in personnel requirements may be expected for the same period. (This method can be applied to specific positions as well as to the work force in general. It is not, however, a very precise forecasting method.) At the other extreme are elaborate, computer-based personnel planning models used by some large firms such as Exxon Corporation.

Forecasting Human Resources Supply

The forecast of the supply of human resources must take into account both the present work force and any changes that may occur within it. For example, suppose that planners project that in five years a firm that currently employs 100 engineers will need to employ a total of 200 engineers. Planners simply cannot assume that they will have to hire 100 engineers; during that period, some of the firm's present engineers are

2 LEARNING OBJECTIVE
Identify the steps in human resources planning.

human resources planning the development of strategies to meet a firm's future human resources needs

likely to be promoted, leave the firm, or move to other jobs within the firm. Thus planners may project the supply of engineers in five years at 87, which means that the firm will have to hire a total of 113 new engineers. When forecasting supply, planners should analyze the organization's existing employees to determine who can be retrained to perform the required tasks.

Two useful techniques for forecasting human resources supply are the replacement chart and the skills inventory. A **replacement chart** is a list of key personnel and their possible replacements within a firm. The chart is maintained to ensure that top-management positions can be filled fairly quickly in the event of an unexpected death, resignation, or retirement. Some firms also provide additional training for employees who might eventually replace top managers.

replacement chart a list of key personnel and their possible replacements within a firm

A **skills inventory** is a computerized data bank containing information on the skills and experience of all present employees. It is used to search for candidates to fill available positions. For a special project, a manager may be seeking a current employee with specific information technology skills, at least six years of experience, and fluency in French. The skills inventory can quickly identify employees who possess such qualifications. Skill-assessment tests can be administered inside an organization, or they can be provided by outside vendors. For example, SkillView Technologies, Inc., and Bookman Testing Services TeckChek are third-party information technology skill-assessment providers.

skills inventory a computerized data bank containing information on the skills and experience of all present employees

Matching Supply with Demand

Once they have forecasted the supply and demand for personnel, planners can devise a course of action for matching the two. When demand is predicted to be greater than supply, plans must be made to recruit new employees. The timing of these actions depends on the types of positions to be filled. Suppose that we expect to open another plant in five years. Along with other employees, a plant manager and twenty-five maintenance workers will be needed. We probably can wait quite a while before we begin to recruit maintenance personnel. However, because the job of plant manager is so critical, we may start searching for the right person for that position immediately.

When supply is predicted to be greater than demand, the firm must take steps to reduce the size of its work force. When the oversupply is expected to be temporary, some employees may be *laid off*—dismissed from the work force until they are needed again.

Perhaps the most humane method for making personnel cutbacks is through attrition. *Attrition* is the normal reduction in the work force that occurs when employees leave a firm. If these employees are not replaced, the work force eventually shrinks to the point where supply matches demand. Of course, attrition may be a very slow process—often too slow to help the firm. AutoNation, the U.S.'s largest new and used car retailer, recently achieved the desired cost cuts needed through employee attrition. Attrition reduced the work force by about 1,500. Through the resulting cost reductions and measures to increase revenues, AutoNation was able to increase its earnings.[3]

Early retirement is another option. Under early retirement, people who are within a few years of retirement are permitted to retire early with full benefits. Depending on the age makeup of the work force, this may or may not reduce the staff enough.

As a last resort, unneeded employees are sometimes simply *fired*. However, because of its negative impact, this method generally is used only when absolutely necessary.

3 LEARNING OBJECTIVE
Describe cultural diversity and understand some of the challenges and opportunities associated with it.

Cultural Diversity in Human Resources

Today's work force is made up of many types of people. Firms can no longer assume that every employee has similar beliefs or expectations. Whereas North American white males may believe in challenging authority, Asians tend to respect and defer to it. In Hispanic cultures, people often bring music, food, and family members to work, a custom that U.S. businesses traditionally have not allowed. A job applicant who will

The value of cultural diversity. Organizations that are dedicated to diversity, such as American Airlines, gain significant benefits from their efforts. American Airlines received one of the 40 Best Companies for Diversity awards presented by *Black Enterprise Magazine.*

not make eye contact during an interview may be rejected for being unapproachable, when, according to his or her culture, he or she was just being polite.

Since a larger number of women, minorities, and immigrants have entered the U.S. work force, the workplace is more diverse. It is estimated that women make up about 46 percent of the U.S. work force, and African Americans and Hispanics each account for about 11 percent.[4]

Cultural (or **workplace**) **diversity** refers to the differences among people in a work force owing to race, ethnicity, and gender. Increasing cultural diversity is forcing managers to learn to supervise and motivate people with a broader range of value systems. The high proportion of women into the work force, combined with a new emphasis on participative parenting by men, has brought many family-related issues to the workplace. Today's more educated employees also want greater independence and flexibility. In return for their efforts, they want both compensation and a better quality of life.

cultural (workplace) diversity differences among people in a work force owing to race, ethnicity, and gender

Although cultural diversity presents a challenge, managers should view it as an opportunity rather than a limitation. When managed properly, cultural diversity can provide competitive advantages for an organization. Table 10.1 shows several benefits that creative management of cultural diversity can offer. A firm that manages diversity properly can develop cost advantages over other firms. Moreover, organizations that manage diversity creatively are in a much better position to attract the best personnel. A culturally diverse organization may gain a marketing edge because it understands different cultural groups. Proper guidance and management of diversity in an organization also can improve the level of creativity. Culturally diverse people frequently are more flexible in the types of positions they will accept.

Bilingual skills bring numerous benefits to an organization. Toyota, for example, recently decided to locate its sixth North American manufacturing facility in San Antonio, Texas, with one of the primary factors in the decision being the tremendous bilingual labor available in the area.

SPOTLIGHT

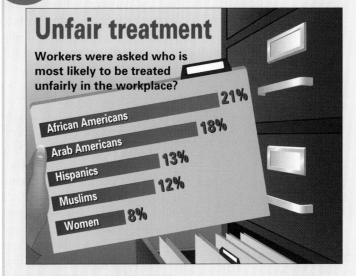

Unfair treatment

Workers were asked who is most likely to be treated unfairly in the workplace?

African Americans — 21%
Arab Americans — 18%
Hispanics — 13%
Muslims — 12%
Women — 8%

Source: *USA Today,* April 10, 2002, p. B1.

>> TABLE 10.1

COMPETITIVE ADVANTAGES OF CULTURAL DIVERSITY

Cost	As organizations become more diverse, the cost of a poor job in integrating workers will increase. Companies that handle this well thus can create cost advantages over those that do a poor job. In addition, companies also experience cost savings by hiring people with knowledge of various cultures as opposed to having to train Americans, for example, about how German people do business.
Resource acquisition	Companies develop reputations as being favorable or unfavorable prospective employers for women and ethnic minorities. Those with the best reputations for managing diversity will win the competition for the best personnel.
Marketing edge	For multinational organizations, the insight and cultural sensitivity that members with roots in other countries bring to marketing efforts should improve these efforts in important ways. The same rationale applies to marketing subpopulations domestically.
Flexibility	Culturally diverse employees often are open to a wider array of positions within a company and are more likely to move up the corporate ladder more rapidly, given excellent performance.
Creativity	Diversity of perspectives and less emphasis on conformity to norms of the past should improve the level of creativity.
Problem solving	Differences within decision-making and problem-solving groups potentially produce better decisions through a wider range of perspectives and more thorough critical analysis of issues.
Bilingual skills	Cultural diversity in the workplace brings with it bilingual and bicultural skills, which are very advantageous to the ever-growing global marketplace. Employees with knowledge about how other cultures work not only can speak to them in their language but also can prevent their company from making embarrassing moves owing to a lack of cultural sophistication. Thus companies seek job applicants with perhaps a background in cultures in which the company does business.

Sources: Taylor H. Cox and Stacy Blake, "Managing Cultural Diversity: Implications for Organizational Competitiveness," *Academy of Management Executive* 5(3):46, 1991; Graciela Kenig, "Yo Soy Ingeniero: The Advantages of Being Bilingual in Technical Professions," *Diversity Monthly,* February 28, 1999, p. 13; and "Dialogue Skills in the Multicultural Workplace," *North American Post,* March 19, 1999, p. 2

This factory will manufacture Toyota trucks and bring economic growth to the San Antonio area.[5]

Because cultural diversity creates challenges along with advantages, it is important for an organization's employees to understand it. To accomplish this goal, numerous U.S. firms have trained their managers to respect and manage diversity. Diversity training programs may include recruiting minorities, training minorities to be managers, training managers to view diversity positively, teaching English as a second language, and facilitating support groups for immigrants. Many organizations are realizing the necessity of having diversity training. Universities and colleges across the nation have ramped up efforts to increase faculty diversity. These government-funded schools are realizing that a valid education includes cultural diversity.[6] Many companies are realizing the necessity of having diversity training spanning beyond just racial issues. Eaton Corp., which manufactures engine parts for cars, has invested in diversity training and encourages its employees to consider religion, gender, and nationality in addition to race. Other companies add age, religious practices, weight, sexual orientation, and even hobbies to this list.[7] Owing to the high quality of its program, Texas Instruments has received several awards for being one of the best places in America for minorities to work. Texas Instruments' cultural diversity program involves training and education, employee diversity groups, and corporate policies that support advancement of minorities. Thousands of managers, supervisors, and employees from all parts of the company have attended diversity training programs that taught them to value the cultural differences in Texas Instruments. One of the reasons for this program's success is the strong commitment that senior management at Texas Instruments has made to this program.[8]

A diversity program will be successful only if it is systematic, ongoing, and has a strong, sustained commitment from top leadership. Cultural diversity is here to stay. Its impact on organizations is widespread and will continue to grow within corporations. Management must learn to overcome the obstacles and capitalize on the advantages associated with culturally diverse human resources.

Job Analysis

There is no sense in hiring people unless we know what we are hiring them for. In other words, we need to know the nature of a job before we can find the right person to do it.

Job analysis is a systematic procedure for studying jobs to determine their various elements and requirements. Consider the position of clerk, for example. In a large corporation, there may be fifty kinds of clerk positions. They all may be called "clerks," but each position may differ from the others in the activities to be performed, the level of proficiency required for each activity, and the particular set of qualifications that the position demands. These distinctions are the focus of job analysis. Some companies such as ManTech International specialize in developing job-analysis materials and conducting the analysis for companies and government entities alike; in fact, ManTech won a contract worth $76 million to provide their services to the U.S. Navy.[9]

The job analysis for a particular position typically consists of two parts—a job description and a job specification. A **job description** is a list of the elements that make up a particular job. It includes the duties to be performed, the working conditions, responsibilities, and the tools and equipment that must be used on the job (see Figure 10.1).

A **job specification** is a list of the qualifications required to perform a particular job. Included are the skills, abilities, education, and experience the jobholder must have. When attempting to hire a financial analyst, Bank of America used the following job specification: "Requires 8–10 years of financial experience, a broad-based financial background, strong customer focus, the ability to work confidently with the client's management team, strong analytical skills. Must have strong Excel and Word skills. Personal characteristics should include strong desire to succeed, impact performer (individually and as a member of a team), positive attitude, high energy level and ability to influence others"[10]

The job analysis is not only the basis for recruiting and selecting new employees; it is also used in other areas of HRM, including evaluation and the determination of equitable compensation levels.

Recruiting, Selection, and Orientation

In an organization with jobs waiting to be filled, HRM personnel need to (1) find candidates for those jobs and (2) match the right candidate with each job. Three activities are involved: recruiting, selection, and new employee orientation.

Recruiting

Recruiting is the process of attracting qualified job applicants. Because it is a vital link in a costly process (the cost of hiring an employee can be several thousand dollars), recruiting needs to be a systematic process. One goal of recruiters is to attract the "right number" of applicants. The right number is enough to allow a good match between applicants and open positions but not so many that matching them requires too much time and effort. For example, if there are five open positions and five applicants, the firm essentially has no choice. It must hire those five applicants (qualified or not), or the positions will remain open. At the other extreme, if several hundred job seekers apply for the five positions, HRM personnel will have to spend weeks processing their applications.

Recruiters may seek applicants outside the firm, within the firm, or both. The source used depends on the nature of the position, the situation within the firm, and sometimes the firm's established or traditional recruitment policies.

4 LEARNING OBJECTIVE
Explain the objectives and uses of job analysis.

job analysis a systematic procedure for studying jobs to determine their various elements and requirements

job description a list of the elements that make up a particular job

job specification a list of the qualifications required to perform a particular job

5 LEARNING OBJECTIVE
Describe the processes of recruiting, employee selection, and orientation.

recruiting the process of attracting qualified job applicants

>> **FIGURE 10.1**

JOB DESCRIPTION AND JOB SPECIFICATION

This job description explains the job of sales coordinator and lists the responsibilities of the position. The job specification is contained in the last paragraph.

HOUGHTON MIFFLIN COMPANY

JOB DESCRIPTION

TITLE:	Georgia Sales Coordinator	**DATE:**	3/25/05
DEPARTMENT:	College, Sales	**GRADE:**	12
REPORTS TO:	Regional Manager	**EXEMPT/NON-EXEMPT:**	Exempt

BRIEF SUMMARY:

Supervise one other Georgia-based sales representative to gain supervisory experience. Captain the 4 members of the outside sales rep team that are assigned to territories consisting of colleges and universities in Georgia. Oversee, coordinate, advise, and make decisions regarding Georgia sales activities. Based upon broad contact with customers across the state and communication with administrators of schools, the person will make recommendations regarding issues specific to the needs of higher education in the state of Georgia such as distance learning, conversion to the semester system, potential statewide adoptions, and faculty training.

PRINCIPLE ACCOUNTABILITIES:

1. Supervises/manages/trains one other Atlanta-based sales rep.

2. Advises two other sales reps regarding the Georgia schools in their territories.

3. Increases overall sales in Georgia as well as individual sales territory.

4. Assists regional manager in planning and coordinating regional meetings and Atlanta conferences.

5. Initiates a dialogue with campus administrators, particularly in the areas of the semester conversion, distance learning, and faculty development.

DIMENSIONS:

This position will have one direct report in addition to the leadership role played within the region. Revenue most directly impacted will be within the individually assigned territory, the supervised territory, and the overall sales for the state of Georgia.

KNOWLEDGE AND SKILLS:

Must have displayed a history of consistently outstanding sales in personal territory. Must demonstrate clear teamwork and leadership skills and be willing to extend beyond the individual territory goals. Should have a clear understanding of the company's systems and product offerings in order to train and lead other sales representatives. Must have the communication skills and presence to communicate articulately with higher education administrators and to serve as a bridge between the company and higher education in the state.

Source: Used with permission of Houghton Mifflin Company.

external recruiting the attempt to attract job applicants from outside an organization

External Recruiting   **External recruiting** is the attempt to attract job applicants from outside an organization. External recruiting may include newspaper advertising, employment agencies, recruiting on college campuses, soliciting recommendations from present employees, conducting "open houses," and online employment organizations. The biggest of the online job-search sites is Monster.com, which has as clients about 490 of the *Fortune* 500 companies.[11] In addition, many people simply apply at a firm's employment office.

Clearly, it is best to match the recruiting means with the kind of applicant being sought. For example, private employment agencies most often handle professional people, whereas public employment agencies (operated by state or local governments) are more concerned with operations personnel. We might approach a private agency when looking for a vice president but contact a public agency to hire a machinist. Pulte Homes, a custom home builder, tries to focus on college recruitment centers to recruit

2,500 new hires per year. Pulte feels that college graduates are more likely to have the qualifications to become part of the company culture. Pulte has a low turnover rate of only 11% compared with 29% for the industry.[12]

The primary advantage of external recruiting is that it brings in people with new perspectives and varied business backgrounds. A disadvantage of external recruiting is that it is often expensive, especially if private employment agencies must be used. External recruiting also may provoke resentment among present employees.

Internal Recruiting **Internal recruiting** means considering present employees as applicants for available positions. Generally, current employees are considered for *promotion* to higher-level positions. However, employees may be considered for *transfer* from one position to another at the same level. Among leading companies, 85 percent of CEOs are promoted from within. In the companies that hire CEOs from outside, 40 percent of the CEOs are gone after eighteen months.[13]

Promoting from within provides strong motivation for current employees and helps the firm to retain quality personnel. General Electric, Exxon, and Eastman Kodak are companies dedicated to promoting from within. The practice of *job posting*, or informing current employees of upcoming openings, may be a company policy or required by union contract. The primary disadvantage of internal recruiting is that promoting a current employee leaves another position to be filled. Not only does the firm still incur recruiting and selection costs, but it also must train two employees instead of one.

In many situations it may be impossible to recruit internally. For example, a new position may be such that no current employee is qualified. Or the firm may be growing so rapidly that there is no time to reassign positions that promotion or transfer requires.

The new Yahoo! HotJobs is the only job board that uses Yahoo's renowned search technology to make it easier to find the perfect candidate or the perfect job.

Only Yahoo! HotJobs offers innovative products like HotJobs Direct, our permission-based email service, which can access over 80 million candidates via the Yahoo! network. That's over 1/2 of the U.S. labor force!

Find out how Yahoo! HotJobs can help you find the right one for your job.

Call 1.877.HOTJOBS today or visit us at www.hotjobs.com

YAHOO! hotjobs
Find the right one.

External recruiting tools. Some organizations use employment agencies like Yahoo! HotJobs for recruiting purposes.

internal recruiting considering present employees as applicants for available positions

selection the process of gathering information about applicants for a position and then using that information to choose the most appropriate applicant

Selection

Selection is the process of gathering information about applicants for a position and then using that information to choose the most appropriate applicant. Note the use of the word *appropriate*. In selection, the idea is not to hire the person with the *most* qualifications but rather the applicant who is *most appropriate*. The selection of an applicant is made by line managers responsible for the position. However, HRM personnel usually help by developing a pool of applicants and by expediting the assessment of these applicants. Common means of obtaining information about applicants' qualifications are employment applications, interviews, references, and assessment centers.

Employment Applications An employment application is useful in collecting factual information on a candidate's education, work experience, and personal history (see Figure 10.2). The data obtained from applications usually are used for two purposes: to identify applicants who are worthy of further scrutiny and to familiarize interviewers with their backgrounds.

Many job candidates submit résumés, and some firms require them. A *résumé* is a one- or two-page summary of the candidate's background and qualifications. It may include a description of the type of job the applicant is seeking. A résumé may be sent to a firm to request consideration for available jobs, or it may be submitted along with an employment application.

To improve the usefulness of information, HRM specialists ask current employees about factors in their backgrounds most related to their current jobs. Then these

>> **FIGURE 10.2**

TYPICAL EMPLOYMENT APPLICATION

Employers use applications to collect factual information on a candidate's education, work experience, and personal history.

3M Contribution and Development Summary
FORM 37450 - B

Employee Name	Employee Number	Job Title
Department		Location
Coach/Supervisor(s) Name(s)		Review Period From :

Major Job Responsibilities

Goals/Expectations	Contributions/Results

Contribution (To be completed by coach/supervisor)

☐ Good Level of Contribution for this year   ☐ Exceptional Level of Contr

☐ Unsatisfactory Level of Contribution for this year

Development Summary

Areas of Strength	Development Priorities

Career Interests

Next job	Longer Range

Current Mobility

☐ **0** - Currently Unable to Relocate   ☐ **3** - Position Within O.U.S. Area (ex: Europe, Asia)

☐ **1** - Position In Home Country Only (Use if Home Country is Outside U.S.)   ☐ **4** - Position In U.S.

☐ **2** - Position Within O.U.S. Region (e: Nordic, SEA...)   ☐ **5** - Position Anywhere In The World

Development

☐ **W** - Well placed. Development plans achievable in current role for at least the next year   ☐ **X** - Not well placed. Action required to resolve placement issues.

☐ **C** - Ready now for a move to a different job for career broadening experience   **Comments on Development**

☐ **I** - Ready now for a move to a different job involving increased responsibility

Employee Comments

Coach/Supervisor Comments	Other Supervisor (if applicable) and/or Reviewer

Signatures

Coach/Supervisor	Date	Other Coach/Supervisor or Reviewer	Date
Employee			Date

page 4

Source: Courtesy of 3M.

factors are included on the applications and may be weighted more heavily when evaluating new applicants' qualifications.

Employment Tests   Tests administered to job candidates usually focus on aptitudes, skills, abilities, or knowledge relevant to the job. Such tests (basic computer skills tests, for example) indicate how well the applicant will do the job. Occasionally, companies use general intelligence or personality tests, but these are seldom helpful in predicting specific job performance. However, *Fortune* 500 companies, as well as an increasing number of medium- and small-sized companies, are using predictive-behavior personality tests as administration costs decrease. Darden Restaurants, parent company of The Olive Garden and Red Lobster, uses a work-style inventory in its hiring process for all positions, whereas firms such as Disney and Hampton Inn use similar tests for management positions.[14]

Recruiting at job fairs. At job fairs, recruiters and job applicants can meet to discuss job opportunities and applicants' qualifications.

At one time, a number of companies were criticized for using tests that were biased against certain minority groups—in particular, African Americans. The test results were, to a great extent, unrelated to job performance. Today, a firm must be able to prove that a test is not discriminatory by demonstrating that it accurately measures one's ability to perform. Applicants who believe that they have been discriminated against through an invalid test may file a complaint with the Equal Employment Opportunity Commission (EEOC).

Interviews   The interview is perhaps the most widely used selection technique. Job candidates are interviewed by at least one member of the HRM staff and by the person for whom they will be working. Candidates for higher-level jobs may meet with a department head or vice president over several interviews.

Interviews provide an opportunity for applicants and the firm to learn more about each other. Interviewers can pose problems to test the candidate's abilities, probe employment history, and learn something about the candidate's attitudes and motivation. The candidate has a chance to find out more about the job and potential coworkers.

Unfortunately, interviewing may be the stage at which discrimination begins. For example, suppose that a female applicant mentions that she is the mother of small children. Her interviewer may assume that she would not be available for job-related travel. In addition, interviewers may be unduly influenced by such factors as appearance. Or they may ask different questions of different applicants so that it becomes impossible to compare candidates' qualifications.

Some of these problems can be solved through better interviewer training and use of structured interviews. In a *structured interview*, the interviewer asks only a prepared set of job-related questions. The firm also may consider using several different interviewers for each applicant, but this is likely to be costly.

References   A job candidate generally is asked to furnish the names of references—people who can verify background information and provide personal evaluations. Naturally, applicants tend to list only references who are likely to say good things. Thus personal evaluations obtained from references may not be of much value. However, references are often contacted to verify such information as previous job responsibilities and the reason an applicant left a former job.

Assessment Centers   An assessment center is used primarily to select current employees for promotion to higher-level positions. Typically, a group of employees is sent to the center a few days. While there, they participate in activities designed to simulate the management environment and to predict managerial effectiveness.

YOUR CAREER

Here's How to Negotiate for Higher Compensation

Consider making a case for higher compensation if you've taken on more responsibilities, completed a challenging assignment, or achieved exceptionally high performance. Consider the following negotiating tips:

- *Do your homework.* Research typical salaries for your job by checking classified ads, websites, and other sources. This is a starting point for your negotiation.
- *List your accomplishments.* Document how you've contributed to your firm's success or completed tasks beyond those in your job description. Susan

Hackley, head of Harvard Law School's Program on Negotiation, advises: "This is the one chance you've got to convey to your boss that you deserve everything you're asking for."

- *Approach your boss.* Make an appointment with your boss, and go in prepared. Be positive but not pushy, and be patient. Your manager may need higher-level approval to grant a raise. Finally, be flexible. Incentive pay may be a possibility, if a raise is not.

Trained observers make recommendations regarding promotion possibilities. Although this technique is gaining popularity, the expense involved limits its use.

Orientation

Once all information about job candidates has been collected and analyzed, a job offer is extended. If it is accepted, the candidate becomes an employee.

Soon after a candidate joins a firm, he or she goes through the firm's orientation program. **Orientation** is the process of acquainting new employees with an organization. Orientation topics range from the location of the company cafeteria to career paths within the firm. The orientation itself may consist of a half-hour informal presentation by a human resources manager. Or it may be an elaborate program involving dozens of people and lasting several days or weeks.

orientation the process of acquainting new employees with an organization

Compensation and Benefits

6 LEARNING OBJECTIVE
Discuss the primary elements of employee compensation and benefits.

An effective employee reward system must (1) enable employees to satisfy basic needs, (2) provide rewards comparable with those offered by other firms, (3) be distributed fairly within the organization, and (4) recognize that different people have different needs.

A firm's compensation system can be structured to meet the first three of these requirements. The fourth is more difficult because it must account for many variables. Most firms offer a number of benefits that, taken together, generally help to provide for employees' varying needs.

Compensation Decisions

compensation the payment employees receive in return for their labor

Compensation is the payment employees receive in return for their labor. Its importance to employees is obvious. And because compensation may account for up to 80 percent of a firm's operating costs, it is equally important to management. The firm's

compensation system, the policies and strategies that determine employee compensation, therefore must be designed carefully to provide for employee needs while keeping labor costs within reasonable limits. For most firms, designing an effective compensation system requires three separate management decisions—wage level, wage structure, and individual wages.

compensation system the policies and strategies that determine employee compensation

Wage Level

Management first must position the firm's general pay level relative to pay levels of comparable firms. Most firms choose a pay level near the industry average. A firm that is not in good financial shape may pay less than average, and large, prosperous organizations may pay more than average.

To determine what the average is, the firm may use wage surveys. A **wage survey** is a collection of data on prevailing wage rates within an industry or a geographic area. Such surveys are compiled by industry associations, local governments, personnel associations, and (occasionally) individual firms.

wage survey a collection of data on prevailing wage rates within an industry or a geographic area

Wage Structure

Next, management must decide on relative pay levels for all the positions within the firm. Will managers be paid more than secretaries? Will secretaries be paid more than custodians? The result of this set of decisions is often called the firm's *wage structure.*

The wage structure almost always is developed on the basis of a job evaluation. **Job evaluation** is the process of determining the relative worth of the various jobs within a firm. Most observers probably would agree that a secretary should make more money than a custodian, but how much more? Job evaluation should provide the answer to this question.

job evaluation the process of determining the relative worth of the various jobs within a firm

A number of techniques may be used to evaluate jobs. The simplest is to rank all the jobs within the firm according to value. A more frequently used method is based on the job analysis. Points are allocated to each job for each of its elements and requirements. For example, "college degree required" might be worth fifty points, whereas the need for a high school education might count for only twenty-five points. The more points a job is allocated, the more important it is presumed to be (and the higher its level in the firm's wage structure).

Individual Wages

Finally, the specific payments individual employees will receive must be determined. Consider the case of two secretaries working side by side. Job evaluation has been used to determine the relative level of secretarial pay within the firm's wage structure. However, suppose that one secretary has fifteen years of experience and can type eighty words per minute accurately. The other has two years of experience and can type only fifty-five words per minute. In most firms these two people would not receive the same pay. Instead, a wage range would be established for the secretarial position. In this case, the range might be $7 to $9.50 per hour. The more experienced and proficient secretary then would be paid an amount near the top of the range (say, $8.90 per hour); the less experienced secretary would receive an amount that is lower but still within the range (say, $7.75 per hour).

Two wage decisions come into play here. First, the employee's initial rate must be established. It is based on experience, other qualifications, and expected performance. Later, the employee may be given pay increases based on seniority and performance.

Comparable Worth

One reason women in the work force are paid less may be that a proportion of women occupy female-dominated jobs—nurses, secretaries, and medical records analysts, for example—that require education, skills, and training equal to higher-paid positions but are undervalued. **Comparable worth** is a concept that seeks equal compensation for jobs that require about the same level of education, training, and skills. Several states have enacted laws requiring equal pay for comparable work in government positions. Critics of comparable worth argue that the market has determined the worth of jobs and laws should not tamper with the pricing mechanism of the market. The

comparable worth a concept that seeks equal compensation for jobs requiring about the same level of education, training, and skills

EXAMINING ETHICS

CEO Compensation: How Much Is Too Much?

Are CEOs overpaid? Although the CEO of Yahoo! earned $230 million in total compensation during one recent year, not all CEOs enjoy such a hefty pay package. Still, CEO compensation has increased 146 percent in the past decade, raising a number of questions:

- *Should CEO compensation be based on performance?* Ideally, yes—in practice, not always. If the company's profits are flat or the stock price barely budges, should the CEO receive a big raise?
- *What does compensation include?* CEOs often receive club memberships and other extras. Should stockholders know about these extras? The Securities and Exchange Commission thinks so and now requires more complete disclosure.
- *Should the CEO's salary be hundreds of times greater than an average worker's salary?* The organic grocery chain Whole Foods is against such a huge pay disparity. Its CEO's total compensation cannot be more than fourteen times that of the average employee. Will more companies follow its lead in capping CEO pay?

Equal Pay Act, discussed later in this chapter, does not address the issue of comparable worth. Critics also argue that artificially inflating salaries for female-dominated occupations encourages women to keep these jobs rather than seek out higher-paying jobs.

Types of Compensation

Compensation can be paid in a variety of forms. Most forms of compensation fall into the following categories: hourly wage, weekly or monthly salary, commissions, incentive payments, lump-sum salary increases, and profit sharing.

Hourly Wage   An **hourly wage** is a specific amount of money paid for each hour of work. People who earn wages are paid their hourly wage for the first forty hours worked in any week. They are then paid one and one-half times their hourly wage for time worked in excess of forty hours. (That is, they are paid "time and a half" for overtime.) Workers in retailing and fast-food chains, on assembly lines, and in clerical positions usually are paid an hourly wage.

Weekly or Monthly Salary   A **salary** is a specific amount of money paid for an employee's work during a set calendar period, regardless of the actual number of hours worked. Salaried employees receive no overtime pay, but they do not lose pay when they are absent from work. Most professional and managerial positions are salaried.

hourly wage a specific amount of money paid for each hour of work

salary a specific amount of money paid for an employee's work during a set calendar period, regardless of the actual number of hours worked

commission a payment that is a percentage of sales revenue

incentive payment a payment in addition to wages, salary, or commissions

Commissions   A **commission** is a payment that is a percentage of sales revenue. Sales representatives and sales managers often are paid entirely through commissions or through a combination of commissions and salary.

Incentive Payments   An **incentive payment** is a payment in addition to wages, salary, or commissions. Incentive payments are really extra rewards for outstanding job performance. They may be distributed to all employees or only to certain employees. Some firms distribute incentive payments to all employees annually. The size of the payment depends on the firm's earnings and, at times, on the particular employee's length of service with the firm. Firms sometimes offer incentives to employees who exceed specific sales or production goals, a practice called *gain sharing*.

To avoid yearly across-the-board salary increases, some organizations reward outstanding workers individually through *merit pay*. This pay-for-performance approach allows management to control labor costs while encouraging employees to work more efficiently. An employee's merit pay depends on his or her achievements relative to those of others.

lump-sum salary increase an entire pay raise taken in one lump sum

Lump-Sum Salary Increases   In traditional reward systems, an employee who receives an annual pay increase is given part of the increase in each pay period. For example, suppose that an employee on a monthly salary gets a 10 percent annual pay hike. He or she actually receives 10 percent of the former monthly salary added to each month's paycheck for a year. Companies that offer a **lump-sum salary increase** give the employee the option of taking the entire pay raise in one lump sum. The employee then draws his or her "regular" pay for the rest of the year. The lump-sum payment typically is treated as an interest-free loan that must be repaid if the employee leaves the firm during the year.

Profit Sharing   **Profit sharing** is the distribution of a percentage of a firm's profit among its employees. The idea is to motivate employees to work effectively by giving them a stake in the company's financial success. Some firms—including Sears, Roebuck—have linked their profit-sharing plans to employee retirement programs; that is, employees receive their profit-sharing distributions, with interest, when they retire.

Employee Benefits

An **employee benefit** is a reward in addition to regular compensation that is provided indirectly to employees. Employee benefits consist mainly of services (such as insurance) that are paid for partially or totally by employers and employee expenses (such as college tuition) that are reimbursed by employers. Currently, the average cost of these benefits is 28 percent of an employee's total compensation, which includes wages plus benefits. Thus a person who received total compensation (including benefits) of $40,000 a year earned $28,000 in wages and received an additional $11,200 in benefits.[15] A recent online survey conducted by TrueCareers found that 84 percent of employees would rather receive better benefits than higher salaries. These findings are significant to employers as they try to attract and retain good employees. Increased desire for benefits is partially the result of increasing health care insurance costs.[16]

Employee benefits.
Companies that are named one of the 100 Best Companies to Work For, such as Ernst & Young, often provide employee benefit packages that result in employee satisfaction.

Types of Benefits   Employee benefits take a variety of forms. *Pay for time not worked* covers such absences as vacation time, holidays, and sick leave. *Insurance packages* may include health, life, and dental insurance for employees and their families. Some firms pay the entire cost of the insurance package, and others share the cost with the employee. The costs of *pension and retirement programs* also may be borne entirely by the firm or shared with the employee.

Some benefits are required by law. For example, employers must maintain *workers' compensation insurance*, which pays medical bills for injuries that occur on the job and provides income for employees who are disabled by job-related injuries. Employers also must pay for *unemployment insurance* and contribute to each employee's federal *Social Security* account.

Other benefits provided by employers include tuition-reimbursement plans, credit unions, child care, company cafeterias, exercise rooms, and broad stock-option plans available to all employees. Some companies offer special benefits to U.S. military reservists who are called up for active duty. IBM offers to make up the difference between a reservist's military pay and his or her regular pay so that overall pay remains at the IBM level. In addition, normal benefits are still given when reservists are called, and employees can continue to contribute to their 401(k) plans and receive contributions from IBM. When reservists return from active duty, they come back to their same positions, and their active-duty times counts toward their years of service with IBM.[17]

Some companies offer unusual benefits in order to attract and retain employees. DaimlerChrysler makes available to every salaried, non–United Auto Workers Union worker a one-time $4,000 work-family account that can be used for child care, adoption costs, elder care, college tuition, or extra retirement funds. Compuware Corporation, a software company, makes cheap meals available to workers to take home after a workout in the company gym. Dayton Hudson not only provides employees with discounts on airfares, rental cars, and hotels for vacations but also allows employees to customize work schedules to fit their personal needs. Worthington Industries, a metal-processing company located in Columbus, Ohio, offers employees on-site haircuts for just $3.00. At BP Exploration in Anchorage, Alaska, employees are given vacation allowances ($800 per family member) annually.[18]

Flexible Benefit Plans   Through a **flexible benefit plan,** an employee receives a predetermined amount of benefit dollars and may allocate those dollars to various

profit sharing the distribution of a percentage of a firm's profit among its employees

employee benefit a reward in addition to regular compensation that is provided indirectly to employees

flexible benefit plan compensation plan whereby an employee receives a predetermined amount of benefit dollars to spend on a package of benefits he or she has selected to meet individual needs

categories of benefits in the mix that best fits his or her needs. Some flexible benefit plans offer a broad array of benefit options, including health care, dental care, life insurance, accidental death and dismemberment coverage for both the worker and dependents, long-term disability coverage, vacation benefits, retirement savings, and dependent-care benefits. Other firms offer limited options, primarily in health and life insurance and retirement plans.

Although the cost of administering flexible plans is high, a number of organizations, including Quaker Oats and Coca-Cola, have implemented this option for several reasons. Because employees' needs are so diverse, flexible plans help firms to offer benefit packages that more specifically meet their employees' needs. Flexible plans can, in the long run, help a company to contain costs because a specified amount is allocated to cover the benefits of each employee. Furthermore, organizations that offer flexible plans with many choices may be perceived as being employee-friendly. Thus they are in a better position to attract and retain qualified employees.

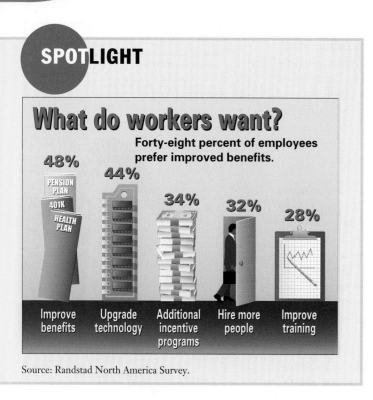

SPOTLIGHT

What do workers want?

Forty-eight percent of employees prefer improved benefits.

48% — Improve benefits (PENSION PLAN, 401K, HEALTH PLAN)
44% — Upgrade technology
34% — Additional incentive programs
32% — Hire more people
28% — Improve training

Source: Randstad North America Survey.

Training and Development

7 LEARNING OBJECTIVE
Explain the purposes and techniques of employee training, development, and performance appraisal.

employee training the process of teaching operations and technical employees how to do their present jobs more effectively and efficiently

management development the process of preparing managers and other professionals to assume increased responsibility in both present and future positions

Training and development are extremely important at the Container Store. Because great customer service is so important, every first-year full-time salesperson receives about 185 hours of formal training as opposed to the industry standard, which is approximately seven hours. Training and development continue throughout a person's career. Each store has a full-time trainer called the *super sales trainer* (SST). This trainer provides product training, sales training, and employee development training. Top management believes that the financial and human resources invested in training and development are well worth it.[19]

Both training and development are aimed at improving employees' skills and abilities. However, the two are usually differentiated as either employee training or management development. **Employee training** is the process of teaching operations and technical employees how to do their present jobs more effectively and efficiently. **Management development** is the process of preparing managers and other professionals to assume increased responsibility in both present and future positions. Thus training and development differ in who is being taught and the purpose of the teaching. Both are necessary for personal and organizational growth. Companies that hope to stay competitive typically make huge commitments to employee training and development. For example, Edward Jones, the stockbroker with nearly 8,000 branches, spends 3.8 percent of its payroll on training. These expenditures average out to be 146 hours per year for each employee, with new hires receiving about four times this amount of training. This dedication to its employees has helped Edward Jones claim the rating as the best company to work for by *Fortune* magazine for two consecutive years.[20] Internet-based e-learning is growing. Driven by cost, travel, and time savings, online learning alone (and in conjunction with face-to-face situations) is a strong alternative strategy. Development of a training program usually has three components: analysis of needs, determination of training and development methods, and creation of an evaluation system to assess the program's effectiveness.

Sources of training. Training occurs both internally and externally. Timken provides its distributors with product training that includes information about how and where its products are used and how they should be properly installed.

Analysis of Training Needs

When thinking about developing a training program, managers first must determine if training is needed and, if so, what types of training needs exist. At times, what at first appears to be a need for training is actually, on assessment, a need for motivation. Training needs can vary considerably. For example, some employees may need training to improve their technical skills, or they may need training about organizational procedures. Training also may focus on business ethics, product information, or customer service. Because training is expensive, it is critical that the correct training needs be identified.

Training and Development Methods

A number of methods are available for employee training and management development. Some of these methods may be more suitable for one or the other, but most can be applied to both training and management development.

- *On-the-job methods.* The trainee learns by doing the work under the supervision of an experienced employee.
- *Simulations.* The work situation is simulated in a separate area so that learning takes place away from the day-to-day pressures of work.
- *Classroom teaching and lectures.* You probably already know these methods quite well.

BizTech

Employee Training Goes Virtual

Videogame-style training is catching on as organizations seek new ways to educate and engage their employees. Pilots have trained on flight simulators for years. Military recruits play specialized videogames to practice combat skills; firefighters learn to handle hazardous materials by playing the Hazmat Hotzone videogame. Pfizer and Unilever are among the growing number of firms using virtual training to teach employees about

important internal processes. Top managers of Humana, a health insurance firm, recently used virtual training to practice strategy and teamwork. As videogames become increasingly realistic, watch for more organizations to play the virtual training game.

Videogame-style training is being used as follows:

- To simulate hands-on experiences
- To teach and test product knowledge
- To reinforce rules and regulations
- To brush up skills as needed
- To train many employees in a short time
- To actively involve employees in learning

- *Conferences and seminars.* Experts and learners meet to discuss problems and exchange ideas.
- *Role playing.* Participants act out the roles of others in the organization for better understanding of those roles (primarily a management development tool).

Evaluation of Training and Development

Training and development are very expensive. The training itself costs quite a bit, and employees are usually not working—or are working at a reduced load and pace—during training sessions. To ensure that training and development are cost-effective, the managers responsible should evaluate the company's efforts periodically.

The starting point for this evaluation is a set of verifiable objectives that are developed *before* the training is undertaken. Suppose that a training program is expected to improve the skills of machinists. The objective of the program might be stated as follows: "At the end of the training period, each machinist should be able to process thirty parts per hour with no more than one defective part per ninety parts completed." This objective clearly specifies what is expected and how training results may be measured or verified. Evaluation then consists of measuring machinists' output and the ratio of defective parts produced after the training.

The results of training evaluations should be made known to all those involved in the program—including trainees and upper management. For trainees, the results of evaluations can enhance motivation and learning. For upper management, the results may be the basis for making decisions about the training program itself.

Performance Appraisal

performance appraisal the evaluation of employees' current and potential levels of performance to allow managers to make objective human resources decisions

Performance appraisal is the evaluation of employees' current and potential levels of performance to allow managers to make objective human resources decisions. The process has three main objectives. First, managers use performance appraisals to let workers know how well they are doing and how they can do better in the future. Second, a performance appraisal provides an effective basis for distributing rewards, such as pay raises and promotions. Third, performance appraisal helps the organization monitor its employee selection, training, and development activities. If large numbers of employees continually perform below expectations, the firm may need to revise its selection process or strengthen its training and development activities.

Common Evaluation Techniques

The various techniques and methods for appraising employee performance are either objective or judgmental in nature.

Objective Methods   Objective appraisal methods use some measurable quantity as the basis for assessing performance. Units of output, dollar volume of sales, number of defective products, and number of insurance claims processed are all objective, measurable quantities. Thus an employee who processes an average of twenty-six insurance claims per week is given a higher evaluation than one whose average is nineteen claims per week.

Such objective measures may require some adjustment for the work environment. Suppose that the first of our insurance-claims processors works in New York City, and the second works in rural Iowa. Both must visit each client because they are processing homeowners' insurance claims. The difference in their average weekly output may be due entirely to the long distances the Iowan must travel to visit clients. In this case, the two workers may very well be equally competent and motivated. Thus a manager must take into account circumstances that may be hidden by a purely statistical measurement.

Judgmental Methods Judgmental appraisal methods are used much more frequently than objective methods. They require that the manager judge or estimate the employee's performance level. However, judgmental methods are not capricious. These methods are based on employee ranking or rating scales. When ranking is used, the manager ranks subordinates from best to worst. This approach has a number of drawbacks, including the lack of any absolute standard. Rating scales are the most popular judgmental appraisal technique. A *rating scale* consists of a number of statements; each employee is rated on the degree to which the statement applies (see Figure 10.3). For example, one statement might be, "This employee always does high-quality work." The supervisor would give the employee a rating, from 5 down to 1, corresponding to gradations ranging from "strongly agree" to "strongly disagree." The ratings on all the statements are added to obtain the employee's total evaluation.

▶▶ FIGURE 10.3

PERFORMANCE APPRAISAL

Judgmental appraisal methods are used much more often than objective methods. Using judgmental methods requires the manager to estimate the employee's performance level relative to some standard.

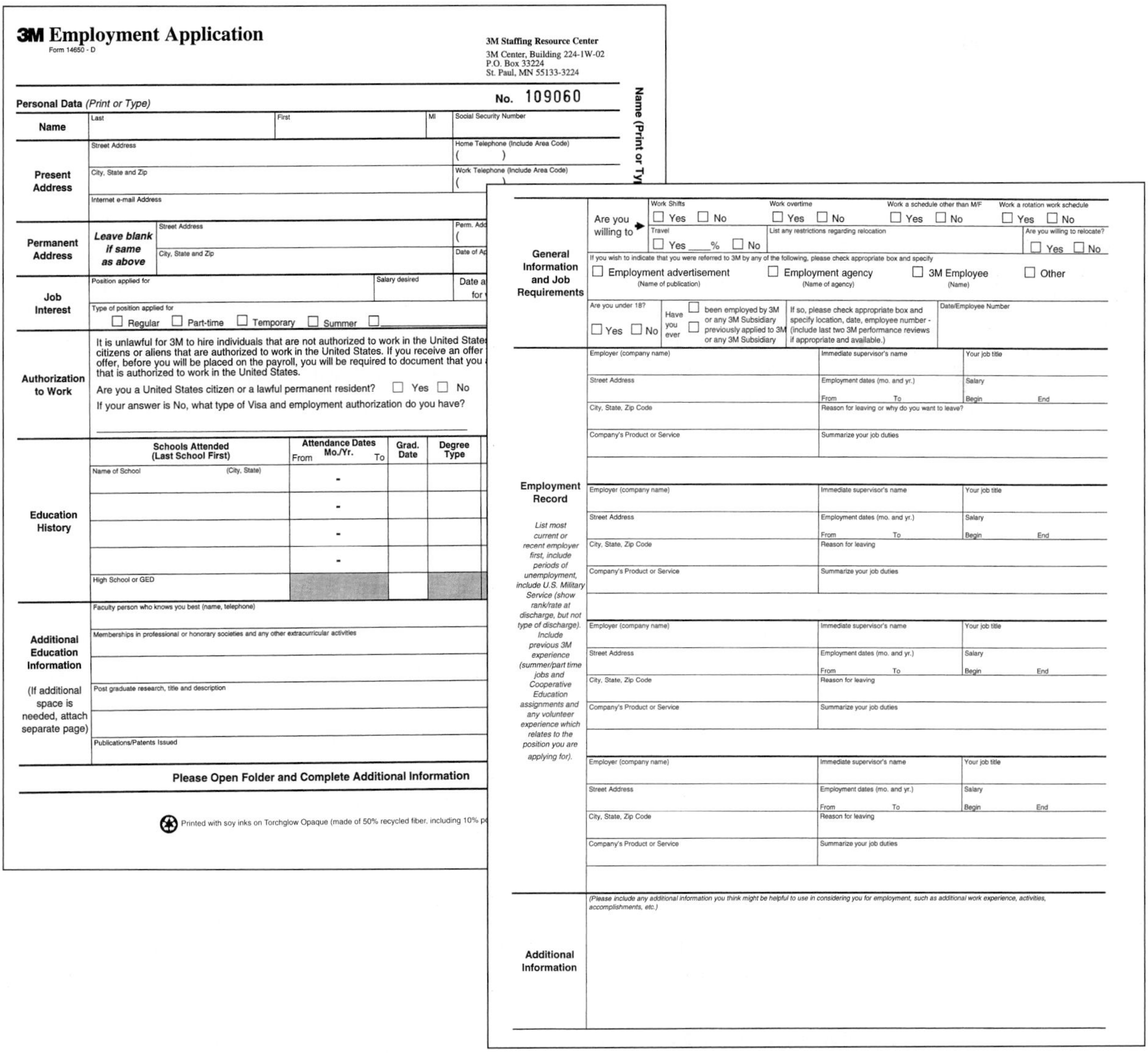

Source: Courtesy of 3M.

Avoiding Appraisal Errors   Managers must be cautious if they are to avoid making mistakes when appraising employees. It is common to overuse one portion of an evaluation instrument, thus overemphasizing some issues and underemphasizing others. A manager must guard against allowing an employee's poor performance on one activity to influence his or her judgment of that subordinate's work on other activities. Similarly, putting too much weight on recent performance distorts an employee's evaluation. For example, if the employee is being rated on performance over the last year, a manager should not permit last month's disappointing performance to overshadow the quality of the work done in the first eleven months of the year. Finally, a manager must guard against discrimination on the basis of race, age, gender, religion, national origin, or sexual orientation.

Performance Feedback

No matter which appraisal technique is used, the results should be discussed with the employee soon after the evaluation is completed. The manager should explain the basis for present rewards and should let the employee know what he or she can do to be recognized as a better performer in the future. The information provided to an employee in such discussions is called a *performance feedback*, and the process is known as a *performance feedback interview*.

There are three major approaches to performance feedback interviews: tell and sell, tell and listen, and problem solving. In a *tell-and-sell* feedback interview, the superior tells the employee how good or bad the employee's performance has been and then attempts to persuade the employee to accept this evaluation. Since the employee has no input into the evaluation, the tell-and-sell interview can lead to defensiveness, resentment, and frustration on the part of the subordinate. The employee may not accept the results of the interview and may not be committed to achieving the goals that are set.

With the *tell-and-listen* approach, the supervisor tells the employee what has been right and wrong with the employee's performance and then gives the employee a chance to respond. The subordinate simply may be given an opportunity to react to the supervisor's statements or may be permitted to offer a full self-appraisal, challenging the supervisor's assessment.

In the *problem-solving* approach, employees evaluate their own performance and set their own goals for future performance. The supervisor is more a colleague than a judge and offers comments and advice in a noncritical manner. An active and open dialogue ensues in which goals for improvement are established mutually. The problem-solving interview is more likely to result in the employee's commitment to the established goals.

To avoid some of the problems associated with the tell-and-sell interview, a mixed approach sometimes is used. The mixed interview uses the tell-and-sell approach to communicate administrative decisions and the problem-solving approach to discuss employee-development issues and future performance goals.[21]

An appraisal approach that has become popular is called a *360-degree evaluation*. A 360-degree evaluation collects anonymous reviews about an employee from his or her peers, subordinates, and supervisors and then compiles these reviews into a feedback report that is given to the employee. Companies that invest significant resources in employee-development efforts are especially likely to use 360-degree evaluations. An employee should not be given a feedback report without first having a one-on-one meeting with his or her supervisor. The most appropriate way to introduce a 360-degree evaluation system in a company is to begin with upper-level management. Then managers should be trained on how to interpret feedback reports so that they can coach their employees on how to use the feedback to achieve higher-level job-related skills and behaviors.[22]

Finally, we should note that many managers find it difficult to discuss the negative aspects of an appraisal. Unfortunately, they may ignore performance feedback altogether or provide it in a very weak and ineffectual manner. In truth, though, most employees have strengths that can be emphasized to soften the discussion of their weaknesses. An employee may not even be aware of weaknesses and their consequences. If such weaknesses are not pointed out through performance feedback, they cannot possibly be eliminated. Only through tactful, honest communication can the results of an appraisal be fully utilized.

The Legal Environment of HRM

Legislation regarding HRM practices has been passed mainly to protect the rights of employees, to promote job safety, and to eliminate discrimination in the workplace. The major federal laws affecting HRM are described in Table 10.2.

National Labor Relations Act and Labor-Management Relations Act

These laws are concerned with dealings between business firms and labor unions. This general area is, in concept, a part of HRM. However, because of its importance, it is often treated as a separate set of activities. We discuss both labor-management relations and these two acts in detail in Chapter 12.

8 LEARNING OBJECTIVE
Outline the major legislation affecting human resources management.

>> **TABLE 10.2**

FEDERAL LEGISLATION AFFECTING HUMAN RESOURCES MANAGEMENT

Law	Purpose
National Labor Relations Act (1935)	Established a collective-bargaining process in labor-management relations as well as the National Labor Relations Board (NLRB)
Fair Labor Standards Act (1938)	Established a minimum wage and an overtime pay rate for employees working more than forty hours per week
Labor-Management Relations Act (1947)	Provided a balance between union power and management power; also known as the Taft-Hartley Act
Equal Pay Act (1963)	Specified that men and women who do equal jobs must be paid the same wage
Title VII of the Civil Rights Act (1964)	Outlawed discrimination in employment practices based on sex, race, color, religion, or national origin
Age Discrimination in Employment Act (1967–1986)	Outlawed personnel practices that discriminate against people aged 40 and older; the 1986 amendment eliminated a mandatory retirement age
Occupational Safety and Health Act (1970)	Regulated the degree to which employees can be exposed to hazardous substances and specified the safety equipment that the employer must provide
Employment Retirement Income Security Act (1974)	Regulated company retirement programs and provided a federal insurance program for retirement plans that go bankrupt
Worker Adjustment and Retraining Notification (WARN) Act (1988)	Required employers to give employees sixty days notice regarding plant closure or layoff of fifty or more employees
Americans with Disabilities Act (1990)	Prohibited discrimination against qualified individuals with disabilities in all employment practices, including job-application procedures, hiring, firing, advancement, compensation, training, and other terms, conditions, and privileges of employment
Civil Rights Act (1991)	Facilitated employees' suing employers for sexual discrimination and collecting punitive damages
Family and Medical Leave Act (1993)	Required an organization with fifty or more employees to provide up to twelve weeks of leave without pay on the birth (or adoption) of an employee's child or if an employee or his or her spouse, child, or parent is seriously ill

Fair Labor Standards Act

This act, passed in 1938 and amended many times since, applies primarily to wages. It established minimum wages and overtime pay rates. Many managers and other professionals, however, are exempt from this law. Managers, for example, seldom get paid overtime when they work more than forty hours a week.

Equal Pay Act

Passed in 1963, this law overlaps somewhat with Title VII of the Civil Rights Act (see below). The Equal Pay Act specifies that men and women who are doing equal jobs must be paid the same wage. Equal jobs are jobs that demand equal effort, skill, and responsibility and that are performed under the same conditions. Differences in pay are legal if they can be attributed to differences in seniority, qualifications, or performance. However, women cannot be paid less (or more) for the same work solely because they are women.

Civil Rights Acts

Title VII of the Civil Rights Act of 1964 applies directly to selection and promotion. It forbids organizations with fifteen or more employees to discriminate in those areas on the basis of sex, race, color, religion, or national origin. The purpose of Title VII is to ensure that employers make personnel decisions on the basis of employee qualifications only. As a result of this act, discrimination in employment (especially against African Americans) has been reduced in this country.

The Equal Employment Opportunity Commission (EEOC) is charged with enforcing Title VII. A person who believes that he or she has been discriminated against can file a complaint with the EEOC. The EEOC investigates the complaint, and if it finds that the person has, in fact, been the victim of discrimination, the commission can take legal action on his or her behalf.

The Civil Rights Act of 1991 facilitates an employee's suing and collecting punitive damages for sexual discrimination. Discriminatory promotion and termination decisions as well as on-the-job issues, such as sexual harassment, are covered by this act.

Age Discrimination in Employment Act

The general purpose of this act, which was passed in 1967 and amended in 1986, is the same as that of Title VII—to eliminate discrimination. However, as the name implies, the Age Discrimination in Employment Act is concerned only with discrimination based on age. It applies to companies with twenty or more employees. In particular, it outlaws personnel practices that discriminate against people aged 40 or older. (No federal law forbids discrimination against people younger than age 40, but several states have adopted age discrimination laws that apply to a variety of age groups.) Also outlawed are company policies that specify a mandatory retirement age. Employers must base employment decisions on ability and not on a number. The EEOC recently settled an age discrimination suit with Foot Locker when it found evidence that older workers had been laid off and then quickly replaced with younger employees at Foot Locker. The EEOC determined that this discrimination was nationwide and ordered payment of $3.5 million to 678 former employees all age 40 or older.[23]

Occupational Safety and Health Act

Passed in 1970, this act is concerned mainly with issues of employee health and safety. For example, the act regulates the degree to which employees can be exposed to hazardous substances. It also specifies the safety equipment that the employer must provide.

The Occupational Safety and Health Administration (OSHA) was created to enforce this act. Inspectors from OSHA investigate employee complaints regarding unsafe working conditions. They also make spot checks on companies operating in particularly hazardous industries, such as chemicals and mining, to ensure compliance with the law. A firm found to be in violation of federal standards can be heavily fined or shut down. Many people feel that issuing OSHA violations is not enough to protect workers from harm. McWane Industries, a large manufacturer of pipes and other products, has been cited for nearly 1,000 safety and environmental violations since 1995. Yet it has still had nine employees killed in its plants during this time. Although the company has paid about $10 million in fines for violations and has three criminal convictions, safety continues to be a major concern. Workers at one of McWane's plants have been seen with bumper stickers saying, "Pray for me. I work at Kennedy Valve." Although OSHA has made much progress, workplace safety is still a major concern.[24]

Employee Retirement Income Security Act

This act was passed in 1974 to protect the retirement benefits of employees. It does not require that firms provide a retirement plan. However, it does specify that *if* a retirement plan is provided, it must be managed in such a way that the interests of employees are protected. It also provides federal insurance for retirement plans that go bankrupt.

Affirmative Action

Affirmative action is not one act but a series of executive orders issued by the president of the United States. These orders established the requirement for affirmative action in personnel practices. This stipulation applies to all employers with fifty or more employees holding federal contracts in excess of $50,000. It prescribes that such employers (1) actively encourage job applications from members of minority groups and (2) hire qualified employees from minority groups not fully represented in their organizations. Many firms that do not hold government contracts voluntarily take part in this affirmative action program.

Protecting workers. This OSHA poster affirms the right of workers to a safe and healthful workplace. Employers are expected to post this sign in a location visible to employees.

Americans with Disabilities Act

The Americans with Disabilities Act (ADA) prohibits discrimination against qualified individuals with disabilities in all employment practices—including job-application procedures, hiring, firing, advancement, compensation, training, and other terms and conditions of employment. All private employers and government agencies with fifteen or more employees are covered by the ADA. Defining who is a qualified individual with a disability is, of course, difficult. Depending on how *qualified individual with a disability* is interpreted, up to forty-three million Americans can be included under this law. This law also mandates that all businesses that serve the public must make their facilities accessible to people with disabilities.

Not only are individuals with obvious physical disabilities protected under the ADA, but also safeguarded are those with less visible conditions such as heart disease, diabetes, epilepsy, cancer, AIDS, and mental illnesses. Because of this law, many organizations no longer require job applicants to pass physical examinations as a condition of employment.

Employers are required to provide disabled employees with reasonable accommodation. *Reasonable accommodation* is any modification or adjustment to a job or work environment that will enable a qualified employee with a disability to perform a central job function. Examples of reasonable accommodation include making existing facilities readily accessible to and usable by an individual confined to a wheelchair. Reasonable accommodation also might mean restructuring a job, modifying work schedules, acquiring or modifying equipment, providing qualified readers or interpreters, or changing training programs.

RETURN TO Inside Business

A diverse work force is important for bottom-line reasons, says Rudy Mendez, McDonald's vice president of diversity initiatives. "We've learned to frame our discussions about diversity around business opportunities, rather than ethical and social [responsibilities]," he says. "We can talk very competently about the business opportunities it brings us and how, in a respectful way, we may be able to bring in a business opportunity within a demographic."

Today, McDonald's is looking for employees from all backgrounds who want a career with ad-

vancement potential, not just a part-time job. The company recently aired a Spanish-language television commercial in which a businessman paying a McDonald's cashier explains that he was once an employee in the fast-food chain—and now owns one of its franchises. Food for thought: CEO Jim Skinner started as an hourly employee in a local McDonald's restaurant, and 70 percent of the company's executives followed a similar career path.

Questions

1. Do you agree with Pat Harris that diversity is "a business imperative" for McDonald's? Explain your answer.
2. Why would McDonald's advertise that it offers career advancement opportunities, not just part-time employment?

▶▶ CHAPTER REVIEW

Summary

Describe the major components of human resources management.

Human resources management (HRM) is the set of activities involved in acquiring, maintaining, and developing an organization's human resources. Responsibility for HRM is shared by specialized staff and line managers. HRM activities include human resources planning, job analysis, recruiting, selection, orientation, compensation, benefits, training and development, and performance appraisal.

2

Identify the steps in human resources planning.

Human resources planning consists of forecasting the human resources that a firm will need and those that it will

have available and then planning a course of action to match supply with demand. Layoffs, attrition, early retirement, and (as a last resort) firing are ways to reduce the size of the work force. Supply is increased through hiring.

3

Describe cultural diversity and understand some of the challenges and opportunities associated with it.

Cultural diversity refers to the differences among people in a work force owing to race, ethnicity, and gender. With an increasing number of women, minorities, and immigrants entering the U.S. work force, management is faced with both challenges and competitive advantages. Some organizations are implementing diversity-related training programs and working to make the most of cultural diversity. With the proper guidance and management, a culturally diverse organization can prove beneficial to all involved.

4

Explain the objectives and uses of job analysis.

Job analysis provides a job description and a job specification for each position within a firm. A job description is a list of the elements that make up a particular job. A job specification is a list of qualifications required to perform a particular job. Job analysis is used in evaluation and in determining compensation levels and serves as the basis for recruiting and selecting new employees.

5

Describe the processes of recruiting, employee selection, and orientation.

Recruiting is the process of attracting qualified job applicants. Candidates for open positions may be recruited from within or outside a firm. In the selection process, information about candidates is obtained from applications, résumés, tests, interviews, references, or assessment centers. This information then is used to select the most appropriate candidate for the job. Newly hired employees then will go through a formal or informal orientation program to acquaint them with the firm.

6

Discuss the primary elements of employee compensation and benefits.

Compensation is the payment employees receive in return for their labor. In developing a system for paying employees, management must decide on the firm's general wage level (relative to other firms), the wage structure within the firm, and individual wages. Wage surveys and job analyses are useful in making these decisions. Employees may be paid hourly wages, salaries, or commissions. They also may receive incentive payments, lump-sum salary increases, and profit-sharing payments. Employee benefits, which are nonmonetary rewards to employees, add about 28 percent to the cost of compensation.

7

Explain the purposes and techniques of employee training, development, and performance appraisal.

Employee training and management-development programs enhance the ability of employees to contribute to a firm. When developing a training program, training needs should be analyzed. Then training methods should be selected. Because training is expensive, an organization should evaluate the effectiveness of its training programs periodically.

Performance appraisal, or evaluation, is used to provide employees with performance feedback, to serve as a basis for distributing rewards, and to monitor selection and training activities. Both objective and judgmental appraisal techniques are used. Their results are communicated to employees through three performance feedback approaches: tell and sell, tell and listen, and problem solving.

8

Outline the major legislation affecting human resources management.

A number of laws have been passed that affect HRM practices and that protect the rights and safety of employees. Some of these are the National Labor Relations Act of 1935, the Labor-Management Relations Act of 1947, the Fair Labor Standards Act of 1938, the Equal Pay Act of 1963, Title VII of the Civil Rights Act of 1964, the Age Discrimination in Employment Acts of 1967 and 1986, the Occupational Safety and Health Act of 1970, the Employment Retirement Income Security Act of 1974, the Worker Adjustment and Retraining Notification Act of 1988, the Americans with Disabilities Act of 1990, the Civil Rights Act of 1991, and the Family and Medical Leave Act of 1993.

Key Terms

You should now be able to define and give an example relevant to each of the following terms:

human resources management (HRM) (314)
human resources planning (315)
replacement chart (316)
skills inventory (316)
cultural (workplace) diversity (317)
job analysis (319)
job description (319)
job specification (319)
recruiting (319)
external recruiting (320)
internal recruiting (321)
selection (321)
orientation (324)
compensation (324)
compensation system (325)
wage survey (325)
job evaluation (325)
comparable worth (325)
hourly wage (326)
salary (326)
commission (326)
incentive payment (326)
lump-sum salary increase (326)
profit sharing (327)
employee benefit (327)
flexible benefit plan (327)
employee training (328)
management development (328)
performance appraisal (330)

Review Questions

1. List the three main HRM activities and their objectives.
2. In general, on what basis is responsibility for HRM divided between line and staff managers?
3. How is a forecast of human resources demand related to a firm's organizational planning?
4. How do human resources managers go about matching a firm's supply of workers with its demand for workers?
5. What are the major challenges and benefits associated with a culturally diverse work force?
6. How are a job analysis, job description, and job specification related?
7. What are the advantages and disadvantages of external recruiting? Of internal recruiting?
8. In your opinion, what are the two best techniques for gathering information about job candidates?
9. Why is orientation an important HRM activity?
10. Explain how the three wage-related decisions result in a compensation system.
11. How is a job analysis used in the process of job evaluation?
12. Suppose that you have just opened a new Ford sales showroom and repair shop. Which of your employees would be paid wages, which would receive salaries, and which would receive commissions?
13. What is the difference between the objective of employee training and the objective of management development?
14. Why is it so important to provide feedback after a performance appraisal?

Discussion Questions

1. How accurately can managers plan for future human resources needs?
2. How might an organization's recruiting and selection practices be affected by the general level of employment?
3. Are employee benefits really necessary? Why?
4. As a manager, what actions would you take if an operations employee with six years of experience on the job refused ongoing training and ignored performance feedback?
5. Why are there so many laws relating to HRM practices? Which are the most important laws, in your opinion?

►► VIDEO CASE 10.1

People Make the Difference at the New England Aquarium

From porpoises and penguins to seals and sea turtles, the nonprofit New England Aquarium houses an incredibly diverse array of the world's sea life. The aquarium's official mission statement is "to present, promote, and protect the world of water." It also wants to appeal to the broadest possible audience and build a work force of paid and unpaid staff that reflects the diversity of the Boston community.

Volunteers are a major resource for the New England Aquarium. Its staff of 1,000 volunteers—one of the nonprofit world's largest—contributes 100,000 hours of service yearly. Many high school and college students volunteer to try out possible career choices. Adults with and without specialized college degrees (in fields such as marine biology and environmental affairs) volunteer their time as well. And the New England Aquarium's internships offer college students and recent graduates hands-on experience in veterinary services, communications, and other key areas.

Maureen C. Hentz, director of volunteer programs, is a champion for workplace diversity. Most organizations "are good at putting diversity in their mission statements and talking about it, but not actually accomplishing it," she observes. In contrast, she and her New England Aquarium colleagues aggressively reach out to recruit volunteers, interns, and employees of different races, ethnicities, socioeconomic levels, physical abilities, and ages. In addition, they welcome people of diverse educational backgrounds, personalities, and viewpoints because of the new ideas these differences can bring to the organization's opportunities and challenges.

One reason the New England Aquarium needs to constantly recruit and train new volunteers (and employees) is that it attracts more visitors every year. Also, like most nonprofits, the New England Aquarium has a very limited budget and must manage its payroll expenses carefully. Therefore, Hentz is always looking for volunteers to assist paid staff in various departments, including education, administration, and animal rescue.

The New England Aquarium must plan for employees, volunteers, or interns to handle certain tasks whenever the facility is open. For example, it needs cashiers to collect admission fees during daytime, evening, and weekend hours. Volunteers are often available to work during weekend hours, but filling daytime positions can be difficult. This is another reason why Hentz and her staff attend community meetings and find other ways to encourage volunteerism.

The internet is an important and cost-effective recruiting tool for the New England Aquarium. Prospective volunteers can browse its website to find open positions, read job descriptions and specifications, and download an application form to complete and submit. Hentz and her staff members read all the applications and ask those who seem the most qualified to come in for a personal interview. Once the final selections are made, volunteers are notified about their assignments and working hours. They receive training in the organization's procedures and learn their specific duties before they start their jobs.

Candidates for internships must send a letter expressing interest in working as an intern and include a résumé plus two academic or professional references. As an option, candidates can send a letter of reference and a college transcript to support the application letter. The New England Aquarium's internship coordinators interview the most promising candidates and make the final selections. Interns, like volunteers, gain valuable experience and can list their New England Aquarium positions on their résumés when looking for future employment.

Paid employees receive a full package of valuable benefits, including paid holidays and sick days, insurance, and tuition reimbursement. Just as important, employees gain an opportunity to make a difference. When hired,

they become part of an organization that protects the underwater environment, educates the public, and saves the lives of whales and other marine life.[25]

For more information about this organization, go to **www.neaq.org.**

Questions

1. Why would the New England Aquarium require people to apply in writing for unpaid volunteer and internship positions?
2. In addition to using the web and attending community meetings, what other external recruiting techniques would you suggest that Hentz use? Why?
3. Do you think that the New England Aquarium should evaluate the performance of its volunteers periodically? Support your answer.

▶▶ CASE 10.2

Can the U.S. Army Recruit 6,600 a Month to "Go Army"?

Imagine having to recruit 80,000 new employees every year while increasing the size of the full-time work force from 482,000 to 512,000. This is the challenge facing the U.S. Army, which must match supply with demand on a huge scale. As the largest employer of 17- to 24-year-olds in the United States, the Army has job descriptions and job specifications for 150 jobs in ten categories. In addition to combat jobs, soldiers are needed for technical and support positions such as mechanics, computers and technology, medical and emergency, engineering, and administration.

Many of the 150 jobs are entry-level. "We need more privates than we do sergeants or captains," says Major Elizabeth Robbins. Month in and month out, the Army must replace soldiers who are promoted, discharged, changed to a different position, or moved from active duty to the Army Reserves. Because the Army does not have enough soldiers to fill certain jobs, it must find qualified and interested candidates among the 6,600 new recruits it seeks to attract every month.

Recruits must have a high school diploma and be in good mental and physical shape. Only one in three young American adults meets these qualifications, which narrows the pool of possible candidates to approximately three million. In reality, the pool is even smaller because some of these potential recruits will choose to continue their education or work for other employers rather than join up. Among those who are qualified and willing to consider enlisting, some may be unsure about the military life, and some simply may wonder what they would gain. In fact, some may decide to join one of the other branches of the armed forces, not the Army.

As a result, recruiting is not just a challenge but also a top priority for the Army. With an annual recruiting budget topping $300 million, the Army uses a lot of advertising plus a variety of less traditional techniques to attract potential recruits. For example, it sponsors NASCAR driver Joe Nemechek, hot rod racers, and drag-strip motorcycles to give the Army "brand" high visibility at racing events. Potential recruits can experience the thrill of flying in Army flight simulators or check under the hood of specially equipped Hummers that tour high schools, colleges, and shopping centers. The Army's recruiting effort extends to cable television as well. One example is the ESPN reality show *Bound for Glory: The Montour Spartans,* in which a high school football team gets new direction from a veteran football player and a retired Army drill sergeant.

The Go Army website is designed to engage web-savvy young adults in a number of ways. Visitors can watch Army commercials, download computer games and screensavers, search job descriptions, learn about benefits such as financial incentives, request more information, locate or chat with a recruiter, and more. One section gives potential recruits a sense of Army life, and another addresses the concerns of parents.

Increasingly, the Army is addressing recruitment messages to parents, who often play a pivotal role in a young adult's decision to enlist. Colonel Thomas Nickerson, the Army's chief recruiting marketer, observes that many parents "grew up during the Vietnam War and have different ideas about the military than the grandparents of today's recruits." Although Army commercials still touch on patriotism, they also focus on the benefits of military service and encourage a dialogue between parents and their children.

Because the Army must meet its monthly recruitment goals to be fully staffed, it analyzes the effectiveness of each recruitment technique. Even with $300 million to spend, the Army has to choose carefully. In determining how to recruit, says Colonel Nickerson, the Army relies on "the best practices of corporate America to make an informed business decision."[26]

For more information about this organization, go to **www.goarmy.com** and **www.army.mil.**

Questions

1. Assuming that enlistment bonuses can't be increased, what might the Army do to appeal to prospective recruits?

2. If the Army is unable to attract the number of recruits needed to fill the forecasted demand for six consecutive months, what are the likely consequences for the organization?

3. What are the advantages and disadvantages of the Army reaching out to parents to influence the enlistment decisions of their children?

→ **CHAPTER 10: JOURNAL EXERCISE**

Discovery statement: This chapter discussed human resource management from an organizational and business perspective.

Assuming that you are currently in school and that you plan to begin a new job when you have completed your studies, at what point will you begin looking for a job? Explain why.

_____

_____

_____

_____

_____

How will you find out about job openings?

_____

_____

_____

_____

What types of information will be important to you when considering whether or not to interview for a specific position?

_____

_____

_____

_____

_____

What sources of information will you use to prepare for an interview with a specific organization?

_____

_____

_____

_____

BUILDING SKILLS FOR CAREER SUCCESS

1. Exploring the Internet

Although you may believe that your formal learning will end when you graduate and enter the working world, it won't. Companies both large and small spend billions of dollars annually in training employees and updating their knowledge and skills. Besides supporting employees who attend accredited continuing-education programs, companies also may provide more specialized in-house course work on new technologies, products, and markets for strategic planning. The Internet is an excellent search tool to find out about course work offered by private training organizations, as well as by traditional academic institutions. Learning online is a fast-growing alternative, especially for busy employees requiring updates to skills in the information technology (IT) field, where software knowledge must be refreshed continuously. Visit the text website for updates to this exercise.

Assignment

1. Visit the websites of several academic institutions and examine their course work offerings. Also examine the offerings of some of the following private consulting firms:

   Learning Tree International:
   www.learningtree.com
   Accenture: **www.accenture.com**
   KPMG: **www.kpmg.com**
   Ernst & Young: **www.ey.com/global**

2. What professional continuing-education training and services are provided by one of the academic institutions whose site you visited?

3. What sort of training is offered by one of the preceding consulting firms?

4. From the company's point of view, what is the total real cost of a day's worth of employee training? What is the money value of one day of study for a full-time college student? Can you explain why firms are willing to pay higher starting salaries for employees with higher levels of education?

5. The American Society for Training and Development (**www.astd.org/**) and the Society for Human Resource Management (**www.shrm.org/**) are two good sources for information about online training pro-

grams. Describe what you found out at these and other sites providing online learning solutions.

2. Developing Critical-Thinking Skills

Suppose that you are the manager of the six supervisors described in the following list. They have all just completed two years of service with you and are eligible for an annual raise. How will you determine who will receive a raise and how much each will receive?

- Joe Garcia has impressed you by his above-average performance on several difficult projects. Some of his subordinates, however, do not like the way he assigns jobs. You are aware that several family crises have left him short of cash.

- Sandy Vance meets her goals, but you feel that she could do better. She is single, likes to socialize, and at times arrives late for work. Several of her subordinates have low skill levels, but Sandy feels that she has explained their duties to them adequately. You believe that Sandy may care more about her friends than about coaching her subordinates. Her workers never complain and appear to be satisfied with their jobs.

- Paul Steiberg is not a good performer, and his work group does not feel that he is an effective leader. You also know that his group is the toughest one to manage. The work is hard and dirty. You realize that it would be very difficult to replace him, and you therefore do not want to lose him.

- Anna Chen runs a tight ship. Her subordinates like her and feel that she is an excellent leader. She listens to them and supports them. Recently, her group won the TOP (The Outstanding Performance) Award. Anna's husband is CEO of a consulting firm, and as far as you know, she is not in financial need.

- Jill Foster has completed every assignment successfully. You are impressed by this, particularly since she has a very difficult job. You recently learned that she spends several hours every week on her own taking classes to improve her skills. Jill seems to be motivated more by recognition than by money.

- Fred Hammer is a jolly person who gets along with everyone. His subordinates like him, but you do not think that he is getting the job done to your expectations. He has missed a critical delivery date twice, and this cost the firm over $5,000 each time. He recently divorced his wife and is having an extremely difficult time meeting his financial obligations.

Assignment

1. You have $25,000 available for raises. As you think about how you will allot the money, consider the following:

   a. What criteria will you use in making a fair distribution?

   b. Will you distribute the entire $25,000? If not, what will you do with the remainder?

2. Prepare a four-column table in the following manner:

   a. In column 1, write the name of the employee.

   b. In column 2, write the amount of the raise.

   c. In column 3, write the percentage of the $25,000 the employee will receive.

   d. In column 4, list the reasons for your decision.

3. Building Team Skills

The New Therapy Company is soliciting a contract to provide five nursing homes with physical, occupational, speech, and respiratory therapy. The therapists will float among the five nursing homes. The therapists have not yet been hired, but the nursing homes expect them to be fully trained and ready to go to work in three months. The previous therapy company lost its contract because of high staff turnover owing to "burnout" (a common problem in this type of work), high costs, and low-quality care. The nursing homes want a plan specifying how the New Therapy Company will meet staffing needs, keep costs low, and provide high-quality care.

Assignment

1. Working in a group, discuss how the New Therapy Company can meet the three-month deadline and still ensure that the care its therapists provide is of high quality. Also discuss the following:

   a. How many of each type of therapist will the company need?

   b. How will it prevent therapists from "burning out"?

   c. How can it retain experienced staff and still limit costs?

   d. Are promotions available for any of the staff? What is the career ladder?

   e. How will the company manage therapists at five different locations? How will it keep in touch with them (computer, voice mail, monthly meetings)? Would it make more sense to have therapists work permanently at each location rather than rotate among them?

   f. How will the company justify the travel costs? What other expenses might it expect?

2. Prepare a plan for the New Therapy Company to present to the nursing homes.

4. Researching Different Careers

A résumé provides a summary of your skills, abilities, and achievements. It also may include a description of the type of job you want. A well-prepared résumé indicates that you know what your career objectives are, shows that you have given serious thought to your career, and tells a potential employer what you are qualified to do. The way a résumé is prepared can make a difference in whether you are considered for a job.

Assignment

1. Prepare a résumé for a job that you want using the information in Appendix A (see text website).

   a. First, determine what your skills are and decide which skills are needed to do this particular job.

   b. Decide which type of format—chronological or functional—would be most effective in presenting your skills and experience.

   c. Keep the résumé to one page, if possible (definitely no more than two pages). (Note that portfolio items may be attached for certain types of jobs, such as artwork.)

2. Have several people review the résumé for accuracy.

3. Ask your instructor to comment on your résumé.

5. Improving Communication Skills

Workplaces in the United States are becoming more culturally diverse. Employees from other countries bring their customs, traditions, values, and language with them to the workplace. It can be difficult for some employees who have worked in a business for a long time to adjust to the changes that accompany cultural diversity. The work environment may become tense and full of distrust and hostility as conflicts erupt among employees. This appears to be the situation at the Zire Company, which manufactures fence posts from recycled plastic. As the company's human resources manager, you are faced with the job of changing this environment into one that encourages cooperation, trust, and mutual respect among employees.

Assignment

1. Putting yourself in the role of the Zire Company's human resources manager, address the following questions:

   a. What are the issues and problems associated with cultural diversity in your company?

   b. What benefits and opportunities could this diversity have for your company?

   c. How can you encourage employees to be more understanding and have greater empathy toward workers who are different from themselves?

2. On the basis of your answers to these questions, prepare a plan for creating an environment that will foster cooperation, trust, and mutual respect among the employees of the Zire Company.

→ PREP TEST

Matching Questions

____ 1. Jobs are studied to determine specific tasks.

____ 2. People are acquired, maintained, and developed for the firm.

____ 3. Personal qualifications required in a job are described.

____ 4. Potential applicants are made aware of available positions.

____ 5. The reward employees receive for their labor.

____ 6. The process for teaching employees to do their job more efficiently.

____ 7. An employee's work performance is evaluated.

____ 8. Gain sharing is an example.

____ 9. It seeks equal compensation for similar jobs.

____ 10. Employees may choose from a wide array of benefit options.

a. comparable worth

b. compensation

c. employee training

d. flexible benefit plan

e. human resources management

f. incentive payment

g. job analysis

h. job specification

i. performance appraisal

j. recruiting

True/False Questions

T F

11. ○ ○ Recruiting is an activity of human resources acquisition.

12. ○ ○ Transfers involve moving employees into higher-level positions.

13. ○ ○ In a structured interview, the interviewer uses a prepared set of questions.

14. ○ ○ The most widely used selection technique is the employment test.

15. ○ ○ Staffing, personnel management, and human resources management are synonymous terms.

16. ○ ○ Attrition is the process of acquiring information on applicants.

T F

17. ○ ○ The selection process matches the right candidate with each job.

18. ○ ○ Employee benefits such as vacation and sick leave are required by law.

19. ○ ○ The purpose of Title VII is to ensure that employers make personnel decisions on the basis of employee qualifications.

20. ○ ○ The Employee Retirement Income Security Act requires firms to provide a retirement plan for their employees.

Multiple-Choice Questions

21. Required retirement before age 70 was outlawed in the
    a. Age Discrimination in Employment Act.
    b. Equal Pay Act.
    c. Fair Labor Standards Act.
    d. Employee Retirement Income Security Act.
    e. Civil Rights Act.

22. A one-page summary of an applicant's qualifications is known as a(n)
    a. application form.
    b. data sheet.
    c. summary sheet.
    d. résumé.
    e. qualification sheet.

23. Melinda walked into the First National Bank to pick up an application for an administrative assistant position. When she asked about the duties and working conditions, the busy receptionist handed her a job
    a. description.
    b. inventory.
    c. analysis.
    d. orientation.
    e. specification.

24. Human resources planning requires the following steps *except*
    a. using the firm's strategic plan.
    b. forecasting the firm's future demand.
    c. determining availability of human resources.
    d. acquiring funds for implementation.
    e. matching supply with demand.

25. Larry was hurt while playing football in his senior year in high school. Since then, he has been confined to a wheel chair. After receiving his college diploma, he applied for a supervision job in a local warehouse. Under ADA, the employer must provide *reasonable accommodation* for disabled employees. Which activity will not legally cover Larry?
    a. Providing adequate home medical care
    b. Making existing facilities accessible
    c. Modifying work schedules
    d. Providing qualified readers
    e. Changing examinations

Fill-in-the-Blank Questions

26. A _____ inventory is a computerized data bank containing information on employee's qualifications.

27. Internet websites and employment agencies are examples of _____ recruiting sources.

28. Acquainting new employees with an organization is the process of _____.

29. The process for preparing managers to assume greater responsibility is accomplished through _____ development.

30. Money paid for work accomplished during a calendar period is _____.

Online Study Center

FOR MORE **test practice, use the interactive ACE quizzes available at the Online Student Center:**
www.college.hmco.com/PIC/pridebusiness9e.

Answers on p. PT1.

Motivating and Satisfying Employees and Teams

LEARNING OBJECTIVES

WHAT you will be able to do once you complete this chapter:

1 Explain what motivation is.

2 Understand some major historical perspectives on motivation.

3 Describe three contemporary views of motivation: equity theory, expectancy theory, and goal-setting theory.

4 Explain several techniques for increasing employee motivation.

5 Understand the types, development, and uses of teams.

WHY this chapter matters

As you move up into management positions or operate your own business, you will need to understand what motivates others in an organization.

FOR HELP with studying this chapter, visit the Online Student Center:

www.college.hmco.com/PIC/pridebusiness9e

Online Study Center

How can managers encourage employee dedication and good performance? FedEx offers employees free flights to any place in the United States served by its cargo jets. At each Four Seasons Hotel, one outstanding employee is rewarded with a week-long getaway, all-expenses-paid—plus a $1,000 bonus for shopping. Cisco Systems' employees get a special treat on the day of the Academy Awards, when the technology company's cafés serve up fun, film-themed lunches. At the financial services firm First Horizon National Corp., employees can take time off whenever they need to visit their children's schools.

So many employees of these firms say "I love my job" that *Fortune* magazine has included all four on its yearly list of "The 100 Best Companies to Work For." The companies on this list are known for how well they treat their employees. Depending on the company, employees may enjoy generous tuition reimbursement, holiday bonuses and parties, on-site day care or dental services, financial assistance with adoption costs, free or low-cost health care coverage, or other benefits.

Wegmans Food Markets, a supermarket chain based in Rochester, New York, recently captured the top spot on the *Fortune* list because of its "employees first" philosophy. The family-owned company rings up $3.4 billion in yearly revenue and employs 30,000 people in four states. Its knowledgeable, enthusiastic work force is a key competitive tool in a high-pressure industry. "If we don't show our customers what to do with our products, they won't buy them," says CEO Danny Wegman. "So the first pump we have to prime is our own people."

In the past 20 years, Wegmans has given employees $54 million worth of college scholarships. It provides extensive training, excellent medical coverage, and an environment in which employees have the authority to do whatever it takes to satisfy customers. Employees like the company so much that 20 percent of the work force has been on the payroll for at least a decade. Lower turnover keeps costs down, yet another reason for Wegmans to invest in its employees.[1]

DID YOU KNOW?
FedEx offers employees free U.S. flights on its cargo jets.

Wegmans
helping you make great meals easy

For more information about this topic, go to http://money.cnn.com/magazines/fortune/fortune_archive/, www.fedex.com, www.fourseasons.com, www.cisco.com, www.firsthorizon.com, and www.wegmans.com.

To achieve its goals, any organization—whether it's FedEx, Four Seasons Hotels, Wegmans, or a local convenience store—must be sure that its employees have more than the right raw materials, adequate facilities, and equipment that works. The organization also must ensure that its employees are *motivated*. To some extent, a high level of employee motivation derives from effective management practices.

In this chapter, after first explaining what motivation is, we present several views of motivation that have influenced management practices over the years: Taylor's ideas of scientific management, Mayo's Hawthorne Studies, Maslow's hierarchy of needs, Herzberg's motivation-hygiene theory, McGregor's Theory X and Theory Y, Ouchi's Theory Z, and reinforcement theory. Then, turning our attention to contemporary ideas, we examine equity theory, expectancy theory, and goal-setting theory. Finally, we discuss specific techniques managers can use to foster employee motivation and satisfaction.

What Is Motivation?

A *motive* is something that causes a person to act. A successful athlete is said to be "highly motivated." A student who avoids work is said to be "unmotivated." We define **motivation** as the individual internal process that energizes, directs, and sustains behavior. It is the personal "force" that causes you or me to act in a particular way. For example, job rotation may increase your job satisfaction and your enthusiasm for your work so that you devote more energy to it, but perhaps job rotation would not have the same impact on me.

    Morale is an employee's attitude or feelings about the job, about superiors, and about the firm itself. To achieve organizational goals effectively, employees need more than the right raw materials, adequate facilities, and equipment that works. High morale results mainly from the satisfaction of needs on the job or as a result of the job. One need that might be satisfied on the job is the need *to be recognized* as an important contributor to the organization. A need satisfied as a result of the job is the need for *financial security*. High morale, in turn, leads to dedication and loyalty, as well as to the desire to do the job well. Low morale can lead to shoddy work, absenteeism, and high turnover rates as employees leave to seek more satisfying jobs with other firms. A study conducted by the Society for Human Resource Management (SHRM) showed that 75 percent of all employees are actively or passively seeking new employment opportunities. To offset this turnover trend, companies are creating retention plans focused on employee morale.[2] Sometimes creative solutions are needed to motivate people and boost morale. This is especially true where barriers to change are deeply rooted in cultural stereotypes of the job and in the industry.

    Motivation, morale, and the satisfaction of employees' needs are thus intertwined. Along with productivity, they have been the subject of much study since the end of the nineteenth century. We continue our discussion of motivation by outlining some landmarks of that early research.

Historical Perspectives on Motivation

Researchers often begin a study with a fairly narrow goal in mind. After they develop an understanding of their subject, however, they realize that both their goal and their research should be broadened. This is exactly what happened when early research into productivity blossomed into the more modern study of employee motivation.

Scientific Management

Toward the end of the nineteenth century, Frederick W. Taylor became interested in improving the efficiency of individual workers. This interest stemmed from his own experiences in manufacturing plants. It eventually led to **scientific management,** the application of scientific principles to management of work and workers.

1 LEARNING OBJECTIVE
Explain what motivation is.

motivation the individual internal process that energizes, directs, and sustains behavior; the personal "force" that causes you or me to behave in a particular way

morale an employee's feelings about his or her job and superiors and about the firm itself

2 LEARNING OBJECTIVE
Understand some major historical perspectives on motivation.

scientific management the application of scientific principles to management of work and workers

Motivating employees. Whether 100 years ago or today, employee motivation sometimes occurs through direct supervision.

One of Taylor's first jobs was with the Midvale Steel Company in Philadelphia, where he developed a strong distaste for waste and inefficiency. He also observed a practice he called "soldiering." Workers "soldiered," or worked slowly, because they feared that if they worked faster, they would run out of work and lose their jobs. Taylor realized that managers were not aware of this practice because they had no idea what the workers' productivity levels *should* be.

Taylor later left Midvale and spent several years at Bethlehem Steel. It was there that he made his most significant contribution. In particular, he suggested that each job should be broken down into separate tasks. Then management should determine (1) the best way to perform these tasks and (2) the job output to expect when the tasks were performed properly. Next, management should carefully choose the best person for each job and train that person to do the job properly. Finally, management should cooperate with workers to ensure that jobs were performed as planned.

Taylor also developed the idea that most people work only to earn money. He therefore reasoned that pay should be tied directly to output. The more a person produced, the more he or she should be paid. This gave rise to the **piece-rate system**, under which employees are paid a certain amount for each unit of output they produce. Under Taylor's piece-rate system, each employee was assigned an output quota. Those exceeding the quota were paid a higher per-unit rate for *all* units they produced (see Figure 11.1). Today, the piece-rate system is still used by some manufacturers and by farmers who grow crops that are harvested by farm laborers.

When Taylor's system was put into practice at Bethlehem Steel, the results were dramatic. Average earnings per day for steel handlers rose from $1.15 to $1.88. (Don't let the low wages that prevailed at the time obscure the fact that this was an increase of better than 60 percent!) The average amount of steel handled per day increased from sixteen to fifty-seven tons.

Taylor's revolutionary ideas had a profound impact on management practice. However, his view of motivation soon was recognized as overly simplistic and narrow. It is true that most people expect to be paid for their work, but it is also true that people work for a variety of reasons other than pay. Simply increasing a person's pay may not increase that person's motivation or productivity.

The Hawthorne Studies

Between 1927 and 1932, Elton Mayo conducted two experiments at the Hawthorne plant of the Western Electric Company in Chicago. The original objective of these

piece-rate system a compensation system under which employees are paid a certain amount for each unit of output they produce

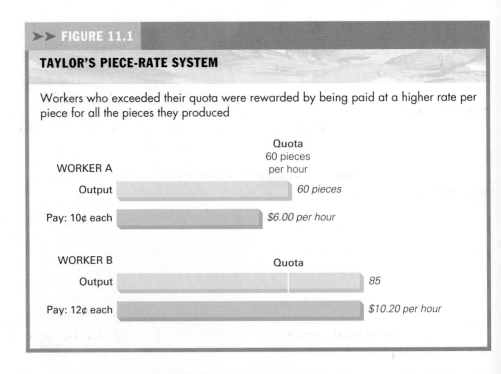

>> FIGURE 11.1

TAYLOR'S PIECE-RATE SYSTEM

Workers who exceeded their quota were rewarded by being paid at a higher rate per piece for all the pieces they produced

WORKER A — Quota 60 pieces per hour
Output: 60 pieces
Pay: 10¢ each — $6.00 per hour

WORKER B — Quota
Output: 85
Pay: 12¢ each — $10.20 per hour

studies, now referred to as the *Hawthorne Studies*, was to determine the effects of the work environment on employee productivity.

In the first set of experiments, lighting in the workplace was varied for one group of workers but not for a second group. Then the productivity of both groups was measured to determine the effect of the light. To the amazement of the researchers, productivity increased for *both* groups. And for the group whose lighting was varied, productivity remained high until the light was reduced to the level of moonlight!

The second set of experiments focused on the effectiveness of the piece-rate system in increasing the output of *groups* of workers. Researchers expected that output would increase because faster workers would put pressure on slower workers to produce more. Again, the results were not as expected. Output remained constant no matter what "standard" rates management set.

The researchers came to the conclusion that *human factors* were responsible for the results of the two experiments. In the lighting experiments, researchers had given both groups of workers a *sense of involvement* in their jobs merely by asking them to participate in the research. These workers—perhaps for the first time—felt as though they were an important part of the organization. In the piece-rate experiments, each group of workers informally set the acceptable rate of output for the group. To gain or retain the *social acceptance* of the group, each worker had to produce at that rate. Slower or faster workers were pressured to maintain the group's pace.

The Hawthorne Studies showed that such human factors are at least as important to motivation as pay rates. From these and other studies, the *human relations movement* in management was born. Its premise was simple: Employees who are happy and satisfied with their work are motivated to perform better. Hence management would do best to provide a work environment that maximizes employee satisfaction.

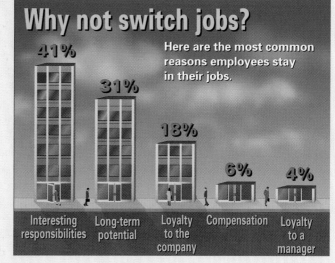

SPOTLIGHT

Why not switch jobs?

Here are the most common reasons employees stay in their jobs.

- 41% Interesting responsibilities
- 31% Long-term potential
- 18% Loyalty to the company
- 6% Compensation
- 4% Loyalty to a manager

Source: Fortune Personnel Consultants survey.

Maslow's Hierarchy of Needs

Abraham Maslow, an American psychologist whose best-known works were published in the 1960s and 1970s, developed a theory of motivation based on a hierarchy of needs. A **need** is a personal requirement. Maslow assumed that humans are "wanting" beings who seek to fulfill a variety of needs. He observed that these needs can be arranged according to their importance in a sequence now known as **Maslow's hierarchy of needs** (see Figure 11.2).

At the most basic level are **physiological needs,** the things we require to survive. They include food and water, clothing, shelter, and sleep. In the employment context, these needs usually are satisfied through adequate wages.

At the next level are **safety needs,** the things we require for physical and emotional security. Safety needs may be satisfied through job security, health insurance, pension plans, and safe working conditions. During a time of falling corporate profits, many companies are facing increasing insurance premiums for employee health care. Both General Electric (GE) and Hershey recently endured strikes centered on the issue of increased health care costs. Reduced health care coverage is a threat to employees' need for safety. Some companies are trying to find unique solutions. For example, SAS, a software company, maintains its own health care center that offers free physical examinations, emergency treatment, immunizations, and care for chronic illnesses.[3]

Next are the **social needs,** the human requirements for love and affection and a sense of belonging. To an extent, these needs can be satisfied through relationships in

need a personal requirement

Maslow's hierarchy of needs a sequence of human needs in the order of their importance

physiological needs the things we require for survival

safety needs the things we require for physical and emotional security

social needs the human requirements for love and affection and a sense of belonging

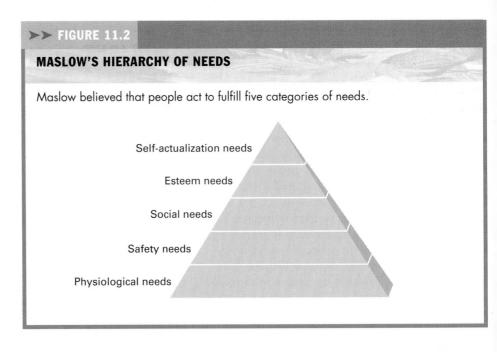

> **► ► FIGURE 11.2**
>
> **MASLOW'S HIERARCHY OF NEEDS**
>
> Maslow believed that people act to fulfill five categories of needs.
>
> Self-actualization needs
>
> Esteem needs
>
> Social needs
>
> Safety needs
>
> Physiological needs

the work environment and the informal organization. However, social networks beyond the workplace—with family and friends, for example—usually are needed too. Casino operator Isle of Capri Casinos, Inc., uses unique methods to help employees meet their social needs. The company holds an annual retreat for managers that is fun and exciting. The latest retreat was called "Isle Survive" and featured a *Survivor*-like game where employees were teamed up and given money and other resources and sent on a sort of scavenger hunt. This is just one of the ways Isle of Capri motivates its workers, and the company seems to be successful in meeting its employees' needs, as evidenced by the lowest employee turnover in the industry.[4]

esteem needs our need for respect, recognition, and a sense of our own accomplishment and worth

At the level of **esteem needs** we require respect and recognition from others and a sense of our own accomplishment and worth (self-esteem). These needs may be sat-

EXAMINING ETHICS

Keeping Employees Safe

Violence on the job is a growing threat for Americans, as these issues show:

● Every year, nearly 2 million employees deal with physical threats from coworkers, customers, or others.

● Managers and employees who travel abroad may be attractive targets for kidnapping or robbery.

● Although the possibility of terrorist attack may seem remote, employees who work in certain cities, buildings, or industries might be at higher risk.

What should companies do to keep employees safe? A growing number of firms offer anger man-

agement courses to help employees prevent feelings from boiling over and learn to handle conflict constructively. Many multinational firms teach employees who travel internationally to vary their daily routines, avoid calling attention to themselves, and identify warning signals of dangerous situations. American Express is one of many companies that notify employees when the terror alert level changes, when security rules are changed, and when specific information about threats are available.

isfied through personal accomplishment, promotion to more responsible jobs, various honors and awards, and other forms of recognition.

At the top of the hierarchy are our **self-actualization needs,** the need to grow, develop, and become all that we are capable of being. These are the most difficult needs to satisfy, and the means of satisfying them tend to vary with the individual. For some people, learning a new skill, starting a new career after retirement, or becoming "the best there is" at some endeavor may be the way to realize self-actualization.

Maslow suggested that people work to satisfy their physiological needs first, then their safety needs, and so on up the "needs ladder." In general, they are motivated by the needs at the lowest level that remain unsatisfied. However, needs at one level do not have to be satisfied completely before needs at the next-higher level come into play. If the majority of a person's physiological and safety needs are satisfied, that person will be motivated primarily by social needs. But any physiological and safety needs that remain unsatisfied also will be important.

Maslow's hierarchy of needs provides a useful way of viewing employee motivation, as well as a guide for management. By and large, American business has been able to satisfy workers' basic needs, but the higher-order needs present more of a challenge. These needs are not satisfied in a simple manner, and the means of satisfaction vary from one employee to another.

Esteem needs. Employee recognition helps to satisfy esteem needs. Recognition of this type shows respect for an individual and his or her accomplishments.

Herzberg's Motivation-Hygiene Theory

In the late 1950s, Frederick Herzberg interviewed approximately two hundred accountants and engineers in Pittsburgh. During the interviews, he asked them to think of a time when they had felt especially good about their jobs and their work. Then he asked them to describe the factor or factors that had caused them to feel that way. Next, he did the same regarding a time when they had felt especially bad about their work. He was surprised to find that feeling good and feeling bad resulted from entirely different sets of factors; that is, low pay may have made a particular person feel bad, but it was not high pay that had made that person feel good. Instead, it was some completely different factor.

self-actualization needs the need to grow and develop and to become all that we are capable of being

Satisfaction and Dissatisfaction   Before Herzberg's interviews, the general assumption was that employee satisfaction and dissatisfaction lay at opposite ends of the same scale. People felt satisfied, dissatisfied, or somewhere in between. But Herzberg's interviews convinced him that satisfaction and dissatisfaction may be different dimensions altogether. One dimension might range from satisfaction to no satisfaction, and the other might range from dissatisfaction to no dissatisfaction. In other words, the opposite of satisfaction is not dissatisfaction. The idea that satisfaction and dissatisfaction are separate and distinct dimensions is referred to as the **motivation-hygiene theory** (see Figure 11.3).

The job factors that Herzberg found most frequently associated with satisfaction are achievement, recognition, responsibility, advancement, growth, and the work itself. These factors generally are referred to as **motivation factors** because their presence increases motivation. However, their absence does not necessarily result in feelings of dissatisfaction. When motivation factors are present, they act as *satisfiers*.

Job factors cited as causing dissatisfaction are supervision, working conditions, interpersonal relationships, pay, job security, company policies and administration. These factors, called **hygiene factors,** reduce dissatisfaction when they are present to an acceptable degree. However, they do not necessarily result in high levels of motivation. When hygiene factors are absent, they act as *dissatisfiers*.

motivation-hygiene theory the idea that satisfaction and dissatisfaction are separate and distinct dimensions

motivation factors job factors that increase motivation but whose absence does not necessarily result in dissatisfaction

hygiene factors job factors that reduce dissatisfaction when present to an acceptable degree but that do not necessarily result in high levels of motivation

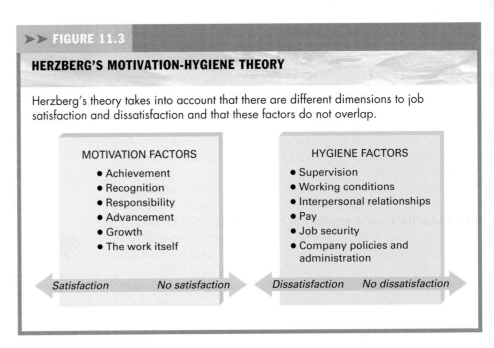

>> FIGURE 11.3

HERZBERG'S MOTIVATION-HYGIENE THEORY

Herzberg's theory takes into account that there are different dimensions to job satisfaction and dissatisfaction and that these factors do not overlap.

MOTIVATION FACTORS	HYGIENE FACTORS
• Achievement	• Supervision
• Recognition	• Working conditions
• Responsibility	• Interpersonal relationships
• Advancement	• Pay
• Growth	• Job security
• The work itself	• Company policies and administration

Satisfaction   No satisfaction   *Dissatisfaction*   No dissatisfaction

Theory X a concept of employee motivation generally consistent with Taylor's scientific management; assumes that employees dislike work and will function only in a highly controlled work environment

Which motivation factors?
This crewmember celebrates after winning the National Pit Crew Championship. Which motivation factors would be most likely to produce a highly effective NASCAR pit crew?

Using Herzberg's Motivation-Hygiene Theory Herzberg provides explicit guidelines for using the motivation-hygiene theory of employee motivation. He suggests that the hygiene factors must be present to ensure that a worker can function comfortably. He warns, however, that a state of *no dissatisfaction* never exists. In any situation, people always will be dissatisfied with something.

According to Herzberg, managers should make hygiene as positive as possible but then should expect only short-term, not long-term, improvement in motivation. Managers must focus instead on providing those motivation factors that presumably *will* enhance motivation and long-term effort.

We should note that employee pay has more effect than Herzberg's theory indicates. He suggests that pay provides only short-term change and not true motivation. Yet, in many organizations, pay constitutes a form of recognition and reward for achievement—and recognition and achievement are both motivation factors. The effect of pay may depend on how it is distributed. If a pay increase does not depend on performance (as in across-the-board or cost-of-living raises), it may not motivate people. However, if pay is increased as a form of recognition (as in bonuses or incentives), it may play a powerful role in motivating employees to higher performance.

Theory X and Theory Y

The concepts of Theory X and Theory Y were advanced by Douglas McGregor in his book *The Human Side of Enterprise*.[5] They are, in essence, sets of assumptions that underlie management's attitudes and beliefs regarding worker behavior.

Theory X is a concept of employee motivation generally consistent with Taylor's scientific management. Theory X assumes that employees dislike work and will function effectively only in a highly controlled work environment.

Theory X is based on the following assumptions:

1. People dislike work and try to avoid it.
2. Because people dislike work, managers must coerce, control, and frequently threaten employees to achieve organizational goals.
3. People generally must be led because they have little ambition and will not seek responsibility; they are concerned mainly with security.

The logical outcome of such assumptions will be a highly controlled work environment—one in which managers make all the decisions and employees take all the orders.

On the other hand, **Theory Y** is a concept of employee motivation generally consistent with the ideas of the human relations movement. Theory Y assumes that employees accept responsibility and work toward organizational goals, and by so doing they also achieve personal rewards. Theory Y is based on the following assumptions:

1. People do not naturally dislike work; in fact, work is an important part of their lives.
2. People will work toward goals to which they are committed.
3. People become committed to goals when it is clear that accomplishing the goals will bring personal rewards.
4. People often seek out and willingly accept responsibility.
5. Employees have the potential to help accomplish organizational goals.
6. Organizations generally do not make full use of their human resources.

Theory Y a concept of employee motivation generally consistent with the ideas of the human relations movement; assumes that employees accept responsibility and work toward organizational goals if by so doing they also achieve personal rewards

Obviously, this view is quite different from—and much more positive than—that of Theory X. McGregor argued that most managers behave in accordance with Theory X. But he maintained that Theory Y is more appropriate and effective as a guide for managerial action (see Table 11.1).

The human relations movement and Theories X and Y increased managers' awareness of the importance of social factors in the workplace. However, human motivation is a complex and dynamic process to which there is no simple key. Neither money nor social factors alone can provide the answer. Rather, a number of factors must be considered in any attempt to increase motivation.

Theory Z

William Ouchi, a management professor at UCLA, studied business practices in American and Japanese firms. He concluded that different types of management systems dominate in these two countries.[6] In Japan, Ouchi found what he calls *type J* firms. They are characterized by lifetime employment for employees, collective (or group) decision making, collective responsibility for the outcomes of decisions, slow

>> **TABLE 11.1**

THEORY X AND THEORY Y CONTRASTED

Area	Theory X	Theory Y
Attitude toward work	Dislike	Involvement
Control systems	External	Internal
Supervision	Direct	Indirect
Level of commitment	Low	High
Employee potential	Ignored	Identified
Use of human resources	Limited	Not limited

evaluation and promotion, implied control mechanisms, nonspecialized career paths, and a holistic concern for employees as people.

American industry is dominated by what Ouchi calls *type A* firms, which follow a different pattern. They emphasize short-term employment, individual decision making, individual responsibility for the outcomes of decisions, rapid evaluation and promotion, explicit control mechanisms, specialized career paths, and a segmented concern for employees only as employees.

A few very successful American firms represent a blend of the type J and type A patterns. These firms, called *type Z* organizations, emphasize long-term employment, collective decision making, individual responsibility for the outcomes of decisions, slow evaluation and promotion, informal control along with some formalized measures, moderately specialized career paths, and a holistic concern for employees.

Theory Z the belief that some middle ground between Ouchi's type A and type J practices is best for American business

Ouchi's **Theory Z** is the belief that some middle ground between his type A and type J practices is best for American business (see Figure 11.4). A major part of Theory Z is the emphasis on participative decision making. The focus is on "we" rather than on "us versus them." Theory Z employees and managers view the organization as a family. This participative spirit fosters cooperation and the dissemination of information and organizational values.

Reinforcement Theory

reinforcement theory a theory of motivation based on the premise that behavior that is rewarded is likely to be repeated, whereas behavior that is punished is less likely to recur

Reinforcement theory is based on the premise that behavior that is rewarded is likely to be repeated, whereas behavior that is punished is less likely to recur. A *reinforcement* is an action that follows directly from a particular behavior. It may be a pay raise following a particularly large sale to a new customer or a reprimand for coming to work late.

Reinforcements can take a variety of forms and can be used in a number of ways. A *positive reinforcement* is one that strengthens desired behavior by providing a reward. For example, many employees respond well to praise; recognition from their supervisors for a job well done increases (strengthens) their willingness to perform well in the future. A *negative reinforcement* strengthens desired behavior by eliminating an undesirable task or situation. Suppose that a machine shop must be cleaned thoroughly every month—a dirty, miserable task. During one particular month when the workers do a less-than-satisfactory job at their normal work assignments, the boss requires the workers to clean the factory rather than bringing in the usual private maintenance

---

>> FIGURE 11.4

THE FEATURES OF THEORY Z

The best aspects of Japanese and American management theories combine to form the nucleus of Theory Z.

TYPE J FIRMS (Japanese)	TYPE Z FIRMS (Best choice for American firms)	TYPE A FIRMS (American)
• Lifetime employment • Collective decision making • Collective responsibility • Slow promotion • Implied control mechanisms • Nonspecialized career paths • Holistic concern for employees	• Long-term employment • Collective decision making • Individual responsibility • Slow promotion • Informal control • Moderately specialized career paths • Holistic concern for employees	• Short-term employment • Individual decision making • Individual responsibility • Rapid promotion • Explicit control mechanisms • Specialized career paths • Segmented concern for employees

service. The employees will be motivated to work harder the next month to avoid the unpleasant cleanup duty again.

Punishment is an undesired consequence of undesirable behavior. Common forms of punishment used in organizations include reprimands, reduced pay, disciplinary lay-offs, and termination (firing). Punishment often does more harm than good. It tends to create an unpleasant environment, fosters hostility and resentment, and suppresses undesirable behavior only until the supervisor's back is turned.

Managers who rely on *extinction* hope to eliminate undesirable behavior by not re-sponding to it. The idea is that the behavior eventually will become "extinct." Suppose, for example, that an employee has the habit of writing memo after memo to his or her manager about insignificant events. If the manager does not respond to any of these memos, the employee probably will stop writing them, and the behavior will have been squelched.

The effectiveness of reinforcement depends on which type is used and how it is timed. One approach may work best under certain conditions, but some situations lend themselves to the use of more than one approach. Generally, positive reinforcement is considered the most effective, and it is recommended when the manager has a choice.

Continual reinforcement can become tedious for both managers and employees, especially when the same behavior is being reinforced over and over in the same way. At the start, it may be necessary to reinforce a desired behavior every time it occurs. However, once a desired behavior has become more or less established, occasional re-inforcement seems to be most effective.

Contemporary Views on Motivation

Maslow's hierarchy of needs and Herzberg's motivation-hygiene theory are popular and widely known theories of motivation. Each is also a significant step up from the relatively narrow views of scientific management and Theories X and Y. But they do have one weakness: Each attempts to specify *what* motivates people, but neither ex-plains *why* or *how* motivation develops or is sustained over time. In recent years, man-agers have begun to explore three other models that take a more dynamic view of mo-tivation. These are equity theory, expectancy theory, and goal-setting theory.

3 LEARNING OBJECTIVE
Describe three contemporary views of motivation: equity the-ory, expectancy theory, and goal-setting theory.

Equity Theory

The **equity theory** of motivation is based on the premise that people are motivated to obtain and preserve equitable treatment for themselves. As used here, *equity* is the dis-tribution of rewards in direct proportion to the contribution of each employee to the organization. Everyone need not receive the *same* rewards, but the rewards should be in accordance with individual contributions.

equity theory a theory of motivation based on the premise that people are motivated to obtain and preserve equitable treat-ment for themselves

According to this theory, we tend to implement the idea of equity in the following way: First, we develop our own input-to-outcome ratio. *Inputs* are the time, effort, skills, education, experience, and so on that we contribute to the organization. *Outcomes* are the rewards we get from the organization, such as pay, benefits, recogni-tion, and promotions. Next, we compare this ratio with what we perceive as the input-to-outcome ratio for some other person. It might be a coworker, a friend who works for another firm, or even an average of all the people in our organization. This person is called the *comparison other*. Note that our perception of this person's input-to-out-come ratio may be absolutely correct or completely wrong. However, we believe that it is correct.

If the two ratios are roughly the same, we feel that the organization is treating us equitably. In this case we are motivated to leave things as they are. However, if our ra-tio is the higher of the two, we feel under-rewarded and are motivated to make changes. We may (1) decrease our own inputs by not working so hard, (2) try to in-crease our total outcome by asking for a raise in pay, (3) try to get the comparison other to increase some inputs or receive decreased outcomes, (4) leave the work situation, or (5) do a new comparison with a different comparison other.

Equity theory is most relevant to pay as an outcome. Because pay is a very real measure of a person's worth to an organization, comparisons involving pay are a natural part of organizational life. Managers can try to avoid problems arising from inequity by making sure that rewards are distributed on the basis of performance and that everyone clearly understands the basis for his or her own pay.

Expectancy Theory

expectancy theory a model of motivation based on the assumption that motivation depends on how much we want something and on how likely we think we are to get it

Expectancy theory, developed by Victor Vroom, is a very complex model of motivation based on a deceptively simple assumption. According to expectancy theory, motivation depends on how much we want something and on how likely we think we are to get it (see Figure 11.5). Consider, for example, the case of three sales representatives who are candidates for promotion to one sales manager's job. Bill has had a very good sales year and always gets good performance evaluations. However, he isn't sure that he wants the job because it involves a great deal of travel, long working hours, and much stress and pressure. Paul wants the job badly but doesn't think he has much chance of getting it. He has had a terrible sales year and gets only mediocre performance evaluations from his present boss. Susan wants the job as much as Paul, and she thinks that she has a pretty good shot at it. Her sales have improved significantly this past year, and her evaluations are the best in the company.

Expectancy theory would predict that Bill and Paul are not very motivated to seek the promotion. Bill doesn't really want it, and Paul doesn't think that he has much of a chance of getting it. Susan, however, is very motivated to seek the promotion because she wants it *and* thinks that she can get it.

Expectancy theory is complex because each action we take is likely to lead to several different outcomes; some we may want, and others we may not want. For example, a person who works hard and puts in many extra hours may get a pay raise, be promoted, and gain valuable new job skills. However, that person also may be forced to spend less time with his or her family and be forced to cut back on his or her social life.

For one person, the promotion may be paramount, the pay raise and new skills fairly important, and the loss of family and social life of negligible importance. For someone else, the family and social life may be most important, the pay raise of moderate importance, the new skills unimportant, and the promotion undesirable because of the additional hours it would require. The first person would be motivated to work hard and put in the extra hours, whereas the second person would not be at all motivated to do so. In other words, it is the entire bundle of outcomes—and the individual's evaluation of the importance of each outcome—that determines motivation.

Expectancy theory is difficult to apply, but it does provide several useful guidelines for managers. It suggests that managers must recognize that (1) employees work for a

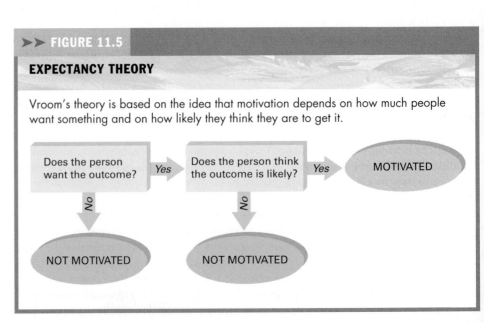

> **FIGURE 11.5**

EXPECTANCY THEORY

Vroom's theory is based on the idea that motivation depends on how much people want something and on how likely they think they are to get it.

variety of reasons, (2) these reasons, or expected outcomes, may change over time, and (3) it is necessary to clearly show employees how they can attain the outcomes they desire.

Goal-Setting Theory

Goal-setting theory suggests that employees are motivated to achieve goals that they and their managers establish together. The goal should be very specific, moderately difficult, and one the employee will be committed to achieve.[7] Rewards should be tied directly to goal achievement. Using goal-setting theory, a manager can design rewards that fit employee needs, clarify expectations, maintain equity, and provide reinforcement. A major benefit of this theory is that it provides a good understanding of the goal the employee is to achieve and the rewards that will accrue to the employee if the goal is accomplished.

goal-setting theory a theory of motivation suggesting that employees are motivated to achieve goals that they and their managers establish together

Key Motivation Techniques

Today, it takes more than a generous salary to motivate employees. Increasingly, companies are trying to provide motivation by satisfying employees' less tangible needs. In this section we discuss several specific techniques that help managers to boost employee motivation and job satisfaction.

4 LEARNING OBJECTIVE
Explain several techniques for increasing employee motivation.

Management by Objectives

Management by objectives (MBO) is a motivation technique in which managers and employees collaborate in setting goals. The primary purpose of MBO is to clarify the roles employees are expected to play in reaching the organization's goals. For example, Daymark Solutions has put MBO to use by establishing short-term goals for every employee. These quarterly objectives may be achieving a high level of customer satisfaction or receiving specific certifications. These smaller goals directly correlate with the larger company objectives, such as cost containment or revenue goals.[8] By allowing individuals to participate in goal setting and performance evaluation, MBO increases their motivation. Most MBO programs consist of a series of five steps.

management by objectives (MBO) a motivation technique in which managers and employees collaborate in setting goals

The first step in setting up an MBO program is to secure the acceptance of top management. It is essential that top managers endorse and participate in the program if others in the firm are to accept it. The commitment of top management also provides a natural starting point for educating employees about the purposes and mechanics of MBO.

Next, preliminary goals must be established. Top management also plays a major role in this activity because the preliminary goals reflect the firm's mission and strategy. The intent of an MBO program is to have these goals filter down through the organization.

The third step, which actually consists of several smaller steps, is the heart of MBO:

1. The manager explains to each employee that he or she has accepted certain goals for the group (the manager as well as the employees) and asks the individual to think about how he or she can help to achieve these goals.
2. The manager later meets with each employee individually. Together they establish goals for the employee. Whenever possible, the goals should be measurable and should specify the time frame for completion (usually one year).
3. The manager and the employee decide what resources the employee will need to accomplish his or her goals.

As the fourth step, the manager and each employee meet periodically to review the employee's progress. They may agree to modify certain goals during these meetings if circumstances have changed. For example, a sales representative may have accepted a goal of increasing sales by 20 percent. However, an aggressive competitor may have entered the marketplace, making this goal unattainable. In light of this circumstance, the goal may be revised downward to 10 or 15 percent.

The fifth step in the MBO process is evaluation. At the end of the designated time period, the manager and each employee meet again to determine which of the individual's goals were met, which were not met, and why. The employee's reward (in the form of a pay raise, praise, or promotion) is based primarily on the degree of goal attainment.

As with every other management method, MBO has advantages and disadvantages. MBO can motivate employees by involving them actively in the life of the firm. The collaboration on goal setting and performance appraisal improves communication and makes employees feel that they are an important part of the organization. Periodic review of progress also enhances control within an organization. A major problem with MBO is that it does not work unless the process begins at the top of an organization. In some cases MBO results in excessive paperwork. Also, a manager may not like sitting down and working out goals with subordinates and may instead just assign them goals. Finally, MBO programs prove difficult to implement unless goals are quantifiable.

job enrichment a motivation technique that provides employees with more variety and responsibility in their jobs

job enlargement expanding a worker's assignments to include additional but similar tasks

Job Enrichment

Job enrichment is a method of motivating employees by providing them with variety in their tasks while giving them some responsibility for, and control over, their jobs. At the same time, employees gain new skills and acquire a broader perspective about how their individual work contributes to the goals of the organization. Earlier in this chapter we noted that Herzberg's motivation-hygiene theory is one rationale for the use of job enrichment; that is, the added responsibility and control that job enrichment confers on employees increases their satisfaction and motivation. Employees at 3M get to spend 15 percent of their time at work on whatever projects they choose regardless of the relationship of these "pet projects" to the employees' regular duties. This type of enrichment can motivate employees and create a variety of benefits for the company.[9] At times, **job enlargement,** expanding a worker's assignments to include additional but similar tasks, can lead to job enrichment. Job enlargement might mean that a worker on an assembly line who used to connect three wires to components moving down the line, now connects five wires. Unfortunately, the added tasks often are just as routine as those the worker performed before the change. In such cases, enlargement may not be effective.

Whereas job enlargement does not really change the routine and monotonous nature of jobs, job enrichment does. Job enrichment requires that added tasks give an employee more responsibility for what he or she does. It provides workers with both more tasks to do and more control over how they perform them. In particular, job enrichment removes many controls from jobs, gives workers more authority, and assigns work in complete, natural units. Moreover, employees frequently are given fresh and challenging job assignments. By blending more planning and decision making into jobs, job

Make Your Job Application Stand Out

You want your job application, résumé, and cover letter to stand out—but so does every other applicant. So how do you catch the eye of a prospective employer?

- *Add a little personality.* Alison Hager sent her résumé to twenty advertising agencies but got no response until she wrote in one cover letter, "It would be a dream for me" to work at a small agency. She was called for an interview—and landed the job.

- *Show what you can do.* Show that you understand the challenges the company is facing, and suggest how you might help. Lisa Jacobson, who owns a tutoring company, received dozens of applications for a recent job opening but interviewed (and hired) the one candidate who explained "what she was going to do to make my company better."

- *Be creative but don't go overboard.* Depending on the position you want, an outlandish attention-getting technique might hurt your chances. However, consider an imaginative approach when the job requires creativity. One applicant impressed the head of human resources by submitting his résumé along with a home video about marketing the company's product—and he marketed himself into a marketing job.

Job enrichment. Employees at this New Balance plant are enrolled in a job enrichment program. Each person on this work team has been cross-trained to do other team members' jobs.

enrichment gives work more depth and complexity.

Job redesign is a type of job enrichment in which work is restructured in ways that cultivate the worker-job match. Job redesign can be achieved by combining tasks, forming work groups, or establishing closer customer relationships. Employees often are more motivated when jobs are combined because the increased variety of tasks presents more challenge and therefore more reward. Work groups motivate employees by showing them how their jobs fit within the organization as a whole and how they contribute to its success. Establishing client relationships allows employees to interact directly with customers. Not only does this type of redesign add a personal dimension to employment, but it also provides workers with immediate and relevant feedback about how they are doing their jobs.

Job enrichment works best when employees seek more challenging work. Of course, not all workers respond positively to job-enrichment programs. Employees must desire personal growth and have the skills and knowledge to perform enriched jobs. Lack of self-confidence, fear of failure, or distrust of management's intentions are likely to lead to ineffective performance on enriched jobs. In addition, some workers do not view their jobs as routine and boring, and others even prefer routine jobs because they find them satisfying. Companies that use job enrichment as an alternative to specialization also face extra expenses, such as the cost of retraining. Another motivation for job redesign is to reduce employees' stress at work. A job redesign that carefully matches worker to job can prevent stress-related injuries, which constitute about 60 to 80 percent of all work-related injuries. The reduced stress also creates greater motivation.[10]

job redesign a type of job enrichment in which work is restructured to cultivate the worker-job match

behavior modification a systematic program of reinforcement to encourage desirable behavior

Behavior Modification

Behavior modification is a systematic program of reinforcement to encourage desirable behavior. Behavior modification involves both rewards to encourage desirable actions and punishments to discourage undesirable actions. However, studies have shown that rewards, such as compliments and expressions of appreciation, are much more effective behavior modifiers than punishments, such as reprimands and scorn.

When applied to management, behavior modification strives to encourage desirable organizational behavior. Use of this technique begins with identification of a *target behavior*—the behavior that is to be changed. (It might be low production levels or a high rate of absenteeism, for example.) Existing levels of this behavior then are measured. Next, managers provide positive reinforcement in the form of a reward when employees exhibit the *desired behavior* (such as increased production or less

SPOTLIGHT

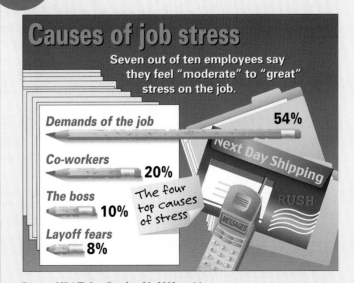

Causes of job stress

Seven out of ten employees say they feel "moderate" to "great" stress on the job.

Demands of the job — 54%

Co-workers — 20%

The boss — 10%

The four top causes of stress

Layoff fears — 8%

Source: *USA Today*, October 29, 2002, p. A1.

absenteeism). The reward might be praise or a more tangible form of recognition, such as a gift, meal, or trip. Finally, the levels of the target behavior are measured again to determine whether the desired changes have been achieved. If they have, the reinforcement is maintained. However, if the target behavior has not changed significantly in the desired direction, the reward system must be changed to one that is likely to be more effective. John Kotter, a renowned Harvard Business School professor, states that this is difficult; the kind of emotional persuasion needed for these changes is not taught in business schools and is not often properly considered in many business settings.[11] The key is to devise effective rewards that not only will modify employees' behavior in desired ways but also will motivate them. To this end, experts suggest that management should reward quality, loyalty, and productivity.

Flextime

To most people, a work schedule means the standard nine-to-five, forty-hour workweek. In reality, though, many people have work schedules that are quite different from this. Police officers, firefighters, restaurant personnel, airline employees, and medical personnel usually have work schedules that are far from standard. Some manufacturers also rotate personnel from shift to shift. Many professional people—such as managers, artists, and lawyers—need more than forty hours each week to get their work done.

The needs and lifestyles of today's work force are changing. Dual-income families make up a much larger share of the work force than ever before, and women are one of its fastest-growing sectors. Additionally, more employees are responsible for the care of elderly relatives. Recognizing that these changes increase the demand for family time, many employers are offering flexible work schedules that not only help employees to manage their time better but also increase employee motivation and job satisfaction.

flextime a system in which employees set their own work hours within employer-determined limits

Flextime is a system in which employees set their own work hours within certain limits determined by employers. Typically, the firm establishes two bands of time: the *core time*, when all employees must be at work, and the *flexible time*, when employees may choose whether to be at work. The only condition is that every employee must work a total of eight hours each day. For example, the hours between 9 and 11 a.m. and 1 and 3 p.m. might be core time, and the hours between 6 and 9 a.m., between 11 a.m. and 1 p.m., and between 3 and 6 p.m. might be flexible time. This would give employees the option of coming in early and getting off early, coming in later and leaving later, or taking an extralong lunch break. But flextime also ensures that everyone is present at certain times, when conferences with supervisors and department meetings can be scheduled. Another type of flextime allows employees to work a forty-hour work week in four days instead of five. Workers who put in ten hours a day instead of eight get an extra day off each week. According to a survey conducted by the Society for Human Resource Management, approximately 56 percent of firms offer flextime.[12] At times, smaller firms use flextime to attract and retain employees, especially when they cannot match the salaries and benefit package provided by larger companies. For example, independent accounting firm Jefferson Wells uses flexible schedules as an incentive when recruiting high-quality candidates. By offering a customized work schedule and part-time positions with full-time benefits, the firm is able to remain competitive with larger companies.[13]

The sense of independence and autonomy employees gain from having a say in what hours they work can be a motivating factor. In addition, employees who have enough time to deal with nonwork issues often work more productively and with greater satisfaction when they are on the job. Approximately 29 percent of U.S. workers participate in determining their own work schedules, thus experiencing some form of flextime.[14] Two common problems associated with using flextime are (1) supervisors sometimes find their jobs complicated by having employees who come and go at different times, and (2) employees without flextime sometimes resent coworkers who have it.

Part-Time Work and Job Sharing

Part-time work is permanent employment in which individuals work less than a standard work week. The specific number of hours worked varies, but part-time jobs are structured so that all responsibilities can be completed in the number of hours an employee works. Part-time work is of special interest to parents who want more time with their children and people who simply desire more leisure time. One disadvantage of part-time work is that it often does not provide the benefits that come with a full-time position. This is not, however, the case at Starbucks, where approximately 80 percent of its employees work part time. Starbucks does not treat its part-time employees any differently from its full-time employees; all receive the same access to numerous benefits, which even includes a free pound of coffee every week.[15]

Job sharing (sometimes referred to as *work sharing*) is an arrangement whereby two people share one full-time position. One job sharer may work from 8 a.m. to noon, and the other may work from 1 to 5 p.m., or they may alternate work days. For example, at the BBC, two women share the same job. By communicating daily through telephone, voice mail, and fax machines, these announcers are able to handle a challenging administrative position and still have time for their families. Through their partnership at work, they have been able to share a position for more than six years.[16] Job sharing combines the security of a full-time position with the flexibility of a part-time job. Among the "100 Best Companies for Working Mothers," ninety-four offer job sharing because it allows these companies to retain highly talented professionals.[17]

For firms, job sharing provides a unique opportunity to attract highly skilled employees who might not be available on a full-time basis. In addition, companies can save on expenses by reducing the cost of benefits and avoiding the disruptions of employee turnover. For employees, opting for the flexibility of job sharing may mean giving up some of the benefits received for full-time work. In addition, job sharing is difficult if tasks are not easily divisible or if two people do not work or communicate well with one another.

Part-time work. At Starbucks, part-time employees receive the same level of benefits as full-time employees.

part-time work permanent employment in which individuals work less than a standard work week

job sharing an arrangement whereby two people share one full-time position

Telecommuting

A growing number of companies allow **telecommuting,** working at home all the time or for a portion of the work week. Personal computers, modems, fax machines, voice mail, cellular phones, and overnight couriers all facilitate the work-at-home trend. Working at home means that individuals can set their own hours and have more time with their families. Even the federal government is recognizing the benefits of telecommuting in that 90 percent of the U.S. Treasury Inspector General for Tax Administration (TIGTA) workers and over 100 lawyers for the U.S. Trademark Office telecommute at least three days a week.[18]

Companies that allow telecommuting experience several benefits, including increased productivity, lower real estate and travel costs, reduced employee absenteeism and turnover, increased work/life balance, improved morale, and access to additional labor pools. Pitney Bowes reports that an additional benefit gained when employees work from home is the company's image as a good corporate citizen because the program helps to decrease pollution and traffic congestion.[19] Among the disadvantages to telecommuting are feelings of isolation, putting in longer hours, and being distracted by family or household responsibilities. In addition, some supervisors have difficulty monitoring productivity. Although most bosses say that they trust their staff to work from home, many think that home workers are work-shy and less productive than office-based staff. A survey conducted in the United Kingdom found that up to

telecommuting working at home all the time or for a portion of the work week

BizTech

Telecommuting: By the Numbers

Aided by ever-better communication technology, telecommuting is on the rise. Here's a look at some key statistics:

- 30 percent of large companies now offer telecommuting as an alternative.
- 13 percent of all U.S. employees telecommute at least once a week.
- Fewer than 10 percent of U.S. government employees currently telecommute.

- Government transportation spending could drop by $3,000 for each employee who switches to telecommuting.
- 90 percent of telecommuters say that their morale is higher when they work from home.

- 85 percent of managers say that telecommuting does not hurt productivity—and some say that it increases productivity by up to 20 percent.

Employees equipped with the right technology can work for companies around the corner or around the world. Companies generally require telecommuters to participate in regular teleconference or videoconference meetings, file weekly e-mail reports, and stay in close touch by phone or instant messaging as needed.

38 percent of managers surveyed believe that home workers are less productive, and 22 percent think that working from home is an excuse for time off. In addition, some supervisors have difficulty monitoring productivity.[20]

Sun Microsystems, for example, is an industry leader at providing a virtual work environment. Approximately 80 percent of the company's 20,000-member workforce connects to the company remotely. Sun was awarded the Optimas Award for Global Outlook because of its new iWork Program that allows employees to connect to Sun all over the globe. The program has boosted employee satisfaction, reduced turnover, and saved the company $255 million on real estate over the past four years.[21]

Employee Empowerment

empowerment making employees more involved in their jobs by increasing their participation in decision making

Many companies are increasing employee motivation and satisfaction through the use of empowerment. **Empowerment** means making employees more involved in their jobs and in the operations of the organization by increasing their participation in decision making. With empowerment, control no longer flows exclusively from the top levels of the organization downward. Empowered employees have a voice in what they do and how and when they do it. In some organizations, employees' input is restricted to individual choices, such as when to take breaks. In other companies, their responsibilities may encompass more far-reaching issues. For example, at Wegmans grocery stores, employees are empowered to ensure that the store achieves its primary objective: No customer leaves unhappy. Employees are allowed to make any concessions or decisions necessary to provide a good shopping experience. Anything is possible—from baking a family's Thanksgiving turkey in the store's oven to traveling to a customer's home to fix a botched order. Not only are Wegmans employees empowered to make on-the-spot customer-service decisions, but they also receive extensive training in the products they sell so as to guarantee that they can answer customers' questions about recipes, exotic items, and even food preparation.[22]

For empowerment to work effectively, management must be involved. Managers should set expectations, communicate standards, institute periodic evaluations, and guarantee follow-up. Effectively implemented, empowerment can lead to increased job satisfaction, improved job performance, higher self esteem, and increased organizational commitment. Obstacles to empowerment include resistance on the part of management, distrust of management on the part of workers, insufficient training, and poor communication between management and employees.

Employee Ownership

Some organizations are discovering that a highly effective technique for motivating employees is **employee ownership**— that is, employees own the company they work for by virtue of being stockholders. Employee-owned businesses directly reward employees for success. When the company enjoys increased sales or lower costs, employees benefit directly. The National Center for Employee Ownership, an organization that studies employee-owned American businesses, reports that employee stock ownership plans (ESOPs) provide considerable employee incentive and increase employee involvement and commitment. In the United States today, about 8.5 million employees participate in 11,500 ESOPs and stock bonus plans.[23] As a means to motivate top executives and, frequently, middle-ranking managers who are working long days for what are generally considered poor salaries, some firms provide stock options as part of the employee compensation package. The option is simply the right to buy shares of the firm within a prescribed time at a set price. If the firm does well and its stock price rises past the set price (presumably because of all the work being done by the employee), the employee can exercise the option and immediately sell the stock and cash in on the company's success.

The difficulties of such companies as United Airlines have damaged the idea of employee ownership. United's ESOP has failed to solve problems between employees and management. In addition, Lowe's, the home-improvement retailer, recently stopped its long-running and mostly successful ESOP and transferred remaining money into 401(k) plans.[24]

employee ownership a situation in which employees own the company they work for by virtue of being stockholders

Teams and Teamwork

The concepts of teams and teamwork may be most commonly associated with sports, but they also are integral parts of business organizations. This organizational structure is popular because it encourages employees to participate more fully in business decisions.

The growing number of companies organizing their work forces into teams reflects an effort to increase employee productivity and creativity, because team members are working on specific goals and are given greater autonomy. This leads to greater job satisfaction as employees feel more involved in the management process.[25] America Funds has been using the team structure since 1958. This mutual fund company employs a team of managers and a team of analysts that each handle a portion of the fund's investments. This approach prevents egotism and fad stocks from damaging a fund's performance.[26]

5 LEARNING OBJECTIVE
Understand the types, development, and uses of teams.

What Is a Team?

In a business organization, a **team** is a group of workers functioning together as a unit to complete a common goal or purpose. A team may be assigned any number of tasks or goals, from development of a new product to selling that product.[27] Jones Walker, a New Orleans–based law firm, recently assembled a team of business students, alumni, and faculty advisors from Harvard University to assist Mayor C. Ray Nagin's Bring New Orleans Back Commission.[28] While teamwork may seem like a simple concept learned on soccer or football fields, teams function as a microcosm of the larger organization, and it is important to understand the types, development, and general nature of teams.

team a group of workers functioning together as a unit to complete a common goal or purpose

Types of Teams

There are several types of teams within businesses that function in specific ways to achieve different purposes, including problem-solving teams, self-managed teams, cross-functional teams, and virtual teams.

What type of team is this?
At New Balance, team members discuss ideas for improving efficiency during a bi-weekly meeting of workers and supervisors. Ideas from factory workers have led to improved performance and, in turn, have helped the employees keep their jobs from going overseas.

problem-solving team a team of knowledgeable employees brought together to tackle a specific problem

virtuoso team a team of exceptionally highly skilled and talented individuals brought together to produce significant change

self-managed teams groups of employees with the authority and skills to manage themselves

cross-functional team a team of individuals with varying specialties, expertise, and skills that are brought together to achieve a common task

Problem-Solving Teams The most common type of team in business organizations is the **problem-solving team.** It is generally used temporarily in order to bring knowledgeable employees together to tackle a specific problem. Once the problem is solved, the team typically is disbanded. For example, when General Motors (GM) announced its plans to close an assembly plant in Wilmington, Delaware, employees formed problem-solving teams with managers to improve quality control and reduce costs. The teams' suggested changes were so effective that within two years, the factory became the lowest-cost producer of all General Motors' factories. This prompted GM to keep the plant open, and the employees' jobs were saved.[29]

In some extraordinary cases, an expert team may be needed to generate groundbreaking ideas. A **virtuoso team** consists of exceptionally highly skilled and talented individuals brought together to produce significant change. As with other kinds of problem-solving teams, virtuoso teams usually are assembled on a temporary basis. Instead of being task-oriented, they focus on producing ideas and provoking change that could have an impact on the company and its industry. Because of the high skill level of their members, virtuoso teams can be difficult to manage. And unlike traditional teams, virtuoso teams place an emphasis on individuality over teamwork, which can cause further conflict. However, their conflicts usually are viewed as competitive and therefore productive in generating the most substantial ideas.[30]

Self-Managed Work Teams **Self-managed teams** are groups of employees with the authority and skills to manage themselves. Experts suggest that workers on self-managed teams are more motivated and satisfied because they have more task variety and job control. On many work teams, members rotate through all the jobs for which the team is responsible. Some organizations cross-train the entire team so that everyone can perform everyone else's job. In a traditional business structure, management is responsible for hiring and firing employees, establishing budgets, purchasing supplies, conducting performance reviews, and taking corrective action. When self-managed teams are in place, they take over some or all of these management functions. Xerox, Procter & Gamble, and Ferrari have used self-managed teams successfully. At its factory, Ferrari uses work teams designed to let each team perform a variety of tasks for about an hour and a half before the vehicle moves on to the next team. Employees learn more job skills, are more interested in their work, and develop a greater sense of pride in and loyalty to Ferrari.[31] The major advantages and disadvantages of self managed teams are mentioned in Figure 11.6.

Cross-Functional Teams Traditionally, businesses have organized employees into departments based on a common function or specialty. However, increasingly, business organizations are faced with projects that require a diversity of skills not available within a single department. A **cross-functional team** consists of individuals with varying specialties, expertise, and skills that are brought together to achieve a common task. For example, a purchasing agent might create a cross-functional team with representatives from various departments to gain insight into useful purchases for the company. This structure avoids departmental separation and allows greater efficiency when there is a single goal. Although cross-functional teams aren't necessarily self-managed, most self-managed teams are cross-functional. They also can be crossdivisional, such as at Mercedes Benz, which has begun assembling cross-functional teams to improve quality and cut costs in research and development. Instead of a single team per model, cross-functional teams will be developing standard parts to be used

> **FIGURE 11.6**

ADVANTAGES AND DISADVANTAGES OF SELF-MANAGED TEAMS

While self-managed teams provide benefits, managers must recognize their limitations.

ADVANTAGES	DISADVANTAGES
• Boosts employee morale	• Additional training costs
• Increases productivity	• Teams may be disorganized
• Aids innovation	• Conflicts may arise
• Reduces employee boredom	• Leadership role may be unclear

across different types of Mercedes' vehicles.[32] Cross-functional teams also can include a variety of people from outside the company, such as the cross-functional team of ergonomists, users, and university scientists that developed the new natural ergonomic keyboard for Microsoft.[33] Owing to their speed, flexibility, and increased employee satisfaction, it is likely that the use of cross-functional teams will increase.

Virtual Teams   With the advent of sophisticated communications technology, it is no longer necessary for teams to be geographically close. A **virtual team** consists of members who are geographically dispersed but communicate electronically. In fact, team members may never meet in person but rely solely on e-mail, teleconferences, faxes, voice mail, and other technologic interactions. In the modern global environment, virtual teams connect employees on a common task across continents, oceans, time zones, and organizations. Oracle recruited former U.S. Army Lieutenant General Keith Kellogg to lead a virtual team to develop technology to address homeland security solutions.[34] In some cases, the physical distances between participants and the lack of face-to-face interaction can be difficult when deadlines approach or communication is not clear.

virtual team a team consisting of members who are geographically dispersed but communicate electronically

Developing and Using Effective Teams

When a team is first developed, it takes time for the members to establish roles, relationships, delegation of duties, and other attributes of an effective team. As a team matures, it passes through five stages of development, as shown in Figure 11.7.

Forming   In the first stage, *forming*, team members are introduced to one another and begin to develop a social dynamic. The members of the team are still unsure how to relate to one another, what behaviors are considered acceptable, and what the ground rules for the team are. Through group member interaction over time, team members become more comfortable, and a group dynamic begins to emerge.

Storming   During the *storming* stage, the interaction may be volatile, and the team may lack unity. Because the team is still relatively new, this is the stage at which goals and objectives begin to develop. Team members will brainstorm to develop ideas and plans and establish a broad-ranging agenda. It is important at this stage for team members to grow more comfortable around the others so that they can contribute openly. At this time, the leadership role likely will be formally undefined. A team member may emerge as the informal leader. The success or failure of the ideas in storming determines how long until the team reaches the next stage.

Norming   After storming and the first large burst of activity, the team begins to stabilize during the *norming* stage. During this process, each person's role within the group starts to become apparent, and members begin to recognize the roles of others. A sense of unity will become stronger. If it hasn't already occurred, an identified leader

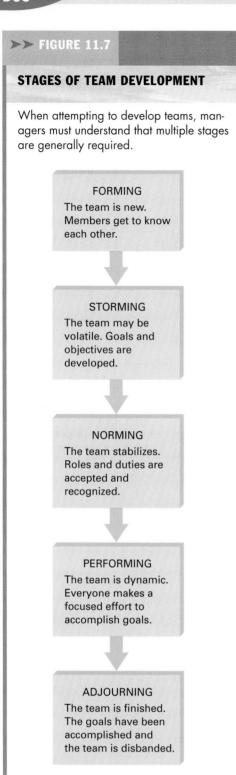

➤➤ **FIGURE 11.7**

STAGES OF TEAM DEVELOPMENT

When attempting to develop teams, managers must understand that multiple stages are generally required.

FORMING
The team is new. Members get to know each other.

STORMING
The team may be volatile. Goals and objectives are developed.

NORMING
The team stabilizes. Roles and duties are accepted and recognized.

PERFORMING
The team is dynamic. Everyone makes a focused effort to accomplish goals.

ADJOURNING
The team is finished. The goals have been accomplished and the team is disbanded.

will emerge. The group still may be somewhat volatile at this point and may regress back to the second stage if any conflict, especially over the leadership role, occurs.

Performing   The fourth stage, *performing*, is when the team achieves its full potential. It is usually slow to develop and occurs when the team begins to focus strongly on the assigned task and away from team-development issues. The members of the team work in harmony under the established roles to accomplish the necessary goals.

Adjourning   In the final stage, *adjourning*, the team is disbanded because the project has been completed. Team members may be reassigned to other teams or tasks. This stage does not always occur if the team is placed together for a task with no specific date of completion. For example, a marketing team for Best Buy may continue to develop promotional efforts for a store even after a specific promotional task has been accomplished. This stage is especially common in problem-solving teams that are dismantled after the assigned problem has been resolved.

Roles Within a Team

Within any team, each member has a role to play in helping the team attain its objectives. Each of these roles adds important dimensions to team member interactions. The group member who pushes forward toward goals and places the objective first is playing the *task-specialist role* by concentrating fully on the assigned task. In a cross-functional team this might be the person with the most expertise relating to the current task. The *socioemotional role* is played by the individual who supports and encourages the emotional needs of the other members. This person places the team members' personal needs over the task of the team. While this may sound unimportant, the socioemotional member's dedication to team cohesiveness will lead to greater unity and higher productivity. The leader of the team, and possibly others as well, will play a *dual role*. This dual role is a combination of both the socioemotional and task-specialist roles because this individual focuses on both the task and the team. The team leader might not always play a dual role, but the team is likely to be most successful when he or she does. Sometimes an individual assumes the *nonparticipant role*. This role behavior is characterized by a person who does not contribute to accomplishing the task and does not provide favorable input with respect to team members' socioemotional needs.

Team Cohesiveness

Developing a unit from a diverse group of personalities, specialties, backgrounds, and work styles can be challenging and complicated. In a cohesive team, the members get along and are able to accomplish their tasks effectively. There are factors that affect cohesiveness within a team. Teams generally are ideal when they contain five to twelve people. Fewer than five people is too few to accomplish tasks and generate a variety of ideas. More than twelve is too large because members do not develop relationships, may feel intimidated to speak, or may disconnect. It also may be beneficial to have team members introduce themselves and describe their past work experiences. This activity will foster familiarity and shared experiences. One of the most reliable ways to build cohesiveness within a team is through competition with other teams. When two teams are competing for a single prize or recognition, they are forced to put aside conflict and accomplish their goal. By adding an incentive to finishing the task, the team automatically becomes more goal-oriented. Also, a favorable appraisal from an outsider may strengthen team cohesiveness. Since the team is being praised as a group, team members recognize their contribution as a unit. Teams are also more successful when goals have become agreed on. A team that is clear about its objective will focus more on accomplishing it. Frequent interaction also builds cohesiveness as relationships strengthen and familiarity increases.

Team Conflict and How to Resolve It

Conflict occurs when a disagreement arises between two or more team members. Conflict traditionally has been viewed as negative, but if handled properly, conflict can work to improve a team. For example, if two team members disagree about a certain decision, both may analyze the situation more closely to determine the best choice. As long as conflict is handled in a respectful and professional manner, it can improve the quality of work produced. If conflict turns hostile and affects the work environment, then steps must be taken to arrive at a suitable compromise. Compromises can be difficult in a business organization because neither party ends up getting everything he or she wants. The best solution is a middle-ground alternative in which each party is satisfied to some degree. It is best to avoid attempting to minimize or ignore conflicts within a group because this may cause the conflict to grow as members concentrate on the problem instead of the task. However the conflict is resolved, it is important to remember that conflict must be acknowledged if it is to be either resolved or serve a constructive purpose.

Benefits and Limitations of Teams

Teamwork within a company has been credited as a key to reducing turnover and costs and increasing production, quality, and customer service. There is also evidence that working in teams leads to higher levels of job satisfaction among employees and a harmonious work environment. Thus an increasingly large number of companies are considering teams as a viable organizational structure. However, the process of reorganizing into teams can be stressful and time-consuming with no guarantee that the team will develop effectively. If a team lacks cohesiveness and is unable to resolve conflict, the company may experience lower productivity.

@ USING THE INTERNET

Sense of Delight considers itself the "fairy godmother" of employee motivation. This California based company offers fun and unique activities for teambuilding. Sense of Delight has created a DaVinci Conspiracy activity in which employees unravel hidden codes to boost creativity and develop team solving-problem skills. It also offers a "Gilligan's Island" outdoor activity and "Mission: Impossible" – a mix of clue and The Amazing Race. For more information and photos, visit **senseofdelight.com.**

Team-building exercises. Employees at AT&T participate in team-building exercises that will help them improve their overall abilities to engage in productive teamwork.

RETURN TO   Inside Business

How far should a company go to keep employees happy and motivated? Medtronic, which makes medical products, allows employees to spend one-fourth of their day experimenting with new technology. A.G. Edwards, a brokerage firm, sponsors running clubs and yoga classes. Chip-maker Intel has a spa at its Dallas headquarters. Wegmans has sent employees to Europe to learn first hand about fancy cheeses.

Employee absenteeism remains a problem for some firms. Royal Mail, the United Kingdom's postal service, now enters employees in a drawing for prizes such as new cars and vacations if they take no sick leave for six months. Although some experts question

Wegmans
helping you make great meals easy

whether companies will see a solid return on investment from such programs, Royal Mail's managers are happy with the results. In the first seven months of the program, employee sick leave fell by 11 percent.

Questions

1. Is Wegmans motivating its employees according to Theory X or Theory Y? How do you know?
2. Which of the motivation theories does Royal Mail's sick-leave-reduction program exemplify? Why do you think it works?

▶▶ CHAPTER REVIEW

Summary

1

Explain what motivation is.

Motivation is the individual internal process that energizes, directs, and sustains behavior. Motivation is affected by employee morale—that is, the employee's feelings about the job, superiors, and the firm itself. Motivation, morale, and job satisfaction are closely related.

2

Understand some major historical perspectives on motivation.

One of the first approaches to employee motivation was Frederick Taylor's scientific management, the application of scientific principles to the management of work and workers. Taylor believed that employees work only for money and that they must be closely supervised and managed. This thinking led to the piece-rate system, under which employees are paid a certain amount for each unit they produce. The Hawthorne Studies attempted to determine the effects of the work environment on productivity. Results of these studies indicated that human factors affect productivity more than do physical aspects of the workplace.

Maslow's hierarchy of needs suggests that people are motivated by five sets of needs. In ascending order of importance, these motivators are physiological, safety, social, esteem, and self-actualization needs. People are motivated by the lowest set of needs that remains unfulfilled. As needs at one level are satisfied, people try to satisfy needs at the next level.

Frederick Herzberg found that job satisfaction and dissatisfaction are influenced by two distinct sets of factors. Motivation factors, including recognition and responsibility, affect an employee's degree of satisfaction, but their absence does not necessarily cause dissatisfaction. Hygiene factors, including pay and working conditions, affect an employee's degree of dissatisfaction but do not affect satisfaction.

Theory X is a concept of motivation that assumes that employees dislike work and will function effectively only in a highly controlled work environment. Thus, to achieve an organization's goals, managers must coerce, control, and threaten employees. This theory generally is consistent with Taylor's scientific management. Theory Y is more in keeping with the results of the Hawthorne Studies and the human relations movement. It suggests that employees can be motivated to behave as responsible members of the organization. Theory Z emphasizes long-term employment, collective decision making, individual responsibility for the outcomes of decisions, informal control, and a holistic concern for employees. Reinforcement theory is based on the idea that people will repeat behavior that is rewarded and will avoid behavior that is punished.

3

Describe three contemporary views of motivation: equity theory, expectancy theory, and goal-setting theory.

Equity theory maintains that people are motivated to obtain and preserve equitable treatment for themselves. Expectancy theory suggests that our motivation depends on how much we want something and how likely we think we are to get it. Goal-setting theory suggests that employees are motivated to achieve a goal that they and their managers establish together.

4

Explain several techniques for increasing employee motivation.

Management by objectives (MBO) is a motivation technique in which managers and employees collaborate in setting goals. MBO motivates employees by getting them more involved in their jobs and in the organization as a whole. Job enrichment seeks to motivate employees by varying their tasks and giving them more responsibility for and control over their jobs. Job enlargement, expanding a worker's assignments to include additional tasks, is one aspect of job enrichment. Job redesign is a type of job enrichment in which work is restructured to improve the worker-job match.

Behavior modification uses reinforcement to encourage desirable behavior. Rewards for productivity, quality, and loyalty change employees' behavior in desired ways and also increase motivation.

Allowing employees to work more flexible hours is another way to build motivation and job satisfaction. Flextime is a system of work scheduling that allows workers to set their own hours as long as they fall within limits established by employers. Part-time work is permanent employment in which individuals work less than a standard work week. Job sharing is an arrangement whereby two people share one full-time position. Telecommuting allows employees to work at home all or part of the work week. All these types of work arrangements give employees more time outside the workplace to deal with family responsibilities or to enjoy free time.

Employee empowerment, self-managed work teams, and employee ownership are also techniques that boost employee motivation. Empowerment increases employees' involvement in their jobs by increasing their decision-making authority. Self-managed work teams are groups of employees with the authority and skills to manage themselves. When employees participate in ownership programs such as employee stock ownership plans (ESOPs), they have more incentive to make the company succeed and therefore work more effectively.

5

Understand the types, development, and uses of teams.

A large number of companies use teams to increase their employees' productivity. In a business organization, a team is a group of workers functioning together as a unit to complete a common goal or purpose.

There are several types of teams within businesses that function in specific ways to achieve different purposes. A problem-solving team is a team of knowledgeable employees brought together to tackle a specific problem. A virtuoso team is a team of highly skilled and talented individuals brought together to produce significant change A virtual team is a team consisting of members who are geographically dispersed but communicate electronically. A cross-functional team is a team of individuals with varying specialties, expertise, and skills.

The five stages of team development are forming, storming, norming, performing, and adjourning. As a team develops, it should become more productive and unified. The four roles within teams are task specialist, socioemotional, dual, and nonparticipative. Each of these roles plays a specific part in the team's interaction. For a team to be successful, members must learn how to resolve and manage conflict so that the team can work cohesively to accomplish goals.

Key Terms

You should now be able to define and give an example relevant to each of the following terms:

motivation (349)
morale (349)
scientific management (349)
piece-rate system (350)
need (351)
Maslow's hierarchy of needs (351)
physiological needs (351)
safety needs (351)
social needs (351)
esteem needs (352)
self-actualization needs (353)
motivation-hygiene theory (353)
motivation factors (353)
hygiene factors (353)
Theory X (354)
Theory Y (355)
Theory Z (356)
reinforcement theory (356)
equity theory (357)
expectancy theory (358)
goal-setting theory (359)
management by objectives (MBO) (359)
job enrichment (360)
job enlargement (360)
job redesign (361)
behavior modification (361)

flextime (362)
part-time work (363)
job sharing (363)
telecommuting (363)
empowerment (364)
employee ownership (365)
team (365)
problem-solving team (366)
virtuoso team (366)
self-managed teams (366)
cross-functional team (366)
virtual team (367)

8. Identify and describe the major techniques for motivating employees.
9. Describe the steps involved in the MBO process.
10. What are the objectives of MBO? What do you think might be its disadvantages?
11. How does employee participation increase motivation?
12. Describe the steps in the process of behavior modification.
13. Identify and describe the major types of teams.
14. What are the major benefits and limitations associated with the use of self-managed teams?
15. Explain the major stages of team development.

Review Questions

1. How do scientific management and Theory X differ from the human relations movement and Theory Y?
2. How did the results of the Hawthorne Studies influence researchers' thinking about employee motivation?
3. What are the five sets of needs in Maslow's hierarchy? How are a person's needs related to motivation?
4. What are the two dimensions in Herzberg's theory? What kinds of elements affect each dimension?
5. What is the fundamental premise of reinforcement theory?
6. According to equity theory, how does an employee determine whether he or she is being treated equitably?
7. According to expectancy theory, what two variables determine motivation?

Discussion Questions

1. How might managers make use of Maslow's hierarchy of needs in motivating employees? What problems would they encounter?
2. Do the various theories of motivation contradict each other or complement each other? Explain.
3. What combination of motivational techniques do you think would result in the best overall motivation and reward system?
4. Reinforcement theory and behavior modification have been called demeaning because they tend to treat people "like mice in a maze." Do you agree?
5. In what ways are team cohesiveness and team conflict related?

▶▶ VIDEO CASE 11.1

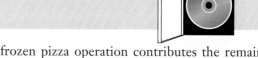

American Flatbread Fires Up Employees

George Schenk's passion is making work meaningful, sustainable, and personal. He learned about wood-fired cooking from his grandmother in Vermont and, years later, rekindled his love of cooking with fire when he founded the American Flatbread Company. His company produces frozen wood-fired flatbread pizzas from all-natural, locally grown ingredients, handmade by 100 employees in Waitsfield and Middlebury, Vermont.

On Mondays, Tuesdays, Wednesdays, and Thursdays, two shifts of employees stoke the bakeries' wood-fired ovens to a temperature of 800°F and prepare the flatbreads. After the products are baked, frozen, and wrapped, they are shipped to grocery and specialty stores such as Whole Foods supermarkets. Both bakeries are transformed into casual pizza restaurants on Friday and Saturday nights, where diners sit in view of the gigantic ovens to enjoy salads and flatbreads. Schenk also has licensed American Flatbread's brand and wood-fired cooking methods to bakeries and restaurants in New England and in Los Alamos, California. One-third of American Flatbread's annual revenue comes from the licensing deals and restaurant receipts, whereas the whole-

sale frozen pizza operation contributes the remaining two-thirds.

Schenk's enthusiasm for wood-fired cooking is matched by his enthusiasm for building a business in which the work has long-term significance to the employees and the community. Among American Flatbread's goals are to "create a pleasant, fulfilling, sustainable, and secure workplace" and "to trust one another and practice respectful relationships with everyone involved in this work."

Another goal mentioned in the mission statement is to be grateful, respectful, and forgiving—and to encourage the same in others. In line with this goal, Schenk has worked hard to avoid what he calls "founder's syndrome," the notion that the founder can do nothing wrong. Because Schenk is quick to admit that he's not perfect, his managers and employees know they can speak up about their mistakes and not lose the opportunity to try new things.

Jennifer Moffroid, the company's director of marketing, stresses that the founder has created an environment in which employees can do work that is in keeping with what they want for their lives. Making the workday fun is one of Schenk's priorities, as is making the workplace an inviting place to be. Moffroid also notes that

Schenk not only delegates, but he also "empowers employees and celebrates their work." The company's seven senior managers are involved in decision making, and every suggestion is evaluated on its merit, not on its source. "We're all in this together," Schenk says.

Since the beginning, American Flatbread has supported local food producers and given back to the community in a variety of ways. For example, the restaurants hold "benefit bakes" to raise money for causes such as public health clinics and habitat preservation. In turn, the community has come to the company's aid on more than one occasion. When flood waters inundated American Flatbread's bakery, people came from miles around to clean and rebuild the facility. Thanks to this outpouring of support, the bakery was able to reopen in only seven days. Without the help of the community, Schenk observes, the company might well have failed. Today, the Vermont bakeries turn out 10,000 flatbreads every week; the California bakery produces another 4,000 for distribution in western states. Schenk keeps the

company's values in the spotlight by writing a dedication for each week's menu. These dedications focus employees on what's important and provide "food for thought" for restaurant customers. Sharing values, being "a good neighbor," and building trusting, respectful relationships with stakeholders have enabled American Flatbread to keep employees happy and productive, minimize turnover, and strengthen financial performance.[35]

For more information about this company, go to **www.americanflatbread.com.**

Questions

1. Does George Schenk manage American Flatbread as a type A or a type Z firm? Support your answer.
2. Would you recommend that American Flatbread offer bakery and restaurant employees flextime arrangements? Explain.
3. How has George Schenk paved the way for empowerment at his company?

▶▶ CASE 11.2

Borders Group Asks Employees What They Value—and Delivers

Book lovers, music lovers, and movie lovers wanted— Borders Group looks for employees who are as passionate about the retailer's merchandise as its customers are. Based in Ann Arbor, Michigan, Borders is the second-largest book retailer in the United States, behind market-leader Barnes & Noble. With annual revenue of $4 billion, the company's work force exceeds 34,000. Unlike its competitor Barnes & Noble, Borders has expanded beyond North America and now has more than 1,200 stores worldwide, including a 60,000-square-foot store in Malaysia's largest shopping center.

Some of Borders' stores are open more than 12 hours a day, some are open 7 days a week, and some are open on holidays as well. Nearly 500 are superstores featuring 150,000 books, DVDs, CDs, gifts, and stationery products. Because two-thirds of shoppers have no specific item in mind when they arrive at a Borders store, they depend on knowledgeable employees for suggestions and assistance. Even when employees are enthusiastic about the products they sell and enjoy meeting the public, however, keeping them motivated and satisfied day after day is an ongoing challenge.

To address this challenge, Borders conducted internal surveys to learn what employees value. This feedback formed the basis of programs focused on seven areas: health, family, future, time, finances, life, and training and development. For health, the company offers medical, dental, and vision coverage, plus discounts on fitness-center memberships. It helps employees to balance

family and work responsibilities through flextime schedules, family medical leave, and more.

By matching employees' contributions to the company savings plan, inviting employees to buy insurance through the company, and offering college scholarships, Borders provides the tools for future financial security. It allows for time away from work through paid vacation, holiday, sick, personal, and bereavement days. The retailer also offers discounts on store merchandise and has negotiated for discounts on other goods and services from minivans to money-market accounts. Its "promotion from within" policy leads to advancement opportunities throughout the organization. Finally, Borders runs dozens of training courses to develop employees' knowledge of store operations, leadership, professional skills, and technical skills.

The retailer began recruiting seniors after studies showed that in the United States, half of all books sold are bought by customers over 45 years old. "We found that they better related to our customers," notes human resources executive Dan Smith. Within seven years, employees over the age of 50 made up 16 percent of Borders' work force. Changing the composition of the work force gave Borders the added benefit of lowering annual turnover by 30 percent because older employees tend to stay longer than younger employees. "These workers have a great passion to be connected to the community, and our bookstores provide them with that venue," Smith says.

Soon Borders had a new challenge: How to retain senior employees who live in one state during the winter and another during the summer. It found that some older employees from the Northeast, for example, were going to Florida during the snowy months and returning to the Northeast after snow season ended. Those who wanted to work for Borders year-round wound up searching for local stores in both areas and making arrangements on their own. Now Borders has a corporate "passport" plan that enables employees to work for a number of months at one store and transfer to a second store for the rest of the year. Through an internal website, store managers can find the names of employees who will be moving to their area and call to discuss arrival dates and convenient working schedules. This system works well for both sides—and is another reason why Borders' turnover remains low.[36]

For more information about this company, go to **www.bordersgroupinc.com.**

Questions

1. Borders has created a variety of programs based on what employees say they value. Which of the needs in Maslow's hierarchy do these programs aim to satisfy?
2. Does Borders' corporate passport program address Herzberg's motivation factors or his hygiene factors?
3. Is Borders' policy of promoting from within consistent with Theory X or Theory Y? Support your answer.

→ CHAPTER 11: JOURNAL EXERCISE

Discovery statement: Many managers use special techniques to foster employee motivation and satisfaction.

Thinking about your current job (or your most recent job), what types of motivation techniques are being used?

_____

_____

_____

_____

_____

How well does each technique work on you and on your coworkers?

_____

_____

_____

_____

Thinking about the first job that you will take after completing your studies, what types of motivation techniques will be most effective in motivating you to truly excel in your new position? Explain why.

_____

_____

_____

_____

Do you expect that most of your coworkers will be motivated by the same techniques that motivate you? Explain.

_____

_____

_____

_____

_____

BUILDING SKILLS FOR CAREER SUCCESS

1. Exploring the Internet

There are few employee incentives as motivating as owning "a piece of the action." Either through profit sharing or equity, many firms realize that the opportunity to share in the wealth generated by their effort is a primary force to drive employees toward better performance and a sense of ownership. The Foundation for Enterprise Development (www.fed.org/) is a nonprofit organization dedicated to helping entrepreneurs and executives use employee ownership and equity compensation as a fair and effective means of motivating the work force and improving corporate performance. You can learn more about this approach at the foundation's website. Visit the text website for updates to this exercise.

Assignment

1. Describe the content and services provided by the Foundation for Enterprise Development through its website.
2. Do you agree with this orientation toward motivation of employees/owners, or does it seem contrived to you? Discuss.
3. How else might employees be motivated to improve their performance?

2. Developing Critical-Thinking Skills

This chapter has described several theories managers can use as guidelines in motivating employees to do the best job possible for the company. Among these theories are Maslow's hierarchy of needs, equity theory, expectancy theory, and goal-setting theory. How effective would each of these theories be in motivating you to be a more productive employee?

Assignment

1. Identify five job needs that are important to you.
2. Determine which of the theories mentioned above would work best to satisfy your job needs.
3. Prepare a two-page report explaining how you reached these conclusions.

3. Building Team Skills

By increasing employees' participation in decision making, empowerment makes workers feel more involved in their jobs and the operations of the organization. While empowerment may seem like a commonsense idea, it is a concept not found universally in the workplace. If you had empowerment in your job, how would you describe it?

Assignment

1. Use brainstorming to explore the concept of empowerment.
   a. Write each letter of the word *empowerment* in a vertical column on a sheet of paper or on the classroom chalkboard.
   b. Think of several words that begin with each letter.
   c. Write the words next to the appropriate letter.
2. Formulate a statement by choosing one word from each letter that best describes what empowerment means to you.
3. Analyze the statement.
   a. How relevant is the statement for you in terms of empowerment? Or empowerment in your workplace?
   b. What changes must occur in your workplace for you to have empowerment?
   c. How would you describe yourself as an empowered employee?
   d. What opportunities would empowerment give to you in your workplace?
4. Prepare a report of your findings.

4. Researching Different Careers

Because a manager's job varies from department to department within firms, as well as among firms, it is virtually impossible to write a generic description of a manager's job. If you are contemplating becoming a manager, you may find it very helpful to spend time on the job with several managers learning first hand what they do.

Assignment

1. Make an appointment with managers in three firms, preferably firms of different sizes. When you make the appointments, request a tour of the facilities.

2. Ask the managers the following questions:

   a. What do you do in your job?

   b. What do you like most and least about your job? Why?

   c. What skills do you need in your job?

   d. How much education does your job require?

   e. What advice do you have for someone thinking about pursuing a career in management?

3. Summarize your findings in a two-page report. Include answers to these questions:

   a. Is management a realistic field of study for you? Why?

   b. What might be a better career choice? Why?

5. Improving Communication Skills

Suppose that you and a friend went into the auto repair business some years ago. You had the technical expertise, and he had the business knowledge. Although funds were tight for the first three years, your customer base grew, and you were able to hire extra help and expand business hours. Your business is now six years old and very successful. You have five people working under you. Henry, your most productive employee, wants to be promoted to a supervisory position. However, two other employees, Jack and Fred, have seniority over Henry, and you anticipate much dissension and poor morale if you go ahead and promote Henry. Henry clearly deserves the supervisory position because of his hard work and superior skills, but you stand to lose the other two employees if you promote him.

Assignment

1. Analyze the scenario, and answer these questions:

   a. Will you promote Henry? If so, why?

   b. How can you motivate Jack and Fred to stay with you if you promote Henry?

2. Refer to specific motivational techniques or theories to explain your reasoning in resolving the situation with Henry, Jack, and Fred.

3. Prepare a three-page report outlining and justifying your decision.

→ PREP TEST

Matching Questions

_____ 1. A force that causes people to behave in a particular way.

_____ 2. Based on an assumption that people dislike work.

_____ 3. Employees believe they will receive the rewards.

_____ 4. When not provided, they become dissatisfiers.

_____ 5. Needs that can be met by health care benefits.

_____ 6. Promotions and rewards can fulfill these needs.

_____ 7. Behavior that is rewarded is likely to be repeated.

_____ 8. Employees become more involved in the decision-making process.

_____ 9. Employees are given more variety and responsibility in their jobs.

_____ 10. Groups that have more task variety and greater job control.

a. empowerment
b. esteem needs
c. expectancy theory
d. hygiene factors
e. job enrichment
f. motivation
g. reinforcement theory
h. self-managed work teams
i. safety needs
j. Theory X

True/False Questions

T F

11. ○ ○ Giving an employee recognition builds employee morale.

12. ○ ○ The Hawthorne Studies concluded that human factors were responsible for the results.

13. ○ ○ Maslow's higher-level needs are the easiest to satisfy.

14. ○ ○ MBO is an inflexible system that requires all goals to be met; if not, the employee is fired.

15. ○ ○ Theory Y is a set of assumptions that are consistent with the human relations movement.

16. ○ ○ Frederick W. Taylor made his most significant contribution to management practice by his involvement with the Hawthorne Studies.

T F

17. ○ ○ According to the expectancy theory, motivation depends on how much we want something and how likely we think we are to get it.

18. ○ ○ Self-actualization needs are the most basic needs that Maslow discovered.

19. ○ ○ Herzberg's theory suggests that pay is a strong motivator.

20. ○ ○ A systematic program of reinforcement that encourages desirable behavior is called behavior modification.

Multiple-Choice Questions

21. Herzberg cited _____ as a cause of dissatisfaction.
    a. working conditions
    b. promotions
    c. pay for special projects
    d. rewards
    e. challenging work

22. According to Theory Y, which type of behavior would a supervisor expect from an employee?
    a. Delegate most of the work to others.
    b. Avoid working too hard.
    c. Spend time discussing job security.
    d. Ask to leave early several times a month.
    e. Seek opportunities to learn new skills.

23. Developing an input-to-output ratio is the basis of the _____ theory.
    a. equity
    b. expectancy
    c. reward
    d. reinforcement
    e. quality circles

24. If Delta Airlines ticket agents discovered that they were being paid a lot less per ticket sold than Northwest Airlines ticket agents, we might expect the Delta ticket agents to
    a. increase their sales so that they will make as much as their Northwest peers.
    b. think their outcome-to-input ratios are lower than those of the Northwest ticket agents.
    c. have as a group very different personal needs than Northwest ticket agents.
    d. be very satisfied because they work for a great airline.
    e. feel that rewards are being distributed fairly and equitably.

25. Randi Wood wants to become the best manager in the firm. She takes every available opportunity to learn new skills and improve her knowledge about management. Which need is Randi attempting to satisfy?
    a. Social
    b. Esteem
    c. Self-actualization
    d. Physiological
    e. Safety

Fill-in-the-Blank Questions

26. The idea that satisfaction and dissatisfaction are distinct dimensions is part of the _____ theory.

27. Giving public recognition to an employee who has done an excellent job on a project is an example of _____ reinforcement.

28. Pay directly ties to output uses the _____ system.

29. The stockholders of ESOPs are the _____.

30. When supervisors assume that employees accept responsibility, they are relying on Theory _____.

Online Study Center

FOR MORE **test practice, use the interactive ACE quizzes available at the Online Student Center:**
www.college.hmco.com/PIC/pridebusiness9e.

Answers on p. PT1.

Enhancing Union-Management Relations

www.college.hmco.com/PIC/pridebusiness9e

LEARNING OBJECTIVES

WHAT you will be able to do once you complete this chapter:

1 **Explain** how and why labor unions came into being.

2 **Discuss** the sources of unions' negotiating power and trends in union membership.

3 **Identify** the main focus of several major pieces of labor-management legislation.

4 **Enumerate** the steps involved in forming a union and show how the National Labor Relations Board is involved in the process.

5 **Describe** the basic elements in the collective-bargaining process.

6 **Identify** the major issues covered in a union-management contract.

7 **Explain** the primary bargaining tools available to unions and management.

WHY this chapter matters

As you move into management, you will better understand the roles played by unions and how to work with union members.

FOR HELP with studying this chapter, visit the Online Student Center:

www.college.hmco.com/PIC/pridebusiness9e

Online Study Center

Labor disputes in the major leagues can cause major headaches. Sometimes the players or referees disagree with the owners of hockey, baseball, basketball, and football teams about salaries. Sometimes the two sides disagree about when players are considered free agents. And sometimes the two sides disagree about when salary disputes should be resolved by a third party. Labor strife in sports is nothing new—but with multiyear contracts, multimillion-dollar team budgets, and millions of fans watching, the stakes are higher every year.

The latest in a series of National Hockey League (NHL) labor disputes started in 2004 when the owners called for a salary cap to rein in team payrolls—an issue that had divided labor and management for more than a decade. The owners insisted, the players resisted, talks grew heated, and the owners postponed game after game, month after month—eventually canceling the entire season. The two sides continued talking as the 2005–2006 season approached. The resulting 600-page agreement included a salary cap as well as new playing rules to make the game more exciting and bring fans back. In the past, NHL players have

DID YOU KNOW?

Some professional sports players believe that they don't make enough money and thus choose to not play.

gone on strike over free-agent rules, referees have gone on strike over salaries and pensions, and owners have locked out players over salary restrictions.

Major League Baseball players went on strike in the summer of 1994 because team owners wanted to impose a salary cap to improve the financial situation of some teams. Even the White House tried to help end the standoff. After 235 days, countless meetings, and the involvement of federal labor regulators, the union called off the strike, and the 1995 season got underway. Meanwhile, the umpires' contract had expired. Their union bargained for a big pay raise. When talks were unproductive, the owners hired replacement umpires to get the season underway. Four months later, the two sides came to terms, and the umpires returned to work. Although the unions and management always have settled their differences, how do the fans feel about labor disputes involving professional sports teams?[1]

For more information about this topic, go to **www.nhlpa.com** and **www.mlbpa.com.**

Professional sports teams, like some other business organizations, have been unionized for years, and both management and the unions have experienced ups and downs. Many businesses today have highly cooperative relationships with labor unions. A **labor union** is an organization of workers acting together to negotiate their wages and working conditions with employers. In the United States, nonmanagement employees have the legal right to form unions and to bargain, as a group, with management. The result of the bargaining process is a *labor contract*, a written agreement that is in force for a set period of time (usually one to three years). The dealings between labor unions and business management, both in the bargaining process and beyond it, are called **union-management relations** or, more simply, **labor relations.**

Because labor and management have different goals, they tend to be at odds with each other. However, these goals must be attained by the same means—through the production of goods and services. At contract bargaining sessions, the two groups must work together to attain their goals. Perhaps mainly for this reason, antagonism now seems to be giving way to cooperation in union-management relations.

We open this chapter by reviewing the history of labor unions in this country. Then we turn our attention to organized labor today, noting current membership trends and union-management partnerships and summarizing important labor-relations laws. We discuss the unionization process, why employees join unions, how a union is formed, and what the National Labor Relations Board does. Collective-bargaining procedures then are explained. Next, we consider issues in union-management contracts, including employee pay, working hours, security, management rights, and grievance procedures. We close with a discussion of various labor and management negotiating techniques: strikes, slowdowns and boycotts, lockouts, mediation, and arbitration.

labor union an organization of workers acting together to negotiate their wages and working conditions with employers

union-management (labor) relations the dealings between labor unions and business management both in the bargaining process and beyond it

The Historical Development of Unions

Until the middle of the nineteenth century, there was very little organization of labor in this country. Groups of workers occasionally did form a **craft union,** an organization of skilled workers in a single craft or trade. These alliances usually were limited to a single city, and they often lasted only a short time. In 1786, the first known strike in the United States involved a group of Philadelphia printers who stopped working over demands for higher wages. When the employers granted the printers a pay increase, the group disbanded.

1 LEARNING OBJECTIVE
Explain how and why labor unions came into being.

craft union an organization of skilled workers in a single craft or trade

Early History

In the mid-1800s, improved transportation opened new markets for manufactured goods. Improved manufacturing methods made it possible to supply those markets, and American industry began to grow. The Civil War and the continued growth of the railroads after the war led to further industrial expansion.

Large-scale production required more and more skilled industrial workers. As the skilled labor force grew, craft unions emerged in the more industrialized areas. From these craft unions, three significant labor organizations evolved. (See Figure 12.1 for a historical overview of unions and their patterns of membership.)

Knights of Labor The first significant national labor organization to emerge was the Knights of Labor, which was formed as a secret society in 1869 by Uriah Stephens, a utopian reformer and abolitionist from Philadelphia. Membership reached approximately 700,000 by 1886. One major goal of the Knights was to eliminate the depersonalization of the worker that resulted from mass-production technology. Another was to improve the moral standards of both employees and society. To the detriment of the group, its leaders concentrated so intently on social and economic change that they did not recognize the effects of technological change. Moreover, they assumed that all employees had the same goals as the Knights' leaders—social and moral reform. The major reason for the demise of the Knights was the Haymarket riot of 1886.

>> **FIGURE 12.1**

HISTORICAL OVERVIEW OF UNIONS

The total number of members for all unions generally rose between 1869, when the first truly national union was organized, and 1980. The dates of major events in the history of labor unions are singled out along the line of membership change.

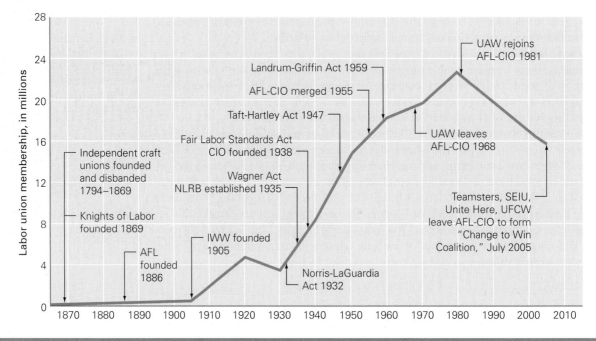

Sources: U.S. Bureau of Labor Statistics, Union Membership 2005, **www.hls.gov; www.aflcio.org;** *Statistical Abstract of the United States, 2001.*

At a rally (called to demand a reduction in the length of a work day from ten to eight hours) in Chicago's Haymarket Square, a bomb exploded. Several police officers and civilians were killed or wounded. The Knights were not implicated directly, but they quickly lost public favor.

American Federation of Labor   In 1886, several leaders of the Knights of Labor joined with independent craft unions to form the *American Federation of Labor* (AFL). Samuel Gompers, one of the AFL's founders, became its first president. Gompers believed that the goals of the union should be those of its members rather than those of its leaders. The AFL did not seek to change the existing business system, as the Knights of Labor had. Instead, its goal was to improve its members' living standards within that system.

    Another major difference between the Knights of Labor and the AFL was in their positions regarding strikes. A **strike** is a temporary work stoppage by employees, calculated to add force to their demands. The Knights did not favor the use of strikes, whereas the AFL strongly believed that striking was an effective labor weapon. The AFL also believed that organized labor should play a major role in politics. As we will see, the AFL is still very much a part of the American labor scene.

strike a temporary work stoppage by employees, calculated to add force to their demands

Industrial Workers of the World   The *Industrial Workers of the World* (IWW) was created in 1905 as a radical alternative to the AFL. Among its goals was the overthrow of capitalism. This revolutionary stance prevented the IWW from gaining much of a foothold. Perhaps its major accomplishment was to make the AFL seem, by comparison, less threatening to the general public and to business leaders.

Testifying about working conditions. Samuel Gompers, one of the founders of the American Federation of Labor, testifies during hearings of the Federal Industrial Relations Commission about the need for better working conditions.

Evolution of Contemporary Labor Organizations

Between 1900 and 1920, both business and government attempted to keep labor unions from growing. This period was plagued by strikes and violent confrontations between management and unions. In steelworks, garment factories, and auto plants, clashes took place in which striking union members fought bitterly against nonunion workers, police, and private security guards.

The AFL continued to be the major force in organized labor. By 1920, its membership included 75 percent of all those who had joined unions. Throughout its existence, however, the AFL had been unsure of the best way to deal with unskilled and semiskilled workers. Most of its members were skilled workers in specific crafts or trades. However, technological changes during World War I had brought about a significant increase in the number of unskilled and semiskilled employees in the work force. These people sought to join the AFL, but they were not well received by its established membership.

Some unions within the AFL did recognize the need to organize unskilled and semiskilled workers, and they began to penetrate the auto and steel industries. The type of union they formed was an **industrial union,** an organization of both skilled and unskilled workers in a single industry. Soon workers in the rubber, mining, newspaper, and communications industries also were organized into unions. Eventually, these unions left the AFL and formed the *Congress of Industrial Organizations* (CIO).

industrial union an organization of both skilled and unskilled workers in a single industry

During this same time (the late 1930s), there was a major upswing in rank-and-file membership in the AFL, the CIO, and independent unions. Strong union leadership, the development of effective negotiating tactics, and favorable legislation combined to increase total union membership to nine million in 1940. At this point the CIO began to rival the AFL in size and influence. There was another bitter rivalry: The AFL and CIO often clashed over which of them had the right to organize and represent particular groups of employees.

Since World War II, the labor scene has gone through a number of changes. For one thing, during and after the war years there was a downturn in public opinion regarding unions. A few isolated but very visible strikes during the war caused public sentiment to shift against unionism. Perhaps the most significant occurrence, however, was the merger of the AFL and the CIO. After years of bickering, the two groups recognized that they were wasting effort and resources by fighting each other and that a merger would greatly increase the strength of both. The merger took place on December 5, 1955. The resulting organization, called the *AFL-CIO,* had a membership of as many as sixteen million workers, which made it the largest labor organization of its kind in the world. Its first president was George Meany, who served until 1979.

Organized Labor Today

2 LEARNING OBJECTIVE
Discuss the sources of unions' negotiating power and trends in union membership.

The power of unions to negotiate effectively with management is derived from two sources. The first is their membership. The more workers a union represents within

SPOTLIGHT

Who employs the most union members?

Public sector	36.5%
Transportation & utilities	24.0%
Information	13.6%
Construction	13.1%
Manufacturing	13.0%
Education & health services	9.4%
Mining	8.5%
Wholesale & retail sales	5.9%

Union membership in 2005 was highest in the public sector.

Source: Bureau of Labor Statistics, 2005.

an industry, the greater is its clout in dealing with firms operating in that industry. The second source of union power is the group of laws that guarantee unions the right to negotiate and, at the same time, regulate the negotiating process.

Union Membership

At present, union members account for a relatively small portion of the American work force: Approximately 15.5 percent of the nation's workers belong to unions.[2] Union membership is concentrated in a few industries and job categories. Within these industries, though, unions wield considerable power.

The AFL-CIO is still the largest union organization in this country, boasting approximately nine million members. Those represented by the AFL-CIO include actors, barbers, construction workers, carpenters, retail clerks, musicians, teachers, postal workers, painters, steel and iron workers, firefighters, bricklayers, and newspaper reporters.

One of the largest unions not associated directly with the AFL-CIO is the *Teamsters Union*. The Teamsters originally were part of the AFL-CIO, but in 1957 they were expelled for corrupt and illegal practices. The union started out as an organization of professional drivers, but it has begun recently to recruit employees in a wide variety of jobs. Current membership is about 1.4 million workers.

The *United Steelworkers* (USW) and the *United Auto Workers* (UAW) are two of the largest industrial unions. The USW membership has risen to over 850,000 workers. It is known as the dominant union in paper and forestry products, steel, aluminum, tire and rubber, mining, glass, chemicals, petroleum, and other basic resource industries.[3] The UAW represents employees in the automobile industry. The UAW, too, originally was part of the AFL-CIO, but it left the parent union—of its own accord—in 1968. Currently, the UAW has about 640,000 members. For a while, the Teamsters and the UAW formed a semistructured partnership called the *Alliance for Labor Action*. This partnership was dissolved eventually, and the UAW again became part of the AFL-CIO in 1981.

Membership Trends

The proportion of union members relative to the size of the nation's work force has declined over the last thirty years. Moreover, total union membership has dropped since 1980 despite steadily increasing membership in earlier years (see Figure 12.1). To a great extent, this decline in membership is caused by changing trends in business, such as the following:

- Heavily unionized industries either have been decreasing in size or have not been growing as fast as nonunionized industries. For example, cutbacks in the steel industry have tended to reduce union membership. At the same time, the growth of high-tech industries has increased the ranks of nonunion workers.
- Many firms have moved from the heavily unionized Northeast and Great Lakes regions to the less unionized Southeast and Southwest—the so-called Sunbelt. At the relocated plants, formerly unionized firms tend to hire nonunion workers.
- The largest growth in employment is occurring in the service industries, and these industries typically are not unionized.
- Some U.S. companies have moved their manufacturing operations to other countries where less unionized labor is employed.

- Management is providing benefits that tend to reduce employees' need for unionization. Increased employee participation and better wages and working conditions are goals of unions. When these benefits are already supplied by management, workers are less likely to join existing unions or start new ones. The number of elections to vote on forming new unions has declined. The unions usually win about half the elections.

- According to Alan Greenspan, former chairman of the Federal Reserve, American labor laws and culture allow for the quicker displacement of unneeded workers and their replacement with those in demand, whereas labor laws in other countries tend to take longer for the change to occur.

Union-Management partnerships. At General Motors' Saturn plant in Springhill, Tennessee, the UAW and Saturn management have forged a partnership that has resulted in a high level of productivity, and in a comfortable and satisfying work environment for employees.

It remains to be seen whether unions will be able to regain the prominence and power they enjoyed between the world wars and during the 1950s. There is little doubt, however, that they will remain a powerful force in particular industries.

Union-Management Partnerships

For most of the twentieth century, unions represented workers with respect to wages and working conditions. To obtain rights for workers and recognition for themselves, unions engaged in often-antagonistic collective-bargaining sessions and strikes. At the same time, management traditionally protected its own rights of decision making, workplace organization, and strategic planning. Increasingly, however, management has become aware that this traditionally adversarial relationship does not result in the kind of high-performance workplace and empowered work force necessary to succeed in today's highly competitive markets. For their part, unions and their members acknowledge that most major strikes result in failures that cost members thousands of jobs and reduce the unions' credibility. Today, instead of maintaining an "us versus them" mentality, many unions are becoming partners with management, cooperating to enhance the workplace, empower workers, increase production, improve quality, and reduce costs. According to the Department of Labor, the number of union-management partnerships in the United States is increasing.

Union-management partnerships can be initiated by union leaders, employees, or management. *Limited partnerships* center on accomplishing one specific task or project, such as the introduction of teams or the design of training programs. For example, Levi Strauss formed a limited partnership with its employees who are members of the Amalgamated Clothing and Textile Workers Union to help the company in setting up team operations in its nonunion plants. *Long-range strategic partnerships* focus on sharing decision-making power for a whole range of workplace and business issues. Long-range partnerships sometimes begin as limited ones and develop slowly over time.

Although strategic union-management partnerships vary, most of them have several characteristics in common. First, strategic partnerships focus on developing cooperative relationships between unions and management instead of arguing over contractual rights. Second, partners work toward mutual gain, in which the organization becomes more competitive, employees are better off, and unions are stronger as a result of the partnership. Finally, as already noted, strategic partners engage in joint decision making on a broad array of issues.[4] These issues include performance expectations, organizational structure, strategic alliances, new technology, pay and benefits, employee security and involvement, union-management roles, product development, and education and training.

Good labor-management relations can help everyone to deal with new and difficult labor issues as they develop. For example, many companies hope that their union-management partnerships will be strong enough to deal with the critical issue of rising health care costs. Unions work hard to protect their members from having to pay an increased percentage of health care costs, and they have experienced some success, in that an average union worker pays about 16 percent of his or her health care premiums compared with a nonunion worker's contribution of about 32 percent.[5] Strong union-management partnerships will play a vital role in resolving health care issues.

Union-management partnerships have many potential benefits for management, workers, and unions. For management, partnerships can result in lower costs, increased revenue, improved product quality, and greater customer satisfaction. For workers, benefits may include increased response to their needs, more decision-making opportunities, less supervision, more responsibility, and increased job security. Unions can gain credibility, strength, and increased membership.

Among the many organizations that have found union-management partnerships beneficial is Saturn. The labor-management partnership between the Saturn Corporation and the UAW is one of the boldest experiments in U.S. industrial relations today. It was created through a joint design effort that included the UAW as a full partner in decisions regarding product, technology, suppliers, retailers, site selection, business planning, training, quality systems, job design, and manufacturing systems. This partnership has resulted in a dense communications network throughout the company's management system as well as improvement in quality performance.[6]

Labor-Management Legislation

3 LEARNING OBJECTIVE
Identify the main focus of several major pieces of labor-management legislation.

As we have noted, business opposed early efforts to organize labor. The federal government generally supported anti-union efforts through the court system, and in some cases federal troops were used to end strikes. Gradually, however, the government began to correct this imbalance through the legislative process.

Norris-LaGuardia Act

The first major piece of legislation to secure rights for unions, the *Norris-LaGuardia Act* of 1932, was considered a landmark in labor-management relations. This act made it difficult for businesses to obtain court orders that banned strikes, picketing, or union membership drives. Previously, courts had issued such orders readily as a means of curbing these activities.

National Labor Relations Act

The *National Labor Relations Act*, also known as the *Wagner Act*, was passed by Congress in 1935. It established procedures by which employees decide whether they want to be represented by a union. If workers choose to be represented, the Wagner Act requires management to negotiate with union representatives. Before this law was passed, union efforts sometimes were interpreted as violating the Sherman Act (1890) because they were viewed as attempts to monopolize. The Wagner Act also forbids certain unfair labor practices on the part of management, such as firing or punishing workers because they are pro-union, spying on union meetings, and bribing employees to vote against unionization.

National Labor Relations Board (NLRB) the federal agency that enforces the provisions of the Wagner Act

Finally, the Wagner Act established the **National Labor Relations Board (NLRB)** to enforce the provisions of the law. The NLRB is concerned primarily with (1) overseeing the elections in which employees decide whether they will be represented by a union and (2) investigating complaints lodged by unions or employees. For example, New York University (NYU) graduate teaching and research assistants organized themselves as a union under the UAW. Initially, the NLRB voted to recognize the union, and the students negotiated a 40 percent stipend increase and gained health care benefits. The NLRB later reversed its decision, stating that the graduate students were not employees of the college and should not be recognized as a union. The students went on strike when NYU chose not to renew their union contract and extended offers to students on an individual basis.[7] In another example, the NLRB ruled in favor of a local carpenters union that filed charges of unfair labor practices against United Builder Services. The carpenters claimed to have been promised $25 per hour and living expenses by the company to relocate from California to Nevada. When they arrived in Nevada, the carpenters' pay was cut to $17 per hour, and they were not compensated for the move. The NLRB's decision led to a $12,000 settlement in back pay for the workers.[8]

@ USING THE INTERNET

The U.S. Department of Labor website (**www.dol.gov/**) provides a good overview of the major issues concerning labor news, legislation, and statistics. There are also links to other websites focusing on labor issues.

Fair Labor Standards Act

In 1938, Congress enacted the *Fair Labor Standards Act*. One major provision of this act permits the federal government to set a minimum wage. The first minimum wage, which was set in the late 1930s and did not include farm workers and retail employees, was $0.25 an hour. Today, the minimum wage is $5.15 an hour. Some employees, such as farm workers, are still exempt from the minimum-wage provisions. The act also requires that employees be paid overtime rates for work in excess of forty hours a week. Finally, it prohibits the use of child labor.

Labor-Management Relations Act

The legislation of the 1930s sought to discourage unfair practices on the part of employers. Recall from Figure 12.1 that union membership grew from approximately two million in 1910 to almost twelve million by 1945. Unions represented over 35 percent of all nonagricultural employees in 1945. As union membership and power grew, however, the federal government began to examine the practices of labor. Several long and bitter strikes, mainly in the coal mining and trucking industries, in the early 1940s led to a demand for legislative restraint on unions. As a result, in 1947 Congress passed the *Labor-Management Relations Act*, also known as the *Taft-Hartley Act*, over President Harry Truman's veto.

The objective of the Taft-Hartley Act is to provide a balance between union power and management authority. It lists unfair labor practices that unions are forbidden to use. These include refusal to bargain with management in good faith, charging excessive membership dues, harassing nonunion workers, and using various means of coercion against employers.

The Taft-Hartley Act also gives management more rights during union organizing campaigns. For example, management may outline for employees the advantages and disadvantages of union membership, as long as the information it presents is accurate. The act gives the president of the United States the power to obtain a temporary injunction to prevent or stop a strike that endangers national health and safety. An **injunction** is a court order requiring a person or group either to perform some act or to refrain from performing some act. President George W. Bush invoked the Taft-Hartley Act when union representatives could not reach an agreement with the Pacific Maritime Association. This ten-day shutdown delayed more than $12 billion worth of goods at a critical time for most retailers preparing for the holiday season. President Bush was the first to issue an injunction under this law since 1978.[9] Finally, the Taft-Hartley Act authorized states to enact laws to allow employees to work in a unionized firm without joining the union. About twenty states (many in the South) have passed such *right-to-work laws*.

injunction a court order requiring a person or group either to perform some act or to refrain from performing some act

Business Around the World

China's Labor Movement: Is It Helping Workers?

Relations between management and labor in China are evolving as employees, activists, and companies add their voices to calls for change:

- *Employees.* Employee demonstrations by the thousands have successfully pressured local factories to raise wages and improve working conditions.
- *Activists.* Luo Guangfu is one of many activists who help factory coworkers assert their rights. Liu Kaiming, a former teacher, founded the Migrant Workers Community College to train employees in job skills and encourage companies such as Nokia to "expand their business through being responsible corporations" in China.
- *Companies.* Many multinational firms have, in fact, already demonstrated good corporate citizenship by improving conditions in their Chinese factories.

The nation's only officially sanctioned union is the All-China Federation of Trade Unions. However, labor experts say that the union is part of the Communist party and doesn't fight vigorously for members' rights. Still, China's employee-rights movement is gaining momentum year by year, fueled by employees, activists, and companies.

Landrum-Griffin Act

In the 1950s, Senate investigations and hearings exposed racketeering in unions and uncovered cases of bribery, extortion, and embezzlement among union leaders. It was discovered that a few union leaders had taken union funds for personal use and accepted payoffs from employers for union protection. Some were involved in arson, blackmail, and murder. Public pressure for reform resulted in the 1959 *Landrum-Griffin Act.*

This law was designed to regulate the internal functioning of labor unions. Provisions of the law require unions to file annual reports with the U.S. Department of Labor regarding their finances, elections, and various decisions made by union officers. The Landrum-Griffin Act also ensures that each union member has the right to seek, nominate, and vote for each elected position in his or her union. It provides safeguards governing union funds, and it requires management and unions to report the lending of management funds to union officers, union members, or local unions.

The various pieces of legislation we have reviewed here effectively regulate much of the relationship between labor and management after a union has been established. The next section demonstrates that forming a union is also a carefully regulated process.

4 LEARNING OBJECTIVE

Enumerate the steps involved in forming a union and show how the National Labor Relations Board is involved in the process.

The Unionization Process

For a union to be formed at a particular firm, some employees of the firm first must be interested in being represented by a union. Then they must take a number of steps to formally declare their desire for a union. To ensure fairness, most of the steps in this unionization process are supervised by the NLRB.

Additional union benefits. UnionPlus is a program made available to all AFL-CIO members. The program provides additional benefits to union members, including education benefits and benefits associated with special purchases.

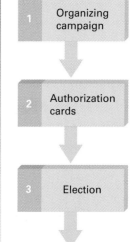
Why Some Employees Join Unions

Obviously, employees start or join a union for a variety of reasons. One commonly cited reason is to combat alienation. Some employees—especially those whose jobs are dull and repetitive—may perceive themselves as merely parts of a machine. They may feel that they lose their individual or social identity at work. Union membership is one way to establish contact with others in a firm.

Another common reason for joining a union is the perception that union membership increases job security. No one wants to live in fear of arbitrary or capricious dismissal from a job. Unions actually have only limited ability to guarantee a member's job, but they can help to increase job security by enforcing seniority rules.

Employees also may join a union because of dissatisfaction with one or more elements of their jobs. If they are unhappy with their pay, benefits, or working conditions, they may look to a union to correct the perceived deficiencies.

Some people join unions because of their personal backgrounds. For example, a person whose parents are strong believers in unions might be inclined to feel just as positive about union membership.

In some situations, employees *must* join a union to keep their jobs. Many unions try, through their labor contracts, to require that a firm's new employees join the union after a specified probationary period. Under the Taft-Hartley Act, states may pass right-to-work laws prohibiting this practice.

Steps in Forming a Union

The first step in forming a union is the *organizing campaign* (see Figure 12.2). Its primary objective is to develop widespread employee interest in having a union. To kick off the campaign, a national union may send organizers to the firm to stir this interest. Alternatively, the employees themselves may decide that they want a union. Then they contact the appropriate national union and ask for organizing assistance.

The organizing campaign can be quite emotional, and it may lead to conflict between employees and management. On the one hand, the employees who want the union will be dedicated to its creation. On the other hand, management will be extremely sensitive to what it sees as a potential threat to its power and control.

At some point during the organizing campaign, employees are asked to sign *authorization cards* (see Figure 12.3) to indicate—in writing—their support for the union. Because of various NLRB rules and regulations, both union organizers and company management must be very careful in their behavior during this authorization drive. For example, employees cannot be asked to sign the cards when they are supposed to be working. And management may not indicate in any way that employees' jobs or job security will be in jeopardy if they *do* sign the cards.

If at least 30 percent of the eligible employees sign authorization cards, the organizers generally request that the firm recognize the union as the employees' bargaining representative. Usually the firm rejects this request, and a *formal election* is held to decide whether to have a union. This election usually involves secret ballots and is conducted by the NLRB. The outcome of the election is determined by a simple majority of eligible employees who choose to vote.

If the union obtains a majority, it becomes the official bargaining agent for its members, and the final step, *NLRB certification*, takes place. The union immediately

▶▶ FIGURE 12.2

STEPS IN FORMING A UNION

The unionization process consists of a campaign, signing of authorization cards, a formal election, and certification of the election by the NLRB.

1. Organizing campaign
2. Authorization cards
3. Election
4. NLRB certification

>> **FIGURE 12.3**

SAMPLE AUTHORIZATION CARD

Unions must have written authorization to represent employees.

OBLIGATION OF

"I _____ , in the presence of
(PLEASE PRINT NAME)

members of the _____

promise and agree to conform to and abide by the Constitution

and laws of the _____ and its Local Unions. I will further the

purpose for which the _____ is instituted. I will bear true

allegiance to it and will not sacrifice its interest in any manner."

_____
(TO BE SIGNED BY APPLICANT — PLEASE DO NOT PRINT)

PRINT OR TYPE IN BLACK INK ONLY

SEX – MALE ☐ FEMALE ☐

LAST NAME	FIRST	INITIAL	SOCIAL SECURITY NO.
ADDRESS (STREET & NUMBER)			DATE OF BIRTH
CITY & STATE (OR PROVINCE)	POSTAL CODE		TELEPHONE NO.
PRESENT EMPLOYER			DATE HIRED
CLASSIFICATION			DATE OF THIS APPLICATION

Have you ever been   YES ☐
a member of   ?   NO ☐   If so, where?   LOCAL NO. _____   STATE _____

PORTION BELOW TO BE FILLED IN BY L.U. SECRETARY

LOCAL UNION NO.	DATE OF INITIATION	TYPE OF MEMBERSHIP	CARD NO.

may begin the process of negotiating a labor contract with management. If the union is voted down, the NLRB will not allow another election for one year.

Several factors can complicate the unionization process. For example, the **bargaining unit,** which is the specific group of employees that the union is to represent, must be defined. Union organizers may want to represent all hourly employees at a particular site (such as all workers at a manufacturing plant). Or they may wish to represent only a specific group of employees (such as all electricians in a large manufacturing plant).

bargaining unit the specific group of employees represented by a union

Another issue that may have to be resolved is that of **jurisdiction,** which is the right of a particular union to organize particular groups of workers (such as nurses). When jurisdictions overlap or are unclear, the employees themselves may decide who will represent them. In some cases, two or more unions may be trying to organize some or all of the employees of a firm. Then the election choices may be union A, union B, or no union at all.

jurisdiction the right of a particular union to organize particular groups of workers

The Role of the NLRB

As we have demonstrated, the NLRB is heavily involved in the unionization process. Generally, the NLRB is responsible for overseeing the organizing campaign, conducting the election (if one is warranted), and certifying the election results.

During the organizing campaign, both employers and union organizers can take steps to educate employees regarding the advantages and disadvantages of having a union. However, neither is allowed to use underhanded tactics or to distort the truth. If violations occur, the NLRB can stop the questionable behavior, postpone the election, or set aside the results of an election that has already taken place.

The NLRB usually conducts the election within forty-five days of receiving the required number of signed authorization cards from the organizers. A very high percentage of the eligible voters generally participates in the election, and it is held at the workplace during normal working hours. In certain cases, however, a mail ballot or other form of election may be called for.

Certification of the election involves counting the votes and considering challenges to the election. After the election results are announced, management and the union organizers have five days in which to challenge the election. The basis for a challenge might be improper conduct prior to the election or participation by an ineligible voter. After considering any challenges, the NLRB passes final judgment on the election results.

When union representation is established, union and management get down to the serious business of contract negotiations.

Collective Bargaining

Once certified by the NLRB, a new union's first task is to establish its own identity and structure. It immediately signs up as many members as possible. Then, in an internal election, members choose officers and representatives. A negotiating committee is also chosen to begin **collective bargaining,** the process of negotiating a labor contract with management.

The First Contract

To prepare for its first contract session with management, the negotiating committee decides on its position on the various contract issues and determines the issues that are most important to the union's members. For example, the two most pressing concerns might be a general wage increase and an improved benefits package.

The union then informs management that it is ready to begin negotiations, and the two parties agree on a time and location. Both sides continue to prepare for the session up to the actual date of the negotiations.

Negotiations occasionally are held on company premises, but it is more common for the parties to meet away from the workplace—perhaps in a local hotel. The union typically is represented by the negotiating committee and one or more officials from the regional or national union office. The firm normally is represented by managers from the industrial-relations, operations, human resources management, and legal departments. Each side is required by law to negotiate in good faith and not to stall or attempt to extend the bargaining proceedings unnecessarily.

The union normally presents its contract demands first. Management then responds to the demands, often with a counterproposal. The bargaining may move back and forth, from proposal to counterproposal, over a number of meetings. Throughout the process, union representatives constantly keep their members informed of what is going on and how the negotiating committee feels about the various proposals and counterproposals.

Each side clearly tries to "get its own way" as much as possible, but each also recognizes the need for compromise. For example, the union may begin the negotiations by demanding a wage increase of $1 per hour but may be willing to accept 60 cents per hour. Management initially may offer 40 cents but may be willing to pay 75 cents. Eventually, the two sides will agree on a wage increase of between 60 and 75 cents per hour.

If an agreement cannot be reached, the union may strike. Strikes are rare during a union's first contract negotiations. In most cases, the negotiating teams are able to

5 LEARNING OBJECTIVE
Describe the basic elements in the collective-bargaining process.

collective bargaining the process of negotiating a labor contract with management

A WORLD CLASS OFFER

· Full-Time Wages —
  $114,500 to $137,5

· Zero Cost Health C
  NO PREMIUMS , N

· $50,000 per Year Pension Be

· Job Protection Guarantee

Offers by management.
The CEO of the Pacific
Maritime Association
provides the details of an
offer to union members.

ratification approval of a labor contract by a vote of
the union membership

agree on an initial contract without re-
course to a strike.

The final step in collective bargaining
is **ratification,** which is approval of the
contract by a vote of the union membership. If the membership accepts the terms
of the contract, it is signed and becomes a
legally binding agreement. If the contract
is not ratified, the negotiators must go
back and try to iron out a more acceptable
agreement.

Later Contracts

A labor contract may cover a period of one
to three years or more, but every contract
has an expiration date. As that date approaches, both management and the
union begin to prepare for new contract
negotiations. Now, however, the entire
process is likely to be much thornier than the first negotiation.

For one thing, the union and the firm have "lived with each other" for several
years, during which some difficulties may have emerged. Each side may see certain issues as being of critical importance—issues that provoke a great deal of emotion at the
bargaining table and often are difficult to resolve. Also, each side has learned from the
earlier negotiations. Each may take a harder line on certain issues and be less willing
to compromise.

The contract deadline itself also produces tension. As the expiration date of the existing contract draws near, each side feels pressure—real or imagined—to reach an
agreement. This pressure may nudge the negotiators toward agreement, but it also can
have the opposite effect, making an accord more difficult to reach. Moreover, at some
point during the negotiations, union leaders are likely to take a *strike vote*. This vote reveals whether union members are willing to strike in the event that a new contract is
not negotiated before the old one expires. In almost all cases this vote supports a strike.
Thus the threat of a strike may add to the pressure mounting on both sides as they go
about the business of negotiating.

Union-Management Contract Issues

LEARNING OBJECTIVE
Identify the major issues covered in a union-
management contract.

As you might expect, many diverse issues are negotiated by unions and management
and are incorporated into a labor contract. Unions tend to emphasize issues related to
members' income, their standard of living, and the strength of the union.
Management's primary goals are to retain as much control as possible over the firm's
operations and to maximize its strength relative to that of the union. The balance of
power between union and management varies from firm to firm.

Employee Pay

An area of bargaining central to union-management relations is employee pay. Three
separate issues usually are involved: the forms of pay, the magnitude of pay, and the
means by which the magnitude of pay will be determined.

Forms of Pay   The primary form of pay is direct compensation—the wage or salary
and benefits an employee receives in exchange for his or her contribution to the organization. Because direct compensation is a fairly straightforward issue, negotiators
often spend much more of their time developing a benefits package for employees. And

as the range of benefits and their costs have escalated over the years, this element of pay has become increasingly important and complex.

We discussed the various employee benefits in Chapter 10. Of these, health, life, disability, and dental insurance are important benefits that unions try to obtain for their members. As the costs of health care continue to increase, insurance benefits are costing employers more, and many are trying to pass a portion of this increased cost on to their employees. Unions do not take these increased burdens lightly, and health care benefits recently led to the first General Electric strike in over thirty years. Many large companies such as General Motors, Ford, Lucent, and Goodyear will face these issues as they negotiate new union contracts in the near future.[10] Deferred compensation, in the form of pension or retirement programs, is also a common focal point. Decisions about deferred compensation can have a long-lasting impact on a company. General Motors is still suffering from the hefty compensation payments that it agreed to back in 1990 to appease the UAW. These payments add an extra $1,350 in costs to every car General Motors manufactures compared with a Japanese car built at a nonunion U.S. plant. General Motors will spend many years and billions of dollars paying these retired UAW employees.[11]

Other benefits commonly dealt with in the bargaining process include paid vacation time, holidays, and a policy on paid sick leave. Obviously, unions argue for as much paid vacation and holiday time as possible and for liberal sick-leave policies. Management naturally takes the opposite position.

SPOTLIGHT

Union vs. nonunion pay

Data from the AFL-CIO indicate that union membership has pay benefits for many workers.

Median weekly pay

	Union	Nonunion
All workers	$740	$587
Women	$667	$510
African American	$615	$447
Latino	$623	$408

Source: **www.aflcio.org/aboutunions/joinunions/whyjoin/uniondifference.**

Magnitude of Pay   Of considerable importance is the *magnitude*, or amount, of pay that employees receive as both direct and indirect compensation. The union attempts to ensure that pay is on par with that received by other employees in the same or similar industries, both locally and nationally. The union also attempts to include in the contract clauses that provide pay increases over the life of the agreement. The most common is the *cost-of-living clause*, which ties periodic pay increases to increases in the cost of living, as defined by various economic statistics or indicators.

Of course, the magnitude of pay is also affected by the organization's ability to pay. If the firm has posted large profits recently, the union may expect large pay increases for its members. If the firm has not been very profitable, the union may agree to smaller pay hikes or even to a pay freeze. In an extreme situation (e.g., when the firm is bordering on bankruptcy), the union may agree to pay cuts. Very stringent conditions usually are included in any agreement to a pay cut.

Bargaining with regard to magnitude also revolves around employee benefits. At one extreme, unions seek a wide range of benefits, entirely or largely paid for by the firm. At the other extreme, management may be willing to offer the benefits package but may want its employees to bear most of the cost. Again, factors such as equity (with similar firms and jobs) and ability to pay enter into the final agreement.

Pay Determinants   Negotiators also address the question of how individual pay will be determined. For management, the ideal arrangement is to tie wages to each employee's productivity. As we saw, this method of payment tends to motivate and reward effort. Unions, on the other hand, feel that this arrangement can create unnecessary competition among employees. They generally argue that employees should be paid— at least in part—according to seniority. **Seniority** is the length of time an employee has worked for an organization.

seniority the length of time an employee has worked for an organization

Determinants regarding benefits also are negotiated. For example, management may want to provide profit-sharing benefits only to employees who have worked for the firm for a specified number of years. The union may want these benefits provided to all employees.

Working Hours

Working hours are another important issue in contract negotiations. The matter of overtime is of special interest. Federal law defines **overtime** as time worked in excess of forty hours in one week. And it specifies that overtime pay must be at least one and one-half times the normal hourly wage. Unions may attempt to negotiate overtime rates for all hours worked beyond eight hours in a single day. Similarly, the union may attempt to obtain higher overtime rates (say, twice the normal hourly wage) for weekend or holiday work. Still another issue is an upper limit to overtime, beyond which employees can refuse to work.

In firms with two or more work shifts, workers on less desirable shifts are paid a premium for their time. Both the amount of the premium and the manner in which workers are chosen for (or choose) particular shifts are negotiable issues. Other issues related to working hours are the work starting times and the length of lunch periods and coffee breaks.

overtime time worked in excess of forty hours in one week (under some union contracts, time worked in excess of eight hours in a single day)

Security

Security actually covers two issues. One is the job security of the individual worker; the other is the security of the union as the bargaining representative of the firm's employees.

Job security is protection against the loss of employment. It is a major concern of individuals. As we noted earlier, the desire for increased job security is a major reason for joining unions in the first place. In the typical labor contract, job security is based on seniority. If employees must be laid off or dismissed, those with the least seniority are the first to go. Some of the more senior employees may have to move to lower-level jobs, but they remain employed.

Union security is protection of the union's position as the employees' bargaining agent. Union security is frequently a more volatile issue than job security. Unions strive for as much security as possible, but management tends to see an increase in union security as an erosion of its control.

Union security arises directly from its membership. The greater the ratio of union employees to nonunion employees, the more secure the union is. In contract negotiations, unions thus attempt to establish various union membership conditions. The most restrictive of these is the **closed shop,** in which workers must join the union before they are hired. This condition was outlawed by the Taft-Hartley Act, but several other arrangements, including the following, are subject to negotiation:

job security protection against the loss of employment

union security protection of the union's position as the employees' bargaining agent

closed shop a workplace in which workers must join the union before they are hired; outlawed by the Taft-Hartley Act

union shop a workplace in which new employees must join the union after a specified probationary period

- The **union shop,** in which new employees must join the union after a specified probationary period

- The **agency shop,** in which employees can choose not to join the union but must pay dues to the union anyway (The idea is that nonunion employees benefit from union activities and should help to support them.)
- The **maintenance shop,** in which an employee who joins the union must remain a union member as long as he or she is employed by the firm

agency shop a workplace in which employees can choose not to join the union but must pay dues to the union anyway

maintenance shop a workplace in which an employee who joins the union must remain a union member as long as he or she is employed by the firm

Management Rights

Of particular interest to the firm are those rights and privileges that are to be retained by management. For example, the firm wants as much control as possible over whom it hires, how work is scheduled, and how discipline is handled. The union, in contrast, would like some control over these and other matters affecting its members. It is interesting that some unions are making progress toward their goal of playing a more direct role in corporate governance. Some union executives have, in fact, been given seats on corporate boards of directors.

Grievance Procedures

A **grievance procedure** is a formally established course of action for resolving employee complaints against management. Virtually every labor contract contains a grievance procedure. Procedures vary in scope and detail, but they may involve all four steps described below (see Figure 12.4).

grievance procedure a formally established course of action for resolving employee complaints against management

Original Grievance   The process begins with an employee who believes that he or she has been treated unfairly in violation of the labor contract. For example, an employee may be entitled to a formal performance review after six months on the job. If no such review is conducted, the employee may file a grievance. To do so, the employee explains the grievance to a **shop steward,** an employee elected by union

shop steward an employee elected by union members to serve as their representative

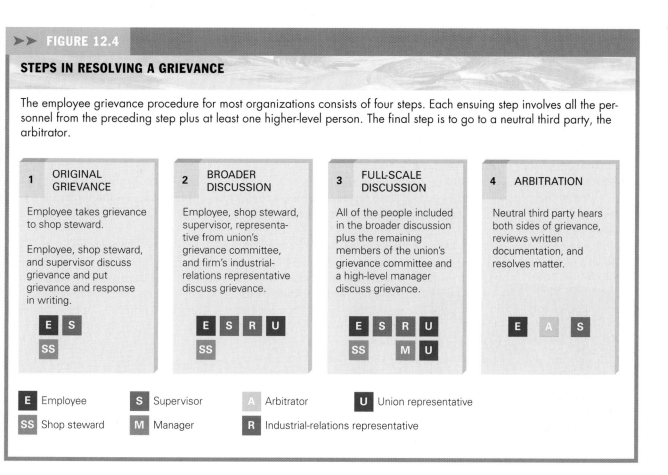

>> **FIGURE 12.4**

STEPS IN RESOLVING A GRIEVANCE

The employee grievance procedure for most organizations consists of four steps. Each ensuing step involves all the personnel from the preceding step plus at least one higher-level person. The final step is to go to a neutral third party, the arbitrator.

1 ORIGINAL GRIEVANCE

Employee takes grievance to shop steward.

Employee, shop steward, and supervisor discuss grievance and put grievance and response in writing.

E S
SS

2 BROADER DISCUSSION

Employee, shop steward, supervisor, representative from union's grievance committee, and firm's industrial-relations representative discuss grievance.

E S R U
SS

3 FULL-SCALE DISCUSSION

All of the people included in the broader discussion plus the remaining members of the union's grievance committee and a high-level manager discuss grievance.

E S R U
SS M U

4 ARBITRATION

Neutral third party hears both sides of grievance, reviews written documentation, and resolves matter.

E A S

E Employee   **S** Supervisor   **A** Arbitrator   **U** Union representative

SS Shop steward   **M** Manager   **R** Industrial-relations representative

members to serve as their representative. The employee and the steward then discuss the grievance with the employee's immediate supervisor. Both the grievance and the supervisor's response are put in writing.

Broader Discussion

In most cases the problem is resolved during the initial discussion with the supervisor. If it is not, a second discussion is held. Now the participants include the original parties (employee, supervisor, and steward), a representative from the union's grievance committee, and the firm's industrial-relations representative. Again, a record is kept of the discussion and its results.

Full-Scale Discussion

If the grievance is still not resolved, a full-scale discussion is arranged. This discussion includes everyone involved in the broader discussion, as well as all remaining members of the union's grievance committee and another high-level manager. As usual, all proceedings are put in writing. All participants are careful not to violate the labor contract during this attempt to resolve the complaint.

arbitration the step in a grievance procedure in which a neutral third party hears the two sides of a dispute and renders a binding decision

Arbitration

The final step in a grievance procedure is **arbitration,** in which a neutral third party hears the two sides of a dispute and renders a binding decision. As in a court hearing, each side presents its case and has the right to cross-examine witnesses. In addition, the arbitrator reviews the written documentation of all previous steps in the grievance procedure. Both sides may then give summary arguments and/or present briefs. The arbitrator then decides whether a provision of the labor contract has been violated and proposes a remedy. The arbitrator cannot make any decision that would add to, detract from, or modify the terms of the contract. If it can be proved that the arbitrator exceeded the scope of his or her authority, either party may appeal the decision to the courts.

What actually happens when union and management "lock horns" over all the issues we have mentioned? We can answer this question by looking now at the negotiating tools each side can wield.

 ## BizTech

Who's Blogging—And Why?

Union-management relations have taken a high-tech turn with the rise of the blog. Short for web log, a *blog* is an Internet site where people post thoughts or complaints and invite comments. Here are a few examples:

- *Unions.* On the United Federation of Teachers' unofficial blog (**www.edwize.com**), members, education advocates, and others comment on contract issues, teaching, and related topics. The Service International Employees Union's blog (**www.weiu.org**) features comments on organizing activities, labor laws, and more.
- *Employees and management.* Sun Microsystems, which makes networking systems, encour-

ages everyone on staff to blog (**www.blogs.sun.com**) about almost anything as long as they follow guidelines, including a disclaimer that posts are each writer's personal opinion. Sun's blog has caught the eye of potential employees, recruiters, industry analysts, and competitors.

What's on the minds of employees, managers, union members, and union officials? Blogs—including unauthorized blogs that criticize or compliment—offer valuable clues.

Union and Management Negotiating Tools

Management and unions can draw on certain tools to influence each other during contract negotiations. Both sides may use advertising and publicity to gain support for their respective positions. The most extreme tools are strikes and lockouts, but there are other, milder techniques as well.

Strikes

Unions go out on strike only in a very few instances and almost always only after an existing labor contract has expired. (In 2004, there were only seventeen major strikes in the private sector—*major* meaning those involving over 1,000 workers.[12]) Even then, if new contract negotiations seem to be proceeding smoothly, a union does not actually start a strike. The union does take a strike vote, but the vote may be used primarily to show members' commitment to a strike if negotiations fail.

Using a strike to negotiate. A strike can increase public support for a union's position and decrease a firm's ability to operate effectively.

The main objective of a strike is to put financial pressure on the company to encourage management to meet union demands. When union members do go out on strike, it is usually because negotiations seem to be stalled. A strike is simply a work stoppage: The employees do not report for work. In addition, striking workers engage in **picketing,** marching back and forth in front of a place of employment with signs informing the public that a strike is in progress. In doing so, they hope that (1) the public will be sympathetic to the strikers and will not patronize the struck firm, (2) nonstriking employees of the firm will honor the picket line and not report to work either, and (3) members of other unions will not cross the picket line (e.g., to make deliveries) and thus will further restrict the operations of the struck firm. Unions also may engage in informational picketing to let companies know of their dissatisfaction. New York, the city that never sleeps, came to a crashing halt when 33,000 members of the Transport Workers Union went on a three-day strike. The strike shut down the city's 243 bus routes and 26 subway lines, forcing its seven million daily commuters to rely on taxis, cars, and their own feet. The striking workers were angry over contract negotiations that reduced pensions and raised the price of their health care.[13]

Obviously, strikes are expensive to both the firm and the strikers. The firm loses business and earnings during the strike, and the striking workers lose the wages they would have earned if they had been at their jobs. During a strike, unions try to provide their members with as much support as possible. Larger unions are able to put a portion of their members' dues into a *strike fund.* The fund is used to provide financial support for striking union members. At times, workers may go out on a **wildcat strike,** which is a strike that has not been approved by the union. In this situation, union leaders typically work with management to convince the strikers to return to work.

7 LEARNING OBJECTIVE
Explain the primary bargaining tools available to unions and management.

picketing marching back and forth in front of a place of employment with signs informing the public that a strike is in progress

wildcat strike a strike not approved by the strikers' union

Slowdowns and Boycotts

Almost every labor contract contains a clause that prohibits strikes during the life of the contract. (This is why strikes, if they occur, usually take place after a contract has expired.) However, a union may strike a firm while the contract is in force if members believe that management has violated its terms. Workers also may engage in a **slowdown,** a technique whereby workers report to their jobs but work at a pace that is slower than normal.

A **boycott** is a refusal to do business with a particular firm. Unions occasionally bring this strategy to bear by urging members (and sympathizers) not to purchase the

slowdown a technique whereby workers report to their jobs but work at a slower pace than normal

boycott a refusal to do business with a particular firm

products of a firm with which they are having a dispute. Teachers' unions have organized "back to school" boycotts to protest labor practices of retailing giant Wal-Mart. The National Education Association, the largest union in the United States with 2.7 million members, and the 1.3-million-member American Federation of Teachers urged consumers to join the boycott by holding rallies, distributing fliers, and holding news conferences. The boycott was strategically planned during the "back to school" season, the second largest for Wal-Mart aside from the Christmas holiday.[14] A *primary boycott*, aimed at the employer directly involved in the dispute, can be a powerful weapon. A *secondary boycott*, aimed at a firm doing business with the employer, is prohibited by the Taft-Hartley Act. Cesar Chavez, a migrant worker who founded the United Farm Workers Union, used boycotts to draw attention to the low pay and awful conditions endured by produce pickers.

Lockouts and Strikebreakers

lockout a firm's refusal to allow employees to enter the workplace

strikebreaker a nonunion employee who performs the job of a striking union member

mediation the use of a neutral third party to assist management and the union during their negotiations

Management's most potent weapon is the lockout. In a **lockout,** the firm refuses to allow employees to enter the workplace. Like strikes, lockouts are expensive for both the firm and its employees. For this reason, they are used rarely and then only in certain circumstances. A firm that produces perishable goods, for example, may use a lockout if management believes that its employees will soon go on strike. The idea is to stop production in time to ensure minimal spoilage of finished goods or work in process.

Management also may attempt to hire strikebreakers. A **strikebreaker** is a nonunion employee who performs the job of a striking union member. Hiring strikebreakers can result in violence when picketing employees confront the nonunion workers at the entrance to the struck facility. The firm also faces the problem of finding qualified replacements for the striking workers. Sometimes management personnel take over the jobs of strikers. Managers at telephone companies have handled the switchboards on more than one occasion.

Mediation and Arbitration

Strikes, strikebreaking, lockouts, and boycotts all pit one side against the other. Ultimately, one side "wins" and the other "loses." Unfortunately, the negative effects of such actions—including resentment, fear, and distrust—may linger for months or years after a dispute has been resolved.

More productive techniques that are being used increasingly are mediation and arbitration. Either one may come into play before a labor contract expires or after some other strategy, such as a strike, has proved ineffective.

Mediation is the use of a neutral third party to assist management and the union during their negotiations. This third party (the mediator) listens to both sides, trying to find common ground for agreement. The mediator also tries to facilitate communication between the two sides, to promote compromise, and generally to keep the negotiations moving. At first the mediator may meet privately with each side. Eventually, however, his or her goal is to get the two to settle their differences. The Federal Mediation and Conciliation Service (FMCS) is an independent government agency that handles mediation for labor disputes. The FMCS resolved the strike of 60,000

Kroger, Albertson's, and Vons employees in southern California. The FMCS also mediated a labor dispute between SBD Communications and the Communications Workers of America (CWA). The agency handles 4,700 collective bargaining negotiations per year, with 80-percent of those mediations reaching an agreement from both parties.[15] The agency reports to have saved businesses and workers approximately $9 billion dollars during 1999–2004, showing the benefits of mediation for both parties.[16]

Unlike mediation, the *arbitration* step is a formal hearing. Just as it may be the final step in a grievance procedure, it also may be used in contract negotiations (perhaps after mediation attempts) when the two sides cannot agree on one or more issues. Here, the arbitrator hears the formal positions of both parties on outstanding, unresolved issues. The arbitrator then analyzes these positions and makes a decision on the possible resolution of the issues. If both sides have agreed in advance that the arbitration will be *binding*, they must accept the arbitrator's decision.

If mediation and arbitration are unsuccessful, then, under the provisions of the Taft-Hartley Act, the president of the United States can obtain a temporary injunction to prevent or stop a strike if it would jeopardize national health or security.

This chapter ends our discussion of human resources. Next, we examine the marketing function of business. We begin in Chapter 13 by discussing the meaning of the term *marketing*.

RETURN TO   Inside Business

The players, owners, and fans aren't the only people affected by labor disputes in professional sports. Restaurants, souvenir sellers, equipment manufacturers, and all manner of sports-related businesses lose revenue when teams don't play. During the NHL lockout, a sports apparel store owner complained, "Without hockey, it's been a horrible year." Restaurants that bustle with hundreds of fans on game night stand empty when labor disputes keep nearby stadiums or arenas dark.

Until the recent NHL lockout, no professional sport had ever called off an entire season. Would fans return? Consider that baseball attendance plummeted at many stadiums when teams resumed play in 1995 after the lengthy strike that canceled

the 1994 World Series. Similarly, attendance at many basketball games declined after the National Basketball Association (NBA) lockout that ended in 1999. Although hockey fans did come back, how will major league sports cope with the long-term effects of labor strife?

Questions

1. If you had been heading the NHL Players' Association, what negotiating tools would you have used to influence management before the team owners locked out the players?
2. If you had been a labor advisor to Major League Baseball after the four-month dispute with the umpires' union, what would you have suggested to improve relations with umpires before the start of the next season?

➤➤ CHAPTER REVIEW

Summary

1

Explain how and why labor unions came into being.

A labor union is an organization of workers who act together to negotiate wages and working conditions with their employers. Labor relations are the dealings between labor unions and business management.

The first major union in the United States was the Knights of Labor, formed in 1869 to eliminate the depersonalization of workers. The Knights were followed in 1886 by the American Federation of Labor (AFL). The goal of the AFL was to improve its members' living standards without changing the business system. In 1905 the radical Industrial Workers of the World (IWW) was formed; its goal was the overthrow of capitalism. Of these three, only the AFL remained when the Congress of Industrial Organizations (CIO) was founded as a body of industrial unions between World War I and World War II. After years of competing, the AFL and CIO merged in 1955. The largest union not affiliated with the AFL-CIO is the Teamsters Union.

2

Discuss the sources of unions' negotiating power and trends in union membership.

The power of unions to negotiate with management comes from two sources. The first is the size of their membership. The second is the groups of laws that guarantee unions the right to negotiate and that regulate the negotiation process. At present, union membership accounts for less than 15 percent of the American work force, and it seems to be decreasing for various reasons. Nonetheless, unions wield considerable power in many industries—those in which their members comprise a large proportion of the work force.

Many unions today are entering into partnerships with management rather than maintaining their traditional adversarial position. Unions and management cooperate to increase production, improve quality, lower costs, empower workers, and enhance the workplace. Limited partnerships center on accomplishing one specific task or project. Long-range strategic partnerships focus on sharing decision-making power for a range of workplace and business matters.

3

Identify the main focus of several major pieces of labor-management legislation.

Important laws that affect union power are the Norris-LaGuardia Act (limits management's ability to obtain injunctions against unions), the Wagner Act (forbids certain unfair labor practices by management), the Fair Labor Standards Act (allows the federal government to set the minimum wage and to mandate overtime rates), the Taft-Hartley Act (forbids certain unfair practices by unions), and the Landrum-Griffin Act (regulates the internal functioning of labor unions). The National Labor Relations Board (NLRB), a federal agency that oversees union-management relations, was created by the Wagner Act.

4

Enumerate the steps involved in forming a union and show how the National Labor Relations Board is involved in the process.

Attempts to form a union within a firm begin with an organizing campaign to develop widespread employee interest in having a union. Next, employees sign authorization cards indicating in writing their support for the union. The third step is to hold a formal election to decide whether to have a union. Finally, if the union obtains a majority, it receives NLRB certification, making it the official bargaining agent for its members. The entire process is supervised by the NLRB, which oversees the organizing campaign, conducts the election, and certifies the election results.

5

Describe the basic elements in the collective-bargaining process.

Once a union is established, it may negotiate a labor contract with management through the process of collective bargaining. First, the negotiating committee decides on its position on the various contract issues. The union informs management that it is ready to begin negotiations, and a time and place are set. The union is represented by the negotiating committee, and the organization is represented by managers from several departments in the company. Each side is required to negotiate in good faith and not to stall or attempt to extend the bargaining unnecessarily. The final step is ratification, which is approval of the contract by a vote of the union membership.

6

Identify the major issues covered in a union-management contract.

As the expiration date of an existing contract approaches, management and the union begin to negotiate a new contract. Contract issues include employee pay and benefits, working hours, job and union security, management rights, and grievance procedures.

7

Explain the primary bargaining tools available to unions and management.

Management and unions can use certain tools to sway one another—and public opinion—during contract negotiations. Advertising and publicity help each side to gain support. When contract negotiations do not run smoothly, unions may apply pressure on management through strikes, slowdowns, or boycotts. Management may counter by imposing lockouts or hiring strikebreakers. Less drastic techniques for breaking contract deadlocks are mediation and arbitration. In both, a neutral third party is involved in the negotiations.

Key Terms

You should now be able to define and give an example relevant to each of the following terms:

labor union (381)
union-management (labor) relations (381)
craft union (381)
strike (382)
industrial union (383)
National Labor Relations Board (NLRB) (386)
injunction (387)
bargaining unit (390)
jurisdiction (390)
collective bargaining (391)
ratification (392)
seniority (393)
overtime (394)
job security (394)
union security (394)
closed shop (394)
union shop (394)
agency shop (395)
maintenance shop (395)
grievance procedure (395)
shop steward (395)
arbitration (396)
picketing (397)
wildcat strike (397)
slowdown (397)
boycott (397)
lockout (398)
strikebreaker (398)
mediation (398)

Review Questions

1. Briefly describe the history of unions in the United States.
2. Describe the three characteristics common to most union-management partnerships. Discuss the benefits of union-management partnerships to management, unions, and workers.
3. How has government regulation of union-management relations evolved during this century?
4. For what reasons do employees start or join unions?
5. Describe the process of forming a union, and explain the role of the National Labor Relations Board (NLRB) in that process.
6. List the major areas that are negotiated in a labor contract.
7. Explain the three issues involved in negotiations concerning employee pay.
8. What is the difference between job security and union security? How do unions attempt to enhance union security?
9. What is a grievance? Describe the typical grievance procedure.
10. What steps are involved in collective bargaining?
11. For what reasons are strikes and lockouts relatively rare nowadays?
12. What are the objectives of picketing?
13. In what ways do the techniques of mediation and arbitration differ?

Discussion Questions

1. Do unions really derive their power mainly from their membership and labor legislation? What are some other sources of union power?
2. Which labor contract issues are likely to be the easiest to resolve? Which are likely to be the most difficult?
3. Discuss the following statement: Union security means job security for union members.
4. How would you prepare for labor contract negotiations as a member of management? As head of the union negotiating committee?
5. Under what circumstances are strikes and lockouts justified in place of mediation or arbitration?

▶▶ VIDEO CASE 12.1

Is Wal-Mart Waging War on Its Workers?

The world's largest retailer, Wal-Mart, is also one of organized labor's largest unionization targets. The United Food and Commercial Workers Union (UFCW) says that Wal-Mart's employees would benefit from collective bargaining, citing the retailer's low wages, inadequate benefits, huge profits, and anti-union attitudes. However, Wal-Mart's management says that its 1.3 million associates (the company's term for employees) are treated well and need no outside representation to communicate with the company.

The UFCW uses pro-union literature, meetings, and media releases to fuel organizing campaigns among Wal-Mart employees. "Americans can't live on a Wal-Mart paycheck," states Greg Denier, the UFCW's communications director. "Yet it's the dominant employer, and what they pay will be the future of working America." The union charges that Wal-Mart brainwashes its employees into believing that they can speak up without union help and uses surveillance, interrogation, intimidation, and termination to stay union-free.

In addition, the UFCW is sponsoring "Wake Up Wal-Mart," a nationwide campaign to put the spotlight on the retailer's wages, benefits, and business practices. Through a website, television commercials, press releases, local demonstrations, and other activities, the union wants to pressure the retailer into boosting wages, improving benefits, and keeping jobs in America rather than buying from Chinese suppliers. Wal-Mart notes that it has long offered benefits such as health insurance, retirement plans, incentive bonuses, stock purchase plans, and merchandise discounts. It is also known for promotion from within. Still, stung by growing criticism, Wal-Mart has begun offering more affordable health insurance plans and will match up to $1,000 when employees contribute to a new health care spending account.

Some current and former employees and managers are supporting the UFCW's fight by publicly discussing their experiences. Gretchen Adams, a former Wal-Mart co-manager, stresses that many employees complained about the high premiums for health insurance through the retailer's benefit plan. Linda Gruen was so upset about the insurance issue that she left her job at Sam's Club to become a UFCW organizer.

Wal-Mart denies the UFCW's allegations. "It's our approach with our associates to treat them right and have a genuine partnership with them," responds Wal-Mart spokesperson Bill Wertz. "We need a lot of people to conduct our business and fill our existing stores. We couldn't do that if we mistreated our people." In fact, Wertz says, "The question our people have is what the unions' real intent is. It doesn't seem like a genuine membership drive. It seems like more of an effort to discredit the company and protect those companies that do employ union members."

Legally, Wal-Mart can call employees together for anti-union meetings, show anti-union videos, and distribute anti-union literature. According to an academic study, 92 percent of companies use anti-union meetings, and 70 percent send workers anti-union literature when faced with an organizing campaign. The executive vice president of Wal-Mart's People Division says that it uses labor experts to "educate associates about how these [union election] processes work." On the other hand, according to former Wal-Mart "people" manager Stan Fortune, the actions he took years ago as a self-described company "union buster" were not legal.

Wal-Mart's nonunion stance keeps it at odds with organized labor. And the recent movie *Wal-Mart: The High Cost of Low Price* has stirred up even more controversy about the retailer. Is Wal-Mart waging war on its workers, as the UFCW asserts? Or is the union using rhetoric to stir up pro-union feelings among Wal-Mart's work force? The debate continues as each side turns up the heat to get its story out to the public.[17]

For more information about this topic, go to **www.walmartstores.com** and **www.wakeupwalmart.com**.

Questions

1. Why does the UFCW want to unionize and represent Wal-Mart employees? What types of obstacles does the UFCW face in this effort?
2. If management believes that its benefit plans are acceptable to employees, why would Wal-Mart engage in strong anti-union activities?
3. What role does public opinion play in the fight between Wal-Mart and the UFCW?

▶▶ CASE 12.2

Can Striking Workers Be Replaced?

Strikes are costly to both the union members walking the picket line and the company whose employees are off the job. Companies may lose business and struggle to get things done properly and on time. Often they try to minimize the disruption by assigning managers and hiring workers to fill in. Meanwhile, those on strike don't earn what they would if they were at work. But can striking workers be replaced?

In general, U.S. companies can legally replace workers temporarily or permanently during a strike. Consider what happened when the union representing 1,730 nurses at Stanford University Medical Center and Lucile Salter Packard Children's Hospital wanted to get members a raise in the next contract. The union asked for more than 17 percent, but management initially offered 8 percent. The two sides couldn't agree on the size of the raise, so the union notified the hospitals that a strike was imminent.

The hospitals quickly arranged for U.S. Nursing Corp. to fly in hundreds of temporary replacements. "We're not strikebreakers; we're not scab nurses," said Daniel Mordecai, who founded U.S. Nursing. "We're a company that performs an emergency staffing service. If we didn't, the hospital would not be able to care for its patients and the community." The American Nurses Association, an organization of unions representing nurses around the country, countered that the company "undermines the nurses who go out on the picket line, and it encourages lengthy strikes" because the hospitals are less motivated to continue negotiations. In this case, the nurses went back to work after a seven-week strike ended in a new contract with pay raises of up to 12 percent.

Although companies are allowed to hire permanent replacements for employees on strike, few actually do so. Northwest Airlines decided to hire permanent replacements when its mechanics went on strike to protest the financially ailing airline's demand for significant pay cuts. As the dispute dragged on, Northwest intensified its cost-cutting efforts and finally filed for bankruptcy reorganization. The airline kept its jets in the air even as it continued to hire permanent replacements for the striking mechanics.

Opponents say that companies should not be allowed to hire permanent replacements because the practice puts unions at a severe negotiating disadvantage. The unions have far less bargaining power if companies simply can replace workers who strike. Moreover, the striking workers suffer because they lose their jobs—not by being fired but by being replaced. Critics also observe that companies in Canada, Mexico, and many other countries are not legally allowed to hire permanent replacement workers. If so many nations outlaw this practice, should it be legal in the United States?

Until U.S. legislators take action on this issue, unions are looking more closely at other ways of pressuring companies without prolonged strikes. One approach is to hold demonstrations and publicity strikes to call attention to the situation and to try to gain public support. Another approach is to strike intermittently or strike different facilities at different times. Instead of striking, some unions may use slowdowns or file large numbers of grievances to put pressure on management without endangering workers' jobs.

Professor Richard Lippke of James Madison University cites four alternatives to a total ban on permanent replacements. One option is to use permanent replacements only after a strike has lasted for a certain period. A second option is to enact laws discouraging but not forbidding permanent replacements, such as disqualifying companies from receiving government contracts for a specified period. A third option is to ban the practice but permit a company to ask an independent arbitrator to make an exception if warranted. A fourth option is to force both sides to go to arbitration and have both pay penalties for each day they fail to reach an agreement.[18]

For more information about this topic, go to **www.nursingworld.org** and **www.usnursing.com**.

Questions

1. How might management and the public react to a union publicizing a company's use of temporary or permanent replacement workers during a strike?
2. Should U.S. lawmakers forbid all companies from hiring permanent replacements for striking workers? Support your answer.
3. Should U.S. lawmakers forbid all unions from striking unless mediation and arbitration fail to resolve their disputes with management?

→ CHAPTER 12: JOURNAL EXERCISE

Discovery statement: This chapter focused on the unionization process and why employees join unions.

What are the major reasons for joining and being a part of a labor union?

_____

_____

_____

_____

_____

Under what conditions would you like to be a union member?

_____

_____

_____

_____

Are there any circumstances under which a striking union member should cross a picket line and go back to work? Explain.

_____

_____

_____

_____

_____

Will the unions in the United States grow or decline over the next decade? Why?

_____

_____

_____

_____

_____

BUILDING SKILLS FOR CAREER SUCCESS

1. Exploring the Internet

Union websites provide a wealth of information about union activities and concerns. Just as a corporate home page gives a firm the opportunity to describe its mission and goals and present its image to the world, so too does a website allow a union to speak to its membership as well as to the public at large. Visit the text website for updates to this exercise.

Assignment

1. Visit the following websites:

   AFL-CIO: **www.aflcio.com**
   United Auto Workers: **www.uaw.org**

2. What are the mission statements of these unions?

3. Briefly describe your impression of the areas of interest to union members.
4. What is your impression of the tone of these websites? Do they differ in any way from a typical business website?

2. Developing Critical-Thinking Skills

Recently, while on its final approach to an airport in Lubbock, Texas, a commercial airliner encountered a flock of ducks. The flight crew believed that one or more of the ducks hit the aircraft and were ingested into the plane's main engine. The aircraft landed safely and taxied to the terminal. The flight crew advised the maintenance and operations crews of the incident. Operations grounded the plane until it could be inspected, but because of the time of day, maintenance personnel available to perform the inspection were in short supply. The airline had to call in two off-duty mechanics. A supervisor, calling from an overtime list, made calls until contacting two available mechanics. They worked on overtime pay to perform the inspection and return the aircraft to a safe flying status. Several days after the inspection, a mechanic on the overtime list who was not home when the supervisor called complained that she had been denied overtime. This union member believed that the company owed her overtime pay for the same number of hours worked by a mechanic who performed the actual inspection. The company disagreed. What options are available to resolve this conflict?

Assignment

1. Using the following questions as guidelines, determine how this dispute can be resolved.

   a. What options are available to the unhappy mechanic? What process must she pursue? How does this process work?

   b. Do you believe that the mechanic should receive pay for time she did not work? Justify your answer.

   c. What do you think was the final outcome of this conflict?

2. Prepare a report describing how you would resolve this situation.

3. Building Team Skills

For more than a century, American unions have played an important role in the workplace, striving to improve the working conditions and quality of life of employees. Today, federal laws cover many of the workers' rights that unions first championed. For this reason, some people believe that unions are no longer necessary. According to some experts, however, as technology changes the workplace and as cultural diversity and the number of part-time workers increase, unions will increase their memberships and become stronger as we move into the new century. What do you think?

Assignment

1. Form a "pro" group and a "con" group and join one of them.

2. Debate whether unions will be stronger or weaker in the next century.

3. Record the key points for each side.

4. Summarize what you learned about unions and their usefulness in a report, and state your position on the debated issue.

4. Researching Different Careers

When applying for a job, whether mailing or faxing in your résumé, you should always include a letter of application, or a cover letter, as it is often called. A well-prepared cover letter should convince the prospective employer to read your résumé and to phone you for an interview. The letter should describe the job you want and your qualifications for the job. It also should let the firm know where you can be reached to set up an appointment for an interview.

Assignment

1. Prepare a letter of application to use with the résumé you prepared in Chapter 10. (An example appears in Appendix A online).

2. After having several friends review your letter, edit it carefully.

3. Ask your instructor to comment on your letter.

5. Improving Communication Skills

A union contract is an agreement between a company and its employees who are union members. The contract sets forth the procedures that both parties must use to resolve disputes. Sometimes, however, the disputed issues become so complex that they cannot be resolved easily by union and management. At this point, mediators usually step in to help move both sides closer to resolving their issues. At times, even this measure is not enough, and the union calls a strike.

Assignment

1. Read recent newspaper articles about issues that divide a firm's management and its union employees.

2. Find answers to the following questions:

   a. What are the disputed issues?

   b. Which issues are the most difficult to resolve? Why?

   c. Where does each party stand on the issues?

   d. How are the issues being resolved, or if they are already resolved, how were they resolved?

   e. What might be the effect of this dispute on union-management relations?

3. Summarize your findings and what you learned about unions in a report.

→ PREP TEST

Matching Questions

_____ 1. A union is given the right to organize a particular group of workers.

_____ 2. It is a court order.

_____ 3. After completing their probationary period, new employees must join a union.

_____ 4. All the workers in a single industry are eligible to join the union.

_____ 5. It is the group of employees that the union represents.

_____ 6. It is the final step in the grievance procedure.

_____ 7. The process helps employees resolve work-related complaints.

_____ 8. A process to negotiate labor contracts.

_____ 9. The Taft-Hartley Act declared it illegal.

_____ 10. A neutral third party offers suggestions for settling a dispute.

a. arbitration
b. bargaining unit
c. closed shop
d. collective bargaining
e. grievance procedure
f. industrial union
g. injunction
h. jurisdiction
i. mediation
j. union shop

True/False Questions

T F

11. ○ ○ A labor union is a group of organized workers.

12. ○ ○ The first step in the grievance process involves securing a mediator.

13. ○ ○ A labor contract is the result of the bargaining process.

14. ○ ○ Today, union members account for a large proportion of the total American work force.

15. ○ ○ The Wagner Act made it difficult for businesses to ban strikes, picketing, or union membership drives.

T F

16. ○ ○ The Wagner Act requires management to negotiate with union representatives.

17. ○ ○ The union has the responsibility to ensure that pay is equitable with that received by other employees in the same or similar industries.

18. ○ ○ Arbitrators sit in the capacity of a judge who has final authority.

19. ○ ○ Job security and union security are interchangeable terms.

20. ○ ○ A craft union is one composed of both skilled and unskilled workers.

Multiple-Choice Questions

21. Joe, an employee in an engine-repair shop, feels that he has been unfairly treated because he was not called during the weekend to work overtime. His name was the first name on the official overtime call list; instead, another person was called. Who should Joe talk to about his situation?

    a. mediator
    b. bargainer
    c. shop steward
    d. arbitrator
    e. negotiator

22. The NLRB is primarily concerned with

    a. establishing procedures for obtaining an injunction.
    b. setting a minimum-wage policy.
    c. monitoring the process for preparing a union's annual report.
    d. overseeing the process for creating a union.
    e. providing safeguards governing union funds.

23. What is the main objective of a strike?

    a. Show support to the community
    b. Gain sympathy for management
    c. Put financial pressure on the firm
    d. Promote the firm's products
    e. Allow employees time off from work

24. Union employees in a local production plant have been without a contract for six months. Management has presented its final offer, which was not accepted by the union. Management believes that the employees are about to go on strike. What is the *most* potent tool that management can use against these employees?

    a. Declare a strike
    b. Issue a slowdown
    c. Go into a lockout
    d. Exercise a boycott
    e. Picketing

25. The practice of requiring employees to join a union after a probation period might violate

    a. the right-to-work laws in that state.
    b. the minimum-wage part of the Fair Labor Standards Act.
    c. an injunction.
    d. unfair labor practices under the Wagner Act.
    e. the provisions of the law establishing the NLRB.

Fill-in-the-Blank Questions

26. A vote that reveals whether union members are willing to strike is called a _____ vote.

27. The _____ Act authorized states to enact "right to work" laws that allow employees to work in a unionized firm without joining the union.

28. A written agreement that sets forth issues between labor and management is called a _____ contract.

29. Job security under union contracts is based on _____.

30. The act that requires management to negotiate with union representatives is the _____ Act.

⟅Online Study Center

FOR MORE **test practice, use the interactive ACE quizzes available at the Online Student Center: www.college.hmco.com/PIC/pridebusiness9e.**

Answers on p. PT1.

Inside the People Business at Finagle A Bagel

People are a vital ingredient in Finagle A Bagel's recipe for success. As a quick-serve business, the company strives for high turnover in food, not employees. In fact, careful attention to human resources management has enabled Finagle A Bagel to continue expanding its market share without spending money on advertising. Low work force turnover means less money and time spent on recruiting and training—an important financial consideration for a fast-growing business. It also means that Finagle A Bagel has the human resources strength to combine super service with fresh food for a distinctive competitive advantage in a crowded marketplace.

The Right People in the Right Place

"We depend on our crew at the store level—who are interacting with our guests every day—to know their jobs, to understand the company mission, and to communicate with the guests," says Heather Robertson, who directs the company's marketing, human resources, and research and development. "And once we get them on board, people don't leave our company. They just stay. They realize that it can be a career for them."

A sizable number of Finagle A Bagel's managers and employees (including Robertson) were hired years ago and became so excited about the product, the company, and the customers that they simply stayed. Many remain with Finagle A Bagel because they prefer the more personal atmosphere of a 320-employee business over the relatively faceless anonymity of a gigantic corporation. "It's really unusual to have one-on-one interaction on a daily basis with the president of the company or any senior executive member of the company," Robertson states. "Our cashiers, our café attendants, our bakers, and our managers know they can pick up the phone at any point and call anybody here and say, 'Here's my problem. How do I fix it?' or 'I need your help.' The size of our company allows us to do that, and the culture of the company encourages that."

Because bagels are an integral part of every menu item, employees who join Finagle A Bagel must "love" bagels, regardless of any other skills or experiences they bring to their jobs. When Robertson advertises to fill an open position in Finagle A Bagel's headquarters, for example, she always mentions this requirement. As résumés come in, she sorts them according to whether the candidates indicate a fondness for bagels. Those who fail to mention it are automatically disqualified from consideration.

Different Kinds of Managers for Different Locations

Alan Litchman, Finagle A Bagel's copresident, says that selecting a candidate to manage one of the Boston stores is easier than selecting one for a suburban store. Given the inner-city location of the company's support center, he or another executive can get to the Boston stores more quickly if a problem arises. Moreover, the city stores compete by providing speedy, accurate service to busy customers who have little time to waste waiting in line. Paulo Pereira, general manager of the Harvard Square store in Cambridge, has become an expert at squeezing inefficiencies from the city stores so that customers are in and out more quickly. By increasing the number of customers served each day and slashing the number of bagels left over at closing, Pereira boosts both sales revenues and profits.

When selecting a manager for a suburban store, Litchman looks for people with an "owner-operator mentality" who have the drive, initiative, and know-how to build business locally. His message to a potential general manager is: "If you want to be a franchisee but don't have the capital, or if you want to own your own business, we're going to put you in business. You don't have to give us any money to do that. And if your store achieves more than a certain level of sales or profits, we'll start splitting the bottom line with you in a bonus program." Consider Nick Cochran, who worked his way up from assistant manager to general manager of the store in Wayland, an affluent Boston suburb. Cochran's enthusiasm for quality and service has drawn a highly loyal customer following and contributed to the Wayland store's success.

Hiring and Motivating Store Personnel

General managers such as Cochran and Pereira are responsible for recruiting, interviewing, hiring, training, motivating, and evaluating store-level personnel. They assign job responsibilities according to the skills and strengths of each manager and employee, but they also expect everyone to work as a team during extremely busy periods. In addition to motivating general managers by offering bonuses based on meeting revenue and profit goals, Finagle A Bagel encourages crew members to take advantage of extra training and internal promotions.

"In a company our size," stresses co-president Laura Trust, "there is always opportunity. You just have to find the right fit for the individual." In fact, says her husband, "The best supervisors, coordinators, assistant managers, or managers in any unit—by far—are the ones who have started with us at a lower level and worked their way up."

Diverse Work Force, Family Business

Finagle A Bagel has an extremely diverse work force made up of people originally from Latin America, Europe, western Africa, and many other areas. Over the years, the company has served as a sponsor for new Americans who need government-issued work permits so that they can legally remain in the United States for work reasons. Despite diversity's many advantages—including creativity, flexibility, and the ability to relate to a broader customer base—it also can create communications challenges when English is not an employee's native language. To avoid confusion, Litchman and Trust insist that employees speak only in English when addressing customers.

As a small, family-run business, Finagle A Bagel sees its work force as a group of unique individuals, not interchangeable cogs in an impersonal corporate machine. Trust feels strongly that "there's a responsibility that you have to your employees and to your colleagues. These people work for you—they work hard to try and move your company forward—and their efforts need to be recognized." Because the business is still small, she adds, "the people who have become a part of the management team are very much like family to Alan and me. If you run your company that way,

then you'll be successful because everybody believes that you care about not only the work they do but everything they do, and every part of their lives affects their job."

Questions

1. What effect has diversity had on Finagle A Bagel?
2. If you were the general manager of a downtown Finagle A Bagel store, what job description and job specification would you prepare for a cashier? Based on these, what kinds of questions would you ask when interviewing candidates for this position?
3. Which of Herzberg's motivation factors are Trust and Litchman emphasizing for general managers?
4. Would it be feasible for Finagle A Bagel to apply the concept of flextime to store employees? To senior managers at the headquarters facility? Explain.

BUILDING A BUSINESS PLAN PART IV

In this section of your business plan you will expand on the type and quantity of employees that will be required to operate the business. Your human resources requirements are determined by the type of business and by the size and scale of your operation. From the preceding section, you should have a good idea of how many people you will need. And Part 4 of your textbook, "Human Resources," especially Chapters 10 and 11, should help you in answering some of the questions in this part of the business plan.

The Human Resources Component

To ensure successful performance by employees, you must inform workers of their specific job requirements. Employees must know what is expected on the job, and they are entitled to expect regular feedback on their work. It is vital to have a formal job description and job specification for every position in your business. Also, you should establish procedures for evaluating performance.

The labor force component should include the answers to at least the following questions:

4.1. How many employees will you require, and what are their qualifications—including skills, experience, and knowledge? How many jobs will be full time? Part time?

4.2. Will you have written job descriptions for each position?

4.3. Have you prepared a job-application form? Do you know what can legally be included in it?

4.4. What criteria will you use in selecting employees?

4.5. Have you made plans for the orientation process?

4.6. Who will do the training?

4.7. What can you afford to pay in wages and salaries? Is this in line with the going rate in your region and industry?

4.8. Who will evaluate your employees?

4.9. Will you delegate any authority to employees?

4.10. Have you developed a set of disciplinary rules?

4.11. Do you plan to interview employees when they resign?

Review of Business Plan Activities

Remember that your employees are the most valuable and important resource. Therefore, make sure that you expend a great deal of effort to acquire and make full use of this resource. Check and resolve any issues in this component of your business plan before beginning Part 5. Again, make sure that your answers to the questions in each part are consistent with the entire business plan. Finally, write a brief statement that summarizes all the information for this part of the business plan.

Part 5

Marketing

The business activities that make up a firm's marketing efforts are those most directly concerned with satisfying customers' needs. In this part we explore these activities in some detail. Initially, we discuss markets, marketing mixes, marketing environment forces, marketing plans, and buying behavior. Then, in turn, we discuss the four elements that together make up a marketing mix: product, price, distribution, and promotion.

Building Customer Relationships Through Effective Marketing

LEARNING OBJECTIVES

WHAT you will be able to do once you complete this chapter:

1 Understand the meaning of *marketing* and the importance of management of customer relationships.

2 Explain how marketing adds value by creating several forms of utility.

3 Trace the development of the marketing concept and understand how it is implemented.

4 Understand what markets are and how they are classified.

5 Identify the four elements of the marketing mix and be aware of their importance in developing a marketing strategy.

6 Explain how the marketing environment affects strategic market planning.

7 Understand the major components of a marketing plan.

8 Describe how market measurement and sales forecasting are used.

9 Distinguish between a marketing information system and marketing research.

10 Identify the major steps in the consumer buying decision process and the sets of factors that may influence this process.

WHY this chapter matters

Marketers are concerned about building long-term customer relationships. To develop competitive product offerings that will satisfy customer needs, business people must be able to identify acceptable target customer groups and understand customer behavior.

FOR HELP with studying this chapter, visit the Online Student Center:

www.college.hmco.com/PIC/pridebusiness9e

Online Study Center

In today, out tomorrow—the quest for cool drives much of the buying done by teenagers and young adults. Companies that offer products based on the newest trend or latest pop culture development know that they have to move quickly, before a sales frenzy becomes a fizzle. This is why many companies hire trend consultants or specialized researchers to help them spot the new, new thing before it becomes the old, old thing.

Often what teenagers think is cool is heavily influenced by media. "Each season, teens get more fashionable," says Erin Conroy of Brown Shoe, a fashion shoe company. "They are tuned in to MTV and Hollywood and follow celebrities and other trend setters rather than setting the trends." Yet media coverage contributes to the speedy death of trends as well as to their birth. As soon as a celebrity wears a new style, the word spreads through the Internet, television, magazines, and newspapers. Teens want what's cool right now, not what was cool yesterday. Trend analyst Irma Zandl stresses the importance

DID YOU KNOW?

Teens determine "what's cool," and they influence people slightly younger and people slightly older than them.

of timing: Being the first to introduce a product in the hope of making it trendy is just as risky as being the last to market.

Moreover, teen tastes influence what preteens and young adults will buy. As other groups start to buy what teens in the vanguard are buying, trendy products become mainstream and much less appealing to the superhip. This is the signal for companies to put once-cool items on sale and gear up for the next trend.

Keeping up with cool also means keeping advertising up to date. Andrew Keller, creative director at ad agency CP+B, says that "advertising is disposable," and yet, he adds, "the faster we react to fads, the faster they'll go away." The bottom line for businesses is that the quest for cool never ends. Now more than ever, companies need to know their customers and look carefully for clues to the next cool thing.[1]

For more information about this topic, go to **www.pbs.org/wgbh/pages/frontline/shows/cool/themes/symbiotic.html.**

Marketing efforts are directed toward providing customer satisfaction. Understanding customers' needs, such as "what's cool," is crucial to providing customer satisfaction. Although marketing encompasses a diverse set of decisions and activities performed by individuals and by both business and nonbusiness organizations, marketing always begins and ends with the customer. The American Marketing Association defines **marketing** as "an organizational function and a set of processes for creating, communicating, and delivering value to customers [and] for managing customer relationships in ways that benefit the organization and its stakeholders."[2] The marketing process involves eight major functions and numerous related activities (see Table 13.1). All these functions are essential if the marketing process is to be effective.

In this chapter we examine marketing activities that add value to products. We trace the evolution of the marketing concept and describe how organizations practice it. Next, our focus shifts to market classifications and marketing strategy. We analyze the four elements of a marketing mix and also discuss uncontrollable factors in the marketing environment. Then we examine the major components of a marketing plan. We consider tools for strategic market planning, including market measurement, sales forecasts, marketing information systems, and marketing research. Last, we look at the forces that influence consumer and organizational buying behavior.

marketing an organizational function and a set of processes for creating, communicating, and delivering value to customers and for managing customer relationships in ways that benefit the organization and its stakeholders

> > **TABLE 13.1**

MAJOR MARKETING FUNCTIONS

Exchange functions: All companies—manufacturers, wholesalers, and retailers—buy and sell to market their merchandise.

1. **Buying** includes obtaining raw materials to make products, knowing how much merchandise to keep on hand, and selecting suppliers.

2. **Selling** creates possession utility by transferring the title of a product from seller to customer.

Physical distribution functions: These functions involve the flow of goods from producers to customers. Transportation and storage provide time utility and place utility and require careful management of inventory.

3. **Transporting** involves selecting a mode of transport that provides an acceptable delivery schedule at an acceptable price.

4. **Storing** goods is often necessary to sell them at the best selling time.

Facilitating functions: These functions help the other functions take place.

5. **Financing** helps at all stages of marketing. To buy raw materials, manufacturers often borrow from banks or receive credit from suppliers. Wholesalers may be financed by manufacturers, and retailers may receive financing from the wholesaler or manufacturer. Finally, retailers often provide financing to customers.

6. **Standardizing** sets uniform specifications for products or services. **Grading** classifies products by size and quality, usually through a sorting process. Together, standardization and grading facilitate production, transportation, storage, and selling.

7. **Risk taking**—even though competent management and insurance can minimize risks—is a constant reality of marketing because of such losses as bad-debt expense, obsolescence of products, theft by employees, and product-liability lawsuits.

8. **Gathering market information** is necessary for making all marketing decisions.

Managing Customer Relationships

Marketing relationships with customers are the lifeblood of all businesses. Maintaining positive relationships with customers is an important goal for marketers. The term **relationship marketing** refers to establishing "long-term, mutually beneficial arrangements in which both the buyer and seller focus on value enhancement through the creation of more satisfying exchanges."[3] Relationship marketing continually deepens the buyer's trust in the company, which, as the customer's loyalty grows, increases a company's understanding of the customer's needs and desires. Successful marketers respond to customer needs and strive to continually increase value to buyers over time. Eventually, this interaction becomes a solid relationship that allows for cooperation and mutual dependency. For example, customers depend on the Coca-Cola Company to provide a standardized, reliable, satisfying soft drink or beverage anyplace in the world. Owing to its efforts to expand distribution to every possible location, Coca-Cola sells 33 percent of its volume in Europe and the Middle East, 31 percent in North America, 22 percent in the Asian/Pacific region, 10 percent in Latin America, and 5 percent in Africa.[4] The company continues to introduce new products, expand distribution, and maintain high-quality products. Coca-Cola is also a good "corporate citizen," donating millions of dollars to education, health and human services, and disaster-plagued regions each year.

To build long-term customer relationships, marketers increasingly are turning to marketing research and information technology. **Customer relationship management (CRM)** focuses on using information about customers to create marketing strategies that develop and sustain desirable customer relationships. By increasing customer value over time, organizations try to retain and increase long-term profitability through customer loyalty.[5]

Relationship marketing. Opteum Financial Services indicates in its advertisements that it wants to develop long-term relationships with customers based on trust. Opteum advertises that it lives by the promises it makes.

WE PROMISE YOU A FIVE-STAR MORTGAGE EXPERIENCE.
IF YOU CLOSE YOUR LOAN WITH US
AND WE DON'T DELIVER, WE'LL PAY YOU $500.

Managing customer relationships requires identifying patterns of buying behavior and using that information to focus on the most promising and profitable customers.[6] Companies must be sensitive to customers' requirements and desires, and establish communication to build customers' trust and loyalty. In some instances it may be more profitable for a company to focus on satisfying a valuable existing customer than to attempt to attract a new one who may never develop the same level of loyalty. This involves determining how much the customer will spend over his or her lifetime. The **customer lifetime value** is a combination of purchase frequency, average value of purchases, and brand-switching patterns over the entire span of a customer's relationship with a company.[7] However, there are also intangible benefits of retaining lifetime-value customers, such as their ability to provide feedback to a company and referring new customers of similar value. The amount of money a company is willing to spend to retain such customers is also a factor. In general, when marketers focus on customers chosen for their lifetime value, they earn higher profits in future periods than when they focus on customers selected for other reasons.[8] Because the loss of a potential lifetime customer can result in lower profits, managing customer relationships has become a major focus of marketers.

Utility: The Value Added by Marketing

As defined in Chapter 9, **utility** is the ability of a good or service to satisfy a human need. A lunch at a Pizza Hut, an overnight stay at a Holiday Inn, and a Mercedes S500L all satisfy human needs. Thus each possesses utility. There are four kinds of utility.

Form utility is created by converting production inputs into finished products. Marketing efforts may influence form utility indirectly because the data gathered as part of marketing research frequently are used to determine the size, shape, and features of a product.

The three kinds of utility that are created directly by marketing are place, time, and possession utility. **Place utility** is created by making a product available at a location where customers wish to purchase it. A pair of shoes is given place utility when it is shipped from a factory to a department store.

Time utility is created by making a product available when customers wish to purchase it. For example, Halloween costumes may be manufactured in April but not displayed until late September, when consumers start buying them. By storing the costumes until they are wanted, the manufacturer or retailer provides time utility.

Possession utility is created by transferring title (or ownership) of a product to a buyer. For a product as simple as a pair of shoes, ownership usually is transferred by means of a sales slip or receipt. For such products as automobiles and homes, the transfer of title is a more complex process. Along with the title to its products, the seller transfers the right to use that product to satisfy a need (see Figure 13.1).

Place, time, and possession utility have real value in terms of both money and convenience. This value is created and added to goods and services through a wide variety of marketing activities—from research indicating what customers want to product warranties ensuring that customers get what they pay for. Overall, these marketing activities account for about half of every dollar spent by consumers. When they are part of an integrated marketing program that delivers maximum utility to the customer, many would agree that they are worth the cost.

Place, time, and possession utility are only the most fundamental applications of marketing activities. In recent years, marketing activities have been influenced by a broad business philosophy known as the *marketing concept*.

customer lifetime value a combination of purchase frequency, average value of purchases, and brand-switching patterns over the entire span of a customer's relationship with a company

2 LEARNING OBJECTIVE

Explain how marketing adds value by creating several forms of utility.

utility the ability of a good or service to satisfy a human need

form utility utility created by converting production inputs into finished products

place utility utility created by making a product available at a location where customers wish to purchase it

time utility utility created by making a product available when customers wish to purchase it

possession utility utility created by transferring title (or ownership) of a product to a buyer

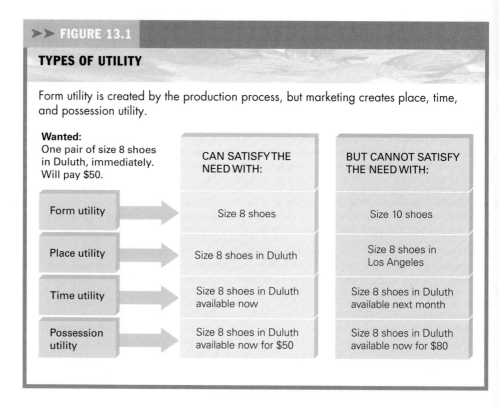

>> FIGURE 13.1

TYPES OF UTILITY

Form utility is created by the production process, but marketing creates place, time, and possession utility.

Wanted: One pair of size 8 shoes in Duluth, immediately. Will pay $50.	CAN SATISFY THE NEED WITH:	BUT CANNOT SATISFY THE NEED WITH:
Form utility	Size 8 shoes	Size 10 shoes
Place utility	Size 8 shoes in Duluth	Size 8 shoes in Los Angeles
Time utility	Size 8 shoes in Duluth available now	Size 8 shoes in Duluth available next month
Possession utility	Size 8 shoes in Duluth available now for $50	Size 8 shoes in Duluth available now for $80

The Marketing Concept

3 LEARNING OBJECTIVE

Trace the development of the marketing concept and understand how it is implemented.

marketing concept a business philosophy that a firm should provide goods and services that satisfy customers' needs through a coordinated set of activities that allows the firm to achieve its objectives

The **marketing concept** is a business philosophy that a firm should provide goods and services that satisfy customers' needs through a coordinated set of activities that allows the firm to achieve its objectives. Thus, initially, the firm must communicate with potential customers to assess their product needs. Then the firm must develop a good or service to satisfy those needs. Finally, the firm must continue to seek ways to provide customer satisfaction. This process is an application of the marketing concept, or marketing orientation. Ben & Jerry's, for example, constantly assesses customer demand for ice cream and sorbet. On its website, it maintains a "flavor graveyard" listing combinations that were tried and ultimately failed. It also notes its top ten flavors each month. Thus the marketing concept emphasizes that marketing begins and ends with customers.

Evolution of the Marketing Concept

From the start of the Industrial Revolution until the early twentieth century, business effort was directed mainly toward the production of goods. Consumer demand for manufactured products was so great that manufacturers could almost bank on selling everything they produced. Business had a strong *production orientation*, in which emphasis was placed on increased output and production efficiency. Marketing was limited to taking orders and distributing finished goods.

In the 1920s, production caught up with and began to exceed demand. Now producers had to direct their efforts toward selling goods rather than just producing goods that consumers readily bought. This new *sales orientation* was characterized by increased advertising, enlarged sales forces, and occasionally, high-pressure selling techniques. Manufacturers produced the goods they expected consumers to want, and marketing consisted primarily of promoting products through personal selling and advertising, taking orders, and delivering goods.

During the 1950s, however, business people started to realize that even enormous advertising expenditures and the most thoroughly proven sales techniques were not enough. Something else was needed if products were to sell as well as expected. It was then that business managers recognized that they were not primarily producers or sell-

ENTREPRENEURIAL CHALLENGE

Building a Business on eBay

Thinking of building a small business by buying and selling on the auction website eBay? Here are some of the pros and cons:

Pros:

- *Work from home or anywhere.* "I just need a post office and a phone line," says rare coin dealer Mark Goldberg. Still, entrepreneurs should be ready to rent more space as their businesses grow.
- *Find out what works—fast.* Entrepreneurs can test new products, find new markets, and change prices quickly and easily.
- *Be the boss.* "I own my own business, and I make my own hours," says Jody Rogers, who co-owns a business that auctions hand-made sandals.

Cons:

- *Lots of details.* Somebody has to photograph and describe items for sale, answer bidders'

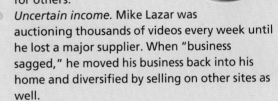

questions, and ship products out. In fact, some entrepreneurs make their living handling these details for others.
- *Uncertain income.* Mike Lazar was auctioning thousands of videos every week until he lost a major supplier. When "business sagged," he moved his business back into his home and diversified by selling on other sites as well.
- *Lots of competition.* Millions of users buy and sell on eBay, which means competition can be fierce.

---

ers but rather were in the business of satisfying customers' needs. Marketers realized that the best approach was to adopt a customer orientation—in other words, the organization had to first determine what customers need and then develop goods and services to fill those particular needs (see Table 13.2).

All functional areas—research and development (R&D), production, finance, human resources, and of course, marketing—are viewed as playing a role in providing customer satisfaction.

Implementing the Marketing Concept

The marketing concept has been adopted by many of the most successful business firms. Some firms, such as Ford Motor Company and Apple Computer, have gone through minor or major reorganizations in the process. Because the marketing concept is essentially a business philosophy, anyone can say, "I believe in it." To make it work, however, management must fully adopt and then implement it.

To implement the marketing concept, a firm first must obtain information about its present and potential customers. The firm must determine not only what customers' needs are but also how well those needs are being satisfied by products currently on the market—both its own products and those of competitors. It must ascertain how its products might be improved and what opinions customers have about the firm and its marketing efforts.

The firm then must use this information to pinpoint the specific needs and potential customers toward which it will direct its marketing activities and resources. (Obviously, no firm can expect to satisfy all needs. And not every individual or firm can be considered a potential customer for every product manufactured or sold by a firm.) Next, the firm must mobilize its marketing resources to (1) provide a product that will satisfy its customers, (2) price the product at a level that is acceptable to buyers and that

> > **TABLE 13.2**

EVOLUTION OF CUSTOMER ORIENTATION

Business managers recognized that they were not primarily producers or sellers but rather were in the business of satisfying customers' wants.

Production Orientation	Sales Orientation	Customer Orientation
Take orders	Increase advertising	Determine customer needs
Distribute goods	Enlarge sales force	Develop products to fill these needs
	Intensify sales techniques	Achieve the organization's goals

will yield an acceptable profit, (3) promote the product so that potential customers will be aware of its existence and its ability to satisfy their needs, and (4) ensure that the product is distributed so that it is available to customers where and when needed.

Finally, the firm again must obtain marketing information—this time regarding the effectiveness of its efforts. Can the product be improved? Is it being promoted properly? Is it being distributed efficiently? Is the price too high or too low? The firm must be ready to modify any or all of its marketing activities based on information about its customers and competitors. Toyota, for example, has taken the lead in the American automotive industry through its promise of high quality yet sensible cars. But Toyota isn't satisfied with producing practical cars and is launching a new campaign to make consumers passionate about its product. Toyota is revamping its relationship with customers by forgoing traditional advertising and bringing its cars straight to the consumer. The Toyota Camry, the no. 1 selling car in America, is being redesigned to integrate a flashier grill and a sportier body to add fun to its proven quality. When the hybrid version of the new Camry debuts, Toyota will team up with medical doctors to promote the vehicle as asthma-friendly. Toyota will test out its new FJ Cruiser sport-utility vehicle (SUV) at off-road and trail events instead of using more traditional television advertising. As for its truck line, Toyota will focus on fishing and hunting events.[9]

4 LEARNING OBJECTIVE

Understand what markets are and how they are classified.

market a group of individuals or organizations, or both, that need products in a given category and that have the ability, willingness, and authority to purchase such products

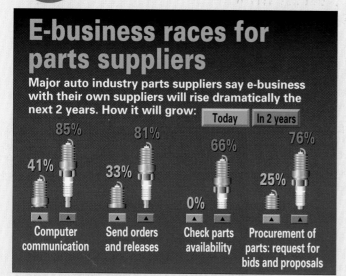

SPOTLIGHT

E-business races for parts suppliers

Major auto industry parts suppliers say e-business with their own suppliers will rise dramatically the next 2 years. How it will grow:

Today | In 2 years

Computer communication: 41% | 85%
Send orders and releases: 33% | 81%
Check parts availability: 0% | 66%
Procurement of parts: request for bids and proposals: 25% | 76%

Source: *USA Today*, October 18, 2001, p. B1.

Markets and Their Classification

A **market** is a group of individuals or organizations, or both, that need products in a given category and that have the ability, willingness, and authority to purchase such products. The people or organizations must want the product. They must be able to purchase the product by exchanging money, goods, or services for it. They must be willing to use their buying power. Finally, they must be socially and legally authorized to purchase the product.

Markets are broadly classified as consumer or business-to-business markets. These classifications are based on the characteristics of the individuals and organizations within each market. Because marketing efforts vary depending on the intended market, marketers should understand the general characteristics of these two groups.

Consumer markets consist of purchasers and/or household members who intend to consume or benefit from the purchased products and who do not buy products to make profits. *Business-to-business markets,* also called *industrial markets,* are grouped broadly into producer, reseller, governmental, and institutional categories. These markets purchase specific kinds of products for use in making other products for resale or for day-to-day operations. *Producer markets* consist of individuals and business organizations that buy certain products to use in the manufacture of other products. *Reseller markets* consist of intermediaries such as wholesalers and retailers that buy finished products and sell them for a profit. *Governmental markets* consist of federal, state, county, and local governments. They buy goods and services to maintain internal operations and to provide citizens with such products as highways, education, water, energy, and national defense. Governmental purchases total billions of dollars each year. *Institutional markets* include churches, not-for-profit private schools and hospitals, civic clubs, fraternities and sororities, charitable organizations, and foundations. Their goals are different from such typical business goals as profit, market share, or return on investment.

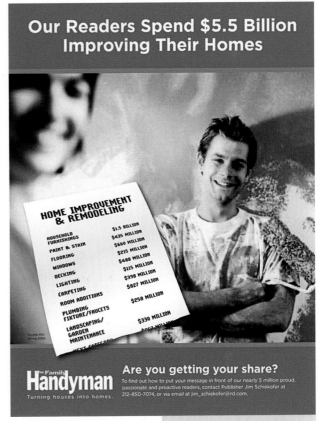

Reaching a target market.
A company's marketing efforts for a brand or product group are aimed at a specific target market. This advertisement for *Family Handyman* magazine indicates that the magazine can help a company reach a target market of customers who do their own home improvement projects.

Developing Marketing Strategies

A **marketing strategy** is a plan that will enable an organization to make the best use of its resources and advantages to meet its objectives. A marketing strategy consists of (1) the selection and analysis of a target market and (2) the creation and maintenance of an appropriate **marketing mix,** a combination of product, price, distribution, and promotion developed to satisfy a particular target market.

Target Market Selection and Evaluation

A **target market** is a group of individuals or organizations, or both, for which a firm develops and maintains a marketing mix suitable for the specific needs and preferences of that group. In selecting a target market, marketing managers examine potential markets for their possible effects on the firm's sales, costs, and profits. The managers attempt to determine whether the organization has the resources to produce a marketing mix that meets the needs of a particular target market and whether satisfying those needs is consistent with the firm's overall objectives. They also analyze the strengths and numbers of competitors already marketing to people in this target market. Marketing managers may define a target market as a vast number of people or a relatively small group. Rolls-Royce, for example, targets its automobiles toward a small, very exclusive market: wealthy people who want the ultimate in prestige in an automobile. Other companies target multiple markets with different products, prices, distribution systems, and promotion for each one. Nike uses this strategy, marketing different types of shoes to meet specific needs of cross-trainers, rock climbers, basketball players, aerobics enthusiasts, and other athletic-shoe buyers. When selecting a target market, marketing managers generally take either the undifferentiated approach or the market segmentation approach.

Undifferentiated Approach   A company that designs a single marketing mix and directs it at the entire market for a particular product is using an **undifferentiated approach** (see Figure 13.2). This approach assumes that individual customers in the

marketing strategy a plan that will enable an organization to make the best use of its resources and advantages to meet its objectives

marketing mix a combination of product, price, distribution, and promotion developed to satisfy a particular target market

target market a group of individuals or organizations, or both, for which a firm develops and maintains a marketing mix suitable for the specific needs and preferences of that group

undifferentiated approach directing a single marketing mix at the entire market for a particular product

>> **FIGURE 13.2**

GENERAL APPROACHES FOR SELECTING TARGET MARKETS

The undifferentiated approach assumes that individual customers have similar needs and that most customers can be satisfied with a single marketing mix. When customers' needs vary, the market segmentation approach—either concentrated or differentiated—should be used.

UNDIFFERENTIATED APPROACH

Organization → Single marketing mix → Target market

CONCENTRATED MARKET SEGMENTATION APPROACH

Organization → Single marketing mix → Target market

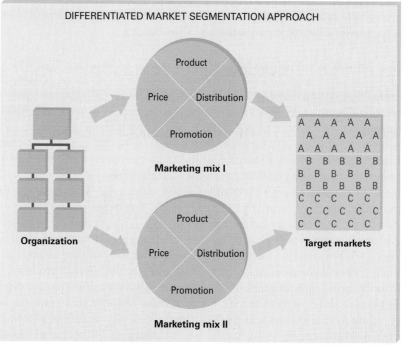

DIFFERENTIATED MARKET SEGMENTATION APPROACH

Organization → Marketing mix I, Marketing mix II → Target markets

NOTE: The letters in each target market represent potential customers. Customers that have the same letters have similar characteristics and similar product needs.

Source: William M. Pride and O. C. Ferrell, *Marketing: Concepts and Strategies,* 13th ed. (Boston: Houghton Mifflin, 2006). Copyright © 2006 by Houghton Mifflin Company. Adapted with permission.

target market for a specific kind of product have similar needs and that the organization therefore can satisfy most customers with a single marketing mix. This single marketing mix consists of one type of product with little or no variation, one price, one promotional program aimed at everyone, and one distribution system to reach all customers in the total market. Products that can be marketed successfully with the undifferentiated approach include staple food items, such as sugar and salt, and certain kinds of farm produce. An undifferentiated approach is useful in only a limited number of situations because for most product categories, buyers have different needs. When customers' needs vary, a company should use the market segmentation approach.

Market Segmentation Approach   A firm that is marketing forty-foot yachts would not direct its marketing effort toward every person in the total boat market. Some might want a sailboat or a canoe. Others might want a speedboat or an outboard-powered fishing boat. Still others might be looking for something resembling a small ocean liner. Marketing efforts directed toward such boat buyers would be wasted.

Instead, the firm would direct its attention toward a particular portion, or *segment*, of the total market for boats. A **market segment** is a group of individuals or organizations within a market that shares one or more common characteristics. The process of dividing a market into segments is called **market segmentation.** As shown in Figure 13.2, there are two types of market-segmentation approaches: concentrated and differentiated. When an organization uses *concentrated* market segmentation, a single marketing mix is directed at a single market segment. If *differentiated* market segmentation is employed, multiple marketing mixes are focused on multiple market segments.

In our boat example, one common characteristic, or *basis*, for segmentation might be "end use of a boat." The firm would be interested primarily in that market segment whose uses for a boat could lead to the purchase of a forty-foot yacht. Another basis for segmentation might be income; still another might be geographic location. Each of these variables can affect the type of boat an individual might purchase. When choosing a basis for segmentation, it is important to select a characteristic that relates to differences in people's needs for a product. The yacht producer, for example, would not use religion to segment the boat market because people's needs for boats do not vary based on religion.

Marketers use a wide variety of segmentation bases. Those bases most commonly applied to consumer markets are shown in Table 13.3. Each may be used as a single

market segment a group of individuals or organizations within a market that shares one or more common characteristics

market segmentation the process of dividing a market into segments and directing a marketing mix at a particular segment or segments rather than at the total market

>> **TABLE 13.3**

COMMON BASES OF MARKET SEGMENTATION

Demographic	Psychographic	Geographic	Behavioristic
Age	Personality attributes	Region	Volume usage
Gender	Motives	Urban, suburban, Rural	End use
Race	Lifestyles	Market density	Benefit expectations
Ethnicity		Climate	Brand loyalty
Income		Terrain	Price sensitivity
Education		City size	
Occupation		County size	
Family size		State size	
Family life cycle			
Religion			
Social class			

Source: William M. Pride and O. C. Ferrell, *Marketing: Concepts and Strategies,* 13th ed. (Boston: Houghton Mifflin, 2006). Copyright © 2006 by Houghton Mifflin Company. Adapted with permission.

GET **10** YEARS BACK

I'm 40

RoC® RETINOL CORREXION®
DEEP WRINKLE SERUM

NEW

CLINICALLY PROVEN TO GIVE **10 YEARS BACK** TO THE LOOK OF YOUR SKIN*

• concentrated moisturizing fluid contains a unique mineral complex
• pure, active Retinol helps to stimulate skin renewal
• in 12 weeks, even deep wrinkles are visibly diminished
• works under makeup or while you sleep

RoC
FRANCE, 1957

WE KEEP OUR PROMISES.

Available at a drugstore near you. For more information visit rocskincare.com.
*Diminished appearance of wrinkles after 12 weeks use in clinical testing

Is this ad aimed at all women? The maker of RoC Retinol Correxion is not aiming its product at all women, but is using market segmentation. This product is targeted to women aged 40 and older.

5 LEARNING OBJECTIVE

Identify the four elements of the marketing mix and be aware of their importance in developing a marketing strategy.

basis for market segmentation or in combination with other bases. For example, Vertu, a part of mobile phone maker Nokia, has segmented the market for cellular phones and is using a concentrated targeting strategy. The segment Vertu is after is very wealthy customers who want luxurious, social-status possessions. The company's mobile phones are made from precious materials, including gold, platinum, and sapphire crystal. The phones include a button that connects the owner to a personal assistant twenty-four hours a day. To reach its wealthy target market, Vertu sells its phones in private suites in select large cities (e.g., New York, London, Paris, Tokyo, and of course, Beverly Hills) and at Nieman Marcus department stores for a price ranging from just under $5,000 to almost $20,000 per phone. Such stars as Gwyneth Paltrow and Madonna are some of Vertu's customers.[10]

Creating a Marketing Mix

A business firm controls four important elements of marketing that it combines in a way that reaches the firm's target market. These are the *product* itself, the *price* of the product, the means chosen for its *distribution*, and the *promotion* of the product. When combined, these four elements form a marketing mix (see Figure 13.3).

A firm can vary its marketing mix by changing any one or more of these ingredients. Thus a firm may use one marketing mix to reach one target market and a second, somewhat different marketing mix to reach another target market. For example, most automakers produce several different types and models of vehicles and aim them at different market segments based on age, income, and other factors.

For example, Toyota's marketing research about Generation Y drivers found that they practically live in their cars, and many even keep a change of clothes handy in their vehicles. As a result of this research, Toyota designed its Scion as a "home on wheels," with a 15-volt outlet for plugging in a computer, reclining front seats for napping, and a powerful audio system for listening to MP3 music files, all for a $12,500 price tag.[11]

The *product* ingredient of the marketing mix includes decisions about the product's design, brand name, packaging, warranties, and the like. When McDonald's decides on brand names, package designs, sizes of orders, flavors of sauces, and recipes, these choices are all part of the product ingredient.

The *pricing* ingredient is concerned with both base prices and discounts of various kinds. Pricing decisions are intended to achieve particular goals, such as to maximize profit or even to make room for new models. The rebates offered by automobile manufacturers are a pricing strategy developed to boost low auto sales. Product and pricing are discussed in detail in Chapter 14.

The *distribution* ingredient involves not only transportation and storage but also the selection of intermediaries. How many levels of intermediaries should be used in the distribution of a particular product? Should the product be distributed as widely as possible? Or should distribution be restricted to a few specialized outlets in each area? These and other questions related to distribution are considered in Chapter 15.

The *promotion* ingredient focuses on providing information to target markets. The major forms of promotion are advertising, personal selling, sales promotion, and public relations. These four forms are discussed in Chapter 16.

These ingredients of the marketing mix are controllable elements. A firm can vary each of them to suit its organizational goals, marketing goals, and target markets. As we extend our discussion of marketing strategy, we will see that the marketing environment includes a number of *uncontrollable* elements.

>> **FIGURE 13.3**

THE MARKETING MIX AND THE MARKETING ENVIRONMENT

The marketing mix consists of elements that the firm controls—product, price, distribution, and promotion. The firm generally has no control over forces in the marketing environment.

Source: William M. Pride and O. C. Ferrell, *Marketing: Concepts and Strategies*, 13th ed. (Boston: Houghton Mifflin, 2006). Copyright © 2006 by Houghton Mifflin Company. Adapted with permission.

Marketing Strategy and the Marketing Environment

The marketing mix consists of elements that a firm controls and uses to reach its target market. In addition, the firm has control over such organizational resources as finances and information. These resources, too, may be used to accomplish marketing goals. However, the firm's marketing activities are also affected by a number of external—and generally uncontrollable—forces. As Figure 13.3 illustrates, the forces that make up the external *marketing environment* are

- *Economic forces*—the effects of economic conditions on customers' ability and willingness to buy
- *Sociocultural forces*—influences in a society and its culture that result in changes in attitudes, beliefs, norms, customs, and lifestyles
- *Political forces*—influences that arise through the actions of elected and appointed officials
- *Competitive forces*—the actions of competitors, who are in the process of implementing their own marketing plans
- *Legal and regulatory forces*—laws that protect consumers and competition and government regulations that affect marketing
- *Technological forces*—technological changes that, on the one hand, can create new marketing opportunities or, on the other, can cause products to become obsolete almost overnight

These forces influence decisions about marketing-mix ingredients. Changes in the environment can have a major impact on existing marketing strategies. In addition,

6 LEARNING OBJECTIVE
Explain how the marketing environment affects strategic market planning.

Marketing Me

Whether you're looking for an entry-level job or a new job with more responsibilities, developing a marketing plan can keep your search on course.

- *Environmental analysis.* What industries are growing, and what types of careers do these industries offer? What environmental forces could affect jobs in these industries? Narrow the list to specific companies you want to target, and "put all of your energy into those," advises JetBlue Airways' head of human resources.

- *Strengths and weaknesses, opportunities and threats.* How do your skills, education, abilities, and interests match the companies and positions you're targeting? What might prevent you from applying or qualifying for these positions? Where are the best job opportunities for you?

- *Objectives, strategies, and implementation.* What job objective will you list on your résumé? How will you organize your job search? What, exactly, will you do to find promising jobs—and when?

- *Evaluation and control.* How can you improve your job search and your career marketing plan?

7 LEARNING OBJECTIVE
Understand the major components of a marketing plan.

marketing plan a written document that specifies an organization's resources, objectives, strategy, and implementation and control efforts to be used in marketing a specific product or product group

changes in environmental forces may lead to abrupt shifts in customers' needs. Technological forces, for example, are having a major impact at Intel, the world's largest producer of computer microchips. With competition from iPods, Blackberrys, cell phones, and other handheld devices, the PC industry is slowing, and Intel is revamping its focus and its brand in an effort to remain relevant. Intel is launching more new products than at any time in the company's history. The Viiv will be a new chip designed to replace your TiVo, stereo, and potentially, cable or satellite box. It can download first-run movies, music, and games. In addition to its expanding product range, Intel is hiring software developers, sociologists, ethnographers, and even doctors for product development.[12]

Developing a Marketing Plan

A **marketing plan** is a written document that specifies an organization's resources, objectives, marketing strategy, and implementation and control efforts to be used in marketing a specific product or product group. The marketing plan describes the firm's current position or situation, establishes marketing objectives for the product, and specifies how the organization will attempt to achieve these objectives. Marketing plans vary with respect to the time period involved. Short-range plans are for one year or less, medium-range plans cover from over one year up to five years, and long-range plans cover periods of more than five years.

Although time-consuming, developing a clear, well-written marketing plan is important. The plan will be used for communication among the firm's employees. It covers the assignment of responsibilities, tasks, and schedules for implementation. It specifies how resources are to be allocated to achieve marketing objectives. It helps marketing managers monitor and evaluate the performance of the marketing strategy. Because the forces of the marketing environment are subject to change, marketing plans have to be updated frequently. Disney, for example, recently made changes to its marketing plans by combining all activities and licensing associated with the Power Rangers, Winnie the Pooh, and Disney Princess into one marketing plan with a $500 million budget. The primary goal is to send consistent messages about branding to customers. As the new marketing plan is implemented, Disney will have to respond quickly to customers' reactions and make adjustments to the plan.[13] The major components of a marketing plan are shown in Table 13.4.

Market Measurement and Sales Forecasting

8 LEARNING OBJECTIVE
Describe how market measurement and sales forecasting are used.

Measuring the sales potential of specific types of market segments helps an organization to make some important decisions. It can evaluate the feasibility of entering new segments. The organization also can decide how best to allocate its marketing resources and activities among market segments in which it is already active. All such

> > **TABLE 13.4**

COMPONENTS OF THE MARKETING PLAN

Plan Component	Component Summary	Highlights
Executive summary	One- to two-page synopsis of the entire marketing plan	
Environmental analysis	Information about the company's current situation with respect to the marketing environment	1. Assessment of marketing environment factors 2. Assessment of target market(s) 3. Assessment of current marketing objectives and performance
SWOT analysis	Assessment of the organization's strengths, weaknesses, opportunities, and threats	1. Strengths 2. Weaknesses 3. Opportunities 4. Threats
Marketing objectives	Specification of the firm's marketing objectives	Qualitative measures of what is to be accomplished
Marketing strategies	Outline of how the firm will achieve its objectives	1. Target market(s) 2. Marketing mix
Marketing implementation	Outline of how the firm will implement its marketing strategies	1. Marketing organization 2. Activities and responsibilities 3. Implementation timetable
Evaluation and control	Explanation of how the firm will measure and evaluate the results of the implemented plan	1. Performance standards 2. Financial controls 3. Monitoring procedures (audits)

Source: William M. Pride and O. C. Ferrell, *Marketing: Concepts and Strategies,* 13th ed. (Boston: Houghton Mifflin, 2006). Copyright © 2006 by Houghton Mifflin Company. Reprinted with permission.

estimates should identify the relevant time frame. As with marketing plans, these estimates may be short range, covering periods of less than one year; medium range, covering one to five years; or long range, covering more than five years. The estimates also should define the geographic boundaries of the forecast. For example, sales potential can be estimated for a city, county, state, or group of nations. Finally, analysts should indicate whether their estimates are for a specific product item, a product line, or an entire product category.

A **sales forecast** is an estimate of the amount of a product that an organization expects to sell during a certain period of time based on a specified level of marketing effort. Managers in different divisions of an organization rely on sales forecasts when they purchase raw materials, schedule production, secure financial resources, consider plant or equipment purchases, hire personnel, and plan inventory levels. Because the accuracy of a sales forecast is so important, organizations often use several forecasting methods, including executive judgments, surveys of buyers or sales personnel, time-series analyses, correlation analyses, and market tests. The specific methods used depend on the costs involved, type of product, characteristics of the market, time span of the forecast, purposes for which the forecast is used, stability of historical sales data, availability of the required information, and expertise and experience of forecasters.

sales forecast an estimate of the amount of a product that an organization expects to sell during a certain period of time based on a specified level of marketing effort

Marketing Information

The availability and use of accurate and timely information are critical to making effective marketing decisions. A wealth of marketing information is obtainable. There are two general ways to obtain it: through a marketing information system and through marketing research.

9 LEARNING OBJECTIVE
Distinguish between a marketing information system and marketing research.

Marketing information provider. Many organizations, such as Abacus, a division of DoubleClick, Inc., provide information to help marketers develop, implement, and manage marketing strategies effectively.

marketing information system a system for managing marketing information that is gathered continually from internal and external sources

marketing research the process of systematically gathering, recording, and analyzing data concerning a particular marketing problem

Marketing Information Systems

A **marketing information system** is a system for managing marketing information that is gathered continually from internal and external sources. Most of these systems are computer-based because of the amount of data the system must accept, store, sort, and retrieve. *Continual* collection of data is essential if the system is to incorporate the most up-to-date information.

In concept, the operation of a marketing information system is not complex. Data from a variety of sources are fed into the system. Data from *internal* sources include sales figures, product and marketing costs, inventory levels, and activities of the sales force. Data from *external* sources relate to the organization's suppliers, intermediaries, and customers; competitors' marketing activities; and economic conditions. All these data are stored and processed within the marketing information system. Its output is a flow of information in the form that is most useful for making marketing decisions. This information might include daily sales reports by territory and product, forecasts of sales or buying trends, and reports on changes in market share for the major brands in a specific industry. Both the information outputs and their form depend on the requirements of the personnel in the organization.

Marketing Research

Marketing research is the process of systematically gathering, recording, and analyzing data concerning a particular marketing problem. Thus marketing research is used in specific situations to obtain information not otherwise available to decision makers. It is an intermittent, rather than a continual, source of marketing information. With the help of a new software company, Dunkin' Donuts is using marketing research to remain competitive against Krispy Kreme and Starbucks, as well as McDonald's, which recently entered the espresso-drink market. A survey of Dunkin' Donuts customers revealed that they welcomed menu changes such as iced beverages, espresso drinks, and scrambled eggs and cheese on a bagel. The firm's research also suggested that it should continue its strategy of targeting workday on-the-go customers and not taking on Starbucks directly.[14]

Table 13.5 outlines a six-step procedure for conducting marketing research. This procedure is particularly well suited to testing new products, determining various characteristics of consumer markets, and evaluating promotional activities. Food-processing companies, such as Kraft Foods and Kellogg's, use a variety of marketing research methods to avoid costly mistakes in introducing the wrong products or products in the wrong way or at the wrong time. They have been particularly interested in using marketing research to learn more about the African-American and Hispanic markets. Understanding of the food preferences, loyalties, and purchase motivators of these groups enables these companies to serve them better.

Using Technology to Gather and Analyze Marketing Information

Technology is making information for marketing decisions increasingly accessible. The ability of firms to track the purchase behaviors of customers electronically and to better determine what they want is changing the nature of marketing. The integration of telecommunications with computing technology provides marketers with access to accurate information not only about customers and competitors but also about industry forecasts and business trends. Among the communication tools that are radically changing the way marketers obtain and use information are databases, online information services, and the Internet.

➤➤ TABLE 13.5

THE SIX STEPS OF MARKETING RESEARCH

1. Define the problem	In this step, the problem is stated clearly and accurately to determine what issues are involved in the research, what questions to ask, and what types of solutions are needed. This is a crucial step that should not be rushed.
2. Make a preliminary investigation	The objective of preliminary investigation is to develop both a sharper definition of the problem and a set of tentative answers. The tentative answers are developed by examining internal information and published data and by talking with persons who have some experience with the problem. These answers will be tested by further research.
3. Plan the research	At this stage, researchers know what facts are needed to resolve the identified problem and what facts are available. They make plans on how to gather needed but missing data.
4. Gather factual information	Once the basic research plan has been completed, the needed information can be collected by mail, telephone, or personal interviews; by observation; or from commercial or government data sources. The choice depends on the plan and the available sources of information.
5. Interpret the information	Facts by themselves do not always provide a sound solution to a marketing problem. They must be interpreted and analyzed to determine the choices available to management.
6. Reach a conclusion	Sometimes the conclusion or recommendation becomes obvious when the facts are interpreted. However, in other cases, reaching a conclusion may not be so easy because of gaps in the information or intangible factors that are difficult to evaluate. If and when the evidence is less than complete, it is important to say so.

Marketing research. Marketing research service companies, such as AC Nielsen, provide a variety of marketing research services to organizations that have information needs.

A *database* is a collection of information arranged for easy access and retrieval. Using databases, marketers tap into internal sales reports, newspaper articles, company news releases, government economic reports, bibliographies, and more. Many marketers use commercial databases, such as LEXIS-NEXIS, to obtain useful information for marketing decisions. Many of these commercial databases are available in printed form (for a fee), online (for a fee), or on purchasable CD-ROMs. Other marketers develop their own databases in-house. Some firms sell their databases to other organizations. *Reader's Digest*, for example, markets a database that provides information on 100 million households. Dunn & Bradstreet markets a database that includes information on the addresses, phone numbers, and contacts of businesses located in specific areas.

Information provided by a single firm on household demographics, purchases, television viewing behavior, responses to

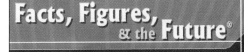

Facts, Figures & the Future is the monthly e-publication focused on delivering the latest consumer data and trend information to members of the Food Marketing Institute and clients of ACNielsen. Facts, Figures & the Future is published jointly by FMI, ACNielsen and The Lempert Report.

Send this report to a friend

Phil Lempert,
editor

Telephone: 323-860-3070

Plempert@FactsFiguresFuture.com

May 16, 2006

The family that eats together...

One of the most important announcements that came out of Chicago last week was the FMI's support of "Family Day".

This event, celebrated each year on the fourth Monday in September, will be heavily promoted in supermarkets throughout the nation, and is the brainchild of the National Center on Addiction and Substance Abuse, headed up by Joe Califano Jr., the former U.S. Secretary of Health, Education and Welfare.

Michael Sansolo
Senior VP
Food Marketing
Institute

Getting to Know Today's Shopper
Assembling a single picture of today's supermarket shopper is a near impossibility.

Growing diversity in background, shopping needs, outlook and feelings make the picture of today's shopper more muddled than ever, giving the industry a powerful challenge of understanding how to provide the best possible shopping experience to a large enough group.

Phil Lempert
Editor
Facts, Figures &
the Future

360: A Holistic Approach to Shoppers
I find myself sitting this morning with over 1,000 CPG brand managers and retailers at this year's Consumer 360 conference in Palm Desert. "Today is the first day of the rest of your life" comes to mind. Sitting here, I think it's apropos to suggest a slight variation: "Today is the first day of the rest of your consumers' shopping lives".

promotions such as coupons and free samples is called *single-source data*. For example, Behavior Scan, offered by Information Resources, Inc., screens about 60,000 households in twenty-six U.S. markets. This single-source information service monitors household televisions and records the programs and commercials viewed. When buyers from these households shop in stores equipped with scanning registers, they present Hotline cards (similar to credit cards) to cashiers. This enables each customer's identification to be coded electronically so that the firm can track each product purchased and store the information in a database.

Online information services offer subscribers access to e-mail, websites, files for downloading (such as with Acrobat Reader), news, databases, and research materials. By subscribing to mailing lists, marketers can receive electronic newsletters and participate in online discussions with other network users. This ability to communicate online with customers, suppliers, and employees improves the capability of a firm's marketing information system and helps the company track its customers' changing desires and buying habits.

The *Internet* has evolved as a powerful communication medium, linking customers and companies around the world via computer networks with e-mail, forums, web pages, and more. Growth in Internet use has given rise to an entire industry that makes marketing information easily accessible to both companies and customers. Among the many web pages useful for marketing research are the home pages of Nielsen marketing research and *Advertising Age*. While most web pages are open to all Internet users, some companies, such as U.S. West and Turner Broadcasting System, also maintain internal web pages, called *intranets*, that allow employees to access internal data and facilitate communication among departments.

Table 13.6 lists a number of websites that may serve as valuable resources for marketing research. The Bureau of the Census, for example, uses the Internet to disseminate information that may be useful to marketing researchers, particularly through the *Statistical Abstract of the United States* and data from the most recent Census. The "Census Lookup" option allows marketing researchers to create their own customized information. With this online tool, researchers can select tables by clicking boxes to select a state and then, within the state, the county, place, and urbanized area or metropolitan statistical area to be examined.

10 LEARNING OBJECTIVE
Identify the major steps in the consumer buying decision process and the sets of factors that may influence this process.

buying behavior the decisions and actions of people involved in buying and using products

consumer buying behavior the purchasing of products for personal or household use, not for business purposes

business buying behavior the purchasing of products by producers, resellers, governmental units, and institutions

Types of Buying Behavior

Buying behavior may be defined as the decisions and actions of people involved in buying and using products.[15] **Consumer buying behavior** refers to the purchasing of products for personal or household use, not for business purposes. **Business buying**

> > **TABLE 13.6**

INTERNET SOURCES OF MARKETING INFORMATION

Government sources	Commercial sources	Periodicals and books
census.gov	acnielsen.com	adage.com
state.gov	Infores.com	salesandmarketing.com
fedworld.gov	gallup.com	Fortune.com
	arbitron.com	inc.com
	chamber-of-commerce.com	businessweek.com
	bloomberg.com	

Source: William M. Pride and O. C. Ferrell, *Marketing: Concepts and Strategies,* 13th ed. (Boston: Houghton Mifflin, 2006). Copyright © 2006 by Houghton Mifflin Company. Reprinted with permission.

behavior is the purchasing of products by producers, resellers, governmental units, and institutions. Since a firm's success depends greatly on buyers' reactions to a particular marketing strategy, it is important to understand buying behavior. Marketing managers are better able to predict customer responses to marketing strategies and to develop a satisfying marketing mix if they are aware of the factors that affect buying behavior.

Consumer Buying Behavior

Consumers' buying behaviors differ when they buy different types of products. For frequently purchased low-cost items, a consumer employs routine response behavior involving very little search or decision-making effort. The buyer uses limited decision making for purchases made occasionally or when more information is needed about an unknown product in a well-known product category. When buying an unfamiliar, expensive item or one that is seldom purchased, the consumer engages in extensive decision making.

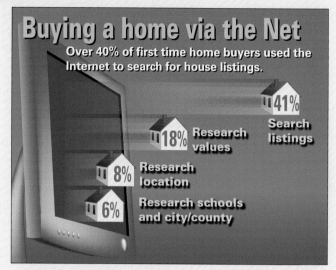

SPOTLIGHT

Buying a home via the Net

Over 40% of first time home buyers used the Internet to search for house listings.

41% Search listings

18% Research values

8% Research location

6% Research schools and city/county

Source: **Real Estate.com** survey.

A person deciding on a purchase goes through some or all of the steps shown in Figure 13.4. First, the consumer acknowledges that a problem exists. A problem is usually the lack of a product or service that is desired or needed. Then the buyer looks for information, which may include brand names, product characteristics, warranties, and other features. Next, the buyer weighs the various

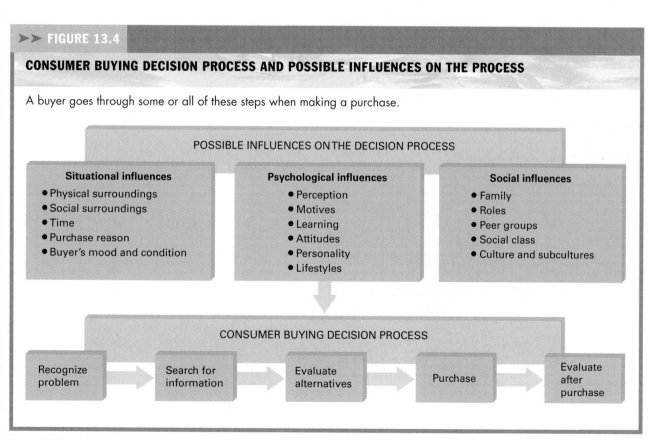

>> **FIGURE 13.4**

CONSUMER BUYING DECISION PROCESS AND POSSIBLE INFLUENCES ON THE PROCESS

A buyer goes through some or all of these steps when making a purchase.

POSSIBLE INFLUENCES ON THE DECISION PROCESS

Situational influences
- Physical surroundings
- Social surroundings
- Time
- Purchase reason
- Buyer's mood and condition

Psychological influences
- Perception
- Motives
- Learning
- Attitudes
- Personality
- Lifestyles

Social influences
- Family
- Roles
- Peer groups
- Social class
- Culture and subcultures

CONSUMER BUYING DECISION PROCESS

Recognize problem → Search for information → Evaluate alternatives → Purchase → Evaluate after purchase

Source: William M. Pride and O. C. Ferrell, *Marketing: Concepts and Strategies*, 13th ed. (Boston: Houghton Mifflin, 2006). Copyright © 2006 by Houghton Mifflin Company. Adapted with permission.

personal income the income an individual receives from all sources *less* the Social Security taxes the individual must pay

disposable income personal income *less* all additional personal taxes

discretionary income disposable income *less* savings and expenditures on food, clothing, and housing

alternatives he or she has discovered and then finally makes a choice and acquires the item. In the after-purchase stage, the consumer evaluates the suitability of the product. This judgment will affect future purchases. As Figure 13.4 shows, the buying process is influenced by situational factors (physical surroundings, social surroundings, time, purchase reason, and buyer's mood and condition), psychological factors (perception, motives, learning, attitudes, personality, and lifestyle), and social factors (family, roles, peer groups, social class, culture, and subculture).

Consumer buying behavior is also affected by ability to buy or buying power, which is largely determined by income. As every taxpayer knows, not all income is available for spending. For this reason, marketers consider income in three different ways. **Personal income** is the income an individual receives from all sources *less* the Social Security taxes the individual must pay. **Disposable income** is personal income *less* all additional personal taxes. These taxes include income, estate, gift, and property taxes levied by local, state, and federal governments. About 3 percent of all disposable income is saved. **Discretionary income** is disposable income *less* savings and expenditures on food, clothing, and housing. Discretionary income is of particular interest to marketers because consumers have the most choice in spending it. Consumers use their discretionary income to purchase items ranging from automobiles and vacations to movies and pet food.

Business Buying Behavior

Business buyers consider a product's quality, its price, and the service provided by suppliers. Marketers at GraniteRock Company understand the value of customer service and thus concentrate their efforts on on-time delivery to distinguish GraniteRock from its competitors.[16] Business buyers usually are better informed than consumers about products and generally buy in larger quantities. In a business, a committee or group of people, rather than just one person, often decides on purchases. Committee members must consider the organization's objectives, purchasing policies, resources, and personnel. Business buying occurs through description, inspection, sampling, or negotiation. A number of organizations buy a variety of products online.

Recognizing a problem. Some advertisements, such as this one for Uni-Ball pens, are aimed at a particular stage of the consumer's buying-decision process. This Uni-Ball pen ad is meant to stimulate the problem-recognition stage of the buying-decision process.

EXAMINING ETHICS

A Matter of Trust: Dell Rebuilds Customer Relationships

Dell, once the darling of the computer industry, is counting on a three-pronged program to regain customers' trust after a dip in satisfaction ratings and global publicity about some of the company's laptop batteries catching fire.

- *Emphasize product safety.* Dell recalled and replaced 4.1 million laptop batteries made by Sony. This program has cost more than $200 million but demonstrates Dell's strong commitment to safety.

- *Improve customer service.* Dell is spending $115 million to expand its service centers, hire additional representatives, and train staff to handle more technical questions.
- *Launch new products.* To compete more effectively with Hewlett-Packard and other rivals, Dell is introducing faster computers and lighter laptops that will meet customers' needs.

RETURN TO   Inside Business

From colas to cars, jeans to jerseys, music to mobile phones, cool makes a difference in many product categories—especially when young adults are the target market. Firms that cater to trendy teens cannot afford the luxury of waiting months for items to be manufactured and shipped from the Far East or other distant places because the window of opportunity closes much sooner these days. When teens want a cool product, they want it now. Price is a secondary consideration.

Many companies use the Internet to keep their brands cool. Coca-Cola, for example, sponsors an interactive website called MyCoke.com. Millions of teens have registered to create music mixes, record songs, play games, download screensavers, and more. The head of Coke's online agency explains that companies are particularly keen to keeping teens interested because "if you can be cool, then you're going to be talked about, and that's going to produce results."

Questions

1. MyCoke.com members are asked to list their birth date and e-mail address (but not their names) when they register. How might this information be valuable to Coca-Cola's marketers?
2. How does the concept of time utility apply to trendy products?

►► CHAPTER REVIEW

Summary

1

Understand the meaning of *marketing* and the importance of management of customer relationships.

Marketing is an organizational function and a set of processes for creating, communicating, and delivering value to customers and for managing customer relationships in ways that benefit the organization and its stakeholders. Maintaining positive relationships with customers is crucial. Relationship marketing is establishing long-term, mutually satisfying buyer-seller relationships. Customer relationship management uses information about customers to create marketing strategies that develop and sustain desirable customer relationships. Managing customer relationships requires identifying patterns of buying behavior and focusing on the most profitable customers. Customer lifetime value is a combination of purchase frequency, average value of purchases, and brand-switching patterns over the entire span of a customer's relationship with the company.

2

Explain how marketing adds value by creating several forms of utility.

Marketing adds value in the form of utility or the power of a product or service to satisfy a need. It creates place utility by making products available where customers want them, time utility by making products available when customers want them, and possession utility by transferring the ownership of products to buyers.

3

Trace the development of the marketing concept and understand how it is implemented.

From the Industrial Revolution until the early twentieth century, business people focused on the production of goods; from the 1920s to the 1950s, the emphasis moved to the selling of goods. During the 1950s, however, business people recognized that their enterprises involved not only producing and selling products but also satisfying customers' needs. They began to implement the marketing concept, a business philosophy that involves the entire organization in the dual processes of meeting the customers' needs and achieving the organization's goals.

Implementation of the marketing concept begins and ends with customers—first to determine what customers' needs are and later to evaluate how well the firm is meeting those needs.

4

Understand what markets are and how they are classified.

A market consists of people with needs, the ability to buy, and the desire and authority to purchase. Markets are classified as consumer and industrial (producer, reseller, governmental, and institutional) markets.

5

Identify the four elements of the marketing mix and be aware of their importance in developing a marketing strategy.

A marketing strategy is a plan for the best use of an organization's resources to meet its objectives. Developing a marketing strategy involves selecting and analyzing a target market and creating and maintaining a marketing mix that will satisfy that target market. A target market is chosen through either the undifferentiated approach or the market-segmentation approach. A market segment is a group of individuals or organizations within a market that have similar characteristics and needs. Businesses that use an undifferentiated approach design a single marketing mix and direct it at the entire market for a particular product. The market-segmentation approach directs a marketing mix at a segment of a market.

The four elements of a firm's marketing mix are product, price, distribution, and promotion. The product ingredient includes decisions about the product's design, brand name, packaging, and warranties. The pricing ingredient is concerned with both base prices and various types of discounts. Distribution involves not only transportation and storage but also the selection of intermediaries. Promotion focuses on providing information to target markets. The elements of the marketing mix can be varied to suit broad organizational goals, marketing objectives, and target markets.

6

Explain how the marketing environment affects strategic market planning.

To achieve a firm's marketing objectives, marketing-mix strategies must begin with an assessment of the marketing environment, which, in turn, will influence decisions about marketing-mix ingredients. Marketing activities are affected by a number of external forces that make up the marketing environment. These forces include economic forces, sociocultural forces, political forces, competitive forces, legal and regulatory forces, and technological forces. Economic forces affect customers' ability and willingness to buy. Sociocultural forces are societal and cultural factors, such as attitudes, beliefs, and lifestyles, that affect customers' buying choices. Political forces and legal and regulatory forces influence marketing planning through laws that protect consumers and regulate competition. Competitive forces are the actions of competitors who are implementing their own marketing plans. Technological forces can create new marketing opportunities or quickly cause a product to become obsolete.

7

Understand the major components of a marketing plan.

A marketing plan is a written document that specifies an organization's resources, objectives, strategy, and implementation and control efforts to be used in marketing a specific product or product group. The marketing plan describes a firm's current position, establishes marketing objectives, and specifies the methods the organization will use to achieve these objectives. Marketing plans can be short range, covering one year or less; medium range, covering two to five years; or long range, covering periods of more than five years.

8

Describe how market measurement and sales forecasting are used.

Market measurement and sales forecasting are used to estimate sales potential and predict product sales in specific market segments.

9

Distinguish between a marketing information system and marketing research.

Strategies are monitored and evaluated through marketing research and the marketing information system that stores and processes internal and external data in a form that aids marketing decision making. A marketing information system is a system for managing marketing information that is gathered continually from internal and external sources. Marketing research is the process of systematically gathering, recording, and analyzing data concerning a particular marketing problem. It is an intermittent rather than a continual source of marketing information. Technology is making information for marketing decisions more accessible. Electronic communication tools can be very useful for accumulating accurate information with minimal customer interaction. Information technologies that are changing the way marketers obtain and use information are databases, online information services, and the Internet.

10

Identify the major steps in the consumer buying decision process and the sets of factors that may influence this process.

Buying behavior consists of the decisions and actions of people involved in buying and using products. Consumer buying behavior refers to the purchase of products for personal or household use. Organizational buying behavior is the purchase of products by producers, resellers, governments, and institutions. Understanding buying behavior helps marketers to predict how buyers will respond to marketing strategies. The consumer buying decision process consists of five steps, including recognizing the problem, searching for information, evaluating alternatives, purchasing, and evaluating after purchase. Factors affecting the consumer buying decision process fall into three categories: situational influences, psychological influences, and social influences.

Key Terms

You should now be able to define and give an example relevant to each of the following terms:

marketing (413)
relationship marketing (414)
customer relationship management (CRM) (414)
customer lifetime value (415)
utility (415)
form utility (415)
place utility (415)
time utility (415)
possession utility (415)
marketing concept (416)
market (418)
marketing strategy (419)
marketing mix (419)
target market (419)
undifferentiated approach (419)
market segment (421)
market segmentation (421)
marketing plan (424)
sales forecast (425)
marketing information system (426)
marketing research (426)
buying behavior (428)
consumer buying behavior (428)
business buying behavior (428)
personal income (430)
disposable income (430)
discretionary income (430)

Review Questions

1. How, specifically, does marketing create place, time, and possession utility?
2. What is relationship marketing?
3. How is a marketing-oriented firm different from a production-oriented firm or a sales-oriented firm?
4. What are the major requirements for a group of individuals and organizations to be a market? How does a consumer market differ from a business-to-business market?
5. What are the major components of a marketing strategy?

6. What is the purpose of market segmentation? What is the relationship between market segmentation and the selection of target markets?

7. What are the four elements of the marketing mix? In what sense are they "controllable"?

8. Describe the forces in the marketing environment that affect an organization's marketing decisions.

9. What is a marketing plan, and what are its major components?

10. What major issues should be specified before conducting a sales forecast?

11. What is the difference between a marketing information system and a marketing research project? How might the two be related?

12. What new information technologies are changing the ways that marketers keep track of business trends and customers?

13. Why do marketers need to understand buying behavior?

14. How are personal income, disposable income, and discretionary income related? Which is the best indicator of consumer purchasing power?

Discussion Questions

1. Are there any problems for a company that focuses mainly on the most profitable customers?

2. In what way is each of the following a marketing activity?
   a. The provision of sufficient parking space for customers at a suburban shopping mall
   b. The purchase by a clothing store of seven dozen sweaters in assorted sizes and colors
   c. The inclusion of a longer and more comprehensive warranty on an automobile

3. How might adoption of the marketing concept benefit a firm? How might it benefit the firm's customers?

4. Is marketing information as important to small firms as it is to larger firms? Explain.

5. How does the marketing environment affect a firm's marketing strategy?

►► VIDEO CASE 13.1

New Balance Races for Customer Relationships

New Balance is racing to build relationships with consumers who are less interested in superstar endorsements than in superperformance shoes. The brand is, as company ads proclaim, "endorsed by no one," which sets it apart from competitors that sign high-profile sports stars to promote their athletic shoes. Yet New Balance regularly racks up $1.5 billion in annual sales and is speeding along to gain ground on much larger competitors such as Nike and Reebok.

Rather than chase the teen market, New Balance appeals to a variety of segments of 21- to 55-year-old adults who want to achieve their personal best. Its marketers begin by studying customer needs in a specific category—for instance, running—and ask questions such as: For what type of runner will the shoe be designed? How many miles is that person likely to run every day or week? What is the runner's body makeup? The company also hires an outside firm to prepare a marketing brief with more details about the target customer, special features the shoe should have, estimated sales forecasts, and potential profit levels.

Next, marketing experts start adding up the costs of producing each new product so that they can estimate the retail price. Upscale high-performance shoes may contain more expensive materials and technology and thus sell for higher prices. Lower-end products may employ less technology and use different materials that perform at a different level. By varying both materials and technology, New Balance can offer a variety of products at different prices for various segments in each sports category, such as running shoes or basketball sneakers. Still, most New Balance shoes are priced at $60 and above, reinforcing the brand's reputation for high quality and high performance.

When New Balance is developing an $80 cushioning shoe, its marketers examine $80 cushioning shoes from competitors, comparing features as well as appearance and color. They often buy competing shoes to see what else is on the market and how New Balance products match up. Then the company will either make a prototype in one of its New England plants or, if the shoe is to be manufactured abroad, have one of the overseas factories make a prototype. This gives marketers a more realistic picture of costs so that they can determine the actual selling price and the expected profit.

Now New Balance is expanding beyond athletic shoes to target other markets. For example, it makes women's shoes under the Aravon brand. The Office line of Aravon shoes targets women who want fashion footwear, the Sandals line targets women who want casual footwear, and the Everyday line targets women who want comfortable footwear. All Aravon shoes use the foot-cushioning technology that New Balance builds into its sports shoes. In addition, New Balance markets high-performance sports apparel for men and women and has licensed its brand for parkas, jackets, and other outwear apparel.

New Balance's decision to continue producing shoes in the United States is a smart competitive move for two reasons. First, the company has modernized and reorganized its U.S. factories to cut the production cycle from eight days to just eight hours. This means that it can get by with much less inventory. More important, it can start production immediately when retailers order or reorder merchandise. Second, New Balance has the manufacturing flexibility to fill special orders for unusual sizes and widths quickly. This strengthens its relationships with retailers, who are key players in the company's marketing mix. Because purchasing patterns can and do change at any time, New Balance has to be fast on its feet to stay ahead of the trends and win the race for customer relationships.[17]

For more information about this company, go to **www.newbalance.com.**

Questions

1. Is there evidence that New Balance is applying the marketing concept? Support your answer.
2. Is New Balance using an undifferentiated approach, a concentrated approach, or a differentiated approach to selecting target markets?
3. Why does New Balance pay close attention when retailers reorder a particular item?

▶▶ CASE 13.2

IKEA Targets Do-It Yourselfers

Every day, more than 1 million customers visit IKEA stores worldwide to buy everything from beds and baskets to bookcases and bathmats. The Swedish-based retailer has grown to more than 225 stores worldwide with annual sales of $18 billion by offering 7,000 home furnishings that are well designed, functional, and affordably priced. Its customers like the contemporary look of IKEA's products—and they don't mind assembling their purchases to save money.

IKEA is always driving costs down in manufacturing, marketing, warehousing, and raw materials so that it can pass the savings along to customers. Year after year, the retailer lowers its prices by an average of 2 to 3 percent by buying in bulk, searching for the most efficient suppliers, and sticking to simple, contemporary styles. For a company that buys from 1,700 suppliers, including some that are thousands of miles from company headquarters, even small efficiencies quickly add up to significant savings.

Although IKEA's customers are frugal, they want fashionable furniture that fits their personalities and lifestyles. In fact, the store's appeal cuts across demographic lines. Some customers who can well afford to shop at posh emporiums come to IKEA because they like the combination of chic design, down-to-earth functionality, and speedy assembly. Any item that must be assembled at home is accompanied by clear step-by-step instructions and illustrations, reassuring to even the most inexperienced do-it-yourselfer.

Customers in many countries have responded enthusiastically to IKEA's formula. After expanding beyond Sweden to Norway and Denmark, the company opened stores in Europe, Australia, and North America. More recently, IKEA has come to Russia, Japan, and China. By 2010, fifty IKEA stores will dot the United States from coast to coast.

Product names such as Billy bookcases and Klippan sofas are standard throughout the world and reflect the company's Swedish origins. However, IKEA's designers are careful to modify products for local tastes. "Americans want more comfortable sofas, higher-quality textiles, bigger glasses, more spacious entertainment units," says the head of IKEA North America. Designers and researchers visit customers' homes to observe how they use furniture. As a result, when IKEA makes bedroom furniture for the U.S. market, it adds deeper drawers because "Americans prefer to store most of their clothes folded," notes the product manager. In Europe, product measurements are provided in centimeters, whereas in the United States, measurements are provided in inches.

IKEA translates its catalogs into thirty-six languages and distributes 160 million copies every year. Here again, IKEA looks for ways to minimize expenses. It has all products photographed at a large European studio and transmits the images electronically to printing plants in the different regions where catalogs will be distributed, saving on shipping and mailing costs. Every detail, from paper quality to type size, is scrutinized to identify new cost efficiencies.

IKEA's formula of fashionable, affordable, and functional furniture has won it a loyal following. Customers have been known to line up a week ahead of opening day for a chance to win prizes and fifteen minutes of local fame as the first to see the new store. If customers get hungry while they shop, they can drop into the informal store restaurant for a quick snack or a light meal of Scandinavian delicacies. The most popular dish is Swedish meatballs: Customers devour 150 million of these tiny meatballs every year.

As popular as IKEA has become, CEO Anders Dahlvig sees plenty of room for growth because "awareness of our brand is much bigger than the size of our company." Still, no matter how large and fast IKEA grows, its focus will remain on keeping costs low to satisfy the target market's need for reasonably priced, well-designed assemble-it-yourself home furnishings.[18]

For more information about this company, go to **www.ikea.com.**

Questions

1. Is IKEA's targeting strategy concentrated or undifferentiated? Explain your answer.
2. Which of the variables for segmenting consumer markets is IKEA using, and why are these variables appropriate?
3. What combination of techniques might IKEA apply when preparing sales forecasts for North America?

→ CHAPTER 13: JOURNAL EXERCISE

Discovery statement: This chapter emphasized the importance of keeping the customer at the core of every marketing decision.

Think about the businesses from which you've purchased goods or services. Select the organization that you believe has adopted the marketing concept. Discuss the reasons why you believe that this company has adopted the marketing concept.

_____

_____

_____

_____

_____

Describe the marketing mix this company has created for the brand that you purchase from this company.

_____

_____

_____

_____

Which two companies are the strongest competitors of this organization? Explain why.

_____

_____

_____

_____

_____

Besides competition, which environmental forces have the greatest impact on this company for which you are a customer?

_____

_____

_____

_____

Calculate your customer lifetime value to this company. After recording your customer lifetime value, describe how you calculated it.

_____

_____

_____

_____

_____

BUILDING SKILLS FOR CAREER SUCCESS

1. Exploring the Internet

Consumer products companies with a variety of famous brand names known around the world are making their presence known on the Internet through websites and online banner advertising. The giants in consumer products include U.S.-based Procter & Gamble (**www.pg.com/**), Swiss-based Nestlé (**www.nestle.com/**), and British-based Unilever (**www.unilever.com/**).

According to a spokesperson for the Unilever Interactive Brand Center in New York, the firm is committed to making the Internet part of its marketing strategy. The center carries out research and development (R&D) and serves as a model for others now in operation in the Netherlands and Singapore. Information is shared with interactive marketers assigned to specific business units. Eventually, centers will be established globally, reflecting the fact that most of Unilever's $52 billion in sales takes place in about 100 countries around the world.

Unilever's view that online consumer product sales are the way of the future was indicated by online alliances established with Microsoft Network, America Online, and NetGrocer.com. Creating an online dialogue with consumers on a global scale is no simple task. Cultural differences often are subtle and difficult to explain but nonetheless are perceived by the viewers interacting with a site. Unilever's website, which is its connection to customers all over the world, has a global feel to it. The question is whether or not it is satisfactory to each target audience.[19] Visit the text website for updates to this exercise.

Assignment

1. Examine the Unilever, Procter & Gamble, and Nestlé sites and describe the features that you think would be most interesting to consumers.

2. Describe those features you do not like and explain why.

3. Do you think that the sites can contribute to better consumer buyer behavior? Explain your thinking.

2. Developing Critical-Thinking Skills

Market segmentation is the process of breaking down a larger target market into smaller segments. One common base of market segmentation is demographics. Demographics for the consumer market, which consists of individuals and household members who buy goods for their own use, include such criteria as age, gender, race, religion, income, family size, occupation, education, social class, and marital status. Liz Claiborne, Inc., retailer of women's apparel, uses demographics to target a market it calls *Liz Lady.* The company knows Liz Lady's age, income range, professional status, and family status, and it uses this profile to make marketing decisions.

Assignment

1. Identify a company that markets to the consumer.

2. Identify the company's major product.

3. Determine the demographics of one of the company's markets.

   a. From the list that follows, choose the demographics that apply to this market. (Remember that the demographics chosen must relate to the interest, need, and ability of the customer to purchase the product.)

   b. Briefly describe each demographic characteristic.

Consumer Market	Description
Age _____	_____
Income _____	_____
Gender _____	_____
Race _____	_____
Ethnicity _____	_____
Income _____	_____
Occupation _____	_____
Family size _____	_____
Education _____	_____
Religion _____	_____
Home owner _____	_____
Marital status _____	_____
Social class _____	_____

4. Summarize your findings in a statement that describes the target market for the company's product.

3. Building Team Skills

Review the text definitions of *market* and *target market*. Markets can be classified as consumer or industrial. Buyer behavior consists of the decisions and actions of those involved in buying and using products or services. By examining aspects of a company's products, you usually can determine the company's target market and the characteristics important to members of that target market.

Assignment

1. Working in teams of three to five, identify a company and its major products.
2. List and discuss characteristics that customers may find important. These factors may include price, quality, brand name, variety of services, salespeople, customer service, special offers, promotional campaign, packaging, convenience of use, convenience of purchase, location, guarantees, store/office decor, and payment terms.
3. Write a description of the company's primary customer (target market).

4. Researching Different Careers

Before interviewing for a job, you should learn all you can about the company. With this information, you will be prepared to ask meaningful questions about the firm during the interview, and the interviewer no doubt will be impressed with your knowledge of the business and your interest in it. To find out about a company, you can conduct some market research.

Assignment

1. Choose at least two local companies for which you might like to work.

2. Contact your local Chamber of Commerce. (The Chamber of Commerce collects information about local businesses, and most of its services are free.) Ask for information about the companies.
3. Call the Better Business Bureau in your community and ask if there are any complaints against the companies.
4. Prepare a report summarizing your findings.

5. Improving Communication Skills

Each year *Sales and Marketing Management* magazine publishes an issue called "Survey of Buying Power." It contains data on every county in the United States and cities with populations over 10,000. Included are

- Total population
- Number of households
- Median cash income per household
- Population percentage breakdown by income
- Total retail sales for each of the following businesses: automotive, drug, food, furniture, general merchandise, and household appliances

Assignment

1. Choose one of the businesses whose total retail sales are given in *Sales and Marketing Management* magazine's annual "Survey of Buying Power."
2. Use the magazine to evaluate trends in the industry. Is demand for the product increasing or decreasing?
3. Report to the class on total retail sales and potential demand.
4. Summarize your findings in a report.

→ PREP TEST

Matching Questions

____ 1. The process of planning and executing the conception, pricing, promotion, and distribution of ideas, goods, and services.

____ 2. A business philosophy that involves the satisfying of customer's needs while achieving a firm's goals.

____ 3. Value is added through converting raw materials into finished goods.

____ 4. It is the individuals in a market who share common characteristics.

____ 5. Income that is left after savings, food, clothing, and housing are paid.

____ 6. It is a combination of marketing elements designed to reach a target market.

____ 7. It is a plan of actions intended to accomplish a marketing goal.

____ 8. The decision-making process that is used when purchasing personal-use items.

____ 9. Marketing activities that focus on a particular group such as teenagers.

____ 10. The marketing objectives for a product are established.

a. consumer buying behavior
b. discretionary income
c. form utility
d. market segment
e. marketing
f. marketing concept
g. marketing mix
h. marketing plan
i. marketing strategy
j. target market

True/False Questions

T F

11. ○ ○ Marketing is a process that fulfills consumers' needs.

12. ○ ○ The first step in implementing the marketing concept is to provide a product that satisfies customers.

13. ○ ○ The marketing mix is composed of product, price, distribution, and promotion.

14. ○ ○ Markets are classified as consumer markets or business-to-business markets.

15. ○ ○ Financing and risk taking are physical distribution functions of marketing.

16. ○ ○ The four common bases of market segmentation are demographic, strategic, geographic, and discretionary.

T F

17. ○ ○ The Internet, *Advertising Age,* and the *Statistical Abstract of the United States* are important resources for marketing research.

18. ○ ○ When the Ford Motor Company focuses its advertising for the Explorer on the population between the ages of twenty and thirty-four, it is targeting a market.

19. ○ ○ Understanding factors that affect buying behavior helps marketing managers to predict consumer responses to marketing strategies and helps to develop a market mix.

20. ○ ○ Pricing is an uncontrollable element of the marketing environment.

Multiple-Choice Questions

21. The three major categories of marketing functions are
    a. place, time, and possession.
    b. form, buying, and exchange.
    c. risk taking, selling, and form.
    d. physical distribution, facilitating, and possession.
    e. exchange, physical distribution, and facilitating.

22. Older Americans have more discretionary income to spend than younger people. As a result, firms are focusing their attention on developing new products and services for this market. What type of market is this?
    a. Industrial b. Producer c. Governmental
    d. Consumer e. Institutional

23. Robin Wallace owns a frozen yogurt shop. She has decided to concentrate her marketing efforts on health-conscious customers. What type of approach is Robin practicing?
    a. Product differentiation   b.Total market
    c. Market segmentation   d. Target market
    e.Marketing mix

24. Scott and Lindsey, a young married couple, just purchased their first house. They are excited to have a yard for their dog to play. The title company had their warranty deed recorded in the county court records. What type of utility does this process add to the value of the property?
    a. Possession   b. Form   c. Target   d. Time
    e. Place

25. Measuring the sales potential for specific types of market segments helps a firm to make important decisions. All the following are viable reasons for measuring the sales potential *except*
    a. evaluating the feasibility of entering new segments.
    b. deciding how best to allocate its marketing resources.
    c. designing the product.
    d. defining the geographic boundaries of the sales.
    e. estimating relevant time frames.

Fill-in-the-Blank Questions

26. Sales forecasting methods include _____ given to buyers.

27. Goods purchased to use in making other products for resale make up the _____ market.

28. A group of individuals or organizations with the authority to purchase products make up a _____.

29. When products are available in the store when customers need them, _____ value is created.

30. Systematically gathering, recording, and analyzing data about products and markets is the process of conducting marketing _____.

Online Study Center

FOR MORE test practice, use the interactive ACE quizzes available at the Online Student Center: **www.college.hmco.com/PIC/pridebusiness9e.**

Answers on p. PT2.

Creating and Pricing Products that Satisfy Customers

WHAT you will be able to do once you complete this chapter:

1 **Explain** what a product is and how products are classified.

2 **Discuss** the product life cycle and how it leads to new product development.

3 **Define** *product line* and *product mix* and distinguish between the two.

4 **Identify** the methods available for changing a product mix.

5 **Explain** the uses and importance of branding, packaging, and labeling.

6 **Describe** the economic basis of pricing and the means by which sellers can control prices and buyers' perceptions of prices.

7 **Identify** the major pricing objectives used by businesses.

8 **Examine** the three major pricing methods that firms employ.

9 **Explain** the different strategies available to companies for setting prices.

10 **Describe** three major types of pricing associated with business products.

WHY this chapter matters

To be successful, a business person must understand how to develop and manage a mix of appropriately priced products and to recognize that over time a firm's mix of products will have to be changed because customers change and so do their needs.

FOR HELP with studying this chapter, visit the Online Student Center:

www.college.hmco.com/PIC/pridebusiness9e

Online Study Center

The Apple brand is shinier than ever, thanks to a never-ending stream of high-tech products with the human touch. A pioneer in the computer industry in the 1980s, Apple has long concentrated on developing cutting-edge products that are good looking and user-friendly. Its easy-to-use Macintosh computers have a loyal customer following. Still, they account for only a small share of the PC market, which is dominated by PCs that run on Microsoft Windows systems.

However, the company's iPod portable digital media players have really polished Apple's reputation for breaking new ground. When the iPod was introduced, it faced considerable competition from established products—yet its stylish design and innovative features immediately captured the public imagination. The original iPod was designed specifically for music; the next-generation model accommodated photos, followed by models that also allowed viewing of videos. Today, the iPod product line holds a commanding lead in digital media players,

DID YOU KNOW?

The iPod's stylish product design is a major characteristic that has made this product successful.

with an estimated 75 percent share of the U.S. market.

A key part of Apple's product mix is its popular web-based iTunes Music Store. Here, songs sell for 99 cents each, and episodes of television programs such as *Desperate Housewives* sell for $1.99 each. Customers also can choose from thousands of music videos and short movies. Each downloaded song nets Apple just 10 cents in profits, but it helps sell iPods.

Both iPod and iTunes face an ever-more-crowded field of competitors. For example, Wal-Mart's website sells music downloads for just 88 cents each. As another example, the U.S. cell phone carrier Sprint Nextel has teamed up with the South Korean electronics firm Samsung to challenge Apple. The Sprint Music store offers hundreds of thousands of songs and video clips that can be downloaded directly to Samsung cell phones or to PCs. Can Apple remain at the top of the tree?[1]

For more information about this topic, go to **www.apple.com**.

---

1 LEARNING OBJECTIVE

Explain what a product is and how products are classified.

product everything one receives in an exchange, including all tangible and intangible attributes and expected benefits; it may be a good, service, or idea

A **product** is everything one receives in an exchange, including all tangible and intangible attributes and expected benefits. An Apple iPod purchase, for example, includes not only the iPod itself but also earphones, instructions, and a warranty. A car includes a warranty, an owner's manual, and perhaps free emergency road service for a year. Some of the intangibles that may go with an automobile include the status associated with ownership and the memories generated from past rides. Developing and managing products effectively are crucial to an organization's ability to maintain successful marketing mixes.

A product may be a good, a service, or an idea. A *good* is a real, physical thing that we can touch, such as a Classic Sport football. A *service* is the result of applying human or mechanical effort to a person or thing. Basically, a service is a change we pay others to make for us. A real estate agent's services result in a change in the ownership of real property. A barber's services result in a change in your appearance. An *idea* may take the form of philosophies, lessons, concepts, or advice. Often ideas are included with a good or service. Thus we might buy a book (a good) that provides ideas on how to lose weight. Or we might join Weight Watchers for ideas on how to lose weight and for help (services) in doing so.

We look first in this chapter at products. We examine product classifications and describe the four stages, or life cycle, through which every product moves. Next, we illustrate how firms manage products effectively by modifying or deleting existing products and by developing new products. We also discuss branding, packaging, and labeling of products. Then our focus shifts to pricing. We explain competitive factors that influence sellers' pricing decisions and also explore buyers' perceptions of prices. After considering organizational objectives that can be accomplished through pricing, we outline several methods for setting prices. Finally, we describe pricing strategies by which sellers can reach target markets successfully.

Classification of Products

Different classes of products are directed at particular target markets. A product's classification largely determines what kinds of distribution, promotion, and pricing are appropriate in marketing the product.

Products can be grouped into two general categories: consumer and business (also called *business-to-business* or *industrial products*). A product purchased to satisfy personal and family needs is a **consumer product.** A product bought for resale, for making other products, or for use in a firm's operations is a **business product.** The buyer's use of the product determines the classification of an item. Note that a single item can be both a consumer and a business product. A broom is a consumer product if you use it in your home. However, the same broom is a business product if you use it in the maintenance of your business. After a product is classified as a consumer or business product, it can be categorized further as a particular type of consumer or business product.

> **consumer product** a product purchased to satisfy personal and family needs
>
> **business product** a product bought for resale, for making other products, or for use in a firm's operations
>
> **convenience product** a relatively inexpensive, frequently purchased item for which buyers want to exert only minimal effort
>
> **shopping product** an item for which buyers are willing to expend considerable effort on planning and making the purchase

Consumer Product Classifications

The traditional and most widely accepted system of classifying consumer products consists of three categories: convenience, shopping, and specialty products. These groupings are based primarily on characteristics of buyers' purchasing behavior.

A **convenience product** is a relatively inexpensive, frequently purchased item for which buyers want to exert only minimal effort. Examples include bread, gasoline, newspapers, soft drinks, and chewing gum. The buyer spends little time in planning the purchase of a convenience item or in comparing available brands or sellers.

A **shopping product** is an item for which buyers are willing to expend considerable effort on planning and making the purchase. Buyers allocate ample time for comparing stores and brands with respect to prices, product features, qualities, services, and perhaps warranties. Appliances, upholstered furniture, men's suits, bicycles, and cellular phones are examples of shopping products. These products are expected to last for a fairly long time and thus are purchased less frequently than convenience items.

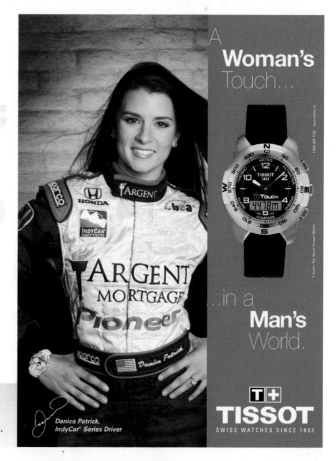

Shopping products. Most brands of watches are shopping products. However, very expensive watches that are sold in few outlets across the U.S. are classified as specialty products.

Danica Patrick,
IndyCar® Series Driver

specialty product an item
that possesses one or more
unique characteristics for
which a significant group of
buyers is willing to expend
considerable purchasing
effort

A **specialty product** possesses one or more unique characteristics for which a group of buyers is willing to expend considerable purchasing effort. Buyers actually plan the purchase of a specialty product; they know exactly what they want and will not accept a substitute. In searching for specialty products, purchasers do not compare alternatives. Examples include unique sports cars, a specific type of antique dining table, a rare imported beer, or perhaps special handcrafted stereo speakers.

One problem with this approach to classification is that buyers may behave differently when purchasing a specific type of product. Thus a single product can fit into more than one category. To minimize this problem, marketers think in terms of how buyers are most likely to behave when purchasing a specific item.

Business Product Classifications

Based on their characteristics and intended uses, business products can be classified into the following categories: raw materials, major equipment, accessory equipment, component parts, process materials, supplies, and services.

raw material a basic material
that actually becomes part
of a physical product;
usually comes from mines,
forests, oceans, or recycled
solid wastes

A **raw material** is a basic material that actually becomes part of a physical product. It usually comes from mines, forests, oceans, or recycled solid wastes. Raw materials usually are bought and sold according to grades and specifications.

major equipment large tools
and machines used for
production purposes

Major equipment includes large tools and machines used for production purposes. Examples of major equipment are lathes, cranes, and stamping machines. Some major equipment is custom-made for a particular organization, but other items are standardized products that perform one or several tasks for many types of organizations.

accessory equipment
standardized equipment
used in a firm's production
or office activities

Accessory equipment is standardized equipment used in a firm's production or office activities. Examples include hand tools, fax machines, fractional-horsepower motors, and calculators. Compared with major equipment, accessory items are usually much less expensive and are purchased routinely with less negotiation.

component part an item that
becomes part of a physical
product and is either a
finished item ready for
assembly or a product
that needs little processing
before assembly

A **component part** becomes part of a physical product and is either a finished item ready for assembly or a product that needs little processing before assembly. Although it becomes part of a larger product, a component part often can be identified easily. Clocks, tires, computer chips, and switches are examples of component parts.

process material a material
that is used directly in the
production of another
product but is not readily
identifiable in the finished
product

A **process material** is used directly in the production of another product. Unlike a component part, however, a process material is not readily identifiable in the finished product. Like component parts, process materials are purchased according to industry standards or to the specifications of the individual purchaser. Examples include industrial glue and food preservatives.

supply an item that facilitates production and operations but does not become
part of a finished product

A **supply** facilitates production and operations but does not become part of a finished product. Paper, pencils, oils, and cleaning agents are examples.

business service an intangible
product that an organization
uses in its operations

A **business service** is an intangible product that an organization uses in its operations. Examples include financial, legal, online, janitorial, and marketing research services. Purchasers must decide whether to provide their own services internally or to hire them from outside the organization.

The Product Life Cycle

2 LEARNING OBJECTIVE
Discuss the product life
cycle and how it leads
to new product
development.

product life cycle a series of
stages in which a product's
sales revenue and profit
increase, reach a peak, and
then decline

In a way, products are like people. They are born, they live, and they die. Every product progresses through a **product life cycle,** a series of stages in which a product's sales revenue and profit increase, reach a peak, and then decline. A firm must be able to launch, modify, and delete products from its offering of products in response to changes in product life cycles. Otherwise, the firm's profits will disappear, and the firm will fail. Depending on the product, life-cycle stages will vary in length. In this section we discuss the stages of the life cycle and how marketers can use this information.

Stages of the Product Life Cycle

Generally, the product life cycle is assumed to be composed of four stages—introduction, growth, maturity, and decline—as shown in Figure 14.1. Some products progress through these stages rapidly, in a few weeks or months. Others may take years to go through each stage. The Rubik's Cube had a relatively short life cycle. Parker Brothers' Monopoly game, which was introduced over seventy years ago, is still going strong.

Introduction   In the *introduction stage*, customer awareness and acceptance of the product are low. Sales rise gradually as a result of promotion and distribution activities, but initially, high development and marketing costs result in low profit or even in a loss. There are relatively few competitors. The price is sometimes high, and purchasers are primarily people who want to be "the first" to own the new product. The marketing challenge at this stage is to make potential customers aware of the product's existence and its features, benefits, and uses.

A new product is seldom an immediate success. Marketers must watch early buying patterns carefully and be prepared to modify the new product promptly if necessary. The product should be priced to attract the particular market segment that has the greatest desire and ability to buy the product. Plans for distribution and promotion should suit the targeted market segment. As with the product itself, the initial price, distribution channels, and promotional efforts may need to be adjusted quickly to maintain sales growth during the introduction stage.

Growth   In the *growth stage*, sales increase rapidly as the product becomes well known. Other firms probably have begun to market competing products. The competition and lower unit costs (owing to mass production) result in a lower price, which reduces the profit per unit. Note that industry profits reach a peak and begin to decline during this stage. To meet the needs of the growing market, the originating firm offers modified versions of its product and expands its distribution. The 3M Company, the maker of Post-it Notes, has developed a variety of sizes, colors, and designs.

➤➤ **FIGURE 14.1**

PRODUCT LIFE CYCLE

The graph shows sales volume and profits during the life cycle of a product.

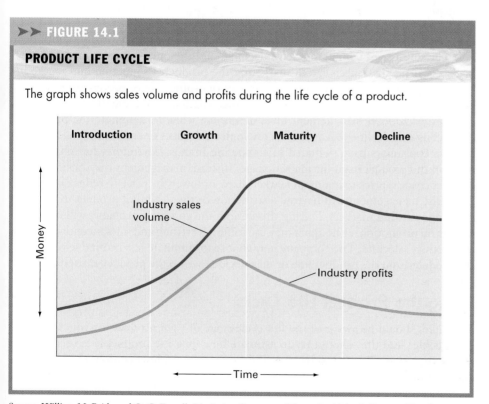

Source: William M. Pride and O. C. Ferrell, *Marketing: Concepts and Strategies*, 13th ed. (Boston: Houghton Mifflin, 2006). Copyright © 2006 by Houghton Mifflin Company. Adapted with permission.

Management's goal in the growth stage is to stabilize and strengthen the product's position by encouraging brand loyalty. To beat the competition, the company may further improve the product or expand the product line to appeal to additional market segments. Apple, for example, has introduced several variations on its wildly popular iPod MP3 player. The iPod Mini is a smaller, more colorful device, and the iPod Shuffle, is a more affordable version. The iPod Nano is a pencil-thin device that weighs barely over 1 ounce. The Video iPod can store and play movies, television shows, and music videos. Apple has expanded its iTunes Music Store to include downloadable versions of popular shows such as *Saturday Night Live, Desperate Housewives,* and *Lost,* as well as exclusive music videos from artists such as U2. Continuous product innovation and service expansion have helped to expand Apple's market penetration in the competitive MP3 player industry.[2] Management also may compete by lowering prices if increased production efficiency has resulted in savings for the company. As the product becomes more widely accepted, marketers may be able to broaden the network of distributors. Marketers also can emphasize customer service and prompt credit for defective products. During this period, promotional efforts attempt to build brand loyalty among customers.

Maturity Sales are still increasing at the beginning of the *maturity stage,* but the rate of increase has slowed. Later in this stage the sales curve peaks and begins to decline. Industry profits decline throughout this stage. Product lines are simplified, markets are segmented more carefully, and price competition increases. The increased competition forces weaker competitors to leave the industry. Refinements and extensions of the original product continue to appear on the market.

During a product's maturity stage, its market share may be strengthened by redesigned packaging or style changes. Also, consumers may be encouraged to use the product more often or in new ways. Pricing strategies are flexible during this stage. Markdowns and price incentives are not uncommon, although price increases may work to offset production and distribution costs. Marketers may offer incentives and assistance of various kinds to dealers to encourage them to support mature products, especially in the face of competition from private-label brands. New promotional efforts and aggressive personal selling may be necessary during this period of intense competition.

Decline During the *decline stage,* sales volume decreases sharply. Profits continue to fall. The number of competing firms declines, and the only survivors in the marketplace are firms that specialize in marketing the product. Production and marketing costs become the most important determinant of profit.

When a product adds to the success of the overall product line, the company may retain it; otherwise, management must determine when to eliminate the product. A product usually declines because of technological advances or environmental factors or because consumers have switched to competing brands. Therefore, few changes are made in the product itself during this stage. Instead, management may raise the price to cover costs, reprice to maintain market share, or lower the price to reduce inventory. Similarly, management will narrow distribution of the declining product to the most profitable existing markets. During this period, the company probably will not spend heavily on promotion, although it may use some advertising and sales incentives to slow the product's decline. The company may choose to eliminate less profitable versions of the product from the product line or may decide to drop the product entirely.

Using the Product Life Cycle

Marketers should be aware of the life-cycle stage of each product for which they are responsible. And they should try to estimate how long the product is expected to remain in that stage. Both must be taken into account in making decisions about the marketing strategy for a product. If a product is expected to remain in the maturity stage for a long time, a replacement product might be introduced later in the maturity stage. If the maturity stage is expected to be short, however, a new product should be introduced much earlier. For example, Logitech, a leading manufacturer of computer mice, faces a short product life cycle with its technology-driven accessories. In an industry with powerful competitors such as Microsoft, Logitech must introduce new products frequently with the current trend toward everything wireless. Logitech also has introduced its Laser Mouse, engineered specifically for use in gaming. The company has made strides against the competition with significant growth in sales in recent years.[3] In some cases a firm may be willing to take the chance of speeding up the decline of existing products. In other situations a company will attempt to extend a product's life cycle. For example, General Mills has extended the life of Bisquick baking mix (launched in the mid-1930s) by improving the product's formulation significantly and creating and promoting a variety of uses.

Product Line and Product Mix

A **product line** is a group of similar products that differ only in relatively minor characteristics. Generally, the products within a product line are related to each other in the way they are produced, marketed, or used. Procter & Gamble, for example, manufactures and markets several shampoos, including Prell, Head & Shoulders, Pert Plus, and Ivory.

Many organizations tend to introduce new products within existing product lines. This permits them to apply the experience and knowledge they have acquired to the production and marketing of new products. Other firms develop entirely new product lines.

An organization's **product mix** consists of all the products the firm offers for sale. For example, Procter & Gamble, which recently acquired Gillette, has over 300 brands that fall into one of twenty-two product lines ranging from deodorants to paper products.[4] Two "dimensions" are often applied to a firm's product mix. The *width* of the mix is the number of product lines it contains. The *depth* of the mix is the average number of individual products within each line. These are general measures; we speak of a *broad* or a *narrow* mix rather than a mix of exactly three or five product lines. Some organizations provide broad product mixes to be competitive. For example, GE Financial Network (GEFN), a comprehensive Internet-based consumer-friendly financial services resource, provides an extensive product mix of financial services, including home mortgages, mutual funds, stock price quotes, annuities, life insurance, auto insurance, long-term care insurance, credit cards, and auto warranty plans.[5]

3 LEARNING OBJECTIVE
Define *product line* and *product mix* and distinguish between the two.

product line a group of similar products that differ only in relatively minor characteristics

product mix all the products a firm offers for sale

Managing the Product Mix

To provide products that satisfy people in a firm's target market or markets and that also achieve the organization's objectives, a marketer must develop, adjust, and maintain an effective product mix. Seldom can the same product mix be effective for long. Because customers' product preferences and attitudes change, their desire for a product may diminish or grow. In some cases a firm needs to alter its product mix to adapt to competition. A marketer may have to eliminate a product from the mix because one or more competitors dominate that product's specific market segment. Similarly, an organization may have to introduce a new product or modify an existing one to compete more effectively. A marketer may expand the firm's product mix to take advantage of excess marketing and production capacity. For example, both Coca-Cola and Pepsi have expanded their lines by adding the bottled-water brands Dasani and Aquafina. More recently, they have launched berry- and citrus-flavored waters. The bottled-water category leader, Nestle, is planning to release its own four-flavor line of water called Pure Life Splash in direct response to Coca-Cola and Pepsi's latest line extensions.[6] For whatever reason a product mix is altered, the product mix must be managed to bring about improvements in the mix. There are three major ways to improve a product mix: change an existing product, delete a product, or develop a new product.

4 LEARNING OBJECTIVE
Identify the methods available for changing a product mix.

Managing Existing Products

A product mix can be changed by deriving additional products from existing ones. This can be accomplished through product modifications and by line extensions.

Product Modifications   **Product modification** refers to changing one or more of a product's characteristics. For this approach to be effective, several conditions must be met. First, the product must be modifiable. Second, existing customers must be able to perceive that a modification has been made, assuming that the modified item is still directed at the same target market. Third, the modification should make the product more consistent with customers' desires so that it provides greater satisfaction. For example, Ford modified its popular F-150 pickup by adding more interior room, better safety features, and an optional DVD player built in. The company designed these modifications for 80 percent of its F-150 customers who use the truck as family transportation.[7]

Existing products can be altered in three primary ways: in quality, function, and aesthetics. *Quality modifications* are changes that relate to a product's dependability and durability and usually are achieved by alterations in the materials or production process. *Functional modifications* affect a product's versatility, effectiveness, convenience, or safety; they usually require redesign of the product. Typical product categories that have undergone extensive functional modifications include home appliances, office and farm equipment, and consumer electronics. *Aesthetic modifications* are directed at changing the sensory appeal of a product by altering its taste, texture, sound, smell, or visual characteristics. Because a buyer's purchasing decision is affected by how a product looks, smells, tastes, feels, or sounds, an aesthetic modification may have a definite impact on purchases. Through aesthetic modifications, a firm can differentiate its product from competing brands and perhaps gain a sizable market share if customers find the modified product more appealing.

Line Extensions   A **line extension** is the development of a product closely related to one or more products in the existing product line but designed specifically to meet somewhat different customer needs. For example, Nabisco extended its cookie line to include Reduced Fat Oreos and Double Stuf Oreos.

Many of the so-called new products introduced each year are in fact line extensions. Line extensions are more common than new products because they are a less expensive, lower-risk alternative for increasing sales. A line extension may focus on a different market segment or be an attempt to increase sales within the same market segment by more precisely satisfying the needs of people in that segment. Line extensions are also used to take market share from competitors.

Line extensions. Gatorade Endurance Formula products are line extensions. These products are available in three ready-to-drink flavors and instant mixes.

product modification the process of changing one or more of a product's characteristics

line extension development of a new product that is closely related to one or more products in the existing product line but designed specifically to meet somewhat different customer needs

Deleting Products

To maintain an effective product mix, an organization often has to eliminate some products. This is called **product deletion.** A weak product costs a firm time, money, and resources that could be used to modify other products or develop new ones. Also, when a weak product generates an unfavorable image among customers, the negative image may rub off on other products sold by the firm.

Most organizations find it difficult to delete a product. Some firms drop weak products only after they have become severe financial burdens. A better approach is some form of systematic review of the product's impact on the overall effectiveness of a firm's product mix. Such a review should analyze a product's contribution to a company's sales for a given period. It should include estimates of future sales, costs, and

product deletion the elimination of one or more products from a product line

profits associated with the product and a consideration of whether changes in the marketing strategy could improve the product's performance.

A product-deletion program definitely can improve a firm's performance. Long-time rivals Coke and Pepsi went head to head when they both introduced their own midcalorie soft drinks: C2 and Pepsi Edge. Both were meant to appeal to regular soda drinkers who wanted fewer calories without diet taste. While neither product was successful, Pepsi was quick to cut its losses and deleted Edge, whereas Coke continued producing C2.[8]

Developing New Products

Developing and introducing new products is frequently time-consuming, expensive, and risky. Thousands of new products are introduced annually. Depending on how we define it, the failure rate for new products ranges between 60 and 75 percent. Although developing new products is risky, failing to introduce new products can be just as hazardous. New products generally are grouped into three categories on the basis of their degree of similarity to existing products. *Imitations* are products designed to be similar to—and to compete with—existing products of other firms. Examples are the various brands of whitening toothpastes that were developed to compete with Rembrandt. *Adaptations* are variations of existing products that are intended for an established market. For example, with increasing concerns nationwide about health issues such as diabetes and obesity, Hershey decided to introduce product adaptations with the launching of its sugar-free versions of twenty-four of its major chocolate brands in conjunction with a partnership with the American Diabetes Association. Instead of sugar, these candy bars contain Splenda.[9] Product refinements and extensions are the adaptations considered most often, although imitative products also may include some refinement and extension. *Innovations* are entirely new products. They may give rise to a new industry or revolutionize an existing one. The introduction of CDs, for example, has brought major changes to the recording industry. Innovative products take considerable time, effort, and money to develop. They are therefore less common than adaptations and imitations. As shown in Figure 14.2, the process of developing a new product consists of seven phases.

EXAMINING ETHICS

Cookie Monster

Is it ethical for online marketers to use cookies—software sent by websites to track a user's activities? So many consumers are concerned about the potential for invasion of privacy that an estimated four in ten delete cookies from their computers every month. Some of the pros and cons of cookies are as follows:

Pros:

- Cookies can personalize the site for individual users. AskJeeves builds loyalty by using cookies to save a user's favorite search words.
- Cookies help marketers to target appropriate audiences. As a result, consumers who search skiing information would see ads for ski equipment, not coffeepots.

Cons:

- Consumers may be wary unless sites explain how and why cookies are used. Even full disclosure may be confusing; however, Yahoo! says that thirty-four advertising networks and servers might send cookies to users' computers.
- Unless deleted, cookies can track user activities for a long time. Google's cookies, for instance, expire in 2038.

"While it seems scary, the reality is most Internet advertisers don't really care about your identity—they care about sending you an ad that will get you to buy something," says one privacy expert. "[But] most people don't see cookies as something that helps them."

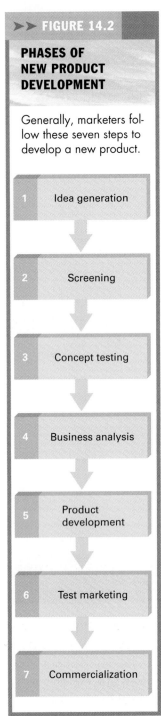

FIGURE 14.2

PHASES OF NEW PRODUCT DEVELOPMENT

Generally, marketers follow these seven steps to develop a new product.

1. Idea generation
2. Screening
3. Concept testing
4. Business analysis
5. Product development
6. Test marketing
7. Commercialization

Source: William M. Pride and O. C. Ferrell, *Marketing: Concepts and Strategies*, 13th ed. (Boston: Houghton Mifflin, 2006). Copyright © 2006 by Houghton Mifflin Company. Adapted with permission.

Idea Generation   Idea generation involves looking for product ideas that will help a firm to achieve its objectives. Although some organizations get their ideas almost by chance, firms trying to maximize product-mix effectiveness usually develop systematic approaches for generating new product ideas. Ideas may come from managers, researchers, engineers, competitors, advertising agencies, management consultants, private research organizations, customers, salespersons, or top executives.

Screening   During screening, ideas that do not match organizational resources and objectives are rejected. In this phase, a firm's managers consider whether the organization has personnel with the expertise to develop and market the proposed product. Management may reject a good idea because the company lacks the necessary skills and abilities. The largest number of product ideas are rejected during the screening phase.

Concept Testing   Concept testing is a phase in which a product idea is presented to a small sample of potential buyers through a written or oral description (and perhaps a few drawings) to determine their attitudes and initial buying intentions regarding the product. For a single product idea, an organization can test one or several concepts of the same product. Concept testing is a low-cost means for an organization to determine consumers' initial reactions to a product idea before investing considerable resources in product research and development (R&D). Product development personnel can use the results of concept testing to improve product attributes and product benefits that are most important to potential customers. The types of questions asked vary considerably depending on the type of product idea being tested. The following are typical questions:

- Which benefits of the proposed product are especially attractive to you?
- Which features are of little or no interest to you?
- What are the primary advantages of the proposed product over the one you currently use?
- If this product were available at an appropriate price, how often would you buy it?
- How could this proposed product be improved?

Business Analysis   Business analysis provides tentative ideas about a potential product's financial performance, including its probable profitability. During this stage, the firm considers how the new product, if it were introduced, would affect the firm's sales, costs, and profits. Marketing personnel usually work up preliminary sales and cost projections at this point, with the help of R&D and production managers.

Product Development   In the product development phase, the company must find out first if it is technically feasible to produce the product and then if the product can be made at costs low enough to justify a reasonable price. If a product idea makes it to this point, it is transformed into a working model, or *prototype*.

Test Marketing   Test marketing is the limited introduction of a product in several towns or cities chosen to be representative of the intended target market. Its aim is to determine buyers' probable reactions. The product is left in the test markets long enough to give buyers a chance to repurchase the product if they are so inclined. Marketers can experiment with advertising, pricing, and packaging in different test areas and can measure the extent of brand awareness, brand switching, and repeat purchases that result from alterations in the marketing mix.

Commercialization   During commercialization, plans for full-scale manufacturing and marketing must be refined and completed, and budgets for the project must be prepared. In the early part of the commercialization phase, marketing management analyzes the results of test marketing to find out what changes in the marketing mix are needed before the product is introduced. The results of test marketing may tell the marketers, for example, to change one or more of the product's physical attributes, to modify the distribution plans to include more retail outlets, to alter promotional efforts, or to change the product's price. Products usually are not introduced nationwide overnight. Most new products are marketed in stages, beginning in selected geographic areas and expanding into adjacent areas over a period of time.

Why Do Products Fail? Despite this rigorous process for developing product ideas, most new products end up as failures. In fact, many well-known companies have produced market failures (see Table 14.1).

Why does a new product fail? Mainly because the product and its marketing program are not planned and tested as completely as they should be. For example, to save on development costs, a firm may market-test its product but not its entire marketing mix. Or a firm may market a new product before all the "bugs" have been worked out. Or, when problems show up in the testing stage, a firm may try to recover its product development costs by pushing ahead with full-scale marketing anyway. Finally, some firms try to market new products with inadequate financing.

Branding, Packaging, and Labeling

Three important features of a product (particularly a consumer product) are its brand, package, and label. These features may be used to associate a product with a successful product line or to distinguish it from existing products. They may be designed to attract customers at the point of sale or to provide information to potential purchasers. Because the brand, package, and label are very real parts of the product, they deserve careful attention during product planning.

Will this product succeed?
Developing a new product involves considerable risk, because a significant portion of new products fail. However, failure to create new products is also very risky.

5 LEARNING OBJECTIVE
Explain the uses and importance of branding, packaging, and labeling.

>> **TABLE 14.1**

EXAMPLES OF PRODUCT FAILURES

Company	Product
Orajel	Toddler training toothpaste
3M	Floptical storage disk
IncrEdibles Breakaway Foods	Push n' Eat
General Mills	Betty Crocker MicroRave Singles
Adams (Pfizer)	Body Smarts nutritional bars
General Motors Corp.	Cadillac Allante luxury sedan
Anheuser-Busch Companies	Bud Dry and Michelob Dry beer
Coca-Cola	Surge Citrus drink
Heinz	Ketchup Salsa
Noxema	Noxema Skin Fitness

Sources: **www.newproductworks.com**; accessed January 23, 2006; Robert M. McMath, "Copycat Cupcakes Don't Cut It," *American Demographics*, January 1997, p. 60; Eric Berggren and Thomas Nacher, "Why Good Ideas Go Bust," *Management Review*, February 2000, pp. 32–36.

What Is a Brand?

brand a name, term, symbol, design, or any combination of these that identifies a seller's products as distinct from those of other sellers

brand name the part of a brand that can be spoken

brand mark the part of a brand that is a symbol or distinctive design

trademark a brand name or brand mark that is registered with the U.S. Patent and Trademark Office and thus is legally protected from use by anyone except its owner

trade name the complete and legal name of an organization

manufacturer (or producer) brand a brand that is owned by a manufacturer

store (or private) brand a brand that is owned by an individual wholesaler or retailer

A **brand** is a name, term, symbol, design, or any combination of these that identifies a seller's products as distinct from those of other sellers.[10] A **brand name** is the part of a brand that can be spoken. It may include letters, words, numbers, or pronounceable symbols, such as the ampersand in *Procter & Gamble*. A **brand mark,** on the other hand, is the part of a brand that is a symbol or distinctive design, such as the Nike "swoosh." A **trademark** is a brand name or brand mark that is registered with the U.S. Patent and Trademark Office and thus is legally protected from use by anyone except its owner. A **trade name** is the complete and legal name of an organization, such as Pizza Hut or Houghton Mifflin Company (the publisher of this text).

Types of Brands

Brands often are classified according to who owns them: manufacturers or stores. A **manufacturer** (or **producer**) **brand,** as the name implies, is a brand that is owned by a manufacturer. Many foods (Frosted Flakes), major appliances (Whirlpool), gasolines (Exxon), automobiles (Honda), and clothing (Levis) are sold as manufacturers' brands. Some consumers prefer manufacturer brands because they usually are nationally known, offer consistent quality, and are widely available.

A **store** (or **private**) **brand** is a brand that is owned by an individual wholesaler or retailer. Among the better-known store brands are Kenmore and Craftsman, both owned by Sears, Roebuck. Owners of store brands claim that they can offer lower prices, earn greater profits, and improve customer loyalty with their own brands. Some companies that manufacture private brands also produce their own manufacturer brands. They often find such operations profitable because they can use excess capacity and at the same time avoid most marketing costs. Many private-branded grocery products are produced by companies that specialize in making private-label products. About 20 percent of products sold in supermarkets are private-branded items.[11]

Consumer confidence is the most important element in the success of a branded product, whether the brand is owned by a producer or by a retailer. Because branding identifies each product completely, customers can easily repurchase products that provide satisfaction, performance, and quality. And they can just as easily avoid or ignore products that do not. In supermarkets, the products most likely to keep their shelf space are the brands with large market shares and strong customer loyalty.

generic product (or brand) a product with no brand at all

A **generic product** (sometimes called a **generic brand**) is a product with no brand at all. Its plain package carries only the name of the product—applesauce, peanut butter, potato chips, or whatever. Generic products, available in supermarkets since 1977, sometimes are made by the major producers that manufacture name brands. Even though generic brands may have accounted for as much as 10 percent of all grocery sales several years ago, they currently represent less than one-half of 1 percent.

Benefits of Branding

Both buyers and sellers benefit from branding. Because brands are easily recognizable, they reduce the amount of time buyers must spend shopping; buyers can quickly identify the brands they prefer. Choosing particular brands, such as Tommy Hilfiger, Polo, Nautica, and Nike, can be a way of expressing oneself. When buyers are unable to evaluate a product's characteristics, brands can help them to judge the quality of the product. For example, most buyers are not able to judge the quality of stereo components but may be guided by a well-respected brand name. Brands can symbolize a certain quality level to a customer, allowing that perception of quality to represent the actual quality of the item. Brands thus help to reduce a buyer's perceived risk of purchase. Finally, customers may receive a psychological reward that comes from owning a brand that symbolizes status. The Lexus brand is an example.

Because buyers are already familiar with a firm's existing brands, branding helps a firm to introduce a new product that carries the same brand name. For example, Unilever, the company that produces the Dove brand as well as many others, has continued to expand its Dove product line. Originally, Dove made bar soap and then extended to deodorant, facial cleansing products, and body soap. The latest additions are Dove shampoos and conditioners. Unilever hopes to gain market share quickly because of customers' favorable perceptions of Dove products.[12] Branding aids sellers in their promotional efforts because promotion of each branded product indirectly promotes other products of the same brand. H.G. Heinz, for example, markets many products with the Heinz brand name, such as ketchup, vinegar, vegetarian beans, gravies, barbecue sauce, and steak sauce. Promotion of one Heinz product indirectly promotes the others.

One chief benefit of branding is the creation of **brand loyalty,** the extent to which a customer is favorable toward buying a specific brand. The stronger the brand loyalty, the greater is the likelihood that buyers will consistently choose the brand. There are three levels of brand loyalty: recognition, preference, and insistence. *Brand recognition* is the level of loyalty at which customers are aware that the brand exists and will purchase it if their preferred brands are unavailable or if they are unfamiliar with available brands. This is the weakest form of brand loyalty. *Brand preference* is the level of brand loyalty at which a customer prefers one brand over competing brands. However, if the preferred brand is unavailable, the customer is willing to substitute another brand. *Brand insistence* is the strongest level of brand loyalty. Brand-insistent customers strongly prefer a specific brand and will not buy substitutes. Brand insistence is the least common type of brand loyalty. Partly owing to marketers' increased dependence on discounted prices, coupons, and other short-term promotions, and partly because of the enormous array of new products with similar characteristics, brand loyalty in general seems to be declining.

Brand equity is the marketing and financial value associated with a brand's strength in a market. Although difficult to measure, brand equity represents the value of a brand to an organization. Some of the world's most valuable brands include Coca-Cola, Microsoft, IBM, General Electric, and Intel.[13] The four major factors that contribute to brand equity are brand awareness, brand associations, perceived brand quality, and brand loyalty. Brand awareness leads to brand familiarity, and buyers are more likely to select a familiar brand than an unfamiliar one. The associations linked to a brand can connect a personality type or lifestyle with a particular brand. For example, consumers may associate De Beers diamonds with loving, long-lasting relationships. When consumers are unable to judge for themselves the quality of a product, they may rely on their perception of the quality of the product's brand. Finally, brand loyalty is a valued element of brand equity because it reduces both a brand's vulnerability to competitors and the need to spend tremendous resources to attract new customers; it also provides brand visibility and encourages retailers to carry the brand. New companies, for example, have much work to do in establishing new brands to compete with well-known brands. For example, China's Beijing Li Ning Sports Goods Company, started by the gymnastic gold medalist Li Ning, is establishing itself as a rival brand to Nike in shoes and sporting goods. Building brand equity will take both time and large investments of capital. Currently, Li Ning Company spends 11 percent of its revenues on marketing efforts to increase brand recognition and loyalty. The company is expanding internationally, and its "L" logo that resembles a wavy check mark is set up to rival the Nike swoosh in China and beyond.[14]

Marketing on the Internet sometimes is best done in collaboration with a better-known web brand. For instance, Weight Watchers, Tire Rack, wine.com, Office Depot, Toys "R" Us, and Shutterfly all rely on partnerships with Internet retail giant Amazon to increase their sales. Amazon provides special sections on its website to

SPOTLIGHT

Consumers often choose the store brand

Percentage of total product sales derived from store brand products:

57.8% Sugar
50.9% Powdered milk
51.7% Dry beans/vegetables
53.4% Marshmallows
45.4% Coffee creamer

Source: *PLMA's 2003 Private Label Yearbook: A Statistical Guide to Today's Store Brands, p,63.*

brand loyalty extent to which a customer is favorable toward buying a specific brand

brand equity marketing and financial value associated with a brand's strength in a market

Building brand equity. The Jolly Green Giant is a trade character. Companies employ trade characters to elicit positive brand associations in consumers' minds.

promote its partners and their products. As with its own products, Amazon gives users the ability to post online reviews of its partners' products or to add them to an Amazon "wish list" that can be saved or e-mailed to friends. Amazon even labels its partners as "Amazon Trusted" when customers browse their sites, giving even these well-known real-world companies credibility in the online marketplace.[15]

Choosing and Protecting a Brand

A number of issues should be considered when selecting a brand name. The name should be easy for customers to say, spell, and recall. Short, one-syllable names such as *Tide* often satisfy this requirement. The brand name should suggest, in a positive way, the product's uses, special characteristics, and major benefits and should be distinctive enough to set it apart from competing brands. Choosing the right brand name has become a challenge because many obvious product names already have been used.

It is important that a firm select a brand that can be protected through registration, reserving it for exclusive use by that firm. Some brands, because of their designs, are infringed more easily on than others. Although registration protects trademarks domestically for ten years and can be renewed indefinitely, a firm should develop a system for ensuring that its trademarks will be renewed as needed. To protect its exclusive right to the brand, the company must ensure that the selected brand will not be considered an infringement on any existing brand already registered with the U.S. Patent and Trademark Office. This task may be complicated by the fact that infringement is determined by the courts, which base their decisions on whether a brand causes consumers to be confused, mistaken, or deceived about the source of the product. Starbucks, the Seattle-based coffee company, recently took legal action against companies using similar brand names, including Sambuck's Coffeehouse, Black Bear's Charbucks Blend, and A&D Cafe's Warbucks coffee.[16]

A firm must guard against a brand name's becoming a generic term that refers to a general product category. Generic terms cannot be legally protected as exclusive brand names. For example, names such as *yo-yo*, *aspirin*, *escalator*, and *thermos*—all exclusively brand names at one time—eventually were declared generic terms that refer to product categories. As such, they could no longer be protected. To ensure that a brand name does not become a generic term, the firm should spell the name with a capital letter and use it as an adjective to modify the name of the general product class, as in Jell-O Brand Gelatin. An organization can deal directly with this problem by advertising that its brand is a trademark and should not be used generically. Firms also can use the registered trademark symbol ® to indicate that the brand is trademarked.

Branding Strategies

The basic branding decision for any firm is whether to brand its products. A producer may market its products under its own brands, private brands, or both. A retail store may carry only producer brands, its own brands, or both. Once either type of firm decides to brand, it chooses one of two branding strategies: individual branding or family branding.

Individual branding is the strategy in which a firm uses a different brand for each of its products. For example, Procter & Gamble uses individual branding for its

individual branding the strategy in which a firm uses a different brand for each of its products

Business Around the World

Accept No Imitations: Fighting Fakes

Illegal imitations of reputable brands make up nearly 9 percent of the world's trade and cost legitimate businesses more than $400 billion in lost sales every year, according to the International Chamber of Commerce. Here's how a few U.S. companies are battling the problem of counterfeiting abroad:

- Time Warner releases some movies on DVD in China on the same day that the films debut in U.S. theaters; it also has cut DVD prices to the equivalent of $2 to $4 (a counterfeit sells for about $1).
- TaylorMade Golf's lawyers scour the web looking for counterfeits of its golf clubs and pressure authorities in other countries to seize the fakes.
- Philip Morris and other tobacco manufacturers mount sting operations and sue retailers to cut down on the sale of counterfeits of Marlboro and other well-known cigarette brands.
- Universal Music Group has developed music-related products that are not easily counterfeited, such as talent-search television shows for Asian markets, and sells advertising time on the shows to other businesses.

---

line of bar soaps, which includes Ivory, Camay, Zest, Safeguard, Coast, and Oil of Olay. Individual branding offers two major advantages. A problem with one product will not affect the good name of the firm's other products, and the different brands can be directed toward different market segments. For example, Marriotts' Fairfield Inns are directed toward budget-minded travelers and Marriott Hotels toward upscale customers.

Family branding is the strategy in which a firm uses the same brand for all or most of its products. Sony, Dell, IBM, and Xerox use family branding for their entire product mixes. A major advantage of family branding is that the promotion of any one item that carries the family brand tends to help all other products with the same brand name. In addition, a new product has a head start when its brand name is already known and accepted by customers.

family branding the strategy in which a firm uses the same brand for all or most of its products

Brand Extensions A **brand extension** occurs when an organization uses one of its existing brands to brand a new product in a different product category. For example, Procter & Gamble employed a brand extension when it named a new product Ivory Body Wash. A brand extension should not be confused with a line extension. A *line extension* refers to using an existing brand on a new product in the same product category, such as a new flavor or new sizes. For example, when the makers of Tylenol introduced Extra Strength Tylenol PM, the new product was a line extension because it was in the same product category. One thing marketers must be careful of, however, is extending a brand too many times or extending too far outside the original product category, which may weaken the brand.

brand extension using an existing brand to brand a new product in a different product category

Packaging

Packaging consists of all the activities involved in developing and providing a container with graphics for a product. The package is a vital part of the product. It can make the product more versatile, safer, or easier to use. Through its shape, appearance, and printed message, a package can influence purchasing decisions.

packaging all the activities involved in developing and providing a container with graphics for a product

Packaging Functions

Effective packaging means more than simply putting products in containers and covering them with wrappers. The basic function of packaging materials is to protect the product and maintain its functional form. Fluids such as milk, orange juice, and hair spray need packages that preserve and protect them; the packaging should prevent damage that could affect the product's usefulness and increase costs. Since product tampering has become a problem for marketers of many types of goods, several packaging techniques have been developed to counter this danger. Some packages are also designed to foil shoplifting.

Another function of packaging is to offer consumer convenience. For example, small, aseptic packages—individual-serving boxes or plastic bags that contain liquids and do not require refrigeration—appeal strongly to children and to young adults with active lifestyles. The size or shape of a package may relate to the product's storage, convenience of use, or replacement rate. Small, single-serving cans of vegetables, for instance, may prevent waste and make storage easier. A third function of packaging is to promote a product by communicating its features, uses, benefits, and image. Sometimes a firm develops a reusable package to make its product more desirable. For example, the Cool Whip package doubles as a food-storage container.

Package Design Considerations

Many factors must be weighed when developing packages. Obviously, one major consideration is cost. Although a number of packaging materials, processes, and designs are available, some are rather expensive. While U.S. buyers have shown a willingness to pay more for improved packaging, there are limits.

Marketers also must decide whether to package the product in single or multiple units. Multiple-unit packaging can increase demand by increasing the amount of the product available at the point of consumption (in the home, for example). However, multiple-unit packaging does not work for infrequently used products because buyers do not like to tie up their dollars in an excess supply or to store those products for a long time. However, multiple-unit packaging can make storage and handling easier (as in the case of six-packs used for soft drinks); it also can facilitate special price offers, such as two-for-one sales. In addition, multiple-unit packaging may increase consumer acceptance of a product by encouraging the buyer to try it several times. On the other hand, customers may hesitate to try the product at all if they do not have the option to buy just one.

Marketers should consider how much consistency is desirable among an organization's package designs. To promote an overall company image, a firm may decide that all packages must be similar or include one major element of the design. This approach, called *family packaging*, is sometimes used only for lines of products, as with

Package design. McDonald's has changed its package designs, which now feature images of people enjoying life's simple pleasures. One of McDonald's goals is to do a better job of connecting with customers worldwide.

Campbell's soups, Weight Watchers entrees, and Planters nuts. The best policy is sometimes no consistency, especially if a firm's products are unrelated or aimed at vastly different target markets.

Packages also play an important promotional role. Through verbal and nonverbal symbols, the package can inform potential buyers about the product's content, uses, features, advantages, and hazards. Firms can create desirable images and associations by choosing particular colors, designs, shapes, and textures. Many cosmetics manufacturers, for example, design their packages to create impressions of richness, luxury, and exclusiveness. The package performs another promotional function when it is designed to be safer or more convenient to use if such features help to stimulate demand.

Packaging also must meet the needs of intermediaries. Wholesalers and retailers consider whether a package facilitates transportation, handling, and storage. Resellers may refuse to carry certain products if their packages are cumbersome.

Finally, firms must consider the issue of environmental responsibility when developing packages. Companies must balance consumers' desires for convenience against the need to preserve the environment. About one-half of all garbage consists of discarded plastic packaging, such as plastic soft drink bottles and carryout bags. Plastic packaging material is not biodegradable, and paper necessitates destruction of valuable forest lands. Consequently, many companies are exploring packaging alternatives and recycling more materials.

Labeling

Labeling is the presentation of information on a product or its package. The *label* is the part that contains the information. This information may include the brand name and mark, the registered trademark symbol ®, the package size and contents, product claims, directions for use and safety precautions, a list of ingredients, the name and address of the manufacturer, and the Universal Product Code (UPC) symbol, which is used for automated checkout and inventory control.

A number of federal regulations specify information that *must* be included in the labeling for certain products. For example,

labeling the presentation of information on a product or its package

- Garments must be labeled with the name of the manufacturer, country of manufacture, fabric content, and cleaning instructions.
- Food labels must contain the most common term for ingredients.
- Any food product for which a nutritional claim is made must have nutrition labeling that follows a standard format.
- Food product labels must state the number of servings per container, the serving size, the number of calories per serving, the number of calories derived from fat, and amounts of specific nutrients.
- Nonedible items such as shampoos and detergents must carry safety precautions as well as instructions for their use.

Such regulations are aimed at protecting customers from both misleading product claims and the improper (and thus unsafe) use of products.

Labels also may carry the details of written or express warranties. An **express warranty** is a written explanation of the responsibilities of the producer in the event that a product is found to be defective or otherwise unsatisfactory. As a result of consumer discontent (along with some federal legislation), firms have begun to simplify the wording of warranties and to extend their duration. The L. L. Bean warranty states, "Our products are guaranteed to give 100 percent satisfaction in every way. Return anything purchased from us at any time if it proves otherwise. We will replace it, refund your purchase price or credit your credit card, as you wish."

express warranty a written explanation of the responsibilities of the producer in the event that a product is found to be defective or otherwise unsatisfactory

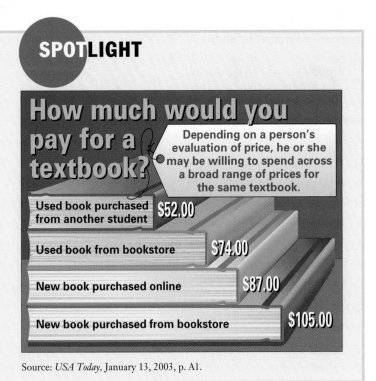

SPOT**LIGHT**

How much would you pay for a textbook?

Depending on a person's evaluation of price, he or she may be willing to spend across a broad range of prices for the same textbook.

Used book purchased from another student $52.00

Used book from bookstore $74.00

New book purchased online $87.00

New book purchased from bookstore $105.00

Source: *USA Today*, January 13, 2003, p. A1.

Pricing Products

A product is a set of attributes and benefits that has been carefully designed to satisfy its market while earning a profit for its seller. No matter how well a product is designed, however, it cannot help an organization to achieve its goals if it is priced incorrectly. Few people will purchase a product with too high a price, and a product with too low a price will earn little or no profit. Somewhere between too high and too low there is a "proper," effective price for each product. Let's take a closer look at how businesses go about determining a product's right price.

The Meaning and Use of Price

The **price** of a product is the amount of money a seller is willing to accept in exchange for the product at a given time and under given circumstances. At times, the price results from negotiations between buyer and seller. In many business situations, however, the price is fixed by the seller. Suppose that a seller sets a price of $10 for a particular product. In essence, the seller is saying, "Anyone who wants this product can have it here and now in exchange for $10."

Each interested buyer then makes a personal judgment regarding the utility of the product, often in terms of some dollar value. A particular person who feels that he or she will get at least $10 worth of want satisfaction (or value) from the product is likely to buy it. If that person can get more want satisfaction by spending $10 in some other way, however, he or she will not buy the product.

Price thus serves the function of *allocator*. First, it allocates goods and services among those who are willing and able to buy them. (As we noted in Chapter 1, the answer to the economic question "For whom to produce?" depends primarily on prices.) Second, price allocates financial resources (sales revenue) among producers according to how well they satisfy customers' needs. And third, price helps customers to allocate their own financial resources among various want-satisfying products.

Supply and Demand Affects Prices

In Chapter 1 we defined the **supply** of a product as the quantity of the product that producers are willing to sell at each of various prices. We can draw a graph of the supply relationship for a particular product, say, jeans (see the left graph in Figure 14.3). Note that the quantity supplied by producers *increases* as the price increases along this *supply curve*.

As defined in Chapter 1, the **demand** for a product is the quantity that buyers are willing to purchase at each of various prices. We also can draw a graph of the demand relationship (see the center graph in Figure 14.3). Note that the quantity demanded by purchasers *increases* as the price decreases along the *demand curve*. The buyers and sellers of a product interact in the marketplace. We can show this interaction by superimposing the supply curve onto the demand curve for our product, as shown in the right graph in Figure 14.3. The two curves intersect at point *E*, which represents a quantity of fifteen million pairs of jeans and a price of $30 per pair. Point *E* is on the *supply curve;* thus producers are willing to supply fifteen million pairs at $30 each. Point *E* is also on the demand curve; thus buyers are willing to purchase fifteen million pairs at $30 each. Point *E* represents *equilibrium*. If fifteen million pairs are produced and priced at $30, they all will be sold. And everyone who is willing to pay $30 will be able to buy a pair of jeans.

6 LEARNING OBJECTIVE

Describe the economic basis of pricing and the means by which sellers can control prices and buyers' perceptions of prices.

price the amount of money a seller is willing to accept in exchange for a product at a given time and under given circumstances

supply the quantity of a product that producers are willing to sell at each of various prices

demand the quantity of a product that buyers are willing to purchase at each of various prices

>> **FIGURE 14.3**

SUPPLY AND DEMAND CURVES

Supply curve (*left*): The upward slope means that producers will supply more jeans at higher prices. **Demand curve** (*center*): The downward slope (to the right) means that buyers will purchase fewer jeans at higher prices. **Supply and demand curves together** (*right*): Point *E* indicates equilibrium in quantity and price for both sellers and buyers.

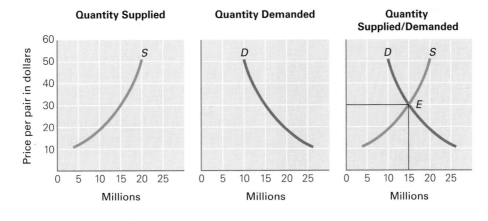

Price and Nonprice Competition

Before the price of a product can be set, an organization must decide on the basis on which it will compete—on the basis of price alone or some combination of factors. The choice influences pricing decisions as well as other marketing-mix variables.

Price competition occurs when a seller emphasizes the low price of a product and sets a price that equals or beats competitors' prices. To use this approach most effectively, a seller must have the flexibility to change prices often and must do so rapidly and aggressively whenever competitors change their prices. Price competition allows a marketer to set prices based on demand for the product or in response to changes in the firm's finances. Competitors can do likewise, however, which is a major drawback of price competition. They, too, can quickly match or outdo an organization's price cuts. In addition, if circumstances force a seller to raise prices, competing firms may be able to maintain their lower prices.

The Internet makes price comparison relatively easy for users. This ease of price comparison helps to drive competition. Examples of websites where customers can compare prices include mysimon.com, pricescan.com, bizrate.com, pricegrabber .com, pricecomparison.com, shopping.yahoo.com, nextag.com, and froogle.google.com.

price competition an emphasis on setting a price equal to or lower than competitors' prices to gain sales or market share

Price competition. Sam's Club engages in price competition for its Soy Infant Formula.

IN CASE OF HEARTBURN
BREAK GLASS

FOR RELIEF
NOW

FOR FULL EFFECT
IN 1-4 DAYS

When the alarm sounds for heartburn, think fast. Prilosec OTC® is not intended for immediate relief. It can take 1 to 4 days for full effect. But Tums neutralizes acid on contact. There's nothing faster. And Tums has calcium.

TUMS.

Nonprice competition. Tums competes with Prilosec on the basis of product attributes. There is no mention of price in this advertisement.

Nonprice competition is competition based on factors other than price. It is used most effectively when a seller can make its product stand out from the competition by distinctive product quality, customer service, promotion, packaging, or other features. Buyers must be able to perceive these distinguishing characteristics and consider them desirable. Once customers have chosen a brand for nonprice reasons, they may not be attracted as easily to competing firms and brands. In this way, a seller can build customer loyalty to its brand. A method of nonprice competition is **product differentiation** which is the process of developing and promoting differences between one's product and all similar products.

Buyers' Perceptions of Price

In setting prices, managers should consider the price sensitivity of people in the target market. How important is price to them? Is it always "very important"? Members of one market segment may be more influenced by price than members of another. For a particular product, the price may be a bigger factor to some buyers than to others. For example, buyers may be more sensitive to price when purchasing gasoline than when purchasing running shoes.

nonprice competition competition based on factors other than price

product differentiation the process of developing and promoting differences between one's product and all similar products

Buyers will accept different ranges of prices for different products; that is, they will tolerate a narrow range for certain items and a wider range for others. Consider the wide range of prices that consumers pay for soft drinks—from 15 cents per ounce at the movies down to 1.5 cents per ounce on sale at the grocery store. Management should be aware of these limits of acceptability and the products to which they apply. The firm also should take note of buyers' perceptions of a given product in relation to competing products. A premium price may be appropriate if a product is considered superior to others in its category or if the product has inspired strong brand loyalty. On the other hand, if buyers have even a hint of a negative view of a product, a lower price may be necessary.

Sometimes buyers relate price to quality. They may consider a higher price to be an indicator of higher quality. Managers involved in pricing decisions should determine whether this outlook is widespread in the target market. If it is, a higher price may improve the image of a product and, in turn, make the product more desirable. For example, German automobile manufacturer Porsche has always worked to keep its quality and image as a luxury sports car maker. In addition to its traditional 911 model and more recently the Boxster model, Porsche recently added a new model called the Cayenne. Porsche hopes this SUV-like vehicle will be very desirable to customers, equally for those who are willing to pay the $88,900.[17]

Pricing Objectives

7 LEARNING OBJECTIVE
Identify the major pricing objectives used by businesses.

Before setting prices for a firm's products, management must decide what it expects to accomplish through pricing. That is, management must set pricing objectives that are in line with both organizational and marketing objectives. Of course, one objective of pricing is to make a profit, but this may not be a firm's primary objective. One or more of the following factors may be just as important.

BizTech

Talk Is Cheap: Online Telephone Services

Internet technology is making talk so cheap that traditional phone companies are reeling from the price competition. Some major players in this telephone service revolution include

Skype. More than fifty million people worldwide talk for free using Skype's software for PC-to-PC phone calls. Because calls are routed over the Internet, "we don't have any cost per user," says a Skype cofounder. Customers pay pennies per

minute for PC-to-telephone or telephone-to-PC calls. Seeing a bright future for Skype, eBay acquired it for $2.6 billion.

Vonage. One of the largest of the U.S. voice-over-Internet Protocol (VoIP) companies, Vonage has one million subscribers who pay a flat monthly fee for telephone-to-telephone calls anywhere in the United States, Canada, and Puerto Rico. Rates on international calls run less than 10 cents per minute.

Time Warner and Cablevision. These giant cable companies have jumped on the VoIP bandwagon by bundling low-price phone service with television and pay-per-view subscription packages.

All this competition puts pricing pressure on traditional phone companies. AT&T, for instance, is vulnerable because voice calls account for more than half its revenue. What will ever-lower prices do to the telephone industry?

Survival

A firm may have to price its products to survive—either as an organization or as a player in a particular market. This usually means that the firm will cut its price to attract customers, even if it then must operate at a loss. Obviously, such a goal hardly can be pursued on a long-term basis, for consistent losses would cause the business to fail.

Profit Maximization

Many firms may state that their goal is to maximize profit, but this goal is impossible to define (and thus impossible to achieve). What, exactly, is the *maximum* profit? How does a firm know when it has been reached? Firms that wish to set profit goals should express them as either specific dollar amounts or percentage increases over previous profits.

Target Return on Investment

The *return on investment* (ROI) is the amount earned as a result of that investment. Some firms set an annual percentage ROI as their pricing goal. ConAgra, the company that produces Healthy Choice meals and a multitude of other products, has a target after-tax ROI of 20 percent.

Market-Share Goals

A firm's *market share* is its proportion of total industry sales. Some firms attempt, through pricing, to maintain or increase their share of the market. To gain market share, Netzero priced unlimited hours of service for $6.95.[18]

Status-Quo Pricing

In pricing their products, some firms are guided by a desire to avoid "making waves," or to maintain the status quo. This is especially true in industries that depend on price

8 LEARNING OBJECTIVE

Examine the three major pricing methods that firms employ.

markup the amount a seller adds to the cost of a product to determine its basic selling price

breakeven quantity the number of units that must be sold for the total revenue (from all units sold) to equal the total cost (of all units sold)

total revenue the total amount received from sales of a product

fixed cost a cost incurred no matter how many units of a product are produced or sold

variable cost a cost that depends on the number of units produced

total cost the sum of the fixed costs and the variable costs attributed to a product

stability. If such a firm can maintain its profit or market share simply by meeting the competition—charging about the same price as competitors for similar products—then it will do so.

Pricing Methods

Once a firm has developed its pricing objectives, it must select a pricing method to reach that goal. Two factors are important to every firm engaged in setting prices. The first is recognition that the market, and not the firm's costs, ultimately determines the price at which a product will sell. The second is awareness that costs and expected sales can be used only to establish some sort of *price floor*, the minimum price at which the firm can sell its product without incurring a loss. In this section we look at three kinds of pricing methods: cost-based, demand-based, and competition-based pricing.

Cost-Based Pricing

Using the simplest method of pricing, *cost-based pricing*, the seller first determines the total cost of producing (or purchasing) one unit of the product. The seller then adds an amount to cover additional costs (such as insurance or interest) and profit. The amount that is added is called the **markup.** The total of the cost plus the markup is the selling price of the product.

A firm's management can calculate markup as a percentage of its total costs. Suppose, for example, that the total cost of manufacturing and marketing 1,000 DVD players is $100,000, or $100 per unit. If the manufacturer wants a markup that is 20 percent above its costs, the selling price will be $100 plus 20 percent of $100, or $120 per unit.

Markup pricing is easy to apply, and it is used by many businesses (mostly retailers and wholesalers). However, it has two major flaws. The first is the difficulty of determining an effective markup percentage. If this percentage is too high, the product may be overpriced for its market; then too few units may be sold to return the total cost of producing and marketing the product. In contrast, if the markup percentage is too low, the seller is "giving away" profit it could have earned simply by assigning a higher price. In other words, the markup percentage needs to be set to account for the workings of the market, and that is very difficult to do.

The second problem with markup pricing is that it separates pricing from other business functions. The product is priced *after* production quantities are determined, *after* costs are incurred, and almost without regard for the market or the marketing mix. To be most effective, the various business functions should be integrated. *Each* should have an impact on *all* marketing decisions.

Cost-based pricing also can be facilitated through the use of breakeven analysis. For any product, the **breakeven quantity** is the number of units that must be sold for the total revenue (from all units sold) to equal the total cost (of all units sold). **Total revenue** is the total amount received from the sales of a product. We can estimate projected total revenue as the selling price multiplied by the number of units sold.

The costs involved in operating a business can be broadly classified as either fixed or variable costs. A **fixed cost** is a cost incurred no matter how many units of a product are produced or sold. Rent, for example, is a fixed cost; it remains the same whether 1 or 1,000 units are produced. A **variable cost** is a cost that depends on the number of units produced. The cost of fabricating parts for a stereo receiver is a variable cost. The more units produced, the higher is the cost of parts. The **total cost** of producing a certain number of units is the sum of the fixed costs and the variable costs attributed to those units.

If we assume a particular selling price, we can find the breakeven quantity either graphically or by using a formula. Figure 14.4 graphs the total revenue earned and the

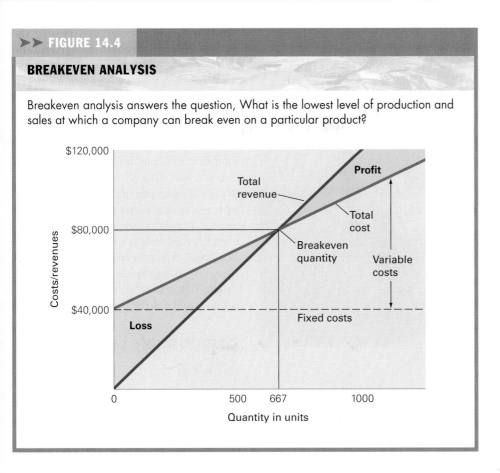

➤➤ FIGURE 14.4

BREAKEVEN ANALYSIS

Breakeven analysis answers the question, What is the lowest level of production and sales at which a company can break even on a particular product?

total cost incurred by the sale of various quantities of a hypothetical product. With fixed costs of $40,000, variable costs of $60 per unit, and a selling price of $120, the breakeven quantity is 667 units. To find the breakeven quantity, first deduct the variable cost from the selling price to determine how much money the sale of one unit contributes to offsetting fixed costs. Then divide that contribution into the total fixed costs to arrive at the breakeven quantity. (The breakeven quantity in Figure 14.4 is the quantity represented by the intersection of the total revenue and total cost axes.) If the firm sells more than 667 units at $120 each, it will earn a profit. If it sells fewer units, it will suffer a loss.

Demand-Based Pricing

Rather than basing the price of a product on its cost, companies sometimes use a pricing method based on the level of demand for the product: *demand-based pricing*. This method results in a high price when product demand is strong and a low price when demand is weak. Some long-distance telephone companies use demand-based pricing. Buyers of new cars that are in high demand, such as Hummer H3, Pontiac Solstice, Dodge Charger, Ford Mustang GT, and Toyota Prius, pay sticker prices plus a premium. To use this method, a marketer estimates the amount of a product that customers will demand at different prices and then chooses the price that generates the highest total revenue. Obviously, the effectiveness of this method depends on the firm's ability to estimate demand accurately.

A firm may favor a demand-based pricing method called *price differentiation* if it wants to use more than one price in the marketing of a specific product. Price differentiation can be based on such considerations as time of the purchase, type of customer, or type of distribution channel. For example, Florida hotel accommodations are more expensive in winter than in summer; a home owner pays more for air-conditioner filters than does an apartment complex owner purchasing the same size filters in greater quantity; and Christmas tree ornaments usually are cheaper on December 26 than on December 16. For price differentiation to work correctly, the company first

Demand-based pricing.
Airlines employ demand-based pricing. When demand for a particular flight is high, prices are elevated. When demand for a particular flight is low, airfare is less expensive. Airlines also employ competition-based pricing, especially on routes on which competing airlines offer very low fares.

must be able to segment a market on the basis of different strengths of demand and then must be able to keep the segments separate enough so that segment members who buy at lower prices cannot sell to buyers in segments that are charged a higher price. This isolation could be accomplished, for example, by selling to geographically separated segments.

Compared with cost-based pricing, demand-based pricing places a firm in a better position to attain higher profit levels, assuming that buyers value the product at levels sufficiently above the product's cost. To use demand-based pricing, however, management must be able to estimate demand at different price levels, which may be difficult to do accurately.

Competition-Based Pricing

In using *competition-based pricing*, an organization considers costs and revenue secondary to competitors' prices. The importance of this method increases if competing products are quite similar and the organization is serving markets in which price is the crucial variable of the marketing strategy. A firm that uses competition-based pricing may choose to be below competitors' prices, slightly above competitors' prices, or at the same level. The price that your bookstore paid to the publishing company of this text was determined using competition-based pricing. Competition-based pricing can help to attain a pricing objective to increase sales or market share. Competition-based pricing may be combined with other cost approaches to arrive at profitable levels.

Pricing Strategies

9 LEARNING OBJECTIVE
Explain the different strategies available to companies for setting prices.

A *pricing strategy* is a course of action designed to achieve pricing objectives. Generally, pricing strategies help marketers to solve the practical problems of setting prices. The extent to which a business uses any of the following strategies depends on its pricing and marketing objectives, the markets for its products, the degree of product differentiation, the life-cycle stage of the product, and other factors. Figure 14.5 contains a list of the major types of pricing strategies. We discuss these strategies in the remainder of this section.

New Product Strategies

The two primary types of new product pricing strategies are price skimming and penetration pricing. An organization can use either one or even both over a period of time.

price skimming the strategy of charging the highest possible price for a product during the introduction stage of its life cycle

Price Skimming   Some consumers are willing to pay a high price for an innovative product either because of its novelty or because of the prestige or status that ownership confers. **Price skimming** is the strategy of charging the highest possible price for a product during the introduction stage of its life cycle. The seller essentially "skims the cream" off the market, which helps to recover the high costs of R&D more quickly. Also, a skimming policy may hold down demand for the product, which is helpful if the firm's production capacity is limited during the introduction stage. The greatest disadvantage is that a skimming price may make the product appear lucrative to potential competitors, who then may attempt to enter that market.

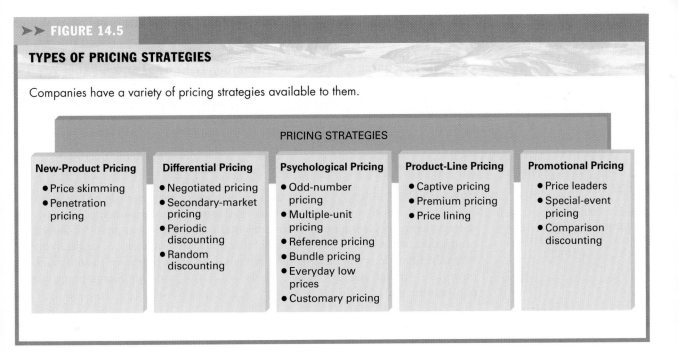

>> **FIGURE 14.5**

TYPES OF PRICING STRATEGIES

Companies have a variety of pricing strategies available to them.

PRICING STRATEGIES

New-Product Pricing	Differential Pricing	Psychological Pricing	Product-Line Pricing	Promotional Pricing
• Price skimming • Penetration pricing	• Negotiated pricing • Secondary-market pricing • Periodic discounting • Random discounting	• Odd-number pricing • Multiple-unit pricing • Reference pricing • Bundle pricing • Everyday low prices • Customary pricing	• Captive pricing • Premium pricing • Price lining	• Price leaders • Special-event pricing • Comparison discounting

Penetration Pricing   At the opposite extreme, **penetration pricing** is the strategy of setting a low price for a new product. The main purpose of setting a low price is to build market share for the product quickly. The seller hopes that the building of a large market share quickly will discourage competitors from entering the market. If the low price stimulates sales, the firm also may be able to order longer production runs, which result in lower production costs per unit. A disadvantage of penetration pricing is that it places a firm in a less flexible position. It is more difficult to raise prices significantly than it is to lower them.

penetration pricing the strategy of setting a low price for a new product

Differential Pricing

An important issue in pricing decisions is whether to use a single price or different prices for the same product. A single price is easily understood by both employees and customers, and since many salespeople and customers do not like having to negotiate a price, it reduces the chance of a marketer developing an adversarial relationship with a customer.

 Differential pricing means charging different prices to different buyers for the same quality and quantity of product. For differential pricing to be effective, the market must consist of multiple segments with different price sensitivities. When this method is employed, caution should be used to avoid confusing or antagonizing customers. Differential pricing can occur in several ways, including negotiated pricing, secondary-market pricing, periodic discounting, and random discounting.

Negotiated Pricing   **Negotiated pricing** occurs when the final price is established through bargaining between the seller and the customer. Negotiated pricing occurs in a number of industries and at all levels of distribution. Even when there is a predetermined stated price or a price list, manufacturers, wholesalers, and retailers still may negotiate to establish the final sales price. Consumers commonly negotiate prices for houses, cars, and used equipment.

negotiated pricing establishing a final price through bargaining

Secondary-Market Pricing   **Secondary-market pricing** means setting one price for the primary target market and a different price for another market. Often the price charged in the secondary market is lower. However, when the costs of serving a secondary market are higher than normal, secondary-market customers may have to pay a higher price. Examples of secondary markets include a geographically isolated domestic market, a market in a foreign country, and a segment willing to purchase a prod-

secondary-market pricing setting one price for the primary target market and a different price for another market

uct during off-peak times (such as "early bird" diners at restaurants and off-peak users of cellular phones).

Periodic Discounting   **Periodic discounting** is the temporary reduction of prices on a patterned or systematic basis. For example, many retailers have annual holiday sales, and some women's apparel stores have two seasonal sales each year—a winter sale in the last two weeks of January and a summer sale in the first two weeks of July. From the marketer's point of view, a major problem with periodic discounting is that customers can predict when the reductions will occur and may delay their purchases until they can take advantage of the lower prices.

periodic discounting temporary reduction of prices on a patterned or systematic basis

Random Discounting   To alleviate the problem of customers' knowing when discounting will occur, some organizations employ **random discounting.** That is, they reduce their prices temporarily on an nonsystematic basis. When price reductions of a product occur randomly, current users of that brand are not likely to be able to predict when the reductions will occur and so will not delay their purchases in anticipation of buying the product at a lower price. Marketers also use random discounting to attract new customers.

random discounting temporary reduction of prices on an unsystematic basis

Psychological Pricing Strategies

Psychological pricing strategies encourage purchases based on emotional responses rather than on economically rational responses. These strategies are used primarily for consumer products rather than business products.

Odd-Number Pricing   Many retailers believe that consumers respond more positively to odd-number prices such as $4.99 than to whole-dollar prices such as $5. **Odd-number pricing** is the strategy of setting prices using odd numbers that are slightly below whole-dollar amounts. Nine and five are the most popular ending figures for odd-number prices.

odd-number pricing the strategy of setting prices using odd numbers that are slightly below whole-dollar amounts

Sellers who use this strategy believe that odd-number prices increase sales. The strategy is not limited to low-priced items. Auto manufacturers may set the price of a car at $11,999 rather than $12,000. Odd-number pricing has been the subject of various psychological studies, but the results have been inconclusive.

Multiple-Unit Pricing   Many retailers (and especially supermarkets) practice **multiple-unit pricing,** setting a single price for two or more units, such as two cans for 99 cents rather than 50 cents per can. Especially for frequently purchased products, this strategy can increase sales. Customers who see the single price and who expect eventually to use more than one unit of the product regularly purchase multiple units to save money.

multiple-unit pricing the strategy of setting a single price for two or more units

Reference Pricing   **Reference pricing** means pricing a product at a moderate level and positioning it next to a more expensive model or brand in the hope that the customer will use the higher price as a reference price (i.e., a comparison price). Because of the comparison, the customer is expected to view the moderate price favorably. When you go to Sears to buy a DVD recorder, a moderately priced DVD recorder may appear especially attractive because it offers most of the important attributes of the more expensive alternatives on display and at a lower price.

reference pricing pricing a product at a moderate level and positioning it next to a more expensive model or brand

Bundle Pricing   **Bundle pricing** is the packaging together of two or more products, usually of a complementary nature, to be sold for a single price. To be attractive to customers, the single price usually is considerably less than the sum of the prices of the individual products. Being able to buy the bundled combination of products in a single transaction may be of value to the customer as well. Bundle pricing is used commonly for banking and travel services, computers, and automobiles with option packages. Bundle pricing can help to increase customer satisfaction. Bundling slow-moving products with ones with a higher turnover, an organization can stimulate sales and in-

bundle pricing packaging together two or more complementary products and selling them for a single price

crease its revenues. Selling products as a package rather than individually also may result in cost savings. As regulations in the telecommunications industry continue to evolve, many experts agree that telecom services will be provided together using bundled pricing in the near future. The new term *all-distance* has emerged, but the bundling of services goes beyond just combined pricing for local and long-distance services. Verizon, for example, is offering the Verizon Freedom Package plan that gives customers unlimited local, long-distance, wireless, DSL, and Direct TV for a bundled price of about $112 per month.[19]

Everyday Low Prices (EDLPs)

To reduce or eliminate the use of frequent short-term price reductions, some organizations use an approach referred to as **everyday low prices (EDLPs).** When EDLPs are used, a marketer sets a low price for its products on a consistent basis rather than setting higher prices and frequently discounting them. EDLPs, though not deeply discounted, are set far enough below competitors' prices to make customers feel confident that they are receiving a fair price. EDLPs are employed by retailers such as Wal-Mart and by manufacturers such as Procter & Gamble. A company that uses EDLPs benefits from reduced promotional costs, reduced losses from frequent mark downs, and more stability in its sales. A major problem with this approach is that customers have mixed responses to it. In some instances, customers simply do not believe that EDLPs are what they say they are but are instead a marketing gimmick.

everyday low prices (EDLPs) setting a low price for products on a consistent basis

Customary Pricing

In **customary pricing,** certain goods are priced primarily on the basis of tradition. Examples of customary, or traditional, prices would be those set for candy bars and chewing gum.

customary pricing pricing on the basis of tradition

Product-Line Pricing

Rather than considering products on an item-by-item basis when determining pricing strategies, some marketers employ product-line pricing. *Product-line pricing* means establishing and adjusting the prices of multiple products within a product line. Product-line pricing can provide marketers with flexibility in price setting. For example, marketers can set prices so that one product is quite profitable, whereas another increases market share by virtue of having a lower price than competing products.

When marketers employ product-line pricing, they have several strategies from which to choose. These include captive pricing, premium pricing, and price lining.

Captive Pricing

When **captive pricing** is used, the basic product in a product line is priced low, but the price on the items required to operate or enhance it are set at a higher level. For example, a manufacturer of cameras and film may price a camera at a low level to attract customers but price the film at a relatively high level because customers must continue to purchase film in order to use their cameras.

captive pricing pricing the basic product in a product line low, but pricing related items at a higher level

Premium Pricing

Premium pricing occurs when the highest-quality product or the most-versatile version of similar products in a product line is given the highest price. Other products in the line are priced to appeal to price-sensitive shoppers or to those who seek product-specific features. Marketers that use premium pricing often realize a significant portion of their profits from premium-priced products. Examples of product categories in which premium pricing is common are small kitchen appliances, beer, ice cream, and television cable service.

premium pricing pricing the highest-quality or most-versatile products higher than other models in the product line

Price Lining

Price lining is the strategy of selling goods only at certain predetermined prices that reflect definite price breaks. For example, a shop may sell men's ties only at $22 and $37. This strategy is used widely in clothing and accessory stores. It eliminates minor price differences from the buying decision—both for customers and for managers who buy merchandise to sell in these stores.

price lining the strategy of selling goods only at certain predetermined prices that reflect definite price breaks

Promotional Pricing

Price, as an ingredient in the marketing mix, often is coordinated with promotion. The two variables sometimes are so interrelated that the pricing policy is promotion-oriented. Examples of promotional pricing include price leaders, special-event pricing, and comparison discounting.

price leaders products priced below the usual markup, near cost, or below cost

Price Leaders   Sometimes a firm prices a few products below the usual markup, near cost, or below cost, which results in prices known as **price leaders.** This type of pricing is used most often in supermarkets and restaurants to attract customers by giving them especially low prices on a few items. Management hopes that sales of regularly priced products will more than offset the reduced revenues from the price leaders.

special-event pricing advertised sales or price cutting linked to a holiday, season, or event

Special-Event Pricing   To increase sales volume, many organizations coordinate price with advertising or sales promotions for seasonal or special situations. **Special-event pricing** involves advertised sales or price cutting linked to a holiday, season, or event. If the pricing objective is survival, then special sales events may be designed to generate the necessary operating capital.

comparison discounting setting a price at a specific level and comparing it with a higher price

Comparison Discounting   **Comparison discounting** sets the price of a product at a specific level and simultaneously compares it with a higher price. The higher price may be the product's previous price, the price of a competing brand, the product's price at another retail outlet, or a manufacturer's suggested retail price. Customers may find comparative discounting informative, and it can have a significant impact on them. However, because this pricing strategy on occasion has led to deceptive pricing practices, the Federal Trade Commission has established guidelines for comparison discounting. If the higher price against which the comparison is made is the price formerly charged for the product, sellers must have made the previous price available to customers for a reasonable period of time. If sellers present the higher price as the one charged by other retailers in the same trade area, they must be able to demonstrate that this claim is true. When they present the higher price as the manufacturer's suggested retail price, then the higher price must be similar to the price at which a reasonable proportion of the product was sold. Some manufacturers' suggested retail prices are so high that very few products actually are sold at those prices. In such cases, it would be deceptive to use comparison discounting.

Pricing Business Products

10 LEARNING OBJECTIVE
Describe three major types of pricing associated with business products.

Many of the pricing issues discussed thus far in this chapter deal with pricing in general. Setting prices for business products can be different from setting prices for consumer products owing to several factors such as size of purchases, transportation considerations, and geographic issues. We examine three types of pricing associated with business products, including geographic pricing, transfer pricing, and discounting.

Geographic Pricing

Geographic pricing strategies deal with delivery costs. The pricing strategy that requires the buyer to pay the delivery costs is called *FOB origin pricing*. It stands for "free on board at the point of origin," which means that the price does not include freight charges, and thus the buyer must pay the transportation costs from the seller's warehouse to the buyer's place of business. *FOB destination* indicates that the price does include freight charges, and thus the seller pays these charges.

Transfer Pricing

transfer pricing prices charged in sales between an organization's units

When one unit in an organization sells a product to another unit, **transfer pricing** occurs. The price is determined by calculating the cost of the product. A transfer price can vary depending on the types of costs included in the calculations. The choice of the costs to include when calculating the transfer price depends on the company's management strategy and the nature of the units' interaction. An organization also must ensure that transfer pricing is fair to all units involved in the purchases.

Discounting

A **discount** is a deduction from the price of an item. Producers and sellers offer a wide variety of discounts to their customers, including the following:

discount a deduction from the price of an item

- *Trade discounts* are discounts from the list prices that are offered to marketing intermediaries, or middlemen. A furniture retailer, for example, may receive a 40 percent discount from the manufacturer. The retailer then would pay $60 for a lamp carrying a list price of $100. Intermediaries, discussed in Chapter 15, perform various marketing activities in return for trade discounts.
- *Quantity discounts* are discounts given to customers who buy in large quantities. The seller's per-unit selling cost is lower for larger purchases. The quantity discount is a way of passing part of these savings on to the buyer.
- *Cash discounts* are discounts offered for prompt payment. A seller may offer a discount of "2/10, net 30," meaning that the buyer may take a 2 percent discount if the bill is paid within ten days and that the bill must be paid in full within thirty days.
- A *seasonal discount* is a price reduction to buyers who purchase out of season. This discount lets the seller maintain steadier production during the year. For example, automobile rental agencies offer seasonal discounts in winter and early spring to encourage firms to use automobiles during the slow months of the automobile rental business.
- An *allowance* is a reduction in price to achieve a desired goal. Trade-in allowances, for example, are price reductions granted for turning in used equipment when purchasing new equipment. This type of discount is popular in the aircraft industry. Another example is a promotional allowance, which is a price reduction granted to dealers for participating in advertising and sales-support programs intended to increase sales of a particular item.

RETURN TO Inside Business

The Apple brand has become so desirable that non-competing firms are lining up to link their products and brands with the Apple image. JBL and Bose are just two of many companies that make speaker systems specifically for docking with iPod models. BMW and Volvo are among the growing list of automakers that offer iPod connections as options on new vehicles.

Although iTunes downloads are inexpensive, new iPod models are premium-priced to reinforce their trendy, up-to-the-minute positioning and attract

buyers who must have the latest "cool" product. At the same time, Apple has slowly lowered prices on older iPod models to maintain overall sales momentum by appealing to more cost-conscious buyers. Look for more innovations ahead as Apple continues to polish its brand through innovative new products.

Questions

1. Why would Apple use family branding rather than individual branding for the iPod and the Macintosh?
2. Do you think Apple is using cost-based pricing, demand-based pricing, or competition-based pricing for iPod products? Explain your answer.

➤➤ CHAPTER REVIEW

Summary

1

Explain what a product is and how products are classified.

A product is everything one receives in an exchange, including all attributes and expected benefits. The product may be a manufactured item, a service, an idea, or some combination of these.

Products are classified according to their ultimate use. Classification affects a product's distribution, promotion, and pricing. Consumer products, which include convenience, shopping, and specialty products, are purchased to satisfy personal and family needs. Business products are purchased for resale, for making other products, or for use in a firm's operations. Business products can be classified as raw materials, major equipment, accessory equipment, component parts, process materials, supplies, and services.

2

Discuss the product life cycle and how it leads to new product development.

Every product moves through a series of four stages—introduction, growth, maturity, and decline—which together form the product life cycle. As the product progresses through these stages, its sales and profitability increase, peak, and then decline. Marketers keep track of the life-cycle stage of products in order to estimate when a new product should be introduced to replace a declining one.

3

Define *product line* **and** *product mix* **and distinguish between the two.**

A product line is a group of similar products marketed by a firm. The products in a product line are related to each other in the way they are produced, marketed, and used. The firm's product mix includes all the products it offers for sale. The width of a mix is the number of product lines it contains. The depth of the mix is the average number of individual products within each line.

4

Identify the methods available for changing a product mix.

Customer satisfaction and organizational objectives require marketers to develop, adjust, and maintain an effective product mix. Marketers may improve a product mix by changing existing products, deleting products, and developing new products.

New products are developed through a series of seven steps. The first step, idea generation, involves the accumulation of a pool of possible product ideas. Screening, the second step, removes from consideration those product ideas that do not mesh with organizational goals or resources. Concept testing, the third step, is a phase in which a small sample of potential buyers is exposed to a proposed product through a written or oral description in order to determine their initial reaction and buying intentions. The fourth step, business analysis, generates information about the potential sales, costs, and profits. During the development step, the product idea is transformed into mock-ups and actual prototypes to determine if the product is technically feasible to build and can be produced at reasonable costs. Test marketing is an actual launch of the product in several selected cities. Finally, during commercialization, plans for full-scale production and marketing are refined and implemented. Most product failures result from inadequate product planning and development.

5

Explain the uses and importance of branding, packaging, and labeling.

A brand is a name, term, symbol, design, or any combination of these that identifies a seller's products as distinct from those of other sellers. Brands can be classified as manufacturer brands, store brands, or generic brands. A firm can choose between two branding strategies—individual branding or family branding. Branding strategies are used to associate (or *not* associate) particular products with existing products, producers, or intermediaries. Packaging protects goods, offers consumer convenience, and enhances marketing efforts by communicating product features, uses, benefits, and image. Labeling provides customers with product information, some of which is required by law.

6

Describe the economic basis of pricing and the means by which sellers can control prices and buyers' perceptions of prices.

Under the ideal conditions of pure competition, an individual seller has no control over the price of its products. Prices are determined by the workings of supply and demand. In our real economy, however, sellers do exert some control, primarily through product differentiation. Product differentiation is the process of developing and promoting differences between one's product and all similar products. Firms also attempt to gain some control over pricing through advertising. A few large sellers have considerable control over prices because each controls a large proportion of the total supply of the product. Firms must consider the relative importance of price to buyers in the target market before setting prices. Buyers' perceptions of prices are affected by the importance of the product to them, the range of prices they consider acceptable, their perceptions of competing products, and their association of quality with price.

7

Identify the major pricing objectives used by businesses.

Objectives of pricing include survival, profit maximization, target return on investment, achieving market goals, and maintaining the status quo. Firms sometimes have to price products to survive, which usually requires cutting prices to attract customers. Return on investment (ROI) is the amount earned as a result of the investment in developing and marketing the product. The firm sets an annual percentage ROI as the pricing goal. Some firms use pricing to maintain or increase their market share. And in industries in which price stability is important, firms often price their products by charging about the same as competitors.

8

Examine the three major pricing methods that firms employ.

The three major pricing methods are cost-based pricing, demand-based pricing, and competition-based pricing. When cost-based pricing is employed, a proportion of the cost is added to the total cost to determine the selling price. When demand-based pricing is used, the price will be higher when demand is higher, and the price will be lower when demand is lower. A firm that uses competition-based pricing may choose to price below competitors' prices, at the same level as competitors' prices, or slightly above competitors' prices.

9

Explain the different strategies available to companies for setting prices.

Pricing strategies fall into five categories: new product pricing, differential pricing, psychological pricing, product-line pricing, and promotional pricing. Price skimming and penetration pricing are two strategies used for pricing new products. Differential pricing can be accomplished through negotiated pricing, secondary-market pricing, periodic discounting, and random discounting. The types of psychological pricing strategies are odd-number pricing, multiple-unit pricing, reference pricing, bundle pricing, everyday low prices, and customary pricing. Product-line pricing can be achieved through captive pricing, premium pricing, and price lining. The major types of promotional pricing are price-leader pricing, special-event pricing, and comparison discounting.

10

Describe three major types of pricing associated with business products.

Setting prices for business products can be different from setting prices for consumer products as a result of several factors, such as size of purchases, transportation considerations, and geographic issues. The three types of pricing associated with the pricing of business products are geographic pricing, transfer pricing, and discounting.

Key Terms

You should now be able to define and give an example relevant to each of the following terms:

product (442)
consumer product (443)
business product (443)
convenience product (443)
shopping product (443)
specialty product (444)
raw material (444)
major equipment (444)
accessory equipment (444)
component part (444)
process material (444)
supply (444)
business service (444)
product life cycle (444)
product line (447)
product mix (447)
product modification (448)
line extension (448)
product deletion (448)
brand (452)
brand name (452)
brand mark (452)
trademark (452)
trade name (452)
manufacturer (or producer) brand (452)
store (or private) brand (452)
generic product (or brand) (452)
brand loyalty (453)
brand equity (453)
individual branding (454)
family branding (455)
brand extension (455)
packaging (455)
labeling (457)
express warranty (457)
price (458)
supply (458)
demand (458)
price competition (459)
nonprice competition (460)
product differentiation (460)
markup (462)
breakeven quantity (462)

total revenue (462)

fixed cost (462)

variable cost (462)

total cost (462)

price skimming (464)

penetration pricing (465)

negotiated pricing (465)

secondary-market pricing (465)

periodic discounting (466)

random discounting (466)

odd-number pricing (466)

multiple-unit pricing (466)

reference pricing (466)

bundle pricing (466)

everyday low prices (EDLPs) (467)

customary pricing (467)

captive pricing (467)

premium pricing (467)

price lining (467)

price leaders (468)

special-event pricing (468)

comparison discounting (468)

transfer pricing (468)

discount (469)

Review Questions

1. What does the purchaser of a product obtain besides the good, service, or idea itself?
2. What are the products of (a) a bank, (b) an insurance company, and (c) a university?
3. What major factor determines whether a product is a consumer or a business product?
4. Describe each of the classifications of business products.
5. What are the four stages of the product life cycle? How can a firm determine which stage a particular product is in?
6. What is the difference between a product line and a product mix? Give an example of each.
7. Under what conditions does product modification work best?
8. Why do products have to be deleted from a product mix?
9. Why must firms introduce new products?
10. Briefly describe the seven new product development stages.
11. What is the difference between manufacturer brands and store brands? Between family branding and individual branding?
12. What is the difference between a line extension and a brand extension?

13. How can packaging be used to enhance marketing activities?
14. For what purposes is labeling used?
15. What is the primary function of prices in our economy?
16. Compare and contrast the characteristics of price and nonprice competition.
17. How might buyers' perceptions of price influence pricing decisions?
18. List and briefly describe the five major pricing objectives.
19. What are the differences among markup pricing, pricing by breakeven analysis, and competition-based pricing?
20. In what way is demand-based pricing more realistic than markup pricing?
21. Why would a firm use competition-based pricing?
22. What are the five major categories of pricing strategies? Give at least two examples of specific strategies that fall into each category.
23. Identify and describe the main types of discounts that are used in the pricing of business products.

Discussion Questions

1. Why is it important to understand how products are classified?
2. What factors might determine how long a product remains in each stage of the product life cycle? What can a firm do to prolong each stage?
3. Some firms do not delete products until they become financially threatening. What problems may result from relying on this practice?
4. Which steps in the evolution of new products are most important? Which are least important? Defend your choices.
5. Do branding, packaging, and labeling really benefit consumers? Explain.
6. To what extent can a firm control its prices in our market economy? What factors limit such control?
7. Under what conditions would a firm be most likely to use nonprice competition?
8. Can a firm have more than one pricing objective? Can it use more than one of the pricing methods discussed in this chapter? Explain.
9. What are the major disadvantages of price skimming?
10. What is an "effective" price?
11. Under what conditions would a business most likely decide to employ one of the differential pricing strategies?
12. For what types of products are psychological pricing strategies most likely to be used?

►► VIDEO CASE 14.1

Flying High with Low Prices at JetBlue

How long can JetBlue Airways stay in the black while offering low airfares, lots of flights, and lots of legroom? Founded by David Neeleman, a savvy entrepreneur who sold his regional airline to Southwest Airlines in 1994, JetBlue sent its first flight into the skies in 2000. The airline quickly attained profitability and built a loyal customer base on the winning combination of customer-friendly service and low airfares. In recent years, however, JetBlue's high-flying profitability has lost a little altitude owing to high fuel costs.

CEO Neeleman knows that price is one of the top considerations for travelers. Major carriers typically quote dozens of fares between two locations, depending on time of day and other factors. By comparison, JetBlue's everyday pricing structure is generally lower, far simpler, and avoids complicated requirements such as Saturday-night stayovers. The CEO says that the fares are based on demand and that JetBlue uses pricing to equalize the loads on the flights so that no jet takes off empty while another is completely full. Thus fares for Sunday-night flights tend to be higher because of higher demand, whereas Tuesday-night flights may be priced lower owing to lower demand. Whenever the airline inaugurates a new route, it grabs travelers' attention with even lower promotional fares.

Price is not the only way that JetBlue sets itself apart from competing airlines. Although many new carriers buy used jets, JetBlue flies new Airbus A320 and Embraer 190 jets with seat-back video screens showing satellite television programming. Rather than squeeze in the maximum 180 seats that A320s can hold, JetBlue flies with only 156, giving passengers more legroom. In addition, the jets are outfitted with roomier leather seats, which cost twice as much as ordinary seats but last twice as long and make passengers feel pampered.

Another advantage of new jets is higher fuel efficiency. A320s can operate on 60 percent of the amount of fuel burned by an equivalent jet built decades before. Even so, JetBlue's profit margin drops when fuel costs skyrocket. "It's all about the fuel," the CEO says. Nonetheless, the airline's total costs of 6.5 cents per mile remain well below the per-mile costs of most major competitors. In part, this is so because JetBlue's technicians work on only two types of jets, which means they gain proficiency at maintenance tasks and therefore save the airline time and money. Also, newer jets are under warranty, which keeps maintenance expenses down.

CEO Neeleman decided to base his airline in New York City for two main reasons. First, he knew that New York travelers departing from nearby LaGuardia Airport faced crowds and delays unless they were willing to venture eight miles farther to fly from John F. Kennedy (JFK) International Airport. Second, JFK was not a regional hub for major airlines or for low-fare carriers such as Southwest. Seizing an opportunity to trade off a slightly less convenient location for lower competition and better on-time performance, Neeleman secured enough space to accommodate JetBlue's growth for years to come.

From its first day of operation, JetBlue has relied on Internet bookings to minimize sales costs. Travelers who buy tickets directly through the company's website get a special discount and are also eligible for online specials. JetBlue books about half its fares on the web and saves about $5 in transaction costs for each ticket booked online. Now, as Neeleman accepts delivery of one new jet every three weeks and hires 1,700 new employees per year, he must keep travelers coming back, rein in costs, and keep JetBlue's prices competitive without grounding profits.[20]

For more information about this company, go to **www.jetblue.com.**

Questions

1. In an industry where pricing has driven many firms out of business or into bankruptcy protection, why does JetBlue compete so successfully on the basis of price?
2. How would you use the airplane and other physical aspects of the business to build the JetBlue brand?
3. How does JetBlue use pricing to deal with demand fluctuations?

➤➤ CASE 14.2

XM: 4 U 24/7/365

Satellite radio is gaining customers more quickly than any other new consumer technology in history—and XM Satellite Radio is leading the way. The company started on the road to static-free radio in 1997, when it paid more than $80 million for a federal license to broadcast digital radio. Until then, AM and FM radio stations had been free to all listeners mainly because of commercial sponsorship. However, XM believed that commuters—and anyone traveling by car for long periods—would pay for perfect 24-hour radio reception and dozens of channel choices anywhere in the United States. After all, millions of viewers were paying for cable television service, even though in many geographic areas they could watch broadcast television for free.

Turning the concept of digital radio into reality cost XM more than $1 billion. First, the company had to design and launch two satellites into orbit over the United States. It set up satellite dishes to beam radio signals to the satellites and erected antennas on 800 buildings in major cities to reach local listeners across the country. In addition, XM created a vast library of digital recordings and built two performance studios to broadcast and record live musical performances.

Another big challenge was developing the radio equipment for customers' cars. XM planned to encode its satellite signals to prevent noncustomers from listening to its channels. The radio had to be capable of receiving and decoding the satellite signals yet compact enough to fit in a car. After building and testing prototypes, XM began manufacturing a radio about the size of a suitcase, to be connected to an antenna on the car's roof for proper reception. Initially, customers had to retrofit their cars with XM radios. Then General Motors, Honda, Toyota, and several other big automakers began offering factory-installed XM radios as options in new cars.

Meanwhile, XM was conducting marketing research to determine the target market's listening tastes. Based on this research, the company decided to devote most of its radio stations to specific types of music, such as country, rap, jazz, blues, rock and roll, classic rock, international pop, instrumental classical music, and movie soundtracks. For more variety, it planned news-only, sports-only, talk-only, comedy-only, and children's stations, among other special-interest stations. XM also has become the exclusive satellite radio home of Major League Baseball, the National Hockey League, and celebrities such as Ellen DeGeneres.

Pricing involved a delicate balancing act. On the one hand, XM wanted to build a sizable base of subscribers, so its pricing had to be within customers' reach. On the other hand, the company was planning for long-term profitability and wanted to recoup some of its high start-up costs. Initially, XM set a monthly subscription fee of $9.95 and priced its first radios at $300 or less. Within a year, the company launched smaller, less expensive radios for the home and for listening on the go. "We are an entertainment company, but we also recognized that if we were going to be successful, we had to rapidly drive down the cost of the equipment people needed to get our service," recalls an XM marketing analyst.

XM's new product introduction has been successful. Even though XM has raised its monthly subscription fee to $12.95, more than six million subscribers already have signed up. Its only competitor, New York–based Sirius Satellite Radio, also charges a monthly subscription fee of $12.95 and has signed three million subscribers. Sirius channels are entirely commercial-free, whereas some XM channels broadcast commercials as well as music. To draw listeners with exclusive programming, Sirius has signed radio personality Howard Stern, lifestyle guru Martha Stewart, and other well-known names. DaimlerChrysler, BMW, and Ford all offer Sirius radio receivers as new-car options.

Today, XM customers must have its radio equipment to receive XM channels, just as Sirius customers must have its equipment to receive Sirius channels. This will change when new radios capable of receiving either company's channels become available. Still, XM's CEO expects to continue his company's market dominance by putting the emphasis on program content. "The technology is only the facilitator," he says. "Music connects so personally to people. We're putting the passion back into radio."[21]

For more information about this company, go to **www.xmradio.com.**

Questions

1. At what stage of the product life cycle is satellite radio? What factors are likely to affect satellite radio's movement into the next stage?
2. Evaluate the brand names of XM Satellite Radio and Sirius Satellite Radio. What are the strengths and weaknesses of each brand? Which do you think is the better brand name—and why?
3. Why is XM Satellite Radio relying on nonprice competition rather than price competition? Do you agree with this choice? Explain.

→ CHAPTER 14: JOURNAL EXERCISE

Discovery statement: This chapter explained the importance of product branding.

Thinking about the brands of products that you use, to which brand are you the most loyal? Explain the functional benefits of this brand.

_____

_____

_____

_____

_____

Beyond the functional benefits, what does this brand mean to you?

_____

_____

_____

_____

_____

Under what set of circumstances would you be willing to change to another competing brand?

_____

_____

_____

_____

Discuss how you first began to use this brand.

_____

_____

_____

_____

_____

BUILDING SKILLS FOR CAREER SUCCESS

1. Exploring the Internet

The Internet has quickly taken comparison shopping to a new level. Several websites such as bizrate.com, pricescan.com, and mysimon.com have emerged boasting that they can find the consumer the best deal on any product. From computers to watches, these sites offer unbiased price and product information to compare virtually any product. Users may read reviews about products as well as provide their own input from personal experience. Some of these sites also offer special promotions and incentives in exchange for user information. Visit the text website for updates to this exercise.

Assignment

1. Search all three of the websites listed above for the same product.
2. Did you notice any significant differences between the sites and the information they provide?
3. What percentage of searches do you think lead to purchases as opposed to browsing? Explain your answer.
4. Which site are you most likely to use on a regular basis? Why?
5. In what ways do these websites contribute to price competition?

2. Developing Critical-Thinking Skills

A feature is a characteristic of a product or service that enables it to perform its function. Benefits are the results a person receives from using a product or service. For example, a toothpaste's stain-removing formula is a feature; the benefit to the user is whiter teeth. While features are valuable and enhance a product, benefits motivate people to buy. The customer is more interested in how the product can help (the benefits) than in the details of the product (the features).

Assignment

1. Choose a product and identify its features and benefits.
2. Divide a sheet of paper into two columns. In one column, list the features of the product. In the other column, list the benefits each feature yields to the buyer.
3. Prepare a statement that would motivate you to buy this product.

3. Building Team Skills

In his book, *The Post-Industrial Society,* Peter Drucker wrote:

> Society, community, and family are all conserving institutions. They try to maintain stability and to prevent, or at least slow down, change. But the organization of the post-capitalist society of organizations is a destabilizer. Because its function is to put knowledge to work—on tools, processes, and products; on work; on knowledge itself—it must be organized for constant change. It must be organized for innovation.
>
> New product development is important in this process of systematically abandoning the past and building a future. Current customers can be sources of ideas for new products and services and ways of improving existing ones.

Assignment

1. Working in teams of five to seven, brainstorm ideas for new products or services for your college.
2. Construct questions to ask currently enrolled students (your customers). Sample questions might include
   a. Why did you choose this college?
   b. How can this college be improved?
   c. What products or services do you wish were available?
3. Conduct the survey and review the results.
4. Prepare a list of improvements and/or new products or services for your college.

4. Researching Different Careers

Standard & Poor's Industry Surveys, designed for investors, provides insight into various industries and the companies that compete within those industries. The "Basic Analysis" section gives overviews of industry trends and issues. The other sections define some basic industry terms, report the latest revenues and earnings of more than 1,000 companies, and occasionally list major reference books and trade associations.

Assignment

1. Identify an industry in which you might like to work.
2. Find the industry in *Standard & Poor's.* (*Note: Standard & Poor's* uses broad categories of industry. For example, an apparel or home-furnishings store would be included under "Retail" or "Textiles.")
3. Identify the following:
   a. Trends and issues in the industry
   b. Opportunities and/or problems that might arise in the industry in the next five years
   c. Major competitors within the industry (These companies are your potential employers.)
4. Prepare a report of your findings.

5. Improving Communication Skills

One often-overlooked source of business information is the Yellow Pages of the local telephone directory. The Yellow Pages can give you insight into the nature and scope of local companies.

Assignment

1. Choose a product and look it up in the Yellow Pages.
2. Telephone three companies that provide the product and ask for directions from your campus.
3. Evaluate the quality of the directions given and your impression of each company's service.
4. Report on your findings.

→ PREP TEST

Matching Questions

____ 1. A brand name that is legally protected for the owner's use only.

____ 2. A series of stages reflecting a product's sales.

____ 3. It is owned by a manufacturer, such as Honda and Whirlpool.

____ 4. A unique sports car for which no substitution will be accepted is an example.

____ 5. Buyers are concerned about prices, product features, qualities, and services.

____ 6. It is a written explanation of the producer's responsibilities.

____ 7. It involves the process of promoting differences between products.

____ 8. It is determined by the seller.

____ 9. Its purpose is to attract customers by giving them especially low prices on a few items.

____ 10. A strategy that is used when products are introduced at a high price.

a. express warranty
b. manufacturer brand
c. price
d. price leaders
e. price skimming
f. product differentiation
g. product life cycle
h. shopping product
i. specialty product
j. trademark

True/False Questions

T F

11. ○ ○ In the introduction stage of the product life cycle, consumer awareness and acceptance of the product are generally low.

12. ○ ○ Imitations are products designed for an established market.

13. ○ ○ A design or symbol that distinguishes a product from its competitor is called packaging.

14. ○ ○ Cheerios, Wheaties, and Total cereals are considered a product mix.

15. ○ ○ The majority of new products entering the marketplace are successful.

T F

16. ○ ○ A generic product has no brand.

17. ○ ○ The equilibrium point occurs when all units of a product are sold at the highest price, meeting the expectations of both buyers and sellers.

18. ○ ○ Differential pricing means charging different prices to different buyers.

19. ○ ○ The minimum price at which a product can be sold without incurring a loss is called the *price floor*.

20. ○ ○ The breakeven quantity includes the desired profit level.

Multiple-Choice Questions

21. IBM and Xerox use a strategy that helps promote all their products. This strategy is called
   a. family branding.
   b. generic brands.
   c. store brands.
   d. individual branding.
   e. none of the above.

22. A cost determined by the number of units produced is called _____ cost.
   a. variable
   b. selling
   c. differentiation
   d. fixed
   e. penetration

23. The manager of a local restaurant wants to add new desserts to the menu. Customers were asked to complete a survey about what they like. The restaurant is in which stage of the new product development process?
   a. Test marketing
   b. Product development
   c. Idea generation
   d. Screening
   e. Business analysis

24. Product modification makes changes to existing products in three primary ways. They are
   a. screening, testing, and changing.
   b. growth, maturity, and decline.
   c. quality, function, and aesthetics.
   d. quantity, description, and appearance.
   e. product, price, and service.

25. Western Day was a special day at the office. Janice wanted to dress in the latest western fashion, but she had limited funds. She visited several shops before finding the right outfit. For Janice, what type of product is the clothing?
   a. Specialty product
   b. Major equipment
   c. Industrial product
   d. Shopping product
   e. Convenience product

Fill-in-the-Blank Questions

26. A basic function of packing is to communicate the product's _____.

27. Three classifications of consumer goods are shopping, _____, and specialty.

28. The largest number of product ideas is rejected in the _____ stage.

29. The sum of fixed costs and variable costs is the _____ costs.

30. The legal name of a firm is its _____ name.

Online Study Center

FOR MORE **test practice, use the interactive ACE quizzes available at the Online Student Center: www.college.hmco.com/PIC/pridebusiness9e.**

Answers on p. PT2.

Wholesaling, Retailing, and Physical Distribution

LEARNING OBJECTIVES

WHAT you will be able to do once you complete this chapter:

1 Identify the various channels of distribution that are used for consumer and industrial products.

2 Explain the concept of market coverage.

3 Understand how supply-chain management facilitates partnering among channel members.

4 Describe what a vertical marketing system is and identify the types of vertical marketing systems.

5 Discuss the need for wholesalers and describe the services they provide to retailers and manufacturers.

6 Identify and describe the major types of wholesalers.

7 Distinguish among the major types of retailers.

8 Identify the categories of shopping centers and the factors that determine how shopping centers are classified.

9 Explain the five most important physical distribution activities.

WHY this chapter matters

Being able to create and maintain a mix of products that satisfies customers is important. A company also must be able to make these products available at the right place and time.

FOR HELP with studying this chapter, visit the Online Student Center:

www.college.hmco.com/PIC/pridebusiness9e

Online Study Center

Dell has achieved a global market share of nearly 19 percent by marketing directly to customers—but are distribution changes on the horizon? Founder and CEO Michael Dell realized early in the life of his Texas-based business that he could keep costs low and profits high by bypassing the traditional distribution network through which personal computers are sold. Customers simply log onto the company's website, specify the features they want, and arrange for payment. The new built-to-order PC arrives at the customer's home or office within a few days. If they prefer, customers can browse Dell's printed catalog and call toll free to place an order.

Instead of developing every component in-house, Dell saves time and money by choosing among the best components available on the market. The company strengthens relationships with suppliers by guaranteeing certain purchasing volumes in exchange for on-time delivery and expedited transactions. Because parts are available precisely when needed, Dell can maintain ultralow inventory levels of components, minimize warehousing costs, and gear up for higher sales quickly.

DID YOU KNOW?

Dell does not always sell direct.

Dell's control over its marketing channel gives it more flexibility to try different marketing ideas. As an example, Dell has sparked sales by offering low-interest-rate financing on expensive products. The build-to-order approach also eliminates excess inventory, which in the very dynamic PC industry can become obsolete overnight. In contrast, competitors that market through retailers must assemble PCs in advance, ship them to stores, and have sufficient inventory to fill reorders quickly.

Not long ago, however, Dell began selling older-model PCs and laptops through Costco's website and stores. The company had tested retail store distribution in the 1990s but determined that direct marketing offered better control and profit. Asked about the Costco deal, a Dell spokesperson stressed that it was not a return to full-scale retail store distribution but "just another way to get product in front of customers." Is Dell planning to diversify its channels of distribution?[1]

For more information about this topic, go to **www.dell.com.**

Some companies, like Dell, use a particular approach to distribution and marketing channels that gives them a sustainable competitive advantage. More than two million firms in the United States help to move products from producers to consumers. Store chains such as Dollar General Stores, Starbucks, Sears, and Wal-Mart operate retail outlets where consumers make purchases. Some retailers, such as Avon Products and Amway, send their salespeople to the homes of customers. Other retailers, such as Lands' End and L. L. Bean, sell through catalogs or through both catalogs and online. Still others, such as Amazon, sell online to customers.

In addition, there are more than half a million wholesalers that sell merchandise to other firms. Most consumers know little about these firms, which work "behind the scenes" and rarely sell directly to consumers. These and other intermediaries are concerned with the transfer of both products and ownership. They thus help to create the time, place, and possession utilities that are critical to marketing. As we will see, they also perform a number of services for their suppliers and their customers.

In this chapter we initially examine various channels of distribution that products follow as they move from producer to ultimate user. Then we discuss wholesalers and retailers within these channels. Next, we examine the types of shopping centers. Finally, we explore the physical distribution function and the major modes of transportation that are used to move goods.

Channels of Distribution

A **channel of distribution,** or **marketing channel,** is a sequence of marketing organizations that directs a product from the producer to the ultimate user. Every marketing channel begins with the producer and ends with either the consumer or the business user.

A marketing organization that links a producer and user within a marketing channel is called a **middleman,** or **marketing intermediary.** For the most part, middlemen are concerned with the transfer of *ownership* of products. A **merchant middleman** (or, more simply, a *merchant*) is a middleman that actually takes title to products by buying them. A **functional middleman,** on the other hand, helps in the transfer of ownership of products but does not take title to the products.

Different channels of distribution generally are used to move consumer and business products. The six most commonly used channels are illustrated in Figure 15.1.

Channels for Consumer Products

Producer to Consumer   This channel, often called the *direct channel,* includes no marketing intermediaries. Practically all services and a few consumer goods are distributed through a direct channel. Examples of marketers that sell goods directly to consumers include Dell Computer, Mary Kay Cosmetics, and Avon Products.

Producers sell directly to consumers for several reasons. They can better control the quality and price of their products. They do not have to pay (through discounts) for the services of intermediaries. And they can maintain closer ties with customers.

Producer to Retailer to Consumer   A **retailer** is a middleman that buys from producers or other middlemen and sells to consumers. Producers sell directly to retailers when retailers (such as Wal-Mart) can buy in large quantities. This channel is used most often for products that are bulky, such as furniture and automobiles, for which additional handling would increase selling costs. It is also the usual channel for perishable products, such as fruits and vegetables, and for high-fashion products that must reach the consumer in the shortest possible time.

Producer to Wholesaler to Retailer to Consumer   This channel is known as the *traditional channel* because many consumer goods (especially convenience goods) pass through wholesalers to retailers. A **wholesaler** is a middleman that sells products

LEARNING OBJECTIVE
Identify the various channels of distribution that are used for consumer and industrial products.

channel of distribution (or marketing channel) a sequence of marketing organizations that directs a product from the producer to the ultimate user

middleman (or marketing intermediary) a marketing organization that links a producer and user within a marketing channel

merchant middleman a middleman that actually takes title to products by buying them

functional middleman a middleman that helps in the transfer of ownership of products but does not take title to the products

retailer a middleman that buys from producers or other middlemen and sells to consumers

wholesaler a middleman that sells products to other firms

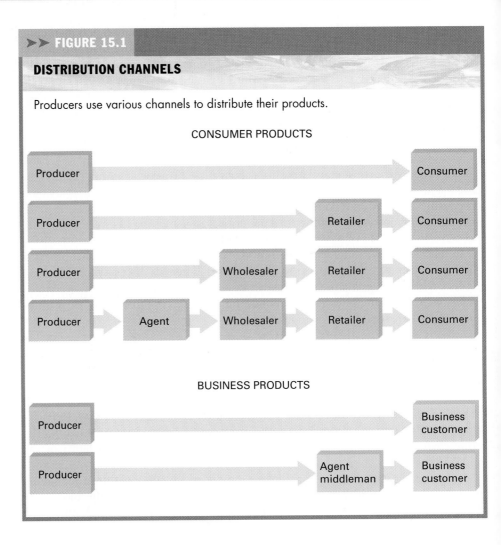

▶▶ FIGURE 15.1

DISTRIBUTION CHANNELS

Producers use various channels to distribute their products.

CONSUMER PRODUCTS

Producer	→				Consumer
Producer	→		Retailer	→	Consumer
Producer	→	Wholesaler	→ Retailer	→	Consumer
Producer	→ Agent	→ Wholesaler	→ Retailer	→	Consumer

BUSINESS PRODUCTS

| Producer | → | | Business customer |
| Producer | → | Agent middleman | → Business customer |

to other firms. These firms may be retailers, industrial users, or other wholesalers. A producer uses wholesalers when its products are carried by so many retailers that the producer cannot deal with all of them. For example, the maker of Wrigley's gum uses this type of channel.

Producer to Agent to Wholesaler to Retailer to Consumer Producers may use agents to reach wholesalers. Agents are functional middlemen that do not take title to products and that are compensated by commissions paid by producers. Often these products are inexpensive, frequently purchased items. For example, to reach a large number of potential customers, a small manufacturer of gas-powered lawn edgers might choose to use agents to market its product to wholesalers, which, in turn, sell the lawn edgers to a large number of retailers. This channel is also used for highly seasonal products (such as Christmas tree ornaments) and by producers that do not have their own sales forces.

Multiple Channels for Consumer Products Often a manufacturer uses different distribution channels to reach different market segments. A manufacturer uses multiple channels, for example, when the same product is sold to consumers and business customers. Multiple channels are also used to increase sales or to capture a larger share of the market. With the goal of selling as much merchandise as possible, Firestone markets its tires through its own retail outlets as well as through independent dealers.

ENTREPRENEURIAL CHALLENGE

Entrepreneurs Break into the Big Time

Many small-business owners dream of getting their products onto the shelves of Target, Wal-Mart, Staples, or other retail giants. With competition so fierce, how can entrepreneurs break into the big chains?

- *Know the retailer's customers.* When Mickey Miladinov was with Kmart, she purchased only products that would appeal to most of the chain's shoppers. "If not, I'd have to pass on that product," she remembers.
- *Build a track record.* Wal-Mart prefers products "to be sold somewhere else first, even if it's just a downtown boutique," says the director of supplier development.
- *Be ready.* Arden Beverage Co. had to gear up for large-scale production before selling vitamin-

enhanced soft drinks through Target. Be ready to customize the product or the packaging and to ship in quantity when and where needed.
- *Get help.* A food broker helped get Arden Beverage sodas into Target. Not every big chain will work with intermediaries, however.

Even though Wal-Mart accepts only 2 percent of the suppliers who apply, it is open to new sources because "we don't have all the suppliers we need," says a senior vice president.

Channels for Business Products

Producers of business products generally tend to use short channels. We will outline the two that are used most commonly.

Producer to Business User In this direct channel, the manufacturer's own sales force sells directly to business users. Heavy machinery, airplanes, and major equipment usually are distributed in this way. The very short channel allows the producer to provide customers with expert and timely services, such as delivery, machinery installation, and repairs.

Producer to Agent Middleman to Business User Manufacturers use this channel to distribute such items as operating supplies, accessory equipment, small tools, and standardized parts. The agent is an independent intermediary between the producer and the user. Generally, agents represent sellers.

Market Coverage

How does a producer decide which distribution channels (and which particular intermediaries) to use? As with every other marketing decision, this one should be based on all relevant factors. These include the firm's production capabilities and marketing resources, the target market and buying patterns of potential customers, and the product itself. After evaluating these factors, the producer can choose a particular *intensity of market coverage.* Then the producer selects channels and intermediaries to implement that coverage.

Intensive distribution is the use of all available outlets for a product. The producer that wants to give its product the widest possible exposure in the marketplace chooses intensive distribution. The manufacturer saturates the market by selling to any intermediary of good financial standing that is willing to stock and sell the product. For the consumer, intensive distribution means being able to shop at a convenient store and spend minimum time buying the product. Many convenience goods, including

2 LEARNING OBJECTIVE
Explain the concept of market coverage.

intensive distribution the use of all available outlets for a product

Selective distribution. Home appliances, such as those manufactured by Whirlpool, are usually distributed through selective distribution.

selective distribution the use of only a portion of the available outlets for a product in each geographic area

exclusive distribution the use of only a single retail outlet for a product in a large geographic area

candy, gum, and soft drinks, are distributed intensively. In fact, PepsiCo, with its soft drinks and Frito Lay snack foods, traditionally focused its intensive distribution on convenience stores and supermarkets. Experts believe that the future success for PepsiCo's use of intensive distribution will include greater focus on outlets such as Blockbuster, Auto Zone, Starbucks, and Dollar General Stores.[2]

Selective distribution is the use of only a portion of the available outlets for a product in each geographic area. Manufacturers of goods such as furniture, major home appliances, and clothing typically prefer selective distribution. Franchisors also use selective distribution in granting franchises for the sale of their goods and services in a specific geographic area. Levi Strauss, like most clothing companies, uses selective distribution to get its products to consumers. The company recently decided to expand the distribution of its denim products beyond its usual choices of department and specialty stores. It launched its new Type One jeans for its regular distribution outlets and is expanding through the introduction of its Levi Strauss Signature line in Wal-Mart stores. Levi is counting on this less selective approach to distribution to boost its sales significantly. Some executives are concerned about the effect this tactic will have on sales of Levi's higher-priced department-store denim products.[3]

Exclusive distribution is the use of only a single retail outlet for a product in a large geographic area. Exclusive distribution usually is limited to very prestigious products. It is appropriate, for instance, for specialty goods such as upscale pianos, fine china, and expensive jewelry. The producer usually places many requirements (such as inventory levels, sales training, service quality, and warranty procedures) on exclusive dealers.

Partnering Through Supply-Chain Management

Supply-chain management is a long-term partnership among channel members working together to create a distribution system that reduces inefficiencies, costs, and redundancies while creating a competitive advantage and satisfying customers. Supply-chain management requires cooperation throughout the entire marketing channel, including manufacturing, research, sales, advertising, and shipping. Supply chains focus not only on producers, wholesalers, retailers, and customers but also on component-parts suppliers, shipping companies, communication companies, and other organizations that participate in product distribution. Suppliers are having a greater impact on determining what items retail stores carry. This phenomenon, called *category management*, is becoming common for mass merchandisers, supermarkets, and convenience stores. Through category management, the retailer asks a supplier in a particular category how to stock the shelves. For example, Borders asked publisher HarperCollins what books it should sell, which includes both HarperCollins' books and competitors' books. Many retailers and suppliers claim this process delivers maximum efficiency.[4]

Traditionally, buyers and sellers have been adversarial when negotiating purchases. Supply-chain management, however, encourages cooperation in reducing the costs of inventory, transportation, administration, and handling; in speeding order-cycle times; and in increasing profits for all channel members. When buyers, sellers, marketing intermediaries, and facilitating agencies work together, customers' needs regarding delivery, scheduling, packaging, and other requirements are better met. Home Depot, North America's largest home-improvement retailer, is working to help its suppliers improve productivity and thereby supply Home Depot with better-quality products at lower costs. The company has even suggested a cooperative partnership with its competitors so that regional trucking companies making deliveries to all these organizations can provide faster, more efficient delivery.

Technology has enhanced the implementation of supply-chain management significantly. Through computerized integrated information sharing, channel members reduce costs and improve customer service. At Wal-Mart, for example, supply-chain management has almost eliminated the occurrence of out-of-stock items. Using barcode and electronic data interchange (EDI) technology, stores, warehouses, and suppliers communicate quickly and easily to keep Wal-Mart's shelves stocked with items customers want. Furthermore, there are currently about four hundred electronic trading communities made up of businesses selling to other businesses, including auctions, exchanges, e-procurement hubs, and multisupplier online catalogs. As many major industries transform their processes over the next five to ten years, the end result will be increased productivity by reducing inventory, shortening cycle time, and removing wasted human effort.

Vertical Marketing Systems

Vertical channel integration occurs when two or more stages of a distribution channel are combined and managed by one firm. A **vertical marketing system (VMS)** is a centrally managed distribution channel resulting from vertical channel integration. This merging eliminates the need for certain intermediaries. One member of a marketing channel may assume the responsibilities of another member, or it actually may purchase the operations of that member. For example, a large-volume discount retailer that ships and warehouses its own stock directly from manufacturers does not need a wholesaler. Total vertical integration occurs when a single management controls all operations from production to final sale. Oil companies that own wells, transportation facilities, refineries, terminals, and service stations exemplify total vertical integration.

There are three types of VMSs: administered, contractual, and corporate. In an *administered VMS*, one of the channel members dominates the other members, perhaps because of its large size. Under its influence, the channel members collaborate on production and distribution. A powerful manufacturer, such as Procter & Gamble, receives a great deal of cooperation from intermediaries that carry its brands. Although the goals of the entire system are considered when decisions are made, control rests with individual channel members, as in conventional marketing channels. Under a *contractual VMS*, cooperative arrangements and the rights and obligations of channel members are defined by contracts or other legal measures. In a *corporate VMS*, actual ownership is the vehicle by which production and distribution are joined. For example, Benetton manufactures clothing, which it then ships to its own retail outlets. Most vertical marketing systems are organized to improve distribution by combining individual operations.

Marketing Intermediaries: Wholesalers

Wholesalers may be the most misunderstood of marketing intermediaries. Producers sometimes try to eliminate them from distribution channels by dealing directly with retailers or consumers. Yet wholesalers provide a variety of essential marketing

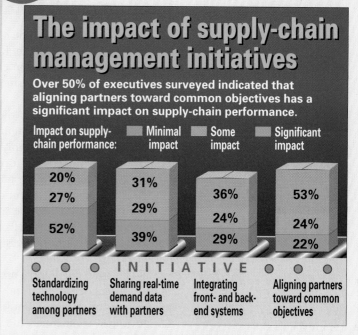

SPOTLIGHT

The impact of supply-chain management initiatives

Over 50% of executives surveyed indicated that aligning partners toward common objectives has a significant impact on supply-chain performance.

Impact on supply-chain performance:

| | Minimal impact | Some impact | Significant impact |

Standardizing technology among partners	Sharing real-time demand data with partners	Integrating front- and back-end systems	Aligning partners toward common objectives
20%	31%	36%	53%
27%	29%	24%	24%
52%	39%	29%	22%

INITIATIVE

Source: Tim Stevens, "View from on High," *Industry Week*, November 1, 2001; accesses from **IndustryWeek.com**, June 7, 2002.

4 LEARNING OBJECTIVE
Describe what a vertical marketing system is and identify the types of vertical marketing systems.

vertical channel integration the combining of two or more stages of a distribution channel under a single firm's management

vertical marketing system (VMS) a centrally managed distribution channel resulting from vertical channel integration

5 LEARNING OBJECTIVE
Discuss the need for wholesalers and describe the services they provide to retailers and manufacturers.

services. Although wholesalers can be eliminated, their functions cannot be eliminated. These functions *must* be performed by other channel members or by consumers. Eliminating a wholesaler may or may not cut distribution costs.

Justifications for Marketing Intermediaries

The press, consumers, public officials, and other marketers often charge wholesalers, at least in principle, with inefficiency and parasitism. Consumers in particular feel strongly that the distribution channel should be made as short as possible. They assume that the fewer the intermediaries in a distribution channel, the lower the price of the product will be.

Those who believe that the elimination of wholesalers would bring about lower prices, however, do not recognize that the services wholesalers perform still would be needed. Those services simply would be provided by other means, and consumers would still bear the costs. Moreover, all manufacturers would have to keep extensive records and employ enough personnel to deal with a multitude of retailers individually. Even with direct distribution, products might be considerably more expensive because prices would reflect the costs of producers' inefficiencies. Figure 15.2 shows that sixteen contacts could result from the efforts of four buyers purchasing the products of four producers. With the assistance of an intermediary, only eight contacts would be necessary.

To illustrate further the useful role of wholesalers in the marketing system, assume that all wholesalers in the candy industry were abolished. With thousands of candy retailers to contact, candy manufacturers would be making an extremely large number of sales calls just to maintain the present level of product visibility. Hershey Foods, for example, would have to set up warehouses all over the country, organize a fleet of trucks, purchase and maintain thousands of vending machines, and deliver all its own candy. Sales and distribution costs for candy would soar. Candy producers would be contacting and shipping products to thousands of small businesses instead of to a limited number of large wholesalers and retailers. The outrageous costs of this inefficiency would be passed on to consumers. Candy bars would be more expensive and likely available through fewer retailers.

Wholesalers often are more efficient and economical not only for manufacturers, but also for consumers. Because pressure to eliminate them comes from both ends of

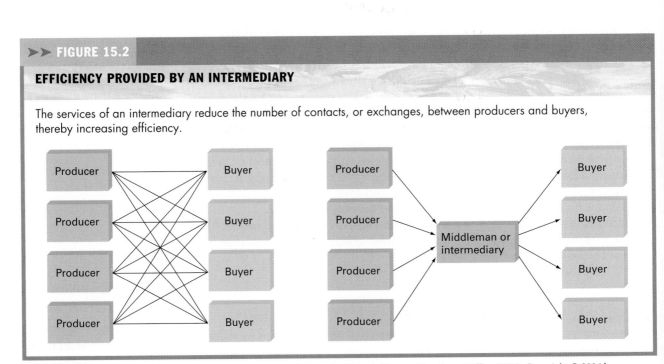

>> FIGURE 15.2

EFFICIENCY PROVIDED BY AN INTERMEDIARY

The services of an intermediary reduce the number of contacts, or exchanges, between producers and buyers, thereby increasing efficiency.

Source: William M. Pride and O. C. Ferrell, *Marketing: Concepts and Strategies,* 13th ed. (Boston: Houghton Mifflin, 2006). Copyright © 2006 by Houghton Mifflin Company. Adapted with permission.

the marketing channel, wholesalers should perform only those functions that are genuinely in demand. To stay in business, wholesalers also should take care to be efficient and productive and to provide high-quality services to other channel members.

Wholesalers' Services to Retailers

Wholesalers help retailers by buying in large quantities and then selling to retailers in smaller quantities and by delivering goods to retailers. They also stock—in one place—the variety of goods that retailers otherwise would have to buy from many producers. And wholesalers provide assistance in three other vital areas: promotion, market information, and financial aid.

Promotion   Some wholesalers help to promote the products they sell to retailers. These services are usually either free or performed at cost. Wholesalers, for example, are major sources of display materials designed to stimulate impulse buying. They also may help retailers to build effective window, counter, and shelf displays; they even may assign their own employees to work on the retail sales floor during special promotions.

Market Information   Wholesalers are a constant source of market information. Wholesalers have numerous contacts with local businesses and distant suppliers. In the course of these dealings, they accumulate information about consumer demand, prices, supply conditions, new developments within the trade, and even industry personnel. This information may be relayed to retailers informally through the wholesaler's sales force. Some wholesalers also provide information to their customers through websites.

Information regarding industry sales and competitive prices is especially important to all firms. Dealing with a number of suppliers and many retailers, a wholesaler is a natural clearinghouse for such information. And most wholesalers are willing to pass information on to their customers.

Financial Aid   Most wholesalers provide a type of financial aid that retailers often take for granted. By making prompt and frequent deliveries, wholesalers enable retailers to keep their own inventory investments small in relation to sales. Such indirect financial aid reduces the amount of operating capital that retailers need.

Wholesalers' Services to Manufacturers

Some of the services that wholesalers perform for producers are similar to those they provide to retailers. Others are quite different.

Providing an Instant Sales Force   A wholesaler provides its producers with an instant sales force so that producers' sales representatives need not call on retailers. This can result in enormous savings for producers. For example, Lever Brothers and General Foods would have to spend millions of dollars each year to field a sales force large enough to call on all the retailers that sell their numerous products. Instead, these producers rely on wholesalers to sell and distribute their products to many retailers. These producers do have sales forces, though, that call on wholesalers and large retailers.

Reducing Inventory Costs   Wholesalers purchase goods in sizable quantities from manufacturers and store these goods for resale. By doing so, they reduce the amount of finished-goods inventory that producers must hold and thereby reduce the cost of carrying inventories.

Assuming Credit Risks   When producers sell through wholesalers, it is the wholesalers who extend credit to retailers, make collections from retailers, and assume the risks of nonpayment. These services reduce the producers' cost of extending credit to customers and the resulting bad-debt expense.

LEARNING OBJECTIVE

6 Identify and describe the major types of wholesalers.

merchant wholesaler a middleman that purchases goods in large quantities and then sells them to other wholesalers or retailers and to institutional, farm, government, professional, or industrial users

full-service wholesaler a middleman that performs the entire range of wholesaler functions

general-merchandise wholesaler a middleman that deals in a wide variety of products

limited-line wholesaler a middleman that stocks only a few product lines but carries numerous product items within each line

specialty-line wholesaler a middleman that carries a select group of products within a single line

limited-service wholesaler a middleman that assumes responsibility for a few wholesale services only

commission merchant a middleman that carries merchandise and negotiates sales for manufacturers

agent a middleman that expedites exchanges, represents a buyer or a seller, and often is hired permanently on a commission basis

broker a middleman that specializes in a particular commodity, represents either a buyer or a seller, and is likely to be hired on a temporary basis

Furnishing Market Information   Just as they do for retailers, wholesalers supply market information to the producers they serve. Valuable information accumulated by wholesalers may concern consumer demand, the producers' competition, and buying trends.

Types of Wholesalers

Wholesalers generally fall into three categories: merchant wholesalers; commission merchants, agents, and brokers; and manufacturers' sales branches and sales offices. Of these, merchant wholesalers constitute the largest portion. They account for about four-fifths of all wholesale establishments and employees.

Merchant Wholesalers   A **merchant wholesaler** is a middleman that purchases goods in large quantities and then sells them to other wholesalers or retailers and to institutional, farm, government, professional, or industrial users. Merchant wholesalers usually operate one or more warehouses at which they receive, take title to, and store goods. These wholesalers are sometimes called *distributors* or *jobbers*.

Most merchant wholesalers are businesses composed of salespeople, order takers, receiving and shipping clerks, inventory managers, and office personnel. The successful merchant wholesaler must analyze available products and market needs. It must be able to adapt the type, variety, and quality of its products to changing market conditions.

Merchant wholesalers may be classified as full-service or limited-service wholesalers depending on the number of services they provide. A **full-service wholesaler** performs the entire range of wholesaler functions described earlier in this section. These functions include delivering goods, supplying warehousing, arranging for credit, supporting promotional activities, and providing general customer assistance.

Under this broad heading are the general-merchandise wholesaler, limited-line wholesaler, and specialty-line wholesaler. A **general-merchandise wholesaler** deals in a wide variety of products, such as drugs, hardware, nonperishable foods, cosmetics, detergents, and tobacco. A **limited-line wholesaler** stocks only a few product lines but carries numerous product items within each line. A **specialty-line wholesaler** carries a select group of products within a single line. Food delicacies such as shellfish represent the kind of product handled by this type of wholesaler.

In contrast to a full-service wholesaler, a **limited-service wholesaler** assumes responsibility for a few wholesale services only. Other marketing tasks are left to other channel members or consumers. This category includes cash-and-carry wholesalers, truck wholesalers, drop shippers, and mail-order wholesalers.

Commission Merchants, Agents, and Brokers   Commission merchants, agents, and brokers are functional middlemen. Functional middlemen do not take title to products. They perform a small number of marketing activities and are paid a commission that is a percentage of the sales price.

A **commission merchant** usually carries merchandise and negotiates sales for manufacturers. In most cases, commission merchants have the power to set the prices and terms of sales. After a sale is made, they either arrange for delivery or provide transportation services.

An **agent** is a middleman that expedites exchanges, represents a buyer or a seller, and often is hired permanently on a commission basis. When agents represent producers, they are known as *sales agents* or *manufacturer's agents*. As long as the products represented do not compete, a sales agent may represent one or several manufacturers on a commission basis. The agent solicits orders for the manufacturers within a specific territory. As a rule, the manufacturers ship the merchandise and bill the customers directly. The manufacturers also set the prices and other conditions of the sales. What do the manufacturers gain by using a sales agent? The sales agent provides immediate entry into a territory, regular calls on customers, selling experience, and a known, predetermined selling expense (a commission that is a percentage of sales revenue).

A **broker** is a middleman that specializes in a particular commodity, represents either a buyer or a seller, and is likely to be hired on a temporary basis. However, food brokers, which sell grocery products to resellers, generally have long-term relationships with their clients. Brokers may perform only the selling function, or both buying and selling, using established contacts or special knowledge of their fields.

Manufacturers' Sales Branches and Sales Offices

A **manufacturer's sales branch** is, in essence, a merchant wholesaler that is owned by a manufacturer. Sales branches carry inventory, extend credit, deliver goods, and offer help in promoting products. Their customers are retailers, other wholesalers, and industrial purchasers.

Because sales branches are owned by producers, they stock primarily the goods manufactured by their own firms. Selling policies and terms usually are established centrally and then transmitted to branch managers for implementation.

A **manufacturer's sales office** is essentially a sales agent owned by a manufacturer. Sales offices may sell goods manufactured by their own firms as well as certain products of other manufacturers that complement their own product lines. For example, Hiram Walker & Sons imports wine from Spain to increase the number of products its sales offices can offer to customers.

@ USING THE INTERNET

The National Retail Federation (**www.nrf.com**) and the American Wholesale Marketers Association (**www.awmanet.org**) are two industry gateways for information about their respective distribution channels. Each site provides access to online journals and links to related websites of interest to retailers and wholesalers.

manufacturer's sales branch essentially a merchant wholesaler that is owned by a manufacturer

manufacturer's sales office essentially a sales agent owned by a manufacturer

Marketing Intermediaries: Retailers

Retailers are the final link between producers and consumers. Retailers may buy from either wholesalers or producers. They sell not only goods but also such services as auto repairs, haircuts, and dry cleaning. Some retailers sell both. Sears, Roebuck and Company sells consumer goods, financial services, and repair services for home appliances bought at Sears.

Of approximately 2.6 million retail firms in the United States, about 90 percent have annual sales of less than $1 million. On the other hand, some large retail organizations realize well over $1 million in sales revenue per day. Table 15.1 lists the twenty largest retail organizations and their approximate sales revenues and yearly profits.

7 LEARNING OBJECTIVE
Distinguish among the major types of retailers.

Classes of In-Store Retailers

One way to classify retailers is by the number of stores owned and operated by the firm. An **independent retailer** is a firm that operates only one retail outlet. Approximately three-fourths of retailers are independent. One-store operators, like all small businesses, generally provide personal service and a convenient location.

A **chain retailer** is a company that operates more than one retail outlet. By adding outlets, chain retailers attempt to reach new geographic markets. As sales increase, chains usually buy merchandise in larger quantities and thus take advantage of quantity discounts. They also wield more power in their dealings with suppliers. About one-fourth of retail organizations operate chains.

Another way to classify in-store retailers is by store size and the kind and number of products carried. Let's take a closer look at store types based on these dimensions.

independent retailer a firm that operates only one retail outlet

chain retailer a company that operates more than one retail outlet

Department Stores

These large retail establishments consist of several sections, or departments, that sell a wide assortment of products. According to the U.S. Bureau of the Census, a **department store** is a retail store that (1) employs twenty-five or more persons and (2) sells at least home furnishings, appliances, family apparel, and household linens and dry goods, each in a different part of the store. Marshall Field's in Chicago (and several other cities), Harrods in London, and Au Printemps in Paris are examples of large department stores. Sears, Roebuck and JC Penney are also department stores. Traditionally, department stores have been service-oriented. Along with the goods they sell, these retailers provide credit, delivery, personal assistance, liberal return policies, and pleasant shopping atmospheres.

department store a retail store that (1) employs twenty-five or more persons and (2) sells at least home furnishings, appliances, family apparel, and household linens and dry goods, each in a different part of the store

>> TABLE 15.1

THE TWENTY LARGEST RETAIL FIRMS IN THE UNITED STATES

Rank	Company	Annual Sales (000)	Annual Profits (000)	Number of Stores
1	Wal- Mart Inc.	$285,222	$10,267	5,200
2	The Home Depot	73,094	5,001	2,000
3	Kroger	56,434	−100	2,532
4	Costco	47,146	882	400
5	Target	45,682	3,198	1,249
6	Albertson's	39,897	444	2,500
7	Walgreen's	37,508	1,350	5,240
8	Lowe's	36,464	2,176	2,300
9	Safeway	35,823	560	1,700
10	Sears	35,718	−507	2,400
11	CVS	30,594	919	4,122
12	Best Buy	27,433	984	750
13	Kmart	19,701	1,106	1,479
14	Publix	18,554	819	875
15	JC Penney	18,424	524	1,017
16	RiteAid	16,816	302	3,300
17	Gap	16,267	1,150	3,000
18	Federated Dept. Stores	15,630	689	459
19	TJX Cos. Inc.	14,913	664	1,900
20	May Inc.	14,441	524	1,229

Source: 2006 Global Powers of Retailing. Copyright © 2006 by Deloitee Touche Tohmatsu, **www.deloitte.com**; accessed January 20, 2006. Reprinted with permission.

discount store a self-service general-merchandise outlet that sells products at lower-than-usual prices

Discount Stores

A **discount store** is a self-service general-merchandise outlet that sells products at lower-than-usual prices. These stores can offer lower prices by operating on smaller markups, by locating large retail showrooms in low-rent areas, and by offering minimal customer services. To keep prices low, discount stores operate on the basic principle of high turnover of such items as appliances, toys, clothing, automotive products, and sports equipment. To attract customers, many discount stores also offer some food and household items at low prices. Popular discount stores include K Mart, Wal-Mart, Dollar General, and Target.

As competition among discount stores has increased, some discounters have improved their services, store environments, and locations. As a consequence, many of the better-known discount stores have assumed the characteristics of department stores. This upgrading has boosted their prices and blurred the distinction between some discount stores and department stores.[5]

catalog showroom a retail outlet that displays well-known brands and sells them at discount prices through catalogs within the store

warehouse showroom a retail facility in a large, low-cost building with a large on-premises inventory and minimal service

Catalog and Warehouse Showrooms

A **catalog showroom** is a retail outlet that displays well-known brands and sells them at discount prices through catalogs within the store. Colorful catalogs are available in the showroom (and sometimes by mail). The customer selects the merchandise, either from the catalog or from the showroom display. The customer fills out an order form provided by the store and hands the form to a clerk. The clerk retrieves the merchandise from a warehouse room that is adjacent to the selling area. Service Merchandise is a catalog showroom.

A **warehouse showroom** is a retail facility with five basic characteristics: (1) a large, low-cost building, (2) warehouse materials-handling technology, (3) vertical merchandise displays, (4) a large on-premises inventory, and (5) minimal service. Some of the best-known showrooms are operated by big furniture retailers. These operations employ few personnel and offer few services. Most customers carry away purchases in the manufacturer's carton, although some warehouse showrooms will deliver for a fee.

Convenience Stores

A **convenience store** is a small food store that sells a limited variety of products but remains open well beyond normal business hours. Almost 70 percent of convenience store customers live within a mile of the store. White Hen Pantry, 7-Eleven, Circle K, and Open Pantry stores, for example, are found in some areas, as are independent convenience stores. There are over 138,205 convenience stores in the United States, and two-thirds of Americans visit at least one of these locations every month. Convenience stores are the fastest-growing category of retailer, with a 5.8 percent growth in sales over the past year compared with an 8 percent decline in overall retail sales.[6] Their limited product mixes and higher prices keep convenience stores from becoming a major threat to other grocery retailers.

Supermarkets

A **supermarket** is a large self-service store that sells primarily food and household products. It stocks canned, fresh, frozen, and processed foods; paper products; and cleaning supplies. Supermarkets also may sell such items as housewares, toiletries, toys and games, drugs, stationery, books and magazines, plants and flowers, and a few clothing items.

Supermarkets are large-scale operations that emphasize low prices and one-stop shopping for household needs. A supermarket has annual sales of at least $2 million. Current top-ranking supermarkets include Kroger, Albertson's, Safeway, Winn-Dixie, and A&P. Many of these supermarket chains are finding it difficult to compete with superstores such as Wal-Mart Supercenters and are experiencing minuscule profit margins. Albertsons, Safeway, and Ahold's divisions, including BI-LO and Giant, are choosing to use funds set aside for expansion to remodel existing stores instead. They are emphasizing a neighborhood theme designed to meet the unique needs of local shoppers and to differentiate these supermarkets from superstores.[7]

Superstores

A **superstore** is a large retail store that carries not only food and nonfood products ordinarily found in supermarkets but also additional product lines—housewares, hardware, small appliances, clothing, personal-care products, garden products, and automotive merchandise. Superstores also provide a number of services to entice customers. Typically, these include automotive repair, snack bars and restaurants, film developing, and banking.

Warehouse Clubs

The **warehouse club** is a large-scale members-only establishment that combines features of cash-and-carry wholesaling with discount retailing. For a nominal annual fee (about $25), small retailers may purchase products at wholesale prices for business use or for resale. Warehouse clubs also sell to ultimate consumers. Instead of paying a membership fee, individual consumers pay about 5 percent more on each item than do small-business owners. Individual purchasers usually can choose to pay yearly dues for membership cards that allow them to avoid the 5 percent additional charge.

convenience store a small food store that sells a limited variety of products but remains open well beyond normal business hours

supermarket a large self-service store that sells primarily food and household products

superstore a large retail store that carries not only food and nonfood products ordinarily found in supermarkets but also additional product lines

warehouse club a large-scale members-only establishment that combines features of cash-and-carry wholesaling with discount retailing

Traditional specialty stores.
This Swatch store is an example of a traditional specialty store.

Warehouse clubs offer the same types of products offered by discount stores but in a limited range of sizes and styles. Because their product lines are shallow and sales volumes are high, warehouse clubs can offer a broad range of merchandise, including perishable and nonperishable foods, beverages, books, appliances, housewares, automotive parts, hardware, furniture, and sundries. The sales volume of most warehouse clubs is four to five times that of a typical department store. With stock turning over at an average rate of eighteen times each year, warehouse clubs sell their goods before manufacturers' payment periods are up, thus reducing their need for capital.

To keep their prices 20 to 40 percent lower than those of supermarkets and discount stores, warehouse clubs provide few services. They generally advertise only through direct mail. Their facilities often have concrete floors and aisles wide enough for forklifts. Merchandise is stacked on pallets or displayed on pipe racks. Usually customers must transport purchases themselves. Although at one time there were about twenty competing warehouse clubs, only two major competitors remain: Sam's Club and Costco.

traditional specialty store a store that carries a narrow product mix with deep product lines

Traditional Specialty Stores   A **traditional specialty store** carries a narrow product mix with deep product lines. Traditional specialty stores are sometimes called *limited-line retailers.* If they carry depth in one particular product category, they may be called *single-line retailers.* Specialty stores usually sell such products as clothing, jewelry, sporting goods, fabrics, computers, flowers, baked goods, books, and pet supplies. Examples of specialty stores include the Gap, Radio Shack, Bath and Body Works, and Foot Locker.

Specialty stores usually offer deeper product mixes than department stores. They attract customers by emphasizing service, atmosphere, and location. Consumers who are dissatisfied with the impersonal atmosphere of large retailers often find the attention offered by small specialty stores appealing.

off-price retailer a store that buys manufacturers' seconds, overruns, returns, and off-season merchandise for resale to consumers at deep discounts

Off-Price Retailers   An **off-price retailer** is a store that buys manufacturers' seconds, overruns, returns, and off-season merchandise at below-wholesale prices and sells them to consumers at deep discounts. Off-price retailers sell limited lines of national-brand and designer merchandise, usually clothing, shoes, or housewares. Examples of off-price retailers include T.J. Maxx, Burlington Coat Factory, and Marshalls. Off-price stores charge up to 50 percent less than department stores do for comparable merchandise but offer few customer services. They often include community dressing rooms and central checkout counters, and some off-price retailers have a no-returns, no-exchanges policy.

category killer a very large specialty store that concentrates on a single product line and competes on the basis of low prices and product availability

Category Killers   A **category killer** is a very large specialty store that concentrates on a single product line and competes by offering low prices and an enormous number of products. These stores are called *category killers* because they take business away from smaller, high-cost retail stores. Examples of category killers include Home Depot (building materials), Office Depot (office supplies and equipment), and Best Buy (electronics), all of which are leaders in their niche. Toys "R" Us, one of the original category killers, has a bleak future; the inability to maintain high sales year round with a market that focuses on the holidays has had its effect on the toy retailer. Some experts

Category killers. Home Depot is a category killer for home improvement products.

are predicting a decrease in the number of large-scale category killers in the not so distant future owing to other stores focusing on even smaller niches.[8]

Kinds of Nonstore Retailing

Nonstore retailing is selling that does not take place in conventional store facilities; consumers purchase products without visiting a store. This form of retailing accounts for an increasing percentage of total retail sales. Nonstore retailers use direct selling, direct marketing, and vending machines.

Direct Selling **Direct selling** is the marketing of products to customers through face-to-face sales presentations at home or in the workplace. Traditionally called *door-to-door selling*, direct selling in the United States began with peddlers more than a century ago and has since grown into a sizable industry that generates about $30 billion in U.S. sales annually.[9] Instead of the door-to-door approach, many companies today—such as Mary Kay, Kirby, Amway, and Avon—use other approaches. They identify customers by mail, telephone, the Internet, or at shopping malls and then set up appointments. Direct selling sometimes involves the "party plan," which can occur in the customer's home or workplace. One customer will act as a host and invite friends and coworkers to view merchandise in a group setting where the salesperson demonstrates the products. Direct selling through the party plan requires effective salespeople who can identify potential hosts and provide encouragement and incentives for them to organize a gathering of friends and associates. Companies that commonly use the party plan are Tupperware, Stanley Home Products, Pampered Chef, and Sarah Coventry. Mary Kay also uses the party plan by holding group pajama parties, makeovers, and girls' nights out.

Direct selling has both benefits and limitations. It gives the marketer an opportunity to demonstrate the product in an environment—usually customers' homes—where it most likely would be used. Some companies, such as Kirby Vacuums, will even clean the carpet in your home while they demonstrate their product. The direct seller can give the customer personal attention, and the product can be presented to the customer at a convenient time and location. Personal attention to the customer is the foundation on which some direct sellers have built their businesses. For example, your Mary Kay salesperson can recommend beauty and skin products tailored to your special needs. Because commissions are so high, ranging from 30 to 50 percent of the sales price, and great effort is required to isolate promising prospects, overall costs of direct selling make it a very expensive form of retailing. Furthermore, some customers view direct selling negatively owing to unscrupulous and fraudulent practices used by some direct sellers in the past. Some communities even have local ordinances that control or, in some cases, prohibit door-to-door selling.

Direct Marketing **Direct marketing** is the use of the telephone, Internet, and nonpersonal media to communicate product and organizational information to customers, who then can purchase products via mail, telephone, or the Internet. Direct marketing is one type of nonstore retailing. Direct marketing can occur through catalog marketing, direct-response marketing, telemarketing, television home shopping, and online marketing.

In **catalog marketing,** an organization provides a catalog from which customers make selections and place orders by mail, telephone, or the Internet. Catalog market-

nonstore retailing a type of retailing whereby consumers purchase products without visiting a store

direct selling the marketing of products to customers through face-to-face sales presentations at home or in the workplace

direct marketing the use of the telephone, Internet, and nonpersonal media to introduce products to customers, who then can purchase them via mail, telephone, or the Internet

catalog marketing a type of marketing in which an organization provides a catalog from which customers make selections and place orders by mail, telephone, or the Internet

ing began in 1872, when Montgomery Ward issued its first catalog to rural families. Today, there are more than 7,000 catalog marketing companies in the United States, as well as a number of retail stores, such as JC Penney, that engage in catalog marketing. Some organizations, including Spiegel and JC Penney, offer a broad array of products spread over multiple product lines. Catalog companies such as Lands' End, Pottery Barn, and J. Crew offer considerable depth in one major line of products. Still other catalog companies specialize in only a few products within a single line. The advantages of catalog marketing include efficiency and convenience for customers. The retailer benefits by being able to locate in remote, low-cost areas, save on expensive store fixtures, and reduce both personal selling and store operating expenses. On the other hand, catalog marketing is inflexible, provides limited service, and is most effective for only a selected set of products.

Even though the cost of mailing catalogs continues to rise, catalog sales are growing at double the rate of in-store retailing. Williams-Sonoma, for example, sells kitchenware and home and garden products through five catalogs, including Pottery Barn and Gardeners' Eden. Catalog sales have been increasing owing to the convenience of catalog shopping. Product quality is often high, and because consumers can call toll free 24 hours a day or order online, charge purchases to a credit card, and have the merchandise delivered to their door in one to two days, such shopping is much easier than going to a store.

direct-response marketing a type of marketing in which a retailer advertises a product and makes it available through mail, telephone, or online orders

Direct-response marketing occurs when a retailer advertises a product and makes it available through mail, telephone, or online orders. Examples of direct-response marketing include a television commercial offering a recording artist's musical collection, a newspaper or magazine advertisement for a series of children's books, and even a billboard promoting floral services available by calling 1-800-Flowers. Direct-response marketing is also conducted by sending letters, samples, brochures, or booklets to prospects on a mailing list and asking that they order the advertised products by mail, telephone, or online.

telemarketing the performance of marketing-related activities by telephone

Telemarketing is the performance of marketing-related activities by telephone. Some organizations use a prescreened list of prospective clients. Telemarketing can help generate sales leads, improve customer service, speed up payments on past-due accounts, raise funds for nonprofit organizations, and gather marketing data.

Currently, the laws and regulations regarding telemarketing, while in a state of flux, are becoming more restrictive. Several states have established do-not-call lists of customers who do not want to receive telemarketing calls from companies. On October 1, 2003, the U.S. Congress implemented the national do-not-call registry for consumers who do not want to receive telemarketing calls. After the first two years, the do-not-call registry listed over 100 million phone numbers. Regulations associated with the national do-not-call registry are enforced by the Federal Trade Commission (FTC). Companies are subject to fines of up to $12,000 for each call made to consumers listed on the national do-not-call registry.[10] For example, DirecTV recently was ordered to pay $5.3 million in fines by the FTC for violating the do-not-call list.[11] Certain exceptions apply to no-call lists. A company still can use telemarketing to communicate with existing customers. In addition, charitable, political, and telephone survey organizations are not restricted by the national registry.

television home shopping a form of selling in which products are presented to television viewers, who can buy them by calling a toll-free number and paying with a credit card

Television home shopping presents products to television viewers, encouraging them to order through toll-free numbers and pay with credit cards. Home Shopping Network (HSN) originated and popularized this format. The most popular products sold through television home shopping are jewelry (40 percent of total sales), clothing, housewares, and electronics. Home shopping channels have grown so rapidly in recent years that more than 60 percent of U.S. households have access to home shopping programs. HSN and QVC are two of the largest home shopping networks. With the growing popularity of this medium, new channels are being added, even ones that specialize on one specific product category, such as Jewelry Television. Approximately 60 percent of home shopping sales revenues come from repeat purchasers.

The television home shopping format offers several benefits. Products can be demonstrated easily, and an adequate amount of time can be spent showing the product so as to make viewers well informed. The length of time a product is shown depends not only on the time required for doing the demonstration but also on whether the product is selling. Once the calls peak and begin to decline, a new product is shown. Another benefit is that customers can shop at their convenience from the comfort of their homes. HSN has made this even easier by teaming up with GoldPocket Interactive to equip television remotes with buying power. Users with a special settop box and an HSN account will be able to charge the items being displayed to their accounts by pressing a button on their remote instead of calling by phone.[12]

Online retailing makes products available to buyers through computer connections. Most bricks-and-mortar retailers have websites to sell products, provide information about their company, or distribute coupons. Consumers also can bid on anything from concert tickets, automobiles, or even a wedge of cheese shaped like Elvis on eBay. Netflix has changed the video rental industry by offering its completely online movie rental service. Customers pay a monthly fee for unlimited rentals and browse the Netflix site to compose a list of videos they want to rent. Selections are mailed to their home, and customers are free to keep the rental as long as they want without the late fees typically charged by traditional stores.[13] Brokerage firms have established websites to give their customers direct access to manage their accounts and enable them to trade online. With advances in computer technology continuing and consumers ever more pressed for time, online retailing will continue to escalate. Although online retailing represents a major retailing venue, security remains an issue. In a recent survey conducted by the Business Software Alliance, some Internet users still expressed concerns about shopping online. The major issues are identity theft and credit card theft.

online retailing retailing that makes products available to buyers through computer connections

SPOTLIGHT

Benefits of online marketing

Researchers report that the four major advantages of online marketing are increased revenue, greater visibility, cost savings, and reaching new customers.

Increased revenue ▶ 73%

Greater visibility ▶ 58%

Cost savings ▶ 56%

Reaching new customers ▶ 54%

Search [____] GO   Clothing Footwear Accessories Home

Source: Mutlichannel Marketing 2005 Report, DMA

Automatic Vending **Automatic vending** is the use of machines to dispense products. It accounts for less than 2 percent of all retail sales. Video game machines provide an entertainment service, and many banks offer automatic teller machines (ATMs), which dispense cash and perform other services.

automatic vending the use of machines to dispense products

Automatic vending is one of the most impersonal forms of retailing. Small, standardized, routinely purchased products (e.g., chewing gum, candy, newspapers, cigarettes, soft drinks, and coffee) can be sold in machines because consumers usually buy them at the nearest available location. Machines in areas of heavy traffic provide efficient and continuous service to consumers. Such high-volume areas may have more diverse product availability—for example, hot and cold sandwiches, DVD rentals, or even iPods (yes, $200 iPods are available in machines with coin slots). San Francisco–based company Zoom Systems has expanded its vending machine offerings from snacks to digital cameras. But their number one seller is the iPod vending machine that offers Apple's popular MP3 players as well as accessories such as headphones, speakers, and battery chargers.[14]

Since vending machines need only a small amount of space and no sales personnel, this retailing method has some advantages over stores. These advantages are partly offset, however, by the high costs of equipment and frequent servicing and repairs.

Planned Shopping Centers

8 LEARNING OBJECTIVE
Identify the categories of shopping centers and the factors that determine how shopping centers are classified.

The planned shopping center is a self-contained retail facility constructed by independent owners and consisting of various stores. Shopping centers are designed and promoted to serve diverse groups of customers with widely differing needs. The

Lifestyle shopping centers.
The Village of Rochester Hills shopping center is one example of a lifestyle shopping center.

management of a shopping center strives for a coordinated mix of stores, a comfortable atmosphere, adequate parking, pleasant landscaping, and special events to attract customers. The convenience of shopping for most family and household needs in a single location is an important part of shopping-center appeal.

A planned shopping center is one of four types: lifestyle, neighborhood, community, or regional. Although shopping centers vary, each offers a complementary mix of stores for the purpose of generating consumer traffic.

Lifestyle Shopping Centers

lifestyle shopping center an open-air-environment shopping center with upscale chain specialty stores

A **lifestyle shopping center** is a shopping center that has an open-air configuration and is occupied by upscale national chain specialty stores. The lifestyle center is more convenient than a traditional enclosed mall and offers the same quality of upscale retail, department stores, movie theaters, and dining. A strong emphasis is placed on the architecture of the center and creating a pleasant and "hip" shopping environment. Most lifestyle centers are found in affluent neighborhoods.[15]

Neighborhood Shopping Centers

neighborhood shopping center a planned shopping center consisting of several small convenience and specialty stores

A **neighborhood shopping center** typically consists of several small convenience and specialty stores. Businesses in neighborhood shopping centers might include small grocery stores, drugstores, gas stations, and fast-food restaurants. These retailers serve consumers who live less than ten minutes away, usually within a two- to three-mile radius of the stores. Because most purchases in the neighborhood shopping center are based on convenience or personal contact, these retailers generally make only limited efforts to coordinate promotional activities among stores in the shopping center.

Community Shopping Centers

community shopping center a planned shopping center that includes one or two department stores and some specialty stores, along with convenience stores

A **community shopping center** includes one or two department stores and some specialty stores, along with convenience stores. It attracts consumers from a wider geographic area who will drive longer distances to find products and specialty items unavailable in neighborhood shopping centers. Community shopping centers, which are carefully planned and coordinated, generate traffic with special events such as art exhibits, automobile shows, and sidewalk sales. The management of a community shopping center maintains a balance of tenants so that the center can offer wide product mixes and deep product lines.

Regional Shopping Centers

A **regional shopping center** usually has large department stores, numerous specialty stores, restaurants, movie theaters, and sometimes even hotels. It carries most of the merchandise offered by a downtown shopping district. Downtown merchants, in fact, often have renovated their stores and enlarged their parking facilities to meet the competition of successful regional shopping centers. Urban expressways and improved public transportation also have helped many downtown shopping areas to remain vigorous.

Regional shopping centers carefully coordinate management and marketing activities to reach the 150,000 or more customers in their target market. These large centers usually advertise, hold special events, and provide transportation to certain groups of customers. They also maintain a suitable mix of stores. National chain stores can gain leases in regional shopping centers more easily than small independent stores because they are better able to meet the centers' financial requirements.

regional shopping center a planned shopping center containing large department stores, numerous specialty stores, restaurants, movie theaters, and sometimes even hotels

9 LEARNING OBJECTIVE
Explain the five most important physical distribution activities.

physical distribution all those activities concerned with the efficient movement of products from the producer to the ultimate user

inventory management the process of managing inventories in such a way as to minimize inventory costs, including both holding costs and potential stock-out costs

Physical Distribution

Physical distribution is all those activities concerned with the efficient movement of products from the producer to the ultimate user. Physical distribution therefore is the movement of the products themselves—both goods and services—through their channels of distribution. It is a combination of several interrelated business functions. The most important of these are inventory management, order processing, warehousing, materials handling, and transportation.

Not too long ago each of these functions was considered distinct from all the others. In a fairly large firm, one group or department would handle each function. Each of these groups would work to minimize its own costs and to maximize its own effectiveness, but the result was usually high physical distribution costs.

Various studies of the problem emphasized both the interrelationships among the physical distribution functions and the relationships between physical distribution and other marketing functions. Long production runs may reduce per-unit product costs, but they can cause inventory-control and warehousing costs to skyrocket. A new automated warehouse may reduce materials-handling costs, but if the warehouse is not located properly, transportation time and costs may increase substantially. Because of such interrelationships, marketers now view physical distribution as an integrated effort that provides important marketing functions: getting the right product to the right place at the right time and at minimal overall cost.

Inventory Management

In Chapter 9 we discussed inventory management from the standpoint of operations. We defined **inventory management** as the process of managing inventories in such a way as to minimize inventory costs, including both

Inventory management technology. This handheld inventory management device allows employees to have an instant overview of every item—and its price—in the warehouse at any given time.

EXAMINING ETHICS

Too Much Information

A growing number of businesses are using radio frequency identification (RFID) tags, computer chips equipped with a radio transmitter, for inventory management. Pacific Cycle, maker of Schwinn bicycles, tags each bike so that it can track products from factory to warehouse to store. However, critics worry about the potential for invasion of privacy. What does RFID mean to each side?

Businesses can use RFID to do the following:

- Quickly verify shipment receipt, contents, and location
- Fill orders more accurately
- Reduce out-of-stock situations
- Protect expensive items from theft

Privacy advocates worry that

- Everything that individual consumers buy will be recorded and monitored.
- Data about how, where, and when a product is used could be collected indefinitely.
- Consumers cannot control how companies use data collected through RFID.
- Data could be collected without consumers' awareness or consent.

So is RFID an aid to inventory management or a threat to privacy?

holding costs and potential stock-out costs. Both the definition and the objective of inventory control apply here as well.

Holding costs are the costs of storing products until they are purchased or shipped to customers. *Stock-out costs* are the costs of sales lost when items are not in inventory. Of course, holding costs can be reduced by minimizing inventories, but then stock-out costs could be financially threatening to the organization. And stock-out costs can be minimized by carrying very large inventories, but then holding costs would be enormous.

Inventory management therefore is a sort of balancing act between stock-out costs and holding costs. The latter include the cost of money invested in inventory, the cost of storage space, insurance costs, and inventory taxes. Often even a relatively small reduction in inventory investment can provide a relatively large increase in working capital. And sometimes this reduction can best be accomplished through a willingness to incur a reasonable level of stock-out costs.

Companies frequently rely on technology and software to help manage inventory on a regular basis and for special situations. For example, Wal-Mart used Retail Link, predictive technology based on past customer purchases, to prepare its stores for Hurricane Frances. By analyzing purchases made before the arrivals of other hurricanes, Wal-Mart was able to effectively anticipate its customers' special needs, from flashlights to Pop-Tarts. Most of the products that Wal-Mart specifically stocked in anticipation of the storm were sold out.[16]

Order Processing

order processing activities involved in receiving and filling customers' purchase orders

Order processing consists of activities involved in receiving and filling customers' purchase orders. It may include not only the means by which customers order products but also procedures for billing and for granting credit.

Fast, efficient order processing is an important marketing service—one that can provide a dramatic competitive edge. The people who purchase goods for intermediaries are especially concerned with their suppliers' promptness and reliability in order processing. To them, promptness and reliability mean minimal inventory costs as well as the ability to order goods when they are needed rather than weeks in advance. The Internet is providing new opportunities for improving services associated with order processing.

Warehousing

warehousing the set of activities involved in receiving and storing goods and preparing them for reshipment

Warehousing is the set of activities involved in receiving and storing goods and preparing them for reshipment. Goods are stored to create time utility; that is, they are held until they are needed for use or sale. Warehousing includes the following activities:

- *Receiving goods*—The warehouse accepts delivered goods and assumes responsibility for them.
- *Identifying goods*—Records are made of the quantity of each item received. Items may be marked, coded, or tagged for identification.

- *Sorting goods*—Delivered goods may have to be sorted before being stored.
- *Dispatching goods to storage*—Items must be moved to specific storage areas, where they can be found later.
- *Holding goods*—The goods are kept in storage under proper protection until needed.
- *Recalling, picking, and assembling goods*—Items that are to leave the warehouse must be selected from storage and assembled efficiently.
- *Dispatching shipments*—Each shipment is packaged suitably and directed to the proper transport vehicle. Shipping and accounting documents are prepared.

A firm may use its own warehouses or rent space in public warehouses. A *private warehouse*, owned and operated by a particular firm, can be designed to serve the firm's specific needs. However, the organization must take on the task of financing the facility, determining the best location for it, and ensuring that it is used fully. Generally, only companies that deal in large quantities of goods can justify private warehouses. With a total of almost ninety million square feet in warehouse space, United Parcel Service (UPS) owns the largest amount of private warehouse space in the world. Wal-Mart is second with sixty-five million, and Target is third with thirty-five million.[17]

Public warehouses offer their services to all individuals and firms. Most are huge one-story structures on the outskirts of cities, where rail and truck transportation are easily available. They provide storage facilities, areas for sorting and assembling shipments, and office and display spaces for wholesalers and retailers. Public warehouses also will hold—and issue receipts for—goods used as collateral for borrowed funds.

Many organizations locate and design their warehouses not only to be cost-efficient but also to provide excellent customer service.

Materials Handling

Materials handling is the actual physical handling of goods—in warehouses as well as during transportation. Proper materials-handling procedures and techniques can increase the usable capacity of a warehouse or that of any means of transportation. Proper handling can reduce breakage and spoilage as well.

Modern materials handling attempts to reduce the number of times a product is handled. One method is called *unit loading*. Several smaller cartons, barrels, or boxes are combined into a single standard-size load that can be handled efficiently by forklift, conveyer, or truck.

materials handling the actual physical handling of goods, in warehouses as well as during transportation

Transportation

As a part of physical distribution, **transportation** is simply the shipment of products to customers. The greater the distance between seller and purchaser, the more important is the choice of the means of transportation and the particular carrier.

A firm that offers transportation services is called a **carrier.** A *common carrier* is a transportation firm whose services are available to all shippers. Railroads, airlines, and most long-distance trucking firms are common carriers. A *contract carrier* is available for hire by one or several shippers. Contract carriers do not serve the general public. Moreover, the number of firms they can handle at any one time is limited by law. A *private carrier* is owned and operated by the shipper.

In addition, a shipper can hire agents called *freight forwarders* to handle its transportation. Freight forwarders pick up shipments from the shipper, ensure that the goods are loaded on selected carriers, and assume responsibility for safe delivery of the shipments to their destinations. Freight forwarders often can group a number of small shipments into one large load (which is carried at a lower rate). This, of course, saves money for shippers.

The U.S. Postal Service offers *parcel post* delivery, which is used widely by mail-order houses. The Postal Service provides complete geographic coverage at the lowest rates, but it limits the size and weight of the shipments it will accept. UPS, a

transportation the shipment of products to customers

carrier a firm that offers transportation services

Waterways. Waterway transportation is used to move heavy, non-perishable products, such as large equipment, grain, motor vehicles, and chemicals.

privately owned firm, also provides small-parcel services for shippers. Other privately owned carriers, such as Federal Express, DHL, and Airborne, offer fast—often overnight—parcel delivery both within and outside the United States. There are also many local parcel carriers, including specialized delivery services for various time-sensitive industries, such as publishing.

The six major criteria used for selecting transportation modes are compared in Table 15.2. Obviously, the *cost* of a transportation mode is important to marketers. At times, marketers choose higher-cost modes of transportation because of the benefits they provide. *Speed* is measured by the total time that a carrier possesses the products, including time required for pickup and delivery, handling, and movement between point of origin and destination. Usually there is a direct relationship between cost and speed; that is, faster modes of transportation are more expensive. A transportation mode's *dependability* is determined by the consistency of service provided by that mode. *Load flexibility* is the degree to which a transportation mode can provide appropriate equipment and conditions for moving specific kinds of products and can be adapted for moving other kinds of products. For example, certain types of products may need controlled temperatures or humidity levels. *Accessibility* refers to a transportation mode's ability to move goods over a specific route or network. *Frequency* refers to how often a marketer can ship products by a specific transportation mode. Whereas pipelines provide continuous shipments, railroads and waterways follow specific schedules for moving products from one location to another. In Table 15.2, each transportation mode is rated on a relative basis for these six selection criteria. Figure 15.3 shows recent trends and a breakdown by use of the five different modes of transportation.

Railroads   In terms of total freight carried, railroads are America's most important mode of transportation. They are also the least expensive for many products. Almost all railroads are common carriers, although a few coal-mining companies operate their own lines.

> ▶▶ **TABLE 15.2**

RELATIVE RATINGS OF TRANSPORTATION MODES BY SELECTION CRITERIA

	Selection Criteria					
Mode	Cost	Speed	Dependability	Load Flexibility	Accessibility	Frequency
Railroads	Moderate	Average	Average	High	High	Low
Trucks	High	Fast	High	Average	Very high	High
Airplanes	Very high	Very fast	High	Low	Average	Average
Waterways	Very low	Very slow	Average	Very high	Limited	Very low
Pipelines	Low	Slow	High	Very low	Very limited	Very high

>> **FIGURE 15.3**

CHANGES IN TON-MILES FOR VARIOUS TRANSPORTATION MODES

Between 1980 and 2005, ton-miles for airlines, railroads, and trucks increased significantly, whereas pipeline and waterway usage remained steady. Examples of typical products carried by the various modes are shown here.

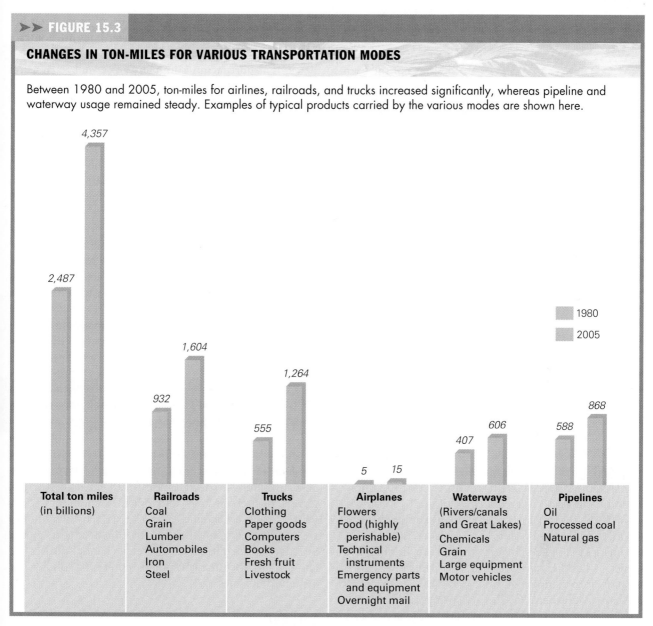

Total ton miles (in billions)	Railroads	Trucks	Airplanes	Waterways	Pipelines
	Coal	Clothing	Flowers	(Rivers/canals	Oil
	Grain	Paper goods	Food (highly	and Great Lakes)	Processed coal
	Lumber	Computers	perishable)	Chemicals	Natural gas
	Automobiles	Books	Technical	Grain	
	Iron	Fresh fruit	instruments	Large equipment	
	Steel	Livestock	Emergency parts	Motor vehicles	
			and equipment		
			Overnight mail		

Legend: 1980, 2005

Source: U.S. Bureau of Transportation Statistics, *National Transportation Statistics 2005*, **www.bts.gov**; accessed January 30, 2006.

Many commodities carried by railroads could not be transported easily by any other means. They include a wide range of foodstuffs, raw materials, and manufactured goods. Coal ranks first by a considerable margin. Other major commodities carried by railroads include grain, paper and pulp products, liquids in tank-car loads, heavy equipment, and lumber.

Trucks   The trucking industry consists of common, contract, and private carriers. It has undergone tremendous expansion since the creation of a national highway system in the 1920s. Trucks can move goods to suburban and rural areas not served by railroads. They can handle freight quickly and economically, and they carry a wide range of shipments. Many shippers favor this mode of transportation because it offers door-to-door service, less stringent packaging requirements than ships and airplanes, and flexible delivery schedules.

Railroad and truck carriers have teamed up to provide a form of transportation called *piggyback*. Truck trailers are carried from city to city on specially equipped railroad flatcars. Within each city, the trailers are then pulled in the usual way by truck tractors.

Airplanes   Air transport is the fastest but most expensive means of transportation. All certified airlines are common carriers. Supplemental or charter lines are contract carriers.

Because of the high cost, lack of airport facilities in many areas, and reliance on weather conditions, airlines carry less than 1 percent of all intercity freight. Only high-value or perishable items, such as flowers, aircraft parts, and pharmaceuticals or goods that are needed immediately, usually are shipped by air.

Waterways   Cargo ships and barges offer the least expensive, but slowest, form of transportation. They are used mainly for bulky nonperishable goods such as chemicals, grain, motor vehicles, and large equipment. Of course, shipment by water is limited to cities located on navigable waterways. But ships and barges account for about 14 percent of all intercity freight hauling.

Pipelines   Pipelines are a highly specialized mode of transportation. They are used primarily to carry petroleum and natural gas. Pipelines have become more important as the nation's need for petroleum products has increased. Such products as semiliquid coal and wood chips also can be shipped through pipelines continuously, reliably, and with minimal handling.

In the next chapter we discuss the fourth element of the marketing mix—promotion.

RETURN TO   Inside Business

Thanks to an efficient and effective direct-marketing strategy, Dell's revenue tops $50 billion, and it enjoys a 32 percent share of the U.S. PC market. In many cases the company can book an order, build the PC, and receive payment before it must pay suppliers for the components in that product. When PC sales are slow, the firm's low costs allow it to compete on price and increase its market share. And when PC sales are strong, Dell can introduce new models at attractive prices to keep orders and profits rolling in.

Dell's main target market these days is the business customer who needs not just PCs but also servers, printers, storage systems, and technology services. These customers are less price sensitive and are accustomed to buying directly from producers. Still, Dell may continue to test retail channels for certain products because consumers represent a solid 15 percent of its sales.

Questions

1. Why would Costco agree to carry a few Dell products for a limited time?
2. How important is physical distribution to Dell's profitability? Explain your answer.

▶▶ CHAPTER REVIEW

Summary

1

Identify the various channels of distribution that are used for consumer and industrial products.

A marketing channel is a sequence of marketing organizations that directs a product from producer to ultimate user. The marketing channel for a particular product is concerned with the transfer of ownership of that product. Merchant middlemen (merchants) actually take title to products, whereas functional middlemen simply aid in the transfer of title.

The channels used for consumer products include the direct channel from producer to consumer; the channel from producer to retailer to consumer; the channel from producer to wholesaler to retailer to consumer; and the channel from producer to agent to wholesaler to retailer to consumer. There are two major channels of industrial products: (1) producer to user and (2) producer to agent middleman to user.

2

Explain the concept of market coverage.

Channels and intermediaries are chosen to implement a given level of market coverage. Intensive distribution is the use of all available outlets for a product, providing the widest market coverage. Selective distribution uses only a portion of the available outlets in an area. Exclusive distribution uses only a single retail outlet for a product in a large geographic area.

3

Understand how supply-chain management facilitates partnering among channel members.

Supply-chain management is a long-term partnership among channel members working together to create a distribution system that reduces inefficiencies, costs, and redundancies while creating a competitive advantage and satisfying customers. Cooperation is required among all channel members, including manufacturing, research, sales, advertising, and shipping. When all channel partners work together, delivery, scheduling, packaging, and other customer requirements are better met. Technology, such as bar coding and electronic data exchange (EDI), makes supply-chain management easier to implement.

4

Describe what a vertical marketing system is and identify the types of vertical marketing systems.

A vertical marketing system (VMS) is a centrally managed system. It results when two or more channel members from different levels combine under one management. Administered, contractual, and corporate systems represent the three major types of VMSs.

5

Discuss the need for wholesalers and describe the services they provide to retailers and manufacturers.

Wholesalers are intermediaries that purchase from producers or other intermediaries and sell to industrial users, retailers, or other wholesalers. Wholesalers perform many functions in a distribution channel. If they are eliminated, other channel members—such as the producer or retailers—must perform these functions. Wholesalers provide retailers with help in promoting products, collecting information, and financing. They provide manufacturers with sales help, reduce their inventory costs, furnish market information, and extend credit to retailers.

6

Identify and describe the major types of wholesalers.

Merchant wholesalers buy and then sell products. Commission merchants and brokers are essentially agents and do not take title to the goods they distribute. Sales branches and offices are owned by the manufacturers they represent and resemble merchant wholesalers and agents, respectively.

7

Distinguish among the major types of retailers.

Retailers are intermediaries that buy from producers or wholesalers and sell to consumers. In-store retailers include department stores, discount stores, catalog and warehouse showrooms, convenience stores, supermarkets, superstores, warehouse clubs, traditional specialty stores, off-price retailers, and category killers. Nonstore retailers do not sell in conventional store facilities. Instead, they use direct selling, direct marketing, and automatic vending. Types of direct marketing include catalog marketing, direct-response marketing, telemarketing, television home shopping, and online retailing.

8

Identify the categories of shopping centers and the factors that determine how shopping centers are classified.

There are three major types of shopping centers: neighborhood, community, and regional. A center fits one of these categories based on its mix of stores and the size of the geographic area it serves.

9

Explain the five most important physical distribution activities.

Physical distribution consists of activities designed to move products from producers to ultimate users. Its five major functions are inventory management, order processing, warehousing, materials handling, and transportation. These interrelated functions are integrated into the marketing effort.

Key Terms

You should now be able to define and give an example relevant to each of the following terms:

channel of distribution (or marketing channel) (481)
middleman (or marketing intermediary) (481)
merchant middleman (481)
functional middleman (481)
retailer (481)
wholesaler (481)
intensive distribution (483)
selective distribution (484)
exclusive distribution (484)
supply-chain management (484)
vertical channel integration (485)
vertical marketing system (VMS) (485)
merchant wholesaler (488)
full-service wholesaler (488)
general-merchandise wholesaler (488)
limited-line wholesaler (488)
specialty-line wholesaler (488)
limited-service wholesaler (488)
commission merchant (488)
agent (488)
broker (488)
manufacturer's sales branch (489)
manufacturer's sales office (489)
independent retailer (489)
chain retailer (489)
department store (489)
discount store (490)
catalog showroom (490)
warehouse showroom (490)
convenience store (491)
supermarket (491)

superstore (491)
warehouse club (491)
traditional specialty store (492)
off-price retailer (492)
category killer (492)
nonstore retailing (493)
direct selling (493)
direct marketing (493)
catalog marketing (493)
direct-response marketing (494)
telemarketing (494)
television home shopping (494)
online retailing (495)
automatic vending (495)
lifestyle shopping center (496)
neighborhood shopping center (496)
community shopping center (496)
regional shopping center (497)
physical distribution (497)
inventory management (497)
order processing (498)
warehousing (498)
materials handling (499)
transportation (499)
carrier (499)

Review Questions

1. In what ways is a channel of distribution different from the path taken by a product during physical distribution?
2. What are the most common marketing channels for consumer products? For industrial products?
3. What are the three general approaches to market coverage? What types of products are each used for?
4. What is a vertical marketing system? Identify examples of the three types of VMSs.
5. List the services performed by wholesalers. For whom is each service performed?
6. What is the basic difference between a merchant wholesaler and an agent?
7. Identify three kinds of full-service wholesalers. What factors are used to classify wholesalers into one of these categories?
8. Distinguish between (a) commission merchants and agents and (b) manufacturers' sales branches and manufacturers' sales offices.
9. What is the basic difference between wholesalers and retailers?
10. What is the difference between a department store and a discount store with regard to selling orientation and philosophy?
11. How do (a) convenience stores, (b) traditional specialty stores, and (c) category killers compete with other retail outlets?
12. What can nonstore retailers offer their customers that in-store retailers cannot?
13. Compare and contrast community shopping centers and regional shopping centers.
14. What is physical distribution? Which major functions does it include?
15. What activities besides storage are included in warehousing?

16. List the primary modes of transportation and cite at least one advantage of each.

Discussion Questions

1. Which distribution channels would producers of services be most likely to use? Why?
2. Many producers sell to consumers both directly and through middlemen. How can such a producer justify competing with its own middlemen?
3. In what situations might a producer use agents or commission merchants rather than its own sales offices or branches?
4. If a middleman is eliminated from a marketing channel, under what conditions will costs decrease? Under what conditions will costs increase? Will the middleman's functions be eliminated? Explain.
5. Which types of retail outlets are best suited to intensive distribution? To selective distribution? To exclusive distribution? Explain your answer in each case.
6. How are the various physical distribution functions related to each other? To the other elements of the marketing mix?

►► VIDEO CASE 15.1

REI: The Great Indoors

Few retailers allow customers to test ride mountain bikes on special indoor trails or let them pour water through different filtration devices before they decide which model to purchase. An open invitation to "try it before you buy it" is just one reason why Recreational Equipment, Inc. (REI), stands out in the world of retailing.

REI was founded in 1938 by twenty-five mountain climbers who pooled their buying power to get a better deal on ice axes and other climbing gear. From the start, REI was a consumer cooperative: a retail business that shares some of its profits with members. Today, the retailer sells a vast array of outdoor sporting goods and apparel through eighty stores in twenty-four states, a printed catalog, and a website, as well as by telephone.

The in-store shopping experience is an adventure in itself. Every REI store contains a two-story climbing wall where customers can try gear before buying. For example, the store in Sandy, Utah, features a twenty-two-foot-high climbing wall modeled after the granite walls of a local canyon. Like other stores in the chain, the Sandy store has demonstration areas devoted to camp stoves, water-filter testing, and hiking boots. Surrounding these special areas are acres and acres of items that one employee calls "grown-up toys," from kayaks and canteens to snow shoes and sleeping bags.

REI's retail website features page after page of details about 50,000 products in stock, as well as how-to articles about outdoor sports and equipment. Customers can shop the site from home or order from Internet kiosks set up in each store. More than one-third of REI.com's customers arrange to pick up their online orders at a nearby REI store, which eliminates shipping fees. And when customers pick up their orders in the store, they keep shopping—spending as much as $85 more per visit.

Customers can become members of the REI cooperative by paying a one-time fee of $15. They are then eligible for refund vouchers of up to 10 percent on their total annual purchases from REI stores, catalogs, and websites. They also pay lower prices for equipment rented or repaired in REI stores.

One of REI's core values is its ongoing commitment to protecting the natural environment by donating to nature centers, open-space projects, youth recreation programs, land conservation, and related activities in local communities. Moreover, as REI's president notes, store employees invest a great deal of "sweat equity" in the local community by volunteering their time to maintain hiking trails, clean up rivers, and preserve the environment in many other ways.

The market for outdoor sporting goods and apparel is highly competitive. One key rival is Bass Pro Shops, which targets customers who like fishing, hunting, and boating. Another is Eastern Mountain Sports (EMS), which operates 100 stores in eastern and midwestern states. In addition, REI competes with many independent stores and chain retailers that carry clothing and gear for the active lifestyle.

REI now generates more than $885 million in revenue and serves two million customers yearly. Its eighty stores range in size from 10,000 to 95,000 square feet, so no two stores carry exactly the same merchandise. "Even though we don't have a lot of stores, we have a lot of variety in our stores," says REI's inventory planning manager, "and that creates merchandising challenges for us." REI's solution: Analyze the profitability and sales per square foot of each product category in each store, and then eliminate the weakest categories to make room for the strongest. This helps the retailer to manage inventory more efficiently and choose the most profitable assortment for each store.[18]

For more information about this company, go to **www.rei.com.**

Questions

1. Knowing that it incurs transportation costs to ship merchandise to each store, what are the advantages and disadvantages of REI waiving shipping fees for merchandise ordered online that is picked up in a store?
2. How would you classify REI as an in-store retailer? Support your answer.
3. REI opens a handful of new stores every year. Would you recommend that the company invest more heavily in online retailing than in-store retailing? Why?

►►CASE 15.2

Grainger Gets It Done

W. W. Grainger ships 80,000 orders every day to business customers who call, click, or stop by to purchase maintenance, repair, and operating (MRO) supplies. Grainger is an industrial distributor offering virtually one-stop shopping for producer, government, and institutional markets. With more than 575 distribution branches and 13 distribution centers spread across North America, the company can time shipments to arrive quickly when business customers place orders.

William W. Grainger founded the Illinois-based company in the 1920s as a wholesaler of electric motors. In less than a decade, the firm was operating fifteen U.S. sales branches and serving business customers from coast to coast. By 1949, the branch network had expanded to thirty states. Today, Grainger offers 2.5 million products, rings up more than $5.5 billion in annual sales, and prints 1.5 million copies of its red-cover catalog every year.

The company puts a high priority on using technology to streamline the supply chain. In the early 1990s, it put a satellite dish on the roof of every branch to communicate with headquarters about sales and orders, inventory levels, and other operational details. In 1995, it launched Grainger.com as a comprehensive catalog site for businesses seeking the convenience of browsing and buying online. Since then, the company has continued to refine its Internet presence by adding live-chat customer assistance, a virtual tour of the site for new customers, special international services, and web-only price promotions. In its first ten years of operation, Grainger.com sold $2 billion worth of merchandise—and it continues to generate revenue increases year after year.

Despite its success with online distribution, Grainger is not abandoning its branch system. It is closing less productive branches, opening larger branches near major metropolitan centers, and hiring more sales staff. The company also has opened convenient on-site branches for two big customers, Florida State University and Langley Air Force Base. "Our customers are trying to keep a business running," notes Grainger's vice president of branch services. "It's imperative that we have products and services available when and where the customer needs them."

To prepare for future growth, Grainger has opened nine additional automated distribution centers and im-

plemented a new logistics network. These steps have cut the company's inventory investment by $100 million and strengthened its ability to serve a larger customer base. Grainger also has hired a logistics service company to manage the 350 delivery firms that transport orders to customers in North America. As a result, the company receives a single report about delivery performance rather than 350 separate reports—which simplifies the process of managing outbound transportation.

Grainger is showing major customers such as the U.S. Postal Service how to better manage their supply chains and cut costs throughout the procurement process. It is also helping businesses of all sizes plan and budget for the estimated 40 percent of MRO purchases that are unexpected and infrequent. For example, customers often need parts right away to repair machines that break down without warning. In such cases, the customers want to minimize equipment down time without budgeting to have all replacement parts on hand at all times. Grainger uses sophisticated software to analyze how often business customers of similar sizes buy spare parts and related products and then suggests how individual businesses can achieve an appropriate balance of inventory and planned purchasing for these products.

Supply-chain management is enabling Grainger to achieve more efficiencies, keep physical distribution costs in check, and help customers to better manage their buying as well. Already the largest industrial distributor in North America, Grainger is continuing to push hard for higher future market share, revenue, and profits.[19]

For more information about this company, go to **www.grainger.com.**

Questions

1. How does Grainger benefit by helping its customers to improve their inventory management?
2. What are the cost and pricing implications of Grainger being able to buy directly from producers and sell directly to business customers?
3. If you owned a manufacturing firm that makes parts for industrial equipment, would you distribute your products exclusively through Grainger? Explain your answer.

→ CHAPTER 15: JOURNAL EXERCISE

Discovery statement: In this chapter you learned that retailers are marketing intermediaries and part of the distribution channel.

Thinking about bricks-and-mortar retail stores, in which store have you had your most enjoyable shopping experience? Describe this retail store.

_____

_____

_____

_____

_____

Discuss this shopping experience and why it was such a great shopping experience.

_____

_____

_____

_____

At what bricks-and-mortar store did you have your worst experience? Describe this store.

_____

_____

_____

_____

_____

Discuss this worst shopping experience and be sure to mention the reasons why this shopping experience was the worst one for you.

_____

_____

_____

_____

_____

BUILDING SKILLS FOR CAREER SUCCESS

1. Exploring the Internet

One reason the Internet has generated so much excitement and interest among both buyers and distributors of products is that it is a highly effective method of direct marketing. Already a multibillion dollar industry, e-commerce is growing as more businesses recognize the power of the Internet to reach customers twenty-four hours a day anywhere in the world. In addition to using the Internet to provide product information to potential customers, businesses can use it to process orders and accept payment from customers. Quick delivery from warehouses or stores by couriers such as UPS and FedEx adds to the convenience of Internet shopping.

Businesses whose products traditionally have sold well through catalogs are clear leaders in the electronic marketplace. Books, CDs, clothing, and other frequently purchased, relatively low-cost items sell well through both the Internet and catalogs. As a result, many successful catalog companies are including the Internet as a means of communicating about products. And many of their customers are finding that they prefer the more dynamic online versions of the catalogs.

Assignment

1. Explore the websites listed below, or just enter "shopping" on one of the web search engines—then stand back! Also visit the text website for updates to this exercise.

   www.llbean.com
   www.jcpenney.com
   www.sears.com
   www.landsend.com
   www.barnesandnoble.com
   www.amazon.com

2. Which website does the best job of marketing merchandise? Explain your answer.

3. Find a product that you would be willing to buy over the Internet and explain why you would buy it. Name the website and describe the product.

4. Find a product that you would be unwilling to buy over the Internet and, again, explain your reasoning. Name the website and describe the product.

2. Developing Critical-Thinking Skills

According to the wheel of retailing hypothesis, retail businesses begin as low-margin, low-priced, low-status operations. As they successfully challenge established retailers for market share, they upgrade their facilities and offer more services. This raises their costs and forces them to increase their prices so that eventually they become like the conventional retailers they replaced. As they move up from the low end of the wheel, new firms with lower costs and prices move in to take their place. For example, Kmart started as a low-priced operation that competed with department stores. Over time, it upgraded its facilities and products; big Kmart stores now offer such exclusive merchandise as Martha Stewart's bed-and-bath collection, full-service pharmacies, café areas, and "pantry" areas stocked with frequently bought grocery items, including milk, eggs, and bread. In consequence, Kmart has become a higher-cost, higher-priced operation and, as such, is vulnerable to lower-priced firms entering at the low end of the wheel.

Assignment

1. Investigate the operations of a local retailer.

2. Explain how this retailer is evolving on the wheel of retailing.

3. Prepare a report on your findings.

3. Building Team Skills

Surveys are a commonly used tool in marketing research. The information they provide can reduce business risk and facilitate decision making. Retail outlets often survey their customers' wants and needs by distributing comment cards or questionnaires. The customer survey (on p. 509) is an example of a survey that a local photography shop might distribute to its customers.

Assignment

1. Working in teams of three to five, choose a local retailer.

2. Classify the retailer according to the major types of retailers.

3. Design a survey to help the retailer to improve customer service. (You may find it beneficial to work with the retailer and actually administer the survey to the retailer's customers. Prepare a report of the survey results for the retailer.)

4. Present your findings to the class.

4. Researching Different Careers

When you are looking for a job, the people closest to you can be extremely helpful. Family members and friends may be able to answer your questions directly or put you in touch with someone else who can. This type of "networking" can lead to an "informational interview," in which you can meet with someone who will answer your questions about a career or a company and who also can provide inside information on related fields and other helpful hints.

Assignment

1. Choose a retailer or wholesaler and a position within the company that interests you.

2. Call the company and ask to speak to the person in that particular position. Explain that you are a college student interested in the position, and ask to set up an "informational interview."

3. Prepare a list of questions to ask in the interview. The questions should focus on

   a. The type of training recommended for the position

   b. How the person entered the position and advanced in it

   c. What he or she likes and dislikes about the work

4. Present your findings to the class.

5. Improving Communication Skills

As the first step in finding a home, an increasing number of people are turning to the Internet rather than to a realtor. The National Association of Realtors (NAR) lists over one million homes each month. However, over the past five years, the NAR has lost many members. Home buyers can search the Internet for demographic information about a particular town or region, including school quality, crime rates, and income level, and can use relocation calculators, which estimate how much the cost of living differs from one region to another.

Assignment

1. Compare shopping for a home over the Internet with the traditional experience of shopping for a home with a realtor. (Be sure to consider the time required to gather information on housing, prices, order processing, and payment methods.)

2. Prepare a brief position paper entitled, "A Perspective: Nonstore Retailers Are/Are Not a Threat to Traditional Retailers."

Customer Survey

To help us to serve you better, please take a few minutes while your photographs are being developed to answer the following questions. Your opinions are important to us.

1. Do you live/work in the area? (Circle one or both if they apply.)

2. Why did you choose us? (Circle all that apply.)

   Close to home
   Close to work
   Convenience
   Good service
   Quality
   Full-service photography shop
   Other

3. How did you learn about us? (Circle one.)

   Newspaper
   Flyer/coupon
   Passing by
   Recommended by someone
   Other

4. How frequently do you have film developed? (Please estimate.)
   _____ Times per month
   _____ Times per year

5. Which aspects of our photography shop do you think need improvement?

6. Our operating hours are from 8:00 A.M. to 7:00 P.M. weekdays and Saturdays from 9:30 A.M. to 6:00 P.M. We are closed on Sundays and legal holidays. If changes in our operating hours would serve you better, please specify how you would like them changed.

7. Age (Circle one.)
   Under 25
   26–39
   40–59
   Over 60

Comments:

→ PREP TEST

Matching Questions

____ 1. This strategy provides the widest possible exposure in the marketplace.

____ 2. Its primary goal is to transfer ownership of products.

____ 3. It is a middleman that buys and resells products.

____ 4. A middleman often hired on a commission basis.

____ 5. This middleman carries a few lines with many products within each line.

____ 6. A low-cost building is used to display large inventories.

____ 7. The process involves receiving and filling customers' purchase orders.

____ 8. Marketing-related activities are performed by phone.

____ 9. Manufacturer's seconds or off-season merchandise are examples of products sold.

____ 10. A hypothesis that suggests that new retail operations usually begin at the bottom.

a. agent
b. intensive distribution
c. limited-line wholesaler
d. merchant wholesaler
e. middleman
f. off-price retailer
g. order processing
h. telemarketing
i. warehouse showroom
j. wheel of retailing

True/False Questions

T F

11. ○ ○ A direct channel of distribution includes both wholesalers and retailers.

12. ○ ○ Exclusive distribution makes use of all available outlets for a product.

13. ○ ○ Agents who represent producers are called manufacturer's agents.

14. ○ ○ Piggyback service is unique to air freight.

15. ○ ○ A retailer buys and sells merchandise.

16. ○ ○ Warehousing creates possession utility.

T F

17. ○ ○ Inventory holding costs consist of money invested in inventory, cost of storage space, insurance costs, and inventory taxes.

18. ○ ○ Community shopping centers strive to reach 150,000 or more customers in their target market.

19. ○ ○ The direct channel of distribution for business products includes retailers.

20. ○ ○ All certified airlines are contract carriers.

Multiple-Choice Questions

21. Which activity combines inventory management, order processing, warehousing, materials handling, and transportation?
    a. Marketing
    b. Merchandising
    c. Warehousing
    d. Physical distribution
    e. Transporting

22. Haley is shopping for a new outfit to wear to an awards banquet where she will be honored. She has found a beautiful outfit at The Gap and a new pair of shoes at the Foot Locker. What type of stores are these?
    a. Warehouse
    b. Convenience
    c. Specialty
    d. Department
    e. Wholesale

23. Margie recently was invited to a Pampered Chef party held at the local high school. The hostess prepared a meal using kitchen utensils and bowls made by the Pampered Chef Company. During the meal preparation, she explained how to use the items properly. Which selling techniques is the Pampered Chef Company using?
    a. Direct selling
    b. Party plan of selling
    c. Face-to-face sales presentations
    d. Nonstore retailing
    e. All of the above

24. Total vertical channel integration occurs when
    a. the goods move from the retailer to the consumer.
    b. wholesalers are eliminated from the distribution process.
    c. a single management controls all operations from production to final sale.
    d. retailers take on the financing function.
    e. intensive distribution is the goal.

25. The job of a freight forwarder is to
    a. ensure that each shipment travels alone to receive the best rate.
    b. assume responsibility for the safe delivery of the shipments.
    c. ask the sender to bring the shipment to a central location.
    d. allow the shipper to supervise loading selected carriers.
    e. ensure that the shipper selects a private carrier.

Fill-in-the-Blank Questions

26. A _____ middleman buys goods and takes title to the products.

27. When only one store is located in each geographic area, the type of distribution used is known as _____ distribution.

28. The actual physical handling of goods, in warehouses as well as during transportation, is the process of _____ handling.

29. All activities concerned with the efficient movement of products from the producer to the ultimate consumer is known as _____ distribution.

30. A middleman likely to be hired on a temporary basis is a _____.

Online Study Center

FOR MORE test practice, use the interactive ACE quizzes available at the Online Student Center: www.college.hmco.com/PIC/pridebusiness9e.

Answers on p. PT2.

Developing Integrated Marketing Communications

LEARNING OBJECTIVES

WHAT you will be able to do once you complete this chapter:

1 Describe integrated marketing communications.

2 Understand the role of promotion.

3 Explain the purposes of the three types of advertising.

4 Describe the advantages and disadvantages of the major advertising media.

5 Identify the major steps in developing an advertising campaign.

6 Recognize the various kinds of salespersons, the steps in the personal-selling process, and the major sales management tasks.

7 Describe sales promotion objectives and methods.

8 Understand the types and uses of public relations.

9 Identify the factors that influence the selection of promotion-mix ingredients.

WHY this chapter matters

It is absolutely crucial that a business communicate with customers about products, prices, and where and when those products are available. Without effective marketing communication, a firm's other marketing efforts will not be effective.

FOR HELP with studying this chapter, visit the Online Student Center:

www.college.hmco.com/PIC/pridebusiness9e

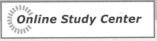

Online Study Center

wned by Yum! Brands, which also owns KFC and Taco Bell, Pizza Hut has gobbled up more than 40 percent of the U.S. pizza market with nearly 7,500 locations and $5.2 billion in annual revenue. Competition in the pizza business is heating up, however, with lots of special products, promotions, and pricing by challengers Domino's and Papa John's. Therefore, to maintain its dominance and keep customers coming back for more, Pizza Hut is cooking up an ever-expanding menu of creative promotions.

Every time the chain launches a new type of pizza, it blankets the nation with advertising supplemented by direct mail and signage in each Pizza Hut restaurant. When introducing the sixteen-inch Big New Yorker pizza, for example, Pizza Hut aired splashy television commercials geared to the "family dinner" market. The direct-mail campaign created excitement about the pizza by offering prizes such as a family holiday in Europe. When introducing the 3Cheese Stuffed Crust Pizza, Pizza Hut showcased the new menu item in both television and print advertising.

DID YOU KNOW?

Pizza Hut sells over $5 billion worth of pizza annually.

Competition is so intense that despite higher costs for cheese and other ingredients, Pizza Hut and its rivals frequently offer money-saving coupons. In fact, visitors to Pizza Hut's website can click to print coupons for selected products. Moreover, to reward repeat purchasing, Pizza Hut now invites customers to join the Very Into Pizza (VIP) program. For a $14.99 annual fee, members receive one free large pizza when they enroll and free breadsticks once a month for a year. When they place two or more $10 orders in a month, VIP members are eligible for a free large pizza.

Pizza Hut also appeals to racing fans by sponsoring a NASCAR team and airing television commercials featuring Jeff Gordon and other well-known drivers. It continues the NASCAR theme with the Family Race Pack meal, a complete package of pizza, breadsticks, cinnamon sticks, soda, napkins, cups, and plates. Watch for more promotions ahead as Pizza Hut pushes for higher share—and higher profits.[1]

For more information about this company, go to **www.pizzahut.com**.

Marketers at Pizza Hut employ multiple promotional methods to create very favorable company and product images in the minds of customers. Skillful use of promotion is of great benefit to Pizza Hut.

Promotion is communication about an organization and its products that is intended to inform, persuade, or remind target-market members. The promotion with which we are most familiar—advertising—is intended to inform, persuade, or remind us to buy particular products. But there is more to promotion than advertising, and it is used for other purposes as well. Charities use promotion to inform us of their need for donations, to persuade us to give, and to remind us to do so in case we have forgotten. Even the Internal Revenue Service uses promotion (in the form of publicity) to remind us of its April 15 deadline for filing tax returns.

A **promotion mix** (sometimes called a *marketing-communications mix*) is the particular combination of promotional methods a firm uses to reach a target market. The makeup of a mix depends on many factors, including the firm's promotional resources and objectives, the nature of the target market, the product characteristics, and the feasibility of various promotional methods.

In this chapter we introduce four promotional methods and describe how they are used in an organization's marketing plans. First, we examine the role of advertising in the promotion mix. We discuss different types of advertising, the process of developing an advertising campaign, and social and legal concerns in advertising. Next, we consider several categories of personal selling, noting the importance of effective sales management. We also look at sales promotion—why firms use it and which sales promotion techniques are most effective. Then we explain how public relations can be used to promote an organization and its products. Finally, we illustrate how these four promotional methods are combined in an effective promotion mix.

promotion communication about an organization and its products that is intended to inform, persuade, or remind target-market members

promotion mix the particular combination of promotion methods a firm uses to reach a target market

What Is Integrated Marketing Communications?

Integrated marketing communications is the coordination of promotion efforts to ensure maximal informational and persuasive impact on customers. A major goal of integrated marketing communications is to send a consistent message to customers. Integrated marketing communications provides an organization with a way to coordinate and manage its promotional efforts to ensure that customers do receive consistent messages. This approach fosters not only long-term customer relationships but also the efficient use of promotional resources.

The concept of integrated marketing communications has been increasingly accepted for several reasons. Mass-media advertising, a very popular promotional method in the past, is used less today because of its high costs and less predictable audience sizes. Marketers now can take advantage of more precisely targeted promotional tools, such as cable TV, direct mail, DVDs, the Internet, special-interest magazines, and podcasts. Database marketing is also allowing marketers to be more precise in targeting individual customers. Until recently, suppliers of marketing communications were specialists. Advertising agencies provided advertising campaigns, sales promotion companies provided sales promotion activities and materials, and public-relations organizations engaged in public-relations efforts. Today, a number of promotion-related companies provide one-stop shopping to the client seeking advertising, sales promotion, and public relations, thus reducing coordination problems for the sponsoring company. Because the overall costs of marketing communications are significant, management demands systematic evaluations of communications efforts to ensure that promotional resources are being used efficiently. Although the fundamental role of promotion is not changing, the specific communication vehicles employed and the precision with which they are used are changing.

1 LEARNING OBJECTIVE
Describe integrated marketing communications.

integrated marketing communications coordination of promotion efforts to ensure maximal informational and persuasive impact on customers

Podcasting – Not Just for Big Business

Organizations like CNN and NPR are using podcasts; the New York City Transit system uses its TransitTrax podcast as a tool to communicate with riders. Podcasts—digital files that distribute audio or video programs over the Internet—can be downloaded and played on digital music players or PCs. Podcasting is such an affordable marketing technique that even entrepreneurs and small businesses can use it to connect with their audiences.

Two Pros in a Pod. Entrepreneurs Cinda Donovan and Janet McGlynn make their podcasting site available for brief interviews with political candidates. "The politicians have been enthusiastic," Donovan says, because podcasting is a unique media option that allows them to get their message out to voters in the 18-24 age bracket.

Aspenbloom Pet Care. Kim Bloomer, who owns Aspenbloom Pet Care, is passionate about animals. Her online business provides podcasts in order to build relationships with customers, offering tips on proper pet care while promoting a variety of pet products.

---

2 LEARNING OBJECTIVE

Understand the role of promotion.

The Role of Promotion

Promotion is commonly the object of two misconceptions. Often people take note of highly visible promotional activities, such as advertising and personal selling, and conclude that these make up the entire field of marketing. People also sometimes consider promotional activities to be unnecessary, expensive, and the cause of higher prices. Neither view is accurate.

The role of promotion is to facilitate exchanges directly or indirectly by informing individuals, groups, or organizations and influencing them to accept a firm's products or to have more positive feelings about the firm. To expedite changes directly, marketers convey information about a firm's goods, services, and ideas to particular market segments. To bring about exchanges indirectly, marketers address interest groups (such as environmental and consumer groups), regulatory agencies, investors, and the general public concerning a company and its products. The broader role of promotion, therefore, is to maintain positive relationships between a company and various groups in the marketing environment.

Marketers frequently design promotional communications, such as advertisements, for specific groups, although some may be directed at wider audiences. Several different messages may be communicated simultaneously to different market segments. For example, ExxonMobil Corporation may address customers about a new motor oil, inform investors about the firm's financial performance, and update the general public on the firm's environmental efforts.

Marketers must plan, implement, and coordinate promotional communications carefully to make the best use of them. The effectiveness of promotional activities depends greatly on the quality and quantity of informtion available to marketers about the organization's marketing environment (see Figure 16.1). If a marketer wants to influence customers to buy acertain product, for example, the firm must know who these customers are andhow they make purchase decisions for that type of product. Marketers must gather and use information about particular audiences to communicate successfully with them. At times, two or more firms partner in joint promotional

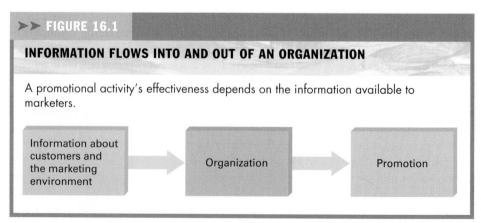

▶▶ FIGURE 16.1

INFORMATION FLOWS INTO AND OUT OF AN ORGANIZATION

A promotional activity's effectiveness depends on the information available to marketers.

| Information about customers and the marketing environment | → | Organization | → | Promotion |

Source: William M. Pride and O. C. Ferrell, *Marketing: Concepts and Strategies*, 13th ed. (Boston: Houghton Mifflin, 2006). Copyright © 2006 by Houghton Mifflin Company. Adapted with permission.

efforts. For example, Kraft Foods has teamed up with popular cable channel Nickelodeon to market healthy foods to kids. With consumer advocacy groups complaining about the skyrocketing levels of childhood obesity, Kraft is introducing a whole-grain version of its famous macaroni and cheese, called SuperMac. SuperMac will feature popular Nickolodeon characters Sponge Bob Square Pants and The Fairly Odd Parents both on the box and as noodle shapes. SuperMac also will be reinforced with calcium and several vitamins.[2]

The Promotion Mix: An Overview

Marketers can use several promotional methods to communicate with individuals, groups, and organizations. The methods that are combined to promote a particular product make up the promotion mix for that item.

Advertising, personal selling, sales promotion, and public relations are the four major elements in an organization's promotion mix (see Figure 16.2). While it is possible that one ingredient may be used, it is likely that two, three, or four of these ingredients will be used in a promotion mix depending on the type of product and target market involved.

Advertising is a paid nonpersonal message communicated to a select audience through a mass medium. Advertising is flexible enough that it can reach a very large target group or a small, carefully chosen one. **Personal selling** is personal communication aimed at informing customers and persuading them to buy a firm's products. It is more expensive to reach a consumer through personal selling than through advertising, but this method provides immediate feedback and often is more persuasive than advertising. **Sales promotion** is the use of activities or materials as direct inducements to customers or salespersons. It adds extra value to the product or increases the customer's incentive to buy the product. **Public relations** is a broad set of communication activities used to create and maintain favorable relationships between an organization and various public groups, both internal and external. There are a variety of public relations activites that can be very effective.

advertising a paid nonpersonal message communicated to a select audience through a mass medium

personal selling personal communication aimed at informing customers and persuading them to buy a firm's products

sales promotion the use of activities or materials as direct inducements to customers or salespersons

public relations communication activities used to create and maintain favorable relations between an organization and various public groups, both internal and external

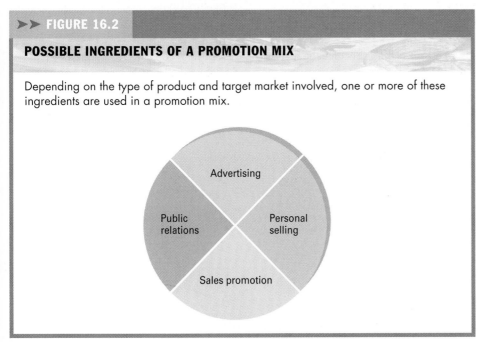

▶▶ FIGURE 16.2

POSSIBLE INGREDIENTS OF A PROMOTION MIX

Depending on the type of product and target market involved, one or more of these ingredients are used in a promotion mix.

Source: William M. Pride and O. C. Ferrell, *Marketing: Concepts and Strategies*, 13th ed. (Boston: Houghton Mifflin, 2006). Copyright © 2006 by Houghton Mifflin Company. Adapted with permission.

Advertising

3 LEARNING OBJECTIVE
Explain the purposes of
the three types of
advertising.

In 2005, organizations spent $276 billion on advertising in the United States.[3] Figure 16.3 shows how advertising expenditures are distributed across major media categories.

Types of Advertising by Purpose

Depending on its purpose and message, advertising may be classified into one of three groups: primary demand, selective demand, or institutional.

primary-demand advertising
advertising whose purpose
is to increase the demand
for *all* brands of a product
within a specific industry

Primary-Demand Advertising **Primary-demand advertising** is advertising aimed at increasing the demand for *all* brands of a product within a specific industry. Trade and industry associations, such as the California Milk Processor Board ("Got Milk?"), are the major users of primary-demand advertising. Their advertisements promote broad product categories, such as beef, milk, pork, potatoes, and prunes, without mentioning specific brands.

selective-demand (or brand)
advertising advertising that
is used to sell a particular
brand of product

Selective-Demand Advertising **Selective-demand** (or **brand**) **advertising** is advertising that is used to sell a particular brand of product. It is by far the most common type of advertising, and it accounts for the lion's share of advertising expenditures. Producers use brand-oriented advertising to convince us to buy everything from Bubble Yum to Buicks.

Selective advertising that aims at persuading consumers to make purchases within a short time is called *immediate-response advertising*. Most local advertising is of this type. Often local advertisers promote products with immediate appeal. Selective advertising aimed at keeping a firm's name or product before the public is called *reminder advertising*.

Comparative advertising, which has become more popular over the last three decades, compares specific characteristics of two or more identified brands. Of course, the comparison shows the advertiser's brand to be as good as or better than the other

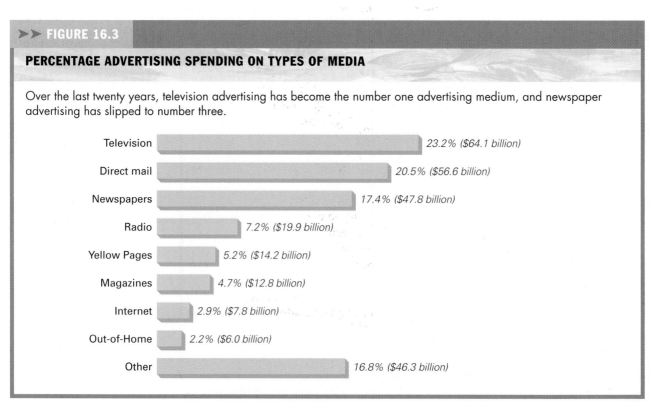

>> FIGURE 16.3

PERCENTAGE ADVERTISING SPENDING ON TYPES OF MEDIA

Over the last twenty years, television advertising has become the number one advertising medium, and newspaper advertising has slipped to number three.

Media	Percentage (Amount)
Television	23.2% ($64.1 billion)
Direct mail	20.5% ($56.6 billion)
Newspapers	17.4% ($47.8 billion)
Radio	7.2% ($19.9 billion)
Yellow Pages	5.2% ($14.2 billion)
Magazines	4.7% ($12.8 billion)
Internet	2.9% ($7.8 billion)
Out-of-Home	2.2% ($6.0 billion)
Other	16.8% ($46.3 billion)

Sources: "Ad Spending Totals by Media," *Advertising Age*, June 27, 2005, p. S-21.

identified competing brands. Comparisons often are based on the outcome of surveys or research studies. Although competing firms act as effective watchdogs against each other's advertising claims, consumers themselves sometimes become rather guarded concerning claims based on "scientific studies" and various statistical manipulations. Comparative advertising is unacceptable or illegal in a number of other countries.

Institutional Advertising Institutional advertising is advertising designed to enhance a firm's image or reputation. Many public utilities and larger firms, such as AT&T and the major oil companies, use part of their advertising dollars to build goodwill rather than to stimulate sales directly. A positive public image helps an organization to attract not only customers but also employees and investors.

Advertising Media

The **advertising media** are the various forms of communication through which advertising reaches its audience. The major media are newspapers, magazines, direct mail, Yellow Pages, out-of-home, television, radio, and the Internet. Figure 16.3 shows how organizations allocate their advertising expenditures among the various media. Note that television and radio account for less than one-third of all media expenditures.

Milk mustaches don't last long when you're a sponge.

Which means I may have to drink another glass of yummy chocolate milk.

Or two.

Or three.

Or four.

CHOCOLATE
got milk?

Newspapers Newspaper advertising accounts for about 17.4 percent of all advertising expenditures. Approximately 85 percent is purchased by local retailers. Retailers use newspaper advertising extensively because it is relatively inexpensive compared with other media. Moreover, since most newspapers provide local coverage, advertising dollars are not wasted in reaching people outside the organization's market area. It is also timely. Ads usually can be placed just a few days before they are to appear.

There are some drawbacks, however, to newspaper advertising. It has a short life span; newspapers generally are read through once and then discarded. Color reproduction in newspapers is usually not high quality; thus most ads are run in black and white. Finally, marketers cannot target specific demographic groups through newspaper ads because newspapers are read by such a broad spectrum of people.

Magazines The advertising revenues of magazines have been almost flat over the last few years. In 2005 they reached $12.8 billion, or about 4.7 percent of all advertising expenditures.

Advertisers can reach very specific market segments through ads in special-interest magazines. A boat manufacturer has a ready-made consumer audience in subscribers to *Yachting* or *Sail*. Producers of photographic equipment advertise in *Travel & Leisure* or *Popular Photography*. A number of magazines such as *Time* and *Cosmopolitan* publish regional editions, which provide advertisers with geographic flexibility as well.

Magazine advertising is more prestigious than newspaper advertising, and it allows for high-quality color reproduction. In addition, magazine advertisements have a longer life span than those in other media. Issues of *National Geographic*, for example, may be kept for months or years, and the ads they contain may be viewed repeatedly.

The major disadvantages of magazine advertising are high cost and lack of timeliness. Because magazine ads normally must be prepared two to three months in advance, they cannot be adjusted to reflect the latest market conditions. Magazine ads—especially full-color ads—are also expensive. Although the cost of reaching a thousand

Generating primary demand. Several milk industry associations promote milk in order to stimulate primary demand. Rather than promote a specific brand, the familiar "Got Milk?" ad campaigns are meant to increase demand for milk in general.

institutional advertising advertising designed to enhance a firm's image or reputation

4 LEARNING OBJECTIVE
Describe the advantages and disadvantages of the major advertising media.

advertising media the various forms of communication through which advertising reaches its audience

USING THE INTERNET

people may compare favorably with that of other media, the cost of a full-page four-color ad can be very high—$246,000 in *Time*.[4]

Direct Mail   **Direct-mail advertising** is promotional material mailed directly to individuals. Direct mail is the most selective medium; mailing lists are available (or can be compiled) to reach almost any target audience, from airplane enthusiasts to zoologists. The effectiveness of direct-mail advertising can be measured because the advertiser has a record of who received the advertisements and can track who responds to the ads.

Some organizations are using direct e-mail. To avoid customers receiving unwanted e-mail, a firm should ask customers to complete a request form in order to receive promotional e-mail from the company.

The success of direct-mail advertising depends to some extent on appropriate and current mailing lists. A direct-mail campaign may fail if the mailing list is outdated and the mailing does not reach the right people. In addition, this medium is relatively costly. Direct-mail advertising expenditures in 2005 amounted to more than $56 billion, almost 20.5 percent of the total.

direct-mail advertising promotional material mailed directly to individuals

Yellow Pages advertising simple listings or display advertisements presented under specific product categories appearing in print and online telephone directories

Yellow Pages Advertising   **Yellow Pages advertising,** appearing in print and online telephone directories, is presented under specific product categories and may appear as simple listings or as display advertisements. In 2005, advertisers spent $14 billion on Yellow Pages advertising, which represented approximately 5.2 percent of total advertising expenditures. Yellow Pages advertising appears in over 6,000 editions of telephone directories that are distributed to millions of customers annually. Approximately 85 percent of Yellow Pages advertising is used by local advertisers as opposed to national advertisers.

Customers use Yellow Pages advertising to save time in finding products, to find information quickly, and to learn about products and marketers. It is estimated that approximately 60 percent of adults read Yellow Pages advertising at least once a week. Unlike other types of advertising media, Yellow Pages advertisements are purchased for one year and cannot be changed. Advertisers often pay for their Yellow Pages advertisements through monthly charges on their telephone statements.

out-of-home advertising short promotional messages on billboards, posters, signs, and transportation vehicles

Out-of-Home Advertising   **Out-of-home advertising** consists of short promotional messages on billboards, posters, signs, and transportation vehicles. In 2005, advertisers spent $6 billion, or 2.2 percent of total advertising expenditures, on out-of-home advertising.

Sign and billboard advertising allows the marketer to focus on a particular geographic area; it is also fairly inexpensive. However, because most outdoor promotion is directed toward a mobile audience, the message must be limited to a few words. The medium is especially suitable for products that lend themselves to pictorial display.

Television   Television ranks number one in total advertising revenue. In 2005, almost one-fourth of all advertising expenditures, about $64 billion, went to television. Approximately 99 percent of American homes have at least one television set that is watched an average of seven hours and forty minutes each day. The average U.S. household can receive twenty-eight TV channels, including cable and pay stations, and about 80 percent of households receive basic cable/satellite television. Television obviously provides advertisers with considerable access to consumers.

Television advertising is the primary medium for larger firms whose objective is to reach national or regional markets. A national advertiser may buy *network time*, which means that its message usually will be broadcast by hundreds of local stations affiliated with the network. However, the opportunity to reach extremely large television audiences has been reduced by the increased availability and popularity of cable channels and home videos. Both national and local firms may buy *local time* on a single station that covers a particular geographic area.

Advertisers may *sponsor* an entire show, participate with other sponsors of a show, or buy *spot time* for a single 10-, 20-, 30-, or 60-second commercial during or between programs. To an extent, they may select their audience by choosing the day of the week and the approximate time of day their ads will be shown. Anheuser-Busch advertises Budweiser Beer during TV football games because the majority of viewers are men, who are likely to buy beer.

Marketers also can employ *product placement*, which is paying a fee to have a product appear in a television program or movie. The product might appear on a table or counter, or one or more of the actors might be using it. Through channel switching and personal video recorders such as TiVo, television viewers can avoid watching regular television commercials. By placing the product directly into the program, viewers are likely to be exposed to the product. For example, after Oprah Winfrey gave 276 audience members new Pontiac G6s, it generated tremendous publicity for both *Oprah* and Pontiac. More than 600 media outlets commented on the giveaway in the days following the show, and sales of the G6 rose above its closest competitor by 20 percent. Reality programming in particular has been a natural fit for product placement because of the close interchange between the participants and the product. Sears home-improvement products are heavily promoted and used on *Extreme Makeover Home Edition*. Aspiring Donald Trumps work on projects for Levi's, Burger King, Marquis Jet, and Dove on *The Apprentice*; people appearing on *Survivor* compete for Pringles; and each year's winner of *American Idol* receives a new Ford vehicle.[5]

Another option available to television advertisers is the infomercial. An **infomercial** is a program-length televised commercial message resembling an entertainment or consumer affairs program. Infomercials for products such as exercise equipment tell customers why they need the product, what benefits it provides, in what ways it outperforms its competitors, and how much it costs. Infomercials have turned two-time heavyweight champion boxer George Foreman into his own brand. In 1995, Foreman starred in an infomercial promoting the George Foreman Lean and Mean Grilling Machine. The fat-fighting electric grill was a sensation, with sales of over 70 million units. The incredible success of the original infomercial led to a line expansion that includes rotisserie ovens, outdoor propane grills, griddles, and even companion cookbooks that Foreman cheerfully endorses in new spots. Foreman is now the reigning champion of infomercials, with a cleaning solutions line called George Foreman's Knock Out and a successful line of Big and Tall clothing for men.[6] Although infomercials initially were aired primarily over cable television, today they are becoming more common on other types of television. Currently, infomercials are responsible for marketing over $1 billion worth of products annually. Even some *Fortune* 500 companies are now using them.

Television advertising rates are based on the number of people expected to be watching when the commercial is aired. In 2006, the cost of a 30-second Super Bowl commercial was $2.5 million.[7] Advertisers spend over $500,000 for a 30-second television commercial during a top-rated prime-time program.

Radio   Advertisers spent $19.9 billion, or 7.4 percent of total expenditures, on radio advertising in 2005. Like magazine advertising, radio advertising offers selectivity.

infomercial a program-length televised commercial message resembling an entertainment or consumer affairs program

Super Bowl ad prices climb

**Super Bowl ad prices have grown steadily.
Price of a 30-second ad.**

I	1967	$42,000
X	1976	$125,000
XX	1986	$550,000
XXX	1996	$1,100,000
XL	2006	$2,500,000

Sources: Brooks Barnes, "Super Bowl Draws 6% More Viewers than Last Year," *Wall Street Journal*, February 7, 2006, p. B10; "Super Bowl Statistics," *Advertising Age*, www.adage.com/page.cms?pageId=684; accessed February 7, 2006; *CBS News*, February 7, 2005, www.cbsnews.com/stories2005/02/07/earlyshow/main672016.shtml.

Radio stations develop programming for—and are tuned in by—specific groups of listeners. There are almost half a billion radios in the United States (about six per household), which makes radio the most accessible medium.

Radio advertising can be less expensive than in other media. Actual rates depend on geographic coverage, the number of commercials contracted for, the time period specified, and whether the station broadcasts on AM, FM, or both. Even small retailers are able to afford radio advertising. A radio advertiser can schedule and change ads on short notice. The disadvantages of using radio are the absence of visual images and (because there are so many stations) the small audience size.

Internet　Spending on Internet advertising has increased significantly. In 2005, U.S. advertisers spent $7.8 billion on Internet advertising compared with $5.8 billion three years earlier. Internet advertising accounts for 2.9 percent of the total advertising expenditures. Internet advertising can take a variety of forms. The *banner ad* is a rectangular graphic that appears at the top of a website. A lot of websites are able to offer free services because they are supported by banner advertisements. Advertisers can use animation and interactive capabilities to draw more attention to their ads. Yahoo! even invites its users to participate in surveys evaluating the banner ads on its home page. Another type is *sponsorship* (or *cobranded* ads). These ads integrate a company's brand with editorial content. The goal of this type of ad is to get users to strongly identify the advertiser with the site's mission. For example, many food brands such as Kraft advertise on Allrecipes.com. This site allows users to share and browse thousands of recipes. Kraft offers its own recipes on the site, and they all include its products. There are also banner ads for Kraft on other recipes, reminding the user of Kraft cheese while they read a recipe for cheese dip. Many Internet advertisers choose to purchase keywords on popular search engines such as Google, Yahoo!, and MSN. For example, Kellogg purchased the word *cereal* on Google so that every time someone conducts a search using that word, a link to Kellogg's website appears. *Interstitial* ads pop up to display a product. For example, users can gain access to online magazine Salon.com by watching a commercial that will grant them a twenty-four-hour pass to all of Salon's content, or they can bypass the ad altogether by paying a monthly subscription fee for an ad-free version.

Major Steps in Developing an Advertising Campaign

**5 LEARNING OBJECTIVE
Identify** the major steps in developing an advertising campaign.

An advertising campaign is developed in several stages. These stages may vary in number and the order in which they are implemented depending on the company's resources, products, and audiences. The development of a campaign in any organization, however, will include the following steps in some form:

1. Identify and Analyze the Target Audience　The target audience is the group of people toward which a firm's advertisements are directed. To pinpoint the organization's target audience and develop an effective campaign, marketers must analyze such information as the geographic distribution of potential customers; their age, sex, race, income, and education; and their attitudes toward both the advertiser's product and competing products. How marketers use this information will be influenced by the features of the product to be advertised and the nature of the competition. Precise identification of the target audience is crucial to the proper development of subsequent stages and, ultimately, to the success of the campaign itself.

2. Define the Advertising Objectives   The goals of an advertising campaign should be stated precisely and in measurable terms. The objectives should include the current position of the firm, indicate how far and in what direction from that original reference point the company wishes to move, and specify a definite period of time for the achievement of the goals. Advertising objectives that focus on sales will stress increasing sales by a certain percentage or dollar amount or expanding the firm's market share. Communication objectives will emphasize increasing product or brand awareness, improving consumer attitudes, or conveying product information.

3. Create the Advertising Platform   An advertising platform includes the important selling points or features that an advertiser wishes to incorporate into the advertising campaign. These features should be important to customers in their selection and use of a product, and if possible, they should be features that competing products lack. Although research into what consumers view as important issues is expensive, it is the most productive way to determine which issues to include in an advertising platform.

4. Determine the Advertising Appropriation
The advertising appropriation is the total amount of money designated for advertising in a given period. This stage is critical to the success of the campaign because advertising efforts based on an inadequate budget will understimulate customer demand, and a budget too large will waste a company's resources. Advertising appropriations may be based on last year's (or next year's forecasted) sales, on what competitors spend on advertising, or on executive judgment.

Target audience—Is this ad aimed at everyone? Most advertisements are not aimed at everyone. This Harlequin Enterprises advertisement asks women: "Is your man too good to be true? Hot, gorgeous, and romantic?" Then the company indicates that he could be a Harlequin Blaze cover model or win prizes.

5. Develop the Media Plan   A media plan specifies exactly which media will be used in the campaign and when advertisements will appear. Although cost-effectiveness is not easy to measure, the primary concern of the media planner is to reach the largest number of persons in the target audience for each dollar spent. In addition to cost, media planners must consider the location and demographics of people in the advertising target, the content of the message, and the characteristics of the audiences reached by various media. The media planner begins with general media decisions, selects subclasses within each medium, and finally chooses particular media vehicles for the campaign.

6. Create the Advertising Message   The content and form of a message are influenced by the product's features, the characteristics of people in the target audience, the objectives of the campaign, and the choice of media. An advertiser must consider these factors to choose words and illustrations that will be meaningful and appealing to persons in the advertising target. The copy, or words, of an advertisement will vary depending on the media choice but should attempt to move the audience through attention, interest, desire, and action. Artwork and visuals should complement copy by attracting the audience's attention and communicating an idea quickly. Creating a cohesive advertising message is especially difficult for a company such as eBay that offers such a broad mix of products. eBay developed a "whatever it is" campaign that features a variety of consumers of every age using a variety of products (a car, a television, a dress, and a laptop) all shaped like the letters "it." The tagline, "Whatever *it* is, you can get it on eBay," emphasizes the massive range of products available from the site and showcases the service that the company provides effectively.

7. Execute the Campaign Execution of an advertising campaign requires extensive planning, scheduling, and coordinating because many tasks must be completed on time. The efforts of many people and firms are involved. Production companies, research organizations, media firms, printers, photoengravers, and commercial artists are just a few of the people and firms that may contribute to a campaign. Advertising managers constantly must assess the quality of the work and take corrective action when necessary. In some instances, advertisers make changes during the campaign to meet objectives more effectively.

8. Evaluate Advertising Effectiveness A campaign's success should be measured in terms of its original objectives before, during, and/or after the campaign. An advertiser should at least be able to estimate whether sales or market share went up because of the campaign or whether any change occurred in customer attitudes or brand awareness. Data from past and current sales and responses to coupon offers and customer surveys administered by research organizations are some of the ways in which advertising effectiveness can be evaluated.

Advertising Agencies

advertising agency an independent firm that plans, produces, and places advertising for its clients

Advertisers can plan and produce their own advertising with help from media personnel, or they can hire advertising agencies. An **advertising agency** is an independent firm that plans, produces, and places advertising for its clients. Many large ad agencies offer help with sales promotion and public relations as well. The media usually pay a commission of 15 percent to advertising agencies. Thus the cost to the agency's client can be quite moderate. The client may be asked to pay for selected services that the agency performs. Other methods for compensating agencies are also used.

Firms that do a lot of advertising may use both an in-house advertising department and an independent agency. This approach gives the firm the advantage of being able to call on the agency's expertise in particular areas of advertising. An agency also can bring a fresh viewpoint to a firm's products and advertising plans.

Table 16.1 lists the nation's twenty leading advertisers in all media. In 2004, the number one spot went to General Motors.

Social and Legal Considerations in Advertising

Critics of U.S. advertising have two main complaints—that it is wasteful and that it can be deceptive. Although advertising (like any other activity) can be performed inefficiently, it is far from wasteful. Let's look at the evidence:

- Advertising is the most effective and least expensive means of communicating product information to a large number of individuals and organizations.
- Advertising encourages competition and is, in fact, a means of competition. It thus leads to the development of new and improved products, wider product choices, and lower prices.
- Advertising revenues support our mass-communications media—newspapers, magazines, radio, and television. This means that advertising pays for much of our news coverage and entertainment programming.
- Advertising provides job opportunities in fields ranging from sales to film production.

A number of government and private agencies scrutinize advertising for false or misleading claims or offers. At the national level, the Federal Trade Commission (FTC), the Food and Drug Administration (FDA), and the Federal Communications Commission (FCC) oversee advertising practices. The FDA conducted a survey of doctors about the impact of direct-to-consumer advertising for prescription drugs and found that 92 percent could recall a patient initiating conversation about a drug he or she had seen advertised. A controversial type of advertising, direct-to-consumer prescription ads make patients more aware of potential treatments according to 72 per-

>> TABLE 16.1

ADVERTISING EXPENDITURES AND SALES VOLUME FOR THE TOP TWENTY NATIONAL ADVERTISERS

Rank	Company	Advertising Expenditures (in millions)	Sales (in millions)	Advertising Expenditures as Percentage of Sales
1	General Motors	$3,997	$134,380	3.0
2	Procter & Gamble	3,919	23,688	16.5
3	Time Warner	3,283	33,572	9.8
4	Pfizer	2,957	29,539	10.0
5	SBC Communications	2,686	40,787	6.6
6	DaimlerChrysler	2,462	80,224	3.1
7	Ford Motor	2,458	100,208	2.5
8	Walt Disney Co.	2,241	24,012	9.3
9	Verizon Communications	2,197	69,269	3.2
10	Johnson & Johnson	2,175	27,770	7.8
11	Glaxo Smith Kline	1,828	17,513	10.4
12	Sears Holdings Corp.	1,823	31,230	5.8
13	Toyota Motor Corp.	1,821	55,007	3.3
14	General Electric Co.	1,819	90,954	2.0
15	Sony Corp.	1,665	19,741	8.4
16	Nissan Motor Co.	1,539	34,709	4.4
17	Altria Group	1,399	39,966	3.5
18	McDonald's Corp.	1,388	24,390	5.7
19	L'Oreal	1,341	4,711	28.5
20	Unilever	1,319	11,231	11.7

Source: Reprinted with permission from the June 27, 2005 issue of *Advertising Age.* Copyright © Crain Communications, Inc., 2005.

cent of the physicians surveyed, and it also caused 47 percent of these doctors to feel pressured into prescribing a particular drug.[8] Advertising also may be monitored by state and local agencies, Better Business Bureaus, and industry associations.

Personal Selling

Personal selling is the most adaptable of all promotional methods because the person who is presenting the message can modify it to suit the individual buyer. However, personal selling is also the most expensive method of promotion.

Most successful salespeople are able to communicate with others on a one-to-one basis and are strongly motivated. They strive to have a thorough knowledge of the products they offer for sale. And they are willing and able to deal with the details involved in handling and processing orders. Sales managers tend to emphasize these qualities when recruiting and hiring.

Many selling situations demand the face-to-face contact and adaptability of personal selling. This is especially true of industrial sales, in which a single purchase may amount to millions of dollars. Obviously, sales of that size must be based on carefully planned sales presentations, personal contact with customers, and thorough negotiations.

6 LEARNING OBJECTIVE
Recognize the various kinds of salespersons, the steps in the personal-selling process, and the major sales management tasks.

Kinds of Salespersons

Because most businesses employ different salespersons to perform different functions, marketing managers must select the kinds of sales personnel that will be most effective in selling the firm's products. Salespersons may be identified as order getters, order takers, and support personnel. A single individual can, and often does, perform all three functions.

order getter a salesperson who is responsible for selling a firm's products to new customers and increasing sales to present customers

creative selling selling products to new customers and increasing sales to present customers

Order Getters   An **order getter** is responsible for what is sometimes called **creative selling**— selling a firm's products to new customers and increasing sales to current customers. An order getter must perceive buyers' needs, supply customers with information about the firm's product, and persuade them to buy the product. Order-getting activities may be separated into two groups. In current-customer sales, sales-people concentrate on obtaining additional sales or leads for prospective sales from customers who have purchased the firm's products at least once. In new-business sales, sales personnel seek out new prospects and convince them to make an initial purchase of the firm's product. The real estate, insurance, appliance, heavy industrial machinery, and automobile industries in particular depend on new-business sales.

order taker a salesperson who handles repeat sales in ways that maintain positive relationships with customers

Order Takers   An **order taker** handles repeat sales in ways that maintain positive relationships with customers. An order taker sees that customers have products when and where they are needed and in the proper amounts. *Inside order takers* receive incoming mail and telephone orders in some businesses; salespersons in retail stores are also inside order takers. *Outside* (or *field*) *order takers* travel to customers. Often the buyer and the field salesperson develop a mutually beneficial relationship of placing, receiving, and delivering orders. Both inside and outside order takers are active salespersons and often produce most of their companies' sales.

sales support personnel employees who aid in selling but are more involved in locating prospects, educating customers, building goodwill for the firm, and providing follow-up service

missionary salesperson a salesperson—generally employed by a manufacturer—who visits retailers to persuade them to buy the manufacturer's products

trade salesperson a salesperson—generally employed by a food producer or processor—who assists customers in promoting products, especially in retail stores

technical salesperson a salesperson who assists a company's current customers in technical matters

Support Personnel   **Sales support personnel** aid in selling but are more involved in locating *prospects* (likely first-time customers), educating customers, building goodwill for the firm, and providing follow-up service. The most common categories of support personnel are missionary, trade, and technical salespersons.

A **missionary salesperson,** who usually works for a manufacturer, visits retailers to persuade them to buy the manufacturer's products. If the retailers agree, they buy the products from wholesalers, who are the manufacturer's actual customers. Missionary salespersons often are employed by producers of medical supplies and pharmaceuticals to promote these products to retail druggists, physicians, and hospitals.

A **trade salesperson,** who generally works for a food producer or processor, assists customers in promoting products, especially in retail stores. A trade salesperson may obtain additional shelf space for the products, restock shelves, set up displays, and distribute samples. Because trade salespersons usually are order takers as well, they are not strictly support personnel.

A **technical salesperson** assists a company's current customers in technical matters. He or she may explain how to use a product, how it is made, how to install it, or how a system is designed. A technical salesperson should be formally educated in science or engineering. Computers, steel, and chemicals are some of the products handled by technical salespeople.

Marketers usually need sales personnel from several of these categories. Factors that affect hiring and other personnel decisions include the number of customers and their characteristics; the product's attributes, complexity, and price; the distribution channels used by the company; and the company's approach to advertising.

The Personal-Selling Process

No two selling situations are exactly alike, and no two salespeople perform their jobs in exactly the same way. Most salespeople, however, follow the six-step procedure illustrated in Figure 16.4.

Prospecting The first step in personal selling is to research potential buyers and choose the most likely customers, or prospects. Sources of prospects include business associates and customers, public records, telephone and trade-association directories, and company files. The salesperson concentrates on those prospects who have the financial resources, willingness, and authority to buy the product.

Approaching the Prospect First impressions are often lasting impressions. Thus the salesperson's first contact with the prospect is crucial to successful selling. The best approach is one based on knowledge of the product, of the prospect's needs, and of how the product can meet those needs. Salespeople who understand each customer's particular situation are likely to make a good first impression—and to make a sale.

Making the Presentation The next step is actual delivery of the sales presentation. In many cases this includes demonstrating the product. The salesperson points out the product's features, its benefits, and how it is superior to competitors' merchandise. If the product has been used successfully by other firms, the salesperson may mention this as part of the presentation.

During a demonstration, the salesperson may suggest that the prospect try out the product personally. The demonstration and product trial should underscore specific points made during the presentation.

Answering Objections The prospect is likely to raise objections or ask questions at any time. This gives the salesperson a chance to eliminate objections that might prevent a sale, to point out additional features, or to mention special services the company offers.

Closing the Sale To close the sale, the salesperson asks the prospect to buy the product. This is considered the critical point in the selling process. Many experienced salespeople make use of a *trial closing*, in which they ask questions based on the assumption that the customer is going to buy the product. The questions "When would you want delivery?" and "Do you want the standard model or the one with the special options package?" are typical of trial closings. They allow the reluctant prospect to make a purchase without having to say, "I'll take it."

Following Up The salesperson must follow up after the sale to ensure that the product is delivered on time, in the right quantity, and in proper operating condition. During follow-up, the salesperson also makes it clear that he or she is available in case problems develop. Follow-up leaves a good impression and eases the way toward future sales. Hence it is essential to the selling process. The salesperson's job does not end with a sale. It continues as long as the seller and the customer maintain a working relationship.

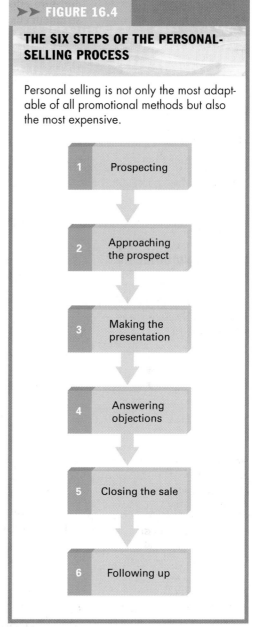

▶▶ FIGURE 16.4

THE SIX STEPS OF THE PERSONAL-SELLING PROCESS

Personal selling is not only the most adaptable of all promotional methods but also the most expensive.

1. Prospecting
2. Approaching the prospect
3. Making the presentation
4. Answering objections
5. Closing the sale
6. Following up

Source: William M. Pride and O. C. Ferrell, *Marketing: Concepts and Strategies*, 13th ed. (Boston: Houghton Mifflin, 2006). Copyright © 2006 by Houghton Mifflin Company. Adapted with permission.

Managing Personal Selling

A firm's success often hinges on the competent management of its sales force. Although some companies operate efficiently without a sales force, most firms rely on a strong sales force—and the sales revenue it brings in—for their success.

Sales managers have responsibilities in a number of areas. They must set sales objectives in concrete, quantifiable terms and specify a certain period of time and a certain geographic area. They must adjust the size of the sales force to meet changes in the firm's marketing plan and the marketing environment. Sales managers must attract and hire effective salespersons. For example, Guitar Center, the largest musical instrument chain in the United States, has only one requirement for members of its sales force—that they be able to play a musical instrument. The company believes that a rocking sales force will care more deeply about the product and sell it more effectively to customers.[9] Sales managers must develop a training program and decide where, when, how, and for whom to conduct the training. They must formulate a fair and adequate compensation plan to keep qualified employees. They must motivate salespersons to boost their productivity. They must define sales territories and determine scheduling and routing of the sales force. Finally, sales managers must evaluate the operation as a whole through sales reports, communications with customers, and invoices.

Sales Promotion

7 **LEARNING OBJECTIVE**
Describe sales promotion objectives and methods.

Sales promotion consists of activities or materials that are direct inducements to customers or salespersons. Are you a member of an airline frequent-flyer program? Did you recently receive a free sample in the mail or at a supermarket? Have you recently received a rebate from a manufacturer? Do you use coupons? All these are examples of sales promotion efforts. Sales promotion techniques often are used to enhance and supplement other promotional methods. They can have a significant impact on sales.

The dramatic increase in spending for sales promotion shows that marketers have recognized the potential of this promotional method. Many firms now include numerous sales promotion efforts as part of their overall promotion mix.

Sales Promotion Objectives

Sales promotion activities may be used singly or in combination, both offensively and defensively, to achieve one goal or a set of goals. Marketers use sales promotion activities and materials for a number of purposes, including

1. To attract new customers
2. To encourage trial of a new product
3. To invigorate the sales of a mature brand
4. To boost sales to current customers
5. To reinforce advertising
6. To increase traffic in retail stores
7. To steady irregular sales patterns
8. To build up reseller inventories
9. To neutralize competitive promotional efforts
10. To improve shelf space and displays[10]

Any sales promotion objectives should be consistent with the organization's general goals and with its marketing and promotional objectives.

Sales Promotion Methods

consumer sales promotion method a sales promotion method designed to attract consumers to particular retail stores and to motivate them to purchase certain new or established products

trade sales promotion method a sales promotion method designed to encourage wholesalers and retailers to stock and actively promote a manufacturer's product

Most sales promotion methods can be classified as promotional techniques for either consumer sales or trade sales. A **consumer sales promotion method** attracts consumers to particular retail stores and motivates them to purchase certain new or established products. A **trade sales promotion method** encourages wholesalers and retailers to stock and actively promote a manufacturer's product. Incentives such as money, merchandise, marketing assistance, and gifts are commonly awarded to resellers who buy products or respond positively in other ways. Of the combined dollars spent on sales promotion and advertising last year, about one-half was spent on trade promotions, one-fourth on consumer promotions, and one-fourth on advertising.

A number of factors enter into marketing decisions about which and how many sales promotion methods to use. Of greatest importance are the objectives of the promotional effort. Product characteristics—size, weight, cost, durability, uses, features, and hazards—and target market profiles—age, gender, income, location, density, usage rate, and buying patterns—likewise must be considered. Distribution channels and availability of appropriate resellers also influence the choice of sales promotion methods, as do the competitive and regulatory forces in the environment. Let's now discuss a few important sales promotion methods.

Rebates

A **rebate** is a return of part of the purchase price of a product. Usually the refund is offered by the producer to consumers who send in a coupon along with a specific proof of purchase. Rebating is a relatively low-cost promotional method. Once used mainly to help launch new product items, it is now applied to a wide variety of products. Some automakers offer rebates on their vehicles because they have found that many car customers are more likely to purchase a car with a rebate than the same car with a lower price and no rebate. One problem with rebates is that many people perceive the redemption process as too complicated. Only about half of individuals who purchase rebated products actually apply for the rebates.

Coupons

A **coupon** reduces the retail price of a particular item by a stated amount at the time of purchase. Coupons may be worth anywhere from a few cents to a few dollars. They are made available to customers through newspapers, magazines, direct mail, online, and shelf dispensers in stores. Some coupons are precisely targeted at customers. For example, All Online Coupons is an Internet site that provides visitors with links to all online coupons currently being offered. Customers can find coupons by category or store name. Other companies, such as Old Navy and The Gap, offer coupons

SPOTLIGHT

Redeeming loyalty
What types of rewards do loyal customers prefer?

Gift certificates — Rewards Card **57%**

Cash back, and lower or no fees — Rewards Card **37%**

2.7% Travel

2.6% Merchandise

Source: Maritz Loyalty Marketing.

rebate a return of part of the purchase price of a product

coupon reduces the retail price of a particular item by a stated amount at the time of purchase

---

BizTech

Coupon Trends: Click or Clip?

More than 75 percent of consumers save money with coupons. Although businesses traditionally distribute coupons in newspaper inserts, in printed ads, or on packages, a growing number are offering coupons online. Here's a look at coupon statistics:

- Each year, consumers save approximately $3 billion by using coupons.
- More than 251 billion coupons are distributed yearly through newspaper inserts.

- Fewer than 1 percent of all coupons distributed come from online sources.
- Just under 2 percent of all the coupons distributed in a year are redeemed.

- Online coupons are redeemed at a rate 15 times that of coupons from newspaper inserts.

  Businesses such as General Mills and General Electric are cutting the cost of distributing coupons and targeting more effectively through online coupons. Just as important, they can easily test different coupon values and determine how a coupon program affects sales of specific products.

Handing out samples. In this photo, NBA stars hand out free samples of McDonald's chicken-strip products.

sample a free product given to customers to encourage trial and purchase

premium a gift that a producer offers a customer in return for buying its product

frequent-user incentive a program developed to reward customers who engage in repeat (frequent) purchases

point-of-purchase display promotional material placed within a retail store

trade show an industry-wide exhibit at which many sellers display their products

buying allowance a temporary price reduction to resellers for purchasing specified quantities of a product

cooperative advertising an arrangement whereby a manufacturer agrees to pay a certain amount of a retailer's media cost for advertising the manufacturer's product

on their websites that can be used online or in stores. Billions of coupons are distributed annually. Of these, just under 2 percent are redeemed by consumers. Still, 73 percent of consumers say that coupons save them a lot of money.[11] The largest number of coupons distributed are for household cleaners, condiments, frozen foods, medications and health aids, and paper products. Stores in some areas even deduct double or triple the value of manufacturers' coupons from the purchase price as a sales promotion technique of their own. Coupons also may offer free merchandise, either with or without an additional purchase of a product.

Samples   A **sample** is a free product given to customers to encourage trial and purchase. Marketers use free samples to stimulate trial of a product, increase sales volume in the early stages of a product's life cycle, and obtain desirable distribution. Samples may be offered via online coupons, direct mail, or in stores. Many customers prefer to receive their samples by mail. It is the most expensive sales promotion technique, and while it is used often to promote new products, it can be used to promote established brands, too, such as cosmetics companies that use samples to attract customers. In designing a free sample, organizations must consider such factors as seasonal demand for the product, market characteristics, and prior advertising.

Distribution of free samples through websites such as StartSampling.com is growing. Consumers choose the free samples they would like to receive and request delivery. The online company manages the packaging and distribution of the samples.

Premiums   A **premium** is a gift that a producer offers a customer in return for buying its product. They are used to attract competitors' customers, introduce different sizes of established products, add variety to other promotional efforts, and stimulate consumer loyalty. Creativity is essential when using premiums; to stand out and achieve a significant number of redemptions, the premium must match both the target audience and the brand's image. Premiums also must be easily recognizable and desirable. Premiums are placed on or inside packages and also can be distributed through retailers or through the mail.

Frequent-User Incentives   A **frequent-user incentive** is a program developed to reward customers who engage in repeat (frequent) purchases. Such programs are used commonly by service businesses such as airlines, hotels, and auto rental agencies. Frequent-user incentives foster customer loyalty to a specific company or group of cooperating companies because the customer is given an additional reason to continue patronizing the business.

Point-of-Purchase Displays   A **point-of-purchase display** is promotional material placed within a retail store. The display is usually located near the product being promoted. It actually may hold merchandise (as do L'eggs hosiery displays) or inform customers about what the product offers and encourage them to buy it. Most point-of-purchase displays are prepared and set up by manufacturers and wholesalers.

Trade Shows   A **trade show** is an industry-wide exhibit at which many sellers display their products. Some trade shows are organized exclusively for dealers—to permit manufacturers and wholesalers to show their latest lines to retailers. Others are promotions designed to stimulate consumer awareness and interest. Among the latter are boat shows, home shows, and flower shows put on each year in large cities.

EXAMINING ETHICS

Subway Closes the Club

Subway, the 21,000-outlet fast-food chain known for its sandwiches, decided to put its Sub Club frequent-user incentive program out of commission not long ago. Under the Sub Club system, every customer who bought a six-inch sandwich was rewarded with a stamp (two stamps for a foot-long sandwich). After collecting eight stamps, the customer received a free six-inch sandwich with the purchase of a soda. Why shutter the Sub Club?

- *Fraud.* Counterfeiters were cheating Subway franchisees by selling thousands of fake cards and stamps.
- *Age.* The Sub Club was more than twenty years old, almost ancient compared with newer reward programs offered by Starbucks and other chains.

Franchisees have been evaluating Sub Club alternatives. One is the plastic Subway Card, which can be loaded with up to $100 for purchases at any Subway. In initial tests, customers bought more and completed purchases faster with the card than with cash. Subway is also able to print targeted promotional offers on each cardholder's receipt. But will the new program achieve Subway's promotion objectives?

Buying Allowances A **buying allowance** is a temporary price reduction to resellers for purchasing specified quantities of a product. For example, a laundry detergent manufacturer might give retailers $1 for each case of detergent purchased. A buying allowance may serve as an incentive to resellers to handle new products and may stimulate purchase of items in large quantities. While the buying allowance is simple, straightforward, and easily administered, competitors can respond quickly by offering a better buying allowance.

Cooperative Advertising **Cooperative advertising** is an arrangement whereby a manufacturer agrees to pay a certain amount of a retailer's media cost for advertising the manufacturer's products. To be reimbursed, a retailer must show proof that the advertisements actually did appear. A large percentage of all cooperative advertising dollars are spent on newspaper advertisements. Not all retailers take advantage of available cooperative advertising offers because they cannot afford to advertise or do not choose to do so.

Trade shows. This 40-foot-tall, 24 ton chair is a part of the NeoCon Trade Show held at Chicago's Merchandise Mart. This trade show is for businesses involved with the contract furnishings industry.

Public Relations

As noted earlier, public relations is a broad set of communication activities used to create and maintain favorable relationships between an organization and various public groups, both internal and external. These groups can include customers, employees, stockholders, suppliers, educators, the media, government officials, and society in general.

Types of Public-Relations Tools

Organizations use a variety of public-relations tools to convey messages and to create images. Public-relations professionals prepare written materials such as brochures, newsletters, company magazines, annual reports, and news releases. They also create corporate-identity materials such as logos, business cards, signs, and stationery. Speeches are another public-relations tool. Speeches can affect an organization's image and therefore must convey the desired message clearly.

Another public-relations tool is event sponsorship, in which a company pays for all or part of a special event such as a concert, sports competition, festival, or play. Sponsoring special events is an effective way for organizations to increase brand recognition and receive media coverage with comparatively little investment. For example, pharmaceutical company Bristol-Myers Squibb sponsored the Tour of Hope, a nine-day bike trek from San Diego, California, to Washington, D.C., to raise money for cancer research. Bristol-Myers spokesman, seven-time Tour de France winner and cancer survivor Lance Armstrong, led twenty-four other bikers on the tour.[12]

Some public-relations tools traditionally have been associated specifically with publicity, which is a part of public relations. **Publicity** is communication in news-story form about an organization, its products, or both. Publicity is transmitted through a mass medium, such as newspapers or radio, at no charge. Organizations use publicity to provide information about products; to announce new product launches, expansions, or research; and to strengthen the company's image. Public-relations personnel sometimes organize events, such as grand openings with prizes and celebrities, to create news stories about a company.

The most widely used type of publicity is the **news release.** It is generally one typed page of about 300 words provided by an organization to the media as a form of publicity. The release includes the firm's name, address, phone number, and contact person. Table 16.2 lists some of the issues news releases can address. There are also several other kinds of publicity-based public-relations tools. A **feature article,** which may run as long as 3,000 words, is usually written for inclusion in a particular publication. For example, a software firm might send an article about its new product to a computer magazine. A **captioned photograph,** a picture accompanied by a brief explanation, is an effective way to illustrate a new or improved

publicity communication in news-story form about an organization, its products, or both

news release a typed page of about 300 words provided by an organization to the media as a form of publicity

feature article a piece (of up to 3,000 words) prepared by an organization for inclusion in a particular publication

captioned photograph a picture accompanied by a brief explanation

Event sponsorship. The various names shown on these NASCAR drivers' clothing, and on their cars, are of companies and brands engaged in event sponsorship. The highest proportion of funds spent on event sponsorship is for sporting events.

> > **TABLE 16.2**

POSSIBLE ISSUES FOR NEWS RELEASES

Use of new information technology	Packaging changes
Support of a social cause	New products
Improved warranties	Creation of new software
Reports on industry conditions	Research developments
New uses for established products	Company's history and development
Product endorsements	Launching of new website
Winning of quality awards	Award of contracts
Company name changes	Opening of new markets
Interviews with company officials	Improvements in financial position
Improved distribution policies	Opening of an exhibit
Global business initiatives	History of a brand
Sponsorship of athletic events	Winners of company contests
Visits by celebrities	Logo changes
Reports of new discoveries	Speeches of top management
Innovative marketing activities	Merit awards to the organization
Economic forecasts	Anniversaries of inventions

product. A **press conference** allows invited media personnel to hear important news announcements and to receive supplementary textual materials and photographs. Finally, letters to the editor, special newspaper or magazine editorials, films, and tapes may be prepared and distributed to appropriate media for possible use.

press conference a meeting at which invited media personnel hear important news announcements and receive supplementary textual materials and photographs

The Uses of Public Relations

Public relations can be used to promote people, places, activities, ideas, and even countries. Public relations focuses on enhancing the reputation of the total organization by making people aware of a company's products, brands, or activities and by creating specific company images such as that of innovativeness or dependability. For example, ice-cream maker Ben and Jerry's uses news stories and other public-relations efforts to reinforce its reputation as a socially responsible company. By getting the media to report on a firm's accomplishments, public relations helps a company to maintain positive public visibility. Effective management of public-relations efforts also can reduce the unfavorable effects of negative events.

9 LEARNING OBJECTIVE
Identify the factors that influence the selection of promotion-mix ingredients.

Promotion Planning

A **promotional campaign** is a plan for combining and using the four promotional methods—advertising, personal selling, sales promotion, and public relations—in a particular promotion mix to achieve one or more marketing goals. When selecting promotional methods to include in promotion mixes, it is important to coordinate promotional elements to maximize total informational and promotional impact on customers. Integrated marketing communication requires a marketer to look at the broad perspective when planning promotional programs and coordinating the total set of communication functions.

promotional campaign a plan for combining and using the four promotional methods—advertising, personal selling, sales promotion, and publicity—in a particular promotion mix to achieve one or more marketing goals

In planning a promotional campaign, marketers must answer these two questions:

- What will be the role of promotion in the overall marketing mix?
- To what extent will each promotional method be used in the promotion mix?

The answer to the first question depends on the firm's marketing objectives because the role of each element of the marketing mix—product, price, distribution, and promotion—depends on these detailed versions of the firm's marketing goals. The answer to the second question depends on the answer to the first, as well as on the target market.

Promotion and Marketing Objectives

Promotion naturally is better suited to certain marketing objectives than to others. For example, promotion can do little to further a marketing objective such as "reduce delivery time by one-third." It can, however, be used to inform customers that delivery is faster. Let's consider some objectives that *would* require the use of promotion as a primary ingredient of the marketing mix.

Providing Information This is, of course, the main function of promotion. It may be used to communicate to target markets the availability of new products or product features. It may alert them to special offers or give the locations of retailers that carry a firm's products. In other words, promotion can be used to enhance the effectiveness of each of the other ingredients of the marketing mix. For example, as H&R Block continues to expand beyond tax preparation services, it attempts to inform potential customers of its additional offerings. H&R Block also offers mortgages, investment advising, and other financial services and has nearly doubled its advertising budget in order to communicate the availability of all its services.[13]

Increasing Market Share Promotion can be used to convince new customers to try a product while maintaining the product loyalty of established customers. Comparative advertising, for example, is directed mainly at those who might—but presently do not—use a particular product. Advertising that emphasizes the product's features also assures those who *do* use the product that they have made a smart choice.

Positioning the Product The sales of a product depend, to a great extent, on its competition. The stronger the competition, the more difficult it is to maintain or increase sales. For this reason, many firms go to great lengths to position their products in the marketplace. **Positioning** is the development of a product image in buyers' minds relative to the images they have of competing products.

positioning the development of a product image in buyers' minds relative to the images they have of competing products

Promotion is the prime positioning tool. A marketer can use promotion to position a brand away from competitors to avoid competition. For example, Hardee's, the nation's sixth-largest hamburger chain, is seeking to position itself as the place to go for big beef. Its new approach includes dropping about forty items from its menu and offering more Thickburgers ranging from one-third to two-thirds pound of beef per burger. This positioning is designed to avoid the value-menu wars of McDonald's and Burger King. The new positioning was launched with a promotional campaign that actually pokes fun at Hardee's.[14] Promotion also may be used to position one product directly against another product. For example, Coca-Cola and Pepsi position their products to compete head to head against each other.

Stabilizing Sales Special promotional efforts can be used to increase sales during slack periods, such as the "off season" for certain sports equipment. By stabilizing sales in this way, a firm can use its production facilities more effectively and reduce both capital costs and inventory costs. Promotion is also used frequently to increase the sales of products that are in the declining stage of their life cycle. The objective is to keep them going for a little while longer.

Developing the Promotion Mix

Once the role of promotion is established, the various methods of promotion may be combined in a promotional campaign. As in so many other areas of business, promotion planning begins with a set of specific objectives. The promotion mix then is designed to accomplish these objectives.

Marketers often use several promotion mixes simultaneously if a firm sells multiple products. The selection of promotion-mix ingredients and the degree to which they are used depend on the organization's resources and objectives, the nature of the target market, the characteristics of the product, and the feasibility of various promotional methods.

The amount of promotional resources available in an organization influences the number and intensity of promotional methods that marketers can use. A firm with a limited budget for promotion probably will rely on personal selling because the effectiveness of personal selling can be measured more easily than that of advertising. An organization's objectives also have an effect on its promotional activities. A company wishing to make a wide audience familiar with a new convenience item probably will depend heavily on advertising and sales promotion. If a company's objective is to communicate information to consumers—on the features of countertop appliances, for example—then the company may develop a promotion mix that includes some advertising, some sales promotion to attract consumers to stores, and much personal selling.

The size, geographic distribution, and socioeconomic characteristics of the target market play a part in the composition of a product's promotion mix. If the market is small, personal selling probably will be the most important element in the promotion mix. This is true of organizations that sell to small industrial markets and businesses that use only a few wholesalers to market their products. Companies that need to contact millions of potential customers, however, will emphasize sales promotion and advertising because these methods are relatively inexpensive. The age, income, and education of the target market also will influence the choice of promotion techniques. For example, with less-educated consumers, personal selling may be more effective than ads in newspapers or magazines.

In general, industrial products require a considerable amount of personal selling, whereas consumer goods depend on advertising. This is not true in every case, however. The price of the product also influences the composition of the promotion mix. Because consumers often want the advice of a salesperson on an expensive product, high-priced consumer goods may call for more personal selling. Similarly, advertising and sales promotion may be more crucial to marketers of seasonal items because having a year-round sales force is not always appropriate.

The cost and availability of promotional methods are important factors in the development of a promotion mix. Although national advertising and sales promotion activities are expensive, the cost per customer may be quite small if the campaign succeeds in reaching large numbers of people. In addition, local advertising outlets—newspapers, magazines, radio and television stations, and outdoor displays—may not be that costly for a small local business. In some situations, a firm may find that no available advertising medium reaches the target market effectively.

RETURN TO   Inside Business

Every year, Pizza Hut spends more than $200 million on advertising to support new product introductions and to keep its brand in front of consumers. The chain's sales promotion programs are designed to encourage trial, increase sales, combat competitive moves, retain market leadership, and reinforce advertising messages. In addition, Pizza Hut burnishes its image and reputation through other promotion efforts.

For example, Pizza Hut once arranged for product placement on the reality television show *Three Wishes*, in which host Amy Grant makes someone's wish come true. When a young teenager wished for a new library in her Ohio town, Pizza Hut donated 500 books and hosted a town-wide pizza party, spotlighting both its brand and its community involvement. Media coverage mentioned that the company has donated $300 million worth of books and instructional materials to U.S. schools during the past two decades—a public-relations plus.

Questions

1. Why would Pizza Hut print an expiration date and a promotion code on coupons available for download from its website?
2. How much emphasis do you think Pizza Hut should put on public relations? Explain your answer.

▶▶ CHAPTER REVIEW

Summary

1

Describe integrated marketing communications.

Integrated marketing communications is the coordination of promotion efforts to achieve maximum informational and persuasive impact on customers.

2

Understand the role of promotion.

Promotion is communication about an organization and its products that is intended to inform, persuade, or remind target-market members. The major ingredients of a promotion mix are advertising, personal selling, sales promotion, and public relations. The role of promotion is to facilitate exchanges directly or indirectly and to help an organization maintain favorable relationships with groups in the marketing environment.

3

Explain the purposes of the three types of advertising.

Advertising is a paid nonpersonal message communicated to a specific audience through a mass medium. Primary-demand advertising promotes the products of an entire industry rather than just a single brand. Selective-demand advertising promotes a particular brand of product. Institutional advertising is image-building advertising for a firm.

4

Describe the advantages and disadvantages of the major advertising media.

The major advertising media are newspapers, magazines, direct mail, outdoor displays, television, radio, and the Internet. Television accounts for the largest share of advertising expenditures, with newspapers running a close second. Newspapers are relatively inexpensive compared with other media, reach only people in the market area, and are timely. Disadvantages include a short life span, poor color reproduction, and an inability to target specific demographic groups. Magazine advertising can be quite prestigious. In addition, it can reach very specific market segments, can provide high-quality color reproduction, and has a relatively long life span. Major disadvantages are high cost and lack of timeliness. Direct mail is the most selective medium, and its effectiveness is measured easily. The disadvantage of direct mail is that if the mailing list is outdated and the advertisement does not reach the right people, then the campaign cannot be successful. An advantage of Yellow Pages advertising is that customers use it to save time in finding products, to find information quickly, and to learn about products and marketers. Unlike other types of advertising media, Yellow Pages advertisements are purchased for one year and cannot be changed. Out-of-home advertising allows marketers to focus on a particular geographic area and is relatively inexpensive. Messages, though, must be limited to a few words because the audience is usually moving. Television offers marketers the opportunity to broadcast a firm's message nationwide. However, television advertising can be very expensive and has a short life span, and the advent of cable channels and home videos has reduced the likelihood of reaching extremely large audiences. Radio advertising offers selectivity, can be less expensive than other media, and is flexible for scheduling purposes. Radio's limitations include no visual presentation and fragmented, small audiences. Benefits of using the Internet as an advertising medium include the growing number of people using the Internet, which means a growing audience, and the ability to precisely target specific customers. Disadvantages include the relatively simplistic nature of the ads that can be produced, especially in comparison with television, and the lack of evidence that net browsers actually pay attention to the ads.

5

Identify the major steps in developing an advertising campaign.

An advertising campaign is developed in several stages. A firm's first task is to identify and analyze its advertising target. The goals of the campaign also must be clearly defined. Then the firm must develop the advertising platform, or statement of important selling points, and determine the size of the advertising budget. The next steps are to develop a media plan, to create the advertising message, and to execute the campaign. Finally, promotion managers must evaluate the effectiveness of the advertising efforts before, during, and/or after the campaign.

6

Recognize the various kinds of salespersons, the steps in the personal-selling process, and the major sales management tasks.

Personal selling is personal communication aimed at informing customers and persuading them to buy a firm's products. It is the most adaptable promotional method be-cause the salesperson can modify the message to fit each buyer. Three major kinds of salespersons are order getters, order takers, and support personnel. The six steps in the personal-selling process are prospecting, approaching the prospect, making the presentation, answering objections, closing the sale, and following up. Sales managers are involved directly in setting sales force objectives; recruiting, selecting, and training salespersons; compensating and motivating sales personnel; creating sales territories; and evaluating sales performance.

7

Describe sales promotion objectives and methods.

Sales promotion is the use of activities and materials as direct inducements to customers and salespersons. The primary objective of sales promotion methods is to enhance and supplement other promotional methods. Methods of sales promotion include rebates, coupons, samples, premiums, frequent-user incentives, point-of-purchase displays, trade shows, buying allowances, and cooperative advertising.

8

Understand the types and uses of public relations.

Public relations is a broad set of communication activities used to create and maintain favorable relationships between an organization and various public groups, both internal and external. Organizations use a variety of public-relations tools to convey messages and create images. Brochures, newsletters, company magazines, and annual reports are written public-relations tools. Speeches, event sponsorship, and publicity are other public-relations tools. Publicity is communication in news-story form about an organization, its products, or both. Types of publicity include news releases, feature articles, captioned photographs, and press conferences. Public relations can be used to promote people, places, activities, ideas, and even countries. It can be used to enhance the reputation of an organization and also to reduce the unfavorable effects of negative events.

9

Identify the factors that influence the selection of promotion-mix ingredients.

A promotional campaign is a plan for combining and using advertising, personal selling, sales promotion, and publicity to achieve one or more marketing goals. Campaign objectives are developed from marketing objectives. Then the promotion mix is developed based on the organization's promotional resources and objectives, the nature of the target market, the product characteristics, and the feasibility of various promotional methods.

Key Terms

You should now be able to define and give an example relevant to each of the following terms:

promotion (515)
promotion mix (515)
integrated marketing communications (515)
advertising (517)
personal selling (517)
sales promotion (517)
public relations (517)
primary-demand advertising (518)
selective-demand (or brand) advertising (518)
institutional advertising (519)
advertising media (519)
direct-mail advertising (520)
Yellow Pages advertising (520)
out-of-home advertising (520)
infomercial (521)
advertising agency (524)
order getter (526)
creative selling (526)
order taker (526)
sales support personnel (526)
missionary salesperson (526)
trade salesperson (526)
technical salesperson (526)
consumer sales promotion method (528)
trade sales promotion method (528)
rebate (529)
coupon (529)
sample (530)
premium (530)
frequent-user incentive (530)
point-of-purchase display (530)
trade show (530)
buying allowance (530)
cooperative advertising (530)
publicity (532)
news release (532)
feature article (532)
captioned photograph (532)
press conference (533)
promotional campaign (533)
positioning (534)

Review Questions

1. What is integrated marketing communications, and why is it becoming increasingly accepted?
2. Identify and describe the major ingredients of a promotion mix.
3. What is the major role of promotion?
4. How are selective-demand, institutional, and primary-demand advertising different from one another? Give an example of each.
5. List the four major print media, and give an advantage and a disadvantage of each.
6. Which types of firms use radio, television, and the Internet?
7. Outline the main steps involved in developing an advertising campaign.
8. Why would a firm with its own advertising department use an ad agency?
9. Identify and give examples of the three major types of salespersons.
10. Explain how each step in the personal-selling process leads to the next step.
11. What are the major tasks involved in managing a sales force?
12. What are the major differences between consumer and trade sales promotion methods? Give examples of each.
13. What is cooperative advertising? What sorts of firms use it?
14. What is the difference between publicity and public relations? What is the purpose of each?
15. Why is promotion particularly effective in positioning a product? In stabilizing or increasing sales?
16. What factors determine the specific promotion mix that a firm should use?

Discussion Questions

1. Discuss the pros and cons of comparative advertising from the viewpoint of (a) the advertiser, (b) the advertiser's competitors, and (c) the target market.
2. Which kinds of advertising—in which media—influence you most? Why?
3. Which kinds of retail outlets or products require mainly order taking by salespeople?
4. A number of companies have shifted a portion of their promotion dollars from advertising to trade sales promotion methods? Why?
5. Why would a producer offer refunds or cents-off coupons rather than simply lowering the price of its products?
6. How can public-relations efforts aimed at the general public help an organization?
7. Why do firms use event sponsorship?
8. What kind of promotion mix might be used to extend the life of a product that has entered the declining stage of its product life cycle?

➤➤ VIDEO CASE 16.1

BMW: Promoting the Ultimate Driving Machine

Careful targeting, consistent positioning, and a good match between message and media all have helped Bayerische Motoren Werke (better known as BMW) accelerate sales revenue on a relatively small advertising budget. The company, based in Munich, Germany, markets such well-known global brands as BMW, Mini, and Rolls-Royce, as well as BMW motorcycles. Although other multibrand automobile manufacturers offer a range of vehicles for mass-market and upscale segments, BMW has taken a different route to profitability. The automaker focuses exclusively on high-end vehicles, targeting drivers who are affluent, successful, demanding of themselves and their cars, and interested in the time-saving convenience of automotive technology.

BMW uses television and magazine advertising to reinforce its brand image and give the target audience a feeling for what the company calls "The Ultimate Driving Machine." Because its advertising budget is not as large as its competitors' ad budgets, BMW looks for ways to stand out in the crowd. For example, it likes to air television commercials supported by brief yet intense bursts of newspaper advertising; more than once, it has signed on as the lone sponsor of television programs favored by its target audience. "TV advertising plays a vital role for us in building brand awareness, image, and desirability among members of the general public," notes a BMW marketing executive. "Without that type of broad appeal, a brand such as BMW would have less desirability within its target consumer groups."

The point of every commercial is to help viewers to envision themselves on the open road behind the wheel of a BMW; the car, not the driver or the scenery, is the star of the advertising show. The camera lingers on the vehicle's sleek lines, comfortable interior, high-tech features, and the familiar blue-and-white brand symbol. From commercial to commercial, the vehicle may change and the scenery may shift, but the ultimate objective is to motivate consumers to test drive a BMW.

Movies play a key role in BMW's promotions. The company has garnered huge waves of publicity from having the Mini featured in *The Italian Job* and arranging for James Bond to drive new BMWs. To reach Internet-savvy car buyers, BMW also hired top directors to make short films especially for web viewing. Although the films ran online for only four years, they were viewed more than 100 million times, won numerous awards, and were later issued on DVD for free distribution to prospective buyers.

BMW's sales promotion efforts include samples—in the form of extended test drives—as well as participating in major automotive trade shows. Eye-catching point-of-purchase displays in dealer showrooms support the overall marketing effort by echoing the company's advertising. Price promotions are rare, although the company held its first end-of-year clearance sale on select U.S. models not long ago. The company also has offered special leasing deals to spark sales of its X3 model.

After a long stretch as head of marketing for BMW of North America, Jim McDowell switched jobs with Jack Pitney, who directed marketing for the company's Mini brand. Pitney has begun infusing BMW's marketing with some of the Mini's most successful promotional ideas. He plans to retain "The Ultimate Driving Machine" slogan for BMW's marketing communications because it resonates with the target audience and differentiates the brand from other premium competitors. BMW's worldwide positioning will not change but, with the launch of new models every year, the company will continue refining the promotion mix to attract new buyers, maintain brand image, and keep profits high.[15]

For more information about this company, go to **www.bmw.usa.com.**

Questions

1. What marketing reason could BMW have for limiting the run of its popular web-based movie series to four years only?
2. Why would BMW avoid offering rebates on its vehicles, even though this is a popular sales promotion method among automakers?
3. How does BMW's promotion mix facilitate the personal-selling process when customers visit a BMW dealership?

►► CASE 16.2

Harry Potter and the Wizards of Public Relations

Public-relations magic has catapulted every Harry Potter book to the top of the best-seller lists and transformed every Harry Potter movie into a box-office hit. Worldwide, nearly 300 million copies of J. K. Rowling's Harry Potter books and more than $1 billion worth of tickets to Harry Potter movies have been sold to date. The enormous popularity of the series has made reading "an event with the glitz of a movie premiere," in the words of one children's literature expert. It also has made the author an instant celebrity—and now a billionaire.

The magic started with the U.K. release of *Harry Potter and the Philosopher's Stone* (published by Scholastic in the United States as *Harry Potter and the Sorcerer's Stone*). Sales of this first book picked up quickly, fueled by publicity about Hogwarts and wizardry, the author's background, and even the hefty length of the book. As the buzz carried across the Atlantic, Scholastic started by printing 50,000 copies for the U.S. market. However, the publisher was unprepared for the unprecedented demand and had to reprint this debut book again and again. Readers remained enchanted with the young wizard's adventures, boosting sales of each successive book in the series. In all, Scholastic has sold twenty-six million copies of the first book, twenty-four million of the second, nineteen million of the third, eighteen million of the fourth, and sixteen million of the fifth.

To build anticipation and excitement for the sixth book, *Harry Potter and the Half-Blood Prince*, none of the eleven million copies printed for the U.S. market were sold before midnight on the official launch date. Advertising and sales promotion not only boosted sales, but they also provoked considerable media coverage as well. Bookstores invited readers to preorder the new book and show up at 12:01 A.M.—dressed up as Harry, Hermione, or another character from the series—to pick up their purchases. Barnes & Noble, the country's largest book retailer, offered the book at a 40 percent discount and sold 1.3 million copies in the first forty-eight hours. Amazon.com discounted the book by 43 percent and delivered 1.5 million copies to customers on the launch date. Borders sold 850,000 copies in the twenty-four hours following the launch, with a few stores staying open around the clock. Libraries and schools kept enthusiasm high with Harry Potter parties, parades, and trivia contests.

In addition, all kinds of people connected with the book made public appearances, including author Rowling and Jim Dale, the Shakespearean actor who narrated the audiobook. Reporters sought out children and parents, educators, librarians, literacy professionals, and child psychologists to discuss the "Harry Potter phenomenon." Media coverage continued for weeks as a prelude to the holiday-season release of the *Harry Potter and the Goblet of Fire* movie, just a few months away.

As the premiere date approached, Warner Bros. briefed reporters on every detail of the production. The studio also posted movie previews, games, newsletters, and more on its Harry Potter website (**www .harry potter.com**). The film's teenage stars made news everywhere as they met fans, reporters, and television personalities. The public-relations barrage paid off: *Harry Potter and the Goblet of Fire* smashed box-office records, with $400 million worth of movie tickets sold worldwide in the first ten days.

Warner Bros. kept its public-relations activities going to bring fans back to movie houses a second and third time. For example, it sent Katie Leung, who plays Cho Chang, to visit China. "China is not a market that is used to frequent talent visits, so having Katie Leung there during our second week of release will contribute to maintaining the momentum on the movie," said a studio executive. Clearly, Harry Potter knows the power of public relations.[16]

For more information about this topic, go to **www .harrypotter.com, www.scholastic.com/harrypotter/ home.asp,** and **www.jkrowling.com.**

Questions

1. What would you suggest that Scholastic do to increase sales of earlier Harry Potter books through public relations?
2. How might Warner Bros. use event sponsorship to promote sales of Harry Potter movies on DVD?
3. From the retailer's perspective, what are the advantages and disadvantages of running ads that trumpet sizable discounts on a new Harry Potter book or DVD?

→ CHAPTER 16: JOURNAL EXERCISE

Discovery statement: As this chapter showed, advertising is an important part of an organization's promotional mix.

During the last year, you have been exposed to a number of television advertisements. Identify and describe what you believe to be the best TV commercial that you have experienced over the last year.

_____

_____

_____

_____

Why did you feel that this ad is the very best?

_____

_____

_____

_____

_____

Describe the content of this advertisement in as much detail as possible, and explain what you can recall about this television advertisement.

_____

_____

_____

_____

_____

BUILDING SKILLS FOR CAREER SUCCESS

1. Exploring the Internet

As a promotional tool, the Internet stands alone among all media for cost-effectiveness and variety. A well-designed company website can enhance most of the promotional strategies discussed in this chapter. It can provide consumers with advertising copy and sales representatives with personal-selling support services and information anytime on demand. In addition, many companies use the Internet for sales promotion. For instance, most newspapers and magazines provide sample articles in the hope that interested readers eventually will become subscribers. And virtually all software companies present demonstration editions of their products for potential customers to explore and test.

Assignment

1. Visit two of the following websites and examine the promotional activities taking

place there. Note the sort of promotion being used and its location within the site. Also visit the text website for updates to this exercise.

www.wsj.com
www.businessweek.com
www.forbes.com

2. Describe the promotional tools exhibited on one of these sites.

3. What would you recommend the company do to improve the site?

2. Developing Critical-Thinking Skills

Obviously, salespeople must know the products they are selling, but to give successful sales presentations, they also must know their competition. Armed with information about competing products, they are better able to field prospective customers' questions and objectives regarding their own products.

Assignment

1. Choose a product or service offered by one company and gather samples of the competitors' sales literature.
2. After examining the competitors' sales literature, answer the following questions:
   a. What type of literature do the competitors use to advertise their product or service? Do they use full-color brochures?
   b. Do they use videotapes?
   c. Do they offer giveaways or special discounts?
3. Compare the product or service you chose with what the competition is selling.
4. Compile a list of all the strengths and weaknesses you have discovered.

3. Building Team Skills

The cost of promotional methods is an important factor in a promotional campaign. Representatives who sell advertising space for magazines, newspapers, radio stations, and television stations can quote the price of the medium to the advertiser. The advertiser then can use cost per thousand persons reached (CPM) to compare the cost efficiency of vehicles in the same medium.

Assignment

1. Working in teams of five to seven, choose one of these media: local television stations, newspapers, or radio stations. You can choose magazines if your library has a copy of *Standard Rate and Data Service.*
2. Using the following equation, compare the CPM of advertising in whatever local medium you chose:

$$CPM = \frac{\text{price of the medium to the advertiser} \times 1000}{\text{circulation}}$$

3. To compare different newspapers' rates, use the milline rate (the cost of a unit of advertising copy):

$$Milline = \frac{1{,}000{,}000 \times \text{line rate}}{\text{circulation}}$$

4. Report your team's findings to the class.

4. Researching Different Careers

Most public libraries maintain relatively up-to-date collections of occupational or career materials. Begin your library search by looking at the computer listings under "vocations" or "careers" and then under specific fields. Check the library's periodicals section, where you will find trade and professional magazines and journals about specific occupations and industries. (*Business Periodicals Index,* published by H. W. Wilson, is an index to articles in major business publications. Arranged alphabetically, it is easy to use.) Familiarize yourself with the concerns and activities of potential employers by skimming their annual reports and other information they distribute to the public. You also can find occupational information on videocassettes, in kits, and through computerized information systems.

Assignment

1. Choose a specific occupation.
2. Conduct a library search of the occupation.
3. Prepare an annotated bibliography for the occupation.

5. Improving Communication Skills

The basis for a sales presentation is the prospect's needs. Successful salespeople divide their presentations into components, each of which is an important element in making the sale. Sales presentations typically include an introduction, definition of the need, benefits of the product or service, and the cost of the product or service. One of the most important components of the sales presentation is the demonstration. Commonly used presentation aids include the product itself, videotapes, slides, overheads, flip charts, and computers. A well-planned presentation turns prospects into customers.

Assignment

1. Choose a product that you can demonstrate.
2. Select the audiovisuals most appropriate for the demonstration.
3. Acting the part of a salesperson, explain step by step how the product works. Ask a classmate to play a skeptical customer who questions the reliability of the product. (This presentation may be videotaped or conducted before your classmates.)
4. Summarize what you learned about being a salesperson.

→ PREP TEST

Matching Questions

____ 1. The process includes any nonpersonal, paid form of communication.

____ 2. Advertising that informs, persuades, or reminds potential users.

____ 3. The purpose is to increase demand for all brands of a product.

____ 4. A program-length commercial message placed on television.

____ 5. The job involves explaining benefits of products, creating goodwill, and persuading retailers to buy.

____ 6. It is the most selective medium for advertising products.

____ 7. The main focus is to process the repeat purchases of customers.

____ 8. News stories about products, employees, or a company that appear in the newspaper are examples.

____ 9. The device that holds merchandise for promotional purposes.

____ 10. JC Penney advertises men's sport shirts in a local newspaper.

a. advertising
b. consumer sales promotion method
c. direct-mail advertising
d. infomercial
e. missionary salesperson
f. order taker
g. point-of-purchase display
h. primary-demand advertising
i. promotion
j. publicity

True/False Questions

T F

11. ○ ○ The characteristics of a target market determine the promotion mix.

12. ○ ○ Institutional advertising promotes specific brands of products and services.

13. ○ ○ Most nationally advertised products use immediate-response advertising.

14. ○ ○ A major disadvantage of magazines is their lack of timeliness.

15. ○ ○ Critics argue that advertising is wasteful.

16. ○ ○ Promotion planning begins with a set of specific objectives.

T F

17. ○ ○ Advertisers can reach very specific market segments through ads in special-interest magazines.

18. ○ ○ Radio advertising offers a high degree of selectivity.

19. ○ ○ News releases are the least used type of publicity.

20. ○ ○ Advertising can be broadly classified into three groups: selective-demand, institutional, and primary-demand.

Multiple-Choice Questions

21. Every week the HEB Grocery Store runs a full-page advertisement in the local newspaper. The advertisement focuses on specials for the week, gives easy recipes, and offers special prices on combinations of food products. Which type of advertising is HEB using?

    a. Immediate response

    b. Comparative

    c. Institutional

    d. Primary-demand

    e. Reminder

22. Promotion and marketing objectives include

    a. positioning the product.

    b. stabilizing sales.

    c. increasing the market share.

    d. improving consumer attitudes.

    e. all of the above.

23. Closing the sale is considered the critical point in the selling process. Many salespeople use a trial closing. Based on an assumption that the customer is going to buy, which of the following statements is an appropriate trial closing?

    a. "Will you be placing an order, Mrs. Johnston?"

    b. "Do you want the standard or the deluxe model?"

    c. "Here's my card. Give me a call if you would like to place an order."

    d. "Shall I give you a week to consider the offer?"

    e. "I'll put you down for the deluxe model. Is that your natural hair color?"

24. Deloitte & Touche, a public accounting firm, helps to underwrite the musical production "Mama Mia" currently playing at the Theater Center. Why would the accounting firm do this? What is Deloitte & Touche creating?

    a. Point-of-purchase activity

    b. Sales promotion

    c. Public-relations activity

    d. Community-service activity

    e. Cooperative advertising

25. Which statement is *not* true about advertising?

    a. Most advertising is deceptive and wasteful.

    b. Advertising encourages competition.

    c. Advertising revenues support our mass-communications media.

    d. Advertising is the least expensive means of communicating product information to millions of consumers.

    e. Advertising provides job opportunities in fields ranging from sales to film production.

Fill-in-the-Blank Questions

26. A Coca-Cola advertisement on television is an example of _____ advertising.

27. When a producer such as Revlon and a retailer such as Macy's share the cost of advertising a cosmetic product, they are using _____ advertising.

28. The process of developing an image for a product is called _____.

29. A _____ promotion may include cash refunds, samples, and coupons as inducements.

30. An independent firm that plans, produces, and places advertising is known as an advertising _____.

Online Study Center

FOR MORE test practice, use the interactive ACE quizzes available at the Online Student Center: www.college.hmco.com/PIC/pridebusiness9e.

Answers on p. PT2.

Finagle A Bagel's Approach to Marketing

Round, flat, seeded, plain, crowned with cheese, or cut into croutons, bagels form the basis of every menu item at Finagle A Bagel. "So many other shops will just grab onto whatever is hot, whatever is trendy, in a 'me-too' strategy," observes Heather Robertson, the director of marketing, human resources, and research and development. In contrast, she says, "We do bagels—that's what we do best. And any menu item in our stores really needs to reaffirm that as our core concept." That's the first of Finagle A Bagel's marketing rules.

In addition to its retailing activities, the company wholesales its bagels in bulk to hospitals, schools, and other organizations. It also wholesales a line of Finagle A Bagel–branded bagels for resale in Shaw's Market stores. Whether selling wholesale or retail, the company is always hunting for new product ideas involving bagels.

Product Development: Mix, Bake, Bite, and Try Again

To identify a new product idea, Robertson and her colleagues conduct informal research by talking with both customers and employees. They also browse food magazines and cookbooks for ideas about out-of-the-ordinary flavors, taste combinations, and preparation methods. When developing a new bagel variety, for example, Robertson says that she looks for ideas that are uncommon and innovative yet appealing: "If someone else has a sun-dried tomato bagel, that's all the more reason for me not to do it. People look at Finagle A Bagel as kind of the trendsetter."

Once the marketing staff comes up with a promising idea, the next step is to write up a formula or recipe, walk downstairs to the dough factory, and mix up a test batch. Through trial and error, they refine the idea until they like the way the bagel or sandwich looks and tastes. Occasionally, Finagle A Bagel has to put an idea on hold until it can find just the right ingredients.

For example, when Robertson was working on a new bagel with jalapeno peppers and Cheddar cheese, she had difficulty finding a cheese that would melt during baking but not dissolve and disappear into the batter. Ultimately, she found a supplier willing to cook up cheese formulas especially for Finagle A Bagel. The supplier would send a batch of cheese overnight for Robertson to incorporate into the next day's test batch of bagels. After baking, Robertson would send some of the bagels overnight to the supplier so that the two of them could discuss the flavor, consistency, and other details.

The cheeses and bagels flew back and forth for eight months until Finagle A Bagel hit on a recipe that worked well. "When we finally got it done," Robertson says, "we shipped test batches to our stores, three stores at a time. And we just gave the product away. We'd make several batches during the week, and guess who would come back wanting to buy dozens of these bagels?" That's when she knew the new product was going to be a hit. Not every new flavor becomes popular, however. Dark chocolate bagels with white chocolate chips sold poorly, as did pineapple-mango-coconut bagels. Today, plain bagels remain the best-selling flavor, followed by sesame.

Samples and Coupons Spark Word-of-Mouth Communication

The story of the jalapeno-and-cheese bagel illustrates another of Finagle A Bagel's marketing rules: Spend nothing on advertising. Many quick-serve food companies use television and radio commercials, newspaper advertisements, and other mass-media messages to build brand awareness, promote products, and attract customers. However, Robertson and her colleagues believe that the best way to build the Finagle A Bagel brand and whet customers' appetites for a new menu item is to give them a free taste.

Consider what happened when Finagle A Bagel used samples and coupons to build lunchtime sales by promoting bagel sandwiches in one of the suburban stores. Instead of placing an ad in the local newspaper, Robertson and her staff went to the store and prepared 100 bagel sandwiches. They cut each in half and wrapped the halves individually. Then they set up 200 Finagle A Bagel bags, put a half-sandwich into each, and added a coupon for a free bagel sandwich without any risk. They piled all the bags into a big basket, attached a sign reading, "Free Bagel Sandwiches," and headed to a large intersection just a block from the store.

"Every time the light turned red, we would run out into the middle of the street and throw a bag through someone's car window," Robertson recalls. "We got a lot of strange looks. A few people would roll up their car windows . . . but a lot of people just thought it was hysterically funny. They would be motioning, waving us over, saying, 'What have you got?' And then they'd go back to their office and tell their coworkers, 'Hey, you know what happened to me today? Some crazy lady threw a bagel through my car window, and it was great. You should check it out.'" The entire effort cost $100—and convinced a large number of customers to look around the store, try a sandwich risk-free, and talk up the experience to colleagues, friends, and family.

The popular Finagle A Bagel headquarters tour has become an effective public-relations tool. Community groups, students, and bagel lovers of all ages can visit the "World Headquarters" building and walk through exhibits representing the company's successes and mistakes. In the factory area, visitors watch through a huge window as hundreds of pounds of dough are mixed, cut, and shaped into bagels. The window is set low so even the youngest visitors can get a great view of the process.

Buy a Branded Bagel—Again and Again

Although some restaurant companies want each unit to look distinctly different, Finagle A Bagel uses consistency to reinforce the brand image—another of its marketing rules. "We believe the stores should have a very similar look and feel so that you can walk into any Finagle A Bagel and know what to expect," says copresident Alan Litchman. For example, every Finagle A Bagel store sports an eye-catching burgundy-and-yellow sign featuring an oversized bagel with a few bites taken out. This bagel icon is repeated on posters highlighting menu items as well as on other store decorations.

Still, the suburban stores are not exactly like the downtown stores. Many of the suburban stores have children's furniture and cushiony chairs so that families can sit and relax. Free weekly concerts by the "Music Man"—a local musician—make these stores decidedly family friendly. The city stores have no children's furniture because they cater to busy working people who want to be in and out in a hurry. The Harvard Square store is unique: It has a liquor license and attracts a large student crowd, which means it is busier on weekends than on weekdays.

One of the most effective sales promotion techniques the company uses is the Frequent Finagler loyalty card, which rewards customers for making repeat purchases. For every dollar customers spend on bagels or other menu items, they receive Frequent Finagler points that can be redeemed for free coffee, free sandwiches, and so on. Customers are pleased because they receive extra value for the money they spend—and Finagle A Bagel is pleased because its average sale to loyal customers is higher.

Pricing a Bagel

Pricing is an important consideration in the competitive world of quick-serve food. This is where another of Finagle A Bagel's marketing rules comes in. Regardless of cost, the company will not compromise quality. Therefore, the first step in pricing a new product is to find the best possible ingredients and then examine the costs and calculate an approximate retail price. After thinking about what a customer might expect to pay for such a menu item, shopping the competition, and talking with some customers, the company settles on a price that represents "a great product for a fair value," says Robertson.

Although Finagle A Bagel's rental costs vary, the copresidents price menu items the same in higher-rent stores as in lower-rent stores. "We have considered adjusting prices based upon the location of the store, but we haven't done it because it can backfire in a very significant way," copresident Laura Trust explains. "People expect to be treated fairly, regardless of where they live."

Questions

1. Does Finagle A Bagel apply all seven phases of the new product development process when working on a new menu item such as the jalapeno-and-cheese bagel? Explain.
2. Do you agree with Laura Trust's assessment that adjusting prices based on store location can backfire? What arguments can you offer for and against Finagle A Bagel raising prices in higher-rent stores?
3. Finagle A Bagel is both a wholesaler and a retailer. Which of these two marketing intermediary roles do you think the company should develop more aggressively in the next few years? Why?
4. Should Finagle A Bagel continue to spend nothing on media advertising and rely instead primarily on sales promotion techniques such as samples and coupons?

This part is one of the most important components of your business plan. In this part you will present the facts that you have gathered on the size and nature of your market(s). State market size in dollars and units. How many units and what is the dollar value of the products you expect to sell in a given time period? Indicate your primary and secondary sources of data and the methods you used to estimate total market size and your market share. Part 5 of your textbook covers all marketing-related topics. These chapters should help you to answer the questions in this part of the business plan.

The Marketing Plan Component

The marketing plan component is and should be unique to your business. Many assumptions or projections used in the analysis may turn out differently; therefore, this component should be flexible enough to be adjusted as needed. The marketing plan should include answers to at least the following questions:

5.1. What are your target markets, and what common identifiable need(s) can you satisfy?

5.2. What are the competitive, legal, political, economic, technological, and sociocultural factors affecting your marketing efforts?

5.3. What are the current needs of each target market? Describe the target market in terms of demographic, geographic, psychographic, and product-usage characteristics. What changes in the target market are anticipated?

5.4. What advantages and disadvantages do you have in meeting the target market's needs?

5.5. How will your product distribution, promotion, and price satisfy customer needs?

5.6. How effectively will your products meet these needs?

5.7. What are the relevant aspects of consumer behavior and product use?

5.8. What are your company's projected sales volume, market share, and profitability?

5.9. What are your marketing objectives? Include the following in your marketing objectives:

- Product introduction, improvement, or innovation
- Sales or market share
- Profitability
- Pricing
- Distribution
- Advertising (Prepare advertising samples for the Appendix.)

Make sure that your marketing objectives are clearly written, measurable, and consistent with your overall marketing strategy.

5.10. How will the results of your marketing plan be measured and evaluated?

Review of Business Plan Activities

Remember that even though it will be time-consuming, developing a clear, well-written marketing plan is important. Therefore, make sure that you have checked the plan for any weaknesses or problems before proceeding to Part 6. Also make certain that all your answers to the questions in this and other parts are consistent throughout the business plan. Finally, write a brief statement that summarizes all the information for this part of the business plan.

Part 6

Information for Business Strategy and Decision Making

In this part of the book we focus on information, one of the four essential resources on which all businesses rely. First, we discuss the information necessary for effective decision making, where it can be found, how it is organized, and how it can be used throughout an organization by those who need it. We then examine the role of accounting and how financial information is collected, stored, processed, presented, and used to better control managerial decision making.

17 Acquiring, Organizing, and Using Information

18 Using Accounting Information

Acquiring, Organizing, and Using Information

LEARNING OBJECTIVES

WHAT you will be able to do once you complete this chapter:

1 Examine how information can reduce risk when making a decision.

2 Discuss management's information requirements.

3 Outline the five functions of an information system.

4 Explain how different research methods can be used to obtain information.

5 Analyze how computers and technology change the way information is acquired, organized, and used.

6 Describe how the Internet helps employees to make decisions and communicate, assists a firm's sales force, trains and recruits employees, and tracks employee expenses.

7 Understand how software can be used to collect and distribute information.

WHY this chapter matters

Question: How important is information for a successful business?

Answer: It would be extremely difficult to manage even a small business without information. Although information always has been around, never before has it been so important. With useful information, a manager or employee can make more informed decisions that can improve both a firm's competitive edge and its bottom-line profit amount.

FOR HELP with studying this chapter, visit the Online Student Center:

www.college.hmco.com/PIC/pridebusiness9e

Online Study Center

Harrah's Entertainment, Inc., never gambles with information systems. The company has spent heavily on technology to manage its 90,000 employees, revenue from 40,000 hotel rooms, and 47 casino properties around the world. "Investments in information technology help sustain our position as the industry leader," notes Chuck Atwood, Harrah's chief financial officer.

When an upper-level manager proposes a company-wide technology project to generate additional information, executives use sophisticated software to evaluate how that project would support the firm's overall strategy, how it would affect the product mix, and how it would affect long-term financial goals. This software also looks at the technology staffing, skills, and resources available to complete the project. Then top managers take into account the risks associated with potential problems such as costly delays. Even though a project is in the planning stage, managers also think about what data must be collected to evaluate whether the project lives up to expectations. After projects are approved, the management team relies on software to track progress so that they can identify when projects are running behind or over budget. As a result, 88 percent of Harrah's technology projects wind up costing less than the original estimates.

DID YOU KNOW?

Harrah's Entertainment, Inc., uses information to manage 90,000 employees, 40,000 hotel rooms, and 47 casino properties around the world.

One recent project, dubbed the Revenue Management System (RMS), was designed to gather, store, and process data for making decisions about how to attract more high-spending customers to ten of Harrah's hotels. Simply put, the goal was to increase by 3 percent the amount of revenue generated per room by attracting higher-spending customers. The RMS project, which cost Harrah's $8 million, examined numerous factors, including how much individual customers spent and how many nights each stayed at a Harrah's hotel, along with each customer's profitability.

The RMS was a huge success. Renting rooms to more profitable customers boosted revenue by 15 percent, or $50 million, in the first year. Now the system is Internet-based so that it can be used in dozens of Harrah's hotels. "It's the gift that keeps on giving," says Heath Daughtrey, vice president of information technology services.[1]

For more information about this company, go to **www.harrahs.com**.

How do you manage 90,000 employees, 40,000 hotel rooms, and 47 casino properties around the world? Good question! For Harrah's Entertainment, Inc., the answer is technology. Since this Nevada-based firm operates in a very competitive industry, it is essential that Harrah's have information that not only is accurate but also is up-to-date. To provide information to meet these needs, Harrah's has invested heavily on technology. In turn, the technology generates information that provides both management and employees with the information they need to do their job while increasing both revenues and profits for the entertainment giant. And Harrah's is not alone. In fact, information is so important that every successful business firm needs information.

While some believe that we may be reaching an information saturation point, individuals enjoy having the information that can make life easier and more enjoyable. You, for example, can use computers or cell phones to access information about when a new Harry Potter movie is playing at a local Cinemark theater. With the help of technology, you also can obtain up-to-the-minute news, flight information for a vacation trip to Florida, or the latest weather forecast. Like individuals, business firms use computers and the Internet to find information about their customers, suppliers, competitors, and even new products available in the marketplace.

To improve the decision-making process, the information used by both individuals and business firms must be relevant or useful to meet a specific need. When individuals and business firms use relevant information, the result is better decisions, as illustrated below:

Relevant information → better intelligence and knowledge → better decisions

For businesses, better intelligence and knowledge that lead to better decisions are especially important because they can provide a competitive edge when compared with competitors and improve a firm's profits.

We begin this chapter by describing why employees need information. Just for a moment, assume that you graduated from college three years ago and are now working as an entry-level supervisor for an electronics firm. Consider how the answers to the following three questions could have an impact on you—the entry-level supervisor—on a daily basis.

1. How can information reduce risk when making a decision?
2. What is an information system?
3. How do employees use an information system?

These questions provide the headings for the first three major sections in this chapter. In fact, a practical understanding of what information is and how an information system provides answers to important questions is the first step. The next step is to obtain the information you need. In the last part of this chapter we discuss how employees use business research methods, computers, the Internet, and software—all topics covered in this chapter—to obtain the information needed to make decisions on a daily basis. To learn more about how information can reduce risk when making decisions, read the information in the next section.

How Can Information Reduce Risk When Making a Decision?

As we noted in Chapter 1, information is one of the four major resources (along with material, human, and financial resources) managers must have to operate a business. While a successful business uses all four resources efficiently, it is information that helps managers reduce risk when making a decision.

Information and Risk

Theoretically, with accurate and complete information, there is no risk whatsoever. On the other hand, a decision made without any information is a gamble. These two extreme situations are rare in business. For the most part, business decision makers see themselves located someplace between either extreme. As illustrated in Figure 17.1, when the amount of available information is high, there is less risk; when the amount of available information is low, there is more risk.

For example, suppose that a marketing manager for Procter & Gamble responsible for the promotion of a well-known shampoo such as Pantene Pro-V has called a meeting of her department team to consider the selection of a new magazine advertisement. The company's advertising agency has submitted two new advertisements in sealed envelopes. Neither the manager nor any of her team has seen them before. Only one selection will be made for the new advertising campaign. Which advertisement should be chosen?

Without any further information available to the group, any selection is equally risky, and the team might as well make the decision by flipping a coin. If, however, team members were allowed to open the envelopes and examine the advertisements, they would have more information with which to form an opinion and make an informed recommendation. If, in addition to allowing them to examine the advertisements, the marketing manager circulated a report containing the reaction of a group of target consumers toward each of the two advertisements, the team would have even more information with which to work. Thus information, when understood properly, produces knowledge and empowers managers and employees to make better decisions.

Information Rules

Marketing research continues to show that discounts influence almost all car buyers. Simply put, if dealers lower their prices, they will sell more cars. This relationship between buyer behavior and price can be thought of as an *information rule* that usually will guide the marketing manager correctly. An information rule emerges when research confirms the same results each time that it studies the same or a similar set of circumstances. Because of the volume of information they receive each day and their need to make decisions on a daily basis, business people try to accumulate information rules to shorten the time they spend analyzing choices.

Information rules are the "great simplifiers" for all decision makers. Business research is continuously looking for new rules that can be put to good use and looking to discredit old ones that are no longer valid. This ongoing process is necessary because business conditions rarely stay the same for very long.

> **1 LEARNING OBJECTIVE**
> **Examine** how information can reduce risk when making a decision.

The Difference Between Data and Information

Many people use the terms *data* and *information* interchangeably, but the two differ in important ways. **Data** are numerical or verbal descriptions that usually result from

data numerical or verbal descriptions that usually result from some sort of measurement

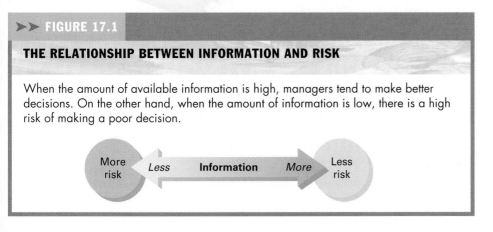

> **▶▶ FIGURE 17.1**
>
> **THE RELATIONSHIP BETWEEN INFORMATION AND RISK**
>
> When the amount of available information is high, managers tend to make better decisions. On the other hand, when the amount of information is low, there is a high risk of making a poor decision.

some sort of measurement. (The word *data* is plural; the singular form is *datum*.) Your current wage level, the amount of last year's after-tax profit for Hewlett Packard, and the current retail prices of Honda automobiles are all data. Most people think of data as being numerical only, but they can be nonnumerical as well. A description of an individual as a "tall, athletic person with short, dark hair" certainly would qualify as data.

information data presented in a form that is useful for a specific purpose

Information is data presented in a form that is useful for a specific purpose. Suppose that a human resources manager wants to compare the wages paid to male and female employees over a period of five years. The manager might begin with a stack of computer printouts listing every person employed by the firm, along with each employee's current and past wages. The manager would be hard pressed to make any sense of all the names and numbers. Such printouts consist of data rather than information.

Now suppose that the manager uses a computer to graph the average wages paid to men and to women in each of the five years. As Figure 17.2 shows, the result is information because the manager can use it for the purpose at hand—to compare wages paid to men with those paid to women over the five-year period. When sum-

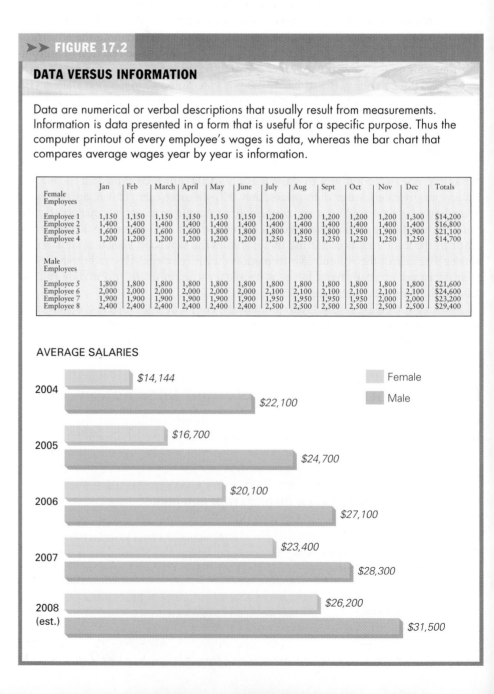

>> FIGURE 17.2

DATA VERSUS INFORMATION

Data are numerical or verbal descriptions that usually result from measurements. Information is data presented in a form that is useful for a specific purpose. Thus the computer printout of every employee's wages is data, whereas the bar chart that compares average wages year by year is information.

	Jan	Feb	March	April	May	June	July	Aug	Sept	Oct	Nov	Dec	Totals
Female Employees													
Employee 1	1,150	1,150	1,150	1,150	1,150	1,150	1,200	1,200	1,200	1,200	1,200	1,300	$14,200
Employee 2	1,400	1,400	1,400	1,400	1,400	1,400	1,400	1,400	1,400	1,400	1,400	1,400	$16,800
Employee 3	1,600	1,600	1,600	1,600	1,800	1,800	1,800	1,800	1,800	1,900	1,900	1,900	$21,100
Employee 4	1,200	1,200	1,200	1,200	1,200	1,200	1,250	1,250	1,250	1,250	1,250	1,250	$14,700
Male Employees													
Employee 5	1,800	1,800	1,800	1,800	1,800	1,800	1,800	1,800	1,800	1,800	1,800	1,800	$21,600
Employee 6	2,000	2,000	2,000	2,000	2,000	2,000	2,100	2,100	2,100	2,100	2,100	2,100	$24,600
Employee 7	1,900	1,900	1,900	1,900	1,900	1,900	1,950	1,950	1,950	1,950	2,000	2,000	$23,200
Employee 8	2,400	2,400	2,400	2,400	2,400	2,400	2,500	2,500	2,500	2,500	2,500	2,500	$29,400

AVERAGE SALARIES

Female | Male

2004 $14,144 $22,100

2005 $16,700 $24,700

2006 $20,100 $27,100

2007 $23,400 $28,300

2008 (est.) $26,200 $31,500

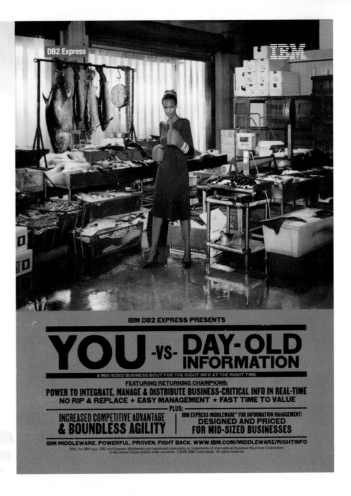

marized in the graph, the wage data from the printouts become information. For a manager, information presented in a practical, useful form such as a graph simplifies the decision-making process.

Large sets of data often must be summarized if they are to be useful, but this is not always the case. If the manager in our example had wanted to know only the wage history of a specific employee, that information would be contained in the original computer printout. That is, the data (the employee's name and wage history) already would be in the most useful form for the manager's purpose; they would need no further processing.

The average company maintains a great deal of data that can be transformed into information. Typical data include records pertaining to personnel, inventory, sales, and accounting. Often each type of data is stored in individual departments within an organization. However, the data can be used more effectively when they are organized into a database. A **database** is a single collection of data stored in one place that can be used by people throughout an organization to make decisions. Today, most companies have several different types of databases. While databases are important, the way the data and information are used is even more important—and more valuable to the firm. As a result, management information experts now use the term **knowledge management (KM)** to incorporate a firm's procedures for generating, using, and sharing the data and information contained in the firm's databases. While there are many advantages to the knowledge management approach, one of the most important is the ability to see the "big picture" and how individual pieces of information fit together. Typically, data, information, databases, and knowledge management all become important parts of a firm's management information system.

database a single collection of data stored in one place that can be used by people throughout an organization to make decisions

knowledge management a firm's procedures for generating, using, and sharing the data and information contained in the firm's databases

What Is an Information System?

Just for a moment, think back to the terrorist attacks on September 11, 2001. Everyone was watching their television sets, listening to the radio, or reading news stories on the Internet in order to obtain the information they needed to determine what was going on and what to expect. Now, years after the terrorist attacks, a new federal Department of Homeland Security uses information to track terrorist activities and hopefully to prevent future attacks that have the potential to kill and destroy. Where does the information come from? In many organizations, including the government and business firms, the answer lies in a management information system (MIS). A **management information system (MIS)** is a system that provides managers and employees with the information they need to perform their jobs as effectively as possible (see Figure 17.3).

The purpose of an MIS (sometimes referred to as an *information technology system* or simply *IT system*) is to distribute timely and useful information from both internal and external sources to the managers and employees who need it. Today, most medium-sized to large business firms have an information technology (IT) officer. An

management information system (MIS) a system that provides managers and employees with the information they need to perform their jobs as effectively as possible

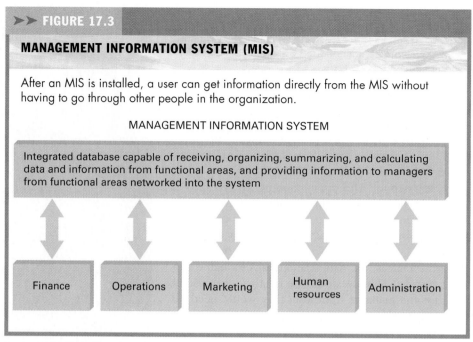

>> **FIGURE 17.3**

MANAGEMENT INFORMATION SYSTEM (MIS)

After an MIS is installed, a user can get information directly from the MIS without having to go through other people in the organization.

MANAGEMENT INFORMATION SYSTEM

Integrated database capable of receiving, organizing, summarizing, and calculating data and information from functional areas, and providing information to managers from functional areas networked into the system

| Finance | Operations | Marketing | Human resources | Administration |

Source: Ricky W. Griffin, *Management*, 8th ed. (Boston: Houghton Mifflin Company, 2005). Copyright © 2005 by Houghton Mifflin Company. Adapted with permission.

information technology (IT) officer a manager at the executive level who is responsible for ensuring that a firm has the equipment necessary to provide the information the firm's employees and managers need to make effective decisions

information technology (IT) officer is a manager at the executive level who is responsible for ensuring that a firm has the equipment necessary to provide the information the firm's employees and managers need to make effective decisions.

Today's typical MIS is built around a computerized system of record-keeping and communications software. In many firms, the MIS is combined with a marketing information system (discussed in Chapter 13) so that it can provide information based on a wide variety of data. In fact, it makes little sense to have separate information systems for

ENTREPRENEURIAL CHALLENGE

The Rise of Craigslist

Started by Craig Newmark in 1995, Craigslist (**www.craigslist.org**) features data for everyday living, such as job openings, real estate listings, personal ads, and more. The original Craigslist focused on the San Francisco area; today, local sites are available for nearly 200 communities worldwide. How did Newmark build his information empire?

- *Standardize.* No blinking or animated ads here—just all-text, easy-to-read listings organized into categories so that users can find what they want quickly.
- *Focus on users.* Newmark spends most of his day reading users' comments, investigating their

complaints, and policing the site to keep scammers out.
- *Provide value.* Businesses in selected cities, for example, pay a nominal fee to post job openings, but users have access to listings for free.

Already, Craigslist sites hold more than six million listings and generate annual revenue topping $20 million. New features are on the drawing board, and even more profits are ahead for this fast-growing business.

the various functional areas within a business. After all, the goal is to provide needed information to all managers and employees.

Managers' Information Requirements

Managers have to plan for the future, implement their plans in the present, and evaluate results against what has been accomplished in the past. Of course, the specific types of information they need depend on their area of management and on their level within the firm.

In Chapter 7 we identified five areas of management: finance, operations, marketing, human resources, and administration. *Financial* managers obviously are most concerned with their firm's finances. They study its debts and receivables, cash flow, future capitalization needs, financial statements, and other accounting information. Of equal importance to financial managers is information about the present state of the economy, interest rates, and predictions of business conditions in the future.

Operations managers are concerned with present and future sales levels, current inventory levels of work in process and finished goods, and the availability and cost of the resources required to produce goods and services. And they are involved with new product planning. They also must keep abreast of any innovative production technology that might be useful to the firm.

Marketing managers need to have detailed information about their firm's product mix and the products offered by competitors. Such information includes prices and pricing strategies, new promotional campaigns, and products that competitors are test marketing. Information concerning target markets, current and projected market share, new and pending product legislation, and developments within channels of distribution is also important to marketing managers.

Human resources managers must be aware of anything that pertains to the firm's employees. Key examples include current wage levels and benefits packages both within the firm and in firms that compete for valuable employees, current legislation and court decisions that affect employment practices, union activities, and the firm's plans for growth, expansion, or mergers.

Administrative managers are responsible for the overall management of the organization. Thus they are concerned with the coordination of information—just as they are concerned with the coordination of material, human, and financial resources. First, administrators must ensure that all employees have access to the information they need to do their jobs. Second, they must ensure that the information is used in a consistent manner throughout the firm. Suppose, for example, that General Electric (GE) is designing a new plant that will open in five years and be devoted to manufacturing consumer electronic products. GE's management will want answers to many questions: Is the capacity of the plant consistent with marketing plans based on sales projections? Will human resources managers be able to staff the plant on the basis of employment forecasts? And do sales projections indicate enough income to cover the expected cost of the plant?

Third, administrative managers must make sure that all managers and employees are able to use the information technology that is available. Certainly this requires that all employees receive the skills training required to use the firm's MIS. Finally, administrative managers also must commit to the costs of updating the firm's MIS and providing additional training when necessary.

Who would think that this CompactFlash card could store more than 45,000 images? In order to meet the needs of both professionals and consumers, Lexar Media developed a CompactFlash card that can store lots of photographs. Now it's the job—some would say opportunity—of Jim Gustke and other marketing professionals at Lexar Media to get information about their new product to the customers who can use it.

2 LEARNING OBJECTIVE
Discuss management's information requirements.

Size and Complexity of the System

An MIS must be tailored to the needs of the organization it serves. In some firms, a tendency to save on initial costs may result in a system that is too small or overly sim-

YOUR CAREER

Employee Alumni Stay in Touch

Should you stay in touch with a former employer after you leave the job? Some high-tech businesses such as Texas Instruments and Hewlett Packard and nontech firms such as Ernst & Young and Fidelity Investments take the initiative to communicate with employee "alumni" through special websites, meetings, or newsletters. As one of these alumni, you may

- Hear about career opportunities by networking with other alumni
- Be asked to refer qualified candidates for job openings
- Be invited to apply for a new job with your former employer

Your former employer may see you as an attractive job candidate because you're already familiar with the company's culture, policies, and management—and because you now have more experience. At the very least, maintaining good relationships with former employers can't hurt when you need references later in your career.

3 LEARNING OBJECTIVE
Outline the five functions of an information system.

ple. Such a system generally ends up serving only one or two management levels or a single department. Managers in other departments "give up" on the system as soon as they find that it cannot process their data. Often they look elsewhere for information, process their own data, or simply do without.

Almost as bad is an MIS that is too large or too complex for the organization. Unused capacity and complexity do nothing but increase the cost of owning and operating the system. In addition, a system that is difficult to use probably will not be used at all. Obviously, much is expected of an effective MIS system. Let's examine the functions an MIS system must perform to provide the information managers need.

How Do Employees Use an Information System?

To provide information, an MIS must perform five specific functions. It must collect data, store the data, update the data, process the data into information, and present information to users (see Figure 17.4).

Collecting Data

A firm's employees, with the help of an MIS system, must gather the data needed to establish the firm's *data bank*. The data bank should include all past and current data that may be useful in managing the firm. Because of the abundance of information available today, only useful information should be entered into the data bank. Data that are obsolete and serve no useful purpose must be filtered out. Clearly, the data entered into the system must be *relevant* to the needs of the firm's managers. And perhaps most important, the data must be *accurate*. Irrelevant data are simply useless; inaccurate data can be disastrous. The data can be obtained from within the firm and from outside sources.

Internal Sources of Data   Typically, most of the data gathered for an MIS comes from internal sources. The most common internal sources of information are managers and employees, company records and reports, and minutes of meetings.

Past and present accounting data also can provide information about the firm's customers, creditors, and suppliers. Sales reports are a source of data on sales, pricing strategies, and the effectiveness of promotional campaigns. Human resources records are useful as a source of data on wage and benefits levels, hiring patterns, employee turnover, and other personnel variables.

Present and past production forecasts also should be included in the firm's data bank, along with data indicating how well these forecasts predicted actual events. And specific plans and management decisions—regarding capital expansion and new product development, for example—should be incorporated into the MIS system.

External Sources of Data   External sources of data include customers, suppliers, bankers, trade and financial publications, industry conferences, online computer services, and firms that specialize in gathering data for organizations. For example, a marketing research company may acquire forecasts pertaining to product demand, consumer tastes, and other marketing variables. Suppliers are also an excellent source of information about the future availability and costs of raw materials and compo-

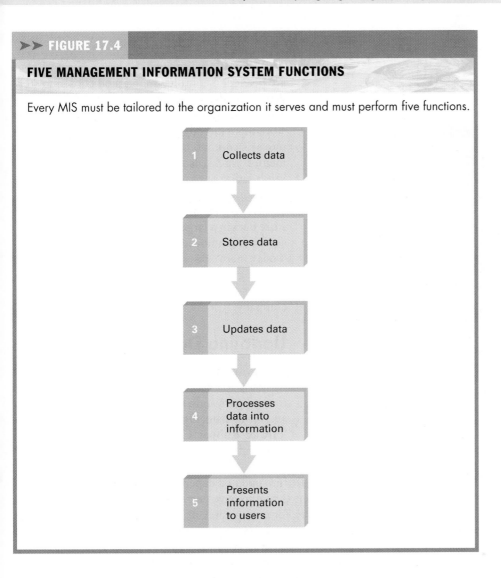

➤➤ **FIGURE 17.4**

FIVE MANAGEMENT INFORMATION SYSTEM FUNCTIONS

Every MIS must be tailored to the organization it serves and must perform five functions.

1 Collects data

2 Stores data

3 Updates data

4 Processes data into information

5 Presents information to users

nent parts. Bankers often can provide valuable economic insights and projections. And the information furnished by trade publications and industry conferences usually is concerned as much with future projections as with present conditions.

Legal issues and court decisions that may affect a firm are discussed occasionally in local newspapers and, more often, in specialized publications such as the *Wall Street Journal, Fortune,* and *BusinessWeek.* Government publications such as the *Monthly Labor Review* and the *Federal Reserve Bulletin* also are quite useful as sources of external data, as are a number of online computer services.

Cautions in Collecting Data   Three cautions should be observed in collecting data for a firm's data bank. First, the cost of obtaining data from some external sources, such as marketing research firms, can be quite high. In all cases, the cost of obtaining data should be weighed against the potential benefits that having the data will confer on the firm.

Second, although computers generally do not make mistakes, the people who use them can make or cause errors. Simply by pushing the wrong key on a computer keyboard, you can change an entire set of data, along with the information it contains. When data (or information) and your judgment disagree, always check the data.

Third, outdated or incomplete data usually yield inaccurate information. Data collection is an ongoing process. New data must be added to the data bank either as they are obtained or in regularly scheduled updates.

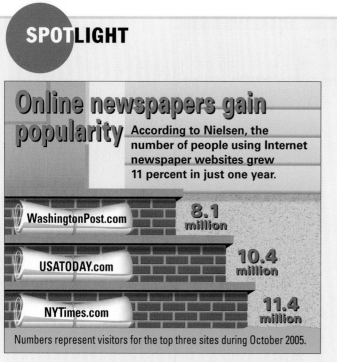

SPOTLIGHT

Online newspapers gain popularity

According to Nielsen, the number of people using Internet newspaper websites grew 11 percent in just one year.

WashingtonPost.com — **8.1 million**

USATODAY.com — **10.4 million**

NYTimes.com — **11.4 million**

Numbers represent visitors for the top three sites during October 2005.

Source: Data from Nielsen/NetRatings website: **Nielsen-netratings.com/news.jsp**; accessed November 11, 2005.

Storing Data

An MIS must be capable of storing data until they are needed. Typically, the method chosen to store data depends on the size and needs of the organization. Small businesses may enter data and then store them directly on the hard drive inside an employee's computer. Floppy disks, CD-ROMs, and memory sticks also can be used to store important information or to move data and information from one computer to another.

Generally, medium-sized to large businesses store data in a larger computer system and provide access to employees through a computer network. Today, networks take on many configurations and are designed by specialists who work with a firm's IT personnel to decide on what's best for the company.

Updating Data

Today, an MIS must be able to update stored data regularly to ensure that the information presented to managers and employees is accurate, complete, and up-to-date. Operations managers at Goodyear Tire & Rubber Company, for instance, cannot produce tires with last week's raw materials inventory. They need to know what is available today.

The frequency with which data are updated depends on how fast they change and how often they are used. When it is vital to have current data, updating may occur as soon as the new data are available. For example, Giant Food, a grocery-store chain operating in the eastern part of the United States, has cash registers that automatically transmit data on each item sold to a central computer. The computer adjusts the store's inventory records accordingly. At any time of the day, a manager can get precise, up-to-the-minute information on the inventory of every item the store sells. In some systems the computer even may be programmed to reorder items whose inventories fall below some specified level.

Data and information also may be updated according to a predetermined time schedule. Data on paper documents, for instance, may be entered into a firm's data bank at certain intervals—every twenty-four hours, weekly, or monthly.

Processing Data

Data are collected, stored in an MIS, and updated under the assumption that they will be of use to managers and employees. Some data are used in the form in which they are stored. This is especially true of verbal data—a legal opinion, for example. Other data require processing to extract, highlight, or summarize the information they contain. **Data processing** is the transformation of data into a form that is useful for a specific purpose. For verbal data, this processing consists mainly of extracting the pertinent material from storage and combining it into a report.

data processing the transformation of data into a form that is useful for a specific purpose

Most business data, however, are in the form of numbers—large groups of numbers, such as daily sales totals or production costs for a specific product. Such groups of numbers are difficult to handle and to comprehend, but their contents can be summarized through the use of statistics.

statistic a measure that summarizes a particular characteristic of an entire group of numbers

Statistics as Summaries   A **statistic** is a measure that summarizes a particular characteristic of an entire group of numbers. In this section we discuss the most commonly used statistics, using the data given in Figure 17.5. This figure contains only

>> **FIGURE 17.5**

STATISTICS

Managers often examine statistics that describe trends in employee compensation.

Sky Cloud Manufacturing
Employee Salaries for April 2007

Employee	Monthly Salary
Thomas P. Ouimet	$ 3,500
Marina Ruiz	3,500
Ronald F. Washington	3,000
Sarah H. Abrams	3,000
Kathleen L. Norton	3,000
Martin C. Hess	2,800
Jane Chang	2,500
Margaret S. Fernandez	2,400
John F. O'Malley	2,000
Robert Miller	2,000
William G. Dorfmann	1,800
Total	$29,500

eleven items of data, which simplifies our discussion, but most business situations involve hundreds or even thousands of items. Fortunately, computers can be programmed to process such large volumes of numbers quickly.

Developing a frequency distribution can reduce the number of items in a set of data. A **frequency distribution** is a listing of the number of times each value appears in the set of data. For the data in Figure 17.5, the frequency distribution is as follows:

frequency distribution a listing of the number of times each value appears in a set of data

Monthly Salary	Frequency
$3,500	2
3,000	3
2,800	1
2,500	1
2,400	1
2,000	2
1,800	1

It is also possible to obtain a grouped frequency distribution:

Salary Range	Frequency
$3,000–3,500	5
2,500–2,999	2
2,000–2,499	3
1,500–1,999	1

Note that summarizing the data into a grouped frequency distribution has reduced the number of data items by approximately 65 percent.

Measures of Size and Dispersion The arithmetic mean, median, and mode are statistical measures used to describe the size of numerical values in a set of data. Perhaps the most familiar statistic is the arithmetic mean, commonly called the *average*.

The **arithmetic mean** of a set of data is the total of all the values divided by the number of items. The sum of employee salaries given in Figure 17.5 is $29,500. The average (arithmetic mean) of employee salaries is $2,681.82 ($29,500 ÷ 11 = $2,681.82).

The **median** of a set of data is the value at the exact middle of the data when they are arranged in order. The data in Figure 17.5 are already arranged from the *highest* value to the *lowest* value. Their median thus is $2,800, which is exactly halfway between the top and bottom values.

The **mode** of a set of data is the value that appears most frequently in the set. In Figure 17.5, the $3,000 monthly salary appears three times, more often than any other salary amount appears. Thus $3,000 is the mode for this set of data.

Although the arithmetic mean, or average, is the most commonly used statistical measure, it may be distorted by a few extremely small or large values. In this case a manager may want to rely on the median or mode, or both, to describe the values. For example, managers often use the median to describe dollar values or income levels when the arithmetic mean for the same numbers is distorted. In a similar fashion, marketers often use the mode to describe a firm's most successful or popular product when average sales amounts for a group of products would be inaccurate or misleading.

Another characteristic of the items within a set of values is the dispersion, or spread. The simplest measure of dispersion is the **range,** which is the difference between the highest value and the lowest value in a set of data. The range of the data in Figure 17.5 is $3,500 − $1,800 = $1,700.

With the proper software, a computer can provide these and other statistical measures almost as fast as a user can ask for them. How they are used is then up to the manager. Although statistics provide information in a more manageable form than raw data, they can be interpreted incorrectly. Note, for example, that the average of the employee salaries given in Figure 17.5 is $2,681.82, yet not one of the employee salaries is exactly equal to this amount. This distinction between actual data and the statistics that describe them is an important one that you should never disregard.

Presenting Information

An MIS must be capable of presenting information in a usable form. That is, the method of presentation—reports, tables, graphs, or charts, for example—must be appropriate for the information itself and for the uses to which it will be put.

Verbal information may be presented in list or paragraph form. Employees often are asked to prepare formal business reports. A typical business report includes (1) an introduction, (2) the body of the report, (3) the conclusions, and (4) the recommendations.

The *introduction*, which sets the stage for the remainder of the report, describes the problem to be studied in the report, identifies the research techniques that were used, and previews the material that will be presented in the report. The *body of the report* should objectively describe the facts that were discovered in the process of completing the report. The body also should provide a foundation for the conclusions and the recommendations. The *conclusions* are statements of fact that describe the findings contained in the report. They should be specific, practical, and based on the evidence contained in the report. The *recommendations* section presents suggestions on how the problem might be solved. Like the conclusions, the recommendations should be specific, practical, and based on the evidence.

Visual and tabular displays may be necessary in a formal business report. For example, numerical information and combinations of numerical and verbal information may be easier to understand if presented in charts and tables.

---

arithmetic mean the total of all the values in a set of data divided by the number of items

median the value at the exact middle of a set of data when the data are arranged in order

mode the value that appears most frequently in a set of data

range the difference between the highest value and the lowest value in a set of data

Visual Displays A *visual display* is a diagram that represents several items of information in a manner that makes comparison easier. *Graphs* are most effective for presenting information about one variable that changes with time (such as variations in sales figures for a business over a five- or ten-year period). Graphs tend to emphasize trends as well as peaks and low points in the value of the variable. Figure 17.6 illustrates examples of visual displays generated by a computer.

In a *bar chart*, each value is represented as a vertical or horizontal bar. The longer the bar, the greater is the value. This type of display is useful for presenting values that are to be compared. The eye can quickly pick out the longest or shortest bar or even those that seem to be of average size.

A *pie chart* is a circle ("pie") divided into "slices," each of which represents a different item. The circle represents the whole—for example, total sales. The size of each slice shows the contribution of that item to the whole. By their nature, pie charts are most effective in displaying the relative size or importance of various items of information.

>> **FIGURE 17.6**

TYPICAL VISUAL DISPLAYS USED IN BUSINESS PRESENTATIONS

Visual displays help business people to present information in a form that can be understood easily.

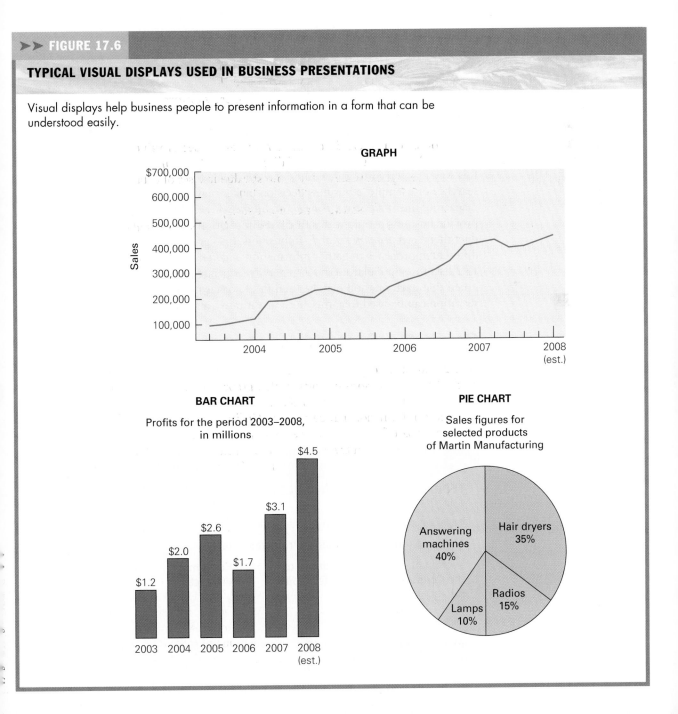

Tabular Displays   A tabular display is used to present verbal or numerical information in columns and rows. It is most useful in presenting information about two or more related variables. A table, for example, can be used to illustrate the number of salespeople in each region of the country, sales for different types of products, and total sales for all products (see Table 17.1). And information that is to be manipulated—for example, to calculate loan payments—also usually is displayed in tabular form.

Tabular displays generally have less impact than visual displays. However, displaying the information that could be contained in a multicolumn table such as Table 17.1 would require several bar or pie charts. In such cases, the items of information are easier to compare when they are presented in a table.

Until now we have discussed why information is important and how an MIS can help both employees and managers function on a daily basis. While it would be nice if information "magically" appeared in a firm's MIS, the truth is that someone has to obtain the information. In the remainder of this chapter we discuss methods that can be used to gather and use the information that employees and managers need to make decisions.

Using Business Research to Obtain Information

4 LEARNING OBJECTIVE
Explain how different research methods can be used to obtain information.

For information about important issues that affect their ability to make decisions, business people use external sources and read trade journals and professional publications, attend conferences, and talk to experts outside their firms. Gathering information in this way is referred to as *secondary research* because someone else did the original research. For example, a business decision maker may read articles published in *Fortune* magazine, the *Wall Street Journal*, or *BusinessWeek*. When secondary sources do not provide business people with sufficient information to make decisions, they may conduct their own *primary research*. In business, primary research uses two fundamentally different approaches to gather information: *qualitative* and *quantitative research*. Table 17.2 lists three popular methods generally associated with each category. It should be noted that each method may be used in the other category as well. For instance, observation can be used to gather both quantitative and qualitative data.

Qualitative Research

qualitative research a process that involves the descriptive or subjective reporting of information discovered by a researcher

Qualitative research involves the descriptive or subjective reporting of information discovered by a researcher. Generally, qualitative research is conducted in one of three ways: observation, interviews, or focus groups. For example, *observation* may be used to

>> **TABLE 17.1**

TYPICAL THREE-COLUMN TABLE USED IN BUSINESS PRESENTATIONS

Tables are most useful for displaying information about two or more variables.

All-Star Landscaping Products Projected Sales

Section of the Country	Number of Salespeople	Consumer Products	Industrial Products
Eastern territory	15	$1,500,000	$ 3,500,000
Midwestern territory	20	$2,000,000	$ 5,000,000
Western territory	10	$1,000,000	$ 4,000,000
TOTALS	45	$4,500,000	$12,500,000

> > **TABLE 17.2**

METHODS USED BY BUSINESS RESEARCHERS

A number of different methods can be used to conduct qualitative and quantitative research.

Qualitative Research Methods	Quantitative Research Methods
1. *Observation.* The act of noting or recording something, such as the facial expressions of shoppers in a retail store.	1. *Survey.* A research method that relies on asking the same questions to a large number of people to obtain responses and information.
2. *Interview.* A conversation conducted by a researcher with an individual to obtain responses and information.	2. *Experiment.* A research method that involves the use of two or more groups of people to determine how people in each group react.
3. *Focus group.* A conversation conducted by a researcher with a small group of people to obtain responses and information.	3. *Content analysis.* A research method that involves measuring particular items in a written publication, television program, or radio program.

better understand retail shoppers' levels of satisfaction. The researcher simply may walk around a JC Penney department store observing the facial expressions and mannerisms of shoppers. Several researchers also may study the behavior of the same group of subjects so that a consensus of opinion can develop. The researchers then create a formal report detailing each researcher's observations.

Business researchers also conduct *interviews* with individuals as well as group interviews. Group interviews, which usually involve six to ten subjects, are called *focus groups.* A researcher for Dell Computer, for instance, may form a focus group to discuss features that should be incorporated in a new laptop computer. By posing questions to the focus group and then recording their responses and concerns, the researcher gathers information that can be used to "fine tune" the product. Based on the information provided by this and other focus groups, Dell can manufacture a product that more closely meets the needs of its customers.

The basic problem with qualitative research is that it is only as good as the ability of the researcher to "read" the situation under study. Given that two people observing the same event may interpret the event quite differently, it is little wonder that some researchers are hesitant to place too great a value on qualitative research without knowing the credentials of the researchers involved.

quantitative research a process that involves the collection of numerical data for analysis through a survey, experiment, or content analysis

Quantitative Research

Quantitative research involves the collection of numerical data for analysis through a *survey, experiment,* or *content analysis.* Many researchers believe that the statistical information that results from analysis of

Where does information come from? For most business firms, the answer is from business research. Typically, business firms can use qualitative or quantitative research methods to find the information used to manage a business. In this photo, Edmunds.com, a leading source of research information for both automobile manufacturers and consumers, provides information about the true cost of automobile incentive programs in an easy-to-understand graph.

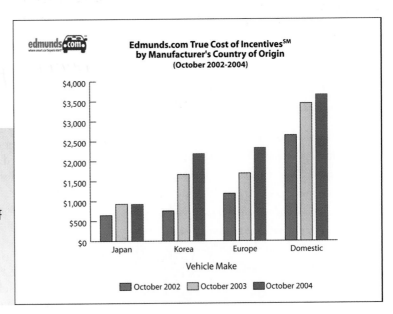

Edmunds.com True Cost of Incentives℠
by Manufacturer's Country of Origin
(October 2002-2004)

Vehicle Make

October 2002   October 2003   October 2004

numerical data represents a more objective and unbiased picture than the subjective interpretation used in qualitative research. To gather numerical data through a *survey*, a researcher might approach shoppers in a Target discount store with a list of questions to determine their degree of satisfaction with store service, personnel, and prices. A response scale often is used to simplify this process. For example, the researcher might ask customers to rank the following statements on a scale of 1 to 5, 5 indicating strong agreement with the statement, 4 indicating agreement, 3 indicating indecision, 2 indicating disagreement, and 1 indicating strong disagreement:

1. The store personnel are friendly and courteous.
2. The store personnel are informed about their merchandise.
3. The store's prices are competitive with prices charged by other retailers in the same area.

A trained researcher walking around the store with a clipboard can easily ask such questions and record customers' responses. However, validity is a concern with this method, too. Some people might not want to speak to a stranger walking about with a clipboard. If this is the case, the data will be heavily biased. To avoid bias, researchers should use several different methods to test the validity of their data. Consistency among the test results can help to alleviate management's concerns about the accuracy of the research.

Experiments typically involve comparison studies of two or more groups of people. Suppose that managers at Southwest Airlines want to know which of three television advertisements is the best choice for the company's target market. Researchers might select three groups of people believed to be representative of the target market. Each group would be shown a film of only one advertisement, and a variety of measurements would be taken after they finished watching it. If the managers were interested in knowing the level of "brand awareness" among the target market, and the level of brand awareness was significantly higher among one group than among the other two, they likely would select the advertisement that was shown to that group. Researchers also might measure brand preferences *before* each group watched the advertisement and then immediately *after*. In this way, the effect of watching the advertisement would be more clearly evident.

Content analysis is a simple technique that involves measuring particular items in a written publication, television program, or radio program. For instance, suppose that footwear manufacturer Adidas wants to know the extent to which its competitors use a specific sports magazine to advertise their products. To determine how much competing manufacturers use the magazine, researchers would examine back issues of the magazine over the last twelve months and count the number and size of advertisements bought by competitors. Based on how much competitors are using the magazine, Adidas might decide to begin an advertising campaign in the same magazine.

Which Research Method to Choose

The decision about which research method or methods to use often is based on a combination of factors, including limitations on time and money and the need for accuracy. In general, managers and employees rely on the results of proven research methods until those methods no longer work well.

Nielsen Media Research, for example, traditionally has led the research industry in measuring the viewing behavior of television audiences. The firm uses a variety of techniques, including "people meters" placed in nearly 10,000 households for nationwide audience measurement. The meter measures three things—when a television is turned on, what station is being viewed, and who is watching. Who is watching television is measured by the "people" part of the people meter. Each member of the household is assigned a personal viewing button. These personal buttons allow Nielsen Media Research to determine which family member is watching which program. Once the data are collected, Nielsen then sells the information to advertisers who want to know when their target audience watches television and, in particular, which programs they watch. The people meter technique is a relatively recent response to the problems associated with earlier methods, such as the diary reports written by people paid to record their television viewing habits.[2]

Using Computers and the Internet to Obtain Information

We live in a rapidly changing **information society**—that is, a society in which large groups of employees generate or depend on information to perform their jobs. The need for more and better information will only continue to grow. Most experts predict that in the future, computers will affect every aspect of our lives. In fact, it would be very difficult to find a person not affected in some way by a computer or the information generated by a computer.

Although much needed information can be obtained by using both qualitative and quantitative methods, business research does take time and effort to obtain needed information. Another source of information is the Internet. Today, businesses are using the Internet to find and distribute information to global users. Currently, the primary business use of the Internet is e-business. In Chapter 4, *e-business* was defined as the organized effort of individuals to produce and sell, for a profit, the goods and services that satisfy society's needs *through the facilities available on the Internet.* The Internet is also used for communicating between the firm's employees and its customers. Finally, businesses use the Internet to gather information about competitors' products, prices, and other business strategies readily available on corporate websites and through online publications and newsletters. Clearly, the Internet is here to stay.

The Internet, the Intranet, and Networks

The **Internet** is a worldwide network of computers linked through telecommunications. Enabling users around the world to talk with each other electronically, the Internet provides access to a huge array of information sources. The Internet's most commonly used network for finding information is the *World Wide Web.* The web contains numerous *sites*—documents whose pages include text, graphics, and sound. To get on the Internet, you need a computer, a modem, and an *Internet service provider* (ISP), such as America Online, AT&T, or other companies that provide a connection to the World Wide Web. Today, connections to the Internet include simple telephone lines or faster digital subscriber lines (DSLs) and cabled broadband that carry larger amounts of data at quicker transfer speeds. **Broadband technology** is a general term referring to higher-speed Internet connections that deliver data, voice, and video material. And with new wireless technology it is possible to access the Internet by using your cellular phone and other wireless communications devices. (Wireless technology is especially attractive for many people because not only does it enable them to access the Internet, but it also enables computers and other electronic components to communicate with each other without the multitude of cables and wires common in many offices and homes.)

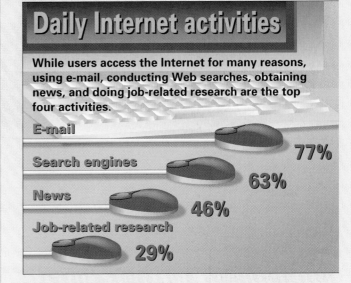

SPOTLIGHT

Daily Internet activities

While users access the Internet for many reasons, using e-mail, conducting Web searches, obtaining news, and doing job-related research are the top four activities.

E-mail — **77%**
Search engines — **63%**
News — **46%**
Job-related research — **29%**

Source: Enid Burns, "Search Usage Spikes as a Daily Online Habit," The Click Z Network website: **www.clickz.com;** accessed November 20, 2005.

5 LEARNING OBJECTIVE
Analyze how computers and technology change the way information is acquired, organized, and used.

information society a society in which large groups of employees generate or depend on information to perform their jobs

Internet a worldwide network of computers linked through telecommunications

broadband technology a general term referring to higher-speed Internet connections that deliver data, voice, and video material

glide

Introducing glide mobile™

The new laws of physics.

As tools such as cellular telephones, pagers, and fax machines have converged with computer technology, inexpensive telecommunications services have become the norm in business. Consider the tools a salesperson for a clothing manufacturer might use during a typical sales call to a nationwide retailer such as the Gap. After discussing the customer's needs, the salesperson opens his or her laptop computer and, using a cellular phone or a convenient phone jack in the office, dials the local phone number of his or her ISP. Once the salesperson is on the Internet, *web browser* software helps the user to navigate around the World Wide Web and connect to the firm's website.

Now the site's *home page* (first page) offers the salesperson several choices, including access to the firm's MIS. By clicking on the appropriate *icons*, or graphic symbols, the salesperson is able to see invoicing records, the present status of outstanding orders, inventory at warehouses located around the globe, and photographs of all available products. Although the salesperson brought a few samples to show the client the quality of the workmanship and fabrics, he or she can generate images on the laptop computer's screen showing the color, pattern, and fabric of any of the firm's products. Furthermore, the latest fashion accessories are flashed on the side of the screen for the customer and sales representative to consider.

As the salesperson enters the customer's order into the computer, a new icon appears on his or her screen indicating that the volume of buying entered thus far requires a credit check before the sale can be closed. While he or she completes the sales presentation, software automatically calculates the allowable credit limit for the customer and provides credit authorization.

In addition to corporate sites, the World Wide Web has a wide array of government and institutional sites that provide information to a firm's employees and the general public. There are also online sites available for most of the popular business periodicals. See Table 17.3 for a listing of favorite websites that managers and employees use to obtain information.

An **intranet** is a smaller version of the Internet for use within a firm. Using a series of customized web pages, employees can quickly find information about their firm as well as connect to external sources. For instance, an employee might use the intranet to access the firm's policy documents on customer warranties or even take a company-designed course on new products and how to introduce them to customers. Generally, intranet sites are protected, and users must supply both a user name and a password to gain access to a company's intranet site.

Both the Internet and intranets are examples of a computer network. A **computer network** is a group of two or more computers linked together that allows users to share data and information. Today, two basic types of networks affect the way employees and the general public obtain data and information. A **wide-area network (WAN)** is a network that connects computers over a large geographic area, such as a state, province, or country. The world's most popular WAN is the Internet.[3] In addition to the Internet, other WANs include private corporate networks (sometimes referred to as *virtual private networks*, or VPNs) and research networks. A **local-area network (LAN)** is a network that connects computers that are in close proximity to each other, such as an office building or a college campus. LANs allow users to share files, printers, games, or other applications.[4] Typically, LANs also will allow users to connect to the Internet.

What will they think of next? With improved technology from Glide Mobile, it is now possible to manage all of your videos, music, documents, photos, contacts, and email from your cell phone. Your phone can now also be your primary tool for accessing and sharing files and information. For more information, go to **www.glidemobile.com**.

intranet a smaller version of the Internet for use within a firm

computer network a group of two or more computers linked together that allows users to share data and information

wide-area network (WAN) a network that connects computers over a large geographic area, such as a state, province, or country

local-area network (LAN) is a network that connects computers that are in close proximity to each other, such as an office building or a college campus

> > **TABLE 17.3**

FAVORITE WEBSITES USED BY MANAGERS AND EMPLOYEES TO OBTAIN INFORMATION ABOUT BUSINESS AND THE ECONOMY

Sponsor and Description	Web Address
1. Bureau of Labor Statistics	**www.bls.gov**
The Bureau of Labor Statistics provides statistical information about all facets of the economy.	
2. Department of Commerce	**www.commerce.gov**
The Department of Commerce is the primary source of government-generated business information.	
3. Federal Reserve Bank of New York	**www.ny.frb.org**
The Federal Reserve Bank of New York provides information about banking and the economy.	
4. American Marketing Association	**www.marketingpower.com**
The association uses its site to provide marketing information and services useful both to its members and to the general public.	
5. *BusinessWeek Online*	**www.businessweek.com**
This site provides articles about business, finance, and economic issues that affect businesses and investors.	
6. *Fortune Magazine Online*	**www.fortune.com**
This site provides articles about business, finance, and economic issues that affect businesses and investors.	
7. *Wall Street Journal Online*	**www.wsj.com**
This site provides current business news along with detailed coverage of the financial markets.	
8. *CEOExpress*	**www.ceoexpress.com**
This site provides an exhaustive collection of well-organized links to a wide variety of business websites.	

Accessing the Internet

In order to access the Internet or an intranet, computers and software must be standardized. **Standardization** is defined as the guidelines that let products, services, materials, and processes achieve their purposes. Establishing standards is vital to ensure that a Hewlett Packard computer in McPherson, Kansas, can "talk" with a Dell computer in San Francisco, California. It is just as important for software to be standardized if businesses and individuals are going to use computers to communicate and conduct business activities through the Internet. The search for available information often begins with a specific website address or a search engine.

standardization the guidelines that let products, services, materials, and processes achieve their purposes

Website Addresses Every website on the Internet is identified by its *Uniform Resource Locator (URL)*, which acts as its address. To connect to a site, you enter its URL in your web browser. The URLs of most corporate sites are similar to the organizations' real names. For instance, you can reach IBM by entering **http://www.ibm.com.** The first part of the entry, "http," sets the software protocols for proper transfer of information between your computer and the one at the site to which you are connecting. "http" stands for *HyperText Transfer Protocol* and frequently is omitted from a URL because your computer adds it automatically when you enter the rest of the address.

Hypertext refers to words or phrases highlighted or underlined on a web page; when you select these, they link you to other websites.

Web Search Engines To find a particular website, you can take advantage of several free search programs available on the web, such as Yahoo!, Google, and AltaVista. While many Internet users are annoyed by the pop-up ads and advertising banners that are common on most search engines, the services provided by search engines are free of charge because advertisers buy space on their screens. Thus the services provided by a search engine are paid for in much the same way advertisements pay for television and radio broadcasts. To locate a search engine, enter its URL in your browser. Some URLs for popular search engines are

> www.altavista.com
> www.google.com
> www.yahoo.com

The home page for many search engines provides a short list of primary topic divisions, such as *careers, finance, news, travel, health,* and *weather,* as well as a search window where you can enter the particular topic you are looking for.

Software for Creating Web Pages

Today, employees and the general public connect to the Internet, enter a web address, or use a web search engine in order to access information. That information is presented on a website created and maintained by business firms; agencies of federal, state, or local governments; or educational or similar organizations. Because a website should provide accurate information, great care is required when creating a website. Generally, once a *template* or structure for the web page has been created, content such as text or images can be inserted or changed readily, allowing the site to remain current.

The design of a firm's website should be carefully thought out. The web page is, after all, the global image distributed to customers, suppliers, and other parties interested in knowing more about the firm and possibly doing business with the firm. What the website says about a company is important and should be developed carefully to portray the "right" image. Therefore, it is understandable that a firm without the internal human resources to design and launch its website will turn to the talents of creative experts available through web consulting firms. Regardless of whether the website is developed by the firm's employees or outside consultants, the suggestions listed in Table 17.4 should be considered when creating materials for a firm's website.

Once a website is established, most companies prefer to manage their sites on their own computers. An alternative approach is to pay a hosting service that often will provide guaranteed user accessibility, e-commerce shopping software, site-updating services, and other specialized services.

6 LEARNING OBJECTIVE
Describe how the Internet helps employees to make decisions and communicate, assists a firm's sales force, trains and recruits employees, and tracks employee expenses.

Improving Productivity with the Help of Computers and Technology

Today, many employees use computers and the Internet to improve productivity and performance and communicate with other employees while at the office or away from the office. In this section we examine several solutions to problems created when a firm or its employees use the Internet. In each case a solution is always evaluated in terms of its costs and compared with the benefits a firm receives, generally referred to as a *cost/benefit analysis.* Typical areas of concern for a business include decision making, communications, sales, training and recruiting, and accounting and finance.

> > **TABLE 17.4**

TIPS FOR WEBSITE DEVELOPMENT

Whether you build your site from scratch, use a web design software program, or hire outside professionals, make sure that your website conveys not only the "right" image but also useful information about your company or organization.

1. Develop a theme	A website is like a book and needs a theme to tie ideas together and tell an interesting story.
2. Determine how much information to include on your site	Get a handle on the type and amount of information that will be contained on your site. Although it is tempting to include "everything," you must be selective.
3. Plan the layout of your site	Think about how you want your site to look. Websites that combine color, art, and links to narrative material are the most useful.
4. Add graphics	Obtain graphics that illustrate the types of data and information contained on your site. Choose colors and photos carefully to make sure that they add rather than detract from the site.
5. Outline the material for each page	Generally, the opening, or home, page contains basic information with links to additional pages that provide more detailed information.
6. Develop plans to update the site	It is important to develop a plan to update your site on a regular basis. Too often sites are "forgotten" and contain dated or inaccurate material.
7. Make sure that your site is easy to use	Stand back and take a look at your site. Is your site confusing, or does it provide a roadmap to get from point A to point B? If you have trouble getting information, others will too.

Making Smart Decisions

With so much information available today, it's no wonder that managers feel pressured to use information to improve the decision-making process. And yet, how do you sort out relevant and useful information from the spam, junk mail, and useless data that employees must deal with on a regular basis in a typical office setting? Three different applications actually can help to improve and speed the decision-making process for people at different levels within an organization. First, a **decision-support system (DSS)** is a type of computer program that provides relevant data and information to help a firm's employees make decisions and choose different courses of action. It also can be used to determine the effect of changing different variables and answer "what if" type questions. For example, a manager at California-based KB Homes may use a DSS to determine prices for new homes built in an upscale, luxury subdivision. By entering the number of homes that will be built along with different costs associated with land, labor, materials, building permits, promotional costs, and all other costs, a DSS can help to determine a base price for each new home. It is also possible to increase or decrease the building costs and determine new home prices for each set of assumptions with a DSS.

Although similar to a DSS, an **executive information system (EIS)** is a computer-based system that facilitates and supports the decision-making needs of top managers and senior executives by providing easy access to both internal and external information. With an EIS, executives can obtain information by touching a computer screen, using a mouse, or using voice recognition and simply talking to the computer. Needed data and information can be displayed in graphs, charts, and spreadsheets.

An **expert system** is a type of computer program that uses artificial intelligence to imitate a human's ability to think. An expert system uses a set of rules that analyzes in-

decision-support system (DSS) a type of computer program that provides relevant data and information to help a firm's employees make decisions and choose different courses of action

executive information system (EIS) a computer-based system that facilitates and supports the decision-making needs of top managers and senior executives by providing easy access to both internal and external information

expert system a type of computer program that uses artificial intelligence to imitate a human's ability to think

"Gotcha!" Because of computers and wireless technology, employees such as this police officer in Flint Michigan can now access information without having to go to the office. For police officers on patrol, the ability to obtain needed information helps them to do a better job of protecting the public and makes their jobs safer.

groupware one of the latest types of software that facilitates the management of large projects among geographically dispersed employees as well as such group activities as problem solving and brainstorming

collaborative learning system a work environment that allows problem-solving participation by all team members

formation supplied by the user about a particular activity or problem. Based on the information supplied, the expert system then provides recommendations or suggests specific actions in order to help make decisions. Expert systems, for example, have been used to schedule manufacturing tasks, diagnose illnesses, determine credit limits for credit card customers, and develop electronic games. And the number of business applications is growing as experts develop new ways to use this high-level type of artificial intelligence.

Helping Employees Communicate

One of the first business applications of computer technology was e-mail. Once software was chosen and employees trained, communications could be carried out globally within and outside a firm at any time, twenty-four hours a day, seven days a week. The firm's costs for software, training, and Internet connection services were small compared with the benefits of being able to communicate with all the firm's employees without having to use traditional pencil-and-paper methods or the telephone.

Today, e-mail solutions are available to firms of all sizes and are used for more than just communicating within a company. e-Mail is being used as a direct link between business and customer. When investment bank Putnam Lovell Securities, for example, sent research reports to clients by e-mail instead of printing, packaging, and shipping the reports, the firm saved over $500,000 a year.[5] **Groupware** is one of the latest type of software that facilitates the management of large projects among geographically dispersed employees, as well as such group activities as problem solving and brainstorming. For example, suppose that the home office of a software development firm in a major city has been hired to prepare customized software for a client in another city. The project team leader uses groupware to establish guidelines for the project, check availability of employees around the world, give individuals specific work assignments, and set up a schedule for work completion, testing, and final installation on the client's computer. As work progresses, the program automatically signals team members for their input. The team leader is also able to monitor work progress and may intervene if asked or if problems develop. When needed, people from various locations, possessing an array of knowledge and skills, can be called to the "workspace" created on the computer system for their contribution. When the work is finally completed, it can be forwarded to the client's computer and installed.

Besides being useful in project management, groupware provides an opportunity for establishing a collaborative learning system to help solve a specific problem. A **collaborative learning system** is a work environment that allows problem-solving participation by all team members. By posting a question or problem on the groupware site, the team leader invites members, who may be located anywhere in the world, to submit messages that can help to move the group toward a solution.

Assisting the Firm's Sales Force

In addition to general communications programs that may be used by all of a firm's employees, there are also Internet-based software application programs sometimes referred to as *customer-relationship management* (CRM) programs that focus on the special informational needs of sales personnel. For example, sales force automation programs support sales representatives with organized databases of information such as names of clients, status of pending orders, and sales leads and opportunities, as well as any related advice or recommendations from other company personnel.

BizTech

Log on and Learn

Just a few years ago, attending employee training meant bringing a pad and pencil to the company classroom or traveling to a special seminar. Now employees are increasingly logging on to learn. According to the American Society for Training and Development,

- Average percentage of learning hours spent in technology-based training: 29

- Average percentage of learning hours spent in classroom training: 42

- Average percentage of learning hours spent in a blend of training methods: 29

The Union Pacific railroad blends web-based training with classroom programs. "If you're training maintenance work-ers, for example, it's hard to torque a wrench on a computer," says the director of technical training. On the other hand, the corporate training director of Trustmark National Bank in Jackson, Mississippi, uses online training because it is cost-efficient and "everybody hears the same message."

Consider what happens when a sales representative for a pharmaceutical company such as Johnson & Johnson is planning to visit doctors, health care providers, and hospitals in the Chicago area. A sales force automation software program can help to map out which clients should be visited by providing useful information such as how long it has been since they were last contacted. The software also can provide information about how clients were approached, what the results were of the last contacts, who else in the pharmaceutical firm has interacted with the client, and previous purchases the client has made.

As sales representatives complete their visits, information about what was learned should be entered into the sales force automation system as soon as possible so that everyone can use the latest information. For instance, a sales representative might learn from an individual within the client's organization that another department is seeking information about a product that could provide a sales opportunity. Although the sales representative may not be involved directly in that field, the information can be entered into the firm's database of information. At the same time, a message can be sent to the sales manager or sales representative in the appropriate department that a new opportunity has been identified. Then a sales representative in the appropriate department can provide information to the potential customer and ultimately increase sales of the firm's products or services.

Training Employees

Large and midsize companies spend a great deal of money on educational and training programs for employees. By distributing information about the firm, the organization, products and services, new procedures, and general information to employees through the Internet for reading and study at convenient times and places, firms can reduce training costs dramatically. For example, new employees generally are required to attend an intensive training program in which a wide variety of information about the firm is presented in a classroom setting. Online training then may be used on a number of topics to provide additional information and keep both new and experienced employees up-to-date on the latest information about the firm and its products and services.

Information on a wide range of topics ranging from ethical behavior to sexual harassment to discrimination also can be distributed to a firm's employees. Often these sites may be needed only on rare occasions; however, it is important that employees

Yet another use for technology. Imagine trying to maintain the information submitted by job applicants who want to work for a firm like Boeing, one of the world's leading aerospace companies. In order to attract skilled candidates, Boeing has a career website at **www.boeing.com/employment/careers.** In fact, most large corporations have a "career hot button" on their corporate home page where both existing and aspiring employees can obtain information about job opportunities within the firm.

know that the information exists and where it is. Furthermore, revision and distribution of important changes to this type of information are much easier if the information is provided on the company's website.

Recruiting Employees

A common icon on most corporate websites is a link to "careers" or "employment opportunities." Firms looking for people with specialized skills can post their employee needs on their websites and reach potential candidates from around the globe. This is an extremely important method of recruiting employees for positions where labor shortages are common, and individuals with the *right* skills are in high demand.

Furthermore, software programs can help large firms such as General Electric, ExxonMobil, and Citigroup to establish a database of potential employees. This is an especially important function for a firm that receives thousands of unsolicited employment applications from people all over the world. The cost of organizing and processing this information is high, but software can reduce this expense when compared with a paper-based system. As a bonus, the software can organize data in a way most useful to the firm. Critical data, such as an applicant's knowledge about IBM's p5 eServer, for example, may be identified quickly by managers using the database.

In addition to individual corporate websites, would-be employees also can access online recruiting websites that can help to match up job seekers with businesses seeking to hire additional employees. Perhaps the best known of these is Monster.com (**www.monster.com**), which recognized the advantages of providing a clearinghouse for job seekers and employers. This type of online service helps to resolve the problems that a person living in one city encounters when searching for employment in another city. On the other hand, this type of online service also can help employers attract job applicants who presently reside in other cities or countries.

Tracking Employee Expenses

The use of expense-tracking software provides an opportunity for firms to improve the way they process employee expense requests. Web-based applications available from Necho Systems Corporation (**www.necho.com**) allow employees such as sales representatives, who regularly pay for many expenses that are part of their job, to report their expenses through the Internet. Expenses then are charged to the appropriate accounts in the firm's accounting system, and sales representatives are issued a refund. Because Necho's software uses the Internet, sales representatives can input data whenever they want and wherever they happen to be in the world. The information they input will be transferred securely to appropriate company personnel, and once expenses are approved, reimbursement checks may be issued quickly. Clients such as American

Electric Power, Honda, Visa, and 7-Eleven, Inc. have been able to reduce expenses while simplifying expense accounting and reducing internal financial management costs by using Necho software.[6]

Business Applications Software

Early software typically performed a single function. Today, however, *integrated software* combines many functions in a single package. Integrated packages allow for the easy *linking* of text, numerical data, graphs, photos, and even audiovisual clips. A business report prepared using the Microsoft Office package, for instance, can include all these components, and the report then may be disseminated electronically through the firm's MIS or the Internet or printed and delivered through more traditional channels, including the U.S. Postal Service or messenger.

Integration offers at least two other benefits. Once data have been entered into an application in an integrated package, the data can be used in another integrated package without having to reenter the data again. Also, once a user learns one application, it is much easier to learn another application in an integrated package.

7 LEARNING OBJECTIVE
Understand how software can be used to collect and distribute information.

Current Business Applications

Software has been developed to satisfy almost every business need. Today the most common types of software for business applications focus on the following functions:

- Database management
- Graphics
- Spreadsheets
- Word processing
- Desktop publishing
- Accounting

From a career standpoint, you should realize that firms will assume that you possess, or will possess after training, a high degree of working comfort with several of these programs, particularly word processing, spreadsheets, and graphics.

Database Management   A **database management program** allows users to store large amounts of data electronically and to transform the data into information. Data can be sorted by different criteria. For example, a firm's personnel department may sort by each worker's gender, salary, and years of service. If management needs to know the names of workers who have at least fifteen years of experience, an employee using database management software can print a list of such employees in a matter of minutes. The same type of manipulation of data for other departments within a business is possible with database management software. In addition to building its own database, a company can subscribe to online computer services that enable users to access large external databases.

database management program software that allows users to store large amounts of data electronically and to transform the data into information

Graphics   A **graphics program** enables users to display and print pictures, drawings, charts, and diagrams. In business, graphics are used for oral or written presentations of financial analyses, budgets, sales projections, and the like.

With the aid of a graphics program, the computer can generate drawings in seconds. Typically, graphics software allows the user to select a type of visual aid from a menu of options. The user enters the numerical data, such as sales figures, to be illustrated. The computer program then converts the data into a graph, bar chart, or pie chart.

graphics program software that enables users to display and print pictures, drawings, charts, and diagrams

Spreadsheets   A **spreadsheet program** is a software package that allows the user to organize numerical data into a grid of rows and columns. With a spreadsheet

spreadsheet program a software package that allows users to organize numerical data into a grid of rows and columns

program such as Microsoft Excel, the computer performs mathematical calculations automatically. For example, a manager at a Macy's Department Store may want to project sales and expenses for the next three-month period. The manager enters numerical data for both sales and expenses, and the spreadsheet software calculates the dollar amount of profit or loss based on the data. If the manager wanted to calculate the firm's profits based on projections that sales will increase by 5, 10, and 15 percent, three additional spreadsheets could be prepared based on each set of assumptions. In fact, a spreadsheet user can change any variable and, within seconds, have new information to aid in the decision-making process.

word-processing program software that allows a user to prepare and edit written documents and to store them in the computer or in a memory device

Word Processing

A **word-processing program** allows a user to prepare and edit letters, memos, reports, and other written documents and to store them in the computer or in a memory device. Text revision is greatly simplified because the user can make changes where necessary without having to retype the entire document. In addition, word-processing programs can be used to send personalized copies of form letters. For example, most firms use a standard collection letter to urge prompt payment of past-due amounts. With a word-processing program, the letter can be personalized by adding an individual's name and address to each letter that is sent to all customers with overdue accounts. To appeal to customers, mail-order firms and direct-mail marketing firms make extensive use of word-processing programs to personalize their sales letters. Thousands of letters—each addressed to a particular individual—can be prepared from one master document.

desktop publishing program a software package that enables users to combine text and graphics in reports, newsletters, and pamphlets

Desktop Publishing

A **desktop publishing program** is a software package that enables users to combine text and graphics in reports, newsletters, and pamphlets. Most desktop publishing programs go beyond word-processing programs to give the user more control over complex designs and page layout. With the aid of a state-of-the-art printer, the user can prepare documents almost as professional looking as those produced by a printing company.

accounting program a software package that enables users to record, process, and report financial information

Accounting

An **accounting program** is a software package that enables the user to record, process, and report financial information. Almost all commercially available accounting packages contain three basic modules: general ledger and financial reporting, accounts receivable, and accounts payable. The general ledger and financial reporting module processes routine daily accounting entries and prepares financial statements at the end of each accounting period. The accounts receivable module prepares customer invoices, maintains customer balances, allows different payment terms to different customers, and generates past-due notices to slow-paying customers. The accounts payable module records and monitors invoices from a firm's suppliers. It also should take advantage of cash discounts offered by suppliers for prompt payment. The better accounting packages also prepare checks to pay suppliers, vendors, and employees.

Other Business Applications

Although it is impossible to describe all the software business firms use today, three programs described in Chapter 9 deserve special mention here. Computer-aided design (CAD) programs use computers to aid in the development of products. Computer-aided manufacturing (CAM) programs use computers to plan and control manufacturing processes. And computer-integrated manufacturing (CIM) not only helps to design products but also controls the machinery needed to produce finished products. Each of these programs streamlines the manufacturing process and ultimately makes a manufacturer more productive. As a result, programs such as these have become an integral part of business firms involved in manufacturing.

In this chapter we have explored some of the functions and requirements of a business firm's MIS and how a computer, the Internet, and technology can help people to obtain the information they need to be effective employees. In Chapter 18 we examine the accounting process, which is a major source of information for business.

RETURN TO   Inside Business

Accurate, up-to-date data about how its millions of customers behave helps Harrah's managers make better decisions about everything from hotel room rates to the mix of slot machines and gaming tables in each casino. To get these data, the company invites customers to join its Total Rewards customer loyalty program. Every time a customer visits a Harrah's casino and presents a Total Rewards card, the company records how much is spent and on what. The more customers spend, the more rewards they earn—rewards such as free meals, merchandise, hotel stays, and travel.

Information generated by Harrah's Total Rewards card and other technology-based initiatives is no accident. To maintain Harrah's state-of-the-art information systems, updates and upgrades to its computer-based information system must be planned and executed carefully. For example, when it was necessary to upgrade the computers at the Horseshoe Casino in Hammond, Indiana, the system used to verify winning slot machine tickets had to be interrupted for brief periods.

Casino management minimized the disruption by having additional staff on hand to manually verify winning tickets for customers while the computer upgrades were accomplished without inconveniencing customers.

Questions

1. Harrah's Total Rewards customer loyalty program generates a great deal of specific information about its customers. How could this information be used to increase revenues and profits?
2. Although Harrah's has invested heavily in technology, it must continue to invest in order to maintain its state-of-the-art information system. Is the investment worth it? Why?

►► CHAPTER REVIEW

Summary

1

Examine how information can reduce risk when making a decision.

The more information a manager has, the less risk there is that a decision will be incorrect. Information produces knowledge and empowers managers and employees to make better decisions. Without correct and timely information, individual performance will be undermined and, consequently, so will the performance of the entire organization. Because of the volume of information they receive each day and their need to make decisions on a daily basis, business people use information rules to shorten the time spent analyzing choices. Information rules emerge when business research confirms the same results each time it studies the same or a similar set of circumstances. Although many people use the terms *data* and *information* interchangeably, there is a difference. Data are numerical or verbal descriptions that usually result from some sort of measurement. Information is data presented in a form that is useful for a specific purpose. A database is a single collection of data stored in one place that can be used by people throughout an organization to make decisions. While databases are important, the way the data and information are used is even more important. As a result, management information experts now use the term knowledge management (KM) to incorporate a firm's procedures for generating, using, and sharing the data and information contained in the firm's databases.

2

Discuss management's information requirements.

A management information system (MIS) is a means of providing managers with the information they need to perform their jobs as effectively as possible. The purpose of an MIS is to distribute timely and useful information from both internal and external sources to the decision makers who need it. The specific types of information managers need depend on their area of management and level within the firm. The size and complexity of an MIS must be tailored to the information needs of the organization it serves.

3

Outline the five functions of an information system.

The five functions performed by an MIS system are collecting data, storing data, updating data, processing data into information, and presenting information to users. Data may be collected from such internal sources as company records, reports, and minutes of meetings, as well as from the firm's managers. External sources include customers, suppliers, bankers, trade and financial publications, industry conferences, online computer services, and information-gathering organizations. An MIS must be able to store data until they are needed and to update them regularly to ensure that the information presented to managers is accurate, complete, and timely. Data processing is the MIS function that transforms stored data into a form useful for a specific purpose. Large groups of numerical data usually are processed into summary numbers called statistics. The most commonly used statistics are the arithmetic mean, median, and mode. Other statistics are the frequency distribution and the range, which is a measure of the dispersion, or spread, of data values. Finally, the processed data (which now can be called information) must be presented for use. Verbal information generally is presented in the form of a report. Numerical information most often is displayed in graphs, charts, or tables.

4

Explain how different research methods can be used to obtain information.

When secondary sources do not provide business people with sufficient information to make decisions with acceptable levels of risk, they may undertake primary research. Primary research in business employs two fundamentally different approaches to information gathering and analysis. Qualitative research involves the descriptive or subjective reporting of information discovered by research. Generally, qualitative research is conducted in one of three ways: observation, interviews, or focus groups. Quantitative research involves the collection of numerical data for analysis through a survey, experiment, or content analysis. The decision about which research method to use often is based on a combination of factors, including limitations on time and money and the need or concern for accuracy. In general, managers rely on the results of proven research methods until those methods no longer work well.

5

Analyze how computers and technology change the way information is acquired, organized, and used.

We live in an information society—one in which large groups of employees generate or depend on information to perform their jobs. To find needed information, many businesses and individuals use the Internet. The Internet is a worldwide network of computers linked through telecommunications. Firms also can use an intranet to distribute information within the firm. Both the Internet and intranets are examples of a computer network. A computer network is a group of two or more computers linked together to allow users to share data and information. Today, two basic types—local-area networks (LANs) and wide-area networks (WAN)—affect the way employees and the general public obtain data and information. Standardization is also important because it allows computers to interact with other computers. Because of standardization, it is possible to use the Internet to access websites, search engines, and web pages to obtain a wealth of information with the click of a computer's mouse.

6

Describe how the Internet helps employees to make decisions and communicate, assists a firm's sales force, trains and recruits employees, and tracks employee expenses.

Today, many employees use computers and the Internet to improve productivity and performance and communicate with other employees while at the office or away from the office. Three different applications—decision-support systems, executive information systems, and expert systems—can help managers and employees to speed and improve the decision-making process. Another application in the workplace is electronic mail, or simply e-mail, which provides for communication within and outside the firm at any time, twenty-four hours a day, seven days a week. An extension of e-mail is groupware, which is software that facilitates the management of large projects among geographically dispersed employees as well as such group activities as problem solving and brainstorming. The Internet and a sales force automation software program can provide a database of information that can be used to assist a sales representative. The Internet also can be used to improve employee training and recruitment while lowering costs. Finally, the Internet can help firms to track employee expenses.

7

Understand how software can be used to collect and distribute information.

Software has been developed to satisfy almost every business need. Today, integrated software combines many functions in a single package. Integrated packages also allow for the easy linking of text, numerical data, graphs, photos, and even audiovisual clips. And once data have been entered into an application, the data can be used in another integrated package without having to be reentered into the system. The most common programs for business applications include database management, graphics, spreadsheets, word processing, desktop publishing, and accounting. Although it is impossible to describe all the software business firms use today, computer-aided design (CAD), computer-aided manufacturing (CAM), and computer-integrated manufacturing (CIM) should be mentioned because they are used to help manufacture the products a firm sells in the marketplace. From a career standpoint, you should realize that firms will assume that you possess, or will possess after training, a high degree of working comfort with several of these programs, particularly word processing, spreadsheets, and graphics.

Key Terms

You should now be able to define and give an example relevant to each of the following terms:

data (553)
information (554)
database (555)
knowledge management (555)
management information system (MIS) (555)
information technology (IT) officer (556)
data processing (560)
statistic (560)
frequency distribution (561)
arithmetic mean (562)
median (562)
mode (562)
range (562)
qualitative research (564)
quantitative research (565)
information society (567)
Internet (567)
broadband technology (567)
intranet (568)
computer network (568))
wide-area network (WAN) (568)
local-area network (LAN) (568)
standardization (569)
decision-support system (DSS) (571)
executive information system (EIS) (571)
expert system (571)
groupware (572)
collaborative learning system (572)
database management program (575)
graphics program (575)
spreadsheet program (575)
word-processing program (576)
desktop publishing program (576)
accounting program (576)

Review Questions

1. In your own words, describe how information reduces risk when you make a personal or work-related decision.
2. What are information rules? How do they simplify the process of making decisions?

3. What is the difference between data and information? Give one example of accounting data and one example of accounting information.
4. How do the information requirements of managers differ by management area?
5. Why must a management information system (MIS) be tailored to the needs of the organization it serves?
6. List five functions of an MIS.
7. What are the differences among the mean, median, and mode of a set of data? How can a few extremely small or large numbers affect the mean?
8. What are the components of a typical business report?
9. What is the difference between qualitative research and quantitative research?
10. Describe the methods used to conduct qualitative research and quantitative research.
11. Explain the differences between the Internet and an intranet. What types of information does each of these networks provide?
12. What is the difference between a wide-area network (WAN) and a local-area network (LAN)?
13. Why is standardization necessary for computers and the Internet to operate properly?
14. How can a web search engine such as Yahoo!, AltaVista, or Google help you to find information on a business topic such as interest rates or the consumer price index?
15. What factors should be considered when a firm is developing a web page?
16. How do business firms use groupware to encourage collaborative learning systems?
17. Describe how the Internet and software can help a firm's employees make decisions, train and recruit employees, and track expenses.
18. Describe how businesses use database management programs, graphics programs, spreadsheet programs, word-processing programs, desktop publishing programs, and accounting programs.

Discussion Questions

1. How can confidential data and information (such as the wages of individual employees) be kept confidential and yet still be available to managers who need them?
2. Do managers really need all the kinds of information discussed in this chapter? If not, which kinds can they do without?
3. Why are computers so well suited to management information systems (MISs)? What are some things computers *cannot* do in dealing with data and information?
4. Assume that you have been out of college for ten years, are unemployed, and your computer skills are seriously outdated. How would you go about updating your computer skills?
5. How could the Internet help you to find information about employment opportunities at Coca-Cola, Johnson & Johnson, or Microsoft? Describe the process you would use to access this information.

➤➤ VIDEO CASE 17.1

Lextant's Research Helps Managers Make Decisions

Good management decisions start with good information because today's business world is more complex, changeable, and competitive than ever before. Executives must have solid, up-to-date information to identify problems or opportunities correctly, assess and select suitable solutions, and evaluate the results of their decisions. Quantitative research provides information that can help managers to determine the "what" of product usage, such as what features appeal to different groups of customers. Qualitative research goes beyond "what" to uncover the "why" of product usage by studying how customers actually use certain products and by learning how customers think and feel about specific products and brands.

Lextant Corp., based in Columbus, Ohio, specializes in qualitative research. Its experts are experienced in using observation and focus groups to understand customers' behavior, needs, attitudes, and reactions. For example, Lextant researchers traveled to China to observe surgeons at work so that they could help a manufacturer develop superpremium medical equipment for hospital operating rooms. The researchers made detailed notes on how much space was available in the operating room, who participated in the surgery and for how long, what role each participant played, how participants interacted, and whether the surgical equipment presented any constraints to efficient and effective medical attention.

After returning from China, the researchers processed the data to pinpoint meaningful patterns. They had no preconceived ideas about what the data might reveal; instead, they were looking for clues to patterns that were representative of customer attitudes or that indicated a particular problem in the operating room. Based on their analysis of the data, the Lextant researchers were able to recommend a number of product design enhancements to address the specific needs of surgical teams in Chinese hospitals.

The Hard Rock Café also has hired Lextant to conduct business research as input for decisions about the company's e-commerce activities. Top management wanted to use the website to boost online sales, increase customer retention, and attract new customers. Lextant's specialists dug deep to learn why consumers were visiting the site, what their expectations were, and what they thought of their online experience at hardrock.com. Armed with this knowledge, the researchers created prototype pages and navigation flows so that the Hard Rock Café could test and refine new areas of the site before making them available to the public. This research helped the Hard Rock Café increase its online revenues, turn visitors into buyers, and encourage customers to return to the site more frequently.

Another client, Wilson Leather, recently was searching for ways to strengthen brand awareness. The retail chain's executives wondered whether customers viewed the brand the way management viewed it. Lextant used qualitative research to collect data about the customers' perspective. Researchers conducted a focus group to check brand awareness among consumers. They also conducted research to find out what customers consider the ideal leather-shopping experience and to learn how Wilson Leather measures up to that ideal. As a result, the chain's executives discovered that their view of the brand was not the same as the customers' view. The executives then were able to use the information provided by Lextant to make marketing decisions that moved Wilson Leather closer to the ideal leather-shopping experience.

Many software manufacturers have asked Lextant's experts to identify specific changes that would make their products easier to use. Chris Rockwell, Lextant's president and CEO, says that "sometimes the best thing to do is to just watch somebody trying to use the software." Observation is particularly valuable because it allows the researcher to see first hand the environment in which the software is being used and the minute-by-minute reaction of users trying to accomplish specific tasks.

The point of such usability testing is to reveal whether software users actually can complete typical tasks and whether they tend to make certain kinds of mistakes. If research shows that a number of users are experiencing similar problems with a software product, it's time for management to make changes. Similarly, usability testing for websites can provide the information managers need for decisions about how to improve the online experience for customers while helping the company achieve its e-commerce objectives.[7]

For more information about this company, go to **www.lextantcorp.com**.

Questions

1. A firm such as Lextant charges its clients to conduct research. At a time when most corporations are trying to reduce marketing costs and business expenses, is the cost of obtaining information from outside research firms such as Lextant worthwhile? Explain your answer.
2. Why do Lextant's researchers use qualitative rather than quantitative research to understand how and why people use software products?
3. What are the possible advantages and disadvantages of using only focus groups to gather data for management decisions about developing a new product?
4. Lextant's research helps marketing managers to develop and refine products such as surgical equipment. Why would finance, operations, and administrative managers also want access to the research results?

➤➤ CASE 17.2

The Blog's the Thing at IBM

"Other companies have fired people for blogging, but IBM is encouraging it," states Christopher Barger, the tech giant's "blogger in chief." Blogging (short for *web logging*) means posting comments on an Internet site known as a blog (or *web log*). Like a growing number of companies—tech and nontech alike—IBM sees blogging as a way to stay in touch informally with a community of interested people, share ideas, and gauge responses to issues and products. In the course of blogging, IBM employees pick up valuable information about what customers want, how they think, how they use tech products, and what others in the industry are doing.

More than 15,000 IBMers contribute to the company's internal blog. In addition, 2,200 employees have blogs that are open to the public, regularly attracting comments from customers, colleagues, and business partners. For example, 14,000 people check Ed Brill's blog (**www.edbrill.com**) every day to see what the head of IBM's Lotus Notes software division is up to. Brill has been blogging since 2002, and his blog is so popular that it rates among the top 5,000 in the "blogosphere." Although he spends an hour or more on his daily blogging, investing this kind of time has paid off. "I found that the one-to-one community interactions became incredibly powerful for decision making in my own job and for feedback in my own organization," he explains. "It also keeps me up on competitive trends."

In the past, when Brill wanted to learn about customers' reactions to something Lotus Notes was doing, he'd ask company salespeople to ask their customers and report back. Getting answers in this fashion took time. Today, he can talk directly (and unofficially) to customers through his blog. Recently, Brill posted a question on his blog seeking reaction to a Lotus Notes ad. By the next day, he had thirty-six responses. "I can take a pulse on anything I am working on. It's not a random sample, but it doesn't take three months to get feedback," he says.

IBM gives all employees access to blogging software, along with basic blogging guidelines. The company requires employees to identify themselves by name and title or role when blogging about IBM-related matters. At the same time, employees must clarify that they are blogging as individuals and not as official IBM representatives. They are expected to comply with IBM's code of business conduct, respect their audience, maintain the confidentiality of trade secrets, and follow copyright laws. IBM also tells employees: "Don't pick fights, be the first to correct your own mistakes, and don't alter previous posts without indicating that you have done so."

Monitoring nonemployee blogs gives IBM managers a good sense of market trends and shifts in customer needs and concerns. Instead of clicking from one blog to the next, which is tedious and time-consuming, IBMers use sophisticated blog-search tools to track mentions of the company and its products. These tools also help IBM to follow postings about the industry and its technology.

IBM continues to conduct hundreds of traditional marketing research studies every year, covering everything from customer satisfaction to brand image. While blogging is no substitute for these types of statistically valid surveys, it does help IBM to do more than simply acquire data for management decisions. "This is a way to get our expertise out there, not by shoving it down people's throats, but by just starting conversations," states Christopher Barger.[8]

For more information about this company, go to **www.ibm.com**.

Questions

1. Compared with more traditional research methods used to gather information, what are the advantages of using blogging to obtain information for a corporation such as IBM?

2. Why would IBM encourage blogging for internal audiences as well as for external audiences?

3. What are the advantages and disadvantages of IBM allowing its employees to post messages on blogs maintained by outsiders?

4. Considering the corporation's reputation for ethical business practices, IBM employees are given guidelines of what is acceptable behavior when blogging. What could happen if a company didn't provide similar guidelines and "left it up to an employee's own judgment"?

→ CHAPTER 17: JOURNAL EXERCISE

Discovery statement: Before making a decision to buy a product or service, many consumers use the Internet to obtain information that helps them to make a purchase decision. Choose one of the following products and use the Internet to obtain information about that product. Then record your answers to the questions below.

- A movie that was released within the last two weeks
- A laptop computer that costs between $500 and $995
- A new automobile that costs between $20,000 and $24,000

What website did you use to obtain information about the product you chose?

_____

What type of information was contained on the website? Was there enough information to persuade you to buy this product?

_____

_____

_____

_____

_____

Take another look at the website. Describe any missing information that you could have used to make your buying decision.

_____

_____

_____

_____

_____

What specific suggestions would you make to improve the website?

_____

_____

_____

_____

_____

BUILDING SKILLS FOR CAREER SUCCESS

1. Exploring the Internet

Computer technology is a fast-paced, highly competitive industry in which product life cycles sometimes are measured in months or even weeks. To keep up with changes and trends in hardware and software, MIS managers routinely must scan computer publications and websites that discuss new products.

A major topic of interest among MIS managers is groupware, software that facilitates the management of large projects among geo-graphically dispersed employees, as well as group activities such as problem solving and brainstorming.

Assignment

1. Use a search engine and enter the keyword *groupware* to locate companies that provide this type of software. Try the demonstration edition of the groupware if it is available.

2. Based on your research of this business application, why do you think groupware is growing in popularity?

3. Describe the structure of one of the groupware programs you examined as well as your impressions of its value to users.

2. Developing Critical-Thinking Skills

To stay competitive in the marketplace, businesses must process data into information and make that information readily available to decision makers. For this, many businesses rely on a management information system (MIS). The purpose of an MIS is to provide managers with accurate, complete, and timely information so that they can perform their jobs as effectively as possible. Because an MIS must fit the needs of the firm it serves, these systems vary in the way they collect, store, update, and process data and present information to users.

Assignment

1. Select a local company large enough to have an MIS. Set up an interview with the person responsible for managing the flow of information within the company.

2. Prepare a list of questions you will ask during the interview. Structure the questions around the five basic functions of an MIS. Some sample questions follow:

   a. *Collecting data.* What type of data are needed? How often are data collected? What sources produce the data? How do you ensure that the data are accurate?

   b. *Storing data.* How are data stored?

   c. *Updating data.* What is the process for updating?

   d. *Processing data.* Can you show me some examples of the types of data that will be processed into information? How is the processing done?

   e. *Presenting information.* Would you show me some examples (reports, tables, graphs, charts) of how the information is presented to various decision makers and tell me why that particular format is used?

3. At the end of the interview, ask the interviewee to predict how the system will change in the next three years.

4. In a report, describe what you believe the strengths and weaknesses of this firm's MIS are and make recommendations for improving the system. Also describe the most important thing you learned from the interview.

3. Building Team Skills

To provide marketing managers with information about consumers' reactions to a particular product or service, business researchers often conduct focus groups. The participants in these groups are representative of the target market for the product or service under study. The leader poses questions and lets members of the group express their feelings and ideas about the product or service. The ideas are recorded, transcribed, and analyzed.

Assignment

1. Working in a small team, select a product or service to research—for example, your college's food service or bookstore or a new item you would like to see stocked in your local grocery store.

2. Create a list of questions that can be used to generate discussion about the product or service with focus-group members.

3. Form a focus group of five to seven people representative of the market for the product or service your team has selected.

4. During the group sessions, record the input. Later, transcribe it into printed form, analyze it, and process it into information. On the basis of this information, make recommendations for improving the product or service.

5. In a report, describe your team's experiences in forming the focus groups and the value of focus groups in collecting data. Use the report as the basis for a five- to ten-minute class presentation.

4. Researching Different Careers

Firms today expect employees to be proficient in using computers and computer software. Typical business applications include e-mail, word processing, spreadsheets, and graphics. By improving your skills in these areas, you can increase your chances not only of being employed but also of being promoted once you are employed.

Assignment

1. Assess your computer skills by placing a check in the appropriate column in the following table:

Software	Skill Level			
	None	Low	Average	High
Database management				
Graphics				
Spreadsheet				
Word processing				
Desktop publishing				
Accounting				
Groupware				

2. Describe your self-assessment in a written report. Specify the software programs in which you need to become more proficient, and outline a plan for doing this.

5. Improving Communication Skills

Over the past decade, computers have changed the way we do business and conduct our daily lives. As computer technology continues to improve over the next decade, it will affect our lives in new and very different ways.

Assignment

1. Research articles that predict how computers will be used in the next decade and how their use will change the way we live.

2. Write a paper focusing on the future use of computers in two or more of the following areas: health care, genetics, travel, communications, manufacturing, transportation, management, farming, or meal preparation. Conclude your paper with a discussion of how you think computers will affect your life over the next ten years.

→ PREP TEST

Matching Questions

____ 1. Data that have been processed.

____ 2. It is numerical or verbal descriptions that result from taking a measurement.

____ 3. It incorporates a firm's procedures for generating, using, and sharing the data and information contained in the firm's database.

____ 4. It transforms data into useful information.

____ 5. It can access a firm's policy documents.

____ 6. Employees at various locations can keep track as work progresses.

____ 7. The collection of numerical data is involved.

____ 8. It is a work environment that allows groups to solve problems.

____ 9. The most frequently used statistical measure.

____ 10. This tool organizes numerical data in grids of rows and columns.

a. arithmetic mean
b. collaborative learning system
c. data
d. data processing
e. groupware
f. information
g. intranet
h. knowledge management
i. quantitative research
j. spreadsheet program

True/False Questions

T F

11. ○ ○ Information rules help consumers to make purchasing decisions.

12. ○ ○ Information rules can reduce the time business people spend analyzing choices.

13. ○ ○ The recommendation section of a business report lists the findings.

14. ○ ○ Most data gathered for an MIS come from external sources.

15. ○ ○ Information gathered from trade journals is considered primary data.

T F

16. ○ ○ A major way to conduct quantitative research is to use focus groups.

17. ○ ○ MIS is defined as a system of connected computers revolving around a mainframe or minicomputer.

18. ○ ○ A pie chart is a circle divided into slices, each of which represents a different item.

19. ○ ○ One of the first business applications of computer technology was e-mail.

20. ○ ○ Frequency distribution increases the number of data items.

Multiple-Choice Questions

21. You are a purchasing manager in a large firm and are responsible for deciding on and ordering the appropriate software program that allows the user to prepare and edit letters and store them on a disk. What type of program will you order?

    a. Spreadsheet

    b. Word processing

    c. Graphics

    d. Communications

    e. Database

22. Management information systems

    a. collect data, hire personnel, and compensate workers.

    b. store data, present data to users, and make final decisions.

    c. collect, store, update, process, and present data.

    d. supervise personnel, reprimand workers, and conduct follow-ups.

    e. collect relevant information.

23. As an MIS manager, you are charged with establishing a management information system that is capable of presenting information in a usable form. Which item below do you feel is *not* appropriate for presenting information in business-report format?

    a. The introduction describes the problem and techniques used to gather data.

    b. The body of the report describes the facts.

    c. The conclusions describe the findings.

    d. The recommendations present suggestions for solving the problem.

    e. The database of research methods used by the author of the report..

24. As an information manager, you must ensure that

    a. information is protected from employees.

    b. information is used in a consistent manner.

    c. the smart group receives the data first.

    d. the promotional campaigns are aired on time.

    e. new product planning is on schedule.

25. A single collection of data stored in one place and used by employees throughout an organization is called a(n)

    a. data collection.

    b. information center.

    c. database.

    d. data center.

    e. management data center.

Fill-in-the-Blank Questions

26. The value that appears the most times in a data set is called the _____.

27. Descriptive or subjective information is the result of _____ research.

28. A visual that is most effective for presenting information about one variable that changes over time is a _____.

29. The goal of a management information system is to provide needed _____ to all managers.

30. In the following data set—5, 8, 9, 5, 3, 4, 5, 2, 3, 6—the arithmetic mean is _____.

Online Study Center

FOR MORE test practice, use the interactive ACE quizzes available at the Online Student Center: **www.college.hmco.com/PIC/pridebusiness9e.**

Answers on p. PT2.

Using Accounting Information

LEARNING OBJECTIVES

WHAT you will be able to do once you complete this chapter:

1 Explain why accurate accounting information and audited financial statements are important.

2 Identify the people who use accounting information and possible careers in the accounting industry.

3 Discuss the accounting process.

4 Read and interpret a balance sheet.

5 Read and interpret an income statement.

6 Describe business activities that affect a firm's cash flow.

7 Summarize how managers evaluate the financial health of a business.

WHY this chapter matters

Although lenders, suppliers, stockholders, and government agencies all rely on the information generated by a firm's accounting system, the primary users of accounting information are managers. It is impossible to manage a business without accurate and up-to-date information supplied by the firm's accountants.

FOR HELP with studying this chapter, visit the Online Student Center:

www.college.hmco.com/PIC/pridebusiness9e

Online Study Center

Most of America's largest 1,000 corporations count on one of the "Big Four" U.S. accounting firms to double-check internal accounting procedures, review financial records, and sign off on annual reports. The Big Four consist of Deloitte Touche Tohmatsu, Ernst & Young, PricewaterhouseCoopers, and KPMG, each employing tens of thousands of accounting and tax experts. The fifth- and sixth-largest U.S. accounting firms, Grant Thornton and BDO Seidman, also handle accounting services for major corporations.

The number of big accounting firms has dropped in the past two decades as firms merged to gain economies of scale and diversify their services. High-profile legal problems have brought even more dramatic changes to the industry. Arthur Andersen, for example, was convicted of obstructing justice in the government investigation of client Enron's sudden (and massive) bankruptcy. This effectively put Andersen out of business, even though the Supreme Court eventually overturned the conviction. Then, months after Enron's collapse, WorldCom filed for bankruptcy following the disclosure of accounting frauds involving billions of dollars.

DID YOU KNOW?

Most of America's largest 1,000 corporations count on one of the "Big Four" U.S. accounting firms to double-check internal accounting procedures, review financial records, and sign off on annual reports.

In the wake of these and other big-money scandals, the U.S. Congress tightened key accounting and financial reporting rules. As a result, corporations have put in place more stringent controls to ensure that the accounting process runs smoothly and that their financial records are both accurate and complete. Now the biggest accounting firms are busier than ever, conducting in-depth audits for clients and complying with the government's tougher documentation requirements.

All this extra work is generating extra revenue but also putting extra pressure on the employees of major accounting firms. "Public accounting firms have just been inundated with work," confirms the head of the accounting department at Ohio State University in Columbus. And who's auditing these busy auditors? An independent board has been established to investigate how well the big accounting firms handle their reviews of corporate clients' accounting practices and financial statements.[1]

For more information about these companies, go to **www.deloitte.com**, **www.ey.com**, **www .pwcglobal.com**, and **www.kpmg.com**.

For investors, corporate executives and employees, lenders, and government regulators, the financial reporting problems at Enron and WorldCom were a wake-up call for more exacting accounting standards. After these financial horror stories, the U.S. Congress tightened key accounting and financial reporting rules. As a result, corporations have enacted more stringent controls to ensure that the accounting process runs smoothly and that their financial records are both accurate and complete. And the "Big Four," along with smaller U.S. accounting firms, that are responsible for auditing a corporation's accounting records and signing off on annual reports are busier than ever. The message now is clear: Accounting and financial information is too important and the penalties too severe to "doctor" the books and report inflated revenues and phony earnings.

We begin this chapter by looking at why accounting information is important, the recent problems in the accounting industry, and attempts to improve financial reporting. Then we look at how managers, employees, individuals, and groups outside a firm use accounting information. We also identify different types of accountants and career opportunities in the accounting industry. Next, we focus on the accounting process and the basics of an accounting system. We also examine the three most important financial statements: the balance sheet, the income statement, and the statement of cash flows. Finally, we show how ratios are used to measure specific aspects of a firm's financial health.

Why Accounting Information Is Important

Accounting is the process of systematically collecting, analyzing, and reporting financial information. Today it is impossible to manage a business without accurate and up-to-date information supplied by the firm's accountants. Just for a moment, think about the following three questions:

1. How much profit did a business earn last year?
2. How much tax does a business owe the Internal Revenue Service?
3. How much cash does a business have on hand?

In each case, the firm's accountants and its accounting system provide the answers to these questions and many others. And while accounting information can be used to answer questions about what has happened in the past, it also can be used to help make decisions about the future. For these reasons, accounting is one of the most important areas within a business organization.

Because the information provided by a firm's accountants and its accounting system is so important, managers and other groups interested in a business firm's financial records must be able to "trust the numbers." Unfortunately, a large number of accounting scandals have caused people to doubt not only the numbers but also the accounting industry.

Recent Accounting Problems for Corporations and Their Auditors

Today, much of the pressure on corporate executives to "cook" the books is driven by the desire to look good to Wall Street analysts and investors. Every three months companies report their revenues, expenses, profits, and projections for the future. If a company meets or exceeds "the street's" expectations, everything is usually fine. However, if a company reports financial numbers that are lower than expected, the company's stock value can drop dramatically. An earnings report that is lower by even a few pennies per share than what is expected can cause a company's stock value to drop immediately by as much as 30 to 40 percent or more. Greed—especially when salary and bonuses are tied to a company's stock value—is another factor that can lead some corporate executives to

1 LEARNING OBJECTIVE
Explain why accurate accounting information and audited financial statements are important.

accounting the process of systematically collecting, analyzing, and reporting financial information

Accounting problems at Enron. For employees like Meredith Stewart, the accounting problems at Enron reached a personal level when they lost their jobs. In addition to those who lost their jobs when the one-time energy giant failed, investors, retirees, and creditors also lost millions of dollars.

use questionable accounting methods to inflate a firm's financial performance.

In a perfect world, the accountants who inspect the corporate books would catch mistakes and disclose questionable accounting practices. Unfortunately, we do not live in a perfect world. Consider the part that auditors for the accounting firm Arthur Andersen played in the Enron meltdown. When the Securities and Exchange Commission (SEC) launched its inquiry into Enron's financial affairs, Andersen employees shredded the documents related to the audit. As a result, both the SEC and the Department of Justice began to investigate Andersen's role in the failure of Enron. Eventually, Andersen was convicted of obstruction of justice and was forced to cease auditing public companies. Simply put, Andersen—the once-proud accounting firm—was found guilty.[2] Less than a month after admitting accounting errors that inflated earnings by almost $600 million since 1994, Enron filed for bankruptcy.[3] Other high-profile companies, including Adelphia, Quest Communications, and Tyco International, have been hauled into court to explain their accounting practices. And more accounting firms—including KPMG and PricewaterhouseCoopers—have been targeted by trial lawyers, government regulators, and in some cases the Internal Revenue Service (IRS) for providing questionable audit work for major corporate clients.[4] Make no mistake, the penalties for what some critics call "executive crime" are real. Consider the following:

- Bernard Ebbers, WorldCom CEO, was sentenced to twenty-five years in prison for his part in defrauding investors, employees, pension holders, and other groups that lost money on WorldCom stock.[5]
- Former Tyco CEO Dennis Kozlowski was found guilty of looting more than $600 million from the company.[6]
- Enron executives Ken Lay and Jeff Skilling were convicted of conspiracy to commit securities and wire fraud in May 2006.[7]

While there will be appeals for many of these individuals, the cases show that corporate executives can't escape responsibility for reporting inaccurate or misleading accounting information. Unfortunately, the ones hurt often are not the high-paid corporate executives. In many cases it's the employees who lose their jobs and often the money they invested in the company's retirement program and investors, lenders, and suppliers who relied on fraudulent accounting information in order to make a decision to invest in or lend money to the company.

In an indirect way, the recent accounting scandals underscore how important accurate accounting information is for a corporation. To see how the auditing process can improve accounting information, read the next section.

Why Audited Financial Statements Are Important

Assume that you are a bank officer responsible for evaluating loan applications. How do you make a decision to approve or reject a loan request? In this situation, most bank officers rely on the information contained in the firm's balance sheet, income statement, and statement of cash flows, along with other information provided by the prospective borrower. In fact, most lenders insist that these financial statements be audited by a certified public accountant (CPA). An **audit** is an examination of a company's financial statements and the accounting practices that produced them. The purpose of an audit is to make sure that a firm's financial statements have been prepared in accordance with generally accepted accounting principles. Today, **generally**

audit an examination of a company's financial statements and the accounting practices that produced them

accepted accounting principles (GAAPs) have been developed to provide an accepted set of guidelines and practices for companies reporting financial information and the accounting profession. Today, three organizations—the Financial Accounting Standards Board (FASB), the American Institute of Certified Public Accountants (AICPA), and the International Accounting Standards Committee (IASC)—have greatly influenced the methods used by the accounting profession.

If an accountant determines that a firm's financial statements present financial information fairly and conform to GAAPs, then he or she will issue the following statement:

> In our opinion, the financial statements . . . present fairly, in all material respects . . . in conformity with generally accepted accounting principles.

While an audit and the resulting report do not *guarantee* that a company has not "cooked" the books, it does imply that, on the whole, the company has followed GAAPs. Bankers, creditors, investors, and government agencies are willing to rely on an auditor's opinion because of the historically ethical reputation and independence of auditors and accounting firms. Even with the recent scandals involving corporations and their accountants that falsified or misled the general public, most of the nation's accountants still abide by the rules. And while it is easy to indict an entire profession because of the actions of a few, there are many more accountants who adhere to the rules and are honest, hard-working professionals. Finally, it should be noted that without the audit function and GAAPs, there would be very little oversight or supervision. The validity of a firm's financial statements and its accounting records would drop quickly, and firms would find it difficult to obtain debt financing, acquire goods and services from suppliers, find investor financing, or prepare documents requested by government agencies.

EXAMINING ETHICS

Why Fudge the Figures?

What drives executives to "cook" the corporate books? While there are many reasons, greed is one of the strongest motivations behind manipulating corporate financial statements. Regardless of the reasons, huge amounts of money are at stake. Consider what happened at WorldCom and Tyco International:

WorldCom. Former CEO Bernard Ebbers and former CFO Scott D. Sullivan were convicted of fraud and conspiracy in manipulating revenue and expense numbers to mask problems and prop up the share price. The $11 billion fraud pushed WorldCom into bankruptcy.

Tyco International. Former CEO Dennis Kozlowski and former CFO Mark Swartz were convicted of hiding millions of dollars in improper stock gains and unauthorized bonuses. Disclosure of the fraud drove the share price down more than 70 percent in 12 months, hurting large and small investors alike.

Lower-level managers may go along with dubious accounting schemes because they stand to profit from cooperating, because they fear retaliation from senior executives, or because they worry about losing their jobs—especially when new employment opportunities are scarce.

Reform: The Sarbanes-Oxley Act of 2002

According to John Bogle, founder of Vanguard Mutual Funds, "Investing is an act of faith. Without that faith—that reported numbers reflect reality, that companies are being run honestly, that Wall Street is playing it straight, and that investors aren't being hoodwinked—our capital markets simply can't function."[8] In reality, what Mr. Bogle says is true. To help ensure that corporate financial information is accurate and in response to the many accounting scandals that surfaced in the last part of the 1990s and the first part of the twenty-first century, Congress enacted the Sarbanes-Oxley Act. Key components include the following:

- The SEC is required to establish a full-time five-member federal oversight board that will police the accounting industry.
- Chief executive and financial officers are required to certify periodic financial reports and are subject to criminal penalties for violations of securities reporting requirements.

generally accepted accounting principles (GAAPs) an accepted set of guidelines and practices for companies reporting financial information and for the accounting profession

- Accounting firms are prohibited from providing many types of non-audit and consulting services to the companies they audit.
- Auditors must maintain financial documents and audit work papers for five years.
- Auditors, accountants, and employees can be imprisoned for up to twenty years for destroying financial documents and willful violations of the securities laws.
- A public corporation must change its lead auditing firm every five years.
- There is added protection for whistle-blowers who report violations of the Sarbanes-Oxley Act.

While most people welcome the Sarbanes-Oxley Act, complex rules make compliance more expensive and time-consuming for corporate management and more difficult for accounting firms. And yet, most people agree that the cost of compliance is justified. As you read the next section, you will see just how important accurate accounting information is.

Who Uses Accounting Information

2 LEARNING OBJECTIVE
Identify people who use accounting information and possible careers in the accounting industry.

Managers and employees, lenders, suppliers, stockholders, and government agencies all rely on the information contained in three financial statements, each no more than one page in length. These three reports—the balance sheet, the income statement, and the statement of cash flows—are concise summaries of a firm's activities during a specific time period. Together they represent the results of perhaps tens of thousands of transactions that have occurred during the accounting period. Moreover, the form of the financial statements is pretty much the same for all businesses, from a neighborhood video store or small dry cleaner to giant conglomerates such as Home Depot, Boeing, and Bank of America. This information has a variety of uses both within the firm and outside it. However, first and foremost, accounting information is management information.

The People Who Use Accounting Information

The primary users of accounting information are *managers*. The firm's accounting system provides information that can be compiled for the entire firm—for each product; for each sales territory, store, or salesperson; for each division or department; and generally in any way that will help those who manage the organization. At a company such as Kraft Foods, for example, financial information is gathered for all

How did he get so rich? Although there are many reasons why Warren Buffett, chairman of the board of Berkshire Hathaway, has become one of the wealthiest people in America, his ability to understand accounting information has enabled him to identify investments that are extremely profitable. This same appreciation for numbers is one reason why Berkshire Hathaway subsidiary companies are known to have lower operating costs and larger bottom-line profits than their competitors.

its hundreds of food products: Maxwell House Coffee, A1 Steak Sauce, Post Cereals, Jell-O Desserts, Kool Aid, and so on. The president of the company would be interested in total sales for all these products. The vice president for marketing would be interested in national sales for Post Cereals and Jell-O Desserts. The northeastern sales manager might want to look at sales figures for Kool Aid in New England. For a large, complex organization like Kraft, the accounting system must enable managers to get the information they need.

Much of this accounting information is *proprietary;* it is not divulged to anyone outside the firm. This type of information is used by a firm's managers and employees to plan and set goals, organize, lead, motivate, and control—all the management functions that were described in Chapter 7.

To see how important accounting is, just think about what happens when an employee or manager asks a supervisor for a new piece of equipment or a salary increase. Immediately, everyone involved in the decision begins discussing how much it will cost and what effect it will have on the firm's profits, sales, and expenses. It is the firm's accounting system that provides the answers to these important questions. In addition to proprietary information used inside the firm, certain financial information must be supplied to individuals and organizations outside the firm (see Table 18.1).

YOUR CAREER

Knowing the Numbers

Knowing a little about your company's numbers can do a lot for your career. Why? Understanding your company's financial position gives you a sense of its financial health and competitive situation and helps you to see how you contribute. Here's how two companies encourage employees to study accounting information:

Development Counsellors International. Employees take turns presenting financial reports at this public-relations firm's staff meetings. The "chief financial officer" of the day presents sales figures, explains trends, and compares actual with planned profits to focus the work force on the goals that matter.

Trinity Products. Employees of this construction supply company take a financial literacy course and attend twice-monthly finance meetings to learn what drives return on sales and other key ratios. "It's a form of ownership, and it's a way to get people invested" in overall performance, says Trinity's president.

Be aware that if you work for a private company, you'll probably be asked to keep all financial information confidential.

- *Lenders* require information contained in the firm's financial statements before they will commit themselves to either short- or long-term loans. *Suppliers* who provide the raw materials, component parts, or finished goods a firm needs also generally ask for financial information before they will extend credit to a firm.
- *Stockholders and potential investors* are concerned not only about a company's current financial health but also about the financial risk associated with an investment in its stock.
- *Government agencies* require a variety of information about the firm's tax liabilities, payroll deductions for employees, and new issues of stocks and bonds.

>> **TABLE 18.1**

USERS OF ACCOUNTING INFORMATION

The primary users of accounting information are a company's managers, but individuals and organizations outside the company also require information on its finances.

Management	Lenders and Suppliers	Stockholders and Potential Investors	Government Agencies
Plan and set goals	Evaluate credit risks before committing to short- or long-term financing	Evaluate the financial health of the firm before purchasing stocks or bonds	Confirm tax liabilities
Organize			Confirm payroll deductions
Lead and motivate			Approve new issues of stocks and bonds
Control			

An important function of accountants is to ensure that such information is accurate and thorough enough to satisfy these outside groups.

Different Types of Accounting

While many people think that all accountants do the same tasks, there are special areas of expertise within the accounting industry. In fact, accounting usually is broken down into two broad categories: managerial and financial.

Managerial accounting provides managers and employees with the information needed to make decisions about a firm's financing, investing, and operating activities. By using managerial accounting information, both managers and employees can evaluate how well they have done in the past and what they can expect in the future. **Financial accounting**, on the other hand, generates financial statements and reports for interested people outside of an organization. Typically, stockholders, financial analysts, bankers, lenders, suppliers, government agencies, and other interested groups use the information provided by financial accounting to determine how well a business firm has achieved its goals. In addition to managerial and financial accounting, additional special areas of accounting include the following:

- *Cost accounting*—determining the cost of producing specific products or services.
- *Tax accounting*—planning tax strategy and preparing tax returns for the firm
- *Government accounting*—providing basic accounting services to ensure that tax revenues are collected and used to meet the goals of state, local, and federal agencies.
- *Not-for-profit accounting*—helping not-for-profit organizations to account for all donations and expenditures.

Careers in Accounting

Wanted: An individual with at least two years of college accounting courses. Must be honest, dependable, and willing to complete all routine accounting activities for a manufacturing business. Salary dependent on experience.

Want a job? Positions such as the one described in this newspaper advertisement increasingly are becoming available to those with the required training. According to the *Occupational Outlook Handbook*, published by the Department of Labor, job opportunities for accountants, auditors, and managers in the accounting area are expected to experience average growth between now and the year 2012.[9]

Many people have the idea that accountants spend their day working with endless columns of numbers in a small office locked away from other people. In fact, accountants do spend a lot of time at their desks, but their job entails far more than just adding or subtracting numbers. Accountants are expected to share their ideas and the information they possess with people who need the information. Accounting can be an exciting and rewarding career—one that offers higher-than-average starting salaries. To be successful in the accounting industry, employees must

managerial accounting provides managers and employees with the information needed to make decisions about a firm's financing, investing, and operating activities

financial accounting generates financial statements and reports for interested people outside an organization

Accounting information you can use. The website for the American Institute of Certified Public Accountants (AICPA) provides a wealth of career information for people who are interested in becoming certified public accountants (CPAs). Why not check it out at **www.aicpa.org**?

- Be responsible, honest, and ethical.
- Have a strong background in financial management.
- Know how to use a computer and software to process data into accounting information.
- Be able to communicate with people who need accounting information.

Today, accountants generally are classified as either private accountants or public accountants. A *private accountant* is employed by a specific organization. A medium-sized or large firm may employ one or more private accountants to design its accounting information system, manage its accounting department, and provide managers with advice and assistance.

Individuals, self-employed business owners, and smaller firms that do not require their own full-time accountants can hire the services of public accountants. A *public accountant* works on a fee basis for clients and may be self-employed or be the employee of an accounting firm. Accounting firms range in size from one-person operations to huge international firms with hundreds of accounting partners and thousands of employees. Today, the largest accounting firms, sometimes referred to as the "Big Four," are PricewaterhouseCoopers, Ernst & Young, KPMG, and Deloitte Touche Tohmatsu.

Typically, public accounting firms include on their staffs at least one **certified public accountant (CPA),** an individual who has met state requirements for accounting education and experience and has passed a rigorous accounting examination prepared by the AICPA. The AICPA uniform CPA examination covers four areas: (1) taxation, business law, and professional responsibilities, (2) auditing, (3) business environment and concepts, and (4) financial accounting and reporting. More information about general requirements and the CPA profession can be obtained by contacting the AICPA at **www.aicpa.org.**[10] State requirements usually include a college degree or a specified number of hours of college coursework and generally from one to three years of on-the-job experience. Details regarding specific state requirements for practice as a CPA can be obtained by contacting the state's board of accountancy.

Once an individual becomes a CPA, he or she must participate in continuing-education programs to maintain state certification. These specialized programs are designed to provide the current training needed in today's changing business environment. CPAs also must take an ethics course to satisfy the continuing-education requirement.

Certification as a CPA brings both status and responsibility. Only an independent CPA can audit the financial statements contained in a corporation's annual report and express an opinion—as required by law—regarding the acceptability of the corporation's accounting practices. In addition to auditing a corporation's financial statements, typical services performed by CPAs include planning and preparing tax returns, determining the true cost of producing and marketing a firm's goods or services, and compiling the financial information needed to make major management decisions. Fees for the services provided by CPAs generally range from $50 to $300 an hour.

In addition to certified public accountants, there are also certified management accountants. A **certified management accountant (CMA)** is an accountant who has met the requirements for education and experience, passed a rigorous exam, and is certified by the Institute of Management

certified public accountant (CPA) an individual who has met state requirements for accounting education and experience and has passed a rigorous two-day accounting examination prepared by the AICPA

certified management accountant (CMA) an accountant who has met the requirements for education and experience, passed a rigorous exam, and is certified by the Institute of Management Accountants

SPOTLIGHT

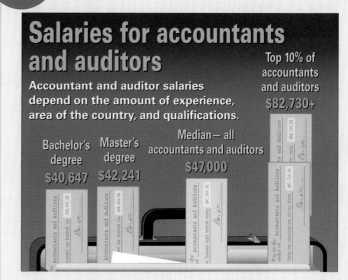

Salaries for accountants and auditors

Accountant and auditor salaries depend on the amount of experience, area of the country, and qualifications.

Top 10% of accountants and auditors
$82,730+

Bachelor's degree
$40,647

Master's degree
$42,241

Median— all accountants and auditors
$47,000

Source: The Bureau of Labor Statistics website: **www.bls.gov;** accessed December 5, 2005.

Accountants. The CMA exam is designed to develop and measure not only accounting skills but also decision-making and critical-thinking skills. For more information about the CMA exam, visit the Institute of Management Accountants website at **www.imanet.org.** While both CPAs and CMAs can work for the public, a CMA is more likely to work within a large organization. Also, both types of accountants are excellent career choices.

The Accounting Process

3 LEARNING OBJECTIVE
Discuss the accounting process.

In Chapter 17, *information* was defined as data presented in a form that is useful for a specific purpose. In this section we examine accounting as the system for transforming raw financial *data* into useful financial *information*. Then, in the next sections we describe the three most important financial statements provided by the accounting process.

The Accounting Equation

The accounting equation is a simple statement that forms the basis for the accounting process. This important equation shows the relationship between a firm's assets, liabilities, and owners' equity.

assets the resources that a business owns

liabilities a firm's debts and obligations

owners' equity the difference between a firm's assets and its liabilities

accounting equation the basis for the accounting process: *assets = liabilities + owners' equity*

- **Assets** are the resources a business owns—cash, inventory, equipment, and real estate.
- **Liabilities** are the firm's debts—what it owes to others.
- **Owners' equity** is the difference between total assets and total liabilities—what would be left for the owners if the firm's assets were sold and the money used to pay off its liabilities.

The relationship between assets, liabilities, and owners' equity is shown by the following **accounting equation:**

$$\text{Assets} = \text{liabilities} + \text{owners' equity}$$

Whether a business is a small corner grocery store or a giant corporation such as General Motors, its assets must equal the sum of its liabilities and owners' equity. To use this equation, a firm's accountants must record raw data—that is, the firm's day-to-day financial transactions—using the double-entry system of bookkeeping. The **double-entry bookkeeping system** is a system in which each financial transaction is recorded as two separate accounting entries to maintain the balance shown in the accounting equation. With the double-entry system, an accountant can use the steps in the accounting cycle to generate accounting information and financial statements.

double-entry bookkeeping system a system in which each financial transaction is recorded as two separate accounting entries to maintain the balance shown in the accounting equation

The Accounting Cycle

In the typical accounting system, raw data are transformed into financial statements in five steps. The first three—analyzing, recording, and posting—are performed on a regular basis throughout the accounting period. The last two—preparation of the trial balance and of the financial statements and closing the books—are performed at the end of the accounting period.

Analyzing Source Documents   Basic accounting data are contained in *source documents*, the receipts, invoices, sales slips, and other documents that show the dollar amounts of day-to-day business transactions. The accounting cycle begins with the analysis of each of these documents. The purpose of the analysis is to determine which accounts are affected by the documents and how they are affected.

Recording Transactions   Every financial transaction then is recorded in a journal—a process called *journalizing*. Transactions must be recorded in the firm's general journal or in specialized journals. The *general journal* is a book of original entry in which typical transactions are recorded in order of their occurrence. An accounting system also may include *specialized journals* for specific types of transactions that occur frequently. Thus a retail store might have journals for cash receipts, cash disbursements, purchases, and sales in addition to its general journal.

Posting Transactions   After the information is recorded in the general journal and specialized journals, it is transferred to the general ledger. The *general ledger* is a book of accounts containing a separate sheet or section for each account. Today, most businesses use a computer and software to post accounting entries from the general journal or specialized journals to the general ledger.

Preparing the Trial Balance   A **trial balance** is a summary of the balances of all general ledger accounts at the end of the accounting period. To prepare a trial balance, the accountant determines and lists the balances for all ledger accounts. If the trial balance totals are correct and the accounting equation is still in balance, the accountant can prepare the financial statements. If not, a mistake has occurred somewhere, and the accountant must find it and correct it before proceeding.

> **trial balance** a summary of the balances of all general ledger accounts at the end of the accounting period

Preparing Financial Statements and Closing the Books   The firm's financial statements are prepared from the information contained in the trial balance. This information is presented in a standardized format to make the statements as accessible as possible to the various people who may be interested in the firm's financial affairs—managers, employees, lenders, suppliers, stockholders, potential investors, and government agencies. A firm's financial statements are prepared at least once a year and included in the firm's annual report. An **annual report** is a report distributed to stockholders and other interested parties that describes a firm's operating activities and its financial condition. Most firms also have financial statements prepared semiannually, quarterly, or monthly.

> **annual report** a report distributed to stockholders and other interested parties that describes a firm's operating activities and its financial condition

Once these statements have been prepared and checked, the firm's books are "closed" for the accounting period, and a *postclosing* trial balance is prepared. Although, like the trial balance just described, the postclosing trial balance generally is prepared after *all* accounting work is completed for one accounting period. If the postclosing trial balance totals agree, the accounting equation is still in balance at the end of the cycle. Only then can a new accounting cycle begin for the next accounting period.

With this brief information about the steps of the accounting cycle in mind, let's now examine the three most important financial statements generated by the accounting process: the balance sheet, the income statement, and the statement of cash flows.

The Balance Sheet

Question: *Where could you find the total amount of assets, liabilities, and owners' equity for Hershey Foods Corporation?*

Answer: The firm's balance sheet.

> **4 LEARNING OBJECTIVE**
> Read and interpret a balance sheet.

A **balance sheet** (sometimes referred to as a **statement of financial position**) is a summary of the dollar amounts of a firm's assets, liabilities, and owners' equity accounts at the end of a specific accounting period. The balance sheet must demonstrate that assets are equal to liabilities plus owners' equity. Most people think of a balance sheet as a statement that reports the financial condition of a business firm such as Hershey Foods Corporation, but balance sheets apply to individuals, too. For example, Marty Campbell graduated from college three years ago and obtained a position as a sales representative for an office supply firm. After going to work, he established a checking and savings account and purchased an automobile, stereo, television, and a few pieces of furniture. Marty paid cash for some purchases, but he had to borrow

> **balance sheet (or statement of financial position)** a summary of the dollar amounts of a firm's assets, liabilities, and owners' equity accounts at the end of a specific accounting period

money to pay for the larger ones. Figure 18.1 shows Marty's current personal balance sheet.

Marty Campbell's assets total $26,500, and his liabilities amount to $10,000. While the difference between total assets and total liabilities is referred to as *owners' equity* or *stockholders' equity* for a business, it is normally called *net worth* for an individual. As reported on Marty's personal balance sheet, net worth is $16,500. The total assets ($26,500) and the total liabilities *plus* net worth ($26,500) are equal.

Figure 18.2 shows the balance sheet for Northeast Art Supply, a small corporation that sells picture frames, paints, canvases, and other artists' supplies to retailers in New England. Note that assets are reported at the top of the statement, followed by liabilities and stockholders' equity. Let's work through the different accounts in Figure 18.2 from top to bottom.

Assets

On a balance sheet, assets are listed in order from the *most liquid* to the *least liquid.* The **liquidity** of an asset is the ease with which it can be converted into cash.

liquidity the ease with which an asset can be converted into cash

current assets assets that can be converted quickly into cash or that will be used in one year or less

Current Assets   **Current assets** are assets that can be converted quickly into cash or that will be used in one year or less. Because cash is the most liquid asset, it is listed first. Next are *marketable securities*—stocks, bonds, and other investments—that can be converted into cash in a matter of days.

Next are the firm's receivables. Its *accounts receivables*, which result from allowing customers to make credit purchases, generally are paid within thirty to sixty days. However, the firm expects that some of these debts will not be collected. Thus it has

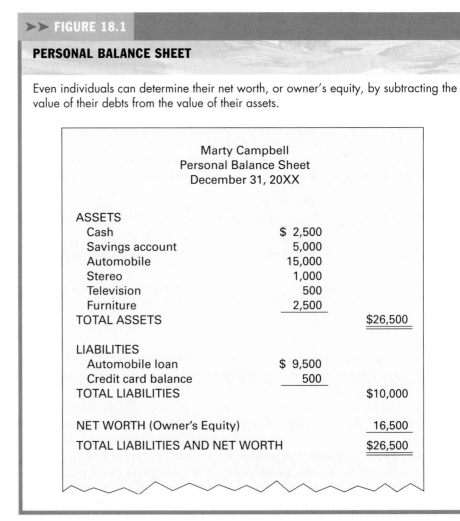

>> **FIGURE 18.1**

PERSONAL BALANCE SHEET

Even individuals can determine their net worth, or owner's equity, by subtracting the value of their debts from the value of their assets.

Marty Campbell
Personal Balance Sheet
December 31, 20XX

ASSETS		
Cash	$ 2,500	
Savings account	5,000	
Automobile	15,000	
Stereo	1,000	
Television	500	
Furniture	2,500	
TOTAL ASSETS		$26,500
LIABILITIES		
Automobile loan	$ 9,500	
Credit card balance	500	
TOTAL LIABILITIES		$10,000
NET WORTH (Owner's Equity)		16,500
TOTAL LIABILITIES AND NET WORTH		$26,500

>> FIGURE 18.2

BUSINESS BALANCE SHEET

A balance sheet summarizes a firm's accounts at the end of an accounting period, showing the various dollar amounts that enter into the accounting equation. Note that assets ($340,000) equal liabilities plus owners' equity ($340,000).

NORTHEAST ART SUPPLY, INC.

Balance Sheet
December 31, 20XX

ASSETS

Current assets

Cash		$ 59,000	
Marketable securities		10,000	
Accounts receivable	$ 40,000		
Less allowance for doubtful accounts	2,000	38,000	
Notes receivable		32,000	
Merchandise inventory		41,000	
Prepaid expenses		2,000	
Total current assets			$182,000

Fixed assets

Delivery equipment	$110,000		
Less accumulated depreciation	20,000	$ 90,000	
Furniture and store equipment	62,000		
Less accumulated depreciation	15,000	47,000	
Total fixed assets			137,000

Intangible assets

Patents		$ 6,000	
Goodwill		15,000	
Total intangible assets			21,000
TOTAL ASSETS			$340,000

LIABILITIES AND STOCKHOLDERS' EQUITY

Current liabilities

Accounts payable	$ 35,000		
Notes payable	25,675		
Salaries payable	4,000		
Taxes payable	5,325		
Total current liabilities		$ 70,000	

Long-term liabilities

Mortgage payable on store equipment	$ 40,000		
Total long-term liabilities		$ 40,000	
TOTAL LIABILITIES			$110,00

Stockholders's equity

Common stock		$150,000	
Retained earnings		80,000	
TOTAL OWNERS'S EQUITY			$230,000
TOTAL LIABILITIES AND OWNERS' EQUITY			$340,000

reduced its accounts receivables by a 5 percent *allowance for doubtful accounts.* The firm's *notes receivables* are receivables for which customers have signed promissory notes. They generally are repaid over a longer period of time than the firm's accounts receivables.

Sometimes inventory is cute! As part of their regular inventory process, employees at the Hanover, Germany zoo must count, weigh, and measure more than 2000 animals and 200 different species. In this photo, a zoo employee checks the length of a small neo-tropical animal named "Diego." For retailers, wholesalers, and manufacturers, inventory procedures are important to ensure that there is enough inventory for customers who want to purchase their products.

fixed assets assets that will be held or used for a period longer than one year

depreciation the process of apportioning the cost of a fixed asset over the period during which it will be used

intangible assets assets that do not exist physically but that have a value based on the rights or privileges they confer on a firm

Northeast's *merchandise inventory* represents the value of goods on hand for sale to customers. Since Northeast Art Supply is a wholesale operation, the inventory listed in Figure 18.2 represents finished goods ready for sale to retailers. For a manufacturing firm, merchandise inventory also may represent raw materials that will become part of a finished product or work that has been partially completed but requires further processing.

Northeast's last current asset is *prepaid expenses,* which are assets that have been paid for in advance but have not yet been used. An example is insurance premiums. They are usually paid at the beginning of the policy year. The unused portion (say, for the last four months of the time period covered by the policy) is a prepaid expense. For Northeast Art, all current assets total $182,000.

Fixed Assets **Fixed assets** are assets that will be held or used for a period longer than one year. They generally include land, buildings, and equipment used in the continuing operation of the business. Although Northeast owns no land or buildings, it does own *delivery equipment* that originally cost $110,000. It also owns *furniture and store equipment* that originally cost $62,000.

Note that the values of both fixed assets are decreased by their *accumulated depreciation.* **Depreciation** is the process of apportioning the cost of a fixed asset over the period during which it will be used, that is, its useful life. The depreciation amount allotted to each year is an expense for that year, and the value of the asset must be reduced by the amount of depreciation expense. Although the actual methods used to calculate the dollar amounts for depreciation expense reported on a firm's financial statements are beyond the scope of this text, you should know that there are a number of different methods that can be used. In the case of Northeast's delivery equipment, $20,000 of its value has been depreciated (or used up) since it was purchased. Its value at this time is thus $110,000 less $20,000, or $90,000. In a similar fashion, the original value of furniture and store equipment ($62,000) has been reduced by depreciation totaling $15,000. Furniture and store equipment now has a reported value of $47,000. For Northeast Art, all fixed assets total $137,000.

Intangible Assets **Intangible assets** are assets that do not exist physically but that have a value based on the rights or privileges they confer on a firm. They include patents, copyrights, trademarks, franchises, and goodwill. By their nature, intangible assets are long-term assets—they are of value to the firm for a number of years.

Northeast Art Supply lists two intangible assets. The first is a *patent* for a special oil paint that the company purchased from the inventor. The firm's accountants estimate that the patent has a current market value of $6,000. The second intangible asset, *goodwill,* is the value of a firm's reputation, location, earning capacity, and other intangibles that make the business a profitable concern. Goodwill normally is not listed on a balance sheet unless the firm has been purchased from previous owners. In such a case, the new owners actually have paid an additional amount over and above the fair market value of the firm's assets for goodwill. Goodwill exists because most businesses are worth more as going concerns than as a collection of assets. Northeast Art's accountants included a $15,000 amount for goodwill. The firm's intangible assets total $21,000. Now it is possible to total all three types of assets for Northeast Art. As calculated in Figure 18.2, total assets are $340,000.

Liabilities and Owners' Equity

The liabilities and the owners' equity accounts complete the balance sheet. The firm's liabilities are separated into two categories—current and long term.

Current Liabilities

A firm's **current liabilities** are debts that will be repaid in one year or less. Northeast Art Supply purchased merchandise from its suppliers on credit. Thus its balance sheet includes an entry for accounts payable. *Accounts payable* are short-term obligations that arise as a result of a firm making credit purchases.

Notes payable are obligations that have been secured with promissory notes. They are usually short-term obligations, but they may extend beyond one year. Only those that must be paid within the year are listed under current liabilities.

Northeast also lists *salaries payable* and *taxes payable* as current liabilities. These are both expenses that have been incurred during the current accounting period but will be paid in the next accounting period. For Northeast Art, current liabilities total $70,000.

current liabilities debts that will be repaid in one year or less

Long-Term Liabilities

Long-term liabilities are debts that need not be repaid for at least one year. Northeast lists only one long-term liability—a $40,000 *mortgage payable* for store equipment. Bonds and other long-term loans would be included here as well, if they existed. As you can see in Figure 18.2, Northeast's current and long-term liabilities total $110,000.

long-term liabilities debts that need not be repaid for at least one year

Owners' or Stockholders' Equity

For a sole proprietorship or partnership, the owners' equity is shown as the difference between assets and liabilities. In a partnership, each partner's share of the ownership is reported separately in each owner's name. For a corporation, the owners' equity usually is referred to as *stockholders' equity.* The dollar amount reported on the balance sheet is the total value of stock plus retained earnings that have accumulated to date. **Retained earnings** are the portion of a business's profits not distributed to stockholders.

retained earnings the portion of a business's profits not distributed to stockholders

The original investment by the owners of Northeast Art Supply was $150,000. In addition, $80,000 of Northeast's earnings have been reinvested in the business since it was founded. Thus owners' equity totals $230,000.

As the two grand totals in Figure 18.2 show, Northeast's assets and the sum of its liabilities and owners' equity are equal—at $340,000. The accounting equation (assets = liabilities + owners' equity) is still in balance.

The Income Statement

Question: *Where can you find the profit or loss amount for The Gap, Inc.?*

Answer: The firm's income statement.

An **income statement** is a summary of a firm's revenues and expenses during a specified accounting period—one month, three months, six months, or a year. The income statement is sometimes called the *earnings statement* or the *statement of income and expenses.* Let's begin our discussion by constructing a personal income statement for Marty Campbell. Having worked as a sales representative for an office supply firm for the past three years, Marty now earns $33,600 a year, or $2,800 a month. After deductions, his take-home pay is $1,900 a month. As illustrated in Figure 18.3, Marty's typical monthly expenses include payments for an automobile loan, credit-card purchases, apartment rent, utilities, food, clothing, and recreation and entertainment.

While the difference between income and expenses is referred to as *profit* or *loss* for a business, it is normally referred to as a *cash surplus* or *cash deficit* for an individual. Fortunately for Marty, he has a surplus of $250 at the end of each month. He can use this surplus for savings, investing, or paying off debts.

Figure 18.4 shows the income statement for Northeast Art Supply. Generally, revenues *less* cost of goods sold *less* operating expenses equals net income.

5 LEARNING OBJECTIVE
Read and interpret an income statement.

income statement a summary of a firm's revenues and expenses during a specified accounting period

Revenues

revenues the dollar amounts earned by a firm from selling goods, providing services, or performing business activities

gross sales the total dollar amount of all goods and services sold during the accounting period

Revenues are the dollar amounts earned by a firm from selling goods, providing services, or performing business activities. Like most businesses, Northeast Art obtains its revenues solely from the sale of its products or services. The revenues section of its income statement begins with gross sales. **Gross sales** are the total dollar amount of all goods and services sold during the accounting period. From this amount are deducted the dollar amounts of

- *Sales returns*—merchandise returned to the firm by its customers
- *Sales allowances*—price reductions offered to customers who accept slightly damaged or soiled merchandise
- *Sales discounts*—price reductions offered to customers who pay their bills promptly

net sales the actual dollar amounts received by a firm for the goods and services it has sold after adjustment for returns, allowances, and discounts

The remainder is the firm's net sales. **Net sales** are the actual dollar amounts received by the firm for the goods and services it has sold after adjustment for returns, allowances, and discounts. For Northeast Art, net sales are $451,000.

Cost of Goods Sold

cost of goods sold the dollar amount equal to beginning inventory *plus* net purchases *less* ending inventory

The standard method of determining the **cost of goods sold** by a retailing or wholesaling firm can be summarized as follows:

Cost of goods sold = beginning inventory + net purchases − ending inventory

A manufacturer must include raw materials inventories, work in progress, and direct manufacturing costs in this computation.

▶▶ FIGURE 18.3

PERSONAL INCOME STATEMENT

By subtracting expenses from income, anyone can construct a personal income statement and determine if they have a surplus or deficit at the end of the month.

Marty Campbell
Personal Income Statement
For the month ended December 31, 20XX

INCOME (Take-home pay)		$1,900
LESS MONTHLY EXPENSES		
Automobile loan	$ 250	
Credit card payment	100	
Apartment rent	500	
Utilities	200	
Food	250	
Clothing	100	
Recreation & entertainment	250	
TOTAL MONTHLY EXPENSES		1,650
CASH SURPLUS (or profit)		$ 250

>> FIGURE 18.4

BUSINESS INCOME STATEMENT

An income statement summarizes a firm's revenues and expenses during a specified accounting period. For Northeast Art, net income after taxes is $30,175.

NORTHEAST ART SUPPLY, INC.

Income Statement
For the Year Ended
December 31, 20XX

Revenues			
Gross sales		$465,000	
Less sales returns and allowances	$ 9,500		
Less sales discounts	4,500	14,000	
Net sales			$451,000
Cost of goods sold			
Beginning inventory, January 1, 20XX		$ 40,000	
Purchases	$346,000		
Less purchase discounts	11,000		
Net purchases		335,000	
Cost of goods available for sale		$375,000	
Less ending inventory December 31, 20XX		41,000	
Cost of goods sold			334,000
Gross profit			$117,000
Operating expenses			
Selling expenses			
Sales salaries	$ 22,000		
Advertising	4,000		
Sales promotion	2,500		
Depreciation—store equipment	3,000		
Depreciation—delivery equipment	4,000		
Miscellaneous selling expenses	1,500		
Total selling expenses		$ 37,000	
General expenses			
Office salaries	$ 28,500		
Rent	8,500		
Depreciation—office furniture	1,500		
Utilities expense	2,500		
Insurance expense	1,000		
Miscellaneous expense	500		
Total general expense		42,500	
Total operating expenses			$ 79,500
Net income from operations			$ 37,500
Less interest expense			2,000
NET INCOME BEFORE TAXES			$ 35,500
Less federal income taxes			5,325
NET INCOME AFTER TAXES			$ 30,175

According to Figure 18.4, Northeast began its accounting period on January 1 with a merchandise inventory that cost $40,000. During the next twelve months, the firm purchased merchandise valued at $346,000. After taking advantage of *purchase discounts*, however, it paid only $335,000 for this merchandise. Thus, during the year, Northeast had total *goods available for sale* valued at $40,000 plus $335,000, or $375,000.

Twelve months later, at the end of the accounting period on December 31, Northeast had sold all but $41,000 worth of the available goods. The cost of goods sold by Northeast was therefore $375,000 less ending inventory of $41,000, or $334,000. It is now possible to calculate gross profit. A firm's **gross profit** is its net sales *less* the cost of goods sold. For Northeast, gross profit was $117,000.

gross profit a firm's net sales *less* the cost of goods sold

Sometimes a firm must spend money to make money. The cost of this Red Lobster advertisement is reported on the firm's income statement as a marketing expense. Marketing expenses—along with all other expenses—are deducted from sales revenue to determine if the restaurant chain earned a profit during a specific accounting period.

Operating Expenses

A firm's **operating expenses** are all business costs other than the cost of goods sold. Total operating expenses generally are divided into two categories: selling expenses or general expenses.

Selling expenses are costs related to the firm's marketing activities. For Northeast Art, selling expenses total $37,000. *General expenses* are costs incurred in managing a business. For Northeast Art, general expenses total $42,500. Now it is possible to total both selling and general expenses. As Figure 18.4 shows, total operating expenses for the accounting period are $79,500.

Net Income

When revenues exceed expenses, the difference is called **net income.** When expenses exceed revenues, the difference is called **net loss.** As Figure 18.4 shows, Northeast Art's *net income from operations* is computed as gross profit ($117,000) *less* total operating expenses ($79,500). For Northeast Art, net income from operations is $37,500. From this amount, *interest expense* of $2,000 is deducted to obtain a *net income before taxes* of $35,500. The interest expense is deducted in this section of the income statement because it is not an operating expense. Rather, it is an expense that results from financing the business.

Northeast's *federal income taxes* are $5,325. Although these taxes may or may not be payable immediately, they are definitely an expense that must be deducted from income. This leaves Northeast Art with a *net income after taxes* of $30,175. This amount may be used to pay a dividend to stockholders, it may be retained or reinvested in the firm, it may be used to reduce the firm's debts, or all three.

operating expenses all business costs other than the cost of goods sold

net income occurs when revenues exceed expenses

net loss occurs when expenses exceed revenues

The Statement of Cash Flows

Cash is the lifeblood of any business. In 1987, the SEC and the Financial Accounting Standards Board required all publicly traded companies to include a statement of cash flows, along with their balance sheet and income statement, in their annual report. The **statement of cash flows** illustrates how the operating, investing, and financing activities of a company affect cash during an accounting period. A statement of cash flows for Northeast Art Supply is illustrated in Figure 18.5. It provides information concerning the company's cash receipts and cash payments and is organized around three different activities: operations, investing, and financing.

- *Cash flows from operating activities.* This is the first section of a statement of cash flows. It addresses the firm's primary revenue source—

providing goods and services. The amounts paid to suppliers, employees, interest, taxes, and other expenses are deducted from the amount received from customers. Finally, the interest and dividends received by the firm are added to determine the total. After all adjustments are made, the total represents a true picture of cash flows from operating activities.

- *Cash flows from investing activities.* The second section of the statement is concerned with cash flow from investments. This includes the purchase and sale of land, equipment, and other assets and investments.
- *Cash flows from financing activities.* The third and final section deals with the cash flow from all financing activities. It reports changes in debt obligation and owners' equity accounts. This includes loans and repayments, the sale and repurchase of the company's own stock, and cash dividends.

The totals of all three activities are added to the beginning cash balance to determine the ending cash balance. For Northeast Art Supply, the ending cash balance is

LEARNING OBJECTIVE
Describe business activities that affect a firm's cash flow.

statement of cash flows a statement that illustrates how the operating, investing, and financing activities of a company affect cash during an accounting period

---

▶▶ FIGURE 18.5

STATEMENT OF CASH FLOWS

A statement of cash flows summarizes how a firm's operating, investing, and financing activities affect its cash during a specified period—one month, three months, six months, or a year. For Northeast Art, the amount of cash at the end of the year reported on the statement of cash flows is $59,000—the same amount reported for the cash account on the firm's balance sheet.

NORTHEAST ART SUPPLY, INC.

Statement of Cash Flows
For the Year Ended
December 31, 20XX

Cash flows from operating activities		
Cash received from customers	$ 451,000	
Cash paid to suppliers and employees	(385,500)	
Interest paid	(2,000)	
Income taxes paid	(5,325)	
Net cash provided by operating activities		$ 58,175
Cash flows from investing activities		
Purchase of equipment	$(2,000)	
Purchase of investments	(10,000)	
Sale of investments	10,000	
Net cash provided by investing activities		$(2,000)
Cash flows from financing activities		
Payment of short-term debt	$(9,000)	
Payment of long-term debt	(17,000)	
Payment of dividends	(15,000)	
Net cash provided by financing activities		$(41,000)
NET INCREASE (DECREASE) IN CASH		$ 15,175
Cash at beginning of year		43,825
CASH AT END OF YEAR		$ 59,000

$59,000. Note that this is the same amount reported for the cash account on the firm's balance sheet. Together the cash flow statement, balance sheet, and income statement illustrate the results of past business decisions and reflect the firm's ability to pay debts and dividends and to finance new growth.

Evaluating Financial Statements

7 LEARNING OBJECTIVE
Summarize how managers evaluate the financial health of a business.

All three financial statements—the balance sheet, the income statement, and the statement of cash flows—can provide answers to a variety of questions about a firm's ability to do business and stay in business, its profitability, its value as an investment, and its ability to repay its debts. Even more information can be obtained by comparing present financial statements with those prepared for past accounting periods.

Using Annual Reports to Compare Data for Different Accounting Periods

Typically, an annual report contains a great deal of information about the company, its operations, current financial statements, and its past and current financial health. The following five suggestions can help you get to the "bottom line" of a corporation's annual report.

1. Look at the firm's income statement to determine whether the company is profitable or not.
2. Read the letters from the chairman of the board and chief executive officer (CEO) that describe the corporation's operations, prospects for the future, new products or services, financial strengths, *and* any potential problems.
3. Compare the corporation's current income statement and balance sheet with previous financial statements. Look at trends for sales, expenses, profits or losses, assets, liabilities, and owners' equity.
4. Examine the footnotes closely, and look for red flags that may be in the fine print. Often the footnotes contain (and sometimes hide) important information about the company and its finances.
5. Learn how to calculate financial ratios. Some of the most important financial ratios are discussed in the last part of this section.

Most corporations include in their annual reports comparisons of the important elements of their financial statements for recent years. Figure 18.6 shows such comparisons—of revenue, research and development (R&D), operating income, and sales and marketing expenses—for Microsoft Corporation, a world leader in the computer software industry. By examining these data, an operating manager can tell whether R&D expenditures are increasing or decreasing over the past three years. The vice president of marketing can determine if the total amount of sales and marketing expenses is changing. Stockholders and potential investors, on the other hand, may be more concerned with increases or decreases in Microsoft's revenues and operating income over the same time period.

What's so big about GE?
To answer that question, look at General Electric's "BIG" annual report. For investors, an annual report provides a great deal of information about the company, its operations, and its current financial statements. General Electric's annual report is yet another tool that can be used to showcase how the company continues to earn profits, as well as the respect of customers, employees, and investors.

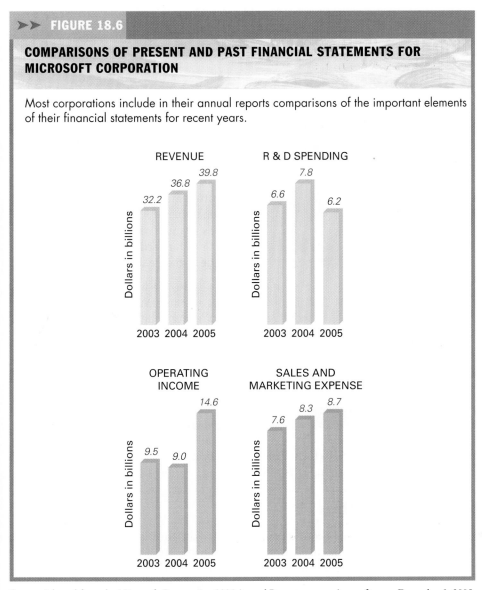

>> FIGURE 18.6

COMPARISONS OF PRESENT AND PAST FINANCIAL STATEMENTS FOR MICROSOFT CORPORATION

Most corporations include in their annual reports comparisons of the important elements of their financial statements for recent years.

Source: Adapted from the Microsoft Corporation 2005 Annual Report, **www.microsoft.com**, December 3, 2005.

Comparing Data with Other Firms' Data

Many firms also compare their financial results with those of competing firms and with industry averages. Comparisons are possible as long as accountants follow generally accepted accounting principles.

Except for minor differences in format and terms, the balance sheet and income statement of Procter & Gamble, for example, will be similar to those of other large corporations, such as Alberto-Culver, Clorox, Colgate-Palmolive, and Unilever, in the consumer goods industry. Comparisons among firms give managers a general idea of a firm's relative effectiveness and its standing within the industry. Competitors' financial statements can be obtained from their annual reports—if they are public corporations. Industry averages are published by reporting services such as D&B (formerly Dun & Bradstreet) and Standard & Poor's, as well as by some industry trade associations.

Still another type of analysis of a firm's financial health involves computation of financial ratios. A **financial ratio** is a number that shows the relationship between two elements of a firm's financial statements. Among the most useful ratios are profitability ratios, short-term financial ratios, activity ratios, and the debt-to-owners'-equity ratio. Like the individual elements in financial statements, these ratios can be compared with the firm's past ratios, with those of competitors, and with industry averages.

financial ratio a number that shows the relationship between two elements of a firm's financial statements

Business Around the World

Accounting Standards Go Global

Just as U.S. corporations that sell stock in other countries must meet each nation's financial reporting standards, any foreign corporation selling stock in the United States has to report financial data in accordance with U.S. generally accepted accounting practices (often referred to as GAAPs). Now accounting standards are on the verge of going global:

- The Financial Accounting Standards Board, which establishes and improves accounting standards for U.S. companies, is working toward standards convergence with the London-based International Accounting Standards Board.

- Issues to be reconciled include how to report the details of mergers and acquisitions and how to account for minority stakes in corporations.
- U.S., Japanese, and Canadian companies often must report additional information before selling stock in Europe because of differences in accounting standards—but this may change in the near future.

For multinational firms, the benefits of global accounting standards are huge. With 24-hour global securities trading a reality, multinational firms will save time and money when they can meet just one accounting standard in order to offer shares on stock exchanges around the world.

The information required to form these ratios is found in a firm's balance sheet and income statement (in our examples for Northeast Art Supply, Figures 18.2 and 18.4).

Profitability Ratios

A firm's net income after taxes indicates whether the firm is profitable. It does not, however, indicate how effectively the firm's resources are being used. For this latter purpose, three ratios can be computed.

return on sales (or profit margin) a financial ratio calculated by dividing net income after taxes by net sales

Return on Sales

Return on sales, sometimes called *profit margin*, is a financial ratio calculated by dividing net income after taxes by net sales. For Northeast Art Supply,

$$\text{Return on sales} = \frac{\text{net income after taxes}}{\text{net sales}} = \frac{\$30,175}{\$451,000}$$

$$= 0.067, \text{ or } 6.7 \text{ percent}$$

The return on sales indicates how effectively the firm is transforming sales into profits. A higher return on sales is better than a low one. Today, the average return on sales for all business firms is between 4 and 5 percent. With a return on sales of 6.7 percent, Northeast Art Supply is above average. A low return on sales can be increased by reducing expenses, increasing sales, or both.

return on owners' equity a financial ratio calculated by dividing net income after taxes by owners' equity

Return on Owners' Equity

Return on owners' equity is a financial ratio calculated by dividing net income after taxes by owners' equity. For Northeast Art Supply,

$$\text{Return on owners' equity} = \frac{\text{net income after taxes}}{\text{owners' equity}} = \frac{\$30,175}{\$230,000}$$

$$= 0.13, \text{ or } 13 \text{ percent}$$

Return on owners' equity indicates how much income is generated by each dollar of equity. Northeast is providing income of 13 cents per dollar invested in the business. The average for all businesses is between 12 and 15 cents. A higher return on owners' equity is better than a low one, and the only practical ways to increase return on owners' equity is to reduce expenses, increase sales, or both.

Earnings per Share   From the point of view of stockholders, **earnings per share** is one of the best indicators of a corporation's success. It is calculated by dividing net income after taxes by the number of shares of common stock outstanding. If we assume that Northeast Art Supply has issued 25,000 shares of stock, then its earnings per share are

$$\text{Earnings per share} = \frac{\text{net income after taxes}}{\text{common stock shares outstanding}} = \frac{\$30,175}{25,000}$$

$$= \$1.21 \text{ per share}$$

earnings per share a financial ratio calculated by dividing net income after taxes by the number of shares of common stock outstanding

There is no meaningful average for this ratio mainly because the number of outstanding shares of a firm's stock is subject to change as a result of stock splits and stock dividends. Also, some corporations choose to issue more stock than others. As a general rule, however, an increase in earnings per share is a healthy sign for any corporation.

Short-Term Financial Ratios

Two short-term financial ratios permit managers (and lenders) to evaluate the ability of a firm to pay its current liabilities. Before we discuss these ratios, we should examine one other easily determined measure: working capital.

Working Capital   **Working capital** is the difference between current assets and current liabilities. For Northeast Art,

Current assets	$182,000
Less current liabilities	$ 70,000
Equals working capital	$112,000

working capital the difference between current assets and current liabilities

Working capital indicates how much would remain if a firm paid off all current liabilities with cash and other current assets. The "proper" amount of working capital depends on the type of firm, its past experience, and its particular industry. A firm with too little working capital may have to borrow money to finance its operations.

Current Ratio   A firm's **current ratio** is computed by dividing current assets by current liabilities. For Northeast Art Supply,

$$\text{Current ratio} = \frac{\text{current assets}}{\text{current liabilities}} = \frac{\$182,000}{\$70,000} = 2.6$$

current ratio a financial ratio computed by dividing current assets by current liabilities

This means that Northeast Art Supply has $2.60 of current assets for every $1 of current liabilities. The average current ratio for all industries is 2.0, but it varies greatly from industry to industry. A high current ratio indicates that a firm can pay its current liabilities. A low current ratio can be improved by repaying current liabilities, by reducing dividend payments to increase the firm's cash balance, or by obtaining additional cash from investors.

Acid-Test Ratio   This ratio, sometimes called the *quick ratio*, is a measure of the firm's ability to pay current liabilities *quickly*—with its cash, marketable securities, and receivables. The **acid-test ratio** is calculated by adding cash, marketable securities and receivables and dividing the total by current liabilities. The value of inventory and other current assets are "removed" from current assets because these assets are not converted into cash as easily as cash, marketable securities, and receivables. For Northeast Art Supply,

acid-test ratio a financial ratio calculated by adding cash, marketable securities and receivables and dividing the total by current liabilities

$$\text{Acid-test ratio} = \frac{\text{cash + marketable securities + receivables}}{\text{current liabilities}} = \frac{\$139,000}{\$70,000}$$

$$= 1.99$$

For all businesses, the desired acid-test ratio is 1.0. Northeast Art Supply is above average with a ratio of 1.99, and the firm should be well able to pay its current liabilities. To increase a low acid-test ratio, a firm would have to repay current liabilities, reduce dividend payments to increase the firm's cash balance, or obtain additional cash from investors.

Activity Ratios

Two activity ratios permit managers to measure how many times each year a company collects its accounts receivables or sells its inventory.

accounts receivable turnover a financial ratio calculated by dividing net sales by accounts receivable

Accounts Receivable Turnover   A firm's **accounts receivable turnover** is the number of times the firm collects its accounts receivable in one year. If the data are available, this ratio should be calculated using a firm's net credit sales. Since data for Northeast Art Supply's credit sales are unavailable, this ratio can be calculated by dividing net sales by accounts receivable. For Northeast Art,

$$\text{Accounts receivable turnover} = \frac{\text{net sales}}{\text{accounts receivable}} = \frac{\$451{,}000}{\$38{,}000}$$

$$= 11.9 \text{ times per year}$$

Northeast Art Supply collects its accounts receivables 11.9 times each year, or about every thirty days. If a firm's credit terms require customers to pay in twenty-five days, a collection period of thirty days is considered acceptable. There is no meaningful average for this measure mainly because credit terms differ among companies. A high accounts receivable turnover is better than a low one. As a general rule, a low accounts receivable turnover ratio can be improved by pressing for payment of past-due accounts and by tightening requirements for prospective credit customers.

inventory turnover a financial ratio calculated by dividing the cost of goods sold in one year by the average value of the inventory

Inventory Turnover   A firm's **inventory turnover** is the number of times the firm sells its merchandise inventory in one year. It is approximated by dividing the cost of goods sold in one year by the average value of the inventory.

The average value of the inventory can be found by adding the beginning inventory value and the ending inventory value (given on the income statement) and dividing the sum by 2. For Northeast Art Supply, average inventory is $40,500. Thus

$$\text{Inventory turnover} = \frac{\text{cost of goods sold}}{\text{average inventory}} = \frac{\$334{,}000}{\$40{,}500}$$

$$= 8.2 \text{ times per year}$$

Northeast Art Supply sells its merchandise inventory 8.2 times each year, or about once every forty-five days. The average inventory turnover for all firms is about 9 times per year, but turnover rates vary widely from industry to industry. For example, supermarkets may have turnover rates of 20 or higher, whereas turnover rates for furniture stores are generally well below the national average. The quickest way to improve inventory turnover is to order merchandise in smaller quantities at more frequent intervals.

Debt-to-Owners'-Equity Ratio

Our final category of financial ratios indicates the degree to which a firm's operations are financed through borrowing. Although other ratios can be calculated, the debt-to-owners'-equity ratio is used often to determine whether a firm has too much debt. The **debt-to-owners'-equity ratio** is calculated by dividing total liabilities by owners' equity. For Northeast Art Supply,

debt-to-owners'-equity ratio a financial ratio calculated by dividing total liabilities by owners' equity

$$\text{Debt-to-owners' equity ratio} = \frac{\text{total liabilities}}{\text{owner's equity}} = \frac{\$110{,}000}{\$230{,}00}$$

$$= 0.48, \text{ or } 48 \text{ percent}$$

A debt-to-owners'-equity ratio of 48 percent means that creditors have provided about 48 cents of financing for every dollar provided by the owners. The higher this ratio, the riskier the situation is for lenders. A high debt-to-owners'-equity ratio may make borrowing additional money from lenders difficult. It can be reduced by paying off debts or by increasing the owners' investment in the firm.

Northeast's Financial Ratios: A Summary

Table 18.2 compares the financial ratios of Northeast Art Supply with the average financial ratios for all businesses. It also lists the formulas we used to calculate Northeast's ratios. Northeast seems to be in good financial shape. Its return on sales, current ratio, and acid-test ratio are all above average. Its other ratios are about average, although its inventory turnover and debt-to-equity ratio could be improved.

This chapter ends our discussion of accounting information. In Chapter 19 we begin our examination of business finances by discussing money, banking, and credit.

> > **TABLE 18.2**

FINANCIAL RATIOS OF NORTHEAST ART SUPPLY COMPARED WITH AVERAGE RATIOS FOR ALL BUSINESSES

Ratio	Formula	Northeast Ratio	Average Business Ratio	Direction for Improvement
Profitability Ratios				
Return on sales	$\dfrac{\text{net income after taxes}}{\text{net sales}}$	6.7%	4–5%	Higher
Return on owner's equity	$\dfrac{\text{net income after taxes}}{\text{owners' equity}}$	13%	12–15%	Higher
Earnings per share	$\dfrac{\text{net income after taxes}}{\text{common stock shares outstanding}}$	$1.21 per share	—	Higher
Short-Term Financial Ratios				
Working capital	current assets − current liabilities	$112,000	—	Higher
Current ratio	$\dfrac{\text{current assets}}{\text{current liabilities}}$	2.6	2.0	Higher
Acid-test ratio	$\dfrac{\text{cash + marketable securities + receivables}}{\text{current liabilities}}$	1.99	1.0	Higher
Activity Ratios				
Accounts receivable turnover	$\dfrac{\text{net sales}}{\text{accounts receivable}}$	11.9	—	Higher
Inventory turnover	$\dfrac{\text{cost of goods sold}}{\text{average inventory}}$	8.2	9	Higher
Debt-to-owners'-equity ratio	$\dfrac{\text{total liabilities}}{\text{owners' equity}}$	48 percent	—	Lower

RETURN TO Inside Business

Accounting firms, like their corporate clients, have assets, liabilities, and owners' equity. The big firms were organized originally as traditional partnerships, with partners contributing toward expenses and sharing in profits. Many accounting firms today are organized as limited-liability partnerships (sometimes referred to as LLPs), which means that each firm's assets are used to cover its liabilities. Unless the partners are convicted individually of business-related crimes such as fraud, generally their personal assets are protected. As a result, partners in an LLP lose

their owners' equity but not their homes, cars, or other personal assets.

More changes are ahead for the accounting industry. The Sarbanes-Oxley Act requires corporations to switch their lead auditing firms every five years. This means even more competition among accounting firms—at a time when the Big Four face regular reviews by the Public Company Accounting Oversight Board. Which firms will survive if the Big Four give way to the Big Three?

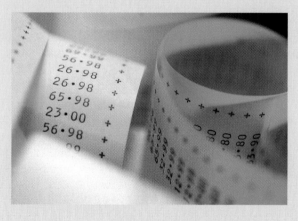

Questions

1. In the wake of phony earnings and fraudulent accounting practices, the U.S. Congress tightened key accounting and financial reporting rules. Why would investors, managers and employees, lenders, and government regulators care about the validity of the financial information reported by corporations?
2. If an accounting firm fails to detect major accounting irregularities that cause a corporation to file for bankruptcy protection, do you think individual partners should be held accountable? Why or why not?

►► CHAPTER REVIEW

Summary

1

Explain why accurate accounting information and audited financial statements are important.

Accounting is the process of systematically collecting, analyzing, and reporting financial information. It can be used to answer questions about what has happened in the past; it also can be used to help make decisions about the future. In fact, it's the firm's accountants and its accounting system that often translates goals, objectives, and plans into dollars and cents to help determine if a decision or plan of action makes "financial sense." Unfortunately, a large number of accounting scandals have caused people to doubt not only the financial information reported by a corporation but also the accounting industry. In a perfect world, accountants and auditors would catch mistakes and disclose questionable accounting practices in a firm's audit. The purpose of an audit is to make sure that a firm's financial statements have been prepared in accordance

with generally accepted accounting principles (GAAPs). To help ensure that corporate financial information is accurate and in response to the many accounting scandals that surfaced in the last part of the 1990s and the first part of the twenty-first century, the Sarbanes-Oxley Act was signed into law. This law contains a number of provisions designed to restore public confidence in the accounting industry.

2

Identify the people who use accounting information and possible careers in the accounting industry.

To be successful in the accounting industry, employees must be responsible, honest, and ethical; have a strong background in financial management; know how to use a computer and software to process data into accounting information; and be able to communicate with people who need accounting information. Primarily management uses accounting information, but it is also demanded by lenders, suppliers, stockholders, potential investors, and government agencies. While many people think that all account-ants do the same tasks, there are special areas of expertise within the accounting industry. Typical areas of expertise include managerial, financial, cost, tax, government, and not-for-profit accounting. A private accountant is employed by a specific organization to operate its accounting system. A public accountant performs these functions for various in-dividuals or firms on a fee basis. Most accounting firms in-clude on their staffs at least one certified public accountant (CPA). In addition to CPAs, there are also certified man-agement accountants (CMAs). While both CPAs and CMAs can work for the public, a CMA is more likely to work within a large organization. Also, both types of ac-countants are excellent career choices.

3

Discuss the accounting process.

The accounting process is based on the accounting equa-tion: Assets = liabilities + owners' equity. Double-entry bookkeeping ensures that the balances shown by the ac-counting equation is maintained. The accounting process involves five steps: (1) source documents are analyzed, (2) each transaction is recorded in a journal, (3) each journal entry is posted in the appropriate general ledger accounts, (4) at the end of each accounting period, a trial balance is prepared to make sure that the accounting equation is in balance, and (5) financial statements are prepared from the trial balance. A firm's financial statements are included in its annual report. An annual report is a report distributed to stockholders and other interested parties that describes a firm's operating activities and its financial condition. Once statements are prepared, the books are closed. A new ac-counting cycle then is begun for the next accounting period.

4

Read and interpret a balance sheet.

A balance sheet is a summary of a firm's assets, liabilities, and owners' equity accounts at the end of an accounting pe-riod. This statement must demonstrate that the accounting equation is in balance. On the balance sheet, assets are cat-egorized as current, fixed, or intangible. Similarly, liabilities can be divided into current liabilities and long-term ones. For a sole proprietorship or partnership, owners' equity is shown as the difference between assets and liabilities. For corporations, the owners' equity section reports the values of stock and retained earnings.

5

Read and interpret an income statement.

An income statement is a summary of a firm's financial op-erations during the specified accounting period. On the in-come statement, the company's gross profit is computed by subtracting the cost of goods sold from net sales. Operating expenses and interest expense then are deducted to compute

net income before taxes. Finally, income taxes are deducted to obtain the firm's net income after taxes.

6

Describe business activities that affect a firm's cash flow.

Since 1987, the Securities and Exchange Commission (SEC) and the Financial Accounting Standards Board (FASB) have required all publicly traded companies to in-clude a statement of cash flows in their annual reports. This statement illustrates how the operating, investing, and fi-nancing activities of a company affect cash during an ac-counting period. Together the cash flow statement, balance sheet, and income statement illustrate the results of past de-cisions and the business's ability to pay debts and dividends and to finance new growth.

7

Summarize how managers evaluate the financial health of a business.

The firm's financial statements and its accounting informa-tion become more meaningful when compared with corre-sponding information for previous years, for competitors, and for the industry in which the firm operates. Such com-parisons permit managers and other interested people to pick out trends in growth, borrowing, income, and other business variables and to determine whether the firm is on the way to accomplishing its long-term goals. A number of financial ratios can be computed from the information in a firm's financial statements. These ratios provide a picture of the firm's profitability, its short-term financial position, its activity in the area of accounts receivable and inventory, and its debt financing. Like the information on the firm's finan-cial statements, these ratios can and should be compared with those of past accounting periods, those of competitors, and those representing the average of the industry as a whole.

Key Terms

You should now be able to define and give an example rele-vant to each of the following terms:

accounting (589)
audit (590)
generally accepted accounting principles (GAAPs) (591)
managerial accounting (594)
financial accounting (594)
certified public accountant (CPA) (595)
certified management accountant (CMA) (595)
assets (596)
liabilities (596)
owners' equity (596)
accounting equation (596)
double-entry bookkeeping system (596)
trial balance (597)

annual report (597)
balance sheet (or statement of financial position) (597)
liquidity (598)
current assets (598)
fixed assets (600)
depreciation (600)
intangible assets (600)
current liabilities (601)
long-term liabilities (601)
retained earnings (601)
income statement (601)
revenues (602)
gross sales (602)
net sales (602)
cost of goods sold (602)
gross profit (603)
operating expenses (604)
net income (604)
net loss (604)
statement of cash flows (605)
financial ratio (607)
return on sales (or profit margin) (608)
return on owners' equity (608)
earnings per share (609)
working capital (609)
current ratio (609)
acid-test ratio (609)
accounts receivable turnover (610)
inventory turnover (610)
debt-to-owners'-equity ratio (610)

Review Questions

1. What purpose do audits and generally accepted accounting principles (GAAPs) serve in today's business world?
2. How do the major provisions of the Sarbanes-Oxley Act affect a public company's audit procedures?
3. List four groups that use accounting information, and briefly explain why each group has an interest in this information.
4. What is the difference between a private accountant and a public accountant? What are certified public accountants and certified management accountants?
5. State the accounting equation, and list two specific examples of each term in the equation.
6. How is double-entry bookkeeping related to the accounting equation?
7. Briefly describe the five steps of the accounting cycle in order.
8. What is the principal difference between a balance sheet and an income statement?

9. How are current assets distinguished from fixed assets? Why are fixed assets depreciated on a balance sheet?
10. Explain how a retailing firm would determine the cost of goods sold during an accounting period.
11. How does a firm determine its net income after taxes?
12. What is the purpose of a statement of cash flows?
13. For each of the accounts listed below, indicate if the account should be included on a firm's balance sheet, income statement, or statement of cash flows.

Type of Account	Statement Where Reported
Assets	_____
Income	_____
Expenses	_____
Operating activities	_____
Liabilities	_____
Investing activities	_____
Owners' equity	_____

14. What type of information is contained in an annual report? How does the information help to identify financial trends?
15. Explain the calculation procedure for and significance of each of the following:
    a. One of the profitability ratios
    b. A short-term financial ratio
    c. An activity ratio
    d. Debt-to-owners'-equity ratio

Discussion Questions

1. Why do you think there have been so many accounting scandals involving public companies in recent years?
2. Bankers usually insist that prospective borrowers submit audited financial statements along with a loan application. Why should financial statements be audited by a CPA?
3. What can be said about a firm whose owners' equity is a negative amount? How could such a situation come about?
4. Do the balance sheet, income statement, and statement of cash flows contain all the information you might want as a potential lender or stockholder? What other information would you like to examine?
5. Why is it so important to compare a firm's current financial statements with those of previous years, those of competitors, and the average of all firms in the industry in which the firm operates?
6. Which do you think are the two or three most important financial ratios? Why?

➤➤ VIDEO CASE 18.1

The Ethics of "Making the Numbers"

Will sales and profits meet the expectations of investors and Wall Street analysts? Managers at public corporations must answer this vitally important question quarter after quarter, year after year. In an ideal world—one in which the economy never contracts, expenses never go up, and customers never buy competing products—the corporation's share price would soar, and investors would cheer as every financial report showed ever-higher sales revenues, profit margins, and earnings.

In the real world, however, many uncontrollable and unpredictable factors can affect a corporation's performance. Customers may buy fewer units or postpone purchases, competitors may introduce superior products, energy costs and other expenses may rise, interest rates may climb, and buying power may plummet. Faced with the prospect of releasing financial results that fall short of Wall Street's expectations, managers may feel intense pressure to "make the numbers" using a variety of accounting techniques.

For example, some executives at WorldCom made earnings look better by booking billions of dollars in ordinary expenses as capital investments. The company was forced into bankruptcy a few weeks after the accounting scam was exposed. As another example, top managers at the drug retailer Rite Aid posted transactions improperly to inflate corporate earnings. Ultimately, Rite Aid had to lower its earnings figures by $1.6 billion, and investors fled, driving the share price down.

Under the Sarbanes-Oxley Act, the CEO and CFO now must certify the corporation's financial reports. This has led hundreds of companies to restate their earnings in recent years, a sign that stricter controls on accounting practices are having the intended effect. "I don't mean to sugarcoat the figure on restatements," says Steve Odland, CEO of Office Depot, "but I think it is positive—it shows a healthy system." Yet not all earnings restatements are due to accounting irregularities. "The general impression of the public is that accounting rules are black and white," Odland adds. "They are often anything but that, and in many instances the changes in earnings came after new interpretations by the chief accountant of the SEC."

Because accounting rules are open to interpretation, managers sometimes find themselves facing ethical dilemmas when a corporation feels pressure to live up to Wall Street's expectations. Consider the hypothetical situation at Commodore Appliances, a fictional company that sells to Home Depot, Lowe's, and other major retail chains. Margaret, the vice president of sales, has told Rob, a district manager, that the company's sales are down 10 percent in the current quarter. She points out that sales in Rob's district are down 20 percent and states that higher-level managers want him to improve this month's figures using "book and hold," which means recording future sales transactions in the current period.

Rob hesitates, saying that the company is gaining market share and that he needs more time to get sales momentum going. He thinks "book and hold" is not good business practice, even if it is legal. Margaret hints that Rob will lose his job if his sales figures don't look better and stresses that he will need the book-and-hold approach for one month only. Rob realizes that if he doesn't go along, he won't be working at Commodore for very much longer.

Meeting with Kevin, one of Commodore's auditors, Rob learns that book and hold meets generally accepted accounting principles. Kevin emphasizes that customers must be willing to take title to the goods before they're delivered or billed. Any book-and-hold sales must be real, backed by documentation such as e-mails to and from buyers, and the transactions must be completed in the near future.

Rob is at a crossroads: His sales figures must be higher if Commodore is to achieve its performance targets, yet he doesn't know exactly when (or if) he actually would complete any book-and-hold sales he might report this month. He doesn't want to mislead anyone, but he also doesn't want to lose his job or put other people's jobs in jeopardy by refusing to do what he is being asked to do. Rob is confident that he can improve his district's sales over the long term. On the other hand, Commodore's executives can't wait—they are pressuring Rob to make the sales figures look better right now. What should he do?[11]

For more information about the Sarbanes-Oxley Act, go to **www.aicpa.org** (This is the website for the American Institute of Certified Public Accountants and is a good source of information about the act.)

Questions

1. What are the ethical and legal implications of using accounting practices such as the book-and-hold technique to inflate corporate earnings?
2. Why would Commodore's auditor insist that Rob document any sales booked under the book-and-hold technique?
3. If you were in Rob's situation, would you agree to use the book-and-hold technique this month? Justify your decision.
4. Imagine that Commodore has taken out a multi-million-dollar loan that must be repaid next year. How might the lender react if it learned that Commodore was using the book-and-hold method to make revenues look higher than they really are?

➤➤ CASE 18.2

Software Stands Guard over Accounting at Kimberly-Clark

Kimberly-Clark, famous for making Kleenex and Scott paper products, has automated its accounting controls playbook for compliance with the Sarbanes-Oxley Act. This multinational manufacturer generates annual revenues of more than $15 billion and employs 60,000 people in 200 facilities spread across fifty countries. Enforcing strict, consistent controls on accounting information in all locations has long been a top priority for Kimberly-Clark's finance department. Nonetheless, testing and documenting internal controls to bring the company into complete compliance with Sarbanes-Oxley were a major challenge because of the "different languages, cultures, time zones, and systems," remembers Jerry Rehfuss, the finance director who spearheaded the compliance effort. This is why the company decided to have software stand guard over accounting.

The basis of Kimberly-Clark's compliance initiative was its five-book set of corporate financial instructions, a detailed playbook for avoiding fraud and manipulation in accounting procedures. "From location to location, country to country, the actual controls might vary," says Rehfuss. "But the basic principles—say, for each transaction, one person needs to prepare it, and another person needs to authorize it—have been in place for each process."

Next, Rehfuss hired an outside accounting firm to specify the individual accounting processes and controls that could have the greatest impact on accuracy in Kimberly-Clark's financial statements. He also had internal experts review this list with an eye toward adding new controls where needed. The completed list was sent to coordinators in the company's 200 facilities, who, in turn, identified the employees responsible for applying these processes and controls. The objective was to determine the number and type of accounting elements that would have to be tested and documented in each location to comply with Sarbanes-Oxley. In the end, the company tested approximately 4,000 controls worldwide and assembled the information into a "control map" indicating what guidelines were being used in which locations.

To automate these controls, Rehfuss turned to software that allowed or restricted access to accounting systems based on the playbook's rules. The software also alerted employees electronically when it was time to document their processes and controls for legal purposes. Outside auditors used the software on a "read-only" basis to check that problems actually were resolved but not to make changes to the system. Kimberly-Clark managers used the software to obtain problem reports, learn what auditors were testing, and track test results. The company found no fraud, although Rehfuss says that it uncovered some mistakes caused by "human error," such as when a new employee was unaware of certain control details. Finally, special software was installed to prevent employees from handling more aspects of an accounting transaction than the playbook allowed.

Using software to automate the playbook and document controls for compliance is especially important because Kimberly-Clark has thousands of employees tapping into local or corporate systems to post transactions, prepare financial statements, and handle other accounting tasks. Rehfuss says that this "could create the potential for widespread errors and, in the worst case, intentional fraud [without proper control over access] because so much of our business and transactions are run by computers."

Electronically restricting access to authorized personnel only, electronically enforcing the playbook's controls, and electronically reviewing documentation are cost-effective ways for Kimberly-Clark to stand guard over accounting information. In one year, the company was able to slash more than $2 million (25 percent) off the annual cost of complying with the Sarbanes-Oxley Act. The technology also saves the company about forty hours per audit per location while strengthening its protection against accounting fraud.[12]

For more information about this company, go to **www.kimberly-clark.com.**

Questions

1. According to Jerry Rehfuss, Kimberly-Clark uses a basic accounting principle of having more than one person involved in accounting processes to uncover mistakes or fraud. How can getting more people involved in the accounting process act as a safeguard against fraud and mistakes?

2. It would seem that one important goal for a good accounting system would be to provide financial information to any of Kimberly-Clark's 60,000 employees. And yet Kimberly-Clark has restricted access to its accounting system so that only a limited number of people can access certain information. Why is restricted access important?

3. Do you think Kimberly-Clark's outside auditors should be allowed to make changes to the company's accounting software if they discover a serious problem? Why or why not?

4. Today, most large corporations such as Kimberly-Clark spend millions of dollars to ensure that their accounting information is accurate and complies with the Sarbanes-Oxley Act. Is the expense worth it? Why?

→ CHAPTER 18: JOURNAL EXERCISE

Discovery statement: Today, more and more people are using computers and personal finance and accounting software to manage their finances. To complete this journal entry, use the Internet to research the Quicken *and* Microsoft Money software packages. If there is a demonstration video, view the video. Then answer the questions below.

Describe the specific types of activities that you can accomplish with the help of your computer and the software packages.

_____

_____

_____

_____

_____

Both the Quicken and Microsoft Money are popular software packages used by millions of people. Based on your initial research, which software package do you prefer? Explain your answer.

_____

_____

_____

_____

_____

After examining both packages, do you think that either software package could help you to manage your finances? Why?

_____

_____

_____

_____

_____

BUILDING SKILLS FOR CAREER SUCCESS

1. Exploring the Internet

To those unacquainted with current activities and practices in larger accounting firms, there is often some surprise at just how varied the accounting work involved actually is. Although setting up and maintaining accounting software for clients are standard, accounting firms also can provide a wide range of specialized services. For example, research into mergers or acquisitions of other firms, investment advice, and solutions to financial problems are now common strategies for revenue growth within accounting firms. Most websites for large accounting firms also will post information about current employment opportunities.

Assignment

1. Visit the website of a major accounting firm such as Deloitte Touche Tohmatsu (**www.deloitte.com**), KPMG (**www.kpmg.com**), PricewaterhouseCoopers (**www.pwc.com**), or Ernst & Young (**www.ey.com**). Describe in general terms how the website is used to communicate with clients and prospective clients. Visit the text website for updates to this exercise.

2. What are some of the content items presented on the site? What do these tell you about the firm and its clients?

3. Search the site for career information. Often the firm will post descriptions of employment opportunities along with

educational and experience requirements. Describe what you find.

2. Developing Critical-Thinking Skills

According to the experts, you must evaluate your existing financial condition before establishing an investment plan. As pointed out in this chapter, a personal balance sheet provides a picture of your assets, liabilities, and net worth. A personal income statement will tell you whether you have a cash surplus or cash deficit at the end of a specific period.

Assignment

1. Using your own financial information from last month, construct a personal balance sheet and personal income statement.
2. Based on the information contained in your personal financial statements, answer the following:
   a. What is your current net worth?
   b. Do you have a cash surplus or a cash deficit at the end of the month?
   c. What specific steps can you take to improve your financial condition?
3. Based on your findings, prepare a plan for improving your financial condition over the next six months.

3. Building Team Skills

This has been a bad year for Miami-based Park Avenue Furniture. The firm increased sales revenues to $1,400,000, but total expenses ballooned to $1,750,000. Although management realized that some of the firm's expenses were out of control, including cost of goods sold ($700,000), salaries ($450,000), and advertising costs ($140,000), it could not contain expenses. As a result, the furniture retailer lost $350,000. To make matters worse, the retailer applied for a $350,000 loan at Fidelity National Bank and was turned down. The bank officer, Mike Nettles, said that the firm already had too much debt. At that time, liabilities totaled $420,000; owners' equity was $600,000.

Assignment

1. In groups of three or four, analyze the financial condition of Park Avenue Furniture.
2. Discuss why you think the bank officer turned down Park Avenue's loan request.

3. Prepare a detailed plan of action to improve the financial health of Park Avenue Furniture over the next twelve months.

4. Researching Different Careers

As pointed out in this chapter, job opportunities for accountants and managers in the accounting area are expected to experience average growth between now and the year 2012. Employment opportunities range from entry-level positions for clerical workers and technicians to professional positions that require a college degree in accounting, management consulting, or computer technology. Typical job titles in the accounting field include bookkeeper, corporate accountant, public accountant, auditor, managerial accountant, and controller.

Assignment

1. Answer the following questions based on information obtained from interviews with people employed in accounting, from research in the library or by using the Internet, or from information gained from your college's career center.
   a. What types of activities would a person employed in one of the accounting positions listed above perform on a daily basis?
   b. Would you choose this career? Why or why not?
2. Summarize your findings in a report.

5. Improving Communication Skills

One of the best resources for determining the soundness of an investment opportunity is a corporation's annual report. An annual report will tell you about a company's management, its past performance, and its future goals. Most annual reports contain a letter from the chairman of the board, as well as photographs of smiling employees. While these are nice to look at, it is the financial statements and footnotes in an annual report that give the true picture of a corporation's financial health.

Assignment

1. Obtain a printed copy of an annual report or use the Internet to access a corporation's annual report for a company that you consider a "promising investment."

2. Use the report to answer the following questions:

   a. What does the CEO/president say about the company's past performance and future projections?

   b. Is the firm profitable? Are profits increasing or decreasing?

   c. Most annual reports contain graphs or illustrations that show trends for sales, profits, earnings per share, and other important financial measures over a five- or ten-year period. What significant trends for this company are illustrated in its annual report?

3. On the basis of your examination of its annual report, would you invest in this company? Prepare a brief report justifying your decision.

→ PREP TEST

Matching Questions

____ 1. It is the process of collecting, analyzing, and reporting data.

____ 2. All the firm's debts are included.

____ 3. It is the difference between a firm's assets and its liabilities.

____ 4. A person who is employed by PricewaterhouseCoopers.

____ 5. Inventories are an example.

____ 6. The ease with which assets can be converted into cash.

____ 7. This statement reveals the financial position of the firm.

____ 8. It illustrates how operating, investing, and financing activities affect cash.

____ 9. A promissory note secures this obligation.

____ 10. The result of dividing current assets by current liabilities.

a. accounting

b. assets

c. balance sheet

d. current ratio

e. liabilities

f. liquidity

g. notes payable

h. owner's equity

i. public accountant

j. statement of cash flows

True/False Questions

T F

11. ○ ○ The accounting equation is assets + liabilities = owners' equity.

12. ○ ○ Cash receipts journal is a specialized journal.

13. ○ ○ Return on owners' equity indicates a measure of the amount earned per share.

14. ○ ○ An acid-test ratio is a measure of the firm's ability to pay current liabilities.

15. ○ ○ Working capital is the amount remaining after a firm has paid its current liabilities with cash and other current assets.

16. ○ ○ The debt-to-owners'-equity ratio is used to indicate the degree to which a firm's operations are financed through borrowing.

T F

17. ○ ○ Recording transactions in the general ledger is the first step in the accounting cycle.

18. ○ ○ Marketable securities can be converted into cash in a matter of days.

19. ○ ○ Stockholder's equity represents the total value of a corporation's stock plus retained earnings that have accumulated to date.

20. ○ ○ A low current ratio can be improved by increasing its current liabilities.

Multiple-Choice Questions

21. Which statement is *not* true about a balance sheet?

    a. It provides proof that assets = liabilities + owners' equity.

    b. It lists the current, fixed, and intangible assets.

    c. It summarizes the firm's revenues and expenses during one accounting period.

    d. It gives the liabilities of the firm.

    e. It shows the owners' equity in the business.

22. The board of directors decided to pay 50 percent of the $460,000 earnings in dividends to the stockholders. The firm has retained earnings of $680,000 on the books. After the dividends are paid, which of the following statements is true about the total owners' equity?

    a. The current value of the firm's retained earnings is $910,000.

    b. The current value of the firm's retained earnings is $450,000.

    c. The firm failed to reach its profit goal.

    d. Each shareholder will receive more than he or she received last year.

    e. The firm's retained earnings are too high.

23. A firm had gross profits from sales in the amount of $180,000, operating expenses of $90,000, and federal income taxes of $20,000. What was the firm's net income after taxes?

    a. $10,000

    b. $20,000

    c. $70,000

    d. $90,000

    e. $200,000

24. The Sarbanes-Oxley Act

    a. requires the SEC to police the accounting industry.

    b. requires CEOs to certify periodic financial statements.

    c. subjects CEOs to criminal penalties for violations of security reporting.

    d. prohibits many types of consulting services by accounting firms.

    e. All the above are true.

25. A high debt-to-owners' equity ratio

    a. reduces the risk for lenders.

    b. will increase as debts are paid off.

    c. will increase the owner's investment.

    d. makes borrowing money from lenders difficult.

    e. All the above are true.

Fill-in-the-Blank Questions

26. The accounting equation is assets equal liabilities plus _____.

27. An income statement is sometimes called the _____ statement.

28. When a company reports financial numbers that are lower than expected, the company's stock value can _____ dramatically.

29. Net income after taxes that is divided by the number of shares of common stock outstanding results in _____ per share.

30. Selling expenses are an example of _____ expenses.

Online Study Center

FOR MORE test practice, use the interactive ACE quizzes available at the Online Student Center: **www.college.hmco.com/PIC/pridebusiness9e.**

Answers on p. PT2.

▶▶ RUNNING A BUSINESS PART VI

Information Systems and Accounting at Finagle A Bagel

Like the hole in a bagel, any hole in Finagle A Bagel's information and accounting systems means less dough for the company. Copresidents Alan Litchman and Laura Trust and their management team could not make timely, informed decisions to build the business profitably without reliable systems for collecting data, processing them, and presenting the results in a meaningful way.

Putting Technology to Work

Regina Jerome is Finagle A Bagel's director of information systems. She and her assistant are responsible for running the computerized accounting system in the company support center, as well as the management information and marketing information systems. As a small business, Finagle A Bagel can't afford to spend money for the sake of having the fastest computer equipment or the flashiest software. Having a limited budget means that "it's absolutely imperative that every piece of technology that we invest in directly supports our business," she says.

One of Jerome's biggest challenges has been implementing a point-of-sale system that supports the information needs of the stores as well as of the senior managers. Unlike restaurant chains that sell standard menu items, Finagle A Bagel customizes everything to the individual customer's taste. Thus store employees must be able to record, prepare, and serve complicated orders. "We designed our point-of-sale system so that when a customer orders, the system follows our menu and enables our cashiers to deliver exactly what the customer ordered," Jerome says. "At the same time, the system collects all the pertinent financial information. Every transaction is recorded and can be retrieved by minute, by day, by store, by cashier, and by terminal." With information from the point-of-sale system, general managers can analyze detailed sales patterns before making decisions about store staffing levels, food orders, and other day-to-day operational issues.

Tracking Cash, Calculating Profits

The copresidents use the financial data drawn from every cash register connected to this point-of-sale system to reconcile daily store sales with daily bank deposits. As a result, copresident Litchman knows by 7:30 each morning how much money was deposited on the previous day and the total amount the company has to cover payroll, food purchases, and other expenses. He also knows if a store's reported sales match its bank deposit. If not, a senior manager immediately looks into the discrepancy, which usually turns out to be some kind of error. Once in a while, however, the discrepancy is a sign of store-level theft that requires further investigation and—when warranted—legal action.

Finagle A Bagel's managers use the company's accounting system to make other important decisions. For every dollar of sales, a food service business makes only a few cents in profit. Finagle A Bagel makes about 8 cents in profit from every sales dollar, but Litchman is aiming to make a profit of 10 cents per dollar. He and his team need timely reports showing retailing and wholesaling revenues, the cost of goods sold, and operating expenses to calculate the company's pretax profit and measure progress toward this profit goal. Food and labor costs constitute more than two-thirds of Finagle A Bagel's costs—so the faster managers can see these numbers, the faster they can act if expenses are higher than expected.

Technology Drives the Frequent Finagler Card

Thanks to new software running on the point-of-sale system, Finagle A Bagel has been able to introduce a new and improved Frequent Finagler customer loyalty card. Customers pay $1 to buy this card, which is activated immediately at the store. From that point on, the cardholder receives one point for every dollar spent in any Finagle A Bagel store. Points can be redeemed for free food, such as a cup of coffee, a bagel sandwich, or a bottle of fruit juice.

The Frequent Finagler card is an excellent way for the company to learn more about the buying habits of its most valuable customers. Managers can see which menu items loyal customers buy, in which store, and at what time of day. Going a step further, Finagle A Bagel is using the card to start a dialogue with loyal customers. The company's website (**www.finagleabagel.com**) plays a key role in this initiative. When cardholders log on and register personal data such as address, phone number, and e-mail address, they re-

ceive five points on their new Frequent Finagler card. Finagle A Bagel receives a wealth of customer data to analyze and use in targeting its marketing efforts more precisely.

Add a Product, Drop a Product

The technologies driving the Frequent Finagler card and the point-of-sale system help Finagle A Bagel to gather sufficient data to support decisions about changing the product line. "We add products to categories that are doing well, we eliminate things that are not selling, and we bring back products that have done well," says Trust. "Being able to know that a product isn't selling so we can get it off the menu and try something new is a vital piece of information."

For example, says Trust, "We just introduced a new sausage bagel pizza based on the fact that our pepperoni pizza sells very well—better than our veggie pizza." When sales data confirmed the popularity of sausage, Finagle A Bagel began introducing it in a breakfast bagel sandwich. Now the company is looking at incorporating sausage into other menu items to delight customers' taste buds and boost sales. However, Trust and her management team won't make any product decisions without first consulting reports based on data collected by the Frequent Finagler card and the point-of-sale system.

Questions

1. Is Finagle A Bagel collecting data from internal sources, external sources, or both? What cautions apply to the sources of its data?
2. Finagle A Bagel uses information to track cash, sales revenues, and expenses on a daily basis. How does this type of accounting system encourage effective decision making and discourage store-level theft?
3. As a small business, which of the financial ratios might Finagle A Bagel want to track especially closely? Why?
4. Do you think the Frequent Finagler card has any effect on Finagle A Bagel's customer loyalty? For the firm, what are the benefits of the loyalty program?

Now that you have a marketing plan, the next big and important step is to prepare a financial plan. One of the biggest mistakes an entrepreneur makes when faced with a need for financing is not being prepared. Completing this section will show you that if you are prepared and you are creditworthy, the task may be easier than you think. Remember, most lenders and investors insist that you submit current financial statements that have been prepared by an independent certified public accountant (CPA). Chapter 18, "Using Accounting Information," should help you to answer the questions in this part of the business plan.

The Financial Plan Component

Your financial plan should answer at least the following questions about the investment needed, sales and cash-flow forecasts, breakeven analysis, and sources of funding.

6.1. What is the actual amount of money you need to open your business (start-up budget) and the amount needed to keep it open (operating budget)? Prepare a realistic budget.
6.2. How much money do you have, and how much money will you need to start your business and stay in business?

6.3. Prepare a projected income statement by month for the first year of operation and by quarter for the second and third years.
6.4. Prepare projected balance sheets for each of the first three years of operation.
6.5. Prepare a breakeven analysis. How many units of your products or service will have to be sold to cover your costs?
6.6. Reinforce your final projections by comparing them with industry averages for your chosen industry.

Review of Business Plan Activities

Throughout this project you have been investigating what it takes to open and run a business, and now you are finally at the bottom line: What it is going to cost to open your business, and how much money you will need to keep it running for a year? Before tackling the last part of the business plan, review your answers to the questions in each part to make sure that all your answers are consistent throughout the entire business plan. Then write a brief statement that summarizes all the information for this part of the business plan.

Part 7

Finance and Investment

In this part we look at another business resource—money. First we discuss the functions of money and the financial institutions that are part of our banking system. Then we examine the concept of financial management and investing for both firms and individuals.

Understanding Money, Banking, and Credit

WHAT you will be able to do once you complete this chapter:

1 Identify the functions and characteristics of money.

2 Summarize how the Federal Reserve System regulates the money supply.

3 Describe the organizations involved in the banking industry.

4 Identify the services provided by financial institutions.

5 Understand how financial institutions are changing to meet the needs of domestic and international customers.

6 Explain how deposit insurance protects customers.

7 Discuss the importance of credit and credit management.

WHY this chapter matters

You've heard the old saying, "Money makes the world go around!" And it's true because it takes money to function in today's economy. In this chapter we take a look at financial institutions and how important banking activities are for both individuals and business firms.

FOR HELP with studying this chapter, visit the Online Student Center:

www.college.hmco.com/PIC/pridebusiness9e

Online Study Center

"America's Most Convenient Bank," as Commerce Bank calls itself, is wooing customers up and down the eastern seaboard with "wow" banking. The New Jersey–based bank was founded in 1973 and now has more than 350 branches (which it calls "stores") stretching from Connecticut to Florida. Before the end of this decade, Commerce Bank plans to have 700 branches and grow its deposits from $36 billion to more than $100 billion.

In many ways Commerce Bank operates more like a retailer than an up-and-coming financial institution. Its branches sport a big red "C" and are open Monday through Sunday. Not only do its branches stay open in the evening, a few keep their doors open until midnight on weekdays. The extended banking hours actually are longer than posted because, says John Tolomer, a Commerce Bank senior vice president, "We open ten minutes early and stay ten minutes late."

People—not computers—answer phone calls at the branches, usually just a few seconds after the first ring. Loan specialists and customer service representatives can be reached by phone at any hour, day or night. The teller at the drive-through window gives customers red lollipops for their children and treats for their dogs. At a time when banks charge for many services, Commerce Bank offers free personal checking accounts. And each branch has a free "Penny Arcade" coin-counting machine for use by customers and noncustomers alike.

Although Commerce Bank has automated teller machines (ATMs), customers enjoy visiting branches in person to cash a check, apply for credit, or make a deposit because "we create an experience, not just a transaction," says Heather Newcomb, an assistant vice president. "We call it our 'wow' experience." The bank is also a good neighbor in the communities where it does business, making generous donations to local nonprofit organizations.

Even as Commerce Bank continues its aggressive expansion, competitors are fighting back with new branches, new services, and longer business hours. Can Commerce Bank ride the "wow" factor to meet its long-term growth goals?[1]

For more information about this company, go to **www .commerceonline .com**.

DID YOU KNOW?

"America's Most Convenient Bank," as Commerce Bank calls itself, is attracting new customers by using "wow" banking and plans to expand from 350 branches to 700 branches by the end of this decade.

In Chapter 1 we defined a *business* as the organized effort of individuals to produce, and sell for a profit, the products and services that satisfy society's needs. Commerce Bank fulfils the last part of this definition by accepting deposits, making loans, and providing other financial services to its customers. And yet Commerce Bank is different! Words such as "America's Most Convenient Bank" and "wow banking" describe this East Coast bank's daily operations. Extended hours, real people answering the phones, free personal checking, and employees who care about customer service create an atmosphere where customers actually look forward to visiting the branches to cash a check, apply for credit, or make a deposit. But how does Commerce Bank—or for that matter any bank—earn profits?

Most people regard a bank, savings and loan association, or similar financial institution as a place to deposit or borrow money. When you deposit money, you *receive* interest. When you borrow money, you must *pay* interest. You may borrow to buy a home, a car, or some other high-cost item. In this case the resource that will be transformed into money to repay the loan is the salary you receive for your labor.

Businesses also transform resources into money. A business firm (even a new one) may have a valuable asset in the form of an idea for a product or service. If the firm (or its founder) has a good credit history and the idea is a good one, a bank or other lender probably will lend it the money to develop, produce, and market the product or service. The loan—with interest—will be repaid out of future sales revenue. In this way, both the firm and the lender will earn a reasonable profit.

In each of these situations, the borrower needs the money now and will have the ability to repay it later. But also in each situation, the borrowed money will be repaid through the use of *resources*. And while the decision to borrow money from a bank or other financial institution always should be made after careful deliberation, the fact is that responsible borrowing enables both individuals and business firms to meet specific needs.

In this chapter we begin by outlining the functions and characteristics of money that make it an acceptable means of payment for products, services, and resources. Then we consider the role of the Federal Reserve System in maintaining a healthy economy. Next, we describe the banking industry—commercial banks, savings and loan associations, credit unions, and other institutions that offer banking services. Then we turn our attention to how banking practices meet the needs of customers. We also describe the safeguards established by the federal government to protect depositors against losses. In closing, we examine credit transactions, sources of credit information, and effective collection procedures.

What Is Money?

The members of some societies still exchange goods and services through barter, without using money. A **barter system** is a system of exchange in which goods or services are traded directly for other goods or services. One family may raise vegetables and herbs, and another may weave cloth. To obtain food, the family of weavers trades cloth for vegetables, provided that the farming family is in need of cloth.

The trouble with the barter system is that the two parties in an exchange must need each other's products at the same time, and the two products must be roughly equal in value. Thus even very isolated societies soon develop some sort of money to eliminate the inconvenience of trading by barter.

Money is anything a society uses to purchase products, services, or resources. Historically, different groups of people have used all sorts of objects as money—whales' teeth, stones, beads, copper crosses, clamshells, and gold and silver, for example. Today, the most commonly used objects are metal coins and paper bills, which together are called *currency*.

The Functions of Money

Money aids in the exchange of goods and services. However, this is a rather general (and somewhat theoretical) way of stating money's function. Let's look instead at three *specific* functions money serves in any society.

Money as a Medium of Exchange A **medium of exchange** is anything accepted as payment for products, services, and resources. This definition looks very much like the definition of money. It is meant to be because the primary function of money is to serve as a medium of exchange. The key word here is *accepted*. As long as the owners of products, services, and resources *accept* money in an exchange, it is performing this function. For example, if you want to purchase a Hewlett Packard Photosmart printer that is priced at $229 in a Circuit City store, you must give the store the correct amount of money. In return, the store gives you the product.

medium of exchange anything accepted as payment for products, services, and resources

Money as a Measure of Value A **measure of value** is a single standard or "yardstick" used to assign values to and compare the values of products, services, and resources. Money serves as a measure of value because the prices of all products, services, and resources are stated in terms of money. It is thus the "common denominator" we use to compare products and decide which we will buy.

measure of value a single standard or "yardstick" used to assign values to and compare the values of products, services, and resources

store of value a means of retaining and accumulating wealth

Money as a Store of Value Money received by an individual or firm need not be used immediately. It may be held and spent later. Hence money serves as a **store of value,** or a means of retaining and accumulating wealth. This function of money comes into play whenever we hold onto money—in a pocket, a cookie jar, a savings account, or whatever.

Value that is stored as money is affected by *inflation*. Remember from Chapter 1 that *inflation* is a general rise in the level of prices. As prices go up in an inflationary period, money loses purchasing power. Suppose that you can buy a Sony home theater system for $1,000. Your $1,000 has a value equal to the value of that home theater system. But suppose that you wait and do not buy the home theater system immediately. If the price goes up to $1,050 in the meantime because of inflation, you can no longer buy the home theater system with your $1,000. Your money has *lost* purchasing power because it is now worth less than the home theater system.

It's all money! Regardless of what their money looks like, people around the world know that their currency serves as a medium of exchange, a measure of value, and a store of value. In this photo, a bank clerk exchanges Chinese yuan for U.S. dollars.

To determine the effect of inflation on the purchasing power of a dollar, economists often refer to a consumer price index such as the one illustrated in Figure 19.1. The consumer price index measures the changes in prices of a fixed basket of goods purchased by a typical consumer, including food, transportation, housing, utilities, clothing, medical care, entertainment, and other items. The base amount for the consumer price index is 100 and was established by averaging the cost of the items included in the consumer price index over a 36-month period from 1982 to 1984. In November 2005, it took approximately $198 to purchase the same goods that could have been purchased for $100 in the base period 1982–1984.

Important Characteristics of Money

Money must be easy to use, trusted, and capable of performing the three functions just mentioned. To meet these requirements, money must possess the following five characteristics.

Divisibility The standard unit of money must be divisible into smaller units to accommodate small purchases as well as large ones. In the United States, our standard is the dollar, and it is divided into pennies, nickels, dimes, quarters, and

>> **FIGURE 19.1**

THE CONSUMER PRICE INDEX AND THE PURCHASING POWER OF THE CONSUMER DOLLAR (BASE PERIOD 1982–1984 = 100)

Inflation causes a loss of money's stored value. As the consumer price index goes up, the purchasing power of the consumer's dollar goes down.

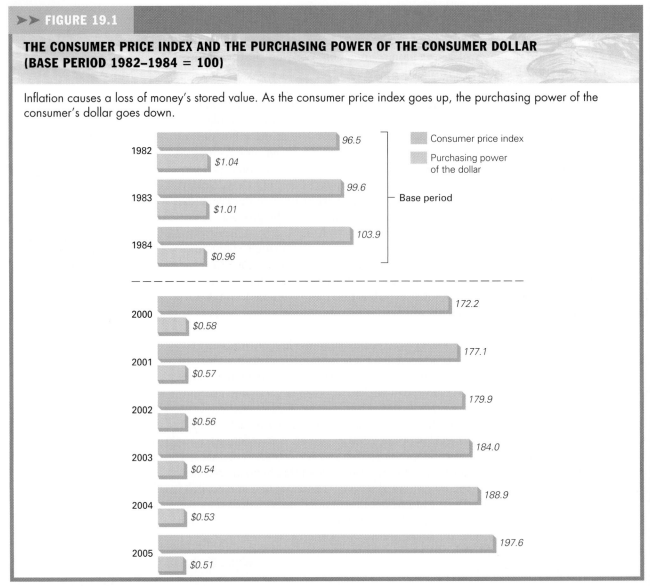

Source: The U.S. Bureau of Labor Statistics website, **www.bls.gov,** December 16, 2005.

half-dollars. These coins allow us to make purchases of less than a dollar and of odd amounts greater than a dollar. Other nations have their own divisible currencies: the euro in European nations, the rupee in India, and the yen in Japan, to mention a few.

Portability Money must be small enough and light enough to be carried easily. For this reason, paper currency is issued in larger *denominations*—multiples of the standard dollar unit. Five-, ten-, twenty-, fifty-, and hundred-dollar bills make our money convenient for almost any purchase.

Stability Money should retain its value over time. When it does not, people tend to lose faith in their money. When money becomes extremely unstable, people may turn to other means of storing value, such as gold and jewels, works of art, and real estate. They even may use such items as a medium of exchange in a barter system. During upheavals in Eastern Europe including Russia in the 1990s, farmers traded farm products for cigarettes because the value of cigarettes was more stable than each nation's money.

Durability The objects that serve as money should be strong enough to last through reasonable usage. No one would appreciate (or use) dollar bills that disintegrated as they were handled or coins that melted in the sun. To increase the life expectancy of paper currency, most nations use special paper with a high fiber content.

Difficulty of Counterfeiting If a nation's currency were easy to counterfeit—that is, to imitate or fake—its citizens would be uneasy about accepting it as payment. Thus countries do their best to ensure that it is very hard to reproduce their currency. In an attempt to make paper currency more difficult to counterfeit, the U.S. government periodically redesigns its paper currency. Typically, countries use special paper and watermarks and print intricate designs on their currency to discourage counterfeiting.

The Supply of Money: M_1 and M_2

How much money is there in the United States? Before we can answer this question, we need to define a couple of concepts. A **demand deposit** is an amount on deposit in a checking account. It is called a *demand* deposit because it can be claimed immediately—on demand—by presenting a properly made out check, withdrawing cash from an automated teller machine (ATM), or transferring money between accounts.

> **demand deposit** an amount on deposit in a checking account

A **time deposit** is an amount on deposit in an interest-bearing savings account. Financial institutions generally permit immediate withdrawal of money from savings accounts. However, they can require advance written notice prior to withdrawal. The time between notice and withdrawal is what leads to the name *time* deposit. For this reason, they are called *near-monies*. Other near-monies include short-term government securities, money-market mutual fund shares, and the cash surrender values of insurance policies.

> **time deposit** an amount on deposit in an interest-bearing savings account

Now we can discuss the question of how much money there is in the United States. There are two main measures of the supply of money: M_1 and M_2.

The M_1 *supply of money* is a narrow definition and consists only of currency, demand and other checkable deposits, and traveler's checks. By law, currency must be accepted as payment for products, services, and resources. Checks (demand deposits) are accepted as payment because they are convenient, convertible to cash, and generally safe.

The M_2 *supply of money* consists of M_1 (currency and demand deposits) plus savings accounts, certain money-market securities, and small-denomination time deposits or certificates of deposit (CDs) of less than $100,000. The M_2 definition of money is based on the assumption that time deposits can be converted to cash for spending. Figure 19.2 shows the elements of the M_1 and M_2.

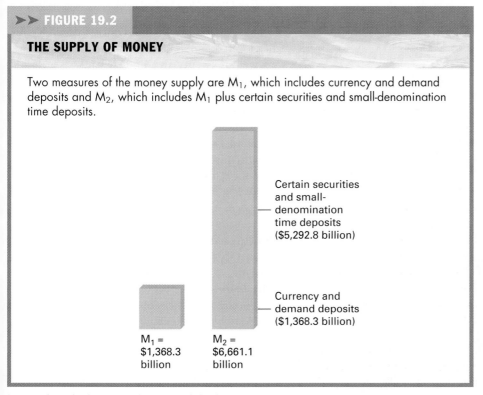

▶▶ FIGURE 19.2

THE SUPPLY OF MONEY

Two measures of the money supply are M_1, which includes currency and demand deposits and M_2, which includes M_1 plus certain securities and small-denomination time deposits.

Certain securities and small-denomination time deposits ($5,292.8 billion)

Currency and demand deposits ($1,368.3 billion)

$M_1 =$ $1,368.3 billion

$M_2 =$ $6,661.1 billion

Source: The Federal Reserve website, **www.federalreserve.gov,** December 15, 2005.

We have, then, at least two measures of the supply of money. (Actually, there are other measures as well, which may be broader or narrower than M_1 and M_2.) Therefore, the answer to our original question is that the amount of money in the United States depends very much on how we measure it. Generally, economists, politicians, and bankers tend to focus on M_1 or some variation of M_1.

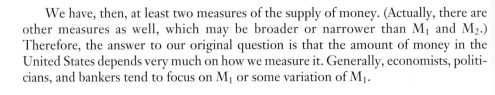

2 LEARNING OBJECTIVE

Summarize how the Federal Reserve System regulates the money supply.

Federal Reserve System the central bank of the United States responsible for regulating the banking industry

The nation's No. 1 banker. As chairman of the Federal Reserve Board, Ben Bernanke and the Fed's other board members are responsible for maintaining a healthy economy. In order to regulate the nation's money supply, the board controls bank reserve requirements, regulates the discount rate, and buys and sells U.S. government securities through open-market operations.

The Federal Reserve System

How do Federal Reserve actions affect me? What is the Federal Reserve System? These are both good questions, and now for some answers. Lately, it seems like the Federal Reserve Board, often referred to as the *Fed*, has been in the news more than usual. Part of the reason is that the Fed lowered interest rates that banks pay to borrow money from the Fed in an effort to shore up a sagging economy after an economic downturn that began in 2000 and the terrorist attacks on September 11. When the Fed lowers rates, banks pay less to borrow money from the Fed. In turn, they often lower the interest rates they charge for business loans, home mortgages, car loans, and even credit cards. Lower rates often provide an incentive for both business firms and individuals to buy goods and services, which, in turn, helps to restore the economic health of the nation. Rate cuts continued until June 2004, when the Federal Reserve began to increase rates that banks pay to borrow money from the Fed. Rate increases were designed to sustain economic growth while controlling inflation. When the Fed raises rates, banks must pay more to borrow money from the Fed. And the banks, in turn, charge higher rates for both consumer and business loans.

Now let's answer the second question. The **Federal Reserve System** is the central bank of the United States and is responsible for regulating the banking industry. Created by Congress on December 23, 1913, its mission is to maintain an economically healthy and financially sound business environment in which banks can operate.

The Federal Reserve System is controlled by its seven-member board of governors, who meet in Washington, D.C. Each governor is appointed by the president and confirmed by the Senate for a fourteen-year term. The president also selects the chairman and vice chairman of the board from among the board members for four-year terms.

The Federal Reserve System consists of twelve district banks located in major cities throughout the United States, as well as twenty-five branch banks (see Figure 19.3). All national (federally chartered) banks must be members of the Fed. State banks may join if they choose to and if they meet membership requirements. For more information about the Federal Reserve System, visit its website at **www.federalreserve.gov.**

The most important function of the Fed is to use monetary policy to regulate the nation's supply of money in such a way as to maintain a healthy economy. In Chapter 1, *monetary policy* was defined as the Federal Reserve's decisions that determine the size of the supply of money in the nation and the level of interest rates. The goals of monetary policy are continued economic growth, full employment, and stable prices. Three methods—controlling bank reserve requirements, regulating the discount rate, and running open-market operations—are used to implement the Fed's monetary policy.

>> **FIGURE 19.3**

FEDERAL RESERVE SYSTEM

The Federal Reserve System consists of twelve district banks and twenty-five branch banks.

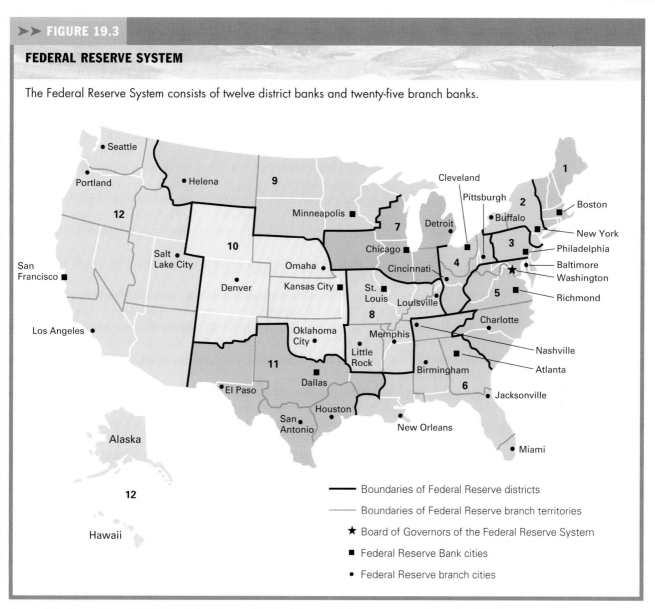

Source: "91st Annual Report, 2004," The Federal Reserve Board website: **www.federalreserve.gov**, December 17, 2005.

Regulation of Reserve Requirements

When money is deposited in a bank, the bank must retain a portion of it to satisfy customers who may want to withdraw money from their accounts. The remainder is available to fund loans. By law, the Federal Reserve sets the reserve requirement for financial institutions, whether or not they are members of the Federal Reserve System. The **reserve requirement** is the percentage of its deposits a bank *must* retain, either in its own vault or on deposit with its Federal Reserve district bank. For example, if a bank has deposits of $20 million and the reserve requirement is 10 percent, the bank must retain $2 million. The present reserve requirements range from 0 to 10 percent depending on such factors as the total amount individual banks have on deposit, average daily deposits, and the location of the particular member bank.[2]

> **reserve requirement** the percentage of its deposits a bank *must* retain, either in its own vault or on deposit with its Federal Reserve district bank

Once reserve requirements are met, banks can use remaining funds to create more money and make more loans through a process called *deposit expansion*. In the preceding example, the bank must retain $2 million in a reserve account. It can use the remaining $18 million to fund consumer and business loans. Assume that the bank lends all $18 million to different borrowers. Also assume that before using any of the borrowed funds, all borrowers deposit the $18 million in their bank accounts at the lending institution. Now the bank's deposits have increased by an additional $18 million. Since these deposits are subject to the same reserve requirement described earlier, the bank must maintain $1.8 million in a reserve account, and the bank can lend the additional $16.2 million to other bank customers. Of course, the bank's lending potential becomes steadily smaller and smaller as it makes more loans. And we should point out that since bankers usually are very conservative by nature, they will not use deposit expansion to maximize their lending activities; they will take a more middle-of-the-road approach.

The Fed's board of governors sets the reserve requirement. *When it increases the requirement, banks have less money available for lending.* Fewer loans are made, and the economy tends to slow. *On the other hand, by decreasing the reserve requirement, the Fed can make additional money available for lending to stimulate a slow economy.* Because this means of controlling the money supply is so very potent and has such far-reaching effects on both consumers and financial institutions, the Fed seldom changes the reserve requirement.

Regulation of the Discount Rate

discount rate the interest rate the Federal Reserve System charges for loans to member banks

Member banks may borrow money from the Fed to satisfy the reserve requirement. The interest rate the Federal Reserve charges for loans to member banks is called the **discount rate.** It is set by the Fed's board of governors. For the period from January 2003 to December 2005, the discount rate has been as low as 2 percent and as high as 5.25 percent.[3] In May 2006, the Federal Reserve raised the discount rate to 6.0 percent.[4]

When the Fed *lowers* the discount rate, it is easier and cheaper for banks to obtain money. Member banks feel free to make more loans and to charge lower interest rates. This action generally stimulates the nation's economy. When the Fed *raises* the discount rate, banks begin to restrict loans. They increase the interest rates they charge and tighten their own loan requirements. The overall effect is to slow the economy. Although the discount rate has increased slowly to the rate of 6.0 percent over the past three years, you should remember that the Fed can decrease rates in an effort to maintain a healthy economy.

Open-Market Operations

open-market operations the buying and selling of U.S. government securities by the Federal Reserve System for the purpose of controlling the supply of money

The federal government finances its activities partly by buying and selling securities issued by the U.S. Treasury (Treasury bills, notes, and bonds) and federal agency securities. These securities, which pay interest, may be purchased by any individual, firm, or organization—including the Fed. **Open-market operations** are the buying and selling of U.S. government securities by the Federal Reserve System for the purpose of controlling the supply of money.

The Federal Open Market Committee (FOMC) is charged with carrying out the Federal Reserve's open-market operations by buying and selling securities through the trading desk of the Federal Reserve Bank of New York. To reduce the nation's money supply, the FOMC simply *sells* government securities on the open market. The money it receives from purchasers is taken out of circulation. Thus less money is available for investment, purchases, or lending. To increase the money supply, the FOMC *buys* government securities. The money the FOMC pays for securities goes back into circulation, making more money available to individuals and firms.

Because the major purchasers of government securities are banking and financial institutions, open-market operations tend to have an immediate effect on lending and investment.

federal funds rate the interest rate at which a bank lends immediately available funds to another bank overnight in order to meet the borrowing bank's reserve requirements

Of the three tools used to influence monetary policy, the use of open-market operations is the most important. When the Federal Reserve buys and sells securities, the goal is to affect the federal funds rate. The **federal funds rate** is the interest rate at which a bank lends immediately available funds to another bank overnight in order to meet the borrowing bank's reserve requirements. While the FOMC sets a target for the federal funds rate, it does not actually set the rate because it is determined by the open market.[5] (*Note:* There is a difference between the federal funds rate and the discount rate discussed earlier in this section. The *federal funds rate* is the interest rate paid by a bank to borrow funds from other banks. The *discount rate* is the interest rate paid by a bank to borrow funds from the Federal Reserve.) Table 19.1 summarizes the effects of open-market operations and the other tools used by the Fed to regulate the money supply and control the economy.

Other Fed Responsibilities

In addition to its regulation of the money supply, the Fed is also responsible for serving as the government's bank, clearing checks and electronic transfers, inspecting currency, and applying selective credit controls.

Serving as Government Bank   The Federal Reserve is the bank for the U.S. government. As the government's bank, it processes a variety of financial transactions involving trillions of dollars each year. For example, the Federal Reserve provides financial services for the U.S. Treasury, including accounts through which incoming tax deposits and outgoing government payments are handled.

Clearing Checks and Electronic Transfers   Today, people use checks to pay for nearly everything they buy. A check written by a customer of one bank and presented for payment to another bank in the same town may be processed through a local clearinghouse. The procedure becomes more complicated, however, when the banks are not in the same town. This is where the Federal Reserve System comes in. The Fed is responsible for the prompt and accurate collection of almost fourteen billion checks each year.[6] Banks that use the Fed to clear checks are charged a fee for this service. Through the use of electronic equipment, most checks can be cleared within two or three days.

Inspection of Currency   As paper currency is handled, it becomes worn or dirty. The typical one-dollar bill has a life expectancy of less than two years. Fifty- and one-hundred dollar bills usually last longer because they are handled less. When member banks deposit their surplus cash in a Federal Reserve Bank, the currency is inspected. Bills unfit for further use are separated and destroyed.

Selective Credit Controls   The Federal Reserve System has the responsibility for enforcing the Truth-in-Lending Act, which Congress passed in 1968. This act

> > **TABLE 19.1**

METHODS USED BY THE FEDERAL RESERVE SYSTEM TO CONTROL THE MONEY SUPPLY AND THE ECONOMY

Method Used	Immediate Result	End Result
Regulating Reserve Requirement		
1. Fed *increases* reserve requirement	Less money for banks to lend to customers—reduction in overall money supply	Economic slowdown
2. Fed *decreases* reserve requirement	More money for banks to lend to customers—increase in overall money supply	Increased economic activity
Regulating the Discount Rate		
1. Fed *increases* the discount rate	Less money for banks to lend to customers—reduction to overall money supply	Economic slowdown
2. Fed *decreases* the discount rate	More money for banks to lend to customers—increase in overall money supply	Increased economic activity
Open-Market Operations		
1. Fed *sells* government securities	Reduction in overall money supply	Economic slowdown
2. Fed *buys* government securities	Increase in overall money supply	Increased economic activity

Business Around the World

Microloans Help Launch Microbusinesses

Microloans of as little as $25 have helped fifty million grass-roots entrepreneurs worldwide escape poverty by turning their small-business dreams into reality. Among the institutions involved in microloans are

- Oikocredit, which has made microloans totaling $281 million in sixty-seven countries
- Compartamos, which helped 400,000 clients in Mexico go into business with a microloan
- The Bangladesh Rural Action Committee, which serves 3.5 million microloan borrowers in Bangladesh

- Opportunity International, an Illinois-based organization that has made microloans to 500,000 entrepreneurs in twenty-seven nations

Sometimes a group of entrepreneurs—often women—borrows money and apportions the proceeds to members for small businesses such as pig farming. Members make payments until the debt is repaid, and then the group applies for another microloan to continue building members' businesses. Although borrowers with home appliances or other collateral can qualify for larger loans, even a tiny microloan can start an entrepreneur on the road to self-sufficiency.

---

requires lenders to state clearly the annual percentage rate and total finance charge for a consumer loan. The Federal Reserve System is also responsible for setting the margin requirements for stock transactions. The *margin* is the minimum amount (expressed as a percentage) of the purchase price that must be paid in cash or eligible securities. (The investor may borrow the remainder.) The current margin requirement is 50 percent. Thus, if an investor purchases $4,000 worth of stock, he or she must pay at least $2,000 in cash or its equivalent in securities. The remaining $2,000 may be borrowed from the brokerage firm. Although the minimum margin requirements are regulated by the Federal Reserve, margin requirements and the interest charged on the loans used to fund margin transactions may vary among brokerage firms and different security exchanges. For example, although an initial investment of at least $2,000 is required to open a margin account, some brokerage firms require more than $2,000.

The American Banking Industry

3 LEARNING OBJECTIVE
Describe the organizations involved in the banking industry.

The economic problems that both individuals and business firms have encountered in the last three to four years have caused a ripple effect for banks, savings and loan associations, and other financial institutions. Simply put, individuals worried about losing their jobs and businesses with reduced sales revenues are reluctant or unable to borrow more money. While bankers are in business to make loans, they also want to make sure that the loans will be repaid. As a result, lenders have begun to screen potential borrowers more carefully before approving loans. Fortunately, an improving economy has encouraged borrowers with the financial resources needed to pay back borrowed money to obtain loans to purchase all kinds of consumer products and to finance business needs.

In addition, competition among banks, savings and loan associations, credit unions, and other business firms that want to perform banking activities has never been greater. And banks from Japan, Canada, France, and other foreign nations have thrown their hat into U.S. banking circles. As a result, major banks such as Bank of America, Chase, Wells Fargo, and Washington Mutual have begun to provide innovative services for their customers, including electronic and online banking. Even smaller banks have adopted the full-service banking philosophy and compete aggressively for customers, who expect more services than ever before. As you read the material in this section, keep in mind that banking will become even more competitive as bankers offer more services to attract new customers. Let's begin this section with some information about one of the major players in the banking industry—the commercial bank.

Commercial Banks

A **commercial bank** is a profit-making organization that accepts deposits, makes loans, and provides related services to its customers. Like other businesses, the bank's primary goal—its mission—is to meet the needs of its customers while earning a profit. In a nutshell, here is how a bank earns its profit: It accepts money in the form of deposits, for which it pays interest. Once money is deposited in the bank, the bank lends it to qualified individuals and businesses that pay interest for the use of borrowed money. If the bank is successful, its income is greater than its expenses, and it will show a profit.

Because they deal with money belonging to individuals and other business firms, banks are carefully regulated. They also must meet certain requirements before they receive a charter, or permission to operate, from either federal or state banking authorities. A **national bank** is a commercial bank chartered by the U.S. Comptroller of the Currency. There are approximately 1,900 national banks, accounting for about 57 percent of all bank assets.[7] These banks must conform to federal banking regulations and are subject to unannounced inspections by federal auditors.

A **state bank** is a commercial bank chartered by the banking authorities in the state in which it operates. State banks outnumber national banks by about three to one, but they tend to be smaller than national banks. They are subject to unannounced inspections by both state and federal auditors.

Table 19.2 lists the seven largest banks in the United States. All are classified as national banks.

commercial bank a profit-making organization that accepts deposits, makes loans, and provides related services to its customers

national bank a commercial bank chartered by the U.S. Comptroller of the Currency

state bank a commercial bank chartered by the banking authorities in the state in which it operates

>> TABLE 19.2

THE SEVEN LARGEST U.S. BANKS, RANKED BY TOTAL REVENUES

Rank	Commercial Bank	Revenues (in millions)	Number of Employees
1	Citigroup	$108,276	290,500
2	Bank of America Corp.	63,324	175,742
3	J.P. Morgan Chase & Co.	56,931	160,968
4	Wells Fargo	33,876	145,500
5	Wachovia Corp.	28,067	96,030
6	U.S. Bancorp	14,706	48,831
7	MBNA	12,327	26,292

Source: *Fortune*, April 18, 2005, p. F48.

Other Financial Institutions

In addition to commercial banks, at least eight other types of financial institutions perform either full or limited banking services for their customers.

Savings and Loan Associations

savings and loan association (S&L) a financial institution that offers checking and savings accounts and CDs and that invests most of its assets in home mortgage loans and other consumer loans

A **savings and loan association (S&L)** is a financial institution that offers checking and savings accounts and CDs and that invests most of its assets in home mortgage loans and other consumer loans. Originally, S&Ls were permitted to offer their depositors *only* savings accounts. However, since Congress passed the Depository Institutions Deregulation and Monetary Control Act in 1980, they have been able to offer other services to attract depositors.

Today there are approximately 1,300 S&Ls in the United States.[8] Federal associations are chartered under provisions of the Home Owners' Loan Act of 1933 and are supervised by the Office of Thrift Supervision, a branch of the U.S. Treasury. S&Ls also can be chartered by state banking authorities in the state in which they operate. State-chartered S&Ls are subject to unannounced audits by state authorities.

Credit Unions

credit union a financial institution that accepts deposits from and lends money to only those people who are its members

Today there are approximately 9,300 credit unions in the United States.[9] A **credit union** is a financial institution that accepts deposits from and lends money to only those people who are its members. Usually the membership consists of employees of a particular firm, people in a particular profession, or those who live in a community served by a local credit union. Credit unions generally pay higher interest on deposits than commercial banks and S&Ls, and they may provide loans at lower cost. The National Credit Union Administration regulates federally chartered credit unions and many state credit unions. State authorities also may regulate credit unions with state charters.

Organizations That Perform Banking Functions

Six other types of financial institutions are involved in limited banking activities. Although not actually full-service banks, they offer customers limited banking services.

- *Mutual savings banks* are financial institutions that are owned by their depositors and offer many of the same services offered by banks, S&Ls, and credit unions, including checking accounts, savings accounts, and CDs. Like other financial institutions, they also fund home mortgages, commercial loans, and consumer loans. Unlike other types of financial institutions, the profits of a mutual savings bank go to the depositors, usually in the form of dividends or slightly higher interest rates on savings. Today there are approximately 450 savings banks in operation, primarily in the Northeast.[10]
- *Insurance companies* provide long-term financing for office buildings, shopping centers, and other commercial real estate projects throughout the United States. The funds used for this type of financing are obtained from policyholders' insurance premiums.
- *Pension funds* are established by employers to guarantee their employees a regular monthly income on retirement. Contributions to the fund may come from the employer, the employee, or both. Pension funds earn additional income through generally conservative investments in corporate stocks, corporate bonds, and government securities, as well as through financing real estate developments.

- *Brokerage firms* offer combination savings and checking accounts that pay higher-than-usual interest rates (so-called money-market rates). Many people have switched to these accounts because they are convenient and to get the higher rates, but banks have instituted similar types of accounts, hoping to lure their depositors back.
- *Finance companies* provide financing to individuals and business firms that may not be able to get financing from banks, S&Ls, or credit unions. Firms such as Ford Motor Credit, GE Capital, and General Motors Acceptance Corporation provide loans to both individuals and business firms. Lenders such as Household Finance Corporation and Ace Cash Express, Inc., provide short-term loans to individuals. The interest rates charged by these lenders may be higher than the interest rates charged by other financial institutions.
- *Investment banking firms* are organizations that assist corporations in raising funds, usually by helping sell new issues of stocks, bonds, or other financial securities. Although these firms do not accept deposits or make loans like traditional banking firms, they do help companies raise millions of dollars. More information about investment banking firms and the role they play in American business is provided in Chapters 20 and 21.

Careers in the Banking Industry

Take a second look at Table 19.2. The seven largest banks in the United States employ approximately 944,000 people. If you add to this amount the people employed by smaller banks not listed in Table 19.2 and those employed by S&Ls, credit unions, and other financial institutions, the number of employees grows dramatically. But be warned: According to the *Career Guide to Industries*, published by the U.S. Department of Labor, banking employment is projected to grow more slowly than jobs in the economy between now and the year 2012. Even though employment within the industry is expected to increase more slowly when compared with other industries, there will be job growth for management and professional jobs, customer service representatives, and securities and financial services sales representatives. It also should be noted that job openings for tellers arising from replacement needs should be plentiful because turnover is high and the occupation is large.[11]

To be successful in the banking industry, you need a number of different skills. For starters, employees for a bank, S&L, credit union, or other financial institution must possess the following traits:

The perfect match. Without the help of her First Union banker and loan officer, Marie Bartholomew (right) would not have been able to start her own small business, Tampa Vending. In addition to approving the loan that enabled Bartholomew to purchase equipment and inventory, First Union provided a number of banking services that helped her manage the day-to-day operations needed for a new business venture.

1. *You must be honest.* Because you are handling other people's money, many financial institutions go to great lengths to discover dishonest employees.
2. *You must be able to interact with people.* A number of positions in the banking industry require that you possess the interpersonal skills needed to interact not only with other employees but also with customers.
3. *You need a strong background in accounting.* Many of the routine tasks performed by employees in the banking industry are basic accounting functions. For example, a teller must post deposits or withdrawals to a customer's account and then balance out at the end of the day to ensure accuracy.
4. *You need to appreciate the relationship between banking and finance.* Bank officers must interview loan applicants and determine if their request for money is based on sound financial principles. Above all, loan officers must be able

to evaluate applicants and their loan requests to determine if the borrower will be able to repay a loan.

5. *You should possess basic computer skills.* Almost all employees in the banking industry use a computer for some aspect of their work on a daily basis.

Depending on qualifications, work experience, and education, starting salaries generally are between $15,000 and $30,000 a year, but it is not uncommon for college graduates to earn $35,000 a year or more.

If banking seems like an area you might be interested in, why not do more career exploration? You could take a banking course if your college or university offers one, or you could obtain a part-time job during the school year or a summer job in a bank, S&L, or credit union.

Traditional Services Provided by Financial Institutions

4 LEARNING OBJECTIVE
Identify the services provided by financial institutions.

To determine how important banking services are to you, ask yourself the following questions:

- How many checks did you write last month?
- Do you have a major credit card? If so, how often do you use it?
- Do you have a savings account or a CD?
- Have you ever financed the purchase of a new or used automobile?
- How many times did you visit an ATM last month?

If you are like most people and business firms, you would find it hard to live a normal life without the services provided by banks and other financial institutions. Typical services provided by a bank or other financial institution are illustrated in Figure 19.4.

The most important traditional banking services for both individuals and businesses are described in this section. Online banking, electronic transfer of funds, and other significant and future developments are discussed in the next section.

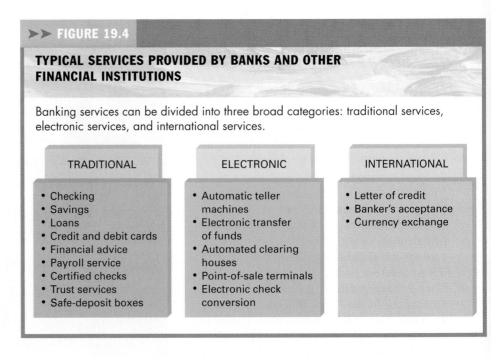

▶▶ FIGURE 19.4

TYPICAL SERVICES PROVIDED BY BANKS AND OTHER FINANCIAL INSTITUTIONS

Banking services can be divided into three broad categories: traditional services, electronic services, and international services.

TRADITIONAL	ELECTRONIC	INTERNATIONAL
• Checking	• Automatic teller machines	• Letter of credit
• Savings	• Electronic transfer of funds	• Banker's acceptance
• Loans	• Automated clearing houses	• Currency exchange
• Credit and debit cards	• Point-of-sale terminals	
• Financial advice	• Electronic check conversion	
• Payroll service		
• Certified checks		
• Trust services		
• Safe-deposit boxes		

Checking Accounts

Imagine what it would be like living in today's world without a checking account. Although a few people do not have one, most of us like the convenience a checking account offers. Firms and individuals deposit money in checking accounts (demand deposits) so that they can write checks to pay for purchases. A **check** is a written order for a bank or other financial institution to pay a stated dollar amount to the business or person indicated on the face of the check. In order to attract new customers, many financial institutions offer free checking; others charge activity fees (or service charges) for checking accounts. Fees and charges generally range between $5 and $20 per month for individuals. For businesses, monthly charges are based on the average daily balance in the checking account and/or the number of checks written. Typically, charges for business checking accounts are higher than those for individual accounts.

Today, most financial institutions offer interest-paying checking accounts, often called *NOW accounts*. A **NOW account** is an interest-bearing checking account. (*NOW* stands for *negotiable order of withdrawal*.) For these accounts, the usual interest rate is between 0.25 and 1 percent. However, individual banks may impose certain restrictions on their NOW accounts, including the following:

- A minimum balance before any interest is paid
- Monthly fees for accounts whose balances fall below a set minimum amount
- Restrictions on the number of checks that may be written each month

Although banks and other financial institutions may pay low interest rates on checking accounts, even small earnings are better than no earnings. In addition to interest rates, be sure to compare monthly fees before opening a checking account.

check a written order for a bank or other financial institution to pay a stated dollar amount to the business or person indicated on the face of the check

NOW account an interest-bearing checking account; *NOW* stands for *negotiable order of withdrawal*

Savings Accounts

Savings accounts (time deposits) provide a safe place to store money and a very conservative means of investing. The usual *passbook savings account* earns between 0.50 and 2 percent in commercial banks and S&Ls and slightly more in credit unions.

A depositor who is willing to leave money on deposit with a bank for a set period of time can earn a higher rate of interest. To do so, the depositor buys a certificate of deposit. A **certificate of deposit (CD)** is a document stating that the bank will pay the depositor a guaranteed interest rate on money left on deposit for a specified period of time. The interest rates paid on CDs change weekly; they once briefly exceeded 11 percent in 1980. Recently, interest rates have ranged from 2 to 5 percent. The rate always depends on how much is invested and for how long. Generally, the rule is: The longer the period of time until maturity, the higher is the rate. Depositors are penalized for early withdrawal of funds invested in CDs.

certificate of deposit (CD) a document stating that the bank will pay the depositor a guaranteed interest rate on money left on deposit for a specified period of time

Short- and Long-Term Loans

Banks, S&Ls, credit unions, and other financial institutions provide short- and long-term loans to both individuals and businesses. *Short-term business loans* must be repaid within one year or less. Typical uses for the money obtained through short-term loans include solving cash-flow problems, purchasing inventory, financing promotional needs, and meeting unexpected emergencies.

To help ensure that short-term money will be available when needed, many firms establish a line

Savings growth over time

Dollar amounts assume that you invest $1,000 each year at 5 percent.

	Total savings	Savings + earnings
5 years	$5,000	$5,526
10 years	$10,000	$12,578
15 years	$15,000	$21,579
20 years	$20,000	$33,066

line of credit a loan that is approved before the money is actually needed

of credit. A **line of credit** is a loan that is approved before the money is actually needed. Because all the necessary paperwork is already completed and the loan is preapproved, the business can obtain the money later without delay, as soon as it is required. Even with a line of credit, a firm may not be able to borrow money if the bank does not have sufficient funds available. For this reason, some firms prefer a **revolving credit agreement**, which is a guaranteed line of credit.

revolving credit agreement a guaranteed line of credit

Long-term business loans are repaid over a period of years. The average length of a long-term business loan is generally three to seven years but sometimes as long as fifteen years. Long-term loans are used most often to finance the expansion of buildings and retail facilities, mergers and acquisitions, replacement of equipment, or product development.

collateral real estate or property pledged as security for a loan

Most lenders require some type of collateral for long-term loans. **Collateral** is real estate or property (stocks, bonds, equipment, or any other asset of value) pledged as security for a loan. For example, when an individual obtains a loan to pay for a new Chevrolet Monte Carlo, the automobile is the collateral for the loan. If the borrower fails to repay the loan according to the terms specified in the loan agreement, the lender can repossess the car.

Repayment terms and interest rates for both short- and long-term loans are arranged between the lender and the borrower. For businesses, repayment terms may include monthly, quarterly, semiannual, or annual payments. Repayment terms (and interest rates) for personal loans vary depending on how the money will be used and what type of collateral, if any, is pledged. However, individuals typically make monthly payments to repay personal loans. Borrowers always should "shop" for a loan, comparing the repayment terms and interest rates offered by competing financial institutions.

Credit-Card and Debit-Card Transactions

Over 173 million Americans use credit cards to pay for everything from tickets on American Airlines to Zebco fishing gear.[12] And the number of cardholders increases every month. In fact, most Americans receive at least two or three credit-card applications in the mail every month. Why have credit cards become so popular?

For a merchant, the answer is obvious. By depositing charge slips in a bank or other financial institution, the merchant can convert credit-card sales into cash. In return for processing the merchant's credit-card transactions, the bank charges a fee that

BizTech

eMoney Cashes In with Paperless Payments

Although cash, checks, credit cards, and debit cards are still commonplace, paperless payments in small amounts have become big business these days. Here's an overview of two popular paperless payment methods:

● *PayPal.* Owned by eBay, PayPal processes 600,000 payments daily and transfers $26 billion

yearly among eighty million users. Consumers and businesses around the world can use PayPal to send money to someone else or to pay for a purchase.

● *BitWallet.* A joint venture of Sony, Toyota, NTT DoCoMo, All Nippon Airways, and two major banks, BitWallet allows four million consumers in Japan to leave their coins home and make small purchases using specially equipped cell phones. Users transmit electronic cash through their cell phones to buy from vending machines, newsstands, and other businesses.

generally ranges between 1.5 and 5 percent. Typically, small, independent businesses pay more than larger stores or chain stores. Let's assume that you use a Visa credit card to purchase a microwave oven for $300 from Richardson Appliance, a small retailer in Richardson, Texas. At the end of the day, the retailer deposits your charge slip, along with other charge slips, checks, and currency collected during the day, at its bank. If the bank charges Richardson Appliance 5 percent to process each credit-card transaction, the bank deducts a processing fee of $15 ($300 × 0.05 = $15) for your credit-card transaction and immediately deposits the remainder ($285) in Richardson Appliance's account. The number of credit-card transactions, the total dollar amount of credit sales, and how well the merchant can negotiate the fees the bank charges determine actual fees.

For the consumer, credit cards permit the purchase of goods and services even when funds are low. Today, most major credit cards are issued by banks or other financial institutions in cooperation with Visa International or MasterCard International. The unique feature of bank credit cards is that they extend a line of credit to the cardholder, much as a bank's consumer loan department does. Thus credit cards provide immediate access to short-term credit for the cardholder. Of course, the ability to obtain merchandise immediately and pay for it later can lead to credit-card misuse. Today, the average college student has a credit-card balance of approximately $2,400.[13] With typical finance charges ranging from 1 to 1.5 percent a month (that's 12 to 18 percent a year), you can end up paying large finance charges. And the monthly finance charges continue until you manage to pay off your credit-card debt. If you find yourself getting deeper into debt, the first step is to *stop shopping!* Next, contact your creditors and discuss options for reducing your finance charges and repaying your debts with lower monthly payments. If you do need assistance, organizations such as a local chapter of the Consumer Credit Counseling Service (**www.cccsintl.org**) or Myvesta (**www.myvesta.org**) or a local support group such as Debtors Anonymous is there to help you.

Do not confuse debit cards with credit cards. Although they may look alike, there are important differences. A **debit card** electronically subtracts the amount of your purchase from your bank account at the moment the purchase is made. (By contrast, when you use your credit card, the credit-card company extends short-term financing, and you do not make payment until you receive your next statement.) Debit cards are used most commonly to obtain cash at ATMs and to purchase products and services from retailers. The use of debit cards is expected to increase because many people feel that they are more convenient than writing checks.

debit card a card that electronically subtracts the amount of your purchase from your bank account at the moment the purchase is made

Innovative Banking Services

Samantha Wood used an ATM three times this week. Why? She needed cash and did not have time to make a trip to the bank and wait in line. When Bart Jones, owner of Aquatic Pools, needed a short-term $50,000 loan to solve some of his firm's cash-flow problems, he turned to LendingTree.com (**www.lendingtree.com**), an online loan-matching service. He answered some questions, and within an hour, three financial institutions had bid on his loan. He got approval (and the money he needed) without leaving his office. Like Samantha Wood and Bart Jones, many individuals, financial managers, and business owners are finding it convenient to do their banking electronically. Let's begin by looking at how banking has changed over the last five years. Then we will discuss how those changes may provide a foundation for change in the future.

5 LEARNING OBJECTIVE
Understand how financial institutions are changing to meet the needs of domestic and international customers.

Recent Changes in the Banking Industry

In 1999, Congress enacted the Financial Services Modernization Banking Act. This act allowed banks to establish one-stop financial supermarkets where customers can bank, buy and sell securities, and purchase insurance coverage. Now, as a result of this legislation and the increasing use of technology in the banking industry, even the experts are asking the question: How will banking change in the next five to ten years?

Is this a place for a latte, or a place to save your money? If you visit one of ING Direct's cafes, you can sip a latte while talking with a bank officer about savings programs and other banking services. You can even surf the Internet for free! It's all part of a plan created by ING Direct, a Delaware-based Internet bank, to make banking more enjoyable by creating offices that customers look forward to visiting.

What is this place anyway?
It's a place to sip a latte, surf the Internet for free, and talk to us about simple ways to save your money.

While the experts may not be able to predict with 100 percent accuracy the changes that will affect banking, they all agree that banking *will* change. The most obvious changes the experts do agree on are

- A reduction in the number of banks, S&Ls, credit unions, and financial institutions because of consolidation and mergers
- Globalization of the banking industry
- The importance of customer service as a way to keep customers from switching to competitors
- Increased use of credit and debit cards and a decrease in the number of written checks
- Increased competition from nonbank competitors that provide many of the same services as banks, S&Ls, credit unions, and other financial institutions
- Spectacular growth in online banking[14]

Online Banking and International Banking

Online banking allows you to access your bank's computer system from home, the office, or even while you are traveling. For the customer, online banking offers a number of advantages, including the following:

- The ability to obtain current account balances
- The convenience of transferring funds from one account to another
- The ability to pay bills
- The convenience of seeing which checks have cleared
- Easy access to current interest rates
- Simplified loan application procedures

Banks such as Chase (**www.chase.com**), Citibank (**www.citibank.com**), and Commerce Bank (**www.commerceonline.com**) are a few good examples for insight into this sector.

For people who bank online, the largest disadvantage is not being able to discuss financial matters with their "personal banker." To overcome this problem, many larger banks are investing huge amounts on electronic customer relationship management systems that will provide the type of service and financial advice that customers used to get when they walked through the doors of their financial institution.[15]

Online banking provides a number of advantages for the financial institution. Probably the most important advantage is the lower cost of processing large numbers of transactions. As you learned in Chapter 18, lower costs often lead to larger profits. In addition to lower costs and increased profits, financial institutions believe that online banking offers increased security because fewer people handle fewer paper documents.

Electronic Funds Transfer (EFT)   Although electronic funds transfer systems have been used for years, their use will increase dramatically as we continue through the twenty-first century. An **electronic funds transfer (EFT) system** is a means of performing financial transactions through a computer terminal or telephone hookup. The following three EFT applications are changing how banks do business:

> **electronic funds transfer (EFT) system** a means of performing financial transactions through a computer terminal or telephone hookup

1. *Automatic teller machines (ATMs).* An ATM is an electronic bank teller—a machine that provides almost any service a human teller can provide. Once the customer is properly identified, the machine dispenses cash from the customer's checking or savings account or makes a cash advance charged to a credit card. ATMs are located in bank parking lots, supermarkets, drugstores, and even gas stations. Customers have access to them at all times of the day or night. Generally, there is a fee for each transaction.
2. *Automated clearinghouses (ACHs).* Designed to reduce the number of paper checks, automated clearinghouses process checks, recurring bill payments, Social Security benefits, and employee salaries. For example, large companies use ACHs to transfer wages and salaries directly into their employees' bank accounts, thus eliminating the need to make out individual paychecks. The ACH system saves time and effort for both employers and employees and adds a measure of security to the transfer of these payments.
3. *Point-of-sale (POS) terminals.* A POS terminal is a computerized cash register located in a retail store and connected to a bank's computer. At the cash register, you pull your bank credit or debit card through a magnetic card reader. A central processing center notifies a computer at your bank that you want to make a purchase. The bank's computer immediately adds the amount to your account for a credit-card transaction. In a similar process, the bank's computer deducts the amount of the purchase from your bank account if you use a debit card. Finally, the amount of your purchase is added to the store's account. The store then is notified that the transaction is complete, and the cash register prints out your receipt.

A similar process occurs when a store uses electronic check conversion to process a paper check. **Electronic check conversion (ECC)** is a process used to convert information from a paper check into an electronic payment for merchandise, services, or bills. Here's how ECC works. When you give your completed check to a store cashier, the check is processed through an electronic system that captures your banking information and the dollar amount of the check. Once the check is processed, you are asked to sign a receipt, and you get a voided (canceled) check back for your records. Finally, the funds to pay for your transaction are transferred into the business firm's account. ECC also can be used for checks you mail to pay for a purchase or to pay on an account. *Be warned:* Because the check is processed electronically, money is withdrawn immediately from your account. There is no "float time" for your check. This means that if you write a check, you need to have funds in your account to cover it. If you don't, your check may bounce, and you may be charged a fee by the merchant, your financial institution, or both.

> **electronic check conversion (ECC)** a process used to convert information from a paper check into an electronic payment for merchandise, services, or bills

Bankers and business owners generally are pleased with online banking and EFT systems. Both online banking and EFT are fast, and they eliminate the costly processing of checks. However, many customers are reluctant to use online banking or EFT systems. Some simply do not like "the technology," whereas others fear that the computer will garble their accounts. Early on, in 1978, Congress responded to such fears by passing the Electronic Funds Transfer Act, which protects the customer in case the bank makes an error or the customer's personal identification number is stolen.

International Banking Services For international businesses, banking services are extremely important. Depending on the needs of an international firm, a bank can help by providing a letter of credit or a banker's acceptance.

A **letter of credit** is a legal document issued by a bank or other financial institution guaranteeing to pay a seller a stated amount for a specified period of time—usually thirty to sixty days. (With a letter of credit, certain conditions, such as delivery of the merchandise, may be specified before payment is made.)

A **banker's acceptance** is a written order for a bank to pay a third party a stated amount of money on a specific date. (With a banker's acceptance, no conditions are specified. It is simply an order to pay without any strings attached.)

Both a letter of credit and a banker's acceptance are popular methods of paying for import and export transactions. For example, imagine that you are a business owner in the United States who wants to purchase some leather products from a small business in Florence, Italy. You offer to pay for the merchandise with your company's check drawn on an American bank, but the Italian business owner is worried about payment. To solve the problem, your bank can issue either a letter of credit or a banker's acceptance to guarantee that payment will be made. In addition to a letter of credit and a banker's acceptance, banks also can use EFT technology to speed international banking transactions.

One other international banking service should be noted. Banks and other financial institutions provide for currency exchange. If you place an order for Japanese merchandise valued at $50,000, how do you pay for the order? Do you use U.S. dollars or Japanese yen? To solve this problem, you can use a bank's currency-exchange service. To make payment, you can use either currency, and if necessary, the bank will exchange one currency for the other to complete your transaction.

letter of credit a legal document issued by a bank or other financial institution guaranteeing to pay a seller a stated amount for a specified period of time

banker's acceptance a written order for a bank to pay a third party a stated amount of money on a specific date

The FDIC and NCUA

6 LEARNING OBJECTIVE
Explain how deposit insurance protects customers.

During the Depression, which began in 1929, a number of banks failed, and their depositors lost all their savings. To make sure that such a disaster does not happen again and to restore public confidence in the banking industry, Congress enacted legislation that created the *Federal Deposit Insurance Corporation (FDIC)* in 1933. The primary purpose of the FDIC is to insure deposits against bank failures. Then, in 1989, Congress passed legislation to bail out a large number of failed S&Ls and extend FDIC insurance coverage to deposits in S&Ls. As a result of the 1989 legislation, the FDIC was reorganized into two insurance units: the Bank Insurance Fund (BIF) and the Savings Association Insurance Fund (SAIF). BIF members are predominantly commercial and savings banks. SAIF members are predominantly savings and loan associations.

Today, the FDIC provides deposit insurance of $100,000 for non-retirement accounts. Deposits maintained in different categories of legal ownership are insured separately. Thus you can have coverage for more than $100,000 in a single institution. The most common categories of ownership are single (or individual) ownership and joint ownership. Deposit insurance is also available for funds held for retirement purposes in self-directed individual retirement accounts (up to $250,000) and certain employee benefit plans and pension plans that are not self-directed. A depositor also may obtain additional coverage by opening separate accounts in different banks or S&Ls.[16] To determine if your deposits are insured or if your bank or S&L is insured, visit the FDIC website at **www.fdic.gov.**

To obtain coverage, banks and S&Ls must pay insurance premiums to the FDIC. In a similar manner, the National Credit Union Association (NCUA) insures deposits in member credit unions for up to $100,000 for non-retirement accounts and $250,000 for retirement accounts.

The FDIC and NCUA have improved banking in the United States. When either of these organizations insures a financial institution's deposits, they reserve the right to examine that institution's operations periodically. If a bank, S&L, savings bank, or credit union is found to be poorly managed, it is reported to the proper banking authority.

Lending to individuals and firms is a vital function of banks. And deciding wisely to whom it will extend credit is one of the most important activities of any financial institution or business. The material in the next section explains the different factors used to evaluate credit applicants.

Effective Credit Management

Credit is immediate purchasing power that is exchanged for a promise to repay borrowed money, with or without interest, at a later date. A credit transaction is a two-sided business activity that involves both a borrower and a lender. The borrower is most often a person or business that wishes to make a purchase. The lender may be a bank, some other lending institution, or a business firm selling merchandise or services on credit.

For example, suppose that you obtain a bank loan to buy a $100,000 home. You, as the borrower, obtain immediate purchasing power. In return, you agree to certain terms imposed by the bank, S&L, or home mortgage company. The lender requires that you make a down payment, make monthly payments, pay interest, and purchase insurance to protect your home until the loan is paid in full.

Banks and other financial institutions lend money because they are in business for that purpose. The interest they charge is what provides their profit. Other businesses extend credit to their customers for at least three reasons. First, some customers simply cannot afford to pay the entire amount of their purchase immediately, but they *can* repay credit in a number of smaller payments stretched out over some period of time. Second, some firms are forced to sell goods or services on credit to compete effectively when other firms offer credit to their customers. Finally, firms can realize a profit from interest charges that a borrower pays on some credit arrangements.

How Do You Get Money from a Bank or Lender?

Many individuals and business owners are nervous when applying for a loan. They are not sure what information they need. And what happens if they are turned down? Let's begin with the basics. While lenders need interest from loans to help pay their business expenses and earn a profit, they also want to make sure that the loans they make will be repaid. Your job is to convince the lender that you are able and willing to repay the loan.

For individuals, the following suggestions may be helpful when applying for a loan:

- Although it may pay to shop around for lower interest rates, you usually have a better chance of obtaining a loan at a bank, S&L, or credit union where you already have an account.
- Obtain a loan application and complete it at home. At home, you have the information needed to answer *all* the questions on the loan application.
- Be prepared to describe how you will use the money and how the loan will be repaid.
- For most loans, an interview with a loan officer is required. Here again, preparation is the key. Think about how you would respond to questions a loan officer might ask.

7 LEARNING OBJECTIVE
Discuss the importance of credit and credit management.

credit immediate purchasing power that is exchanged for a promise to repay borrowed money, with or without interest, at a later date

This banker wants to help. Bob Harvey, a branch manager for Seattle Metropolitan Credit Union, likes to help people and business owners achieve their financial goals. Still, like most bankers, Harvey is concerned with two questions: What will the loan money be used for, and can the applicant repay the loan as scheduled? The answers to these questions often determine if a loan will be approved.

Americans love credit cards

In 2005, 173 million Americans possessed at least 1 credit card.

2000 — 159 million cardholders

2002 — 163 million cardholders

2005 — 173 million cardholders

Source: *Statistical Abstract of the United States, 2004–2005*, Table 1185, p. 747.

- If your loan request is rejected, try to analyze what went wrong. Ask the loan officer why you were rejected. If the rejection is based on incorrect information, supply the correct information and reapply.

Business owners in need of financing may find the following additional tips helpful:

- It is usually best to develop a relationship with your banker before you need financing. Help the banker understand what your business is and how you may need future financing for expansion, cash-flow problems, or unexpected emergencies.
- Apply for a preapproved line of credit or revolving credit agreement even if you do not need the money. View the application as another way to showcase your company and its products or services.
- In addition to the application, supply certified public accountant (CPA)–prepared financial statements and business tax returns for the last three years and your own personal financial statements and tax returns for the same period.
- Write a cover letter describing how much experience you have, whether you are operating in an expanding market, or any other information that would help convince the banker to provide financing.

From the lender's viewpoint, the major pitfall in granting credit is the possibility of nonpayment. However, if a lender follows the five Cs of credit management, it can minimize this possibility.

The Five Cs of Credit Management

When a business extends credit to its customers, it must face the fact that some customers will be unable or unwilling to pay for their credit purchases. With this in mind, lenders must establish policies for determining who will receive credit and who will not. Most lenders build their credit policies around the five Cs of credit.

Character   *Character* means the borrower's attitude toward credit obligations. Experienced lenders often see this as the most important factor in predicting whether a borrower will make regular payments and ultimately repay a credit obligation. Typical questions to consider in judging a borrower's character include the following:

1. Is the borrower prompt in paying bills?
2. Have other lenders had to dun the borrower with overdue notices before receiving payment?
3. Have lenders been forced to take the borrower to court to obtain payment?
4. Has the customer ever filed for bankruptcy? If so, did the customer make an attempt to repay debts voluntarily?

Although it is illegal to discriminate, personal factors such as drinking or gambling habits may affect a lender's decision to loan money or extend credit to an individual.

Capacity   *Capacity* means the borrower's financial ability to meet credit obligations—that is, to make regular loan payments as scheduled in the credit or loan agreement. If the customer is a business, the lender looks at the firm's income statement.

For individuals, the lender checks salary statements and other sources of income, such as dividends and interest. The borrower's other financial obligations and monthly expenses are also taken into consideration before credit is approved.

Capital The term *capital* as used here refers to the borrower's assets or net worth. In general, the greater the capital, the greater is the borrower's ability to repay a loan. The capital position of a business can be determined by examining its balance sheet. For individuals, information on net worth can be obtained by requiring that the borrower complete a credit application such as the one illustrated in Figure 19.5. The borrower also must authorize employers and financial institutions to release information to confirm the claims made in the credit application.

Collateral For large amounts of credit—and especially for long-term loans—the lender may require some type of collateral. As mentioned earlier, collateral is real estate or property (stocks, bonds, equipment, or any other asset of value) pledged as security for a loan. If the borrower fails to live up to the terms of the credit agreement, the lender can repossess the collateral and then sell it to satisfy the debt.

Conditions *Conditions* refers to the general economic conditions that can affect a borrower's ability to repay a loan or other credit obligation. How well a business firm can withstand an economic storm may depend on the particular industry the firm is in, its relative strength within that industry, the type of products it sells, its earnings history, and its earnings potential. For individuals, the basic question focuses on security—of both the applicant's job and the firm for which he or she works. For example, if the economy takes a downturn, some employees may lose their jobs. Even though these former employees lost their jobs, they still have mortgage payments, car payments, and credit-card payments that must be paid.

Checking Credit Information

The five Cs of credit are concerned mainly with information supplied by the applicant. But how can a lender determine whether this information is accurate? This depends on whether the potential borrower is a business or an individual consumer.

Credit information concerning businesses can be obtained from the following four sources:

- *Global credit-reporting agencies.* D&B (formerly Dun & Bradstreet) is the most widely used credit-reporting agency in the world. D&B reports present detailed credit information about specific companies. For more information on D&B services, visit the company's website at **www.dnb.com.**
- *Local credit-reporting agencies*, which may require a monthly or yearly fee for providing information on a continual basis.
- *Industry associations*, which may charge a service fee.
- *Other firms* that have given the applicant credit.

Various credit bureaus provide credit information concerning individuals. The following are the three major consumer credit bureaus:

- Experian—at **www.experian.com** or toll free at 888–397–3742
- TransUnion—at **www.transunion.com** or toll free at 800–888–4213
- Equifax Credit Information Services—at **www.equifax.com** or toll free at 800–685–1111

Note: With the recent rise in identity theft, experts recommend that you check your credit report at least once a year.

Consumer credit bureaus are subject to the provisions of the Fair Credit Reporting Act. This act safeguards consumers' rights in two ways. First, every consumer has the right to know what information is contained in his or her credit bureau

➤➤ FIGURE 19.5

CREDIT APPLICATION FORM

Lenders use the information on credit application forms to help determine which customers should be granted credit.

Apply today! Just complete this application or call 1-800-438-9222.

Citizens Bank Customer Credit Card Application

Branch # _____

This offer is for existing Citizens Bank Customers applying for a new credit card account

Existing Citizens Bank cardholders should call 1-800-438-9222 for special cardholder rate information.

Citizens Bank VISA® (Code: BVCFNU)

Please tell us about yourself

First Name   Middle Initial   Last Name

Address (street)

(City, state, zip)

Date of Birth   Social Security Number

❑ Own   ❑ Rent   ❑ Live with Parents
Years/Months at Present Address

$ (   )
Monthly Housing Payment   Home Telephone

Previous Address   Years/Months There
(if less than 2 years at present address)

Mother's Maiden Name

Citizens Bank Account Information

❑ Checking   ❑ Savings   ❑ Loan   ❑ Citizens Circle℠ Checking

account # _____

Please tell us about your employment

Present Employer   Position

                                   (   )
Years/Months Employed There   Business Telephone

Previous Employer   Years/Months There
(if less than 2 years at present employer)

$ $
Gross Monthly Household Income   Other Monthly Income*

*Alimony, child support, or separate maintenance income need not be revealed if you do not wish it to be considered as a basis for repaying this obligation.

24-hour banking convenience

Your card(s) can be encoded with a four-digit personal identification number (PIN) to obtain cash advances at automated teller machines. This four-digit PIN will be known only to you. So that we may properly encode your card(s), please select the four digits of your choice and enter them in the spaces below:

_____ _____ _____ _____

Please send a second card at no cost for

First Name   Middle Initial   Last Name

Please read and sign

Your Signature   Date

All information on this application is true and complete, and Citizens Bank of Rhode Island, the card issuer, is authorized to obtain further credit and employment information from any source. I understand that you will retain this application whether or not it is approved. You may share with others, only for valid business reasons, any information relating to me, this application, and any of my banking relationships with you. I request issuance of a Citizens credit card and agree to be bound by the terms and conditions of the Agreement received with the card(s). I understand that Citizens Bank of Rhode Island will assign a credit line based on information provided and information obtained from any other source; and the issuance of a Gold card is subject to a minimum annual income of $35,000 and qualification for a minimum $5,000 credit line.

Transfer balances and save

Citizens will transfer your high interest rate balances to your new Citizens Bank VISA Card at no extra charge. Use the form below to indicate the amount(s) to be transferred in order of priority. (Citizens Bank will not transfer balances from existing Citizens Bank accounts.) (see reverse side for balance transfer disclosure)

Creditor Name	Account Number	Amount
		$
Creditor Name	Account Number	Amount
		$
Creditor Name	Account Number	Amount
		$

Bank Use Only   Bank Code: ❑ CBMA ❑ CBRI ❑ CBCT   Sales ID# _____   Application code: 1122

Source: Courtesy of Citizens Financial Group, Inc., Providence, Rhode Island.

file. A recent amendment to the federal Fair Credit Reporting Act requires each of the nationwide credit reporting companies—Equifax, Experian, and TransUnion—to provide you with a free copy of your credit report, at your request, once every 12 months. To obtain your free credit report, go to **www.annualcreditreport.com.** (*Note:* Beware of other sites that may look and sound similar to this site.[17]) In other situations, the consumer may obtain the information for a fee that is usually about $8 to $15 per request. It is also possible to obtain credit reports on a monthly or quarterly basis by subscribing to a credit-reporting service, which usually charges higher fees.

Second, a consumer who feels that some information in the file is inaccurate, misleading, or vague has the right to request that the credit bureau verify it. If the disputed information is found to be correct, the consumer can provide a brief explanation, giving his or her side of the dispute. This explanation must become part of the consumer's credit file. If the disputed information is found to be inaccurate, it must be deleted or corrected. Furthermore, you may request that any lender that has been supplied an inaccurate credit report in the last six months be sent a corrected credit report.

ENTREPRENEURIAL CHALLENGE

Collection Practices That Pay Off

What can a small business owner do to collect from a credit customer who doesn't make payments as scheduled? Experts suggest

- *Call as soon as a payment is missed.* Check whether the customer has a problem with the goods or services. If so, arrange to correct the problem and then firmly but politely ask for the overdue payment.
- *Follow up with a letter.* Reiterate the credit terms and set a short deadline for making the overdue payment.
- *Push for repayment, full or partial.* Getting even a small payment is a first step toward complete repayment—and it establishes that the customer acknowledges the debt.
- *Make collections a priority.* The founder of OpenSystems Publishing has set aside one morning every week for making collection calls.

Sound Collection Procedures

The vast majority of borrowers follow the lender's repayment terms exactly. However, some accounts inevitably become overdue for a variety of reasons. Experience shows that such accounts should receive immediate attention.

Some firms handle their own delinquent accounts; others prefer to use a professional collection agency. (Charges for a collection agency's services are usually high—up to half the amount collected.) Both tend to use the following techniques, generally in the order in which they are listed:

1. Subtle reminders, such as duplicate statements marked "Past Due"
2. Telephone calls to urge prompt payment
3. Personal visits to business customers to stress the necessity of paying overdue amounts immediately
4. Legal action, although the time, expense, and uncertain outcome of a lawsuit make this action a last resort

Good collection procedures should be firm, but they also should allow for compromise. Harassment is both illegal and bad business. Ideally, the customer will be convinced to make up missed payments, and the firm will retain the customer's goodwill.

In the next chapter you will see why firms need financing, how they obtain the money they need, and how they ensure that funds are used efficiently, in keeping with their organizational objectives.

RETURN TO   Inside Business

Commerce Bank provides all the traditional services customers expect from a financial institution—with the personal touch. The bank has a staff of 260 "mystery shoppers" who travel to different branches and pose as customers to assess the level of service they receive. The next day, bank management receives a full report about what the mystery shoppers found. Employees who go above and beyond receive "wow" awards, and the best of the best are honored at the bank's annual party.

In addition, Commerce Bank offers online banking for customers who want the convenience of transferring money, paying bills, checking balances, or trading securities from home or office. In its branches and online, Commerce Bank is banking on the "wow" factor to attract new customers, keep current customers, and live up to its billing as "America's Most Convenient Bank."

Questions

1. As pointed out in this chapter, there are thousands of banks, savings and loan associations, credit unions, and other financial institutions in the United States. What makes Commerce Bank different from other financial institutions that perform banking activities?
2. Would you like to work for Commerce Bank—America's Most Convenient Bank? Explain your answer.

▶▶ CHAPTER REVIEW

Summary

1

Identify the functions and characteristics of money.

Money is anything a society uses to purchase products, services, or resources. Money must serve as a medium of exchange, a measure of value, and a store of value. To perform its functions effectively, money must be divisible into units of convenient size, light and sturdy enough to be carried and used on a daily basis, stable in value, and difficult to counterfeit. The M_1 supply of money is made up of coins and bills (currency) and deposits in checking accounts (demand deposits). The M_2 supply includes M_1 plus savings accounts, certain money-market securities and small-denomination time deposits.

2

Summarize how the Federal Reserve System regulates the money supply.

The Federal Reserve System is responsible for regulating the U.S. banking industry and maintaining a sound economic environment. Banks with federal charters (national banks) must be members of the Fed. State banks may join if they choose to and if they can meet the requirements for membership. Twelve district banks and twenty-five branch banks compose the Federal Reserve System, whose seven-member board of governors is headquartered in Washington, D.C.

To control the supply of money, the Federal Reserve System regulates the reserve requirement, or the percentage of deposits a bank must keep on hand. It also regulates the discount rate, or the interest rate the Fed charges member banks for loans from the Federal Reserve. And it engages in open-market operations, in which it buys and sells government securities. Of the three tools used to influence monetary policy, the use of open-market operations is the most important. When the Federal Reserve buys and sells securities, the goal is to increase or decrease the federal funds rate. The federal funds rate is the interest rate at which a bank lends immediately available funds to another bank overnight in order to meet the borrowing bank's reserve requirements. The Fed serves as the government's bank and is also responsible for clearing checks and electronic transfers, inspecting currency, enforcing the Truth-in-Lending Act, and setting margin requirements for stock transactions.

3

Describe the organizations involved in the banking industry.

A commercial bank is a profit-making organization that accepts deposits, makes loans, and provides related services to customers. Commercial banks are chartered by the federal government or state governments. Savings and loan associations and credit unions offer the same basic services that commercial banks provide. Mutual savings banks, insurance companies, pension funds, brokerage firms, finance companies, and investment banking firms provide some limited banking services. A large number of people work in the banking industry because of the number of banks and other financial institutions. To be successful in the banking industry, you must be honest, be able to interact with people, have a strong background in accounting, appreciate the relationship between banking and finance, and possess basic computer skills.

4

Identify the services provided by financial institutions.

Banks and other financial institutions offer today's customers a tempting array of services. Among the most important and attractive banking services for both individuals and businesses are checking accounts, savings accounts, short- and long-term loans, and credit-card and debit-card transactions. Other traditional services include financial advice, payroll services, certified checks, trust services, and safe-deposit boxes.

5

Understand how financial institutions are changing to meet the needs of domestic and international customers.

Among the laws enacted during the last thirty years to deregulate the banking industry, probably the most important is the Financial Services Modernization Banking Act. This act allowed banks to establish one-stop financial supermarkets where customers can bank, buy and sell securities, and purchase insurance coverage. Because of this act, competition among banks, brokerage firms, and insurance companies has increased. As we enter the twenty-first century, an increasing use of technology and the need for bankers to help American businesses compete in the global marketplace will change the way banks and other financial institutions do business. The use of technology will increase as financial institutions continue to offer online banking. Increased use of electronic funds transfer systems (automated teller machines, automated clearinghouses, point-of-sale terminals, and electronic check conversion) also will change the way people bank. For firms in the global marketplace, a bank can provide letters of credit and banker's acceptances that will reduce the risk of nonpayment for sellers. Banks and financial institutions also can provide currency exchange to reduce payment problems for import or export transactions.

6

Explain how deposit insurance protects customers.

The Federal Deposit Insurance Corporation (FDIC) and the National Credit Union Association (NCUA) insure accounts in member commercial banks, S&Ls, savings banks, and credit unions for up to $100,000 for non-retirement accounts and $250,000 for some types of retirement accounts. Deposits maintained in different categories of legal ownership are insured separately. Thus you can have coverage for more than $100,000 in a single institution. The most common ownership categories are single ownership and joint ownership. It is also possible to obtain additional coverage by opening separate accounts in different banks, S&Ls, or credit unions. The FDIC and NCUA have improved banking in the United States. When either of these organizations insures a financial institution's deposits, they reserve the right to examine that institution's operations periodically. If a bank, S&L, or credit union is found to be poorly managed, it is reported to the proper banking authority.

7

Discuss the importance of credit and credit management.

Credit is immediate purchasing power that is exchanged for a promise to repay borrowed money, with or without interest, at a later date. Banks lend money because they are in business for that purpose. Businesses sell goods and services on credit because some customers cannot afford to pay cash and because they must keep pace with competitors who offer credit. Businesses also may realize a profit from interest charges.

Decisions on whether to grant credit to businesses and individuals usually are based on the five Cs of credit: character, capacity, capital, collateral, and conditions. Credit information can be obtained from various credit-reporting agencies, credit bureaus, industry associations, and other firms. The techniques used to collect past-due accounts should be firm enough to prompt payment but flexible enough to maintain the borrower's goodwill.

Key Terms

You should now be able to define and give an example relevant to each of the following terms:

barter system (628)
money (628)
medium of exchange (629)
measure of value (629)

store of value (629)
demand deposit (631)
time deposit (631)
Federal Reserve System (632)
reserve requirement (633)
discount rate (634)
open-market operations (634)
federal funds rate (634)
commercial bank (637)
national bank (637)
state bank (637)
savings and loan association (S&L) (638)
credit union (638)
check (641)
NOW account (641)
certificate of deposit (CD) (641)
line of credit (642)
revolving credit agreement (642)
collateral (642)
debit card (643)
electronic funds transfer (EFT) system (645)
electronic check conversion (ECC) (645)
letter of credit (646)
banker's acceptance (646)
credit (647)

Review Questions

1. How does the use of money solve the problems associated with a barter system of exchange?
2. What are three functions money must perform in a sound monetary system?
3. Explain why money must have each of the following characteristics:
   a. Divisibility
   b. Portability
   c. Stability
   d. Durability
   e. Difficulty of counterfeiting
4. What is included in the definition of the M_1 supply of money? Of the M_2 supply?
5. What is the Federal Reserve System? How is it organized?
6. Explain how the Federal Reserve System uses each of the following to control the money supply:
   a. Reserve requirements
   b. The discount rate
   c. Open-market operations

7. The Federal Reserve is responsible for enforcing the Truth-in-Lending Act. How does this act affect you?
8. What is the difference between a national bank and a state bank? What other financial institutions compete with national and state banks?
9. Describe the major banking services provided by financial institutions today.
10. For consumers, what are the major advantages of online banking? What is its major disadvantage?
11. How do automated teller machines, automated clearing houses, and point-of-sale terminals affect how you bank?
12. How can a bank or other financial institution help American businesses to compete in the global marketplace?
13. What is the basic function of the FDIC, SAIF, BIF, and NCUA? How do they perform this function?
14. List and explain the five Cs of credit management.
15. How would you check the information provided by an applicant for credit at a department store? By a business applicant at a heavy-equipment manufacturer's sales office?

Discussion Questions

1. It is said that financial institutions "create" money when they make loans to firms and individuals. Explain what this means.
2. Is competition among financial institutions good or bad for the following:
   a. The institutions themselves
   b. Their customers
   c. The economy in general
3. Why does the Fed use indirect means of controlling the money supply instead of simply printing more money or removing money from circulation when necessary?
4. Why would banks pay higher interest on money left on deposit for longer periods of time (e.g., on CDs)?
5. How could an individual get in financial trouble by using a credit card? If you were in trouble because of credit-card debt, what steps could you take to reduce your debts?
6. Lenders generally are reluctant to extend credit to individuals with no previous credit history (and no outstanding debts). Yet they willingly extend credit to individuals who are in the process of repaying debts. Is this reasonable? Is it fair? Explain your answer.
7. Assume that you want to borrow $10,000. What can you do to convince the loan officer that you are a good credit risk?

▶▶ VIDEO CASE 19.1

Financial Fusion Banks on the Internet

Web-based and wireless banking is "really revolutionizing the way that banks process transactions," says Michon Schenck, former president of Financial Fusion. Based in Concord, Massachusetts, Financial Fusion's software is the firepower behind this revolution. Its technology drives online banking systems and securities trading systems for more than 200 banks and financial institutions around the world. California Federal Bank, eMarquette Holdings, and First Citizens Bank are just three of Financial Fusion's bank customers.

The company's Consumer e-Finance Suite provides the technology for offering a full range of banking services that individual customers can access from any web-enabled device, not just personal computers. Knowing that the needs of business customers differ from those of individuals, Financial Fusion also has developed a separate Business e-Finance Suite for banks to offer their small-business customers. Financial institutions involved in securities trading can buy TradeForce Suite, a system for managing the communication of trade and payment transactions.

Financial Fusion customizes a system for each bank or institution, backing up the technology with personalized service through four regional offices in North America. Owned by high-tech Sybase, Inc., Financial Fusion implements customer systems through alliances with its parent company as well as with IBM and Sun Microsystems. The goal is not only to address each customer's current needs but also to allow for changes and future developments. The result is a system that grows as each financial services firm grows.

Consider how Financial Fusion helped First Citizens Bank. Headquartered in Raleigh, North Carolina, First Citizens is an $11 billion regional bank operating about 350 branches in North Carolina, Virginia, West Virginia, and other states. The bank originally offered online banking through another technology supplier. When First Citizen's executives learned that its online banking technology was about to become obsolete, they decided to evaluate other suppliers and technologies. "We really distinguish ourselves by providing outstanding customer service in our branches and contact center," explains Executive Vice President Jeff Ward, "and we wanted to use this occasion to take our online service to the next level."

In particular, First Citizens was interested in making the online banking system easier to use and in expanding its capabilities for consumers and small to medium-sized businesses. At the same time, the bank wanted to ensure that any system it chose would be able to keep pace with expansion plans in Texas, Arizona, and other states. To start, its executives sent a detailed listing of its criteria to six technology suppliers. They eliminated three suppliers and entered discussions with three finalists, including Financial Fusion. The First Citizens team carefully looked at the ability of the finalists to provide a system that was user-friendly and customizable.

Ultimately, First Citizens chose Financial Fusion's Consumer e-Finance Suite. Then Financial Fusion's technical specialists went to work integrating the suite with the bank's existing IBM system. They also tailored the look and functionality to First Citizens' specific requirements. Once the system was operational, First Citizens and its customers were so satisfied that top management decided to expand into a new revenue-producing venture: offering online services for other banks. As installed, the Financial Fusion system can easily accommodate many more transactions, and it needs only minimal adaptation for each bank that First Citizens serves.

As the online banking revolution continues, Financial Fusion will have considerable opportunity to increase its customer base, product line, and profits. Today, about half the largest U.S. financial services firms use their own software to operate their online banking sites. However, experts foresee a trend away from "home grown" systems and toward systems provided by suppliers such as Financial Fusion and its competitors, including Corillian and S1 Corp. Watch for even more high-tech financial services innovations in the coming years—and more high-tech systems from Financial Fusion.[18]

For more information about this company, go to **www.financialfusion.com.**

Questions

1. From a management standpoint, describe the process that First Citizens Bank used to choose Financial Fusion to develop its current online banking system.
2. To establish an online banking system, a bank, S&L, or credit union must be willing to invest both time and money in technology. From a practical standpoint, what are the advantages and disadvantages of online banking for the financial institution? For the customer?
3. Although most online banking systems are seamless, and a growing number of customers are using them, what fears might customers have about online banking? As a bank executive, how could you reduce those fears?
4. In the interest of security, some banks are considering giving each customer an electronic fingerprint pad that easily connects to any desktop or laptop computer. The customer would gain access to the online banking system only if the fingerprint made by pressing on the pad matches the fingerprint on file. If you worked for a bank, what points would you make to convince customers to participate in a test of this identification system?

>> CASE 19.2

Citigroup Banks on Credit and More

When more than 150 million people around the world open their wallets to pay for a purchase, they take out a Citigroup card. Citigroup is the largest U.S. financial services organization and the global leader in credit cards. It offers numerous varieties of Visa, MasterCard, American Express, and Diners Club credit cards, each geared to the needs of a particular group of consumers or businesses. Citigroup also handles the credit-card operations of Sears, Home Depot, May Department Stores, and many other major retailers. And its CitiFinancial unit has loaned money to four million borrowers throughout North America.

Credit cards are only one of the many banking services that Citigroup offers for individuals and businesses. Its Citibank unit maintains an extensive network of bank branches and ATMs stretching across North America and around the world from Norway and Nigeria to New Zealand and the Netherlands. Citibank pioneered the CD during the 1960s and was one of the driving forces behind the development of 24-hour ATM banking in the 1970s. The Citigroup Private Bank specializes in banking and investment services for wealthy customers. Finally, the Corporate and Investment Banking unit helps companies to manage and enhance their financial resources.

No two Citigroup cards are exactly alike in features or benefits. Some of its credit cards allow customers (consumers or business people) to earn rewards such as cash rebates, free hotel stays, and free flights when they charge purchases. Its American Express cards give customers early access to excellent seats for concerts and sporting events. Its series of no-frills credit cards carry no annual fees and low finance charges. At the other end of the spectrum, the Citigroup Chairman Card comes with a generous line of credit, special travel privileges, and other services valued by high-income executives.

Simplicity, one of Citigroup's newer credit cards, "is designed to address key complaints" about issues such as complex legal jargon, says an executive vice president. As part of this card's streamlined credit agreement, customers who charge at least one purchase per month will not have late fees added to their accounts if a payment arrives after the deadline. Simplicity also eliminates the frustration and delays involved in using automated telephone response systems to reach a customer service representative. Cardholders who have questions or want assistance can call and press "0" to speak with a representative right away.

Citigroup is also starting to think small with new initiatives to encourage customers to use credit or debit cards instead of cash when paying for small, everyday purchases. The total annual value of all consumer purchases under $5 is estimated to be $1.3 trillion, according to research conducted by a MasterCard International unit. Small wonder that Citibank (and competitors such as J.P. Morgan Chase) are highly interested in pursuing this huge market. The key to profits in small transactions, however, is to make the purchase as convenient as possible for customers while making the processing as efficient as possible for the bank.

This is why "contactless payment technology" is fast becoming big business. Citibank's debit cardholders have already received key fobs containing tiny computer chips embedded with their account information. Instead of fishing around in a wallet or purse for plastic and signing for each purchase, customers just wave their fobs at the checkout or in front of special readers to complete small purchases, typically under $25. Contactless payments make routine transactions such as buying a movie ticket or paying for a latte faster and easier than ever—opening up new profit possibilities for Citibank and its parent, Citigroup.[19]

For more information about this company, go to **www.citigroup.com.**

Questions

1. Today, over 170 million Americans possess at least one credit card? And yet most people get one or more credit-card offers in the mail each week. Why do you think banks encourage consumers to sign up for more credit cards? How can consumers get "in trouble" by having a wallet full of credit cards?
2. How are changes in the Fed discount rate likely to affect Citigroup's profitability and the pace at which it acquires new credit customers?
3. If you worked for Citigroup and were responsible for approving credit applicants, which of the five Cs of credit would carry the most weight in your decision to approve or reject a customer's credit application? Why?
4. What are the advantages and disadvantages of Citibank's contactless payment technology for consumers? For banks and retailers?

→ CHAPTER 19: JOURNAL EXERCISE

Discovery statement: You could be one in a million—the one million Americans who fall victim to the crime of identity theft every year. Crooks who steal your name, birth date, credit-card numbers, bank account numbers, and Social Security number can withdraw money from your bank accounts, charge merchandise in your name, or contract for cell phone service.

Use the Internet to obtain information about how to prevent identity theft. Then, according to the professionals, describe the steps someone should take to protect their identity.

_____

_____

_____

_____

_____

Complete a "security audit" of your personal information and financial records. Based on your audit and the recommendations from professionals, what should you do now to protect your identity?

_____

_____

_____

_____

It always helps to have a plan in case your identity is stolen. Based on the information you obtained from your Internet research, what immediate steps should you take if your identity is stolen?

_____

_____

_____

_____

_____

BUILDING SKILLS FOR CAREER SUCCESS

1. Exploring the Internet

Internet-based banking is no longer a new concept. For many Americans, technology has changed the way they conduct their banking transactions. For example, most people no longer carry their paychecks to the bank to be deposited; instead, the money is deposited directly into their accounts. And an increasing number of individuals and businesses are using computers and the Internet to handle their finances, apply for loans, and pay their bills. Banking from a home computer is continually being made easier, giving bank customers access to their accounts twenty-four hours a day and seven days a week. As a result, you have more control over your money.

Assignment

1. Examine the websites of several major banks with which you are familiar. Describe their online banking services. Are they worthwhile in your opinion?

2. In the past three years, how has technology changed the way you handle your money and conduct your banking transactions, such as depositing your paychecks, paying

your monthly bills, obtaining cash, paying for purchases, and applying for loans?

3. In the next five to ten years, what will the banking industry be like? How will these changes affect you and the way you do your banking? How readily will you adapt to change? The Internet and the library can help you to learn what is in the forefront of banking technology.

4. Prepare a report explaining your answers to these questions.

2. Developing Critical-Thinking Skills

Every year your grandmother in Seattle, Washington, sends you a personal check for $100 for your birthday. You live in Monticello, Georgia, seventy-five miles southeast of Atlanta. You either cash the check or deposit it in your savings account at a local bank. Your banker does not return the canceled check directly to your grandmother, but somehow it ends up back in your grandmother's hands in Seattle. How does this happen? *Hint:* For information about the process used to clear checks, go to **http://federalreserve.gov/paymentsystems/checkservices.**

Assignment

1. Research the process that your bank uses to collect a check that is from an individual located in another city and state.

2. Summarize what you learned and how this information might be helpful to you in the future.

3. Building Team Skills

Three years ago, Ron and Ginger were happy to learn that on graduation, Ron would be teaching history in a large high school, making $30,000 a year, and Ginger would be working in a public accounting firm, starting at $34,000. They married immediately after graduation and bought a new home for $110,000. Since Ron had no personal savings, Ginger used her savings for the down payment. They soon began furnishing their home, charging their purchases to three separate credit cards, and that is when their debt began to mount. When the three credit cards reached their $10,000 limits, Ron and Ginger signed up for four additional credit cards with $10,000 limits that were offered through the mail, and they started using them. Soon their monthly payments were more than

their combined take-home pay. To make their monthly payments, Ron and Ginger began to obtain cash advances on their credit cards. When they reached the credit ceilings on their seven credit cards, they could no longer get the cash advances they needed to cover their monthly bills. Stress began to mount as creditors called and demanded payment. Ron and Ginger began to argue over money and just about everything else. Finally, things got so bad they considered filing for personal bankruptcy, but ironically, they could not afford the legal fees. What options are available to this couple?

Assignment

1. Working in teams of three or four, use your local library, the Internet, and personal interviews to investigate the following:

   a. Filling for personal bankruptcy.
      - What is involved in filing for personal bankruptcy?
      - How much does it cost?
      - How does bankruptcy affect individuals?

   b. The Consumer Credit Counseling Service at **www.cccsintl.org** or Myvesta at **www.myvesta.org**.
      - What services do these organizations provide?
      - How could they help Ron and Ginger?
      - What will it cost?

2. Prepare a specific plan for repaying Ron and Ginger's debt.

3. Outline the advantages and disadvantages of credit cards, and make the appropriate recommendations for Ron and Ginger concerning their future use of credit cards.

4. Summarize what you have learned about credit-card misuse.

4. Researching Different Careers

It has long been known that maintaining a good credit record is essential to obtaining loans from financial institutions, but did you know that employers often check credit records before offering an applicant a position? This is especially true of firms that handle financial accounts for others. Information contained in your credit report can tell an employer a lot about how responsible you are with money and how well you manage it. Individuals have the right to know what is in their credit bureau files and to have the credit bureau verify any inaccurate, misleading, or vague information. Before you apply for a job or a loan, you should check with a credit bureau to learn what is in your file.

Assignment

1. Using information in this chapter, use the Internet or call a credit bureau and ask for a copy of your credit report. A small fee may be required depending on the bureau and circumstances.
2. Review the information.
3. Have the bureau verify any information that you feel is inaccurate, misleading, or vague.
4. If the verification shows that the information is correct, prepare a brief statement explaining your side of the dispute, and send it to the bureau.
5. Prepare a statement summarizing what the credit report says about you. Based on your credit report, would a firm hire you as its financial manager?

5. Improving Communication Skills

Often loan applicants—especially individuals—are afraid to talk with a loan officer about borrowing money. A number of suggestions were made in this chapter that could help you to obtain money from a bank or lender. Assume that you are a business owner who has been operating a small manufacturing business. Also assume that your business is profitable and needs to expand and purchase new equipment to remain competitive in your region. Finally, assume that the equipment will cost $50,000.

Assignment

1. Describe the type of information that a loan officer at your bank would want to document this loan request.
2. Assume that for loans of this size, your bank requires an interview with a loan officer. Prepare a list of questions that you think the loan officer will ask.
3. How would you, as a business owner in need of financing, answer the questions that you just developed?
4. Based on the questions you prepared (as loan officer) and your answers to those questions (as a business owner in need of financing), describe your chances of getting approval and the money you need to expand your small manufacturing business in a one- to two-page report.

→ PREP TEST

Matching Questions

___ 1. Deposits that are made to interest-bearing savings accounts.

___ 2. It is a system in which goods and services are exchanged.

___ 3. Money in checking accounts is an example.

___ 4. A financial institution created to serve its members.

___ 5. A loan that is approved before the money is actually needed.

___ 6. It is pledged as security against a loan.

___ 7. A bank must retain a percentage of its deposits.

___ 8. It is a guaranteed line of credit from a bank.

___ 9. Banking authorities within each state are the chartering agents.

___ 10. It is a legal document guaranteeing payment for a specific time.

a. barter system
b. collateral
c. credit union
d. demand deposit
e. letter of credit
f. line of credit
g. revolving credit agreement
h. reserve requirement
i. state bank
j. time deposits

True/False Questions

T F

11. ○ ○ Spending money on a new car is an example of how money creates a store of value.

12. ○ ○ Savings and loan associations have checking accounts, savings accounts, and home-mortgage loans.

13. ○ ○ Demand deposits are called near-monies.

14. ○ ○ When the Fed raises the discount rate, banks begin to restrict loans.

15. ○ ○ Through a process called deposit expansion, commercial banks can fund more loans.

T F

16. ○ ○ The standard unit of money must be capable of division into smaller units.

17. ○ ○ There are twenty-two Federal Reserve District Banks in the United States that make up the Federal Reserve System.

18. ○ ○ Enforcing the Truth-in-Lending Act is the responsibility of The Fed.

19. ○ ○ Congress first created the Federal Reserve System in 1929.

20. ○ ○ Debit cards are used most commonly at ATMs and to purchase products and services from retailers.

Multiple-Choice Questions

21. Coins, paper bills, checking accounts, and traveler's checks make up the
    a. M_1 supply of money.
    b. M_2 supply of money.
    c. M_3 supply of money.
    d. open-market operations.
    e. barter system.

22. What are the terminals called when you pull a bank card through a magnetic card reader, enter an identification number, and the amount of the purchase is added to the store's account?
    a. Automated teller machines
    b. Automated clearinghouse terminals
    c. Electronic bank tellers
    d. Point-of-sale (POS) terminals
    e. Revolving credits

23. When the Fed lowers the discount rate, what happens?
    a. There is less money for banks to lend.
    b. There is a decrease in the overall money supply.
    c. There is decreased economic activity.
    d. There is an economic slowdown.
    e. Money is cheaper and the bank makes more loans.

24. If you have been denied credit on the basis of information provided by a credit bureau and you feel that some information in your file is inaccurate, what can you do? Which of the following is *not* an option?
    a. You have a right to know what is in the file.
    b. You can request a copy of your credit record.
    c. You can ask the credit bureau to verify any inaccurate, misleading, or vague information.
    d. You can pay to have the information removed.
    e. You can write an explanation and ask that it be made a part of your file.

25. Sonya has $1,000 she will not need in the next year, and she wants to deposit it in a bank. Which of the following services is *best* for Sonya?
    a. Certificate of deposit
    b. Passbook savings account
    c. Super NOW account
    d. NOW account
    e. Regular checking account

Fill-in-the-Blank Questions

26. The fund established to guarantee employees a regular monthly income at retirement is known as a _____ fund.

27. The interest rate that banks pay for money they borrow from the Federal Reserve Bank is called a _____ rate.

28. The primary purpose of the FDIC is to insure _____ against bank failure.

29. An interest-bearing checking account with limited privileges is a _____ account.

30. A penalty for early withdrawal of funds is imposed on _____ of deposits.

Online Study Center

FOR MORE **test practice, use the interactive ACE quizzes available at the Online Student Center:**
www.college.hmco.com/PIC/pridebusiness9e.

Answers on p. PT2.

Mastering Financial Management

LEARNING OBJECTIVES

WHAT you will be able to do once you complete this chapter:

1 **Explain** the need for financial management in business.

2 **Summarize** the process of planning for financial management.

3 **Describe** the advantages and disadvantages of different methods of short-term debt financing.

4 **Evaluate** the advantages and disadvantages of equity financing.

5 **Evaluate** the advantages and disadvantages of long-term debt financing.

WHY this chapter matters

The old saying goes, "Money makes the world go around." For both individuals and business firms, the saying is true. The fact is that it's hard to live in this world or operate a business without money. In this chapter we discuss how financial management can be used to obtain money and then to make sure that it is used effectively.

FOR HELP with studying this chapter, visit the Online Student Center:

www.college.hmco.com/PIC/pridebusiness9e

Online Study Center

"Bowie Bonds," named for British rock-and-roll legend David Bowie, started stars and investors down a new financial path. Thanks to decades of hit songs such as "Ziggy Stardust," "Space Oddity," and "Changes," Bowie's concert tours sell out all over the world, and his acting credits are as stellar as his music credits. He played the title role in the 1976 cult-movie classic *The Man Who Fell to Earth* and also has appeared in *The Last Temptation of Christ* and dozens of other films. On Broadway, his star turn as John Merrick in *The Elephant Man* garnered rave reviews.

Because musical tastes constantly change, however, even a prolific songwriter such as Bowie can never predict with certainty how much he'll make from song royalties in the future. This is why Bowie worked with investment banker David Pullman to turn his hefty catalog of past hits into immediate cash. Bowie pledged ten years of royalties on 287 songs as security, and in exchange, he borrowed an upfront lump sum of $55 million by issuing bonds.

DID YOU KNOW?

David Bowie, the British rock-and-roll legend, raised $55 million by selling bonds that pay investors 8 percent each year until maturity.

The annual interest rate on Bowie Bonds was 8 percent. At the end of ten years, Bowie would have to repay the $55 million, but he would regain ownership of future earnings on his songs' royalties. If total song royalties for the decade were lower than expected, Bowie still had the use of the $55 million for the full ten years.

The insurance firm Prudential bought all the Bowie Bonds as a long-term investment. One risk it faced was the possibility of finding no willing buyers if it decided to sell the bonds before the end of the ten-year term. Another risk was that royalties would be lower than expected, and the company might not receive all payments due during the investment's ten-year term. Would Bowie Bonds pay off?[1]

For more information about this story, go to **www.pullmanco.com/dbb.htm.**

While you may recognize the name David Bowie, there's a good chance that you didn't know you could invest in Bowie Bonds. Mr. Bowie, like most people *and most business firms*, needed cash. To meet this need, he sold bonds valued at $55 million and promised to repay the borrowed money in ten years. He also agreed to pay 8 percent annual interest each year until the bonds were repaid at maturity. But where would the money come from to repay bondholders and to pay the annual interest? For Bowie, the answer was simple: He pledged his future royalties from the 287 songs he had written during his career as collateral for the bonds. While this may seem like an unusual method of raising cash for an entertainer, the truth is that Bowie possessed a valuable asset that would continue to generate royalty income in the future. In a similar fashion, corporations own assets that, when managed properly, generate sales revenues and profits for the business. These corporate assets, just like Bowie's song hits, can be used to secure immediate cash. Selling corporate bonds—along with selling stock, obtaining short- and long-term loans, and other financing methods—are used on a regular basis to help firms obtain the financing needed to operate in today's competitive business environment.

In this chapter we focus on how firms find the financing required to meet two needs of all business organizations: first, the need for money to start a business and keep it going, and second, the need to manage that money effectively. We also look at how firms develop financial plans and evaluate financial performance. Then we compare various methods of obtaining short-term financing. We also examine sources of long-term financing.

What Is Financial Management?

Financial management consists of all the activities concerned with obtaining money and using it effectively. Within a business organization, the financial manager not only must determine the best way (or ways) to raise money, but he or she also must ensure that projected uses are in keeping with the organization's goals.

1 LEARNING OBJECTIVE
Explain the need for financial management in business.

financial management all the activities concerned with obtaining money and using it effectively

The Need for Financing

Money is needed both to start a business and to keep it going. The original investment of the owners, along with money they may have borrowed, should be enough to open the doors. After that, it would seem that sales revenues could be used to pay the firm's expenses and to provide a profit as well.

This is exactly what happens in a successful firm—over the long run. However, income and expenses may vary from month to month or from year to year. Temporary financing may be needed when expenses are high or sales are low. Then, too, situations such as the opportunity to purchase a new facility or expand an existing plant may require more money than is currently available within a firm. In either case, the firm must look for outside sources of financing.

Short-Term Financing **Short-term financing** is money that will be used for one year or less. Many financial managers define short-term financing as money that will be used for one year *or* one operating cycle of the business, whichever is longer. The *operating cycle of a business* may be longer than one year and is the amount of time between the purchase of raw materials and the sale of finished products to wholesalers, retailers, or consumers.

As illustrated in Table 20.1, there are many short-term financing needs, but two deserve special attention. First, certain business practices may affect a firm's cash flow and create a need for short-term financing. **Cash flow** is the movement of money into and out of an organization. The ideal is to have sufficient money coming into the firm in any period to cover the firm's expenses during that period. The ideal, however, is not always achieved. For example, California-based Callaway Golf offers credit to retailers and wholesalers that carry the firm's golf clubs and balls. Credit purchases made by Callaway's retailers generally are not paid until thirty to sixty days (or more) after

short-term financing money that will be used for one year or less

cash flow the movement of money into and out of an organization

> ≫ **TABLE 20.1**

COMPARISON OF SHORT- AND LONG-TERM FINANCING

Whether a business seeks short- or long-term financing depends on what the money will be used for.

Corporate Cash Needs

Short-Term Financing Needs	Long-Term Financing Needs
Cash-flow problems	Business start-up costs
Current inventory needs	Mergers and acquisitions
Monthly expenses	New product development
Speculative production	Long-term marketing activities
Short-term promotional needs	Replacement of equipment
Unexpected emergencies	Expansion of facilities

the transaction. Callaway therefore may need short-term financing to pay its bills until its customers have paid theirs.

A second major need for short-term financing is inventory. For most manufacturers, wholesalers, and retailers, inventory requires considerable investment. Moreover, most goods are manufactured four to nine months before they are actually sold to the ultimate customer. This type of manufacturing is often referred to as *speculative production.* **Speculative production** refers to the time lag between the actual production of goods and when the goods are sold. Consider what happens when a firm such as Black & Decker begins to manufacture electric tools and small appliances for sale during the Christmas season. Manufacturing begins in February, March, and April, and Black & Decker negotiates short-term financing to buy materials and supplies, to pay wages and rent, and to cover inventory costs until its products eventually are sold to wholesalers and retailers later in the year. Take a look at Figure 20.1. Although Black & Decker manufactures and sells finished products all during the year, expenses peak during the first part of the year. During this same period, sales revenues are low. Once

speculative production the time lag between the actual production of goods and when the goods are sold

Inventory management: A complex problem. For retailers like Sears, managing inventory can be a problem, especially before Christmas and other peak selling periods. Although retailers don't want to get stuck with unsold inventory, they must have the right mix and amount of inventory to meet consumer demand. Despite the problems associated with inventory, it's a good feeling to see customers at the cash register purchasing the products they need.

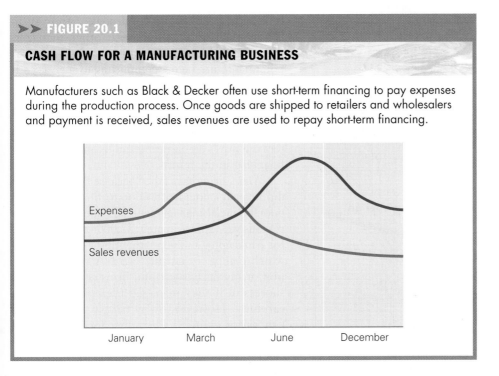

➤➤ FIGURE 20.1

CASH FLOW FOR A MANUFACTURING BUSINESS

Manufacturers such as Black & Decker often use short-term financing to pay expenses during the production process. Once goods are shipped to retailers and wholesalers and payment is received, sales revenues are used to repay short-term financing.

the firm's finished products are shipped to retailers and wholesalers and payment is received (usually within thirty to sixty days), sales revenues are used to repay short-term financing.

Retailers that range in size from Wal-Mart to the neighborhood drugstore also need short-term financing to build up their inventories before peak selling periods. For example, Dallas-based Bruce Miller Nurseries must increase the number of shrubs, trees, and flowering plants that it makes available for sale during the spring and summer growing seasons. To obtain this merchandise inventory from growers or wholesalers, it uses short-term financing and repays the loans when the merchandise is sold.

Long-Term Financing **Long-term financing** is money that will be used for longer than one year. Long-term financing obviously is needed to start a new business. As Table 20.1 shows, it is also needed for business mergers and acquisitions, new product development, long-term marketing activities, replacement of equipment that has become obsolete, and expansion of facilities.

The amounts of long-term financing needed by large firms can seem almost unreal. Exxon spends about $10 million to drill an exploratory offshore oil well—without knowing for sure whether oil will be found. And Merck invested $4 billion in research and development (R&D) to create new or improved prescription drugs in 2004—the last year that complete dollar amounts are available at the time of this publication.[2]

The Need for Financial Management

To some extent, financial management can be viewed as a two-sided problem. On one side, the uses of funds often dictate the type or types of financing needed by a business. On the other side, the activities a business can undertake are determined by the types of financing available. Financial managers must ensure that funds are available when needed, that they are obtained at the lowest possible cost, and that they are used as efficiently as possible. Financial managers also must consider the risk-return ratio when making decisions. The **risk-return ratio** is based on the principle that a high-risk decision should generate higher financial returns for a business. On the other hand, more conservative decisions (with less risk) often generate lesser returns. While financial managers want higher returns, they often must strive for a balance between risk and return. For example, American Electric Power may consider investing millions of dollars to fund research into new solar technology that could enable the company to use

long-term financing money that will be used for longer than one year

risk-return ratio a ratio based on the principle that a high-risk decision should generate higher financial returns for a business and more conservative decisions often generate lesser returns

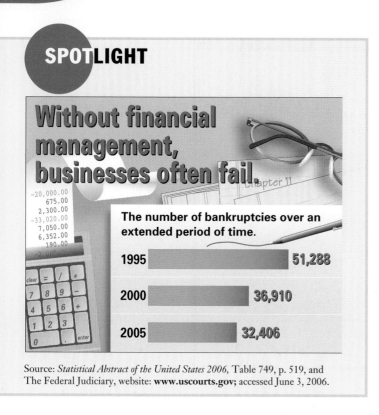

SPOTLIGHT

Without financial management, businesses often fail.

−20,000.00
675.00
2,300.00
−33,020.00
7,050.00
6,352.00
190.00

The number of bankruptcies over an extended period of time.

1995	51,288
2000	36,910
2005	32,406

Source: *Statistical Abstract of the United States 2006*, Table 749, p. 519, and The Federal Judiciary, website: **www.uscourts.gov;** accessed June 3, 2006.

the sun to generate electrical power. And yet, financial managers (along with other managers throughout the organization) must determine the potential return before committing to such a costly research project. And finally, financial managers must ensure that funds are available for the repayment of debts in accordance with lenders' financing terms. Prompt repayment is essential to protect the firm's credit rating and its ability to obtain financing in the future.

Many firms have failed because their managers did not pay enough attention to finances. In fact, poor financial management was one of the major reasons why approximately 32,000 businesses filed for bankruptcy in 2005—the most recent year for which complete statistics are available.[3] In addition, many fairly successful firms could be highly successful if they managed their finances more carefully. However, many people often take finances for granted. Their first focus may be on production or marketing. As long as there is sufficient financing today, they don't worry about how well it is used or whether it will be there tomorrow. Proper financial management can ensure that

- Financing priorities are established in line with organizational goals and objectives.
- Spending is planned and controlled.
- Sufficient financing is available when it is needed, both now and in the future.
- A firm's credit customers pay their bills on time, and the number of past-due or delinquent accounts is reduced.
- Bills are paid promptly to protect the firm's credit rating and its ability to borrow money.
- The funds required for paying the firm's taxes are available when needed to meet tax deadlines.
- Excess cash is invested in certificates of deposit (CDs), government securities, or conservative, marketable securities.

These functions define effective management as applied to a particular resource—money. And like all effective management, financial management begins with people who must set goals and plan for the future.

Careers in Finance

When you hear the word *finance*, you may think of highly paid executives who determine what a

A career in finance can mean handling a lot of money. Anna Escobedo Cabral is the Treasurer of the United States, one of the top positions in the U.S. government. Cabral has held a number of leadership positions, which include serving as director of the Smithsonian Institution's Center for Latino Initiatives and as deputy staff director for the United States Senate Judiciary Committee. A native of California, she majored in political science and earned a master's degree with an emphasis in international trade and finance.

corporation can afford to do and what it can't. At the executive level, most large business firms have a chief financial officer for financial management. A **chief financial officer (CFO)** is a high-level corporate executive who manages a firm's finances and reports directly to the company's chief executive officer or president. Some firms prefer to use the titles vice president of financial management, treasurer, or controller instead of the CFO title for executive-level positions in the finance area.

While some executives in finance do make $300,000 a year or more, many entry-level and lower-level positions that pay quite a bit less are available. Banks, insurance companies, and investment firms obviously have a need for workers who can manage and analyze financial data. So do businesses involved in manufacturing, services, and marketing. Colleges and universities, not-for-profit organizations, and government entities at all levels also need finance workers.

People in finance must have certain traits and skills. After the scandals that have occurred in the last few years that involve accountants, auditors, and corporate executives, one of the most important priorities for someone interested in a finance career is honesty. Be warned: Investors, lenders, and other corporate executives expect financial managers to be above reproach. And both federal and state government entities have enacted legislation to ensure that corporate financial statements reflect the "real" status of a firm's financial position. In addition to honesty, managers and employees in the finance area must

1. Have a strong background in accounting or mathematics.
2. Know how to use a computer to analyze data.
3. Be an expert at both written and oral communication.

Typical job titles in finance include bank officer, consumer credit officer, financial analyst, financial planner, loan officer, insurance analyst, and investment account executive. Depending on qualifications, work experience, and education, starting salaries generally begin at $20,000 to $30,000 a year, but it is not uncommon for college graduates to earn $35,000 a year or more. In addition to salary, many employees have attractive benefits and other perks that make a career in financial management attractive.

YOUR CAREER

Is Fundraising a Career Fit

Pursuing a career in nonprofit fundraising can bring a special sense of satisfaction along with a paycheck. Public television executive Paula Kerger observes that people who choose this type of career "go home at the end of the day and feel they've made the world a better place." Is a career in nonprofit fundraising for you? Ask yourself:

- Are you motivated to make a difference by helping a charity, cultural organization, or another worthwhile nonprofit group achieve its goals?
- Are you ready to hone your leadership and communication skills by dealing with contributors, colleagues, clients, and volunteers?
- Are you prepared to meet and build relationships with people at all levels inside and outside the organization?
- Do you prefer working in smaller organizations where you can have considerable responsibility and your accomplishments can shine?
- Do you have a positive attitude? "Fundraisers can often receive more rejections than donations, so it's vital that you don't get downhearted," says the fundraiser for a performing arts center.

chief financial officer (CFO) a high-level corporate executive who manages a firm's finances and reports directly to the company's chief executive officer or president

Planning—The Basis of Sound Financial Management

In Chapter 7 we defined a *plan* as an outline of the actions by which an organization intends to accomplish its goals. A **financial plan,** then, is a plan for obtaining and using the money needed to implement an organization's goals.

Developing the Financial Plan

Financial planning (like all planning) begins with establishing a set of valid goals and objectives. Financial managers next must determine how much money is needed to accomplish each goal and objective. Finally, financial managers must identify available

2 LEARNING OBJECTIVE
Summarize the process of planning for financial management.

financial plan a plan for obtaining and using the money needed to implement an organization's goals

sources of financing and decide which to use. The three steps involved in financial planning are illustrated in Figure 20.2.

Establishing Organizational Goals and Objectives   As pointed out in Chapter 7, a *goal* is an end result that an organization expects to achieve over a one- to ten-year period. *Objectives* are specific statements detailing what the organization intends to accomplish within a shorter period of time. If goals and objectives are not specific and measurable, they cannot be translated into dollar costs, and financial planning cannot proceed. Goals and objectives also must be realistic. Otherwise, they may be impossible to finance or achieve. For large corporations, goals and objectives can be expensive. For example, when communications giant SBC merged with AT&T, it wanted to use one brand—the older and more recognized AT&T brand—to represent both companies. To fulfill this objective, SBC management planned to spend at least $500 million beginning in 2006.[4]

Budgeting for Financial Needs   Once planners know what the firm's goals and objectives are for a specific period—say, the next calendar year—they can budget the costs the firm will incur and the sales revenues it will receive. Specifically, a **budget** is a financial statement that projects income and/or expenditures over a specified future period.

> **budget** a financial statement that projects income and/or expenditures over a specified future period

Usually the budgeting process begins with the construction of budgets for sales and various types of expenses. (A typical sales budget—for Stars and Stripes Clothing, a California-based retailer—is shown in Figure 20.3.) Financial managers can easily combine each department's budget for sales and expenses into a company-wide cash budget. A **cash budget** estimates cash receipts and cash expenditures over a specified period. Notice in the cash budget for Stars and Stripes Clothing, shown in Figure 20.4, that cash sales and collections are listed at the top for each calendar quarter. Payments for purchases and routine expenses are listed in the middle section. Using this infor-

> **cash budget** a financial statement that estimates cash receipts and cash expenditures over a specified period

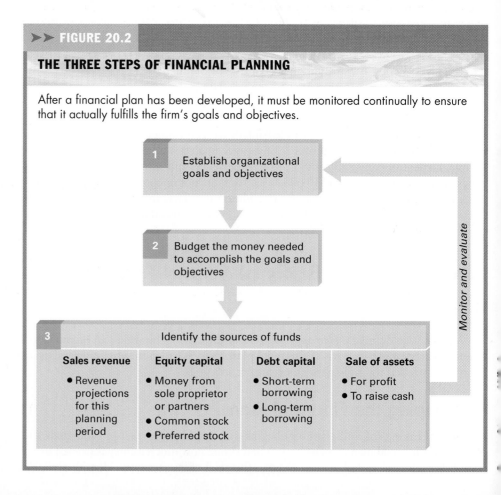

> ➤➤ **FIGURE 20.2**

THE THREE STEPS OF FINANCIAL PLANNING

After a financial plan has been developed, it must be monitored continually to ensure that it actually fulfills the firm's goals and objectives.

1 Establish organizational goals and objectives

2 Budget the money needed to accomplish the goals and objectives

3 Identify the sources of funds

Sales revenue	Equity capital	Debt capital	Sale of assets
• Revenue projections for this planning period	• Money from sole proprietor or partners • Common stock • Preferred stock	• Short-term borrowing • Long-term borrowing	• For profit • To raise cash

Monitor and evaluate

>> **FIGURE 20.3**

SALES BUDGET FOR STARS AND STRIPES CLOTHING

Usually the budgeting process begins with the construction of departmental budgets for sales and various expenses.

STARS AND STRIPES CLOTHING
Sales Budget   For January 1, 2008 to December 31, 2008

Department	First Quarter	Second Quarter	Third Quarter	Fourth Quarter	Totals
Infants'	$ 50,000	$ 55,000	$ 60,000	$ 70,000	$235,000
Children's	45,000	45,000	40,000	40,000	170,000
Women's	35,000	40,000	35,000	50,000	160,000
Men's	20,000	20,000	15,000	25,000	80,000
Totals	$150,000	$160,000	$150,000	$185,000	$645,000

mation, it is possible to calculate the anticipated cash gain or loss at the end of each quarter.

Most firms today use one of two approaches to budgeting. In the *traditional* approach, each new budget is based on the dollar amounts contained in the budget for the preceding year. These amounts are modified to reflect any revised goals and objectives, and managers are required to justify only new expenditures. The problem with this approach is that it leaves room for padding budget items to protect the (sometimes selfish) interests of the manager or his or her department.

This problem is essentially eliminated through zero-base budgeting. **Zero-base budgeting** is a budgeting approach in which every expense in every budget must be justified. It can reduce unnecessary spending dramatically because every budget item must stand on its own merits. However, some managers oppose zero-base budgeting because it requires entirely too much time-consuming paperwork.

To develop a plan for long-term financing needs, managers often construct a capital budget. A **capital budget** estimates a firm's expenditures for major assets,

zero-base budgeting a budgeting approach in which every expense in every budget must be justified

capital budget a financial statement that estimates a firm's expenditures for major assets and its long-term financing needs

>> **FIGURE 20.4**

CASH BUDGET FOR STARS AND STRIPES CLOTHING

A company-wide cash budget projects sales, collections, purchases, and expenses over a specified period to anticipate cash surpluses and deficits.

STARS AND STRIPES CLOTHING
Cash Budget   For January 1, 2008 to December 31, 2008

	First Quarter	Second Quarter	Third Quarter	Fourth Quarter	Totals
Cash sales and collections	$150,000	$160,000	$150,000	$185,000	$645,000
Less payments					
Purchases	$110,000	$ 80,000	$ 90,000	$ 60,000	$340,000
Wages/salaries	25,000	20,000	25,000	30,000	100,000
Rent	10,000	10,000	12,000	12,000	44,000
Other expenses	4,000	4,000	5,000	6,000	19,000
Taxes	8,000	8,000	10,000	10,000	36,000
Total payments	$157,000	$122,000	$142,000	$118,000	$539,000
Cash gain or (loss)	$ (7,000)	$ 38,000	$ 8,000	$ 67,000	$106,000

including new product development, expansion of facilities, replacement of obsolete equipment, and mergers and acquisitions. For example, Bank of America constructed a capital budget to determine the best way to finance the $35 billion acquisition of MBNA Corporation.[5]

Identifying Sources of Funds The four primary sources of funds, listed in Figure 20.2, are sales revenue, equity capital, debt capital, and proceeds from the sale of assets. Future sales revenue generally provides the greatest part of a firm's financing. Figure 20.4 shows that for Stars and Stripes Clothing, sales for the year are expected to cover all expenses and to provide a cash gain of $106,000, or about 16 percent of sales. However, Stars and Stripes has a problem in the first quarter, when sales are expected to fall short of expenses by $7,000. In fact, one of the primary reasons for financial planning is to provide management with adequate lead time to solve this type of cash-flow problem.

A second type of funding is **equity capital.** For a sole proprietorship or partnership, equity capital is provided by the owner or owners of the business. For a corporation, equity capital is money obtained from the sale of shares of ownership in the business. Equity capital is used almost exclusively for long-term financing. Thus it might be used to start a business and to fund expansions or mergers. It would not be considered for short-term financing needs, such as Stars and Stripes Clothing's first-quarter $7,000 shortfall.

A third type of funding is **debt capital,** which is borrowed money. Debt capital may be borrowed for either short- or long-term use—and a short-term loan seems made to order for Stars and Stripes Clothing's shortfall problem. The firm probably would borrow the needed $7,000 (or perhaps a bit more) at some point during the first quarter and repay it from second-quarter sales revenue. Stars and Stripes Clothing already may have established a line of credit at a local bank to cover just such short-term needs. As discussed in Chapter 19, a *line of credit* is a prearranged short-term loan.

Proceeds from the sale of assets are the fourth type of funding. Selling assets is a drastic step. However, it may be a reasonable last resort when neither equity capital nor debt capital can be found. Assets also may be sold when they are no longer needed or do not "fit" with the company's core business. To concentrate on its core business and to raise financing, General Motors sold its 8.7 percent stake in Japan's Fuji Heavy Industries, the maker of Subaru cars, to Toyota Motor Corporation for $315 million. General Motors also plans to sell its remaining 11.4 percent in Fuji on the open market in an effort to raise an additional $500 million.[6]

Monitoring and Evaluating Financial Performance

It is important to ensure that financial plans are being implemented properly and to catch potential problems before they become major ones. For example, many Internet-based businesses have reduced various expenses in order to become profitable. Even so, many of these high-tech companies have failed in the past few years. Pets.com is an example of a dot-com start-up that lost control of its finances. Backed by Amazon, the firm spent $27 million on television and other media advertising to generate awareness and sales. The funny advertisements presented by the famous talking-dog sock-puppet could not create the critical mass of buyers quickly enough to offset the advertising and other operational costs.

equity capital money received from the owners or from the sale of shares of ownership in a business

debt capital borrowed money obtained through loans of various types

It takes more than a cute advertising gimmick. Although most people enjoyed seeing the Pets.com sock puppet, they didn't buy the firm's products. Pets.com, a dot-com start-up backed by Amazon, spent millions of dollars on television and other media advertising, but failed to generate enough sales revenue to avoid the cash crisis that eventually led to the company's failure.

As a result, the firm lost $5 for every dollar of pet supplies revenue received. This quickly created a cash crisis and eventually led to failure.

To prevent problems such as those just described, financial managers should establish a means of monitoring financial performance. Interim budgets (weekly, monthly, or quarterly) may be prepared for comparison purposes. These comparisons point up areas that require additional or revised planning—or at least areas calling for a more careful investigation. Budget comparisons also can be used to improve the firm's future budgets.

Sources of Short-Term Debt Financing

The decision to borrow money does not necessarily mean that a firm is in financial trouble. On the contrary, astute financial management often means regular, responsible borrowing of many different kinds to meet different needs. In this section we examine the sources of *short-term debt financing* available to businesses. In the next two sections we look at long-term financing options: equity capital and debt capital.

Sources of Unsecured Short-Term Financing

Short-term debt financing (money repaid in one year or less) is usually easier to obtain than long-term debt financing for three reasons:

1. For the lender, the shorter repayment period means less risk of nonpayment.
2. The dollar amounts of short-term loans usually are smaller than those of long-term loans.
3. A close working relationship normally exists between the short-term borrower and the lender.

Most lenders do not require collateral for short-term financing. When they do, it is usually because they are concerned about the size of a particular loan, the borrowing firm's poor credit rating, or the general prospects of repayment.

Unsecured financing is financing that is not backed by collateral. A company seeking unsecured short-term financing has several options.

Trade Credit Manufacturers and wholesalers often provide financial aid to retailers by allowing them thirty to sixty days (or more) in which to pay for merchandise. This delayed payment, known as **trade credit,** is a type of short-term financing extended by a seller who does not require immediate payment after delivery of merchandise. It is the most popular form of short-term financing; 70 to 90 percent of all transactions between businesses involve some trade credit.

Let's assume that a Barnes & Noble bookstore receives a shipment of books from a publisher. Along with the merchandise, the publisher sends an invoice that states the terms of payment. Barnes & Noble now has two options for payment. First, the book retailer may pay the invoice promptly and take advantage of any cash discount the publisher offers. Cash-discount terms are specified on the invoice. For instance, "2/10, net 30" means that the customer—Barnes & Noble—may take a 2 percent discount if it pays the invoice within ten days of the invoice date. Cash discounts can generate substantial savings and lower the cost of purchasing merchandise for a retailer such as Barnes & Noble. Let's assume that the dollar amount of the invoice is $140,000. In this case, the cash discount is $2,800 ($140,000 × 0.02 = $2,800).

A second option is to wait until the end of the credit period before making payment. If payment is made between eleven and thirty days after the date of the invoice, the customer must pay the entire amount. As long as payment is made before the end of the credit period, the customer maintains the ability to purchase additional merchandise using the trade-credit arrangement.

3 LEARNING OBJECTIVE
Describe the advantages and disadvantages of different methods of short-term debt financing.

unsecured financing financing that is not backed by collateral

trade credit a type of short-term financing extended by a seller who does not require immediate payment after delivery of merchandise

When automakers don't sell cars, financial troubles build. In this photo, a group of demonstrators attempts to convince Ford to increase its research efforts to develop automobiles that operate on alternative fuels. For the automaker, this protest couldn't have come at a worse time. Because of lower sales revenues and operating losses, Ford has less money for research and development projects. In addition, financial analysts have lowered the firm's credit rating. Ford's lower credit rating reduces the availability of credit financing and increases the cost of borrowing money.

promissory note a written pledge by a borrower to pay a certain sum of money to a creditor at a specified future date

prime interest rate the lowest rate charged by a bank for a short-term loan

Promissory Notes Issued to Suppliers A **promissory note** is a written pledge by a borrower to pay a certain sum of money to a creditor at a specified future date. Suppliers uneasy about extending trade credit may be less reluctant to offer credit to customers who sign promissory notes. Unlike trade credit, however, promissory notes usually require the borrower to pay interest. Although repayment periods may extend to one year, most short-term promissory notes are repaid in 60 to 180 days.

A promissory note offers two important advantages to the firm extending the credit. First, a promissory note is a legally binding and enforceable document that has been signed by the individual or business borrowing the money. Second, most promissory notes are negotiable instruments, and the supplier (or company extending credit) may be able to discount, or sell, the note to its own bank. If the note is discounted, the dollar amount the supplier would receive is slightly less than the maturity value because the bank charges a fee for the service. The supplier would recoup most of its money immediately, and the bank would collect the maturity value when the note matured.

Unsecured Bank Loans Banks and other financial institutions offer unsecured short-term loans to businesses at interest rates that vary with each borrower's credit rating. The **prime interest rate,** sometimes called the *reference rate*, is the lowest rate charged by a bank for a short-term loan. Figure 20.5 traces the fluctuations in the average prime rate charged by U.S. banks from 1997 to 2005. This lowest rate generally is reserved for large corporations with excellent credit ratings. Organizations with good

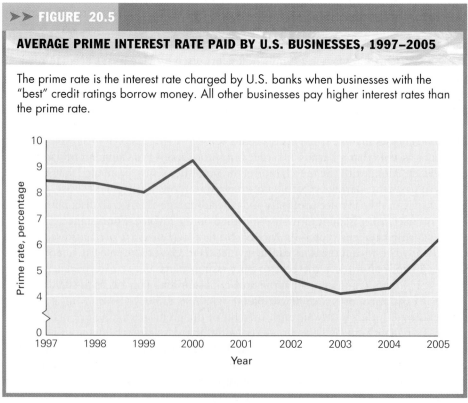

>> FIGURE 20.5

AVERAGE PRIME INTEREST RATE PAID BY U.S. BUSINESSES, 1997–2005

The prime rate is the interest rate charged by U.S. banks when businesses with the "best" credit ratings borrow money. All other businesses pay higher interest rates than the prime rate.

Source: Federal Reserve Bank website: **www.federalreserve.gov,** accessed January 5, 2006.

to high credit ratings may pay the prime rate plus 2 percent. Firms with questionable credit ratings may have to pay the prime rate plus 4 percent. (The fact that a banker charges a higher interest rate for a higher-risk loan is a practical application of the risk-return ratio discussed earlier in this chapter.) Of course, if the banker believes that loan repayment may be a problem, the borrower's loan application may well be rejected.

Banks generally offer unsecured short-term loans through promissory notes, a line of credit, or a revolving credit agreement. A bank promissory note is similar to the promissory note issued by suppliers described in the preceding section. For both types of promissory notes, interest rates and repayment terms may be negotiated between the borrower and a bank or supplier. A bank that offers a promissory note or line of credit may require that a *compensating balance* be kept on deposit at the bank. This balance may be as much as 20 percent of the borrowed funds. Assume that Bank of America requires a 20 percent compensating balance on a short-term promissory note or a line of credit. If you borrow $50,000, at least $10,000 ($50,000 × 0.20 = $10,000) of the loan amount must be kept on deposit at the bank. In this situation, the effective interest rate you must pay on the original $50,000 loan increases because you have the use of only $40,000. The bank also may require that every commercial borrower *clean up* (pay off completely) its short-term promissory note or line of credit at least once each year and not use it again for a period of thirty to sixty days.

Even with a line of credit, a firm may not be able to borrow on short notice if the bank does not have sufficient funds available. For this reason, some firms prefer a *revolving credit agreement*, which is a *guaranteed* line of credit. Under this type of agreement, the bank guarantees that the money will be available when the borrower needs it. In return for the guarantee, the bank charges a commitment fee ranging from 0.25 to 1.0 percent of the *unused* portion of the revolving credit agreement. The usual interest is charged for the portion that *is* borrowed.

Commercial Paper   **Commercial paper** is a short-term promissory note issued by a large corporation. Commercial paper is secured only by the reputation of the issuing firm; no collateral is involved. It is usually issued in large denominations, ranging from $5,000 to $100,000. Corporations issuing commercial paper pay interest rates slightly below the interest rates charged by banks for short-term loans. Thus, issuing commercial paper is cheaper than getting short-term financing from a bank. The interest rate a corporation pays when it issues commercial paper is tied to its credit rating and its ability to repay the commercial paper. For example, when the major U.S. credit-reporting agencies raised the credit ratings of Edison International and Starwood Hotels, these firms paid less to borrow money.[7]

Large firms with excellent credit reputations can raise large sums of money quickly by issuing commercial paper. General Motors Acceptance Corporation (GMAC) and GE Capital, for example, may issue commercial paper totaling millions of dollars. However, commercial paper is not without risks. If a corporation has severe financial problems, it may not be able to repay commercial paper. Enron Corporation, for instance, had issued commercial paper worth millions of dollars at the time of its bankruptcy.[8]

commercial paper a short-term promissory note issued by a large corporation

Sources of Secured Short-Term Financing

If a business cannot obtain enough capital through unsecured financing, it must put up collateral to obtain additional short-term financing. Almost any asset can serve as collateral. However, *inventories* and *accounts receivable* are the assets most commonly pledged for short-term financing. Even when it is willing to pledge collateral to back up a loan, a firm that is financially weak may have difficulty obtaining short-term financing.

Loans Secured by Inventory   Normally, manufacturers, wholesalers, and retailers have large amounts of money invested in finished goods. In addition, manufacturers carry raw materials and work-in-process inventories. All three types of inventory may be pledged as collateral for short-term loans. However, lenders prefer the much more salable finished merchandise to raw materials or work-in-process inventories.

A lender may insist that inventory used as collateral be stored in a public warehouse. In such a case, the receipt issued by the warehouse is retained by the lender. Without this receipt, the public warehouse will not release the merchandise. The lender releases the warehouse receipt—and the merchandise—to the borrower when the borrowed money is repaid. In addition to paying the interest on the loan, the borrower must pay for storage in the public warehouse. As a result, this type of loan is more expensive than an unsecured short-term loan.

A special type of financing called *floor planning* is used by automobile, furniture, and appliance dealers. **Floor planning** is a method of financing in which title to merchandise is given to lenders in return for short-term financing. The major difference between floor planning and other types of secured short-term financing is that the borrower maintains control of the inventory. As merchandise is sold, the borrower repays the lender a portion of the loan, and the lender returns the title to the merchandise sold.

floor planning method of financing in which title to merchandise is given to lenders in return for short-term financing

Loans Secured by Receivables As defined in Chapter 18, *accounts receivable* are amounts owed to a firm by its customers. They are created when trade credit is given to customers and usually are due within thirty to sixty days. A firm can pledge its accounts receivable as collateral to obtain short-term financing. A lender may advance 70 to 80 percent of the dollar amount of the receivables. First, however, it conducts a thorough investigation to determine the *quality* of the receivables. (The quality of the receivables is the credit standing of the firm's customers, coupled with the customers' ability to repay their credit obligations.) If a favorable determination is made, the loan is approved. When the borrowing firm collects from a customer whose account has been pledged as collateral, it must turn the money over to the lender as partial repayment of the loan. An alternative approach is to notify the borrower's credit customers to make their payments directly to the lender.

Factoring Accounts Receivable

factor a firm that specializes in buying other firms' accounts receivable

Accounts receivable may be used in one other way to help raise short-term financing: They can be sold to a factoring company (or factor). A **factor** is a firm that specializes in buying other firms' accounts receivable. The factor buys the accounts receivable for less than their face value, but it collects the full dollar amount when each account is due. The factor's profit thus is the difference between the face value of the accounts receivable and the amount the factor has paid for them. Generally, the amount of profit the factor receives is based on the risk the factor assumes. Risk, in this case, is the probability that the accounts receivable will not be repaid when they mature.

Even though the firm selling its accounts receivable gets less than face value, it does receive needed cash immediately. Moreover, it has shifted both the task of collecting and the risk of nonpayment to the factor, which now owns the accounts receivable. In many cases the factor may purchase only selected accounts receivable—usually those with the highest potential of repayment. In other cases, the firm selling its accounts receivable must obtain approval from the factor *before* selling merchandise to a credit customer. Thus the firm receives instant feedback on whether the factor will purchase the credit customer's account. Generally, customers whose accounts receivable have been factored are given instructions to make their payments directly to the factor.

Cost Comparisons

Table 20.2 compares the various types of short-term financing. As you can see, trade credit is the least expensive. Factoring of accounts receivable is typically the highest-cost method shown.

For many purposes, short-term financing suits a firm's needs perfectly. At other times, however, long-term financing may be more appropriate. In this case, a business may try to raise equity capital or long-term debt capital.

>> **TABLE 20.2**

COMPARISON OF SHORT-TERM FINANCING METHODS

Type of Financing	Cost	Repayment Period	Businesses That May Use It	Comments
Trade credit	Low, if any	30–60 days	All businesses	Usually no finance charge
Promissory note issued to suppliers	Moderate	1 year or less	All businesses	Usually unsecured but requires legal document
Unsecured bank loan	Moderate	1 year or less	All businesses	Promissory note, a line of credit,or revolving credit agreement generally required
Commercial paper	Moderate	1 year or less	Large corporations with high credit ratings	Available only to large firms
Secured loan	High	1 year or less	Firms with questionable credit ratings	Inventory or accounts receivable often used as collateral
Factoring	High	None	Firms that have large numbers of credit customers	Accounts receivable sold to a factor

Sources of Equity Financing

Sources of long-term financing vary with the size and type of business. As mentioned earlier, a sole proprietorship or partnership acquires equity capital (sometimes referred to as *owner's equity*) when the owner or owners invest money in the business. For corporations, equity-financing options include the sale of stock and the use of profits not distributed to owners. All three types of businesses also can obtain venture capital.

4 **LEARNING OBJECTIVE**
Evaluate the advantages and disadvantages of equity financing.

Selling Stock

Some equity capital is used to start every business—sole proprietorship, partnership, or corporation. In the case of corporations, stockholders who buy shares in the company provide equity capital.

Initial Public Offerings An **initial public offering (IPO)** occurs when a corporation sells common stock to the general public for the first time. To raise money, the search engine Google used an IPO and raised over $2 billion that it could use to fund expansion and other business activities.[9] Established companies that plan to raise capital by selling subsidiaries to the public also can use IPOs. For example, at the time of publication, McDonald's was planning to sell shares in its Chipotle casual restaurant subsidiary. The Chipotle

initial public offering (IPO) when a corporation sells common stock to the general public for the first time

You recognize their credit card, but did you know that they just sold stock for the first time? That's right; MasterCard sold stock for the first time in 2006. Although the company has been issuing credit cards for years, its long-awaited initial public offering (IPO) created quite a stir on Wall Street and was one of the largest in the past two years.

SPOTLIGHT

Investment bankers raise billions for corporations

IPO statistics for 2005

Total capital raised $35 billion

Dollar amount raised per deal $173.3 million

Number of IPOs 202

STOCK

Source: The Red Herring website: **www.redherring.com;** accessed January 1, 2006.

IPO could be worth $100 million or more. McDonald's will use the money to fund capital expenditures and expansion of its current business activities. Also, selling off Chipotle will allow McDonald's to concentrate on its core fast-food business.[10] Generally, corporations sell off subsidiaries for two reasons. First, the sale of a subsidiary can boost the value of the firm's core business by shedding a unit that is growing more slowly. Second, the sale of a subsidiary also can bolster corporate finances and improve the parent company's balance sheet if the money is used to reduce corporate debt.

A corporation selling stock often will use an **investment banking firm**— an organization that assists corporations in raising funds, usually by helping to sell new issues of stocks, bonds, or other financial securities. The investment banking firm generally charges a fee of 2 to 20 percent of the proceeds received by the corporation issuing the securities. The size of the commission depends on the financial health of the corporation issuing the new securities and the size of the new security issue.

Although a corporation can have only one IPO, it can sell additional stock after the IPO, assuming that there is a market for the company's stock. Even though the cost of selling stock (often referred to as *flotation costs*) is high, the *ongoing* costs associated with this type of equity financing are low for two reasons. First, the corporation does not have to repay money obtained from the sale of stock because the corporation is under no legal obligation to do so. If you purchase corporate stock and later decide to sell your stock, you may sell it to another investor—not the corporation.

A second advantage of selling stock is that a corporation is under no legal obligation to pay dividends to stockholders. As noted in Chapter 5, a *dividend* is a distribution of earnings to the stockholders of a corporation. For any reason (if a company has a bad year, for example), the board of directors can vote to omit dividend payments. Earnings then are retained for use in funding business operations. Of course, corporate management may hear from unhappy stockholders if expected dividends are omitted too frequently.

There are two types of stock: common and preferred. Each type has advantages and drawbacks as a means of long-term financing.

investment banking firm an organization that assists corporations in raising funds, usually by helping to sell new issues of stocks, bonds, or other financial securities

Common Stock   A share of **common stock** represents the most basic form of corporate ownership. In return for the financing provided by selling common stock, management must make certain concessions to stockholders that may restrict or change corporate policies. By law, every corporation must hold an annual meeting, at which the holders of common stock may vote for the board of directors and approve or disapprove major corporate actions. Among such actions are

common stock stock whose owners may vote on corporate matters but whose claims on profits and assets are subordinate to the claims of others

1. Amendments to the corporate charter or by-laws
2. Sale of certain assets
3. Mergers and acquisitions
4. New issues of preferred stock or bonds
5. Changes in the amount of common stock issued

Few investors will buy common stock unless they believe that their investment will increase in value. Information on the reasons why investors purchase stocks and how to evaluate stock investments is provided in Chapter 21.

Preferred Stock   As noted in Chapter 5, the owners of **preferred stock** must receive their dividends before holders of common stock receive theirs. And preferred stockholders have first claim (after creditors) on assets if the corporation is dissolved or declares bankruptcy. Even so, as with common stock, the board of directors must approve dividends on preferred stock, and this type of financing does not represent a debt that must be legally repaid. In return for preferential treatment, preferred stockholders generally give up the right to vote at a corporation's annual meeting.

The dividend on a share of preferred stock is stated on the stock certificate either as a percent of the par value of the stock or as a specified dollar amount. The **par value** of a stock is an assigned (and often arbitrary) dollar value printed on the stock certificate. For example, Pitney Bowes—a U.S. manufacturer of office and business equipment—issued 4 percent preferred stock with a par value of $50. The annual dividend amount is $2 per share ($50 par value × 0.04 = $2 annual dividend).

Although a corporation usually issues only one type of common stock, it may issue many types of preferred stock with varying dividends or dividend rates. For example, New York–based Consolidated Edison has one common-stock issue but two preferred-stock issues with different dividend amounts for each type of preferred stock.

When a corporation believes that it can issue new preferred stock at a lower dividend rate (or common stock with no specified dividend), it may decide to "call in," or buy back, an earlier stock issue. In this case, management has two options. First, it can buy shares in the market—just like any other investor. Second, it can exercise a call provision because practically all preferred stock is *callable*. When considering the two options, management naturally will obtain the preferred stock in the less costly way.

To make preferred stock more attractive to investors, some corporations include a conversion feature. **Convertible preferred stock** is preferred stock that an owner may exchange for a specified number of shares of common stock. The Textron Corporation—a manufacturer of component parts for the automotive and aerospace industries—has issued convertible preferred stock. Each share of Textron preferred stock is convertible to 4.4 shares of the firm's common stock. This conversion feature provides the investor with the safety of preferred stock and the hope of greater speculative gain through conversion to common stock.

Retained Earnings

Most large corporations distribute only a portion of their after-tax earnings to stockholders. The portion of a corporation's profits not distributed to stockholders is called **retained earnings.** Because they are undistributed profits, retained earnings are considered a form of equity financing.

The amount of retained earnings in any year is determined by corporate management and approved by the board of directors. Most small and growing corporations pay no cash dividend—or a very small dividend—to their stockholders. All or most earnings are reinvested in the business for R&D, expansion, or the funding of major projects. Reinvestment tends to increase the value of the firm's stock while it provides essentially cost-free financing for the business. More mature corporations may distribute 40 to 60 percent of their after-tax profits as dividends. Utility companies and other corporations with very stable earnings often pay out as much as 80 to 90 percent of what they earn. For a large corporation, retained earnings can amount to a hefty bit of financing. For example, in 2004, the total amount of retained earnings for General Electric was almost $91 billion.[11]

Venture Capital and Private Placements

To establish a new business or expand an existing one, an entrepreneur may try to obtain venture capital. In Chapter 6 we defined *venture capital* as money invested in small

preferred stock stock whose owners usually do not have voting rights but whose claims on dividends and assets are paid before those of common-stock owners

par value an assigned (and often arbitrary) dollar value printed on a stock certificate

convertible preferred stock preferred stock that an owner may exchange for a specified number of shares of common stock

retained earnings the portion of a corporation's profits not distributed to stockholders

Computer electrical engineer or venture capitalist? Five years after engineering a better computer chip, Win-Mei Hwu is teaching at the University of Illinois while his company sells the improved technology to other high-tech companies. Because his invention was developed from university research, the University of Illinois gets a cut of the profits, which it has used to finance a venture capital fund to help other entrepreneurs start new businesses.

(and sometimes struggling) firms that have the potential to become very successful. Most venture capital firms do not invest in the typical small business—a neighborhood convenience store or a local dry cleaner—but in firms that have the potential to become extremely profitable. And while venture capital firms are willing to take chances, they are also more selective about where they invest their money after the high-tech bust that occurred in the last part of the 1990s and first part of the twenty-first century.

Generally, a venture capital firm consists of a pool of investors, a traditional partnership established by a wealthy family, or a joint venture formed by corporations with money to invest. In return for financing, these investors generally receive an equity position in the business and share in its profits. Venture capital firms vary in size and scope of interest. Some offer financing for start-up businesses, whereas others finance only established businesses. In addition to venture capital firms, smaller boutique private equity groups also provide financing for entrepreneurs. For more information about private equity boutiques, read the Entrepreneurial Challenge.

ENTREPRENEURIAL CHALLENGE

Finding the Money

How can an entrepreneur find the money for expansion, an important acquisition, or a new R&D initiative? Obtaining financing from a boutique private equity group can be a good alternative. Boutique private equity groups are like venture capital firms but much, much smaller. They often provide financing for companies too small to go public or attract the interest of the large venture capital firms.

Advantages

- The owner gets an infusion of funding without selling the business or going into debt.
- The owner benefits from the boutique's specialization, expertise, and advice.
- The boutique can provide a reality check on the owner's financial management skills.

Disadvantages

- Some boutiques insist on a majority interest in exchange for a sizable investment.
- The owner may chafe at the boutique's close scrutiny of company affairs.
- The owner may have to give control to the boutique if the investment doesn't achieve a specified rate of return.

Another method of raising capital is through a private placement. A **private placement** occurs when stock and other corporate securities are sold directly to insurance companies, pension funds, or large institutional investors. When compared with selling stocks and other corporate securities to the public, there are often fewer government regulations and the cost is generally less when the securities are sold through a private placement. Typically, terms between the buyer and seller are negotiated when a private placement is used to raise capital.

private placement occurs when stock and other corporate securities are sold directly to insurance companies, pension funds, or large institutional investors

Sources of Long-Term Debt Financing

As we pointed out earlier in this chapter, businesses borrow money on a short-term basis for many valid reasons other than desperation. There are equally valid reasons for long-term borrowing. In addition to using borrowed money to meet the long-term needs listed in Table 20.1, successful businesses often use the financial leverage it creates to improve their financial performance. **Financial leverage** is the use of borrowed funds to increase the return on owners' equity. The principle of financial leverage works as long as a firm's earnings are larger than the interest charged for the borrowed money.

To understand how financial leverage can increase a firm's return on owners' equity, study the information for Texas-based Cypress Springs Plastics presented in Table 20.3. Pete Johnston, the owner of the firm, is trying to decide how best to finance a $100,000 purchase of new high-tech manufacturing equipment. He could borrow the money and pay 9 percent annual interest. As a second option, Johnston could invest an additional $100,000 in the firm. Assuming that the firm earns $95,000 a year and that annual interest for this loan totals $9,000 ($100,000 × 0.09 = $9,000), the return on owners' equity for Cypress Springs Plastics would be higher if the firm borrowed the additional financing. Return on owners' equity—a topic covered in Chapter 18—is determined by dividing a firm's net income by the dollar amount of owners' equity. For Cypress Springs Plastics, return on owners' equity equals 17.2 percent ($86,000 ÷ $500,000 = 0.172, or 17.2 percent) if Johnston borrows the additional $100,000. The firm's return on owners' equity would decrease to 15.8 percent ($95,000 ÷ $600,000 = 0.158, or 15.8 percent) if Johnston invests an additional $100,000 in the business.

5 LEARNING OBJECTIVE
Evaluate the advantages and disadvantages of long-term debt financing.

financial leverage the use of borrowed funds to increase the return on owners' equity

> > **TABLE 20.3**

ANALYSIS OF THE EFFECT OF ADDITIONAL CAPITAL FROM DEBT OR EQUITY FOR CYPRESS SPRINGS PLASTICS, INC.

Additional Debt		Additional Equity	
Owners' equity	$ 500,000	Owners' equity	$ 500,000
Additional equity	+0	Additional equity	+100,000
Total equity	$ 500,000	Total equity	$ 600,000
Loan (@ 9 percent)	+100,000	No loan	+0
Total capital	$ 600,000	Total capital	$ 600,000
Year-End Earnings			
Gross profit	$ 95,000	Gross profit	$ 95,000
Less loan interest	− 9,000	No interest	− 0
Operating profit	$ 86,000	Operating profit	$ 95,000
Return on owners' equity	17.2%	Return on owners' equity	15.8%
($86,000 ÷ $500,000 = 17.2%)		($95,000 ÷ $600,000 = 15.8%)	

The most obvious danger when using financial leverage is that the firm's earnings may be less than expected. If this situation occurs, the fixed interest charge actually works to reduce or eliminate the return on owners' equity. Of course, borrowed money eventually must be repaid. Finally, because lenders always have the option to turn down a loan request, many managers are reluctant to rely on borrowed money.

A company that cannot obtain a long-term loan to acquire property, buildings, and equipment may be able to lease these assets. A **lease** is an agreement by which the right to use real estate, equipment, or other assets is transferred temporarily from the owner to the user. The owner of the leased item is called the *lessor*; the user is called the *lessee*. With the typical lease agreement, the lessee makes regular payments on a monthly, quarterly, or yearly basis. Even when a firm is able to obtain long-term debt financing, it may choose to lease assets because, under the right circumstances, a lease can have tax advantages.

For a small business, long-term debt financing generally is limited to loans. Large corporations have the additional option of issuing corporate bonds.

Long-Term Loans

Many businesses finance their long-range activities such as those listed in Table 20.1 with loans from commercial banks, insurance companies, pension funds, and other financial institutions. Manufacturers and suppliers of heavy machinery also may provide long-term debt financing by granting extended credit to their customers.

lease an agreement by which the right to use real estate, equipment, or other assets is transferred temporarily from the owner to the user

term-loan agreement a promissory note that requires a borrower to repay a loan in monthly, quarterly, semiannual, or annual installments

Term-Loan Agreements　When the loan repayment period is longer than one year, the borrower must sign a term-loan agreement. A **term-loan agreement** is a promissory note that requires a borrower to repay a loan in monthly, quarterly, semiannual, or annual installments. Although repayment may be as long as fifteen to twenty years, long-term business loans normally are repaid in three to seven years.

Assume that Pete Johnson, the owner of Cypress Springs Plastics, decides to borrow $100,000 and take advantage of the principle of financial leverage illustrated in Table 20.3. Although the firm's return on owners' equity does increase, interest must be paid each year, and eventually, the loan must be repaid. To pay off a $100,000 loan over a three-year period with annual payments, Cypress Springs Plastics must pay $33,333 on the loan balance plus $9,000 annual interest, or a total of $42,333 the first year. While the amount of interest decreases each year because of the previous year's payment on the loan balance, annual payments of this amount are still a large commitment for a small firm such as Cypress Springs Plastics.

The interest rate and repayment terms for term loans often are based on such factors as the reasons for borrowing, the borrowing firm's credit rating, and the value of collateral. Although long-term loans occasionally may be unsecured, the lender usually requires some type of collateral. Acceptable collateral includes real estate, machinery, and equipment. Lenders also may require that borrowers maintain a minimum amount of working capital. Finally, lenders

EXAMINING ETHICS

Bank Lending Goes Green

Under pressure from activists and investors, major banks now take into account both environmental effects and financial criteria when evaluating commercial loan applications. Many major international banks have adopted the Equator Principles. In banking and financial circles, the Equator Principles refer to guidelines used to manage environmental and social issues in project financing. In addition to the Equator Principles, some lenders use the term *green lending* to reflect environmental and social concerns. Here's a sample of how some major lenders have adapted their lending policies to include environmental and social concerns:

● *JPMorgan Chase* now checks the environmental impact of all loans over $50 million, as well as loans exceeding $10 million made to energy, forestry, and mining companies.
● *Bank of America* refuses to finance logging projects that might endanger sensitive forest areas around the world.
● *Wells Fargo Bank* pledges to provide $1 billion worth of financing for sustainable forestry and other ecologically friendly projects.

Green lending is a priority for HSBC Bank because "everyone is interested in the balance between sustainability and economic development," says a senior executive. "We believe you can do well and do good."

may consider the environmental and social impact of the projects they are asked to finance before funding a loan request.

The Basics of Getting a Loan   According to many financial experts, preparation is the key when applying for a long-term business loan. In reality, preparation begins before you ever apply for the loan. To begin the process, you should get to know potential lenders before requesting debt financing. While there may be many potential lenders that can provide the money you need, the logical place to borrow money is where your business does its banking. This fact underscores the importance of maintaining adequate balances in the firm's bank accounts. Before applying for a loan, you also may want to check your firm's credit rating with a national credit bureau such as D&B (formerly known as Dun & Bradstreet).

Typically, you will be asked to fill out a loan application. In addition to the loan application, the lender also will want to see your current business plan. Be sure to explain what your business is, how much funding you require to accomplish your goals and objectives, and how the loan will be repaid. Next, have your certified public accountant (CPA) prepare financial statements. Most lenders insist that you submit current financial statements that have been prepared by an independent CPA along with your business plan. Then compile a list of references that includes your suppliers, other lenders, or the professionals with whom you are associated. Once you submit your application, business plan, and supporting financial documents, a bank officer or a loan committee will examine the loan application. You also may be asked to discuss the loan request with a loan officer. Hopefully, your loan request will be approved. If not, try to determine why your loan request was rejected. Think back over the loan process and determine what you could do to improve your chances of getting a loan the next time you apply.

Corporate Bonds

In addition to loans, large corporations may choose to issue bonds in denominations of $1,000 to $50,000. Although the usual face value for corporate bonds is $1,000, the total face value of all the bonds in an issue usually amounts to millions of dollars. In fact, one of the reasons why corporations sell bonds is that they can borrow a lot of money from a lot of different bondholders and raise larger amounts of money than could be borrowed from one lender. A **corporate bond** is a corporation's written pledge that it will repay a specified amount of money with interest. Figure 20.6 shows a corporate bond for the American & Foreign Power Company. Note that it includes the interest rate (5 percent) and the maturity date. The **maturity date** is the date on which the corporation is to repay the borrowed money. The bond also has spaces for the amount of the bond, the registration number, and the bond owner's name. Today, many corporations do not issue actual bonds like the one illustrated in Figure 20.6. Instead, the bonds are recorded electronically, and the specific details regarding the bond issue, along with the current owner's name and address, are maintained by computer. While some people like to have physical possession of their corporate bonds, computer entries are easier to transfer when a bond is sold. Computer entries also are safer because they cannot be stolen, misplaced, or destroyed—all concerns that you must worry about if you take physical possession of a corporate bond.

Until a bond's maturity, a corporation pays interest to the bond owner at the stated rate. Owners of the American & Foreign Power Company bond receive 5 percent per year for each bond. Because interest for corporate bonds is usually paid semi-annually, bond owners receive a payment every six months for each bond they own.

Types of Bonds   Today, most corporate bonds are registered bonds. A **registered bond**—like the American & Foreign Power Company bond—is a bond registered in the owner's name by the issuing company. Until the maturity date, the registered owner receives periodic interest payments. On the maturity date, the owner returns a registered bond to the corporation and receives cash equaling the face value.

Corporate bonds generally are classified as debentures, mortgage bonds, or convertible bonds. Most corporate bonds are debenture bonds. A **debenture bond** is a

corporate bond a corporation's written pledge that it will repay a specified amount of money with interest

maturity date the date on which a corporation is to repay borrowed money

registered bond a bond registered in the owner's name by the issuing company

debenture bond a bond backed only by the reputation of the issuing corporation

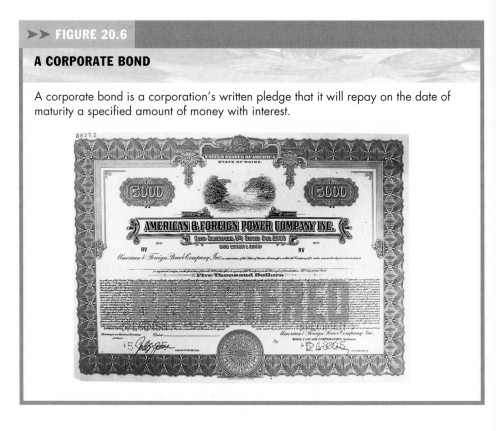

▶▶ FIGURE 20.6

A CORPORATE BOND

A corporate bond is a corporation's written pledge that it will repay on the date of maturity a specified amount of money with interest.

---

mortgage bond a corporate bond secured by various assets of the issuing firm

convertible bond a bond that can be exchanged, at the owner's option, for a specified number of shares of the corporation's common stock

bond backed only by the reputation of the issuing corporation. To make its bonds more appealing to investors, a corporation may issue mortgage bonds. A **mortgage bond** is a corporate bond secured by various assets of the issuing firm. Typical corporate assets that are used as collateral for a mortgage bond include real estate, machinery, and equipment that is not pledged as collateral for other debt obligations. The corporation also can issue convertible bonds. A **convertible bond** can be exchanged, at the owner's option, for a specified number of shares of the corporation's common stock. Kerr McGee's bond that matures in 2010 is convertible: Each bond can be converted to 16.373 shares of Kerr McGee common stock. A corporation can gain in three ways by issuing convertible bonds. First, convertibles usually carry a lower interest rate than nonconvertible bonds. Second, the conversion feature attracts investors who are interested in the speculative gain that conversion to common stock may provide. Third, if the bondholder converts to common stock, the corporation no longer has to redeem the bond at maturity.

Repayment Provisions for Corporate Bonds   Maturity dates for bonds generally range from ten to thirty years after the date of issue. If the interest is not paid or the firm becomes insolvent, bond owners' claims on the assets of the corporation take precedence over the claims of both common and preferred stockholders. Some bonds are callable before the maturity date; that is, a corporation can buy back, or redeem, them. For these bonds, the corporation may pay the bond owner a call premium. The amount of the call premium is specified, along with other provisions, in the bond indenture. The **bond indenture** is a legal document that details all the conditions relating to a bond issue.

bond indenture a legal document that details all the conditions relating to a bond issue

Before deciding if bonds are the best way to obtain corporate financing, managers must determine if the company can afford to pay the interest on the corporate bonds. It should be obvious that the larger the bond issue, the higher the dollar amount of interest will be. For example, assume that American Express issues bonds with a face value of $100 million. If the interest rate is 4.875 percent, the interest on this bond issue is $4,875,000 ($100 million × 0.04875 = $4,875,000) each year until the bonds are repaid. In addition, corporate bonds must be redeemed for their face value at maturity. If the corporation defaults on (does not pay) either interest payments or repayment of the bond at maturity, owners of bonds can force the firm into bankruptcy.

A corporation may use one of three methods to ensure that it has sufficient funds available to redeem a bond issue. First, it can issue the bonds as **serial bonds,** which are bonds of a single issue that mature on different dates. For example, a company may use a twenty-five-year $50 million bond issue to finance its expansion. None of the bonds mature during the first fifteen years. Thereafter, 10 percent of the bonds mature each year until all the bonds are retired at the end of the twenty-fifth year. Second, the corporation can establish a sinking fund. A **sinking fund** is a sum of money to which deposits are made each year for the purpose of redeeming a bond issue. When Pacific Gas & Electric Company sold a $200 million bond issue, the company agreed to contribute to a sinking fund twice a year until the bond's maturity in the year 2024. Third, a corporation can pay off an old bond issue by selling new bonds. Although this may appear to perpetuate the corporation's long-term debt, a number of utility companies and railroads use this repayment method.

A corporation that issues bonds also must appoint a **trustee,** an individual or an independent firm that acts as the bond owners' representative. A trustee's duties are handled most often by a commercial bank or other large financial institution. The corporation must report to the trustee periodically regarding its ability to make interest payments and eventually redeem the bonds. In turn, the trustee transmits this information to the bond owners, along with its own evaluation of the corporation's ability to pay.

serial bonds bonds of a single issue that mature on different dates

sinking fund a sum of money to which deposits are made each year for the purpose of redeeming a bond issue

trustee an individual or an independent firm that acts as a bond owners' representative

Cost Comparisons

Table 20.4 compares some of the methods that can be used to obtain long-term equity *and* debt financing. Although the initial cost of issuing stock is high, selling common stock generally is the first choice for most financial managers. Once the stock is sold and upfront costs are paid, the *ongoing* costs of using stock to finance a business are low. The type of long-term financing that generally has the highest *ongoing* costs is a long-term loan (debt).

To a great extent, firms are financed through the investments of individuals— money that people have deposited in banks or have used to purchase stocks, mutual funds, and bonds. In Chapter 21 we look at securities markets and how they help people to invest their money in business.

>> **TABLE 20.4**

COMPARISON OF LONG-TERM FINANCING METHODS

Type of Financing	Repayment	Repayment Period	Cost/Dividends Interest	Businesses That May Use It
Equity				
Common stock	No	None	High initial cost; low ongoing costs because dividends not required	All corporations that sell stock to investors
Preferred stock	No	None	Dividends not required but must be paid before common stockholders receive any dividends	Large corporations that have an established investor base of common stockholders
Debt				
Long-term loan	Yes	Usually 3–7 years	Interest rates between 7 and 13 percent depending on economic conditions and the financial stability of the company requesting the loan	All firms that can meet the lender's repayment and collateral requirements
Corporate bond	Yes	Usually 10–30 years	Interest rates between 5 and 10 percent depending on economic conditions and the financial stability of the company issuing the bonds	Large corporations that investors trust

RETURN TO   Inside Business

Bowie Bonds were the first long-term investments to be secured by future earnings of song royalties. James Brown, Ashford & Simpson, and the Isley Brothers also have issued bonds secured by their hit-song royalties. Although some experts predicted an upswing in celebrity bonds secured by athletes' endorsement earnings, for example, or authors' book royalties, few such asset-based securities have emerged since Bowie Bonds were created in the late 1990s.

A few years ago, Bowie Bonds were downgraded by Moody's Investors Service "due to weakness in sales for recorded music" as free song downloads and music swapping became popular. Nonetheless, Bowie Bonds have continued paying Prudential the promised 8 percent annual interest. Now the enormous success of iTunes and other online music stores could pave the way for new investments based on future royalty earnings from the sale of downloaded songs and cell phone ringtones.

Questions

1. Based on Internet or library research, determine how the bond ratings issued by Moody's Investors Service affect the investment value of a bond.
2. Do you think Prudential should have sold its holdings in Bowie Bonds after the Moody's downgrade? Explain your answer.

▶▶ CHAPTER REVIEW

Summary

1

Explain the need for financial management in business.

Financial management consists of all activities concerned with obtaining money and using it effectively. Short-term financing is money that will be used for one year or less. There are many short-term needs, but cash flow and inventory are two for which financing is often required. Long-term financing is money that will be used for more than one year. Such financing may be required for a business start-up, for a merger or acquisition, for new product development, for long-term marketing activities, for replacement of equipment, or for expansion of facilities. Financial management can be viewed as a two-sided problem. On one side, the uses of funds often dictate the type or types of financing needed by a business. On the other side, the activities a business can undertake are determined by the types of financing available. Financial managers also must consider the risk-return ratio when making decisions. The risk-return ratio is based on the

principle that a high-risk decision should generate higher financial returns for a business. On the other hand, more conservative decisions generate lesser returns. Financial managers must ensure that funds are available when needed, that they are obtained at the lowest possible cost, and that they are available for the repayment of debts.

2

Summarize the process of planning for financial management.

A financial plan begins with an organization's goals and objectives. Next, these goals and objectives are "translated" into departmental budgets that detail expected income and expenses. From these budgets, which may be combined into an overall cash budget, the financial manager determines what funding will be needed and where it may be obtained. Whereas departmental and cash budgets emphasize short-term financing needs, a capital budget can be used to estimate a firm's expenditures for major assets and its long-term financing needs. The four principal sources of financing are sales revenues, equity capital, debt capital, and proceeds from the sale of assets. Once the needed funds have been obtained, the financial manager is responsible for ensuring that they are used properly. This is accomplished through a system of monitoring and evaluating the firm's financial activities.

3

Describe the advantages and disadvantages of different methods of short-term debt financing.

Most short-term financing is unsecured; that is, no collateral is required. Sources of unsecured short-term financing include trade credit, promissory notes issued to suppliers, unsecured bank loans, and commercial paper. Sources of secured short-term financing include loans secured by inventory and accounts receivable. A firm also may sell its receivables to factors. Trade credit is the least expensive source of short-term financing. The cost of financing through other sources generally depends on the source and on the credit rating of the firm that requires the financing. Factoring generally is the most expensive approach.

4

Evaluate the advantages and disadvantages of equity financing.

A corporation can raise equity capital by selling either common or preferred stock. Common stock is voting stock; holders of common stock elect the corporation's directors and must approve changes to the corporate charter. Holders of preferred stock must be paid dividends before holders of common stock are paid any dividends. Another source of equity funding is retained earnings, which is the portion of a business's profits not distributed to stockholders. Venture capital—money invested in small (and sometimes struggling) firms that have the potential to become very successful—is yet another source of equity funding. Generally, the venture capital is provided by investors, partnerships established by wealthy families, or a joint venture formed by corporations with money to invest. In return, they receive an equity position in the firm and share in the profits of the business. Finally, a private placement can be used to sell stocks and other corporate securities.

5

Evaluate the advantages and disadvantages of long-term debt financing.

For a small business, debt financing generally is limited to loans. Large corporations have the additional option of issuing corporate bonds. Regardless of whether the business is small or large, it can take advantage of financial leverage. Financial leverage is the use of borrowed funds to increase the return on owners' equity. The rate of interest for long-term loans usually depends on the financial status of the borrower, the reason for borrowing, and the kind of collateral pledged to back up the loan. Long-term business loans normally are

repaid in three to seven years but can be as long as fifteen to twenty years. Money realized from the sale of corporate bonds must be repaid when the bonds mature. In addition, the corporation must pay interest on that money from the time the bonds are sold until maturity. Maturity dates for bonds generally range from ten to thirty years after the date of issue. Three types of bonds—debentures, mortgage bonds, and convertible bonds—are sold to raise debt capital. When comparing the cost of equity and debt long-term financing, the ongoing costs of using stock (equity) to finance a business are low. The most expensive is a long-term loan (debt).

Key Terms

You should now be able to define and give an example relevant to each of the following terms:

financial management (665)
short-term financing (665)
cash flow (665)
speculative production (666)
long-term financing (667)
risk-return ratio (667)
chief financial officer (CFO) (669)
financial plan (669)
budget (670)
cash budget (670)
zero-base budgeting (671)
capital budget (671)
equity capital (672)
debt capital (672)
unsecured financing (673)
trade credit (673)
promissory note (674)
prime interest rate (674)
commercial paper (675)
floor planning (676)
factor (676)
initial public offering (IPO) (677)
investment banking firm (678)
common stock (678)
preferred stock (679)
par value (679)
convertible preferred stock (679)
retained earnings (679)
private placement (681)
financial leverage (681)
lease (682)
term-loan agreement (682)
corporate bond (683)
maturity date (683)
registered bond (683)
debenture bond (683)
mortgage bond (684)
convertible bond (684)
bond indenture (684)
serial bonds (685)
sinking fund (685)
trustee (685)

Review Questions

1. How does short-term financing differ from long-term financing? Give two business uses for each type of financing.
2. In your own words, describe the risk-return ratio.
3. What is the function of a cash budget? A capital budget?
4. What is zero-base budgeting? How does it differ from the traditional concept of budgeting?
5. What are four general sources of funds?
6. How does a financial manager monitor and evaluate a firm's financing?
7. How important is trade credit as a source of short-term financing?
8. Why would a supplier require a customer to sign a promissory note?
9. What is the prime rate? Who gets the prime rate?
10. What is the difference between a line of credit and a revolving credit agreement?
11. Explain how factoring works. Of what benefit is factoring to a firm that sells its receivables?
12. What are the advantages of financing through the sale of stock?
13. From a corporation's point of view, how does preferred stock differ from common stock?
14. Where do a corporation's retained earnings come from? What are the advantages of this type of financing?
15. What is venture capital?
16. Describe how financial leverage can increase return on owners' equity.

17. For a corporation, what are the advantages of corporate bonds over long-term loans?
18. Describe the three methods used to ensure that funds are available to redeem corporate bonds at maturity.

Discussion Questions

1. What does a financial manager do? How can he or she monitor a firm's financial success?
2. If you were the financial manager of Stars and Stripes Clothing, what would you do with the excess cash that the firm expects in the second and fourth quarters? (See Figure 20.4.)
3. Develop a *personal* cash budget for the next six months. Explain what you would do if there are budget shortfalls or excess cash amounts at the end of any month during the six-month period.
4. Why would a supplier offer both trade credit and cash discounts to its customers?
5. Why would a lender offer unsecured loans when it could demand collateral?
6. How can a small-business owner or corporate manager use financial leverage to improve the firm's profits and return on owners' equity?
7. In what circumstances might a large corporation sell stock rather than bonds to obtain long-term financing? In what circumstances would it sell bonds rather than stock?

▶▶ VIDEO CASE 20.1

Gilford Securities' Financial Matchmaking: Easier Than Dating

Companies need money for operations and growth, and investors need good investments. This is where Gilford Securities comes in. Since 1979, employee-owned Gilford has served as an investment matchmaker, helping small and midsized companies to raise money through IPOs and private debt placements. In addition to investment banking expertise, it has a full-service brokerage unit to buy and sell securities for individual and institutional investors. And to enhance its matchmaking capabilities, Gilford maintains a staff of expert research analysts who search out and study undervalued securities to identify good investment opportunities for the investors who use its brokerage services.

In a twenty-four-month period, matchmaker Gilford helped fifteen companies obtain capital. Its initial and secondary public offerings range in size from $5 million to $25 million; its private placements range from $5 million to $20 million. Although such numbers generally are too small to capture the attention of giant Wall Street investment banking firms, they are the right size for Gilford. Its specialists know that preparing for an IPO can be traumatic for a growing company and its

management team. This is why they work closely with companies during every step in the process, from compiling and filing the necessary financial information to scheduling the offering, setting the initial share price, and arranging for the stock to begin and continue trading. After a transaction, Gilford tracks the performance of the companies it has taken public and issues regular research reports for current and prospective investors. Rather than hopping from deal to deal, Gilford carefully follows up after every transaction to be sure that each company's needs have been satisfied properly. This approach has earned the firm a reputation for building long-term relationships.

The first contact some companies have with Gilford is through its research analysts. For example, the CEO of Pennsylvania Enterprises was extremely impressed after a Gilford analyst researched his company and wrote a report demonstrating a thorough understanding of the company and the industry. Since that contact, Pennsylvania Enterprises has become an enthusiastic customer.

Casey Alexander, a senior vice president, explains that researching companies is challenging and time-consuming but essential if Gilford is to unearth potential investment opportunities for its institutional and individual brokerage customers. One clue he uses is whether managers and directors are buying their own company's stock and the level of their purchases. If insiders are buying heavily, then he digs deeper to find the catalyst prompting these investments so that he can alert Gilford's brokerage customers to the opportunity. Does the company have a new product, a new process, or a new patent? What special circumstances might induce insiders to make sizable investments that clearly are not guaranteed to pay off? Alexander and his team do not stop researching until they come up with answers.

By analyzing companies that few other firms research and recognizing stocks that seem poised to increase in value, Gilford helps its brokerage customers wring the most from their investment dollars. In some cases the firm even can arrange for large investors to meet with the management of companies whose stock its analysts are recommending for purchase. However, not every recommendation is a "buy." When they uncover emerging problems owing to the environment, competition, or other factors that affect a corporation, Gilford's analysts will issue reports explaining their reasoning and suggesting that customers consider selling the stock.

Yet, having an investment banking group to advise companies and a research team to advise customers on the brokerage side of the business is a delicate balancing act these days. Gilford's Howard Perkins stresses that the company upholds the highest ethical standards as part of its commitment to professionalism and customer service. In fact, top brokers join Gilford because they know that they will have the freedom to do what's right for their customers. Over time, Gilford's customer orientation has helped Gilford to build a loyal customer base and to expand nationwide despite intense competition in the brokerage business. The firm now has 150 employees spread across offices in New York City and other locations.[12]

For more information about this company, go to **www.gilfordsecurities.com.**

Questions

1. Imagine you're an analyst researching a toy manufacturer that relies on speculative production to prepare for the year-end holiday sales period. What questions would you ask the company before determining whether to recommend its stock to investors?
2. In addition to significant insider buying, what other clues might Casey Alexander use in identifying companies that could be profitable investments for Gilford's brokerage customers?
3. Why do you think going public can be traumatic for a company's management team? How does Gilford make the process easier for a firm selling a new securities issue?
4. If you were the owner of a growing business in need of capital, what questions would you ask when choosing an investment bank to take your company public?

►► CASE 20.2

The Mountain Thyme Inn Buys the Farm

Mike and Rhonda Hicks dreamed of opening their own bed-and-breakfast business after vacationing in cozy New England inns during one colorful fall season. The would-be entrepreneurs lived in Dallas, where Mike worked in the software industry. Although the two talked and talked about running a bed-and-breakfast, they didn't actually pursue the idea until pushed by Polly Felker, Rhonda's mother.

Felker had retired to Hot Springs, Arkansas, and was working on an herb farm twenty miles out of town in rural Jessieville, at the edge of the Ouachita National Forest. After listening to her daughter and son-in-law kick around the bed-and-breakfast concept any number of times, Felker told them to get down to business. The couple sought permission to buy nine scenic acres from the herb farm. Then they hired an architect to design an attractive country inn with eight spacious guest rooms, an old-fashioned wraparound porch, and private quarters for the owners. The Hickses estimated that purchasing the land, building the inn, buying furniture, and landscaping the property would cost nearly $600,000.

The next step was to get financing for what would be called the Mountain Thyme Bed & Breakfast Inn. The entrepreneurs approached bank after bank, explaining their idea and showing their plans, but could not get their loan application past worried bankers. Was the inn located too far from the well-known spa town of Hot Springs? Would guests find their way through the back roads and down the secluded gravel driveway to the inn? What about the size of the loan? "When you're used to doing simple little home mortgages, funding a project with that kind of price tag was indeed a scary thing," Mike Hicks observes.

After eighteen months of searching, the couple located a financial institution in California that agreed to approve part of the funding as a Small Business Administration loan. The couple also was introduced to the Arkansas Certified Development Corp. (ACDC), part of the nonprofit Arkansas Capital Corporation Group, which specializes in financing small businesses within the state. When an ACDC loan officer drove to Jessieville to see the site of the proposed inn, "he thought it was a little slice of heaven and fell in love with it," Rhonda Hicks remembers. The ACDC allowed the Hickses to borrow the money they needed at a good rate—and construction on the inn finally could begin.

Polly Felker joined her daughter and son-in-law as a partner in the inn. Chef Felker has been cooking up gourmet breakfasts and late-night treats since Mountain Thyme opened in 1998. The inn's comfortable rooms, beautiful surroundings, and delectable food have brought it nationwide acclaim. Moreover, the owners have been listed among the Top 10 Friendliest Innkeepers in the United States.

Now that their dream of operating an inn has come true, the owners host seminars so that others can learn all about the business of inn ownership. They're always improving the inn with new snacks, new services, new gift items, and more. Although the inn isn't always full, its occupancy rate is high enough to make Mountain Thyme a financial success—and to allow the three partners to take a little time off now and then. Despite the years of planning and hard work, Mike Hicks says, "There'd be no bed-and-breakfast" without the funding approved by the ACDC. "But other than the trouble we had finding some money in the beginning, it'd be hard for this to be working out any better."[13]

For more information about this company, go to **www.mountainthyme.com**.

Questions

1. If you were a banker, would you have approved the loan the Hickses needed to build their bed-and-breakfast? Explain your answer.
2. How can establishing realistic goals and objectives, budgeting, and monitoring and evaluating financial performance help the Hickses to manage the Mountain Thyme Inn?
3. Why would the owners need a capital budget for Mountain Thyme years after its opening?
4. Often small businesses such as this bed-and-breakfast struggle to make ends meet. And yet there is no shortage of people who want to become entrepreneurs. After reading this case and how difficult it was for the Hickses to obtain financing, were the benefits of a small business such as this bed-and-breakfast worth the effort? Justify your answer.

→ CHAPTER 20: JOURNAL EXERCISE

Discovery statement: Do you feel like your financial affairs are always in a mess? Have you ever been turned down for a loan? Have you ever run out of money before the next payday? If you answered yes to any of these questions, you may need to take corrective action and do a better job of managing your finances.

Today, many people spend more than they make on a regular basis. To make matters worse, they often use credit cards to make routine daily purchases. As a result, the amount they owe on credit cards increases each month, and there is no money left to begin a savings or investment program. This exercise will help you to understand (1) how you manage your credit cards and (2) what steps you can take to improve your personal finances. To begin, answer the following three questions.

How many credit cards do you have?

_____

Based on the information on your monthly credit-card statements, what types of credit-card purchases do you make?

_____

_____

_____

_____

_____

Do you pay your balance in full each month *or* make minimum payments on your credit cards?

_____

_____

_____

_____

Now read the following information.

Most experts recommend that you have one or two credit cards that you use only if you are in an emergency situation. The experts also recommend that you avoid using credit cards to make inexpensive purchases on a daily basis. Finally, the experts recommend that you pay your credit-card balance in full each month.

Based on the preceding information, what steps can you take to better manage your finances?

_____

_____

_____

_____

_____

BUILDING SKILLS FOR CAREER SUCCESS

1. Exploring the Internet

Finding capital for new business start-ups is never an easy task. Besides a good business plan, those seeking investor funds must be convincing and clear about how their business activities will provide sufficient revenue to pay back investors who help to get them going in the first place. To find out what others have done, it is useful to read histories of successful start-ups as well as failures in journals that specialize in this area. Visit the text website for updates to this exercise.

Assignment

1. Examine articles that profile at least three successes or failures in the following publications and highlight the main points that led to either result.

   American Venture magazine (**www.avce.com**)
   Business 2.0 (**www.business2.com**)
   Red Herring (**www.redherring.com**)
   Fast Company (**www.fastcompany.com**)

2. What are the shared similarities?

3. What advice would you give to a start-up venture after reading these stories?

2. Developing Critical-Thinking Skills

Financial management involves preparing a plan for obtaining and using the money needed to accomplish a firm's goals and objectives. After a financial plan has been developed, it must be monitored continually to ensure that it actually fulfills these goals and objectives. To accomplish your own goals, you should prepare a *personal* financial plan. Determine what is important in your life and what you want to accomplish, budget the amount of money required to get it, and identify sources for acquiring the funds. You should monitor and evaluate the results regularly and make changes when necessary.

Assignment

1. Using the three steps shown in Figure 20.2, prepare a personal financial plan.

2. Prepare a three-column table to display it.

   a. In column 1, list at least two objectives under each of the following areas:

   Financial (savings, investments, retirement)
   Education (training, degrees, certificates)
   Career (position, industry, location)
   Family (children, home, education, trips, entertainment)

   b. In column 2, list the amount of money it will take to accomplish your objectives.

   c. In column 3, identify the sources of funds for each objective.

3. Describe what you learned from doing this exercise in a comments section at the bottom of the table.

3. Building Team Skills

Suppose that for the past three years you have been repairing lawn mowers in your garage.

Your business has grown steadily, and recently, you hired two part-time workers. Your garage is no longer adequate for your business; it is also in violation of the city code, and you have been fined twice for noncompliance. You have decided that it is time to find another location for your shop and that it also would be a good time to expand your business. If the business continues to grow in the new location, you plan to hire a full-time employee to repair small appliances. You are concerned, however, about how you will get the money to move your shop and get it established in a new location.

Assignment

1. With all class members participating, use brainstorming to identify the following:
   a. The funds you will need to accomplish your business goals
   b. The sources of short-term financing available to you
   c. Problems that might prevent you from getting a short-term loan
   d. How you will repay the money if you get a loan
2. Have a classmate write the ideas on the board.
3. Discuss how you can overcome any problems that might hamper your current chances of getting a loan and how your business can improve its chances of securing short-term loans in the future.
4. Summarize what you learned from participating in this exercise.

4. Researching Different Careers

Financial managers are responsible for determining the best way to raise funds, for ensuring that the funds are used to accomplish their firm's goals and objectives, and for developing and implementing their firm's financial plan. Their decisions have a direct impact on the firm's level of success. When managers do not pay enough attention to finances, a firm is likely to fail.

Assignment

1. Investigate the job of financial manager by searching the library or Internet and/or by interviewing a financial manager.

2. Find answers to the following questions:
   a. What skills do financial managers need?
   b. How much education is required?
   c. What is the starting salary? Top salary?
   d. What will the job of financial manager be like in the future?
   e. What opportunities are available?
   f. What types of firms are most likely to hire financial managers? What is the employment potential?
3. Prepare a report on your findings.

5. Improving Communication Skills

Trade credit is a source of short-term financing extended by a seller who does not require immediate payment on delivery of merchandise. The bill, or invoice, states the credit terms, often offering a cash discount for prompt payment. Many managers and owners, however, fail to take advantage of these discounts, which can save a business hundreds and even thousands of dollars each year.

Assignment

1. Prepare an invoice that offers the buyer a 2 percent cash discount if the bill is paid within ten days.
2. Using the data in the following table, calculate how much a business would save per transaction and in the course of a year, based on six transactions, if it took advantage of trade credit that offered a 2 percent cash discount.

Invoice Amount	Amount Saved per Transaction	Amount Saved Annually (Based on Six Transactions)
$1,000		
$2,300		
$5,600		
$11,000		
$22,500		
TOTAL		

3. Discuss why you think businesses fail to take advantage of cash discounts.
4. Summarize what you have learned about trade credit from this exercise.

→ PREP TEST

Matching Questions

____ 1. It is the movement of money into and out of an organization.

____ 2. Determining a firm's financial needs is one of its important functions.

____ 3. Every budgeted expense must be justified.

____ 4. Funding that comes from the sale of stock.

____ 5. Payments are delayed until later.

____ 6. Must receive dividends before common stockholders.

____ 7. It is an arbitrary dollar value printed on a stock certificate.

____ 8. A method of financing that is a legally binding and enforceable and often issued to suppliers.

____ 9. The deposits are used for redeeming a bond issue.

____ 10. This investment is backed by the reputation of the issuing corporation.

a. cash flow
b. debenture bond
c. equity capital
d. financial management
e. par value
f. preferred stock
g. promissory note
h. sinking fund
i. trade credit
j. zero-base budgeting

True/False Questions

T F

11. ○ ○ Equity financing can be used to fund openings and operations of new businesses.

12. ○ ○ A budget is a historical record of the previous year's financial activities.

13. ○ ○ Most lenders do not require collateral for short-term financing.

14. ○ ○ A revolving credit agreement is a guaranteed line of credit.

15. ○ ○ Factoring of accounts receivable typically is the highest-cost method of short-term financing.

16. ○ ○ Bonds usually are issued in units of $25.

17. ○ ○ Most corporate bonds are backed by assets of the firm.

T F

18. ○ ○ A prearranged short-term loan is called a line of credit.

19. ○ ○ A capital budget estimates a firm's expenditures for labor costs.

20. ○ ○ Sole proprietorships often use short-term debt capital to start a business.

Multiple-Choice Questions

21. An invoice in the amount of $200 carries cash terms of "2/10, net 30." If the buyer takes advantage of the discount terms, how much will the buyer pay?
    a. $100
    b. $120
    c. $140
    d. $160
    e. $196

22. When a firm sells its accounts receivable to raise short-term cash, it is engaging in a strategy called
    a. factoring.
    b. financial planning.
    c. debt financing.
    d. drafting.
    e. retaining earnings.

23. Retained earnings, as a form of equity financing, are
    a. gross earnings.
    b. profits before taxes.
    c. profits after taxes.
    d. undistributed profits.
    e. total owners' equity.

24. Which statement is true about floor planning?
    a. Title of merchandise is given to lenders in return for short-term financing.
    b. The lender controls the inventory.
    c. The borrower checks periodically to ensure that the collateral is still available.
    d. As merchandise is sold, the lender repays a portion of the loan.
    e. It is a special type of financing used only in the apparel industry.

25. Since prices are extremely low, the Pipeline Supply Company wants to purchase a special line of pipes from a company going out of business. Pipeline, however, will need to borrow money to make this deal. Which assets will Pipeline *most commonly* pledge as collateral for this short-term loan?
    a. Cash and accounts receivable
    b. Accounts and notes payable
    c. Manufacturing equipment
    d. Marketable securities and owners' equity
    e. Inventory and accounts receivable

Fill-in-the-Blank Questions

26. A type of investment that carries voting rights is called _____ stock.

27. Trade credit may offer _____ discounts.

28. A _____ bond can be exchanged for shares of common stock.

29. The time when a corporation repays a bond is called the _____ date.

30. A short-term promissory note issued by large corporations is known as _____ paper.

Answers on p. PT2.

Understanding Personal Finances and Investments

WHY this chapter matters

Too often people spend years in school learning how to make money but very little time learning how to manage money and invest. As a result, these same people never have enough money to do the things in life that are really important. While reading this chapter won't magically make you a millionaire and solve your money problems, it does provide some of the tools you need to manage your personal finances and begin an investment program.

FOR HELP with studying this chapter, visit the Online Student Center:

www.college.hmco.com/PIC/pridebusiness9e

Online Study Center

Charles Schwab has been helping to educate investors for more than thirty years. The brokerage firm was originally "a transactional company for people to make their own choices," recalls founder Charles Schwab. Do-it-yourself investors—those who were willing to make their own decisions about buying stocks and bonds—paid lower commissions to trade through Schwab than they would pay at a full-service brokerage firm, where stockbrokers offered personalized assistance and investment guidance.

However, it didn't take long for the founder to realize that "85 percent of people need help" determining what and when to buy and sell. The company responded to this need by launching the first in a long series of educational seminars. From the start, Schwab invested heavily in technology to service its fast-growing customer base and support ever-higher trading volume. Now—more than thirty years later—the brokerage firm is still teaching investors how to use technology to manage their nest eggs.

Today, the firm is a recognized leader in the brokerage industry for its ability

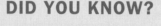

DID YOU KNOW?

Charles Schwab has been helping to educate investors for more than thirty years. Today, the firm is a recognized leader in the brokerage industry for its ability to meet the needs of both beginning and experienced investors.

to meet the needs of both beginning and experienced investors. And yet, like most successful firms, Schwab has an interesting history. By the time Schwab celebrated its tenth birthday, it had attracted one million customers. Two years later, Schwab went public to fuel future expansion. It opened a Latin American Center in the early 1990s and held customer assets totaling $100 billion before its twentieth birthday. The company took another technological leap forward with Schwab.com, which brought fast, low-cost trading within reach of any investor with a PC and an Internet connection.

Since the start, the Schwab.com website has featured an array of informative articles plus interactive tools to help customers analyze their finances and calculators for assessing progress toward long-term goals such as paying for college or having money for retirement. Now customers can ask questions or seek advice online, by phone, in person at a Schwab branch, or at one of the firm's local educational seminars. The stock market may go up and down, but Schwab knows that its customers are always in the market for sound ideas about how to invest wisely.[1]

For more information about this company, go to **www.schwab.com**.

The old saying goes, "I've been rich and I've been poor, but believe me, rich is better." And yet, just dreaming of being rich doesn't make it happen. While being rich doesn't guarantee happiness, managing your personal finances and beginning an investment program are both worthy goals. Firms such as Charles Schwab offer an array of services to help people manage their personal finances, research investments, and buy and sell stocks, bonds, mutual funds, and other securities. Still, you must be willing to invest the time and effort required to become a good money manager and a good investor. And don't underestimate how important you are when it comes to managing your money. No one is going to make you manage your money. No one is going to make you save the money you need to fund an investment program. These are your decisions—important decisions that literally can change your life.

Many people ask the question: Why begin an investment program now? The answer is simple: The sooner you start an investment program, the more time your investments have to work for you. So why do people wait to begin investing? In most cases there are two reasons. First, they don't have the money needed to fund an investment program. And yet, once you begin managing your personal finances and get your spending under control, you will be able to save the money needed to fund an investment program. The second reason people don't begin investing is because they don't know anything about investing. Again, this chapter provides the basics to get you started. We begin this chapter by examining everyday money management activities and outlining the reasons for developing a personal investment plan. Next, we examine the process of buying and selling securities. Then we discuss both traditional and high-risk (or speculative) investments. Finally, we explain how to obtain and interpret financial information. It is time! Take the first step, and begin managing your personal finances.

Preparing for an Investment Program

While it would be nice if you could accumulate wealth magically, it's not magic. For most people, the first step is to make sure that their "financial house" is in order. In the next section we examine several steps for effective money management that will help you to prepare for an investment program.

Managing Your Personal Finances

Many personal finance experts recommend that you begin the process of managing your money by determining your current financial condition. The first step often is to construct a personal balance sheet and a personal income statement. A *personal balance sheet* lists your assets and liabilities on a specific date. By subtracting the total amount of liabilities from the total amount of assets, you can determine your net worth. A *personal income statement* lists your income and your expenses for a specific period of time—usually a month. By subtracting expenses from income, you can determine if you have a surplus or a deficit at the end of the time period. (*Note:* Both personal balance sheets and personal income statements were examined in more detail in Chapter 18.) Based on the information contained in these statements, you can determine your current financial condition and where you spent your money. You also can take the next step: Construct a personal budget.

A **personal budget** is a specific plan for spending your income. You begin by estimating your income for a specific period—for example, next month. For most people, their major source of income is their salary. The second step is to list expenses for the same time period. Typical expenses include savings and investments, housing, food, transportation, entertainment, and so on. For most people, this is the area where you can make choices and increase or decrease the amount spent on different items listed in your budget. For example, you may decide to reduce the dollar amount spent on entertainment in order to increase the amount for savings. Above all, it is important to balance your budget so that your income is equal to the money you spend or invest each month. Unfortunately, many individuals spend more than they make. They

LEARNING OBJECTIVE

1 Explain why you should manage your personal finances and develop a personal investment program.

personal budget a specific plan for spending your income

THE ORGANIZATION TO CHOOSE
FOR A SECURE RETIREMENT.

For over 85 years, families and businesses have relied on the
insurance and financial solutions of the AIG companies. Over
50 million customers know the strength and experience of the
AIG companies can help secure your financial future.

AIG
INSURANCE | LOANS | RETIREMENT
www.aig.com

Do you need help planning your retirement? Many companies, such as AIG, offer retirement advice and investment and insurance products. It's important for you to be involved in your own investment program, especially when you're young. The sooner you start saving and investing, the more time your money and investments have to work for you.

personal investment the use of your personal funds to earn a financial return

financial planner an individual who has had at least two years of training in investments, insurance, taxation, retirement planning, and estate planning and has passed a rigorous examination

purchase items on credit and then must make monthly payments and pay finance charges ranging from 10 to 21 percent. It makes no sense to start an investment program until payments for credit-card and installment purchases, along with the accompanying finance charges, are reduced or eliminated. By reducing or eliminating credit purchases, eventually the amount of cash remaining after the bills are paid will increase and can be used to start a savings program or finance investments.

Investment Goals

Personal investment is the use of your personal funds to earn a financial return. Thus, in the most general sense, the goal of investing is to earn money with money. However, such a goal is completely useless for the individual because it is so vague and so easily attained. If you put $1,000 in a savings account paying 2 percent annual interest, your money will earn $1.67 in one month. If your goal is simply to earn money with your $1,000, you will have attained that goal at the end of the month. If your goals are somewhat more ambitious, you will find the material in this section helpful.

In reality, an investment goal must be specific and measurable. It must be tailored to you so that it takes into account your particular financial needs. It also must be oriented toward the future because investing is usually a long-term undertaking. Finally, an investment goal must be realistic in terms of current economic conditions and available investment opportunities.

Some financial planners suggest that investment goals should be stated in terms of money: "By January 1, 2014, I will have total assets of $80,000." Others believe that people are more motivated to work toward goals that are stated in terms of the particular things they desire: "By May 1, 2015, I will have accumulated enough money so that I can take a year off from work to travel around the world." Like the goals themselves, the way they are stated depends on you. The following questions can be helpful in establishing valid investment goals:

1. What financial goals do you want to achieve?
2. How much money will you need, and when?
3. What will you use the money for?
4. Is it reasonable to assume that you can obtain the amount of money you will need to meet your investment goals?
5. Do you expect your personal situation to change in a way that will affect your investment goals?
6. What economic conditions could alter your investment goals?
7. Are you willing to make the necessary sacrifices to ensure that your investment goals are met?
8. What are the consequences of not obtaining your investment goals?

A Personal Investment Program

Once you have formulated specific goals, investment planning is similar to planning for a business. It begins with the evaluation of different investment opportunities—including the potential return and risk involved in each. At the very least, this process requires some careful study and maybe some expert advice. Investors should beware of people who call themselves "financial planners" but who are in reality nothing more than salespersons for various financial investments, tax shelters, or insurance plans.

A true **financial planner** has had at least two years of training in investments, insurance, taxation, retirement planning, and estate planning and has passed a rigorous examination. As evidence of training and successful completion of the qualifying examination, the Certified Financial Planners Board of Standards in Denver allows individuals to use the designation Certified Financial Planner (CFP). Similarly, the American College in Bryn Mawr, Pennsylvania, allows individuals who have completed the necessary requirements to use the designation Chartered Financial Consultant (ChFC). Most CFPs and ChFCs do not sell a particular investment product or receive commissions for their investment recommendations. Instead, they charge consulting fees that range from $100 to $250 an hour.

Many financial planners suggest that you begin an investment program by accumulating an "emergency fund"—a certain amount of money that can be obtained quickly in case of immediate need. The amount of money that should be salted away in a savings account varies from person to person. However, most financial planners agree that an amount equal to at least three months' living expenses is reasonable.

After the emergency account is established, you may invest additional funds according to your investment program. Some additional funds already may be available, or money for further investing may be saved out of earnings. For suggestions to help you obtain the money needed to fund your investment program, see Table 21.1.

Once your program has been put into operation, you must monitor it and, if necessary, modify it. Your circumstances and economic conditions are both subject to change. Therefore, all investment programs should be re-evaluated regularly.

Important Factors in Personal Investment

How can you (or a financial planner) tell which investments are "right" for an investment program and which are not? One way to start is to match potential investments with your investment goals in terms of safety, risk, income, growth, and liquidity.

Safety and Risk   Safety and risk are two sides of the same coin. *Safety* in an investment means minimal risk of loss; *risk* in an investment means a measure of uncertainty about the outcome. If you want a steady increase in value over an extended period of time, choose safe investments, such as certificates of deposit (CDs), highly rated corporate and municipal bonds, and the stocks of highly regarded corporations—sometimes called *blue-chip stocks.* A **blue-chip stock** is a safe investment that generally attracts conservative investors. Blue-chip stocks generally are issued by corporations that often are industry leaders and have provided their stockholders with stable earn-

2 LEARNING OBJECTIVE
Describe how the factors of safety, risk, income, growth, and liquidity affect your investment program.

blue-chip stock a safe investment that generally attracts conservative investors

> >> **TABLE 21.1**

SUGGESTIONS TO HELP YOU ACCUMULATE THE MONEY NEEDED TO FUND AN INVESTMENT PROGRAM

1. *Pay yourself first.* Many financial experts recommend that you (1) pay your monthly bills, (2) save a reasonable amount of money, and (3) use whatever money is left over for personal expenses.

2. *Take advantage of employer-sponsored retirement programs.* Many employers will match part or all of the contributions you make to a 401(k) or 403(b) retirement account. (*Hint:* When looking for a new job, check out the retirement plan offered by the employer.)

3. *Participate in an elective savings program.* Elect to have money withheld from your paycheck each payday and automatically deposited in a savings account.

4. *Make a special savings effort one or two months each year.* By cutting back to the basics, you can obtain money for investment purposes.

5. *Take advantage of gifts, inheritances, and windfalls.* During your lifetime, you likely will receive gifts, inheritances, salary increases, year-end bonuses, or federal income tax returns. Instead of spending these windfalls, invest these funds.

Source: Jack R. Kapoor, Les R. Dlabay, and Robert J. Hughes, *Personal Finance,* 8th ed. Copyright © 2007 by The McGraw Hill Companies Inc. Reprinted with permission of The McGraw Hill Companies Inc., p. 411.

ings and dividends over a number of years. Selected mutual funds and real estate also may be very safe investments.

To implement goals that stress higher dollar returns on investments, you generally must give up some safety. In general, *the potential return should be directly related to the assumed risk.* That is, the greater the risk assumed by the investor, the greater the potential monetary reward should be. As you will see shortly, there are a number of risky—and potentially profitable—investments. They include some stocks, mutual funds, bonds and commodities and stock options. The securities issued by new and growing corporations usually fall in this category.

Often beginning investors are afraid of the risk associated with many investments. But it helps to remember that without risk, it is impossible to obtain larger returns that really make an investment program grow. In fact, some investors often base their investment decision on projections for rate of return. You also can use the same calculation to determine how much you actually earn on an investment over a specific period of time. To calculate **rate of return,** the total income you receive on an investment over a specific period of time is divided by the amount invested. For example, assume that you invest $5,000 in Home Depot stock. Also assume that you receive $50 in dividends, and the stock is worth $5,500 at the end of one year. Your rate of return is 11 percent, as illustrated below.

rate of return the total income you receive on an investment over a specific period of time divided by the amount invested

Step 1: Subtract the investment's initial value from the investment's value at the end of the year.

$$\$5,500 - 5,000 = \$500$$

Step 2: Add the annual income to the amount calculated in step 1.

$$\$50 + \$500 = \$550$$

Step 3: Divide the total dollar amount of return calculated in step 2 by the original investment.

$$\$550 \div \$5,000 = 0.11 = 11\%$$

Note: If an investment decreases in value, the steps used to calculate the rate of return are the same, but the answer is a negative number. With this information, it is possible to compare the rate of return for different investment alternatives that offer more or less risk.

Investment Income CDs, corporate and government bonds, and certain stocks pay a predictable amount of interest or dividends each year. Some mutual funds and real estate also may offer steady income potential. Such investments generally are used by conservative investors who need a predictable source of income.

Investors in CDs and bonds know exactly how much income they will receive each year. The dividends paid to stockholders can and do vary, even for the largest and most stable corporations. As with dividends from stock, the income from mutual funds and real estate also may vary from one year to the next.

Investment Growth To investors, *growth* means that their investments will increase in value. For example, growing corporations such as Wal-Mart and The Gap usually pay a small cash dividend or no dividend at all. Instead, profits are reinvested in the business (as retained earnings) to finance additional expansion. In this case the value of their stock increases as the corporation expands. For investors who choose their investments carefully, both mutual funds and real estate may offer substantial growth possibilities.

liquidity the ease with which an investment can be converted into cash

Investment Liquidity **Liquidity** is the ease with which an investment can be converted into cash. Investments range from cash or cash equivalents (such as investments in government securities or money-market accounts) to the other extreme of frozen investments, which you cannot convert easily into cash.

Although you may be able to sell stock, mutual-fund, and corporate-bond investments quickly, you may not regain the amount of money you originally invested because of market conditions, economic conditions, or many other reasons. It also may be difficult to find buyers for real estate. And finding a buyer for investments in certain types of collectibles also may be difficult.

How Securities Are Bought and Sold

To purchase a Geoffrey Beene sweater, you simply walk into a store that sells these sweaters, choose one, and pay for it. To purchase stocks, bonds, mutual funds, and many other investments, you often work through a representative—your account executive or stockbroker. In turn, your account executive must buy or sell for you in either the primary or secondary market.

The Primary Market

The **primary market** is a market in which an investor purchases financial securities (via an investment bank) directly from the issuer of those securities. As mentioned in Chapter 20, an *investment banking firm* is an organization that assists corporations in raising funds, usually by helping sell new issues of stocks, bonds, or other financial securities. Typically, this type of stock or security offering is referred to as an *initial public offering* (IPO). An example of an IPO sold through the primary market is the common-stock issue sold by Google that raised over $2 billion.[2] *Caution:* The promise of quick profits often lures investors to purchase an IPO. Investors should be aware, however, that an IPO generally is classified as a **high-risk investment**—one made in the uncertain hope of earning a relatively large profit in a short time. Depending on the corporation selling the new security, IPOs may be too speculative for most people.

For a large corporation, the decision to sell securities often is complicated, time-consuming, and expensive. Such companies usually choose one of two basic methods. Large firms that need a lot of financing often use an investment banking firm to sell the new security issue. If the analysts for the investment banking firm are satisfied that the new security issue is a good risk, the bank will buy the securities and then resell them to its customers—institutional investors or individuals. **Institutional investors** are pension funds, insurance companies, mutual funds, banks, and other organizations that trade large quantities of securities.

The second method used by a corporation trying to obtain financing through the primary market is to sell directly to current stockholders. Usually, promotional materials describing the new security issue are mailed to current stockholders. These stockholders then may purchase securities directly from the corporation.

The Secondary Market

The **secondary market** is a market for existing financial securities that are traded between investors. Usually, secondary-market transactions are completed through a securities exchange or the over-the-counter market.

Securities Exchanges A **securities exchange** is a marketplace where member brokers meet to buy and sell securities. Generally, securities issued by larger corporations are traded at the New York Stock Exchange, the American Stock Exchange, or at *regional exchanges* located in Chicago, Boston, and several other cities. The securities of very large corporations may be traded at more than one of

3 LEARNING OBJECTIVE
Understand how securities are bought and sold.

primary market a market in which an investor purchases financial securities (via an investment bank) directly from the issuer of those securities

high-risk investment an investment made in the uncertain hope of earning a relatively large profit in a short time

institutional investors pension funds, insurance companies, mutual funds, banks, and other organizations that trade large quantities of securities

secondary market a market for existing financial securities that are traded between investors

securities exchange a marketplace where member brokers meet to buy and sell securities

SPOTLIGHT

Value of shares traded

Trading securities is big business! The numbers represent the value of shares of stock for companies listed on organized exchanges in each country.

United States
$19,354.9

United Kingdom
$3,707.2

In billions

Germany
$1,406.1

Japan
$3,430.4

Source: U.S. Census Bureau, *Statistical Abstract of the United States 2006*, 125th Edition, p. 893.

Orderly confusion. What looks like confusion is actually an orderly system that allows investors to buy and sell the more than 2,800 different stocks listed on the New York Stock Exchange. Because the total market value for stocks listed on the exchange exceeds $21 trillion, the NYSE is one of the largest and best-known security exchanges in the world.

these exchanges. Securities of firms also may be listed on foreign securities exchanges—in Tokyo or London, for example.

One of the largest and best-known securities exchanges in the world is the New York Stock Exchange (NYSE). The NYSE lists over 2,800 corporate stocks, with a total market value of $21 trillion.[3] Before a corporation's stock is approved for listing on the NYSE, the firm usually must meet specific criteria. The American Stock Exchange, regional exchanges, and the over-the-counter market have different listing requirements and account for the remainder of securities traded in the United States.

The Over-the-Counter Market Stocks issued by several thousand companies are traded in the over-the-counter market. The **over-the-counter (OTC) market** is a network of dealers who buy and sell the stocks of corporations that are not listed on a securities exchange. The term *over-the-counter* was coined more than 100 years ago when securities actually were sold "over the counter" in stores and banks.

Most OTC securities today are traded through an *electronic* exchange called the **Nasdaq** (pronounced "nazzdack"). The Nasdaq quotation system provides price information on approximately 3,300 different stocks. Begun in 1971 and regulated by the National Association of Securities Dealers, the Nasdaq is now one of the largest securities markets in the world. Today, the Nasdaq is known for its forward-looking, innovative, growth companies. Although most companies that trade are small, the stock of some large firms, including Intel, Microsoft, Cisco Systems, and Dell Computer, is traded through the Nasdaq.

When you want to sell shares of a company that trades on the Nasdaq—for example, Apple Computer—your account executive sends your order into the Nasdaq computer system, where it shows up on the screen, together with all the other orders from people who want to buy or sell Apple Computer. A Nasdaq dealer (sometimes referred to as a *marketmaker*) sits at a computer terminal putting together these buy and sell orders for Apple Computer. Once a match is found, your order is completed.

The Role of an Account Executive

An **account executive**—sometimes called a *stockbroker* or *registered representative*—is an individual who buys and sells securities for clients. Choosing an account executive can be difficult for at least two reasons. First, you must exercise a shrewd combination of trust and mistrust when you approach an account executive. Remember that you are interested in the broker's recommendations to increase your wealth, but the account executive is interested in your investment trading as a means to swell commissions.

over-the-counter (OTC) market a network of dealers who buy and sell the stocks of corporations that are not listed on a securities exchange

Nasdaq computerized electronic exchange system through which most OTC securities are traded

account executive an individual, sometimes called a *stockbroker* or *registered representative*, who buys and sells securities for clients

E*Trade and a computer may be all you need to invest online. Today, more and more investors are choosing to invest and manage their finances online. With a computer and the help of a firm like E*Trade, you can evaluate various investment alternatives, track the value of your investments, and buy and sell stocks and other securities online. Because of competition for new clients, an online brokerage firm will do everything possible to make sure your investment experience is pleasant *and* profitable.

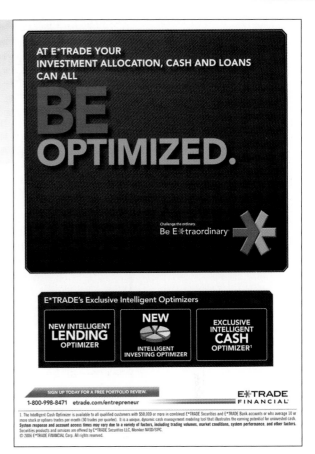

Unfortunately, some account executives are guilty of *churning*—a practice that generates commissions by excessive buying and selling of securities.

Second, you must decide whether you need a *full-service* broker or a *discount* broker. A full-service broker usually charges higher commissions but gives you personal investment advice and provides detailed research information. A discount broker simply executes buy and sell orders, usually over the phone or online. Most discount brokers offer no or very little free investment advice; you must make your own investment decisions. Some discount brokers will supply research reports for a nominal fee—usually $5 to $10.

Before deciding if you should use a full-service or a discount brokerage firm, you should consider how much help you need when making an investment decision. Many full-service brokerage firms argue that you need a professional to help you make important investment decisions. While this may be true for some investors, most account executives employed by full-service brokerage firms are too busy to spend unlimited time with you on a one-on-one basis, especially if you are investing a small amount. On the other side, many discount brokerage firms argue that you alone are responsible for making your investment decisions. And they argue that discount brokerage firms have both the personnel and research materials to help you to become a better investor.

The Mechanics of a Transaction Once investors have decided on a particular security, most simply telephone their account executive and place a market, limit, or discretionary order. A **market order** is a request that a security be purchased or sold at the current market price. Figure 21.1 illustrates one method of executing a market order to sell a stock listed on the NYSE at its current market value. It is also possible for a brokerage firm to match a buy order for a security for one of its customers with a sell order for the same security from another of its customers. Matched orders are not completed through a security exchange or the OTC market. Regardless of how the security is bought or sold, payment for stocks, and many other financial securities generally is required within three business days of the transaction.

A **limit order** is a request that a security be bought or sold at a price equal to or better than (lower for buying, higher for selling) some specified price. Suppose that you place a limit order to *sell* Coca-Cola common stock at $41 per share. Your broker's representative sells the stock only if the price is $41 per share or *more*. If you place a limit order to *buy* Coca Cola at $41, the representative buys it only if the price is $41 per share or *less*. Usually a limit order is good for one day, one week, one month, or good until canceled (GTC).

Investors also can choose to place a discretionary order. A **discretionary order** is an order to buy or sell a security that lets the broker decide when to execute the transaction and at what price. *Caution:* Financial planners advise against using a discretionary order for two reasons. First, a discretionary order gives the account executive a great deal of authority. If the account executive makes a mistake, it is the investor who

market order a request that a security be purchased or sold at the current market price

limit order a request that a security be bought or sold at a price that is equal to or better than some specified price

discretionary order an order to buy or sell a security that lets the broker decide when to execute the transaction and at what price

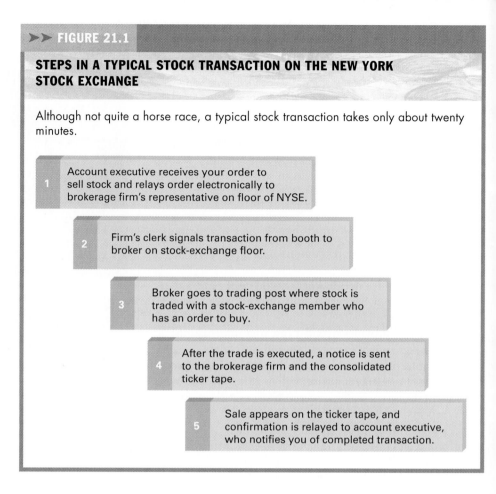

> ➤➤ **FIGURE 21.1**

STEPS IN A TYPICAL STOCK TRANSACTION ON THE NEW YORK STOCK EXCHANGE

Although not quite a horse race, a typical stock transaction takes only about twenty minutes.

1 Account executive receives your order to sell stock and relays order electronically to brokerage firm's representative on floor of NYSE.

2 Firm's clerk signals transaction from booth to broker on stock-exchange floor.

3 Broker goes to trading post where stock is traded with a stock-exchange member who has an order to buy.

4 After the trade is executed, a notice is sent to the brokerage firm and the consolidated ticker tape.

5 Sale appears on the ticker tape, and confirmation is relayed to account executive, who notifies you of completed transaction.

suffers the loss. Second, financial planners argue that only investors (with the help of their account executives) should make investment decisions.

Online Security Transactions   A computer and good investment software can help you to evaluate potential investments, manage your investments, monitor their value more closely, *and* place buy and sell orders online. As a rule of thumb, the more active an investor is, the more it makes sense to use computers and investment software. As you will see in the next section, one very good reason for trading securities online is the lower cost.

program trading a computer-driven program to buy or sell selected stocks

Another kind of computerized transaction is called *program trading.* **Program trading** is a computer-driven program to buy or sell selected stocks. When program trading is used, a computer monitors the market value of stocks and other securities. If security prices increase or decrease to a specified amount, the computer enters an order to buy or sell. Generally, institutional investors such as pension funds, mutual funds, banks, and insurance companies use program trading to monitor the value of their securities.

Commissions   Most full-service brokerage firms have a minimum commission ranging from $25 to $55 for buying and selling stock. Additional commission charges are based on the number of shares and the value of stock bought and sold.

Table 21.2 shows typical commission fees charged by online brokerage firms. Generally, online transactions are less expensive when compared with the costs of trading securities through a full-service or discount brokerage firm. As a rule of thumb, full-service brokerage firms charge as much as 1½ to 2 percent of the transaction amount. Commissions for trading bonds, commodities, and options usually are lower than those for trading stocks.

>> **TABLE 21.2**

TYPICAL COMMISSION COSTS CHARGED BY ONLINE BROKERAGE FIRMS FOR A TRANSACTION IN WHICH 1,000 SHARES ARE BOUGHT OR SOLD

	Internet	Interactive Voice-Response Telephone System	Broker-Assisted
Ameritrade	$10.99	$14.99	$24.99
E*Trade	$12.99	$12.99	$57.99
Fidelity	$19.95	$67.50	$181.00
TD Waterhouse	$17.95	$35.00	$45.00

Source: Ameritrade website: **www.ameritrade.com;** accessed January 14, 2006.

The charge for buying or selling a $1,000 corporate bond typically is $10 to $20. With the exception of most mutual funds, the investor generally pays a commission when buying *and* selling securities.

It should be apparent that vast sums of money are involved in securities trading. In an effort to protect investors from unfair treatment, both federal and state governments have acted to regulate securities trading.

Regulation of Securities Trading

Government regulation of securities was begun as a response to abusive and fraudulent practices in the sale of stocks, bonds, and other financial securities. Today, with so many news reports of corporations that are in "hot water" over financial reporting problems that range from simple mistakes to out-and-out fraud, the concerns of both government officials and investors have grown over the past few years.

Today, a regulatory pyramid consisting of four different levels exists to make sure that investors are protected. The U.S. Congress is at the top of the pyramid. Early on, Congress passed the Securities Act of 1933 (sometimes referred to as the Truth in Securities Act). This act provides for full disclosure. **Full disclosure** means that investors should have access to all important facts about stocks, bonds, and other securities so that they can make informed decisions. This act also requires that corporations issuing new securities file a registration statement and publish a prospectus. A **prospectus** is a detailed, written description of a new security, the issuing corporation, and the corporation's top management. Since 1933, Congress has passed additional legislation that includes creating the Securities Investor Protection Corporation (SIPC) to protect investors. Congress also has passed legislation to curb insider-trading abuses. **Insider trading** occurs when insiders—board members, corporate managers, and employees—buy and sell a corporation's stock. While insiders can buy and sell a corporation's stock, they must disclose their trading activities to the public. And it is illegal for insiders to trade a corporation's stock based on their knowledge of information that has not been made available to the general public. More recently, Congress passed the Sarbanes-Oxley Act to improve corporate accountability and financial reporting (see Chapter 18).

On the next level of the regulatory pyramid is the Security and Exchange Commission (SEC). In 1934, Congress passed the Securities Exchange Act of 1934, which created the SEC. The SEC is the agency that enforces federal securities regulations. The SEC also supervises all national exchanges, investment companies, OTC brokerage firms, and just about every other organization involved in trading securities.

On the next level of the regulatory pyramid is individual states. Today, most states require that new security issues be registered with a state agency and that brokers and securities dealers operating within the state be licensed. Most state regulations also

full disclosure requirement that investors should have access to all important facts about stocks, bonds, and other securities so that they can make informed decisions

prospectus a detailed, written description of a new security, the issuing corporation, and the corporation's top management

insider trading the practice of board members, corporate managers, and employees buying and selling a corporation's stock

provide for the prosecution of individuals accused of the fraudulent sale of stocks, bonds, and other securities.

The foundation and most important level of the regulatory pyramid is self-regulation by securities exchanges and brokerage firms. According to the NYSE, self-regulation—the way the securities industry monitors itself to create a fair and orderly trading environment—begins here.[4] To provide guidelines of ethical behavior, the NYSE has published over 1,000 pages of rules, policies, and standards of conduct. These standards are applied to every member in the NYSE's investment community.[5] In addition, there are more than 300 brokerage firms that buy and sell securities for their customers. These firms are responsible for ensuring that their employees are highly trained and meet rigorous ethical standards.

Traditional Investment Alternatives

4 LEARNING OBJECTIVE
Identify the advantages and disadvantages of savings accounts, bonds, stocks, mutual funds, and real estate investments.

In this section we look at traditional investments. In the next section we explore high-risk investments. A number of the investments listed in Table 21.3 have been discussed. Others have only been mentioned and will be examined in more detail. We begin this section with an overview of how portfolio management can reduce investment risk. Then we describe how specific investments can help you to reach your investment goals.

Portfolio Management

"How can I choose the right investment?" Good question! Unfortunately, there are no easy answers because your investment goals, age, tolerance for risk, and financial resources are different from those of the next person. To help you to decide what investment is right for you, consider the following: Since 1926, stocks have returned approximately 11 percent a year. During the same period, CDs and government bonds have returned about 5 percent.[6] And projections by well-respected Roger Ibbotson, chairman of Ibbotson Associates, an investment consulting, software, and research firm, indicate that these same investments will perform at about the same pace between now and the year 2025.[7] Therefore, why not just invest all your money in stocks or mutual funds that invest in stocks? After all, they offer the largest potential return? In reality, stocks have a place in every investment portfolio, but there is more to investing than just picking a bunch of stocks or stock mutual funds.

>> TABLE 21.3

INVESTMENT ALTERNATIVES

Traditional investments involve less risk than high-risk investments.

Traditional	High Risk
Bank accounts	Short transactions
Corporate and government bonds	Margin transactions
Common stock	Stock options
Preferred stock	Commodities
Mutual funds	Precious metals
Real estate	Gemstones
	Coins/antiques/collectibles

Asset Allocation, the Time Factor, and Your Age

Asset allocation is the process of spreading your money among several different types of investments to lessen risk. While the term *asset allocation* is a fancy way of saying it, simply put, it really means that you need to diversify and avoid the pitfall of putting all of your eggs in one basket—a common mistake made by investors. Asset allocation often is expressed in percentages. For example, what percentage of my assets do I want to put in stocks and mutual funds? What percentage do I want to put in more conservative investments such as CDs and government bonds? In reality, the answers to these questions often are tied to your tolerance for risk.

asset allocation the process of spreading your money among several different types of investments to lessen risk

Two other factors—the time your investments have to work for you and your age—also should be considered before deciding where to invest your money. The amount of time you have before you need your investment money is crucial. If you can leave your investments alone and let them work for five to ten years or more, then you can invest in stocks, mutual funds, and real estate. On the other hand, if you need your investment money in two years, you probably should invest in short-term government bonds, highly rated corporate bonds, or CDs. By taking a more conservative approach for short-term investments, you reduce the possibility of having to sell your investments at a loss because of depressed market value or a staggering economy.

You also should consider your age when developing an investment program. Younger investors tend to invest a large percentage of their nest egg in growth-oriented investments. If their investments take a nosedive, they have time to recover. On the other hand, older investors tend to choose more conservative investments. As a result, a smaller percentage of their nest egg is placed in growth-oriented investments. How much of your portfolio should be in growth-oriented investments? Well-known personal financial expert Suze Orman suggests that you subtract your age from 110, and the difference is the percentage of your assets that should be invested in growth investments. For example, if you are 30 years old, subtract 30 from 110, which gives you 80. Therefore, 80 percent of your assets should be invested in growth-oriented investments, whereas the remaining 20 percent should be kept in safer conservative investments.[8] Now it's time to take a closer look at specific investment alternatives.

Business Around the World

Foreign Investments: Getting Your Share of the World

You don't have to fly to Zurich to buy shares of Nestlé, the Swiss-based international food giant. Nor do you have to travel to Bombay to buy shares of India-based Wipro Technologies. You can own shares in either company by buying their American depositary receipts (ADRs). Here's an overview:

- ADRs are securities traded on U.S. exchanges or in the OTC market in U.S. dollars.
- One ADR may represent a single share, multiple shares, or a fraction of a share in the foreign corporation. Four of Nestlé's ADRs, for example, equal one of its Swiss shares.

- ADR investors don't receive actual stock certificates, which reduces the complexity of the transaction.
- Some ADRs are more highly regulated than others—and with more regulation comes more disclosure under SEC requirements.

Always investigate thoroughly before investing in ADRs or any security. For more information, see the SEC website (**www.sec.gov**).

Bank Accounts

Bank accounts that pay interest—and therefore are investments—include passbook savings accounts, CDs, and interest-bearing accounts. These were discussed in Chapter 19. The interest paid on bank accounts can be withdrawn to serve as income, or it can be left on deposit and increase the value of the bank account and provide for growth. At the time of this publication, one-year CDs were paying between 2 and 5 percent. While CDs and other bank accounts are risk-free for all practical purposes, many investors often choose other investments because of the potential for larger returns.

Corporate and Government Bonds

In Chapter 20 we discussed the issuing of bonds by corporations to obtain financing. The U.S. government and state and local governments also issue bonds for the same reason. Investors generally chose bonds because they provide a predictable source of income.

Corporate Bonds   Because they are a form of long-term debt financing that must be repaid, bonds generally are considered a more conservative investment than either stocks or mutual funds. One of the principal advantages of corporate bonds is that they are primarily long-term, income-producing investments. Between the time of purchase and the maturity date, the bondholder will receive interest payments—usually semiannually, or every six months. For example, assume that you purchase a $1,000 bond issued by GE Capital Corporation and that the interest rate for this bond is 6 percent. In this situation, you receive interest of $60 ($1,000 × 0.06 = $60) a year from the corporation. GE Capital pays the interest every six months in $30 installments.

Most beginning investors think that a $1,000 bond is always worth $1,000. In reality, the price of a bond may fluctuate until its maturity date. Changes in the overall interest rates in the economy are the primary cause of most bond price fluctuations. For example, when overall interest rates in the economy are rising, the market value of existing bonds with a fixed interest rate typically declines. They then may be purchased for less than their face value. By holding such bonds until maturity or until overall interest rates decline (causing the bond's market value to increase), bond owners can sell their bonds for more than they paid for them. In this case, the difference between the purchase price and the selling price is profit and is in addition to annual interest income. However, remember that the price of a corporate bond can decrease and that interest payments and eventual repayment may be a problem for a corporation that encounters financial difficulty. To compare potential risk and return on corporate bond issues, many investors rely on the bond ratings provided by Moody's Investors Service, Inc., and Standard & Poor's Corporation. For a summary of corporate bond ratings provided by these two companies, see Table 21.4. Bond ratings also are provided by Fitch Ratings and are similar to those provided by Moody's and Standard & Poor's.

Convertible Bonds   Some corporations prefer to issue convertible bonds because they carry a lower interest rate than nonconvertible bonds—by about 1 to 2 percent. In return for accepting a lower interest rate, owners of convertible bonds have the opportunity for increased investment growth. For example, assume that you purchase a Walt Disney $1,000 corporate bond that is convertible to 33.9443

Are savings bonds the right investment for you? The answer to this question depends on your tolerance for risk. U.S. savings bonds are often referred to as the safest investment because they are backed by the full faith and credit of the United States government. However, in order to secure this safe investment, investors must relinquish higher returns. In fact, the search for higher returns is why some investors instead choose stocks, mutual funds, real estate, and other investment alternatives.

> > **TABLE 21.4**

BOND RATINGS

The following bond ratings are provided by Moody's Investors Service and Standard & Poor's Corporation.

Quality	Moody's	Standard & Poor's
High grade—Bonds in this category are judged to be of high quality by all standards.	Aaa and Aa	AAA and AA
Medium grade—Bonds in this category possess many favorable attributes.	A and Baa	A and BBB
Speculative—Bonds in this category are judged to have speculative elements, and they may lack characteristics of a desirable investment.	Ba and B	BB and B
Default—Bonds in this category have poor prospects of attaining any real investment standing. The bonds even could be in default and the company in bankruptcy.	Caa, Ca, and C	CCC, CC, C, and D

Source: Moody's Investors Service, **www.moodyseurope.com**, May 15, 2005; Standard & Poor's Corporation, *Standard & Poor's Bond Guide*, April 2005.

shares of the company's common stock. This means that you could convert the bond to common stock whenever the price of the company's stock is $29.46 (1,000 ÷ 33.9443 = $29.46) or higher.[9] However, owners may opt not to convert their bonds to common stock even if the market value of the common stock does increase to $29.46 or more. The reason for not exercising the conversion feature is quite simple. As the market value of the common stock increases, the price of the convertible bond also increases. By not converting to common stock, bondholders enjoy interest income from the bond in addition to the increased bond value caused by the price movement of the common stock.

Government Bonds The federal government sells bonds and securities to finance both the national debt and the government's ongoing activities. Generally, investors choose from four different types of U.S. government bonds:

1. *Treasury bills.* Treasury bills, sometimes called *T-bills*, are sold in minimum units of $1,000, with additional increments of $1,000 above the minimum. Although the maturities may be as long as one year, the Treasury Department currently only sells T-bills with four-, thirteen-, and twenty-six-week maturities. T-bills are sold at a discount, and the actual purchase price is less than $1,000. When the T-bill matures, you receive the $1,000 maturity value.

2. *Treasury notes.* Treasury notes are issued in $1,000 units with a maturity of more than one year but not more than ten years. Typical maturities are two, three, five, and ten years. Treasury notes pay interest every six months until maturity.

3. *Treasury bonds.* Treasury bonds are issued in minimum units of $1,000 and have a thirty-year maturity. Like Treasury notes, Treasury bonds pay interest every six months until maturity.

4. *Savings bonds.* Series EE bonds, often called *U.S. Savings Bonds*, are purchased for one-half their maturity value. Thus a $100 bond costs $50 when purchased. (*Note:* If the interest derived from savings bonds is used to pay qualified college expenses, it may be exempt from federal taxation.)

The main reason investors choose U.S. government bonds is that they consider them risk-free. The other side of the coin is that these bonds pay lower interest than most other investments.

Like the federal government, state and local governments sell bonds to obtain financing. A **municipal bond,** sometimes called a *muni,* is a debt security issued by a state or local government. One of the most important features of municipal bonds is that the interest on them may be exempt from federal taxes. Whether or not the interest on municipal bonds is tax exempt often depends on how the funds obtained from their sale are used. *Caution: It is your responsibility, as an investor, to determine whether or not the interest paid by municipal bonds is taxable. It is also your responsibility to evaluate municipal bonds.* Although most municipal bonds are relatively safe, defaults have occurred in recent years.

municipal bond sometimes called a *muni,* a debt security issued by a state or local government

Common Stock

How do you make money by buying common stock? Basically, there are three ways: through dividend payments, through an increase in the value of the stock, or through stock splits.

Dividend Payments   One of the reasons why many stockholders invest in common stock is *dividend income.* Generally, dividends are paid on a quarterly basis. Although corporations are under no legal obligation to pay dividends, most corporate board members like to keep stockholders happy (and prosperous). A corporation may pay stock dividends in place of—or in addition to—cash dividends. A **stock dividend** is a dividend in the form of additional stock. It is paid to shareholders just as cash dividends are paid—in proportion to the number of shares owned.

stock dividend a dividend in the form of additional stock

capital gain the difference between a security's purchase price and its selling price

market value the price of one share of a stock at a particular time

Increase in Dollar Value   Another way to make money on stock investments is through capital gains. A **capital gain** is the difference between a security's purchase price and its selling price. To earn a capital gain, you must sell when the market value of the stock is higher than the original purchase price. The **market value** is the price of one share of a stock at a particular time. Let's assume that on January 13, 2000, you purchase 100 shares of General Mills at a cost of $33 a share and that you paid $55 in commission charges, for a total investment of $3,355. Let's also assume that you held your 100 shares until January 13, 2006, and then sold the General Mills stock for $50 a share. Your total return on investment is shown in Table 21.5. You realized a profit of $2,203 because you received dividends totaling $6.28 a share and because the stock's market value increased by $17 a share. Of course, if the stock's market value had decreased, or if the firm's board of directors had voted to reduce or omit dividends, your return would have been less than the total dollar return illustrated in Table 21.5.

Why does a stock's value increase? Good question! In most cases, a stock's value increases because the company that issued the stock is selling more products or services and earning larger profits. For example, Citigroup's expansion into markets such as Shanghai, China and other aggressive marketing activities have increased the firm's sales, profits, *and* stock value.

>> **TABLE 21.5**

SAMPLE COMMON-STOCK TRANSACTION FOR GENERAL MILLS

Assumptions: 100 shares of common stock purchased on January 13, 2000, for $33 a share; 100 shares sold on January 13, 2006, for $50 a share; dividends for six years total $6.28 a share.

Cost When Purchased		Return When Sold	
100 shares @ $33	$3,300	100 shares @ $50	$5,000
Plus commission	+ 55	Minus commission	− 70
Total investment	$3,355	Total return	$4,930

Transaction Summary

Total return	$4,930
Minus total investment	−3,355
Profit from stock sale	$1,575
Plus total dividends (6 years)	+ 628
Total return for this transaction	$2,203

Source: Price data and dividend amounts were taken from the Yahoo Finance website: **http://finance.yahoo.com;** accessed January 13, 2006.

Stock Splits   Directors of many corporations feel that there is an optimal price range within which their firm's stock is most attractive to investors. When the market value increases beyond that range, they may declare a *stock split* to bring the price down. A **stock split** is the division of each outstanding share of a corporation's stock into a greater number of shares.

> **stock split** the division of each outstanding share of a corporation's stock into a greater number of shares

   The most common stock splits result in one, two, or three new shares for each original share. For example, in 2006, the board of directors of Papa John's Pizza approved a two-for-one stock split. After this split, a stockholder who originally owned 100 shares owned 200 shares. The value of an original share was proportionally reduced. In the case of Papa John's, the market value per share was reduced to half the stock's value before the two-for-one stock split. *Although there are no guarantees that the stock will increase in value after a split,* the stock is more attractive to the investing public because of the potential for a rapid increase in dollar value. This attraction is based on the belief that most corporations split their stock only when their financial future is improving and on the upswing.

Preferred Stock

As we noted in Chapter 20, a firm's preferred stockholders must receive their dividends before common stockholders are paid any dividend. Moreover, the preferred-stock dividend amount is specified on the stock certificate. And the owners of preferred stock have first claim, after bond owners and general creditors, on corporate assets if the firm is dissolved or enters bankruptcy. These features make preferred stock a more conservative investment with an added degree of safety and a more predictable source of income when compared with common stock.

   In addition, owners of preferred stock may gain through special features offered with certain preferred-stock issues. Owners of *cumulative* preferred stocks are assured that omitted dividends will be paid to them before common stockholders receive any dividends. Owners of *convertible* preferred stock may profit through growth as well as dividends. When the value of a firm's common stock increases, the market value of its *convertible* preferred stock also increases. Convertible preferred stock thus combines the lower risk of preferred stock with the possibility of greater speculative gain through conversion to common stock.

Mutual Funds

For many investors, mutual funds are the investment of choice. And there are plenty of funds from which to choose. In 1970, there were only about 400 mutual funds. In November 2005, there were approximately 8,000 mutual funds.[10]

mutual fund a professionally managed investment vehicle that combines and invests the funds of many individual investors

A **mutual fund** combines and invests the funds of many investors under the guidance of a professional manager. The major advantages of a mutual fund are its professional management and its diversification, or investment in a wide variety of securities. Diversification spells safety because an occasional loss incurred with one security usually is offset by gains from other investments.

Mutual-Fund Basics   There are basically three types of mutual funds: (1) closed-end funds, (2) exchange-traded funds, and (3) open-end funds. A *closed-end fund* sells shares in the fund to investors only when the fund is originally organized. Once all the shares are sold, an investor must purchase shares from some other investor who is willing to sell them. The mutual fund itself is under no obligation to buy back shares from investors. An *exchange-traded fund* (ETF) is a fund that invests in the stocks contained in a specific stock index, such as the Standard & Poor's 500 Stock Index, the Dow Jones Industrial Average, or the Nasdaq Composite Index, and whose shares are traded on a stock exchange. With both a closed-end fund and an ETF, an investor can purchase as little as one share of a fund because both types are traded on a stock exchange or in the OTC market. The investment company sponsoring an *open-end fund* issues and sells new shares to any investor who requests them. It also buys back shares from investors who wish to sell all or part of their holdings.

net asset value (NAV) current market value of a mutual fund's portfolio minus the mutual fund's liabilities and divided by the number of outstanding shares

The share value for any mutual fund is determined by calculating its net asset value. **Net asset value (NAV)** per share is equal to the current market value of the mutual fund's portfolio minus the mutual fund's liabilities and divided by the number of outstanding shares. For most mutual funds, NAV is calculated at least once a day and is reported in newspapers and financial publications and on the Internet.

Mutual-Fund Sales Charges and Fees   With regard to costs, there are two types of mutual funds: load and no-load funds. An individual who invests in a *load fund* pays a sales charge every time he or she purchases shares. This charge may be as high as 8.5 percent. While many exceptions exist, the average load charge for mutual funds is between 3 and 5 percent. Instead of charging investors a fee when they purchase shares in a mutual fund, some mutual funds charge a *contingent deferred sales fee*. Generally, this fee ranges from 1 to 5 percent of the amount withdrawn during the first five to seven years. Typically, the amount of the contingent deferred sales fee declines each year that you own the fund until there is no withdrawal fee. The purchaser of shares in a *no-load fund* pays no sales charges at all. Since no-load funds offer the same type of investment opportunities as load funds, you should investigate them further before deciding which type of mutual fund is best for you.

Retirement accounts and mutual funds can be a perfect match. Because of professional management and diversification, many investors choose to invest the money in their retirement accounts in mutual funds. Mutual fund families like Vanguard do everything possible to make it easy to obtain research about their funds, open an account, and invest and withdraw funds from a retirement account. For more information about Vanguard Funds, go to **www.vanguard.com.**

Mutual funds also collect a yearly management fee of about 0.25 to 2 percent of the total dollar amount of assets in the fund. While fees vary considerably, the average management fee is between 0.50 and 1.25 percent of the fund's assets. Finally, some mutual funds charge a 12b-1 fee (sometimes referred to as a *distribution fee*) to defray the costs of advertising and marketing the mutual fund. Annual 12b-1 fees are calculated on the value of a fund's assets and are generally 1 percent or less of the fund's assets. Unlike the one-time sales fees that some mutual funds charge to purchase *or* sell mutual-fund shares, the management fee and the 12b-1 fee are ongoing fees charged each year.

Today, mutual funds also can be classified as A, B, or C shares. With A shares, investors pay commissions when they purchase shares in the mutual fund. With B shares, investors pay commissions when money is withdrawn or shares are sold during the first five to seven years. With C shares, investors pay no commissions to buy or sell shares but usually must pay higher ongoing management and 12b-1 fees.

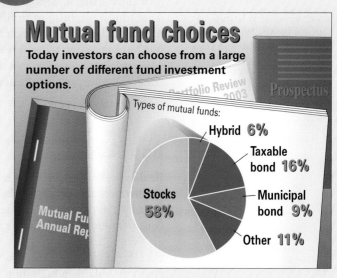

SPOTLIGHT

Mutual fund choices

Today investors can choose from a large number of different fund investment options.

Types of mutual funds:

- Stocks 58%
- Hybrid 6%
- Taxable bond 16%
- Municipal bond 9%
- Other 11%

Source: **www.ici.org**; accessed December 9, 2005.

Managed Funds versus Indexed Funds

Most mutual funds are managed funds. In other words, there is a professional fund manager (or team of managers) who chooses the securities that are contained in the fund. The fund manager also decides when to buy and sell securities in the fund. Ultimately, the fund manager is responsible for the fund's success.

Instead of investing in a managed fund, some investors choose to invest in an index fund. Why? The answer to this question is simple: Over many years, index funds have outperformed managed funds. The exact statistics vary depending on the year, but on average, anywhere from 50 to 80 percent of managed funds are beaten by the index each year.[11] Simply put: It is hard to beat an index such as the Standard & Poor's 500. If the individual securities included in an index increase in value, the index goes up. Because an index mutual fund is a mirror image of a specific index, the dollar value of a share in an index fund also increases when the index increases. Unfortunately, the reverse is true. Index funds, sometimes called *passive funds*, have managers, but they simply buy the stocks or bonds contained in the index. A second reason why investors choose index funds is the lower fees charged by these passively managed funds. (*Note:* Various indexes are discussed later in this chapter.)

Types of Mutual-Fund Investments Based on the type of securities they invest in, mutual funds generally fall into three broad categories: stocks, bonds, and other. The majority of mutual funds are *stock funds* that invest in stocks issued by small, medium-size, and large corporations that provide investors with income, growth, or a combination of income and growth. *Bond funds* invest in corporate, government, or municipal bonds that provide investors with interest income. The third category includes funds that stress asset allocation and money-market investments or strive for a balance between stock and bonds. In most cases, the name of the category gives a pretty good clue to the type of investments included in the fund. Typical fund names include

- Aggressive growth stock funds
- Global stock funds
- Growth stock funds
- High-yield (junk) bond funds
- Income stock funds
- Index funds
- Long-term U.S. bond funds

- Sector stock funds
- Small-cap stock funds

family of funds a group of mutual funds managed by one investment company

To help investors obtain their investment objectives, most investment companies now allow shareholders to switch from one fund to another fund within the same family of funds. A **family of funds** exists when one investment company manages a group of mutual funds. For example, shareholders, at their option, can change from the AIM Global Aggressive Growth Fund to the AIM Basic Value Fund. Generally, investors may give instructions to switch from one fund to another fund within the same family either in writing, over the telephone, or via the Internet. Charges for exchanges, if any, are small for each transaction. For funds that do charge, the fee may be as low as $5 per transaction.

Real Estate

Real estate ownership represents one of the best hedges against inflation, but it—like all investments—has its risks. A piece of property in a poor location, for example, actually can decrease in value. Table 21.6 lists some of the many factors you should consider before investing in real estate.

There are, of course, disadvantages to any investment, and real estate is no exception. If you want to sell your property, you must find an interested buyer with the ability to obtain enough money to complete the transaction. Finding such a buyer can be difficult if loan money is scarce, the real estate market is in a decline, or you overpaid for a piece of property. If you are forced to hold your investment longer than you originally planned, taxes, interest, and installment payments can be a heavy burden. As a rule, real estate increases in value and eventually sells at a profit, but there are no guarantees. The degree of your success depends on how well you evaluate different alternatives.

>> TABLE 21.6

REAL ESTATE CHECKLIST

Although real estate offers one of the best hedges against inflation, not all property increases in value. Many factors should be considered before investing in real estate.

Evaluation of Property	Inspection of the Surrounding Neighborhood	Other Factors
Is the property priced competitively with similar property?	What are the present zoning requirements?	Why are the present owners selling the property?
What type of financing, if any, is available?	Is the neighborhood's population increasing or decreasing?	How long will you have to hold the property before selling it to someone else?
How much are the taxes?	What is the average income of people in the area?	How much profit can you reasonably expect to obtain?
	What is the state of repair of surrounding property? Do most of the buildings and homes need repair?	Is there a chance that the property value will decrease?

High-Risk Investment Techniques

As defined earlier in this chapter, a *high-risk investment* is one made in the uncertain hope of earning a relatively large profit in a short time. (See the high-risk investment category in Table 21.3.) Most high-risk investments become so because of the methods used by investors to earn a quick profit. These methods can lead to large losses as well as to impressive gains. They should not be used by anyone who does not fully understand the risks involved. We begin this section with a discussion of selling short. Then we examine margin transactions and other high-risk investments.

5 LEARNING OBJECTIVE
Describe high-risk investment techniques.

Selling Short

Normally, you buy stocks expecting that they will increase in value and then can be sold at a profit. This procedure is referred to as **buying long.** However, many securities decrease in value for various reasons. Consider what happened to the values of many stocks between 2000 and 2004. Because of the nation's depressed economy and the terrorist attacks of September 11, 2001, many corporations also experienced a financial downturn. These same corporations experienced lower-than-expected sales revenues and profits. In some cases corporations actually posted losses during this same time period. For the firms that were able to weather the economic storm, their stock values were quite a bit lower than they were before the economic downturn began back in 2000. When this type of situation occurs, you can use a procedure called *selling short* to make a profit when the price of an individual stock is falling. **Selling short** is the process of selling stock that an investor does not actually own but has borrowed from a brokerage firm and will repay at a later date. The idea is to sell at today's higher price and then buy later at a lower price. To make a profit from a short transaction, you must proceed as follows:

buying long buying stock with the expectation that it will increase in value and then can be sold at a profit

selling short the process of selling stock that an investor does not actually own but has borrowed from a brokerage firm and will repay at a later date

1. Arrange to borrow a certain number of shares of a particular stock from a brokerage firm.
2. Sell the borrowed stock immediately, assuming that the price of the stock will drop in a reasonably short time.
3. After the price drops, buy the same number of shares that were sold in step 2.
4. Give the newly purchased stock to the brokerage firm in return for the stock borrowed in step 1.

Your profit is the difference between the amount received when the stock is sold in step 2 and the amount paid for the stock in step 3. For example, assume that you think that General Motors stock is overvalued at $27 a share. You also believe that the stock will decrease in value over the next three to four months. You call your broker and arrange to borrow 100 shares of General Motors stock (step 1). The broker then sells your borrowed General Motors stock for you at the current market price of $27 a share (step 2). Also assume that four months later the General Motors stock has dropped to $20 a share. You instruct your broker to purchase 100 shares of General Motors stock at the current lower price (step 3). The newly purchased General Motors stock is given to the brokerage firm to repay the borrowed stock (step 4). In this example, you made $700 by selling short ($2,700 selling price − $2,000 purchase price = $700 profit).[12] Naturally, the $700 profit must be reduced by the commissions you paid to the broker for buying and selling the General Motors stock.

People often ask where the broker obtains the stock for a short transaction. The broker probably borrows the stock from other investors who have purchased General Motors stock and left stock certificates on deposit with the brokerage firm. As a result, the person who is selling short must pay any dividends declared on the borrowed stock. The most obvious danger when selling short, of course, is that a loss can result if the stock's value increases instead of decreases.

Buying Stock on Margin

margin requirement the portion of the price of a stock that cannot be borrowed

An investor buys stock *on margin* by borrowing part of the purchase price, usually from a stock brokerage firm. The **margin requirement** is the portion of the price of a stock that cannot be borrowed. This requirement is set by the Federal Reserve Board.

Today, investors can borrow up to 50 percent of the cost of a stock purchase. Some brokerage firms require that you deposit more cash, which reduces the percentage that can be borrowed. But why would investors want to buy stock on margin? Simply because they can buy up to twice as much stock by buying on margin. Suppose that an investor expects the market price of a share of common stock of TXU Corporation—a global energy company—to increase in the next three to four months. Let's say that this investor has enough money to purchase 200 shares of the stock. However, if the investor buys on margin, he or she can purchase an additional 200 shares for a total of 400 shares. If the price of TXU's stock increases by $8 per share, the investor's profit will be $1,600 ($8 × 200 = $1,600) if he or she pays cash. But it will be $3,200 ($8 × 400 = $3,200) if he or she buys on margin. By buying more shares on margin, the investor will earn double the profit (less the interest he or she pays on the borrowed money and customary commission charges).

Financial leverage—a topic covered in Chapter 20—is the use of borrowed funds to increase the return on an investment. When margin is used as leverage, the investor's profit is earned by both the borrowed money and the investor's own money. The investor retains all the profit and pays interest only for the temporary use of the borrowed funds. Note that the stock purchased on margin serves as collateral for the borrowed funds. Before you become a margin investor, you should consider two factors. First, if the market price of the purchased stock does not increase as quickly as expected, interest costs mount and eventually drain your profit. Second, if the price of the margined stock falls, the leverage works against you. That is, because you have purchased twice as much stock, you lose twice as much money.

If the value of a stock you bought on margin decreases to approximately half its original price, you will receive a *margin call* from the brokerage firm. You then must provide additional cash or securities to serve as collateral for the borrowed money. If you cannot provide additional collateral, the stock is sold, and the proceeds are used to pay off the loan. Any funds remaining after the loan is paid off are returned to you.

Other High-Risk Investments

We have already discussed two high-risk investments—selling short and margin transactions. Other high-risk investments include the following:

- Stock options
- Commodities
- Precious metals
- Gemstones
- Coins
- Antiques and collectibles

Without exception, investments of this kind normally are referred to as high-risk investments for one reason or another. For example, the gold market has many unscrupulous dealers who sell worthless gold-plated lead coins to unsuspecting, uninformed investors. It pays to be careful. *Although investments in this category can lead to large dollar gains, they should not be used by anyone who does not fully understand all the potential risks involved.*

6 LEARNING OBJECTIVE
Use financial information to evaluate investment alternatives.

Sources of Financial Information

A wealth of information is available to investors. Sources include the Internet, newspapers, investors' services, brokerage firm reports, business periodicals, corporate reports, and securities averages.

The Internet

By using the Internet, investors can access a wealth of information on most investment and personal finance topics. For example, you can obtain interest rates for CDs; current price information for stocks, bonds, and mutual funds; and experts' recommendations to buy, hold, or sell an investment. You can even trade securities online just by pushing the right button on your computer keyboard.

Because the Internet makes so much information available, you need to use it selectively. One of the web search engines such as Yahoo! (**www.yahoo.com**), MSN (**www.msn.com**), or Google (**www.google.com**) can help you locate the information you really need. These search engines allow you to do a word search for the personal finance or investment alternative you want to explore. Why not take a look? To access one of the preceding search engines, enter the website address and then type in a key term such as *personal finance* and see the results.

Corporations, investment companies that sponsor mutual funds, and federal, state, and local governments also have home pages where you can obtain valuable investment information. You may want to explore these websites for two reasons. First, they are easily accessible. All you have to do is type in the web address or use one of the above-mentioned search engines to locate the site. Second, the information on these sites may be more up to date than printed material obtained from published sources.

In addition, you can access professional advisory services—a topic discussed later in this section—for information on stocks, bonds, mutual funds, and other investment alternatives. While some of the information provided by these services is free, there is a charge for the more detailed information you may need to evaluate an investment. Although it is impossible to list all the Internet sites related to investments, those described in the accompanying BizTech boxed feature will get you started.

Financial Coverage of Securities Transactions

Most local newspapers carry several pages of business news, including reports of securities transactions. The *Wall Street Journal* (published on weekdays) and *Barron's* (published once a week) are devoted almost entirely to financial and economic news. Both include complete coverage of transactions on all major securities exchanges. (As pointed out in the last section, it is also possible to obtain information about security transactions by using the Internet.)

BizTech

Log On for Investment Help

How can you choose a winning investment from a market filled with thousands of securities? Log on and do your homework with the help of these websites:

MSN's MoneyCentral
(http://moneycentral.msn.com). Here you'll find dozens of tools for analyzing individual securities, checking quotes, and monitoring the value of individual stocks, mutual funds, and other investments.

Yahoo! Finance
(http://finance.yahoo.com). Click here for links to information about investing and personal finance, news that moved the day's markets, and where the main U.S. indices stand.

SmartMoney
(www.smartmoney.com). Chart stock performance, get advice and analysis, and read the top business headlines. Learn the basics at **www.smartmoney.com/university.**

MarketWatch
(www.marketwatch.com). Get an overview of analysts' upgrades and downgrades, read industry and economic reports, and follow the direction of share prices.

Because transactions involving stocks, bonds, and mutual funds are reported differently, we shall examine each type of report separately.

Common and Preferred Stocks Stock transactions are reported in tables that usually look like the top section of Figure 21.2. Stocks are listed alphabetically. Your first task is to move down the table to find the stock you are interested in. To read the *stock quotation*, you read across the table. The highlighted line in Figure 21.2 gives detailed information about common stock issued by home builder Beazer Homes.

If a corporation has more than one stock issue, the common stock is listed first. Then the preferred-stock issues are listed and indicated with the letters *pf* behind the firm's name. (*Exception:* The *Wall Street Journal* has a separate section for preferred-stock listings.)

Bonds While some newspapers and financial publications provide limited information on some corporate and government bonds issues, it is usually easier to obtain more detailed information on more bond issues by accessing the Internet. Regardless of the source, bond prices are quoted as a percentage of the face value, which is usually $1,000. Thus, to find the current price, you must multiply the face value ($1,000) by the quotation. For example, a price quoted as 84 translates to a selling price of $840 ($1,000 × 0.84 = $840). Detailed information obtained from the Yahoo! Finance website for a $1,000 AT&T Broadband corporate bond, which pays 8.375 percent interest and matures in 2013, is provided in Figure 21.3.

➤➤ FIGURE 21.2

READING STOCK QUOTATIONS

Reproduced at the top of the figure is a portion of the stock quotations listed on the NYSE. At the bottom is an enlargement of the same information. The numbers above each of the enlarged columns correspond to the numbered entries in the list of explanations that appears in the middle of the figure.

| YTD | 52 WEEKS | | | | YLD | | VOL | | NET |
% CHG	HI	LO	STOCK (SYM)	DIV	%	PE	100s	CLOSE	CHG
8.6	82.14	43.99	BeazerHm **BZH** s	.40	.5	8	7176	79.12	0.67
4.4	73.35	47.88	BeckmnCoultr **BEC**	.56	.9	21	2802	59.40	− 0.02
2.2	62.38	49.71	BectonDksn **BDX**	.86f	1.4	22	5400	61.43	0.53

1. YTD % Chg reflects the stock price change for the calendar year to date: Beazer Homes has increased 8.6 percent since January 1
2. Highest price paid for one share of Beazer Homes during the past 52 weeks: $82.14
3. Lowest price paid for one share of Beazer Homes during the past 52 weeks: $43.99
4. Name (often abbreviated) of the corporation: Beazer Homes
5. Ticker symbol or letters that identify a stock for trading: BZH
6. Total dividends paid per share over a 12-month period based on the last dividend payment: $0.40
7. Yield percentage, or the percentage of return based on the current dividend and current price of the stock: $0.40 ÷ $79.12 = 0.005 = 0.5%
8. Price earnings (PE) ratio—the price of a share of stock divided by the corporation's earnings per share of stock outstanding over the last 12 months: 8
9. Number of shares of Beazer Homes traded during the day, expressed in hundreds of shares: 717,600
10. Close is the price paid in the last transaction of the day: $79.12
11. Difference between the price paid for the last share sold today and the price paid for the last share sold on the previous day: 0.67 (in Wall Street terms, Beazer Homes "closed up $0.67" on this day).

1	2	3	4	5	6	7	8	9	10	11
YTD % CHG	52 WEEKS HI	LO	STOCK (SYM)		DIV	YLD %	PE	VOL 100s	CLOSE	NET CHG
8.6	82.14	43.99	BeazerHm BZH s		.40	.5	8	7176	79.12	0.67
4.4	73.35	47.88	BeckmnCoultr BEC	.56		.9	21	2802	59.40	− 0.02
2.2	62.38	49.71	BectonDksn BDX		.86f	1.4	22	5400	61.43	0.53

Mutual Funds   Purchases and sales of shares of mutual funds are reported in tables like the one shown in Figure 21.4. As in reading stock quotations, your first task is to move down the table to find the mutual fund you are interested in. Then, to find the mutual-fund price quotation, read across the table. Figure 21.4 gives detailed information for the Icon Health Care mutual fund—a sector fund in the health care industry.

Other Sources of Financial Information

In addition to the Internet and newspaper coverage, other sources, which include investors' services, brokerage firm reports, business periodicals, and corporate reports, offer detailed and varied information about investment alternatives.

Investors' Services   For a fee, various investors' services provide information about investments. Information from investors' services also may be available at university and public libraries.

As illustrated in Table 21.4, Moody's and Standard & Poor's provide information that can be used to determine the quality and risk associated with bond issues. Standard

---

➤➤ FIGURE 21.3

READING BOND QUOTATIONS

Reproduced at the top of the figure is bond information obtained from the Yahoo! Finance website. The numbers beside each line correspond to numbered entries in the list of explanations that appears at the bottom of the figure.

AT&T BROADBAND CORP

OVERVIEW	
1. Price	117.11
2. Coupon (%)	8.375
3. Maturity Date	15-Mar-2013
4. Yield to Maturity (%)	5.449
5. Current Yield (%)	7.151
6. Debt Rating	BBB
7. Coupon Payment Frequency	Semi-Annual
8. First Coupon Date	15-Mar-2003
9. Type	Corporate
10. Industry	Telephone

1. Price quoted as a percentage of the face value: $1000 x 117.11% = $1171.10
2. Coupon (%) is the rate of interest: 8.375 percent
3. Maturity Date is the date when bondholders will receive repayment: March 15, 2013
4. Yield to Maturity (%) takes into account the relationship among a bond's maturity value, the time to maturity, the current price, and the amount of interest: 5.449 percent
5. Current Yield (%) is determined by dividing the dollar amount of annual interest by the current price of the bond: ($83.75 ÷ 1171.10 = 0.07151 = 7.151%)
6. Debt Rating is used to assess risk associated with this bond: BBB
7. Coupon Payment Frequency tells bondholders how often they will receive interest payments: Semi-Annual
8. First Coupon Date: March 15, 2003
9. Type: Corporate
10. Industry: Telephone

Source: The Yahoo! Finance bond website: **http://bonds.yahoo.com;** accessed January 18, 2006.

>> **FIGURE 21.4**

READING MUTUAL-FUND QUOTATIONS

Reproduced at the top of the figure is a portion of the mutual-fund quotations as reported by the *Wall Street Journal.* At the bottom is an enlargement of the same information. The numbers above each of the enlarged columns correspond to numbered entries in the list of explanations that appears in the middle of the figure.

FUND	NAV	NET CHG	YTD %RET	3-YR %RET
ICON Funds				
Energy	35.35	0.44	10.6	44.7
Financial	13.53	0.02	3.3	18.0
HlthCare	18.35	−0.04	2.5	20.2

1. The name of the mutual fund: Icon Health Care Fund
2. The net asset value (NAV) is the value of one share of the Icon Health Care Fund: $18.35
3. The difference between the net asset value today and the net asset value on the previous trading day: −0.04 (in Wall Street terms, the Icon Health Care Fund closed down $0.04 on this day)
4. The YTD % RET gives the total return for Icon Health Care Fund for the year to date: 2.5 percent
5. The 3-YR % RET column gives the annualized return for the Icon Health Care Fund for the past 3 years: 20.2 percent

1	2	3	4	5
FUND	**NAV**	**NET CHG**	**YTD %RET**	**3-YR %RET**
ICON Funds				
Energy	35.35	0.44	10.6	44.7
Financial	13.53	0.02	3.3	18.0
HlthCare	18.35	−0.04	2.5	20.2

Source: *Wall Street Journal,* January 14, 2006, p. B12.

& Poor's, Mergent, Inc., and Value Line also rate the companies that issue common and preferred stock. Each investor service provides detailed financial reports. Take a look at the Mergent's research report for Polo Ralph Lauren illustrated in Figure 21.5. Notice that there are six main sections that provide financial data, information about the company's business operations, recent developments, prospects, and other valuable information. Research reports published by Standard & Poor's and Value Line are like Mergent's report and provide similar information.

A number of investors' services provide detailed information on mutual funds. Morningstar, Inc., Standard & Poor's, Lipper Analytical Services, and Value Line are four widely tapped sources of such information. Although some information may be free, a fee generally is charged for more detailed research reports. In addition, various mutual-fund newsletters supply financial information to subscribers for a fee.

Brokerage Firm Analysts' Reports   Brokerage firms employ financial analysts to prepare detailed reports on individual corporations and their securities. Such reports are based on the corporation's sales, profits or losses, management, and planning, plus other information on the company, its industry, demand for its products, and its efforts to develop new products. The reports, which may include buy or sell recommendations, usually are provided free to the clients of full-service brokerage firms. Firms offering this service include UBS Wealth Management, Smith Barney, Merrill Lynch, and most other full-service brokerage firms. Brokerage firm reports also may be available from discount brokerage firms, but they may charge a fee.

►► FIGURE 21.5

MERGENT'S RESEARCH REPORT FOR POLO RALPH LAUREN

A research report from Mergent is divided into six main parts that describe not only the financial condition of a company but also its history and outlook for the future.

POLO RALPH LAUREN CORP.

Exchange	Symbol	Price	52Wk Range	Yield	P/E
NYS	RL	$49.55 (8/31/2005)	52.60-34.57	0.40	22.73

*7 Year Price Score 131.66 *NYSE Composite Index = 100 *12 Month Price Score 114.52

Interim Earnings (Per Share)

Qtr.	Jun	Sep	Dec	Mar
2002-03	0.07	0.52	0.43	0.74
2003-04	0.05	0.54	0.35	0.75
2004-05	0.13	0.78	0.72	0.20
2005-06	0.48	—	—	—

Interim Dividends (Per Share)

Amt.	Decl	Ex	Rec	Pay
0.05Q	9/20/2004	9/29/2004	10/1/2004	10/15/2004
0.05Q	12/20/2004	12/29/2004	12/31/2004	1/14/2005
0.05Q	3/21/2005	3/30/2005	4/1/2005	4/15/2005
0.05Q	6/14/2005	6/29/2005	7/1/2005	7/15/2005

Indicated Div: $0.20

Valuation Analysis

Forecast P/E	15.64	No. of Institutions
	(9/14/2005)	187
Market Cap	$5.4 Billion	Shares
Book Value	1.7 Billion	58,930,616
Price/Book	3.08	% Held
Price/Sales	1.55	96.83

Business Summary: Apparel (MIC: 4.4 SIC: 2329 NAIC: 315211)

Polo Ralph Lauren designs, licenses, contracts for the manufacture of, markets and distributes men's and women's apparel, accessories, fragrances, skin care products and home furnishings. Co.'s sales are principally to major department and specialty stores located throughout the U.S. and Europe. Also, Co. sells directly to consumers through full-price and outlet Polo Ralph Lauren, Ralph Lauren and Club Monaco stores located throughout the U.S., Canada, Europe, South America and Asia. Co. operates in three integrated business segments: retail, wholesale, and licensing under brand names including Polo by Ralph Lauren, Ralph Lauren Purple Label, Ralph Lauren, Polo Jeans Co., RL and Chaps.

Recent Developments: For the quarter ended July 2, 2005, net income increased 298.5% to $50,707 thousand from net income of $12,725 thousand in the year-earlier quarter. Revenues were $751,942 thousand, up 24.1% from $606,006 thousand the year before. Operating income was $80,221 thousand versus an income of $19,754 thousand in the prior-year quarter. Total direct expense was $337,514 thousand versus $290,478 thousand in the prior-year quarter, an increase of 16.2%. Total indirect expense was $334,207 thousand versus $295,774 thousand in the prior-year quarter, an increase of 13.0%.

Prospects: On July 15, 2005, Co. completed the acquisition of Ralph Lauren Footwear Co., Inc, its global licensee for footwear for men, women, and children for $108.0 million in cash. Looking ahead, Co. expects its fiscal 2006 earnings per share to be in the range of $2.85 to $2.92. These projected results anticipate consolidated revenue growth in the high single-digit and operating margins are expected to increase in a range of 400 to 450 basis points reflecting expansion in its wholesale and retail segments. Co. expects revenue to reflect high single-digit percent growth in wholesale sales and low-teens percent growth in retail sales.

Financial Data
(US$ in Thousands)

	3 Mos.	04/02/2005	04/03/2004	03/29/2003	03/30/2002	03/31/2001	04/01/2000	04/03/1999
Earnings Per Share	2.18	1.83	1.69	1.76	1.75	0.61	1.45	0.91
Cash Flow Per Share	4.62	3.68	2.09	2.74	3.02	1.04	2.46	0.38
Tang Book Value Per Share	10.61	10.38	10.56	8.93	7.38	5.76	5.07	6.60
Dividends Per Share	0.200	0.200	0.200	—	—	—	—	—
Dividend Payout %	9.17	10.93	11.83	—	—	—	—	—
Income Statement								
Total Revenue	751,942	3,305,415	2,649,654	2,439,340	2,363,707	2,225,774	1,955,528	1,726,859
EBITDA	107,923	398,426	355,121	366,533	378,951	201,666	330,191	201,999
Depn & Amortn	27,661	103,633	83,189	78,645	83,919	78,599	66,280	46,414
Income Before Taxes	80,695	299,366	261,932	274,386	275,999	97,954	248,886	152,826
Income Taxes	30,343	107,336	95,055	100,151	103,499	38,692	101,422	62,276
Net Income	50,707	190,425	170,954	174,235	172,500	59,262	143,497	90,550
Average Shares	105,491	101,519	100,960	99,263	98,522	97,446	98,926	99,972
Balance Sheet								
Current Assets	1,447,485	1,413,763	1,271,319	1,166,007	1,008,057	901,721	852,891	679,454
Total Assets	2,743,814	2,726,669	2,270,241	2,038,822	1,749,497	1,626,093	1,620,562	1,104,584
Current Liabilities	591,757	622,410	501,130	500,347	391,771	439,577	406,228	347,972
Long-Term Obligations	269,149	290,960	277,345	248,494	285,414	296,988	342,707	44,217
Total Liabilities	1,000,691	1,050,961	848,168	830,055	751,302	816,784	848,125	445,679
Stockholders' Equity	1,743,123	1,675,708	1,422,073	1,208,767	998,195	809,309	772,437	658,905
Shares Outstanding	108,294	103,118	100,632	98,722	98,227	97,177	97,529	99,779
Statistical Record								
Return on Assets %	9.19	7.64	7.81	9.22	10.25	3.66	10.56	9.23
Return on Equity %	14.30	12.33	12.79	15.83	19.14	7.51	20.11	14.33
EBITDA Margin %	14.35	12.05	13.40	15.03	16.03	9.06	16.89	11.70
Net Margin %	6.74	5.76	6.45	7.14	7.30	2.66	7.34	5.24
Asset Turnover	1.40	1.33	1.21	1.29	1.40	1.37	1.44	1.76
Current Ratio	2.45	2.27	2.54	2.33	2.57	2.05	2.10	1.95
Debt to Equity	0.15	0.17	0.20	0.21	0.29	0.37	0.44	0.07
Price Range	44.11-31.04	42.60-31.04	35.13-22.41	30.64-16.57	30.98-18.41	30.45-13.25	24.63-14.13	31.00-16.00
P/E Ratio	20.23-14.24	23.28-16.96	20.79-13.26	17.41-9.41	17.70-10.52	49.92-21.72	16.98-9.74	34.07-17.58
Average Yield %	0.52	0.54	0.71	—	—	—	—	—

Address: 650 Madison Avenue, New York, NY 10022
Telephone: 212-318-7000
Fax: 212-888-5780

Web Site: www.polo.com
Officers: Ralph Lauren – Chmn., C.E.O.
F. Lance Isham – Vice Chmn.

Auditors: Deloitte & Touche LLP
Investor Contact: 212-813-7862

EXAMINING ETHICS

The Backlash over Backdating

Dozens of public corporations have been caught up in a controversy over the backdating of stock options. Intended as an incentive to improve performance, these options allow managers to buy stock in the future at the share price from a particular day in the past. If the options were backdated to a period when the price was especially low, executives could profit by buying and immediately selling shares. Here's what's happening:

- The SEC and Justice Department are investigating whether some firms improperly backdated options and whether this executive compensation was fully disclosed.
- Former executives of Brocade Communications and Comverse Technology have been charged with securities fraud due to options backdating.
- Apple Computer and dozens of other firms have reexamined their options practices.
- Cheesecake Factory and other corporations have recalculated their past earnings to account for full executive compensation under backdated options.
- Senate hearings are probing how tax laws and securities regulation can curb any manipulation of stock-option dates.

Corporations charged with improper backdating could face costly legal action and hefty financial penalties; which, in turn, will affect their investors.

Business Periodicals Business magazines such as *BusinessWeek*, *Fortune*, and *Forbes* provide not only general economic news but also detailed financial information about individual corporations. Trade or industry publications such as *Advertising Age* and *Business Insurance* include information about firms in a specific industry. News magazines such as *U.S. News & World Report*, *Time*, and *Newsweek* feature financial news regularly. *Money*, *Kiplinger's Personal Finance Magazine*, *Consumer Reports*, and similar magazines provide information and advice designed to improve your investment skills. These periodicals are available at libraries and are sold at newsstands and by subscription. Many of these same periodicals sponsor an online website that may contain all or selected articles that are contained in the print version. Why not check out the investing information available from *BusinessWeek Online* at **www.businessweek.com** or *Kiplinger's Personal Finance Magazine* at **www.kiplinger.com.**

Corporate Reports Publicly held corporations must send their stockholders annual reports. These reports include a description of the company's performance provided by the corporation's top management, information about the firm's products or services, and detailed financial statements that readers can use to evaluate the firm's actual performance. There also should be a letter from the accounting firm that audited the corporation. As mentioned in Chapter 18, an audit does not guarantee that a company hasn't "cooked" the books, but it does imply that the company has followed generally accepted accounting principles to report profits, assets, liabilities, and other financial information.

In addition, a corporation issuing a new security must—by law—prepare a prospectus and ensure that copies are distributed to potential investors. A corporation's prospectus and its annual and quarterly reports are available to the general public.

Security Averages

security average (or security index) an average of the current market prices of selected securities

Investors often gauge the stock market through the security averages reported in newspapers and on television news programs. A **security average** (or **security index**) is an average of the current market prices of selected securities. Over a period of time, these averages indicate price trends, but they do not predict the performance of individual investments. At best, they can give the investor a "feel" for what is happening to investment prices generally.

The *Dow Jones Industrial Average*, established in 1896, is the oldest security index in use today. This average is composed of the prices of the common stocks of thirty leading industrial corporations. In addition, Dow Jones publishes a transportation average, a utility average, and a composite average.

In addition to the Dow Jones' averages, the Standard & Poor 500 Stock Index, the New York Stock Exchange Composite Index, and the Nasdaq Composite Index include more stocks when compared with the Dow averages. Thus they tend to reflect the stock market more fully. In addition to stock averages, there are averages for bonds, mutual funds, real estate, commodities, precious metals, fine art, most collectibles, and many other potential investments.

Before they can start investing, most people have to decide on a career and obtain a job that will provide the money needed to finance an investment program. In Appendix A we provide information that can help you to explore different career options (see text website).

RETURN TO Inside Business

Charles Schwab is a major player in the discount brokerage business, holding customer assets in excess of $1 trillion. It also operates mutual funds, owns a bank, and offers checking accounts, home mortgages, credit cards, CDs, and numerous other financial services. Competing with full-service brokerage firms such as Merrill Lynch, as well as with deep-discount brokerage firms such as E*Trade Financial, Schwab handles accounts for the very wealthy and for first-time investors.

Although do-it-yourself investing remains popular, research shows that 51 percent of the U.S. households with brokerage accounts prefer to double-check their investment decisions

with a financial adviser. This is why Schwab provides customers with a range of options, from participating in live web-based seminars to having an investment expert select specific securities and manage the portfolio. Now, after more than thirty years, Schwab continues to offer investment education for all seasons and all reasons.

Questions

1. Today, investors have a choice. They can use a full-service brokerage firm or a discount brokerage firm. There are also deep-discount firms. Which type of firm do you think could help you to achieve your financial goals? Explain your answer.
2. What are the pros and cons of opening a checking account and having a home mortgage with the brokerage firm that handles all your securities trades?

►► CHAPTER REVIEW

Summary

1

Explain why you should manage your personal finances and develop a personal investment program.

Many personal finance experts recommend that you begin the process of managing your money by determining your current financial condition. The first step often is to con-struct a personal balance sheet and a personal income statement. You also can construct a personal budget. For most people, the next step is to formulate measurable and realistic investment goals. A personal investment program then is designed to implement those goals. Many financial planners also suggest that the investor should establish an emergency fund equivalent to at least three months' living expenses. Then additional funds may be invested according to the investment program. Finally, all investments should be monitored carefully, and if necessary, the investment program should be modified.

2

Describe how the factors of safety, risk, income, growth, and liquidity affect your investment program.

Depending on their particular investment goals, investors seek varying degrees of safety, risk, income, growth, and liquidity from their investments. Safety is, in essence, freedom from the risk of loss. Generally, the greater the risk, the greater should be the potential return on an investment. To determine how much risk you are willing to assume, many investors calculate the rate of return. It is also possible to compare the rate of return for different investments that offer more or less risk. Income is the periodic return from an investment. Growth is an increase in the value of the investment. Liquidity is the ease with which an asset can be converted to cash.

3

Understand how securities are bought and sold.

Securities may be purchased in either the primary or the secondary market. The primary market is a market in which an investor purchases financial securities (via an investment bank) directly from the issuer of those securities. A corporation also can obtain financing by selling securities directly to current stockholders. The secondary market involves transactions for existing securities that are currently traded between investors and usually are bought and sold through a securities exchange or the over-the-counter (OTC) market.

If you invest in securities, chances are that you will use the services of an account executive who works for a brokerage firm. It is also possible to use a discount broker or trade securities online with a computer. Today, a regulatory pyramid consisting of four different levels exists to make sure that investors are protected. The U.S. Congress, the Securities and Exchange Commission (SEC), individual states, and securities exchanges and brokerage firms all are involved in regulating the securities industry.

4

Identify the advantages and disadvantages of savings accounts, bonds, stocks, mutual funds, and real estate investments.

Asset allocation is the process of spreading your money among several different types of investments to lessen risk. Two other factors—the time your investments have to work for you and your age—also should be considered before deciding where to invest your money. Once the factors of asset allocation, time your investments have to work for you, and your age are considered, it is time to examine different investment alternatives. In this section we examined tradi-

tional investments that include bank accounts, corporate bonds, government bonds, common stock, preferred stock, mutual funds, and real estate. Although bank accounts and bonds can provide investment growth, they generally are purchased by investors who seek a predictable source of income. Both corporate and government bonds are a form of debt financing. As a result, bonds generally are considered a more conservative investment than stocks or most mutual funds. With stock investments, investors can make money through dividend payments, an increase in the value of the stock, or stock splits. The major advantages of mutual-fund investments are professional management and diversification. Today there are mutual funds to meet just about any conceivable investment objective. The success of real estate investments is often tied to how well each investment alternative is evaluated.

5

Describe high-risk investment techniques.

High-risk investment techniques can provide greater returns, but they also entail greater risk of loss. You can make money by selling short when the market value of a financial security is decreasing. Selling short is the process of selling stock that an investor does not actually own but has borrowed from a brokerage firm and will repay at a later date. An investor also can buy stock on margin by borrowing part of the purchase price, usually from a stock brokerage firm. Because you can purchase up to twice as much stock by using margin, you can increase your return on investment as long as the stock's market value increases. Other high-risk investments include stock options, commodities, precious metals, gemstones, coins, and antiques and collectibles.

6

Use financial information to evaluate investment alternatives.

Today, there is a wealth of information on stocks, bonds, and other securities and the firms that issue them. There is also a wealth of investment information on other types of investments, including mutual funds, real estate, and high-risk investment alternatives. Two popular sources—the Internet and newspapers—report daily securities transactions. The Internet also can be used to obtain detailed financial information about different investment alternatives. Often the most detailed research information about securities—and the most expensive—is obtained from investors' services. In addition, brokerage firm reports, business periodicals, and corporate reports also can be used to evaluate different investment alternatives. Finally, there are a number of security indexes or averages that indicate price trends but reveal nothing about the performance of individual securities.

Key Terms

You should now be able to define and give an example relevant to each of the following terms:

personal budget (697)
personal investment (698)
financial planner (698)
blue-chip stock (699)
rate of return (700)
liquidity (700)
primary market (701)
high-risk investment (701)
institutional investors (701)
secondary market (701)
securities exchange (701)
over-the-counter (OTC) market (702)
Nasdaq (702)
account executive (702)
market order (703)
limit order (703)
discretionary order (703)
program trading (704)
full disclosure (705)
prospectus (705)
insider trading (705)
asset allocation (707)
municipal bond (710)
stock dividend (710)
capital gain (710)
market value (710)
stock split (711)
mutual fund (712)
net asset value (NAV) (712)
family of funds (714)
buying long (715)
selling short (715)
margin requirement (716)
security average (or security index) (722)

Review Questions

1. How could developing a personal budget help you obtain the money needed to fund your investment program?
2. What is an "emergency fund," and why is it recommended?
3. What is the tradeoff between safety and risk? How do you calculate rate of return?
4. In general, what kinds of investments provide income? What kinds provide growth?
5. What is the difference between the primary market and the secondary market?
6. When a corporation decides to sell stock, what is the role of an investment banking firm?

7. What is the difference between a securities exchange and the over-the-counter market?
8. In what ways could a computer help you to invest?
9. Describe how the securities industry is regulated.
10. How do you think that asset allocation, the time your investments have to work for you, and your age affect the choice of investments for someone who is 25 years old? For someone who is 59 years old?
11. Characterize the purchase of corporate and government bonds as an investment in terms of safety, risk, income, growth, and liquidity.
12. Describe the three methods by which investors can make money with stock investments.
13. An individual may invest in stocks either directly or through a mutual fund. How are the two investment methods different?
14. When would a speculator sell short?
15. What are the risks and rewards of purchasing stocks on margin?
16. How could the Internet help you to research an investment?
17. In what ways are newspaper stock quotations useful to investors? In what ways are security averages useful?
18. In addition to the Internet and newspapers, what other sources of financial information could help you to obtain your investment goals?

Discussion Questions

1. What personal circumstances might lead investors to emphasize income rather than growth in their investment planning? What might lead them to emphasize growth rather than income?
2. Federal laws prohibit corporate managers from making investments that are based on *inside information*—that is, special knowledge about their firms that is not available to the general public. Why are such laws needed?
3. In this chapter it was apparent that stocks have outperformed other investment alternatives over a long period of time. With this fact in mind, why would investors choose to use asset allocation to diversify their investments?
4. What type of individual would invest in government bonds? In global mutual funds? In real estate?
5. Suppose that you have just inherited 500 shares of IBM common stock. What would you do with it, if anything?
6. What kinds of information would you like to have before you invest in a particular common stock or mutual fund? From what sources can you get that information?
7. Take another look at Figure 21.5 (Mergent's research report for Polo Ralph Lauren). Based on the research provided by Mergent's, would you buy stock in Polo Ralph Lauren? Justify your decision by providing specific examples from Figure 21.5.

➤➤ VIDEO CASE 21.1

Is a Bull or Bear Market Ahead for Build-A-Bear Workshop?

Can Build-A-Bear Workshop continue its bear-sized success? Founder Maxine Clark was a retailing executive for twenty-five years before she became an entrepreneur in 1997. Thinking back to her much-loved teddy bear and the magic she remembered in special shopping trips as a child, Clark wanted her new business to combine entertainment and retailing to please children of all ages. The retail company she founded, Build-A-Bear Workshop, Inc., has now blossomed into an international chain of more than 200 stores ringing up $375 million in annual sales.

Master Bear Builders (store employees) help customers choose the types of animals they want. Bears, bunnies, kittens, ponies, and frogs, available in small or large sizes, are just some of the choices. Next, customers select the fake-fur color and the amount of stuffing and then carefully insert the heart. To add a voice, they can insert a prerecorded sound chip or record a personalized sound chip. Then customers help stitch the seams, gently fluff the fur, and name their new friends. If they wish, they can pick out clothing and accessories such as angel wings or miniature cowboy gear. The result is a one-of-a-kind stuffed animal that goes home in a house-shaped package.

As part of the buying procedure, customers enter their animal's names and their own names and addresses, e-mail addresses, gender, and birth dates at computer stations in each store. Build-A-Bear uses this information to generate each toy's birth certificate, signed by Clark as CEB. (By the way, Clark's CEB title stands for Chief Executive Bear.) Then the information is pooled with sales data and other details, analyzed carefully, and used to plan newsletters and other promotional efforts. In addition, because each animal contains a unique bar-coded tag, the company can return lost toys by consulting the database to determine ownership. So far the company has used the system to reunite fifty lost animals with their owners.

Each Build-A-Bear store rings up $600 per square foot in annual sales, roughly twice the average of a typical mall store. The mix of products is constantly evolving to keep customers coming back again and again. "We add new products monthly to stay in step with the latest fashions and trends," she says. "More than 80 percent of our line changes at least twice a year."

To raise millions of dollars for rapid expansion, Clark and her management team decided to take Build-A-Bear public. After filing the legally required forms for an IPO with the SEC, the company was listed on the NYSE, and shares began trading under the BBW symbol on October 28, 2004. First-day trading was brisk: Nearly six million shares changed hands, and the stock closed at $25.05 a share.

Now that Build-A-Bear is a public corporation, its executives present formal financial reports every quarter and every year. They also take questions from brokerage firm analysts during earnings conference calls, industry meetings, and other events. Senior managers have been asked about actual and projected revenue, profit margins, store traffic, new product lines, inventory levels, advertising, new stores, and other issues that shed light on how the business—and, in turn, the stock—is likely to perform in the future. Armed with this information, the analysts then issue recommendations about investing in Build-A-Bear.

Build-A-Bear has been growing by promoting on-line purchasing, opening stores in sports stadiums, and branching out into doll-making products. New advertising campaigns are attracting new customers and repeat business from customers who want to add to their collection. Its investors are watching the company's financial position closely and weighing how the overall economic climate will affect the retailer's future. Is a bull or bear market ahead for Build-A-Bear?[13]

For more information about this company, go to **www.buildabear.com.**

Questions

1. What are the advantages and disadvantages of a corporation such as Build-A-Bear Workshop going public and selling stock?
2. Now, with new stores funded by the money obtained from selling stock, Build-A-Bear has more than 200 stores that generate annual sales revenues of $375 million. Would you buy stock in this company? Explain your answer.
3. What specific information would you want to have before deciding to buy Build-a-Bear stock, and where would you obtain this information?
4. If you were attending Build-A-Bear's annual meeting, what questions would you ask top management—and why?

▶▶ CASE 21.2

Automakers' Bonds Go to the Junkyard

What happens when the long-term bonds issued by major automakers are rated as high-risk rather than blue-chip investments? General Motors and Ford—and their investors—faced this situation when Standard & Poor's, Moody's Investors Services, and Fitch Ratings downgraded the unsecured bonds issued by these corporations to *junk-bond status*. The downgrades signaled that the ratings services viewed the securities as higher risk and lower quality because of the automakers' financial difficulties.

When a bond issue is rated triple A—the best possible rating—there is little risk of the corporation failing to meet its obligations. Moody's rates Toyota's bonds as triple A because the Japanese company is the world's most profitable carmaker and has strong sales, strong cash flow, and strong global market share. Investors who want safe and stable investments seek out the top-rated bonds, even though such bonds don't offer very high returns.

On the other hand, junk bonds that offer higher returns also carry a higher risk that the corporation will fail to meet its financial obligations. Junk bonds are often called *high-yield bonds* because investors receive a higher return in exchange for the higher risk. When Fitch lowered its ratings on Ford's long-term bonds from investment-grade BBB− to junk-grade BB+, the rating service cited a number of reasons for the downgrade. It noted that Ford was struggling to regain market share in North America and pointed to the slowdown in sales of large sport-utility vehicles (SUVs) owing to higher gasoline prices. It also said that Ford's profit margins were being pinched by aggressive competition and raised concerns about the automaker's high pension and health insurance costs.

During the same month that Fitch first downgraded Ford's bonds to junk status, Standard & Poor's downgraded General Motors' bonds for the third time in a year. The securities already were considered junk bonds, but the downgrade from BB− to B represented GM's lowest rating since Standard & Poor's first rated the automaker's bonds in 1953 (giving them a triple-A rating). "This year has witnessed a stunning collapse of GM's financial performance," wrote Robert Schultz, a Standard & Poor's credit analyst, in reporting the downgrade. "We felt we needed to spell it out." Scott Sprinzen, another Standard & Poor's analyst, told the *New York Times* that a bankruptcy filing for GM wasn't "a far-fetched conclusion," given the company's financial deterioration.

GM was still selling more cars and trucks globally than any of its rivals. However, its share of the North American market was dropping, and sales of the Chevrolet Suburban and similarly lucrative SUV models had slumped. During the year when its bonds were downgraded three times, GM lost nearly $4 billion despite plans to lay off 30,000 employees and close several assembly plants. The company's health insurance expenses also were a big financial burden, even though it had come to agreement with the United Automobile Workers union on key cost-cutting measures. GM officials remained confident about the company's business prospects and optimistic about SUV sales in particular. "We are anticipating we will maintain our share of a stable market that is still very profitable," said GM's executive director of global market and industry analysis.

Just a few weeks after it lowered GM's junk-bond rating, Standard & Poor's downgraded Ford's junk-bond rating to BB− amid concern about the company's ability to accelerate North American sales and recapture market share. In fact, the rating service observed that Ford could be hurt by GM's financial problems if the two began an aggressive round of competitive discounting to jump-start auto sales. Investors—and the investors' services—will continue to monitor the financial fortunes of these two large U.S. automakers closely and to evaluate the effect on their long-term unsecured bonds.[14]

For more information about these companies, go to **www.gm.com** and **www.ford.com**.

Questions

1. If you worked for Moody's, Standard & Poor's, or Fitch's Ratings, what questions would you ask General Motors and Ford as you weighed whether to change the ratings on their long-term unsecured bonds?
2. What are the implications for investors who already have GM's or Ford's bonds in their portfolios when these securities are downgraded to lower junk-bond levels?
3. As an investor, what information and criteria would you use when deciding whether to buy GM's or Ford's junk bonds?
4. One bond expert says that individual investors interested in the higher returns offered by junk bonds should choose junk-bond mutual funds because "the professional management and diversification these funds provide can help reduce some of the risks." Do you agree with this statement? Why?

→ CHAPTER 21: JOURNAL EXERCISE

Discovery statement: According to many financial experts, the logical place to begin the search for a quality investment is to examine the products and services you use on a regular basis—products and services that provide a high level of consumer satisfaction.

The preceding statement is based on the assumption that if you like the product or service and you feel that you got excellent value for your money, other consumers will too. And while it may be obvious, a satisfied, growing customer base can mean increased sales revenues, profits, and ultimately, higher stock values for the company that manufactured the product or provided the service.

To begin this journal exercise, think about purchases you made over the last month. Describe one product or service that you feel "was worth the money."

_____

_____

_____

_____

For the product or service you chose, describe the attributes or features that impressed you.

_____

_____

_____

_____

_____

Determine if the company that made the product or provided the service is a public company that has issued stock.* Then go to the library or use the Internet to research the investment potential for this company. In the space below, describe why you feel this would be a good or bad investment at this time.

_____

_____

_____

_____

_____

*If the company that manufactured the product or service you chose is not a public company, choose another product or service.

BUILDING SKILLS FOR CAREER SUCCESS

1. Exploring the Internet

For investors seeking information about individual companies and the industry to which they belong, the Internet is an excellent source. If you find the right website, it provides sales and revenue histories, graphs of recent trading on stock and bond markets, and discussions of anticipated changes within a firm or industry. The interested investor also can look at Internet business reports of stock and bond market activity. Among the many companies that issue these reports are Dow Jones, Standard & Poor's, Moody's, and Value Line—all firms that provide, for a fee, analysis and private research services. Visit the text website for updates to this exercise.

Assignment

1. Suppose that you are interested in investing within a particular industry, such as the semiconductor or computer industry. Explore some of the websites listed below, gathering information about the industry and a few related stocks that are of interest to the "experts."

   BusinessWeek: **www.businessweek.com**
   Fortune: **www.fortune.com**
   Nasdaq: **www.nasdaq.com**
   Standard & Poor's:
   www.standardandpoors.com
   New York Stock Exchange: **www.nyse.com**
   Wall Street Journal: **www.wsj.com**

2. List the stocks the experts recommend and their current trading value. You can use one of the web search engines such as Yahoo! Finance (**http://finance.yahoo.com**) to check the price. Also list several stocks the experts do not like and their current selling prices. Then list your own choices of "good" and "bad" stocks.

3. Explain why you and the experts believe that these stocks are good or poor buys today. (You might want to monitor these same websites over the next six months to see how well your "good" stocks are performing.)

2. Developing Critical-Thinking Skills

One way to achieve financial security is to invest a stated amount of money on a systematic basis.

This investment strategy is called *dollar-cost averaging.* When the cost is lower, your investment buys more shares. When the cost is higher, your investment buys fewer shares. A good way to begin investing is to select a mutual fund that meets your financial objectives and to invest the same amount each month or each year.

Assignment

1. Select several mutual funds from the financial pages of the *Wall Street Journal* or a personal finance periodical such as *Money, Kiplinger's Personal Finance,* or *SmartMoney* that provides information about mutual funds. Call the toll-free number for each fund and ask about its objectives. Also request that the company send you a prospectus and an annual report.

2. Select one fund that meets your financial objectives.

3. Prepare a table that includes the following data:

   a. An initial investment of $2,000 in the mutual fund you have selected

   b. The NAV (net asset value)

   c. The number of shares purchased.

4. Record the investment information on a weekly basis. Look in the *Wall Street Journal* or on the Internet to find the NAV for each week.

5. Determine the value of your investment until the end of the semester.

6. Write a report describing the results. Include a summary of what you learned about investments. Be sure to indicate if you think that dollar-cost averaging (investing another $2,000 next year) would be a good idea.

3. Building Team Skills

Investing in stocks can be a way to beat inflation and accumulate money. Traditionally, stocks have returned on average approximately 11 percent per year. Fixed-rate investments, on the other hand, often earn little more than the inflation rate, making it very difficult to accumulate enough money for retirement. For a better understanding of how investing in stocks works, complete this exercise through the end of the semester.

Assignment

1. Form teams of three people. The teams will compete against each other, striving for the largest gain in investments.

2. Assume that you are buying stock in three companies; some should be listed on the NYSE, and some should be traded in the OTC market.

   a. Research different investments, and narrow your choices to three different stocks.

   b. Divide your total investment of $25,000 into three amounts.

   c. Determine the number of shares of stock you can purchase in each company by dividing the budgeted amount by the price of the stock. Allow enough money to pay for the commission. To find the cost of the stock, multiply the number of shares you are going to purchase by the closing price of the stock.

   d. Assume that the commission is 1 percent. Calculate it by multiplying the cost of the stock by 0.01. Add the dollar amount of commission to the cost of the stock to determine the total purchase price.

3. Set up a table to reflect the following information:

   a. Name of the company

   b. Closing price per share

   c. Number of shares purchased

   d. Amount of the commission

   e. Cost of the stock

4. Record the closing price of the stock on a weekly basis. Prepare a chart to use for this step.

5. Before the end of the semester, assume that you sell the stock.

   a. Take the closing price on the day you sell your stocks and multiply it by the number of shares; then calculate the commission at 1 percent.

   b. Deduct the amount of commission from the selling price of the stock. This is the total return on your investment.

6. Calculate your profit or loss. Subtract the total purchase price of the stock from the total return. If the total return is less than the total purchase price, you have a loss.

7. Prepare a report summarizing the results of the project. Include the table and individual stock charts, as well as a statement describing what you learned about investing in stocks.

4. Researching Different Careers

Account executives (sometimes referred to as *stockbrokers*) are agents who buy and sell securities for clients. After completing this exercise, you will have a better understanding of what account executives do on a daily basis.

Assignment

1. Look in the telephone directory for the names and numbers of financial companies or securities firms that sell stock.

2. Contact an account executive at one of these firms and explain that you would like to set up an interview so that you can learn firsthand about an account executive's job.

3. Summarize the results of your interview in a report. Include a statement about whether the job of account executive appeals to you, and explain your thoughts.

5. Improving Communication Skills

Assessment involves determining the amount of progress relative to a standard. It is a critical part of evaluating results in the workplace, as well as determining what you have learned in a course. In reality, learning often takes place in bits and pieces, and when you take the time for review and assessment as you complete a course, you may be surprised at how much you have learned. Since you are nearing the end of this course, it is time to assess what you have learned about business and business operations.

Assignment

If you have been writing in a journal as suggested in Exercise 5 in Chapter 1, you should refer to your journal notes to complete this exercise. Otherwise, use your class or study notes. Prepare a report reflecting your thoughts on the following questions:

1. What are three things you learned about business that impressed you the most? Or what was the greatest surprise to you?

2. How will you use the information you have learned? Give several examples applicable to your personal life, your career, and your job.

3. Has this course helped you make a decision on a career in business? If so, how did it make a difference?

4. What have you learned about systematically writing your thoughts in a journal? How important is this exercise for personal growth and development?

→ PREP TEST

Matching Questions

___ 1. The share value that is stated for a mutual fund.

___ 2. This technique allows stock to be sold that is not owned.

___ 3. It describes a corporation and its stock issue.

___ 4. A stockbroker who buys and sells securities for clients.

___ 5. A request that a security be sold at a price that is equal to or better than some specified price.

___ 6. Securities activities are regulated by this entity.

___ 7. It is an organized place where listed stocks and bonds are exchanged.

___ 8. Purchasing stock directly from the Exxon Corporation (via an investment bank) creates this market.

___ 9. It involves the ease at which an asset can be converted into cash.

___ 10. It is a computerized electronic exchange system.

a. account executive
b. liquidity
c. Nasdaq
d. net asset value
e. primary market
f. prospectus
g. limit order
h. securities exchange
i. Securities and Exchange Commission
j. selling short

True/False Questions

T F

11. ○ ○ Common stockholders are guaranteed a certain amount of dividends.

12. ○ ○ Asset allocation provides a degree of safety in an investment program.

13. ○ ○ An individual who invests in a no-load fund pays no sales charges.

14. ○ ○ A $1,000 bond always has a market value of $1,000.

15. ○ ○ A difference between a stock purchase price and selling price is its capital gain.

16. ○ ○ Series EE Savings Bonds are purchased for half their maturity value.

T F

17. ○ ○ It is the responsibility of the issuer to inform the investor about the tax status of interest paid on a municipal bond.

18. ○ ○ Potential growth and dividend income are features of convertible preferred stock.

19. ○ ○ The SEC was created by the Maloney Act of 1938.

20. ○ ○ The Dow Jones Industrial Average is comprised of fifteen leading utility stocks.

Multiple-Choice Questions

21. When you allow your account executive to make decisions to buy or sell stocks in your brokerage account, you are using a
    a. market order.
    b. call option.
    c. odd-lot order.
    d. discretionary order.
    e. put order.

22. The regulation that requires a corporation to prepare a prospectus is the
    a. Securities Act of 1933.
    b. Securities Exchange Act of 1934.
    c. Maloney Act of 1938.
    d. Federal Securities Act of 1964.
    e. Truth-in-Lending Act.

23. The group that helps corporations sell new issues of stocks, bonds, or other financial securities on the primary market is
    a. the Securities Exchange Commission.
    b. the National Association of Securities Dealers.
    c. an investment banking firm.
    d. an initial public offering specialist.
    e. a certified financial planner.

24. Which type of mutual fund invests in the stocks contained in a specific index?
    a. 12-b fund
    b. Exchange-traded fund
    c. Contingent fund
    d. No-load fund
    e. Open-end fund

25. Karen has inherited $5,000 from her grandmother and wants to invest it in bonds. She has found a bond quoted at 100 in the *Wall Street Journal* that she likes. What will one bond cost her?
    a. $1
    b. $10
    c. $100
    d. $1,000
    e. $10,000

Fill-in-the-Blank Questions

26. Your tolerance for risk will influence your asset _____.

27. The investment with a high degree of safety is a _____ of deposit.

28. A process that lowers the price of stock is known as a stock _____.

29. A pension fund is an example of a(an) _____ investor.

30. A _____ exchange is a marketplace where member brokers meet to buy and sell securities.

Online Study Center

FOR MORE test practice, use the interactive ACE quizzes available at the Online Student Center: www.college.hmco.com/PIC/pridebusiness9e.

Answers on p. PT2.

Managing Money at Finagle A Bagel

Like many other entrepreneurs, when Laura Trust and Alan Litchman decided to buy a business, they raised some money from friends and family. Unlike many entrepreneurs, however, they were so adamant about retaining full control of the business they bought—Finagle A Bagel—that they would not even consider venture capital financing or selling stock. Instead, Litchman says, "We made the decision to get banks to finance this company, which is a difficult thing."

Bagels, Banking, and Borrowing

Ideally, banks prefer to make loans secured by assets such as inventory or accounts receivable. However, Finagle A Bagel has no inventory aside from each day's raw ingredients and fresh-baked bagels, which cannot be repossessed and resold if the company is unable to repay a loan. Nor does it have significant accounts receivable because most of its revenues come from cash transactions in the twenty stores. The company has commercial ovens and other equipment in its headquarters production facility, but, says copresident Litchman, banks do not consider such assets sufficient collateral for a secured loan. And not every bank is willing to offer an unsecured line of credit to a small, fast-growing company such as Finagle A Bagel.

Fortunately, the copresidents bought Finagle A Bagel after the previous owner (who stayed on for a time after the purchase) had built the business into a highly successful six-store chain. To a bank, a company with a proven record of success and a detailed, practical business plan for continued growth looks less risky as a borrower than a newly established company without customers, assets, or cash flow. Thus Finagle A Bagel was able to negotiate an unsecured line of credit of nearly $4 million. As long as Trust and Litchman could show that the company was healthy and achieving certain financial ratios, they would be allowed to draw on the credit line to open new stores or for other business purposes.

Initially, the copresidents only paid the interest on borrowed money so that they would have more money available for growth. Within a few years, however, they began repaying the principal as well as the interest. This meant less money to fuel growth, but it also lightened the company's debt load.

Twenty Stores, Three Banks, Two Checking Accounts

Even though Finagle A Bagel operates twenty stores plus a wholesale division, it needs only two corporate checking accounts. Here's how the system works. For safety reasons, management does not want general managers or their assistants traveling too far to deposit each day's receipts. Yet no single bank has a branch near every Finagle A Bagel store because the stores are spread throughout downtown Boston and the outlying suburbs. Therefore, the company deals with three New England banks that have local branches located near the stores. For each store, Finagle A Bagel opens an account in the closest branch of one of these three banks. After the day's deposits are made, money is transferred using an electronic funds transfer system to the company's main checking account.

Every morning, Litchman looks at the current balance in the main checking account and examines the report showing the previous day's sales and deposits. That tells him how much money he has to cover the bills to be paid that day. Given the slim profit margin in the food-service business—only pennies per sales dollar—Finagle A Bagel uses most of its cash to pay for food and labor. Clearly, cash flow is critical for a small, fast-growing business. Especially on slower sales days, Litchman observes, "You may be one check away from being cash-negative." If its main checking account balance is too low to cover checks that are presented for payment that day, the company may have to draw on its line of credit with the bank. Once this happens, the company must pay interest on any money it borrows, even for just a day.

Finagle A Bagel uses its second checking account only for payroll. This is a zero-balance account containing no money because its sole function is to clear payroll checks. Having two checking accounts allows the company to separate its payroll payments from its payments for supplies, rent, and other business expenses, a convenience for tax and accounting purposes. It also helps the copresidents maintain tight control over corporate finances: No check can be issued without either Litchman's or Trust's signature.

The Future of Finagle A Bagel

Looking ahead, the copresidents plan to continue growing the Finagle A Bagel brand and opening new stores. They are also working toward franchising their brand and fresh-food concept. Within a few years, however, the firm's future course could take a very different turn. "The opportunity to be bought by, just for an example, a McDonald's or a Wendy's or one of the larger operators becomes more plausible as you start to prove to people that you can survive as a multiunit chain with twenty or more stores," says Trust. Because big companies are always on the lookout for innovative food-service concepts, Finagle A Bagel's owners might receive an acquisition offer that's too good to pass up.

Even if the big companies have not yet noticed Finagle A Bagel's outstanding bagels and great performance, other people have. A few years ago the company was named Greater Boston's Small Business of the Year, and *Boston* magazine put it on the "Best of Boston" list for two consecutive years. As important and gratifying as such honors may be for a small business, money always must be—literally—the bottom line for Finagle A Bagel. "You have to make money," Trust emphasizes. "If you don't make money, you're not in business."

Questions

1. If the copresidents of Finagle A Bagel had approached venture capitalists for funding, they probably would have been able to open more new stores in less time. Instead, they opted to use bank financing that has to be repaid. Do you agree with their decision? Why?

2. Given their growth plans, why would the copresidents repay principal and interest on borrowed money rather than pay interest only? Which repayment plan would Finagle A Bagel's bank prefer?

3. Assuming that Finagle A Bagel decides to raise money through an IPO, what are the advantages and disadvantages of issuing stock to obtain the money needed to start or expand a business?

4. As an investor, would you be willing to buy shares in Finagle A Bagel? Explain why the company's stock would or would not be a good investment for you.

In this last section, provide some information about your exit strategy, and discuss any potential trends, problems, or risks that you may encounter. These risks and assumptions could relate to your industry, markets, company, or personnel. Make sure to incorporate important information not included in other parts of the business plan in an appendix. Now is also the time to go back and prepare the executive summary, which should be placed at the beginning of the business plan.

The Exit Strategy Component

Your exit strategy component should at least include answers to the following questions:

7.1. How do you intend to get yourself (and your money) out of the business?

7.2. Will your children take over the business, or do you intend to sell it later?

7.3. Do you intend to grow the business to the point of an IPO?

7.4. How will investors get their money back?

The Critical Risks and Assumptions Component

Your critical risks and assumptions component should answer at least the following questions:

7.5. What will you do if your market does not develop as quickly as you predicted? What if your market develops too quickly?

7.6. What will you do if your competitors underprice or make your product obsolete?

7.7. What will you do if there is an unfavorable industry-wide trend?

7.8. What will happen if trained workers are not available as predicted?

7.9. What will you do if there is an erratic supply of products or raw materials?

The Appendix Component

Supplemental information and documents often are included in an appendix. Here are a few examples of some documents that can be included:

- Résumés of owners and principal managers
- Advertising samples and brochures
- An organization chart
- Floor plans

Review of Business Plan Activities

As you have discovered, writing a business plan involves a long series of interrelated steps. As with any project involving a number of complex steps and calculations, your business plan should be reviewed carefully and revised before you present it to potential investors.

Remember, there is one more component you need to prepare after your business plan is completed: The executive summary should be written last, but because of its importance, it appears after the introduction.

The Executive Summary Component

In the executive summary, give a one- to two-page overview of your entire business plan. This is the most important part of the business plan and is of special interest to busy bankers, investors, and other interested parties. Remember, this section is a summary; more detailed information is provided in the remainder of your business plan.

Make sure that the executive summary captures the reader's attention instantly in the first sentence by using a key selling point or benefit of the business.

Your executive summary should include answers to at least the following:

7.10. *Company information.* What product or service do you provide? What is your competitive advantage? When will the company be formed? What are your company objectives? What is the background of you and your management team?

7.11. *Market opportunity.* What is the expected size and growth rate of your market, your expected market share, and any relevant market trends?

Once again, review your answers to all the questions in the preceding parts to make sure that they are all consistent throughout the entire business plan.

Although many would-be entrepreneurs are excited about the prospects of opening their own business, remember that it takes a lot of hard work, time, and in most cases a substantial amount of money. While the business plan provides an enormous amount of information about your business, it is only the first step. Once it is completed, it is now your responsibility to implement the plan. Good luck in your business venture.

Glossary

A

absolute advantage   the ability to produce a specific product more efficiently than any other nation (77)

accessory equipment   standardized equipment used in a firm's production or office activities (444)

acid-test ratio   a financial ratio calculated by adding cash, marketable securities, and receivables and dividing the total by current liabilities (609)

accountability   the obligation of a worker to accomplish an assigned job or task (252)

account executive   an individual, sometimes called a stockbroker or registered representative, who buys and sells securities for clients (702)

accounting   the process of systematically collecting, analyzing, and reporting financial information (589)

accounting equation   the basis for the accounting process: assets = liabilities + owners' equity (596)

accounting program   a software package that enables users to record, process, and report financial information (576)

accounts receivable turnover   a financial ratio calculated by dividing net sales by accounts receivable (610)

ad hoc committee   a committee created for a specific short-term purpose (263)

administrative manager   a manager who is not associated with any specific functional area but who provides overall administrative guidance and leadership (228)

advertising   a paid, nonpersonal message communicated to a select audience through a mass medium (517)

advertising agency   an independent firm that plans, produces, and places advertising for its clients (524)

advertising media   the various forms of communication through which advertising reaches its audience (519)

affirmative action program   a plan designed to increase the number of minority employees at all levels within an organization (59)

agency shop   a workplace in which employees can choose not to join the union but must pay dues to the union anyway (395)

agent   a middleman that expedites exchanges, represents a buyer or a seller, and often is hired permanently on a commission basis (488)

alien corporation   a corporation chartered by a foreign government and conducting business in the United States (159)

analytical process   a process in operations management in which raw materials are broken into different component parts (278)

annual report   a report distributed to stockholders and other interested parties that describes a firm's operating activities and its financial condition (597)

arbitration   the step in a grievance procedure in which a neutral third party hears the two sides of a dispute and renders a binding decision (396)

arithmetic mean   the total of all the values in a set of data divided by the number of items (562)

asset allocation   the process of spreading your money among several different types of investments to lessen risk (707)

assets   the resources that a business owns (596)

audit   an examination of a company's financial statements and the accounting practices that produced them (590)

authoritarian leader   one who holds all authority and responsibility, with communication usually moving from top to bottom (231)

authority   the power, within an organization, to accomplish an assigned job or task (252)

automatic vending   the use of machines to dispense products (495)

automation   the total or near-total use of machines to do work (296)

B

balance of payments   the total flow of money into a country minus the total flow of money out of that country over some period of time (80)

balance of trade   the total value of a nation's exports minus the total value of its imports over some period of time (79)

balance sheet (or statement of financial position)   a summary of the dollar amounts of a firm's assets, liabilities, and owners' equity accounts at the end of a specific accounting period (597)

banker's acceptance   a written order for a bank to pay a third party a stated amount of money on a specific date (646)

bargaining unit   the specific group of employees represented by a union (390)

barter   a system of exchange in which goods or services are traded directly for other goods and/or services without using money (23)

barter system   a system of exchange in which goods or services are traded directly for other goods or services (628)

behavior modification   a systematic program of reinforcement to encourage desirable behavior (361)

bill of lading   document issued by a transport carrier to an exporter to prove that merchandise has been shipped (92)

blue-chip stock   a safe investment that generally attracts conservative investors (699)

G1

board of directors   the top governing body of a corporation, the members of which are elected by the stockholders (160)

bond indenture   a legal document that details all the conditions relating to a bond issue (684)

boycott   a refusal to do business with a particular firm (397)

brand   a name, term, symbol, design, or any combination of these that identifies a seller's products as distinct from those of other sellers (452)

brand equity   marketing and financial value associated with a brand's strength in a market (453)

brand extension   using an existing brand to brand a new product in a different product category (455)

brand loyalty   extent to which a customer is favorable toward buying a specific brand (453)

brand mark   the part of a brand that is a symbol or distinctive design (452)

brand name   the part of a brand that can be spoken (452)

breakeven quantity   the number of units that must be sold for the total revenue (from all units sold) to equal the total cost (of all units sold) (462)

broadband technology   a general term referring to higher-speed Internet connections that deliver data, voice, and video material (567)

broker   a middleman that specializes in a particular commodity, represents either a buyer or a seller, and is likely to be hired on a temporary basis (488)

budget   a financial statement that projects income and/or expenditures over a specified future period (670)

bundle pricing   packaging together two or more complementary products and selling them for a single price (466)

bureaucratic structure   a management system based on a formal framework of authority that is outlined carefully and followed precisely (257)

business   the organized effort of individuals to produce and sell, for a profit, the goods and services that satisfy society's needs (9)

business buying behavior   the purchasing of products by producers, resellers, governmental units, and institutions (428)

business cycle   the recurrence of periods of growth and recession in a nation's economic activity (19)

business ethics   the application of moral standards to business situations (41)

business model   represents a group of common characteristics and methods of doing business to generate sales revenues and reduce expenses (125)

business plan   a carefully constructed guide for the person starting a business (194)

business product   a product bought for resale, for making other products, or for use in a firm's operations (443)

business service   an intangible product that an organization uses in its operations (444)

business-to-business (B2B) model   firms that conduct business with other businesses (125)

business-to-consumer (B2C) model   firms that focus on conducting business with individual buyers (126)

buying allowance   a temporary price reduction to resellers for purchasing specified quantities of a product (530)

buying behavior   the decisions and actions of people involved in buying and using products (428)

buying long   buying stock with the expectation that it will increase in value and then can be sold at a profit (715)

C

capacity   the amount of products or services that an organization can produce in a given time (284)

capital budget   a financial statement that estimates a firm's expenditures for major assets and its long-term financing needs (671)

capital gain   the difference between a security's purchase price and its selling price (710)

capital-intensive technology   a process in which machines and equipment do most of the work (285)

capitalism   an economic system in which individuals own and operate the majority of businesses that provide goods and services (13)

captioned photograph   a picture accompanied by a brief explanation (532)

captive pricing   pricing the basic product in a product line low, but pricing related items at a higher level (467)

carrier   a firm that offers transportation services (499)

cash budget   a financial statement that estimates cash receipts and cash expenditures over a specified period (670)

cash flow   the movement of money into and out of an organization (665)

catalog marketing   a type of marketing in which an organization provides a catalog from which customers make selections and place orders by mail, telephone, or the Internet (493)

catalog showroom   a retail outlet that displays well-known brands and sells them at discount prices through catalogs within the store (490)

category killer   a very large specialty store that concentrates on a single product line and competes on the basis of low prices and product availability (492)

caveat emptor   a Latin phrase meaning "let the buyer beware" (52)

centralized organization   an organization that systematically works to concentrate authority at the upper levels of the organization (253)

certificate of deposit (CD)   a document stating that the bank will pay the depositor a guaranteed interest rate on money left on deposit for a specified period of time (641)

certified management accountant (CMA)   an accountant who has met the requirements for education and experience, passed a rigorous exam, and is certified by the Institute of Management Accountants (595)

certified public accountant (CPA)   an individual who has met state requirements for accounting education and experience and has passed a rigorous two-day accounting examination prepared by the AICPA (595)

chain of command   the line of authority that extends from the highest to the lowest levels of an organization (247)

chain retailer   a company that operates more than one retail outlet (489)

channel of distribution (or marketing channel) a sequence of marketing organizations that directs a product from the producer to the ultimate user (481)

check a written order for a bank or other financial institution to pay a stated dollar amount to the business or person indicated on the face of the check (641)

chief financial officer (CFO) a high-level corporate executive who manages a firm's finances and reports directly to the company's chief executive officer or president (669)

closed corporation a corporation whose stock is owned by relatively few people and is not sold to the general public (158)

closed shop a workplace in which workers must join the union before they are hired; outlawed by the Taft-Hartley Act (394)

cluster structure an organization that consists primarily of teams with no or very few underlying departments (259)

code of ethics a guide to acceptable and ethical behavior as defined by the organization (45)

collaborative learning system a work environment that allows problem-solving participation by all team members (572)

collateral real estate or property pledged as security for a loan (642)

collective bargaining the process of negotiating a labor contract with management (391)

command economy an economic system in which the government decides what goods and services will be produced, how they will be produced, for whom available goods and services will be produced, and who owns and controls the major factors of production (15)

commercial bank a profit-making organization that accepts deposits, makes loans, and provides related services to its customers (637)

commercial paper a short-term promissory note issued by a large corporation (675)

commission a payment that is a percentage of sales revenue (326)

commission merchant a middleman that carries merchandise and negotiates sales for manufacturers (488)

common stock stock owned by individuals or firms who may vote on corporate matters, but whose claims on profit and assets are subordinate to the claims of others (159)

common stock stock whose owners may vote on corporate matters, but whose claims on profits and assets are subordinate to the claims of others (678)

community shopping center a planned shopping center that includes one or two department stores and some specialty stores, along with convenience stores (496)

comparable worth a concept that seeks equal compensation for jobs requiring about the same level of education, training, and skills (325)

comparative advantage the ability to produce a specific product more efficiently than any other product (78)

comparison discounting setting a price at a specific level and comparing it with a higher price (468)

compensation the payment employees receive in return for their labor (324)

compensation system the policies and strategies that determine employee compensation (325)

competition rivalry among businesses for sales to potential customers (20)

component part an item that becomes part of a physical product and is either a finished item ready for assembly or a product that needs little processing before assembly (444)

computer-aided design (CAD) the use of computers to aid in the development of products (297)

computer-aided manufacturing (CAM) the use of computers to plan and control manufacturing processes (297)

computer-integrated manufacturing (CIM) a computer system that not only helps to design products but also controls the machinery needed to produce the finished product (297)

computer network a group of two or more computers linked together that allows users to share data and information (568)

computer viruses software codes that are designed to disrupt normal computer operations (131)

conceptual skill the ability to think in abstract terms (229)

consumer buying behavior the purchasing of products for personal or household use, not for business purposes (428)

consumerism all activities undertaken to protect the rights of consumers (55)

consumer price index (CPI) a monthly index that measures the changes in price of a fixed basket of goods purchased by a typical consumer in an urban area (19)

consumer products goods and services purchased by individuals for personal consumption (15)

consumer sales promotion method a sales promotion method designed to attract consumers to particular retail stores and to motivate them to purchase certain new or established products (528)

contingency plan a plan that outlines alternative courses of action that may be taken if an organization's other plans are disrupted or become ineffective (224)

continuous process a manufacturing process in which a firm produces the same product(s) over a long period of time (298)

controlling the process of evaluating and regulating ongoing activities to ensure that goals are achieved (225)

convenience product a relatively inexpensive, frequently purchased item for which buyers want to exert only minimal effort (443)

convenience store a small food store that sells a limited variety of products but remains open well beyond normal business hours (491)

convergence of technologies the overlapping of capabilities and the merging of products and services into one fully integrated interactive system (136)

convertible bond a bond that can be exchanged, at the owner's option, for a specified number of shares of the corporation's common stock (684)

convertible preferred stock preferred stock that an owner may exchange for a specified number of shares of common stock (679)

cookie a small piece of software sent by a website that tracks an individual's Internet use (130)

cooperative an association of individuals or firms whose purpose is to perform some business function for its members (165)

cooperative advertising an arrangement whereby a manufacturer agrees to pay a certain amount of a retailer's media cost for advertising the manufacturer's product (530)

copyright legal right to control content ownership (132)

corporate bond a corporation's written pledge that it will repay a specified amount of money with interest (683)

corporate charter a contract between a corporation and the state in which the state recognizes the formation of the artificial person that is the corporation (159)

corporate culture the inner rites, rituals, heroes, and values of a firm (260)

corporate officers the chairman of the board, president, executive vice presidents, corporate secretary, treasurer, and any other top executive appointed by the board of directors (161)

corporation an artificial person created by law with most of the legal rights of a real person, including the rights to start and operate a business, to buy or sell property, to borrow money, to sue or be sued, and to enter into binding contracts (157)

cost of goods sold the dollar amount equal to beginning inventory plus net purchases less ending inventory (602)

countertrade an international barter transaction (94)

coupon reduces the retail price of a particular item by a stated amount at the time of purchase (529)

craft union an organization of skilled workers in a single craft or trade (381)

creative selling selling products to new customers and increasing sales to present customers (526)

credit immediate purchasing power that is exchanged for a promise to repay borrowed money, with or without interest, at a later date (647)

credit union a financial institution that accepts deposits from and lends money to only those people who are its members (638)

critical path the sequence of production activities that takes the longest time from start to finish (292)

cross-functional team a team of individuals with varying specialties, expertise, and skills that are brought together to achieve a common task (258, 366)

cultural (or workplace) diversity differences among people in a work force owing to race, ethnicity, and gender (6, 317)

currency devaluation the reduction of the value of a nation's currency relative to the currencies of other countries (81)

current assets assets that can be converted quickly into cash or that will be used in one year or less (598)

current liabilities debts that will be repaid in one year or less (601)

current ratio a financial ratio computed by dividing current assets by current liabilities (609)

customary pricing pricing on the basis of tradition (467)

customer lifetime value a combination of purchase frequency, average value of purchases, and brand-switching patterns over the entire span of a customer's relationship with a company (415)

customer relationship management (CRM) using information about customers to create marketing strate-gies that develop and sustain desirable customer relationships (414)

customer relationship management (CRM) software software solutions that incorporate a variety of methods that can be used to manage communication with customers and share important information with all of a firm's employees (122)

D

data numerical or verbal descriptions that usually result from some sort of measurement (553)

database a single collection of data stored in one place that can be used by people throughout an organization to make decisions (555)

database management program software that allows users to store large amounts of data electronically and to transform the data into information (575)

data mining the practice of searching through data records looking for useful information (130)

data processing the transformation of data into a form that is useful for a specific purpose (560)

debenture bond a bond backed only by the reputation of the issuing corporation (683)

debit card a card that electronically subtracts the amount of your purchase from your bank account at the moment the purchase is made (643)

debt capital borrowed money obtained through loans of various types (672)

debt-to-owners'-equity ratio a financial ratio calculated by dividing total liabilities by owners' equity (610)

decentralized organization an organization in which management consciously attempts to spread authority widely in the lower levels of the organization (252)

decisional role a role that involves various aspects of management decision making (230)

decision making the act of choosing one alternative from a set of alternatives (232)

decision-support system (DSS) a type of computer program that provides relevant data and information to help a firm's employees make decisions and choose different courses of action (571)

deflation a general decrease in the level of prices (18)

delegation assigning part of a manager's work and power to other workers (252)

demand the quantity of a product that buyers are willing to purchase at each of various prices (21, 458)

demand deposit an amount on deposit in a checking account (631)

democratic leader one who holds final responsibility but also delegates authority to others, who help to determine work assignments; communication is active upward and downward (231)

departmentalization the process of grouping jobs into manageable units (250)

departmentalization by customer grouping activities according to the needs of various customer populations (251)

departmentalization by function grouping jobs that relate to the same organizational activity (250)

departmentalization by location grouping activities according to the defined geographic area in which they are performed (251)

departmentalization by product grouping activities related to a particular product or service (250)

department store a retail store that (1) employs twenty-five or more persons and (2) sells at least home furnishings, appliances, family apparel, and household linens and dry goods, each in a different part of the store (489)

depreciation the process of apportioning the cost of a fixed asset over the period during which it will be used (600)

depression a severe recession that lasts longer than a recession (20)

design planning the development of a plan for converting a product idea into an actual product or service (283)

desktop publishing program a software package that enables users to combine text and graphics in reports, newsletters, and pamphlets (576)

digitized data that have been converted to a type of signal that computers and telecommunications equipment, that make up the Internet, can understand (120)

directing the combined processes of leading and motivating (224)

direct-mail advertising promotional material mailed directly to individuals (520)

direct marketing the use of the telephone, Internet, and nonpersonal media to introduce products to customers, who then can purchase them via mail, telephone, or the Internet (493)

direct-response marketing a type of marketing in which a retailer advertises a product and makes it available through mail, telephone, or online orders (494)

direct selling the marketing of products to customers through face-to-face sales presentations at home or in the workplace (493)

discount a deduction from the price of an item (469)

discount rate the interest rate the Federal Reserve System charges for loans to member banks (634)

discount store a self-service general-merchandise outlet that sells products at lower-than-usual prices (490)

discretionary income disposable income less savings and expenditures on food, clothing, and housing (430)

discretionary order an order to buy or sell a security that lets the broker decide when to execute the transaction and at what price (703)

disposable income personal income less all additional personal taxes (430)

dividend a distribution of earnings to the stockholders of a corporation (160)

domestic corporation a corporation in the state in which it is incorporated (159)

domestic system a method of manufacturing in which an entrepreneur distributes raw materials to various homes, where families process them into finished goods to be offered for sale by the merchant entrepreneur (23)

double-entry bookkeeping system a system in which each financial transaction is recorded as two separate accounting entries to maintain the balance shown in the accounting equation (596)

draft issued by the exporter's bank, ordering the importer's bank to pay for the merchandise, thus guaranteeing payment once accepted by the importer's bank (92)

dumping exportation of large quantities of a product at a price lower than that of the same product in the home market (80)

E

earnings per share a financial ratio calculated by dividing net income after taxes by the number of shares of common stock outstanding (609)

e-Business the organized effort of individuals to produce and sell through the Internet, for a profit, the products and services that satisfy society's needs (26)

e-business (electronic business) the organized effort of individuals to produce and sell, for a profit, the goods and services that satisfy society's needs through the facilities available on the Internet (116)

e-commerce buying and selling activities conducted online (116)

economic community an organization of nations formed to promote the free movement of resources and products among its members and to create common economic policies (88)

economic model of social responsibility the view that society will benefit most when business is left alone to produce and market profitable products that society needs (53)

economics the study of how wealth is created and distributed (11)

economy the way in which people deal with the creation and distribution of wealth (12)

electronic check conversion (ECC) a process used to convert information from a paper check into an electronic payment for merchandise, services, or bills (645)

electronic funds transfer (EFT) system a means of performing financial transactions through a computer terminal or telephone hookup (645)

embargo a complete halt to trading with a particular nation or in a particular product (81)

employee benefit a reward in addition to regular compensation that is provided indirectly to employees (327)

employee ownership a situation in which employees own the company they work for by virtue of being stockholders (365)

employee training the process of teaching operations and technical employees how to do their present jobs more effectively and efficiently (328)

empowerment making employees more involved in their jobs by increasing their participation in decision making (364)

entrepreneur a person who risks time, effort, and money to start and operate a business (13)

Equal Employment Opportunity Commission (EEOC) a government agency with power to investigate complaints of employment discrimination and power to sue firms that practice it (59)

equity capital money received from the owners or from the sale of shares of ownership in a business (672)

equity theory a theory of motivation based on the premise that people are motivated to obtain and preserve equitable treatment for themselves (357)

esteem needs our need for respect, recognition, and a sense of our own accomplishment and worth (352)

ethics the study of right and wrong and of the morality of the choices individuals make (41)

everyday low prices (EDLPs) setting a low price for products on a consistent basis (467)

exclusive distribution the use of only a single retail outlet for a product in a large geographic area (484)

executive information system (EIS) a computer-based system that facilitates and supports the decision-making needs of top managers and senior executives by providing easy access to both internal and external information (571)

expectancy theory a model of motivation based on the assumption that motivation depends on how much we want something and on how likely we think we are to get it (358)

expert system a type of computer program that uses artificial intelligence to imitate a human's ability to think (571)

Export-Import Bank of the United States an independent agency of the U.S. government whose function it is to assist in financing the exports of American firms (98)

exporting selling and shipping raw materials or products to other nations (78)

express warranty a written explanation of the responsibilities of the producer in the event that a product is found to be defective or otherwise unsatisfactory (457)

external recruiting the attempt to attract job applicants from outside an organization (320)

e-zines small online magazines (124)

F

factor a firm that specializes in buying other firms' accounts receivable (676)

factors of production resources used to produce goods and services (12)

factory system a system of manufacturing in which all the materials, machinery, and workers required to manufacture a product are assembled in one place (25)

family branding the strategy in which a firm uses the same brand for all or most of its products (455)

family of funds a group of mutual funds managed by one investment company (714)

feature article a piece (of up to 3,000 words) prepared by an organization for inclusion in a particular publication (532)

federal deficit a shortfall created when the federal government spends more in a fiscal year than it receives (20)

federal funds rate the interest rate at which a bank lends immediately available funds to another bank overnight in order to meet the borrowing bank's reserve requirements (634)

Federal Reserve System the central bank of the United States responsible for regulating the banking industry (632)

financial accounting generates financial statements and reports for interested people outside an organization (594)

financial leverage the use of borrowed funds to increase the return on owners' equity (681)

financial management all the activities concerned with obtaining money and using it effectively (665)

financial manager a manager who is primarily responsible for an organization's financial resources (227)

financial plan a plan for obtaining and using the money needed to implement an organization's goals (669)

financial planner an individual who has had at least two years of training in investments, insurance, taxation,

retirement planning, and estate planning and has passed a rigorous examination (698)

financial ratio a number that shows the relationship between two elements of a firm's financial statements (607)

first-line manager a manager who coordinates and supervises the activities of operating employees (227)

fiscal policy government influence on the amount of savings and expenditures; accomplished by altering the tax structure and by changing the levels of government spending (20)

fixed assets assets that will be held or used for a period longer than one year (600)

fixed cost a cost incurred no matter how many units of a product are produced or sold (462)

flexible benefit plan compensation plan whereby an employee receives a predetermined amount of benefit dollars to spend on a package of benefits he or she has selected to meet individual needs (327)

flexible manufacturing system (FMS) a single production system that combines robotics and computer-integrated manufacturing (298)

flextime a system in which employees set their own work hours within employer-determined limits (362)

floor planning method of financing in which title to merchandise is given to lenders in return for short-term financing (676)

foreign corporation a corporation in any state in which it does business except the one in which it is incorporated (159)

foreign-exchange control a restriction on the amount of a particular foreign currency that can be purchased or sold (81)

form utility utility created by converting production inputs into finished products (415)

franchise a license to operate an individually owned business as though it were part of a chain of outlets or stores (199)

franchisee a person or organization purchasing a franchise (199)

franchising the actual granting of a franchise (199)

franchisor an individual or organization granting a franchise (199)

free enterprise the system of business in which individuals are free to decide what to produce, how to produce it, and at what price to sell it (4)

frequency distribution a listing of the number of times each value appears in a set of data (561)

frequent-user incentive a program developed to reward customers who engage in repeat (frequent) purchases (530)

full disclosure requirement that investors should have access to all important facts about stocks, bonds, and other securities so that they can make informed decisions (705)

full-service wholesaler a middleman that performs the entire range of wholesaler functions (488)

functional middleman a middleman that helps in the transfer of ownership of products but does not take title to the products (481)

G

Gantt chart   a graphic scheduling device that displays the tasks to be performed on the vertical axis and the time required for each task on the horizontal axis (291)

General Agreement on Tariffs and Trade (GATT)   an international organization of 132 nations dedicated to reducing or eliminating tariffs and other barriers to world trade (86)

general-merchandise wholesaler   a middleman that deals in a wide variety of products (488)

general partner   a person who assumes full or shared responsibility for operating a business (153)

general partnership   a business co-owned by two or more general partners who are liable for everything the business does (153)

generally accepted accounting principles (GAAPs)   an accepted set of guidelines and practices for companies reporting financial information and for the accounting profession (591)

generic product (or brand)   a product with no brand at all (452)

goal   an end result that an organization is expected to achieve over a one- to ten-year period (222)

goal-setting theory   a theory of motivation suggesting that employees are motivated to achieve goals that they and their managers establish together (359)

government-owned corporation   a corporation owned and operated by a local, state, or federal government (164)

grapevine   the informal communications network within an organization (264)

graphics program   software that enables users to display and print pictures, drawings, charts, and diagrams (575)

grievance procedure   a formally established course of action for resolving employee complaints against management (395)

gross domestic product (GDP)   the total dollar value of all goods and services produced by all people within the boundaries of a country during a one-year period (18)

gross profit   a firm's net sales less the cost of goods sold (603)

gross sales   the total dollar amount of all goods and services sold during an accounting period (602)

groupware   one of the latest types of software that facilitates the management of large projects among geographically dispersed employees, as well as such group activities as problem solving and brainstorming (572)

H

hard-core unemployed   workers with little education or vocational training and a long history of unemployment (59)

high-risk investment   an investment made in the uncertain hope of earning a relatively large profit in a short time (701)

hostile takeover   a situation in which the management and board of directors of a firm targeted for acquisition disapprove of the merger (167)

hourly wage   a specific amount of money paid for each hour of work (326)

human resources management (HRM)   all the activities involved in acquiring, maintaining, and developing an organization's human resources (314)

human resources manager   a person charged with managing an organization's human resources programs (228)

human resources planning   the development of strategies to meet a firm's future human resources needs (315)

hygiene factors   job factors that reduce dissatisfaction when present to an acceptable degree but that do not necessarily result in high levels of motivation (353)

I

import duty (tariff)   a tax levied on a particular foreign product entering a country (80)

importing   purchasing raw materials or products in other nations and bringing them into one's own country (79)

import quota   a limit on the amount of a particular good that may be imported into a country during a given period of time (81)

incentive payment   a payment in addition to wages, salary, or commissions (326)

income statement   a summary of a firm's revenues and expenses during a specified accounting period (601)

independent retailer   a firm that operates only one retail outlet (489)

individual branding   the strategy in which a firm uses a different brand for each of its products (454)

industrial union   an organization of both skilled and unskilled workers in a single industry (383)

inflation   a general rise in the level of prices (18)

infomercial   a program-length televised commercial message resembling an entertainment or consumer affairs program (521)

informal group   a group created by the members themselves to accomplish goals that may or may not be relevant to an organization (264)

informal organization   the pattern of behavior and interaction that stems from personal rather than official relationships (264)

information   data presented in a form that is useful for a specific purpose (554)

informational role   a role in which the manager either gathers or provides information (230)

information society   a society in which large groups of employees generate or depend on information to perform their jobs (567)

information technology (IT) officer   a manager at the executive level who is responsible for ensuring that a firm has the equipment necessary to provide the information the firm's employees and managers need to make effective decisions (556)

initial public offering (IPO)   when a corporation sells common stock to the general public for the first time (677)

injunction   a court order requiring a person or group either to perform some act or to refrain from performing some act (387)

insider trading   the practice of board members, corporate managers, and employees buying and selling a corporation's stock (705)

inspection   an examination of the quality of work in process (294)

institutional advertising   advertising designed to enhance a firm's image or reputation (519)

institutional investors pension funds, insurance companies, mutual funds, banks, and other organizations that trade large quantities of securities (701)

intangible assets assets that do not exist physically but that have a value based on the rights or privileges they confer on a firm (600)

integrated marketing communications coordination of promotion efforts to ensure maximal informational and persuasive impact on customers (515)

intensive distribution the use of all available outlets for a product (483)

intermittent process a manufacturing process in which a firm's manufacturing machines and equipment are changed to produce different products (298)

internal recruiting considering present employees as applicants for available positions (321)

international business all business activities that involve exchanges across national boundaries (77)

International Monetary Fund (IMF) an international bank with 184 member nations that makes short-term loans to developing countries experiencing balance-of-payment deficits (99)

International Organization for Standardization a nongovernmental organization in Geneva, Switzerland, with a membership of 156 countries that develops standards for products in order to facilitate trade across national borders (295)

Internet a worldwide network of computers linked through telecommunications (567)

Internet service providers (ISPs) provide customers with a connection to the Internet through various phone plugs and cables (121)

interpersonal role a role in which the manager deals with people (230)

interpersonal skill the ability to deal effectively with other people (230)

intranet a smaller version of the Internet for use within a firm (568)

intrapreneur an employee who pushes an innovative idea, product, or process through an organization (262)

inventory control the process of managing inventories in such a way as to minimize inventory costs, including both holding costs and potential stock-out costs (290)

inventory management the process of managing inventories in such a way as to minimize inventory costs, including both holding costs and potential stock-out costs (497)

inventory turnover a financial ratio calculated by dividing the cost of goods sold in one year by the average value of the inventory (610)

investment banking firm an organization that assists corporations in raising funds, usually by helping to sell new issues of stocks, bonds, or other financial securities (678)

invisible hand a term created by Adam Smith to describe how an individual's own personal gain benefits others and a nation's economy (13)

J

job analysis a systematic procedure for studying jobs to determine their various elements and requirements (319)

job description a list of the elements that make up a particular job (319)

job enlargement expanding a worker's assignments to include additional but similar tasks (360)

job enrichment a motivation technique that provides employees with more variety and responsibility in their jobs (360)

job evaluation the process of determining the relative worth of the various jobs within a firm (325)

job redesign a type of job enrichment in which work is restructured to cultivate the worker-job match (361)

job rotation the systematic shifting of employees from one job to another (250)

job security protection against the loss of employment (394)

job sharing an arrangement whereby two people share one full-time position (363)

job specialization the separation of all organizational activities into distinct tasks and the assignment of different tasks to different people (249)

job specification a list of the qualifications required to perform a particular job (319)

joint venture an agreement between two or more groups to form a business entity in order to achieve a specific goal or to operate for a specific period of time (166)

jurisdiction the right of a particular union to organize particular groups of workers (390)

just-in-time inventory system a system designed to ensure that materials or supplies arrive at a facility just when they are needed so that storage and holding costs are minimized (291)

K

knowledge management a firm's procedures for generating, using, and sharing the data and information contained in the firm's databases (555)

L

labeling the presentation of information on a product or its package (457)

labor-intensive technology a process in which people must do most of the work (285)

labor union an organization of workers acting together to negotiate their wages and working conditions with employers (381)

laissez-faire leader one who gives authority to employees and allows subordinates to work as they choose with a minimum of interference; communication flows horizontally among group members (231)

leadership the ability to influence others (231)

leading the process of influencing people to work toward a common goal (224)

lease an agreement by which the right to use real estate, equipment, or other assets is transferred temporarily from the owner to the user (682)

letter of credit a legal document issued by a bank or other financial institution guaranteeing to pay a seller a stated amount for a specified period of time (646)

leveraged buyout (LBO) a purchase arrangement that

allows a firm's managers and employees or a group of investors to purchase the company (170)

liabilities a firm's debts and obligations (596)

licensing a contractual agreement in which one firm permits another to produce and market its product and use its brand name in return for a royalty or other compensation (90)

lifestyle shopping center an open-air-environment shopping center with upscale chain specialty stores (496)

limited liability a feature of corporate ownership that limits each owner's financial liability to the amount of money that he or she has paid for the corporation's stock (161)

limited-liability company (LLC) a form of business ownership that combines the benefits of a corporation and a partnership while avoiding some of the restrictions and disadvantages of those forms of ownership (164)

limited-line wholesaler a middleman that stocks only a few product lines but carries numerous product items within each line (488)

limited partner a person who contributes capital to a business but has no management responsibility or liability for losses beyond the amount he or she invested in the partnership (153)

limited partnership a business co-owned by one or more general partners who manage the business and limited partners who invest money in it (153)

limited-service wholesaler a middleman that assumes responsibility for a few wholesale services only (488)

limit order a request that a security be bought or sold at a price that is equal to or better than some specified price (703)

line extension development of a new product that is closely related to one or more products in the existing product line but designed specifically to meet different customer needs (448)

line management position a part of the chain of command; a position in which a person makes decisions and gives orders to subordinates to achieve the goals of the organization (255)

line of credit a loan that is approved before the money is actually needed (642)

liquidity the ease with which an asset can be converted into cash (598)

local-area network (LAN) a network that connects computers that are in close proximity to each other, such as in an office building or on a college campus (568)

lockout a firm's refusal to allow employees to enter the workplace (398)

log-file records files that store a record of the websites visited (130)

long-term financing money that will be used for longer than one year (667)

long-term liabilities debts that need not be repaid for at least one year (601)

lump-sum salary increase an entire pay raise taken in one lump sum (326)

M

macroeconomics the study of the national economy and the global economy (12)

maintenance shop a workplace in which an employee

who joins the union must remain a union member as long as he or she is employed by the firm (395)

major equipment large tools and machines used for production purposes (444)

Malcolm Baldrige National Quality Award an award given by the President of the United States to organizations that apply and that are judged to be outstanding in specific managerial tasks that lead to improved quality for both products and services (293)

management the process of coordinating people and other resources to achieve the goals of an organization (220)

management by objectives (MBO) a motivation technique in which managers and employees collaborate in setting goals (359)

management development the process of preparing managers and other professionals to assume increased responsibility in both present and future positions (328)

management information system (MIS) a system that provides managers and employees with the information they need to perform their jobs as effectively as possible (555)

managerial accounting provides managers and employees with the information needed to make decisions about a firm's financing, investing, and operating activities (594)

managerial hierarchy the arrangement that provides increasing authority at higher levels of management (263)

manufacturer (or producer) brand a brand that is owned by a manufacturer (452)

manufacturer's sales branch essentially a merchant wholesaler that is owned by a manufacturer (489)

manufacturer's sales office essentially a sales agent owned by a manufacturer (489)

margin requirement the portion of the price of a stock that cannot be borrowed (716)

market a group of individuals or organizations, or both, that need products in a given category and that have the ability, willingness, and authority to purchase such products (418)

market economy an economic system in which businesses and individuals decide what to produce and buy, and the market determines quantities sold and prices (14)

marketing an organizational function and a set of processes for creating, communicating, and delivering value to customers and for managing customer relationships in ways that benefit the organization and its stakeholders (413)

marketing concept a business philosophy that a firm should provide goods and services that satisfy customers' needs through a coordinated set of activities that allows the firm to achieve its objectives (416)

marketing information system a system for managing marketing information that is gathered continually from internal and external sources (426)

marketing manager a manager who is responsible for facilitating the exchange of products between an organization and its customers or clients (228)

marketing mix a combination of product, price, distribution, and promotion developed to satisfy a particular target market (419)

marketing plan   a written document that specifies an organization's resources, objectives, strategy, and implementation and control efforts to be used in marketing a specific product or product group (424)

marketing research   the process of systematically gathering, recording, and analyzing data concerning a particular marketing problem (426)

marketing strategy   a plan that will enable an organization to make the best use of its resources and advantages to meet its objectives (419)

market order   a request that a security be purchased or sold at the current market price (703)

market price   the price at which the quantity demanded is exactly equal to the quantity supplied (21)

market segment   a group of individuals or organizations within a market that shares one or more common characteristics (421)

market segmentation   the process of dividing a market into segments and directing a marketing mix at a particular segment or segments rather than at the total market (421)

markup   the amount a seller adds to the cost of a product to determine its basic selling price (462)

market value   the price of one share of a stock at a particular time (710)

Maslow's hierarchy of needs   a sequence of human needs in the order of their importance (351)

mass production   a manufacturing process that lowers the cost required to produce a large number of identical or similar products over a long period of time (278)

master limited partnership (MLP)   a business partnership that is owned and managed like a corporation but often taxed like a partnership (153)

materials handling   the actual physical handling of goods, in warehouses as well as during transportation (499)

materials requirements planning (MRP)   a computerized system that integrates production planning and inventory control (290)

matrix structure   an organizational structure that combines vertical and horizontal lines of authority, usually by superimposing product departmentalization on a functionally departmentalized organization (258)

maturity date   the date on which a corporation is to repay borrowed money (683)

measure of value   a single standard, or "yardstick," used to assign values to and compare the values of products, services, and resources (629)

median   the value at the exact middle of a set of data when the data are arranged in order (562)

mediation   the use of a neutral third party to assist management and the union during their negotiations (398)

medium of exchange   anything accepted as payment for products, services, and resources (629)

merchant middleman   a middleman that actually takes title to products by buying them (481)

merchant wholesaler   a middleman that purchases goods in large quantities and then sells them to other wholesalers or retailers and to institutional, farm, government, professional, or industrial users (488)

merger   the purchase of one corporation by another (167)

microeconomics   the study of the decisions made by individuals and businesses (12)

middleman (or marketing intermediary)   a marketing organization that links a producer and user within a marketing channel (481)

middle manager   a manager who implements the strategy and major policies developed by top management (227)

minority   a racial, religious, political, national, or other group regarded as different from the larger group of which it is a part and that is often singled out for unfavorable treatment (57)

mission   a statement of the basic purpose that makes an organization different from others (221)

missionary salesperson   a salesperson—generally employed by a manufacturer—who visits retailers to persuade them to buy the manufacturer's products (526)

mixed economy   an economy that exhibits elements of both capitalism and socialism (14)

mode   the value that appears most frequently in a set of data (562)

monetary policies   Federal Reserve decisions that determine the size of the supply of money in the nation and the level of interest rates (20)

money   anything a society uses to purchase products, services, or resources (628)

monopolistic competition   a market situation in which there are many buyers along with a relatively large number of sellers who differentiate their products from the products of competitors (22)

monopoly   a market (or industry) with only one seller (23)

morale   an employee's feelings about his or her job, superiors, and the firm itself (349)

mortgage bond   a corporate bond secured by various assets of the issuing firm (684)

motivating   the process of providing reasons for people to work in the best interests of an organization (224)

motivation   the individual internal process that energizes, directs, and sustains behavior; the personal "force" that causes you or me to behave in a particular way (349)

motivation factors   job factors that increase motivation but whose absence does not necessarily result in dissatisfaction (353)

motivation-hygiene theory   the idea that satisfaction and dissatisfaction are separate and distinct dimensions (353)

multilateral development bank (MDB)   an internationally supported bank that provides loans to developing countries to help them grow (98)

multinational enterprise   a firm that operates on a worldwide scale without ties to any specific nation or region (94)

multiple-unit pricing   the strategy of setting a single price for two or more units (466)

municipal bond   sometimes called a muni—a debt security issued by a state or local government (710)

mutual fund   a professionally managed investment vehicle that combines and invests the funds of many individual investors (712)

N

Nasdaq   computerized electronic exchange system through which most OTC securities are traded (702)

National Alliance of Business (NAB)　a joint business-government program to train the hard-core unemployed (60)

national bank　a commercial bank chartered by the U.S. Comptroller of the Currency (637)

national debt　the total of all federal deficits (20)

National Labor Relations Board (NLRB)　the federal agency that enforces the provisions of the Wagner Act (386)

natural monopoly　an industry requiring huge investments in capital and within which any duplication of facilities would be wasteful and thus not in the public interest (23)

need　a personal requirement (351)

negotiated pricing　establishing a final price through bargaining (465)

neighborhood shopping center　a planned shopping center consisting of several small convenience and specialty stores (496)

net asset value (NAV)　current market value of a mutual fund's portfolio minus the mutual fund's liabilities and divided by the number of outstanding shares (712)

net income　occurs when revenues exceed expenses (604)

net loss　occurs when expenses exceed revenues (604)

net sales　the actual dollar amount received by a firm for the goods and services it has sold after adjustment for returns, allowances, and discounts (602)

network structure　an organization in which administration is the primary function, and most other functions are contracted out to other firms (260)

news release　a typed page of about 300 words provided by an organization to the media as a form of publicity (532)

nonprice competition　competition based on factors other than price (460)

nonstore retailing　a type of retailing whereby consumers purchase products without visiting a store (493)

nontariff barrier　a nontax measure imposed by a government to favor domestic over foreign suppliers (81)

not-for-profit corporation　a corporation organized to provide a social, educational, religious, or other service rather than to earn a profit (164)

NOW account　an interest-bearing checking account; NOW stands for *negotiable order of withdrawal* (641)

O

objective　a specific statement detailing what an organization intends to accomplish over a short period of time (222)

odd-number pricing　the strategy of setting prices using odd numbers that are slightly below whole-dollar amounts (466)

off-price retailer　a store that buys manufacturers' seconds, overruns, returns, and off-season merchandise for resale to consumers at deep discounts (492)

oligopoly　a market (or industry) in which there are few sellers (22)

online communities　groups of individuals or firms that want to exchange information, products, or services over the Internet (136)

online retailing　retailing that makes products available to buyers through computer connections (495)

open corporation　a corporation whose stock can be bought and sold by any individual (158)

open-market operations　the buying and selling of U.S. government securities by the Federal Reserve System for the purpose of controlling the supply of money (634)

operating expenses　all business costs other than the cost of goods sold (604)

operational plan　a type of plan designed to implement tactical plans (223)

operations management　all activities managers engage in to produce goods and services (277)

operations manager　a manager who manages the systems that convert resources into goods and services (227)

order getter　a salesperson who is responsible for selling a firm's products to new customers and increasing sales to present customers (526)

order processing　activities involved in receiving and filling customers' purchase orders (498)

order taker　a salesperson who handles repeat sales in ways that maintain positive relationships with customers (526)

organization　a group of two or more people working together to achieve a common set of goals (247)

organizational height　the number of layers, or levels, of management in a firm (254)

organization chart　a diagram that represents the positions and relationships within an organization (247)

organizing　the grouping of resources and activities to accomplish some end result in an efficient and effective manner (224)

orientation　the process of acquainting new employees with an organization (324)

out-of-home advertising　short promotional messages on billboards, posters, signs, and transportation vehicles (520)

outsourcing　the process of finding outside vendors and suppliers that provide professional help, parts, or materials at a lower cost (117)

over-the-counter (OTC) market　a network of dealers who buy and sell the stocks of corporations that are not listed on a securities exchange (702)

overtime　time worked in excess of forty hours in one week (under some union contracts, time worked in excess of eight hours in a single day) (394)

owners' equity　the difference between a firm's assets and its liabilities (596)

P

packaging　all the activities involved in developing and providing a container with graphics for a product (455)

partnership　a voluntary association of two or more persons to act as co-owners of a business for profit (152)

part-time work　permanent employment in which individuals work less than a standard work week (363)

par value　an assigned (and often arbitrary) dollar value printed on a stock certificate (679)

penetration pricing　the strategy of setting a low price for a new product (465)

perfect (or pure) competition　the market situation in which there are many buyers and sellers of a product, and no single buyer or seller is powerful enough to affect the price of that product (20)

performance appraisal   the evaluation of employees' current and potential levels of performance to allow managers to make objective human resources decisions (330)

periodic discounting   temporary reduction of prices on a patterned or systematic basis (466)

personal budget   a specific plan for spending your income (697)

personal income   the income an individual receives from all sources less the Social Security taxes the individual must pay (430)

personal investment   the use of personal funds to earn a financial return (698)

personal selling   personal communication aimed at informing customers and persuading them to buy a firm's products (517)

PERT (Program Evaluation and Review Technique)   a scheduling technique that identifies the major activities necessary to complete a project and sequences them based on the time required to perform each one (292)

physical distribution   all those activities concerned with the efficient movement of products from the producer to the ultimate user (497)

physiological needs   the things we require for survival (351)

picketing   marching back and forth in front of a place of employment with signs informing the public that a strike is in progress (397)

piece-rate system   a compensation system under which employees are paid a certain amount for each unit of output they produce (350)

place utility   utility created by making a product available at a location where customers wish to purchase it (415)

plan   an outline of the actions by which an organization intends to accomplish its goals and objectives (223)

planning   establishing organizational goals and deciding how to accomplish them (221)

planning horizon   the period during which an operational plan will be in effect (288)

plant layout   the arrangement of machinery, equipment, and personnel within a production facility (286)

point-of-purchase display   promotional material placed within a retail store (530)

pollution   the contamination of water, air, or land through the actions of people in an industrialized society (60)

positioning   the development of a product image in buyers' minds relative to the images they have of competing products (534)

possession utility   utility created by transferring title (or ownership) of a product to a buyer (415)

preferred stock   stock owned by individuals or firms who usually do not have voting rights but whose claims on dividends are paid before those of common-stock owners (159)

premium   a gift that a producer offers a customer in return for buying its product (530)

premium pricing   pricing the highest-quality or most-versatile products higher than other models in the product line (467)

press conference   a meeting at which invited media personnel hear important news announcements and receive supplementary textual materials and photographs (533)

price   the amount of money a seller is willing to accept in exchange for a product at a given time and under given circumstances (458)

price competition   an emphasis on setting a price equal to or lower than competitors' prices to gain sales or market share (459)

price leaders   products priced below the usual markup, near cost, or below cost (468)

price lining   the strategy of selling goods only at certain predetermined prices that reflect definite price breaks (467)

price skimming   the strategy of charging the highest possible price for a product during the introduction stage of its life cycle (464)

primary-demand advertising   advertising whose purpose is to increase the demand for all brands of a product within a specific industry (518)

primary market   a market in which an investor purchases financial securities (via an investment bank) directly from the issuer of those securities (701)

prime interest rate   the lowest rate charged by a bank for a short-term loan (674)

private placement   occurs when stock and other corporate securities are sold directly to insurance companies, pension funds, or large institutional investors (681)

problem   the discrepancy between an actual condition and a desired condition (232)

problem-solving team   a team of knowledgeable employees brought together to tackle a specific problem (366)

process material   a material that is used directly in the production of another product but is not readily identifiable in the finished product (444)

producer price index (PPI)   an index that measures prices at the wholesale level (19)

product   everything one receives in an exchange, including all tangible and intangible attributes and expected benefits; it may be a good, service, or idea (442)

product deletion   the elimination of one or more products from a product line (448)

product design   the process of creating a set of specifications from which a product can be produced (284)

product differentiation   the process of developing and promoting differences between one's products and all similar products (22, 460)

productivity   the average level of output per worker per hour (17, 295)

product life cycle   a series of stages in which a product's sales revenue and profit increase, reach a peak, and then decline (444)

product line   a group of similar products that differ only in relatively minor characteristics (284, 447)

product mix   all the products a firm offers for sale (447)

product modification   the process of changing one or more of a product's characteristics (448)

profit   what remains after all business expenses have been deducted from sales revenue (11)

profit sharing   the distribution of a percentage of a firm's profit among its employees (327)

program trading   a computer-driven program to buy or sell selected stocks (704)

promissory note   a written pledge by a borrower to pay

a certain sum of money to a creditor at a specified future date (674)

promotion communication about an organization and its products that is intended to inform, persuade, or remind target-market members (515)

promotional campaign a plan for combining and using the four promotional methods—advertising, personal selling, sales promotion, and publicity—in a particular promotion mix to achieve one or more marketing goals (533)

promotion mix the particular combination of promotion methods a firm uses to reach a target market (515)

prospectus a detailed, written description of a new security, the issuing corporation, and the corporation's top management (705)

proxy a legal form listing issues to be decided at a stockholders' meeting and enabling stockholders to transfer their voting rights to some other individual or individuals (160)

proxy fight a technique used to gather enough stockholder votes to control a targeted company (167)

publicity communication in news-story form about an organization, its products, or both (532)

public relations communication activities used to create and maintain favorable relations between an organization and various public groups, both internal and external (517)

purchasing all the activities involved in obtaining required materials, supplies, components, and parts from other firms (289)

Q

qualitative research a process that involves the descriptive or subjective reporting of information discovered by a researcher (564)

quantitative research a process that involves the collection of numerical data for analysis through a survey, experiment, or content analysis (565)

quality circle a team of employees who meet on company time to solve problems of product quality (294)

quality control the process of ensuring that goods and services are produced in accordance with design specifications (293)

R

random discounting temporary reduction of prices on an unsystematic basis (466)

range the difference between the highest value and the lowest value in a set of data (562)

rate of return the total income you receive on an investment over a specific period of time divided by the amount invested (700)

ratification approval of a labor contract by a vote of the union membership (392)

raw material a basic material that actually becomes part of a physical product; usually comes from mines, forests, oceans, or recycled solid wastes (444)

rebate a return of part of the purchase price of a product (529)

recession two or more consecutive three-month periods of decline in a country's GDP (20)

recruiting the process of attracting qualified job applicants (319)

reference pricing pricing a product at a moderate level and positioning it next to a more expensive model or brand (466)

regional shopping center a planned shopping center containing large department stores, numerous specialty stores, restaurants, movie theaters, and sometimes even hotels (497)

registered bond a bond registered in the owner's name by the issuing company (683)

reinforcement theory a theory of motivation based on the premise that behavior that is rewarded is likely to be repeated, whereas behavior that is punished is less likely to recur (356)

relationship marketing establishing long-term, mutually satisfying buyer-seller relationships (414)

replacement chart a list of key personnel and their possible replacements within a firm (316)

research and development (R&D) a set of activities intended to identify new ideas that have the potential to result in new goods and services (282)

reserve requirement the percentage of its deposits a bank must retain, either in its own vault or on deposit with its Federal Reserve district bank (633)

responsibility the duty to do a job or perform a task (252)

retailer a middleman that buys from producers or other middlemen and sells to consumers (481)

retained earnings the portion of a business's profits not distributed to stockholders (601)

return on owners' equity a financial ratio calculated by dividing net income after taxes by owners' equity (608)

return on sales (or profit margin) a financial ratio calculated by dividing net income after taxes by net sales (608)

revenues the dollar amounts earned by a firm from selling goods, providing services, or performing business activities (602)

revenue stream a source of revenue flowing into a firm (118)

revolving credit agreement a guaranteed line of credit (642)

risk-return ratio a ratio based on the principle that a high-risk decision should generate higher financial returns for a business, and that more conservative decisions often generate lesser returns (667)

robotics the use of programmable machines to perform a variety of tasks by manipulating materials and tools (297)

S

safety needs the things we require for physical and emotional security (351)

salary a specific amount of money paid for an employee's work during a set calendar period, regardless of the actual number of hours worked (326)

sales forecast an estimate of the amount of a product that an organization expects to sell during a certain period of time based on a specified level of marketing effort (425)

sales promotion the use of activities or materials as direct inducements to customers or salespersons (517)

sales support personnel employees who aid in selling, but who are more involved in locating prospects, educating customers, building goodwill for the firm, and providing follow-up service (526)

sample a free product given to customers to encourage trial and purchase (530)

Sarbanes-Oxley Act of 2002 provides sweeping new legal protection for employees who report corporate misconduct (45)

savings and loan association (S&L) a financial institution that offers checking and savings accounts and CDs, and that invests most of its assets in home mortgage loans and other consumer loans (638)

scheduling the process of ensuring that materials and other resources are at the right place at the right time (291)

scientific management the application of scientific principles to management of work and workers (349)

secondary market a market for existing financial securities that are traded between investors (701)

secondary-market pricing setting one price for the primary target market and a different price for another market (465)

S-corporation a corporation that is taxed as though it were a partnership (163)

secure electronic transaction (SET) an encryption process developed by MasterCard, Visa, IBM, Microsoft, and Netscape that prevents merchants from ever actually seeing any transaction data, including the customer's credit-card number (132)

securities exchange a marketplace where member brokers meet to buy and sell securities (701)

security average (or security index) an average of the current market prices of selected securities (722)

selection the process of gathering information about applicants for a position and then using that information to choose the most appropriate applicant (321)

selective-demand (or brand) advertising advertising that is used to sell a particular brand of product (518)

selective distribution the use of only a portion of the available outlets for a product in each geographic area (484)

self-actualization needs the need to grow and develop and to become all that we are capable of being (353)

self-managed teams groups of employees with the authority and skills to manage themselves (366)

selling short the process of selling stock that an investor does not actually own but has borrowed from a brokerage firm and will repay at a later date (715)

seniority the length of time an employee has worked for an organization (393)

serial bonds bonds of a single issue that mature on different dates (685)

Service Corps of Retired Executives (SCORE) a group of retired business people who volunteer their services to small businesses through the SBA (196)

service economy an economy in which more effort is devoted to the production of services than to the production of goods (280)

shopping product an item for which buyers are willing to expend considerable effort on planning and making the purchase (443)

shop steward an employee elected by union members to serve as their representative (395)

short-term financing money that will be used for one year or less (665)

sinking fund a sum of money to which deposits are made each year for the purpose of redeeming a bond issue (685)

Six Sigma a disciplined approach that relies on statistical data and improved methods to eliminate defects for a firm's products and services (294)

skills inventory a computerized data bank containing information on the skills and experience of all present employees (316)

slowdown a technique whereby workers report to their jobs but work at a slower pace than normal (397)

small business one that is independently owned and operated for profit and is not dominant in its field (183)

Small Business Administration (SBA) a governmental agency that assists, counsels, and protects the interests of small businesses in the United States (194)

small-business development centers (SBDCs) university-based groups that provide individual counseling and practical training to owners of small businesses (197)

small-business institutes (SBIs) groups of senior and graduate students in business administration who provide management counseling to small businesses (197)

small-business investment companies (SBICs) privately owned firms that provide venture capital to small enterprises that meet their investment standards (199)

social audit a comprehensive report of what an organization has done and is doing with regard to social issues that affect it (65)

social needs the human requirements for love, affection, and a sense of belonging (351)

social responsibility the recognition that business activities have an impact on society and the consideration of that impact in business decision making (48)

socioeconomic model of social responsibility the concept that business should emphasize not only profits but also the impact of its decisions on society (53)

sole proprietorship a business that is owned (and usually operated) by one person (149)

spamming the sending of massive amounts of unsolicited e-mail (131)

span of management (or span of control) the number of workers who report directly to one manager (253)

special-event pricing advertised sales or price cutting linked to a holiday, season, or event (468)

specialization the separation of a manufacturing process into distinct tasks and the assignment of the different tasks to different individuals (25)

specialty-line wholesaler a middleman that carries a select group of products within a single line (488)

specialty product an item that possesses one or more unique characteristics for which a significant group of buyers is willing to expend considerable purchasing effort (444)

speculative production the time lag between the actual production of goods and when the goods are sold (666)

spreadsheet program a software package that allows users to organize numerical data into a grid of rows and columns (575)

staff management position a position created to provide support, advice, and expertise within an organization (255)

stakeholders all of the different people or groups of people who are affected by the policies and decisions made by an organization (11)

standardization the guidelines that let products, services, materials, and processes achieve their purposes (569)

standard of living a loose, subjective measure of how well off an individual or a society is, mainly in terms of want-satisfaction through goods and services (23)

standing committee a relatively permanent committee charged with performing some recurring task (263)

state bank a commercial bank chartered by the banking authorities in the state in which it operates (637)

statement of cash flows a statement that illustrates how the operating, investing, and financing activities of a company affect cash during an accounting period (605)

statistic a measure that summarizes a particular characteristic of an entire group of numbers (560)

statistical process control (SPC) a system that uses sampling to obtain data that are then plotted on control charts and graphs to see if the production process is operating as it should and to pinpoint problem areas (293)

statistical quality control (SQC) a set of specific statistical techniques used to monitor all aspects of the production process to ensure that both work in progress and finished products meet the firm's quality standards (294)

strategic alliance a partnership formed to create competitive advantage on a worldwide basis (93)

strategic plan an organization's broadest plan, developed as a guide for major policy setting and decision making (223)

strategic planning the process of establishing an organization's major goals and objectives and allocating the resources to achieve them (221)

strike a temporary work stoppage by employees, calculated to add force to their demands (382)

strikebreaker a nonunion employee who performs the job of a striking union member (398)

stock the shares of ownership of a corporation (158)

stock dividend a dividend in the form of additional stock (710)

stockholder a person who owns a corporation's stock (158)

stock split the division of each outstanding share of a corporation's stock into a greater number of shares (711)

store (or private) brand a brand that is owned by an individual wholesaler or retailer (452)

store of value a means of retaining and accumulating wealth (629)

supermarket a large self-service store that sells primarily food and household products (491)

superstore a large retail store that carries not only food and nonfood products ordinarily found in supermarkets but also additional product lines (491)

supply the quantity of a product that producers are willing to sell at each of various prices (21, 458)

supply an item that facilitates production and operations but does not become part of a finished product (444)

supply-chain management long-term partnership among channel members working together to create a distribution system that reduces inefficiencies, costs, and redundancies while creating a competitive advantage and satisfying customers (484)

supply-chain management (SCM) software software solutions that focus on ways to improve communication between the suppliers and users of materials and components (122)

syndicate a temporary association of individuals or firms organized to perform a specific task that requires a large amount of capital (166)

synthetic process a process in operations management in which raw materials or components are combined to create a finished product (278)

T

tactical plan a smaller-scale plan developed to implement a strategy (223)

target market a group of individuals or organizations, or both, for which a firm develops and maintains a marketing mix suitable for the specific needs and preferences of that group (419)

task force a committee established to investigate a major problem or pending decision (263)

team a group of workers functioning together as a unit to complete a common goal or purpose (365)

technical salesperson a salesperson who assists a company's current customers in technical matters (526)

technical skill a specific skill needed to accomplish a specialized activity (229)

telecommuting working at home all the time or for a portion of the work week (363)

telemarketing the performance of marketing-related activities by telephone (494)

television home shopping a form of selling in which products are presented to television viewers, who can buy them by calling a toll-free number and paying with a credit card (494)

tender offer an offer to purchase the stock of a firm targeted for acquisition at a price just high enough to tempt stockholders to sell their shares (167)

term-loan agreement a promissory note that requires a borrower to repay a loan in monthly, quarterly, semiannual, or annual installments (682)

Theory X a concept of employee motivation generally consistent with Taylor's scientific management; assumes that employees dislike work and will function only in a highly controlled work environment (354)

Theory Y a concept of employee motivation generally consistent with the ideas of the human relations movement; assumes that employees accept responsibility and work toward organizational goals if by so doing they also achieve personal rewards (355)

Theory Z the belief that some middle ground between Ouchi's type A and type J practices is best for American business (356)

time deposit an amount on deposit in an interest-bearing savings account (631)

time utility utility created by making a product available when customers wish to purchase it (415)

top manager an upper-level executive who guides and controls the overall fortunes of an organization (226)

total cost the sum of the fixed costs and the variable costs attributed to a product (462)

total quality management (TQM) the coordination of efforts directed at improving customer satisfaction, increasing employee participation, strengthening supplier partnerships, and facilitating an organizational atmosphere of continuous quality improvement (234)

total revenue the total amount received from sales of a product (462)

trade credit a type of short-term financing extended by a seller who does not require immediate payment after delivery of merchandise (673)

trade deficit a negative balance of trade (79)

trademark a brand name or brand mark that is registered with the U.S. Patent and Trademark Office and thus is legally protected from use by anyone except its owner (452)

trade name the complete and legal name of an organization (452)

trade salesperson a salesperson—generally employed by a food producer or processor—who assists customers in promoting products, especially in retail stores (526)

trade sales promotion method a sales promotion method designed to encourage wholesalers and retailers to stock and actively promote a manufacturer's product (528)

trade show an industry-wide exhibit at which many sellers display their products (530)

trading company provides a link between buyers and sellers in different countries (94)

traditional specialty store a store that carries a narrow product mix with deep product lines (492)

transfer pricing prices charged in sales between an organization's units (468)

transportation the shipment of products to customers (499)

trial balance a summary of the balances of all general ledger accounts at the end of the accounting period (597)

trustee an individual or an independent firm that acts as a bond owners' representative (685)

U

undifferentiated approach directing a single marketing mix at the entire market for a particular product (419)

union-management (labor) relations the dealings between labor unions and business management both in the bargaining process and beyond it (381)

union security protection of the union's position as the employees' bargaining agent (394)

union shop a workplace in which new employees must join the union after a specified probationary period (394)

unlimited liability a legal concept that holds a business owner personally responsible for all the debts of the business (151)

unsecured financing financing that is not backed by collateral (673)

utility the ability of a good or service to satisfy a human need (279, 415)

V

variable cost a cost that depends on the number of units produced (462)

venture capital money that is invested in small (and sometimes struggling) firms that have the potential to become very successful (198)

vertical channel integration the combining of two or more stages of a distribution channel under a single firm's management (485)

vertical marketing system (VMS) a centrally managed distribution channel resulting from vertical channel integration (485)

virtual team a team consisting of members who are geographically dispersed but communicate electronically (367)

virtuoso team a team of exceptionally highly skilled and talented individuals brought together to produce significant change (366)

W

wage survey a collection of data on prevailing wage rates within an industry or a geographic area (325)

warehouse club a large-scale members-only establishment that combines features of cash-and-carry wholesaling with discount retailing (491)

warehouse showroom a retail facility in a large, low-cost building with a large on-premises inventory and minimal service (490)

warehousing the set of activities involved in receiving and storing goods and preparing them for reshipment (498)

whistle-blowing informing the press or government officials about unethical practices within one's organization (46)

wholesaler a middleman that sells products to other firms (481)

wide-area network (WAN) a network that connects computers over a large geographic area, such as a state, province, or country (568)

wildcat strike a strike not approved by the strikers' union (397)

word-processing program software that allows a user to prepare and edit written documents and to store them in the computer or in a memory device (576)

working capital the difference between current assets and current liabilities (609)

World Trade Organization (WTO) powerful successor to GATT that incorporates trade in goods, services, and ideas (87)

World Wide Web (the web) the Internet's multimedia environment of audio, visual, and text data (120)

Y

Yellow Pages advertising simple listings or display advertisements presented under specific product categories appearing in print and online telephone directories (520)

Z

zero-base budgeting a budgeting approach in which every expense in every budget must be justified (671)

Notes

CHAPTER 1

1. Based on information from Melanie Warner, "California Wants to Serve a Health Warning with That Order," *New York Times*, September 21, 2005, p. C1; Stephanie Thompson, "Frito-Lay Defends Its Snack Turf Against All Comers, Salty or Sweet," *Advertising Age*, May 16, 2005, p. 16; "Frito-Lay Offers 'Health and Wellness Choices,'" *Chain Drug Review*, June 6, 2005, p. 140; "Frito-Lay Ads Reposition Products, Expand Share," *Chain Drug Review*, March 28, 2005, p. 6.
2. The Frito-Lay website at **www.fritolay.com,** September 24, 2005.
3. The Dudley Products, Inc., website at **www.dudleyq.com**, September 25, 2005.
4. The Horatio Alger website at **www.horatioalger.com,** September 25, 2005.
5. Alan Goldstein, "Most Dot.Coms Doomed to Fail, Cuban Tells Entrepreneurs," *Dallas Morning News*, April 7, 2000, p. 1D.
6. Idy Fernandez, "Julie Stav," *Hispanic*, June–July 2005, p. 24.
7. The Wal-Mart website at **www.walmart.com,** September 25, 2005.
8. Amey Stone, "Internet Meltdown, Phase Two," *BusinessWeek Online* at **www.businessweek.com,** April 23, 2001.
9. U.S. Census Bureau, *Statistical Abstract of the United States, 2004–2005*, 124th ed. (Washington: U.S. Government Printing Office, 2005), p. 425.
10. "Gains in U.S. Productivity: Stopgap Measures or Lasting Change?" *FRSBSF Economic Letter*, March 11, 2005, p. 1.
11. The CBS News website at **www.cbsnews.com,** September 30, 2005.
12. "Gains in U.S. Productivity: Stopgap Measures or Lasting Change?" *FRSBSF Economic Letter*, March 11, 2005, p. 1.
13. Bill Weir, "Made in China: Your Job, Your Future, Your Fortune," ABC News website at **www.abcnews.com,** September 20, 2005.
14. The Bureau of Economic Analysis website at **www.bea.gov,** September 28, 2005.
15. The Bureau of Labor Statistics website at **www.bls.gov,** September 29, 2005.
16. The Bureau of Economic Analysis website at **www.bea.gov,** September 28, 2005.
17. U.S. Census Bureau, *Statistical Abstract of the United States, 2004–2005*, 124th ed. (Washington: U.S. Government Printing Office, 2005), p. 308.
18. The Bureau of Labor Statistics website at **www.bls.gov,** October 2, 2005.
19. Bill Weir, "Made in China: Your Job," ABC News website at **www.abcnews.com,** September 21, 2005.
20. Based on information from Andrew Martin, "Stonyfield Farm Yogurt President Oversees Natural Fast-Food Restaurant Chain," *Chicago Tribune*, June 15, 2005, **www.chicagotribune.com;** Jim Johnson, "Yogurt Maker Gets Handle on Recycling Partnership," *Waste News*, January 3, 2005, p. 5; "French Conglomerate Groupe Danone SA Has Increased Its Stake in the Stonyfield Farm," *Food Management*, February 2004, p. 84; David Goodman, "Culture Change," *Mother Jones*, January–February 2003, pp. 52–78; **www.stonyfield.com.**
21. Based on information from "Wipro to Open First Software Development Centre in Beijing," *Asia Africa Intelligence Wire*, September 12, 2005, n.p.; Steve Hamm, "Taking a Page from Toyota's Playbook," *BusinessWeek*, August 22–29, 2005, pp. 69–72; "Wipro to Invest More in Core Outsourcing," *Asia Africa Intelligence Wire*, September 7, 2005, n.p.; Wipro Quarterly Profit Rises 41% on Outsourcing," *InformationWeek*, July 22, 2005, n.p.; "Wipro, Ltd.," *Wall Street Journal*, July 25, 2005, p. C12; Terry Atlas, "Bangalore's Big Dreams," *U.S. News & World Report*, May 2, 2005, pp. 50+.

CHAPTER 2

1. Based on information from Christina Vance, "Store's Workers Give Back," *Bakersfield Californian*, September 21, 2005, n.p.; Jeffrey H. Birnbaum, "Stepping Up: Corporate Efforts for the Stricken Gulf Are Unprecedented," *Washington Post*, September 4, 2005, pp. F1+; "Home Depot's Net Income Rises 15%, Beats Estimates," *Los Angeles Times*, August 17, 2005, p. C3; Brian Grow, Steve Hamm, and Louise Lee, "The Debate Over Doing Good," *BusinessWeek*, August 15, 2005, p. 76; "Home Depot Lends a Helping Hand to Florida," *Industrial Distribution*, October 2004, p. 24; "Home Depot Providing 250,000 Volunteer Hours," *Home Channel News NewsFax*, September 27, 2004, p. 1; Dan Murphy, "'Good Wood' Labeling," *Christian Science Monitor*, August 23, 2001, pp. 1+; **www.homedepot.com.**
2. Carrie Johnson, "Adelphia, U.S. Settle for $75 Million," *Washington Post*, April 26, 2005, p. E1.
3. Charles Haddad and Amy Barrett, "A Whistle-Blower Rocks an Industry," *BusinessWeek*, June 24, 2002, pp. 126–130.
4. Albert B. Crenshaw, "Tax Shelter Leaders Get Jail Time, Must Pay Restitution," *Washington Post*, April 23, 2005, p. E2.
5. *Frontlines* (Washington: U.S. Agency for International Development), September 2005, p. 16.
6. Consumer Protection Laws, **http://nolo.com/lawcenter/ency/article;** accessed January 6, 2003.
7. Anthony Bianco, William Symonds, and Nanette Byrnes, "The Rise and Fall of Dennis Kozlowski," *BusinessWeek*, December 23, 2002, pp. 64–77
8. James Underwood, "Should You Watch Them on the Web," CIO, **www.cio.com/archive/051500_face.html;** accessed May 15, 2000.
9. Paula Dwyer et al., "Year of the Whistleblower," *BusinessWeek*, December 16, 2002, pp. 107–110.
10. **www.whistleblowers.org/;** accessed September 21, 2005.
11. Fiscal 2005 in Review, p. 24; **www.dell.com.**
12. Understanding Our Company: An IBM Prospectus, March 2005, p. 25.
13. GE 2004 Annual Report, p. 44.
14. Merck & Co., Inc., Annual Report 2004, p. 16.
15. 3M Annual Report 2004, p. 14.
16. AT&T Foundation: **www.att.com/foundation/programs;** accessed October 9, 2005.
17. General Mills, 2002 Corporate Citizenship Report, p. 6.
18. 3M, 2004 Annual Report, p. 15.
19. Based on information from "New Belgium Brewing Wins Ethics Award," *Denver Business Journal*, January 2, 2003, **Denver.bizjournals.com/Denver/stories/2002/12/30/daily21.html;** Richard Brandes, "Beer Growth Brands," *Beverage Dynamics*, September–October 2002, pp. 37ff; **www.newbelgium.com.**

20. Based on information from Robert Berner, "Can Wal-Mart Wear a White Hat?" *BusinessWeek Online*, September 22, 2005, **www.businessweek.com;** Robert Berner, "Wal-Mart's Scott: 'We Were Getting Nowhere,'" *BusinessWeek Online*, September 22, 2005, **www.businessweek.com;** Michael Barbaro and Justin Gillis, "Wal-Mart at Forefront of Hurricane Relief," *Washington Post*, September 6, 2005, p. D1.

CHAPTER 3

1. Based on information from Janet Adamy, "Heinz to Overhaul Brands, Ketchup," *Wall Street Journal*, September 20, 2005, p. A6; Teresa F. Lindeman, "H.J. Heinz Profits Beat Expectations," *Pittsburgh Post-Gazette*," August 23, 2005, **www.post-gazette.com;** "The Famous 57," *Retail Merchandiser*, August 2005, p. 22; "How British, How Saucy," *Grocer*, July 2, 2005, p. 57; Sian Harrington, "HP Joins Heinz on Top Table," *Grocer*, June 25, 2005, p. 31; **www.hjheinz.com.**

2. The White House, Office of the Press Secretary, Press Release, August 6, 2002.

3. U.S. Department of Commerce, International Trade Aministration, **www.ita.doc.gov/;** accessed October 12, 2005.

4. Mohanbir Sawhney and Sumant Mandal, "Go Global," *Business 2.0*, **www.business2.com/content/magazine/indepth/2000/05/01/11057,** May 2000.

5. Aaron Steelman, "Steelmakers Receive Protection," *Region Focus*, Federal Reserve of Richmond, Spring 2002, pp. 28–29.

6. *Business Review*, Federal Reserve Bank of Philadelphia, Second Quarter 2005, p. 70.

7. "The Global Economic Outlook and Risks from Global Imbalances," remarks by Rodrigo de Rato, managing director of International Monetary Fund, September 30, 2005.

8. Michael Chriszt and Elena Whisler, "China's Economic Emergence," *Econ South*, First Reserve Bank of Atlanta, Second Quarter 2005, pp. 4–7.

9. William R. Cline, "Doha Can Achieve Much More than Skeptics Expect," *Finance and Development*, March 2005, p. 22.

10. Jesus Cañas and Roberto Coronado, "U.S. – Mexico Trade: Are We Still Connected?" *El Paso Business Frontier* (Federal Reserve Bank of Dallas), Issue 3, 2004, p. 2.

11. **www.whitehouse.gov/news/releases/2005/08/print/20050803-1.html,** September 21, 2005.

12. William M. Pride and O.C. Ferrell, *Marketing*, 12th ed. (Boston: Houghton Mifflin, 2003), p. 122.

13. The U.S. Agency for International Development, "7 More West African Countries Cut Tariffs, Boost Trade Pact," *Frontlines*, September 2005, p. 13.

14. Pride and Ferrell, *Marketing*, p. 127.

15. *Ibid.*, p. 128.

16. *Ibid.*, p. 127.

17. **www.eximbank.gov/about/reports/ar/ar2004/pdf/glance,** accessed October 29, 2005.

18. **www.iadb.org;** accessed November 2, 2005.

19. "ADB Operations," **www.adb.org,** November 2, 2005.

20. **www.ebrd.com;** accessed October 29, 2005.

21. Based on information from "IDG: Ten Years in China," *Asia Africa Intelligence Wire*, September 23, 2005, n.p.; "IDG Develops Partnerships in Vietnam to Expand Its Activities," *Tradeshow Week*, July 18, 2005, p. 5; Sean Callahan, "Publishers Explore Vast Chinese Market," *B to B*, December 9, 2002, p. 3; "'Let Many Gardens Bloom': IDG's Pat Kenealy Sees the Future Everywhere," *Min's B to B*, April 11, 2005, n.p.; **www.idg.com.**

22. Based on information from Chad Terhune, "Coke's Net Rises; Emerging Markets Bolster Revenue," *Wall Street Journal*, July 22, 2005, p. B2; "Coca-Cola to Stick It Out in Zimbabwe," *Africa News Service*, August 8, 2005, n.p.; "Fizzical Facts: Coke Claims 60% Market Share in India," *Asia Africa Intelligence Wire*, August 6, 2005, n.p.; Matthew Forney, "Who's Getting It Right?" *Time International*, November 1, 2004, p. 44; "Coca-Cola Seeks to Increase Its China Presence," *Asia Africa Intelligence Wire*, December 13, 2004, n.p.; Jonathan Wheatley, "Coke Pops the Top Off an Emerging Market," *BusinessWeek*, May 2, 2005, pp. 31; **www.cocacola.com.**

CHAPTER 4

1. Based on information from Jena McGregor, "At Netflix, the Secret Sauce Is Software," *Fast Company*, October 2005, pp. 48+; "McD Rolling out Redbox DVD Rental Machines," *Nation's Restaurant News*, August 15, 2005, p. 3; Michael Liedtke, "Netflix 2Q Profit Nearly Doubles," *InformationWeek*, July 26, 2005, n.p.; "Movies to Go: Face Value," *The Economist*, July 9, 2005, p. 57; Betsy Streisand, "No Pause in DVD Rental Wars," *U.S. News & World Report*, October 18, 2004, pp. 60+; Wendy Wilson, "Online Clicks into DVD," *Video Business*, April 20, 1998, p. 1; **www.netflix.com.**

2. The Forrester Research website: **www.forrester.com;** accessed October 23, 2005.

3. "Telecoms and the Internet," *The Economist*, September 15, 2005 (**www.economist.com/**).

4. Stacy Perman, "Automate or Die," *eCompany Now*, July 2001, pp. 60–67.

5. "Trends & Statistics: The Web's Richest Source," Clickz Network: **www.clickz.com/stats/web_worldwide/;** accessed October 2, 2005.

6. "Small Businesses Buy, but Shy to Sell, Online," Cyberatlas Internet website: **www.cyberatlasinternet.com/markets/professional/article/0,1323,5971_365281.00.html;** accessed March 17, 2000.

7. Robyn Greenspan, "Small Biz Benefits from Internet Tools," Cyberatlas Internet website: **www.cyberatlas.internet.com/markets/smallbiz/article/0,10098_1000171,00.html;** accessed March 28, 2002.

8. Dee-Ann Durbin, *The Cincinnati Post* website: **http://news.cincypost.com/apps/pbcs.dll/article?AID=/20050930/BIZ/509300333/1001;** accessed September 30, 2005.

9. Eric LaRose, "The Pig Delivers for the Picky," *The Sheboygan Press* website: **www.wisinfo.com/sheboyganpress/news/archive/biz_22823331.shtml;** accessed October 2, 2005.

10. Anne Marie Owens, "Mad about Harry," *National Post*, July 10, 2000, p. D1.

11. Associated Press, "Bosses Say They Know Who's Surfing," *Montreal Gazette*, July 16, 2001, p. E2.

12. The Privacy Rights Clearinghouse website: **www.privacyrights.org,** accessed October 19, 2005.

13. Linda Rosencrance, "Survey: Consumers Growing Wary of Buying Online," *Computerworld* website: **www.computerworld.com;** accessed June 24, 2005.

14. "Online Music Sales Will Grow 520% to $6.2 Billion in 2006," Jupiter Media Metrix Press Release, New York, **www.jmm.com/xp/press/2001/pr_072301.xml,** July 23, 2001.

15. Press Release, RIAA website: **www.riaa.com/news/newsletter/100305.asp,** October 3, 2005.

16. "Latest Round of Music Industry Lawsuits Targets Internet Theft at 17 College Campuses," RIAA website: **www.riaa.com/news/newsletter/092905.asp,** September 29, 2005.

17. Charlene Li, Shar VanBoskirk, "U.S. Online Marketing Forecast: 2005 to 2010," Forrester Research, Inc., website: **www.forrester.com/Research/Document/Excerpt/0,7211,36546,00.html,** May 2, 2005.

18. "Worldwide Internet Users Will Top 1 Billion in 2005. USA Remains #1 with 185M Internet Users," *Computer Industry Almanac* website: **www.c-i-a.com/pr0904.htm,** September 3, 2004.

19. Nielsen//NetRatings, "Two Out of Every Five Americans Have Broadband Access at Home," Nielsen//NetRatings website: **www.nielsen-netratings.com/pr/pr_050928.pdf,** September 28, 2005.

20. Enid Burns, "Men Are Media Hogs," Clickz.com website: **www.clickz.com/stats/sectors/traffic_patterns/article.php/3530531,** August 26, 2005.

21. Nielsen//NetRatings, Inc., "U.S. Internet Usage Shows Mature Growth, Forcing Innovation of New Web Offerings, According to Nielsen/NetRatings," Nielsen//NetRatings website: **www.netratings.com/pr/pr_050318.pdf** ; accessed March 18, 2005.

22. Based on information in Dennis Schaal, "Satisfaction 'Guaranteed' by Travelocity," *Travel Weekly*, May 2, 2005, pp. 1+; Suzanne Marta, "Travelocity Trying to Expand Services beyond Lower Prices," *Dallas Morning News*, March 1, 2005, **dallasnews.com;**

Avery Johnson, "Booking a $51 Flight to Fiji Online," The Flyertalk website: **www.flyertalk.com,** April 26, 2005; **www.travelocity .com.**

23. Based on information from Annette Haddad, "Countrywide Buying KB Unit," *Los Angeles Times*, July 1, 2005, p. C2; Sandeep Puri and Serge Ugarte, "User-Friendly Sites," *Mortgage Banking*, May 2005, pp. 36+; "American Dream Builder," *NYSE Magazine*, May 2005, pp. 32–36; James R. Hagerty, "Countrywide Writes Mortgages for the Masses," *Wall Street Journal*, December 21, 2004, pp. C1+; Ted Cornwell, "Hello e-Pay, Bye Snail Mail," *Mortgage Technology*, March 2004, pp. 26+; **www.countrywide .com.**

CHAPTER 5

1. Based on information from Anthony DePalma, "GE Commits to Dredging 43 Miles of Hudson River," *New York Times*, October 7, 2005, p. B3; Diane Brady, "The Immelt Revolution," *BusinessWeek*, March 28, 2005, pp. 63+; Mara Der Hovanesian, "GE: Globetrotting for Real Estate," *BusinessWeek*, October 3, 2005, p. 114; Marc Gunther, "Money and Morals at GE," *Fortune*, November 15, 2004, pp. 176+, and the GE website: **www.ge.com;** accessed October 20, 2005.

2. The Ivy Group website: **www.ivygroupllc.com;** accessed October 13, 2005.

3. The Yahoo! Small Business website: **http://smallbusiness .yahoo.com/resources;** accessed October 12, 2005.

4. The Hispanic PR Wire website: **www.hispanicprwire.com;** accessed October 15, 2005.

5. The Internal Revenue Service website: **www.irs.gov;** accessed October 16, 2005.

6. The Company Corporation website: **www.corporate.com;** accessed October 16, 2005.

7. The Sony Ericsson Mobile Communications website: **www .sonyericsson.com;** accessed October 12, 2005.

8. The Wal-Mart website: **www.walmart.com;** accessed October 16, 2005.

9. The Oracle website: **www.oracle.com;** accessed October 16, 2005.

10. The IBM website: **www.ibm.com;** accessed October 13, 2005.

11. The Procter & Gamble website: **ww.pg.com;** accessed October 15, 2005.

12. Based on information from the Bay Partners website: **www .baypartners.com;** accessed October 18, 2005; Matt Marshall, "Start-ups Getting Venture Funding: 'Healthy' Pace Resumes," *San Jose Mercury News*, February 4, 2003; the Sportvision website: **www. sportvision.com;** accessed October 18, 2005.

13. Based on information from Ronald Grover, "How Eisner Saved the Magic Kingdom," *BusinessWeek Online*, September 30, 2005, **www.businessweek. com;** Ben Fritz, "Mouse Plays Board Games," *Daily Variety*, August 19, 2005, p. 1; Kim Christensen, "Disney Board Gives Shareholders More Clout," *Los Angeles Times*, August 19, 2005, p. C2; Gary Gentile, "Roy Disney, Company Resolve Their Disputes," *Washington Post*, July 9, 2005, p. D1; Merissa Marr, "One Year Later, Disney Attempts Smoother Ride," *Wall Street Journal*, February 7, 2005, pp. B1+; Joann S. Lublin and Bruce Orwall, "Funds Press Disney for Timeline to Replace Eisner," *Wall Street Journal*, May 21, 2004, p. B2.

CHAPTER 6

1. Based on information from Julie Naughton, "Carol's Daughter Gives Birth to New Store," *WWD*, September 16, 2005, p. 20; "Will Smith, Jay-Z Back Beauty Line," *CNN Money*, May 18, 2005, **www.money.cnn.com/2005/05/18/news/newsmakers/ cosmetics;** Erika Kinetz, "DanceAfrica Spills onto Brooklyn Streets in a Bazaar of Goods for Near and Far," *New York Times*, May 27, 2005, pp. E1, E17; Julie Naughton, "Carol's Daughter Poised for Growth," *WWD*, August 5, 2005, p. 6.

2. U.S. Small Business Administration, **www.sba.gov/ size/ summary-whatis.html;** accessed November 1, 2005.

3. U.S. Small Business Administration, **www.sba.gov/advocacy/;** accessed October 29, 2005.

4. *Ibid.*

5. **www.richmondfed.org/community_affairs/;** accessed October 20, 2005.

6. Thomas A. Garrett, "Entrepreneurs Thrive in America," *Bridges*, Federal Reserve Bank of St. Louis, Spring 2005, p. 2.

7. Online Women's Business Center, SBA Success Stories, "Business Was Always Her Passion," **www.onlinewbc.org/docs/success _stories/ss_innovativetech.html,** June 3, 2000.

8. U.S. Small Business Administration, *Small Business's Vital Statistics*, **www.sba.gov/aboutsba/sbastats.html.**

9. Based on information from Rochelle Sharpe, "Teen Moguls," *BusinessWeek*, May 29, 2000, pp. 108–118; "High-Tech Teens," *McLean's*, June 7, 1999, p. 9.

10. U.S. Small Business Administration News Release Number 05-53, September 13, 2005, **www.sba.gov/teens/brian_hendricks.html.**

11. U.S. Small Business Administration, Office of Advocacy Press Release, October 3, 2005, **www.advocacy@sba.gov.**

12. *2004 The Small Economy*, A Report to the President, U.S. Small Business Administration, 2004, p. 2.

13. Kim Girard and Sean Donahue, "Crash and Learn: A Field Manual for e-Business Survival," *Business 2.0*, **www.business2.com/ content/magazine/indepth/2000/06/28/13700,** June 11, 2000.

14. U.S. Small Business Administration, **www.sba.gov/advocacy/ research/sbei/html/;** accessed November 6, 2005.

15. U.S. Small Business Administration, **www.sba.gov/advo/,** accessed October 5, 2005.

16. U.S. Small Business Administration, Office of Advocacy News Release, April 27, 2005, **www.sba. gov/advo/.**

17. U.S. Small Business Administration, "Small Business by the Numbers," **www.sba.gov,** January 11, 2005.

18. U.S. Small Business Administration, "The Digital Divide," **www.sba.gov/classroom/digitaldivide.html,** November 8, 2005.

19. Special Advertising Supplement, *New York Times*, April 25, 2005, p. ZN4.

20. *Ibid.*

21. U.S. Small Business Administration, Office of Advocacy, Frequently Asked Questions, October 2005, p. 1., **www.sba.gov/advo/.**

22. U.S. Small Business Administration, **www.sba.gov/teens/ roadmap.html;** accessed October 4, 2005.

23. Cindy Elmore, "Satisfaction Guarateed," *Marketwise*, Federal Reserve Bank of Richmond, Issue III, 2004, p. 21.

24. U.S. Small Business Administration News Releases, September 12, 2005 and November 8, 2005, **www. sba.gov/news/.**

25. *The New York Times*, April 25, 2005, p. ZN4.

26. U.S. Small Business Administration, **www.sba.gov/ INV/stat/ table1.doc;** accessed November 8, 2005.

27. William M. Pride and O. C. Ferrell, *Marketing*, 12th ed. (Boston: Houghton Mifflin, 2003), p. 414.

28. Cindy Elmore, "Putting the Power into the Hands of Small Business Owners," *Marketwise*, Federal Reserve Bank of Richmond, Issue II, 2005, p. 13.

29. U.S. Small Business Administration, **www.sba.gov/managing/ marketing/intlsales.html;** accessed October 4, 2005.

30. U.S. Small Business Administration, **www.sba.gov/ advo/stats;** accessed January 16, 2003.

31. Based on information from Ed Christman, "Newbury Comics Cuts Staff," *Billboard*, September 10, 2005, p. 8; Wendy Wilson, "Newbury Comics," *Video Business*, December 20, 2004, p. 18; Ed Christman, "'We Have All Had to Grow Up a Little,'" *Billboard*, September 27, 2003, pp. N3ff; **www.newburycomics.com.**

32. Based on information from Thomas Fields-Meyer, "Teen Titans," *People Weekly*, November 8, 2004, pp. 127+; "Actress and Budding Entrepreneur," *Jet*, March 15, 2004, p. 51; Ross Atkin, "Siblings Taste Success, and How Sweet It Is," *Christian Science Monitor*, February 7, 2001, p. 13; **www.manuregourmet.com; www .chocolatefarm.com.**

CHAPTER 7

1. Based on information from Adam Hanft, "Save the Founder," *Inc.*, October 2005, p. 156; Kara Swisher, "Boom Town," *Wall Street Journal*, October 29, 2001, pp. B1+; Cliff Edwards, "The Web's Future Is You," *BusinessWeek*, April 25, 2005, p. 18; Matthew

Boyle, "14 Innovators: Absolutely, Positively, Slow the Hell Down," *Fortune*, November 15, 2004, pp. 192+; **www.fedex.com; www.yahoo.com; www.ebay.com.**

2. Geoff Armstrong, "People Strategies Are Key to Future Success," *Personnel Today*, January 7, 2003, p. 2.

3. Stephanie Mehta and Fred Vogelstein, "AOL: The Relaunch," *Fortune*, November 14, 2005, pp. 78–84.

4. **www.google.com/corporate/.**

5. Curtis Sittenfeld, "Get Well Soon!" *Fast Company*, April 2005, p. 32.

6. Herold Hamprecht, "Chrysler Group Has Big Plans for Europe," *Automotive News Europe* 10(8), April 18, 2005.

7. Lucas Conley, "Climbing Back Up the Mountain," *Fast Company*, April 2005, p. 84.

8. William Diem, "Competitors Look at Nissan's Leadership," *Detroit Free Press Knight Ridder/Tribune Business News*, January 6, 2003, p. 9.

9. Christine Tierney, "Nissan CEO: The Making of a Superstar," *The Detroit News*, February 27, 2005, **www.detnews.com/2005/autosinsider/0502/27/A01-101491.htm.**

10. Scott Morrison, "From Tactics to Strategy," *Financial Times*, January 24, 2003, p. 8.

11. **www.monster.com.**

12. Henry Mintzberg, "The Manager's Job: Folklore and Fact," *Harvard Business Review*, July–August 1975, pp. 49–61.

13. Chana R. Schoenberger, "The Greenhouse Effect," **www.forbes.com/global/2003/0203/030_print.html;** accessed February 3, 2003.

14. Robert Kreitner, *Management*, 9th ed. (Boston: Houghton Mifflin, 2004), p. 505.

15. Ricky W. Griffin, *Fundamentals of Management*, 3d ed. (Boston: Houghton Mifflin, 2003), p. 96.

16. "IBM Announces PC Division's 2005 Plan," *SinoCast China Business Daily News*, London (UK), January 24, 2005, p. 1.

17. Paul R. La Monica, "After Carly, Is HP a Bargain?" *Money*, April 2005, p. 108.

18. Based on information from Mary Naylor, "There's No Place Like Home," *Inc.*, October 2005, **www.inc.com;** Rod Kurtz, "Firms Turn to Perks in Lieu of Bonus Checks," *Inc.*, December 2004, p. 26; Toddi Gutner, "A Dot-Com's Survival Story," *BusinessWeek*, May 2, 2002, **www.businessweek.com;** E. Sandra Simpson, "Get with the Program," *Customer Support Management*, November 1, 2001, **industryclick.com; www.vipdesk.com.**

19. Based on information from Kristen Bellstrom, "Can Mark Hurd Reinvent Hewlett Packard?" *Smart Money*, October 2005, p. 33; "HP Chief Hurd Sees 'Lots of Work' to Change Company," *eWeek*, September 7, 2005, n.p.; Pui-Wing Tam, "Boss Talk," *Wall Street Journal*, April 4, 2005, pp. B1+; Peter Burrows and Ben Elgin, "Memo to HP's Mark Hurd," *BusinessWeek Online*, April 4, 2005, **www.businessweek.com;** "The Word from Hurd," *BusinessWeek Online*, September 1, 2005, **www.businessweek.com; www.hp.com.**

CHAPTER 8

1. Based on information from Barney Gimbel, "Conquer and Divide," *Fortune*, October 17, 2005, pp. 175+; Peter Sanders, "Global Hyatt Joins Industry Rivals with High Style, No-Frills Service," *Wall Street Journal*, September 21, 2005, p. D4; Jay Boehmer, "Hyatt Vertically Realigns Sales Operations," *Business Travel News*, August 15, 2005, p. 14; Joseph Weber, "Hyatt: Quite a Housecleaning," *BusinessWeek*, December 20, 2004, p. 40.

2. "Mercedes-Benz USA selects Workstream," *Business Editors; Automotive Writers*, March 2005.

3. Bill Saporito, "Can Wal-Mart Get Any Bigger? (Yes, a lot Bigger . . . Here's How)," *Time*, January 13, 2003, p. 38.

4. Robert Kreitner, *Foundations of Management: Basics and Best Practices* (Boston: Houghton Mifflin, 2005), pp. 186–187.

5. Paul Kaihla, "Raytheon on Target," *Business 2.0*, **www.business2.com/articles/mag/0,1640,46335,00.html,** February 4, 2003.

6. Stephanie Thompson, "'God Is in the Details: Campbell Soup Chief Energizes Marketing; Fingerman Pushes Innovation Agenda to Stimulate Sleepy Sales," *Advertising Age*, January 27, 2003, p. 3.

7. Robert Kreitner, *Foundations of Management: Basics and Best Practices* (Boston: Houghton Mifflin, 2005), p. 192.

8. Marriott International Fact Sheet, *Hoovers Online*, December 5, 2005.

9. Rob Goffee and Gareth Jones, "The Character of a Corporation: How Your Company's Culture Can Make or Break Your Business," *Jones Harper Business*, p. 182.

10. Paul Sloan, "Dell's Man on Deck," *Business 2.0*, February 2003.

11. "Mergers' Missing Link: Cultural Integration," *PR Newswire*, January 23, 2003.

12. Kreitner, *Management*, p. 49.

13. Jeffrey H. Birnbaum et al., "People to Watch 2003: Moguls! Scapegoats! Insiders! Our Bet? If You Don't Know All These Names Now, You Will Soon," *Fortune*, February 3, 2003, p. 86.

14. Based on information from Tony Baer, "Brewing a New Kind of Connection," *Manufacturing Business Technology*, January 2005, pp. 40–42; Mark Pendergrast, "Green Mountain Coffee Roasters: Doing Well by Doing Good," *Tea & Coffee Trade Journal*, April 20, 2004, pp. 100+; Ellyn Spragins, "The Three-Peat," *Fortune Small Business*, July-August 2003, n.p.; **www.greenmountaincoffee.com.**

15. Based on information from Lindsay Chappell, "GM Just Didn't Get the Magic of Spring Hill," *Automotive News*, July 25, 2005, pp. 14+; Dave Guilford, "Once Different Saturn Looks More Like GM," *Automotive News*, June 14, 2004, p. 30V; Lindsay Chappell, "GM's Saturn Plant May Lose Its Saturns," *Automotive News*, June 27, 2005, pp. 1+; Lee Hawkins, Jr., and Joann S. Lublin, "Emergency Repairman," *Wall Street Journal*, April 6, 2005, pp. B1+; **www.gm.com.**

CHAPTER 9

1. Based on information from Don Hammonds, "Hyundai Gains Share, Plans to Target High-End Vehicle Market," *Pittsburgh Post-Gazette*, October 25, 2005, **www.post-gazette.com;** Michael Schuman, "One for the Road," *Time International*, August 1, 2005, pp. 42+; Jathon Sapsford, Seah Park, and Norihiko Shirouzu, "Hyundai Steers for the Top," *Wall Street Journal*, April 29, 2005, p. B2.

2. The Bureau of Labor Statistics website: **www.bls.gov;** accessed October 28, 2005.

3. Robert Kreitner, *Management*, 9th ed. (Boston: Houghton Mifflin, 2004), pp. 577–578.

4. The Dell website: **www.dell.com;** accessed October 30, 2005.

5. The 3M website: **www.3m.com;** accessed October 31, 2005.

6. The Campbell Soup website: **www.campbellsoup. com;** accessed October 31, 2005.

7. The Kraft Foods website: **www.kraftfoods.com;** accessed November 1, 2005.

8. Berry Plastics website: **www.berryplastics.com;** accessed November 1, 2005.

9. The Boeing website: **www.boeing.com;** accessed November 3, 2005.

10. The SBC Communications website: **www.sbc.com;** accessed November 3, 2005.

11. The National Institute for Standards and Technology (NIST) website: **www.nist.gov;** accessed November 5, 2005.

12. Kim Niles, "What Makes Six Sigma Work?," iSix Sigma website: **www.isixsigma.com.**

13. "Gains in U.S. Productivity: Stopgap Measures or Lasting Change?" *FRSBSF Economic Letter*, March 11, 2005, p. 1.

14. "International Factory Productivity Gains in 2004," The Bureau of Labor Statistics website: **www.bls.gov;** accessed November 5, 2005.

15. David Shook, "A Tool-and-Die Maker for Genesmiths," *BusinessWeek Online* at **www.businessweek.com;** accessed October 15, 2002.

16. The Maxager Technology website: **www.maxager. com;** accessed November 6, 2005.

17. The Dell website: **www.dell.com;** accessed November 6, 2005.

18. Based on information in "Spectrum Brands Names David R. Lumley President, North America," *Business Wire*, January 16, 2006, **www.spectrumbrands.com;** Dick Ahles, "Remington Leaves Bridgeport Site," *New York Times*, January 9, 2005, p. 14CN-2; "Rayovac Corp.: Battery Maker to Change Name and Boost Its

Earnings Target," *Wall Street Journal*, February 15, 2005, p. 1; "Remington Seeks Sexy Image after Court Win," *Marketing*, June 27, 2002, p. 1; "Analysis: What Remington's Ruling Means For Brands," *Marketing*, June 27, 2002, p. 15; **www.remington -products.com** and **www.spectrumbrands.com.**

19. Based on information from Chris Costanzo, "Business Management: BofA Tackles Six Sigma," *U.S. Banker*, June 2005, pp. 22+; Steve Bills, "New Six Sigma Application at B of A: Deposit Deadlines," *American Banker*, September 29, 2004, p. 1; Will Wade, "B of A Touts Six Sigma's Bottom-Line Benefits," *American Banker*, July 28, 2004, p. 1.

CHAPTER 10

1. Based on information from Sakina P. Spruell, "The 30 Best Companies for Diversity," *Black Enterprise*, July 2005, pp. 112+; "Diversity at McDonald's: A Way of Life," *Nation's Restaurant News*, April 11, 2005, pp. S92+; "Human Resources: A Challenge Best Addressed One Unit at a Time," *Nation's Restaurant News*, April 11, 2005, p. S100; Sarah E. Lockyer, "McD Boosts Morale, Ante at Managers' Vegas Confab," *Nation's Restaurant News*, July 4, 2005, pp. 1, 45; **www.mcdonalds.com.**
2. Ivy Schmerken, "The Hiring Game," *Wall Street & Technology*, Spring 2005, pp. 28+.
3. Joseph Mann, "Fort Lauderdale, Florida-Based AutoNation Reports Earnings Increase," *South Florida Sun-Sentinel*, February 7, 2003.
4. Bureau of Labor Statistics website: **www.dol.gov;** accessed October 17, 2005.
5. Travis E. Poling, "Toyota to Build Truck Factory in San Antonio," *San Antonio Express-News*, February 5, 2003.
6. Wendy Killeen, "Colleges Press Issue of Cultural Diversity," *Boston Globe*, March 13, 2005, p. 7.
7. Vicki Lee Parker, "Workers at North Carolina Companies Undergo Diversity Training," *News and Observer*, Raleigh, January 13, 2003, p. 03013039.
8. **www.ti.com/diversity,** accessed January 17, 2003.
9. "ManTech to Provide C4ISR Training Support," *Aerospace Daily & Defense Report*, January 6, 2005, p. 5.
10. **www.bankofamerica.com/careers/index,** accessed January 17, 2003.
11. Linnea Anderson, "Monster Worldwide, Inc.," Hoovers.com, **http://cobrands.hoovers.com/global/cobrands/proquest/ factsheet.xhtml?COID=41617.**
12. Jennifer Kent, "Hiring and Retaining Employees," *Professional Builder*, December 2004, pp. 21–22.
13. Nanette Byrnes, "Start Search," *BusinessWeek*, October 10, 2005, pp. 74–76.
14. Harry Wessel, "Jobs Column," *The Orlando Sentinel*, January 15, 2003, p. 03015055.
15. U.S. Department of Labor, Bureau of Labor Statistics, News Release, June 18, 2002.
16. "Employees, HR Out of Sync," *Employee Benefit News*, January 1, 2003, p. 5.
17. Douglas Harbrecht, "When Active Duty Calls IBM'ers," *BusinessWeek Online*, **www.businessweek .com:/print/careers/ content/feb2003/ca/20030210_9434_ca030.html,** February 10, 2003.
18. **www.readingeagle.com/KRT/business;** accessed January 17, 2003.
19. Kip Tindel, "Who Said the Trash Can Make You Smile? Transcending Value at the Container Store," Arthur Andersen Retailing Issues Letter, Center for Retailing Studies, Texas A&M University, January 2000, p. 3.
20. Robert Levering, Milton Moskowitz, Ann Harrington, and Christopher Tkaczyk, "100 Best Companies to Work For," *Fortune*, January 20, 2003, p. 127.
21. Cynthia D. Fisher, Lyle F. Schoenfeldt, and James B. Shaw, *Human Resource Management* (Boston: Houghton Mifflin, 2003), p. 527.
22. *Ibid.*, pp. 521–523.
23. "Foot Locker to Pay $3.5 Million to Former Woolworth Employees," *Fair Employment Practices Guidelines*, January 15, 2003, p. 8.

24. David Barstow and Lowell Bergman, "Deaths of the Job, Slaps on the Wrist," *New York Times*, January 10, 2003, p. A1.
25. Based on information from Geoff Edgers, "With Eye on Growth, Aquarium Names New Chief," *Boston Globe*, June 15, 2005, **www.bostonglobe.com;** Stephanie Vosk, "It's February, But on Summer Jobs, Hope Springs Eternal," *Boston Globe*, February 20, 2005, p. 3; Jeffrey Krasner, "New England Aquarium Plunges into Financial Turmoil," *Boston Globe*, December 13, 2002, **www.boston.com/global; www.neaq.org.**
26. Based on information from Patrick J. Kiger, "Manpower Mission: Recruitment Battles," *Workforce Management*, October 25, 2005, pp. 1+; Timothy L. O'Brien, "Madison Avenue Wants You," *New York Times*, September 25, 2005, sec. 3, pp. 1, 8; David Kiley, "Uncle Sam Wants You in the Worst Way," *BusinessWeek*, August 22–29, 2005, p. 40; Robert Burns, "Army Appears Headed to Recruiting Shortfall for 2005," *Associated Press*, June 8, 2005, n.p.

CHAPTER 11

1. Based on information from Robert Levering and Milton Moskowitz, "The 100 Best Companies to Work For," *Fortune*, January 24, 2005, pp. 72+; Matthew Boyle, "The Wegmans Way," *Fortune*, January 24, 2005, p. 62; Alison Coleman, "Smiling Workers May Also Be Gritting Teeth," *Employee Benefits*, May 2005, pp. 6–8; Robert L. Whiddon, "Making the Case for Rich Tuition Reimbursement Plans," *Benefit News*, May 2005, pp. 54, 56.
2. Sheree R. Curry, "Retention Getters," *Incentive*, April 2005, pp. 14+.
3. Christopher Bowe and Andrew Hill, "This Month's Strike at General Electric Highlights the Growing Tensions Between Management and Workers over Healthcare and Retirement Benefits," *Financial Times*, January 30, 2003, p. 11.
4. "Isle of Capri Casinos, Inc., Creates Real-Life Employee 'Survivor' Event," *PR Newswire*, January 20, 2003, p. CGM00520012003.
5. Douglas McGregor, *The Human Side of the Enterprise* (New York: McGraw-Hill, 1960).
6. William Ouchi, *Theory Z* (Reading, MA: Addison-Wesley, 1981).
7. Ricky W. Griffin, *Fundamentals of Management*, 3d ed. (Boston: Houghton Mifflin, 2006), p. 334.
8. Rochelle Garner, "Company Growth and Rankings," *Computer Reseller*, January 31, 2005.
9. Alison Overholt, "Power up the People: Economy Stuck in the Doldrums? Morale Stuck There Too? Here Are a Few Things That You Can Do to Jazz Things up in 2003," *Fast Company*, January 2003, p. 50.
10. "Is Job Stress Taking Its Toll in Your Facility?" *Safety Management*, February 2003, p. 3.
11. Alan Deutschman, "Making Change," *Fast Company*, May 2005, pp. 52+.
12. Leah Carlson, "Benefits that Meet Mom's Needs," *Employee Benefits News*, December 1, 2005, n.p.
13. Nanette Byrnes, "Star Search," *BusinessWeek*, October 10, 2005, p. 78.
14. Leigh Strope, "More Workers Have Option of Growing Flex-Time Trend," Associated Press, January 6, 2003.
15. **www.starbucks.com/jobcenter.**
16. Alison Maitland, "Two for the Price of One," *Financial Times Limited*, January 24, 2001, p. 17.
17. *World News This Morning*, Transcript, ABC News, January 10, 2003.
18. "Telework Succeeds for U.S. Agencies," *Work & Family Newsbrief*, January 2003, p. 7.
19. "Boston College Report Presents Challenges and Advantages of Telework," *Work & Family Newsbrief*, January 2003, p. 8.
20. Arif Mohamed, "Bosses Split Over Productivity of Teleworkers," *Computer Weekly*, March 29, 2005, p. 55.
21. Samuel Greengard, "Sun's Shining Example," *Workforce Management*, March 2005, pp. 48+.
22. Matthew Boyle and Ellen Florian Kratz, "The Wegmans Way," *Fortune*, January 24, 2005, p. 62.
23. "A Short History of ESOP," **www.nceo.org,** January 2006.
24. Bruce Upbin, "Work and Buy and Hold," *Forbes*, January 20, 2003, p. 56.

25. Ricky W. Griffin, *Fundamentals of Management* (Boston: Houghton Mifflin, 2006), pp. 428–447.

26. Daniel Kadlec, "Meet the No-Star Team," *Time*, December 19, 2005, p. 58.

27. Barry L. Reece and Rhonda Brandt, *Effective Human Relations: Personal and Organizational Applications* (Boston: Houghton Mifflin, 2005), pp. 280–285.

28. "Jones Walker Law Firm taps Harvard for New Orleans Rebuild Advice," *New Orleans CityBusiness*, News Section, January 3, 2006, n.p.

29. "Case Study: Using the Right Incentive Can Improve Cooperation Among Departments," *Report on Customer Relationship Management*, September 2003, p. 5.

30. Bill Fischer and Andy Boynton, "Virtuoso Teams," *Harvard Business Review*, July–August 2005, pp. 116–123.

31. Milton Moskowitz and Robert Levering, "10 Great Companies to Work For," *Fortune International*, January 20, 2003, p. 26.

32. Jens Meiners, "M-B Changes Product Development," *Automotive News*, September 12, 2005, p. 18.

33. Linda Webb, "Microsoft's New Ergonomic Keyboard More Comfortable," *Cleveland Plain Dealer*, November 7, 2005, p. E4.

34. "Trusted Computer Solutions Names Top Military IT Expert to Advisory Board," *PR Newswire*, October 12, 2004.

35. Based on information from *Pioneering American Flatbread* video by Houghton Mifflin; Andrew Nemethy, "Waitsfield: American Flatbread," *See Vermont*, February 21, 2001, **seevermont.nybor .com/dining/story/20722.html; www.americanflatbread.com.**

36. Based on information from Jessica Marquez, "Novel Ideas at Borders Lure Older Workers," *Workforce Management*, May 2005, pp. 28, 30; Jeffrey A. Trachtenberg, "Borders Looks Beyond Border," *Wall Street Journal*, March 18, 2005, p. C4; **www .bordersgroupinc.com.**

CHAPTER 12

1. Based on information from Gare Joyce, "Will Hockey Fans Return?" *Christian Science Monitor*, September 2, 2005, p. 11; Thomas Heath and Tarik El-Bashir, "NHL Season Put on Ice," *Washington Post*, February 17, 2005, p. D1; Rachel Blount, "NHL Closes Its Doors," *Star Tribune*, February 17, 2005, p. 8c; "NHL Lockout Puts Businesses on Thin Ice," *News-Times* (Danbury, CT), January 27, 2005, p. B8; Larry Wigge, "There Are No Losers with This Settlement," *Sporting News*, December 13, 1993, p. 51; E. M. Swift, "Drop Those Pucks," *Sports Illustrated*, January 23, 1995, pp. 36+; Larry Wigge, "Owners Had a Hammer, and They Used It Well," *Sporting News*, January 23, 1995, p. 47; Mark Starr, "Strike, Uh, Is It Four?" *Newsweek*, April 17, 2005, p. 74.

2. Jane M. Von Bergen, "Union Plan Seeks More for Organizing," *Knight Ridder Tribune Business News*, April 29, 2005, p. 1.

3. Jim McKay, "Merger Makes USW Biggest Industrial Union," *Knight Ridder Tribune Business News*, April 14, 2005, p. 1.

4. "Union and Management Look for New Ways of Doing Business," *Canadian Corporate News*, February 15, 2000.

5. Bureau of Labor Statistics, Survey of Employer Costs, June 2005.

6. Saul A. Rubenstein, "The Impact of Co-Management on Quality Performance: The Case of the Saturn Corporations," *Industrial and Labor Relations Review*, January 2000, pp. 197–218.

7. "NYU Will Not Renew Contract with Graduate Students Union," Associated Press, August 6, 2005; "New York University Issues Ultimatum to Striking Graduate Students," Associated Press, November 29, 2005.

8. Hubble Smith, "Union Accuses Drywall Company of Not Fulfilling Promises for Pay," *Las Vegas Review-Journal*, July 30, 2005, p. 2D.

9. Ari Weinberg, "America's Most Dangerous Unions," *Forbes.com*, **www.forbes.com/2003/01/13/cz_aw_0113union.html,** accessed January 13, 2003.

10. Christopher Bowe and Andrew Hill, "Workers Feeling Sick over Rising Healthcare Costs," *Financial Times*, January 14, 2003, p. 21.

11. David Welch and Kathleen Kerwin, "Rick Wagoner's Game Plan," *BusinessWeek*, February 10, 2003, p. 52.

12. Bureau of Labor Statistics website: **www.bls.gov;** accessed January 5, 2006.

13. Pete Donohue and Corky Siemaszko, "What a Relief, Strike Ends, Riders Thaw, Talks to Resume," *New York Daily News*, December 23, 2005, p.3; Shannon D. Harrington and Soni Sangha, "Back to Normal: Transit Strike Ends in Time for the Morning Commute," *The Record*, December 23, 2005, p. A01; David B. Caruso, "New York Transit Strike Enters Day Two Amid Court Battle," Associated Press State and Local Wire, December 21, 2005.

14. Kim Chapman, "Teachers' Unions Boycott Wal-Mart," *The Houston Chronicle*, August 11, 2005, p. B1.

15. Alvin Hattal, "Organization Case Study: FMCS Boosts Its Reputation through Success," *PR Week*, September 5, 2005.

16. "Study Shows that Federal Mediation Makes Good Business Sense for Labor and Management in Collective Bargaining," PR Newswire, November 17, 2005.

17. Based on information from Holman W. Jenkins, Jr., "Propaganda Clean-up in Aisle Six," *Wall Street Journal*, November 9, 2005, p. A17; Katherine Bowers, "Wal-Mart Unveils New Health Plan For Workers," *HFN*, October 31, 2005, p. 16; Stephanie Armour, "Wal-Mart Takes Hits on Worker Treatment," *USA Today*, February 10, 2003, **www .usatoday.com;** Karen Olsson, "Up Against Wal-Mart," *Mother Jones*, March–April 2003, **www.motherjones.com;** Wendy Zellner, "How Wal-Mart Keeps Unions at Bay," *BusinessWeek*, October 28, 2002, pp. 94+; **www.walmartstores.com; www.wakeupwalmart.com.**

18. Based on information from Martin J. Moylan, "Northwest Resumes Hiring Replacement Mechanics after Union Refuses Vote," *Saint Paul Pioneer Press*, October 22, 2005, **www.twincities.com;** "Nurses at Stanford Hospitals Approve Contract, End Strike," *Los Angeles Times*, July 29, 2000, p. 20; Barbara Feder, "Replacement Nurses at California Hospitals Draw Strikers' Ire, Healthy Pay," *San Jose Mercury News*, June 20, 2000, **www.sjmercury.com;** Richard L. Lippke, "Government Support of Labor Unions and the Ban on Striker Replacements," *Business and Society Review* 109, Summer 2004, pp. 127–151.

CHAPTER 13

1. Based on information from Julie Bosman, "What's Cool Online? Teenagers Render Verdict," *New York Times*, September 29, 2005, p. C14; Mae Anderson, "On the Crest of the Wave," *Adweek*, September 13, 2004, **www.adweek.com;** Matt DeMazza, "Teen Magnets," *Footwear News*, November 17, 2003, p. 15; Lev Grossman, "The Quest for Cool," *Time*, September 8, 2003, pp. 48–54; Irma Zandl, "B-T-S: Anything Hot?" *Marketing Insight from the Zandl Group*, August 2003, n.p.; Barbara White-Sax, "Teens Become Price Savvy in Search for What's Cool," *Drug Store News*, March 23, 2003, pp. 17+.

2. *Marketing News*, September 15, 2004, p. 1.

3. Jagdish N. Sheth and Rajendras Sisodia, "More than Ever Before, Marketing Is under Fire to Account for What It Spends," *Marketing Management*, Fall 1995, pp. 13–14.

4. Coca-Cola 2004 Annual Report, **www2.coca-cola.com/ investors/annualandotherreports/2004/pdf/Coca-Cola _10-K_Item_01.pdf;** accessed January 6, 2006.

5. Lynette Ryals and Adrian Payne, "Customer Relationship Management in Financial Services: Towards Information-Enabled Relationship Marketing," *Journal of Strategic Marketing*, March 2001, p. 3.

6. Werner J. Reinartz and V. Kumark, "On the Profitability of Long-Life Customers in a Noncontractual Setting: an Empirical Investigation and Implications for Marketing," *Journal of Marketing*, October 2000, pp. 17–35.

7. Roland T. Rust, Katherine N. Lemon, and Valarie A. Zeithaml, "Return on Marketing: Using Customer Equity to Focus Marketing Strategy," *Journal of Marketing* 68 (January 2004), pp. 109–127.

8. Rajkumar Venkatesan and V. Kumar, "A Customer Lifetime Value Framework for Customer Selection and Resource Allocation Strategy," *Journal of Marketing* 68 (October 2004), pp. 106–125.

9. Gina Chon, "Toyota's Marketers Get Respect—Now They Want Love," *Wall Street Journal*, January 11, 2006, p. B1.

10. Megan E. Mulligan, "Wireless for the Well Off," *Forbes.com*, **http://forbes.com/2003/01/21/cz_mm_0121tentech_print. html;** accessed January 21, 2003.

11. Michael J. Weiss, "To Be About to Be," *American Demographics*, September 2003, pp. 29–36.

12. Cliff Edwards, "Inside Intel," *BusinessWeek*, January 9, 2006, p. 46.

13. Kenneth Hein, "Disney Puts Pooh, Power Rangers, Princess under Wing with $500M," *Brandweek*, January 27, 2003, p. 6.

14. Mark Jewell, "Dunkin' Donuts Eyes Turn Westward: Chain Evolves from No Frills," *The Coloradoan*, January 17, 2005, p. E1.

15. William M. Pride and O. C. Ferrell, *Marketing: Concepts and Strategies* (Boston: Houghton Mifflin, 2006), p. 233.

16. Chad Kaydo, "A Position of Power," *Sales and Marketing Management*, June 2000, p. 106.

17. Based on information from Stephen Hochman, "Flexibility—Finding the Right Fit," *Supply Chain Management Review*, July–August 2005, p. 10; Naomi Aoki, "New Balance's Latest Ads Celebrate the (Older) Amateur," *Boston Globe*, February 28, 2005, n.p.; Barbara Schneider-Levy, "Woman's Touch: Comfort," *Footwear News*, May 30, 2005, p. 38; Daren Fonda, "Sole Survivor," *Time*, November 8, 2004, p. 48; Thomas J. Ryan, "The Price Is Right," *Footwear Business*, February 2004, n.p.; interviews with Jim Sciabarrasi, Christine Epplett, and Paul Heffernan of New Balance, video, Houghton Mifflin Company, 2003.

18. Based on information from Kerry Capell, Ariane Sains, and Cristina Lindblad, "IKEA: How the Swedish Retailer Became a Global Cult Brand," *BusinessWeek*, November 14, 2005, pp. 96+; "IKEA's Growth Limited by Style Issues, Says CEO," *Nordic Business Report*, January 21, 2004, **www .nordicbusinessreport.com;** "IKEA Sets New Heights with Cat," *Printing World*, August 21, 2003, p. 3; **www.ikea-usa.com.**

19. Kay Parker, "Old-Line Goes Online," *Business 2.0*, **http://www .business2.com/content/magazine/marketing/2000/06/01/ 1270,** June 1, 2000.

CHAPTER 14

1. Based on information from Phil Patton, "Style Meets Function, and Technology Gets a Human Touch," *New York Times*, November 2, 2005, p. G5; Eric A. Taub, "The Small Screen, Redefined," *New York Times*, November 10, 2005, p. C11; Peter Grant and Dionne Searcey, "How to Watch TV," *Wall Street Journal*, November 9, 2005, p. D1; "IPod's Cool Factor May Be Fading," *InformationWeek*, November 7, 2005, **www.informationweek.com.**

2. Peter Lewis, "Play That Funky Music, White Toy," *Fortune*, February 7, 2005, pp. 38–39.

3. William Hall, "Logitech Proves No Mouse Among Men," *Financial Times*, January 6, 2003, p. 15.

4. Procter & Gamble, **www.pg.com** (accessed April 27, 2006). Chennai, *Businessline*, February 6, 2005, p. 1; **www.pg.com/ common/sitemap.jhtml.**

5. **www.gefn.com/search/index;** accessed January 24, 2003.

6. Kate MacArthur, "Drink Your Fruits, Veggies: Water's the New Fitness Fad," *Advertising Age*, January 3, 2005, p. 4.

7. Joseph B. White and Norihiko Shirouzu, "Ford Gambles in Rolling Out New F-150," *Wall Street Journal*, January 6, 2003, p. A15.

8. "10 Worst Strategy Changes," *Advertising Age*, December 19, 2005, p. 10.

9. Mike Beirne, "Hershey Gets Sweet with Sugarfree," *Brandweek*, January 20, 2003, p. 4.

10. Peter D. Bennett (ed.), *Dictionary of Marketing Terms* (Chicago: American Marketing Association and NTC Publishing Group, 1995), p. 27.

11. "Market Profile," **www.plma.com;** accessed January 23, 2006.

12. Deborah Ball and Sarah Ellison, "Two Shampoos Lather Up for Duel," *Wall Street Journal*, January 28, 2003, p. B7.

13. World's Most Valuable Brands," Interbrand, **www.interbrand .com,** July 2005.

14. Gabriel Kahn, "Still Going for the Gold," *Wall Street Journal*, January 28, 2003, pp. B1 and B4.

15. **www.amazon.com;** accessed January 23, 2006.

16. Emily Lambert, "The Buck Stops Here," *Forbes.com*, **www.forbes .com/forbes/2003/ 0106/052.html;** accessed January 6, 2003.

17. Alex Taylor III, "Porsche's Risky Recipe," *Fortune*, **www .fortune.com/fortune/ print/0,15935,418670,00.html;** accessed February 3, 2003.

18. **www.netzero.com.**

19. Verizon, **www.verizon.com,** accessed April 27, 2006.

20. Based on information from "Fuel Costs Hurt Profit at JetBlue," *New York Times*, July 22, 2005, n.p.; Jeremy W. Peters, "Rougher Times Amid Higher Costs at JetBlue," *New York Times*, November 11, 2004, pp. C1+; Chuck Salter, "And Now the Hard Part," *Fast Company*, May 2004, pp. 66+; Amy Goldwasser, "Something Stylish, Something Blue," *Business 2.0*, February 2002, pp. 94–95; "Blue Skies: Is JetBlue the Next Great Airline—Or Just a Little Too Good to Be True?" *Time*, July 30, 2001, p. 24+; Darren Shannon, "Three of a Kind," *Travel Agent*, July 23, 2001, p. 60+; **www.jetblue.com.**

21. Based on information from Adam Aston, "All Bruce, All the Time," *BusinessWeek*, November 7, 2005, p. 92; "Sirius Revenues Soar, But Losses Widen," *InternetWeek*, November 1, 2005, **www .internetweek.com;** Brad Stone, "Greetings, Earthlings: Satellite Radio for Cars Is Taking Off and Adding New Features—Now Broadcasters Are Starting to Fight Back," *Newsweek*, January 26, 2003, p. 55; "In Brief, Radio: XM Radio Ends '03 with 1.36 Million Users," *Los Angeles Times*, January 8, 2004, p. C3; Stephen Holden, "High-Tech Quirkiness Restores Radio's Magic," *New York Times*, December 26, 2003, pp. E1+; David Pogue, "Satellite Radio Extends Its Orbit," *New York Times*, December 18, 2003, p. G1.

CHAPTER 15

1. Based on information from Bob Sechler, "Dell Returns to Retail Shelves with Costco Deal," *Wall Street Journal*, December 1, 2005, p. B5; "Technology's Mr. Predictable," *The Economist*, September 24, 2005, p. 82; Sam Diaz, "Dell Succeeds By Breaking Silicon Valley Rules," *San Jose Mercury News*, December 17, 2003, **www.mercurynews.com;** and J. Bonasia, "Supply Chain Issues Take on New Urgency," *Investor's Business Daily*, February 27, 2002, p. A10.

2. Melanie Wells, "Pepsi's New Challenge," *Forbes*, January 20, 2003.

3. Sally Beatty, "Levi's Strives to Keep a Hip Image," *Wall Street Journal*, January 23, 2003, p. B12.

4. Andrew Raskin, "Who's Minding the Store?" *Business 2.0*, **www .business2.com/articles/mag/0,1640,46334,00.html,** accessed February 2003.

5. William M. Pride and O. C. Ferrell, *Marketing: Concepts and Strategies* (Boston: Houghton Mifflin, 2006), p. 403.

6. "Industry Report 2005," *Convenience Store News*, April 18, 2005.

7. Sandra O'Loughlin and Barry Janoff, "Retailers Seek New Ways to Sell Wares," *Brandweek*, January 6, 2003, p. 12.

8. Michael Barbaro, "Readings," *Washington Post*, January 23, 2005, p. F3; David Moin, "Category Killers' Concerns: Overgrowth and Extinction," *WWD*, January 6, 2005, p. 17.

9. **www.dsa.org;** accessed January 28, 2006.

10. **www.donotcall.gov/FAQ;** accessed January 27, 2006.

11. John Eggerton, "DirecTV Settles $10 Million in Complaints," *Broadcasting & Cable*, December 19, 2005, pp. 4, 30.

12. Nicole Urso, "HSN Viewers Shop with Their Remotes," *Response*, May 2005, p. 8.

13. **www.netflix.com;** accessed January 30, 2006.

14. Robert McMillan, "Got 796 Quarters Handy? Get Yourself an iPod," *PC World*, January 2006, p. 54.

15. Sandra O'Loughlin, "Out with the Old: Malls versus Centers," *Brandweek*, May 9, 2005, p. 30.

16. Constance L. Hays, "What Wal-Mart Knows About Customers' Habits," *New York Times*, November 14, 2005, **www.nytimes.com.**

17. Jeff O'Neil, "Super Warehouses," *Modern Materials Handling*, November 2005, p. 45.

18. Based on information from Denise Power, "REI Woos Customers with Delivery Options," *WWD*, May 18, 2005, pp. 6B+; "REI Climbs Data Mountain to Gain Single View of Customers," *Chain Store Age*, October 2005, p. S7; Ken Clark, "REI Scales New Heights," *Chain Store Age*, July 2004, pp. 26A+; "REI Climbs to New Heights Online," *Chain Store Age*, October 2003, pp. 72+;

www.rei.com; Mike Gorrell, "New REI Store Opens in Salt Lake City Area," *Salt Lake Tribune*, March 28, 2003, **www.sltrib.com.**

19. Based on information from "Grainger Takes New Look at Unplanned MRO Purchases," *Purchasing*, September 1, 2005, pp. 53–55; Perry A. Trunick, "Network in Progress," *Logistics Today*, March 2005, pp. 1, 12–13; Jim Lucy, "The Super Influentials," *Electrical Wholesaling*, April 1, 2004, n.p.; Susan Avery, "Grainger Eases Access to Products for MRO Buyers," *Purchasing*, June 3, 2004, pp. 48+; **www.grainger.com.**

CHAPTER 16

1. Based on information from "Pizza Hut Unveils '50 Per Cent Bigger' Pizza," *Marketing Week*, December 1, 2005, p. 7; Richard Williamson, "Pizza Hut Partakes in 'Three Wishes,'" *Adweek Southwest*, November 11, 2005, n.p.; Richard Williamson, "Pizza Hut Turns Up Heat on Stuffed Crust," *Adweek Southwest*, April 2005, n.p.; Gregg Cebrzynski, "Top Pizza Segment Chains Fight It Out on Familiar Turf," *Nation's Restaurant News*, June 27, 2005, pp. 118+; "Pizza Hut Starts Its Engines for First NASCAR Sponsorship," *Nation's Restaurant News*, May 9, 2005, p. 20; **www.pizzahut.com.**

2. Stephanie Thompson, "Kraft Gets into the Groove," *Advertising Age*, January 23, 2006, p. 25.

3. Robert Coen, "Insider's Report," December 2005, **www .universalmccann.com.**

4. "2006 Rates and Editions," *Time*, **www.time-planner .com/planner/rates/index.html;** accessed January 16, 2006.

5. Andrew Tilin, "The G6 Goes Oprah," *Business 2.0*, January– February 2005, p. 47.

6. Arlene Weintraub, "Marketing Champ of the World," *Entrepreneurship*, December 2004, pp. 64–65.

7. Stuart Elliott, "At $83,333 a Second, Ads Chase Super Bowl Score," *New York Times*, February 2, 2006.

8. "The Impact of Direct-to-Consumer Drug Advertising on Seniors' Health," States News Service, October 10, 2005.

9. Paul Sloan, "The Sales Force that Rocks," *Business 2.0*, July 1, 2005, **cnnmoney.com.**

10. Terence Shimp, *Advertising, Promotion, and Supplemental Aspects of Integrated Marketing Communications*, 2006, Mason, Ohio: Southwestern. p. 527.

11. Natalie Schwartz, "Clipping Path," *Promo's 12th Annual SourceBook 2005*, p. 15.

12. "Berry & Homer Wraps Bus Leading Lance Armstrong and Tour of Hope Team on Cross-Country Trek," *Business Wire*.

13. Todd Wasserman, "H&R Block Takes Diversified Services into Account in Branding Makeover," *Brandweek*, January 13, 2003, p. 9.

14. Kate MacArthur, "Hardee's Shifts to a Big-Beef Menu," *Ad Age*, **www.adage.com/news.cms?newsId=37048;** accessed February 3, 2003.

15. Based on information from Matthew Creamer and Lisa Sanders, "BMW Seeks a 'Holistic' Ad Approach," *Automotive News*, November 21, 2005, p. 10; "50 Years of Fame," *Marketing*, September 21, 2005, p. 25; Neal E. Boudette, "Navigating Curves," *Wall Street Journal*, January 10, 2005, pp. A1+; Neal E. Boudette, "BMW's CEO Just Says 'No' to Protect Brand," *Wall Street Journal*, November 26, 2003, pp. B1+; "The Psychology of Luxury," *USA Today*, December 15, 2003, **www.usatoday.com; www.bmw.usa.com.**

16. Based on information from Vicky Hallett, "The Power of Potter," *U.S. News & World Report*, July 25, 2005, p. 44; Jonathan Landreth, "Harry's Flame Heats Up China," *Washington Post*, November 26, 2005, p. C3; "Latest 'Potter' Spells Magic at Holiday Weekend Box Office," *Wall Street Journal*, November 28, 2005, p. B4; Jeffrey A. Trachtenberg and Deborah Ball, "A Magical Moment for Publishing," *Wall Street Journal*, July 18, 2005, p. B3.

CHAPTER 17

1. Based on information from Damon Hodge, "Harrah's, MGM Mirage Angling to Be World's Top Gaming Company," *Travel Weekly*, November 7, 2005, pp. 42+; Susan Erler, "Horseshoe Computer Upgrade Interrupts Automatic Cashouts," *The Times (Munster, Indiana)*, August 9, 2005, **www.nwitimes.com;** Suzette Parmley, "Gambling Company Boosts Profitability with Customer Tracking," *Philadelphia Inquirer*, April 28, 2005, **www.philly.com;** Kathleen Melymuka, "Betting on IT Value," *Computerworld*, May 3, 2004, pp. 33+; **www.harrahs.com.**

2. The Nielsen Media Research website: **www.nielsenmedia.com;** accessed November 20, 2005.

3. Bradley Mitchell, "Your Guide to Wireless/Networking," About.com website: **www.about.com;** accessed November 22, 2005.

4. *Ibid.*

5. "The Web at Your Service," *BusinessWeek Online*, **www .businessweek.com,** March 18, 2002.

6. Necho Systems website: **www.necho.com;** accessed November 20, 2005.

7. Based on information from Jon Udell, "Art and Science of Usability Analysis," *InfoWorld*, June 4, 2004, **www.infoworld.com;** *Consumer Behavior Research: Lextant*, Houghton Mifflin video; **www .lextantcorp.com.**

8. Based on information from Alison Enhright, "Brill's Blog Builds Community and Gets It Right," *Marketing News*, December 15, 2005, p. 23; Beth Snyder Bulik, "Unemployed Blogger? You Might Apply at IBM," *Advertising Age*, November 14, 2005, p. 12; Michelle Delio, "Enterprise Collaboration with Blogs and Wikis," *InfoWorld*, March 28, 2005, p. 5; William M. Bulkeley, "Marketers Scan Blogs for Brand Insights," *Wall Street Journal*, June 23, 2005, p. B1; "Guidelines for IBM Bloggers," *IBM Blogging Policy and Guidelines*, May 16, 2005, **www.ibm.com.**

CHAPTER 18

1. Based on information from Carrie Johnson, "Regulators Cite Deloitte & Touche," *Washington Post*, October 7, 2005, p. D3; Carrie Johnson, "Overseers Criticize KPMG Audit Quality," *Washington Post*, September 30, 2005, p. D2; Diya Gullapalli, "Take This Job and . . . File It," *Wall Street Journal*, May 4, 2005, p. C1; Claude Solnik, "Compliance with Sarbanes-Oxley Act Creates Big Fees for Big Four Accounting Firms," *Long Island Business News*, March 18, 2005, n.p.; Diya Gullapalli, "BDO Seidman Faces Accounting's New World," *Wall Street Journal*, September 27, 2005, p. C1; Kathy M. Kristof, "Bittersweet Verdict for Firm's Alumni," *Los Angeles Times*, June 1, 2005, p. A12.

2. Jeffrey Kahn, "Do Accountants Have a Future?" *Fortune*, **www.fortune.com,** February 18, 2001.

3. American Institute of Certified Public Accountants (AICPA) website: **www.aicpa.org;** accessed February 25, 2003.

4. Nanette Byrnes and William Symonds, "Is the Avalanche Headed for Pricewaterhouse?" *BusinessWeek*, October 14, 2002, pp. 45–46.

5. Steve Rosenbush, "The Message in Ebbers' Sentence," *BusinessWeek Online*, **www.businessweek.com,** July 14, 2005.

6. "Ex-Tyco CEO Dennis Kozlowski Found Guilty," MSNBC, **www.msnbc.msn.com,** June 17, 2005.

7. Steve Rosenbush, "Key Players in Enron Scandal," *BusinessWeek Online*, **www.businessweek.com,** August 6, 2006.

8. "System Failure," *Fortune*, June 24, 2002, p. 64.

9. Bureau of Labor Statistics website: **www.bls.gov;** accessed December 2, 2005.

10. American Institute of Certified Public Accountants (AICPA) website: **www.aicpa.org;** accessed December 1, 2005.

11. Based on information from Jane Sasseen, "White-Collar Crime: Who Does Time?" *BusinessWeek*, February 6, 2006, **www .businessweek.com;** Stephen Labaton, "Four Years Later, Enron's Shadow Lingers as Change Comes Slowly," *New York Times*, January 5, 2006, p. C1; *Making the Numbers at Commodore Appliance* (Houghton Mifflin video).

12. Based on information from R. Dilip Krishna, "Enterprise Risk Management: Illuminate the Unknown," *Intelligent Enterprise*, December 2005, **www.intelligententerprise.com/showarticle .jhtml?articleID=0174300345;** Cathleen Moore, "Compliance Strives for Automation," *InforWorld*, May 23, 2005, p. 15; Anna Maria Virzi, "Kimberly-Clark: Benefiting from SOX," *Baseline*, September 7, 2005, **www.baseliniemag.com;** Matthew Schwartz, "Q&A: The Future of Security, Control, and SOX Compliance," *Enterprise Systems*, December 13, 2005, **www.esj.com.**

CHAPTER 19

1. Based on information from Jennifer Saranow, "Bankers' Hours Grow Longer as More Branches Extend Days," *Wall Street Journal*, March 17, 2005, p. D2; Chris Bosak, "Commerce Bank Opens Norwalk, Conn., Branch," *The Hour (Norwalk, CT)*, August 17, 2005, **www.thehour.com;** Terence O'Hara, "Area Gets an All-Day Bank Fight," *Washington Post*, June 2, 2005, pp. A1ff; **www.commerceonline.com.**

2. The Federal Reserve Board website: **www.federalreserve.gov;** accessed May 18, 2006.

3. *Ibid.*

4. *Ibid.*

5. The Investopedia website: **www.investopedia.com;** accessed December 16, 2005.

6. The Federal Reserve Bank of San Francisco website: **www.frbsf.org;** accessed December 17, 2005.

7. The Office of the Comptroller of the Currency website: **www.occ.treas.gov;** accessed December 18, 2005.

8. The Federal Deposit Insurance Corporation website: **www.fdic.gov;** accessed December 15, 2005.

9. U.S. Census Bureau, *Statistical Abstract of the United States, 2004–2005*, 124th ed. (Washington: U.S. Government Printing Office, 2004), p. 744.

10. The Federal Deposit Insurance Corporation website: **www.fdic.gov;** accessed December 15, 2005.

11. "Career Guide to Industries," U.S. Department of Labor Bureau of Labor Statistics website: **www.bls.gov;** accessed December 19, 2005.

12. U.S. Census Bureau, *Statistical Abstract of the United States, 2004–2005*, 124th ed. (Washington: U.S. Government Printing Office, 2004), p. 747.

13. "FTC in New York and John Jay College Teach Credit Smarts to NYC Students," The Federal Trade Commission website: **www.ftc.gov;** accessed September 3, 2003.

14. Dr. Patrick Dixon, the Global Change, LTD website: **www.globalchange.com;** accessed January 14, 2003.

15. *Ibid.*

16. The Federal Deposit Insurance Corporation website: **www.fdic.gov;** accessed December 19, 2005.

17. The Federal Trade Commission website: **www.ftc.gov;** accessed December 20, 2005.

18. Based on information from the Financial Fusion website: **www.financialfusion.com;** accessed December 20, 2005; Steve Bills, "Online Banking," *American Banker*, March 11, 2002, p. 23.

19. Based on information from Ron Lieber and Robin Sidel, "Citigroup Unveils Five AmEx Cards," *Wall Street Journal*, December 20, 2005, p. D2; Diya Gullapalli, "Entertainment: Credit Card to Tout No Late Fees," *Wall Street Journal*, October 13, 2005, p. D5; Aleksandra Todorova, "SmartMoney: A Handy New Way to Pay," *Wall Street Journal*, November 27, 2005, p. 3; Robin Sidel, "Credit-Card Firms Go for Small," *Wall Street Journal*, November 1, 2005, pp. C1+; Christopher Wang, "Citigroup to Buy Credit-Card Portfolios," *Reno Gazette-Journal*, June 2, 2005, **www.rgj.com.**

CHAPTER 20

1. Based on information from Karen Richardson, "Street Sleuth: Bankers Hope for a Reprise of 'Bowie Bonds,'" *Wall Street Journal*, August 23, 2005, p. C1; Cora Daniels, "Ground Control to Bowie Bonds," *Fortune*, June 16, 2003, p. 22; "Care to Buy Some Bowie Bonds?" *BusinessWeek*, March 11, 2002, p. 64; Gregory Zuckerman, "James Brown's Got a Brand New Bag," *Wall Street Journal*, May 3, 1999, pp. 1+.

2. The Merck & Company website: **www.merck.com;** accessed December 29, 2005.

3. The Federal Judiciary website: **www.uscourts.gov;** accessed June 3, 2006.

4. The *Ad Age* website: **www.adage.com;** accessed December 30, 2005.

5. The *BusinessWeek Online* website: **www.businessweek.com;** accessed December 30, 2005.

6. Ian Rowley, "Fuji Heavy Trades GM for Toyota," *BusinessWeek Online*, **www.businessweek.com,** October 6, 2005.

7. "Making the Investment Grade," *BusinessWeek Online*, **www.businessweek.com,** December 31, 2005.

8. "Amicus Briefs in Enron Bankruptcy Litigation," BondMarkets.com website, **www.bondmarkets.com,** March 18, 2004.

9. Google IPO Central website: **www.google-ipo.com;** accessed January 1, 2006.

10. Asia Yahoo News website: **www.asia.news.yahoo.com;** accessed January 2, 2006.

11. General Electric website: **www.ge.com;** accessed January 2, 2006.

12. Based on information from the Gilford Securities website: **www.gilfordsecurities.com;** accessed January 3, 2006 and January 21, 2001.

13. Based on information from Nate Hinkel, "Couple's Bed-and-Breakfast Benefits from SBA Loan," *Arkansas Business*, May 16, 2005, p. 22; Farrah Austin, "Thyme Out in Arkansas," *Southern Living*, April 2003, p. 33; **www.mountainthyme.com.**

CHAPTER 21

1. Based on information from Charles Schwab, "In for the Long Term," *New York Times*, August 14, 2005, sec. 3, p. 9; Susanne Craig, "Schwab Again Has Wall Street Fans . . . For Now," *Wall Street Journal*, October 10, 2005, p. C1; Jane J. Kim, "Discount-Broker 'Package' Deal," *Wall Street Journal*, September 17, 2005, p. B5; Jane J. Kim, "Investing Help for Do-It-Yourselfers," *Wall Street Journal*, July 5, 2005, p. D2; **www.schwab. com.**

2. Google IPO Central website: **www.google-ipo.com;** accessed January 1, 2006.

3. New York Stock Exchange website: **www.nyse.com;** accessed January 13, 2006.

4. "Stock Market Savvy: Investing for Your Future," Lifetime Learning Systems, **www.nyse.com/pdfs/ TG_Mech.pdf. 2001.**

5. *Ibid.*

6. Motley Fool website: **www.fool.com;** accessed January 14, 2006.

7. Roger G. Ibbotson, "Predictions of the Past and Forecasts for the Future," Ibbotson Associates website: **www.ibbotson.com;** accessed January 10, 2006.

8. Suze Orman, *The Road to Wealth* (New York: Riverbend Books, 2001), p. 371.

9. *Mergent Bond Record* (New York: Mergent, Inc., October 2005), p. 232.

10. Investment Company Institute website: **www.ici.org;** accessed January 12, 2006.

11. "Index Investing: Index Funds," Investopedia.com website: **www.investopedia.com;** accessed January 15, 2006.

12. Market values for General Motors were obtained from the Yahoo! Finance website: **http://finance.yahoo. com;** accessed January 15, 2006.

13. Sources: Based on information from Lucas Conley, "Customer-Centered Leader: Maxine Clark," *Fast Company*, October 2005, p. 64; "Q3 2005 Build-A-Bear Workshop, Inc., Earnings Conference Call," *America's Intelligence Wire*, October 2, 2005, n.p.; Mary Jo Feldstein, "St. Louis Toy Retailer Build-A-Bear Claws Its Way to Profitable IPO," *St. Louis Post-Dispatch*, October 29, 2004, **www.stltoday.com;** Alyson Grala, "'Bear'ing It All," *License!*, May 2004, pp. 22–24; Allison Fass, "Bear Market," *Forbes*, March 1, 2004, p. 88; Thomas K. Grose, "Teddy Bear Tussle," *U.S. News & World Report*, November 11, 2002, p. 46.

14. Sources: Based on information from Jeffrey McCracken and Joseph B. White, "Ford Woes Mount as S&P Sounds a Louder Alarm," *Wall Street Journal*, January 6, 2006, p. A3; Martin Wolk, "GM Hoping Big SUV Category Still Has Life," MSNBC, January 3, 2006, **www.msnbc.msn.com/id/10499101/;** Dena Aubin, "Fitch Cuts Ford to Junk Status, Outlook Negative," *Reuters*, December 19, 2005, **http://today.reuters. com;** "Update 1-S&P Cuts GM's Debt Rating Deeper into Junk," *Reuters*, December 12, 2005, **http://today.reuters.com;** Tom Walker, "As Rates Rise, Junk Bonds Lose Luster," *Atlanta Journal-Constitution*, October 29, 2005, **www.ajc.com;** Micheline Maynard and Jeremy W. Peters, "S&P Cuts GM Rating to Lowest in 52 Years," *New York Times*, December 13, 2005, p. C4; "Toyota Sees '06 Global Output Up 10 pct," *Reuters*, December 20, 2005, **http://today. reuters.com.**

Credits

BOX CREDITS

Chapter 1 p. 7 **[Your Career]** Based on information in Kristine Conway, "Mentoring: Back to the Basics," *Training*, August 2005, p. 42; Michele Marchetti, "A Helping Hand: Why Mentoring Programs Are Integral to Sales Success," *Sales and Marketing Management*, August 2005, p. 12; Ieva M. Augstums, "Mentoring Can Be a Guide to Success," *Dallas Morning News*, May 22, 2005, **www.dallasnews.com.** **p. 12 [Biz Tech]** Based on information in Jonathan Krim, "eBay's Skype Risk Is a Calculated One," *Washington Post*, September 22, 2005; Mylene Mangalindan, "Outside Merchants Boost Amazon," *Wall Street Journal*, July 27, 2005, p. A3; Monica Soto Ouchi, "Amazon.com Celebrates 10 Years Atop a Turbulent Industry," *Seattle Times*, August 4, 2005, **www.seattletimes.com;** Ben Elgin, "Google's Grand Ambitions," *BusinessWeek*, September 5, 2005, pp. 36+. **p. 27 [Business Around the World]** Based on information in "Fear of Flying," *The Economist*, August 19, 2006; Melanie Trottman, Susan Warren, and Laura Meckler, "New Regulations Further Strain Airlines' Creaky Baggage Systems," *Wall Street Journal*, August 15, 2006, pp. 1ff; Rod Stone, "Ryanair Pushes the U.K. to Relax Rules on Luggage," *Wall Street Journal*, August 28, 2006, p. B2.

Chapter 2 p. 42 **[Examining Ethics]** Based on information in Ivan Schneider, "Lost Data Tapes Likely to Be Costly for Citi," *Bank Systems + Technology*, July 2005, p. 11; Bob Francis, "Security's Weakest Links," *InforWorld*, May 16, 2005, p. 9; Denise Power and Cate T. Corcoran, "POS Safety Under Scrutiny," *WWD*, April 22, 2005, p. 18. **p. 62 [Entrepreneurial Challenge]** Based on information in Tom Spoth, "Helping Farmers Get a Fair Trade," *The Sun (Lowell, Mass.)*, September 9, 2005, **www.lowellsun.com;** Fiona McLelland, "Fair Trade Sector Comes of Age," *Grocer*, May 14, 2005, pp. 55+; **www.starbucks.com. p. 64 [Biz Tech]** Based on information in Elizabeth Royte, "E-Gad!," *Smithsonian*, August 2005, pp. 82+; "Bipartisan Group Raises E-Waste Awareness," *eWeek*, May 24, 2005, **www.eweek.com;** John R. Quain, "How Do I Dump My PC?" *U.S. News & World Report*, April 11, 2005, p. 83.

Chapter 3 p. 95 **[Business Around the World]** Based on information in "Air Deccan to Cover All Airports in Kerala," *Asia Africa Intelligence Wire*, September 28, 2005, n.p.; Eric Torbenson, "Europe's Discount Airline Industry Crowded, Fierce," *Dallas Morning News*, December 2, 2004; **www.dallasnews.com;** "Thai Discount Airline One-Two-Go Weathers Stormy Year," *Knight Ridder/Tribune Business News*, December 3, 2004, n.p.; "Cash Flows," *Flight International*, January 1, 2005, pp. 40+. **p. 83 [Your Career]** Based on information in Jodie Carter, "Globe Trotters," *Training*, August 2005, pp. 22+; Erin White, "For M.B.A. Students, a Good Career Move Means a Job in Asia," *Wall Street Journal*, May 10, 2005, p. B1; David Koeppel, "Working in Switzerland to Ski? No, Just Polishing the Résumé," *New York Times*, August 14, 2005, sec. 10, p. 1. **p. 98 [Entrepreneurial Challenge]** Based on information in Lara L. Sowinski, "Going Global in a Flash," *World Trade*, August 2005, pp. 28+; Kathy Chen, "Chinese E-Commerce Sites Allow Small Firms to Reach Wider Base," *Wall Street Journal*, February 25, 2004, p. A12; **www.export.gov; www.jetro.org;** and **www.buyusa.gov.**

Chapter 4 p. 124 **[Business Around the World]** Based on information in Tara Siegel Bernard, "Building a Luxury Retail Business on the Web," *Wall Street Journal*, July 12, 2005, p. B4; Beckey Bright, "E-Commerce: How Do You Say 'Web'?" *Wall Street Journal*, May 23, 2005, p. R11. **p. 129 [Your Career]** Based on information in Anthony O'Donnell, "Gray Shares Perspective," *Insurance & Technology*, May 2005, p. 50; Brian Murphy, "Census Bureau Names Gerald W. Gates as First Chief Privacy Officer," *America's Intelligence Wire*, March 1, 2005, n.p.; Rene'e Beasley Jones, "Protecting Privacy May Call for a New Office Exec," *San Diego Business Journal*, September 30, 2002, p. 12. **p. 131 [Examining Ethics]** Based on information in Scott Kirsner, "Sweating in the Hot Zone," *Fast Company*, October 2005, pp. 60–65; Cassell Bryan-Low, "Digital Trails," *Wall Street Journal*, September 1, 2005, p. A1; David Bank, "Boss Talk: Keeping Information Safe," *Wall Street Journal*, November 11, 2004, p. B1.

Chapter 5 p. 156 **[Entrepreneurial Challenge]** Based on information in Cristina Rodriguez, "Wetlab Incubator Opens in Science Park," *Shreveport Times*, October 5, 2005, **www.shreveporttimes .com;** Stacy Wong, "Hatching High Tech," *Hartford Courant*, July 31, 2005, p. D1. **p. 162 [Your Career]** Based on information in "Barbara Gasper," *Automotive News*, September 26, 2005, p. 38; S. S. Reynolds, "IR Officer Career Tenets," *Strategic Investor Relations*, Summer 2001, p. 13. **p. 169 [Business Around the World]** Based on information in "Europe's Nascent Merger Boom," *The Economist*, September 3, 2005, p. 56; Jo Wrighton, "France's Stocks Are Very Popular (But You're Not)," *Wall Street Journal*, October 7, 2005, pp. C1, C4; Jad Mouawad, "Foiled Bid Stirs Worry for U.S. Oil," *New York Times*, August 11, 2005, p. C1.

Chapter 6 p. 187 **[Biz Tech]** Based on information in David Colker, "Wi-Fi Phones Are a Cool Way to Go," *Los Angeles Times*, August 31, 2006, p. C6; Matt Richtel and John Markoff, "The Wi-Fi in Your Handset," *New York Times*, July 29, 2006, p. C1. **p. 191 [Entrepreneurial Challenge]** Based on information in Lora Cecere, "So You Want to Outsouce Manufacturing?" *Supply Chain Management Review*, September 2005, pp. 13+; Carolyn Hirschman, "Payroll: In, Out, or In Between?" *HR Magazine*, March 2005, pp. 74+; Don Alleva, "Outsourcing Benefits Small Companies, Too," *Fairfield County Business Journal*, September 20, 2004, p.4. **p. 204 [Business Around the World]** Based on information in Doug Howard, "The Challenges of Importing a Franchise Concept to America," *Franchising World*, June 2005, pp. 66+; Yasser Kouatly, "Expanding to the Gulf Cooperation Council Market: What Are U.S. Franchisors Waiting For?" *Franchising World*, March 2005, pp. 42+; "Borders Vanishing as Franchising's Pace Quickens," *Franchising World*, August 2004, pp. 55; Glenn Baker, "Exporting a Franchise," *NZ Business*, May 2003, pp. 26+.

Chapter 7 p. 225 **[Examining Ethics]** Based on information from "Do the Right Thing," *Management Today*, July 1, 2005, pp. 54+; Robert Phillips, "Ethics and a Manager's Obligations Under Stakeholder Theory," *Ivey Business Journal Online*, March–April 2004, pp. 1+; Kevin McManus, "Are You Ethical?" *Industrial Engineer*, February 2004, p. 18.

C1

p. 229 [Business Around the World] Based on information in "The Pepsi Challenge," *The Economist*, August 19, 2006, pp. 51–52; Amelia Gentleman, "For 2 Giants of Soft Drinks, A Crisis in a Crucial Market," *The New York Times*, August 23, 2006, pp. C3+; "Face Value—The Real Thing," *The Economist*, August 26, 2006, p. 51; Amelia Gentleman, "Coke and Pepsi Try to Reassure India that Drinks are Safe," *The New York Times*, August 8, 2006, p. C7. p. 233 [Your Career] Based on information from Roger L. Martin, "Why Decisions Need Design," *BusinessWeek*, August 31, 2005, www.businessweek.com; Michael Useem and Jerry Useem, "Great Escapes: Nine Decision-Making Pitfalls and Nine Simple Devices to Beat Them," *Fortune*, June 27, 2005, pp. 97+; Thomas A. Stewart, "How to Think with Your Gut," *Business 2.0*, November 2002, pp. 98+.

Chapter 8 p. 253 [Entrepreneurial Challenge] Based on information from Francie Dalton, "Coaching Your CEO Toward Improved Delegation," *Business Credit*, April 2005, pp. 58+; Joel Golden, "Home Plate: Learning How to Let Go by Delegating," *Crain's Detroit Business*, December 8, 2003, p. 18. p. 254 [Business Around the World] Based on information from Miles Socha, "Polet's Gucci Mantra: Decentralize Group to Drive More Growth," *WWD*, September 20, 2005, pp. 1+; William Green and Michiko Tomoya, "Toyota's Tough Boss," *Time*, September 26, 2005, p. A22; Clay Chandler, "Full Speed Ahead," *Fortune*, February 7, 2005, p. 78. p. 262 [Biz Tech] Based on information from Jared Sandberg, "The CEO in the Next Cube," *Wall Street Journal*, June 22, 2005, pp. B1+; Patrick Dillon, "Peerless Leader," *Christian Science Monitor*, March 10, 2004, pp. 11+.

Chapter 9 p. 281 [Your Career] Based on information from Mark Roth, "Consumers Seem to Be Getting Shortchanged on Customer Service," *Pittsburgh Post-Gazette*, October 16, 2005, www.post-gazette.com; "Abide by 12 Laws of Customer Loyalty," *Selling*, October 2005, pp. 6+. p. 283 [Entrepreneurial Challenge] Based on information from "SpinBrush Goes to Church & Dwight," *Chain Drug Review*, September 26, 2005, p. 11; Robert Berner, "Why P&G's Smile Is So Bright," *BusinessWeek Online*, August 2, 2002, www.bw.com. p. 296 [Business Around the World] Based on information from "Harbour Report: U.S. Automakers Boost Factories' Productivity," *Detroit Free Press*, June 3, 2005, www.freep.com; Ron Harbour, "The Best Is Never Good Enough," *Automotive Industries*, October 2002, pp. 12+; "Pushing Carmakers to Rev Up Factories," *BusinessWeek*, February 18, 2002, pp. 28B+. p. 308 [Running a Business Part III] Based on information from Donna Hood Crecca, "Higher Calling," *Chain Leader*, December 2002, p. 14; "While Finagle Flaunts a Breakfast Bagel Pizza," *Restaurant Business Menu Strategies*, November 12, 2002, www.restaurantbusiness.com; Finagle A Bagel website: www.finagleabagel.com; interview with Laura B. Trust and Alan Litchman, February 25, 2003.

Chapter 10 p. 324 [Your Career] Based on information from Matt Villano, "The Smallest Raise in the Office Was Yours," *New York Times*, August 21, 2005, sec. 3, p. 10; Jeff D. Opdyke, "Getting a Bonus Instead of a Raise," *Wall Street Journal*, December 24, 2004, p. D1. p. 326 [Examining Ethics] Based on information from "Survey: CEO Compensation Jumps 30% in 2004," *USA Today*, October 31, 2005, www.usatoday.com; David Silverstein, "Executives Versus Shareholders," *Forbes.com*, October 13, 2005, www.forbes.com; Alan Murray, "New SEC Chief Tackles a Big One: CEO Pay," *Wall Street Journal*, September 21, 2005, pp. A2+; Matthew Boyle, "Ka-Ching! CEOs Grab Record Perks," *Fortune*, May 2, 2005, p. 22; "Why CEOs Haven't Earned Their Pay," *Time*, April 25, 2005, p. A22. p. 329 [Biz Tech] Based on information from "Chasing the Dream," *The Economist*, August 6, 2005, pp. 53–55; Dan Carnevale, "Video Game Helps Firefighters Train for Terrorist Attacks," *Chronicle of Higher Education*, June 24, 2005, pp. A30; Arif Mohamed, "Unilever to Use SAP Simulator to Train Staff," *Computer Weekly*, June 7, 2005, p. 6; Sarah Boehle, "Simulations: The Next Generation of e-Learning," *Training*, January 2005, pp. 22+.

Chapter 11 p. 352 [Examining Ethics] Based on information from Linda Wasmer Andrews, "When It's Time for Anger Management," *HR Magazine*, June 2005, pp. 131+; Michael Bradford, "Focus Needed on Worker Safety Abroad," *Business Insurance*, March 21, 2005, p. 11; "Terror Threats: What to Tell Your Employees and When," *Security Director's Report*, October 2004, pp. 1+. p. 360 [Your Career] Based on information from Erin White, "The Jungle," *Wall Street Journal*, October 12, 2004, p. B8; Joann S. Lublin, "Cover Letters Get You in the Door, So Be Sure Not to Dash Them Off," *Wall Street Journal*, April 6, 2004, p. B1; Stephanie Armour, "Job Seekers Take Creativity to New Level," *USA Today*, September 13, 2002, p. 1B; Fredricka Whitfield and Carolyn Mungo, "Recent College Grad Gets Creative Searching for a Job," *CNN*, July 13, 2002; Davis Bushnell, "Job Hunters Up Antics to Get Noticed," *Boston Globe*, June 9, 2002, p. G1. p. 364 [Biz Tech] Based on information from Claire Kirch, "When the House Is in the Home," *Publishers Weekly*, September 5, 2005, pp. 12+; "Study Finds Everyone Benefits from Telework," *Work & Family Newsbrief*, September 2005, p. 1; "Telework Seen as Helpful to Employers, Yet Full-Time Arrangements Are Rare," *HR Focus*, June 2005, p. 8.

Chapter 12 p. 388 [Business Around the World] Based on information from Dexter Roberts, "Waking Up to Their Rights," *BusinessWeek*, August 22–29, 2005, pp. 123–128; Evelyn Iritani, "Unions Go Abroad in Fight with Wal-Mart," *Los Angeles Times*, August 24, 2005, p. A1. p. 396 [Biz Tech] Based on information from Michael P. Maslanka, "The Right Response to Employee Blogs," *Texas Lawyer*, July 25, 2005, n.p.; Joe Williams, "UFT Gets Blog Rolling to Log Complaints Online," *New York Daily News*, August 21, 2005, n.p. p. 398 [Your Career] Based on information from "Impact Measures of Federal Mediation and Conciliation Service Activities," *Employment Policy Foundation*, November 16, 2005, www.fmcs.gov; "Code of Professional Responsibility for Arbitrators of Labor-Management Disputes," *National Academy of Arbitrators*, June 2003, www.aarb.org/code.html; Federal Mediation and Conciliation Service, www.fmcs.gov.

Chapter 13 p. 417 [Entrepreneurial Challenge] Based on information from Leslie Walker, "EBay Sellers Fell into Careers That Fill Their Lives," *Washington Post*, June 30, 2005, p. D1; Robin Stansbury, "Finding Niche in Online Auction Action," *Hartford Courant*, May 31, 2005, p. B5; Mylene Mangalindan, "And the Opening Bid Is . . .," *Wall Street Journal*, September 26, 2005, p. R9. p. 424 [Your Career] Based on information from Sarah Rubenstein, "For Job Seekers, Tailored Approach Is Best," *Wall Street Journal*, October 18, 2005, p. B10; Mark Rowh, "The Great Online Job Hunt," *Career World*, September 2005, pp. 22+. p. 431 [Examining Ethics] Based on information in Nanette Byrnes, Peter Burrows, and Louise Lee, "Dark Days at Dell," *BusinessWeek*, September 4, 2006, pp. 26+; "Exploding Batteries: Too Hot to Handle," *The Economist*, August 19, 2006, p. 52; Brian Hindo, "Satisfaction Not Guaranteed," *BusinessWeek*, June 19, 2006, pp. 32+.

Chapter 14 p. 449 [Examining Ethics] Based on information from Adam Cohen, "What Google Should Roll Out Next: A Privacy Upgrade," *New York Times*, November 28, 2005, p. A18; Ross Bentley, "Cookies: Picking at Crumbs," *New Media Age*, November 17, 2005, p. 20; Brian Morrissey, "Wary Consumers Ward Off Tracking Cookies," *Adweek*, August 8, 2005, p. 10. p. 455 [Business Around the World] Based on information from Howard W. French, "For U.S., Counterfeiting Problem in China Is Old and Very Real," *New York Times*, September 4, 2005, p. A9; Geoffrey A. Fowler and Jason Dean, "Media Counter Piracy in China in New Ways," *Wall Street Journal*, September 26, 2005, pp. B1, B3; "EU Seizures in War on Fake Goods," *International Herald Tribune*, November 9, 2005, www.iht.com; Myron Levin, "Counterfeit Cigarettes Force Tobacco Firms to Fight Back," *Los Angeles Times*, November 24, 2003, p. A1. p. 461 [Biz Tech] Based on information from Arshad Mohammed, "Internet Phone Subscriptions Up by a Third in 3 Months," *Washington Post*, November 15, 2005, p. D4; Thomas J. Fitzgerald, "How to Make Phone Calls Without a

Telephone," *New York Times*, September 1, 2005, p. C9; "The Meaning of Free Speech," *The Economist*, September 17, 2005, pp. 69–71.

Chapter 15 p. 483 [**Entrepreneurial Challenge**] Based on information from Gwendolyn Bounds, "The Long Road to Wal-Mart," *Wall Street Journal*, September 19, 2005, pp. R1+; April Y. Pennington, Nichole L. Torres, Geoff Williams, and Sara Wilson, "The Real Deal: What's It Really Like to Be Embezzled, Expand Internationally, or Sell Your Product to Target?" *Entrepreneur*, September 2005, pp. 74+; David Orgel, "Executive: Wal-Mart Needs New Vendor Relationships," *Supermarket News*, September 29, 2003, p. 54. **p. 491 [Business Around the World]** Based on information from Laura Heller, "Innovative Thinking Permeates Entire Business Model," *DSN Retailing Today*, April 11, 2005, pp. 40+; Jeffrey Woldt, "Mass Retail Learns That Things Change," *MMR*, June 28, 2004, p. 120; "Target's Global Bazaar Brightens Post-Holiday Retail," *Retail Merchandiser*, March 2005, p. 4. **p. 498 [Examining Ethics]** Based on information from Perry A. Trunick, "Stop Playing the Waiting Game," *Logistics Today*, November 2005, pp. 29+; "Privacy and RFID," *InternetWeek*, November 3, 2005, **www.internetweek.com;** Bill Mongelluzzo, "RFID's Big Bang," *Journal of Commerce*, November 7, 2005, pp. 12+; John S. McClenahen, "Supplier Scenarios," *Industry Week*, April 2005, pp. 47+.

Chapter 16 p. 516 [**Entrepreneurial Challenge**] Based on information in Matt Carroll, "Politicians Discover the iPod Generation," *Boston Globe*, August 24, 2006, p. 1; Thomas J. Lueck, "Riders Encouraged to Plug In For Transit Service Messages," *The New York Times*, August 16, 2006, p. B2; Bill Dyszel, "Assessing the Potential of Podcasts," *PC Magazine*, October 21, 2005, **www.pcmag.com; www.aspenbloompetcare.com. p. 529 [Biz Tech]** Based on information from "Called for Clipping," *Prepared Foods*, August 2005, p. 32; Jeanette Best, "Online Coupons: An Engaging Idea," *Brandweek*, May 2, 2005, p. 20; "Consumer Beat: Couponing Growing at a Fast Clip," *Restaurants & Institutions*, April 1, 2005, p. 22. **p. 531 [Examining Ethics]** Based on information from "Subway Slated to Roll Out Massive Gift Card Program," *Nation's Restaurant News*, July 11, 2005, p. 60; Cara Baruzzi, "Counterfeit 'Sub Club' Cards Force Subway to Cancel Promotion," *New Haven Register*, June 3, 2005, **www.nhregister.com;** "Subway Phases Out Sandwich Promo," *Promo*, June 6, 2005, n.p.

Chapter 17 p. 556 [**Entrepreneurial Challenge**] Based on information in Adam Lashinsky, "Burning Sensation," *Fortune*, December 12, 2005, pp. 55+; "Customer-Centered Leader: Craig Newmark, Founder, Craigslist," *Fast Company*, October 2005, p. 54; **www.craigslist.org. p. 558 [Your Career]** Based on information in "'Boomerang' Hires Slow to Catch On," *America's Intelligence Wire*, September 10, 2005, n.p.; "Company 'Alumni' Networks," *Job-Hunt.org*, n.d., **www.job-hunt.org/employer_alumni_networking.shtml; www.tialumni.org/new. p. 573 [Biz Tech]** Based on information in Michael A. Tucker, "e-Learning Evolves," *HR Magazine*, October 2005, pp. 74+; Chris Costanzo, "An Edge for e-Learning?" *American Banker*, December 10, 2003, p. 1.

Chapter 18 p. 591 [**Examining Ethics**] Based on information from "Bail Denied to Two Tyco Executives," *New York Times*, October 4, 2005, p. C2; Carrie Johnson, "Leniency Sought for WorldCom's Sullivan," *Washington Post*, July 28, 2005, p. D1; Andrew Ross Sorkin, "Court Is Told Tyco Deals Had Backing of Auditors," *New York Times*, February 8, 2003, pp. C2+; "Tyco Gimmicks Inflated Profit, Audit Shows," *Los Angeles Times*, December 31, 2002, p. C3. **p. 593 [Your Career]** Based on information in Nadine Heintz, "Everyone's a CFO," *Inc.*, September 2005, pp. 42+; Robin Seaton Jefferson, "Trinity Products Hangs Success on Open-Book Management," *St. Charles County Business Record*, July 21, 2005, n.p.; Adam Hanft, "These Days, Transparency Is All the Rage," *Inc.*, March 1, 2005, n.p. **p. 608 [Business Around the World]** Based on information in Sylvia Gornik-Tomaszewski, "Convergence of U.S. GAAP with International Financial Reporting Standards," *Bank Accounting & Finance*, October–November 2005, pp. 37+; Arthur Piper, "Graham Ward, CBE, FCA," *Internal Auditor*, October 2005, pp. 62+; Floyd Norris, "Accounting Rules in U.S. a Bit Lacking, Europe Says," *New York Times*, April 28, 2005, p. C4.

Chapter 19 p. 636 [**Business Around the World**] Based on information in G. Jeffrey MacDonald, "Abroad, Women Boost Earnings, But Clout Is Iffy," *Christian Science Monitor*, March 7, 2005, p. 13; Tom Ramstack, "Tsunami Lifted Microloan Industry," *Washington Times*, February 7, 2005, p. C15; Celia W. Dugger, "Debate Stirs Over Tiny Loans for World's Poorest," *New York Times*, February 7, 2005, p. C15; Celia W. Dugger, "Debate Stirs Over Tiny Loans for World's Poorest," *New York Times*, April 29, 2004, p. A1; Pete Engardio, "Small Loan, Big Dream," *BusinessWeek*, October 14, 2002, p. 118. **p. 642 [Biz Tech]** Based on information in "In the Very Near Future," *The Economist*, December 10, 2005, pp. 22+; Anthony Faiola, "Japan Puts Its Money on e-Cash," *Washington Post*, December 12, 2005, p. A1; Rob Garver, "EBay and Banking," *American Banker*, November 16, 2005, p. 10A. **p. 651 [Entrepreneurial Challenge]** Based on information in Paulette Thomas, "Making Them Pay," *Wall Street Journal*, September 19, 2005, p. R6; Laura Bailey, "Cutting to the Chase," *Crain's Detroit Business*, August 12, 2002, p. 11.

Chapter 20 p. 669 [**Your Career**] Based on information from Ann Colin Herbst, "Fund-Raising: Well-Paid Jobs That Sometimes Go Begging," *New York Times*, June 19, 2005, sec. 10, p. 1; "Lorna Christie and Her Team Are the New Driving Force Behind Aberdeen Performing Arts' Fundraising Campaigns," *Europe Intelligence Wire*, March 18, 2005, n.p.; Mary Ellen Slayter, "Doing Well by Doing Good," *Washington Post*, August 22, 2004, p. K1. **p. 680 [Entrepreneurial Challenge]** Based on information from Andrew Blackman, "Money . . . With Strings," *Wall Street Journal*, September 19, 2005, p. R4; David Worrell, "The Right Fit: Looking for Capital?" *Entrepreneur*, September 2005, pp. 58+. **p. 682 [Examining Ethics]** Based on information from Erik Assadourian, "The Evolving Corporation: The Role of Stakeholders," *World Watch*, September–October 2005, pp. 22+; Jim Cole, "In Brief: Wells Lays Out Environmental Strategy," *American Banker*, July 12, 2005, p. 2; Matthew Yeomans, "Banks Go for Green," *Time*, May 30, 2005, p. A13.

Chapter 21 p. 707 [**Business Around the World**] Based on information from Craig Karmin, "The Globe-Trotting Investor," *Wall Street Journal*, September 24, 2005, p. B1; Andrew Bary, "Nestle May Fatten Wallets," *The News-Times (Danbury, CT)*, September 25, 2005, p. B8; Debiprasad Nayak, "Wanna Crack the ADR, GDR Puzzle?" *Asia Africa Intelligence Wire*, May 30, 2005, n.p. **p. 717 [Biz Tech]** Based on information from Diya Gullapalli, "Cranky Consumer: Tracking the Markets Online," *Wall Street Journal*, December 8, 2005, p. D2; David Landis, "Online Allies," *Kiplinger's Personal Finance Magazine*, November 2005, p. 106. **p. 722 [Examining Ethics]** Based on information from "Two Plead Not Guilty in Stock Option Case," *Los Angeles Times*, August 31, 2006, p. C4; "Senate Committees Plan Hearings on Stock-Option Grants," *Los Angeles Times*, August 26, 2006, p. C2; Sarah E. Lockyer, "Groups Sue Cheesecake Factory Amid SEC Options Probe," *Nation's Restaurant News*, August 14, 2006, pp. 1+; Susan Harrigan, "Q & A: Why Backdating Matters," *Newsday*, August 9, 2006, n.p. **Running a Business (Parts I–VII)** Sources: Based on information from Matt Viser, "Small, But Thinking Big," *Boston Globe*, October 27, 2005, **www.boston.com;** "Finagle a Bagel to Move HQ to Newton," *Boston Business Journal*, January 13, 2005, **www.bizjournals.com/boston;** Donna Hood Crecca, "Higher Calling," *Chain Leader*, December 2002, p. 14; "State Fare: Finagle A Bagel, Boston," *Restaurants and Institutions*, October 1, 2002, **www.rimag.com/1902/sr.htm;** "Finagle Sees a Return to More Normal Business Mode," *Foodservice East*, Fall 2002, pp. 1, 17; "Sloan Grads Bet Their Money on Bagels," *Providence Business News*, October 25, 1999, p. 14; interview with Laura B. Trust and Alan Litchman, February 25, 2003.

PHOTO CREDITS

Part 1: © Jose Fuste Raga/Corbis

Chapter 1: p. 3 top, PRNewsFoto/Frito-Lay, Inc.; p. 3 bottom, PRNewsFoto/Frito-Lay North America; p. 6, AP/Wide World /Alaska Journal; p. 7, © Royalty-Free/Corbis; p. 10, AP/Wide World; p. 12 right, AP/Wide World/Michael Probst; p. 12 left, PRNewswire/ eBay, Inc.; p. 15, AP/Wide World; p. 19, AP/Wide World; p. 25, © Bettmann/Corbis; p. 27, AP/Wide World; p. 29 top, PRNewsFoto/ Frito-Lay, Inc.; p. 29 bottom, PRNewsFoto/Frito-Lay North America.

Chapter 2: p. 40, © Royalty-Free/Corbis; p. 42, © Royalty-Free/Corbis; p. 45, AP/Wide World; p. 48, Courtesy Boys and Girls Club and ConAgra Foods' Feeding Children Better Foundation; p. 49, PRNewswire/Marriott International, Inc.; p. 56, PRNewsFoto/ California Pharmacists Association; p. 59, AP/Wide World/Noah Berger; p. 61, AP/Wide World/U.S. Attorney's Office; p. 62, © Royalty-Free/PhotoDisc/Getty; p. 66, © Royalty-Free/Corbis.

Chapter 3: p. 76, BusinessWire/Heinz; p. 77, AP/Wide World/Eric Draper; p. 81, AP/Wide World; p. 83, © Royalty-Free/ Corbis; p. 84, AP/Wide World/Lou Krasky; p. 91, PRNewsFoto/ Samsung Telecommunications America, L.P., MGStudio.com; p. 93, PRNewsFoto/Volkswagen of American, Inc.; p. 95, © Royalty-Free/ Corbis; p. 97, Photo provided by Simpson Strong-Tie, www.strongtie .com; p. 99, BusinessWire/Heinz.

Part 2: AP/Wide World

Chapter 4: p. 115, AP/Wide World/Paul Sakuma; p. 117, AP/Wide World/Ben Curtis; p. 118, Courtesy Sprint PCS; p. 121, AP/Wide World/Harry Cabluck; p. 124, Courtesy Pearl Paradise; p. 127, PRNewsFoto/Scholastic Corporation; p. 131, clipart; p. 132, Courtesy Rhapsody; p. 136, AP/Wide World/Gautam Singh; p. 137, AP/Wide World/Paul Sakuma.

Chapter 5: p. 148, Courtesy GE; p. 152, AP/Wide World/The Daily Record, Heather Marcus; p. 154, AP/Wide World/The Decatur Daily, Emily Saunders; p. 156, AP/Wide World/Lynn Hey; p. 160, AP/Wide World/Greg Baker; p. 162, © Royalty-Free/Corbis; p. 164, AP/Wide World/Ric Field; p. 165, AP/Wide World/Gregory Bull; p. 167, AP/Wide World/The Florida Times-Union, John Pemberton; p. 170, Courtesy GE.

Chapter 6: p. 182, Courtesy Carol's Daughter; p. 186, AP/Wide World/Boca News, Jon Way; p. 187, AP Photo/Jae C. Hong; p. 189, © Bettmann/Corbis; p. 191, © Royalty-Free/Corbis; p. 192, AP/Wide World/The Janesville Gazette, Dan Lassiter; p. 194, 2006 Getty Images; p. 198, Courtesy Little Scoops; p. 199, © Bettmann/ Corbis; p. 205, Courtesy Carol's Daughter.

Part 3: AP/Wide World

Chapter 7: p. 219, AP/Wide World/Marcio Jose Sanchez; p. 222, AP/Wide World/Tony Gutierrez; p. 224, PRNewsFoto/ CareerBuilder.com; p. 227, AP/Wide World/Koji Sasahara; p. 228, AP/Wide World/Nati Harnik; p. 229 top, Courtesy Lee Hecht Harrison; p. 229 bottom, AP/Wide World; p. 233, © Royalty-Free/ Getty; p. 236, AP/Wide World/Marcio Jose Sanchez.

Chapter 8: p. 246, Courtesy Hyatt Hotels and Resorts; p. 250, AP/Wide World/Nicholas Ratzenboeck; p. 253, Getty Images; p. 254 right, PRNewsWire/Toyota North America; p. 254 left, PRNewsFoto/Gucci; p. 258, AP/Wide World/Yakima Herald-Republic, Sandy Summers; p. 260, AP/Wide World/Keith Srakocic; p. 262, AP/Wide World/Paul Sakuma; p. 263, © 2005 T-Mobile USA, Inc.; p. 264, © Randy Faris/Corbis; p. 265, Courtesy Hyatt Hotels and Resorts.

Chapter 9: p. 276, PRNewsFoto/Hyundai Motor America; p. 280, PRNewsFoto/Walt Disney World Resort; p. 281, PRNewsFoto; p. 282, PRNewsFoto/Ford Motor Company; p. 283, PRNewsFoto/Crest; p. 285, PRNewswire/Valmont Industries, Inc.; p. 286, AP/Wide World/Elaine Thompson; p. 294, AP/Wide World/Alexandra Boulat/VII; p. 297, © Brownie Harris/Corbis; p. 299, PRNewsFoto/ Hyundai Motor America.

Part 4: AP/Wide World

Chapter 10: p. 313, PRNewsFoto/McDonald's; p. 315, PRNewsWire/Continental Airlines; p. 317, PRNewsWire/American Airlines, Inc.; p. 321, Courtesy YAHOO Hot Jobs; p. 323, AP/Wide World/Bebeto Matthews; p. 324, © Royalty-Free/Digital Vision/ Getty; p. 327, Courtesy Ernst & Young LLP; p. 329 top, PRNewsWire/The Timken Co.; p. 329 bottom, Courtesy HazMat Hotzone; p. 335, Occupational Safety and Health Administration; p. 336, PRNewsFoto/McDonald's.

Chapter 11: p. 348, Courtesy Wegmans; p. 349, © Bettmann/ Corbis; p. 352, © Royalty-Free/Corbis; p. 353, AP/Wide World; p. 354, AP/Wide World/Chuck Burton; p. 361, AP/Wide World/ Robert F. Bukaty; p. 363, AP/Wide World/Ted S. Warren; p. 364, © Royalty-Free/Corbis; p. 366, AP/Wide World; p. 369, Courtesy AT&T; p. 370, Courtesy Wegmans.

Chapter 12: p. 380, PRNewsWire/XM Satellite Radio; p. 383, © Bettmann/Corbis; p. 385, AP/Wide World/Mark Humphrey; p. 388, AP/Wide World/Elizabeth Dalziel; p. 389, Courtesy unionplus.org; p. 392, AP/Wide World/Ben Margot; p. 394, © Lucy Nicholson/Reuters/Corbis; p. 396, © Royalty-Free/Corbis; p. 397, AP/Wide World/The Oakland Press; p. 399, PRNewsWire/XM Satellite Radio.

Part 5: AP/Wide World

Chapter 13: p. 413, PRNewsWire/Fellowes, Inc.; p. 415, PRNewsWire/Opteum Financial Services; p. 417, PRNewsWire/ Video Professor; p. 419, PRNewsWire/The Reader's Digest; p. 422, Courtesy RoC® Retinol Correxion®; p. 426, Courtesy Abacus -Direct.com; p. 427, Courtesy ACNielsen; p. 430, Courtesy Uni-ball; p. 431, PRNewsWire/Fellowes, Inc.

Chapter 14: p. 442, PRNewsWire/Apple Computer, Inc.; p. 443, PRNewsWire/Tissot Watches; p. 448, PRNewsWire/Gatorade; p. 451, PRNewsWire/Chomp, Inc.; p. 454, PRNewsWire/General Mills; p. 455, AP/Wide World/Greg Baker; p. 456, PRNewsWire/ McDonald's Corporation; p. 459, PRNewsWire/PBM Products; p. 460, © 2005 GlaxoSmithKline; p. 464, PRNewsWire/Connexion by Boeing; p. 469, PRNewsWire/Apple Computer, Inc.

Chapter 15: p. 480, AP/Wide World/Douglas C. Pizac; p. 483, PRNewsWire/Speck Products; p. 484, AP/Wide World/Paul Sancya; p. 491, PRNewsWire/Target; p. 492, PRNewsWire/Swatch Group U.S.; p. 493, AP/Wide World/Ric Field; p. 496, AP/Wide World/Jerry S. Mendoza; p. 497, AP/Wide World/Kevin Rivoli; p. 500, AP/Wide World/Charles Rex Arbogast; p. 502, AP/Wide World/Douglas C. Pizac.

Chapter 16: p. 514, AP/Wide World/Gurinder Osan; p. 519, PRNewsWire/National Dairy Council; p. 521, PRNewsWire/Meijer; p. 523, PRNewsWire/Harlequin Enterprises Ltd.; p. 529, AP/Wide World; p. 530, PRNewsWire/McDonald's; p. 531 top, AP/Wide World; p. 531 bottom, PRNewsWire/The Merchandise Mart; p. 532, AP/Wide World; p. 536, AP/Wide World/Gurinder Osan.

Part 6: AP/Wide World

Chapter 17: p. 551, PRNewsWire/Harrah's Entertainment, Inc.; p. 555, IBM; p. 556, AP/Wide World; p. 557, PRNewsWire/Lexar Media; p. 565, PRNewsWire/Edmunds.com; p. 568, PRNewsWire/Transmedia; p. 572, AP/Wide World; p. 573, PRNewsWire/Kensington Technology Group; p. 574, PRNewsWire/Boeing Shared Services Group; p. 577, PRNewsWire/Harrah's Entertainment, Inc.

Chapter 18: p. 588, RF/PhotoDisc/Getty; p. 590, AP/Wide World; p. 591, © Royalty-Free/PhotoDisc/Getty; p. 592, AP/Wide World; p. 594, Courtesy AICPA; p. 600, AP/Wide World; p. 604, PRNewsWire/Red Lobster; p. 606, AP/Wide World; p. 608, ©Royalty-Free/Digital Vision/Getty; p. 612, RF/PhotoDisc/Getty.

Part 7: AP/Wide World

Chapter 19: p. 627, AP/Wide World; p. 629, © China Daily/Reuters/Corbis; p. 632, AP/Wide World; p. 636, AP/Wide World; p. 638, PRNewsWire/Hancock Holding Co.; p. 639, © Jeffery Allan Salter/Corbis SABA; p. 642, AP/Wide World; p. 644, AP/Wide World; p. 647, PRNewsWire/Seattle Metropolitan Credit Union; p. 652, AP/Wide World.

Chapter 20: p. 664, © Denis O'Regan/Corbis; p. 666, PRNewsWire/Sears, Roebuck and Co.; p. 668, PRNewsWire/Genworth Financial, Inc.; p. 672, Time Life Pictures/Getty Images; p. 674, AP/Wide World; p. 677, AP/Wide World; p. 680 top, AP/Wide World; p. 680 bottom, © Royalty-Free/PhotoDisc/Getty; p. 682, © Royalty-Free/PhotoDisc/Getty; p. 686, © Denis O'Regan/Corbis.

Chapter 21: p. 696, AP/Wide World; p. 698, Courtesy AIG; p. 702, AP/Wide World; p. 703, Courtesy eTrade; p. 707 left, PRNewsWire/Nestle S.A.; p. 707 right, Courtesy Wipro; p. 708, www.treasurydirect.gov; p. 710, AP/Wide World; p. 712, Courtesy Vanguard Family of Funds; p. 717, PRNewsWire/Qwest Communications International, Inc.; p. 723, AP/Wide World.

Answers to Prep Tests

Chapter 1 (page 36)

1. g **2.** c **3.** j **4.** e **5.** d **6.** b **7.** f **8.** a **9.** h
10. i **11.** F **12.** F **13.** T **14.** F **15.** T **16.** T
17. F **18.** T **19.** F **20.** T **21.** a **22.** c **23.** d
24. e **25.** d **26.** domestic **27.** Competition
28. cultural diversity **29.** Microeconomics
30. invisible hand

Chapter 2 (page 73)

1. d **2.** g **3.** e **4.** h **5.** i **6.** b **7.** a **8.** c **9.** f
10. j **11.** F **12.** F **13.** T **14.** F **15.** T **16.** T
17. F **18.** T **19.** F **20.** T **21.** a **22.** b **23.** b
24. b **25.** a **26.** Clayton Antitrust
27. social audit **28.** National Alliance of Business
29. hard-core **30.** pollution

Chapter 3 (page 106)

1. b **2.** a **3.** g **4.** i **5.** e **6.** d **7.** f **8.** j **9.** c
10. h **11.** T **12.** T **13.** F **14.** F **15.** F **16.** F
17. T **18.** T **19.** F **20.** T **21.** c **22.** b **23.** d
24. b **25.** c **26.** absolute **27.** international
28. licensing **29.** draft **30.** embargo

Chapter 4 (page 144)

1. g **2.** h **3.** e **4.** d **5.** a **6.** b **7.** j **8.** f **9.** c
10. i **11.** T **12.** T **13.** F **14.** T **15.** F **16.** F
17. F **18.** F **19.** T **20.** F **21.** e **22.** b **23.** e
24. c **25.** b **26.** World Wide Web **27.** digitized
28. viruses **29.** log-file **30.** supply-chain

Chapter 5 (page 177)

1. h **2.** g **3.** i **4.** e **5.** j **6.** c **7.** b **8.** f **9.** d
10. a **11.** F **12.** F **13.** T **14.** T **15.** T **16.** F
17. T **18.** F **19.** T **20.** T **21.** d **22.** d **23.** c
24. e **25.** e **26.** closed **27.** syndicate
28. proxy fight **29.** partnership **30.** conglomerate

Chapter 6 (page 211)

1. i **2.** g **3.** h **4.** f **5.** a **6.** d **7.** b **8.** j **9.** c
10. e **11.** T **12.** F **13.** T **14.** T **15.** F **16.** F
17. T **18.** F **19.** F **20.** F **21.** e **22.** a **23.** b
24. c **25.** e **26.** Investment **27.** six **28.** franchisee
29. Franchise Mediation **30.** service

Chapter 7 (page 243)

1. g **2.** i **3.** h **4.** e **5.** b **6.** f **7.** d **8.** a **9.** c
10. j **11.** T **12.** F **13.** T **14.** F **15.** T **16.** T
17. F **18.** F **19.** T **20.** T **21.** b **22.** a **23.** b
24. d **25.** a **26.** identifying **27.** human
28. conceptual **29.** operational **30.** strategic plan

Chapter 8 (page 272)

1. h **2.** c **3.** j **4.** b **5.** e **6.** d **7.** i **8.** a **9.** g
10. f **11.** T **12.** F **13.** T **14.** F **15.** T **16.** F
17. T **18.** F **19.** T **20.** T **21.** a **22.** e **23.** c
24. d **25.** c **26.** standing **27.** network
28. cross-functional **29.** culture **30.** line

Chapter 9 (page 306)

1. d **2.** a **3.** f **4.** e **5.** j **6.** b **7.** i **8.** h **9.** c
10. g **11.** F **12.** T **13.** F **14.** F **15.** F **16.** F
17. F **18.** T **19.** F **20.** T **21.** b **22.** b **23.** a
24. d **25.** e **26.** Gantt **27.** flexible
28. purchasing **29.** process **30.** capacity

Chapter 10 (page 343)

1. g **2.** e **3.** h **4.** j **5.** b **6.** c **7.** i **8.** f **9.** a
10. d **11.** T **12.** F **13.** T **14.** F **15.** T **16.** F
17. T **18.** F **19.** T **20.** F **21.** a **22.** d
23. a **24.** d **25.** a **26.** skills **27.** external
28. orientation **29.** management **30.** salary

Chapter 11 (page 377)

1. f **2.** j **3.** c **4.** d **5.** i **6.** b **7.** g **8.** a **9.** e
10. h **11.** T **12.** T **13.** F **14.** F **15.** T **16.** F
17. T **18.** F **19.** F **20.** T **21.** a **22.** e **23.** a
24. b **25.** c **26.** motivation-hygiene **27.** positive
28. piece-rate **29.** employees **30.** Y

Chapter 12 (page 406)

1. h **2.** g **3.** j **4.** f **5.** b **6.** a **7.** e **8.** d **9.** c
10. i **11.** T **12.** F **13.** T **14.** F **15.** F **16.** T
17. T **18.** T **19.** F **20.** F **21.** c **22.** d **23.** c
24. c **25.** a **26.** strike **27.** Taft-Hartley **28.** labor
29. seniority **30.** National Labor Relations

Chapter 13 (page 439)

1. e 2. f 3. c 4. d 5. b 6. g 7. i 8. a 9. j
10. h 11. T 12. F 13. T 14. T 15. F 16. F
17. T 18. T 19. T 20. F 21. e 22. d 23. c
24. a 25. c 26. surveys 27. industrial
28. market 29. time 30. research

Chapter 14 (page 477)

1. j 2. g 3. b 4. i 5. h 6. a 7. f 8. c 9. d
10. e 11. T 12. F 13. F 14. F 15. F 16. T
17. T 18. T 19. T 20. F 21. a 22. a 23. c
24. c 25. d 26. image 27. convenience
28. screening 29. total 30. trade

Chapter 15 (page 510)

1. b 2. e 3. d 4. a 5. c 6. i 7. g 8. h 9. f
10. j 11. F 12. F 13. T 14. F 15. T 16. F
17. T 18. F 19. F 20. F 21. d 22. c 23. e
24. c 25. b 26. merchant 27. exclusive
28. materials 29. physical 30. broker

Chapter 16 (page 543)

1. a 2. i 3. h 4. d 5. e 6. c 7. f 8. j 9. g
10. b 11. T 12. F 13. F 14. T 15. T 16. T
17. T 18. T 19. F 20. T 21. a 22. e 23. b
24. c 25. a 26. reminder 27. cooperative
28. positioning 29. sales 30. agency

Chapter 17 (page 585)

1. f 2. c 3. h 4. d 5. g 6. e 7. i 8. b 9. a
10. j 11. T 12. T 13. F 14. F 15. F 16. F
17. F 18. T 19. T 20. F 21. b 22. c 23. e
24. b 25. c 26. mode 27. qualitative
28. graph 29. information 30. five

Chapter 18 (page 619)

1. a 2. e 3. h 4. i 5. b 6. f 7. c 8. j 9. g
10. d 11. F 12. T 13. F 14. T 15. T 16. T
17. F 18. T 19. T 20. F 21. c 22. a 23. c
24. e 25. d 26. owner's equity 27. earnings
28. drop 29. earnings 30. operating

Chapter 19 (page 660)

1. j 2. a 3. d 4. c 5. f 6. b 7. h 8. g 9. i
10. e 11. F 12. T 13. F 14. T 15. T 16. T
17. F 18. T 19. F 20. T 21. a 22. d 23. e
24. d 25. a 26. pension 27. discount
28. deposits 29. NOW 30. certificates

Chapter 20 (page 693)

1. a 2. d 3. j 4. c 5. i 6. f 7. e 8. g 9. h
10. b 11. T 12. F 13. T 14. T 15. T 16. F
17. F 18. T 19. F 20. F 21. e 22. a 23. d
24. a 25. e 26. common 27. cash
28. convertible 29. maturity 30. commercial

Chapter 21 (page 731)

1. d 2. j 3. f 4. a 5. g 6. i 7. h 8. e 9. b
10. c 11. F 12. T 13. T 14. F 15. T 16. T
17. F 18. T 19. F 20. F 21. d 22. a 23. c
24. b 25. d 26. allocation 27. certificate
28. split 29. institutional 30. securities

Name Index

Subject Index

Effect of Disasters on Business

Introduction to *The Effect of Disasters on Business*

Natural disasters, wars, and, more recently, terrorist acts such as 9/11 have had a significant impact on all phases of society. Beyond the personal tragedy and loss of property, disasters affect infrastructure, culture, the economy, and business, which is the engine that drives the economy. This supplement focuses on the effect that recent disasters have had on business and what companies can do to minimize their impact through proper planning.

Long before the Titanic sank in icy Atlantic waters in 1912, one person was heard to say "God himself could not sink this ship." Obviously, if the ship could not sink, there would be no need to have enough lifeboats for all on board, to conduct drills, to pay attention to iceberg warnings, or to even send a distress signal. Failure to acknowledge risk and uncertainty is not new and sometimes not even uncommon.

More recently, the decimation of New Orleans by Hurricane Katrina was not impossible to predict. In fact, according to the Army Corps of Engineers, the probability of this occurring over a normal person's lifespan of 77 years was 3 in 1. Unfortunately, Katrina will not be the last disaster. A month after Katrina and Rita hit the American gulf coast, Pakistan suffered a major earthquake, which took an estimated 79,000 lives as of October 2005. Unfortunately, the U.N. Office of Emergency Relief has predicted that the total could rise to between 100,000 and 120,000.[1] The human and economic costs of disasters are horrendous, but they can be reduced with the proper planning.

Planning for Trouble

Most major corporations develop contingency plans along with their standard plans. A contingency plan is one that outlines alternative courses of action that may be taken if the organization's other plans are disrupted or become ineffective for whatever reason. Importantly, such plans provide procedures and technical measures to enable the recovery of systems, operations, and data after a disruption. Ideally, it is based on the risks faced not only by the organization itself but those faced by business partners, suppliers, and customers. The objectives of contingency planning include: (1) restoring operations at an alternate site with alternate equipment and (2) performing some or all of the interrupted operations using some other means.[2] First, business continuity must be ensured, and then disaster recovery can follow.

The Importance of a Disaster Management Continuity Plan

When Flight 77 slammed into the Pentagon on September 11, 2001, the 37 employees at Children's World Learning Center, the Pentagon's day-care facility, knew exactly what to do. They calmly led the children out of the building, situated near the Pentagon, to a safe location. It turns out that these day-care employees were just following the evacuation drill they practice once a month. Even though confusion was all around them, they remained "pretty calm, as far as what to do," says Shirley Allen, the day-care center's director. "It helped a lot in a real emergency."

As Allen knows, a little planning can save lives. It can also save businesses. Current estimates suggest that two out of five companies that are hit by a disaster go out of business within five years. It is estimated that 85 percent of large businesses have a disaster management plan. Unfortunately, the equivalent figure for small companies is 25 to 35 percent.[3]

Planning for Disaster

The first step in contingency planning is to recognize the existence of risk and uncertainty. A starting point is to look at those disasters that have occurred in the past.

While all the total costs have yet to be assessed, Hurricane Katrina appears to be the costliest natural disaster the world has seen in recent history. Early estimates run in excess of $200 billion. Other than Katrina, there have been other costly natural disasters within the past 20 years, as listed below.

Beyond natural disasters, wars and terrorist attacks have been enormously destructive and costly to society. The September 11, 2001, attacks on the World Trade Center and the Pentagon inflicted casualties and material damages on a far greater scale than any other aggressive acts in recent history. Lower Manhattan lost approximately 30 percent of its office space, and a number of businesses ceased to exist. Close to 200,000 jobs were destroyed or relocated out of New York City, at least for the foreseeable future. The destruction of physical assets was estimated at $14 billion for private businesses, $1.5 billion for state and local government enterprises, and $0.7 billion for federal enterprises. Rescue, cleanup, and related costs have been estimated to amount to at least $11 billion, for a total direct cost of $27.2 billion.[5]

Focusing on the United States and what the future holds, 150 million people and trillions of dollars worth of buildings and other property are in coastal counties prone to hurricanes. Katrina, Rita, and Wilma did billions of dollars of damage, and hurricanes are just the start. Tornadoes can occur anywhere in the world, from Spain to Wales and from Japan to the USA, but they mostly occur in the United States.

Top 10 Worldwide Natural Disasters[4]				
Rank	Year	Event	Region/Country	Economic Cost U.S. $ Billions
1	2005	Hurricane Katrina	Gulf Coast USA	$200
2	1995	Earthquake	(Kobe) Japan	100
3	1994	Earthquake	(Northridge) USA	44
4	1992	Hurricane Andrew	USA	43
5	1998	Floods	China	31
6	1996	Floods	China	24
7	1993	Flood	(Mississippi) USA	21
8	1999	Winter storms	Europe	19
9	1990	Winter storms	Europe	15
10	1995	Floods	North Korea	15

Tornado Alley and Earthquakes in the U.S.

While tornadoes have hit every state in the union, there is a corridor called Tornado Alley stretching from West Texas to North Dakota, including large pieces of Texas, Kansas, and Nebraska. Due to ideal meteorological circumstances, this area is hit by more tornadoes than any other land mass in the United States. Texas alone experiences more than 100 tornadoes each year.

Then there are the faults—fractures in the earth's crust that can lead to earthquakes. According to David Applegate, the U.S. Department of Interior Senior Science Advisor, earthquakes are the most costly, single-event natural hazard faced by the United States.

A great deal of critical infrastructure is located in seismically active areas of the nation, including homes, schools, hospitals, and other important structures that make up the "built-up" environment. These active areas are populated by 150 million people in 39 states. The most well-known fault is San Andreas, the geological fault that spans roughly 800 miles and is famous for producing large and devastating earthquakes.

The Interior Department's U.S. Geological Survey (USGS) estimates a 62 percent chance of an earthquake of magnitude 6.7 or greater on the Richter scale occurring in the San Francisco region before 2031. The USGS earthquake hazards program devotes approximately 75 percent of its resources to the western United States, primarily because the hazard there is greater. However, history demonstrates that a catastrophic quake could also strike a major city in the eastern United States. Four damaging earthquakes with magnitudes greater than 7 occurred in Missouri, in the Mississippi Valley, in 1811–1812. Charleston, South Carolina, was devastated by a magnitude 6.7 shock in 1886, and a magnitude 6.0 quake struck the Boston area in 1755.

USGS and FEMA studies show that urban areas in the eastern United States would incur far greater damage and far more deaths than a quake of similar magnitude in the west. This is because (1) differences in regional geology produce shaking effects in a much larger area for the same magnitude earthquake, (2) most structures in the east are not designed to resist earthquakes, and (3) population density is high and residents are not routinely educated about seismic safety.[6]

Disease

Disease can also cause economic turmoil. The collapse of export markets following the discovery of a single cow infected with mad cow disease cost Canadian producers about $600 million in 2003 and probably had an overall economic negative impact of $2 billion.[7]

According to health researchers and economists, a worldwide pandemic of bird flu could shut down travel, disrupt supply chains, overwhelm health care systems, and devastate economies, globally. So far, the avian flu does not appear to be transmitted from one human to another. All cases linked to the strain, which has killed 65 people in Asia, have been transmitted from infected birds to humans. However, given the migrations and mobility of birds and the inability of man to control their movements, the consequences of such a disease could be severe.

Dollar estimates of the economic impact of this type of disaster are difficult to quantify but could run in the tens of billions of dollars. An economist at the Center for Disease Control and Prevention estimated in a 1999 article that a pandemic flu could cost the United States alone $71 to $165 billion. "Those economists that have looked at this have likened it to a catastrophic depression," says Michael Osterholm, director of the Center for Infectious Disease Research and Policy at the University of Minnesota. Travel bans, sick workers, and panic could quickly shut down international trade. Industries hardest hit could include airlines, travel-related services, insurance firms, and health care. Soaring death rates could end the housing boom and create a vast oversupply. According to Osterholm, "Depending on its length and severity, its economic impact could be comparable to the Great Depression of the 1930s."[8]

International

Internationally, 3.4 billion of the world's population lives in areas where some form of natural disaster can occur, be it drought, floods, cyclones, earthquakes, volcanoes, or landslides. In a global economy, a disaster in one country can impact many other countries. For example, Taiwan, according to several studies, may be the most vulnerable place on Earth to a natural catastrophe, with 73 percent of its land and people exposed to three or more hazards. Taiwan is a major U.S. trading partner. In the event of a major disaster, the effect on the computer and electronics industry in the United States would be substantial. Too, there are the costs of providing assistance and humanitarian aid. For example, from 1980 to 2003, the World Bank provided US$ 14.4 billion in emergency lending to 20 nations, including India, Bangladesh, Mexico, Brazil, Honduras, and China.[9]

How Should Business Deal with Disasters?

Disasters, natural or man-made, are a fact of life that human beings, society, government, and business have had to deal with throughout history. Unfortunately, disasters won't go away, and man cannot eliminate them. What we can do is prepare for their occurrence and develop plans on how best to deal with them. The success of our ability to deal with disasters is dependent on our ability to plan in advance, the quality of our response to the disaster, and our ability to learn from the situation and apply that learning to preparations for the next disaster. A starting point is contingency planning. There are many approaches to contingency planning. The following is a useful outline in how to develop a contingency plan.

Steps in Contingency Planning

1. *Identify critical functions and resources.* Identify those functions critical to keeping the business running. This would include (1) human resources, such as key personnel, (2) material resources, such as products to sell and ways to get them to consumers, (3) financial resources, such as money to meet payroll, and (4) informational resources, to enable communications and record keeping.
2. *Identify possible emergencies, even the improbable ones.* Often those events that do the most damage are those no one imagined. For example, the possibility of passenger jets crashing into a building such as the World Trade Center had been thought of. What wasn't imagined was that large planes with nearly full fuel tanks crashing at high impact could jar the fireproofing from the supporting girders and thus bring the towers crashing down.
3. *Do the numbers: Assign a probability to each event.* Some companies use 80, 50, or 20 percent. For example, based on an analysis of hurricane patterns, ExxonMobil

might estimate that there is a 20 percent probability that a Category 5 hurricane would hit their oil platforms in the Gulf of Mexico over the next five years. Others try to be more specific. FEMA, for example, suggests using a 1 to 5 ranking where 5 is the emergency most likely to occur and 1 the least likely. While the accuracy of a specific number can be argued, the exercise of estimating the likelihood of an event happening is an important starting point in developing plans to deal with the effect of a disaster.

4. *Assess the potential impact of each emergency on critical functions*. Again, a 1 to 5 ranking could work where 5 is crippling and 1 is no impact at all. Terms such as high, medium, and low would also work. See Exhibit 1 for an example.

5. *Develop alternate plans to deal with an anticipated emergency.*

The scope of preplanning and preparation for disasters can be as wide and diverse as the world of business itself. In an effort to provide useful context, this supplement approaches contingency planning from the structure discussed in the text, *Business*, by Pride, Hughes, and Kapoor. The impact of disasters on the following business areas will be addressed.

- The Environment of Business
- Small Business and e-Business
- Leadership and Human Resource Management

---

1. Critical Functions and Resources:

Material	Human	Financial	Informational
Building	Managers	Income from Sales	Telephones
Machinery	Workers	Payroll	Computers
Paper, Glue	Suppliers	Cost of Goods	Cell Phones
Energy	Maintenance	Time Clocks	Test Equipment

2. Emergency Assessment:

Possible Emergency	Probability	Impact
1. Earthquake	5%	High
2. Ice storm	60%	Medium
3. Terrorist attack	10%	High
4. Flu pandemic	5%	High
5. Power failure	70%	Medium/High

Based on the above, ACME should begin developing plans to respond to power failures and ice storms. This might involve strategies such as:

1. Purchasing back-up generators.

2. Establishing an out-of-town alternative site search in case access to buildings is prevented and/or power outage is long term.

3. Arranging for interim workers for alternative site.

4. Setting up a line of credit to pay for production and payroll while sales income is interrupted.

Exhibit 1

Hypothetical Example: ACME, a small 50-person envelope manufacturing company in Buffalo, New York.

1 The Environment of Business

Business is defined as the organized effort of individuals to produce and sell, for a profit, products and services that satisfy society's needs. For a business to exist, it must combine four kinds of resources:

1. *Material Resources:* Raw materials used in manufacturing processes as well as buildings and machinery.
2. *Human Resources:* Workers who furnish labor in return for wages.
3. *Financial Resources:* Money required to pay employees, purchase materials, and fund operating costs.
4. *Informational Resources:* Data that tells managers how effectively the other resources are being used.

Major disasters such as Hurricanes Katrina, Rita, and Wilma or a terrorist attack such as 9/11 can disrupt the availability of these resources and significantly change the business environment. For example, Hurricane Katrina has had and will continue to have a significant negative impact on each of these resources for businesses both in the United States and abroad.

Material Resources

The Gulf of Mexico produces 30 percent of domestic crude oil, and its ports handle 60 percent of the nation's oil imports. It also produces 20 percent of domestic natural gas.[1] The disruption of operations at these facilities has sent gas prices soaring above $3.00 per gallon, and it is estimated that electrical and heating costs will run 20–35 percent higher this winter across the nation. This increase in the cost of raw materials will significantly impact airlines, the trucking industry, and manufacturers, who in turn will pass on these costs ultimately to consumers.

Beyond the petrochemical industry, the disruption of shipping on the Mississippi River will have a significant impact on raw materials going to and from the United States. The Port of New Orleans is the world's busiest waterway, with more than 6,000 vessels moving through the port annually. It is the largest port in the United States by tonnage and the fifth-largest in the world. It exports more than 52 million tons a year, of which more than half are agricultural products. In addition, nearly 17 million tons of cargo come in through the port—including not only crude oil, but chemicals, fertilizers, coal, concrete, and more.[2] Though Katrina caused widespread damage, the facilities at the Port of New Orleans are repairable. Unfortunately, the storm occurred just prior to the busiest traffic period—the fall harvest, when agricultural products from the Midwest will be shipped down the Mississippi by barge for transfer to ocean-going ships. Certainly, there will be significant delays in the shipment of raw materials through the port.

The specific effect on domestic and foreign business will take time to determine. However, at this point, it is safe to expect that the costs for all sorts of goods made from oil and natural gas byproducts will rise in coming months as petrochemical shortages and high costs left in the wake of the Gulf Coast hurricanes begin filtering throughout the economy.

The diverse list of affected products is almost boundless: polyester shirts, plastic garbage bags, carpets, cleaning supplies, PVC pipe, and parts for automobiles. Then there are the containers: milk jugs, Coke bottles, Styrofoam cups, cheese wrappers, packages for hot dogs, and even those disposable plastic bags most of us carry home from the grocery store.

Finally, there are the indirect effects, such as farmers' higher costs for petroleum-based fertilizer, pesticides, and herbicides that could lead to price increases in the produce aisle. More than 20 percent of North America's plants making important chemicals such as xylene (used in cleaning agents and pesticides) and benzene (used to make rubber, plastic, and dyes), remained out of service, according to Chemical Market Associates, a Houston-based petrochemicals consulting company. Some could remain off-line through the end of the year.

Prices for ethylene, used in plastic film for packaging and a wide variety of other plastics, soared by 118 percent. Prices for propylene and polypropylene, used to make plastic food containers, among other things, jumped by as much as 62 percent. Now, these higher supply costs are beginning to filter down to consumers.

- Kraft Foods said it was exploring additional pricing actions to try to offset soaring costs that included packaging, such as petrochemical-based plastic wraps for its meats and cheeses or containers for coffee and Jell-O.
- Cooper Tire & Rubber Co. said it would raise some prices to help offset rising raw materials costs. It is estimated a tire that cost $60 a few months ago will cost $75 to $80 in a few more months.
- Calhoun-based Mohawk Industries recently said it would boost its carpet prices by 5 to 8 percent because of higher petrochemical and natural gas costs.
- Rohm and Haas Company, which makes everything from home siding to packing tape from petrochemicals, said it plans to quickly implement price increases to offset higher materials and transportation costs. The most widespread price increases for consumers, however, will likely come in everyday goods.
- Dow Chemical and DuPont recently announced they're raising prices on nearly everything they sell, from chemicals used in bathroom cleaners to freezer bags and kitchen countertops, because of high raw materials costs.[3]

Human Resources

Possibly, the most important resource that was affected by Katrina was the human resource, or more specifically, the workforce. It is estimated that more than 500,000 were left homeless in New Orleans and about 300,000 people are out of work and dispersed throughout the South, mostly in contiguous states.[4] The oil fields, pipelines, and ports require a skilled workforce in order to operate. Workers require homes.

They rely on stores to buy food and other supplies. They need hospitals, doctors, dentists, schools, and a myriad of other services to sustain a normal life. At present, New Orleans is still being pumped dry. Most areas of the city do not have electricity, drinkable water, or sewage treatment. It is estimated that up to 50,000 homes in the city will have to be demolished. Obviously, it will take considerable time to replace them. No one knows for certain how long it will take to repair the infrastructure, rebuild the homes, provide the services, rehire the workers and restore productivity to normal at the Port of New Orleans and the petrochemical industry in the area. Certainly, the time frame will be calculated in years rather than months.

Financial Resources

Hurricane Katrina and subsequent flooding in the Southeast could cost the economy more than $200 billion, which would make it the costliest storm ever to hit the United States. The cost in economic activity, which includes losses from interruption and displacement of residents, could set the economy back $100 million a day. That could climb if businesses decide to relocate or are unable to return in a timely fashion, further depressing the long-term economic prospects of New Orleans and surrounding areas.[5]

Locally, New Orleans and its parishes are locked in a painful dilemma. They are unable to lure back exiled residents without services, and they are unable to provide services without taxes from residents. The primary source of revenue in New Orleans is its sales tax, which before the storm covered about one-third of the city's operating budget. "We've gone from about $13 million a month in sales tax to zero," said city finance director Reginald Zeno. He ticks off a long list of other lost revenues, from parking and speeding ticket fines to the tax imposed on utilities that the city can't expect to see for some time. "The level of revenue we might see next year is anyone's guess," Zeno said.[6]

The city has already lost 29 of the 70 conventions that had been scheduled in 2006. Its convention center has yet to reopen and will probably not do so until early next year.

New Orleans has lost $1.5 million in tourist revenues every day since the levees broke, according to the Louisiana Office of Tourism, and less than one-third of its 3,400 restaurants have reopened. Small businesses are struggling to survive because of the lack of residents and tourists, and many large companies have yet to return. Before the hurricane, New Orleans was home to roughly 115,000 small businesses. "Losing half of those businesses is not out of the question," said W. Anthony Patton, a member of the reconstruction commission.[7]

Informational Resources

The effect of disasters on information resources can be a two-edged sword. When telephone lines go down, cellular phones go dead, and Internet communications are lost, it can cause chaos and can contribute to the devastation. However, with proper planning, informational resources can be crucial in saving lives and providing assistance to the stricken. Wal-Mart is a good case in point.

When Hurricane Charlie hit Florida last year, Wal-Mart management was alarmed by the lack of visibility in its affected stores. It was the first time it realized the extent to which the Information Systems Division could lose visibility of the damage at stores and whereabouts of employees in affected areas. It was Wal-Mart's wake-up call to get better prepared to track lost power, network coverage, and cellular phone communications after a disaster strikes.

Before Katrina, Wal-Mart had built what it called an emergency operations center designed to allow employees from different departments to work in close proximity during a disaster. Katrina put it to the test. By having people work in the operations center, it let people from multiple parts of the company make decisions and set priorities on what tasks and systems were most important. "When you go through a crisis similar to Hurricane Katrina, the pharmacy system is as critical as anything else we'll do," Wal-Mart's CIO said. Wal-Mart also utilized a dashboard system developed for the operations center that gives the company the visibility it lacked—showing each store's damage, whether employees were at risk or injured, if the store has communications platforms running, and whether it was running on landlines or satellite systems, utility or generator power. Employees set up mobile pharmacy facilities to fill prescriptions for people dislocated by the storm, and Wal-Mart needed to connect those to a group of pharmacists at its Bentonville, Arkansas, headquarters to fill prescriptions, because the demand at those mobile sites was so high.

Wal-Mart also set up emergency telephone lines for employees to call in, in order to account for all its employees and connect them to family members. Calls quickly exceeded 2,500 daily, swamping the existing call center and forcing the IT team to build a new one, which was accomplished in a matter of hours. Wal-Mart also launched a Web site where employees and others in the affected area could post messages to friends and family. When it proved popular, the company expanded it for use by nonemployees. There have been 40,000 messages posted and more than 2 million hits to the site.[8]

Ethics and the Business Environment

Ethics, specifically business ethics, also plays an important role in defining the business environment. Ethics is the study of right and wrong and of the morality of the choices individuals make. Business ethics is the application of moral standards to business situations. If companies do not employ business ethics in their dealings with investors, customers, employees, creditors, and competitors, they will eventually fail. Enron, WorldCom, and Tyco are painful examples of this simple truth.

Ethics also helps shape how people respond to disasters like Katrina. Dr. Edward Queen, in a discussion of ethical responses to Hurricane Katrina, made the following observation:

> "Incompetence is immorality. This statement has several dimensions. First, to continue in a position that one lacks the competence to fulfill is immoral. For that reason Michael Browne, the discredited director of FEMA, should have resigned . . . but he should have done the honorable thing and fallen on his sword, at least metaphorically, much earlier. Not because he is bad, but because he is a man who, through no fault of his own, had been elevated above his competence. Now, both he and the world know it. He continued in the position of director, knowing that he was unable to meet his obligations; and that was wrong. Please note that I am not referring to mere mistakes, I am talking about the ability to fulfill the overall duties of an office. I am speaking about competence, not perfection.
>
> Second, it is the obligation of systems, their duty, to accomplish the purposes for which they exist, and for those supervising them to ensure that the mechanisms and personnel are there to accomplish those purposes. That is what moral leadership is about: the ability to deliver the goods, as well as the Good. Nothing can be good that does not work; mere good intentions, as the saying has informed us all, pave the road to hell."[9]

Ethics therefore affects the business environment in the manner and competency with which people respond to a disaster. According to several accounts, companies were far more successful than government in their response to Katrina. Home Depot stores were among the first to reopen in the storm's wake, offering rebuilding supplies, electrical generators, and other essential tools. A day after the storm, all but ten of the company's 33 stores in Katrina's impact zone were open. Within a week, it was down to just four closed stores (of nine total) in metropolitan New Orleans.[10]

Wal-Mart began its response six days before the storm hit. The retail giant had studied customer buying patterns in hurricane-prone areas after previous storms. They stocked up on items such as bottled water, flashlights, generators, chain saws, tarps, and mops and shipped them to the disaster areas. In Waveland, Mississippi, a gulf coast town laid to waste by the storm, a Wal-Mart manager salvaged everything she could and handed out food, water, and clothing to people in the parking lot. She even broke into the pharmacy and got insulin and drugs for Aids patients.[11]

FedEx came up with a plan to fix a FedEx radio antenna on top of a 54-story building in New Orleans so that rescuers could have radio contact with each other. Before the storm hit, FedEx positioned 30,000 bags of ice, 30,000 gallons of water, and 85 home generators outside of Baton Rouge and Tallahassee so that it could move in quickly after the storm to relieve employees. Before Katrina, FedEx staged 60 tons of Red Cross provisions (it has since delivered another 440 tons of relief supplies, mostly at no charge).[12]

These companies were more effective than government because they prepared well, responded quickly, and they did so because Katrina was exactly the kind of event for which well-run corporations prepare themselves. The government didn't come through nearly as well. Local and federal officials failed to adequately prepare for the storm and failed to react quickly after it hit. One might conclude that business did a better job of meeting the ethical challenge.

Globalization and the Business Environment

Less than forty years ago, the geographical environment for American business was defined by North and South America, Europe, Japan, and the Middle East (for large oil companies). At that time, only the largest U.S. companies had the scale to market their goods and services to foreign countries. Today, the business environment is global for all companies regardless of their size. In the United States, international trade now accounts for over one-fourth of gross domestic product (GDP). There are several reasons for the rapid expansion of global business: a relatively peaceful political environment, easing of trade barriers, greater availability of capital, more affordable and rapid transportation options, and efficient global information systems. This has spawned the growth of multinational companies, firms that operate on a worldwide scale without ties to any specific nation or region. Though these companies have demonstrated an ability to adapt to changing business environments, their geographical scope makes them increasingly vulnerable to global disasters natural, terrorist-driven, and man-made.

The catastrophe at the Union Carbide Plant in Bhopal, India, is an example of a man-made disaster. Union Carbide's agricultural pesticide plant released approximately 40 tons of methyl isocyanine (MIC) into the atmosphere on December 3, 1984, resulting in the death of as many as 3,000 and injuries to thousands more.[13] The resultant law suits cost the company $470 million in settlement claims and made it economically vulnerable to a takeover. Union Carbide was forced to sell most of its major divisions and was eventually acquired by Dow Chemical Company in 2001.[14] While the Bhopal disaster was the result of poor planning and human error, it reflects the consequences that can befall a company if it does not properly prepare for catastrophic events.

The 1999 Taiwan earthquake was an example of the ripple effect of a natural disaster on business. The earthquake had a significant impact on the worldwide semiconductor industry in that it disrupted the supply of foundry services and increased prices for memories and other products. C-Cube, a manufacturer in Milpitas, California, had 70 to 80 percent of its capacity coming from Taiwan. This manufacturer of chips for products including DVDs and set-top boxes was forced to seek alternative supply sources. Larger companies like Motorola Inc. were able to weather the Taiwan crisis because they had agreements in place with second and third sources. Motorola is a good example of a company that believes in contingency planning.[15]

Terrorist attacks pose a different type of problem for business. Recent history has shown that terrorism is global in scope. Beyond the immediate destruction that terrorist bombings create in lives and property, they have long-term implications on the global economy by raising transaction costs, which results in reductions in potential output. These costs can be broken down as follows:

- *Higher operating costs.* Businesses may experience higher operating costs owing to increased spending on security, higher insurance premiums, and longer wait times for activities.
- *Larger levels of inventories.* Business may be required to hold larger inventories than previously, owing in part to less reliable air and rail transportation. There is anecdotal evidence from the auto industry that production was interrupted because components were not immediately available from suppliers after the September 11 attacks, owing to delays in shipments crossing the U.S.-Canada border.
- *Elevated risk premiums.* As a result of the attack, lenders' appetite for risk may decline, leading to elevated risk premiums that may be passed on to businesses in the form of higher interest rates and lower equity prices, with an adverse effect on business investment, and a smaller capital stock.
- *Shift of resources away from the civilian labor force toward the military.* More resources may be diverted toward the military for use in the containment of terrorism. In addition, research and development (R&D) resources may be shifted way from productive activities and towards the development of new devices to thwart terrorism (although such devices may have beneficial spillover effects elsewhere).
- *Shift away from globalization.* The attack may have effects on firms' investment decisions—in particular, whether to invest domestically or abroad, in part because of potential disruption of cross-border flows of goods and assets. Costs for such transactions may rise owing to closer inspection of transactions and higher insurance premiums.[16]

EXERCISES

1. Contingency Planning Team

The core mission of your college or university is to help students learn and achieve their educational goals. In order to do this, the school has to perform a number of critical functions such as conducting classes, processing grades, collecting tuitions, paying teachers, providing information as to class schedules, and so forth. In order to do this, the school must utilize material resources such as buildings and electricity, human resources such as professors, financial resources to help make payrolls, and informational resources such as email accounts.

Your team has been hired to develop a contingency plan for the school in the event a natural disaster might disrupt operations. As a first step, you need to identify the critical business functions required to keep the school running. List any functions and resources you can think of in addition to the ones listed.

Step 1

School functions and resources:

Material: examples—buildings, heat, light, other? _____

Human: examples—professors, administrators, other? _____

Financial: example—payroll, other? _____

Informational: examples—computer networks, grade processing, registration, other?

_____

Step 2

Develop a list of all the possible emergencies and disasters that might impact the school. Be as detailed as possible in developing your list. Use your imagination; do not be limited by degree of likelihood at this time.

Possible Emergencies/Disasters	Probability	Impact
1. _____		
_____		
2. _____		
_____		
3. _____		
_____		
4. _____		
_____		
5. _____		
_____		

Step 3

Go back and assign a probability of the likelihood of occurrence to each event. This probability will be a number between 0% and 100%.

Step 4

Indicate whether these events will have a high, medium, or low level of impact on critical functions and resources.

Step 5

Develop a list of potential problems your highest probability event might cause on campus. For example, if the power went out in an ice storm, the campus buildings couldn't be used, elevators would not work for the disabled, computer networks would be down, and so forth. Icy roads would keep key personnel from getting to the school. What other problems might you anticipate?

Step 6

Choose one of the major problems you have identified in step 5, and develop a contingency plan. For example, you might decide that getting key personnel to the school to start work on reopening the campus is the most important task. You might wish to suggest that the administration develop a list of such personnel, appoint someone to oversee the process, etc.

2. Pizza Opportunity

You are the owner of a small pizza parlor close to a national university in Tornado Alley. In the past, power outages and damage resulting from tornadoes has left your business closed for up to a week at a time. This has cost you money, especially because demand for pizza and other prepared food tends to be high in such emergencies.

You believe that if you can develop plans to somehow cook and deliver pizzas after a tornado, when others cannot, it will be very beneficial not only in terms of immediate sales but in long-term goodwill. You sit down with your manager and begin brainstorming ideas. One idea is to purchase portable grills, possibly hibachis and Webbers, along with charcoal. At least you could cook something. You also plan to add an emergency cell phone number to your menu so that if the phones go out, your customers could still reach you.

What other ideas might you suggest?

3. Research Assignment

Due to the flooding after Katrina, Tulane University could not physically open its doors to its students. Clearly, its material resources (buildings, infrastructure, and so forth) were not available to its students. How did Tulane respond to the problems faced by its students? What alternative plans were made available to the students? What resources did they bring to bear?

2

How Disasters Affect Small Business and e-Business

As discussed in the text, small businesses are a unique segment of the private sector. They represent about 99 percent of all employers, employ almost 50 percent of the private workforce, and provide roughly two-thirds of the net new jobs added to our economy.[1]

Small businesses are also unique in the fact that disasters have a disproportional impact on them. This is due to many factors. A natural disaster such as a hurricane can completely alter a business district and local shopping patterns. People in the area of the disaster may move away and not return, thereby severely reducing the customer base. If a small business site is inaccessible, the owner usually does not have an additional location to act as a backup site for doing business. When damage is severe, most small business owners do not have the resources to rebuild their businesses. For example, many small businesses in New Orleans wish to return but have found that not only are their customers gone but so, too, are their workers. Even if a company can find its workers, it may not be able to afford them. One small firm affected by the hurricane used to pay an unskilled, common laborer $7 an hour. Today, the same firm cannot hire the same person for even $15 an hour.[2]

According to a recent NFIB National Small Business Poll, man-made disasters affect 10 percent of small businesses, whereas natural disasters have impacted more than 30 percent of all small businesses in the United States. Hurricanes are by far the most destructive force, causing power failure, flooding, customer loss, and the closure of many businesses.

When a major disaster strikes a community, it often will forever change the trading area, leaving many small business owners with few choices but to walk away from the business. The U.S. Department of Labor estimates that over 40 percent of businesses never reopen following a disaster. Of the remaining companies, at least 25 percent will close within two years.[3]

For these reasons, the biggest option for the small business owner is oftentimes survival recovery as opposed to contingency planning. However, there are actions that small business owners can take in anticipation of a disaster to reduce its impact on their business. The following are actions that small business owners should consider in anticipation of and recovery from a disaster.

- *Preplan what can be preplanned.* Maintaining important business information is critical. Records such as customer lists, vendor records, accounts receivables, accounts payables, etc., should be backed up, preferably in an offsite database. (This will be discussed further in the next section.)

- Having a backup site to conduct business in the event your present site is not accessible can be crucial. The ability of a company to use an alternate facility is of course dependent on the nature of its business. For example, a backup location might work well for an assembly plant but may not be feasible for a manufacturing operation that requires bulky and sophisticated machinery. As well, a retail store may not be able to find a location with suitable consumer traffic.
- Help can sometimes come from unexpected sources. When the south tower collapsed in the attacks on the World Trade Center, New York City architectural firm Gruzen Samton saw their offices across the street destroyed. Not only were millions of dollars lost due to burned and broken furnishings and equipment, but so were paper records and computer data, as well as the photographic history of the company's projects. But Gruzen Samton was able to get back up and running thanks to competitors who provided office space. In the face of national tragedy, old rivalries were forgotten.[4]
- Power, heat (or air conditioning), and an alternate water source are critical for most enterprises. Backup generators, heating/cooling options, and water tanks should be investigated. An important preplanning item would be to determine the cost of business interruption insurance. Obviously, the level of contingency planning is dependent on the nature of one's business, one's assessment of the likelihood of a disaster, and the ability and willingness to invest resources in anticipation of a catastrophe.

- *Assess the damage.* After the disaster occurs, companies need to determine the level of damage to their operations. The damage should be quantified and rebuilding/replacement costs estimated utilizing realistic, up-to-date market costs. Obviously, disaster recovery will be more challenging for small businesses with large inventory losses. The timing needed to rebuild, replace, restock, and make the business productive must be carefully estimated, since this will determine financial needs at various points in time.
- *Ensure market viability.* After a disaster, the market will take time to reestablish itself. International, national, and regional businesses will have a much easier time rebuilding following a major disaster than will local businesses. Businesses that rely on heavy foot traffic will have greater challenges in rebuilding. An assessment needs to be done to determine if the firm's previous market segment still has the potential to sustain the business. If not, the business needs to determine whether it can reach out to new markets unaffected by the disaster.

Sometimes the market is still viable, but in order to serve it, the product must change. Kristin Rhyne was nowhere near the twin towers when terrorists crashed airliners into them on September 11. But the 31-year-old Harvard Business School graduate and founder of Boston's Polished Inc. suffered business damage almost as great as those in lower Manhattan. Rhyne owns a chain of airport beauty spas, which among other products sells manicure kits. Because of new airport security regulations, Rhyne was forced to produce manicure tools that were not metal so they could be carried on airplanes by her customers. Additionally, many potential customers stopped traveling immediately after 9/11, and those who did often were delayed in long lines at security checkpoints. Getting business levels back to pre 9/11 levels has been difficult for Ms. Rhyne.[5]

Rebuilding efforts following a disaster can be an economic gain for certain businesses participating in the rebuilding. For example, essential businesses in a disaster zone such as grocery, medical, and construction will be in high demand. On the other hand, if your product or service is not essential to an area's recovery, customers may have very little need or money for what you are offering in the near term. Think of how the disaster will affect your customers' spending habits.

⦿ *Enlist outside support.* To make the best decision to move your business forward, you must have a grasp of how the disaster has impacted those people connected to your business. Contact suppliers, employees, and customers to inform them of your situation. Many will offer support or alternatives for you to consider. Manufacturers might be able to ship directly to your customers, or suppliers can assist in payment schedules. Just knowing these options exist for your small business can help in making the final decision.

⦿ *Assess your financial position.* Vital to the critical decision of how to proceed with your business is assessing your financial position. Insurance agents need to be contacted to determine what and how much will be covered. Another source of funds is the Small Business Association (SBA). The SBA grants loans to businesses that have suffered tangible losses due to a natural disaster. The maximum limit on real estate damage is $200,000, and the amount that can be borrowed depends on the actual cost of repairing or replacing the damage, less any money received from insurance companies, other reimbursements, or grants.[6]

When a 1997 flood put the late Ruby Wyatt and her Falmouth, Kentucky, grocery store out of business, she didn't miss a beat. She just toughened up and rebuilt the family-owned operation. In fact, it was business as usual for the 82-year-old proprietor of Wyatt's SuperValu. "I have not shed a tear, nor will I," she is quoted as saying. "I will rebuild my store and move on with my life."

And within 66 days, that's just what she did. With help from her Minneapolis-based supplier, SuperValu Corp., Wyatt was quickly approved for more than $1.3 million in U.S. Small Business Administration disaster loans.

The never-say-die entrepreneurial spirit of Wyatt and her daughter Dixie Owen caught the attention of federal officials, and the duo was named the winner of the 1998 Phoenix Award for Small Business Disaster Recovery. At the ceremony honoring them in Washington, D.C., Ruby Wyatt announced to the audience that she appreciated the SBA's faith in giving a 30-year loan to an 83-year-old woman and that she was looking forward to living long enough to pay it off.[7]

Small businesses impacted by a disaster might be eligible for tax breaks from the IRS to offset losses, especially if situated in a federally declared disaster area. In general, the IRS allows certain income tax deductions following a casualty for a loss of property resulting from a sudden, unexpected, or unusual event. A taxpayer can deduct the new amount of actual property loss resulting from damage to, or destruction of, property. To qualify for a casualty loss deduction, the taxpayer must prove to the IRS that a loss occurred and that the loss was caused by a casualty.[8]

Once the owner understands all the financial requirements necessary to bring the business back to operation, he or she must decide whether to reinvest in the business or to shut it down. In essence, a business plan should be developed just as if the business were a new startup. In the final analysis, the small business owner who carefully considers options, enlists the support of outside resources, makes new operating plans, and accurately assesses the financial situation will be in the best position to survive a devastating disaster.

e-Business Disasters

e-Business is made up of businesses that use "the facilities available on the Internet" to sell their products and services. Therefore, the discussion of disasters and contingency and recovery planning that affect businesses in general are also relevant to e-business firms. However, given e-businesses' reliance on the Internet and digital information, it is useful to look at a different kind of disaster—the loss of vital business information. Imagine losing your entire customer list, your accounts receivable data, or your inventory records. You could spend weeks, even months, reconstructing this data. In a worst-case scenario, you might not be able to reconstruct it at all.

In today's highly computerized business world, many firms are exposed to the possibility of a sudden loss of information. Natural disasters, computer viruses, mechanical failures, and electronic crime can all result in catastrophic data loss. No matter how hard we try, we can't prevent disasters from occurring. But we can take forceful steps to safeguard data and to ensure that computer information can be retrieved and restored in the event it is lost.[9]

What Causes Data Loss?

Among other causes, data loss can be attributed to system error, human error, virus attacks, sabotage, and natural disasters. See Exhibit 1.

Human causes of data loss include intentional or accidental deletion or overwriting of files. Virus damage, operating system or application software bugs, or failed upgrades may also cause data loss. Common physical causes of data loss include power loss or power surge, overheating, electrostatic discharge, and any kind of physical damage to the storage device or medium.[10]

In 2003, the total cost of U.S. data loss was estimated to be $18.2 billion. This is based on the following computation, which was developed by Dr. David M. Smith of Pepperdine University.[11]

Security breaches of a company's business data can also be quite costly. A recent survey conducted by the Ponemon Institute found that the average cost to a company from a security breach worked out to be about $14 million. According to the survey, that amount included actual costs of internal investigations, outside legal defense fees, notification and call center costs, investor relations efforts, discounted services offered, lost employee productivity, and the financial hit from lost customers.[12]

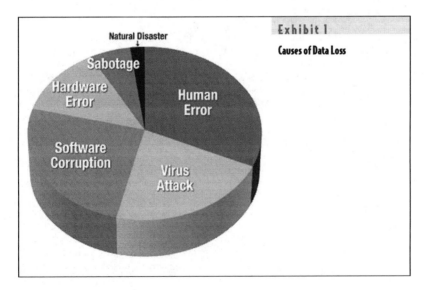

Exhibit 1

Causes of Data Loss

Total U.S. Data Loss Estimates		
Types of Loss		**Average Cost of Each Data Loss**
Value of the Lost Data		$3,400
Technical Services Cost		340
Lost Productivity		217
Total Cost of Each Data Loss		3,957
Number of Data Losses (estimate)	x	4.6 million
Total U.S. Data Loss Cost	=	18.2 million

How Can You Prevent Data Loss?

Companies can do a number of things to prevent data loss.

- Back up all important files. External drives are an excellent choice for this backup task. Then test and verify your backup.
- Use Windows XP System Restore Points before making any significant changes to your system.
- Write a contingency plan and practice restoring your data in case of problems. Your contingency plan should require, at a minimum:
    - Locating all available backups, including dates and types of backup.
    - Listing and locating all original software packages, detailing updates since the original installation.
    - Locating and making ready an alternate computer.
- Never upgrade software or hardware without a complete, verified backup available in case you need to restore data.
- Document your systems and archive original copies of your software in a safe place.
- Ensure proper environmental conditions (stable temperature, controlled humidity, and cleanliness) and proper handling to avoid static discharge and accidental dropping.
- Delete unused files and applications. Use a disc defragmenter.
- Physically secure systems from intruders.
- Deploy firewalls and virus protection.
- Prepare for physical disasters, including use of offsite storage for backup.

In the event you do suffer data loss, there are a number of companies that specialize in data retrieval including retrieving information from hard drive crashes, damaged media repair, virus attacks, data recovery, and Windows 2000 or XP password recovery. These companies can be found through Google, Yahoo!, Ask Jeeves, or other popular search engines.

Resourcefulness is often key to recovering lost data after a disaster. Gerry Nolan, president of disaster recovery consulting firm Eagle Rock Alliance in West Orange, New Jersey, recommends that companies ask clients, vendors, strategic partners, and even employees to scan the disk drives of their undamaged computers to see if useful files may have been stored on them. Gruzen Samton, the architectural firm that lost most of its records in the World Trade Center attacks, did just that, retrieving a number of computerized design files in the form of e-mail attachments that had been sent to consulting engineers. Some disaster survivors have been able to salvage damaged hardware as well as data by having useful information removed from damaged machines, then having the system refurbished, reinstalled, and reloaded with the data.[13]

Disasters come in many forms. It is the obligation of business and companies specifically, to anticipate, plan, and deal with those factors that affect their future. If companies plan sufficiently, they can survive any calamity. If they do not, they will suffer the consequences, which may include their very demise.

EXERCISES

1. Disaster Assessment

After working at the library all afternoon, you return to your dorm room and find the entire building flooded. All papers, notebooks, binders, etc., are destroyed, as is your computer hard drive. Your checks and bank statements are a soggy unreadable shredded mess. Your clothes are in a soaked pile. Your palm pilot is missing, as is your cell phone, which you inadvertently left behind in your hurry to get to the library. Fortunately, you still have your wallet with $50, driver's license, one credit card, and school ID. Everything else is gone. The semester is almost over, and all your work was on your computer. You need to act to save your academic year.

1. Assess the damage by listing all the items that are lost or damaged.
2. Determine which items must be replaced immediately and which can be delayed.
3. Determine the financial implications of repair or replacement. For example, do you need a new computer?
4. Determine sources of loans.
5. Determine any outside sources of help. For example, had you emailed rough drafts of any papers to anyone?

Use the chart below to construct your assessment:

	Item(s)	Importance Level	Degree of Damage (usable/fixable/gone)	Must Be Replaced (now, soon, can wait)	Replacement Source (friends/school, etc.)
1.					
2.					
3.					
4.					
5.					
6.					

6. Having gone through steps 1–5, what plans should you be making right now to minimize losses and damage in case of a real disaster to your living quarters?

2. Personal Document Inventory

Make a list of the ten most important documents you possess. The list might include items such as your birth certificate, passport, etc. Do you know where they are? If so, are they safe from fire, flood, theft, or any other possible mishap?

3. Research Assignment

Security breaches of computerized data cost corporations vast amounts of money. Identify a company that has suffered a security breach and the resulting business consequences both in financial terms and in loss of public trust. What could the company you have identified done differently?

3

The Importance of Leadership in Dealing with Disasters

Disasters require effective leadership. To be truly effective in dealing with a catastrophe, leadership should occur before, during, and after the disaster.

Analyzing Leadership

Management experts such as MIT Sloan Professor Thomas Kochan and his colleagues across MIT have been analyzing leadership as it relates to major disasters to determine what went right, what went wrong, and what needs to change. Kochan spoke recently at a MIT symposium, "Big Questions after Big Hurricanes." In his lecture, he drew comparisons to President Franklin D. Roosevelt's response to the bombing of Pearl Harbor. "FDR instinctively understood the need for cooperation and unity in his time of great crisis," Kochan observed. "Within two weeks of Pearl Harbor, he brought the nation's business and labor leaders together with key government officials and insisted they set aside partisan differences and work together to help the country through its crisis."

In response, they reallocated resources to produce the aircraft, ships, and radar systems needed to win the war. In addition, they worked together to maintain labor relations, train a new generation of workers, and hold inflation in check.

Kochan contends that the present leadership in Washington failed to draw coalitions of critical interests to address the aftermath of recent natural disasters and the terrorist attacks of 9/11. He blames the "go it alone" mindset of the Bush administration resulting in uncoordinated efforts to prepare for and respond to Katrina. "Government leaders must recognize a basic principle: Government cannot and need not manage crises of this magnitude alone. It needs to draw on and work in coordinated fashion with the full range of resources available."

The Issue Is Leadership, Not Technology

MIT supply chain expert Yossi Sheffi thinks many shortfalls led to the crisis in the Gulf Coast recovery effort: "Instead of taking decisive actions, city, state, and federal officials argued with one another, communications broke down, and too many civil servants . . . did not have the urgency or the passion required." Sheffi believes that the troubles in the Gulf Coast weren't about communications technology, as some observers had proposed, but about leadership. "The issues . . . have nothing to do with technology. They entirely have to do with reporting lines, organization lines, agreeing to work together. The technology is there."[1]

Lack of Leadership in New Orleans

Examples of what can happen when there is a leadership void was pointed out in a recent CNN article that stated: "As violence, death, and misery gripped New Orleans and the surrounding parishes in the days after Hurricane Katrina, a leadership vacuum, bureaucratic red tape, and a defensive culture paralyzed volunteers' attempts to help."[2] Consider these events:

- Dr. Bong Mui and his staff evacuated 300 patients after three hellish days at Chalmette Medical Center. When they arrived at the New Orleans airport, they were amazed to see hundreds of sick people. They offered to help, but FEMA officials said they were worried about legal liability. "They told us that, you know, you could help us by mopping the floor." And so they mopped, while people died around them. "I started crying," he recalled. "We felt like we could help and were not allowed to do anything."

- Steve Simpson, sheriff of Loudoun County, Virginia, sent 22 deputies to New Orleans equipped with food and water to last seven days. Their 14-car caravan, including four all-terrain vehicles, was on the road just three hours when they were told to turn back. The reason, Simpson told CNN: A Louisiana state police official told them not to come. "I said, 'what if we just show up?' He says, 'You probably won't get in.'" Simpson said he later learned a dispute over whether state or federal authorities would command the law enforcement effort was being ironed out that night. But no one ever got back to him with the all-clear.

- FEMA halted tractor trailers hauling water to a supply staging area in Alexandria, Louisiana, *The New York Times* quoted William Vines, former mayor of Fort Smith, Arkansas, as saying. "FEMA would not let the trucks unload," he told the newspaper. "The drivers were stuck for several days on the side of the road" because, he said, they did not have a "tasker number." He added, "What in the world is a tasker number? I have no idea. It's just paperwork and it's ridiculous."

- Firefighters who answered a nationwide call for help were sent to Atlanta for FEMA training sessions on community relations and sexual harassment. "On the news every night you hear, 'How come everybody forgot us?'" Pennsylvania firefighter Joseph Manning told *The Dallas Morning News*. "We didn't forget. We're stuck in Atlanta drinking beer."

Distributed Leadership Model

These situations can be avoided with proper leadership. MIT Sloan Professor Deborah Ancona notes that natural disasters call on all of a person's leadership skills. And good leadership requires delegation and dissemination of responsibility. She points to MIT Sloan's pioneering Distributed Leadership Model (DLM). The core of leadership development and research at MIT Sloan, the DLM moves away from "command and control" in favor of "cultivate and coordinate."

Ancona asserts, "What is clear is that during such disasters you need leadership at all levels. Executive leadership to devise overall strategy and people on the ground with the authority and skills to act of their own accord when necessary. During the tsunami, you saw doctors who took it upon themselves to organize." This is the kind of initiative that is needed to deal with circumstances that no one can predict.

This, she notes, is what the DLM model is all about: understanding the context in which one is operating, developing productive relationships and networks, visualizing the desired outcome, and inventing ways of working together to realize that vision. "Natural disasters demand all these skills," Ancona observes. "They are important aspects of a leader's repertoire."

Leadership According to Rudolph Giuliani

An example of a person who has exhibited these qualities is former New York City Mayor Rudolph Giuliani. Dubbed "America's Mayor," Giuliani emerged from 9/11 as a symbol of national strength and resilience. Unlike many in Washington during the 1990s, Giuliani and his associates saw terrorism as "an ongoing threat" and they prepared the city for the inevitable next attack. Among other things, his administration formed a "Mayor's Office of Emergency Management" to coordinate the city's response to potential attacks years prior to 2001. Giuliani created a state of the art emergency command center. His critics mercilessly pounced on the idea, dubbing it "the bunker," and implying that this was the work of a power-hungry and slightly paranoid politician. *The New York Times* said of it: "Some people think it's New York's funniest bunker since Archie." (There was a problem with the "bunker," however. Since it was on the twenty-third floor of Seven World Trade Center, it was destroyed when the building fell.) Nonetheless, it was a tangible example of a leader's preparation for a potential catastrophe. Following the terrorist attack, Giuliani and his management team set up another emergency control center within blocks of ground zero from which they managed the rescue effort.[3] Giuliani has written a book entitled *Leadership* (Hyperion), which provides his philosophy on leadership and what he learned from 9/11. Some of his observations are:

- Leadership Is Learned—While many people appear to have an innate ability to lead, most learn from their life and business experiences and then put those lessons into practice. Giuliani wrote, "The greatest leadership you ever have is the ability to lead your own life."
- Understand Good Leaders, Not Good Leadership—Giuliani wrote, "Read biographies of leaders you admire. That will tell you more about leadership than any leadership book."
- Learn Throughout Life—Education doesn't stop when you quit attending school. In Giuliani's words: "That's how I ended up on the morning of September 12, reading a biography of Churchill. I was thinking, 'I'm going to deal with something I haven't dealt with before. Let me see if I can learn something.'"
- Stand Up to Bullies—It's important to have a sense of justice . . ."to realize you have to stand up to people who take advantage of those who are weaker."
- Discourage Yes-Men/Women—As the saying goes, if we both have the same opinion, one of us is unnecessary. Build your team with people who don't think exactly like you.
- Reflect, Then Decide—Before making important decisions, learn everything you can about the topic. Giuliani said that as soon as he found out he had cancer, he began collecting information and suddenly felt safe, because then he could go to work doing something about it.
- Don't Listen to Critics—Anytime you're in charge, there will be people "chirping" in the background. Giuliani didn't let them distract him from doing what he believed was right.
- Become an Expert—Giuliani wrote: "When people come to you to ask for advice and information because you know more about a subject than they do, that's a sign of great leadership."

- Be Respectful—Use the Golden Rule: treat others as you want to be treated. "People know when you're talking down to them, and they will not respect you," he said.
- Stay Close to Your Customers—In Giuliani's case, this meant being with constituents, New Yorkers, in the weeks after 9/11. Remember him in the NYFD baseball cap and blue jeans, there to provide comfort and determination for all.
- Communicate and Inform—In all of his press conferences and briefings after 9/11, Giuliani provided facts and details, understanding the importance of candid statements at all times. Always let your team know what's going on.[4]

Leadership Lessons from Hurricane Katrina

There are also plenty of examples of what happens when there is a lack of leadership skills when dealing with disasters. Hurricane Katrina is a case in point. It is clear that federal, state, and local governments were slow to react and contributed to the problems in New Orleans following Katrina. The Bush administration has been criticized for underfunding recommended levee repairs. Bush himself has been accused of using FEMA as a dumping ground for political appointees. Michael Brown, the now disgraced former head of FEMA, was severely criticized for FEMA's late and inadequate response. Louisiana Governor Kathleen Blanco seemed by most accounts to be unnerved and uncertain when called upon to take action. When asked what her plans for recovery were, she asked all who were listening to her to join her in prayer. New Orleans mayor Ray Nagin was apparently so overwhelmed by the hurricane that he didn't carry out the city's emergency plan.[5] The picture of over 250 submerged school buses in a New Orleans parking lot that could have been used to carry tens of thousands of people to safety will be his legacy for years to come.

The common thread here is a lack of strong public sector leadership. There was not an assuring, confident, powerful voice amongst them. At a time when the people of the region needed to hear someone tell them that there was a plan, that there was resolve, and that this challenge would be met, they were instead inundated with government officials who reflected anguish and concern but did not bear the burden of leadership. There was no shortage of appropriate outrage, but there was no one who said, "we will fix this." There was no one who said, "we will not let this defeat us." There was no one who was willing to both wade in the water and offer hope. During the first several days after the hurricane hit, there was no sound bite, no film clip that would assure the residents of the region and the citizens of this country that strong people were in charge, that they had resolve for the future, and that those who had responsibility and resources would make this all better.

What can we learn that will help our public sector officials better deal with catastrophes such as Katrina? According to Jeff Coker who has worked with MIT's Distributed Leadership Model, "With the scale and complexity of contemporary disasters, the concept of distributed leadership is essential. One person, one team, one organization is usually not enough to manage all the issues related to such calamities." According to Coker, "Leaders should force themselves out of restrictive command and control hierarchies and bureaucracies that might be effective in controlled crises. Those in charge must build relationships outside their usual networks. In times of crisis, it is these informal relationships that can make the difference. During Katrina, for example, FEMA could have worked with media outlets to get information out quicker and to get the latest news from the affected areas."

The proof of the effectiveness of the distributed leadership model is in its practice. Nathalie Butcher, an MBA student, took the knowledge learned during her first year at MIT Sloan to Indonesia to help victims of the devastating Indian Ocean tsunami. Based in Jakarta, she worked for the Indonesian nongovernmental organization (NGO) United in Diversity helping tsunami victims to rebuild businesses and launch new ones.

Every Disaster Is Different

The challenge, Butcher says, is that every disaster is different and calls for a plan based on the resources and limitations available at that moment in time. She says there's a strategic timeline that must be followed for relief efforts to be productive. "The first step is to get people out of immediate danger. Get them medical attention, food and water, and some form of shelter. Then get people on the ground to survey the situation. Where is the present and future danger? Get communications established. Get people into the unsafe areas to find out what's needed and arrange for the necessary help." The sequence of relief work, Butcher says, is essential: "If you build a school before you've given somebody a tent, your priorities are out of whack." She has seen firsthand the domino effects that hamper relief efforts. "You can't build a house if you can't get the building materials there. You can't get the building materials there if the bridges are out. And you can't get the bridges fixed if you can't get an engineer in to look at them."

The critical flaw in recent disaster relief situations, MIT Professor Otto Scharmer believes, is responding to today's issues based on yesterday's realities—what he calls "downloading." When we are confronted with new challenges, he says, we have to invent new solutions. And the best way to reinvent is to bring together a coalition of individuals with a stake in the outcome. "In disaster relief situations," Scharmer emphasizes, "multiple stakeholders must come together. Business planners, government officials, nongovernmental organization representatives, and all players critical to solutions need to collaborate in jointly addressing the situation on the ground."

Theory U

When it comes to building innovative collaborative systems, Scharmer has plenty of experience putting research into practice. He is cofounder of Project ELIAS (Emerging Leaders for Innovations Across Systems), an alliance of nine global institutions from all sectors that includes BP, Unilever, the UN Global Compact, the World Bank, nongovernmental organization players, and members of the MIT community. Scharmer is also the architect of the pioneering Theory U, which entails sensing and prototyping strategic microcosms of the future. Relative to Theory U, Scharmer sees four essential capabilities for leading disaster management:

1. Be in the moment. Disengage your routine and absorb the situation at hand. Devise new networks of people close to the situation.
2. Reflect deeply. Don't make assumptions. Envision the future. Imagine multiple scenarios.
3. Summon an authentic leadership presence. Be open. Access your deeper sources of intuition.
4. Innovate. Innovate out of the context of the disaster you face. Then improve as you go along.

Scharmer says failure to approach each challenge anew from a multi-stakeholder perspective leads to major breakdowns in the handling of catastrophes. By way of example, he points to issues of sustainability and global warming. "Global climate issues can't be addressed by single institutions or sectors," he says, "but by their root problems." Trying to solve new challenges with antiquated systems, he believes, spells disaster in an era of increasing disasters.

Act on Murphy's Law

According to MIT Sloan Professor Jay Forrester, "Almost every natural disaster, like almost every corporate and social disaster, arises out of a systemic set of policies that created, or at least contributed to the disaster. Usually, the disaster arises from failure to internalize and act on one of 'Murphy's laws,' to the effect that if something can go wrong, it will," he explains. "Regarding the recent New Orleans disaster, it was well known that the levees would likely fail in a major hurricane, but they had not yet, so the hope was that they would not in the future."

Forrester points to the U.S. space shuttle disasters as another case in point. "Such a calamity," he says, "had nearly happened before, but rather than acting to remove the potential causes, managers under budget and political pressures chose to look the other way. Even the Pakistan earthquake disaster is significantly a result of not building for earthquake resistance in an earthquake region."

Forrester observes that while it's the anticipators who deserve credit for disaster averted, it's the disaster managers who attract the attention. "People, politics, and the press are more excited about the hero who copes with a disaster than the people who quietly prevent it."

Leadership in Action

In the wake of Hurricane Katrina, Hands On Network, a network of 52 local nonprofit community service organizations in partnership with the Hands On Network Corporate Service Council, a national alliance of 29 corporate CEOs and civic leaders, has announced an unprecedented initiative to mobilize 6.4 million additional volunteers over the next two years. This represents a 10 percent increase in volunteerism nationwide and includes the training and mobilization of 100,000 volunteer leaders with 10,000 of those leaders focused on long-term Hurricane Katrina relief and rebuilding.

Throughout the two-year effort, each Council member company will set annual volunteerism goals, cultivate project leaders, plan local projects, marshal resources, share best practices, motivate participants and performance, and measure results. Hands On Network will provide on-the-ground project management and a link between the companies and community organizations to achieve real community impact and change.

Spearheaded by Bob Nardelli, chairman, president and CEO of The Home Depot, and Michelle Nunn, co-founder and CEO of Hands On Network, the Council includes CEOs from 3MCompany; AARP; Accenture; Albertson's, Inc.; BellSouth Corporation; The Case Foundation; Cisco Systems, Inc.; Civic Enterprises; The Coca-Cola Company; Dell, Inc.; Delta Air Lines; Discovery Communications, Inc.; Fannie Mae; FedEx Corporation; General Electric Company; The Hitachi Foundation; Home Depot, Inc.; KaBOOM!; Masco Corporation; Nuclear Threat Initiative; PricewaterhouseCoopers LLP; Qwest Communications International, Inc.; Retail Industry Leaders Association; SAP America, Inc.; Starwood Hotels & Resorts Worldwide, Inc.; Turner Broadcasting; U.S. Chamber of Commerce; Young & Rubicam Brands; and Yum! Brands, Inc.[6]

EXERCISES

1. Take Me to Your Leader!

Step 1

Identify someone you know personally who in your opinion is a good leader and someone you would want around in an emergency. List as many personal traits (courageous), characteristics (well-respected), and behaviors (always reading) of that person as you can in the next five minutes.

Personal Traits	Characteristics	Behaviors
_____	_____	_____
_____	_____	_____
_____	_____	_____
_____	_____	_____
_____	_____	_____
_____	_____	_____

Step 2

Compare your lists with those of 3–4 of your classmates. Identify which traits, characteristics, and behaviors these perceived leaders appear to have in common.

Step 3

Based on your comparison, can your group identify a prototypical leader?

2. Personal Evaluation

On a scale of 1 to 5 as detailed below, evaluate yourself on Rudy Giuliani's leadership criteria.

5 = always
4 = mostly
3 = sometimes
2 = rarely
1 = never

1. I try to apply lessons from past successes and failures. _____
2. I read biographies of great leaders and learn from them. _____
3. I stand up to bullies and aggressive people. _____
4. I respect those who disagree with me. _____
5. I get the information I need to make a good decision. _____
6. I do not let naysayers influence me when I know I am right. _____
7. I try to gain expertise in important areas. _____
8. I treat everyone with respect and good manners. _____
9. I maintain relationships with friends and colleagues. _____
10. I am a good communicator. _____

What areas do you need to work on to build your leadership skills?

3. Research Assignment

Wal-Mart was singled out for excellent performance during the Hurricane Katrina disaster. What is the leadership culture like at Wal-Mart and how did it help Wal-Mart respond to the disaster?

4

Disasters and Human Resource Management

Human resource management plays a crucial role in dealing with disasters both in the public sector in helping to restore basic services to a community and in the private sector in helping companies to get back up and running.

Disaster plans typically address in great detail critical aspects of how essential services in a community (such as police and fire protection, public works, and utility services) will be maintained and deployed during and after a disaster. However, oftentimes, the staffing of these services is overlooked if assigned personnel have difficulty responding to a crisis. In these instances, human resources (HR) can play an important role by doing the following:

1. *Maintaining accurate emergency contact information.*
2. *Identifying additional resources for staffing essential services.* The HR professional can assist in addressing this need by:

- Identifying the "special skills" of existing employees. Many employees have skill sets and abilities that they do not utilize in their normally assigned job function. Maintaining an "emergency resource roster" can provide a list of personnel within an organization that can be reassigned during emergency situations to areas of greater need. The focus should be on identifying those skills and abilities that require special training or licensing (e.g., a commercial driver's license).
- Identifying other sources for additional personnel. This may include temporary staffing agencies, union halls, and neighboring communities (assuming they aren't dealing with the same disaster).

3. *Providing flexibility in personnel rules and/or collective bargaining agreements.* In a time of emergency, rules and regulations regarding work jurisdiction, job duty assignments, working hours, etc., will need to be suspended in whole or in part in order to allow the appropriate personnel deployment to occur.[1]

As it relates to the private sector, not only must companies rebuild the physical infrastructure of their businesses, they also must resolve a myriad of workplace challenges. One of the most important and difficult challenges is to restore their workforces. While companies are rebuilding their physical plants or sites and their equipment is being restored, Human Resource Management should be working toward finding the workers who are the backbone of the business. This is not always easy, since many of the original employees may have dispersed to other locations and taken other jobs. Clearly, this is what happened in New Orleans after the destruction caused by Hurricane Katrina.

Consider Tiffany Manning's plight. She had a full-time job as a mental health counselor for adolescents and teenagers with behavioral and psychiatric disorders. But today, she is one of the thousands of evacuees who are no longer getting a paycheck. The situation is creating a surge of displaced and unemployed residents now pouring into job fairs and temporary hiring centers in an anxious search for work.

"I had $40 on me when I left, and now I only have $20," Manning, 25, said in a phone interview. She is no longer getting any income and is staying with her grandmother in Haynesville, Louisiana, and hoping for full-time or temporary work. "I'm thinking about relocating; I'm not sure. But I'm here trying to begin a brand new start." [2]

Many evacuees are struggling to find any type of work in the wake of Katrina. Jenny Bradley, 57, left her home in Terrytown, Louisiana, to stay with her daughter in Memphis before the hurricane struck, thinking she'd be gone only a few days. Instead, she's looking for temporary jobs through Randstad, a staffing firm. She recently got work for four days a week answering phones at a nursing home.

After all she's been through, Bradley says, she wants a permanent job, because she doesn't plan to go back. "Looking for something is really tough," says Bradley, who had worked as a contractor handling accounting and reservations for a Navy Reserve activity center. "I'll flip burgers. I don't care. (Work) keeps my mind off everything." [3]

In light of stories like this, it is important for companies to plan ahead to ensure that they can maintain their current workforces in the face of an emergency. Their first priority should be to keep the employees that have made their business successful, as opposed to starting all over again. They can accomplish this goal in several ways, as follows.

1. *Maintain communication with displaced workers.* After a disaster, many displaced workers may find themselves in unfamiliar locations, without much more than the clothes on their back. Companies should make it easy for their employees to contact them. One approach is to create a web site for employees to make contact with the company from any location. The web site might include a toll-free number that could be passed along to employees without Internet access. Another approach is for employers with operations in cities where evacuees have relocated to establish a communication center that employees can contact.

2. *Continue paying wages.* Government aid may not be available immediately, or in large amounts. To the extent they can, it is in an employer's best interest to continue paying their employees who have been devastated by a disaster. Oftentimes, it will be cheaper for the company to keep their employees on the payroll than go through the process of finding and hiring adequate replacements.

3. *Transfer workers to other operations.* In the aftermath of the 2005 hurricanes, it is becoming evident that thousands of people will not return to the hardest-hit areas until an extensive rebuilding effort is completed or they won't return at all. Employers should consider whether affected employees can be transferred to other operations in surrounding areas so that their valuable skills and experience are not lost. Once the rebuilding is complete, these employees could be an integral part of returning to the impacted area and reestablishing operations.

4. *Institute flexible leave policies.* Most company handbooks make no allowance for the type of disaster that befell the Gulf Coast in 2005. Flexibility and compassion should be the order of the day. Moreover, it is important to note that many employees affected by the storm will qualify for family and medical leave,

bereavement leave, or other types of leave provided under either company policy or federal and state laws. Extreme care should be taken before denying leave or terminating employees for a failure to return to work.

5. *Make medical benefits accessible.* Many affected employees use medical insurance to assist with their recovery after a disaster. Companies should consider providing benefit information on company web sites or through communication centers so that employees are best able to address issues that might arise.

6. *Promote Employee Assistance Programs (EAP).* Most employers have EAPs either separately or as a part of their health insurance benefits. Employers should ensure that their employees understand their benefits in the event of a disaster by making qualified counselors available on site or in areas where a large number of employees have evacuated. These services are invaluable and may facilitate employees returning to normalcy, including the resumption of employment.[4]

TRAINING

It is widely accepted that training is one of the most important tools that human resource managers have in preparing for emergencies and in reducing the impact of disasters. The use of emergency preparedness training can vary significantly from the public sector to the private sector, as well as internationally. The following are some examples of crises training that various organizations engage in.

Public Sector

Eleven years ago, reeling from flawed responses to Hurricanes Hugo and Andrew, the Federal Emergency Management Agency launched the Higher Education Project to ensure that disaster officials at all levels of government were trained to deal with catastrophes. The project consisted of persuading colleges to offer degrees and certificate programs in emergency management, aimed at producing a new breed of professionals who could assume posts often held by ill-equipped appointees. Students in colleges across the country now can take courses in subjects like quarantine and epidemiology; disaster-specific instruction for floods and earthquakes; lectures on politics, planning, and leadership; and onsite experience in everything from community emergencies to the Asian tsunami.

In 1994, there were four college programs in emergency management. Today there are 121 college programs, and 110 more are under consideration. Salaries are rising in the field, to an average of $45,390 annually, according to May 2004 figures from the Bureau of Labor Statistics, though managers in small jurisdictions might make half that and those in the private sector can make double. The U.S. Department of Labor projects emergency management will be one of the fastest-growing fields through 2012.[5]

Wayne Blanchard, who oversees FEMA's Higher Education Project, points out that "disasters are a growth business in this country." One result of that growth is a new breed of emergency managers with far different demographics than a decade ago. More have college degrees and have chosen the field as a first career. They are younger and more diverse.

Why then, with advances in the quality of emergency management and with more qualified people, was the response to Katrina so inept? According to Blanchard, it will take five to ten more years before the true fruits of the program are realized, because the people it attracted are still in lower-level positions without the authority to lead a response to an emergency.

Private Sector

Disaster preparedness training in the private sector can vary widely depending on the nature, size, and location of the company, but it is probably best segmented by large and small organizations. Large companies like IBM are very sophisticated in their preparation for catastrophic events, and in some areas, they are the envy of federal governments. IBM has a Crisis Response Team that has responded to more than 70 critical incidents in 49 countries during the last decade. The team provides immediate, 24/7 assistance, including international humanitarian relief, emergency management and on-site services, as well as business services to government and business entities in the United States and around the world.

After the Tsunami in Southern Asia, IBM deployed its Crisis Response Team and more than 700 employees, business partners, and customer volunteers across the four countries of India, Sri Lanka, Indonesia, and Thailand. It was clear within the first week that the tremendous challenges faced by these governments, as well as relief agencies, businesses, and community organizations could be aided significantly through technology. Among the services that IBM provided were tracking and identifying the missing, dead, and injured, as well as assisting displaced individuals and orphans in finding relatives.

After Hurricane Katrina, IBM deployed its Crisis Response team to Baton Rouge to address critical health and safety needs. Among their contributions were:

- *Missing Person Reunification Project.* IBM developed a number of web sites and local registries to help evacuees and the public locate missing family members, friends, and colleagues.
- *Jobs4Recovery.* In partnership with the U.S. Chamber of Commerce, local chambers in the Gulf region, and nonprofit partners, IBM launched a new job search web site for those people who had an immediate need for employment.
- *American Red Cross Disaster Relief Self-Registration Internet Site.* IBM designed and developed the American Red Cross Disaster Relief Self- Registration Internet Site, which captured and stored demographic and family data in a secure data base. This was particularly helpful for evacuees to apply for benefits online with Red Cross assistance.
- *Centers for Disease Control Support.* IBM provided support to the Centers for Disease Control of the U.S. Department of Health and Human Services to respond to emergency health needs and ensure that evacuees had access to prescriptions and care for chronic illnesses and trauma resulting from the disaster.[6]

It is evident that large companies with technical expertise such as IBM can provide disaster assistance that cannot be duplicated by local and national governments or agencies. Companies with expertise in specialized areas can cover a wide variety of needed assistance including reconstruction (by companies such as Bechtel and Halliburton), medical supplies (Merck and Pfizer), distribution (FedEx and Yellow Freight), and communications (AT&T and Motorola), to name a few. The list of companies with unique capabilities that could be useful in emergencies is quite extensive. It is important that agencies responsible for emergency management identify these companies in their areas, develop relationships with them, and create plans to utilize these private-sector resources in anticipation of crisis situations.

Small companies have their own set of issues. Due to fewer managers and lack of management depth, it is sometimes difficult to separate training from planning. Put another way, if employees in a small firm are familiar with the company's emergency plan, they are in essence trained as to what to do in a crisis situation.

Every business, regardless of its size, should perform some kind of risk assessment and develop a crisis management/business continuity plan. Small businesses, in advance of a problem, should scout backup sites where they can operate, or at least protect key assets, in the event of a major disaster. This could be as simple as renting a motel room and a set of storage lockers in another community. Backup copies of all critical business data, such as insurance policies, incorporation papers, bylaws, and customer and vendor records, should also be stored offsite.

Part 4 Disasters and Human Resource Management

One of the major problems after 9/11 was for companies to account for their employees, to determine who was dead and who was alive. Plans should be developed wherein employees are given a central phone number to call within a specified time after a disaster to acknowledge their condition and location. Communications are another major problem. After 9/11, many landlines and most cell phones didn't work in New York due to traffic overload. Companies should consider purchasing at least a limited number of satellite phones to ensure that they will have uninterrupted communication with their clients, vendors, and other locations in the event of an emergency. Satellite phones are no longer prohibitively expensive and can be deducted as a business expense.

One of the major problems arising after most disasters is the interruption of power. Almost every business enterprise is dependent on electricity. Virtually every emergency planning guide recommends that businesses acquire generators to provide light, heat, and power for their critical equipment.

In the final analysis, disaster planning and preparation begins and ends with individual employees and their families. To this end, every business, small and large alike, should have survival kits, with a first-aid component at every location. As well, employees should be encouraged to have similar, though less extensive, kits at home and in their car.

A major disaster can spell the end for a small business that is heavily damaged or destroyed. Its customers and workforce may drift away, and it may be difficult or impossible to find adequate financial resources to restock its shelves or replace equipment and technology. Indeed, after Hurricane Andrew, two-thirds of all businesses that remained closed for more than three days never reopened their doors. This is why it is so important for small businesses to take necessary and appropriate steps to protect themselves and their employees in the event of a major disaster.[7]

International

Obviously, disaster preparedness training is not unique to the United States. According to Robert Thayer of the U.S. Agency for International Development (USAID), disaster preparedness is particularly needed in Latin America and the Caribbean because the countries in this region are vulnerable to a wide range of natural hazards, including earthquakes, hurricanes, flooding, tsunamis, landslides, volcanoes, and drought. Some countries are also vulnerable to civil unrest resulting from political or economic instability.

Since 1989, USAID's Office of Foreign Disaster Assistance has trained more than 34,000 individuals and certified more than 2,100 instructors in 26 countries. The focus of this program has been on disaster management, training methodologies, technical assistance, and training courses including "collapsed structure" search and rescue, damage and needs assessment, shelter management, and incident command systems. USAID-supported efforts have evolved greatly since 1989. The original emphasis was on "direct training" but then shifted to "training of trainers." The USAID strategy now is moving beyond the training of trainers and focusing more on technical assistance.

Thayer said the international community plays an important role in assisting a nation's relief efforts following a natural disaster. But he emphasized that it is national governments, not foreign governments or international organizations, that have "the local resources, the motivation, the knowledge of local conditions, and of course, the mandate to respond quickly and effectively." He went on to say that "disaster assistance is normally most effective when carried out by the affected countries themselves."[8]

As discussed in a previous section, all disasters are different, and each crisis offers its own set of unique challenges. For this reason, emergency preparedness planning, staffing, and training should be adapted to the geography, local conditions, and the type of disaster that can be reasonably expected. As a philosopher once wrote, "The future belongs to those that prepare for it."

Exercises

1. Research Assignment

The public's attitudes toward institutions that affect their lives often change in the aftermath of a major disaster. For example, faith in government was enhanced after 9/11 and eroded after Katrina. Religious observation increased immediately after 9/11 and then dwindled. What other examples of attitude change in the wake of a disaster have you observed?

2. Class Exercise

Make five copies of the following survey and administer it to five students outside your class. As soon as you have finished surveying, get together in a group with four classmates and combine your results. Analyze your findings. Based on the information you gathered, does it appear that recent disasters have had an impact on the students in your school? If not, what if anything should be done to increase awareness and concern about these events? Report your findings to the class. Indicate if the results were consistent with your expectations.

3. Student Survey

Please rate the following disasters in order of their impact on you personally. Use the following scale:

1. Did not change my attitudes and/or behaviors at all.
2. Minor impact on my attitudes and/or behaviors.
3. Major impact on my attitudes and/or behaviors.
4. Completely changed my attitudes and/or behaviors.

Disasters:	9/11	Katrina/Rita	Asian tsunami
Economic			
My spending habits	_____	_____	_____
Education costs	_____	_____	_____
Food/gas/clothing expenses	_____	_____	_____
My charitable giving	_____	_____	_____
Cultural/social			
Faith in religious institutions	_____	_____	_____
Concern about my fellow man	_____	_____	_____
Feelings about myself	_____	_____	_____
Desire to help others	_____	_____	_____
Political/Legal			
Faith in government	_____	_____	_____
Concern about privacy laws	_____	_____	_____
Desire for world involvement	_____	_____	_____
Technological			
Need for more technology	_____	_____	_____
Concern over privacy	_____	_____	_____

Long-Term Effects of Disasters

Disasters, whether natural or man-made, have a long-term effect on society and business. Not only do disasters change the landscape as infrastructure is replaced, they have a lasting effect on society and the way a country does business.

Effect on the United States

While the ultimate damage is probably months away from being tallied, it is clear that Hurricane Katrina has taken the highest toll—in both lives and property—of any natural disaster in the United States to date. It has wiped out a vibrant city that earlier this year was designated the number one U.S. tourist destination for families. Though the city will be rebuilt, it will take many years before it will regain its status as the leading tourist attraction. The longer-term impact, however, is its effect on workers locally and throughout the United States. The massive exodus of residents out of the New Orleans area is being called the largest redistribution in the country's population since the Dust Bowl. Millions of people are without homes, and hundreds of thousands are potentially without jobs.

Unlike the tragic events of September 11, 2001, Katrina has the potential to affect literally every workplace in the country in one way or another. As well, Katrina and the flooding that followed it have crippled many Gulf Coast oil refineries and the oil industry in general. A large segment of the shipping and trucking industries stalled, and some of the country's most crucial ports closed. Those things can't happen without having an effect on the nation's economy.[1]

9/11 Effect on Consumers

In the wake of the 9/11 terrorist attacks, air travel has gone through a disruption whose effects are still being felt. Continued fear and anxiety on the part of passengers and airlines alike, the creation of a massive new federal bureaucracy (i.e., the Transportation Security Administration), and airport hassles that were once unimaginable are all accepted as common occurrences today. Increased security rules will reportedly cost U.S. airlines $518 million in lost revenues in 2004. A portion if not all of these costs will most likely be passed on to consumers in the form of higher prices. More than three years after the worst terrorist attacks on American soil, the best way to balance passenger safety, privacy, and convenience is far from settled.[2]

9/11 Effect on Products/Services

Beyond passenger hardships, the Department of Homeland Security issued new regulations for all cargo leaving and entering the country to make it harder for terrorists to smuggle nuclear or biological weapons. The new regulations require shippers to provide advance manifest information, much like the advance reporting requirements for ocean cargo. The U.S. Bureau of Customs and Border Protection (CBP) will process advance cargo information into an automated targeting system linked to law enforcement and commercial databases. This will enable CBP to identify high-risk shipments. Prior to this, most nonmaritime inbound shipments entered the United States without being screened by automated targeting systems.[3]

Even with these new regulations, the ability of the U.S. government to adequately screen the majority of incoming shipments especially by water transportation is woefully insufficient. Efforts to improve security in this area will continue at great cost and disruption to the free flow of products between the United States and its trading partners for many years to come.

Industries such as chemical production, fresh water providers, telecommunications companies, oil refineries, and nuclear facilities, to mention a few, will be changing the way they do business and be funding increased security measures because of the 9/11 attacks. The increased costs for these industries eventually will become higher costs for their business partners, communities, and ultimately, their customers.[4]

Global Effect

Disasters are generally geographically confined but often have global effects. The 9/11 terrorist attacks in New York City and Washington D.C. propelled the United States to war with Iraq and has resulted in major political, economic, and social changes in many parts of the world. Specifically, alliances between nations have been altered, the cost of the war has impacted U.S. borrowing and balance of payments, and the relationship between the Muslim and non-Muslim world has been strained.

The sheer magnitude of the devastation of last year's tsunami in the Indian Ocean has changed many peoples' lives forever. The tsunami struck 12 countries and displaced more than two million people, according to the United Nations, destroying their livelihoods, tearing apart families, annihilating entire towns, and leaving at least 183,172 dead.[5] Beyond the obvious consequences that this catastrophe has had for the people involved, it also affects the world community in other ways.

Secretary of State Colin Powell recently pointed out on CNN that long-term developmental assistance for the tsunami-struck region would be required by the United States. He went on to say that food insecurity leads to civil instability and that this can ultimately become a security issue for the United States.[6] Clearly, this is a situation where a natural disaster is dictating a country's national policy.

Psychological Effect

Another long-term effect of disasters is how they impact people psychologically. The 9/11 attacks are affecting not only survivors and their loved ones, but also those who got no closer to the tragedy than their TV sets. "Everyone, everywhere feels vulnerable," says Dr. Carol North, professor of psychiatry at Washington University in St. Louis and an expert on long- and short-term reactions to disasters. Nowhere do people feel more vulnerable than in the workplace. Because the 9/11 attacks struck office buildings, many employees now associate work with terror. "There's a sense of dramatic change everywhere—including the workplace," says Dr. Ian Anderson, deputy chairman of The Global Consulting Partnership, a Dallas consulting firm that helps employees deal with personal and performance-related issues. Employers need to be aware that the disaster has had an impact on the American psyche, one that may go on for years after the initial event. If it's not addressed, it can have a negative impact on the workplace through diminished morale and decreased productivity.

While many workers are likely to experience a sense of disillusionment, some employees will experience post-traumatic stress disorder, a very serious mental condition that, if left untreated, can deeply affect an individual's personal and work life. There's no known time limit for post-traumatic stress disorder. Researchers report that some people are still experiencing symptoms after the Oklahoma City bombing. For those suffering from post-traumatic stress disorder, things may only get worse as time passes. Sufferers may become more isolated and sink further into depression as colleagues slowly return to normal.[7]

Broad Financial Effect

With all the long-term negatives to disasters, there are also some positives from a broad business perspective. Despite the catastrophic damage and unimaginable loss incurred by residents of the Gulf Coast, history shows that natural disasters have little effect on financial markets over the long term. While certain industries such as insurance, transportation, and other regional businesses are impacted negatively by major disasters, the broad financial markets recover swiftly after an initial shock. The economic environment, monetary policy, and technical trends are much more important to the long-term direction of stock prices.

Despite a swift downturn, financial markets have rebounded quickly from major natural disasters. Several reasons account for such rapid bounces. First, large corporations, whose stocks make up the major indexes, are usually insured against business interruption and have the wherewithal to resume operations quickly. While companies might miss a quarterly profit estimate, the long-term financial impact to large companies is miniscule. Second, governments and central banks—like the Federal Reserve—often inject liquidity into the financial system to provide money for the rebuilding effort. Third, the short-term economic disruption caused by a natural disaster is often offset by the long-term economic activity generated from reconstruction. And finally and unfortunately, the majority of the damage is often incurred in poor areas, which have little economic influence to begin with, as was the case in the 2004 Indian Ocean tsunami.[8]

Summary

The purpose of this supplement is to discuss the effects of natural or man-made disasters on business. Business and disasters are connected insofar as they both touch the lives of people in a society. Business involves producing and selling products/services to satisfy people's needs. The business process utilizes a combination of material, human, financial, and information resources. Disasters disrupt these processes both in the short term and long term and, at their worst, result in death and crippling injuries to consumers.

Worldwide pandemics like the bubonic plague that ravaged Europe during the Middle Ages and the 1918 flu that killed millions of Americans generally have been kept in check by modern medical science. However, new crises like mad cow disease and the bird flu pandemic are reminders that global disasters are always a possibility.

The point to be made is that disasters have affected mankind from the beginning of time and there is no reason to believe that they will not continue. As disasters affect society, so, too, will they affect business, which serves society. Since disasters are a fact of life, businesses need to prepare for and develop plans on how best to deal with them. A starting point is contingency planning, which essentially prepares for a disaster based on an analysis of what has occurred and worked in the past. As the saying goes, "those who do not learn from history are doomed to repeat it."

The success of a company's ability to deal with a disaster is dependent on its ability to plan in advance, the quality of its response, and its ability to learn from the situation and apply that learning to preparations for the next disaster. There were several noteworthy examples given of companies like Wal-Mart, Home Depot, and Federal Express (to name a few) who exhibited these qualities.

It was also recognized that every disaster is different and not every contingency can be anticipated—nor is every needed resource to deal with a crisis available at a given point in time. Beyond proper planning, the businesses that will best survive a disaster are those organizations that are most adept at dealing with change. As recognized in the Preface of the Pride/Hughes/Kapoor text, "no other word better describes the current business environment" than change. Disasters are but one of many events that business must deal with to achieve success. The principles and processes needed to deal with these contingencies are discussed in depth in the text.

Notes

Introduction

1. Ron Moreau and Michael Hirsh, "One Crisis Too Many?" *Newsweek,* October 31, 2005.
2. Uday O. Ali Pabrai, "Contingency Planning: Business Impact Analysis," available at **http://www.certman.com/articles/anmviewer.asp?a=1175&print=yes**.
3. Chris Penttilla, "Worst-Case Scenario; Staff Smarts: How Would Your Business Take a September 11-Level Tragedy? Only the Best Preparation Can Ensure It Rises from the Rubble," *Entrepreneur Magazine,* February 2002.
4. Gail Russell Chaddock, "Cost of Katrina Relief Splits Republican Ranks," *Christian Science Monitor,* September 20, 2005; Dr. Gerhard Berz, "Natural Disasters Hit All-Time High in 2000," Geoscience Research Group.
5. Robert Looney, "Economic Costs to the United States Stemming from the 9/11 Attacks," Center for Contemporary Conflict, August, 2002.
6. **http://www.doi.gov/ocl/2004/HR2608.htm,** accessed October 27, 2005.
7. **http://www.cbc.ca/stories/2003/07/14/madcow_030714,** accessed October 27, 2005.
8. Julie Appleby, "Economists Say Avian Flu Could Have Huge Impact," *USA Today,* October 6, 2005.
9. "Risk Analysis Reports Over Half of World's Population Exposed to One or More Major Natural Hazards," The Earth Institute at Columbia University, **http://www.earthinstitute.columbia.edu/news/2005/story03-29-05.html,** October 27, 2005.

Part 1

1. Telis Demos, "Coming Back to Life," *Fortune Magazine,* October 3, 2005.
2. George Freidman, "New Orleans: A Geopolitical Prize," **www.analysis@stratfor.com.**
3. Bob Keefe, "Life's Hidden Energy Costs—High Oil Prices Affect a Long List of Products," *The Atlanta Journal-Constitution,* October 27, 2005.
4. Staff Writers, "Louisiana Counts Storms' Crippling Costs," *Los Angeles Times,* September 28, 2005.
5. "Katrina Could Cost Economy $100B," **http://money.cnn.com,** September 2, 2005.
6. Gary Rivlin, "Left Penniless in Katrina's Wake, Governments Cut Jobs, Services," *San Francisco Chronicle,* October 22, 2005.
7. Jennifer Steinhauer, "New Orleans Is Grappling with the Basics of Rebuilding," *The New York Times,* November 8, 2005.
8. Laurie Sullivan, "Wal-Mart CIO: Hurricane Charlie Paved Way For Katrina Response," *Information Week,* September 19, 2005.
9. Dr. Edward Queen, "Ethics and Incompetence in the Aftermath of Katrina," Center for Ethics—Emory University, September 13, 2005.
10. Justin Fox," A Meditation on Risk," *Fortune Magazine,* October 3, 2005.
11. Devin Leonard, "The Only Lifeline Was the Wal-Mart," *Fortune Magazine,* October 3, 2005.
12. Ellen Florian Kratz, "For FedEx, It Was Time To Deliver," *Fortune Magazine,* October 3, 2005.
13. Case Study, Exportation of Risk: The Case of Bhopal, **http://www4.ncsu.edu,** October 24, 2005.
14. Jack Doyle, "Union Carbide: Outlaw Corporation Acquired by Dow," the Global Pesticide Campaigner, December 2004.
15. Carol Haber, "Effects on Global Semi Market to Linger…," *Electronic News,* September 27, 1999.

16. Robert Looney, "Economic Costs to the United States Stemming from the 9/11 Attacks," Center for Contemporary Conflict, August 2002.

Part 2

1. William Pride, Robert Hughes, Jack Kapoor, *Business, Eighth Edition,* 2005.
2. Ted Griggs, "Cost of Health Care Prohibitive for Many," **http://www.2theadvocate.com/cgi-bin/printme.pl,** accessed November 17, 2005.
3. Darrell Zahorsky, "Disaster Recovery Decision Making for Small Business," **http://sbinformation.about.com,** accessed November 15, 2005.
4. Mark Henricks, "Disastrous Effects: How Does a Business Survive When It's Too Close to a National Crisis for Comfort?" *Entrepreneur,* January 2002, **http://www.findarticles.com/p/articles/mi_m0DTI/is_1_30/ai_83790622,** accessed November 18, 2005.
5. Henricks, Ibid.
6. Small Business Disaster Recovery Loans, **http://www.allbusiness.com,** accessed November 16, 2005.
7. David Miller, "Small Town Kentucky Grocer Able to Rebuild After Devastating Flood: $1.3 Million Disaster Loan Put Wyatt's Super Valu Back in Business in 66 Days," Greater Baton Rouge Business Report, September 16, 2003, **http://www.findarticles.com/p/articles/mi_m5012/is_1_22/ai_108650223/print,** accessed November 18, 2005.
8. Businesses Hit by Natural Disasters Can Get Federal Tax Relief, **http://www.toolkit.cch.com,** accessed November 16, 2005.
9. Data Disaster: Planning for a Computer Meltdown, **http://www.nfib.com,** November 1, 2005.
10. Data Loss Prevention, **http://www.seagate.com,** accessed November 14, 2005.
11. David M. Smith, PhD, "The Cost of Lost Data," **http://gbr.pepperdine.edu,** December 17, 2003.
12. Brian Krebs, "Counting the Cost of Data Loss," **http://blogs.washingtonpost.com,** accessed November 14, 2005.
13. Henricks, Ibid.

Part 3

1. " In Depth: Natural Disasters Leadership: It Takes a Team," MIT Sloan Management, **http://mitsloan.mit.edu/,** accessed November 28, 2005.
2. "Leadership Vacuum Stymied Aid Offers," CNN, **http://www.cnn.com,** September 16, 2005, accessed November 28, 2005.
3. Vincent J. Cannato, "Follow a Leader: Rudy Giuliani Proved that New York Can Be Governed," *The Weekly Standard,* July 25, 2005, **http://www.findarticles.com,** accessed November 29, 2005.
4. David Handler,"11 Things Small Business Owners Can Learn from Rudy Giuliani," April 18, 2005, **http://www.b2bhints.com,** accessed November 29, 2005.
5. Christopher T. Gates, "Special Word on Katrina: An Excess of Blame and a Dearth of Leadership," National Civic League, September 9, 2005, **http://www.ncl.org,** accessed November 29, 2005.
6. "Hands On Network Launches Campaign to Mobilize 6.4 Million Volunteers," **http://www.prnewswire.com/cgi-bin/stories.pl?ACCT=104&STORY=/www/story/09-19-2005/0004110535&EDATE=,** accessed December 7, 2005.

Part 4

1. Alan D. Pennington, "The Role of HR Pros When Disaster Strikes," **http://www.careerjournal.com**, accessed December 6, 2005.
2. Stephanie Armour, "After Searching for Food and Shelter, Now Comes the Job Hunt," *USA Today,* September 7, 2005, **http://www.usatoday.com**, accessed December 6, 2005.
3. Ibid.
4. David L. Barron, Victoria M. Phipps, and Peter A. Steinmeyer, "After the Disaster: Ten Issues for Employers," **http://www.workforce.com**, accessed December 6, 2005.
5. Matt Sedensky, "Expanded Training Seen as Partial Solution to Flawed Disaster Response," *The Associated Press,* September 25, 2005.
6. Stanley S. Litow, "Private Sector Response to Katrina, Senate Homeland Security and Government Affairs Committee," testimony, November 16, 2005, **http://web.lexis-nexis.com.ezproxy.tamu.edu**, accessed December 8, 2005.
7. Neil C. Livingstone, "Small Business and Emergency Preparedness, Committee on House Small Business," testimony, November 1, 2005, **http://web.lexis-nexis.com.ezproxy.tamu.edu**, accessed December 8, 2005.
8. Eric Green, "Value of Disaster Preparedness Training in Americas Cited," *HT Media Ltd.,* September 16, 2005, **http://web.lexis-nexis.com.ezproxy.tamu.edu**, accessed December 7, 2005.

Summary

1. Perkins Coie, "Dealing with Katrina's Impact on Workforces Across the Country," Alaska Employment Law Letter; October 13, 2005; **http://web.lexisnexis.com.ezproxy.tamu.edu:2048/universe/document?_m=27c6a12c9339011f07d253e0edc6a872&_docnum=6&wchp=dGLbVtz-zSkVb&_md5=53111742d04df46b01af05aed7e8e5ef**, accessed December 30, 2005.
2. Robert W. Poole, Jr., and Jim Harper, "Transportation Security Aggravation: Debating the Balance between Privacy and Safety in a Post-9/11 Aviation Industry," *Reason,* March, 2005; **http://www.findarticles.com/p/articles/mi_m1568/is_10_36/ai_n13490360**, accessed December 26, 2005.

3. Brian Albright, "New Cargo Security Regulations . . . ," *Frontline Solutions,* February 2004, **http://www.findarticles.com/p/articles/mi_m0DIS/ is_2_5/ai_113907155**, accessed December 26, 2005.
4. Tom Ramstack, "Terrorism Hurts the Bottom Line . . . ," *Insight on the News,* April 1, 2002, **http://www.findarticles.com/p/articles/mi_m1571/ is_12_18/ai_84396679**, accessed December 26, 2005.
5. Editorial, "One Year after the Tsunami," *New York Times,* December 28, 2005; **http://www.nytimes.com/2005/12/28/opinion/28wed1.html?th&emc=th**, accessed December 29, 2005.
6. Larry Hollon, "The Long-Term Effects of Human Disasters," January 10, 2005; **http://theoblogical.org/movtyp/archives/003794.html**, accessed December 29, 2005.
7. Andrea C. Poe, "Aftershocks of the 11th: Long after the Initial Shock of the September Terrorist Attacks Has Worn Off, Employees May Need Your Continuing Support," *HR Magazine,* December 2001, **http://www.findarticles.com/mi_m3495/is_12_46/ai_81393636**, accessed December 30, 2005.
8. "Natural Disasters Have Little Long-Term Effect on Markets," *ContraHour,* September 3, 2005, **http://www.contrahour.com/contrahour/2005/09/natural_disaste.html**, accessed December 28, 2005.

Career Planning

Career Planning

Stockbyte

We are meant to work in ways that suit us, drawing on our natural talents and abilities as a way to express ourselves and contribute to others. This work, when we find it and do it—even if only as a hobby at first—is a key to our happiness and self-expression.

MARSHA SINETAR

Freedom is the confidence that you can live within the means of something you're passionate about.

PO BRONSON

why
this chapter matters . . .

By discovering your passions and skills, you can plan for a successful career.

what
is included . . .

Choosing who you want to be
You've got a world of choices
Explore vocational assessments
Career planning: Begin the process now
Ways to learn about careers
Test the waters—jump into the job market
Gaining experience as an intern
Financial planning: Meeting your money goals
Take charge of your credit card
Using technology to manage time and money
Choose your conversations
Contributing: The art of selfishness
Keep your career plan alive
Power Process: "Risk being a fool"
Master Student Profile: Fred Smith

how
you can use this chapter . . .

Expand your career options.
Discover a career that aligns with your interests, skills, and values.
Find your place in the world of work through concrete experiences—informational interviews, internships, and more.
Meet your financial goals while contributing to other people.

As you read, ask yourself
what if . . .

I could create the career of my dreams—starting today?

Choosing who you want to be

When people ask about your choice of career, they often pose this question: What do you want to be?

One response is to name a job. "I want to be a computer technician." "I want to be a recording engineer." "I want to be a chef." These answers really suggest what we want to *do*.

Another response is to describe a certain income level or lifestyle. "I want to be rich, with all the free time in the world." "I want to sell all my belongings, move to Hawaii, and live on the beach." These statements are actually about what we'd like to *have*.

Yet another option is to describe what you want your life to stand for—the kind of person you want to become. You could talk about being trustworthy, fun-loving, compassionate, creative, honest, productive, and accountable. These are just a few examples of the core values you can bring to any job or lifestyle that you choose.

Career planning does not begin with grinding out résumés, churning out cover letters, poring over want ads, saving for an MBA, or completing a 100-question vocation interest assessment. Any of those steps can become important or even essential—later. And they can be useless until you take time to exercise your imagination and consider what you want most of all. Career planning starts with dreaming about who you want to *be*.

Dreaming makes sense in a hard-nosed, practical way. Consider people who change careers in midlife. Many of these people have been in the work force for several decades. They've raised families, received promotions, acquired possessions. They've spent a lifetime being "practical." These people are looking for more than just another job. They want a career that pays the bills *and* excites their passions.

There's no need to wait 10, 20, or 30 years to discover your passions. You can start now by reading and completing the exercises in this chapter.

Bring up the subject of career planning and someone might say, "Well, just remember that even if you hate your job, you can always do what you want in your free time." Consider that *all* your time is free time. You give your time freely to your employers or clients, and you do this for your own purposes. All of us are "self-employed," even if we work full-time for someone else.

In this chapter you'll find many suggestions for career planning. Remember that there's more to this process than listing job titles, describing the preferred state of your bank account, or checking off a list of the possessions that you desire. Those are valid concerns—and the foundation for them includes your core values and driving desires. Through career planning, you translate these into transferable skills that are valued by employers. Once you make this translation, your career choices can fall into place like magic.

If you want to be practical, then dream about who you want to be. ▨

journal entry

Discovery/Intention Statement

Recall a time when you felt powerful, competent, and fulfilled. Examples might include writing a paper when the words flowed effortlessly, skillfully leading a bar mitzvah service, or working in a restaurant and creating a new dish that won rave reviews. Mentally re-create this experience and the feelings that came with it.

Now, reflect on this experience. Briefly describe the skills that you were using at that moment, the values you were demonstrating, or both.

I discovered that I . . .

_____

_____

Next, review what you just wrote for an intention that can guide your overall career plan. For example, you might write, "I intend, no matter what job I have, to be an effective leader." Or "I intend to create a career that gives free expression to my creativity."

I intend to . . .

_____

_____

Now scan this chapter for ideas that can help you act on your intention. List at least four ideas here, along with the page numbers where you can read more about them.

Strategy   *Page number*

_____

_____

_____

_____

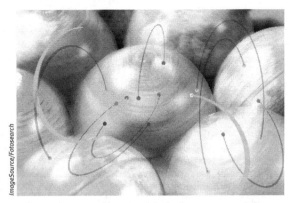

You've got a world of choices

Our society offers a limitless array of careers. You no longer have to confine yourself to a handful of traditional categories, such as business, education, government, or manufacturing.

People are constantly creating new products and services to meet emerging demands. The number of job titles is expanding so rapidly that we can barely track them.

In addition, people are constantly creating new goods and services to meet emerging needs. For instance, there are people who work as *ritual consultants*, helping people to plan weddings, anniversaries, graduations, and other ceremonies. *Space planners* help individuals and organizations to arrange furniture and equipment efficiently. *Auto brokers* will visit dealers, shop around, and buy a car for you. *Professional organizers* will walk into your home or office and advise you on managing time and paperwork. *Pet psychologists* will help you raise a happy and healthy animal. And *life coaches* will assist you to set and achieve goals relating to your career or anything else.

The global marketplace creates even more options for you. Through Internet connections and communication satellites that bounce phone calls across the planet, you can exchange messages with almost anyone, anywhere. Your customers or clients could be located in Colorado or China, Pennsylvania or Panama. You can track packages worldwide in real time and stay on top of investment opportunities as they emerge. Your skills in thinking globally could help you create a new product or service for a new market—and perhaps a career that does not even exist today.

In addition to choosing the *content* of your career, you have many options for integrating work into the context of your life. You can work full-time. You can work part-time. You can commute to a cubicle in a major corporation. Or you can work at home and take the one-minute commute from your bedroom to your desk. You can join a thriving business—or create one of your own.

If the idea of self-employment seems far-fetched, consider that as a student you already *are* self-employed. You are setting your own goals, structuring your time, making your own financial decisions, and monitoring your performance. These are all transferable skills that you could use to become your own boss.

Reading and doing this chapter will help you start gathering information on possible careers. Just remember that there is no reason to limit your choices too soon. You've got the world to choose from. ✖

exercise

DIG OUT THE "LIFE STORY" OF A PRODUCT

All the goods and services in our society result from work done by people. Pondering this fact may give you new possibilities for career planning.

For example, pick up any object near the place where you sit or stand right now—perhaps a computer, notebook, pen, pencil, CD, DVD, or piece of clothing. If possible, choose something that holds a special interest for you.

Next, reflect for a moment on the path that this product took from its creator into your hands. See if you can list the job title of every person who helped to plan, produce, distribute, and sell this item. If you're not sure, just brainstorm answers. After doing this exercise, you can do some research to confirm your answers.

Create your list of job titles in the space below.

_____

_____

_____

Finally, scan this list for any jobs that interest you. To find out more about them, use the resources listed in the article "Ways to learn about careers."

Explore vocational assessments

Vocational assessments can be a helpful resource for self-discovery and career planning. These assessments might also be called vocational aptitude tests, skill inventories, or interest assessments. They provide useful information about personality, comfort with technology, and work preferences.

Your school's career planning, counseling, or job placement center may offer one or more of these assessments. Ask if there is a cost and if anyone will review the results with you.

The following are some better-known vocational assessments. Bear in mind that they are not tests. There are no right or wrong answers to the questions they ask. Take several of these assessments and compare the results. And what you do with the results is always a personal choice. No assessment can dictate your career direction. The choice is always yours.

No assessment can dictate your career direction. The choice is always yours.

California Psychological Inventory. The California Psychological Inventory provides a view of your professional and personal style by measuring a range of individual differences: interpersonal skills, social skills, values, achievement-seeking needs, and stylistic modes. The inventory also measures managerial potential and creative temperament.

Career Ability Placement Survey (CAPS). CAPS provides you with information about your abilities. It helps you understand your potential, and your strengths and weaknesses, and gives you a prediction of success in various types of occupations.

Career Thoughts Inventory. This vocational assessment can help you uncover negative thoughts that may impede effective, successful career planning. The inventory provides suggestions about how to change negative thoughts to positive ones required for good career choices.

Eureka Skills Inventory. This is a card-sorting skills assessment that includes the skills you normally use at work or for daily activities. You select the skills you enjoy using into categories: very satisfying, moderately satisfying, or somewhat satisfying. Your choices are mapped by a computer to show the ways you would prefer to spend your time on the job and types of occupations that use the skills you have selected in the assessment.

Hall Occupational Orientation Inventory (HOOI). This values inventory is designed to help you rank personal factors that are important aspects of choosing your career. The HOOI gives you information about your interests, abilities, needs, and values.

Myers-Briggs Type Indicator® (MBTI) Instrument. The MBTI provides insight about yourself and how someone like you fits into the world of work, working with others of similar and different profiles. Results provide personal awareness and help you identify careers and work environments where you are most likely to thrive and feel fulfilled.

Personal Career Development Profile (PCDP). The PCDP shows you how your personality relates to your career plans and potential job performance. The profile provides you with insights into your choices and preferences, emphasizing your personal strengths, including an analysis of your approach to problem solving and stress management.

The Self-Directed Search (SDS). The SDS asks you to answer a questionnaire about your interests and abilities. Upon completion, you receive a computerized report that provides you with a personality summary code. The report then lists occupations and fields of study that correlate with your personality code. You can begin career exploration with a list of occupations at your fingertips.

Strong Interest Inventory. This inventory helps you identify your interests and matches them with possible occupations. It measures interests rather than abilities and compares your likes and dislikes to those of people who are satisfied in specific careers.

Vocational Preference Inventory (VPI). This inventory is a brief personality test based on the theory that occupations can be based on personality traits. It is especially useful to people who've had ambiguous results on other vocational assessments. ⬢

USE INFORMAL WAYS TO DISCOVER YOURSELF

Vocational assessments offer one path to self-discovery. Another option is to explore your interests in a more informal and playful way. The results can be revealing and useful.

Answer the following questions by writing the first ideas that come to mind. Use additional paper as needed or create a computer file for your writing. Have fun and stay open to new insights.

Imagine that you're at a party and you're having a fascinating conversation with someone you just met. What does this person do for a living? What is your conversation about?

What do you enjoy doing most with your unscheduled time? List any hobby or other activity that you do not currently define as "work."

Think about the kinds of books, newspaper and magazine articles, and television shows that are most likely to capture your attention. What subjects or situations do they involve?

If you bookmark Web sites in your Internet browser, review that list. What interests does it reveal?

What kind of problems do you most enjoy solving—those that involve ideas, people, or products? Give an example.

Finally, reread your answers to the above questions. List three to five interests that are critical to your choice of career.

Career planning

Begin the process now

When you clearly define both your career goal and path to reaching that goal, you can plan your education effectively.

Career planning is an adventure that involves continuous exploration. There are dozens of effective ways to plan your career. You can begin your career-planning adventure now by remembering the following ideas.

Acknowledge what you already know

When people learn study skills and life skills, they usually start with finding out things they don't know. That means discovering new strategies for taking notes, reading, writing, managing time, and other subjects.

Career planning is different. You can begin by realizing how much you know right now. You've already made many decisions about your career. This is true for young people who say, "I don't have any idea what I want to be when I grow up." It's also true for midlife career changers.

Consider the student who can't decide if he wants to be a cost accountant or a tax accountant and then jumps to the conclusion that he is totally lost when it comes to career planning. It's the same with the student who doesn't know if he wants to be a veterinary assistant or a nurse.

These people forget that they already know a lot about their career choices. The person who couldn't decide between veterinary assistance and nursing had already ruled out becoming a lawyer, computer programmer, or teacher. He just didn't know yet whether he had the right bedside manner for horses or for people. The person who was debating tax accounting versus cost accounting already knew he didn't want to be a doctor, playwright, or taxicab driver. He did know he liked working with numbers and balancing books.

In each case, these people have already narrowed their list of career choices to a number of jobs in the same field—jobs that draw on the same core skills. In general, they already know what they want to be when they grow up.

Demonstrate this for yourself. Find a long list of occupations. (One source is the *Occupational Outlook Handbook*, published by the U.S. Department of Labor and available online at **http://www.bls.gov/oco/oco1001.htm**.) Using a stack of 3x5 cards, write down about 100 randomly selected job titles, one title per card. Sort through the cards and divide them into two piles. Label one pile "Careers I've Definitely Ruled Out for Now." Label the other pile "Possibilities I'm Willing to Consider."

It's common for people to go through a stack of 100 such cards and end up with 95 in the "definitely ruled out" pile and five in the "possibilities" pile. This demonstrates that they already have a career in mind.

See your career as your creation

Many people approach career planning as if they were panning for gold. They keep sifting through the dirt, clearing the dust, and throwing out the rocks. They are hoping to strike it rich and discover the perfect career.

Other people believe that they'll wake up one morning, see the heavens part, and suddenly know what they're supposed to do. Many of them are still waiting for that magical day to dawn.

We can approach career planning in a different way. Career planning can be the bridge between our dreams and the reality of our future. Instead of seeing a career as something we discover, we can see it as something we choose. We don't find the right career. We create it.

There's a big difference between these two approaches. Thinking that there's only one "correct" choice for your career can lead to a lot of anxiety: "Did I choose the right one?" "What if I made a mistake?"

Viewing your career as your creation helps you relax. Instead of anguishing over finding the right career, you can stay open to possibilities. You can choose one career today, knowing that you can choose again later.

Suppose that you've narrowed your list of possible careers to five, and you still can't decide. Then just choose one. Any one. You might have several careers during your lifetime. You might be able to do any one of these careers next. The important thing is to choose.

One caution is in order. Choosing your career is not something to do in an information vacuum. Rather, choose after you've done a lot of research. That includes research into yourself—your skills and interests—and a thorough knowledge of what careers are available.

After all of the data has been gathered, there's only one person who can choose your career: you. This choice does not have to be a weighty one. In fact, it can be like going into your favorite restaurant and choosing from a menu that includes all of your favorite dishes. At this point, it's difficult to make a mistake. Whatever your choice, you know you'll enjoy it.

Career planning can be the bridge between our dreams and the reality of our future.

Prepare for an evolving job market

According to one traditional model of career success, the path to prosperity was to do your job well, gradually acquire new skills through training provided by your company, and get along with your coworkers. As long as you met those primary goals, you could expect a long-term relationship with a single employer, along with a stream of promotions and salary raises.

That model is history. In the job market of the twenty-first century, you can get laid off from a job even if you perform well and bond closely with colleagues. When companies merge or acquire their competitors, decisions about hiring and firing are often made on the basis of costs, not employee competence. Evolving technology will render some jobs obsolete. In addition, employers may decide to change their focus or shed certain lines of business. Corporate downsizing and reorganization could take away your job with little, if any, warning.[1]

Even when faced with these realities, you can still take charge of your career with the following strategies:

- Plan for the possibility of several careers within your lifetime—perhaps across several fields.

- Direct your own professional development by listing the transferable skills you want to acquire, creating a specific plan to develop them, and periodically assessing your progress.

- Anticipate changes in your career field and consciously choose your response to those trends.

- Define specifically how your skills contribute to an employer—and carefully document the value you add to an organization.

At any point in your career, ask: "Will my current job exist in five years? If not, what else can I do that aligns with my interests, skills, and values? And even if my job will continue, what can I do to ensure that I'm still enjoying my life's work and meeting my income goals five years from today?" That will give you time to develop new skills and expertise—or even to create a new career.

Plan by naming names

One key to making your career plan real and to ensuring that you can act on it is naming. When you create your career plan, see that you include specific names whenever they're called for:

- *Name your job.* Take the skills you enjoy using and find out which jobs use them. What are those jobs called? List them. Note that the same job might have different names.

- *Name your company—the agency or organization you want to work for.* If you want to be self-employed or start your own business, name the product or service you'd sell. Also list some possible names for your business. If you plan to work for others, name the organizations or agencies that are high on your list.

- *Name your contacts.* Take the list of organizations you just compiled. What people in these organizations are responsible for hiring? List those people and contact them directly. If you choose self-employment, list the names of possible customers or clients. All of these people are job contacts.

Expand your list of contacts by brainstorming with your family and friends. Come up with a list of names—anyone who can help you with career planning and job hunting. Write each of these names on a 3x5 card or Rolodex card. You can also use a spiral-bound notebook or a computer.

Next, call the key people on your list. After you speak with them, make brief notes about what you discussed. Also jot down any actions you agreed to take, such as a follow-up call.

Consider everyone you meet a potential member of your job network, and be prepared to talk about what you do. Develop a "pitch"—a short statement of your career goal that you can easily share with your contacts. For example: "After I graduate, I plan to work in the travel business. I'm looking for an internship in a travel agency for next summer. Do you know of any agencies that take interns?"

- *Name your location.* Ask if your career choices are consistent with your preferences about where to live and work. For example, someone who wants to make a living as a studio musician might consider living in a large city such as New York or Toronto. This contrasts with the freelance graphic artist who conducts his business mainly by phone, fax, and e-mail. He might be able to live anywhere and still pursue his career.

Remember your purpose

While digging deep into the details of career planning, take some time to back up to the big picture. Listing skills, researching jobs, writing résumés—all of this is necessary and useful. At the same time, attending to these tasks can obscure our broadest goals. To get perspective, we can go back to the basics—a life purpose.

Your deepest desire might be to see that hungry children are fed, to make sure that beautiful music keeps getting heard, or to help alcoholics become sober. When such a large purpose is clear, smaller decisions about what to do are often easier.

A life purpose makes a career plan simpler and more powerful. It cuts through the stacks of job data and employment figures. Your life purpose is like the guidance system for a rocket. It keeps the plan on target while revealing a path for soaring to the heights.

Test your career choice—and be willing to change

Career-planning materials and counselors can help you on both counts. Read books about careers and search for career-planning Web sites. Ask career counselors about skills assessments that can help you discover more about your skills and identify jobs that call for those skills. Take career-planning courses and workshops sponsored by your school. Visit the career-planning and job placement offices on campus.

Once you have a possible career choice in mind, run some informal tests to see if it will work for you. For example:

> *Your life purpose is like the guidance system for a rocket. It keeps the plan on target while revealing a path for soaring to the heights.*

- Contact people who are actually doing the job you're researching and ask them what it's like (an *informational interview*).

- Choose an internship or volunteer position in a field that interests you.

- Get a part-time or summer job in your career field.

The people you meet through these experiences are possible sources of recommendations, referrals, and employment in the future.

Career planning is not a once-and-for-all proposition. Rather, career plans are made to be changed and refined as you gain new information about yourself and the world. Career planning never ends. If your present career no longer feels right, you can choose again—no matter what stage of life you're in. The process is the same, whether you're choosing your first career or your fifth.[2]

For more career planning strategies, visit the Houghton Mifflin Career Resource Center at

masterstudent.college.hmco.com

INVENTORY YOUR SKILLS

This exercise about discovering your skills includes three steps. Before you begin, gather at least 100 3x5 cards and a pen or pencil. Allow about one hour to complete the exercise.

Step 1

Recall your activities during the past week or month.

Write down as many activities as you can, listing each one on a separate 3x5 card. Include work-related activities, school activities, and hobbies. Some of your cards might read "washed dishes," "tuned up my car," or "tutored a French class."

In addition to daily activities, recall any rewards you've received or recognition of your achievements during the past year. Examples include scholarship awards, athletic awards, or recognitions for volunteer work. Again, list the activities that were involved.

Spend 20 minutes on this step, listing all of the activities you can recall.

Step 2

Next, look over your activity cards. Then take another 20 minutes to list any specialized knowledge or procedures needed to complete those activities. These are your *content skills*. For example, tutoring a French class requires a working knowledge of that language. Tuning a car requires knowing how to adjust a car's timing and replace spark plugs. You could list several content skills for any one activity. Write each skill on a separate card and label it "Content."

Step 3

Go over your activity cards one more time. Look for examples of *transferable skills*. For instance, giving a speech or working as a salesperson in a computer store requires the ability to persuade people. That's a transferable skill. Tuning a car means that you can attend to details and troubleshoot. Tutoring in French requires teaching, listening, and speaking skills.

Write each of your transferable skills on a separate card.

Congratulations—you now have a detailed picture of your skills. Keep your lists of content and transferable skills on hand when writing your résumé, preparing for job interviews, and other career-planning tasks. As you think of new skills, add them to the lists.

journal entry

Discovery/Intention Statement

Now that you have a detailed picture of your skills, think about your intended career choice. Take a minute to reflect on the skills that you already have in relation to your career plan.

I discovered that I . . .

Now list three specific transferable skills you want to continue to develop in school that will help you prepare for the workplace.

I intend to . . .

Ways to learn about careers

To discover the full range of jobs that exist in our society, you can turn to many sources. These include friends, family members, teachers, classmates, coworkers—and anyone else who's ever held a job. Also check out the following sources of career information. They can lead you to more.

Publications. Visit the career planning and job hunting sections in bookstores and libraries. Look for books, magazines, videos, and other nonprint materials related to career planning. Libraries may subscribe to trade journals and industry newsletters.

Career counseling. Your school may offer career counseling as well as links to similar services in the off-campus community. Private consultants and companies offer career counseling for a fee. Ask around to find someone who's seen a career counselor and get some recommendations.

Before you pay for career counseling, find out exactly what kind of help you'll get and how much it will cost. Read contracts carefully before you sign. Talk directly to a career counselor rather than a salesperson, and see if you can get permission to contact some of the counselor's former clients.

Group sessions led by career counselors are valuable because you get to hear about the problems that other people are facing and work together to create solutions.

The Internet. Through your own searching and suggestions from others, you can find useful Web sites devoted to job hunting and career planning. One place to start is JobHuntersBible.com, which includes links to sites screened by Richard Bolles, author of *What Color Is Your Parachute?* It's online at **http://www.jobhuntersbible.com**. Bolles organizes this site around five ways that the Internet can be used in career planning and job hunting:

- To search for job openings ("want ads") posted online
- To post your résumé online
- To get career counseling
- To research potential careers and places that you might like to work
- To make contacts with people who can provide information or help you get a job interview

Also visit the Occupational Information Network (O*NET) site posted by the U.S. Department of Labor at **http://online.onetcenter.org**. Here you'll find information on hundreds of jobs that you can search by using keywords or browsing a complete list. You'll also find Skills Search, an online tool that helps you list your skills and then matches the list with potential jobs.

Another site that may interest you is CareerOneStop at **http://www.careeronestop.org**. It includes America's Job Bank (where you can search job openings and post your résumé), America's Career InfoNet (information on wages and employment trends), and America's Service Locator (a way to find career planning and job hunting services in your local area).

Of course, your searching may turn up hundreds of other sites. Evaluate them carefully.

Organizations. Professional associations exist for people in almost any career—from the American Institute of Certified Public Accountants to the American Association of Zookeepers. One function of these associations is to publicize career options and job openings of interest to their members. Search the Internet with the key words *professional associations* and follow the links that interest you. Consider joining organizations that interest you. Many offer student rates.

Government agencies at all levels—from local employment agencies to the U.S. Department of Labor—can assist you with learning about the world of work. Search the government listings in your local Yellow Pages under *employment* and *job placement*.

Trade unions, chambers of commerce, and branches of the armed forces are additional sources of information.

Elected representatives. One duty of your congressional representatives, senators, and city council members and school board members is to help create a thriving work force. Contact these people for career planning and job hunting services in your community. ⊠

CREATE YOUR CAREER PLAN—NOW

Write your career plan. Now. Get started with the process of career planning, even if you're not sure where to begin. Your response to this exercise can be just a rough draft of your plan, which you can revise and rewrite many times. The point is to start getting your ideas in writing.

Ultimately, the format of your plan is up to you. You could include many details, such as the next job title you'd like to have, the courses required for your major, and other training that you want to complete. You could list companies to research and people that could hire you. You could also include target dates to complete each of these tasks. Another option is to represent your plan visually through flow charts, timelines, mind maps, or drawings.

For now, experiment with career planning by completing the following sentences. Use the space below and continue on additional paper as needed:

The career I choose for now is . . .

_____

_____

_____

_____

_____

_____

_____

The three major steps that will guide me to this career are . . .

1. _____

_____

_____

_____

2. _____

_____

_____

_____

_____

_____

_____

3. _____

_____

_____

_____

_____

_____

The three immediate steps I will take to pursue this career are . . .

1. _____

_____

_____

_____

2. _____

_____

_____

_____

_____

3. _____

_____

_____

_____

_____

Stockbyte

Test the waters—jump into the job market

Do informational interviews. Talk to people who actually do the kind of work that you'd like to do. Schedule an informational interview to ask them about their work. With their permission, go to their job sites. Spend time with them during a workday. Hang around. Ask questions.

To get the most out of an informational interview, first research the career field you've chosen and the particular business or organization you're going to visit. For example, before you interview a mutual fund manager, be sure you know what a mutual fund is. Also find some basic information about the manager's company, such as its general investment policies and recent financial history.

When scheduling an informational interview, make it clear that your purpose is not job hunting but career research. If you set up an informational interview and then use the occasion to ask for a job, you send mixed messages and risk making a negative impression.

Before your interview, prepare a list of questions, such as:

- How did you enter this line of work?
- What are your major tasks and responsibilities?
- What kind of problems and decisions do you regularly face?
- What do you like most—and least—about your job?
- What changes are occurring in this field?
- What are the salary ranges and opportunities for employment and promotion?

- How can I effectively prepare to work in this field?

While informational interviews are often one-time events, they can also involve multiple visits to several people at the same work site. You might even spend several days or weeks following people on the job. Such extended experience is sometimes referred to as *job-shadowing* or an *externship*.

Volunteer. Volunteering offers another path to work experience that you can list on your résumé. To gain the most from this experience, research and choose volunteer positions as carefully as you would a full-time, salaried job. Identify organizations that are doing the kind of work that excites you. Contact them and ask for the person who supervises volunteers. Then schedule a face-to-face meeting to find out more.

Work. To find out more about working, go to work. Beyond gaining experience, you'll get insights that can change your life. A short-term job assignment can help you define your current skills, develop new ones, refine your career plan, develop contacts, and even lead to doing work that you love.

Cooperative education programs offer one option. These programs combine specific classroom assignments with carefully supervised work experience. In addition to getting academic credit, most "co-op" students get paid and function as productive employees.

Other options include freelancing and "temping." Rather than becoming an employee, a freelancer works for organizations on specific projects. Rates of payment, due dates, and other details are specified by contract. Freelancers typically work "off site" at their own office. A temporary worker ("temp") also works on a contract basis but reports to an organization's work site.

Share the process with others. Consider forming a career planning group. Working in groups allows you to give and receive career coaching. Group members can brainstorm options for each other's careers, research the work world, share information of mutual interest, trade contacts, and pair up for informational interviews. This is one way to raise your energy level for career planning.

Taking part in a group can open you up to your dream career. Others can point out ideas and information you've overlooked. They may alert you to opportunities you never considered or skills you were not aware you had. Working with such a group gives you a firm foundation for networking—building relationships that can lead directly to a job offer. ✍

Gaining experience as an intern

Wonderfile

One way to start your career path is an internship. Internships blend classroom learning with on-the-job experience and let you put your transferable skills into action. As an intern, you work in a job that relates directly to your career interests. Internships often offer academic credit. Some involve paid positions, while other internships are volunteer opportunities. Interns usually prepare for their assignments by completing courses in a specific field.

Note that internships may be called by other names. You might talk to people who use the terms *co-op experience, practicum, externship, field experience*, and *internship* synonymously. The key is to find a program that fits with your courses, your career interests, and your schedule.

Develop job skills now. Through an internship you develop skills specific to your field—as well as transferable skills that you can apply to other jobs in the same field (or even a different field). For instance, you might perform administrative duties that give you professional experience in fielding phone calls, writing correspondence, and serving customers.

Internships are also ways to learn about organizational culture, hone your skills at coping with office politics, and add contacts to your job-hunting network. These are key aspects of the work world that you experience by getting outside the classroom.

Find internships. To find an internship, make an appointment with someone at the career planning and job placement office on your campus. There you can connect with employers in your area who are looking for interns. You will likely submit a résumé and cover letter explaining your career interests. This is valuable in itself as experience in applying for jobs.

You can also locate organizations that interest you and contact them directly about internships. Even companies that do not have formal internship programs may accept applications.

Other suggestions to keep in mind:

- *Start early.* Think two or three terms ahead. During a fall semester, for example, start searching for internships for the spring or summer.

- *Network.* Talk to your friends, parents, family, neighbors, and instructors to discover if they know about internships for you. Mention your career interests and ask for suggestions.

- *Surf the Net.* Use Internet search engines to find employment or internship listings. Research organizations that interest you and contact them via e-mail.

- *Use the library.* Ask a reference librarian to help you find internship guides. Some look like college catalogs, listing popular positions with key contacts, due dates for applications, and information about getting paid.

Cultivate contacts. If the internship offers an experience aligned with your career goals and skills, your role as an intern may help lead to permanent job offers following graduation. Keep in touch with the people you meet through internships. They may be working at another company when you graduate and offer help to get your foot in the door.

Reflect on your internship. After you have completed your internship, review your experience. Write Discovery Statements about what worked well and what you would like to improve.

Internships offer a great way to test a career choice—even if you find out that you don't like a particular field or job. Discovering what you do not want in a career can be just as valuable as gaining any type of work experience. You can benefit from ruling out an inappropriate career choice early on—especially if it involves a major with a lot of required courses.

Even if you find that the workplace setting or tasks involved in your internship did not meet your expectations, you can create a list of criteria that you want your next work experience to include. Be sure to incorporate the skills and experiences from any internship on your résumé—no matter what career field or job you eventually choose. ✹

REVISIT YOUR GOALS

One powerful way to achieve any goal is to assess periodically your progress in meeting it. This is especially important with long-term goals—those that can take years to achieve.

Take your long-term goals and write them in the space below.

I intend to . . .

_____

_____

_____

_____

_____

Next, check in with yourself. How do you feel about this goal? Does it still excite your interest and enthusiasm? On a scale of 1 to 10, how committed are you to achieving this goal? Describe your level of commitment in the space below.

I discovered that I . . .

_____

_____

_____

If your level of commitment is 5 or less, you might want to drop the goal and replace it with a new one. Letting go of one goal creates space in your life to set and achieve a new one.

If you're committed to the goal you just listed, consider whether you're still on track to achieve it. Have you met any of the short-term goals related to this long-term goal? If so, list your completed goals in the space below.

_____

_____

_____

_____

_____

Before going on, take a minute to congratulate yourself and celebrate your success.

Finally, consider any adjustments you'd like to make to your plan. For example, write additional short-term or mid-term goals that will take you closer to your long-term goal. Or cross out any goals that you no longer deem necessary. Make a copy of your current plan in the space below.

Long-term goal (to achieve within your lifetime):

_____

_____

_____

_____

Supporting mid-term goals (to achieve in one to five years):

_____

_____

_____

_____

Supporting short-term goals (to achieve within the coming year):

_____

_____

_____

_____

Financial planning

Meeting your money goals

Ryan McVay/PhotoDisc Green/Getty Images

Some people shy away from setting financial goals. They think that money is a complicated subject.

Yet most money problems result from spending more than is available. It's that simple, even though often we do everything we can to make the problem much more complicated.

The solution also is simple: *Don't spend more than you have.* If you are spending more money than you have, increase your income, decrease your spending, or do both. This idea has never won a Nobel Prize in economics, but you won't go broke applying it.

Starting today, you can take three simple steps to financial independence:

- Tell the truth about how much money you have and how much you spend.
- Make a commitment to spend no more than you have.
- Begin saving money.

If you do these three things consistently, you could meet your monetary goals and even experience financial independence. This does not necessarily mean having all of the money you could ever desire. Rather, you can be free from money worries by living within your means. Soon you will control money instead of letting money control you.

Increase money in

For many of us, making more money is the most appealing way to fix a broken budget. This approach is reasonable—and it has a potential problem: When our income increases, most of us continue to spend more than we make. Our money problems persist, even at higher incomes. You can avoid this dilemma by managing your expenses no matter how much money you make.

There are several ways to increase your income while you go to school. One of the most obvious ways is to get a job. You could also apply for scholarships and grants. You might borrow money, inherit it, or receive it as a gift. You could sell property, collect income from investments, or use your savings. Other options—such as lotteries and gambling casinos—pose obvious risks. Stick to making money the old-fashioned way: Earn it.

If you work while you go to school, you can earn more than money. Working helps you gain experience, establish references, and expand your contacts in the community. Doing well at a work-study position or an internship while you're in school can also help you land a good job after you graduate.

Regular income, even at a lower wage scale, can make a big difference. Look at your monthly budget to see how it would be affected if you worked just 15 hours a week (times 4 weeks a month) for $8 an hour.

If you are currently looking for a job, make a list of several places that you would like to work. Include places that have advertised job openings and those that haven't. Then go to each place on your list and tell someone that you would like a job. This will yield more results than depending on the want ads alone.

The people you speak to might say that there isn't a job available, or that the job is filled. That's OK. Ask to see the person in charge of hiring and tell him that you want to be considered for future job openings. Then ask when you can check back.

Keep your job in perspective. If your current job relates to your major or your career field, great. If it is meaningful and contributes to society, great. If it involves working with people you love and respect, fantastic. If not—well, remember that almost any job can help you reach your career goals. Any job offers a chance to develop a skill that you can transfer to the next career of your choice.

Decrease money out

To control your expenses, you do not have to live like a miser, pinching pennies and saving used dental floss. There are many ways to decrease the amount of money you spend and still enjoy life. Consider the ideas that follow.

Look to the big-ticket items. Your choices about which school to attend, what car to buy, and where to live can save you tens of thousands of dollars. When you look for places to cut expenses, start with the items that cost the most. For example, there are several ways to keep your housing costs reasonable. Sometimes a place a little farther from your school or a smaller house will be much less expensive. You

can cut your housing costs in half by finding a roommate. Also look for opportunities to house-sit rather than paying rent. Some homeowners will even pay a responsible person to live in their house when they are away.

Look to the small-ticket items. Decreasing the money you spend on small purchases can help you balance your budget. A three-dollar cappuccino tastes good, but the amount that some people spend on such treats over the course of a year could give anyone the jitters.

Monitor money out. Each month, review your checkbook, receipts, and other financial records. Sort your expenditures into major categories such as school expenses, housing, personal debt, groceries, eating out, and entertainment. At the end of the month, total up how much you spend in each category. You might be surprised. Once you discover the truth, it might be easier to decrease unnecessary spending.

Create a budget. When you have a budget and stick to it, you don't have to worry about whether you can pay your bills on time. The basic idea is to project how much money is coming in and how much is going out and to make sure that those two amounts balance.

Creating two kinds of budgets is even more useful. A monthly budget includes regularly recurring income and expense items such as paychecks, food costs, and housing. A long-range budget includes unusual monetary transactions such as annual dividends, grants, and tuition payments that occur only a few times a year. With an eye to the future, you can make realistic choices about money today.

Do comparison shopping. Prices vary dramatically on just about anything you want to buy. You can clip coupons and wait for sales or shop around at secondhand stores, mill outlets, or garage sales. When you first go shopping, leave your checkbook and credit cards at home, a sure way to control impulse buying. Look at all of the possibilities, then make your decision later when you don't feel pressured. To save time, money, and gas, you can also search the Internet for sites that compare prices on items.

Use public transportation or car pools. Aside from tuition, a car can be the biggest financial burden in a student's budget. The purchase price is often only the tip of the iceberg. Be sure to consider the cost of parking, insurance, repairs, gas, maintenance, and tires. When you add up all of those items, you might find it makes more sense to car-pool or to take the bus or a cab instead.

Notice what you spend on "fun." Blowing your money on fun is fun. It is also a quick way to ruin your budget. When you spend money on entertainment, ask yourself what the benefits will be and whether you could get the same benefits for less money. You can read or borrow magazines for free at the library. Most libraries also loan CDs, DVDs, and videotapes at no cost. Student councils often sponsor activities, such as dances and music performances, for which there is no fee. Schools with sports facilities set aside times when students can use them for free. Meeting your friends for a pick-up basketball game at the gym can be more fun than meeting at a bar, where there is a cover charge.

Free entertainment is everywhere. However, it usually isn't advertised, so you'll have to search it out. Start with your school bulletin boards and local newspapers.

Redefine money. Think of money as what you accept in exchange for the time and energy that you put into working. When you take this view of money, you might naturally find yourself being more selective about how often you spend it and what you spend it on. It's not just cash you're putting on the line—it's your life energy.

Remember that education is worth it . . .

A college degree is one of the safest and most worthwhile investments you can make. Money invested in land, gold, oil, or stocks can be lost, but your education will last a lifetime. It can't rust, corrode, break down, or wear out. Once you have an education, it becomes a permanent part of you.

Think about all of the services and resources that your tuition money buys: academic advising; access to the student health center and counseling services; career planning and job placement offices; athletic, arts, and entertainment events; and a student center where you can meet people and socialize. If you live on campus, you get a place to stay with meals provided. By the way, you also get to attend classes.

In the long run, education pays off in increased income, job promotions, career satisfaction, and more creative use of your leisure time. These are benefits that you can sustain for a lifetime.

. . . And you can pay for it

Most students can afford higher education. If you demonstrate financial need, you can usually get financial aid. In general, financial need equals the cost of your schooling minus the amount that you can reasonably be expected to pay. Receiving financial assistance has little to

do with "being poor." Your prospects for aid depend greatly on the costs of the school you attend.

Financial aid includes money you don't pay back (grants and scholarships), money you do pay back (low-interest loans), and work-study programs that land you a job while you're in school. Most students receive aid awards that include several of these elements. Visit the financial aid office on campus to find out what's available.

In applying for financial aid, you'll need to fill out a form called the Free Application for Federal Student Aid (FAFSA). You can access it on the World Wide Web at **http://www.fafsa.ed.gov**. For links to a wealth of information about financial aid in general, access **http://www.students.gov**. Create a master plan—a long-term budget listing how much you need to complete your education and where you plan to get the money. Having a plan for paying for your entire education makes completing your degree work a more realistic possibility.

Once you've lined up financial aid, keep it flowing. Find out the requirements for renewing your loans, grants, and scholarships.

Create money for the future

You don't have to wait until you finish school to begin saving and investing. You can start now, even if you are in debt and living on a diet of macaroni.

Start saving. Saving is one of the most effective ways to reach your money goals. Aim to save at least 10 percent of your monthly take-home pay. If you can save more, that's even better.

One possible goal is to have savings equal to at least six months of living expenses. Build this nest egg first as a cushion for financial emergencies. Then save for major, long-term expenses.

Put your money into insured savings accounts, money market funds, savings bonds, or certificates of deposit. These are low-risk options that you can immediately turn into cash. Even a small amount of money set aside each month can grow rapidly. The sooner you begin to save, the more opportunity your money has to grow. Time allows you to take advantage of the power of compound interest.

Invest after you have a cushion. Remember that investing is risky. Invest only money that you can afford to lose. Consider something safe, such as Treasury securities (bills, notes, and bonds backed by the federal government), bonds, no-load mutual funds, or blue chip stocks.

Avoid taking a friend's advice on how to invest your hard-earned money. Be wary, too, of advice from someone who has something to sell, such as a stockbroker or a realtor. See your banker or an independent certified financial planner instead.

Save on insurance. Once you have insured your health or your life, it's usually possible to stay insured, even if you develop a major illness. For that reason, insuring yourself now is a wise investment for the future.

Shop around for insurance. Benefits, premiums, exclusions, and terms vary considerably from policy to policy, so study each one carefully. Buy health, auto, and life insurance with high deductibles to save on premiums. Also ask about safe driver, nonsmoker, or good student discounts.

Be careful with contracts. Before you sign anything, read the fine print. If you are confused, ask questions and keep asking until you are no longer confused. After you sign a contract, policy, or lease, read the entire document again. If you think you have signed something that you will regret, back out quickly and get your release in writing. Purchase contracts in many states are breakable if you act quickly.

Use credit wisely. If you don't already have one, you can begin to establish a credit rating now. Borrow a small amount of money and pay it back on time. Also pay your bills on time. Avoid the temptation to let big companies wait for their money. Develop a good credit rating so that you can borrow large amounts of money if you need to.

Before you take out a loan to buy a big-ticket item, find out what that item will be worth *after* you buy it. A brand-new $20,000 car might be worth only $15,000 the minute you drive it off the lot. To maintain your net worth, don't borrow any more than $15,000 to buy the car.

If you're in trouble. If you find yourself in over your financial head, get specific data about your present situation. Find out exactly how much money you owe, earn, and spend on a monthly basis. If you can't pay your bills in full, be honest with creditors. Many will allow you to pay off a large debt in small installments. Also consider credit counseling with professional advisors who can help you straighten out your financial problems. You can locate these people through your campus or community phone directories. ✉

→ Places to find money for school

- Grants: Pell Grants, Supplemental Educational Opportunity Grants, state government grants

- Scholarships from federal, state, and private organizations

- Loan programs: Perkins Loans, Stafford Loans, Supplemental Loans, Consolidation Loans, Ford Direct Student Loans, and PLUS (Parent Loans for Undergraduate Students)

- Part-time or full-time jobs, including work-study programs

- Military programs: funds from the Veterans Administration and financial aid programs for active military personnel

- Programs to train the unemployed, such as JTPA (Job Training Partnership Act) and WIN (Work Incentive)

- Company assistance programs

- Social security payments

- Relatives

- Personal savings

- Selling a personal possession, such as a car, boat, piano, or house

Note: Programs change constantly. In some cases, money is limited and application deadlines are critical. Be sure to get the most current information from the financial aid office at your school.

desk of ...

from the

MICHAEL TUCKER,
CONSTRUCTION FOREMAN:

Raising a family, holding a full-time job, and attending college part-time was initially a financial burden on my household. My academic advisor suggested I meet with a counselor from the financial aid office. Since that time, I have created a budget that is manageable, and I've even been able to put away some money for my children's education.

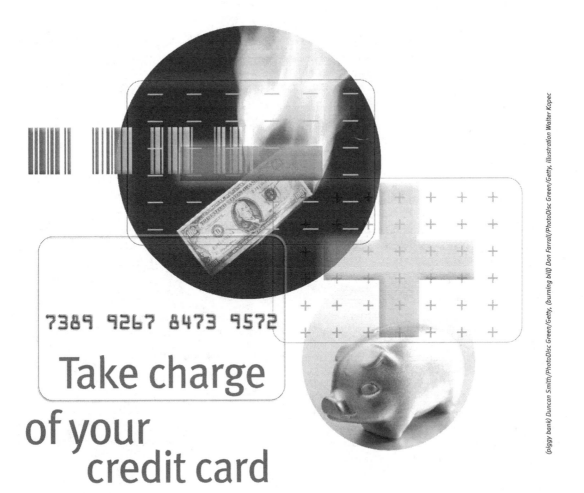

7389 9267 8473 9572

Take charge of your credit card

A credit card is compact and convenient. That piece of plastic seems to promise peace of mind. Low on cash this month? Just whip out your card, slide it across the counter, and relax. Your worries are over—that is, until you get the bill.

Credit cards often come with a hefty interest rate, sometimes as high as 27 percent. That can be over one-fifth of your credit card bill. Imagine working five days a week and getting paid for only four: You'd lose one-fifth of your income. Likewise, when people rely on high-interest credit cards to get by from month to month, they lose one-fifth of their monthly payments to interest charges. In a 2000 survey by Nellie Mae, a student loan corporation, 78 percent of undergraduate students had credit cards. Their average credit card debt was $2,748. Suppose that a student with this debt used a card with an annual percentage rate of 18 percent. Also suppose that he pays only the minimum balance due each month. He'll be making payments for 15 years and will pay an additional $2,748 in interest fees.

Credit cards do offer potential benefits. Getting a card is one way to establish a credit record. Many cards offer rewards, such as frequent flier miles and car rental discounts. Your monthly statement also offers a way to keep track of your expenses.

Used wisely, credit cards can help us become conscious of what we spend. Used unwisely, they can leave us with a load of debt that takes decades to repay. That load can seriously delay other goals—paying off student loans, financing a new car, buying a home, or saving for retirement.

Use the following three steps to take control of your credit cards before they take control of you. Write these steps on a 3x5 card and don't leave home without it.

Do a First Step about money. See your credit card usage as an opportunity to take a financial First Step. If you rely on credit cards to make ends meet every month, tell the truth about that. If you typically charge up to the maximum limit and pay just the minimum balance due each month, tell the truth about that, too.

Write Discovery Statements focusing on what doesn't work—and what does work—about the way you use credit cards. Follow up with Intention Statements regarding steps you can take to use your cards differently. Then take action. Your bank account will directly benefit.

Scrutinize credit card offers. Beware of cards offering low interest rates. These rates are often only temporary. After a few months, they could double or triple. Also look for annual fees and other charges buried in the fine print.

To simplify your financial life and take charge of your credit, consider using only one card. Choose one with no annual fee and the lowest interest rate. Don't be swayed by offers of free T-shirts or coffee mugs. Consider the bottom line and be selective.

Pay off the balance each month. Keep track of how much you spend with credit cards each month. Then save an equal amount in cash. That way, you can pay off the card balance each month and avoid interest charges. Following this suggestion alone might transform your financial life.

If you do accumulate a large credit card balance, ask your bank about a "bill-payer" loan with a lower interest rate. You can use this loan to pay off your credit cards. Then promise yourself never to accumulate credit card debt again. ✖

---

desk of ...

from the

TOMÁS RAMOS,
PHARMACY TECHNICIAN:

Education by the hour is one of the exercises that opened my eyes to getting the most out of my education. Each hour that I am at school or studying is also time away from the workplace where I could be earning money. I discovered that not attending class just to be with my friends was a real mistake. I intend to be in class on time and pay full attention to get the most out of my education.

---

exercise

EDUCATION BY THE HOUR

Determine exactly what it costs you to go to school. Fill in the blanks below using totals for a semester, quarter, or whatever term system your school uses.

Note: Include only the costs that relate directly to going to school. For example, under "Transportation," list only the amount that you pay for gas to drive back and forth to school—not the total amount you spend on gas for a semester.

Tuition	$_____
Books	$_____
Fees	$_____
Transportation	$_____
Clothing	$_____
Food	$_____
Housing	$_____
Entertainment	$_____
Other (such as insurance, medical, childcare)	$_____
Subtotal	$_____
Salary you could earn per term if you weren't in school	$_____
Total (A)	$_____

Now figure out how many classes you attend in one term. This is the number of your scheduled class periods per week multiplied by the number of weeks in your school term. Put that figure below:

Total (B) _____

Divide the **Total (B)** into the **Total (A)** and put that amount here:

$_____

This is what it costs you to go to one class one time.

On a separate sheet of paper, describe your responses to discovering this figure. Also list anything you will do differently as a result of knowing the hourly cost of your education.

Using technology to manage time and money

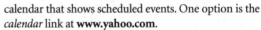

When it comes to managing your time and financial resources, your computer can become as valuable as your calendar and your checkbook. In addition, gaining experience with time management, project planning, and financial software now—while you are in school—can give you additional skills to list on your résumé. Get started with the following options.

Set and meet goals. Take some time to write out your goals—long-term, mid-term, and short-term—and key them into a word processing file or database file. Open up this file every day to review your goals and track your progress toward meeting them.

Since success hinges on keeping goals fresh in your memory, print out a copy of your goals file each time you update it. You might wish to post your printout in a visible place, such as in your study area, on your refrigerator, or even next to a bathroom mirror.

Save yourself a trip or phone call. The Web offers sites that allow you to manage your bank account, get stock quotes, place classified ads for items you want to sell, book airline reservations, and buy almost anything. Use these sites to reduce shopping time, eliminate errands, and get discounts on purchases.

Also employ technology to decrease phone time and avoid long-distance charges. Use e-mail and real time online chatting software to stay in contact with friends, family members, classmates, and teachers.

Manage calendars, contacts, and projects. Software can help you create and edit calendars and to-do lists on your computer. Typically, these applications also allow you to store contact information—mailing addresses, phone numbers, and e-mail addresses—for the key people in your life. To find such products, search the Web using the keywords *contact management, project management, time management,* and *software.*

Also use your computer to prevent the snafus that can result when you want to coordinate your calendar with those of several other people. This is often a necessity in completing group projects. Consider creating an area on the Web where group members can post messages, share files, and access an online calendar that shows scheduled events. One option is the *calendar* link at **www.yahoo.com**.

Crunch numbers and manage money. Many students can benefit from crunching numbers on a computer with spreadsheets such as Excel. This type of computer software allows you to create and alter budgets of any size. By plugging in numbers based on assumptions about the future, you can quickly create many scenarios for future income and expenses. Quicken and similar products include spreadsheets and other features that can help you manage personal and organizational finances.

Employ a personal digital assistant (PDA). These devices—also called *palmtops* or *pocket PCs*—are handheld computers designed to replace paper-based calendars and planning systems. Many PDAs are small enough to fit in a pocket or purse. You can use them to list appointments and view your schedule in a daily, weekly, or monthly format. If you have a recurring event, such as a meeting that takes place at the same time every week, you can just enter it once and watch it show up automatically on your PDA.

Using a PDA, you can also take notes, create contact lists, manage to-do lists, and keep track of personal expenses. Capabilities for connecting to the Internet and sending e-mail are becoming standard features as well. In addition, PDAs come with software for exchanging files with a personal computer. This allows you to store essential information—such as appointments, to-do lists, and contacts—in a form that's even more portable than a laptop computer. ✉

Choose your conversations

This chapter, in particular, aims to engage you in a conversation about career planning. By doing the exercises and journal entries in this chapter and discussing the articles in class, you choose to make this conversation come alive.

The idea of referring to a book as a *conversation* might seem strange to you. If so, consider that conversations can exist in many forms. One involves people talking out loud to each other. At other times, the conversation takes place inside our own heads, and we call it thinking. In this sense, we are even having a conversation when we read a magazine or a book, watch television or a movie, or write a letter or a report. These observations have three implications that wind their way through every aspect of our lives.

Conversations exercise incredible power over what we think, feel, and do. We become our conversations. They shape our attitudes, our decisions, our opinions, our emotions, and our actions. Each of these is primarily the result of what we say over and over again, to ourselves and to others. If you want clues as to what a person will be like tomorrow, listen to what she's talking about today.

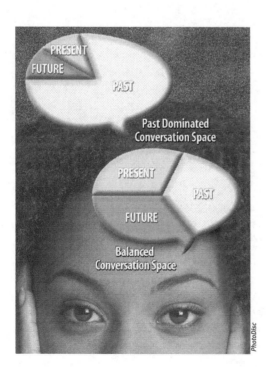

Past Dominated
Conversation Space

Balanced
Conversation Space

PhotoDisc

Conversation is constant

Given that conversations are so powerful, it's amazing that few people act on this fact. Most of us swim in a constant sea of conversations, almost none of which we carefully and thoughtfully choose.

Consider how this works. It begins when we pick up the morning paper. The articles on the front page invite us to a conversation about current events. The advertisements start up a conversation about fantastic products for us to buy. They talk about hundreds of ways for us to part with our money.

That's not all. If we flip on the radio or television, or if we surf the Web, millions of other conversations await us. Thanks to modern digital technology, many of these conversations take place in surround sound, high-resolution images, and living color 24 hours each day.

Something happens when we tune in to conversation in any of its forms. We give someone else permission to dramatically influence our thoughts—the conversation in our heads. It's possible to let this happen dozens of times each day without realizing it.

You have a choice

We can choose our conversations. Certain conversations create real value for us. They give us fuel for reaching our goals. Others distract us from what we want. They might even create lasting unhappiness and frustration.

We can choose more of the conversations that exhilarate and sustain us. Sometimes we can't control the outward circumstances of our lives. Yet no matter what happens, we can retain the right to choose our conversations.

Suppose that you meet with your supervisor at work to ask for help in writing an e-mail that will go out to members of a project team. She launches into a tirade about your writing skills. This presents you with several options. One is to talk about what a jerk the supervisor is and give up on the idea of learning to write well. Another

If you want clues as to what a person will be like tomorrow, listen to what she's talking about today.

option is to refocus the conversation on what you can do to improve your writing skills, such as working with a writing coach or taking a class in writing for the workplace. These two sets of conversations will have vastly different consequences for your success.

The conversations you have are dramatically influenced by the people you associate with. If you want to change your attitudes about almost anything—prejudice, politics, religion, humor—choose your conversations by choosing your community. Spend time with people who speak about and live consistently with the attitudes you value. Use conversations to change habits. Use conversations to create new options in your life.

Consider choosing *not* to participate in certain conversations. Sometimes we find ourselves in conversations that are not empowering—gripe sessions, gossip, and the like. That's a time for us to switch the conversation channel. It can be as simple as changing the topic, politely offering a new point of view, or excusing ourselves and walking away.

Conversations promote success

When we choose our conversations, we discover a tool of unsurpassed power. Career planning is simply a sustained conversation about creating your life's work—and the life of your dreams. Conversation has the capacity to remake our thoughts—and thus our lives. It's as simple as choosing the next article you read or the next topic you discuss with a friend.

Start choosing your conversations and watch what happens.

---

exercise

CREATE A SUPPORT TEAM

To fuel your energy for career planning, create your own support team.

Begin by listing the names of at least five people with whom you can share your frustrations and successes in career planning and job hunting. These can be friends, family members, coworkers, or classmates. Include each person's name, telephone number, and e-mail address. Begin your list in the space below.

From this list, recruit people to be on your support team. Tell each team member your goals and intended actions. Ask them to help in holding you accountable to your plan. Keep touching base with each member of your team and support them in return.

Keep adding to your support team. Post the most current list of members in a conspicuous place. Then use it.

Contributing:
The art of
selfishness

© Corbis Images/ PictureQuest

This chapter is about contributing to yourself—about taking care of yourself, being selfish, and fulfilling your own needs. The techniques and suggestions in these pages focus on ways to get what you want out of school and out of life.

One of the results of all this successful selfishness is the capacity for contributing, for giving to others. Contributing is what's left to do when you're satisfied, when your needs are fulfilled—and it completes the process.

People who are satisfied with life can share that satisfaction with others. It is not easy to contribute to another person's joy until you experience joy yourself. The same is true for love. When people are filled with love, they can more easily contribute love to others.

One way to transform your conversation about career planning is to look at work as a form of contribution. Through your skills and effort, you offer something to the world. You help to create a product or service that can generate value for other people. The work that you do can contribute in some way to reducing human suffering and helping people to create happiness, health, love, and wealth.

Our interdependence calls for contributing. Every day we depend on contributing. We stake our lives on the compassion of other people. When we drive, we depend on others for our lives. If a driver in an oncoming lane should cross into our own lane, we might die. We also depend upon the sensibilities of world leaders for our safety. People everywhere are growing more interdependent. A plunge in the U.S. stock market reverberates in markets across the planet. A decrease in oil prices gives businesses everywhere a shot in the arm. A nuclear war would ignore national boundaries and devastate life on the planet. Successful arms negotiations allow all people to sleep a little easier.

In this interdependent world, there is no such thing as win/lose. If others lose, their loss directly affects us. If we lose, it is more difficult to contribute to others.

The only way to win and to get what we want in life is for others to win, also.

A caution. The idea of contributing is not the same as knowing what is best for other people. We can't know. There are people, of course, who go around "fixing" others: "I know what you need. Here, do it my way." That is not contributing. It often causes more harm than good and can result in dependence on the part of the person we are "helping."

True contributing occurs only after you find out what another person wants or needs and then determine that you can lovingly support his having it.

How you can begin contributing. The world will welcome your gifts of time, money, and talent. The advantages of contributing are clear. When we contribute, the whole human family benefits in a tangible way. Close to home, contributing often means getting involved with other people. This is one way to "break the ice" in a new community and meet people with interests similar to your own.

When you've made the decision to contribute, the next step is knowing how. There are ways to contribute in your immediate surroundings. Visit a neighbor, take a family member to a movie, or offer to tutor a roommate. Look for ways you can contribute by volunteering. An additional benefit of volunteer work is that it offers a way to explore possible career choices. Consider the following organizations, for starters.

Sierra Club, Greenpeace, Audubon Society, World Wildlife Fund, and similar organizations are dedicated to protecting the environment and endangered species.

Amnesty International investigates human rights violations. It assists people who are imprisoned or tortured for peacefully expressing their points of view. You can participate in letter-writing campaigns.

Museums and art galleries need interested people to conduct tours and provide supervision. Performing arts organizations, such as local theater groups or ballet companies, are always in need of volunteers for everything from set decoration to ticket sales.

Hospitals and hospice programs often depend on volunteer help to supplement patient care provided by the professional staff. Nursing homes welcome visitors who are willing to spend time listening to and talking with residents. Most communities have volunteer-based programs for people living with HIV infection or AIDS that provide daily hot meals to men, women, and children too ill to cook for themselves. Political parties, candidates, and special interest groups need volunteers to stuff envelopes, gather petition signatures, and distribute

It is not easy to contribute to another person's joy until you experience joy yourself.

literature. The American Red Cross provides disaster relief. Local community care centers use volunteers to help feed homeless people.

Service organizations such as Jaycees, Kiwanis, Lions, American Association of University Women, Business and Professional Women, and Rotary want members who are willing to serve others.

Tutoring centers offer opportunities for competent students to help non-English-speaking people, grade school and high school students, and illiterate adults. Churches of all denominations want volunteers to assist with projects for the community and beyond. World hunger groups want you to help feed starving people and to inform all of us about the problems of malnutrition, food spoilage, and starvation. These groups include Oxfam America, CARE, and The Hunger Project.

Considering the full scope of our international problems reminds us that there are plenty of opportunities for contributing. For instance, there are still enough nuclear warheads on the planet to end human life. And according to the *Human Development Report 2003*, commissioned by the United Nations, 1,242 million people in the world live on less than one dollar per day.[3]

If they remain unused, the techniques and strategies discussed will make no difference in all this. However, *you* can make a difference. By using these techniques to work with others, you can choose a new future for our planet. ⬛

desk of . . .

from the

MELISSA SILVESTRI,
SPECIAL EVENTS ASSOCIATE:

I had participated in a charity bike ride that benefited my organization. After working on fundraising for this event, I realized nonprofit work was a field I was interested in. Two years later a position opened, and I had a foot in the door due to my past contact. I was able to get an interview and score the job.

THINKING CRITICALLY IN THE WORKPLACE

At the beginning of this chapter, you created a rough draft of your career plan. (If you skipped that exercise, please go back and do it now.) Take the time now to review what you wrote and think critically about your plan. Answer the following questions:

Did you consider the possibility of having several different careers within your lifetime?

_____

_____

_____

Did you list the skills you need for each career that you want—and include a way to develop each skill?

_____

_____

_____

Did you include a way to document the value that you create for an employer—such as new products or services you can develop, sales goals that you can meet, or savings that you can create?

_____

_____

_____

Did you include a way to monitor developments in your career field—especially those that could affect your ability to find employment or meet your income goals?

_____

_____

_____

Did you name the specific jobs that you would like to have?

_____

_____

_____

Did you name specific organizations that you would like to work for, their location, and people at those organizations who could hire you?

_____

_____

_____

In the space below, summarize your answers to these questions. Note any specific changes to make in your career plan.

_____

_____

_____

Keep your career plan alive

You can use a variety of means to remember your goals and continue creating your future, including your career. Following are some suggestions.

Display your goals. Without reminders, even skilled planners can forget their goals. One solution is to post written goals in prominent locations—the bathroom, bedroom, hall mirror, or office door. Also write goals on 3x5 cards and tape them to walls or store them next to your bed. Review the cards every morning and night.

You can make goals even more visible. Create an elaborate poster or collage that displays your life purpose. Use frames, color, graphics, and other visual devices to rivet your attention on your goals.

Add to your plan. Goals might pop into your mind at the oddest moments—while you're waiting in line, riding the bus, or stuck in rush-hour traffic. With a little preparation, you can capture those fleeting goals. Carry around a few 3x5 cards and a pen in your pocket or purse.

As the advertisement said, don't leave home without them. Or pack a small voice recorder with you. Speak your goals and preserve them for the ages.

Schedule time for career planning. Schedule a regular time and place to set and review career goals. This is an important appointment with yourself. Treat it as seriously as an appointment with your doctor.

Remember that planning does not have to take a lot of time. In just one minute you can do the following:

- Reread your life purpose statement.
- Review your career plan.
- Jot down a goal or two.
- Visualize yourself meeting a goal.
- Repeat an affirmation related to your goals.

Advertise your career plan. When it comes to achieving your goals, everyone you know is a potential ally. Take a tip from Madison Avenue and advertise. Tell friends and family members about what you plan to be, do, or have. Make your career plan public.

Enlist support. People might criticize your goals: "You want to promote world peace *and* become a millionaire? That's crazy." Remember that there are ways to deal with resistance.

One is to ask directly for support. Explain how much your goal means to you and what you'll do to achieve it. Mention that you're willing to revise your goal as circumstances change. Also *keep* talking about your vision. Goals that sound outlandish at first can become easier to accept over time.

Get coaching. You can hire a personal life coach to assist with goal setting and achievement. The principle is the same as hiring a personal trainer to set and meet fitness goals. A life coach engages you in a conversation about goals for all areas of your life—work, family, finances, education, spirituality, and more. To find such a person, key the words *life coach* into your favorite search site on the Web. National organizations for life coaches have their own sites, which can link you with resources in your own area.

Teach career planning. There's a saying: We teach what we most want to learn. You can turn this idea into an incentive for creating your future. Explain the process of career planning to friends and family. Volunteer to lead an informal seminar or workshop on this topic. If you have children, help them to set and meet goals.

Enjoy the rewards. Break large, long-term career goals into small tasks that you can finish in one hour or less.

Savor the feeling that comes with crossing items off a to-do list. Experience accomplishment often.

At least once each year, list the career goals that you achieved and celebrate. Do the same with goals in all areas of your life. Let the thrill of meeting one goal lead you to setting more. ☒

TRANSLATE CAREER GOALS INTO ACTION

1. Choose one goal from your career plan. List that goal here:

_____

_____

_____

_____

_____

2. Next, list some follow-up actions. Ask yourself: What will it really take for me to meet this goal? List at least five ideas below:

_____

_____

_____

_____

_____

_____

_____

_____

3. Finally, translate any action you just listed into immediate steps—the kind of items that you would include on a daily to-do list. Think of tasks that you could complete in less than one hour, or start within the next 24 hours.

_____

_____

_____

_____

_____

_____

_____

_____

_____

_____

You can apply this three-step technique to any goal for your career or the rest of your life. The point is to move from ideas into action.

CP-29

power process

Risk being a fool

A powerful person has the courage to take risks. And taking risks means being willing to fail sometimes—even to be a fool. This idea can work for you because you already are a fool.

Don't be upset. All of us are fools at one time or another. There are no exceptions. If you doubt it, think back to that stupid thing you did just a few days ago. You know the one. Yes . . . *that* one. It was embarrassing and you tried to hide it. You pretended you weren't a fool. This happens to everyone.

People who insist that they have never been fools are perhaps the biggest fools of all. We are all fallible human beings. Most of us, however, spend too much time and energy trying to hide our fool-hood. No one is really tricked by this—not even ourselves. And whenever we pretend to be something we're not, we miss part of life.

For example, many of us never dance because we don't want to risk looking ridiculous. We're not wrong. We probably would look ridiculous. That's the secret of risking being a fool.

It's OK to look ridiculous while dancing. It's all right to sound silly when singing to your kids. Sometimes it's OK to be absurd. It comes with taking risks.

Taking risks is not being foolhardy

Sometimes it's not OK to be absurd. This Power Process comes with a warning label: Taking risks does *not* mean escaping responsibility for our actions. "Risk being a fool" is not a suggestion to get drunk at a party and make a fool of yourself. It is not a suggestion to act the fool by disrupting class. It is not a suggestion to be foolhardy or to "fool around."

"Risk being a fool" means recognizing that foolishness—along with dignity, courage, cowardice, grace, clumsiness, and other qualities—is a human characteristic. We all share it. You might as well risk being a fool because you already are one, and nothing in the world can change that. Why not enjoy it once in a while? Consider the case of the person who won't dance because he's afraid he'll look foolish. This same person will spend an afternoon tripping over his feet on a basketball court. If you say that his jump shot from the top of the key looks like a circus accident, he might even agree.

"So what?" he might say. "I'm no Michael Jordan." He's right. On the basketball court, he is willing to risk looking like a fool in order to enjoy the game.

He is no Fred Astaire, either. For some reason, that bothers him. The result is that he misses the fun of dancing. (Dancing badly is as much fun as shooting baskets badly—and maybe a lot more fun.)

There's one sure-fire way to avoid any risk of being a fool, and that's to avoid life. The writer who never finishes a book will never have to worry about getting negative reviews. The center fielder who sits out every game is safe from making any errors. And the comedian who never performs in front of an audience is certain to avoid telling jokes that fall flat. The possibility of succeeding at any venture increases when we're comfortable with making mistakes—that is, with the risk of being a fool.

Look at courage in a new way

Again, remember the warning label. This Power Process does not suggest that the way to be happy in life is to do

Corbis/Royalty Free

The possibility of succeeding at any venture increases when we're comfortable with making mistakes—that is, with the risk of being a fool.

things badly. Courage involves the willingness to face danger and risk failure. Mediocrity is not the goal. The point is that mastery in most activities calls for the willingness to do something new, to fail, to make corrections, to fail again, and so on. On the way to becoming a good writer, be willing to be a bad writer.

Consider these revised clichés: Anything worth doing is worth doing badly at first. Practice makes improvement. If at first you don't fail, try again.

Most artists and athletes have learned the secret of being foolish. Comedians are especially well versed in this art. All of us know how it feels to tell a joke and get complete silence. We truly look and feel like fools. Professional comedians risk feeling that way for a living. Being funny is not enough for success in the comedy business. A comedian must have the courage to face failure.

Courage is an old-fashioned word for an old-fashioned virtue. Traditionally, people have reserved that word for illustrious acts of exceptional people—the campaigns of generals and the missions of heroes.

This concept of courage is fine. At the same time, it can be limiting and can prevent us from seeing courage in everyday actions. Courage is the kindergartner who, with heart pounding, waves good-bye to his parents and boards the bus for his first day of school. Courage is the 40-year-old who registers for college courses after being away from the classroom for 20 years.

For a student, the willingness to take risks means the willingness to experiment with new skills, to achieve personal growth, and sometimes to fail. The rewards of risk taking include expanded creativity, more satisfying self-expression, and more joy.

An experiment for you

Here's an experiment you can conduct to experience the joys of risk taking. The next time you take a risk and end up doing something silly or stupid, allow yourself to be totally aware of your reaction. Don't deny it. Don't cover it up. Notice everything about the feeling, including the physical sensations and thoughts that come with it. Acknowledge the foolishness. Be exactly who you are. Explore all of the emotions, images, and sensations surrounding your experience.

Also remember that we can act independently of our feelings. Courage is not the absence of fear but the willingness to take risks even when we feel fear. We can be keenly homesick and still register for classes. We can tremble at the thought of speaking in public yet still walk up to the microphone.

When we fully experience it, the fear of taking risks loses its power. Then we have the freedom to expand and grow. ◪

desk of ...

from the

HEATHER HOLDREDGE, TEACHER:

I worked in the banking sector post graduation, but did not enjoy it. I quit my job after two years and traveled through Europe for seven weeks by myself. After I returned, I was asked by a relative to volunteer at the local middle school for a computer project. After a month, the principal asked if I wanted to try teaching for the rest of the year. I thought I had nothing to lose. I was hooked by the end of the school year.

career application

Tiana Kabiri earned her BA in computer science and found a job in her field within a month after she graduated.

Royalty-Free/Corbis

She now works as a systems programmer for a large bank with seven local branches. Tiana was the first person in her family to gain a college degree. Her friends and relatives are thrilled with her accomplishments.

While in school, Tiana took part in several workshops on career planning. However, she never did many of the suggested exercises and largely downplayed the concept of career planning. Defining her interests, thinking about the skills she most wanted to develop, and researching employment trends just seemed like too much work.

Besides, according to the National Association of Colleges and Employers, starting salary offers for graduates with a bachelor's degree in computer programming averaged $45,558 a year in 2003. When Tiana heard this, she figured that was all the information she needed in order to choose her career.

One day at work, Tiana received an e-mail from a friend who was still in school—a student majoring in computer science and actively engaged in career planning. The message included these quotations from the online version of the *Occupational Outlook Handbook* published by the U.S. Department of Labor:

> *Employment of programmers is expected to grow about as fast as the average for all occupations through 2012. . . . Employment of programmers, however, is expected to grow much more slowly than that of other computer specialists. With the rapid gains in technology, sophisticated computer software now has the capability to write basic code, eliminating the need for more programmers to do this routine work. . . . Furthermore, as the level of technological innovation and sophistication increases, programmers are likely to face increasing competition from programming businesses overseas, to which much routine work can be contracted out at a lower cost.*

Tiana read this and felt a wave of panic. As an entry-level programmer, she was now worried about her long-term job security. She was happy with her salary and her job seemed secure for the near future. But she worried that her skills would eventually become obsolete or that her job would be "outsourced" and eliminated. ▧

Reflecting on this scenario:

1. Imagine that you are a career counselor and that Tiana has scheduled an appointment with you. You have one hour to give her a crash course on career planning. What are two or three of the major points you would make?

2. Access the online *Occupational Outlook Handbook* at **http://www.bls.gov/oco/ocos110.htm#outlook**. Search the term *computer and mathematical occupations*. Based on the kinds of jobs listed there, what computer skills could you recommend that Tiana develop in order to enhance her long-term job security?

3. Looking beyond Tiana's skills in programming, list five transferable skills that you would recommend Tiana to develop that will help her in the future.

Name _____ Date _____ / _____ / _____

quiz

1. Aside from looking for a specific position on the Internet, name two useful ways to use the Web as a tool for career planning.

2. The chapter suggests that you add specifics to your career plan by "naming names." List three examples of these specifics.

3. Define the traditional model of career success and give one reason why it is changing.

4. Describe two reasons why internships are valuable experiences as you create your career plan.

5. The best way to get useful information from a vocational assessment is to take one and make it a blueprint for choosing your career. True or False? Explain your answer.

6. List three questions that you could ask during an informational interview.

7. List the three steps recommended in this chapter for achieving financial independence.

8. Explain how career planning can be a process of choosing instead of a process of discovery.

9. Contributing to others does *not* involve:
   (A) Telling people what is best for them.
   (B) Finding out what people want or need.
   (C) Determining if you can help people get what they want.
   (D) Giving your time, talent, or money.
   (E) Making sure that you experience satisfaction, also.

10. List three options for decreasing spending.

learning styles application

The questions below will "cycle" you through four styles, or modes, of learning. Each question will help you explore a different mode. You can answer the questions in any order.

what if *Imagine that you will do no career planning. After reading this chapter, do you see any advantages to this approach? How about any disadvantages? Summarize your thoughts in the space below.*

why *Supposed that another student in one of your classes says, "Career planning is irrelevant to me. Besides being in school, I work full-time and have a family. I don't have time to plan a career." In a brief paragraph, sum up your response to this statement.*

how *Name a job you would like to have in the next 3 to 10 years. Then, list the five most important skills you will need to have in order to do that job.*

what *Do a very brief career plan by naming the job titles you would like to hold in 3 years, 5 years, and 10 years from today.*

master student

profile

FRED SMITH

a graduate of Yale and the founder and CEO of Federal Express Corporation.

Frederick W. Smith may have a common last name, but he is a most uncommon man. What other American business leader of today had a revolutionary idea and converted it into a company that, starting from scratch and with heavy early losses, passed the $500 million revenue mark and had a 10 percent net profit margin in a few years?

What other American business leader with so brilliant an idea first wrote it out in a college paper that was graded C? Or says that the people with the greatest impact on him have been a poorly educated sergeant whom he led in combat and a science professor who liked to buzz a university stadium in a fighter plane?

Fred Smith is chairman and chief executive officer of Memphis-based Federal Express Corporation, an air cargo firm that specializes in overnight delivery door-to-door, using its own planes.

To put it another way, Fred Smith is Federal Express.

Smith got his revolutionary idea in the 60's while majoring in economics and political science at Yale. Technological change had opened a radically new transportation market, he decided. . . .

"Steamboats and trains were the logistics arm of the Industrial Revolution's first stage," he says. "Trucks became a good logistics arm later—and still are because of their flexibility. But moving the parts and pieces to support the Electronics Age requires very fast transportation over long distances. I became convinced that a different type of system was going to be a major part of the national economy. . . ."

Smith spelled it out in an overdue economics paper. To cut cost and time, packages from all over the country would be flown to a central point, there to be distributed and flown out again to their destinations—a hub-and-spokes pattern, his company calls it today. The flying would be late at night when air lanes were empty. Equipment and documents from anywhere in the U.S. could be delivered anywhere in the U.S. the next day. . . .

For the benefit of business history, it would be nice to have that college paper today. But who saves college papers, particularly those done in one night and branded mediocre?

He says one reason he was no scholastic superstar was that many courses he had to take didn't interest him. Other things did. He and two faculty members resurrected a long-dormant flying club at Yale. One of his cohorts was Professor Norwood Russell Hansen.

"Russ taught the psychology of science—how science was developed," Smith says. "I was a friend of his, not one of his students. He had a big impact on me because of his outlook on life. He was a great singer and a pianist of virtual concert talent. He rode a motorcycle, and he had a World War II fighter plane that he flew all over the place. He buzzed Yale Bowl from time to time. He marched to the beat of a different drummer. . . ."

Will Smith be successful in future undertakings? Says Arthur C. Bass, vice chairman: "A few years ago, some of us used to let off steam in the afternoon playing basketball on a court behind an apartment house. It was amazing—no matter who had the ball and no matter where Fred was on the court, if Fred's side needed to score to win, he would get the ball and make the winning basket. That's the way he is in the business world."

"A Business Visionary Who Really Delivered" by Henry Altman, from *Nation's Business,* November 1981. Reprinted by permission of *Nation's Business,* November 1981. Copyright ©1981, U.S. Chamber of Commerce.

For more biographical information on Fred Smith, visit the Master Student Hall of Fame on the *Becoming a Master Student* Web site at:

masterstudent.college.hmco.com

end notes

1. Lawrence Mishel, Jared Bernstein, and Heather Boushey, *The State of Working America 2002–03* (Ithaca, NY: Cornell University Press, 2003).
2. Dave Ellis, Stan Lankowitz, Ed Stupka, and Doug Toff, *Career Planning,* Third Edition. Copyright © 2003 by Houghton Mifflin Company. Reprinted by permission.
3. United Nations Development Programme, *Human Development Report* (New York: Oxford University Press, 2003).

Mastering Work

Mastering Work

(collage) Walter Kopec

Passion for what you do is an important ingredient for success, and if you don't love what you do, it's not worth the time and energy.

CARLY FIORINA

By concentrating on a few key efforts such as sharing credit, showing grace under pressure, and promoting your ambition in appropriate ways, your day job can lead to the career of your dreams.

STEPHEN VISCUSI

why
this chapter matters . . .

You can gain strategies to succeed as you transition from master student to master employee.

what
is included . . .

The Master Employee
Use power tools for finding work
Tell everyone you know: The art of networking
Write a résumé that gets noticed
Sell your résumé with an effective cover letter
Creating and using portfolios
Use interviews to hire yourself an employer
Learning on the job
Join a diverse workplace
Decoding corporate culture
Dealing with sexism and sexual harassment
Strategies for working with a mentor
We are all leaders
Loving your next job
Define your values, align your actions
One set of values
Power Process: "Be it"
Master Student Profile: Craig Kielburger

how
you can use this chapter . . .

Learn effective strategies for job hunting.
Create résumés that lead to job interviews.
Go into job interviews fully prepared.
Build satisfying relationships with coworkers.

As you read, ask yourself
what if . . .

I could find work that expresses my core values and connects daily with my passions?

The master employee

The title—*From Master Student to Master Employee*—implies that these two types of mastery have something in common. To some people, this idea sounds half-baked. They separate life into two distinct domains: work and school. One is the "real" world. The other is the place where you attend classes to prepare for the real world.

Consider another point of view—the idea that success in higher education promotes success on the job.

There's some pretty hard-nosed evidence for this idea. One factor is that higher levels of education are correlated with higher levels of income. Another is that mastery in school and in work seem to rest on a common set of transferable skills.

In this chapter you've seen several references to the Secretary's Commission on Achieving Necessary Skills (SCANS) issued by the U.S. Department of Labor. According to this document, one crucial skill for the workplace is a personal quality called responsibility. This is demonstrated by any employee who:

- "Exerts a high level of effort and perseverance toward goal attainment.

- "Works hard to become excellent at doing tasks by setting high standards, paying attention to details, working well, and displaying a high level of concentration even when assigned an unpleasant task.

- "Displays high standards of attendance, punctuality, enthusiasm, vitality, and optimism in approaching and completing tasks."

A better definition of mastery would be hard to find. And if you've ever exerted a high level of effort to complete an assignment, paid attention to the details of a lecture, or displayed a high level of concentration while reading a tough textbook, then you've already demonstrated some key aspects of self-responsibility and mastery.

When you graduate from school, you don't leave your capacity for mastery locked inside a classroom. Excellence in one setting paves the way for excellence in other settings.

For example, a student who knows how to show up for class on time is ready to show up for work on time. The student who knows how to focus attention during a lecture is ready to focus attention during a training session at work. And a student who's worked cooperatively in a study group brings a lot of skills to the table when joining a workplace team.

journal entry

Discovery/Intention Statement

Reflect on all the jobs you've held in your life. What aspect of working would you most like to change? Answers might include job hunting with less frustration, resolving conflicts with coworkers, building a better relationship with your boss, or coping with office politics. Describe the change that would make the biggest positive difference in your job satisfaction over the long run.

I discovered that I . . .

_____

_____

_____

_____

Now preview this chapter for ideas that could help you make the positive change you just described. List three to five suggestions below, along with the page numbers where you can read more about them.

Strategy	Page number

A master employee embraces change, takes risks, and looks for chances to lead others while contributing to the quality of their lives. A master employee completes tasks efficiently, communicates openly and respectfully, and commits to lifelong learning. In developing a mastery of higher education, you'll do all this and more. *Master student* and *master employee* are names for qualities that already exist in you, waiting to be expressed as you embrace new ideas and experiment with new behaviors.

Use power tools for finding work

Tool #1: Upgrade your strategies

When applied to finding work, not all strategies are equal. People often find job searches less effective when they do the following things:

- Rely exclusively on want ads when looking for a job.
- Mail out a stack of résumés and cover letters and simply wait for a reply.
- Wait for a job to open up before contacting potential employers.
- Work only with employment agencies and human resources departments in large companies.
- Rely on a job interview as their only source of information about an employer.

These methods are not all useless. Rather, problems arise when we rely on just one strategy and exclude others.

As an alternative, consider the following ideas. They can greatly increase your chances of finding the work you want:

- Make direct contact with a person who can hire you.
- Make such contacts even when the job you want is not yet open or even conceived.
- Cultivate a list of contacts, join professional associations, and meet people in your field.
- Do thorough research on a company before approaching someone for a job there. Do part of this research via informational interviews.
- Approach a potential employer with a way to solve a problem or achieve a company goal. Talk about what's in it for her—the benefits to the company if you are hired.

- Follow up a résumé with letters and well-timed phone calls.
- Write thank-you notes after an interview.
- Present yourself impeccably—everything from error-free résumés to well-polished shoes.

Tool #2: Consider more than one career

As you begin career planning and job hunting, consider ways to increase your options and stay flexible over the long term. Avoid specializing in a certain field too soon, or becoming so specialized that it's difficult to find work as the market changes.

You can benefit from keeping an overall perspective. Use your education to learn transferable skills and then relate them to several potential careers and jobs. Look for the common threads that unite your courses and your career options.

Tool #3: Develop outside interests

You might find it refreshing to learn about yourself outside the context of your career choices. To do this, break out of ruts. Be creative and open to new activities. Take a course that has nothing to do with your major. Volunteer. Find new ways to invest time and energy in the lives of others.

These kinds of activities promote creative thinking by disrupting old habits and infusing our lives with new possibilities. The potential payoffs include new skills and added career options.

Tool #4: Use spare minutes

The time you spend waiting in line at a grocery store or gas station never needs to be wasted again. Thinking about finding work gives you a way to create value in any spare moment. Many career planning and job hunting tasks can be done in one hour or less.

In fact, there's a lot you can do in a few spare minutes. One option is to take a five-minute career-planning break. Fill that break with "micro-tasks." Do an exercise or journal entry from this chapter. Visit the Web site for a company that interests you. Or call one person to set up an informational interview.

Tool #5: Create your own job

Lists of job openings never include positions that are waiting to be created. With a little imagination and analysis, you can create a job or career where none exists.

Students have a long history of creating self-employment and small businesses to help pay the bills. Some examples are:

- Word processing for papers and theses
- Computer consulting
- Baby sitting and childcare
- Gardening and lawn care
- Doing minor house repairs and odd jobs
- Sewing and mending clothes
- Offering a delivery and errand service
- Pet care and dog walking
- House painting
- Taking photographs or producing videos of weddings and parties
- Working as a singing messenger
- Providing live or recorded music for parties and weddings
- Writing, editing, and proofreading on a freelance basis

You might use creative thinking to create a lifelong career. All it takes is looking for an unmet need that you can respond to with a new product or service.

Another option is to redesign a job you already have. Sometimes companies allow employees to create new positions or businesses "within" a business. Companies may also allow job-sharing, converting a full-time job to a contract position, or working from home.

Tool #6: Attend to the details

The whole process of finding work may hang on details such as getting to appointments on time, respecting an interviewer's schedule, and staying no longer than agreed. Thanking people for their time, dressing appropriately for an interview, and sending follow-up notes can also be crucial.

To make your job search more effective, sweat the small stuff. Ask yourself: "What is one more thing I can do to make my job research more complete or my presentation effective?" Keep taking that next step, however small. Each one takes you closer to finding the work you love.

Tool #7: Use technology to power your job search

Modern technology is creating new ways for you to plan your career and find jobs in the future. On the World Wide Web, you can research companies you'd like to work for, read lists of job openings, and post your résumé and a digital recording of yourself. Through faxes, overnight deliveries, mobile phones, and e-mail, you can stay in continual contact with potential employers. Widespread availability of high-speed Internet access has increased the number of long-distance job interviews being conducted via video conference or in a real time chat room, and has increased the possibility of sending an electronic portfolio attachment with a résumé.

According to one estimate, about two million people go online every month to hunt for jobs. That's a testament to the potential power of the digital medium and to some of its pitfalls as well. When you're looking for a job, the strength of the Internet—the sheer density of data—can also lead to frustration:

- The haphazard organization of the Internet makes it hard for potential employers to find your résumé when you post it online. The organizations you most want to work for might avoid using the Internet to find job applicants.
- Job openings listed on the Internet can be heavily skewed to certain fields, such as jobs for computer professionals or people in other technical fields.
- Across all fields, the majority of job openings are not listed on the Internet (or in newspaper want ads, for that matter).

This is not meant to disparage the Internet as a tool for job hunters and career planners. The point is that posting a résumé on a Web site will not automatically lead to an e-mail in-basket that's bursting to its digital seams with job offers. For an effective job search, view the Internet as just one resource. ✍

REHEARSE YOUR JOB SEARCH

Imagine that you've completed your education as of today. Your next task is to find a job in a field of interest to you. The following questions will help you rehearse this job hunt.

If you are unsure of an answer, write down your best guess. For now, the process of considering the question is more valuable than any particular answer.

Write your answers in the space below each question. Use separate paper as needed.

1. What kind of job will you apply for? If you choose self-employment, what product or service will you offer?

2. Where will you go to find a job? Will you approach an existing company or choose self-employment? If you opt for self-employment, how will you find potential customers or clients?

3. What kind of training, education, and experience is required for the kind of work that you want?

4. If you plan to apply for an existing job, how will you find out who's in charge of hiring?

5. Next, visualize your job interview. Who will interview you? What questions will this person ask? What questions will you ask the interviewer?

6. Will this job be your "dream job"? If not, how long will take you to find that ideal job?

Finally, review what you've just written. Does any of it suggest changes to make in your current course work or major? If so, describe the specific changes you intend to make.

Tell everyone you know
The art of networking

Networking means staying in touch with people to share career planning ideas and track job openings. It's possible that more jobs are filled through networking than through any other method.

When done with persistence over a period of time, networking can lead you effortlessly from one contact to another.

Following are ideas that can help you create a powerful network.

Start by listing people you already know

Start your list of contacts with names of family members and friends who could help you define your career or land a job. List each person's name, phone number, and e-mail address on a separate 3x5 card or Rolodex card. Another option is to keep your list on a computer, using word processing or contact management software.

Whenever you speak to someone on your contact list, make brief notes about what you discussed. Also jot down any further actions you'll take to follow up on your discussion.

Be open to making contacts

Consider everyone you meet to be a potential friend—and a networking partner. Look for things you have in common. If you're both planning a career or looking for a job, that's plenty.

Craft your "pitch"

Develop a short statement of your career goal that you can easily share with people. For example: "After I graduate, I plan to work in the travel business. I'm looking for an internship in a travel agency that helps business people arrange international trips. Do you know of any agencies that take interns?"

Get past the fear of competition

When told about networking, some people feel intimidated. They fear that others will steal or conceal job openings. *Why should I share this information with anybody?* goes the objection. *After all, we're competing with each other for the same jobs.*

In response, remember that few people in any network are actually going after the same jobs. Students majoring in broadcasting, for example, have many different job goals. Some want to be newscasters. Others want to work as video editors or scriptwriters. And even people interested in the same jobs may be looking for positions with different duties or in different parts of the country.

Also, any "competitor" could turn into a friend. Suppose someone in your network lands a job before you. Send a note of congratulations to this person along with your phone number and e-mail address. This person might be in a position to recommend you for another job opening—or even to hire you.

Follow up

Networking uncovers "leads"—companies with job openings and people with the power to hire. Keeping a live list of leads takes action. You might benefit from sending a letter and résumé or making a five-minute call. Any of these steps could bring your name in front of a person who's ready to hire you. 🖂

Write a résumé that gets noticed

Your résumé is a living document that distills an essential part of your overall life plan. The attention you give to your résumé can pay you back hundreds of time over. Use a résumé to find a job that you love and a salary that matches your skills.

Writing an effective résumé creates value in many ways. For one, a résumé can help you discover and express your skills by writing them down. It can serve as a calling card for you to leave with employers. It can remind you of key points to make in a job interview. A résumé can also refresh a potential employer's memory after the interview. If you're applying for a job that's miles away from home, a résumé is essential.

A résumé is a piece of persuasive writing, not a laundry list of previous jobs or dry recitation of facts. This document has a purpose—to get you to the next step in the hiring process, usually an interview. What follows are suggestions for résumés that win attention.

Avoid getting weeded out

Your résumé could be the most important document that you ever write. Yet many résumés fail. They get tossed. They get set aside, lost, or shuffled into oblivion. One goal in résumé writing is to get past the first cut. Several techniques can help you meet this goal.

Start with presentation. Neatness, organization, and correct grammar and punctuation are essential.

Next, leave out irrelevant information that could possibly eliminate you from the hiring process and send your résumé hurtling into the circular file. Some items to delete or question are these:

- Boilerplate language—stock wording from job descriptions or résumé writing services.
- The date you're available to start a new job.
- Salary information, including what you've earned in the past and want to earn now.
- Details about jobs you held over 10 years ago.
- Reasons for leaving previous jobs.

Note that employers cannot legally discriminate against job applicants based on personal information

such as age, national origin, race, religion, disability, and pregnancy status. Including this kind of information on your résumé might even hurt your job prospects. To learn more about types of job discrimination, access the U.S. Equal Employment Opportunity Commission (EEOC) at **http://www.eeoc.gov/types/index.html**. This Web site also explains how to file a charge of discrimination.

Consider a standard format

There is no formula for a perfect résumé, and people have different preferences for what they want to see in one. However, following is one common résumé format.

Begin with contact information—your name, mailing address, e-mail address, and phone number.

Next, you might choose to name your desired job, often called an *objective* or *goal*. This is an optional feature, and not all résumé experts agree on the value of including it.

Follow with the body of your résumé—major headings such as *skills*, *experience*, and *education* with key details. Put those headings in bold print or in the left margin of the page. Whenever possible, use phrases that start with an active verb: "*Supervised* three people." "*Generated* leads for sales calls." "*Wrote* speeches and *edited* annual reports." These verbs refer directly to your skills. Make them relevant to the job you're seeking.

Finish on a strong note. You might end your résumé with an intriguing statement ("I enjoy turning around departments with low morale") or a favorable quote from a coworker ("Julio regularly exceeded the requirements of his job").

Sell your skills as solutions

Every organization has problems to solve—coping with employee turnover, beating the competition, increasing market share and revenues. Do research to discover the typical problems faced by organizations in your career field—and the specific problems faced by individual employers.

In the body of your résumé, show that you know about these problems. Offer your skills as solutions. Give evidence that you've solved similar problems in the past, offering credible numbers whenever possible: "Created a program that reduced training time by 25 percent."

Remember to give a full picture of your skills. This includes content skills—specialized knowledge and abilities that qualify you to do a specific job—along with transferable skills that can help you in *any* job.

Make it easy to skim

Knowing that employers are pressed for time when reading résumés, design yours accordingly. Write your résumé so that key facts leap off the page. Use short paragraphs and short sentences. Use bulleted lists for key points. Also avoid filling the page with ink. Instead, leave some blank space between the major sections of your résumé.

Make it unusual

Sometimes an offbeat approach will attract an employer's attention. If you're applying for a job in public relations, you could write your résumé as a press release formatted to be read by a news announcer. If you're applying for work as an administrator at an art museum, you could design your résumé as a collage.

Before you use such a gimmick, however, carefully consider the ways that it could backfire. When it doubt, stick to a conventional résumé.

Get feedback

Ask friends and family members if your résumé is persuasive and easy to understand. Also get feedback from someone at your school's career planning and job placement office. Revise your résumé based on their comments. Then revise some more. Create sparkling prose that will intrigue a potential employer enough to call you for an interview.

Combine your résumé with other strategies

Do not view a résumé as the core of your job search. Employers might get hundreds of résumés for a single job opening. And interviewers might spend only a few seconds on each résumé. These figures have nothing to do with your skills. They just reflect the constant pressures on people with jobs to fill.

To get the most from your résumé, use it to supplement other job-hunting strategies. Research companies and do informational interviews. Take part in internships and other work experiences in your chosen field. Create a support group and find a mentor.

Go ahead and contact potential employers directly— even if they don't have a job opening at the moment. Use your job contacts to find people within that organization with the power to hire. Then use every job contact you have to introduce yourself to those people and schedule an interview. If you just send out résumés and neglect to make personal contacts, you'll be disappointed.

Each time you meet with someone, leave your résumé

Keys to scannable résumés

Many companies use a computerized scanning program to catalog résumés and fill positions by using keyword searches. Human resources associates can quickly retrieve and route résumés to fill positions by matching their specifications with your qualifications. Including appropriate keywords on your résumé will help you stand out from others. Review job postings to find buzzwords that employers are searching for in your field of interest to include on your résumé. Get recognized by including specific positions and leadership roles you have held, related work experience, and degrees or certifications you have completed. Remember to also include your skills and core competencies.

Some specific things to keep in mind:

- Use enough keywords to define your skills, education, experience, professional affiliations, and so on.
- Describe your experience with concrete terms. For example: "manager of mechanical engineering team" instead of "responsible for managing professionals."
- When in doubt, spell it out. Some systems are programmed with basic abbreviations like BA, MS, Ph.D. But the general rule is if you are not sure, spell it out. You can assume employers will search for standard abbreviations for terms in your field.
- Use common headings such as: Objective, Experience, Education, Professional, Affiliations, and Certifications.
- Remember to describe your interpersonal traits and attitudes. For example: communication skills, leadership, time management, high energy.

Print your scannable résumé on one side of an $8\frac{1}{2} \times$ 11" sheet of plain white paper with an easy-to-read font and layout. If your résumé is more than one page in length, be sure your name and contact information appear on both sheets of paper. Avoid using italics, boldface, or underlining and other special text formatting. Do not staple or fold the résumé. It is best when hand delivered or sent in an oversized envelope.

behind. Then stay in touch. Periodically remind a potential employer of your existence. Send a short personal note: "Here's an updated résumé to put in my file." If the company doesn't have a file on you yet, chances are that somebody will start one. At that point, your name will start to stand out from the crowd. Your résumé is doing its job. ⚒

Sample résumés

Susan Chang
susangeorgia276@aol.com
2500 North Highland Avenue, Atlanta, GA 30306
770-899-8707

Work Experience: **LAND Enterprises, Inc., Atlanta, GA**
Administrative Assistant—January 2004–present
- Responsible for supporting national sales manager and three district managers in creating reports for nationwide sales staff.
- Create, prepare, and maintain Excel spreadsheets with weekly sales data.
- Manage sales representative calendar of events in Lotus Notes database.

Peachtree Bank, Alpharetta, GA
Teller—May 2001–December 2003
- Responsible for receiving cash/checks for deposits, processing withdrawals, and accepting loan payments.
- Communicated with customers and provided account balance and savings and loan information.
- Provided friendly and prompt customer service.

Education: **Macon State Community College, Macon, GA**
AA—Communications and Information Technology; May 2003
Overall GPA–3.0.

Volunteer: **Macon Chamber of Commerce**
Holiday Events Coordinator 2000–2003
- Maintained budget from Chamber of Commerce for annual holiday parties.
- Solicited donations from local businesses to support monthly events.

Computer Skills: Microsoft Word, Microsoft Excel, Microsoft Access, Lotus Notes, Powerpoint.

Personal: Interested in writing poetry, playing team sports, and traveling.

References: Available upon request.

Lamont Jackson
2250 First Avenue, #3 • New York, NY 10029 • (212) 222-5555
Lamont_Jackson44@hotmail.com

Objective

To obtain a position as a public relations associate that allows me to utilize my writing and communication skills.

Education

Rutgers University, New Brunswick, NJ
BA in English, Minor in Business Communication; May 2004
Major GPA — 3.2; Minor GPA — 3.3

Experience

The Medium, Rutgers University, New Brunswick, NJ
Contributing Writer, August 2003–May 2004
• Developed feature articles pertaining to faculty and student issues on campus and community issues.
• Responsible for writing weekly sidebar featuring community service on and off campus.

Shandwick Public Relations, New York, NY
Intern, Summer 2003
• Coordinated mass mailings of press releases to medical community biweekly.
• Conducted health surveys focusing on nutrition habits of senior citizens in the tristate area; organized all retrieved data of 1000 respondents.
• Handled telephone inquiries efficiently from clients and corporations represented by firm.

Activities

• Intramural Soccer Team, Spring 2003
• Habitat for Humanity, *Treasurer*, Fall 2003–Spring 2004
• Rutgers University Orientation Leader, Summer 2002

Skills

• Ability to perform on both PC and Macintosh platforms.
• Software knowledge that includes: Windows NT, Microsoft Office, Lotus Notes, Lotus 1-2-3, Quark, and beginning HTML.
• Fluency in Spanish — oral and written competency.

Honors

Rutgers University Dean's List, Fall 1999, Spring 2004

Sell your résumé with an effective cover letter

An effective cover letter can leave a prospective employer waiting with bated breath to read your résumé. An ineffective letter can propel your résumé to that nefarious stack of papers to be read "later." In some cases, a well-written letter alone can land you an interview.

Many cover letters are little more than a list of stock phrases. In essence, they say: "I want that job you listed. Here's my résumé. Read it."

You can write a more interesting letter that practically demands a response. Remember the primary question in an employer's mind: What do you have to offer us? Using a three-part structure can help you answer this question.

1 In your first sentence, address the person who can hire you and grab that person's attention. Make a statement that appeals directly to her self-interest. Write something that moves potential employer to say, "We can't afford to pass this person up. Call him right away to set up an appointment."

To come up with ideas for your opening, complete the following sentence: "The main benefits that I can bring to your organization are. . . ."

2 Next, build interest. Add a fact or two to back up your opening paragraph. Briefly refer to your experience and highlight one or two key achievements. If you're applying for a specific job opening, state this. If you're not, then offer an idea that will intrigue the employer enough to respond anyway.

3 Finally, take care of business. Refer the reader to your résumé. Then mention that you'll call at a specific point to set up an interview.

Write several drafts of your cover letter. See if you can answer several key questions on a potential employer's mind:

- *Why* should we be interested in this person?
- *What* value can this person add to our organization?
- *How* would we be better off after hiring this person?
- *What if* hiring this person could create the opportunity to expand into new markets or expand the range of services that we offer?

Keep your letter short—two or three paragraphs. Employers are busy people. Reading cover letters is probably not high on their list of fun things to do. Make it easy on them. ✉

Correspondence quick tips

Use these additional suggestions for making your cover letter a "must read."

- Address your letter to a specific individual. Make sure to use the correct title and mailing address. Mistakes in such details could detract from your credibility.
- Use a simple typeface that is easy to read.
- Tailor each letter you write to the specific company and position you are applying for.
- Be honest. During an interview, an employer may choose to ask you questions about information you present in your résumé or cover letter. Be prepared to expand upon and support your statements. The ability to do this enhances your reputation as an ethical employee.

- Thank your reader for her time and consideration.
- Check for typographical, grammatical, and word usage errors. Do not rely on your computer to spell check.
- Ask someone to read over your letter before you send it out. An extra pair of eyes may help you uncover errors.
- Use high-quality paper stock for your hard copy letters.
- When sending cover letters via e-mail, use a meaningful subject header and a professional tone. Do not use emoticons like :-). Be sure to include your phone number in case the contact prefers to follow up with you via phone.
- When faxing a cover letter and résumé, indicate the total number of pages in the transmission.

Sample cover letters

Example 1

My name is Michael Romano and I recently moved to this area. I have worked in the auto industry for the last seventeen years, and I am interested in continuing in that industry as a worker for DWC Radiators. I worked for Angelo's Auto Supplies in Lansing, MI, before moving to Minnesota.

My background is in the repairs department. I played a key role on the team that serviced imported radiators. I have excellent references from my former employer.

I will stop by your office next Wednesday afternoon to fill out a formal application. If you could take a few minutes to see me at that time, I would be very grateful. I will give you a call on Tuesday to see if this can be arranged.

Example 2

As a recent college graduate, I am the perfect candidate for your entry-level position as an editorial assistant for *Seventeen* magazine. During my studies, I have held three positions at my college's magazine, including Features Editor, Campus Correspondent, and Senior Copyeditor. In my senior year, I initiated a new section in our magazine, *Style File*, featuring local clothing and accessories stores. A similar *Style File* in your magazine from different cities across the nation would be an intriguing section for your readers.

I am proficient in using both PC and MAC platforms, and have skills using programs in Microsoft Office Suite and Quark. The enclosed résumé explains how my past positions and other qualifications are a perfect fit for your opening. I will call you in a few days to schedule a time when we can talk in more detail. I would also like the opportunity to share with you my writing portfolio.

Example 3

The flyer announcing the position of Program Coordinator caught my attention immediately. This position interests me because I have the skills required to work on a diverse team. I am fluent in Spanish, French, and English and have had a long-standing interest in working with people from many cultures. My experience as a vendor in an Argentina zoo and my current job as unit manager at the UN Communications Center are two examples of the unique and relevant background I would bring to the position of Program Coordinator at the UC International House.

As a member of the International House, I also have a firsthand understanding about how residents feel about the activities and special events hosted by the office throughout the year. Because of this, I am in an excellent position to help plan a variety of activities residents will appreciate.

As directed in the job announcement, I am requesting an appointment for an interview on March 28, between 2 p.m. and 6 p.m., at a time convenient for you. Please contact me if another time is more appropriate. Thank you very much for your time and consideration.

Example 4

As a recent recipient of an Associates Degree in medical assisting, I am the perfect candidate for the position of team leader for the medical assistant group at Health First Wellness Associates. My experience as a receptionist in the North Shore Medical Center before returning to college has been supplemented by my recent employment in the billing department, where I became proficient using MediSoft.

After you have reviewed my enclosed résumé, I would appreciate the opportunity to discuss with you further my qualifications and explain how I could help create solutions for success with the newly formed MA Team. I can be reached by phone or e-mail as noted above.

Example 5

Your Chief Financial Officer, Elena Perez, told me recently that you were looking for an MIS director. Because of my background, she encouraged me to contact you directly. I am very impressed with the growth your company made in the last two years. With that kind of expansion, I can understand your need to create a separate MIS department.

This position relates well to my current experience at Murphy and Sons, LLP, as you will see from my enclosed résumé. I possess a diversified background that would enable me to serve your organization's MIS needs efficiently. I am a creative and highly motivated individual with good communication and interpersonal skills. I am confident that these qualifications coupled with my work ethic and enthusiasm would allow me to make a positive contribution to your company.

I welcome the opportunity to meet with you to discuss how my qualifications may best meet your needs. Thank you in advance for your time and consideration.

Example 6

When posting your résumé online, include a cover memo such as the example below. Include key information from your résumé and explain your job objective in detail.

Subject: Seeking advertising account position

I am interested in finding a position with a major advertising firm. I have worked in advertising for four years. As a junior advertising assistant, my duties include contract negotiation, lead liaison, and creative development. My present account assignments include Intel, Cisco, Coca-Cola, and Ford.

My attached résumé includes information about my work history, including related internship experiences in advertising. Please e-mail me at mraj212@mindspring.com.

Attached: MRAJ Resume.doc

Creating and using
portfolios

The word *portfolio* derives from two Latin terms: *port,* which means "to move," and *folio,* which means "papers" or "artifacts." True to these ancient meanings, portfolios are movable collections of papers and artifacts.

Portfolios differ from résumés. A résumé lists facts, including your interests, skills, work history, and accomplishments. Although a portfolio might include these facts, it also includes tangible objects to verify the facts—anything from transcripts of your grades to a videotape that you produced. Résumés offer facts; portfolios provide artifacts.

Photographers, contractors, and designers regularly show portfolios filled with samples of their work. Today, employers and educators increasingly see the portfolio as a tool that's useful for everyone. Some schools require students to create them, and some employers expect to see a portfolio before they'll hire a job applicant.

Enjoy the benefits—academic, professional, and personal

A well-done portfolio benefits its intended audience. To an instructor, your portfolio gives a rich, detailed picture of what you did to create value from a class. To a potential employer, your portfolio gives observable evidence of your skills and achievements. In both cases, a portfolio also documents something more intangible—

In medieval times, artisans who wished to join a guild presented samples of their work. Furniture makers showed cabinets and chairs to their potential mentors. Painters presented samples of their sketches and portraits. Centuries later, people still value a purposeful collection of work samples. It is called a portfolio.

you think about the skills you want to develop and ways to showcase those skills. And when you're applying for work, creating a portfolio prepares you for job interviews. Your portfolio can stand out from stacks of letters and résumés and distinguish you from other applicants.

By creating and using portfolios, you also position yourself for the workplace of the future. People such as William Bridges, author of *Jobshift,* have predicted a "jobless economy."[1] In such an economy, work will be done by teams assembled for specific projects instead of by employees in permanent positions. Workers will move from team to team, company to company, and career to career far more often than they do today. If these changes take place on a wide scale, listing your job titles on a résumé will be less useful than documenting your skills in a vivid, detailed way. Creating and using portfolios is a wonderful way to provide that documentation.

In a more general sense, creating a portfolio helps you reflect on your life as a whole. When selecting artifacts to include in your portfolio, you celebrate your levels of energy, passion, and creativity.

Portfolios benefit you in specific ways. When you create a portfolio to document what you learned during a class, you review the content of the entire course. When you're creating a portfolio related to your career,

Artifacts for your portfolio

When looking for items to include in a portfolio, start with the following checklist. Then brainstorm your own list of added possibilities.

- ❏ Brochures describing a product or service you've created, or workshops you've attended
- ❏ Certificates, licenses, and awards
- ❏ Computer disks with sample publications, databases, or computer programs you've created
- ❏ Course descriptions and syllabuses of classes you've taken or taught
- ❏ Formal evaluations of your work
- ❏ Job descriptions of positions you've held
- ❏ Letters of recommendation
- ❏ Lists of grants, scholarships, clients, customers, and organizations you've joined
- ❏ Newspaper and magazine articles about projects you've participated in
- ❏ Objects you've created or received—anything from badges to jewelry
- ❏ Plans—lists of personal and professional values, goals, action plans, completed tasks, project timelines, and lifelines
- ❏ Printouts of e-mail and Web pages (including your personal Web page)
- ❏ Programs from artistic performances or exhibitions
- ❏ Recordings (digital or voice), compact discs, or CD-ROMs
- ❏ Résumés or a curriculum vitae
- ❏ Sheet music or scores
- ❏ Transcripts of grades, test scores, vocational aptitude tests, or learning style inventories
- ❏ Visual art, including drawings, photographs, collages, and computer graphics
- ❏ Writing samples, such as class reports, workplace memos, proposals, policy and mission statements, bids, manuscripts for articles and books, and published pieces or bibliographies of published writing

accomplishments. You discover key themes in your experience. You clarify what's important to you and create goals for the future. Portfolios promote the cycle of discovery, intention, and action presented in the journal entries and exercises. To create a portfolio, experiment with a four-step process:

1. Collect and catalog artifacts.
2. Plan your portfolio.
3. Assemble your portfolio.
4. Present your portfolio.

Collect and catalog artifacts

An artifact is any object that's important to you and that reveals something about yourself. Examples include photographs, awards, recommendation letters, job descriptions for positions you've held, newspaper articles about projects you've done, lists of grants or scholarships you've received, programs from performances you've given, transcripts of your grades, or models you've constructed.

Taken together, your artifacts form a large and visible "database" that gives a picture of you—what you value, what you've done, and what skills you have. You can add to this database during every year of your life. From this constantly evolving collection of artifacts, you can create many portfolios for different purposes and different audiences.

Start collecting now. Write down the kinds of artifacts you'd like to save. Think about what will be most useful to you in creating portfolios for your courses and your job search. In some cases, collecting artifacts requires follow-up. You might call former instructors or employers to request letters of recommendation. Or you might track down newspaper articles about a service-learning project you did. Your responses to the journal entries and exercises in this chapter can also become part of your portfolio. To save hours when you create your next portfolio, start documenting your artifacts. On a 3x5 card, record the "five W's" about each artifact: *who* was involved with it, *what* you did with it, *when* it was created, *where* it was created, and *why* the artifact is important to you. File these cards and update them as you collect new artifacts. Another option is to manage this information with a computer, using word processing or database software.

Plan your portfolio

When you're ready to create a portfolio for a specific audience, allow some time for planning. Begin with your purpose for creating the portfolio—for example, to demonstrate your learning or to document your work experience as you prepare for a job interview.

Also list some specifics about your audience. Write a description of anyone who will see your portfolio. List what each person already knows about you and predict what else these people will want to know. Answer their questions in your portfolio.

Being aware of your purpose and audience will serve you at every step of creating a portfolio. Screen artifacts with these two factors in mind. If a beautiful artifact fails to meet your purpose or fit your audience, leave it out for now. Save the artifact for a future portfolio.

When you plan your portfolio, also think about how to order and arrange your artifacts. One basic option is a chronological organization. For example, start with work samples from your earliest jobs and work up to the present.

Another option is to structure your portfolio around key themes, such as your values or work skills. When preparing this type of portfolio, you can define *work* to include any time you used a job-related skill, whether or not you got paid.

Assemble your portfolio

With a collection of artifacts and a written plan, you're ready to assemble your portfolio. Arranging artifacts according to your design is a big part of this process. Also include elements to orient your audience members and guide them through your portfolio. Such elements can include:

- A table of contents.

- An overview or summary of the portfolio.

- Titles and captions for each artifact.

- An index to your artifacts.

Although many portfolios take their final form as a collection of papers, remember that this is just one possibility. You can also create a bulletin board, a display, or a case that contains your artifacts. You could even create a recording or a digital portfolio in the form of a personal Web site.

You might find it useful to combine your résumé and portfolio into one document. In other cases, you can mention in your résumé that a separate portfolio is available on request.

Present your portfolio

Your audience might ask you to present your portfolio as part of an interview or oral exam. If that's the case,

rehearse your portfolio presentation the way you would rehearse a speech. Write down questions that people might ask about your portfolio. Prepare some answers, then do a dry run. Present your portfolio to friends and people in your career field, and request their feedback.

That feedback will give you plenty of ideas about ways to revise your portfolio. Any portfolio is a living document. Update it as you acquire new perspectives and skills. ◈

For more ideas on portfolios, go online to

masterstudent.college.hmco.com

Use interviews to hire yourself an employer

The young man's palms are sweating, his heart pounding. His hands are shaking so much that it's hard to button his coat. He fumbles for his keys. Locking the door to his apartment, he anticipates returning there later after a disastrous interview. Huddled against the cold, he slouches out the door, eyes cast downward, walking with short, clipped steps. He's got to hurry. Being late for this appointment could dash his already meager chances.

This is the way that some experience their last moments before a job interview. Instead of sensing opportunity, they're acting like they're about to be sentenced for a crime.

Job interviews don't have to be this way. In fact, they can be exhilarating. They offer a way to meet people. They give you a chance to present your skills. They can expand your network of contacts.

If you've written a career plan, developed a network of job contacts, and prepared a résumé, you've already done much of your preparation for a successful interview. You probably have specific ideas about *what* job skills you want to use and *where* you want to use them. By the time you get to a job interview, you'll be able to see if the job is something that you really want. An interview is a chance for you to assess a potential job and work environment. By interviewing, you're "hiring" yourself an employer.

Many of the suggestions for writing résumés also apply to preparing for a job interview. For example, learn everything you can about the organization. Also be able to list your skills and explain how they can benefit the employer. Following are additional ways to get the most out of an interview.

Start on a positive note and stay there

Many interviewers make their decision about an applicant early on. This can happen during the first five minutes of the interview.

With this in mind, start on a strong note. Do everything you can to create a positive impression early in the interview. Even if you're nervous, you can be outgoing and attentive. Explain how your research led you to the company. Focus on how you can contribute to the employer. Talk about skills or experiences that make you stand out from the crowd of other applicants.

One way to create a favorable first impression is through the way you look. Be well groomed. Wear clothing that's appropriate for the work environment.

Also monitor your nonverbal language. Give a firm handshake and make eye contact (without looking like a zombie). Sit in a way that says you're at ease with people and have a high energy level. During the interview, seize opportunities to smile or even tell an amusing story, as long as it's relevant and positive.

As the interview gets rolling, search for common ground. Finding out that you share an interest with an interviewer can make the conversation sail—and put you closer to a job offer. You can demonstrate interest through focused attention. Listen carefully to everything interviewers say. Few of them will mind if you take notes. This might even impress them.

As the interviewer speaks, listen for challenges that the company faces. Then paint yourself as someone who can help meet those challenges. Explain how you've solved similar problems in the past—and what you can do for the employer right now. To support your claims, mention a detail or two about your accomplishments and refer the interviewer to your résumé for more.

Once you hit a positive note, do everything possible to stay there. When speaking about other people, for example, be courteous. If you find it hard to say something positive about a previous coworker or supervisor, shift the focus back to the interviewer's questions.

Show that you know the value of time. If your interview is scheduled to end soon, mention this to the interviewer. Allow this person the option to end the conversation or extend the interview time.

Ask open-ended questions and listen

Come with your own list of questions for the interviewer. Skilled interviewers will leave time for these. Through your questions, find out:

- What qualifications the job requires—and whether your skills and experience offer a match.

- Whether the job meshes with your career plan.

- Whether the job involves contact with people you'd enjoy.

After you ask a question, give the interviewer plenty of time to talk. Listen at least 50 percent of the time.

Keep the key facts at your command

Remembering essential information during an interview can help things go smoothly. Learn everything you can about each organization that interests you. Get a feel for its strong points and know about its successes in the marketplace. Also find out what challenges the organization faces.

As in a résumé, use interviews to present your skills as unique solutions for those challenges. To jog your memory, keep vital information handy. Examples are a list of references, your social security number, and a summary of your work history. To this, add the main points you'd like to get across during the interview.

You can also bring a list of the SCANS skills discussed at the beginning of this chapter as a reminder to mention the key abilities that you will bring to the job. Explain these skills in ways that any potential employer can understand—including those who have never heard of the SCANS report.

You can enter this information in a computer file and print it out on a single sheet of paper. Consider printing extra copies and giving one to the interviewer. After each interview, revise and update the information.

When appropriate, take the initiative

The interviewer might be uncomfortable with her role. Few people have training in this skill. Interviewers may dominate the conversation, interrupt you, or forget what they want to ask.

When things like this happen, take the initiative. Ask for time to get your questions answered. Sum up your qualifications, and ask for a detailed job description.

Some employers do structured interviews. In this case, a group of people meet with each job candidate and ask similar questions each time. The idea behind this tech-nique is to make sure that all job candidates get a hearing and have an equal chance of getting hired.

When done poorly, structured interviews can be artificial or limiting. If you feel this way, remember the key points you want to make about yourself. Seize every opportunity to weave these points into your answers.

Give yourself a raise before you start work

Effective salary discussion can make a huge difference to your financial well-being. Consider the long-term impact of making just an extra $1,000 per year. Over the next decade, that's an extra $10,000 dollars in pretax income, even if you get no other raises.

It's possible to discuss salary too early in the interview. Let the interviewer bring up this topic. In many cases, an ideal time to talk about salary is when the interviewer is ready to offer you a job. At this point, the employer might be willing to part with more money.

Many interviewers use a standard negotiating strategy. They come to the interview with a salary range in mind. Then they offer a starting salary at the lower end of that range.

This strategy holds an important message for you: Salaries are often flexible, especially for upper-level jobs. You usually do not have to accept the first salary offer.

When you finally get down to money, be prepared. Begin by knowing the salary range that you want. First, figure out how much money you need to maintain your desired standard of living. Then add some margin for comfort. If you're working a job that's comparable to the one you're applying for, consider adding 10 percent to your current salary. Also take into account the value of any benefits the employer provides. Consider stating a desired salary range at first rather than a fixed figure.

Sometimes you can look up standard salary ranges for certain jobs. Reference materials such as the *Occupational Outlook Handbook* (available online at **http://www.bls.gov/oco/**) include this information. Also ask friends who work in your field, and review notes from your informational interviews. Another option is the obvious one—asking interviewers what salary range they have in mind.

Once you know that range, aim high. Name a figure toward the upper end and see how the interviewer responds. Starting high gives you some room to negotiate. See if you can get a raise now rather than later.

Use each *no* to come closer to *yes*

Almost everyone who's ever applied for a job knows the

PRACTICE ANSWERING AND ASKING QUESTIONS

Job interviewers ask many questions. Most of them boil down to a few major concerns:

- Would we be comfortable working with you?

- How did you find out about us?

- How can you help us?

- Will you learn to do this job quickly?

- What makes you different from other applicants?

- Will you work for a salary we can afford?

You can prepare your answers to these questions by focusing on key words. In other words, your job during an interview is to explain *why* you are an ideal candidate for the job, *what* skills and experience you bring to the company, *how* well you will get along with other employees, and *what* specific benefits an employer can expect to gain *if* she hires you.

Before your next job interview, also set up situations where you can practice answering common interview questions. Enroll a friend to play the part of an interviewer and ask you the questions listed above or variations of them.

During your practice interview, keep your speaking brief and to the point. See if you can respond to each question in two minutes or less. Also be alert to any inconsistencies in your answers. For example, if you say that you're a "team player" but prefer to work independently, be prepared to explain. When you're done, ask your friend for feedback.

Also list the three most important things that *you* want to find out about a potential job. Phrase these as questions to ask during the interview and write them in the space below.

_____

_____

_____

_____

_____

_____

_____

lines: "We have no job openings right now." "We'll keep your résumé on file." "There were many qualified applicants for this position." "Even though you did not get the job, thanks for applying." "Best of luck to you as you pursue other career opportunities."

Each of those statements is a different way of saying no. And they can hurt.

However, *no* does not have to be the final word. Focus on the future. If you're turned down for one job, consider ways to turn that *no* into a *yes* next time. Could you present yourself differently during the interview? Could you do more thorough research? Can you fine-tune your career goals? You might even ask the interviewer for suggestions. Also ask for referrals to other companies that might be hiring.

Think about what a job rejection really means. It's not an eternal judgment of your character. It only reflects what happened between you and one potential employer, often over just a few hours or even a few minutes. It means no for right now, for this job, for today—not for every job, forever. Every interview is a source of feedback

about what works—and what doesn't work—in meeting with employers. Use that feedback to interview more effectively next time.

Eventually an employer or client will hire you. It's just a matter of time before the inevitable *yes*. When you're turned down for a job, that is just one more *no* that's out of the way.

Follow up

Within 24 hours, send a thank-you note to the person who interviewed you. To personalize your note, mention a detail from your conversation. Also send thank-you's to anyone else who assisted you with the interview— receptionists, assistants, or contacts within the organization. Prompt follow-up can make you stand out in an interviewer's mind. That could make a difference when the next job opens up.[2]

For more interviewing strategies, go online to masterstudent.college.hmco.com

Sample thank-you notes

A thank-you note can be as important as the interview itself—especially if an employer uses your letter as a deciding factor. Include information in your note that will help remind the employer of your conversation. Follow up with any thoughts you had after your interview. Hand-written or word-processed notes are acceptable.

Remember to send thank-you letters to each person who has interviewed you, and highlight specific references to your meeting. This will help them recall your dialogue. After emphasizing your continued interest, be sure to thank the interviewer for her time.

Thank you for the opportunity to interview for the open paralegal position at Robinson, Muñoz, and Martinez. Learning about the day-to-day aspects of the paralegal cohort at your firm has increased my interest in the position with your firm. Thank you also for inviting the paralegal supervisor to speak with me.

I am attaching my references per your request. I hope you will consider contacting my internship coordinator to learn more about how my skills align with your needs. I look forward to hearing from you soon.

Thank you for taking the time to meet with me on Monday. After learning more about EnviroTechnologies and the role of the IT group, I am very excited about the opportunity to work for your company.

As I mentioned in the interview, I would be very interested in the IT Helpdesk position and feel that I could be an asset to your team because of my experience with crystal reports and Microsoft Access.

Thank you for your consideration. I look forward to hearing your decision.

It was very helpful to speak with you and Mr. Qian last Thursday, and I want to thank you for taking the time to show me around your facilities and providing information about Metropolitan Enterprises, Inc. My previous experience as a Marketing Associate at Southwest Communications has prepared me for the role of Account Manager at your company.

I reviewed the internal Web site that you provided me access to; I was impressed with the development that was done to keep your employees informed of company information. I have some ideas for increasing traffic to this Intranet site that I would like to discuss with you. Let me know when would be a good time for us to meet again. I can be available on Tuesday at 10 a.m. or Wednesday at 1 p.m. If these times do not work with your schedule, please suggest another time.

If you have any questions about my résumé, please call me at (617) 662-1234, or e-mail me at jsmarshall@comcast.com.

Imagetoo/Alamy

Learning on the job

Besides a paycheck, the workplace offers constant opportunities for learning. Employers value the person who is a "quick study"—someone who can get up to speed at a new job in minimum time.

In addition, some of the information you acquired in school might become quickly outdated. Learning how to learn—a key transferable skill—is a necessity if you want to survive in the job market and advance in your career.

Let go of old ideas about learning. Educational literature is full of distinctions such as "theory versus application" and "beginning versus advanced." These distinctions are useful. But if you want to learn on the job, you can often benefit by letting them go. In workplace-based learning, for example:

- There is no "finish" line such as a graduation ceremony. Rather, you learn continuously, taking periodic progress checks to assess your current skills.
- Outside of formal training programs, there are no course divisions. A new job might call on you to integrate knowledge of several subjects at once.
- There is no syllabus for learning a subject with assignments carefully laid out in planned sequence. You might learn concepts in an "illogical" order as dictated by the day-to-day demands of a job.

If all this sounds like a prescription for chaos, consider that it reflects the ways you've always learned outside the classroom. Teaching yourself anything from a new golf swing to a new song on the guitar has a lot in common with the way you teach yourself on the job.

Seize informal opportunities to learn. At work, your learning may take place in unplanned, informal ways. Look for opportunities to:

- Do self-directed reading on topics related to new job tasks.
- Observe people who demonstrate a skill that you would like to develop.

- Ask questions on the spot.
- Attend trade shows for new products or services offered by your company's competitors.
- Join professional organizations in your field that offer workshops and seminars.
- Make yourself into the company expert on a new product or procedure by digging into brochures, Web sites, professional journals, technical manuals, and other sources of information that your coworkers may have overlooked.

Create a development plan. Some organizations require their employees to create a professional development plan. If your employer does not require such a plan, create one anyway. You can do this by answering several "W questions":

- **What** skill or specialized base of knowledge is most essential for you to acquire now in order to do your job more effectively?
- **Who** has acquired this knowledge or demonstrated this skill and would be willing to share their expertise? Perhaps one of these people would be willing to mentor you.
- If learning your desired knowledge or skill requires experiences outside your work environment, **where** will you go to pursue those experiences? Answers might include a night class at a local business school or a company-sponsored training session.
- **When** would you like to demonstrate mastery of your new knowledge or skill? Give yourself a due date for meeting each professional development goal.
- In addition, ask **how** you will know that you've mastered the new knowledge or skill. List specifically what you will say or do differently as a result of your development.
- Finally, consider **what if**—what if the job promotions and other career possibilities that you gain help you to meet the goals in your development plan?

As you answer these questions, keep focused. If you try to develop too many skills at once, you might end with few gains over the long run. Consider setting and achieving one major development goal each year.

Act on your plan every day. Remember that the word *learning* is often defined as an enduring change in behavior. Focus on a new work-related behavior—such as creating a to-do list or overcoming procrastination—that will make a significant, positive, and immediate difference in your performance. Then do it. Every day, implement one new behavior or practice one new habit. In the workplace, learning means doing. ✦

In its *Report on the American Workforce 2001*, the U.S. Department of Labor concluded that "the United States likely will continue to be a nation in which increasing racial and ethnic diversity is the rule, not the exception."[3] Translation: Your next boss or coworker could be a person whose life experience and view of the world differ radically from yours.

join a diverse workplace

P eople of all races, ethnicities, and cultures can use several strategies to reach common ground.

Expect differences

To begin, remember an obvious fact: People differ. Obvious as it is, this fact is easy to forget. Most of us unconsciously judge others by a single set of standards—our own. That can lead to communication breakdown. Consider some examples:

- A man in Costa Rica works for a multinational company. He turns down a promotion that would take his family to California. This choice mystifies the company's executives. Yet the man has grandparents who are in ill health, and leaving them behind would be taboo in his country.

- A Native American woman avoids eye contact with her superiors. Her coworkers see her as aloof. However, she comes from a culture where people seldom make eye contact with their superiors.

- A Caucasian woman from Ohio travels to Mexico City on business. She shows up promptly for a 9 a.m. meeting and finds that it starts 30 minutes late and goes an hour beyond its scheduled ending time. She's entered a culture with a flexible sense of time.

- An American executive schedules a meeting over dinner with people from his company's office in Italy. As soon as the group orders food, the executive launches into a discussion of his agenda items. He notices that his coworkers from Italy seem unusually silent, and he wonders if they feel offended. He forgets that they come from a culture where people phase in to business discussions slowly—only after building a relationship through "small talk."

To prevent misunderstandings, remember that culture touches every aspect of human behavior, ranging from

the ways people greet one another to the ways they resolve conflict. Differences in culture could affect any encounter you have with another person. Expecting differences up front helps you keep an open mind and lays the groundwork for all the strategies that follow.

Use language with care

Even people who speak the same language sometimes use simple words that can be confused with each other. For instance, giving someone a "mickey" can mean pulling a practical joke—or slipping a drug into someone's drink. We can find it tough to communicate simple observations, let alone abstract concepts.

You can help by communicating simply and directly. When meeting with people who speak English as a second language, think twice before using figures of speech or slang expressions. Stick to standard English and enunciate clearly.

Also remember that nonverbal language differs across cultures. For example, people from India may shake their head from side to side to indicate agreement, not disagreement. And the hand signal that signifies *OK* to many Americans—thumb and index finger forming a circle—is considered obscene in Brazil.

Put messages in context

When speaking to people of another culture, you might find that words carry only part of an intended message. In many countries, strong networks of shared assumptions form a context for communication.

As an example, people from some Asian and Arabic countries might not include every detail of an agreement in a written contract. These people often place a high value on keeping verbal promises. Spelling out all the details in writing might be considered an insult.

Knowing such facts can help you prevent and resolve conflicts in the workplace.

Test for understanding

To promote cross-cultural understanding, look for signs that your message got through clearly. Ask questions without talking down to your audience: *Am I making myself clear? Is there anything that doesn't make sense?* Watch for nonverbal cues of understanding, such as a nod or smile.

Relate to individuals—not "cultures"

When we see people as faceless representatives of a race or ethnic group, we gloss over important differences. One powerful way to overcome stereotypes is to treat each person as an individual. Remember that the members of any culture can differ widely in beliefs and behaviors.

Discover what you share

The word *communicate* is closely related to *commune* and *common*. This fact points to a useful strategy: When relating to people of another culture, search for what you have in common.

You can start on the job. People from different cultures can share many values related to working: the desire to make more money, to be recognized for achievements, and to win promotions. Cultures often overlap at the level of basic human values—desires for safety, health, and economic security.

Learn about another culture

You can also promote cross-cultural understanding through the path of knowledge. Consider learning everything you can about another culture. Read about that culture and take related classes. Cultivate friends from that culture and take part in their community events. Get a feel for the customs, music, and art that members of the group share. If appropriate, travel abroad to learn more. Also ask about foreign language training your company may offer to the staff.[4]

Follow up with action at work. Join project teams with diverse members. Experiencing diversity firsthand can be a positive experience when you're working with others to meet a common goal.

Expand networks

People with narrow circles of relationships can be at a disadvantage when trying to change jobs or enter a new field. For maximum flexibility in your career path, stay connected to people of your own culture—*and* cultivate contacts with people of other cultures.

Counter bias and discrimination

In the United States, laws dating back to the Equal Pay Act of 1963 and Title VII of the Civil Rights Act of 1964 ban discrimination in virtually all aspects of the work world, from hiring and firing to transfers and promotions. Congress set up the Equal Employment Opportunity Commission (EEOC) to enforce these laws. You can get more information through the EEOC Web site at **http://www.eeoc.gov**.

If you think that you've been the subject of discrimination, take time to examine the facts. Before filing a lawsuit, exhaust other options. Start by bringing the problem to your supervisor, your company's equal employment officer, or someone from the EEOC.

Stereotypes based on race, ethnic group, gender, and disability are likely to fade as the workplace becomes more diverse. As they do, disprove stereotypes through your behavior. Set high standards for yourself and meet them. Seek out key projects that make you visible in the organization, and then perform effectively. These are useful success strategies for anyone in the workplace.

Also keep records of your performance. Log your achievements. Ask for copies of your performance evaluations and make sure they're accurate. Having a stack of favorable evaluations can help you make your case when bringing a complaint or resolving conflict.

Be willing to bridge gaps

Simply being *willing* to bridge culture gaps can be just as crucial as knowing about another group's customs or learning their language. People from other cultures might sense your attitude and be willing to reach out to you.

Begin by displaying some key attributes of a critical thinker. Be open-minded and willing to suspend judgment. Notice when you make assumptions based on another person's accent, race, religion, or gender. Become willing to discover your own biases, listen fully to people with other points of view, enter new cultural territory, and even feel uncomfortable at times.

It's worth it. Bridging to people of other cultures means that you gain new chances to learn, make contacts, increase your career options, and expand your friendships. The ability to work with people of many cultures is a marketable skill—and a way to enlarge your world. ✖

Every organization, large or small, develops its own culture. One way to succeed in the workplace is to "decode" corporate cultures—the basic assumptions and shared values that shape human behavior in the workplace every day.

You can use this knowledge to prevent misunderstanding, resolve conflict, and forge lasting relationships.

ImageSource/Fotosearch

Decoding corporate culture

Start by observing

Being culturally savvy starts with discovering "the way we do things around here"—the beliefs and behaviors that are widely shared by your coworkers. In terms of the cycle of learning, this means that your efforts to decode corporate culture begin with the stage of reflective observation.

In other words, keep your eyes open. See what kind of actions are rewarded and which are punished. Observe what people do and say to gain credibility in your organization.

You may disagree with what you see and find yourself making negative judgments about your coworkers. Start by noticing those judgments and letting them go. You cannot fully observe behaviors and judge them at the same time. Play the role of a social scientist and collect facts impartially.

Create theories about unwritten rules

Next, create theories about how people succeed in your organization. In terms of the learning cycle, this is the stage of abstract conceptualization. In particular, notice the unwritten "rules" that govern your workplace. Your coworkers may behave on the basis of beliefs such as:

- Never make the boss look bad.
- Some commitments are not meant to be kept.
- If you want to get promoted, then be visible.
- Everyone is expected to work some overtime.

Once you understand the norms and standards of your company, you can consciously choose to accept them. Or you can challenge them by actively experimenting with new behaviors and immersing yourself in new experiences. In any case, changing any organization begins with a first step—telling the truth about how it works right now.

Cope with office politics

The unspoken rules for getting recognized and rewarded are usually what people mean when they talk about *office politics*. One way to deal with office politics is to pretend they don't exist. The downfall of this strategy is that politics are a fact of life.

Another option is to be politically savvy—*and* still hold fast to your values. You can move through the echelons of power and meet ethical career goals at the same time. More specifically:

- **Be visible**. To gain credibility in your organization, get involved in a high-profile project that you believe in. Then perform well. Go beyond the minimum standards. Meet the project goals—and deliver even more.

- **Grow "industry-smart."** Read trade journals and newsletters related to your field. Keep up with current developments. Speak the language shared by the decision makers in your organization.

- **Promote your boss.** During your first year with an organization, the single most important person in your work life could be your boss. This is the person who most closely monitors your performance. This is also the person who can become your biggest advocate. Find out what this person needs and wants. Learn about her goals and then assist her to meet them.

- **Get close to the power centers**. People who advance to top positions are often those who know the language of sales, marketing, accounting, and information technology. These departments are power centers. They directly affect the bottom line. However, you can enhance your company's profitability no matter what position you hold. Look for ways to save money and time. Suggest workable ways to streamline procedures or reduce costs. Focus on solutions to problems, no matter how small, and you'll play the ultimate political game—making a contribution. ✄

Dealing with **sexism** and sexual harassment

Sexism and sexual harassment are real. These are events that occur throughout the year at schools and workplaces. Nearly all of these incidents are illegal or violate organizational policies.

Until the early nineteenth century, women in the United States were banned from attending colleges and universities. Today they make up the majority of first-year students in higher education, yet they still encounter bias based on gender.

This bias can take many forms. For example, instructors might gloss over the contributions of women. Students in philosophy class might never hear of a woman named Hypatia, an ancient Greek philosopher and mathematician. Those majoring in computer science might never learn about Rear Admiral Grace Murray Hopper, who pioneered the development of a computer language named COBOL. And your art history textbook might not mention the Mexican painter Frida Kahlo or the American painter Georgia O'Keeffe.

Though men can be subjects of sexism and sexual harassment, women are more likely to experience this form of discrimination. Even the most well-intentioned people might behave in ways that hurt or discount women. Sexism is a factor when:

- Instructors use only masculine pronouns—*he, his,* and *him*—to refer to both men and women.

- Career counselors hint that careers in mathematics and science are not appropriate majors or career fields for women.

- Students pay more attention to feedback from a male teacher than from a female teacher.

- Women are not called on in class, their comments during meetings in the workplace are ignored, or they are overly praised for answering the simplest questions.

- Examples given in a textbook or lecture assign women only to traditionally "female" roles, such as wife, mother, day care provider, elementary school teacher, or nurse.

- People assume that middle-aged women who return to school or the workplace have too many family commitments to study adequately or do well in their jobs.

Many kinds of behavior—both verbal and physical—can be categorized as sexual harassment. This kind of discrimination involves unwelcome sexual conduct. Examples of such conduct in a school setting are:

- Sexual touching or advances.

- Any other unwanted touch.

- Unwanted verbal intimacy.

- Sexual graffiti.

- Displaying or distributing sexually explicit materials.

- Sexual gestures or jokes.

- Pressure for sexual favors.

- Talking about personal sexual activity.

- Spreading rumors about someone's sexual activity or rating someone's sexual performance.

Sexual Harassment: It's Not Academic, a pamphlet from the U.S. Department of Education, quotes a woman who experienced sexual harassment in higher education: "The financial officer made it clear that I could get the money I needed if I slept with him."

That's an example of *quid pro quo harassment.* This legal term applies when students believe that an educational decision depends on submitting to unwelcome sexual conduct. *Hostile environment harassment* takes place when such incidents are severe, persistent, or pervasive.

The feminist movement has raised awareness about discrimination against women. We can now respond to sexism and sexual harassment in the places we live, work, and go to school. Specific strategies follow.

Point out sexist language and behavior. When you see examples of sexism, point them out. Your message can be more effective if you use "I" messages instead of personal attacks. Indicate the specific statements and behaviors that you consider sexist.

For example, you could rephrase a sexist comment so that it targets another group, such as Jews or African Americans. People might spot anti-Semitism or racism more readily than sexism.

Keep in mind that men can also be subjected to sexism, ranging from antagonistic humor to exclusion from jobs that have traditionally been done by women.

Observe your own language and behavior.
Looking for sexist behavior in others is effective. Detecting it in yourself can be just as powerful. Write a Discovery Statement about specific comments that could be interpreted as sexist. Then notice if you say any of these things. Also ask people you know to point out occasions when you use similar statements. Follow up with an Intention Statement that describes how you plan to change your speaking or behavior.

You can also write Discovery Statements about the current level of intimacy (physical and verbal) in any of your relationships at home, work, or school. Be sure that any increase in the level of intimacy is mutually agreed upon.

Encourage support for women.
Through networks, women can work to overcome the effects of sexism. Strategies include study groups for women, women's job networks, and professional organizations, such as Women in Communications. Other examples are counseling services and health centers for women, family planning agencies, and rape prevention centers. Check your school catalog and library to see if any of these services are available at your school.

If your school does not have the women's networks you want, you can help form them. Sponsor a one-day or one-week conference on women's issues. Create a discussion or reading group for the women in your class, department, residence hall, union, or neighborhood.

Set limits.
Women, value yourselves. Recognize your right to an education without the distraction of inappropriate and invasive behavior. Trust your judgment about when your privacy or your rights are being violated. Decide now what kind of sexual comments and actions you're uncomfortable with—and refuse to put up with them.

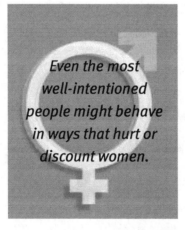

Even the most well-intentioned people might behave in ways that hurt or discount women.

Take action. If you are sexually harassed, take action. Some key federal legislation protects the rights of women. One is Title VII of the Civil Rights Act of 1964. Guidelines for interpreting this law offer the following definition of harassment. *Unwelcome sexual advances, requests for sexual favors, and other verbal or physical conduct of a sexual nature constitute sexual harassment when:*

1. *Submission to this conduct becomes a condition of employment.*

2. *Women's response to such conduct is used as a basis for employment decisions.*

3. *This conduct interferes with work performance or creates an offensive work environment.*[5]

The law also states that schools must take action to prevent sexual harassment.

Another relevant law is Title IX of the Education Amendments of 1972. This act bans discrimination against students and employees on the basis of gender. It applies to any educational program receiving federal funds.

If you believe that you've been sexually harassed, report the incident to a school official. This person can be a teacher, administrator, or campus security officer. Check to see if your school has someone specially designated to handle your complaint, such as an affirmative action officer or Title IX coordinator.

You can also file a complaint with the Office for Civil Rights (OCR), a federal agency that makes sure schools and workplaces comply with Title IX. In your complaint, include your name, address, and daytime phone number, along with the date of the incident and a description of it. Do this within 180 days of the incident. You can contact the OCR at 1-800-421-3481 or go to the agency's Web site at **http://bcol01.ed.gov/CFAPPS/OCR/contactus.cfm**. Your community might also offer resources to protect against sexual discrimination. Examples are public interest law firms, legal aid societies, and unions that employ lawyers. People with these organizations can also advise you about when and how to take action for sexual harass-ment in the workplace to enforce these laws. You can get more information through the Equal Employment Opportunity Commission (EEOC) at **http://www. eeoc.gov.**

Strategies for working with a mentor

One strategy for planning your career and succeeding in the workplace is to find a mentor— a partner in your professional and personal development. Many people will be flattered to take on such a role in your life.

Start with a development plan.

Before you ask someone to mentor you, reflect on your goals for this relationship. Begin with *what* you want to gain rather than *who* to ask for mentoring. List the specific skills that you want to develop with a mentor's involvement. Over time you might work with several mentors, each with different expertise, to develop a variety of skills.

For maximum clarity, put your development plan in writing. Consider using the Discovery and Intention Journal Entry System. Write Discovery Statements to list your current skills, recent examples of how you've used them, and insights from your mentor.

Whenever possible, create a way to measure your progress. For example, you could note the number of times you practice a new habit. Or you could summarize ratings from your performance reviews at work. Include these measurements in your Discovery Statements and share them with your mentor.

Follow up with Intention Statements that describe exactly what new behaviors you want to implement, along with ongoing updates to your development plan.

In your Intention Statements, include a timeline. Use your goal-setting skills to set due dates for acquiring new skills or producing new outcomes in your life. Also state when you want to begin and end the mentoring sessions. Keep in mind that many mentoring relationships are short-term, taking place over weeks or months rather than years.

Approach potential mentors.

Identify several people who have demonstrated competence in the skills you want to gain, along with the energy and desire to take on a mentee—that is, you. If you can find someone at work who has a positive reputation and influence in your organization, that's an added plus.

Next, contact each person on your list and mention that you're seeking a mentor. Summarize your development plan and timetable. Also suggest ways that you can create value for a mentor, such as helping that person complete a project or achieve one of *his* development goals. The more you give to the mentor relationship, the more you'll get out of it.

If a potential mentor is too busy to work with you right now, ask if she can refer you to someone else. After meeting with several people, choose one person to work with.

Accept your mentor's feedback.

Remember that a mentor is not a boss, parent, or taskmaster. Instead, you're looking for coaching. A coach helps you clarify your goals and then offers nonjudgmental observations of your behavior along with suggestions for improvement. However, the responsibility for your day-to-day performance and long-term development lies with you.

Schedule regular meetings with your mentor. During these meetings, put all your listening skills to work. Resist the temptation to debate, argue, or justify your behavior. Simply receive what your mentor has to say. Ask questions to clarify anything you don't understand.

Remember that when you asked for mentoring, you signed on for objective feedback and suggestions—including ideas you may have resisted in the past. A commitment to change implies the willingness to think, speak, and act in new ways. Stay open to suggestion.

Beyond listening, move into action. When your mentor offers an insight, look for an immediate way to apply it. Experiment with a new behavior every day.

Seek closure—and continue.

When you've come to the end of a mentoring relationship, offer your thanks and celebrate your accomplishments. Solidify your learning by listing the top five insights or skills you gained.

In addition, choose your next step. List upcoming opportunities to practice your newly acquired skills. Also consider the benefits of working with a mentor again in the future. This is a development tool that you can use for the rest of your life. ✍

Mrs. Eleanor Roosevelt), (Maria Tallchief, "Firebird") New York City Ballet, (Roberto Clemente), (Frederick Douglass) Charles Phelps Cushing, (Nelson Mandela) © Paul Velasco/Gallo Images/Corbis, (Copernicus), (Thomas A. Edison), (Aung San Suu Kyi) Emmanuel Dunand/Getty, (Winston Churchill), (Queen Elizabeth I), (Albert Einstein) Alan W. Richards/Princeton, (Jesse Owens) © Bettman, (Marian Anderson) New York Public Library, (Golda Meir) © Reuters/Corbis

We are all leaders

Many people mistakenly think that leaders are only those with formal titles such as *supervisor* or *manager*. In fact, some leaders have no such titles. Some have never supervised others. Like Mahatma Gandhi, some people change the face of the world without ever reaching a formal leadership position.

While many of us will never become so well known, we all have the capacity to make significant changes in the world around us. Through our actions and words we constantly influence what happens in our classrooms, offices, communities, and families. We are all conscious leaders, even if sometimes we are unconscious of that fact.

Own your leadership

Let go of the reluctance that many of us feel toward assuming leadership. It's impossible to escape leadership. Every time you speak, you lead others in some small or large way. Every time you take action, you lead others through your example. Every time you ask someone to do something, you are in essence leading that person. Leadership becomes more effective when it is consciously applied.

Take on big projects

Leaders make promises. And effective leaders make big promises. These words—"I will do it. You can count on me"—distinguish a leader.

Look around your world to see what needs to be done and then take it on. Consider taking on the biggest project you can think of—

ending world hunger, eliminating nuclear weapons, wiping out poverty, promoting universal literacy. Think about how you'd spend your life if you knew that you could make a difference regarding these overwhelming problems. Then take the actions you considered. See what a difference they can make for you and for others.

Tackle projects that stretch you to your limits—projects that are worthy of your time and talents.

Provide feedback

An effective leader is a mirror to others. Share what you see. Talk with others about what they are doing effectively—*and* what they are doing ineffectively.

Keep in mind that people might not enjoy your feedback. Some would probably rather not hear it at all.

Two things can help. One is to let people know up front that if they sign on to work with you, they can expect feedback. Also give your feedback with skill. Use "I" messages. Back up any criticisms with specific observations and facts. And when people complete a task with exceptional skill, point that out, too.

Model your values

"Be the change you want to see" is a useful motto for leaders. Perhaps you want to see integrity, focused attention, and productivity in the people around you. Begin by modeling these qualities yourself.

It's easy to excite others about a goal when you are enthusiastic about it yourself. Having fun while being productive is contagious. If you bring these qualities to a project, others might follow suit.

Make requests—lots of them

An effective leader is a request machine. Making requests—both large and small—is an act of respect. When we ask a lot from others, we demonstrate our respect for them and our confidence in their abilities.

At first, some people might get angry when we make requests of them. Over time, many will see that requests are compliments, opportunities to expand their skills. Ask a lot from others, and they might appreciate you for it.

Focus on the problem, not the person

Sometimes projects do not go as planned. Big mistakes

occur. If this happens, focus on the project and the mistakes—not the personal faults of your colleagues. People do not make mistakes on purpose. If they did, we would call them "on-purposes," not mistakes. Most people will join you in solving a problem if your focus is on the problem, not on what they did wrong.

Share credit

As a leader, constantly give away the praise and acknowledgment that you receive. When you're congratulated for your performance, pass it on to others. Share the credit with the group.

When you're a leader, the results you achieve depend on the efforts of many others. Acknowledging that fact often is more than telling the truth—it's essential if you want to continue to count on their support in the future.

Delegate

Ask a coworker or classmate to take on a job that you'd like to see done. Ask the same of your family or friends. Delegate tasks to the mayor of your town, the governor of your state, and the leaders of your country.

Take on projects that are important to you. Then find people who can lead the effort. You can do this even when you have no formal role as a leader.

We often see delegation as a tool that's available only to those above us in the chain of command. Actually, delegating up or across an organization can be just as effective. Consider delegating a project to your boss. That is, ask her to take on a job that you'd like to see accomplished. This might be a job that you cannot do, given your position in the company.

Paint a vision

Help others see the big picture, the ultimate purpose of a project. Speak a lot about the end result and the potential value of what you're doing.

There's a biblical saying: "Without vision, the people perish." Long-term goals usually involve many intermediate steps. Unless we're reminded of the purpose for those day-to-day actions, our work can feel like a grind. Leadership is the art of helping others lift their eyes to the horizon—keeping them in touch with the ultimate value and purpose of a project. Keeping the vision alive helps spirits soar again. ⬥

Loving your next job

Job disappointment has countless symptoms, including statements such as "My boss is a jerk," "I'm so bored," and "This is too hard."

(collage) Walter Kopec

Faced with such sentiments, there's a tempting short-term solution: "I quit." Sometimes that is a reasonable option. In many cases of job dissatisfaction, however, there are solutions that do less damage to your immediate income and your long-term job prospects.

Manage your expectations

Instead of changing jobs, consider changing the way you think. Perhaps you never expected to run the company within six months after joining it. Yet your expectations for your current job might still be unrealistic.

This suggestion can be especially useful if you've just graduated from school and find yourself working in an entry-level position in your field. Students who are used to stimulating class discussions and teachers with a passion for their subject might be shocked by the realities of the workplace: people who hide behind a cubicle and avoid human contact; managers with technical skills but no people skills; coworkers who get promoted on the basis of political favors rather than demonstrated skills.

If you're unhappy at work, review the Power Process: "Notice your pictures and let them go." Then ask which of your work-related pictures might be related to your upset. Perhaps you're operating on the basis of unrealistic "shoulds" such as:

- My first job after graduating *should* draw on all the skills I developed in school.
- Everyone I meet on a job *should* be interesting, competent, and kind.
- Every task that I perform at work *should* be enjoyable.
- My work environment *should* be problem-free.

See if you can replace the should in such statements with *can* or *could*. For example: "Even though I'm not using all my skills, I *can* use this job to learn about corporate culture and coping with office politics." Or "I *could* use this job to develop at least one skill that I can transfer to my next job."

Practice problem solving

Sometimes you can benefit by adjusting more than your attitude. Apply your transferable skills at problem solving. Write Discovery Statements about:

- How you felt when you started the job.
- When you started feeling unhappy with the job.
- Any specific events that triggered your dissatisfaction.

This writing can help you pinpoint the sources of job dissatisfaction. Possibilities include conflict with coworkers, a mismatch between your skills and the job requirements, or a mismatch between your personal values and the values promoted in the workplace.

No matter what the source, you can brainstorm solutions. Ask friends and family members for help. If you're bored with work, propose a project that will create value for your boss and offer to lead it. If your supervisor seems unhappy with your performance, ask for coaching to do it better. If you're in conflict with a coworker, apply strategies for resolving conflict.

Moving into action to solve the problem offers a reminder that you—not your boss or coworkers—are in charge of the quality of your life.

Focus on process

You can also take a cue from the term *Power Process*. Shift your focus from the content of your job to the process you use—from *what* you do to *how* you do it. Even if a task seems boring or beneath you, see if you can do it impeccably and with total attention. As you do, project a professional image in everything from the way you dress to the way you speak. One strategy for handling a dead-end job is to do it so well that you get noticed—and promoted to a new job. ✍

journal entry

Discovery/Intention Statement

You can use this journal entry any time that you feel unhappy at work. Complete the following sentences, using additional paper as needed.

I discovered that:

- If I could change one thing about this job, I would . . .

- Something I *do* like about this job is . . .

- The transferable skills I am learning on this job include . . .

- I intend to make this job—or my next job—more satisfying by . . .

Define your values, align your actions

One key way to choose what's next in your life is to define your values. Values are the things in life that you want for their own sake. Values influence and guide your choices, including your moment-by-moment choices of what to do and what to have. Your values define who you are and who you want to be.

Some people are guided by values that they automatically adopt from others or by values that remain largely unconscious. These people could be missing the opportunity to live a life that's truly of their own choosing.

Investing time and energy to define your values is a pivotal suggestion. This system includes the values of:

- Focused attention
- Self-responsibility
- Integrity
- Risk-taking
- Contributing

You'll find these values and related ones directly stated in the Power Processes throughout the chapter. For instance:

Discover what you want is about the importance of living a purpose-based life.

Ideas are tools points to the benefits of being willing to experiment with new ideas.

Be here now expresses the value of focused attention.

Love your problems (and experience your barriers) is about seeing difficulties as opportunities to develop new skills.

Notice your pictures and let them go is about adopting an attitude of open-mindedness.

I create it all is about taking responsibility for our beliefs and behaviors.

Detach reminds us that our core identity and value as a person does not depend on our possessions, our circumstances, or even our accomplishments.

Find a bigger problem is about offering our lives by contributing to others.

Employ your word expresses the value of making and keeping agreements.

Risk being a fool is about courage—the willingness to take risks for the sake of learning something new.

In addition, most of the study skills and workplace skills you read about in these pages have their source in values. Even the simple act of sharing your notes with a student who missed a class is an example of contributing.

As you begin to define your values, consider those who have gone before you. In creeds, scriptures, philosophies, myths, and sacred stories, the human race has left a vast and varied record of values. Be willing to look everywhere, including sources that are close to home. The creed of your local church or temple might eloquently describe some of your values—so might the mission statement of your school, company, or club. Another way to define your values is to describe the qualities of people you admire.

Also translate your values into behavior. Though defining your values is powerful, it doesn't guarantee any results. To achieve your goals, take actions that align with your values. ✄

One set of values

Following is a sample list of values. Don't read it with the idea that it is the "right" set of values for you. Instead, use this list as a point of departure in creating your own list.

Value: Be accountable

This means being:

- Honest
- Reliable
- Trustworthy
- Operating with integrity
- Dependable
- Responsible
- Making and keeping agreements

Value: Be loving

This means being:

- Affectionate
- Devoted
- Accepting
- Considerate
- Respectful
- Inclusive
- Ethical
- Dedicated
- Equitable
- Gentle
- Forgiving
- Friendly
- Fair

Value: Be promotive

This means being:

- Nurturing
- Contributing—charitable; thrifty; generous with time, money, and possessions
- Frugal—achieving the best results with the fewest possible dollars
- Helpful
- Encouraging
- Reasonable
- Judicious
- Cooperative—working as a member of a team or a community
- Appreciative

Value: Be candid

This means being:

- Honest
- Genuine
- Frank
- Spontaneous
- Free of deceit
- Able to avoid false modesty without arrogance
- Self-disclosing
- Open about strengths and weaknesses
- Authentic
- Self-expressed
- Outspoken
- Sincere

Value: Be detached

This means being:

- Impartial
- Experimental
- Open-minded
- Adaptable
- Trusting
- Joyful
- Unbiased
- Satisfied
- Patient (not resigned)
- Without distress
- Tolerant
- Willing to surrender

Value: Be aware of the possible

This means being:

- Creative
- Resourceful
- Foresighted
- Visionary
- Audacious
- Imaginative
- Inventive
- Holistic
- Inquisitive
- Exploring

THE DISCOVERY WHEEL

Do this exercise online at `masterstudent.college.hmco.com`

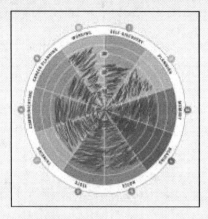

The Discovery Wheel is another opportunity to tell the truth about the kind of student you are and the kind of student you want to become.

This is not a test. There are no trick questions, and the answers will have meaning only for yourself.

Here are two suggestions to make this exercise more effective. First, think of it as the beginning of an opportunity to change. Second, lighten up. A little laughter can make self-evaluations a lot more effective.

Here's how the Discovery Wheel works. By the end of this exercise, you will have filled in a circle similar to the one on this page. The Discovery Wheel circle is a picture of how you see yourself. The closer the shading comes to the outer edge of the circle, the higher the evaluation of a specific skill. In the example to the right, the student has rated her reading skills low and her note-taking skills high.

The terms "high" and "low" are not meant to reflect a negative judgment. The Discovery Wheel is not a permanent picture of who you are. It is a picture of how you view your strengths and weaknesses as a student today. To begin this exercise, read the following statements and award yourself points for each one, using the point system described below. Then add up your point total for each section and shade the Discovery Wheel at the end of this exercise to the appropriate level.

5 points
This statement is always or almost always true of me.

4 points
This statement is often true of me.

3 points
This statement is true of me about half the time.

2 points
This statement is seldom true of me.

1 point
This statement is never or almost never true of me.

1. _____ I enjoy learning.
2. _____ I understand and apply the concept of multiple intelligences.
3. _____ I connect my courses to my purpose for being in school and the benefits I intend to get from my education.
4. _____ I regularly assess my personal strengths and areas for improvement.
5. _____ I am satisfied with how I am progressing toward achieving my goals.
6. _____ I use my knowledge of learning styles to support my success in school and at work.
7. _____ I am willing to consider any idea that can help me succeed in school—even if I initially disagree with that idea.
8. _____ I monitor my habits and change them in ways that support my success.

_____ Total score (1) *Self-Discovery*

1. _____ I set long-term goals and periodically review them.
2. _____ I set midterm and short-term goals to support my long-term goals.
3. _____ I write a plan for each day and each week.
4. _____ I assign priorities to what I choose to do each day.
5. _____ I plan regular recreation time.
6. _____ I adjust my study time to meet the demands of individual courses.

7. _____ I have adequate time each day to accomplish what I plan.

8. _____ I effectively plan projects and manage time in work settings.

_____ Total score (2) *Planning*

1. _____ I am confident of my ability to remember.

2. _____ I can remember people's names.

3. _____ At the end of a presentation, I can summarize what was presented.

4. _____ I apply techniques that enhance my memory skills.

5. _____ I can recall information when I'm under pressure.

6. _____ I remember important information clearly and easily.

7. _____ I can jog my memory when I have difficulty recalling.

8. _____ I can relate new information to what I've already learned.

_____ Total score (3) *Memory*

1. _____ I preview and review reading materials.

2. _____ When reading, I ask myself questions about the material.

3. _____ I underline or highlight important passages when reading.

4. _____ When I read textbooks or reports, I am alert and awake.

5. _____ I relate what I read to my life.

6. _____ I select a reading strategy to fit the type of material I'm reading.

7. _____ I take effective notes when I read.

8. _____ When I don't understand what I'm reading, I note my questions and find answers.

_____ Total score (4) *Reading*

1. _____ When I am in class, I focus my attention.

2. _____ I take notes in class and during meetings.

3. _____ I am aware of various methods for taking notes and choose those that work best for me.

4. _____ I distinguish major ideas from examples and other supporting material.

5. _____ I copy down material that the presenter writes on the board or overhead projector.

6. _____ I can put important concepts into my own words.

7. _____ My notes are valuable for review.

8. _____ I review notes within 24 hours.

_____ Total score (5) *Notes*

1. _____ I feel confident and calm during an exam.

2. _____ I manage my time during exams and am able to complete them.

3. _____ I am able to predict test questions.

4. _____ I adapt my test-taking strategy to the kind of test I'm taking.

5. _____ I create value from any type of evaluation, including performance reviews.

6. _____ I start reviewing for tests at the beginning of the term and continue reviewing throughout the term.

7. _____ I manage stress and maintain my health even when I feel under pressure.

8. _____ My sense of personal worth is independent of my test scores.

_____ Total score (6) *Tests*

1. _____ I have flashes of insight and often think of solutions to problems at unusual times.

2. _____ I use brainstorming to generate solutions to a variety of problems.

3. _____ When I get stuck on a creative project, I use specific methods to get unstuck.

4. _____ I see problems and tough decisions as opportunities for learning and personal growth.

5. _____ I am open to different points of view and diverse cultural perspectives.

6. _____ I can support my points of view with sound logic and evidence.

7. _____ I use critical thinking to resolve ethical dilemmas.

8. _____ As I share my viewpoints with others, I am open to their feedback.

_____ Total score (7) **Thinking**

1. _____ I am candid with others about who I am, what I feel, and what I want.

2. _____ Other people tell me that I am a good listener.

3. _____ I can communicate my upset and resolve conflict without blaming others.

4. _____ I work effectively as a member of a project team.

5. _____ I am learning ways to thrive with diversity—attitudes and behaviors that will support my career success.

6. _____ I can effectively plan, research, draft, and revise a large writing assignment.

7. _____ I learn effectively from materials and activities that are posted online.

8. _____ I prepare and deliver effective speeches and presentations.

_____ Total score (8) **Communicating**

1. _____ I relate school to what I plan to do for the rest of my life.

2. _____ I connect my attitudes, interests, and skills to career possibilities.

3. _____ I use the library, the Internet, and other resources to monitor developments in the job market.

4. _____ I use the career planning and job placement services offered by my school.

5. _____ In work settings, I look for models of success and cultivate mentors.

6. _____ I manage my income and expenses to fund my education and meet other financial goals.

7. _____ I have a written career plan and update it regularly.

8. _____ I use internships and other work experiences to refine my career plans.

_____ Total score (9) **Career Planning**

1. _____ My work contributes something worthwhile to the world.

2. _____ My work creates value for my employer.

3. _____ I see working as a way to pursue my interests, expand my skills, and develop mastery.

4. _____ I support other people in their career planning and job hunting—and am willing to accept their support.

5. _____ I can function effectively in corporate cultures and cope positively with office politics.

6. _____ I create résumés and cover letters that distinguish me from other job applicants.

7. _____ I can accurately predict and prepare responses to questions asked by job interviewers.

8. _____ I see learning as a lifelong process that includes experiences inside and outside the classroom.

_____ Total score (10) **Working**

Filling in your Discovery Wheel

Using the total score from each category, shade in each section of the Discovery Wheel on the next page. Use different colors, if you want. For example, you could use green to denote areas you want to work on. When you have finished, complete the Journal Entry which follows the Wheel.

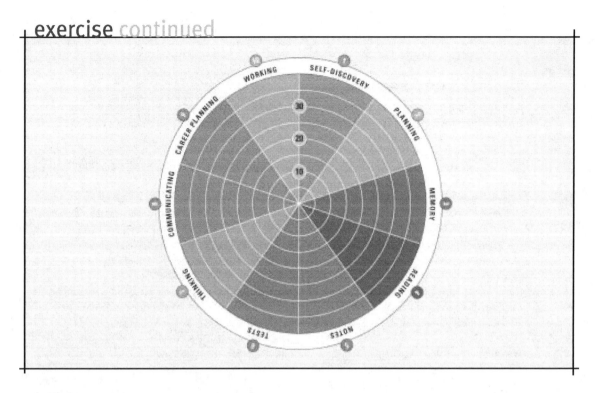

journal entry

Discovery/Intention Statement

Now that you have completed your Discovery Wheel, spend a few minutes with it. Get a sense of its weight, shape, and balance. Can you imagine running your hands around it? If you could lift it, would it feel light or heavy? How would it sound if it rolled down a hill? Would it roll very far? Would it wobble? Make your observations without judging the wheel as good or bad. Simply be with the picture you have created.

After you have spent a few minutes studying your Discovery Wheel, complete the following sentences in the space below. Don't worry if you can't think of something to write. Just put down whatever comes to mind. Remember, this is not a test.

This wheel is an accurate picture of my ability as a student because . . .

_____

_____

This wheel is an accurate picture of my workplace skills because . . .

_____

_____

My self-evaluation surprises me because . . .

_____

_____

The two areas in which I am strongest are . . .

_____

_____

The areas in which I want to improve are . . .

_____

_____

I want to concentrate on improving these areas because . . .

_____

_____

Now, select one of your discoveries and describe how you intend to benefit from it. Complete the following statement: To gain some practical value from this discovery, I will . . .

_____

_____

THINKING CRITICALLY IN THE WORKPLACE

In this exercise you will apply a higher-order thinking skill called *synthesis*—detecting key relationships between ideas and looking for broad patterns in your experiences. You'll also practice a technique for creative thinking. The focus is your experience of job hunting and the assumptions that shape your behaviors.

Recall all the jobs you've had in your life—full-time or part-time, permanent or temporary, contract or freelance. Think about the strategies you typically used to find these jobs. In the space below, list three strategies that you've depended on. Examples might include checking want ads in a newspaper and looking for job openings online.

Next, try some new assumptions on for size. See if you can state three job-hunting strategies that contrast greatly with—or even contradict—the three strategies you just listed. Be willing to think creatively and play with new possibilities, even if you feel resistance to a new idea. If you've depended on want ads, for instance, you might write: "Instead of sending my résumé in response to want ads, I could send a résumé only after meeting face to face with people who can hire me."

List your three new strategies below.

Finally, take the most "outrageous" strategy you just listed and list three potential benefits of using it.

---

journal entry

Discovery/Intention Statement

You've done a lot of writing during this course. To retain your key insights from this experience, review your responses to the exercises and journal entries. Writing in the space below, summarize your key discoveries. List any intentions that call for further action. Write any new Discovery Statements or Intention Statements that seem appropriate.

power process

Be it

All of the techniques in this chapter are enhanced by this Power Process.

To tap into its full benefits, consider that most of our choices in life fall into three categories. We can:

- Increase our material wealth (what we have).
- Improve our skills (what we do).
- Develop our "being" (who we are).

Many people devote their entire lifetime to the first two categories. They act as if they are "human havings" instead of human beings. For them, the quality of life hinges on what they have. They devote most of their waking hours to getting more—more clothes, more cars, more relationships, more degrees, more trophies. "Human havings" define themselves by looking at the circumstances in their lives—what they have.

Some people escape this materialist trap by adding another dimension to their identities. In addition to living as "human havings," they also live as "human doings." They thrive on working hard and doing everything well. They define themselves by how efficiently they do their jobs, how effectively they raise their children, and how actively they participate in clubs and organizations. Their thoughts are constantly about methods, techniques, and skills.

Look beyond doing and having

In addition to focusing on what we have and what we do, we can also focus on our being. While it is impossible to live our lives without having things and doing things, this Power Process suggests that we balance our experience by giving lots of attention to who we are—an aspect of our lives that goes beyond having and doing. Call it soul, passion, purpose, or values. Call it *being*. This word describes how we see ourselves—our deepest commitments, the ground from which our actions spring.

The realm of being is profound and subtle. It is also difficult to capture in words, though philosophers have tried for centuries. Christian theologian Paul Tillich described this realm when he defined faith as "ultimate commitment" and the "ground of being." In the New Testament, Jesus talked about being when he asked his followers to love God with all of their heart, soul, and mind. An ancient Hindu text also touches on being: "You are what your deep, driving desire is."

If all this seems far removed from taking notes or answering test questions, read on. Consider an example of how "Be it" can assist in career choices. In a letter to her father, a young woman wrote:

> We just went to see the Dance Theatre of Harlem. It was great! After the last number, I decided that I want to dance more than anything. I have a great passion to do it, more than anything else I can think or dream of. Dancing is what will make me happy and feel like I can leave this earth when my time comes. It is what I must do. I think that if I never fulfill this passion, I will never feel complete or satisfied with what I have done with my life.

In her heart, this person *is* a dancer now, even before her formal training is complete. From her passion, desire, commitment, and self-image (her *being*) comes her willingness to take classes and rehearse (*doing*). And from her doing she might eventually *have* a job with a professional dance company.

Picture the result as you begin

The example of the dancer illustrates that once you have a clear picture of what you want to *be,* the things you *do* and *have* fall more naturally into place.

The idea is this: Getting where you want to be by what you do or by what you have is like swimming against the current. Have → do → be is a tough journey. It's much easier to go in the other direction: be → do → have.

Usually, we work against nature by trying to have something or do something before being it. That's hard. All of your deeds (what you do) might not get you where you want to be. Getting all of the right things (what you have) might not get you there either.

Take the person who values athletics and wants to master tennis. He buys an expensive racket and a stylish tennis wardrobe. Yet he still can't return a serve. Merely having the right things doesn't deliver what he values.

Suppose that this person takes a year's worth of tennis lessons. Week after week, he practices doing everything "right." Still, his game doesn't quite make it.

What goes wrong is hard to detect. "He lost the match even though he played a good game," people say. "Something seemed to be wrong. His technique was fine, but each swing was just a little off." Perhaps the source of his problem is that he cannot see himself as ever mastering the game. What he has and what he does are at war with his mental picture of himself.

You can see this happen in other areas of life. Two people tell the same joke in what seems to be the same way. Yet one person brings a smile, while the other person has you laughing so hard your muscles hurt. The difference in how they do the joke is imperceptible. When the successful comedian tells a joke, he does it from his experience of already being funny.

To have and do what you want, be it. Picture the result as you begin. If you can first visualize where you want to

(thinking man) Digital Vision/Wonderfile, (graduate) Digital Vision/Wonderfile, (collage) Walter Kopec

be, if you can go there in your imagination, if you can be it today, you set yourself up to succeed.

Demonstrate mastery now

Now relate this Power Process to succeeding in school and at work. All of the techniques discussed can be worthless if you operate with the idea that you are basically ineffective. You might do almost everything this chapter and your course material suggest and still never achieve the success that you desire.

For example, if you believe that you are stupid in math, you are likely to fail at math. If you believe that you are not skilled at remembering, all of the memory techniques in the world might not help you remember the names of coworkers or people in your job-hunting network. Generally, we don't outperform our self-concept.

If you value success, then demonstrate mastery right now. Prepare papers and projects as if you were submitting them to an employer. Imagine that a promotion and raise will be determined by the way that you complete assignments and participate in class. While you are in higher education, reflect and reinforce the view that you are a professional.

Also demonstrate mastery in the work world. If you value a fulfilling career, picture yourself as already being on a path to a job you love. Use affirmations and visualizations to plant this idea firmly in your mind.

While you're at it, remember that "Be it" is not positive thinking or mental cheerleading. This Power Process works well when you take a First Step—when you tell the truth about your current abilities. The very act of accepting who you are and what you can do right now unleashes a powerful force for personal change.

Flow with the natural current of be → do → have. Then watch your circumstances change.

If you want it, be it. ✍

Change the way you see yourself, and watch your actions and results shift as if by magic.

career application

Duane Bigeagle earned his BA in Elementary Education and found a job teaching kindergarten in an urban public school.

Wendy Ashton/Stone/Getty

To his surprise, the hardest thing about the job was not interacting with students—whom he enjoyed greatly—but interacting with his coworkers. Though Duane had heard of office politics, he did not expect them to be so strong in an educational setting.

Duane's greatest concern was a colleague named Reneé, a teacher with 25 years of experience. During weekly staff meetings, the school's principal asked teachers to share any problems they were experiencing with students and collectively brainstorm solutions. Reneé smiled a lot, offered suggestions, and freely offered praise for anyone who was willing to share a problem. During informal conversations with Duane before or after school, however, Reneé complained bitterly about other teachers on staff—including those whom she'd just praised during staff meetings.

Being new to the school and a first-year teacher, Duane decided that he wanted to avoid making enemies. His goal in relating to staff members was simply to learn everything he could from them. With that goal in mind, Duane adopted the habits of carefully observing the classroom strategies used by other teachers and listening without judgment to any coaching they offered him.

Reneé talked with Duane every day and, after gossiping about other teachers, freely offered her advice for managing his classroom. By the end of the school year, Duane had enough of this. He worried that Reneé was taking on the role of a self-appointed mentor to him, and he disagreed with many of her ideas about teaching. He also worried that other teachers would perceive he and Reneé as a "team," and that her reputation for "backstabbing" would reflect negatively on him as well. ⚑

Reflecting on this scenario:

1. Identify a transferable skill that Duane demonstrates.

_____

_____

_____

2. What behaviors lead you to conclude that Duane has this skill?

_____

_____

_____

3. Identify a skill that would be useful for Duane to develop.

_____

_____

_____

4. List two or three suggestions for Duane that could help him cope with office politics and solve his problem with Reneé.

_____

_____

_____

_____

Name _____ Date _____/_____/_____

1. List three examples of unwritten rules that may be part of a corporate culture.

2. Explain the meaning of the suggestion to "promote your boss."

3. List three examples of sexual harassment in a work setting.

4. According to this chapter, the most important function of a leader is to prevent huge mistakes. True or False? Explain your answer.

5. Choose one Power Process from this chapter and briefly explain how it can help you love your next job.

6. List three strategies for keeping your career plan alive.

7. According to this chapter, you can delegate a job to your boss. True or False? Explain your answer.

8. Explain the suggestion to "give yourself a raise before you start work."

9. Using the Power Process: "Be it" eliminates the need to take action. True or False? Explain your answer.

learning styles application

The questions below will "cycle" you through four styles, or modes, of learning. Each question will help you explore a different mode. You can answer the questions in any order.

what if *Consider this statement: "You are on the edge of a universe so miraculous and full of wonder that your imagination at its most creative moment cannot encompass it. Paths are open to lead you to worlds beyond your wildest dreams." If you adopted this statement as a working principle, what would you do differently on a daily basis?*

why *Consider your experience with this chapter and your student success class. Which of your attitudes or actions changed as a result of this experience?*

how *List one suggestion that you would like to apply but have not yet acted upon. Describe exactly how you will implement this suggestion.*

what *List five sugestions from this class that you've already applied. Rate each suggestion for its effectiveness on a scale of 1 to 5 (1 is most effective, 5 is least effective).*

master student profile

CRAIG KIELBURGER

In 1995, at age 12, Craig Kielburger founded Free the Children International, an organization of children helping children who are the victims of poverty and exploitation. He has also served as an ambassador to the Children's Embassy in Sarajevo and was named a Global Leader of Tomorrow at the 1998 World Economic Forum.

I *picked up the* **Toronto Star** *and* put it on the table. But I didn't make it past the front page. Staring back at me was the headline, "BATTLED CHILD LABOUR, BOY, 12, MURDERED." It was a jolt. Twelve, the same age as I was. My eyes fixed on the picture of a boy in a bright-red vest. He had a broad smile, his arm raised straight in the air, a fist clenched....

Riding the bus to school later that morning, I could think of nothing but the article I had read on the front page. What kind of parents would sell their children into slavery at four years of age? And who would ever chain a child to a carpet loom?

Throughout the day I was consumed by Iqbal's story. In my Grade Seven class we had studied the American Civil War, and Abraham Lincoln, and how some of the slaves in the United States had escaped into Canada. But that was history from centuries ago. Surely slavery had been abolished throughout the world by now. If it wasn't, why had I never heard about it?

The school library was no help. After a thorough search I still hadn't found a scrap of information. After school, I decided to make the trek to the public library.

The librarian knew me from my previous visits. Luckily, she had read the same article that morning and was just as intrigued. Together, we searched out more information on child labour. We found a few newspaper and magazine articles, and made copies.

By the time I returned home, images of child labour had imbedded themselves in my mind: children younger than me forced to make carpets for endless hours in dimly lit rooms; others toiling in underground pits, struggling to get coal to the surface; others maimed or killed by explosions raging through fireworks factories. I was angry at the world for letting these things happen to children. Why was nothing being done to stop such cruelty?...

At lunchtime that day, some of us got together and talked about what we could do. I was amazed at how enthusiastic they all were. I told them about the youth fair on Friday.

"Do you think we could put together a display?" I asked. "We haven't got much time."

"Sure. Let's do it."

"We can all meet at my house," I said.

That night, twelve of us got together. It was a very tight deadline, with just two days to prepare. We found an old science fair board, and

we covered it with coloured paper, pasting on all the information I had found on child labour in the library, then drawing pictures to illustrate it.

We had determined that our first objective should be to inform people of the plight of child labourers. Armed with such knowledge, they might be willing to help. We decided to draw up a petition to present to the government, and called on the expertise of a couple of human rights groups to refine the wording for us.

But we were still without a name for our group. For more than an hour we struggled to come up with something suitable. We flipped through the newspaper clippings for inspiration. One of them reported on a demonstration in Delhi, India, where 250 children had marched through the streets with placards, chanting, "We want an education," "We want freedom," "Free the children!"

"That's it!" someone shouted. "Free the Children." 📧

From *Free the Children* by Craig Kielburger with Kevin Major. Copyright © 1998 by Craig Kielburger. Reprinted by permission of HarperCollins Publishers, Inc.

For more biographical information on Craig Kielburger, visit the Master Student Hall of Fame on the *From Master Student to Master Employee* Web site at

masterstudent.college.hmco.com

end notes

1. William Bridges, *Jobshift: How to Prosper in a Workplace Without Jobs* (New York: Perseus, 1995).
2. Dave Ellis, Stan Lankowitz, Ed Stupka, and Doug Toff, *Career Planning*, Third Edition. Copyright © 2003 by Houghton Mifflin Company. Reprinted by permission.
3. U.S. Department of Labor, *Report on the American Workforce 2001*, http://www.bls.gov/opub/rtaw/rtawhome.htm (accessed June 21, 2004).
4. Kathryn Tyler, "I Say Potato, You Say Patata." *HR Magazine*, January 2004, pp. 85–87.
5. U.S. Equal Employment Opportunity Commission, "Sexual Harassment," http://www.eeoc.gov/types/sexual_harassment.html, January 6, 2004 (accessed June 21, 2004).